SOCIAL PSYCHOLOGY

SOCIAL PSYCHOLOGY

Second Edition

ELLIOT ARONSON
University of California, Santa Cruz

TIMOTHY D. WILSON
University of Virginia

ROBIN M. AKERT
Wellesley College

LONGMAN

An imprint of Addison Wesley Longman, Inc.

New York • Reading, Massachusetts • Menlo Park, California • Harlow, England
Don Mills, Ontario • Sydney • Mexico City • Madrid • Amsterdam

Acquisitions Editor: Catherine Woods
Developmental Editor: Ann Marie Kirby
Project Coordination and Text Design: Thompson Steele Production Services
Cover Design: Linda Wade
Cover Illustration: Tina Vey
Art Studio: Alexander Teshin Associates
Photo Researcher: Mira Schachne
Electronic Production Manager: Eric Jorgensen
Manufacturing Manager: Hilda Koparanian
Electronic Page Makeup: Thompson Steele Production Services
Printer and Binder: Courier/Kendallville, Inc.
Cover Printer: Phoenix Color Corp.

For permission to use copyrighted material, grateful acknowledgment is made to the copyright holders on pp. C-1–C-5, which are hereby made part of this copyright page.

Aronson, Elliot.
  Social psychology / Elliot Aronson, Timothy D. Wilson, Robin M. Akert. --2nd ed.
      p.   cm.
    Includes bibliographical references and index.
    ISBN 0-673-99929-7
    1. Social psychology.   I. Wilson, Timothy D.   II. Akert, Robin M.
    III. Title.
    HM251 .A794   1997
    302--dc20   97-2311
                                                                         CIP

0-673-99929-7

1234567910—CRK—99989796

To my family, Vera, Hal, Neal, Julie,
and Joshua Aronson

—E.A.

To my family, Deirdre Smith, Christopher
and Leigh Wilson

—T.D.W.

To my mentor, colleague, and friend,
Dane Archer

—R.M.A.

Brief Contents

I   Introduction

II   Understanding Ourselves and the Social World

III   Social Influence

IV   Social Interaction

V   Social Psychology in Action

DETAILED CONTENTS

I Introduction

CHAPTER 1
Introduction to Social Psychology 2

CHAPTER 2
Methodology: the Process of Doing Research 28

II   Understanding Ourselves and the Social World

Chapter 3
Social Cognition: How We Think About the Social World   64

CHAPTER 4
Social Perception: How We Come to Understand Other People   102

Chapter 5
Self-Understanding: How We Come to Understand Ourselves   142

Chapter 6
Self-Justification and the Need to Maintain Self-Esteem   180

III   Social Influence

CHAPTER 7
Attitudes and Attitude Change:
Influencing Thoughts and Feelings   226

Chapter 8
Conformity: Influencing Behavior   266

Chapter 9
Group Processes: Influence In Social Groups   310

IV   Social Interaction

CHAPTER 10
Interpersonal Attraction: From First Impressions to Close Relationships   354

V Social Psychology in Action

MODULE 1
Social Psychology and Health   524

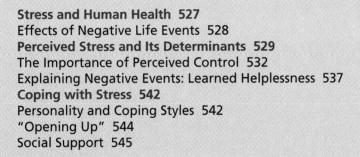

MODULE 2
Social Psychology and the Environment   550

PREFACE

ocial psychology is a broad and complex discipline. No one person can master it all. But we felt that, as a team, we were ideally suited to tell this exciting and engaging story the way it should be told. The three of us had covered broad ranges of this fascinating discipline in our studies and had broken new ground in our research. And our teaching experiences had shown us how to convey the story of social psychology in a way that captures the imagination of the student. Social psychology comes alive for students when they understand the whole context of the field: how theories inspire research, why research is performed as it is, how further research triggers yet new avenues of study. We were confident that we could convey our own fascination with the research process in a down-to-earth, meaningful way, and that we could present the results of the scientific process in terms of the everyday experience of the reader. However, we did not want to "water down" our presentation of the field. In a world where human behavior can be endlessly surprising, and where research results can be surprisingly counterintuitive, it is important to prepare students well by providing a firm foundation on which to build their understanding of this vigorous, challenging discipline.

Following publication of the first edition, we were keenly interested to see how well we succeeded in telling the story of social psychology. We were gratified to learn that we succeeded even beyond our own expectations. Here is what users of the first edition found to be the strengths of this text.

A Storytelling Approach.   Perhaps the most gratifying response we've had to the first edition of *Social Psychology* is overwhelmingly positive feedback from students. Students tell us that our storytelling approach makes the material interesting and memorable. Social psychology is full of good stories, such as how the Kitty Genovese murder prompted research on bystander intervention and how the Holocaust inspired investigations into obedience to

authority. By placing the research in a real-world context, we make the material more familiar, understandable, and memorable.

A Theoretical Synthesis That Pulls It All Together. Many books provide a disjointed set of topics with no clear rationale for why they go together. We've tried to show students how different theories work together in social psychology. In our introductory chapter we provide a framework that organizes and illuminates the entire field. Three key themes are presented: (a) Social psychology is concerned with the power of social influence; (b) social influence is best defined not in objective but in subjective terms—namely, as the way in which people construe their social environments; and (c) to understand how people perceive and construe the social world, we must understand a few basic human motives, such as the need to maintain self-esteem and the desire to form an accurate picture of the social world. We avoid presenting these themes in a manner that is too heavy-handed, leaving room for the instructor to emphasize those themes with which he or she is most comfortable.

The Research Process as Rigorous and Exciting. An important part of the story of social psychology is an understanding of and appreciation for the methods used. After all, what sets social psychology apart from related disciplines, such as philosophy or history, is the ability to test hypotheses empirically. In recent years, the trend has been for textbooks to include only short sections on research methodology and to provide only brief descriptions of the findings of individual studies. In this book, we take a different approach:

First, we devote an entire chapter to the methods of social psychology. To keep students engaged, we present the material in context, describing the way in which important problems can be addressed with different methodologies. Throughout the methods chapter, for example, we discuss whether pornography makes people more likely to commit sexual crimes (see, e.g., pp. 38–39 and 51–52).

Second, throughout the book we describe individual studies in detail. We describe clearly how each study was set up, what the research participants perceived and did, how the research design derives from theoretical issues, and how the findings offer support for the initial hypotheses. We often ask the reader to pretend that he or she was a participant, in order to understand the study from the participants' point of view. Whenever pertinent, we've also included anecdotal information about how a study was done or came to be; these brief stories allow the reader to see the hitherto hidden world of creating research. See, for example, the description of Nisbett and Wilson's (1977) "power saw" study in Chapter 5 (pp. 153–154), or the description of Aronson's jigsaw puzzle technique in Chapter 13 (pp. 516–519).

A Clean, Streamlined Presentation. A cursory glance at our text will reveal that something is missing: There are no boxes interrupting the text. Such boxes are very tempting for textbook writers to use, because they are a means of adding new material that doesn't really fit into the flow of the chapter. However, we believe that such boxes are distracting to readers and detract from the main story of the chapter. Further, placement of such important material as gender differences, cross-cultural research, or applied topics in boxes rather than in running text implies that these issues occur outside the realm of basic social psychology. Rather than marginalizing these important topics in boxes, we integrate cutting-edge research, applied topics, and diversity into the main story line, emphasizing their significance as part of the discipline as a whole. This approach is much more pedagogically sound; students do not have to stop what they are reading, read the material in a box, determine how it relates to what they just read, and then pick up where they left off.

Emphasis on Both Classic and Modern Research. As you will see from flipping through the book, we include a large number of data figures detailing the results of individual experiments. In the second edition, we have added a great deal of new material, describing dozens of major studies done within the past few years. However, in emphasizing what is new, many texts have a tendency to ignore what is old. We have striven to strike a balance between

current, up-to-date research findings and classic research in social psychology. Some older studies deserve their status as classics (e.g., early work in dissonance, conformity, and attribution) and are important cornerstones in the discipline. We showcase many of these studies; examples include our description of the Schachter and Singer (1962) study in Chapter 5, the Festinger and Carlsmith (1959) study in Chapter 6, and the Asch (1956) conformity studies in Chapter 8. We complement such classic research with modern approaches to these same topics, such as research on culture, self, and emotion (e.g., Markus & Kitayama, 1994, in Chapter 5); self-affirmation and stereotype vulnerability (e.g., Steele, 1988, in Chapter 6 and Steele & Aronson, 1995, in Chapter 13); and minority influence (e.g., Wood, Lundgren, Ouellette, Busceme & Blackstone, 1994, in Chapter 8).

Integrated Coverage of Culture and Gender. To understand behavior in a social context, we must consider such influences as culture and gender. Rather than adding a chapter on these important topics, we discuss them in every chapter, as they apply to the topic at hand. In many places, we discuss the wonderful diversity of humankind, by presenting research on the differences between people of different cultures, races, or genders. We also discuss the commonalties people share, by illustrating the applicability of many phenomena across cultures and genders. For example, in Chapter 9 we discuss evidence that social loafing is a pervasive phenomenon; it has been documented in Western and Asian cultures and among men and women. We also note, however, that differences exist in the *degree* of social loafing: Members of Western cultures are more likely to engage in social loafing than members of Asian cultures are, and men are more likely to engage in social loafing than women are.

An Emphasis on Real Life. One of the best ways of capturing students' interest is to point out the real-world significance of the material they are studying. From the vignette that opens each chapter and runs throughout it to the discussions of historical events, current affairs, and our own lives that are embedded in the story line, the narrative is highlighted by real, familiar examples. Often we invite students to apply material to their own lives, as with our discussion in Chapter 5 of how to avoid self-fulfilling prophecies.

Organization of the Second Edition

We have seen a lot of syllabi from social psychology courses and spoken with many colleagues who teach the course, and have been impressed by the different ways in which the course can be taught. To accommodate the diverse ways in which instructors may choose to present topics, we have tried to create a sensible yet flexible organization.

Each chapter of *Social Psychology* is self-contained in terms of topics and concepts. Consequently, instructors can assign the chapters in any order they please; concepts are always explained in clear terms so that students won't have to have read earlier chapters in order to grasp the meanings of later ones. Further, we have designed Part 5, "Social Psychology in Action," as three independent modular chapters on applied topics that instructors can integrate into their course outline however they like. The instructor's manual that accompanies *Social Psychology* includes several alternative outlines, showing how the text can be tailored to fit different syllabi.

Significant Changes to the Second Edition

We have been very pleased by the reception of the first edition. There is always room for improvement, however, and based on feedback from instructors and students, we have made several changes in the second edition. In addition to updated examples, references, figures, and photos that appear throughout the new edition, some of the more significant changes include the following.

- Chapter 2, *Methodology: The Process of Doing Research*, includes updated information on the effects of pornography on sexual aggression, together with new material on cross-cultural research.
- Chapter 3, *Social Cognition: How We Think About the Social World*, has been reorganized to reflect current research and theory in social cognition, including a section titled "The Flexible Social Thinker." New sections on automaticity and controlled social thinking have been added, with discussions of recent work by Gilbert (1993) on "automatic believing" and Wegner (1994) on thought suppression. Other new topics include counterfactual reasoning and cultural determinants of schemas.

- Chapter 4, *Social Perception: How We Come to Understand Other People*, addresses recent theoretical developments concerning the role of language in the actor/observer difference, consensus at zero acquaintance, perceptual salience, and reasons for accuracy or inaccuracy in attributions.
- In Chapter 5, *Self-Understanding: How Do We Understand Ourselves?*, we've updated the section on intrinsic motivation, including a discussion of task-contingent versus performance-contingent rewards, and added a section on cognitive appraisal theories of emotion. New sections on recovered memories and Baumeister's (1991) work on escaping the self have also been added.
- Chapter 6, *Self-Justification and the Need to Maintain Self-Esteem*, is highlighted by a shift in emphasis away from dissonance theory and toward self-justification. We've moved the chapter back in the organization so that it now sits between chapters on the self (Chapter 5) and attitudes (Chapter 7) and can be taught with either. Additions include new discussions of symbolic self-completion (Wicklund & Gollwitzer, 1982) and self-discrepancy theory (Higgins, 1989), along with broadened discussions of such topics as self-verification (Swann, 1995), self-affirmation (Steele, 1988), and self-evaluation maintenance theory (Tesser, 1988)
- Chapter 7, *Attitudes and Attitude Change: Influencing Thoughts and Feelings*, includes new sections on emotion, cultural differences in the self, and attitude change. Coverage of advertising and attitude change has been expanded, including new sections on types of attitudes toward consumer products and a section on subliminal persuasion. An expanded discussion of Chaiken's (1987) heuristic-systematic model of persuasion has also been added.
- Chapter 8, *Conformity: Influencing Behavior*, includes discussions of recent studies on minority influence by Wood and colleagues (1994), treatment of Buehler and Griffin's (1994) work on change in construals after conforming or not conforming, and an expanded section on cross-cultural applications of Asch's (1951) work.
- Chapter 9, *Group Processes: Influence in Social Groups*, includes new material on gender and cultural differences in social loafing, leadership, and conflict between individuals versus groups. A new section on the nature of social groups has

been added, including a discussion of roles and the Zimbardo prison experiment. Recent research addressed includes work on the sharing of information in groups, such as a study by Liang, Moreland, and Argote (1995), and an updated discussion of groupthink, including a meta-analysis by Mullen, Anthony, Salas, and Driskell (1994).

- Chapter 10, *Interpersonal Attraction: From First Impressions to Close Relationships* has been revised substantially. New research includes recent work on close relationships and cross-cultural definitions of beauty.

- Chapter 11, *Prosocial Behavior: Why Do People Help?*, has been updated with a new section on sociobiology, including a discussion of work by Simon (1990) and Burnstein, Crandall, and Kitayama (1994), and Batson's work on the empathy-altruism hypothesis, including an extensive discussion of an experiment by Toi and Batson (1982). The material on gender and helping has been updated, and a new section has been added on communal versus exchange relationships

- Chapter 12, *Aggression: Why We Hurt Other People*, includes new research by Nisbett (1993) on regional and cultural differences in aggression, recent work on transnational differences in violence and homicide by Archer and McDaniel (1995), and recent evidence from the National Academy of Sciences on the effects of punishment on aggression.

- Chapter 13, *Prejudice: Causes and Cures,* includes new experiments by Steele and Aronson (1995) on stereotype vulnerability; Fazio, Jackson, Dunton, and Williams's (1995) work on variability in automatic activation of stereotypes as a measure of racial attitudes; and Bargh and Raymond's (1995) work on automaticity and sexual harassment. An elaborated discussion of the research on the effects of cooperative learning on prejudice reduction and increases in empathy has been added, including work by Gaertner, Hammerman, and Meier.

- In the first edition, we devoted half of a chapter to health; we now discuss it in the first of three independent modular chapters. Module 1, *Social Psychology and Health,* includes new sections on stereotype vulnerability, stress and coping, personality and coping styles, "opening up" and physical health, and social support.

- Module 2, *Social Psychology and the Environment*, includes new discussions of culture and

how it relates to environmental stress and crowding.

- The third and final module, *Social Psychology and the Law,* includes new research by Dunning and Stern (1994) and Schooler and Engstler-Schooler (1990) on the relationship between deliberative thought processes and face recognition, as well as a new section on the own-race bias in face recognition.

Pedagogy: Making It Easy on the Student

We have included a number of pedagogical techniques that make this book "user-friendly" for the student. In addition to a writing style and presentation that keep students reading, we have incorporated functional pedagogical tools into *Social Psychology.*

Chapter opening vignettes. Each chapter opens with a story drawn from a real-life situation, such as a recent news event, a historical incident, a current political debate, or a popular culture phenomenon. These opening vignettes encourage students, from the beginning of the chapter, to examine their daily experiences using a social psychological perspective. We refer back to the opening vignette throughout the chapter, enriching students' understanding of it in light of the theories and research findings they are studying.

Key terms appear boldfaced in the text, where they are explained in context. They are repeated in a marginal glossary to aid study, as well as in the Glossary at the back of the book. Terms are repeated again in boldface in the chapter-ending summaries.

Interim summaries are imbedded within the chapter narrative, to ensure that students understand one concept before moving on to the next.

Author-conceived cartoons. We have created for this book original cartoon art that clarifies difficult or complex social psychological concepts in an eye-catching and amusing visual manner. These cartoons bring difficult concepts to life and help the student experience them firsthand. We're particularly pleased to have had a professional artist turn our amateur renderings into the delightful art you will see.

Data figures sum up research findings in a clear, easy-to-follow manner.

Literary quotations from writers, artists, and philosophers, as well as the common man or woman, appear in the margins throughout the text. The quotes parallel what social psychologists have pondered and discovered through experimentation, and remind students that social life is the province not just of scientists but of artists as well—social psychological phenomena relate to everyone's experience.

Chapter-ending summaries include all of the key terms from that chapter, in boldface type, to facilitate study.

If You're Interested lists at the end of each chapter include not only scholarly books but also novels and films that portray topics raised in the chapter.

Ancillary Package

A really good textbook should become part of the classroom experience, supporting and augmenting the professor's vision for his or her class. *Social Psychology* offers a number of supplements that will enrich both the professor's presentation of social psychology and the student's understanding of it.

For the Instructor Instructor's Resource Kit 0673972844 by Elisa Wurf of Lehigh University.
- Includes lecture ideas, teaching tips, suggested readings, chapter outlines, and a media resource guide. Available to adopters is a three-ring binder.
  Test Bank 0673972852 edited by Marti Hope Gonzales of the University of Minnesota.
- This collection of 2,000 test items comes from text adopters across the country and from the text authors. Each question is referenced to parent page, topic, and skill level. The test bank is also available to adopters in DOS and in Macintosh computerized format. Our test generation TestMaster software program allows professors to customize exams from Test Bank items, new questions, or a combination of both TestMaster DOS 0673972879 and TestMaster Mac 0673972860.

For the Student Study Guide 0673999327 by Kathy Demitrakis of the University of North Carolina–Asheville.
- Contains chapter learning objectives and outlines, study questions, key terms, and practice tests.

Acknowledgments

Elliot Aronson is delighted to acknowledge the general contributions of his best friend (who also happens to be his wife), Vera Aronson. Vera, as usual, provided a great deal of inspiration for his ideas and acted as the sounding board for and supportive critic of many of his semiformed notions, helping to mold them into more sensible analyses. He would also like to thank his son, Joshua Aronson, a brilliant young social psychologist in his own right, for the many stimulating conversations that contributed mightily to the final version of this book.

Tim Wilson would like to thank his graduate mentor, Richard E. Nisbett, who nurtured his interest in the field and showed him the continuity between social psychological research and everyday life. He thanks his graduate students Eric Anderson, Thalia Eliason, Suzanne LaFleur, Samuel Lindsey, and Jay Meyers, who helped keep him a well-balanced professor: a researcher as well as a teacher and author. He thanks his parents, Elizabeth and Geoffrey Wilson, for their comments on chapter drafts and for their overall support. Most of all, he thanks his wife, Deirdre Smith, and his children, Christopher and Leigh, for their love, patience, and understanding, even when the hour was late and the computer was still on.

Robin Akert would like to thank her students and colleagues at Wellesley College for their support and encouragement. In particular, she is beholden to Professors Patricia Berman, Nancy Genero, Jonathan Cheek, and Abigail Panter. Their advice, feedback, and senses of humor were invaluable. She is deeply grateful to her family, Michaela and Wayne Akert, and Linda and Jerry Wuichet; their inexhaustible enthusiasm and boundless support have sustained her on this project as on all the ones before it. Once again she thanks C. Issak for authorial inspiration. Finally, no words can express her gratitude and indebtedness to Dane Archer, mentor, colleague, and friend, who opened the world of social psychology to her and who has been her guide ever since.

No book can be written and published without the help of a great many people working with the authors behind the scenes, and our book is no exception. First, we would like to thank the many colleagues who read chapters in various stages of development and provided extremely valuable feedback: Jeffrey B. Adams, Saint Michael's College; John R. Aiello, Rutgers University; Charles A. Alexander, Rock Valley College; Joan W. Baily, Jersey City State College; Norma Baker, Belmont University; William A. Barnard, University of Northern Colorado; Susan E. Beers, Sweet Briar College; Thomas Blass, University of Maryland, Baltimore County; C. George Boeree, Shippensburg University; Lisa M. Bohon, California State University, Sacramento; Peter J. Brady, Clark State Community College; Kelly A. Brennan, University of Texas at Austin; Thomas P. Cafferty, University of South Carolina–Columbia; Melissa A. Cahoon, Wright State University; Nicholas Christenfeld, University of California at San Diego; Susan D. Clayton, Allegheny College; Brian M. Cohen, University of Texas at San Antonio; Steven G. Cole, Texas Christian University; Eric J. Cooley, Western Oregon State College; Diana Cordova, Yale University; Keith E. Davis, University of South Carolina–Columbia; Karen G. Duffy, State University of New York at Geneseo; Steve L. Ellyson, Youngstown State University; Susan Fiske, University of Massachusetts, Amherst; Robin Franck, Southwestern College; William Rick Fry, Youngstown State University; Frederick X. Gibbons, Iowa State University; Cynthia Gilliland, Louisiana State University; Genaro Gonzalez, University of Texas; Beverly Gray, Youngstown State University; Judith Harackiewicz, University of Wisconsin–Madison; Vicki S. Helgeson, Carnegie Mellon University; Tracy B. Henley, Mississippi State University; Ed Hirt, Indiana University; David E. Hyatt, University of Wisconsin–Oshkosh; James D. Johnson, University of North Carolina–Wilmington; Lee Jussim, Rutgers University; Fredrick Koenig, Tulane University; Alan J. Lambert, Washington University; G. Daniel Lassiter, Ohio University; Joann M. Montepare, Tufts University; Carrie Nance, Stetson University; Todd D. Nelson, Michigan State University; W. Gerrod Parrott, Georgetown University; M. Susan Rowley, Champlain College; Connie Schick, Bloomsburg University; Richard C. Sherman, Miami University of Ohio; Randolph A. Smith, Ouachita Baptist University; Linda Solomon, Marymount Manhattan College; Jakob Steinberg, Fairleigh Dickinson University; T. Gale Thompson, Bethany College; Gary L. Wells, Iowa State University; Paul L. Wienir, Western Michigan University; Kipling D. Williams, University of Toledo; and William H. Zachry, University of Tennessee–Martin.

Especially helpful were the comments from expert reviewers who provided feedback on specific chapters. Many thanks to Richard Moreland, University of Pittsburgh, for his review of Chapter 9 on group processes; Margaret S. Clark, Carnegie Mellon University, for her insights on prosocial behavior (Chapter 11); Leonard Berkowitz, University of Wisconsin–Madison, for his comments on aggression (Chapter 12); Art Aron, State University of New York at Stony Brook, and Steve Duck, University of Iowa, for their input on interpersonal attraction (Chapter 10); and Richard W. Brislin, East-West Center of the University of Hawaii, who looked at the entire manuscript and provided many helpful suggestions on multi- and cross-cultural issues.

We also thank the expert editorial staff of Addison Wesley Longman, especially our dedicated and patient acquisitions editor, Catherine Woods, and our developmental editor, Ann Kirby. We'd also like to thank the staff at Thompson Steele for their ongoing design and production services through their second edition of *Social Psychology*. Finally, we thank Mary Falcon, but for whom we never would have begun this project.

Thank you for inviting us into your classroom. We welcome your suggestions, and we would be delighted to hear your comments about this book.

Elliot Aronson
elliot@cats.ucsc.edu

Tim Wilson
tdw@virginia.edu

Robin Akert
rakert@wellesley.edu.

ABOUT THE AUTHORS

ELLIOT ARONSON

When I was a kid, we were the only Jewish family in a virulently anti-Semitic neighborhood. I had to go to Hebrew school every day, late in the afternoon. Being the only youngster in my neighborhood going to Hebrew school made me an easy target for some of the older neighborhood toughs. On my way home from Hebrew school, after dark, I was frequently waylaid and roughed up by roving gangs shouting anti-Semitic epithets.

I have a vivid memory of sitting on a curb after one of these beatings, nursing a bloody nose or a split lip, feeling very sorry for myself and wondering how these kids could hate me so much when they didn't even know me. I thought about whether those kids were taught to hate Jews or whether, somehow, they were born that way. I wondered if their hatred could be changed; if they got to know me better, would they hate me less? I speculated about my own character. What would I have done if the shoe were on the other foot; that is, if I were bigger and stronger than they, would I be capable of beating them up for no good reason?

I didn't realize it at the time, of course, but eventually I discovered that these were profound questions. And some 30 years later, as an experimental social psychologist, I had the great good fortune to be in a position to answer some of those questions and to invent techniques to reduce the kind of prejudice that had claimed me as a victim.

Elliot Aronson graduated from Brandeis University (where he worked with Abraham Maslow) and received his Ph.D. from Stanford University, working under the guidance of Leon Festinger. He has done pioneering research in the areas of social influence, persuasion, prejudice reduction and AIDS prevention. Aronson has written or edited 15 books, including The Social Animal, The Handbook of Social Psychology, Age of Propaganda, The Jigsaw Classroom, *and* Methods of Research in Social Psychology. *He is among the world's most honored social psychologists, having received major national and international awards for the quality of his teaching, for his experimental research, for his books, and for his contributions to the betterment of society. He has served as president of the Society of Personality and Social Psychology and president of the Western Psychological Association. In 1992, he was elected to the American Academy of Arts and Sciences. He is currently a research professor of psychology at the University of California at Santa Cruz.*

TIM WILSON

When I was 8, a couple of neighborhood friends told me, with great excitement, that they had discovered an abandoned house down a country road. "It's really neat," one of them said. "We broke a window and nobody cared!" My best friend and I decided to investigate. We jumped on our bikes and had no trouble finding the house. As we walked up to it, my friend picked up a baseball-size rock and heaved it through a first-floor window. There was something terribly exciting about the smash-and-tingle of shattering glass, especially when we knew there was nothing wrong with what we were doing; after all, the house was abandoned, wasn't it? We proceeded to break nearly every window in the house, and then climbed through one of the first-floor windows to look around.

It was then that we realized something was terribly wrong. The house certainly did not look abandoned. There were pictures on the wall, nice furniture, books in bookshelves. We went home feeling frightened and confused. We soon learned that the house was not abandoned: It was the residence of an elderly couple who were away on vacation. Eventually my parents found out, and paid a substantial sum to cover the damage I had caused.

For years, I pondered this incident: Why did I do such a terrible thing? Was I a bad kid? I didn't think so, and neither did my parents. But then, how could a good kid do such a bad thing? Even though the neighborhood kids said the house was abandoned, why couldn't my friend and I see the clear signs that someone lived there? How crucial was it that my friend was there and threw the first rock? Though I didn't know it at the time, these reflections touched on several classic social psychological issues, such as whether only bad people do bad things, whether the social situation can be powerful enough to make good people do bad things, and the way in which our expectations about an event can make it difficult to see it as it really is. Fortunately, my career as a vandal ended with this one incident. The incident did, however, mark the beginning of my fascination with basic questions about how people understand themselves and the social world—questions I continue to investigate to this day.

Tim Wilson did his undergraduate work at Williams and Hampshire colleges and received his Ph.D. from the University of Michigan under the guidance of Richard E. Nisbett. Currently a professor of psychology at the University of Virginia, he has published numerous articles in the areas of introspection, judgment, and attitude change. His research has received the support of the National Science Foundation and the National Institute for Mental Health. He has been a member of the Executive Board of the Society for Experimental Social Psychology, a member of the Social and Groups Processes Review Committee at the National Institute of Mental Health, and a member of the editorial boards of several professional journals.

ROBIN AKERT

One fall day, when I was about 16, I was walking with a friend along the shore of the San Francisco Bay. Deep in conversation, I glanced over my shoulder and saw a sailboat capsize. I pointed it out to my friend, who took only a perfunctory interest and went on talking. However, I kept watching as we walked, and I realized that the two sailors were in the water, clinging to the capsized boat. Again I said something to my friend, who replied, "Oh, they'll get it upright, don't worry."

But I *was* worried. Was this an emergency? My friend didn't think so. And I was no sailor; I knew nothing about boats. But I kept thinking, "That water is really cold. They can't stay in that water too long." I remember feeling very confused and unsure. What should I do? Should I do anything? Did they really need help?

We were near a restaurant with a big window overlooking the bay, and I decided to go in and see if anyone had done anything about the boat. Lots of people were watching but not doing anything. This confused me too. Very meekly, I asked the bartender to call for some kind of help. He just shrugged. I went back to the window and watched the two small figures in the water. Why was everyone so unconcerned? Was I crazy?

Years later, I reflected on how hard it was for me to do what I did next: I demanded that the bartender let me use his phone. In those days before "911," it was lucky that I knew there was a Coast Guard station on the bay, and I asked the operator for the number. I was relieved to hear the Guardsman take my message very seriously.

It had been an emergency. I watched as the Coast Guard cutter sped across the bay and pulled the two sailors out of the water. Maybe I saved their lives that day. What really stuck with me over the years was how other people behaved and how it made me feel. The other bystanders seemed unconcerned and did nothing to help. Their reactions made me doubt myself and made it harder for me to decide to take action. When I later studied social psychology in college, I realized that on the shore of the San Francisco Bay that day, I had experienced the "bystander effect" fully: The presence of other, apparently unconcerned bystanders had made it difficult for me to decide if the situation was an emergency and whether it was my responsibility to help.

Robin M. Akert graduated summa cum laude from the University of California at Santa Cruz, where she majored in psychology and sociology. She received her Ph.D. in experimental social psychology from Princeton University. She is currently a professor of psychology at Wellesley College, where she was awarded the Pinanski Prize for Excellence in Teaching. She publishes primarily in the area of nonverbal communication and is the coauthor of the forthcoming book Interpretation and Awareness: Verbal and Nonverbal Factors in Person Perception.

SPECIAL TIPS FOR STUDENTS

There is then creative reading as well as creative writing.

—*Ralph Waldo Emerson, 1837*

I am a kind of burr; I shall stick.

—*William Shakespeare, 1604*

These two quotes, taken together, sum up everything you need to know to be a proficient student: Be an active, creative consumer of information and make sure it sticks! How do you accomplish these two feats? Actually it's not difficult at all. Like everything else in life, it just takes some work—some clever, well-planned, purposeful work. Here are some suggestions about how to do it:

Get to Know the Textbook

Believe it or not, in writing this book we thought very carefully about the organization and structure of each chapter. Things are the way they appear for a reason, and that reason is to help you learn the material in the best way possible. Here are some tips on what to look for in each chapter.

Key terms are in boldface type in the text so that you'll notice them. We define the terms in the text, and that definition appears again in the margin. These marginal definitions are there to help you out if later in the chapter you forget what something means. The marginal definitions are quick and easy to find. You can also look up key terms in the alphabetical Glossary at the end of this textbook.

Make sure you notice the headings and subheadings. The headings are the skeleton that holds a chapter together. They link together like vertebrae. If you ever feel lost, look back to the last heading and the headings before that one—this will give you the "big picture" of where the chapter is going. It should also help you see the connections between sections.

The summary at the end of each chapter is a succinct, shorthand presentation of the chapter information, with the key terms set in boldface. You should read it and make sure there are no surprises when you do so. If anything in the summary doesn't ring a bell, go back to the chapter and reread that section. Most importantly, remember that the summary is purposefully brief, whereas your understanding of the material should be full and complete. Use the summary as a study aid before your exams. When you read it over, everything should be familiar and you should have that wonderful feeling of knowing more than is in the summary (in which case you are ready to take the exam).

At the end of each chapter, we list pertinent books or articles that we think are particularly good. These recommended readings are excellent resources for any papers you may be writing for your course. They are the first place to start in a bibliographic search for further information on the topic of your paper. As is always the case with literature searches, they will lead you to still other references. At the end of each chapter, we also list a few novels and movies that poignantly portray themes from that chapter.

Just Say No to the Couch Potato Within

Because social psychology is about everyday life, you might lull yourself into believing that the material is all common sense. Don't be fooled. The material is more complicated than it might seem. Therefore, we want to emphasize that the best way to learn it is to work with it in an active, not passive, fashion. You can't just read a chapter once and expect it to stick with you. You have to go over the material, wrestle with it, make your own connections to it, question it, and think about it. Actively working with material makes it memorable; it makes it your own. Since it's a safe bet that someone is going to ask you about this material later and you're going to have to pull it out of memory, do what you can to get it into memory now. Here are some techniques to use:

Go ahead and be bold—use a highlighter! Go crazy—write in the margins! If you underline, highlight, circle, or draw little hieroglyphics next to important points, you will remember them better. We recall taking exams in college where we not only remembered the material but could actually see in our minds the textbook page it was written on and the little squiggles and stars we'd drawn in the margin.

Read the textbook chapter before the applicable class lecture, not afterward. This way, you'll get more out of the lecture, which will introduce new material. The chapter will give you the big picture, as well as a lot of detail; the lecture will enhance that information and help you put it all together. If you don't read the chapter first, you may not understand some of the points made in the lecture or realize that they are important.

Here's a good way to study material: Write out a difficult concept or a study (or say it out loud to yourself) in your own words, without looking at the book or your notes. Can you do it? How good was your version? Did you omit anything important? Did you get stuck at some point, unable to remember what comes next? If so, you now know that you need to go over that information in more detail. You can also study with someone else, describing theories and studies to each other and seeing if you're making sense.

If you have trouble remembering the results of an important study, try drawing your own version of a graph of the findings (you can use our data graphs for an idea of how to proceed). If all the various points in a theory are confusing you, try drawing your own flowchart of how it works. You will probably find that you remember the research results much better in pictorial form than in words and that the theory isn't so confusing (or missing a critical part) if you've outlined it. Draw information a few times and it will stay with you.

Remember, the more you work with the material—that is, write it in your own words, talk about it, explain it to others, or draw visual representations of it—the better you will learn and remember it.

Last but not least, remember that this material is a lot of fun. You haven't even started reading the book yet, but we think you're going to like it. In particular, you'll see how much social psychology has to tell you about your real, everyday life. As this course progresses, you might want to remind yourself to observe the events of your daily life with new eyes, the eyes of a social psychologist, and try to apply what you are learning to the behavior of your friends, acquaintances, strangers, and, yes, even yourself. When you read newspapers or magazines or watch the nightly news, think about what social psychology has to say about such events and behaviors; we believe you will find that your understanding of daily life is richer. If you notice a newspaper or magazine article that you think is an especially good example of social psychology "in action," please send it to us, with a full reference to where you found it and on what page. If we decide to use it in the next edition of this book, we'll list your name in the Acknowledgments.

We suspect that ten years from now, you may not remember all the facts, theories, and names you learn now. Although we hope you will remember some of them, our main goal is for you to take with you into your future a great many of the broad social psychological concepts presented herein. If you open yourself to social psychology's magic, we believe it will enrich the way you look at the world and the way you live in it.

SOCIAL
PSYCHOLOGY

Chapter 1

Introduction to Social Psychology

Chapter Outline

The task of the psychologist is to try to understand and predict human behavior. Different kinds of psychologists go about this in different ways, and in this book we will attempt to show you how social psychologists do it. Let's begin with a few examples of human behavior. Some of these might seem important; others might seem trivial; one or two might seem frightening. To a social psychologist, all of them are interesting. As you read these examples, try to think about how you would explain why what happened, happened.

1. In the predawn hours of June, 1981, the residents of a trendy neighborhood in Los Angeles heard desperate cries for help coming from a yellow house. "Please don't kill me!" screamed one woman. Other neighbors reported hearing tortured screams and cries for mercy. And yet, not one neighbor bothered to investigate or help in any way. No one even called the police. One woman, who lived two houses away, went out onto her balcony when she heard the screams, but went back into her house without doing anything. Twelve hours later, an acquaintance arrived at the yellow house, and discovered that four people had been brutally murdered. A fifth person was critically wounded, and spent those 12 hours lying in a bedroom, bleeding from her wounds, waiting in vain for just one neighbor to lift their finger and dial the police (*New York Times,* July 3, 1981).

Why do you think the neighbors failed to do anything after hearing the cries for help? Stop and think for a moment: What kinds of people are these neighbors? Would you like to have them as friends? If you had a small child, would you hire one of these neighbors as a baby-sitter?

2. A few years ago, one of our students, Sally, told us about the following incident. Several months after the election of 1992, Sally was watching TV with a few of her acquaintances. On the tube, President Clinton was making an important policy speech. It was the first time Sally had seen President Clinton in action since his election, and she was favorably impressed. There was a homey quality about

the president; Sally felt he was honest, sincere, and straightforward. As soon as the speech was over, her friend Melinda said, "Boy, what a phony—I wouldn't trust that guy with my dirty laundry, let alone the nation. No wonder they call him Slick Willie!" The others quickly chimed in, voicing their agreement. Sally felt uncomfortable, and was frankly puzzled. Finally, she mumbled, "Yeah, I guess he did come off as a bit insincere."

When people view violence on the street, why are most reluctant to help—or even to call 911?

What do you suppose was going on in Sally's mind? Did she actually come to see President Clinton in a new light, or was she simply trying to go along in order to get along?

3.   We have a friend whom we will call Oscar. Oscar is a middle-aged executive in a computer software company. As a student, Oscar had attended a large state university in the Midwest, where he was a member of a fraternity we will call Delta Nu. He remembers having gone through a severe and somewhat scary hazing ritual in order to become a member but believes it was well worth it. Although he had been terribly frightened by the hazing, he loved his fraternity brothers and was proud to be a member of Delta Nu—easily the best of all fraternities. A few years ago, his son, Sam, was about to enroll in the same university; naturally, Oscar urged Sam to pledge Delta Nu: "It's a great fraternity—always attracts a wonderful bunch of fellows. You'll really love it." Sam did in fact pledge Delta Nu and was accepted. Oscar was relieved to learn that Sam was not required to undergo a severe initiation in order to become a member; times had changed, and hazing was now forbidden. When Sam came home for Christmas break, Oscar asked him how he liked the fraternity. "It's all right, I guess," he said, "but most of my friends are outside the fraternity." Oscar was astonished.

How is it that Oscar had been so enamored of his fraternity brothers and Sam wasn't? Had the standards of old Delta Nu slipped? Was the fraternity now admitting a less desirable group of young men than in Oscar's day? Or was it just one of those inexplicable things? What do you think?

4.   In the mid–1970s, several hundred members of the Peoples Temple, a California-based religious cult, immigrated to Guyana under the guidance of their leader, the Reverend Jim Jones. Their aim was to form a model interracial community, called Jonestown, based on "love, hard work, and spiritual enlightenment." In November 1978, Congressman Leo Ryan of California flew to Jonestown to investigate reports that some of the members were being held against their will. He visited the commune and found that several residents wanted to return with him to the United States. Reverend Jones agreed they could leave, but as Ryan was boarding a plane, he and several other members of his party were shot and killed by a member of the Peoples Temple, apparently on Jones's orders. On hearing that several members of Ryan's party had escaped, Jones grew despondent and began to speak over the public address system about the beauty of dying and the certainty that everyone would meet again in another place. The residents lined up at a pavilion in front of a vat containing a mixture of Kool-Aid and cyanide. According to a survivor, almost all of the residents drank willingly of the deadly solution. At least 80 babies and infants were given the poison by their parents, who then drank it themselves. More than 800 people died, including Reverend Jones.

How is it that people could agree to kill themselves and their own children? Were they crazy? Were they under some kind of hypnotic spell? How would you explain it?

Why did the Los Angeles residents ignore the screams coming from the yellow house, when they might have averted a tragedy? Why did Sally change her opinion about the sincerity of the new president and bring it into line with her acquaintances' opinion? Why did Oscar like his frat brothers so much more than Sam did? And how could large numbers of people be induced to kill their own children and themselves in Jonestown? In this chapter, we will consider what these examples have in common and why they are of interest to social psychologists.

What Is Social Psychology?

Social psychology is about what goes on in the hearts and minds of human beings. Although our examples differ widely, they have one thing in common: The phenomenon called social influence. In one way or another, people's thoughts, feelings, or behaviors were influenced by other people. This is the central topic of **social psychology**, which we can define as the scientific study of the way in which people's thoughts, feelings, and behaviors are influenced by the real or imagined presence of other people (Allport, 1985). But what exactly do we mean by "influenced"? The kinds of examples that probably first come to the reader's mind are direct attempts at persuasion, whereby one person deliberately tries to change someone else's behavior. This is what happens in an advertising campaign, when sophisticated techniques are employed to get us to buy a particular brand of toothpaste or laundry detergent, or just prior to an election, when similar techniques are used to get us to vote for a particular political candidate. Direct attempts at persuasion also occur when our friends try to get us to do something we don't really want to do ("Come on, have another shot of bourbon—everyone is doing it") or when the school-yard bully uses force or threats to get smaller, less aggressive kids to part with their lunch money or homework.

These direct social influence attempts form a major part of social psychology and will be discussed in our later chapters on conformity, attitudes, and group processes. To the social psychologist, however, social influence is broader than attempts by one person to change another person's behavior. First, not only our behavior but also our thoughts and feelings are influenced by others. Second, social influence takes on many forms other than deliberate attempts by others to modify our behavior. As noted earlier, people are often influenced by the imagined or implied presence of others.

Even when we are not in the physical presence of other people, we are still influenced by them; thus, in a sense we carry our mothers, fathers, friends, and teachers around with us, as we attempt to make decisions that would make them proud of us. On a still subtler level, each of us is immersed in a social and cultural context. Social psychologists are interested in studying how and why our thoughts, feelings, and behaviors are shaped by the entire social environment—broadly defined—and what happens when one of these influences comes into conflict with another one. For example, when young people go to college, most of them occasionally find themselves in conflict between the beliefs and values they learned at home and the beliefs and values their professors or peers are expressing. When this occurs, how do you handle it?

As we will see in a moment, other disciplines, like anthropology and sociology, are also interested in how people are influenced by their social environment. Social psychology is distinct, however, in several respects. First, it is concerned not with social situations in any objective sense but with how people are influenced by their interpretation, or **construal**, of the social environment. This means that to understand how a person is influenced by the social environment, it is, social psychologists insist, more important to understand how that person perceives, comprehends, or interprets the environment than it is to understand the objective environment (Lewin, 1943).

Suppose, for example, that Jason is a shy high school student who admires Debbie from afar. As a budding social psychologist, you have the job of predicting whether or not Jason will ask Debbie to the senior prom. One way you might do this is to observe Debbie's objective behavior toward Jason. Does she pay

social psychology: the scientific study of the way in which people's thoughts, feelings, and behaviors are influenced by the real or imagined presence of other people

We are by all odds the most persistently and obsessively social of all species, more dependent on each other than the famous social insects, and really, when you look at us, infinitely more imaginative and deft at social living.
—Lewis Thomas.

construal: the way in which people perceive, comprehend, and interpret the social world attention to him and smile a lot? If so, the casual observer might decide that Jason will ask her out. As a social psychologist, however, you are more interested in viewing Debbie's behavior through Jason's eyes—that is, in seeing how Jason interprets Debbie's behavior. If she smiles at him, does he construe this as mere politeness, the kind of politeness she would extend to any nerd? Or does he view her smile as an encouraging sign, one that inspires him to gather the courage to ask her out? If she ignores him, does Jason figure that she's playing "hard to get"? Or does he take it as a sign that she's not interested in dating him? To predict Jason's behavior, it is not enough to know the details of Debbie's behavior; it is imperative to know how Jason interprets Debbie's behavior.

Given the importance placed on the way people interpret the social world, social psychologists pay special attention to the origins of these interpretations. For example, when construing their environment, are most people concerned with making an interpretation that places them in the most positive light (e.g., Jason believing "Debbie is going to the prom with Eric because she is trying to make me jealous") or with making the most accurate interpretation, even if it is unflattering (e.g., "Painful as it may be, I must admit that Debbie would rather go to the prom with a sea slug than with me")? A great deal of research in social psychology has addressed these and other determinants of people's thoughts and behaviors. We will expand on these determinants later in this chapter.

Needless to say, the importance of construals extends far beyond the saga of Jason and Debbie. Consider an additional, rather prominent example: In a murder trial like that involving O. J. Simpson, the prosecution may present evidence on DNA and hair and fiber samples it believes will have a decisive impact on the verdict. But no matter how powerful the evidence might be, the final verdict will always hinge on precisely how each member of the jury construes that evidence—and these construals may rest on a variety of events and perceptions that may or may not bear objective relevance to the matter at hand. For instance, during cross-examination did a key witness hesitate for a moment before answering, suggesting to some jurors that she might not be certain of her data? Or did some jurors consider her too remote, too arrogant, *too* certain of herself?

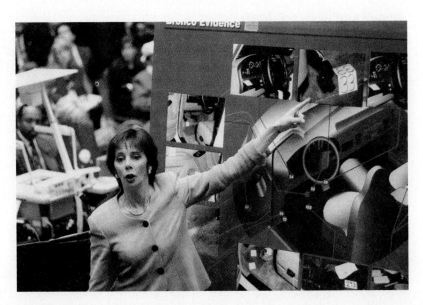

■ Although attorneys do their best to convince a jury, in the end the verdict will depend on how the individual jurors construe the evidence.

Another distinctive feature of social psychology is that it is a science that tests its assumptions, guesses, and ideas about human social behavior empirically, rather than by relying on folk wisdom, common sense, or an appeal to the opinions and insights of philosophers, novelists, political pundits, grandmothers, and others wise in the ways of human beings. Most students, when they think of an experimental science, think of the natural sciences, such as biology and chemistry—of men and women in white lab coats dissecting frogs or mixing chemicals in a beaker. The idea of social psychologists conducting carefully designed and well-controlled experiments on the behavior of human beings does not immediately conjure up available images. Yet in a very real sense, social psychology is no less an experimental science than biology or chemistry. But because, as experimenters, we social psychologists are trying to predict the behavior of highly complex, sophisticated organisms, we are faced with a special array of challenges as we attempt to find answers to important questions—such as what causes aggression, prejudice, and attraction or why certain kinds of political ads work better than others. How experimental social psychologists respond to these challenges will be illustrated throughout this book and discussed in detail in Chapter 2.

We will spend most of this introductory chapter expanding on the issues raised in the above paragraphs—of what social psychology is and how it is distinct from other, related disciplines. A good place to begin is with what social psychology is not.

Social Psychology Compared to Folk Wisdom and Philosophy

Let's take another look at the examples at the beginning of this chapter. Why did people behave the way they did? One way to answer this question might be simply to ask them. We could question the residents in Los Angeles about why they didn't call the police, and ask Sally why she changed her opinion of Bill Clinton. The problem with this approach is that people are not always aware of the origins of their own responses (Nisbett & Wilson, 1977). It is unlikely that the neighbors know exactly why they went back to sleep without calling the police or that Sally knows why she changed her mind about the president.

Folk Wisdom.   Alternatively, we might rely on the wisdom of the ages and sages. Philosophers, journalists, social critics, and novelists might have a great many interesting things to say about these situations, and if they do not, our grandmothers probably do. Such wisdom is generally referred to as common sense. For example, when people fail to intervene in an emergency to help their fellow humans beings, as in the case of the Los Angeles residents who ignored the cries for help from the yellow house, common sense tells us that these people must have some flaw in their personalities—surely a normal, caring human being would take the small step of calling the police. Similarly, the mass suicide at Jonestown received considerable media attention, and explanations of it ranged from an analysis of the so-called diabolic, messianic personal power of Jim Jones to speculation that the people who were attracted to his cult must have been disturbed, self-destructive individuals. These speculations, because they ignore the power of the situation, were almost certainly incorrect—or, at the very least, oversimplified.

Unfortunately, because so-called common sense turns out to be oversimplified, we tend not to learn from previous incidents. For example, in this decade the followers of cult leader David Koresh set fire to their own compound in Waco,

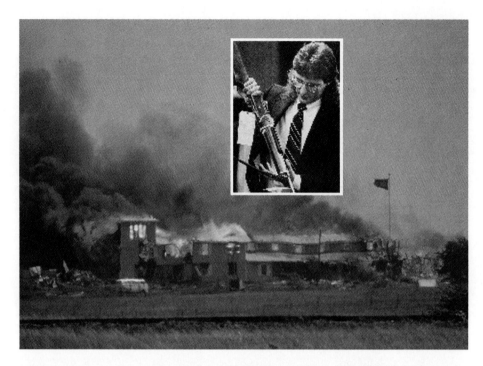

■ Why would any reasonable person blindly follow someone claiming to be Jesus Christ, give up personal freedoms, allow the leader to have sex with her 10-year-old daughter, and dictate which personal relationships will continue? While it may be easy to dismiss the followers of a cult leader like David Koresh as foolish, such oversimplifications and denial of the power of social influence can lead us to blame the victims.

Texas, resulting in the death of 86 people, including several children. In the aftermath of that conflagration, the general population was just as confused as it had been following the Jonestown suicides. It is very difficult for most people to fully grasp just how powerful a cult can be in affecting the hearts and minds of relatively normal people. Accordingly, as in the aftermath of the Jonestown tragedy, the general population—including the U.S. Congress—was eager to find someone to blame for Waco. Some were quick to blame the victims themselves; others focused on the impatience of the FBI, the poor judgment of Janet Reno, or the inadequate leadership of President Clinton. Fixing blame may make us feel better by temporarily assuaging our confusion and may therefore produce some short-term relief in the aftermath of perplexing events—but it is no substitute for understanding the complexities of the situations that produced those events.

Don't get us wrong. We are not opposed to folk wisdom. Far from it; we are convinced that a great deal can be learned about social behavior from journalists, social critics, novelists, and grandmothers—and in this book we will quote liberally from all these sources (with the possible exception of our grandmothers!). There is, however, at least one problem with full reliance on such sources: More often than not, they disagree with one another, and there is no easy way of determining which of them is correct. Consider what folk wisdom has to say about the factors that influence how much we like other people: On the one hand, we know that "birds of a feather flock together," and, with a little effort, each of us could come up with lots of examples where indeed we liked and hung around with people who shared our backgrounds and interests. But then again, folk wisdom also tells us that "opposites attract," and, if we tried, we could also come up with examples where people with different backgrounds and interests did attract us. Which is it?

Similarly, are we to believe that "out of sight is out of mind" or that "absence makes the heart grow fonder," that "haste makes waste" or that "he who hesitates is lost"? And who is to say whether the Jonestown massacre occurred because (a) Reverend Jones succeeded in attracting the kinds of people who were psychologically depressed to begin with; (b) only people with self-destructive tendencies join cults; (c) Jones was such a powerful, messianic, charismatic figure that virtually anyone—even strong, nondepressed individuals like you or us—would have succumbed to his influence; (d) people cut off from society are particularly vulnerable to social influence; (e) all of the above; or (f) none of the above?

Philosophy.   Instead of relying on folk wisdom and adages, perhaps we should turn to philosophers and other great thinkers to answer questions about human nature and the effects of social influence. Throughout the history of psychology, philosophy has been a source of vast insight about human nature. Today there are many exciting examples of philosophers joining with psychologists to tackle such important psychological questions as what the nature of consciousness is (e.g., Dennett, 1991) and how people form beliefs about the social world (e.g., Gilbert, 1991). Sometimes, however, even great thinkers find themselves in disagreement with one another; when this occurs, how is one to know who is right? Are there some situations where philosopher A might be right and other conditions where philosopher B might be right? How would you determine this?

We social psychologists address many of the same questions that philosophers and other purveyors of wisdom do, but we attempt to look at these questions scientifically. Just as a physicist performs experiments to test hypotheses about the nature of the physical world, the social psychologist performs experiments to test hypotheses about the nature of the social world. The major reason we have conflicting philosophical positions and conflicting folk aphorisms is that the world is a complicated place—and apparently small differences in the situation might make for different effects. For example, if we look at the folk wisdom about the kinds of people we like and the relationship between absence and liking, we would suggest that, almost certainly, there are some conditions under which birds of a feather do flock together and other conditions under which opposites do attract; similarly, there are some conditions under which absence does make the heart grow fonder and others under which out of sight does mean out of mind. So both can be true. Good enough? Not really, for if you really want to understand human behavior, knowing that both *can* be true is not sufficient. One of the tasks of the social psychologist is to design experiments sophisticated enough to demonstrate the specific situations under which one or the other applies. This enriches our understanding of human nature and allows us to make accurate predictions once we know the key aspects of the prevailing situation. In Chapter 2, we will discuss in more detail the scientific methods social psychologists use.

Social Psychology Compared to Other Social Sciences

Social psychology's interest in social behavior is shared by several other disciplines in the social sciences, including sociology, economics, and political science. Each of these disciplines is concerned with the influence of social and societal factors on human behavior. There are important differences, however, between social psychology and the other social sciences, most notably in their level of analysis. Social psychology is a branch of psychology and as such is rooted in an interest in individual human beings, with an emphasis on the psychological processes going on in their hearts and minds. For example, to understand why people intentionally hurt one another, the social psychologist focuses on the psychological processes that trigger aggression. To what extent is aggression preceded by a state of frustration? Is frustration necessary? If people are feeling frustrated, under what conditions will they vent their frustration with an overt, aggressive act? What factors might preclude an aggressive response by a frustrated individual? Besides frustration, what other factors might cause aggression? (We will address these questions in Chapter 12.)

Other social sciences are more concerned with broad societal, economic, political, and historical factors that influence human behavior. Sociology, for example, is concerned with such topics as social class, social structure, and social institutions. It goes without saying that, because society is made up of collections of people, some overlap is bound to exist between the domains of sociology and those of social psychology. The major difference is this: Sociology, rather than focusing on the psychology of the individual, tends toward a more macro focus—that of society at large. Although sociologists, like social psychologists, are interested in aggressive behavior, sociologists are more likely to be concerned with why a particular society produces different levels and types of aggression in its members. Why, for example, is the murder rate in the United States so much higher than in Canada? Within the United States, why is the murder rate higher in some social classes than in others? How do changes in society relate to changes in aggressive behavior?

The difference between social psychology and other social sciences in level of analysis reflects another difference between the disciplines—namely, in what they are trying to explain. The goal of social psychology is to identify universal properties of human nature that make everyone—regardless of social class or culture—susceptible to social influence. The laws governing the relationship between frustration and aggression, for example, are hypothesized to be true of most people in most places, not just members of one social class, age-group, or race. Social psychology is a young science that, until recently, has developed mostly in the United States; thus, many of its findings have not yet been tested in other cultures to see if they are indeed universal. Nonetheless, our goal as social psychologists is to come up with such laws. And increasingly, as methods and theories developed by American social psychologists are adopted by European, Asian, African, Middle Eastern, and South American social psychologists, we are learning more about the extent to which these laws are universal. This type of cultural expansion is extremely valuable because it sharpens theories, either by demonstrating their universality or by leading us to discover additional variables whose incorporation will ultimately help us make more accurate predictions of human social behavior. We will encounter several examples of such cross-cultural research in subsequent chapters.

Social Psychology Compared to Personality Psychology

Within the field of psychology are other disciplines that, like social psychology, are interested in studying individuals and why they do what they do; paramount among these is personality psychology. Because personality psychology and social psychology have so much in common, it might be helpful if we try to specify how social psychology and personality psychology differ in their approach and concerns.

If you are like most people, when you read the examples presented at the beginning of this chapter and began to think about how those events might have come about, your first thoughts were about the strengths, weaknesses, flaws, and quirks of the personalities of the individuals involved. When people behave in interesting or unusual ways, it is natural to try to pinpoint what aspects of their personalities led them to respond as they did. Why did the Los Angeles residents fail to call the police when they heard the cries for help? Most of us tend to assume that they possessed some personality flaw or quirk that made them reluctant to respond.

What might these be? Some people are leaders and others are followers; some people are bold and others are timid; some people are public-spirited and others are selfish. That's the way it goes. Think back: How did you answer the question about whether you would want any of these people as a friend or a baby-sitter?

Personality psychologists generally focus their attention on **individual differences** as explanations of social behavior. For example, to explain why the people at Jonestown ended their own lives and those of their children by drinking poison, it seems natural to point to their personalities. Perhaps they were all "conformist types" or weak-willed; maybe they were even psychotic. Yet, although this approach might add something to our understanding of human behavior, social psychologists are convinced that explaining behavior primarily in terms of personality factors can be superficial in that it leads to a serious underestimation of the role played by a principal source of human behavior—social influence. In this context, it is important to bear in mind that it was not just a handful of people who committed suicide at Jonestown but almost 100 percent of the people in the village. While it is conceivable that they were all psychotic, this is highly improbable. If we want a deeper, richer, more thorough explanation of this tragic event, we need to understand what kind of power and influence a charismatic figure like Jim Jones possesses, and what qualities of human beings *in general* make people susceptible to such influence (see Table 1.1).

These two different approaches can best be illustrated by focusing on a more mundane example. Suppose you stop at a roadside restaurant for a cup of coffee and a piece of pie. The waitress comes over to take your order, but you are having

individual differences: the aspects of people's personalities that make them different from other people

Table 1.1

Social psychology compared to related disciplines.		
Sociology	**Social Psychology**	**Personality Psychology**
Provides general laws and theories about societies, not individuals.	Studies the psychological processes people have in common with one another that make them susceptible to social influence.	Studies the characteristics that make individuals unique and different from one another.

a hard time deciding which kind of pie to order. While you are hesitating, the waitress impatiently taps her pen against her order book, rolls her eyes toward the ceiling, scowls at you, and finally snaps, "Hey, I haven't got all day, you know!"

What do you conclude about this event? When faced with such a situation, most people would conclude that the waitress is a nasty or unpleasant person. But suppose we were to tell you that she is a single parent and was kept awake all night by the moaning of her youngest child, who has a painful terminal illness; that her car broke down on her way to work and she has no idea where she will find the money to have it repaired; that when she finally arrived at the restaurant, she learned that her coworker was too drunk to work, requiring her to cover twice the usual number of tables; and that the short-order cook keeps screaming at her because she is not picking up the orders fast enough to please him. Given all that information, you might want to revise your judgment and conclude that she is not necessarily a nasty person—just an ordinary person under enormous stress. But the fact remains that, when trying to account for a person's behavior in a complex situation, the overwhelming majority of people will jump to the conclusion that it had a lot to do with the personality of the individual involved. And this fact—that we often fail to take the situation into account—is important to a social psychologist, for it has a profound impact on how human beings relate to one another. Specifically, the way you relate to the waitress is bound to be affected by how you interpret her behavior toward you.

In sum, to explain social behavior, social psychology is located between its closest cousins, sociology and personality psychology. It shares with sociology an interest in situational and societal influences on behavior but focuses more on the psychological makeup of individuals that renders people susceptible to social influence. It shares with personality psychology an emphasis on the psychology of the individual, but rather than focusing on what makes people different from one another, it emphasizes the psychological processes shared by most people that make them susceptible to social influence.

Such an approach is interesting, of course, only to the extent that social influences actually do affect people's behavior in significant ways. If everyone went on his or her merry or unmerry way, uninfluenced by what other people were doing or thinking, then we would not need a science called social psychology to understand human behavior. It is clear, however, that people are influenced by each other. Nonetheless, the power and extent of this influence are not always obvious to the naked eye—as we shall see.

The Power of Social Influence

fundamental attribution error: the tendency to overestimate the extent to which people's behavior is due to internal, dispositional factors and to underestimate the role of situational factors

When trying to convince people that their behavior is greatly influenced by the social environment, the social psychologist is up against a formidable barrier: the inclination we all have for explaining people's behavior in terms of their personalities (e.g., the case of the waitress discussed above). This barrier has been discussed by several social psychologists, most notably Fritz Heider (1958), E. E. Jones (1979), and Lee Ross (1977). Ross refers to it as the **fundamental attribution error,** or the tendency to explain our own and other people's behavior entirely in terms of personality traits, thereby underestimating the power of social influence.

Because of this tendency to overlook the power of social influence, we, as authors of this book, are fully aware that we face an uphill battle. If you are like most people, when you first encounter the examples of social behavior your initial tendency will be to explain that behavior in terms of the personalities of the people involved. All we ask is that, while reading this book, you try to suspend judgment for a short time and consider the possibility that to understand why people do what they do, it is important to look closely at the nature of the social situation.

Underestimating the Power of Social Influence

Why do people tend to underestimate the power of social influence? There are a great many reasons; we will consider them in detail in Chapter 5. For now, it is important to point out that this tendency constitutes a bias that could lead to dysfunctional attitudes and behaviors; accordingly, it is a bias we should try to overcome. One of the major problems with this bias is that it produces a sense of false security. In a very real sense, by systematically underestimating the power of social influence we increase the risk of succumbing to it. For example, when trying to explain why people do repugnant or bizarre things, such as the people at Jonestown and Waco taking their own lives and those of their children, it is both tempting and comforting to write off the victims as flawed human beings. This gives the rest of us the feeling that it could never happen to us—thus increasing our personal vulnerability to social influence. Moreover, by failing to fully appreciate the power of the situation, we tend to oversimplify complex situations; oversimplification decreases our understanding of the causes of a great deal of human behavior. Among other things, this oversimplification can lead us to blame the victim, as in the Jonestown tragedy, in situations where the individual was overpowered by social forces that were difficult to resist.

Here is an example of the kind of oversimplification we are talking about. Imagine a situation in which people are playing a two-person game wherein each player must choose one of two strategies: They can play competitively, where they try to win as much money as possible and make sure their partner loses as much as possible, or they can play cooperatively, where they try to make sure both they and their partner win some money. We will discuss the details of this game in Chapter 9. For now, it is important to note only that there are these two basic strategies people can use when playing the game: competitive or cooperative. Now think about some of your friends. How do you think they would play this game?

Few people find this question hard to answer; we all have a feeling for the relative competitiveness of our friends. "Well," you might say, "I am certain that my friend Calvin, who is a cutthroat business major, would play this game more competitively than my friend Anna, who is a really caring, loving person." That is, we think of our friends' personalities and answer accordingly. We usually do not think much about the nature of the social situation when making our predictions.

But how accurate are such predictions? Should we think about the social situation? To find out, Lee Ross and Steven Samuels (1993) conducted the following experiment. First, they chose a group of students at Stanford University who were considered by the resident assistants in their dorm to be either especially cooperative or especially competitive. The researchers did this by describing the game to

> The head monkey at Paris puts on a traveller's cap, and all the monkeys in America do the same.
> –Henry David Thoreau, *Walden*, 1854

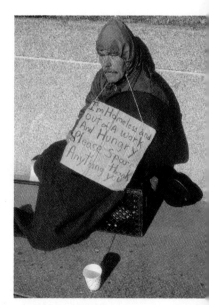

■ Is this person temporarily down on his luck or is he lazy or an addictive personality? How would this affect whether or not you give him money?

the resident assistants and asking them to think of students in their dormitories who would be most likely to adopt the competitive or cooperative strategy. As expected, the resident assistants had no trouble thinking of students who fit each category.

Next, Ross and Samuels invited these students to play the game in a psychology experiment. There was one added twist: The researchers varied a seemingly minor aspect of the social situation—namely, what the game was called. They told half the participants that the name of the game was the Wall Street Game and half that it was the Community Game. Everything else about the game was identical. Thus, people who were judged as either competitive or cooperative played a game that was called either the Wall Street or the Community Game, resulting in four conditions. What do you think happened? How would your friends play this game?

Again, most of us go through life assuming that what really counts is an individual's personality—not something so trivial as what a game is called. Some people seem competitive by nature and would thus relish the opportunity to go head to head with a fellow student. Others seem much more cooperative and would thus achieve the most satisfaction by making sure no one lost too much money and no one's feelings were hurt. Right? Not so fast! As seen in Figure 1.1, even so trivial an aspect of the situation as the name of the game made a tremendous difference in how people behaved. When it was called the Wall Street Game, approximately two-thirds of the people responded competitively, whereas when it was called the Community Game, only a third of the people responded competitively. The name of the game conveyed strong social norms about what kind of behavior was appropriate in this situation, and, as we will see in Chapter 7, social norms can shape people's behaviors in powerful ways.

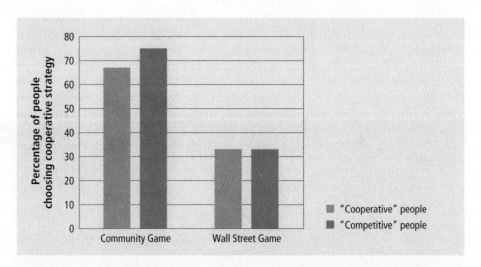

FIGURE 1.1 What influences how cooperative people will be—their personalities or the nature of the social situation? ■ Ross and Samuels (1993) found that college students' personalities, as rated by the resident assistants in their dormitories, did not determine how cooperative or competitive they were in a laboratory game. The name of the game—whether it was called the Wall Street Game or the Community Game—did, however, make a tremendous difference. Such seemingly minor aspects of the social situation can have powerful effects on people's behavior, overwhelming the differences in their personalities. (Adapted from Ross & Samuels, 1993)

In this situation, a student's personality made no measurable difference in how he or she behaved. The students labeled "competitive" were no more likely to adopt the competitive strategy than those labeled "cooperative" were. This pattern of results is one we will encounter frequently in this book: Seemingly minor aspects of the social situation can have powerful effects, overwhelming the differences in people's personalities (Ross & Ward, 1996). This is not to say that personality differences do not exist or are unimportant; they do exist and frequently are of great importance. But we have learned that certain social and environmental situations are so powerful that they have dramatic effects on almost everyone. And this is the domain of the social psychologist.

The Power of Subjective Situations: A Brief History of an Idea

To summarize, the social situation often has surprising and profound effects on human behavior. But what exactly do we mean by the social situation? One strategy for defining it would be to specify the objective properties of the situation, such as how rewarding it is to people, and then document the behaviors that follow from these objective properties.

Behaviorism.   This was the approach taken by **behaviorism,** a school of thought that dominated American psychology in the first half of this century. Behaviorism grew out of research on the lower animals and attempted to show that all learning occurs through *reinforcement*—that is, by associating positive or negative events in the environment with specific behaviors. For example, dogs come when they are called because they have learned that compliance is followed by positive reinforcement (e.g., food or fondling). Psychologists in this tradition, such as John Watson (1924) and B. F. Skinner (1938), suggested that all of human behavior could be understood by examining the rewards and punishments in the organism's environment and that there was no need to study such subjective states as thinking and feeling. Thus, to understand the behavior of the Los Angeles residents who ignored their neighbor's predawn cries for help, a behaviorist would analyze the situation to see what factors were inhibiting any attempts to help. Behaviorists did not use concepts and terms like *cognition, thinking,* and *feeling,* because these were considered too vague and mentalistic and were not directly anchored to observable behavior.

behaviorism: a school of psychology maintaining that to understand human behavior, one need only consider the reinforcing properties of the environment—that is, how positive and negative events in the environment are associated with specific behaviors

Most contemporary social psychologists (including the authors of this book) have come to believe that, while the behaviorist approach has some merit, it is far too simplistic to provide a complete, accurate understanding of social behavior. Moreover, we have learned that, with a certain degree of ingenuity and attention to detail, it is possible for a scientist to be objective and precise even while working with so-called mentalistic concepts like cognition, thinking, and feeling.

In addition, we have learned that social behavior cannot fully be understood by confining our observations to the physical properties of a situation. Instead, we must look at the situation from the viewpoint of the people in it, to see how they construe the world around them (Griffin & Ross, 1991; Ross & Nisbett, 1991). As you know, by construe we mean not what is objectively out there but what human beings make of what's out there. For example, if a person approaches us, slaps us on the back, and asks us how we are feeling, we might construe the meaning differently, depending on whether the question is asked by a close friend of ours who is deeply concerned that we might be working too hard, a casual acquaintance simply passing the time of day, or an automobile salesperson intending to sell us a used car—even if the question is worded the same and asked in the same tone of voice. It is unlikely that, responding to the salesperson's question, we will begin a detailed description of the pains we've been having in our kidney.

Gestalt Psychology.   This emphasis we place on construal has its roots in an approach called **Gestalt psychology.** Initially proposed as a theory of how people perceive the physical word, Gestalt psychology holds that we should study the subjective way in which an object appears in people's minds (the *gestalt*, or whole), rather than the way in which the objective, physical attributes of the object combine. For example, one way to try to understand how people perceive a painting would be to break it down into its individual elements, such as the exact amounts of primary colors applied to the different parts of the canvas, the types of brush strokes used to apply the colors, and the different geometric shapes they form, and to attempt to determine how these elements are combined by the perceiver to form an overall image of the painting. According to Gestalt psychologists, however, it is impossible to understand the way in which an object is perceived simply by studying these building blocks of perception. The whole is different from the sum of its parts. One must focus on the phenomenology of the perceiver—that is, on how an object appears to people—instead of on the individual elements of the objective stimulus.

The Gestalt approach was formulated in Germany in the first part of this century by Kurt Koffka, Wolfgang Kohler, Max Wertheimer, and their students and colleagues. In the late 1930s, several of these psychologists immigrated to the United States to escape the Nazi regime and subsequently had such a major influence on American psychology that one astute observer remarked, "If I were required to name the one person who has had the greatest impact on the field, it would have to be Adolf Hitler" (Cartwright, 1979, p. 84).

Among these was Kurt Lewin, generally considered to be the founding father of modern experimental social psychology. As a young German-Jewish professor, Lewin directly experienced the intolerance for cultural diversity rampant in that country in the 1930s. This experience not only had a major impact on his own thinking but, once he came to America, helped shape American social psychology and directed it toward a deep and abiding interest in the exploration of causes and cures of prejudice and ethnic stereotyping.

As a theorist, Lewin took the bold step of applying Gestalt principles beyond the perception of objects to social perception—how people perceive other people and their motives, intentions, and behaviors. Lewin was the first scientist to fully realize the importance of taking the perspective of the people in any social situation to see how they construe (e.g., perceive, interpret, distort) this social environment. Social psychologists soon began to focus on the importance of considering subjective situations (how they are construed by people). These early social psychologists and their key statements are presented on the following pages.

Such construals can be rather simple, as in the example of the question "How are you feeling?" discussed earlier. They can also be remarkably complex. For example, suppose Maria gives Shawn a kiss on the cheek at the end of their first date. How will Shawn respond to the kiss? We would say that it depends on how he construes the situation: Does he interpret it as a first step—a sign of awakening romantic interest on Maria's part? Or does he see it as an aloof, sisterly expression—a signal that Maria wants to be friends but nothing more? Or does

Gestalt psychology: a school of psychology stressing the importance of studying the subjective way in which an object appears in people's minds, rather than the objective, physical attributes of the object he see it as a sign that Maria is interested in him but wants things to go slow in their developing relationship?

Were Shawn to misconstrue the situation, he might commit a serious blunder; he might turn his back on what could have been the love of his life—or he might express passion inappropriately. In either case, we believe that the best strategy for understanding Shawn's reaction would be to find a way to determine Shawn's construal of Maria's behavior, rather than to dissect the objective nature of the kiss itself (its length, degree of pressure, etc.). But how are these construals formed? Stay tuned.

Where Construals Come From: Basic Human Motives

How will Shawn determine why Maria kissed him? If it is true that subjective and not objective situations influence people, then we need to understand how people arrive at their subjective impressions of the world. What are people trying to accomplish when they interpret the social world? Again, we could address this question from the perspective of people's personalities. What is it about Shawn, including his upbringing, family background, and unique experiences, that makes him view the world the way he does? As we have seen, such a focus on individual differences in people's personalities, while valuable, misses what is usually of far greater importance: the effects of the social situation on people. And to understand these effects, we need to understand the fundamental laws of human nature, common to all, that explain why we construe the social world the way we do.

■ The great theorists emphasized that to predict social behavior, you have to consider how people construe (interpret, perceive) the world.

Fritz Heider—"Generally, a person reacts to what he thinks the other person is perceiving, feeling, and thinking, in addition to what the other person may be doing." (1958)

Leon Festinger—"The way I have always thought about it is that if the empirical world looks complicated, if people seem to react in bewilderingly different ways to similar forces, and if I cannot see the operation of universal underlying dynamics, then that is my fault. I have asked the wrong questions; I have, at a theoretical level, sliced up the world incorrectly. The underlying dynamics are there, and I have to find the theoretical apparatus that will enable me to reveal these uniformities."

Kurt Lewin—"If an individual sits in a room trusting that the ceiling will not come down, should only his 'subjective probability' be taken into account for predicting behavior or should we also consider the 'objective probability' of the ceiling's coming down as determined by engineers? To my mind, only the first has to be taken into account." (1943)

We human beings are complex organisms; at a given moment, myriad intersecting motives underlie our thoughts and behaviors. Over the years, social psychologists have found that two of these motives are of primary importance: the need to be as accurate as possible and the need to justify our thoughts and actions in order to feel good about ourselves.

As we go though life, much of the time each of these motives pulls us in the same direction. For example, suppose our parents' anniversary is coming up and we want to get them the perfect gift. If they are very different kinds of people with different interests and hobbies, getting the perfect gift—one that will delight both of them—requires a great deal of thought and sensitivity to a variety of subtle social cues. If we can achieve this, we not only will have seen the social world accurately but also will feel competent and good about ourselves. Often, however, we find ourselves in situations where these two motives tug us in opposite directions—where to see reality closely is to come to terms with the fact that we have behaved foolishly or immorally.

Leon Festinger, one of social psychology's most innovative theorists, was quick to realize that it is precisely when these two motives tug an individual in opposite directions that we can gain our most valuable insights into the workings of the human heart and mind. An example will clarify. Imagine you are the president of the United States and your country is engaged in a difficult and costly war in Southeast Asia. You have poured hundreds of billions of dollars into that war, and it has consumed tens of thousands of American lives as well as a great many more lives of innocent Vietnamese civilians. The war seems to be at a stalemate; no end is in sight. You frequently wake up in the middle of the night bathed in the cold sweat of conflict: On the one hand, you deplore all the carnage that is going on; on the other hand, you don't want to go down in history as the first American president to lose a war.

Some of your advisers tell you that they can see the light at the end of the tunnel—that if you intensify the bombing, the enemy will soon capitulate and the war will be over. This would be a great outcome for you; not only will you have succeeded in achieving your military and political aims, but history will consider you to have been a hero. Other advisers, however, believe that intensifying the bombing will result only in strengthening the enemy's resolve; they advise you to sue for peace (McNamara, 1995).

■ Social psychology focuses on how even intelligent and powerful individuals can make a grievous error when faced with conflicting advice on a monumental decision.

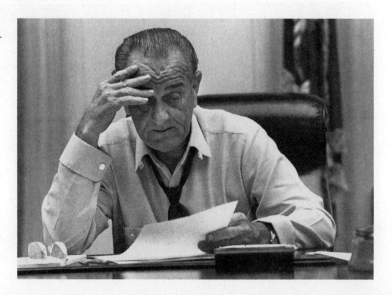

Which advisers are you likely to believe? As we shall see in Chapter 6, President Lyndon Johnson was faced with exactly this dilemma. Not surprisingly, he chose to believe those advisers who suggested that he escalate the war, for if he could succeed in winning the war he would justify his prior behavior as commander in chief, whereas if he withdrew from Vietnam he not only would go down in history as the first president to lose a war but also would have to justify the fact that all those lives and all that money had been spent in vain. This advice, however, proved to be erroneous. Increasing the bombing served only to strengthen the enemy's resolve, thereby needlessly prolonging the war. As this example illustrates, the need for self-justification can fly in the face of the need to be accurate—and can have catastrophic consequences.

Most social psychologists agree that both of these motives are important and that in many situations they can apply with varying degrees of strength. But each has a unique and interesting set of ramifications that is worth considering separately. Let's examine each of these two motives in more detail.

The Self-Esteem Approach: The Desire to Feel Good About Ourselves

Most people have a strong need to view themselves as decent, competent, likable, honorable human beings. The reason people view the world the way they do can often be traced to this underlying need to maintain a favorable image of themselves—in other words, to maintain high **self-esteem** (Aronson, 1992; Baumeister, 1993; Kunda, 1990; Pyszczynski & Greenberg, 1987; Thibodeau & Aronson, 1992). Given the choice between distorting the world in order to feel good about themselves and representing the world accurately, people often take the first option.

self-esteem: people's evaluations of their own self-worth—that is, the extent to which they view themselves as good, competent, and decent

Justifying Past Behavior.   For example, suppose a couple gets divorced after ten years of a marriage made difficult primarily by the husband's irrational jealousy. Suppose the husband blames the breakup of his marriage on the fact that his ex-wife was not sufficiently responsive or attentive to his needs, rather than admitting the truth: that his jealousy and overpossessiveness drove her away. His interpretation serves some purpose, in that it makes him feel better about himself—it is very difficult to own up to major deficiencies in ourselves, even when the cost is seeing the world inaccurately. The consequence of this distortion, of course, is that it decreases the probability of learning from experience; that is, in his next marriage the husband is likely to run into the same problems.

We do not mean to imply that people totally distort reality, denying the existence of all information that reflects badly on them; such extreme behavior is rare outside of mental institutions. Yet it is often possible for normal people like you and us to put a slightly different spin on the existing facts, one that puts us in the best possible light. Consider Roger; everybody knows someone like Roger. He's the guy whose shoes are almost always untied and who frequently has coffee stains on the front of his shirt or mustard stains around his lips. Most observers might consider Roger to be a slob, but Roger might see himself as casual and noncompulsive. Or, if Heather is playing basketball and has missed six or seven easy lay-ups in succession, her teammates might consider her to be untalented and might begin to think twice about passing the ball to her; on the other hand, Heather might simply feel that she hasn't yet gotten into her rhythm.

The fact that people distort their interpretation of reality so that they might feel better about themselves is not surprising, even to the most casual observer of human behavior. The ways in which this motive operates, however, are often startling—and shed a great deal of light on behavior that would otherwise be mystifying.

Suffering and Self-Justification.   Let's go back to one of our early scenarios: the case of Oscar and his son, Sam. Why was Sam less enamored of his fraternity brothers than Oscar had been when he was in college? You will recall that Oscar was quick to form the hypothesis that perhaps his fraternity was not attracting the kinds of wonderful people who were there when he was in college. This might be true. But we would assert that a far more compelling possibility involves the hazing itself. Specifically, we would contend that a major factor that increased Oscar's liking for his fraternity brothers was the unpleasant hazing ritual he underwent, a ritual Sam was able to avoid. That sounds a little strange. Why would something so unpleasant cause Oscar to like his fraternity? Didn't behavioristic psychology teach us that rewards, not punishments, make us like things associated with them? Quite so. But as we indicated earlier, in recent years social psychologists have discovered that this formulation is far too simplistic to account for human thinking and motivation. Unlike rats and pigeons, human beings have a need to justify their past behavior, and this need leads them to thoughts, feelings, and behaviors that don't always fit into the neat categories of the behaviorist.

Here's how it works. If Oscar goes through a severe hazing in order to become a member of the fraternity but later discovers unpleasant things about his fraternity brothers, he will feel like a fool: "Why did I go through all that pain and embarrassment in order to live in a house with a bunch of jerks? Only a moron would do a thing like that." In order to avoid feeling like a fool, he will try to justify his decision to undergo the hazing by distorting his interpretation of his fraternity experience. That is, he will try to put a positive spin on his experiences.

Suppose that, having gone through all that hazing, Oscar moves into the fraternity house and begins to experience things that, to an outside observer, are not very positive: The fraternity dues make a significant dent in Oscar's budget; the frequent parties are mindless and take a toll on the amount of studying he can do, and consequently his grades begin to suffer; most of the meals served in the house are only a small step up from dog chow. While an unmotivated observer—someone who didn't go through the hazing—might consider these experiences to be extremely negative, Oscar is motivated to see them differently; indeed, he considers them to be a small price to pay for the sense of brotherhood he feels toward his fraternity brothers. He focuses on the good parts of living in the fraternity, and he distorts or dismisses the bad parts. The result of all this self-justification is bound to make Oscar more kindly disposed toward the fraternity than Sam was, because Sam, not having gone through the hazing, had no need to justify his behavior and thus no need to see his fraternity experiences in a positive light. The end result? Oscar loved his fraternity; Sam did not.

Does this sound far-fetched? How do we know that the people in the fraternity were not objectively nicer when Oscar was a member than when Sam was a member? In a series of well-controlled laboratory experiments, social psychologists have investigated the phenomenon of hazing, holding constant everything in the situation—including the precise behavior of the fraternity members—except for the severity of the hazing students underwent in order to become members. These experiments demonstrated conclusively that the more unpleasant the procedure the participants underwent to get into a group, the better they liked the group—even though, objectively, the group members were the same people,

■ Our desire to maintain self-esteem can have surprising consequences. Does undergoing a dangerous or embarrassing fraternity hazing increase or decrease people's liking for the fraternity? Social psychological research demonstrates that when people volunteer to undergo a painful or embarrassing initiation in order to join a group, they need to justify the experience to avoid feeling foolish. One way they do this is to decide that the initiation was worth it, because the group is so wonderful.

behaving in the same manner (Aronson & Mills, 1959; Gerard & Mathewson, 1966). This phenomenon will be discussed more thoroughly in Chapter 6. The important points to remember here are that (a) human beings are motivated to maintain a positive picture of themselves, in part by justifying their past behavior, and (b) under certain specifiable conditions, this leads them to do things that at first glance might seem surprising or paradoxical—for example, to prefer those people and things for whom they have suffered to those people and things they associate with easiness and pleasure.

Again, we want to emphasize that the results of this research tradition should not be taken to mean that behaviorist theories are dead wrong; those theories explain some behavior very well (e.g., see our discussion in Chapter 10 of the research on social exchange theory). In our view, however, behavioristic approaches are inadequate to account for a huge subset of important attitudes and behaviors. This will become much clearer as you read on; in future chapters, we will try to specify the precise conditions under which one or the other set of principles is more likely to apply.

The Social Cognition Approach: The Need to Be Accurate

As mentioned earlier, even when people are bending the facts to cast themselves in as favorable a light as they can, they do not completely distort reality. It would not be very adaptive to live in a fantasy world, believing that the car speeding toward us as we step off the curb is really a mirage, or that our future spouse will be Denzel Washington or Kim Basinger, as soon as he or she gets done making movies and arrives at our doorstep. In fact, human beings are quite skilled at thinking, contemplating, and deducing. One of the major hallmarks of being human is the ability to reason, and, as a species, we have highly developed logical and computational abilities that are little short of amazing. We don't have to tell you about the extraordinary achievements people have made in such fields as theoretical physics, philosophy, and mathematics. Pinnacles of the sophisticated reasoning of human beings are occurring in our lifetimes—the invention of computers, the exploration of outer space, the conquering of many human diseases.

Moreover, on a more common (but perhaps more important) level, it is impossible to observe the cognitive development of a child without being awestruck—just think of the vast gains in knowledge and reasoning that occur in the first few years of life. In a relatively short time, we see our child transform from a squirming, helpless newborn, who can do little but eat, cry, and sleep, into a sophisticated, garrulous four-year-old, who can utter complex sentences, hatch diabolic plots to frustrate a younger sibling, and evoke consternation (and pride) in parents.

Social Cognition. Given the incredible cognitive abilities of our species, it makes sense that social psychologists, when formulating theories of social behavior, would take into consideration the way in which human beings think about the world. We call this the cognitive approach to social psychology, or **social cognition** (Fiske & Taylor, 1991; Markus & Zajonc, 1985; Nisbett & Ross, 1980). Those researchers who attempt to understand social behavior from the perspective of social cognition begin with the assumption that all people try to view the world as accurately as possible. Accordingly, human beings are viewed by researchers as amateur sleuths who are doing their best to understand and predict their social world.

But this is by no means as easy or as straightforward as it may seem. We human beings frequently run into problems because we almost never know all the facts we need in order to make the most accurate judgment of a given situation. Whether it is a relatively simple decision, like which breakfast cereal is the best combination of healthfulness and tastiness, or a slightly more complex decision, like our desire to buy the best car we can for under $15,000, or a much more complex decision, like choosing a marriage partner who will make us deliriously happy for the rest of our lives, it is almost never easy to gather all the relevant facts in advance. Moreover, we are making countless decisions every day; even if there was a way to gather all the facts for each decision, we simply lack the time or the stamina to do so.

social cognition: how people think about themselves and the social world; more specifically, how people select, interpret, remember, and use social information

■ Which of these cereals is better for you? The answer may surprise you (see the discussion in the text to find out). Even when we are trying to make accurate judgments about the social world, we often make mistakes.

Does this sound a bit overblown? Aren't most decisions fairly easy? Let's take a closer look. We will begin by asking you a simple question: Which breakfast cereal is better for you, Lucky Charms or 100% Natural from Quaker? If you are like most of our students, you answered "100% Natural from Quaker." After all, everybody knows that Lucky Charms is a kid's cereal, full of sugar and cute little marshmallows. Besides, there is a picture of a leprechaun on the box, for goodness' sake. And 100% Natural has a picture of raw wheat on the box, the box is the color of natural wheat (light tan), and doesn't natural mean "good for you"? If that is the way you reasoned, you have, understandably, –fallen into a common cognitive trap—you have generalized from the cover to the product. A careful reading of the ingredients (printed in small print on the package) will inform you that, although Lucky Charms has a bit more sugar in it than 100% Natural, the latter contains far more fat—so much so that the respected journal Consumer Reports has judged it to be less healthful than Lucky Charms. Things are not always what they appear to be; thus, coming up with an accurate picture of the social world is not always easy.

Expectations About the Social World.   To add to the difficulty, sometimes our expectations about the social world get in the way of perceiving it accurately and even change the nature of the social world. Imagine, for example, that you are an elementary school teacher dedicated to improving the lives of your students as best you can. You are aware at the beginning of the academic year how each student performed on standardized intelligence tests. Early in your career, you were pretty sure but not *entirely* sure that these tests could gauge each child's true potential. But after several years of teaching, you have gradually become absolutely certain that these tests are accurate. Why the change? Almost without fail, you have come to see that the kids who got high scores on these tests are the ones who did the best in your classroom, and the kids who got low scores simply couldn't "cut the mustard."

This scenario doesn't sound all that novel or surprising, except for one key fact: You might be very wrong about the validity of the intelligence tests. It might be that the tests weren't very accurate but that you unintentionally treated the kids with high scores and the kids with low scores differently, making it look like the tests were accurate. This is exactly what Robert Rosenthal and Lenore Jacobson (1968) found in their investigation of a phenomenon called the *self-fulfilling prophecy.* They first entered elementary school classrooms and administered a test. They then informed each teacher that, according to the test, a few specific students were bloomers—that is, they were about to take off and perform extremely well. In actuality, the test showed no such thing; the children labeled as bloomers were chosen by drawing names out of a hat and thus were no different, on average, from any of the other kids. Lo and behold, on returning to the classroom at the end of the school year Rosenthal and Jacobson found that the bloomers were performing extremely well. The mere fact that the teachers were led to expect these students to do well caused a reliable improvement in their performance.

How did this happen? Though this outcome seems almost magical, it is imbedded in an important aspect of human nature. If you were one of those teachers and were led to expect two or three specific students to perform well, you would be more likely to treat those students in special ways—such as paying more attention to them, listening to them with more respect, calling on them more frequently, encouraging them, and trying to teach them more difficult material. This in turn would almost certainly make these students feel happier, more respected, more motivated, and smarter, and—voilà!—a self-fulfilling prophecy. Thus, even when we are trying to perceive the social world as accurately as we can, there are many ways in which we can go wrong, ending up with the wrong impressions. We will see why—and the conditions under which social perception is accurate—in Chapters 3 and 4.

Other Motives

We want to reiterate what we stated earlier: The two major sources of construals we have emphasized here—the need to maintain a positive view of ourselves (the self-esteem approach) and the need to view the world accurately (the social cognition approach)—are the most important of our social motives, but they are certainly not the only motives influencing people's thoughts and behaviors. As noted earlier, we human beings are complex organisms, and under various conditions a variety of motives influence what we think, feel, and do. Biological drives such as hunger and thirst, of course, can be powerful motivators, especially under circumstances of extreme deprivation. At a more psychological level, we can be motivated by fear or by the promise of love, favors, and other rewards involving social exchange. These motives will be discussed at length in Chapters 10 and 11.

Still another significant motive is the need for control. Research has shown that people need to feel they exert some control over their environment (Langer, 1975; Seligman, 1975; Taylor, 1989; Thompson, 1981). When people experience a loss of control, such that they believe they have little or no influence over whether good or bad things happen to them, there are a number of important consequences; we will discuss these further along in this book.

Social Psychology and Social Problems

To recapitulate, social psychology can be defined as the scientific study of social influence. Social influence can best be understood by examining the basic human motives that produce the subjective views people form about their environment. It might have occurred to you to ask why we want to understand social influence in the first place. Who cares? And what difference does it make whether a behavior has its roots in the desire to be accurate or in the desire to bolster our self-esteem?

There are several answers to these questions. The most basic answer is simple: because we are curious. Social psychologists are fascinated by human social behavior and want to understand it on the deepest possible level. And in a sense, all of us are social psychologists. We all live in a social environment, and we all are more than mildly curious about such issues as how we become influenced, how we influence others, and why we fall in love with some people, dislike others, and are indifferent to still others.

Many social psychologists have another reason for studying the causes of social behavior—namely, to contribute to the solution of social problems. From the very beginnings of our young science, social psychologists have been keenly interested in such social problems as the reduction of hostility and prejudice and the increase of altruism and generosity. Contemporary social psychologists have continued this tradition and have broadened the issues of concern to include such

> Understanding does not cure evil, but it is a definite help, inasmuch as one can cope with a comprehensible darkness.
>
> –Carl Jung

■ Among the many kinds of relevant issues social psychologists investigate are these: (a) Does watching violence on TV produce violent behavior in youngsters? (b) Can Joe Camel make cigarette smoking appear attractive? (c) In trying to persuade people to donate organs, will a provocative, humorous appeal be more effective than a straight, no-nonsense appeal?

NEW FRIENDLY MARKET

some people need you inside them.

endeavors as inducing people to conserve natural resources like water and energy, educating people to practice safer sex in order to reduce the spread of AIDS, understanding the relationship between viewing violence on television and the violent behavior of television-watchers, developing effective negotiation strategies for the reduction of international conflict, and helping people adjust to life changes like the entry to college or the death of a loved one (Harris, 1986).

The ability to understand and explain complex and dysfunctional social behavior brings with it the challenge to change it. For example, when our government began to take the AIDS epidemic seriously, it mounted an advertising campaign that seemed intent on frightening people into practicing safer sex. This seems consistent with common sense: If you want people to do something they wouldn't ordinarily do, why not scare the daylights out of them?

This is certainly not a stupid idea. As we shall see in subsequent chapters, there are many dysfunctional acts (e.g., cigarette smoking, drunk driving) for which the induction of fear can and does motivate people to take rational, appropriate action to preserve their health (Levy-Leboyer, 1988; Wilson, Purdon, and Wallston, 1988). But based on years of systematic research on persuasion, social psychologists were quick to realize that, in the specific situation of AIDS, arousing fear would almost certainly not produce the desired effect for most people. The weight of the research evidence suggests that, where sexual behavior is involved, the situation becomes infinitely more murky. Specifically, most people do not want to be thinking about dying or contracting a painful illness while they are getting ready to have sex. Such thoughts can, to say the least, interfere with the romantic aspect of the situation. Moreover, most people do not enjoy using condoms, because they feel that interrupting the sexual act to put on a condom tends to destroy the mood. Given these considerations, when people have been exposed to frightening messages, instead of engaging in rational problem-solving behavior most tend to reduce that fear by engaging in denial ("It can't happen to me," "Surely none of my friends have AIDS," etc.).

The astute reader will see that the process of denial stems not from the desire to be accurate but from the desire to maintain one's self esteem. That is, if people can succeed in convincing themselves that their sexual partners do not have AIDS, then they can continue to enjoy unprotected sex while maintaining a reasonably good picture of themselves as a rational person. By understanding the conditions under which self-esteem maintenance prevails, social psychologists have been able to contribute important insights to AIDS education and prevention, as we shall see (Aronson, Fried, & Stone, 1991; Stone et al., 1994).

Throughout this book, we will examine many similar examples of the applications of social psychology. Likewise, throughout this book we will also discuss some of the underlying human motives and the characteristics of the social situation that produce significant social behaviors, with the assumption that, if we are interested in changing our own or other people's behavior, we must first know something about these fundamental causes. Although most of the studies discussed in these chapters are concerned with such fundamental causes, in the process they also address critical social problems, including the effects of the mass media on attitudes and behavior (Chapter 7), violence and aggression (Chapter 12), and prejudice (Chapter 13). For the benefit of the interested reader, we have also included three separate "modules" centering on the application of social psychology to contemporary issues involving health, the environment, and law. These are briefer and less detailed than regular chapters; the instructor may assign them at any time during the semester or may decide not to assign them at all, allowing that decision to depend on the curiosity of the individual student.

SUMMARY

People are constantly being influenced by other people. **Social psychology** is defined as the scientific study of the way in which people's thoughts, feelings, and behaviors are influenced by the real or imagined presence of other people. Social influence is often very powerful, usually outweighing and frequently overwhelming **individual differences** in people's personalities as determinants of human behavior. To appreciate this fact, we must try to avoid making the **fundamental attribution error**—the tendency to explain our own and others' behavior entirely in terms of personality traits, thus underestimating the power of social influence.

To appreciate the power of social influence, we must understand how people form **construals** of their social environment. We are not computerlike organisms who respond directly and mechanically to environmental stimuli; rather, we are complex human beings who perceive, think about, and sometimes distort information from our environment. By emphasizing the way in which people construe the social world, social psychology has its roots more in the tradition of **Gestalt psychology** than in that of **behaviorism.**

Although human behavior is complex and nonmechanical, it is not unfathomable. A person's construals of the world are rooted primarily in two fundamental motives: the desire to maintain **self-esteem** and the desire to form an accurate picture of oneself and the social world (the **social cognition** approach). Accordingly, to understand how we are influenced by our social environments we must understand how our hearts and minds do the perceiving, thinking, and distorting. Two major concepts in social psychology can thus be stated succinctly: (a) Social influence has a powerful impact on people, and (b) to understand the power of social influence, we must examine the motives that determine how people construe the social environment.

We also discussed another important point about social psychology: It is an empirical science. Social psychologists attempt to find answers to key questions about social influence by designing and conducting research, rather than by relying on common sense or the wisdom of the ages. In Chapter 2, we will discuss the scientific methods social psychologists use when conducting such research.

IF YOU ARE INTERESTED . . .

Aron, A., & Aron, E. (1992). *The heart of social psychology.* Lexington, MA: Lexington Books. A highly readable look behind the scenes at how eminent social psychologists view their discipline.

Festinger, L. (Ed.). (1980). *Retrospections on social psychology.* New York: Oxford University Press. A collection of articles by many of the most eminent scientists in the field of social psychology. Even though this book is more than a decade old, it remains an excellent source of articles about the origins of the field and its current research trends.

Jones, E. E. (1985). Major developments in social psychology during the past five decades. In G. Lindzey & E. Aronson (Eds.), *Handbook of social psychology* (3rd. ed., Vol. 1, pp. 47–107). New York: Random House. A thorough treatment of the history of social psychology from a leading researcher in the field. This chapter discusses the roots of the field, plots the changes in its emphases and trends, and details its intellectual history.

Ross, L., & Nisbett, R. E. (1991). *The person and the situation: Perspectives of social psychology.* New York: McGraw-Hill. An entertaining, insightful look at many of the ideas presented in this chapter, including the importance of considering people's construals of social situations and the ways in which those construals are often more powerful determinants of people's behavior than their personalities are.

Trading Places. This 1993 film stars Dan Aykroyd and Eddie Murphy as pawns in two millionaires' amateur experiment in social psychology. The film takes a light look at the power of social influence and the argument over nature versus nurture.

Chapter 2

Methodology: the Process of Doing Research

Chapter Outline

I love games. I think I could be very happy being a chess player or dealing with some other kinds of games. But I grew up in the Depression. It didn't seem one could survive on chess, and science is also a game. You have very strict ground rules in science and your ideas have to check out with the empirical world. That's very tough and also very fascinating.

—Leon Festinger, 1977

One of the most troubling and pressing social problems today, throughout the world, is violence. Newspaper headlines report murders, assaults, and rapes virtually every day, and local news broadcasts sometimes seem like little more than a recitation of the day's body count. Long-standing conflicts have erupted into war and destruction in many parts of the globe, such as the battles between the Serbs, Croatians, and Muslims in what used to be Yugoslavia. It is obviously of great importance to understand why violent behavior occurs and to find ways of reducing it. Social psychologists have conducted research on aggression and violence from a number of angles, and we will discuss the findings of these studies at several points (see especially Chapter 12). In this chapter, we will address how social psychologists do research, using studies on violence as an example. Once social psychologists decide on a topic of inquiry, such as violence, what tools do they have to unravel its causes?

One possible source of violence—particularly sexual violence against women—has been debated at length: pornography. Does exposure to pornography increase the likelihood that men will assault women? In 1985, the attorney general of the United States, Edwin Meese III, convened a commission to answer this question. This group, which became known as the Meese Commission, reported that pornography is a cause of rape and other violent crimes. Some current social critics have agreed with this conclusion. For example, Catharine MacKinnon (1993) has described horrendous crimes being committed by Serbs against Croatian and Muslim women, including rape, torture, and murder. She points to pornography as one cause of these crimes: "Pornography is the perfect preparation—motivator and instruction manual in one—for the sexual atrocities ordered in this genocide" (p. 28).

Several other experts, however, were quick to disagree with the conclusions of the Meese Commission, claiming that its findings were based more on political and moral concerns than on solid scientific evidence (Vance, 1986). In fact, the commission's conclusions were the opposite of those of the 1970 Presidential Commission on Obscenity and Pornography, which reported that pornography did not contribute significantly to sexual violence (Time, July 21, 1986). Thus, respected experts and social critics disagree on a question of fundamental importance. Who is right? How can we find out if exposure to pornography has negative effects? What sort of research

This is the area where Kitty Genovese was attacked, in full view of her neighbors. Why didn't anyone call the police?

methodologies might we use?

In addition to addressing important questions about the causes of violent behavior, we also need to find ways of stopping violence once it occurs. When will people who witness violent acts try to stop it? Though people might not intervene directly, out of fear for their own safety, we assume that most people will seek help in some fashion, such as by calling the police. It is because of this very assumption that people were so shocked by an incident that occurred in the early 1960s, in the Queens section of New York City. A woman named Kitty Genovese was attacked while walking to her car and brutally murdered in the alley of an apartment complex. The attack lasted 45 minutes. No fewer than 38 of the apartment residents admitted later that they had rushed to their windows after hearing Genovese's screams for help. However, not one of the bystanders attempted in any way to help her—none of them even bothered to telephone the police. As you might imagine, the Kitty Genovese murder received a great deal of publicity. Reporters, commentators, and pundits of all kinds came forward with their personal theories about why the bystanders had done nothing. The most popular explanation was that there is something dehumanizing about living in a metropolis that inevitably leads to apathy, indifference to human suffering, and lack of caring. The blame was laid on New York and New Yorkers; the general belief was that this kind of thing would not have happened in a small town, where people care more about each other (Rosenthal, 1964). Was big-city life the cause of the bystanders' behavior? Or was there some other explanation? Again, how can we find out?

In Chapter 1, we mentioned that it is insufficient to rely on personal beliefs, folk wisdom, or hope when answering questions about human behavior. Many personal observations are astute and accurate reflections of social reality, whereas others are far off the mark. To tell the difference, our observations must be translated into hypotheses that can be tested scientifically. In the case of pornography, respected experts disagree as to its effects, and scientific investigations are the true arbiter of such disputes.

You might think that folk wisdom is a more trustworthy source of social theory and explanation than personal experience. Based on the accumulated observations of many people in a culture over time, these beliefs are not as likely to be biased by one's personal beliefs or experiences. However, folk wisdom can be quite amusingly contradictory. Which best describes a long-distance romantic relationship—"absence makes the heart grow fonder" or "out of sight, out of mind"? Is it true that people are basically selfish and will ultimately put their own self-interest first, or are people basically altruistic, capable of self-sacrifice, and motivated to do well by others? You are probably thinking, "Well, it's both; both are true. It depends." And that is the point: Only by carefully identifying and studying the exact conditions that cause one of these contradictory sayings to be true can we tell that folk wisdom is useful or predictive.

The results of the experiments we will discuss will sometimes seem obvious, because the topic of social psychology is something with which we are all intimately familiar—namely, social behavior and social influence. Note that this fact separates social psychology from other sciences. When you read about an experiment in particle physics, for example, it is unlikely that the results will connect with your personal experiences and have a ring of familiarity to them. We don't know about you, but we have never thought, "Wow! That experiment on quarks was just like what happened to me while I was waiting for the bus yesterday," or "My grandmother always told me to watch out for the interaction of quarks, positrons, and antimatter." When reading about the results of a study on helping behavior, social influence, or aggression, however, it is quite common to think, "Aw, come on, I could have predicted that. That's the same thing that happened to me last Friday."

The thing to remember is that such findings can appear obvious because only in retrospect do most examples of human behavior seem to make sense and to have been easily predictable (Fischhoff, 1975). Given that much of folk wisdom is contradictory, the opposite finding of an experiment might have seemed just as obvious. The trick is to predict what will happen in an experiment before you know how it turned out. To illustrate what we mean when we say that not all obvious findings are easy to predict in advance, take the quiz displayed in Figure 2.1. Each answer is based on social psychological research that we will discuss later in this book. In our experience as teachers, we have found that few of our students get all the answers correct. Findings that seem obvious in retrospect may not be so easy to predict in advance.

Social psychology is an empirical science, with a well-developed set of methods to answer questions about social behavior, such as the ones about violence with which we began this chapter. These methods are of three types: the *observational method,* the *correlational method,* and the *experimental method.* Any of these methods could be used to explore a specific research question; each is a powerful tool in some ways and a weaker tool in others. The creativity in

SOCIAL PSYCHOLOGY QUIZ

1. Suppose an authority figure asks college students to administer near-lethal electric shocks to another student who has not harmed them in any way. What percentage of these students will agree to do it?

2. If you give children a reward for doing something they already enjoy doing, they will subsequently like that activity (a) more, (b) the same, or (c) less.

3. Seeing someone you admire do something rather clumsy or stupid, such as spilling a cup of coffee, will make you like him or her (a) more, (b) the same, or (c) less.

4. Repeated exposure to a stimulus, such as a person, a song, or a painting, will make you like it (a) more, (b) the same, or (c) less

5. You ask an acquaintance to do you a favor—for example, to lend you $10—and he or she agrees. As a result of doing you this favor, the person will probably like you (a) more, (b) the same, or (c) less.

6. True or false: It is most adaptive and beneficial to people's mental health to have a realistic view of the future, an accurate appraisal of their own abilities and traits, and an accurate view of how much control they have over their lives.

7. Suppose that a representative of a community organization knocks on people's doors and asks them to put a small sign in their window promoting auto safety and that most people agree to this request. A couple of weeks later, a different person from a different organization knocks on their doors and asks a much larger favor: to erect an unsightly billboard in their front yard, promoting a clean environment. Do you think that agreeing to the first, smaller request will (a) make people more likely to agree to the second request, (b) make people less likely to agree to the second request, or (c) have no effect on people's agreeing to the second request?

8. Suppose that two elementary school children, Mary and Bob, take an IQ test and Mary gets a higher score than Bob. Which of the following might have contributed to Mary's higher score? (a) On average, girls are smarter than boys; (b) IQ tests are biased so that girls do better than boys; (c) the children's teacher thought Mary was smarter than Bob, even though this is not true; or (d) the children's teacher thought Bob was smarter than Mary, so Mary tried hard to prove her wrong.

9. In public settings, (a) women touch men more, (b) men touch women more, or (c) there is no difference—men and women touch each other equally.

10. True or false: The more you pay people to make a speech against their own beliefs, the more they will change their minds and agree with the speech they made.

ANSWERS

1. In studies conducted by Stanley Milgram (1974), up to 65 percent of participants administered what they thought were near-lethal shocks to another subject. (In fact, no real shocks were administered.)
2. (c) Rewarding people for doing something they enjoy will typically make them like that activity less in the future (e.g., Lepper, Greene, & Nisbett, 1973).
3. (a) More (Aronson, Willerman, & Floyd, 1966).
4. (a) Under most circumstances, repeated exposure increases liking for a stimulus (Zajonc, 1968).
5. (a) More (Jecker & Landy, 1969).
6. False (Taylor & Brown, 1988).
7. (a) People will be more likely to agree to the second request (Freedman & Fraser, 1966).
8. (c) If teachers have a strong expectation about how well a student can do, they can unintentionally treat the child in a way that makes their expectation come true (Rosenthal & Jacobson, 1968).
9. (b) Men touch women more than vice versa (Henley, 1977).
10. False (Festinger & Carlsmith, 1959).

FIGURE 2.1 Social psychology quiz. ■ Take a moment to answer the questions above, each of which is based on social psychological research. Though the correct answers may seem obvious in retrospect, many are hard to guess in advance.

conducting social psychological research involves choosing the right method, maximizing its strengths, and minimizing its weaknesses.

In this chapter, we will discuss these methods in detail. We, the authors of this book, are not primarily textbook writers—we are social scientists who have done a great deal of experimental research in social psychology. As such, we will try to provide you with an understanding of both the joy and the difficulty of doing research. The joy comes in unraveling the clues about the causes of inter-esting and important social behaviors, just as a sleuth gradually unmasks the culprit in a murder mystery. Each of us finds it exhilarating that we have the tools to provide definitive answers to questions philosophers have debated for centuries. At the same time, as seasoned researchers, we have learned to temper this exhilaration with a heavy dose of humility, for the practical and ethical constraints involved in creating and conducting social psychological research are formidable.

Formulating Hypotheses and Theories

The starting point of research is an idea, or hypothesis, that the researcher wants to test. Thus, a good place to begin is with the origin of these hypotheses. There is a lore in science that brilliant insights come all of a sudden, as when Archimedes shouted "Eureka! I have found it!" when the solution to a problem flashed into his mind. Though such insights do sometimes occur suddenly, science is a cumulative process, and people often generate hypotheses from their previous theories and research.

Inspiration from Previous Theories and Research

Leon Festinger was dissatisfied with the ability of behaviorist theories to explain attitude change. He formulated a new approach—dissonance theory—that made specific predictions about when and how people would change their attitudes. As we will see in an upcoming chapter, other researchers were dissatisfied with Festinger's explanation of the results he obtained, and so they conducted further research to test other possible explanations. Social psychologists, like scientists in other disciplines, engage in a continual process of theory refinement: A theory is developed; specific hypotheses derived from that theory are tested; based on the results obtained, the theory is revised and new hypotheses are formulated.

Hypotheses Based on Personal Observations

Theory is not the only way to derive a new hypothesis in social psychology. Researchers often observe a phenomenon in everyday life that they find curious and interesting. These observations can stem from their own personal experience, from literature, or from current events. The researchers then construct a theory about *why* this phenomenon occurred and design a study to see if they are right.

For example, one of us was struck by a curious political phenomenon, lead-ing him to formulate a hypothesis about some of the antecedents of interpersonal attraction. In the early 1960s, Elliot Aronson happened to be glancing through *Time* magazine and was amazed to find that a Gallup poll showed that President John F. Kennedy's personal popularity had undergone a huge increase during the week. What made this startling was that this was the week following the disas-trous attempt by U.S.-sponsored forces to invade Cuba at the Bay of Pigs—known then and forever after as "the Bay of Pigs fiasco." Here was a president who admitted to being responsible for what at the time was considered to be one of our nation's most embarrassing blunders—and his popularity rating had soared. How could this be?

In 1961, John F. Kennedy's personal characteristics and accomplishments made him extraordinarily attractive. Aronson reasoned that Kennedy might have

seemed too wonderful, too talented, and too perfect for people to be able to identify with him; he might have seemed unapproachable. If this were the case, then
perhaps some indication of fallibility—like the blunder of the Bay of Pigs invasion—served to make him more human, more real, more approachable, and
hence more likable. To find out, Aronson conducted an experiment showing that
an attractive person is indeed liked more if he or she commits a blunder
(Aronson, Willerman, & Floyd, 1966).

As another example, consider the murder of Kitty Genovese that we
discussed earlier. As we saw, most people blamed her neighbors' failure to intervene on the apathy, indifference, and callousness that big-city life breeds. Two
social psychologists who taught at universities in New York, however, had a
different idea. Bibb Latané and John Darley got to talking one day about the
Genovese murder. Here is how Latané describes it:

> One evening after [a] downtown cocktail party, John Darley . . . came back with
> me to my 12th Street apartment for a drink. Our common complaint was the
> distressing tendency of acquaintances, on finding that we called ourselves social
> psychologists, to ask why New Yorkers were so apathetic. (Latané, 1987, p. 78)

Instead of focusing on "what was wrong with New Yorkers," Latané and Darley
thought it would be more interesting and more important to examine the social
situation in which Genovese's neighbors found themselves:

> We came up with the insight that perhaps what made the Genovese case so fasci-
> nating was itself what made it happen—namely, that not just one or two, but
> thirty-eight people had watched and done nothing. (Latané, 1987, p. 78)

The researchers had the hunch that, paradoxically, the more people who witness
an emergency, the less likely it is that any given individual will intervene.
Genovese's neighbors might have assumed that someone else had called the

■ Some research hypothe-
ses come from observa-
tions of everyday events.
When Elliot Aronson
observed that John F.
Kennedy's popularity went
up after he admitted
responsibility for the Bay
of Pigs fiasco, Aronson
conceived of the hypothe-
sis that very attractive
people will be liked more
after committing a blun-
der. This hypothesis was
confirmed in a social
psychological experiment
(Aronson, Willerman, &
Floyd, 1966).

police, a phenomenon Latané and Darley (1968) referred to as the *diffusion of responsibility*. Perhaps the bystanders would have been more likely to help had each thought he or she alone was witnessing the murder.

Once a researcher has a hypothesis, whether it comes from a theory, previous research, or an observation of everyday life, how can he or she tell if it is true? How could Latané and Darley tell whether the number of eyewitnesses in fact affects people's likelihood of helping a victim? In science, idle speculation will not do; the researcher must collect data to test his or her hypothesis. Let's look at how the observational method, the correlational method, and the experimental method are used to explore research hypotheses such as Latané and Darley's. These methods are summarized in Table 2.1.

Table 2.1

A summary of research methods.

Method	Questions Answered
1. Observational	Description: What is the nature of the phenomenon?
2. Correlational	Prediction: From knowing X, can we predict Y?
3. Experimental	Causality: Is variable X a cause of variable Y?

The Observational Method: Describing Social Behavior

As its name implies, the **observational method** involves watching people and seeing what they do. It goes without saying that observation is not the exclusive province of social scientists; it is practiced with great success by writers, filmmakers, and journalists interested in a particular social problem or the manner in which an institution works. For example, both Frederick Wiseman and Susan Sheehan spent a considerable amount of time in mental hospitals—not as patients but as observers—Wiseman (1967) recording his observations in a documentary film and Sheehan (1982) in writing. These works had a powerful impact and have been responsible for changing many people's views about the role of mental hospitals in our society.

Sometimes the observation can be in the form of a television camera, placed in a strategic location and used to record what people do in specific situations. For example, in the early days of television Allen Funt produced a show called *Candid Camera* in which people were confronted with strange situations—like a voice coming from inside a mailbox—while a hidden camera simply observed their reactions to the event. As interesting as these observations were, they are of limited value in helping us understand human behavior, because they were not done in a controlled, scientific manner. For example, for every interesting response to the "talking mailbox" that Funt recorded, there were almost certainly dozens of people who, suspecting it was a joke of some kind, simply shrugged and moved on. Since these latter behaviors do not make for interesting television view-

observational method: the technique whereby a researcher observes people and systematically records measurements of their behavior

You see, but you do not observe.
–Sir Arthur Conan Doyle, *The Adventures of Sherlock Holmes*, 1892

ing, Funt discarded them. There's nothing wrong with that—unless you want to draw conclusions about what people in general tend to do in such a situation. As interesting as excerpts from *Candid Camera* might be, they do not provide us with definitive answers about the intricacies of human behavior.

Systematic Observation

systematic observation: a form of the observational method whereby the observer is a trained social scientist who sets out to answer questions about a particular social phenomenon by observing and coding it according to a prearranged set of criteria

With **systematic observation,** the observers are trained social scientists who set out to answer questions about a particular social phenomenon by observing and coding it according to a prearranged set of criteria. This method varies according to the degree to which the observer actively participates in the scene. At one extreme, the observer neither participates nor intervenes in any way; instead, the observer is unobtrusive and tries to blend in with the scenery as much as possible. For example, a researcher interested in children's social behavior might stand outside a playground fence to observe children at play. In this case, the observer would be systematically looking for particular behaviors, such as aggression, cooperation, leadership, or assertiveness. These social behaviors are concretely defined before the observation begins. For instance, cooperation might be defined as a child sharing a toy with another or interacting with others to achieve a goal. The observer then notes when these behaviors occur and makes the appropriate check marks under the type of cooperation observed. If the researcher were interested in exploring possible sex and age differences in social behavior, he or she would also note the child's gender and age.

Participant Observation

participant observation: a form of systematic observation whereby the observer interacts with the people being observed, but tries not to alter the situation in any way

Some situations, by their very nature, require **participant observation.** In these situations, the observer interacts with the people being observed; however, the observer is careful not to alter the situation in any way because of his or her presence. For example, several years ago a group of people in the Midwest predicted that the world would come to an end in a violent cataclysm on a specific date. They also announced that they would be rescued in time by a spaceship that would land in their leader's backyard. Assuming that the end of the world was not imminent, Leon Festinger and his colleagues thought it would be interesting to observe this group closely and chronicle how they reacted when their beliefs and prophecy were disconfirmed (Festinger, Riecken, & Schachter, 1956). However, unlike the case when simply observing children at play, the researchers couldn't stand outside the fence and unobtrusively observe the subtleties of the group members' behavior. In order to monitor the hour-to-hour conversations of this group, the social psychologists found it necessary to join the group and pretend they too believed the world was about to end.

Archival Analysis

archival analysis: a form of systematic observation whereby the researcher observes social behavior by examining the accumulated documents, or archives, of a culture (e.g., diaries, novels, magazines, and newspapers)

A third form of the observational method is **archival analysis.** Much can be learned about social behavior by examining the accumulated documents, or archives, of a culture. For example, diaries, novels, suicide notes, popular music lyrics, television shows, movies, magazine and newspaper articles, and advertising all tell us a great deal about how a society views itself. As long as these written and pictorial traces of the culture have been saved and are available to the researcher, they can be coded on specific variables of interest. Much like in our earlier example, specific, well-defined categories are created and then applied to the archival source. **Interjudge reliability**—the level of agreement between two or more people who independently rate the material—is measured. For example, the content analysis of magazine advertisements should not reflect the subjective opinion of one individual, but should be an objective, scientific rating of what is actually in the source document, agreed on by anyone who analyzes the advertisements.

Archival analysis is a powerful form of observational research because it allows us to examine changes in social behavior over time and across different cultures. For example, Dane Archer, Bonita Iritani, Debra Kimes, and Michael Barrios (1983) and Robin Akert, Judy Chen, and Abigail Panter (1991) have coded portrait art and news and advertising photographs in print and television media for how they portray men and women—specifically, for how much of the pictorial image is devoted to the person's face. Their results indicate that across five centuries, across cultures, and across different forms of media, men are visually presented in a more close-up style (focusing on the head and face), whereas women are visually presented in a more long-shot style (focusing on the body). These researchers interpret their findings as indicating a subtle form of sex-role stereotyping: Men are being portrayed in a stronger style that emphasizes their intellectual achievements, whereas women are being portrayed in a weaker style that emphasizes their total physical appearance. Try doing your own archival analysis the next time you read a magazine or watch television. How are women portrayed differently from men?

Archival Analysis and Pornography.   As another example, think back to the question of the relationship between pornography and violence. One problem with addressing this question is in defining what pornography is. Most of us have come across sexually explicit material at one time or another—for example, the centerfold photographs in magazines like Playboy. Does this constitute pornography? What about nudity in the movies, or newspaper ads for lingerie

interjudge reliability: the level of agreement between two or more people who independently observe and code a set of data; by showing that two or more judges independently come up with the same observations, researchers ensure that the observations are not the subjective, distorted impressions of one individual

THE FAR SIDE   By GARY LARSON

"For crying out loud, gentlemen! That's us! Someone's installed the one-way mirror in backward!"

■ The hazards of the observational method.

that show scantily clad models? For decades, the nation as a whole has been struggling to define pornography; as Supreme Court Justice Potter Stewart put it, "I know it when I see it," but describing its exact content is not easy. What is being portrayed in American "adults-only" literature and photographs?

Archival analysis is a good tool for answering this question, for it enables researchers to describe the content of documents present in the culture—in this case, the photographs and fictional stories that represent currently available pornography in the marketplace. Don Smith (1976) was one of the first researchers to examine the content of pornography, specifically in adults-only fiction paperback books. He purposefully chose for his study locations that were far from the pornography centers of the country (e.g., cities in Nebraska and Tennessee), because he wanted to study the type of pornography that is typically and widely available. For the same reason, he studied books sold at newsstands and regular bookstores, and not those sold at special adults-only bookstores. His method involved choosing every fifth paperback on the shelves at one store in each of eight cities across five states. His content analysis covered many variables, such as how much sex was in the book, what kinds of sex occurred, and what the plots or themes were.

Smith (1976) found that the typical character in these books was young, single, white, physically attractive, and heterosexual. His data strikingly indicated that "the world of pornography is a male's world" (p. 21). Compared to the depictions of women, males' physical characteristics were given little attention; women's bodies were described in minute detail. The most disturbing finding of his study was that almost one-third of all the sex episodes coded in the books involved the use of force (physical, mental, or blackmail) by a male to make a female engage in unwanted sex. Thus, aggression against women was a major theme in these pornographic stories.

A second archival analysis, this time focusing on photographs, also found evidence of sexual violence against women. Park Dietz and Barbara Evans (1982) classified the cover photographs of magazines in adults-only bookstores in the pornography district of Forty-Second Street in New York City. They randomly selected four stores in this area and coded all the magazines that had one or more women on the cover. Their categories reflected the specific sexual acts depicted, the clothes and physical appearance of the women, and so forth. Whereas two people engaged in sexual activity was the most common type of cover photograph (37.3 percent of all covers), the second most common type portrayed bondage and domination (17.2 percent of covers), wherein a woman was shown bound with ropes, handcuffs, chains, shackles, constrictive garments, or other material. As Dietz and Evans (1982) describe this category:

■ Archival studies have shown that news and advertising photographs typically give prominence to men's faces and women's bodies.

> Gags, taped mouths, blindfolds, and hoods were also common. Torture is depicted through clothespins, clamps, and vises attached to the breasts or genitals, burning or dripping hot wax onto the skin, and extreme postures such as hanging by the wrists or ankles. Less frequently, a man is depicted threatening a woman with a gun or knife, raping her, cutting her skin with apparent bleeding, or strangling her. The degree of violence depicted ranges from a stern glance to apparent murder. Some photographs are such that it would take little suspension of belief to imagine that the woman was dead. (p. 1494)

Observational research, in the form of archival analysis, can tell us a great deal about society's values and beliefs. The prevalence in pornography of sexual

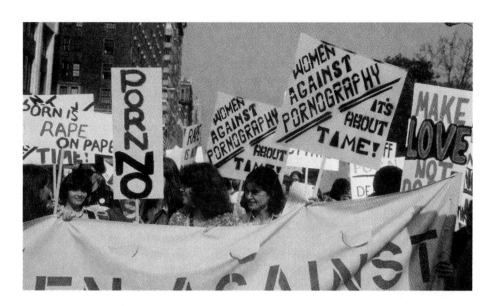

■ Many people believe that there is a causal relationship between the number of publications depicting violent pornography and the rise in sexual violence against women. They believe such publications should be illegal. Do you think reading and looking at pornography can cause people to commit violent sexual crimes against women? How can this question be answered scientifically?

violence against women suggests that these images and stories appeal to many readers (Dietz & Evans, 1982; Lowry, Love, & Kirby, 1981). These disturbing results lead us inexorably to frightening questions: Is pornography associated with sexually violent crimes against women that occur in our society? Do reading and looking at pornography cause some men to commit violent sexual acts? To answer these questions, research methods other than archival analysis must be used. Later in this chapter, we will see how the correlational method and the experimental method have been used to investigate these important questions about sexual violence against women.

Limits of the Observational Method

The observational method is a good one if the researcher's goal is to provide a description of social behavior. This method has some significant drawbacks, however. First, certain kinds of behavior are difficult to observe because they occur only rarely or only in private. For example, had Latané and Darley chosen the observational method to study the effects of the number of bystanders on people's willingness to help a victim, we might still be waiting for an answer. In order to determine how witnesses react to a violent crime, the researchers would have had to linger on street corners throughout the city, wait patiently for assaults to occur, and then keep careful track of the responses of any and all bystanders. Obviously, they would have had to wait a very long time before an assault happened to occur in their presence, and they would have found it difficult to gather data while a real-life emergency occurred at their feet.

Instead, Latané and Darley might have used the archival analysis version of the observational method—for example, by examining newspaper accounts of violent crimes and noting the number of bystanders and how many offered assistance to the victim. Yet here too, the researchers would have quickly run into problems: Did each journalist mention how many bystanders were present? Was the number accurate? Were all forms of assistance noted in the newspaper article? Clearly, these are messy data. As is always the case with archival analysis, the researcher is at the mercy of the original compiler of the material; the journalists had different aims when they wrote their articles and may not have included all the information researchers would later need.

Another limitation of the observational method is that it is confined to one particular group of people, one particular setting, and one particular type of activity—one doomsaying group in the Midwest, or one type of pornography. This can be a problem if the goal is to generalize from what is observed to different populations, settings, and activities. For example, in contrast to archival studies such as Dietz and Parks (1982), other studies have found that the depiction of violence and aggression in pornography is relatively rare (Garcia & Milano, 1990; Scott & Cuvelier, 1993). This may be due to the fact that Dietz and Park looked at "hard-core" pornography sold in adult bookstores in New York City, whereas the other studies looked at "softer" pornography in certain magazines and videos available at video rental stores. Which study best reflects the amount of violence in American pornography in general? It is difficult to tell.

Finally, social scientists usually want to do more than describe social behavior. A goal of social science is to understand relationships between variables and to be able to predict when different kinds of social behavior will occur. For example, what is the relationship between the amount of violence people see on television and how aggressive they are? How do children react when their parents get divorced? Who is most at risk for using drugs? To answer such questions, researchers frequently use a different approach—the correlational method.

The Correlational Method: Predicting Social Behavior

correlational method: the method whereby two or more variables are systematically measured and the relationship between them (i.e., how much one can be predicted from the other) is assessed

The **correlational method** involves systematically measuring two or more variables and seeing if they are related. That is, if you know a person's standing on one variable, how well can you predict his or her standing on the other? This is called assessing the degree of correlation between the two variables. Whereas the goal of the observational method is to describe behavior, the goal of the correlational method is to assess relationships between variables, usually in order to test hypotheses about when and why social behavior occurs.

In correlational research, people's behavior and attitudes can be measured in a variety of ways. Just as with the observational method researchers sometimes make direct observations of people's behavior. For example, using the correlational method researchers might be interested in testing the relationship between children's aggressive behavior and how much violent television they watch. They too might observe children on the playground, but here the goal is to assess the relationship, or correlation, between the children's aggressiveness and other factors, like TV viewing habits, that the researchers also measure.

Surveys

Besides observational data, the correlational method makes heavy use of surveys. Many of the social behaviors of interest to researchers are difficult if not impossible to observe, such as how much pornography people read, how knowledgeable they are about the transmission of AIDS, or how many friends they have. When the variables of interest cannot easily be observed, researchers rely on surveys, wherein people are questioned about their beliefs, attitudes, and behaviors. Here the researcher looks at the relationship between the questions asked on the survey, such as whether people who know a lot about how AIDS is transmitted are more likely than other people to engage in safer sex.

The way researchers look at such relationships is by calculating the correlation between different variables. A **positive correlation** means that increases in the value of one variable are associated with increases in the value of the other variable. Height and weight are positively correlated; the taller people are, the more they tend to weigh. A **negative correlation** means that increases in the value of one variable are associated with decreases in the value of the other. If height and weight were negatively correlated in human beings, we would look very peculiar—short people, such as children, would look like penguins, whereas tall people, like NBA basketball players, would be all skin and bones! It is also possible, of course, for two variables to be completely uncorrelated, so that a researcher cannot predict one variable from the other.

Correlations are expressed as numbers that can range from −1 to +1. A correlation of 1 means that two variables are perfectly correlated in a positive direction; thus, by knowing people's standing on one variable, the researcher can predict exactly where they stand on the other variable. In everyday life, of course, perfect correlations are rare. For example, one study found that the correlation between height and weight was .47, in a sample of men ages 18 to 24 (Freedman, Pisani, Purves, & Adhikari, 1991). This means that, on average, the taller people were heavier than the shorter people, but there were exceptions. A correlation of −1 means that two variables are perfectly correlated in a negative direction, whereas a correlation of zero means that two variables are not correlated.

Surveys have many advantages, not the least of which is the ability to sample representative segments of the population. Answers to a survey are useful only if they reflect the responses of people in general—not just the sample of people actually tested. Survey researchers go to great lengths to ensure that the people they sample are representative. They select samples that are representative of the population on a number of characteristics important to a given research question (e.g., age, educational background, religion, gender, income level). They also make sure to use a **random selection** of people from the population at large; this means that everyone in the population had an equal chance of being selected for the survey. As long as the sample is selected randomly, we can assume that the responses are a reasonable match to those of the population as a whole.

Problems with Survey Data.   Sampling has not always been done successfully. In the fall of 1936, a weekly magazine called the *Literary Digest* conducted a large survey asking people who they planned to vote for in the upcoming presidential election. The magazine obtained the names and addresses of its sample from telephone directories and automobile registration lists. The results of its survey of 2 million people indicated that the Republican candidate, Alf Landon, would win by a landslide. Of course, you know that there never was a President Landon; instead, Franklin Delano Roosevelt won every state in the Union but two. What went wrong with the *Literary Digest*'s poll? In the depths of the Great Depression, many people could not afford telephones or cars. Those who could afford these items were, by definition, doing well financially, were frequently Republican, and overwhelmingly favored Alf Landon. However, the majority of the voters were poor—and overwhelmingly supported the Democratic candidate, Roosevelt. By using a list of names that excluded the less affluent members of the population, the *Literary Digest* created a nonrepresen-

positive correlation: a relationship between two variables wherein increases in the value of one variable are associated with increases in the value of the other variable

negative correlation: a relationship between two variables wherein increases in the value of one variable are associated with decreases in the value of the other variable

random selection: a way of ensuring that a sample of people is representative of a population, by making sure that everyone in the population has an equal chance of being selected for the sample tative sample. (The *Literary Digest* never recovered from this methodological disaster and went out of business shortly after publishing its poll.)

Modern surveys and political polls are not immune from such sampling errors. During the 1984 presidential race, polls conducted by Ronald Reagan's campaign staff found that Reagan had a comfortable lead over Walter Mondale, except when the polls were conducted on Friday nights. After an initial panic, they figured out that because Democrats tend to be poorer than Republicans, they were more likely to be home when the pollsters called on Friday nights (*Newsweek,* September 28, 1992). Despite such notable glitches, or perhaps because of them, surveys have improved enormously over the years and can now accurately detect correlations between many interesting social variables.

Another potential problem with survey data is the accuracy of the responses. Straightforward questions—regarding what people think about an issue or what they typically do—are relatively easy to answer. But, asking survey participants to predict how they might behave in some hypothetical situation or to explain why they behaved as they did in the past is an invitation to inaccuracy (Schuman & Kalton, 1985). Often people simply don't know the answer—but they think they do. Richard Nisbett and Tim Wilson (1977) demonstrated this "telling more than you can know" phenomenon in a number of studies in which people often made inaccurate reports about why they responded the way they did. Their reports about the causes of their responses pertained more to their theories and beliefs about what should have influenced them than to what actually influenced them. (We discuss these studies at greater length in Chapter 5.) Finally, survey researchers have to be careful that they do not influence people's responses by the way they phrase the question (Hippler, Schwarz, & Sudman, 1987).

■ The importance of random selection in surveys. In 1936, the *Literary Digest* obtained a sample of names from telephone directories and automobile registration lists and asked these people whom they planned to vote for in the upcoming presidential election. Based on the results of this survey, the *Literary Digest* predicted that Alf Landon would win by a landslide. In fact, Franklin Roosevelt carried virtually every state in the Union. Why was the *Literary Digest* poll so inaccurate?

Correlation Does Not Equal Causation

The major shortcoming of the correlational method is that it tells us only that two variables are related, whereas the goal of the social psychologist is to identify the psychological processes that explain why people are susceptible to social influence. To obtain this information, we must be able to infer causality. We want to be able to say that A causes B, not just that A is related, or correlated, to B.

If a researcher finds that there is a correlation between two variables, it means that there are three possible causal relationships between these variables. For example, researchers have found a correlation between the amount of violent television children watch and how aggressive they are (Eron, 1982). One explanation of this correlation is that watching the violent TV causes kids to become more violent themselves. It is equally probable, however, that the reverse is true: that kids who are violent to begin with are more likely to watch violent TV. Or there might be no causal relationship between these two variables; instead, both TV watching and violent behavior could be caused by a third variable, such as having neglectful parents who do not pay much attention to their kids. (In Chapter 12, we will present experimental evidence that supports one of these causal relationships.) When we use the correlational method, it is wrong to jump to the conclusion that one variable is causing the other to occur. Correlation does not imply causation.

Unfortunately, one of the most common methodological errors in the social sciences is to forget this adage. Consider, for example, the report of a resident of Los Angeles, following a severe earthquake that rocked Southern California:

> A lot of people probably think that in one way or another they caused the earthquake, but I'm here to tell you that I'm the one who really did it. At seven-forty-two this morning, I pressed the button that raises the door of my garage, and all hell broke loose. The first thing I said to myself was "I've got to get this thing fixed." (*New Yorker*, October 19, 1987)

While this account is clearly tongue-in-cheek, it underscores a trap that is very easy to fall into: concluding that if two variables are correlated, one must have caused the other. Other examples of this error are not nearly so comical or inconsequential, such as the conclusions drawn from a recent study of birth control methods and sexually transmitted diseases (STDs) in women (Rosenberg, Davidson, Chen, Judson, & Douglas, 1992). The researchers examined the records of women who had visited a clinic for STDs, noting which method of birth control they used and whether they had STDs. Surprisingly, the researchers found that women who used condoms had significantly more STDs than women who used diaphragms or contraceptive sponges. This result was widely reported in the popular press, with the conclusion that the use of diaphragms and sponges caused a lower incidence of disease. Some reporters urged women whose partners used condoms to switch to other methods.

Can you see the problem with this conclusion? The fact that the incidence of disease was correlated with the type of contraception women used is open to a number of causal interpretations. Perhaps the women who used sponges and diaphragms had sex with fewer partners. (In fact, condom users were more likely to have had sex with multiple partners in the previous month.) Perhaps the partners of women who relied on condoms were more likely to have STDs than the partners of women who used sponges and diaphragms. There is simply no way of

■ There tends to be a correlation between the watching of violence on television and aggressive behavior in children. What are the different causal relationships that could explain this correlation?

knowing. Thus, the conclusion that any of the three types of birth control was the *cause* of protection against STDs cannot be drawn from this correlational study.

As another example of the difficulty of inferring causality from correlational designs, let's return to the question of whether pornography causes aggressive sexual acts against women, such as rape. To address this question, Larry Baron and Murray Straus (1984) examined the relationship between the amount of pornography sold in different states and the number of rapes reported in those states. To measure the amount of pornography, they chose eight sexually explicit magazines (e.g., *Playboy, Hustler, Chic*) and gathered data on how many issues were sold in 1979 in each state. They compared this information to the incidence of rape in each state, using the FBI *Uniform Crime Reports* publication. (Since rape is an underreported crime, these data are undoubtedly conservative estimates of the actual number of rapes committed.)

The researchers' data revealed a strong, positive correlation of .63 between pornography readership and rape. (Probability theory indicates that there is only 1 chance in 1,000 that a correlation of this size would occur by chance.) In addition, the researchers found that the amount of pornography sold was not as highly correlated with nonsexual violent crimes. Thus, they ruled out the possible explanation that pornography leads to more violent crimes in general, and not just to sexually violent crimes.

As suggestive as these findings are, they do not establish that pornography was a cause of rape. Can you think of alternative explanations for this correlation? Baron and Straus (1984) took pains to acknowledge that causality was not proved in their study. As they noted, the findings could reflect differences between states in a hypermasculine culture pattern that led men both to purchase more pornographic magazines and to commit rape.

Latané and Darley might also have used the correlational method to determine if the number of bystanders affects helping behavior. They might have surveyed victims and bystanders of crimes and then correlated the total number of bystanders at each crime scene with the number of bystanders who helped or tried to help the victims. Let's say that a negative correlation was found in these data: The greater the number of bystanders, the less likely it was that any one of them intervened. Would this be evidence that the number of bystanders caused helping behavior to occur or not? Unfortunately, no. Any number of unknown third variables could be causing both the number of bystanders and the rate of helping to occur. For example, the seriousness of the emergency could be such a third variable, in that serious, frightening emergencies, as compared to minor mishaps, tend to draw large numbers of bystanders and make people less likely to intervene. Other examples of the difficulty of inferring causality from correlational studies are shown in Figure 2.2.

The only way to determine causal relationships is with the **experimental method,** whereby the researcher systematically controls and orchestrates the event so that some people experience it in one way (e.g., they witness an emergency along with other bystanders) and others experience it in another way (e.g., they witness the same emergency but are the sole bystander). As we will see, the experimental method is the method of choice in most social psychological research, because it allows the experimenter to make causal statements. The observational method is extremely useful in helping us describe social behavior; the correlational method is extremely useful in helping us understand what aspects of social behavior are related, or co-occur. However, only the experimental method allows us to make cause-and-effect statements. For this reason, the experimental method is the crown jewel of social psychological research design.

> **experimental method:** the method of choice to study cause-and-effect relationships; the researcher randomly assigns participants to different conditions and ensures that these conditions are identical except for the independent variable (the one thought to have a causal effect on people's responses)

The Experimental Method: Answering Causal Questions

The experimental method always involves a direct intervention on the part of the researcher. The variable (e.g., number of bystanders) thought to be a cause of the behavior of interest (e.g., helping behavior) is controlled by the researcher, so that some participants in the study are exposed to it in one form (e.g., they witness an emergency alone), whereas others are exposed to it in other forms (e.g., they witness the same emergency in a small group, or they witness it in a large group). By carefully changing only one aspect of the situation (e.g., group size), the researcher can see whether this aspect is the cause of the behavior in question.

Sound simple? Actually, it isn't. Stop and think for a moment how you might stage such an experiment to test Latané and Darley's hypothesis about the effects of group size. A moment's reflection will reveal that some rather severe practical and ethical difficulties are involved. What kind of emergency should be used? Ideally (from a scientific perspective), it should be as true to the Genovese case as possible. Accordingly, you would want to stage a murder that passersby could witness. In one condition, you could stage the murder so that only a few onlookers were present; in another condition, you could stage it so that a great many onlookers were present.

Clearly, there are some glaring ethical problems with this scenario. What is ideal from a scientific perspective can be less than ideal from an ethical perspective. It goes without saying that no scientist in his or her right mind would actually commit a murder. Perhaps, instead, we could hire some actors to fake a murder on a city street. This is somewhat better from an ethical perspective, but it is still problematic; it is wrong to subject unsuspecting people to such a disturbing event. A solution might be to compromise further and stage an emergency that is less upsetting and frightening to people. But how can we arrange a realistic situation that is upsetting enough to be similar to the Genovese case without it being too upsetting? In addition, how can we ensure that each bystander experiences the same emergency except for the variable whose effect we want to test—in this case, the number of bystanders?

> Theory is a good thing but a good experiment lasts forever.
> –Peter Leonidovich Kapitsa

FIGURE 2.2   Correlation does not equal causation.
■ It can be rather difficult to remember that correlation does not allow us to make causal inferences, especially when a correlation suggests a particularly compelling cause. It is easy to forget that there are alternative explanations for the obtained correlation; for example, other variables could be causing both of the observed variables to occur. For each of the following examples, think about why the correlation was found. Even if it seems obvious which variable was causing the other, are there alternative explanations?

CORRELATION DOES NOT EQUAL CAUSATION QUIZ

1. Recently, a politician extolled the virtues of the Boy and Girl Scouts organizations. In his salute to the Scouts, the politician mentioned that few teenagers convicted of street crimes had been members of the Scouts. In other words, he was positing a negative correlation between activity in Scouting and frequency of criminal behavior. Why might this be?

2. A research study found that having a pet in childhood is correlated with a reduced likelihood of becoming a juvenile delinquent in adolescence. Why is this?

3. A recent study of soldiers stationed on army bases found that the number of tattoos a soldier had is correlated positively with becoming involved in a motorcycle accident. Why?

4. Officials in the Reagan administration took credit for a reduction in the crime rate, because the crime rate went down after Reagan took office. That is, there was a negative correlation between the onset of the Reagan administration and the crime rate. What are some alternative explanations for this correlation?

5. Recently, it was reported that a correlation exists between people's tendency to eat breakfast in the morning and how long they live, such that people who skip breakfast die younger. Does eating Wheaties lead to a long life?

6. A few years ago, newspaper headlines announced, "Coffee suspected as a cause of heart attacks." Medical studies had found a correlation between the amount of coffee people drank and their likelihood of having a heart attack. Are there any alternative explanations?

7. A positive correlation exists between the viscosity of asphalt in city playgrounds and the crime rate. How can this be? When asphalt becomes viscous (softer), is some chemical released that drives potential criminals wild? When the crime rate goes up, do people flock to the playgrounds, such that the pounding of feet increases the viscosity of the asphalt? What explains this correlation?

ANSWERS

1. The politician ignored possible third variables that could cause both Scout membership and crime, such as socioeconomic class. Traditionally, Scouting has been most popular in small towns and suburbs among middle-class youngsters; it has never been very attractive or even available to youths growing up in densely populated, urban, high-crime areas.

2. Families who can afford or are willing to have a pet might differ in any number of ways from families who neither can afford nor are willing to have one.

3. Did tattoos cause motorcycle accidents? Or, for that matter, did motorcycle accidents cause tattoos? The researchers suggested that a third (unmeasured) variable was in fact the cause of both: A tendency to take risks and to be involved in flamboyant personal displays led to tattooing one's body and to driving a motorcycle recklessly.

4. By chance, the size of the cohort in the population that is most likely to commit crimes—teenagers—went down when Reagan took office.

5. Not necessarily. People who do not eat breakfast might differ from people who do in any number of ways that influence longevity—for example, in how obese they are, in how hard-driving and high-strung they are, or even in how late they sleep in the morning.

6. Coffee drinkers may be more likely to engage in other behaviors that put them at risk, such as smoking cigarettes or not exercising regularly.

7. Both the viscosity of asphalt and the crime rate go up when the temperature is high—for example, on a hot summer day or night.

Let's see how Latané and Darley (1968) dealt with these problems. Imagine you were a participant in their experiment. You arrive at the scheduled time and find yourself in a long corridor with doors to several small cubicles. An experimenter greets you and takes you into one of the cubicles, mentioning that five other students, seated in the other cubicles, will be participating with you. The experimenter leaves after giving you a pair of headphones with an attached microphone. You put on the headphones, and soon you hear the experimenter explaining to everyone that he is interested in learning about the kinds of personal problems college students currently experience. To ensure that people will discuss their problems openly, he explains, each participant will remain anonymous; each will stay in his or her separate room and communicate with the others only via the intercom system. Further, the experimenter says, he will not be listening to the discussion, so that people will feel freer to be open and honest. Finally, the experimenter asks that participants take turns presenting their problems, each speaking for two minutes, after which each person will comment on what the others said. To make sure this procedure is followed, he says, only one person's microphone will be turned on at a time.

The group discussion then begins. You listen as the first participant admits he has found it difficult to adjust to college. With some embarrassment, he mentions that he sometimes has seizures, especially when under stress. When his two minutes are up, you hear the other four participants discuss their problems, after which it is your turn. When you have finished, it is the first person's turn to speak again. To your astonishment, after he makes a few further comments, he begins to experience one of the seizures he mentioned earlier:

> I—er—um—I think I—I need—er—if—if could—er—er—somebody er—er—er—er—er—er—er—give me a little—er—give me a little help here because—er—I—er—I'm—er—er—h—h—having a—a—a real problem—er—right now and I—er—if somebody could help me out it would—it would—er—er s—s—sure be—sure be good . . . because—er—there—er—er—a cause I—er—I—uh—I've got a—a one of the—er—sei—er—er—things coming on and—and—and I could really—er—use some help so if somebody would—er—give me a little h—help—uh—er—er—er—er c—could somebody—er—er—help—er—uh—uh—uh (choking sounds) . . . I'm gonna die—er—er—I'm . . . gonna die—er—help—er—er—seizure—er (chokes, then quiet). (Darley & Latané, 1968, p. 379)

Stop and think for a moment: What would you have done in this situation? If you were like most of the participants in the actual study, you would have remained in your cubicle, listening to your fellow student having a seizure, and done nothing about it. Does this surprise you? Latané and Darley kept track of the number of people who left their cubicle to find the victim or the experimenter before the end of the victim's seizure. Only 31 percent of the participants sought help in this way. Fully 69 percent of the students remained in their cubicles and did nothing—just as Kitty Genovese's neighbors had failed to offer assistance in any way.

Does this finding prove that the failure to help was due to the number of people who witnessed the seizure? How do we know that it wasn't due to some other factor? Here is the major advantage of the experimental method: We know because Latané and Darley included two other conditions in their experiment. In these conditions, the procedure was identical to that described above, with one crucial difference: The size of the discussion group was smaller, meaning that fewer people were witnesses to the seizure. In one condition, the participants were told that there were three other people in the discussion group besides themselves (the victim plus two others). In another condition, participants were told that there was only one other person in their discussion group (namely, the victim). In this latter condition, each participant believed he or she was the only one who could hear the seizure.

Independent and Dependent Variables

independent variable: the variable a researcher changes or varies to see if it has an effect on some other variable; this is the variable the researcher thinks will cause a change in some other variable

The number of people witnessing the emergency was the **independent variable** in the Latané and Darley study. The independent variable is under the direct control of the experimenter; it is the variable that is manipulated (presented in different ways). The independent variable is the one hypothesized to exert a causal effect on the **dependent variable,** which is what the experimenter measures to see if any such effect was present (in this case, whether or not people helped). That is, the dependent variable is hypothesized to depend on the independent variable (see Figure 2.3). Latané and Darley found that their independent variable—the number of bystanders—did have an effect on the dependent variable. When the participants believed that four other people were witnesses to the seizure, only 31 percent offered assistance. When the participants believed that only two other people were aware of the seizure, the amount of helping behavior increased to 62 percent of the participants. When the participants believed that they were the only person listening to the seizure, nearly everyone helped (85 percent of the participants).

dependent variable: the variable a researcher measures to see if it is influenced by the independent variable; the researcher hypothesizes that the dependent variable will depend on the level of the independent variable

Whereas these results indicate that the number of bystanders strongly affects the rate of helping, it does not mean that the size of the group is the only cause of people's decision to help. After all, when there were four bystanders, a third of them still helped; conversely, when participants thought they were the only witness, some of them still failed to help. Obviously, other factors also influence helping behavior—the bystanders' personalities, their prior experience with emergencies, and so on.

Because social behavior is complex, we realize that many variables are typically the cause of any given behavior. Thus, experiments often include more than one independent variable at a time. In addition, because we know that some combinations of independent variables have particularly powerful effects on behavior, we can make sure that all the different versions of the independent variables co-occur with each other. This is called a **factorial design**—an experimental design in which (a) there is more than one independent variable; (b) each independent variable has more than one version, or level; and (c) all possible combinations of these levels occur in one study. In this way, the researcher can determine the independent contribution of more than one independent variable, as well as the unique interaction of different combinations of the independent variables.

factorial design: an experimental design in which there is more than one independent variable; each independent variable has more than one version, or level; and all possible combinations of these levels occur in one study

Establishing Internal Validity in Experiments

How can we be sure that the differences in help across conditions in the Latané and Darley (1968) seizure study were due to the different numbers of bystanders who witnessed the emergency? Could this effect have been caused by some other aspect of the situation? Again, this is the beauty of the experimental method: We can be sure of the causal connection between the number of bystanders and helping because Latané and Darley made sure that everything about the situation was the same in the different conditions except the independent variable, the number of bystanders.

internal validity: making sure that nothing else besides the independent variable can affect the dependent variable; this is accomplished by controlling all extraneous variables and by randomly assigning people to different experimental conditions

Such a study is described as having high **internal validity** (Campbell & Stanley, 1967), meaning that everything was the same in the different conditions of the study except for the independent variable. Latané and Darley were careful to maintain high internal validity in their seizure study in the following ways: All the participants received the same instructions and description of the study; all

Independent Variable	Dependent Variable
The variable that is hypothesized to influence the dependent variable. Participants are treated identically except for this variable.	The response that is hypothesized to depend on the independent variable. All participants are measured on this variable.
Example: Darley and Latané (1968)	
The number of bystanders	**How many subjects helped?**
Participant Victim	85%
Participant Victim Two others	62%
Participant Victim Four others	31%

FIGURE 2.3   Independent and dependent variables in experimental research.

participated in the same set of cubicles; only one person participated in the experiment at a time, so that all other aspects of the situation could be carefully controlled and thus kept the same across participants; and all the comments of the supposed other participants and the victim were prerecorded and played over the intercom system, ensuring that all actual participants heard the same group discussion and witnessed the same emergency.

The astute reader will have noticed, however, that there was a key difference between the conditions of the Latané and Darley experiment other than the number of bystanders: different people participated in the different conditions. Maybe the observed differences in helping were due to characteristics of the participants instead of the independent variable. The people in the sole witness condition might have differed in any number of ways from their counterparts in the other conditions, making them more likely to help. Maybe they were more likely to have had loving parents, to know something about epilepsy, or to have experience helping in emergencies. Were any of these possibilities true, the study's internal validity would be seriously threatened.

Fortunately, there is a technique that allows experimenters to rule out differences among participants as the cause of the results: **random assignment to condition.** This powerful technique is the most important part of the experimental method. It means that each participant in the Latané and Darley study had an equal chance of being assigned to any one of the three conditions. In practice, this is done by flipping coins, drawing names out of a hat, or consulting a random numbers table (lists of numbers that have been randomly generated by a computer). Through random assignment, researchers can be relatively certain that differences in the personalities or backgrounds of their participants are distributed evenly across conditions. For example, since the participants were assigned randomly, probability theory tells us it is very unlikely that the ones who knew the most about epilepsy all ended up in one condition. Knowledge about

random assignment to condition: the process whereby all participants have an equal chance of taking part in any condition of an experiment; through random assignment, researchers can be relatively certain that differences in their participants' personalities or backgrounds are distributed evenly across conditions epilepsy should be randomly (i.e., roughly evenly) dispersed across the three experimental conditions.

However, even with random assignment there is always the (very small) possibility that different characteristics of people did not distribute themselves evenly across conditions. For example, if we randomly divide a group of 40 people into two groups, it is possible that those who know the most about epilepsy will by chance end up more in one group than the other—just as it is possible to get more heads than tails when you flip a coin 40 times. This is a possibility we take seriously in experimental science. Thus, the statistical analyses of our data come with a **probability level (*p*-value)** that the observed findings occurred by chance and not because of our independent variable(s). The convention in science, including social psychology, is to consider results significant if the probability level is less than 5 in 100 that the results might be due to chance factors and not the independent variables studied. For example, if we flipped a coin 40 times and got 40 heads, we would probably assume that this was very unlikely to have occurred by chance and that there was something wrong with the coin (we might check the other side to make sure it wasn't one of those trick coins with heads on both sides!). Similarly, if the results in two conditions of an experiment differ significantly from what we would expect by chance, we assume that the difference was caused by the independent variable (e.g., the number of bystanders present during the emergency). The *p*-value tells us how confident we can be that the difference was due to chance versus the independent variable.

The ability to control extraneous variables that might influence the results and the ability to randomly assign people to conditions are the hallmarks of the experimental method and set it apart from the observational and correlational methods. Only the experimental method can answer causal questions, such as whether exposure to pornography causes men to commit sexually violent acts. For obvious ethical reasons, we cannot conduct experiments in which the dependent variable is the incidence of violent sexual acts. The effects of pornography on attitudes and aggression have been examined, however, in a number of important experiments (e.g., Donnerstein, Linz, & Penrod, 1987; Malamuth, 1986; Malamuth & Donnerstein, 1983; Zillmann, 1994).

Let's take a look at one of these experiments, conducted by Edward Donnerstein (1980). All the participants were male undergraduates. In an experiment purportedly studying the effects of stress on learning, the participant and a confederate (who posed as a real participant) were partners in a learning task that involved one of them administering electric shocks to the other for every wrong answer given. The confederate was always the one who, in another room, received the shocks (no actual electric shocks were given). The gender of the confederate was the first independent variable in the study—the confederate was either a male or a female undergraduate.

Another independent variable was the type of short film the participant saw before delivering the shocks. While the participant was waiting for the confederate to finish studying for his or her upcoming test, the experimenter asked the participant if he would view a film the experimenter was thinking of using in future research and rate it on a number of dimensions. All the participants agreed. They each viewed one of three short films: (a) a film of a man who breaks into a house and rapes a woman at gunpoint (i.e., violent pornography), (b) a film of a male and female in various stages of sexual intercourse, but with no aggressive or violent content, or (c) a neutral film with no sexual or aggressive content.

probability level (*p*-value): a number, calculated with statistical techniques, that tells researchers how likely it is that the results of their experiment occurred by chance (due to the failure of random assignment) and not because of the independent variable(s); the convention in science, including social psychology, is to consider results significant if the probability level is less than 5 in 100 that the results might be due to chance factors and not the independent variable(s) studied

After viewing the film, the participants took part in the learning task. If the confederate gave an incorrect answer, the participant was instructed to deliver an electric shock of an intensity of his choosing—ranging from a shock level of 1 to a shock level of 8. The participants then heard the confederate make several mistakes (actually, this was a tape recording of a male or female accomplice). The dependent measure was the intensity of the shocks the participant chose to deliver. Did those who had just viewed pornography behave more aggressively (give stronger shocks) than those who had not? Did it make a difference whether the pornography was violent or nonviolent? Did the female confederate, or "victim," receive more intense shocks than the male?

The results are shown in Figure 2.4. The most striking finding was that when the male participants saw violent pornography and then had the opportunity to aggress against a female victim, they delivered the most severe electric shocks of all. When the victim was male, seeing either the nonviolent or the violent pornographic film led to a slight increase in aggression, possibly because these films aroused or upset people, which caused them to take it out on the victim. This increase, however, was nowhere near the intensity of the shocks delivered to the female victim by men who saw the violent pornography. This study and others like it (e.g., Linz, Donnerstein, & Penrod, 1984) suggest that when men watch pornography in which women are degraded and treated violently, they become more desensitized to violence toward women, view it as less abhorrent, and become more violent themselves.

We will discuss this issue at greater length in Chapter 12, on aggression. For now, we point out that only studies like Donnerstein's (1980), which are experiments on the effects of pornography, can answer the question of whether pornography causes violence and aggression.

Establishing External Validity in Experiments

For all the advantages of the experimental method, there are some drawbacks. By virtue of gaining enough control over the situation so as to randomly assign people to conditions and rule out the effects of extraneous variables, the situation can become somewhat artificial and distant from real life. For example, one

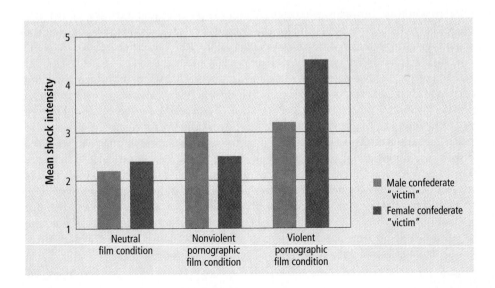

FIGURE 2.4   Effects of watching pornographic films on aggression. ■ Male participants watched a neutral, a nonviolent pornographic, or a violent pornographic film and then chose the intensity of shocks they delivered to a male or female victim. The most severe shocks were delivered to the female victim by males who had seen the violent pornographic films. (Adapted from Donnerstein, 1980)

could argue that Latané and Darley went far astray from the original inspiration for their study, the Kitty Genovese murder. What does witnessing a seizure while participating in a laboratory experiment in a college building have to do with a brutal murder in Queens? How often in everyday life do we have discussions with other people through an intercom system? Did the fact that the participants knew they were in a psychology experiment influence their behavior? Similarly, we might question the extent to which the kind of aggression Donnerstein (1980) examined in his laboratory study—delivering electric shocks to another student— can be generalized to violent sexual crimes, such as rape.

These are important questions that concern the **external validity**, or generalizability, of experiments in psychology. Two kinds of generalizability are at issue: (a) the extent to which we can generalize from the situation constructed by an experimenter to real-life situations (generalizability across *situations*) and (b) the extent to which we can generalize from the kind of people who participated in the experiment to people in general (generalizability across *people*).

Generalizability Across Situations.   A possible criticism of research in social psychology is that it is often conducted in artificial situations that cannot be generalized to real life. To address this problem, social psychologists attempt to increase the generalizability of their results by making their studies as realistic as possible. But it is important to note that there are different ways in which an experiment can be realistic. By one definition—the similarity of an experimental situation to events that occur frequently in everyday life—it is clear that many experiments are decidedly unreal. In many of the experiments we will discuss, people are placed in situations they would rarely if ever encounter in everyday life, such as occurred in Latané and Darley's group discussion of personal problems over an intercom system. We can refer to the extent to which an experiment reflects real-life situations as the **mundane realism** (Aronson & Carlsmith, 1968) of the experiment, which is often low.

A more important kind of realism, however, is how well an experiment captures psychological processes like those occurring in everyday life. We will refer to this as the **psychological realism** of experiments. Even though Latané and Darley staged an emergency that in significant ways was unlike ones encountered in everyday life, was it psychologically similar to real-life emergencies? Were the same psychological processes triggered? Did the participants have the same types of perceptions and thoughts, make the same types of decisions, and choose the same types of behaviors that they would in a real-life situation? If so, then the results of this study are generalizable to everyday life.

Making an experiment realistic, both mundanely and psychologically, is no easy task. It is perhaps where the creative talents of researchers come most into play. For example, the simplest way to study bystander intervention would be to say to people, "Look, we are interested in how people react to emergencies, so at some point during this study we are going to stage an accident, and then we'll see how you respond." We think you will agree, however, that such a procedure would be very low in psychological realism and mundane realism. In everyday life, we do not know when emergencies are going to occur; we do not have time to plan our responses to them; we do not think they are staged for our benefit; and we do not think a researcher is observing our reactions to them. Thus, the situation itself and the kinds of psychological processes triggered would differ widely from those of a real emergency.

external validity: the extent to which the results of a study can be generalized to other situations and other people

mundane realism: the extent to which an experiment is similar to situations encountered in everyday life

psychological realism: the extent to which the psychological processes triggered in an experiment are similar to psychological processes occurring in everyday life; psychological realism can be high in an experiment, even if mundane realism is low

Further, as discussed earlier, people don't always know why they do what they do or even what they will do until it happens. Thus, describing an experimental situation to participants and then asking them to respond normally will produce responses that are at best suspect. For example, after describing the Latané and Darley seizure experiment to our students, we often ask them to predict how they would respond, just as we asked you earlier. Invariably, almost all of our students think they would have helped the victim, even when they know that in the condition where the group size was six, most people did not help. Unfortunately, we cannot depend on people's predictions about what they would do in a hypothetical situation; we can only find out what people will really do when we construct a situation that triggers the same psychological processes as occur in the real world.

To make a study psychologically real, it is often necessary to tell the participants a **cover story**—a description of the purpose of the study that is different from its true purpose. You might have wondered why Latané and Darley told people that the purpose of the experiment was to study the personal problems of college students. It certainly would have been simpler to tell participants that the point of the study was to see how they would react to emergencies. However, this revealing comment would have considerably reduced the study's psychological realism, making it difficult to generalize the results to people's reactions to emergencies in everyday life. Psychological realism is heightened if people find themselves imbedded in a real event. To the extent that they are forewarned, people will plan their response, and this is not how it happens in the real world.

Generalizability Across People. Recall that social psychologists study the way in which people in general are susceptible to social influence. Latané and Darley's experiment documented an interesting, unexpected example of social influence, whereby the mere knowledge that others were present inhibited helping behavior. But what have we learned about people in general? The participants in their study were 52 male and female students at New York University, who received course credit for participating in the experiment. It is reasonable to ask whether the same results would have been found had a different population been used. Would the number of bystanders have influenced helping behavior had the participants been middle-aged blue-collar workers instead of college students? Midwesterners instead of New Yorkers? Japanese instead of American?

The only way to be certain that the results of an experiment represent the behavior of a particular population is to ensure that the participants are randomly selected from that population. Ideally, samples in experiments should be randomly selected, just as they are in surveys. However, it is rare in social psychological experiments for participants to be selected in this way. Latané and Darley, for example, did not attempt to choose a random sample of American citizens, or even New Yorkers, or even students at New York University. As is the case in many of the experiments we will describe in this book, the participants were students who volunteered for the study.

Unfortunately, it is impractical and expensive to select random samples for social psychology experiments. It is difficult enough to convince a random sample of Americans to agree to answer a few questions over the telephone as part of a political poll, and such polls can cost thousands of dollars to conduct. Imagine the difficulty Latané and Darley would have had convincing a random

cover story: a description of the purpose of a study, given to participants, that is different from its true purpose; cover stories are used to maintain psychological realism sample of Americans to board a plane to New York to take part in their study, not to mention the cost of such an endeavor. Even trying to gather a random sample of students at New York University would not have been easy, given that each person contacted would have had to agree to take time out of his or her busy schedule to spend an hour in Latané and Darley's laboratory.

Of course, concerns about practicality and expense are not good excuses for doing poor science. More importantly, given the goal of social psychology it is unnecessary to select random samples for every experiment performed. As noted in Chapter 1, social psychologists attempt to identify the basic psychological processes common to all people that make them susceptible to social influence. If we accept the premise that there are fundamental psychological processes shared by all people in all places and that it is these processes that are being studied in social psychology experiments, then it becomes relatively unimportant to select participants from every corner of the earth. Most social psychologists assume that the processes they study—such as the diffusion of responsibility caused by the presence of others in an emergency—are basic components of human nature, common to New Yorkers, Midwesterners, and Japanese alike.

This is not to say that we should take social psychologists' word for it. How can we be certain that the diffusion of responsibility effect is universal? Ultimately, the extent to which the results of a particular study can be generalized is an empirical question, tested by replicating the study with different populations.

Replications.   Suppose a researcher claims that his or her study is high in psychological realism, that it has thus captured psychological functioning as it occurs in everyday life, and that it doesn't matter that only college sophomores at one university participated, because these psychological processes are universal. Should we believe the researcher?

Not necessarily. The ultimate test of an experiment's external validity is **replication**—conducting the study over again, often with different subject populations or in different settings. Do we think that Latané and Darley found the results they did only because their participants knew they were in a psychology experiment? Then we should try to replicate their study in an experiment conducted outside of the laboratory. Do we think their results are limited to only certain kinds of emergencies? Then we should try to replicate it with an emergency different from an epileptic seizure. Do we think that only New Yorkers would be so unhelpful? Then we should try to replicate it with southerners, Californians, or Germans. Only with such replications can we be certain about how generalizable their results are.

Virtually all findings we will discuss in this book have been replicated in a number of different settings, with different populations, thus proving that they are not phenomena limited to the laboratory or to college sophomores. For example, Latané and Darley's original findings have been replicated in numerous studies. Increasing the number of bystanders has been found to inhibit helping behavior with many kinds of people, including children, college students, and future ministers (Darley & Batson, 1973; Latané & Nida, 1981); in both small towns and large cities (Latané & Dabbs, 1975); in a variety of settings, such as psychology laboratories, city streets, and subway trains (Latané & Darley, 1970; Piliavin, Dovidio, Gaertner, & Clark, 1981; Piliavin & Piliavin, 1972); and with a variety of types of emergencies, such as seizures, potential fires, fights, and accidents (Latané & Darley, 1968; Shotland & Straw, 1976; Staub, 1974), as well as

replication: repetition of a study, often with different subject populations or in different settings

■ Social psychology attempts to study psychological processes that affect all people and make them susceptible to social influence. To see if the results of an experiment are generalizable across people, the study must be replicated with diverse populations.

with less serious events, such as having a flat tire (Hurley & Allen, 1974). Many of these replications have been conducted in real-life settings (e.g., on a subway train) where people could not possibly have known an experiment was being conducted. We will frequently point out similar replications of the major findings we discuss in this book.

Cross-Cultural Research.   As noted in Chapter 1, experimental social psychology began primarily as an American discipline; thus, one limit on the generalizability of the results is that most research in the field has been conducted by Americans with American participants. More and more social psychological experiments are being performed in other cultures, however, and this activity will enrich our understanding of the external validity of many findings. Cross-cultural research has two main goals. The first is to try to demonstrate that a particular psychological process or law is universal, in that it operates the same way in all human beings. This type of research emphasizes what we as human beings have in common, regardless of our backgrounds and culture. For example, Charles Darwin (1872) argued that there is a basic set of human emotions (e.g., anger, happiness) that are expressed and understood throughout the world. Subsequent research has confirmed this, by showing that people in different cultures express emotions on their faces in the same way, even in remote cultures having no contact with the rest of the world (Ekman & Friesen, 1971). As another example, the effects of bystanders on helping behavior have been replicated in at least one other country (Israel; Schwartz & Gottlieb, 1976).

Clearly, however, the diversity of our backgrounds shapes our lives in interesting ways. The second goal of cross-cultural research is to explore the differences between us, by examining how culture influences basic social psychological processes. Some findings in social psychology are culture-dependent, as we will see at many points throughout this book. In Chapter 5, for example, we will see that there are cultural differences in the very way people define themselves. Many Western cultures tend to emphasize individualism and independence, whereas many Asian cultures emphasize collectivism and interdependence (Markus & Kitayama, 1991, 1994; Triandis, 1989). In Chapter 12, we will see that people's cultural and economic backgrounds have intriguing effects on how aggressive they are (Nisbett, 1993).

We do not have the space to discuss how to conduct cross-cultural research and the many nuances involved. Suffice it to say that it is not a simple matter of traveling to another culture, translating materials into the local language, and replicating a study there. Researchers have to be very careful that they are not imposing their own viewpoints and definitions, learned from their culture, onto another culture with which they are unfamiliar. They also have to be sure that their independent and dependent variables are understood in the same way in different cultures (Bond, 1988; Lonner & Berry, 1986).

Suppose, for example, that you wanted to replicate the Latané and Darley (1968) seizure experiment in another culture. Clearly, you could not conduct the exact same experiment somewhere else. The tape-recorded discussion of college life used by Latané and Darley (1968) was specific to the lives of New York University students in the 1960s and could not be used elsewhere. What about more subtle aspects of the study, such as the way people viewed the person who had the seizure? There is considerable variation across cultures in how people define whether another person is a member of their social group, and this factor can be an important determinant of how they behave toward that person (Gudykunst, 1988; Triandis, 1989). If people in one culture view the victim as a member of their social group whereas people in another culture view the victim as a member of a rival social group, you might find very different results in the two cultures—not because the psychological processes of helping behavior are different but because people interpreted the situation differently. It can be quite daunting to conduct a study that is interpreted and perceived similarly in dissimilar cultures. Most cross-cultural researchers are sensitive to these issues, and as more and more cross-cultural research is conducted carefully, we will be able to determine which social psychological processes are universal and which are culture-bound.

field experiments: experiments conducted in real-life settings, rather than in the laboratory

The Basic Dilemma of the Social Psychologist

One of the best ways to increase external validity is by conducting **field experiments.** In a field experiment, people's behavior is studied outside of the labora-

Doonesbury   BY GARRY TRUDEAU tory, in its natural setting. In contrast to systematic observation or the correlational method, however, here the researcher controls the occurrence of an independent variable (e.g., group size) to see what effect it has on a dependent variable (e.g., helping behavior) and randomly assigns people to the different conditions. Thus, a field experiment is identical in design to a laboratory experiment except that it is conducted in a real-life setting, rather than in the relatively artificial laboratory setting. The participants in a field experiment are unaware that the events they experience are in fact an experiment. The external validity of such an experiment is high, since, after all, it is taking place in the real world, with real people who are more diverse than a typical college student sample.

Many such field studies have been conducted in social psychology. For example, Latané and Darley (1970) tested their hypothesis about group size and bystander intervention in a convenience store outside of New York City. Two "robbers" (with full knowledge and permission of the cashier and manager of the store) waited until there were either one or two other customers at the checkout counter. Then they approached the cashier and asked what was the most expensive beer the store carried. The cashier named a brand and said he would check in the back to see how much was in stock. While the cashier was gone, the robbers picked up a case of beer in the front of the store, declared "They'll never miss this," put the beer in their car, and drove off.

Given that the robbers were rather burly fellows, no one attempted to intervene directly to stop their theft. The question was, when the cashier returned, how many people would help by telling him that a theft had just occurred? The number of bystanders had the same inhibiting effect on helping behavior as in the laboratory seizure study: Significantly fewer people reported the theft when there was another witness/customer in the store than when they were alone.

It might have occurred to you to ask why laboratory studies are conducted at all, since field experiments are obviously so much better in terms of external validity. Why not dispense with laboratory studies and do all research in the field? Indeed, it seems to us that the perfect experiment in social psychology would be one that was conducted in a field setting, with a sample randomly selected from a population of interest, and with extremely high internal validity (all extraneous variables controlled; people randomly assigned to the conditions). Sounds good, doesn't it? The only problem is that it is very difficult to satisfy all these conditions in one study—making such studies virtually impossible to conduct.

There is almost always a trade-off between internal and external validity—that is, between (a) having enough control over the situation to ensure that no extraneous variables are influencing the results and randomly assigning people to condition and (b) making sure that the results can be generalized to everyday life. Control is best exerted in a laboratory setting, but the laboratory may be unlike real life. Real life can best be captured by doing a field experiment, but it is very difficult to control all extraneous variables in such studies. For example, the astute reader will have noticed that Latané and Darley's (1970) beer theft study was unlike laboratory experiments in an important respect: People could not be randomly assigned to the alone or in pairs conditions. Were this the only study Latané and Darley had performed, we could not be certain whether the kinds of people who prefer to shop alone, as compared to the kinds of people who prefer to shop with a friend, differ in ways that might influence helping behavior. By randomly assigning people to conditions in their laboratory studies, Latané and Darley were able to rule out such alternative explanations.

The trade-off between internal and external validity has been referred to as the basic dilemma of the social psychologist (Aronson & Carlsmith, 1968). The way to resolve this dilemma is to not try to do it all in a single experiment. Most social psychologists opt first for internal validity, conducting laboratory experiments in which people are randomly assigned to different conditions and all extraneous variables are controlled; here there is little ambiguity about what is causing what. Other social psychologists prefer external validity to control, conducting most of their research in field experiments. And many social psychologists do both. Taken together, both types of studies meet the requirements of our perfect experiment. Through replication, a given research question can thus be studied with maximal internal and external validity.

Basic Versus Applied Research

Now that we have discussed the three major research methodologies in social psychology, there are two remaining issues about research we need to address. First, you might have wondered how people decide which specific topic to study. Why would a social psychologist decide to study helping behavior, cognitive dissonance theory, or the effects of pornography on aggression? Is he or she simply curious? Or does the social psychologist have a specific purpose in mind, such as trying to reduce sexual violence?

In general, we can distinguish between two types of research, each having a different purpose. The goal in **basic research** is to find the best answer to the question of why people behave the way they do, purely for reasons of intellectual curiosity. No direct attempt is made to solve a specific social or psychological problem. In contrast, the goal in **applied research** is to solve a specific problem. Rather than investigating questions for their own sake, constructing theories about why people do what they do, the aim is to find ways of alleviating such problems as racism, sexual violence, and the spread of AIDS.

The difference between basic and applied research is easily illustrated by examples from other sciences. Some biology researchers, for example, are concerned primarily with fundamental theoretical issues, such as the role DNA plays in the transmission of genetic information, without an immediate concern with how these issues can be applied to everyday problems. Other biology researchers are concerned primarily with applied issues, such as how to develop a strain of rice that has more protein and is more resistant to disease, in order to help solve problems of world hunger.

In most sciences, however, the distinction between basic and applied research is fuzzy. Even though many researchers label themselves as either basic or applied scientists, it is clear that the endeavors of one group are not independent of those of the other group. There are countless examples of advances in basic science that at the time had no known applied value but later proved to be the key to solving a significant applied problem. Basic research on DNA and genetics has led to a technology that enables researchers to create new strains of bacteria, with several important real-world applications in medicine and environmental control. For example, genetically engineered bacteria are now used in oil spills to help break up and disperse the oil. The same is true in social psychology. As we will see later in this book, for instance, basic research with dogs, rats, and fish on the effects of feeling in control of one's environment has led to the development of techniques

basic research: studies that are designed to find the best answer to the question of why people behave the way they do and that are conducted purely for reasons of intellectual curiosity

applied research: studies designed specifically to solve a particular social problem; building a theory of behavior is usually secondary to solving a specific problem to improve the health of elderly nursing home residents (Langer & Rodin, 1976; Richter, 1957; Schulz, 1976; Seligman, 1975).

Similarly, advances in applied research often have theoretical implications leading to the revision of basic theories about the physical world. For example, in the mid-1700s James Watt decided to conduct experiments with an applied purpose in mind: to improve the performance of steam engines. Not only did his experiments lead to more efficient engines, but also they provided the foundation for modern theories of thermodynamics.

Most social psychologists would agree that in order to solve a specific social problem, it is vital to have a good understanding of the psychological processes responsible for it. Kurt Lewin (1951), one of the founders of social psychology, coined a phrase that has become a motto for the field: "There is nothing so practical as a good theory." He meant that to solve such difficult social problems as urban violence or racial prejudice, one must first understand the underlying psychological dynamics of human nature and social interaction. In the beginning of social psychology as a discipline, differences emerged in the extent to which researchers focused directly on solving a social problem versus studying basic aspects of human nature. Lewin's own research group fell into these two camps. This dichotomy is present in the field today, with some social psychologists doing basic research primarily in laboratory settings and others doing applied research primarily in field settings.

> There is nothing so practical as a good theory.
> –Kurt Lewin, 1951

This book reflects the first school of social psychologists, those concerned mainly with basic theoretical issues. The subject matter of social psychology, however, is such that even when the goal is to discover the psychological processes underlying social behavior, the findings often have clear applied implications. Thus, throughout this book we will see many examples of research that have direct, applied implications. We also include at the end of the book three modules in which we discuss how social psychology has been applied to important social problems.

Ethical Issues in Social Psychology

Last but not least, it is important to discuss ethical issues that are endemic to research in social psychology. In their quest to create realistic, engaging situations that capture the essence of the process under study, social psychologists frequently face an ethical dilemma. On the one hand, for obvious scientific reasons we want our experiments to resemble the real world as much as possible and to be as sound and well controlled as we can make them. On the other hand, we want to avoid causing our participants undue and unnecessary stress, discomfort, or unpleasantness. These two goals are in a constant state of tension as the researcher goes about his or her business of creating and conducting experiments.

Researchers are concerned about the health and welfare of the individuals participating in their experiments. Researchers are also in the process of discovering important information about human social behavior—such as bystander intervention, prejudice, conformity, aggression, and obedience to authority. Many of these discoveries are bound to be of benefit to society. Indeed, given the fact that social psychologists have developed powerful tools to investigate such issues scientifically, many scholars feel it would be immoral not to conduct these experiments. However, in order to gain insight into such critical issues,

---

ETHICAL PRINCIPLES OF PSYCHOLOGISTS IN THE CONDUCT OF RESEARCH

1. Psychologists must take steps to avoid harming their research participants.

2. When planning research, psychologists must evaluate its ethical acceptability. Because individual researchers might not be objective judges of the ethical acceptability of their studies, they should seek ethical advice from others, including Institutional Review Boards. (Institutional Review Boards are a group of scientists and nonscientists who judge whether the risks to participants outweigh the potential gains of the research.)

3. As much as possible, the researcher should describe the procedures to participants before they take part in a study, and obtain informed consent from participants that documents their agreement to take part in the study as it was described to them.

4. Deception may be used only if there are no other viable means of testing a hypothesis and only if an Institutional Review Board rules that it does not put participants at undue risk. After the study, participants must be provided with a full description and explanation of all procedures, in a postexperimental interview called the debriefing.

5. All participants must be informed that they are free to withdraw from a study at any point.

6. All information obtained from individual participants must be held in strict confidence, unless the consent of the participant is obtained to make it public.

FIGURE 2.5   Procedures for the protection of participants in psychological research. ∎
(Adapted from *Ethical principles of psychologists in the conduct of research,* American Psychological Association, 1992)

researchers must create vivid events that are involving for the participants. Some of these events, by their very nature, are likely to produce a degree of discomfort in the participants. Thus, what is required for good science and what is required for ethical science can be contradictory. The dilemma cannot be resolved by making pious claims that no participant ever experiences any kind of discomfort in an experiment or by insisting that all is fair in science and forging blindly ahead. Clearly, some middle ground is called for.

The dilemma would be less problematic if researchers could obtain **informed consent** from their participants prior to their participation. If the experimenter fully describes to participants the kinds of experiences they are about to undergo and asks them if they are willing to participate, then the ethical dilemma is resolved. In many social psychology experiments, this sort of description is feasible—and where it is feasible, it is done. In other kinds of experiments, however, it is impossible. Suppose Latané and Darley had told their participants that a seizure was about to be staged, that it wouldn't be a real emergency, and that the hypothesis stated they should offer help. As we saw earlier, such a procedure would be bad science. In this kind of experiment, it's essential that the participant experience contrived events as if they were real; this is called a **deception** experiment because the events that transpire differ from what the participants were led to believe would happen. (It is important to note that not all research in social psychology involves deception.)

Over the years, a number of guidelines have been developed to deal with these dilemmas about the ethics of experiments and to ensure that the dignity and safety of research participants are protected. For example, the American Psychological Association has published a list of ethical principles that govern all research in psychology; these ethical guidelines are summarized in Figure 2.5. In addition, all research conducted by psychologists must be reviewed by an Institutional Review Board, or ethics committee. Any aspect of the experimental

informed consent: the procedure whereby the nature of the experiment is explained to participants before it begins and their consent to participate in the experiment is obtained

deception: the procedure whereby participants are misled about the true purpose of a study or the events that will actually transpire

THE FAR SIDE   By GARY LARSON

■ It is unlikely that an Institutional Review Board would have approved this study.

procedure that this committee judges to be stressful or upsetting must be changed or deleted before the study can be conducted. When deception is used, the post-experimental interview, called the **debriefing** session, is crucial and must occur. During the debriefing, the participants are told about the deception and why it was necessary. If they experienced any discomfort, the researchers attempt to undo and alleviate it. Finally, the debriefing session provides an opportunity to inform the participants about the goals and purpose of the research, thereby serving an important educational function. The best researchers question their participants carefully and listen to what they say, regardless of whether or not deception was used in the experiment. (For a detailed description of how debriefing interviews should be conducted, see Aronson, Ellsworth, Carlsmith, & Gonzales, 1989.)

In our experience, virtually all participants understand and appreciate the need for deception, as long as the time is taken in the postexperimental debriefing session to go over the purpose of the research and to explain why alternative procedures could not be used. Several investigators have gone a step further and assessed the impact on people of participating in deception studies (e.g., Christensen, 1988; Gerdes, 1979). These studies have consistently found that people do not object to the kinds of mild discomfort and deceptions typically used in social psychological research. In fact, some studies have found that the vast majority of people who participated in deception experiments said they had learned more and enjoyed the experiments more than those who participated in *non*deception experiments did (Smith & Richardson, 1983). For example, Latané and Darley had this to say about their participants' reactions to their seizure study:

debriefing: the procedure whereby the purpose of the study and exactly what transpired is explained to participants at the end of an experiment

Although the subjects experienced stress and conflict during the experiment, their general reactions to it were highly positive. On a questionnaire administered after the experimenter had discussed the nature and purpose of the experiment, every single subject found the experiment either "interesting" or "very interesting" and was willing to participate in similar experiments in the future. All subjects felt they understood what the experiment was about and indicated that they thought the deceptions were necessary and justified. (Latané & Darley, 1970, p. 101)

We do not mean to imply that all deception is beneficial. Nonetheless, if mild deception is used and time is spent after the study discussing the deception with participants and explaining why it was necessary, the evidence is that people will not be adversely affected.

SUMMARY

The goal of social psychology is to answer questions about social behavior scientifically. The principal research designs used are the observational, correlational, and experimental methods. Each has its strengths and weaknesses and is most appropriate for certain research questions. Each method causes the researcher to make a different type of statement about his or her findings.

The **observational method,** whether it utilizes **systematic observation, participant observation,** or **archival analysis,** primarily fulfills a descriptive function; it allows a researcher to observe and describe a social phenomenon, with the objectivity of the researcher's observations tested through **interjudge reliability.** The **correlational method** allows the researcher to determine if two or more variables are related—that is, whether one can be predicted from the other. If a **positive correlation** exists, increased levels of variable A are related to increased levels of variable B. If a **negative correlation** exists, increased levels of A are related to decreased levels of B. Correlations are often calculated from survey data, in which there is **random selection** of a sample from a larger population. This ensures that the responses of the sample are representative of those of the population. The major drawback of the correlational method is that it cannot determine causality. It is not possible to determine from a correlation whether A causes B, B causes A, or some other variable causes both A and B.

For this reason, the **experimental method** is the preferred design in social psychology; it alone allows the researcher to infer the presence of causality. Experiments can occur in a laboratory setting or in a field setting. The **independent variable** is the one the researcher systematically manipulates; it is the one hypothesized to have a causal effect on behavior. A **factorial design** involves more than one independent variable and more than one level of each; all the various combinations of levels of independent variables are present in the experiment. The **dependent variable** is the measured variable that is hypothesized to be caused or influenced by the independent variable. The researcher makes sure that participants are treated identically except for the independent variable and randomly assigns people to the experimental conditions. **Random assignment to condition,** the hallmark of true experimental design, ensures that different types of people are evenly distributed across conditions. A **probability level** (p-value) is calculated, telling the researcher how likely it is that the results are due to chance versus the independent variable.

Experiments are designed to be as high as possible in **internal validity** (making sure that nothing else besides the independent variables is influencing the results) and in **external validity** (making sure that the results can be generalized across people and situations). **Mundane realism** reflects the extent to which the experimental setting is similar to real-life settings. **Psychological realism** reflects the extent to which the experiment involves psychological responses like those occurring in real life. The best test of external validity is **replication**—repeating the experiment in different settings with different people, to see if the results are the same.

Researchers engage in both **basic research** and **applied**

research. While the line between these is often blurred, basic research aims to gain understanding of human social behavior, without trying specifically to solve a particular problem, whereas applied research aims to solve a specific problem, often one with social policy implications. Finally, a major concern in social psychological research is the ethical treatment of participants. The American Psychological Association's guidelines are followed carefully and include such points as **informed consent,** the ability to leave the experiment at any time, ensured anonymity and confidentiality, and **debriefing** following an experiment, particularly if **deception** (involving a **cover story** about the supposed purpose of the study or the independent or dependent variables) has been used.

IF YOU ARE INTERESTED . . .

Aron, A., & Aron, E. N. (1990). *The heart of social psychology* (2nd. ed.). Lexington, MA: Heath. A behind-the-scenes look at how social psychologists conduct research, based on interviews with leading researchers.

Aronson, E., Ellsworth, P., Carlsmith, J. M., & Gonzales, M. (1989). *Methods of research in social psychology* (2nd. ed.). New York: Random House. An entertaining, thorough treatment of how to conduct social psychological research.

Aronson, E., Wilson, T. D., & Brewer, M. (in press). Experimental methods. In D. Gilbert, S. Fiske, & G. Lindzey (Eds.), *The handbook of social psychology* (4th ed.). New York: Random House. An expanded discussion of many of the same issues discussed in this chapter, for those considering social psychology as a profession.

Ghostbusters (1984). At the beginning of this movie there is a scene in which Bill Murray, playing a psychologist, conducts an experiment on ESP. It is an amusing illustration of how not to do experimental research.

Rosenthal, R., & Rosnow, R. L. (1991). *Essentials of behavioral research: Methods and data analysis* (2nd. ed.). New York: McGraw-Hill. A detailed guide to methodology and statistical analyses, for the advanced student and professionals.

Chapter 3

Social Cognition: How We Think About the Social World

I t's math time in a typical fifth-grade classroom. The teacher, whom we will call Ms. X, is explaining a difficult problem to her students. She asks one of the girls to hold the math book so that everyone can see the problem. She then does something interesting: She turns her back to the girls (who are seated on her right) and explains the problem to the boys (who are seated on her left). Although she occasionally turns to the girls to read an example from the book, she directs virtually all of her attention to the boys, such that the girls can see only the back of her head. "The girl holding the math book had become a prop," noted two observers of this incident. "The teacher . . . had unwittingly transformed the girls into spectators, an audience for the boys" (Sadker & Sadker, 1994, p. 3).

This example of classroom behavior might not seem particularly remarkable or noteworthy. After all, it was just a small exchange between one teacher and her students on a busy school day. Yet according to Myra and David Sadker, who have spent years observing teachers and students in many different classrooms, this incident is typical of the way teachers treat boys and girls in American schools. Most teachers, they argue, do a better job of teaching boys. Boys are more likely to be called on in class, to receive praise for intellectual achievement, and to get help when they do not understand the material.

Here's another real-life example offered by the Sadkers. A fifth-grade social studies class is discussing U.S. presidents, and the teacher has just instructed the class not to shout out their answers but to speak only when called upon. Ignoring these instructions, Stephen blurts out an answer:

Stephen: I think Lincoln was the best president. He held the country together during the war.

Teacher: A lot of historians would agree with you.

Mike (seeing that nothing happened to Stephen, calls out): I don't. Lincoln was okay, but my Dad liked Reagan. He always said that Reagan was a great president.

David (calling out): Reagan? Are you kidding?

Teacher: Who do you think our best president was, Dave?

David: FDR. He saved us from the depression.

Max (calling out): I don't think it's right to pick one best president. There were a lot of good ones.

Teacher: That's interesting.

Kimberly (calling out): I don't think the presidents today are as good as the ones we used to have.

Teacher: Okay, Kimberly. But you forgot the rule. You're supposed to raise your hand. (Sadker & Sadker, 1994, p. 43)

Why is it that, on average, boys do better than girls on many standardized tests? Could it have something to do with the way teachers treat boys versus girls?

Now consider this fact: If you ask teachers which of their current students are most gifted at math, reading, or social studies or which of their students over the years have been most outstanding, an embarrassing truth leaks out: Most of the students they mention are male. Many teachers, even if they are women themselves, believe that males are brighter and more likely to succeed academically than females are (Jussim & Eccles, 1992). Parents hold similar beliefs about the talents of their children, as do adolescents about their own talents (Parsons, Kaczala, & Meece, 1982; Yee & Eccles, 1988).

Few scientists would argue that boys are born smarter than girls or have superior native abilities. For one thing, gender differences in ability are not universal; in fact, in some countries, such as Israel, females do better in math than males do (Bonora & Huteau, 1991; Emanuelson & Fischbein, 1986). In elementary school in the

United States, girls outperform boys on virtually all kinds of standardized tests, including tests of reading, writing, social studies, and math. However, girls begin to fall behind in middle school, and by high school boys surpass girls on many standardized tests (Hedges & Nowell, 1995). On the Scholastic Aptitude Test (SAT), used by many colleges to select students, males outscore females by 50 points on the math section and 10 points on the verbal section. This gap widens by the time college students take the Graduate Record Examination (GRE) for admission to graduate school: Males average 80 points higher on the math section, 26 points higher on the analytical section, and 21 points higher on the verbal section (Sadker & Sadker, 1994).

Why do males outperform females on academic tests? Although there is some evidence that the male and female brains process information differently (Kimura, 1987; Witelson, 1992), it is highly unlikely that the differences in male and female academic performance can be explained by such biological differences. To a social psychologist, the pieces of the puzzle fit together like this: Boys are not inherently smarter than girls. In school, children encounter teachers who believe that boys are smarter. These beliefs may become reality, as a result of the way teachers unwittingly treat their students—as in the example we saw earlier, in which Ms. X paid more attention to boys at math time. Academic differences between boys and girls may be a striking example of the power of social thinking, which is the topic of this chapter. The way in which people think about the social world (e.g., their beliefs about gender differences) can influence their behavior, which can in turn change that world, to the point where beliefs become reality. Sometimes we are sophisticated, accurate thinkers who change things for the better, but other times—as in the case of teachers' beliefs about gender differences—we may make quite costly mistakes.

Why do you think Ms. X treated her male and female students differently? One possibility, as we mentioned in Chapter 1, is that her beliefs and behavior stemmed from a need for self-justification. Perhaps at an early age she was taught that boys do better in school than girls, and now it would be too threatening for her to find out otherwise. People often act in surprising ways to cling to their world views and to avoid threats to their self-esteem. Ms. X may thus have treated the boys more favorably as a way of justifying a deep-seated belief. And the more she behaved consistently with her beliefs about gender differences, the more she would need to justify her actions by strengthening those beliefs.

To us, however, this explanation just doesn't ring true. First, treating boys and girls differently would seem to violate another important part of Ms. X's self-esteem—namely, that she is female and presumably does not want to think of herself as inferior. Second, treating one gender better than another violates another principle that is very important to most teachers: that all students should be given an equal opportunity to grow and learn. Rather than reflecting a need to justify her beliefs, Mrs. X's behavior may stem from something else—something fundamental about the way people think about the social world. Our guess is that Ms. X had formed subtle beliefs and expectations about boys and girls and that, without her even realizing it, these beliefs influenced the way she acted in the classroom. Most importantly, the way she acted may have made her beliefs come true.

How did Ms. X form these beliefs? This is the subject of social cognition; the study of how people select, interpret, and use information to make judgments and decisions about the social world. As noted in Chapter 1, the assumption of the social cognition approach is that people are motivated to understand the social world as accurately as possible. To understand why people do what they do (e.g., why teachers often treat boys and girls differently), it is important to understand the mental strategies the social thinker uses. Under what conditions will these strategies lead to accurate portrayals of the world, and under what conditions will they cause us to make mistakes (e.g., believing boys are smarter than girls)?

> It is the mind which creates the world about us, and even though we stand side by side in the same meadow, my eyes will never see what is beheld by yours.
>
> –George Gissing,
> *The Private Papers of Henry Ryecroft*, 1903

How We Think: The Procedures and Strategies of the Social Thinker

To understand how people think about the social world, we will first consider the procedures, rules, and strategies they use. When faced with an overwhelming amount of information, people rely on a variety of mental shortcuts. We will also consider how flexible these procedures are. Do people always use the same rules when thinking about the social world, or does it depend on what's at stake? As we will see, people are quite pragmatic, adopting different procedures and rules according to their goals and needs in that situation. Even so, human reasoning is not perfect, and in the last section we will consider ways of improving the way people think.

People as Everyday Theorists: Schemas and Their Influence

Scientists develop many theories and hypotheses about their topic of interest, be it the behavior of subatomic particles or of witnesses to an emergency. All of us, in our everyday lives, also have theories about ourselves and the surrounding social world. Social psychologists are interested in these theories because they play a significant role in how people understand and interpret themselves, other people, and all the interactions and social settings in which they find themselves.

Our theories about the social world, called **schemas** (Bartlett, 1932; Markus, 1977; Taylor & Crocker, 1981), profoundly affect what information we notice, think about, and later remember. Schemas are the cognitive structures in our heads that organize information around themes or topics. We have schemas about many things—other people, ourselves, social roles (e.g., what a librarian or an engineer is like), and specific events (e.g., what kinds of things usually happen when people eat a meal in a restaurant). In each case, our schemas contain our basic knowledge and impressions. For example, our schema about the members of the Animal House fraternity might be that they're loud, obnoxious partyers with a propensity for projectile vomiting.

Once people have developed a schema, it has interesting effects on how they process and remember new information. If you see a member of the Animal House acting in a calm, polite, and studious manner, this information will be inconsistent with your schema and under most circumstances you will forget it, ignore it, or fail to even notice it. Thus, schemas act as filters, straining out information that is contradictory to or inconsistent with the prevailing theme (Fiske, 1993; Higgins & Bargh, 1987; Stangor & McMillan, 1992).

Sometimes, of course, a fact can be so inconsistent with a schema that we cannot ignore or forget it. If we encounter a member of the Animal House who is actively campaigning to raise the drinking age to 25 and prefers poetry readings to raucous parties, he is such a glaring exception to our schema that he will stick in our minds—particularly if we spend time pondering how he could ever have ended up in the same house as his party-loving brothers (Hastie, 1980; Stangor & McMillan, 1992). In most cases, however, we are likely to notice and think about the behavior of the Animal House frat members that fits our preconceptions about them. In this way, our schemas become stronger and more impervious to change over time. For example, Claudia Cohen (1981) showed people a videotape of a woman engaged in various activities and identified her as either a librarian or a waitress. When later asked to recall scenes from the video, the participants more accurately recalled information that was consistent with the occupational label, such as the fact that the librarian had been listening to classical music.

In addition, human memory is *reconstructive*. We don't remember exactly what occurred in a given setting, as if our minds were a film camera recording the precise images and sounds. Instead, we remember some information that was there (particularly information our schema leads us to notice and pay attention to) and we remember other information that was never there but that we have unknowingly added later (Darley & Akert, 1991; Markus & Zajonc, 1985). For example, if you ask people what is the most famous line of dialogue in the classic Humphrey Bogart and Ingrid Bergman movie *Casablanca*, they will probably say, "Play it again, Sam." Similarly, if you ask them what is one of the most famous lines from the original (1966–69) *Star Trek* television series, they will probably say, "Beam me up, Scotty."

Here is a piece of trivia that might surprise you: Both of these lines of dialogue are reconstructions—the characters in the movie and the television series never said those lines. Not surprisingly, memory reconstructions tend to be consistent with our schema. For example, in Cohen's (1981) librarian/waitress study, participants misremembered what beverage the librarian had been drink-

schemas: cognitive structures people have to organize their knowledge about the social world by themes or subjects; schemas powerfully affect what information we notice, think about, and remember

> Theory helps us to bear our ignorance of facts.
> –George Santayana,
> *The Sense of Beauty,* 1896

■ "Beam me up, Scotty." Did the characters in the original *Star Trek* television series ever speak this line?

ing in the videotape. They reconstructed the scene in memory so that she was drinking wine, not beer, because that fit their schema of what a librarian would drink. As we will discuss in Chapter 13, the very way in which our schemas operate makes prejudiced attitudes highly resistant to change.

The Function of Schemas: Why Do We Have Them?   If schemas can sometimes make us misperceive the world, why do we have them? Think, for a moment, what it would be like to have no schemas about your social world. What if everything you encountered was inexplicable, confusing, and unlike anything else you'd ever known? Tragically, this is what happens to people who suffer from a neurological disorder called Korsakov's syndrome. They lose the ability to form new memories and must approach every situation as if they were encountering it for the first time—even if they have actually encountered it many times before. This can be so unsettling—even terrifying—that some people with Korsakov's syndrome go to great lengths to try to impose meaning on their experiences. The neurologist Oliver Sacks, for example, gives the following description of a Korsakov patient named Mr. Thompson:

> He remembered nothing for more than a few seconds. He was continually disoriented. Abysses of amnesia continually opened beneath him, but he would bridge them, nimbly, by fluent confabulations and fictions of all kinds. For him they were not fictions, but how he suddenly saw, or interpreted, the world. Its radical flux and incoherence could not be tolerated, acknowledged, for an instant—there was, instead, this strange, delirious, quasi-coherence, as Mr. Thompson, with his ceaseless, unconscious, quick-fire inventions, continually improvised a world around him . . . for such a patient *must literally make himself (and his world) up every moment.* (Sacks, 1987, pp. 109–110; emphasis in original)

In short, it is so important to us to have continuity, to relate new experiences to our past schemas, that people who lose this ability invent schemas where none exist.

Schemas are particularly important when we encounter ambiguous information that can be interpreted in a number of ways, because they provide us with a way of reducing this ambiguity. Consider a classic study by Harold Kelley (1950) in which students in different sections of a college economics class were told that their instructor was out of town and that a guest lecturer would fill in that day. In order to create a schema about what the guest lecturer would be like, Kelley told the students that the economics department was interested in how different classes reacted to different instructors and that the students would thus receive a brief biographical note about the instructor before he arrived. The note contained information about the instructor's age, background, and teaching experience. It also gave one of two descriptions of his personality. One version said, "People who know him consider him to be a rather cold person, industrious, critical, practical, and determined." The other version was identical, except that the phrase "a rather cold person" was replaced with "a very warm person." The students were randomly given one of these personality descriptions.

The guest lecturer then conducted a class discussion for 20 minutes, after which the students rated their impressions of him. How humorous was he? How sociable? How considerate? Given that there was some ambiguity in this situation—after all, the students had seen the instructor for only a brief time—Kelley hypothesized that they would use the schema provided by the biographical note to fill in the blanks. This hypothesis was confirmed: The students who expected the instructor to be warm gave him significantly higher ratings than the students who expected him to be cold, even though all the students had observed the same teacher behaving in the same way. Students who expected the instructor to be warm were also more likely to ask him questions and to participate in the class discussion. Think for a minute if this has ever happened to you. Has what you've known about a professor prior to the first day of class affected your impressions

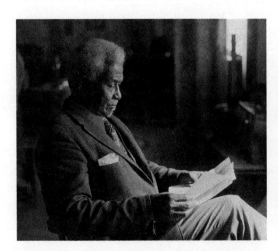

■ People who know him consider him to be a rather cold person, industrious, critical, practical, and determined.

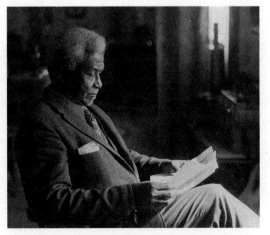

■ People who know him consider him to be a very warm person, industrious, critical, practical, and determined.

of him or her? Did you find, oddly enough, that the professor acted just as you'd expected? Next time, ask a classmate who had a different expectation about the professor what he or she thought. See if the two of you have different perceptions of the instructor based on the different schemas you were using.

Of course, people are not totally blind to what is actually out there in the world. Sometimes what we see is relatively unambiguous and we do not need to use our schemas to help us interpret it. For example, in one of the classes in which Kelley conducted his study, the guest instructor happened to be unambiguously self-confident, even cocky. Given that cockiness is a relatively unambiguous trait, the students did not need to rely on their expectations to fill in the blanks. They rated the instructor as being immodest in both the warm and cold conditions. However, when they rated this instructor's sense of humor, which was less clear-cut, the students relied on their schemas: The students in the warm condition thought he was more humorous than the students in the cold condition did. Thus, people are more likely to use schemas to fill in the blanks when they are not completely sure about what it is they are observing.

It is important to note that there is nothing wrong with what Kelley's students did. As long as people have reason to believe their schemas are accurate, it is perfectly reasonable to use them to resolve ambiguity. If a suspicious-looking character comes up to you in a dark alley and says "Take out your wallet," your schema about such encounters tells you the person wants to steal your money, not admire pictures of your family. This schema helps you avert a serious and perhaps deadly misunderstanding. If you bring to mind the wrong schema you can get yourself into hot water—not many muggers want to ooh and ah over your pictures of Aunt Martha and Uncle Julio.

Note that bringing to mind the wrong schema would not be much of a problem if we could easily and quickly put aside those schemas that are incorrect or inappropriate. The problem is that people often view the world in a way that makes it look like they have invoked the right schema even when they have not—as in the case of teachers who mistakenly believe boys are smarter than girls. We are often overzealous theorists, clinging too long to schemas that are not very accurate representations of the world.

Cultural Determinants of Schemas.   Have you ever met someone from another culture and been amazed at what she or he noticed and remembered about your country? Tim Wilson relates an experience he had when he was a teenager: One Sunday a guest from Iran came to his house for dinner. This man, Mr. Khetabdari, was visiting the United States for the first time and had arrived only a few days before. When he visited the Wilson house, Tim was idly watching a football game on television. As Mr. Khetabdari took off his coat and was introduced to the family, he glanced at the TV and reacted with horror to the sight of the men in weird outfits slamming into each other and throwing each other to the ground. "What are they doing?" he asked. "Why are these people hurting each other?" Mr. Khetabdari knew nothing about football and could not understand why these groups of large, grown men were chasing each other while wearing such strange clothes. Or why Tim and his family were watching them do it. American football was so foreign to Mr. Khetabdari's schemas of the world that he was quite fascinated by the game on television.

Clearly, a very important source of our schemas about the world is the culture in which we grow up. In Chapter 5, we will see that, across cultures, there

> I know that often I would not see a thing unless I thought of it first.
> –Norman Maclean, *A River Runs Through It*

> It is a capital mistake to theorize before you have all the evidence. It biases the judgement.
> –Sherlock Holmes (Sir Arthur Conan Doyle), 1988

are fundamental differences in people's schemas about themselves and the social world, with some interesting consequences. For now, we point out that the schemas our culture teaches us have a large influence on what we notice and remember about the world. Frederic Bartlett (1932), for example, noted that different cultures have schemas about very different things, depending on what is important to that culture, and that these schemas influence what people in different cultures are likely to remember. An aficionado of American football, for instance, can remember many details about a game (e.g., "that third-and-long play in the second quarter when they ran a draw play, completely fooling the defense") that would be lost on Mr. Khetabdari.

To illustrate the relationship between culture, schemas, and memory, Bartlett interviewed a Scottish settler and a local Bantu herdsman in Swaziland, a small country in southeast Africa. Both men had been present at a complicated cattle transaction that had transpired a year earlier. The Scottish man had little memory about the details of the transaction; he had to consult his records to remember how many cattle were bought and sold and for how much. The Bantu man, when asked, promptly recited from memory every detail of the transaction, including from whom each ox and cow had been bought, the color of each ox and cow, and the price of each transaction. The Bantu people's memory for cattle is so good that they do not bother to brand them; if a cow happens to wander away and get mixed up with a neighbor's herd, the owner simply goes over and takes it back—having no trouble distinguishing his cow from the dozens of others.

Perhaps the Bantu simply have better memories overall. Bartlett (1932) argues convincingly, however, that their memories are no better than the memories of people in other cultures. Each of us has a superb memory, he suggests, in the areas that are important to us, areas for which we thus have well-developed schemas. Cattle are a central part of the Bantu economy and culture, and thus the Bantu have well-developed schemas about cattle. To a person who grew up in a different culture, one cow might look like any other. This person, however, might have well-developed schemas about and an excellent memory for things that are quite foreign to the Bantu, such as transactions on the New York Stock Exchange, foreign movies, or, for that matter, American football.

The Problem with Schemas: They Can Distort What We See and Remember. By helping us remember what is important to us, schemas can be of great value. Unfortunately, however, we sometimes distort the evidence so that it will be consistent with our schemas, making it difficult for any truly inconsistent information to register.

A classic demonstration of such distortion was performed by Al Hastorf and Hadley Cantril (1954). They showed a film of a football contest between Dartmouth and Princeton to students from both schools and asked them to record the number of infractions committed by each team. The game had been a particularly rough one, generating heated protests on both campuses; each school blamed the other for the injuries that had occurred. Hastorf and Cantril conjectured that one reason for this difference of opinion was that the students from the two universities noticed different things in the same game, due to their partisanship. This hypothesis was confirmed: The Princeton students who watched the film saw more infractions committed by the Dartmouth team than the Princeton one, whereas the Dartmouth students saw just the reverse. It is important to note

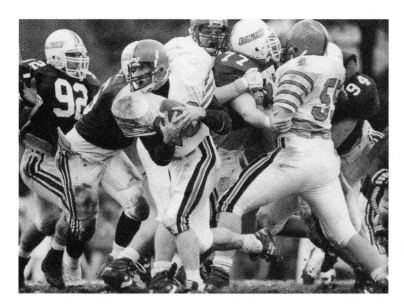

■ People view reality through schema-tinted glasses. Students from Princeton and Dartmouth watched the same film of a rough football game between the two schools. The Princeton students saw more penalties committed by the Dartmouth team, whereas the Dartmouth students saw more penalties committed by the Princeton team.

that the students were perfectly sincere about their perceptions—they really saw two different realities in the same film.

Because of the way in which our schemas bias what we see, there is a tendency for us to view the world in black-and-white terms, wherein our own side is the hero and the other side is the villain. Interestingly, this biased view can make partisans think that most other people are interpreting reality incorrectly. For example, what would have happened had the Princeton and Dartmouth students seen a balanced, neutral newscast reporting that both football teams had exhibited rough, unsportsmanlike behavior? Each side would think the newscast was biased against their school, because it did not present the extreme view they "knew" to be the truth. Vallone, Ross, and Lepper (1985) demonstrated this **hostile media phenomenon**, whereby opposing partisan groups both perceive neutral, balanced media presentations as hostile to their side, because the media have not presented the facts in the one-sided fashion the partisans believe to be true. They showed news broadcasts about conflicts in the Middle East (reporting the massacre of civilians in refugee camps in Lebanon in 1982) to students who were either very pro-Arab or very pro-Israel. As expected, each group believed the newscasts were biased in favor of the other side.

The participants in the Hastorf and Cantril (1954) and Vallone and colleagues (1985) studies were highly involved in the issues and had a substantial investment in viewing their side as the good guys. It is likely that they were motivated to see things in a way that confirmed their view of the world. For example, when the Princeton students saw one of their own players commit a questionable act, they were likely to interpret it as a rough but sportsmanlike play that was well within the rules, due to their investment in the belief that their school was blameless. The students from Dartmouth were likely to interpret the same act as a ruthless, unsportsmanlike attempt to injure one of their players, so that they could maintain the view that their side was blameless. People often interpret the world in a way that is consistent with their self-esteem. One need only attend a

hostile media phenomenon: the finding that two opposing partisan groups both perceive neutral, balanced media presentations as hostile to their side, because the media have not presented the facts in the one-sided fashion the partisans "know" to be true few sessions of divorce court to witness this kind of distortion, whereby two people give conflicting accounts, each swearing that his or her version of reality is true.

There are, however, conditions under which people will interpret the facts as consistent with their schemas and expectations even when they have relatively little investment in the issues. Consider research on what is called the **primacy effect**. Several experiments have demonstrated that first impressions are often very important, because these impressions influence the way in which later information is interpreted. (While there are circumstances under which *recency effects* occur—whereby information received last has the greatest impact—such effects appear to be the exception.) The primacy effect occurs because people form schemas on the basis of the first information they receive, and these schemas then influence the interpretation of later information. That is, people often cling to their first impression, and later information that contradicts it is ignored, discounted, or reinterpreted.

This dominance of first impressions was demonstrated in a simple, elegant experiment by Edward Jones and colleagues (Rock, Shaver, Goethals, and Ward 1968). Participants watched a male student trying to solve 30 multiple-choice analogy questions that were said to be of equal difficulty. The student always solved half the items correctly. The only difference was that in one condition, he started off very well, getting most of the first items right, and then began to do poorly, getting most of the last items wrong. In the other condition, this sequence was reversed: He got most of the first items wrong and then got most of the last ones right. After observing the student, the participants were asked to judge his intelligence and to recall how many items he had solved correctly.

As predicted, the participants were strong theorists who distorted the data to fit their first impressions. Those who observed the student start off well thought he was more intelligent and recalled that he had solved a higher number of items on the test than those who saw him start off poorly. Remember, in both cases the student solved 15 of the 30 items, all of which were of equal difficulty. Even so, the participants exhibited a strong primacy effect: What they saw first dominated their impressions, leading them to discount (and indeed to misrepresent) what came later (see Figure 3.1). Why? It seems unlikely that participants in this study distorted reality in order to feel better about themselves. The participants were judging another student, one who was a stranger to them and whom they would probably never see again. It appears that people's schemas, once formed, take on a life of their own, influencing how new information is viewed, regardless of whether people have an investment in what they see.

There is another way in which schemas can take on a life of their own: Sometimes they persist even after the evidence for them has been completely debunked. Sometimes we hear something about an issue or another person that later turns out not to be true. For example, a jury might hear something in the courtroom about a defendant that is untrue or labeled as inadmissible evidence and be told by the judge to disregard that information. The problem is that, due to the way schemas operate, our beliefs can persist even after the evidence for them proves to be false.

To illustrate this point, imagine you were a participant in a study by Lee Ross, Mark Lepper, and Michael Hubbard (1975). You are given a stack of cards containing both real and fictitious suicide notes. Your job is to guess which ones are real, supposedly to study the effects of physiological processes during decision making. After each guess, the experimenter tells you whether you are right or

primacy effect: the process whereby our first impression of another person causes us to interpret his or her subsequent behavior in a manner consistent with the first impression

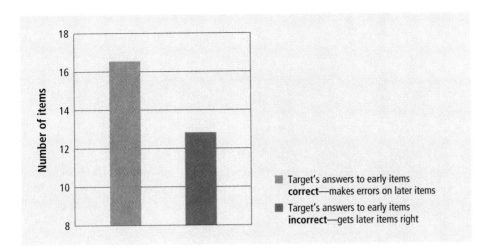

FIGURE 3.1   **The primacy of first impressions.** ■ People observed a student's work on 30 test questions and then recalled how many he answered correctly. Those who saw him get most of the first ones right overestimated the total number, whereas those who saw him get most of the first ones wrong underestimated the total number (in both cases, he got 15 out of 30 correct). (Adapted from Jones et al., 1968)

wrong. As the experiment progresses, you find out that you are pretty good at this task. In fact, you guess right on 24 of the 25 cards, which is much better than the average performance of 16 correct.

At this point, the experimenter tells you that the study is over and explains that it was actually concerned with the effects of success and failure on physiological responses. You learn that the feedback you received was bogus; that is, you had been randomly assigned to a condition in which the experimenter said you were correct on 24 of the cards, regardless of how well you actually did. The experimenter then gives you a final questionnaire, which asks you how many answers you think you *really* got correct and how many times you think you would guess correctly on a second, equally difficult test with new cards. What would you say? Now pretend you were in the other condition of the study. Here everything would be identical, except you would be told that you got only 10 of the 25 answers correct, which is much worse than the average performance of 16 correct. How would you respond to the questionnaire, once you found out that the feedback was bogus?

Depending on which condition you were in, you would have formed a schema that you were either very good or very poor at the task. What happens when the evidence for this schema is discredited? Ross and colleagues (1975) went to some pains to make sure the participants believed the feedback had been randomly determined and had nothing to do with their actual performance. Even though the participants believed this, those who had received the "success" feedback still thought they had gotten more of the items correct and would do better on a second test than people who had received the "failure" feedback did. In addition, when asked how they would do on a new test, success participants said they would do better than failure participants did (see Figure 3.2).

This result is called the **perseverance effect,** because people's beliefs persevered even after the original evidence for them was discredited. When people received the feedback, they explained to themselves why they were doing so well or so poorly, bringing to mind evidence from their past that was consistent with their performance (e.g., "I am really very perceptive. After all, last week I was the only one who realized that Jennifer was depressed" or "Well, I'm not so good at this stuff; my friends always say I'm the last to know"). Even after learning that the feedback was false, these thoughts were still fresh in people's minds, making them think they were particularly good or bad at the task.

perseverance effect: the finding that people's beliefs about themselves and the social world persist even after the evidence supporting these beliefs is discredited

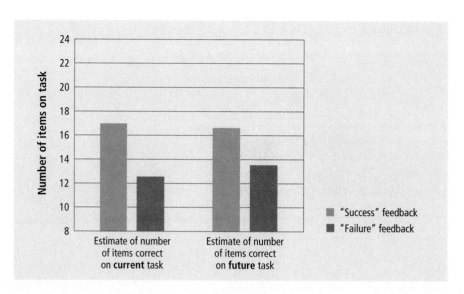

FIGURE 3.2   The perseverance effect. ▪ People were told they had done very well (success feedback) or very poorly (failure feedback) on a test of their social sensitivity. They were then told that the feedback was bogus and had nothing to do with their actual performance. People's impressions that they were good or bad at the task persevered, even after learning that the feedback was bogus. (Adapted from Ross, Lepper, & Hubbard, 1975)

self-fulfilling prophecy: the case whereby people (a) have an expectation about what another person is like, which (b) influences how they act toward that person, which (c) causes that person to behave in a way consistent with people's original expectations

Prophecy is the most gratuitous form of error.

–George Eliot (Mary Ann Evans Cross), 1871

Making Our Schemas Come True: The Self-Fulfilling Prophecy. The preceding studies have shown that when people encounter new evidence or have old evidence discredited, they tend not to revise their schemas as much as we might expect. People are not always passive recipients of information, however. People often act on their schemas and in doing so can change the extent to which their schemas are supported or contradicted. Research on this process—called the **self-fulfilling prophecy**—has found that people sometimes inadvertently behave in a way that creates evidence in support of their schema. Remember the example of teachers' beliefs about boys and girls with which we began this chapter? These beliefs seemed to influence how the teachers acted toward the students, which then influenced how well the students learned—thereby confirming the teachers' erroneous beliefs.

It is difficult to know for sure, in any one case, whether a self-fulfilling prophecy is operating. What came first—the teachers' beliefs or the behavior of the students? What was causing what? To answer these questions, it is necessary to conduct controlled experiments. Robert Rosenthal and Lenore Jacobson (1968) did so in an elementary school, in what has become one of the most famous studies in social psychology. They administered an IQ test to all of the students in the school and told the teachers that some of the students had scored so well that they were sure to "bloom" academically in the upcoming year. In fact, this was not necessarily true: The students identified as "bloomers" were chosen randomly by the researchers. As we discussed in Chapter 2, the use of random assignment means that, on average, the students designated as bloomers were no smarter or more likely to bloom than any of the other kids. The only way in which these students differed from their peers was in the minds of the teachers (neither the students nor their parents were told anything about the results of the test).

After creating the expectations in the teachers that some of the kids would do especially well, Rosenthal and Jacobson waited to see what would happen. They observed the classroom dynamics periodically over the school year, and at the end of the year they tested all of the children again with an actual IQ test. Did the prophecy come true? Indeed it did—the students in each class who had been labeled as bloomers showed significantly higher gains in their IQ scores than the other students did (see Figure 3.3). How could this have happened? How did the teachers' expectations become reality?

It is important to note that the teachers did not callously decide to direct their limited time and resources to the bloomers. Actually, they reported that they spent slightly less time with the students who were labeled as bloomers. In subsequent studies, however, teachers have been found to treat "bloomers" (the students they expect to do better) differently in four general ways: (a) They create a warmer emotional climate for bloomers, giving them more personal attention, encouragement, and support; (b) they give bloomers more material to learn and material that is more difficult; (c) they give bloomers more and better feedback on their work; and (d) they give bloomers more opportunities to respond in class and give them longer to respond (Rosenthal, 1994). Does this last behavior sound familiar? It is exactly how one of the teachers at the beginning of the chapter treated the boys in her class: She let them call out and give answers during the lesson on U.S. presidents, but when a girl called out an answer, the teacher reprimanded her for not raising her hand. Treating "bloomers" in these ways causes them to try harder and to learn more. These favored students respond to the special attention and instructions they receive and in fact do better (Brophy, 1983; Jussim, 1986; Snyder, 1984).

Many studies have reinforced the idea that self-fulfilling prophecies are not the result of a deliberate attempt by people to confirm their schemas; rather, they occur inadvertently and unconsciously. Even when people try to treat others in an evenhanded, unbiased manner, their expectations can creep in and change their behavior, which in turn changes the behavior of the person with whom they are interacting (Darley & Gross, 1983). Consider, for example, the teacher described at the beginning of the chapter who taught math more to the boys than the girls in her class. It is interesting to note that her behavior was being videotaped, with her knowledge and cooperation, for a segment of the NBC television program

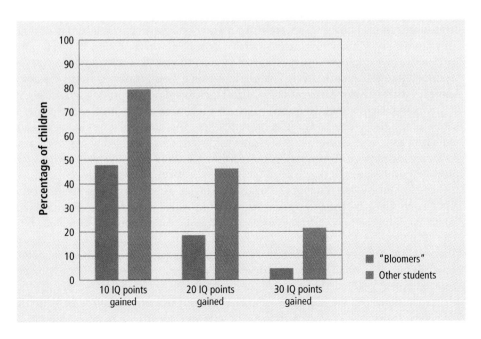

FIGURE 3.3 The self-fulfilling prophecy: Percentage of first- and second-graders who improved on an IQ test over the course of the school year. ■ Those whom the teachers expected to do well actually improved more than the other students. (Adapted from Rosenthal & Jacobson, 1968)

Dateline on sexism in the schools. One would assume, then, that she was trying very hard not to treat the girls any differently from how she treated the boys. Nonetheless, she did. Another example comes from other observations of teachers by Myra and David Sadker (1985). They filmed teachers interacting with their students and asked the teachers, after they viewed the film, who had talked more in class. The teachers said the girls had. In fact, the boys in the film had talked three times as much as the girls, in large part because the teachers were calling on the boys more. Sadker and Sadker (1985) suggest that sex-role stereotypes can be insidious, influencing teachers' perceptions and behaviors without their awareness.

Nor are self-fulfilling prophecies limited to the way teachers treat students. Each of us has all sorts of schemas about what other people are like, and whenever we act on these schemas in a way that makes the schema come true a self-fulfilling prophecy results (Darley & Fazio, 1980). Self-fulfilling prophecies have been found among diverse populations, with diverse expectations, including college students' schemas about what a potential dating partner is like, mothers' schemas about what premature babies are like, and supervisors' expectations about the performance of assembly-line workers (King, 1971; Snyder & Swann, 1978; Stern & Hildebrandt, 1986).

A distressing implication of research on the self-fulfilling prophecy is that our schemas may be resistant to change because we see a good deal of false evidence that confirms them. Suppose a teacher has the schema that boys possess some innate ability that makes them superior in math to girls. "But Mr. Jones," we might say, "how can you hold such a belief? There are plenty of girls who do very well in math." Mr. Jones would probably be unconvinced, because he would have data to support his schema. "In my classes over the years," he might note, "nearly three times as many boys as girls have excelled at math." His error lies not with his characterization of the evidence but in his failure to realize his role in producing it. Robert Merton referred to this process as a "reign of error," whereby people can "cite the actual course of events as proof that [they were] right from the very beginning" (1948, p. 195).

Stop for a moment and examine some of your own schemas and expectations about other social groups, especially ones you don't particularly like. These might be members of a particular race or ethnic group, of a rival fraternity, of a political party, or people with a particular sexual orientation. Why don't you like members of this group? "Well," you might think, "one reason is that whenever I interact with African Americans [substitute whites, Jews, gentiles, gays, straights, Sigma Chis, Democrats, Republicans, or any other social group], they seem cold and unfriendly." And you might be right. Perhaps they do respond to you in a cold and unfriendly fashion. Not, however, because they are this way by nature but because they are responding to the way you have treated them. Figure 3.4 illustrates this sad, self-perpetuating cycle of a self-fulfilling prophecy.

We often ask our students to try this exercise to counteract the self-fulfilling prophecy: The next time you see a member of a group you dislike, try to imagine that this individual is the friendliest, kindest, sweetest person you ever met. Be as charming and outgoing as you can be. You might be surprised by the results. People you thought were inherently cold and unfriendly might suddenly behave in a warm and friendly manner themselves, in response to the way you have treated them.

To summarize, we have seen that the amount of information with which we are faced every day is so vast that we have to reduce it to a manageable size. In

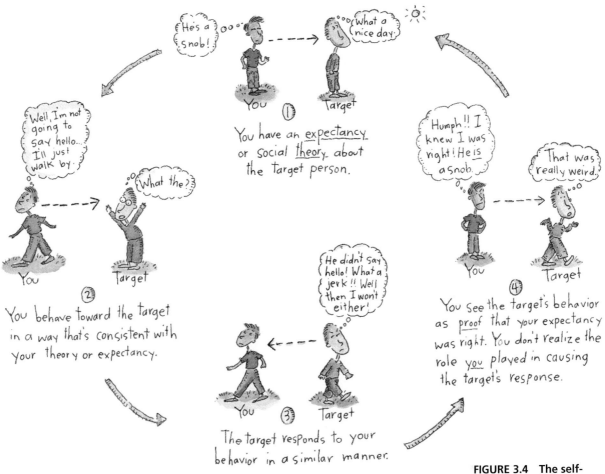

FIGURE 3.4   The self-fulfilling prophecy: A sad cycle in four acts.

addition, much of this information is ambiguous or difficult to decipher. One way we deal with these problems is by relying on schemas, which help us reduce the amount of information we need to take in and help us interpret ambiguous information. We turn now to other, more specific mental shortcuts that people use.

Mental Strategies and Shortcuts

What do you think is the best way to decide where to go to college? One strategy would be to investigate thoroughly every one of the more than 2,000 colleges and universities in the United States. Students could read every catalog from cover to cover, visit every campus, and interview as many faculty members, deans, and students as they could find. Getting tired yet? Such a strategy would, of course, be prohibitively time-consuming and costly. Instead of considering every college and university, most high school students narrow down their choice to a small number of options and find out what they can about those schools.

   This example is analogous to many decisions and judgments we make in everyday life. When deciding what job to accept, what car to purchase, or whom to marry, we usually do not conduct a thorough search of every option ("Ok, it's time for me to get married; I guess I'll consult the Census lists and begin my interviews of every eligible person"). Instead, we use mental strategies and shortcuts that make the decisions easier, allowing us to get on with our lives without turning every decision into a major research project. These shortcuts do not always lead to the best decision. For example, if you had exhaustively studied all 2,000 colleges in the United States, maybe you would have found one that you liked better than the one where you are now. Mental shortcuts are efficient, however, and usually lead to good decisions in a reasonable amount of time.

What shortcuts do people use? One, as we have already seen, is to use schemas to understand new situations. Rather than starting from scratch when examining our options, we often apply our previous knowledge and schemas. We have many such schemas, about everything from colleges and universities (e.g., what Ivy League colleges and big, midwestern universities are like) to other people (e.g., teachers' beliefs about the abilities of boys versus girls). When making specific kinds of judgments and decisions, however, we do not always have a ready-made schema to apply. Other times there are too many schemas that could apply, and it is not clear which one to use. What do we do?

judgmental heuristics: mental shortcuts people use to make judgments quickly and efficiently

At times like this, people often use mental shortcuts called **judgmental heuristics.** The word *heuristic* comes from the Greek word meaning "to discover"; in the field of social cognition, heuristics refer to the rules people follow to make judgments quickly and efficiently. Before discussing these heuristics, we should note that they do not guarantee that people will make accurate inferences about the world. Sometimes heuristics are inadequate for the job at hand or are misapplied, leading to faulty judgments. In fact, a good deal of research in social cognition has focused on just such mistakes in reasoning; we will document many such mental errors in this chapter, such as the case of teachers who mistakenly believed that boys were smarter than girls. As we discuss the mental strategies that sometimes lead to errors, however, it is important to keep in mind that people use heuristics for a reason: Most of the time, they are highly functional and serve us well.

How Easily Does It Come to Mind? The Availability Heuristic.   Suppose you are sitting in a restaurant with several friends one night when it becomes clear that the waiter made a mistake with one of the orders. Your friend Alphonse ordered the Veggie Burger with onion rings but instead got the Veggie Burger with fries. "Oh, well," he says, "I'll just eat the fries." This starts a discussion of whether he should have sent back his order, and some of the gang accuses Alphonse of being unassertive. He turns to you and asks, "Do *you* think I'm an unassertive person?" How would you answer this question?

One way, as we have seen, would be to call on a ready-made schema that provides the answer. If you know Alphonse well and have already formed a picture of how assertive he is, you can recite your answer easily and quickly: "Well, Alphonse, I have to tell you—if I needed someone to help me deal with a car salesperson, you wouldn't be my first choice." Suppose, though, that you've never really thought about how assertive Alphonse is and have to think about your answer. In these situations, we often rely on how easily different examples come to mind. If it is easy to think of times Alphonse acted assertively (e.g., "that time he stopped someone from butting in line in front of him at the movies"), you will conclude that Alphonse is a pretty assertive guy. If it is easier to think of times Alphonse acted unassertively (e.g., "that time he let a phone solicitor talk him into buying a Veg-O-Matic for $29.99"), you will conclude that he is pretty unassertive.

This mental rule of thumb is called the **availability heuristic,** which refers to judgments based on the ease with which we can bring examples to mind (Manis, Shedler, Jonides, & Nelson, 1993; Schwarz et al., 1991; Tversky & Kahneman, 1973). There are many situations in which the availability heuristic is a good strategy to use. If you can easily bring to mind several examples of times Alphonse stood up for his rights, he probably is an assertive person; if you can easily bring to mind several times when people pushed him around, he probably is not. The trouble with the availability heuristic is that sometimes what is easiest to bring to mind is *not* typical of the overall picture, leading to faulty conclusions.

Here are some examples of times when availability leads us astray: Do you think more people die in the United States from shark attacks or from falling airplane parts? From fires or from drowning? Most people report that deaths from shark attacks are more common than those from falling airplane parts and that deaths from fires are more common than those from drowning. Sounds reasonable, doesn't it? In fact, both answers are wrong: More people are killed from falling airplane parts than from shark attacks, and far more people drown than die in fires. It was probably easier to bring to mind examples of deaths from sharks and fires, because these events are more likely to be covered in the news (or shown in movies such as *Jaws*) and thus are more available in people's memory (Plous, 1993; Slovic, Fischhoff, & Lichtenstein, 1976). Similarly, if you ask people to estimate the number of violent crimes committed each year in the United States, you will get very different answers, depending on how much prime-time television they watch. Those who watch a great deal of television—and hence see a great deal of fictionalized violence—vastly overestimate the amount of real crime that occurs in the country (Gerbner, Gross, Morgan, & Signorielli, 1980).

Do people use the availability heuristic to make judgments about themselves? It might seem like we have well-developed ideas about our own personalities, such as how assertive we are. Often, however, people do not have firm schemas about their own traits (Markus, 1977) and thus might make judgments about themselves based on how easily they can bring to mind examples of their own behavior. To see if this is the case, Norbert Schwarz and his colleagues (1991) performed a clever experiment in which they altered how easy it was for people to bring to mind examples of their own past behaviors. In one condition, they asked people to think of 6 times they had acted assertively. Most people found this to be pretty easy; examples came to mind quickly. In another condition, the researchers asked people to think of 12 times they had acted assertively. This was much more difficult; people had to try very hard to think of this many examples. All participants were then asked to rate how assertive they thought they really were.

The question was, did people use the availability heuristic (the ease with which they could bring examples to mind) to infer how assertive they were? As seen on the left-hand side of Figure 3.5, they did. People asked to think of 6 examples rated themselves as relatively assertive, because it was easy to think of this many examples ("Hey, this is easy—I guess I'm a pretty assertive person"). People asked to think of 12 examples rated themselves as relatively unassertive, because it was difficult to think of this many examples ("Hm, this is hard—I must not be a very assertive person"). Other people were asked to think of 6 or 12 times they had acted *un*assertively, and similar results were found. Those asked to think of 6 examples inferred that they were relatively unassertive, because it was easy to think of 6 times they had acted this way. Those asked to think of 12

availability heuristic: a mental rule of thumb whereby people base a judgment on the ease with which they can bring something to mind

■ People overestimate the percentage of people who die in fires and underestimate the percentage of people who perish by drowning. Examples of deaths in fires are more likely to be reported by the media and are thus more available in people's memories.

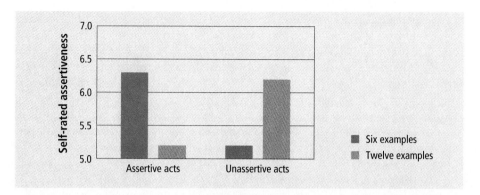

FIGURE 3.5   Availability and how assertive we think we are. ■ People asked to think of 6 times they behaved assertively found it easy to do so and thus concluded that they were pretty assertive people. People asked to think of 12 times they behaved assertively found it difficult to think of so many examples and thus concluded they were not very assertive people (see the left-hand side of the graph). Similar results were found among people asked to think of 6 or 12 times they behaved unassertively. People found it easy to think of 6 examples and thus concluded that they were not very assertive. People found it difficult to think of 12 examples and thus concluded that they must be pretty assertive (see the right-hand side of the graph). These results show that people often base their judgments on availability, or how easily they can bring information to mind. (Adapted from Schwarz et al., 1991)

examples inferred that they were relatively assertive, because it was difficult to think of 12 times they had acted unassertively (see the right-hand side of Figure 3.5). In short, people use the availability heuristic—the ease with which they can bring examples to mind—when making judgments about themselves and other people.

Mentally Undoing the Past: Counterfactual Reasoning.   The ease with which we can think of examples of our own behaviors, then, can influence the kind of person we think we are. The ease with which we can reconstruct the past has also been found to be important in our judgments about ourselves and others. People often engage in **counterfactual thinking**: thinking about how things might have turned out, if only past events had happened differently (Kahneman & Miller, 1986; Kahneman & Tversky, 1982). "If only I hadn't fallen asleep while studying the night before the test," you might think, "I would have gotten a better grade." The ease with which people can mentally undo the past—that is, how easy it is to think of alternative outcomes—can have a large impact on the way in which they explain the past and how they feel about it.

Suppose you learn, for example, about a businesswoman who always took the same plane to Chicago on Monday mornings. Tragically, one day the plane crashed and the woman was killed. Given that taking this plane was a regular part of her routine, it is difficult to imagine how she could have avoided this fate. Suppose, however, you learn that one Monday the woman missed her plane by 60 seconds and thus took the next flight to Chicago. Tragically, this plane crashed and she was killed. In this example, it is easy to mentally undo the outcome: "If only she hadn't gotten that phone call right before she left home; if only she hadn't gotten stuck in traffic on the way to the airport; if, if, if . . ." Even though

counterfactual thinking: mentally changing some aspect of the past as a way of imagining what might have been

■ Imagine that the person who won the lottery was in front of you in line and bought his or her ticket before you bought yours. How would you feel? Logically, you had as much of a chance of winning as that person did, because lottery drawings are random. According to research on counterfactual reasoning, however, you would probably feel pretty bad, because it would be easy to "mentally undo" the outcome, imagining ways you could have bought the winning ticket ("If only I had gotten to the store one minute earlier . . . "). You probably wouldn't feel so bad if the person who won the lottery bought the winning ticket in another part of the state, because it would be harder for you to imagine ways in which you could have purchased that ticket.

the outcome is the same in both cases—she perished in a plane crash, through no fault of her own—the second case, in which she barely missed her regular flight, seems much more tragic, because it is easier to "undo" through counterfactual thinking (Miller, Turnbull, & McFarland, 1990).

As you can see, counterfactual thoughts that are available in memory have a big influence on people's emotional reactions to events. The easier it is to mentally "undo" an outcome, the stronger the emotional reaction to it (Niedenthal, Tangney, & Gavanski, 1994). In a real-life study of counterfactual thinking, Christopher Davis, Darrin Lehman, Camille Wortman, Roxane Silver, and Suzanne Thompson (1995) interviewed people who had suffered the loss of a spouse or child. As expected, the more people imagined ways in which the tragedy could have been averted, by mentally "undoing" the circumstances preceding it, the more distress they reported.

In one sense, these reactions are perfectly rational; if it is true that a tragedy could have been averted, it is logical to feel badly about it. The interesting thing about counterfactual reasoning is that some kinds of outcomes *seem* easy to avoid or change, not because they were but because of the ease with which we can mentally undo them. Think of this example: You go to a basketball game and sit in seat F39 but switch to seat F48 because a really tall person is seated in front of you. At halftime, there is a drawing and prizes are awarded to people sitting in randomly determined seat numbers. Wouldn't you know it, the person who took *your* seat—F39—wins an all-expenses-paid trip for two to the Bahamas. How do you think you would feel? We suspect you would feel a lot more regret and disappointment than if the winning seat was in an entirely different section, because, through counterfactual reasoning, it is so easy to imagine winning ("If only I hadn't changed seats . . . "). At some level, this is illogical, because the drawing was random and in fact the seat you moved to—F48—had as much chance of winning as seat F39 (Johnson, 1986).

How Similar Is A to B? The Representativeness Heuristic.   People use another mental shortcut when trying to categorize something: They judge how similar it is to their idea of the typical case. Suppose, for example, that you attend a state university in New York. At the student union one day, you meet a student named Brian. Brian has blond hair and a dark tan, seems to be very mellow, and likes to go to the beach. What state do you think Brian is from? Because Brian seems similar to many people's stereotype of what Californians are like, you might guess California, or at least seriously entertain this possibility. If so, you would be using the **representativeness heuristic**—that is, classifying things on the basis of their similarity to a typical case (e.g., how similar Brian is to your conception of Californians).

representativeness heuristic:
a mental shortcut whereby
people classify something
according to how similar it
is to a typical case

Categorizing things according to representativeness is often a perfectly reasonable thing to do. If we did not use the representativeness heuristic, how else would we decide where Brian comes from? Should we just randomly choose a state, without making any attempt to judge his similarity to our conception of students from New York State versus out-of-state students? Actually, there is another source of information we might use. If we knew nothing about Brian, it would be wise to guess that he was from New York State, because at state universities there are more in-state than out-of-state students. If we guessed New York State, we would be using what is called **base rate information,** or information about the relative frequency of members of different categories.

base rate information:
information about the
frequency of members of
different categories in the
population

What do people do when they have both base rate information (e.g., knowing that there are more New Yorkers than Californians at a university) and contradictory information about the person in question (e.g., knowing that Brian is blond and mellow and likes to hang out at the beach)? Kahneman and Tversky (1973) found that people underutilize the base rate, paying most attention to how representative the information about the specific person is of the general category (e.g., Californians). While this is not a bad strategy if the information about the person is very reliable, it can get us into trouble when the information is rather flimsy. Given that the base rate of Californians attending state universities in New York is so low, you would need to have very good evidence that this person was a Californian before ignoring the base rate and guessing that he is one of the few exceptions. And given that it is not that unusual to find people from eastern states who have blond hair, are laid-back, and like to go to the beach, you would be wise not to ignore the base rate in this instance.

We don't mean to imply that people totally ignore base rate information (Koehler, 1993). Baseball managers consider the overall likelihood of left-handed batters getting a hit off of left-handed pitchers when deciding who to send up as a pinch hitter, and birdwatchers consider the prevalence of different species of birds in their area when identifying individual birds ("It's unlikely that was a bay-breasted warbler; they've never been seen in this area"). The point is that people often focus too much on individual characteristics of what they observe ("But it did seem to have a chestnut-colored throat; hm, maybe it *was* a bay-breasted warbler") and too little on the base rates.

People's overreliance on the representativeness heuristic can cause problems. Throughout history, for example, people have assumed that the cure for a disease must resemble (be representative of) the symptoms of the disease, even when this isn't the case. At one time, consuming the lungs of a fox was thought to be a cure for asthma, because foxes have a strong respiratory system (Mill, 1974). Such a reliance on representativeness may even impede the discovery of the actual cause of a disease. Around the turn of the century, an editorial in a Washington newspaper denounced the foolhardy use of federal funds on ridiculous, far-fetched ideas about the causes of yellow fever, such as the absurd idea of one Walter Reed that yellow fever was caused by, of all things, a mosquito (Nisbett & Ross, 1980).

Taking Things at Face Value: The Anchoring and Adjustment Heuristic. Suppose you are trying to quit smoking and are sitting around with a group of friends who also smoke. "How likely am I to get cancer anyway?" you say, reaching for a cigarette. "I bet that not all that many people end up with lung cancer. In fact, of all the students at our university, I wonder how many will get cancer in their lifetimes?" One of your friends throws out a number. "I don't know," he says. "I'd guess maybe 4,500." Would your friend's response influence your answer to the question? It would if you use the **anchoring and adjustment heuristic** (Tversky & Kahneman, 1974), a mental shortcut whereby people use a number or value as a starting point and then adjust their answer away from this point. You might begin by saying, "Hm, 4,500—that sounds high; I'd say it's a little lower than that."

Like all the other mental shortcuts we have considered, the anchoring and adjustment heuristic is a good strategy under many circumstances. If you have no idea what the answer is but your friend is a medical student specializing in oncology, it is wise to stick pretty close to his or her answer. But like the other heuristics, this one can get us into trouble. The problem with anchoring and adjustment is that people sometimes use completely arbitrary values as starting points and then stick too close to these values. Suppose, for example, that right before you and your friends were talking about smoking you were chatting about the attendance at a recent concert, which was 4,500 people. The number 4,500 is thus in your head. Would you use it as a starting point when estimating how many students will get cancer? Several studies on anchoring suggest you might. People have been found to stick close to the numbers they start with, even when these numbers are completely arbitrary and have nothing to do with the judgment they are making.

For example, Tim Wilson, Chris Houston, Kate Etling, and Nancy Brekke (1995) asked college students to copy several words or numbers, supposedly as part of a study of handwriting analysis. In one condition, people copied several pages of numbers, all of which happened to be around 4,500. In the other condition, people copied down words, such as "sofa." Then, as part of what was supposedly an unrelated study, everyone was asked how many students at their university would get cancer in the next 40 years. Those who copied down numbers gave much higher estimates (average answer = 3,145) than people who copied words did (average answer = 1,645). Similar anchoring effects have been found in many other studies (e.g., Cervone & Peake, 1986; Quattrone, Lawrence, Finkel, & Andrus, 1984; Slovic & Lichtenstein, 1971; Tversky & Kahneman, 1974).

The examples of anchoring and adjustment we have seen so far have concerned numerical judgments. This process, however, occurs with many other kinds of judgments as well. When we form judgments about the world, we often

anchoring and adjustment heuristic: a mental shortcut that involves using a number or value as a starting point and then adjusting one's answer away from this anchor; people often do not adjust their answer sufficiently allow our personal experiences and observations to anchor our impressions, even when we know our experiences are unusual. Suppose, for example, that you go to a popular restaurant that all your friends rave about. As luck would have it, the waiter is rude and your entree is burned. You know your experience is atypical; after all, your friends have had great meals at this restaurant. Nonetheless, your experiences are likely to anchor your impression of the restaurant, making you reluctant to return. Even when we know our experiences are unusual or atypical, it is hard not to generalize from them.

This tendency to generalize from atypical experiences is interesting because in everyday life people often want their experiences to be "biased" or atypical. When choosing our friends, we do not select a random sample of people out of the phone book; we find people who are kind, fun, and interesting. When sightseeing in Chicago, we do not take out a street map, close our eyes, and visit those locations on which our finger happens to fall; we select a biased sample of sites that are particularly noteworthy. Given that people often deliberately select biased samples, we might expect that they would be reluctant to generalize from these samples. If we know that we have visited only the noteworthy parts of Chicago, presumably we will be careful about assuming that all of Chicago is like what we have seen. To the contrary, people often use values as starting points when making judgments and then adjust insufficiently from these starting points. When generalizing from a sample of information (e.g., one part of Chicago we have visited) to the population of information (e.g., the entire city of Chicago), we are engaging in a process called **biased sampling**. In short, our own experiences serve as anchors when we make generalizations, and we often do not adjust sufficiently from these experiences—even when we know our experiences are atypical or biased.

biased sampling: making generalizations from samples of information that are known to be biased or atypical

For example, one day a social psychologist was eating lunch with several colleagues, one of whom remarked, "Say, did you see the story in the current *New Yorker* about the typical welfare mother? She was a real case, wasn't she?

■ Biased sampling: How would you feel about the entire state of New Jersey if you visited only one of these locations? People have been found to generalize from small samples of information, even when they know that these samples are not typical or representative.

On welfare for years, a terrible mother. Makes you wonder about the welfare system, doesn't it?" Now it just so happened that another person at the lunch table was a prominent economist who was an expert on the welfare system. "What makes you think she is typical?" he asked. "In fact, she is anything but typical. For one thing, the average amount of time on welfare in her state is two years, whereas she has been on welfare for more than a decade."

The fact that the social psychologist had generalized from the woman in the story to the welfare system in general—without considering how typical or unusual she was—was the inspiration for a study by Ruth Hamill, Tim Wilson, and Richard Nisbett (1980). They gave participants a condensed version of the *New Yorker* article, which was written by Susan Sheehan (1975). The article was a vivid portrayal of Carmen Santana, a mother living on welfare in New York City. Though Santana was friendly and warm, she lived a life that was, by most people's standards, irresponsible and bleak. The younger of her eight children (who were the result of relationships with three different men) wore tattered old clothing, and their attendance at school was irregular at best. One had not yet started school, because Ms. Santana did not have a copy of the child's birth certificate. The older children were involved in numbers running, heroin, and prostitution. All in all, it was a sad, depressing picture.

Hamill and colleagues (1980) were curious whether people would become more negative toward welfare recipients as a result of reading the article about Ms. Santana—that is, whether they would draw an inference about the population of welfare recipients based on the sample of one person they read about. Logically, this should depend on how typical people thought Ms. Santana was. To see if people would follow this logic, the researchers explicitly told some of them that Ms. Santana was highly atypical, in that she had been on welfare much longer than the average welfare recipient. They told others that she was typical, in that she had been on welfare for about the same length of time as the average recipient. They then observed whether these two groups changed their attitudes toward welfare, by comparing their views with those of a control group who did not read the story.

Not surprisingly, the people who were told that Ms. Santana was typical became more negative toward welfare recipients in general (see Figure 3.6). Surprisingly, however, people were equally willing to generalize when they knew that Ms. Santana was not typical of welfare recipients. Even though people in this condition were able to recall the fact that she was atypical, this information had little impact on their willingness to generalize from what they had read: They became as negative toward welfare recipients as did the people who believed she was typical.

Even when we know that a piece of information is biased or atypical, it can be hard to ignore it completely. We all know that reporters, television producers, and authors seldom present information that is typical; their job is to present what is unusual, interesting, and attention-grabbing, not what is average. (Imagine that a reporter said, "Leading the news tonight: Barbara Kowalski did not have a car accident on her way to the office, and Jerome Smith had an average day driving his city bus up and down Main Street.") Nonetheless, we seem to find it hard to avoid making generalizations from what we see. Again, this is another example of the anchoring and adjustment heuristic. People have a starting point, or an anchor ("Ms. Santana was really a mess"), from which they should adjust their judgment ("She is not representative of the population at large; therefore, I should not draw inferences about welfare recipients in

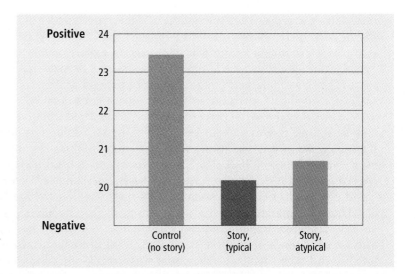

FIGURE 3.6 Attitudes toward welfare recipients. ■ People who read a story about one unlikable welfare recipient had more negative attitudes toward welfare recipients in general, regardless of whether they believed she was typical or atypical. (Adapted from Hamill, Wilson, & Nisbett, 1980)

general"). As with many other kinds of anchoring effects, however, people do not adjust their judgments sufficiently and are influenced too much by the case with which they began.

As a final example of biased sampling, consider this passage from John Steinbeck's book *Travels with Charley*, in which he compares his impressions of Prague with those of a friend who had "sampled" the city quite differently:

> In this report I do not fool myself into thinking I am dealing with constants. A long time ago I was in the ancient city of Prague and at the same time Joseph Alsop, the justly famous critic of places and events, was there. He talked to informed people, officials, ambassadors; he read reports, even the fine print and figures, while I in my slipshod manner roved about with actors, gypsies, vagabonds. Joe and I flew home to America on the same plane, and on the way he told me about Prague, and his Prague had no relation to the city I had seen and heard. It just wasn't the same place, and yet each of us was honest, neither one a liar, both pretty good observers by any standard, and we brought home two cities, two truths. (p. 77)

To summarize, we have discussed two general types of strategies used by the social thinker: schemas and judgmental heuristics. There is a close relationship between these two types of cognitive processing. Schemas are organized bits of knowledge about people and situations, like books in a mental library. When making judgments about the social world, however, it is not always clear which schema is most appropriate to use. The particular schema that is used and how this schema operates depend on the judgmental heuristics we have just considered. The availability heuristic refers to judgments based on the ease with which something can be brought to mind, which, in our library analogy, would refer to how easily a book can be brought up from the stacks. If we're wondering how assertive we are and the easiest "books" to find are examples of assertiveness, we infer we are pretty assertive people. The more a person or situation is representative of a particular schema (the more similar the contents of the book are to the situation we are in), the more likely we are to use it. Once we call up a particular schema, it anchors our judgments. We use it as a starting point to interpret a situation, and we find it difficult to adjust away from this schema (once a book has been retrieved, we apply it to the judgment at hand and it is hard to completely forget it and send it back to the stacks, replacing it with another book).

Thinking on Automatic Pilot

One final property of social thinking is very important, because it greatly facilitates our understanding of the social world: the ability to process information quickly and nonconsciously. Think back to what it was like to learn a new skill, such as riding a bicycle or using in-line skates. The first time you rode a two-wheeler, you probably felt awkward and ungainly as you wobbled across the pavement, and you may have paid for your inexperience with a skinned elbow or knee. You were probably concentrating very hard on what you were doing with your feet, knees, and hands, and it seemed like you would never figure it out. Once you became an experienced rider, however, your actions became automatic, in the sense that you no longer had to think about what you were doing. Now you can probably think about something else entirely while riding your bike. In fact, once a skill becomes well learned, thinking too much about it can make it harder to do ("I wonder exactly how I'm able to keep my balance on a bike? Whoops, look out for that tree!").

Just as our actions can become automatic, so too can the way we think. The more practice we have in thinking in a certain way, the less effortful and the more automatic that kind of thinking becomes, to the point where we can do it unconsciously, with no effort. **Automatic processing** can be defined as thinking that is nonconscious, unintentional, involuntary, and effortless. Though different kinds of automatic thinking meet these criteria to varying degrees (Bargh, 1989), for our purposes we can define automaticity as thinking that satisfies all or most of these criteria.

automatic processing: thinking that is nonconscious, unintentional, involuntary, and effortless

■ Thinking can become automatic, in that it can occur quickly and nonconsciously. For example, we quickly and effortlessly categorize things we see without even intending to do so. Automatic thinking allows us to do two things at the same time, such as painting a fence and talking on the telephone.

Automatic processing is difficult to describe, precisely because it occurs outside of awareness and is thus not very familiar to us. Actually, we have already described some examples of this type of thinking—namely, using schemas to understand the social world. Human beings are programmed to categorize the world quickly and efficiently. When we enter a classroom, we do not see a bunch of objects that have platforms parallel to the floor connected to four legs, with another flat surface at a right angle, that we then mentally assemble to figure out what they are. Instead of having to pause and think "Let's see. Oh, yes, those are chairs," we quickly, unconsciously, and effortlessly categorize the objects into our "chair" schema. The fact that we do this automatically allows us to use our conscious minds for other, more important purposes ("What's going to be on the quiz today?" "Should I strike up a conversation with that cute guy in the third row?"). Similarly, when we encounter other people we categorize them effortlessly into prior schemas. Doing so can be very advantageous, because it allows a great saving in time and effort. Imagine that every time you entered a class, you had to spend the first ten minutes concentrating hard on categorizing everything: "OK, let's see. I'm a student; that's the professor. Oh, yes, these are chairs. And this is a pencil, not a carrot stick." This would not be a very efficient way to spend our time. Instead, the application of categories and schemas occurs automatically.

As with all of the strategies and properties of social cognition we have considered, however, efficiency comes with a cost. If we automatically categorize a thing or person incorrectly, we can get into trouble. Imagine the embarrassment of a friend of ours who drove up to a fancy restaurant and, noticing the sign that said there was valet parking, gave his keys to a young Hispanic man standing by the door. It turned out that the man was not the parking attendant but another customer about to enter the restaurant. Or think back to our example of teachers and the self-fulfilling prophecy. One reason people's expectations can be so consequential is that they operate automatically, without intention, making it difficult for people to know when they are acting on these expectations. We pigeonhole people quickly, such that our schemas based on race, gender, age or physical attractiveness are invoked automatically (Devine, 1989a; Fiske, 1989). This is one reason stereotypes are so difficult to overcome—they often operate without our knowing it, as we will discuss in Chapter 13, on prejudice.

> My thinking is first and last and always for the sake of doing.
> —William James, *The Principles of Psychology*, 1890

The Flexible Social Thinker

So far, our portrayal of the social thinker has not been entirely flattering. True enough, people often use heuristics to their advantage and apply schemas effortlessly and efficiently. We have seen many examples, however, of times when these strategies lead to mistakes and errors in reasoning. People often let their schemas do the talking even in the face of contradictory information and make rash generalizations from atypical experiences. Sometimes these shortcomings in human inference have very unfortunate consequences, as in the case of teachers' expectations about gender differences leading to lower performance among girls. Findings such as these have led some to characterize people as **cognitive misers,** persons who are so limited in their ability to think and make inferences that they take mental shortcuts whenever they can (Taylor, 1981).

But can it really be the case that our thought processes are so flawed? After all, most of us make it through the day quite well, without stumbling too badly.

cognitive misers: a portrayal of people as so limited in their ability to think and make inferences that they take mental shortcuts whenever they can

Some people argue that social psychologists exaggerate the extent to which human reasoning is flawed, and a new view of the social thinker is emerging: people as **motivated tacticians,** those who have a large arsenal of mental rules and strategies and who choose wisely among these strategies, depending on their particular needs and goals (Fiske, 1993; Fiske & Taylor, 1991). A good deal of recent research has suggested that people are flexible thinkers: When little is at stake, they may be "miserly" in the sense that they rely on mental shortcuts that are good enough to get by, but when faced with more important decisions, people choose different and more effective strategies. To examine this question, several studies have increased the consequences of making a bad judgment, to see if people change their strategies. In many cases, they do, as we will now see.

motivated tacticians: a portrayal of people as having a large arsenal of mental rules and strategies and as having the ability to choose wisely among these strategies, depending on their particular needs and goals

Effects of Goals: The Motivated Social Thinker

It may have struck you that in some experiments we have discussed, people have been asked to make judgments that are of little importance to them. In the Jones and colleagues (1968) study on primacy effects, for example, people watched another student work on a test and judged how intelligent he was (see Figure 3.1). The student was not anyone they would see again (or even meet in person); thus, people might not have bothered to make the more effortful, accurate inferences of which they were capable. This point is illustrated by several studies showing that when more consequential tasks are used, people do make more complex and accurate inferences (Borgida & Howard-Pitney, 1983; Chaiken, Liberman, & Eagly, 1989; Hilton & Darley, 1991; Fiske, 1993; Kruglanski, 1989). For example, Allan Harkness, Kenneth DeBono, and Eugene Borgida (1985) gave female participants information about a person named Tom Ferguson, whom they had never met. The participants learned how interested Tom was in dating each of several women and learned several things about these women, such as how good a sense of humor they had. They were asked to judge the relationship between the qualities of the women (e.g., their sense of humor) and Tom's willingness to date them. As with many other studies that have examined people's ability to judge such relationships, Harkness and colleagues (1985) found that the participants used simple strategies that, while not totally wrong, were not particularly accurate.

Unless, that is, they were highly motivated to make careful judgments. Some of the participants thought that they were taking part in a dating study and that they themselves would be dating Tom for several weeks. Now that the women cared more about what Tom liked and disliked in a dating partner, they used more complex mental strategies and made judgments that were more accurate. In general, people have been found to be flexible thinkers, able to choose, at least to some extent, from a variety of mental strategies. When the stakes are high, people use more sophisticated strategies than when the stakes are low, make more accurate judgments, and are more likely to notice facts that conflict with their prior schemas (Dunn & Wilson, 1990; Fiske, 1993; Flink & Park, 1991; Hastie, 1980; Kruglanski, 1989; Neuberg, in press; Petty & Cacioppo, 1986; Stangor & McMillan, 1992; Tetlock, 1992).

Controlled Thinking: Counteracting Automaticity

Another consequence of people's goals is their willingness to rely on automatic processing, versus trying to adjust or correct for this type of thinking. Earlier we argued that a lot of our thinking about the social world occurs automatically—

controlled processing:
thinking that is conscious, intentional, voluntary, and effortful

that is, nonconsciously and without effort or intention. Clearly, however, not all thinking is automatic; like Rodin's statue of the thinker, sometimes we pause and think deeply about ourselves and the social world. This kind of thinking is called **controlled processing**, which is defined as thinking that is conscious, intentional, voluntary, and effortful. An example of controlled processing is the kind of conscious musing people often engage in: "I wonder what's for lunch today?" or "When will the authors get on with it and finish this chapter?" You can "turn on" or "turn off" this type of thinking at will, and you are fully aware of what you are thinking.

One purpose of controlled thinking is to provide a check and balance for automatic processing. As seen earlier, we sometimes make mistakes in our automatic categorizations of people or objects, such as our friend who mistakenly thought the Hispanic man was the parking attendant. Just as an airline captain can turn off the automatic pilot and take control of the plane when trouble occurs, in such situations our controlled thinking takes over. Our friend mumbled an apology to the man and thought a great deal about what he had done and how he might avoid such racist behavior in the future.

Unlike automatic processing, however, controlled thinking requires motivation and effort. We have to want to do it, and we have to have the time and energy to devote to it. Thus, when the stakes are low and we do not particularly care about the accuracy of a decision or judgment, we often let our automatic thinking do the job, without bothering to check or correct it. If we are idly watching television after a long day, for example, we might be judging the people we see on the tube rather mindlessly, without thinking too much about it. As we will discuss in Chapter 13, people must make the effort to engage in controlled processing in order to counteract negative stereotypes that come to mind automatically.

Automatic Believing, Controlled Unbelieving.   There are other interesting ways in which controlled processing acts as a check and balance for automatic processing. As we saw earlier, when people use the anchoring and adjustment heuristic they use starting points in their judgments and fail to adjust sufficiently from these points. One explanation for this process is that we automatically use whatever we encounter as a starting point, without even fully realizing that we are doing so, and then attempt to adjust from this starting point with controlled processing. This characterization of human judgment was made by the philosopher Benedict Spinoza three centuries ago: When people initially see, hear, or learn something, they take it at face value and assume it is true. Only after accepting the veracity of a fact do people go back and decide whether it might be false. Although other philosophers (e.g., René Descartes) have disagreed, recent research by Daniel Gilbert and his colleagues shows that Spinoza was right (Gilbert, 1991, 1993).

Gilbert argues that people are programmed to believe automatically everything they hear and see. This automatic, "seeing is believing" process is built into human beings, he suggests, because pretty much everything people hear and see *is* true. If we had to stop and deliberate about the truthfulness of everything we encountered, life would be difficult indeed ("Let's see, it looks like a car careening toward me down the street, but maybe it's really an illusion . . . CRASH!"). Occasionally, however, what we see or hear is not true; thus, we need a check and balance system to be able to "unaccept" what we have initially believed. When

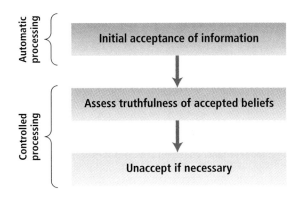

Automatic processing

Controlled processing

FIGURE 3.7   Gilbert's theory of automatic believing. ■ According to Gilbert (1991), people initially believe everything they hear and see. They then assess whether what they heard or saw is really true and "unaccept" it if necessary. The second and third parts of the process, in which people assess and unaccept information, take time and effort. If people are tired or preoccupied these parts of the process are difficult to execute, increasing the likelihood that people will believe false information. (Adapted from Gilbert, 1991)

we hear a candidate for governor say, "If elected, I will lower your taxes, balance the budget, reduce crime, and wash your car every Sunday afternoon," we initially believe what we hear, argues Gilbert (1991), but the "unacceptance" part of the process quickly kicks in, making us doubt the truth of what we've just heard ("Now wait just a minute . . . "). The process is depicted in Figure 3.7.

The interesting thing about this process is that the initial acceptance part occurs automatically, which, as we have seen, means that it occurs nonconsciously and without effort or intention. The assessment and unacceptance part of the process is the product of controlled processing, however, which means that people have to have the energy and motivation to do it. If people are preoccupied, tired, or unmotivated, the acceptance part of the process will operate unchecked, and this can lead to the acceptance of falsehoods.

Consider the following experiment conducted by Gilbert, Tafarodi, and Malone (1993). They asked participants to read crime reports on a computer screen and then to recommend prison sentences for the people who had committed the crimes. They told participants that some of the statements in the reports were false, because there had been a mixup and these statements actually were from other, unrelated crime reports. These statements were printed in red on the computer screen, whereas all of the true statements were printed in black. As it happened, the false statements made the crime seem worse in one condition (e.g., one said that the criminal threatened to sexually assault a clerk). In another condition, the false statements made the crime seem less severe (e.g., one said that the criminal was ashamed of what he had done). After reading the reports, people were asked to recommend a prison sentence for the criminal from 0 to 20 years.

Imagine you were in this study. As you read the reports, you occasionally see one of the false statements printed in red. Although these statements make the crime seem more or less severe, you know they're false and so you don't let them influence the sentence you recommend. This is exactly what happened in some conditions of the study: People who got false attenuating statements recommended about the same sentence as people who got false exacerbating statements (see the left-hand side of Figure 3.8). According to Gilbert, people initially believed the false statements but then rapidly "unaccepted" them, such that these statements had no effect on their recommendations.

How can we tell for sure? These results alone do not show that people went through the process of acceptance and unacceptance. Recall that the second stage, unacceptance, is said to be a more deliberate, controlled process that

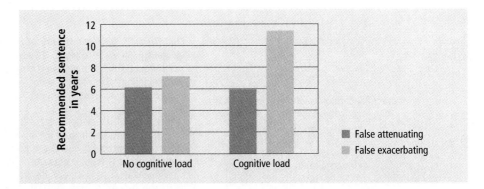

FIGURE 3.8 Cognitive load and the ability to unaccept false statements. ■ People read false information about a criminal that was either attenuating (making his crime seem less severe) or exacerbating (making his crime seem worse). When people were not under cognitive load—they had the time to consider and reject this information—the false information did not influence the sentence they recommended for the criminal. When people were under cognitive load—they had to push a button whenever certain numbers appeared on the computer screen—they had difficulty rejecting the false information. For example, as seen on the right-hand side of the graph, people in the cognitive load condition who heard the exacerbating information recommended much higher sentences—even though they knew the exacerbating information was false. (Adapted from Gilbert et al., 1993).

requires mental effort. If so, then reducing people's ability to concentrate should interrupt this process, allowing automatic acceptance to operate unchecked. To test this hypothesis, Gilbert, Tafarodi, and Malone (1993) gave some participants a second task to do while they were reading the crime reports, thereby increasing their "cognitive load." Similar to an emergency weather bulletin, a string of numbers crawled across the television screen underneath the crime report, and people had to push a button whenever the number 5 appeared in this string of numbers—while reading the crime reports aloud. The number task was designed to reduce people's ability to engage in much controlled processing, thereby disrupting the unacceptance stage of the process. The premise was that this should cause people to recommend longer sentences when the false statements suggested the crime was more severe and shorter sentences when the false statements suggested the crime was less severe, because people would have difficulty unaccepting the false statements. As seen on the right-hand side of Figure 3.8, this is what happened.

In everyday life, of course, we are rarely asked to search for digits on a television screen while performing another task. It is not uncommon, however, to encounter false or misleading information (e.g., extreme claims made in advertisements) while we are preoccupied with some other task (e.g., making sure our three-year-old does not dump her juice on her baby brother). It is under these conditions that people's defenses are down and they are most susceptible to believing false things.

Ironic Processing and Thought Suppression.   There is another interesting consequence of being preoccupied and unable to engage in much controlled processing: It reduces our ability to engage in **thought suppression**—the attempt to avoid thinking about something we would just as soon forget, such as a lost love, an unpleasant encounter with one's boss, or a delectable piece of cheesecake in the

thought suppression: the attempt to avoid thinking about something we would just as soon forget refrigerator. According to Daniel Wegner (1992, 1994), successful thought suppression depends on the interaction of two processes, one relatively automatic and the other relatively controlled. The first, automatic part of the system, called the monitoring process, searches for evidence that the unwanted thought is about to intrude upon consciousness. Once the unwanted thought is detected, the second, more controlled part of the system, called the operating process, comes into play. This is the effortful, conscious attempt to distract oneself by finding something else to think about. These two processes operate in tandem, like two parents conspiring to keep their kids away from junk-food outlets at a mall. One parent's job, akin to the monitoring process, is to keep a watch out for the food joints and let the other one know when they are in the vicinity ("McDonald's alert!"). The other parent's job, akin to the operating process, is then to divert the kids' attention away from the food places ("Hey, kids—look at the picture of Barney in that store!). This system works pretty well as long as each process (parent) does its job, one ever alert for intrusions and the other diverting these intrusions from consciousness.

What happens, though, when the controlled, operating process is unable to do its job, because the person is tired or preoccupied? The monitoring process continues to find instances of the unwanted thought, which then intrude upon consciousness unchecked by the conscious, controlled system. Consequently a state of hyperaccessibility exists, whereby the unwanted thought occurs with high frequency. If the parent whose job it is to distract the children stops doing his or her job, for example, the kids will become even more aware that fast-food joints are in the vicinity, because they will keep hearing the other parent point them out.

To illustrate this process, Daniel Wegner, Ralph Erber, and Robert Bowman (1995) asked people to try not to make sexist responses when completing sentences during a laboratory task. If people had a lot of time to respond they were able to suppress sexist responses, because their monitoring and operating

■ Sometimes we try our best not to think about something, such as fattening foods when we are on a diet. According to research by Daniel Wegner (1994), trying not to think about something can backfire. Particularly when we are under cognitive load, trying to suppress a thought can make that thought come to mind all the more.

processes worked together: one looked for sexist answers and the other suppressed these answers. Another group, however, was instructed not to be sexist and asked to respond immediately. Under these conditions, the operating process did not have time to suppress. The automatic monitoring process that searched for sexist thoughts found many examples and people reported them at a high rate, unchecked by the operating process. Consequently, people in this condition gave the highest number of sexist responses of all. The irony is that, when it is most important to people not to express prejudiced thoughts (e.g., You are on guard not to make any jokes about short people, because your four-foot-eight boss is standing next to you), if you are tired or preoccupied—that is, under cognitive load—these thoughts are especially likely to spill out unchecked.

A Portrayal of Human Judgment

> The greatest of all faults, I should say, is to become conscious of none.
> —Thomas Carlyle

By now we have seen two rather different portraits of the social thinker: Cognitive misers, who take mental shortcuts whenever they can, and motivated tacticians, who choose wisely from an arsenal of mental strategies (e.g., using controlled processing to counteract automatic processing when it is important to do so). Exactly how accurate is social thinking anyway?

A problem in answering this question is defining what a "correct" inference is. Are people at fault for not making inferences in the same way as trained logicians? Should we aspire to be like computers, processing information rationally at all times, devoid of any feeling or emotion? Who is the final arbiter of human thought? These are thorny philosophical issues that cannot be done justice here. (See Cohen, 1981; Gigerenzer, 1993; Kahneman & Tversky, 1983; Nisbett & Ross, 1980; Stich, 1990, for an in-depth discussion of these issues.) We offer what in our view is the best resolution of the debate about how good people are as social thinkers.

We believe that the best portrait of the social thinker lies in between the analogies of people as cognitive misers and motivated tacticians. On the one hand, it is clear that research in the "cognitive miser" tradition has exaggerated the fallibility of human thought. When people are motivated to make careful inferences and have the time and capacity to think, they often think in quite sophisticated ways. No one has yet been able to construct a computer that comes close to matching the power of the human brain. On the other hand, there is plenty of room for improvement in human thought. The fallacies in social thinking we have documented can be quite consequential (Gilovich, 1991; Nisbett & Ross, 1980; Quattrone, 1982; Slusher & Anderson, 1989). For example, in Chapter 13 we will see that racial prejudice can in part be traced back to faulty reasoning processes. The insidious operation of self-fulfilling prophecies, whereby teachers make their false beliefs come true by the way they treat their students, is another example. One of us has gone so far as to use the term *mental contamination* to describe the kinds of biases in our thinking that are pervasive in everyday life (Wilson & Brekke, 1994). Given the evidence that human thinking can sometimes go very wrong, we do not believe that the "motivated tactician" analogy is fully applicable. Perhaps the "flawed scientist" is a better metaphor. Though human beings are brilliant thinkers, people are often blind to truths that don't fit their theories and sometimes even treat others in ways that make their theories come true.

> Modest doubt is called the beacon of the wise.
> —William Shakespeare

Teaching Reasoning Skills

Given that human reasoning is sometimes flawed and can have unpleasant and even tragic consequences, it is important to consider how these mistakes can be corrected. Is it possible to teach people to make better inferences, thereby avoiding some of the mistakes we have discussed in this chapter? If so, what is the best way to do it? Educators, philosophers, and psychologists have debated this question for decades, and recently some fascinating experiments have provided encouraging answers.

One approach is to make people a little more humble about their reasoning abilities. Often we have greater confidence in our judgments than we should (Lichtenstein, Fischhoff, & Phillips, 1982; Vallone, Griffin, Lin, & Ross, 1990). Teachers, for example, sometimes have greater confidence in their beliefs about the abilities of boys versus girls than is warranted. Anyone trying to improve human inference is thus up against an **overconfidence barrier.** Many people seem to think that their reasoning processes are just fine the way they are and hence that there is no need for any remedial action. One approach, then, might be to address this overconfidence directly, getting people to consider the possibility that they might be wrong. This tack was taken by Lord, Lepper, and Preston (1984), who found that when they asked people to consider the opposite point of view to their own, people realized there were other ways to construe the world than their own way and were less likely to make errors in their judgments (see also Anderson, Lepper, & Ross, 1980; Anderson & Sechler, 1986; Koriat, Lichtenstein, & Fischhoff, 1980).

Another approach is to teach people directly some basic statistical and methodological principles about how to reason correctly, with the hope they will apply these principles in their everyday lives. Many of these principles are already taught in courses in statistics and research design, such as the idea that if you want to generalize from a sample of information (e.g., a group of welfare mothers) to a population (e.g., all welfare mothers), you must have a large, unbiased sample. Do people who take these courses apply these principles in their everyday lives? Are they less likely to make the kinds of mistakes we have discussed in this chapter? A recent series of studies by Richard Nisbett and his colleagues have provided encouraging answers to these questions. Nisbett has shown that people's reasoning processes can be improved by college statistics courses, graduate training in research design, and even brief, one-time lessons (Cheng, Holyoak, Nisbett, & Oliver, 1986; Fong, Krantz, & Nisbett, 1986; Nisbett, Fong, Lehman, & Cheng, 1987; Nisbett, Krantz, Jepson, & Kunda, 1983).

One set of studies, for example, examined how different kinds of graduate training influenced people's reasoning on everyday problems involving statistical and methodological reasoning—that is, problems testing mistakes similar to the ones we have considered in this chapter, such as people's understanding of how to generalize from small samples of information (see Figure 3.9 for sample questions). The researchers predicted that students in psychology and medicine would do better on the statistical reasoning problems than students in law and chemistry would, because graduate programs in psychology and medicine include more training in statistics than programs in the other two disciplines do. These predictions were confirmed, as seen in Figure 3.10.

After two years of graduate work, students in psychology and medicine improved on the statistical reasoning problems more than students in law and chemistry did. The improvement among the psychology graduate students was

overconfidence barrier: the finding that people usually have too much confidence in the accuracy of their judgments; people's judgments are usually not as correct as they think they are

> The sign of a first-rate intelligence is the ability to hold two opposed ideas at the same time.
> –F. Scott Fitzgerald

FIGURE 3.9   Sample questions from the test of people's reasoning abilities. ■ (Adapted from Lehman, Lempert, & Nisbett, 1988)

PEOPLE'S REASONING ABILITIES

1. The city of Middleopolis has had an unpopular police chief for a year and a half. He is a political appointee who is a crony of the mayor and he had little previous experience in police administration when he was appointed. The mayor has recently defended the chief in public, announcing that in the time since he took office, crime rates decreased by 12 percent. Which of the following pieces of evidence would most deflate the mayor's claim that his chief is competent? (a) The crime rates of the two cities closest to Middleopolis in location and size have decreased by 18 percent in the same period. (b) An independent survey of the citizens of Middleopolis shows that 40 percent more crime is reported by respondents in the survey than is reported in police records. (c) Common sense indicates that there is little a police chief can do to lower crime rates. These are for the most part due to social and economic conditions beyond the control of officials. (d) The police chief has been discovered to have business contacts with people who are known to be involved in organized crime.

2. After the first two weeks of the major league baseball season, newspapers begin to print the top ten batting averages. Typically, after two weeks, the leading batter has an average of about .450. Yet no batter in major league history has ever averaged .450 at the end of a season. Why do you think this is? (a) A player's high average at the beginning of the season may be just a lucky fluke. (b) A batter who has such a hot streak at the beginning of the season is under a lot of stress to maintain his performance record. Such stress adversely affects his playing. (c) Pitchers tend to get better over the course of the season, as they get more in shape. As pitchers improve, they are more likely to strike out batters, so batters' averages go down. (d) When a batter is known to be hitting for a high average, pitchers bear down more when they pitch to him. (e) When a batter is known to be hitting for a high average, he stops getting good pitches to hit. Instead, pitchers "play the corners" of the plate because they don't mind walking him.

Questions taken from Lehman, D. R., Lempert, R. O., & Nisbett, R. E. (1988). The effects of graduate training on reasoning: Formal discipline and thinking about everyday-life events. *American Psychologist, 43,* 431-442, p. 442.

ANSWERS

1. (a) This question assesses methodological reasoning, namely the recognition that there are several reasons why crime has gone down other than actions taken by the police chief, and that a better "test" of the major's claim is to compare the crime rate in Middleopolis with other, similar cities.
2. (a) This question assesses statistical reasoning, namely the recognition that large samples of information are more likely to reflect true scores and abilities than small samples of information. For example, if you flip a fair coin four times it is not unusual to get all heads or all tails, but if you flip the coin 1000 times it is extremely unlikely that you will get all heads or all tails. Applied to this example, this statistical principle says that when baseball players have small number of at bats it is not unusual to see very high (or very low) averages just by chance. By the end of the season, however, when baseball players have hundreds of at bats, it is very unlikely that they will have a very high average just by luck.

---

particularly impressive. Interestingly, the students in the different disciplines performed equally well on sample items from the Graduate Record Exam, suggesting that they did not differ in overall intelligence. Instead, the different kinds of training they had received appeared to influence how accurately and logically they reasoned on everyday problems (Nisbett, Fong, Lehman, & Cheng, 1987). Thus, there are grounds for being optimistic about people's ability to overcome the kinds of mistakes we have documented in this chapter. And you don't have to go to graduate school to do it. Sometimes it helps simply to consider the

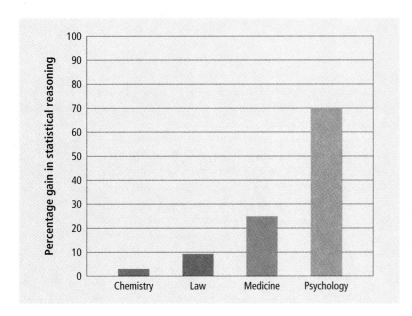

FIGURE 3.10   Performance on a test of statistical reasoning abilities by graduate students in different disciplines. ■ After two years of graduate study, students in psychology and medicine showed more improvement on statistical reasoning problems than students in law and chemistry did. (Adapted from Nisbett et al., 1987)

opposite, as participants in the Lord and colleagues (1984) study did. Beyond this, formal training in statistics helps, at both the graduate and undergraduate levels. So, if you were dreading taking a college statistics course, take heart: It might not only satisfy a requirement for your major but improve your reasoning as well!

SUMMARY

Social cognition is the study of how people select, interpret, and use information to make judgments and decisions. People have developed several strategies and rules to help them understand the social world. **Schemas** are cognitive structures that organize information around themes or subjects. Schemas have a powerful effect on what information we notice, think about, and remember. When we encounter an ambiguous situation, we interpret it according to our schema. Relying on schemas is adaptive and functional up to a point, but people can be overzealous theorists. For example, sometimes we persevere in our beliefs even when they're disproved, as shown in research on the **perseverance effect**. At times, we distort information so that it fits our schemas; for example, the **primacy**

effect shows how our first impression of a person causes us to interpret his or her subsequent behavior in a schema-consistent manner. Because schemas can bias what we see, a **hostile media phenomenon** can result, whereby opposing partisan groups both perceive a neutral, balanced media presentation as hostile to their side. Inasmuch as the media have not presented the facts in the one-sided fashion partisans perceive to be true, each group believes the media are biased against them. Finally, schemas also affect our behavior—we act on the basis of our schemas. The most fascinating example of this is the **self-fulfilling prophecy**, wherein we make our schemas come true by unconsciously treating others in such a way that their response proves to us that our schema about them was right.

In addition to schemas, we use **judgmental heuristics** to help us deal with the large amount of social information with which we are faced. Heuristics are rules of thumb people follow in order to make judgments quickly and efficiently. The **availability heuristic,** the ease with which we can think of something, has a strong effect on how we view the world. One example of the influence of availability is **counterfactual thinking**—that is, mentally changing some aspect of the past as a way of imagining what might have been. The ease with which people can bring to mind alternative scenarios is an example of the use of the availability heuristic, and it can influence people's emotional reactions to events. The **representativeness heuristic** helps us decide how similar one thing is to another; we use it to classify people or situations on the basis of their similarity to a typical case. When using this heuristic, we have a tendency to ignore **base rate information**—the prior probability that something or someone belongs in that classification. People also rely on the **anchoring and adjustment heuristic,** wherein an initial piece of information acts as an anchor, or starting point, for subsequent thoughts on the topic. One example of anchoring and adjustment is **biased sampling,** whereby people make generalizations from samples of information they know are biased or atypical. Whereas all three heuristics are useful, they can also lead to incorrect conclusions. Finally, an important characteristic of social thinking is **automatic processing**—thinking that is nonconscious, unintentional, involuntary, and effortless. Engaging in automatic processing is very efficient, freeing up cognitive resources for other purposes.

Some social psychologists have emphasized the limits of human thinking and the errors people make, referring to people as **cognitive misers**—people with such limited abilities to think that they take mental shortcuts whenever they can. More recently, some have argued that people are **motivated tacticians**—skilled thinkers with a large arsenal of mental rules and strategies, who choose wisely among these strategies, depending on their needs and goals. Consistent with this latter view, people have been found to make fewer errors when the stakes are high—that is, when it is more important to them to be accurate. In addition, people often engage in **controlled processing**—thinking that is conscious, intentional, voluntary, and effortful—to counteract the negative effects of automatic processing. When people are unmotivated or preoccupied, however, controlled processing is difficult to do. In such cases, people are more likely to accept false information and to have difficulty engaging in **thought suppression**: the attempt to avoid thinking about something they would just as soon forget.

Perhaps the best metaphor of the social thinker is that people are like flawed scientists—brilliant thinkers who often blind themselves to truths that don't fit their theories and who sometimes treat others in ways that make those theories come true. Though people often use strategies effectively, there is room for improvement in social thinking. For one thing, people are up against an **overconfidence barrier,** whereby they are too confident in the accuracy of their judgments. Fortunately, recent research has indicated that some of the shortcomings of human reasoning can be improved, particularly by training in statistics.

IF YOU ARE INTERESTED . . .

12 Monkeys (1995), Terry Gilliam, director). In the early 21st century, a convict (Bruce Willis) is sent back in time to investigate the origins of a deadly virus, believed to have been released by an underground terrorist group, called the Army of the Twelve Monkeys, in 1996. A sci-fi thriller with plenty of plot twists, this film explores the way people interpret and process information and the origins of their ideas, memories and beliefs.

Dostoevsky, Fyodor (1945). *Notes from Underground.* A classic disourse on the role of consciousness in human thinking and feeling.

Fiske, S. T., & Taylor, S. E. (1991). *Social cognition* (2nd ed.). New York: McGraw-Hill. A recent, encyclopedic review of the literature on social cognition by two experts in the field.

Gilovich, T. (1991). *How we know what isn't so: The fallibility of human reason in everyday life.* New York: Free Press. An entertaining overview of the many ways in which mental shortcuts can get us into trouble.

Kahneman, D., Slovic, P., & Tversky, A. (1982). *Judgment under uncertainty: Heuristics and biases.* New York: Cambridge University Press. A classic collection of chapters by researchers in the area of human inference.

Nisbett, R. E., & Ross, L. (1980). *Human inference: Strategies and shortcomings of human judgment.* Englewood Cliffs, NJ: Prentice Hall. A lively, poignant review of mental shortcuts and biases in human reasoning by the people who discovered many of them.

Plous, S. (1993). *The psychology of judgment and decision making.* New York: McGraw-Hill. An interesting review of how people form judgments and make decisions, one that expands upon many of the strategies and heuristics we have discussed.

Stand and Deliver (1987). A tough math teacher in an inner-city school challenges his students to do well in calculus. Based on a true story, the teacher expects the students to do well—and they do. An interesting portrayal of the power of social expectations.

Tootsie (1982). An unemployed, male, New York actor finally lands a role on a popular soap opera—as a woman. An amusing, poignant look at the expectations we have about each other based on gender.

Chapter 4

Social Perception: How We Come to Understand Other People

s you've no doubt noticed, other people are not easy to figure out—why are they the way they are? Why do they do what they do? What does it all mean? The frequency and urgency with which we pose these questions are amply demonstrated in this touching story, sent in by a reader to the New York Times:

After ending an office romance, a female friend of mine threw a bag full of her former paramour's love letters, cards and poems into an outside dumpster. The following day he called and wanted to know why she would throw out his letters. She was stunned. He explained that a homeless person going through the garbage read the correspondence and called the number found on a piece of stationery. The homeless man was curious as to why two people who seemed so in love could now be apart. "I would have called you sooner," he told the former boyfriend, "but this was the first quarter I was given today." (DeMarco, 1994)

The homeless man was down on his luck, no home, no money, reduced to rifling through garbage cans—and yet that endless fascination with the human condition still asserted itself. He needed to know why the couple broke up. He even spent his only quarter to find out.

We all have a fundamental fascination with explaining other people's behavior, with piecing together information and coming up with an "answer." It's not an easy job, because the reasons for why others behave as they do are usually hidden from us. All we have to go on is observable behavior: what people do, what they say, their facial expressions, gestures, and tone of voice. Unfortunately, we don't have the ability to read other people's minds—we can't know, truly and completely, who they are and what they mean. Instead, we rely on our impressions and theories, putting them together in as cogent and explanatory a fashion as we can, hoping they will lead to reasonably accurate and useful conclusions.

Our desire to understand other people is so fundamental that we carry it over into our hobbies and recreational lives. We go to movies, read novels, watch soap operas, and "people-watch" at airports because thinking about the behavior of even strangers and fictional characters fascinates us (Weiner, 1985). Advertisers are keenly aware of this fascination and have relied on this aspect of social cognition to mount very successful advertising campaigns for products such as phone services, cigarettes, and coffee.

Undoubtedly, you have seen the ongoing series of commercials for Taster's Choice coffee. The man, the woman, their smouldering gaze and brief conversations laden with innuendo—something more is going on here than just neigh-

Our desire to understand other people is so fundamental that we carry it over into our hobbies and recreational lives.

bors borrowing some instant coffee! The miniseries of commercials was specifically designed to engage viewers' interest in the characters and arouse their curiosity about the couple's budding relationship. "The whole idea of a series is what makes the magic, what makes it so popular," said the president of the advertising agency. "Having wonderful personalities that interact the way they do just makes everybody want to watch what happens to them next" ("Video News," 1995, p. 15). The ad agency recently ran a toll-free phone survey, asking viewers "What's your take on the Taster's Choice couple?" More than 100,000 people responded.

A scene from a Taster's Choice television commercial.

Ad campaigns such as that for Taster's Choice succeed because of our endless curiosity about each other. Why do we expend so much time and energy trying to explain the behavior of others? Because doing so helps us understand and predict our social world (Heider, 1958; Kelley, 1967). In this chapter, we will discuss **social perception**—the study of how we form impressions of other people and how we reach judgments about them. One important source of information that we use is people's nonverbal behavior, such as their facial expressions, body movements, and tone of voice.

social perception: the study of how we form impressions of and make inferences about other people

Nonverbal Behavior

What do we know about people when we first meet them? We know what we can see and hear, and even though we know we should not judge a book by its cover, this kind of easily observable information is critical to our first impressions. Physical characteristics such as people's attractiveness and facial configuration (e.g., a "baby face") influence others' judgments of them (Berry & McArthur, 1986; Hatfield & Sprecher, 1986; McArthur, 1990). We also pay a great deal of attention to what people say. After all, our most noteworthy accomplishment as a species is the development of language; the verbal channel of communication contains an extraordinary amount of information.

But people's words are not the full story. Pretend you are an actor in an improvisational class and say the following sentence out loud in as many different ways as you can: "I don't know her." Try it with an angry tone of voice, a loving one, a sarcastic voice, a fearful tone, and a surprised one. Try emphasizing different words in the sentence, first stressing the word *I*, then the word *her*. The words stay the same, but the message changes dramatically.

This example illustrates that there is a rich source of information about people other than their words: the ways they communicate nonverbally. **Nonverbal communication** refers to a large body of research on different aspects of communication without words. Facial expressions, tone of voice, gestures, body positions and movement, the use of touch, and eye gaze are the most frequently used and diagnostic channels of nonverbal communication (Henley, 1977; Knapp, 1980). Even in a setting where you might think the verbal channel is paramount—a courtroom—various forms of nonverbal communication can prove so powerful and disruptive that a judge is forced to "outlaw" them. For instance, in February 1995 Judge Lance Ito publicly reprimanded all persons attending the trial of O. J. Simpson for displaying their emotions and reactions to courtroom events. Judge Ito said, "Let me remind you that any reactions, gestures . . . facial expressions . . . made during these court sessions, especially when the jury is here, those activities are inappropriate and will result in your expulsion" ("Gestures," 1995, p. 3).

nonverbal communication: the way in which people communicate, intentionally or unintentionally, without words; nonverbal cues include facial expressions, tone of voice, gestures, body position and movement, the use of touch, and eye gaze

How does nonverbal communication work? Nonverbal cues serve many functions in communication. Michael Argyle (1975) describes the primary uses of nonverbal behavior as (a) *expressing emotion* (your eyes narrow, your eyebrows lower, you stare intensely, your mouth is set in a thin, straight line—you're angry), (b) *conveying attitudes* (e.g., "I like you"—smiles, extended eye contact—or "I don't like you"—eyes averted, flat tone of voice, body turned away), (c) *communicating one's personality traits* ("I'm outgoing"—broad gestures, a change in inflection when speaking, an energetic tone of voice), and (d) *facilitating verbal communication* (you lower your voice and look away as you finish your sentence so that your conversational partner knows you are done and it is his or her turn to speak).

In addition, Paul Ekman (1965) notes that some nonverbal cues repeat or complement the spoken message, as when you smile while saying "I'm so happy for you!" Others actually contradict the spoken words. Communicating sarcasm is the classic example of verbal-nonverbal contradiction. Think about how you'd say "I'm so happy for you" sarcastically. (You could use your tone of voice, stressing the word *so* with an ironic twist, or you could roll your eyes as you speak, a sign of sarcasm in North American culture.) Nonverbal cues can also substitute for the verbal message. Hand gestures such as flashing the "OK" sign or drawing a finger across your throat convey clear messages without any words at all.

Nonverbal forms of communication have typically been studied individually, in their separate "channels" (e.g., eye gaze or gestures), even though in everyday life nonverbal cues of many kinds occur all at the same time in a quite dazzling orchestration of information (Archer & Akert, 1980, 1984). Let's focus on a few of these channels and then turn to how we interpret the full symphony of nonverbal information as it naturally occurs.

Facial Expressions of Emotion

Without doubt, the crown jewel of nonverbal communication is the facial expressions channel. This aspect of communication has the longest history of research, beginning with Charles Darwin's (1872) book *The Expression of the Emotions in Man and Animals;* its primacy is due to the exquisite communicativeness of the human face. Look at the photographs on the next page; we bet you can figure out the meaning of these expressions with very little effort.

Darwin's research on facial expressions has had a major impact on the field in many areas; we will focus on his belief that the primary emotions conveyed by the face are universal—all human beings everywhere express (or **encode**) these emotions in the same way, and all human beings can interpret (or **decode**) them with equal accuracy. Given Darwin's (1872) interest in evolution, it is not surprising that he believed nonverbal forms of communication to be "species-specific" and not "culture-specific." He stated that facial expressions were vestiges of once useful physiological reactions—for example, if early hominids ate something that tasted terrible, they would have wrinkled their noses in displeasure (from the bad smell) and expelled the food from their mouths. Note that the photograph on the next page showing the disgusted expression demonstrates this sort of reaction. Darwin (1872) states that such facial expressions then acquired evolutionary significance; being able to communicate such emotional states (e.g., the feeling of disgust, not for food but for another person or a situation) had survival value for the developing species (Hansen & Hansen, 1988; McArthur & Baron, 1983). Was Darwin right? Are facial expressions of emotion universal?

The answer is yes, for the six major emotional expressions: anger, happiness, surprise, fear, disgust, and sadness (Buck, 1984; Ekman, Friesen, & Ellsworth, 1982a, 1982b; Izard, 1977). For example, in a particularly well-designed study, Paul Ekman and Walter Friesen (1971) traveled to New Guinea, where they stud-

> An eye can threaten
> like a loaded and
> leveled gun, or can
> insult like hissing or
> kicking; or, in its
> altered mood, by beams
> of kindness, it can
> make the heart dance
> with joy.
> –Ralph Waldo Emerson,
> *The Conduct of Life*, 1860

encode: to express or emit nonverbal behavior, such as smiling or patting someone on the back

decode: to interpret the meaning of the nonverbal behavior other people express, such as deciding that a pat on the back was an expression of condescension and not kindness ied the decoding ability of the Fore, a preliterate tribe that had had no contact with Western civilization. They told the Fore people brief stories with emotional content and then showed them photographs of American men and women expressing the six emotions; the Fore's job was to match the facial expressions of emotion to the stories. They were as accurate as Western subjects had been. The researchers then asked the Fore people to demonstrate, while being photographed, facial expressions that would match the stories they were told. These photographs, when later shown to American research participants, were also decoded accurately. Thus, there is considerable evidence that the ability to interpret at least the six major emotions is cross-cultural—part of being human and not a product of people's cultural experience (Ekman et al., 1987; Izard, 1969).

Besides the six major emotions, are there other emotional states that are communicated with distinctive and readily identifiable facial expressions? Current research is exploring just this question. For example, recent research by Dacher Keltner (1995) suggests that embarrassment has a distinctive nonverbal display as tested in his sample of Caucasian and African American undergraduates. Keltner's research participants were asked to perform difficult tasks that often made them feel lacking in ability or poise, all the while receiving explicit feedback from the experimenter on how they were doing. Needless to say, they often felt embarrassed (as well as other emotions, e.g., amused). Keltner carefully coded photographs of the various expressions on their faces during the tasks, and

> When the eyes say one thing, and the tongue another, a practiced man relies on the language of the first.
> –Ralph Waldo Emerson, *The Conduct of Life*, 1860

■ These photographs depict facial expressions of the six major emotions. Can you guess the emotion expressed on each face? (Adapted from Ekman & Friesen, 1975)

Answers: (clockwise, beginning with upper-left photo): Anger, fear, disgust, sadness, happiness, and surprise.

■ What emotion is this man feeling? If you said "Embarrassment," you'd be right.

display rules: culturally determined rules about which nonverbal behaviors are appropriate to display

he later asked other research participants to decode them. Keltner concluded that a distinctive expression of embarrassment existed, composed of turning the head away, looking down, shifting the gaze to the side, evincing a controlled smile (e.g., with the lips pressed), and sometimes, touching the face with one's hand—all lasting about four to five seconds in a typical instance. The photograph on this page illustrates this prototypical "embarrassed" nonverbal response. Further research will tell us whether this is a universal expression of embarrassment or one that is found only in American (or Western) society.

While there is ample proof that the six major emotions are expressed the same way by people all over the world, culture does play a role as to when and how people display emotions on their faces. Ekman and Friesen (1969) note that **display rules** are particular to each culture and dictate what kind of emotional expression people are supposed to show. For example, American cultural norms discourage emotional displays in men, such as grief or crying, but allow the facial display of such emotions in women. In Japan, traditional cultural rules dictate that women should not exhibit a wide, uninhibited smile (Ramsey, 1981); Japanese women will often hide their wide smiles behind their hands, while Western women are allowed—indeed encouraged—to smile broadly and often (Henley, 1977). In fact, the cultural display rules that govern Japanese nonverbal expression are surprisingly different from Western ones. Japanese norms lead people to cover up negative facial expressions with smiles and laughter and to display fewer facial expressions in general than is true in the West (Friesen, 1972; Morsbach, 1973). This is undoubtedly what lies behind the Western stereotype that Asians are "inscrutable" and "hard to read."

A final note about decoding facial expressions accurately: This situation is more complicated than it appears, because people frequently display affect blends (Ekman & Friesen, 1975), wherein one part of their face is registering one emotion and another part is registering a different emotion. Take a look at the photographs on this page and see if you can tell which two emotions are being expressed in each face. In the photograph on the left, we see a blend of anger (the eye and eyebrow region) and disgust (the nose and mouth region). (It may help to

■ Often people express more than one emotion at the same time. Can you tell which emotions these people are expressing? The answers are printed below. (Adapted from Ekman & Friesen, 1975)

Answers: The man is expressing a blend of anger and disgust. The woman is expressing a blend of surprise and happiness.

cover half of the photograph with your hand to see each emotional expression clearly.) This is the sort of expression you might display if a person told you something that was both horrible and inappropriate—you'd be disgusted with the content and angry that the person told you.

Other Channels of Nonverbal Communication

There are, of course, other channels of nonverbal communication. Eye contact and gaze are particularly powerful nonverbal cues; we become suspicious when a person doesn't "look us in the eye" while speaking, and people wearing dark sunglasses can be quite disconcerting to talk to. How people use personal space is another form of nonverbal communication. Imagine you are talking to a person who stands too close to you (or too far away); these deviations from "normal" spacing will affect your impressions of him or her. Cultures vary greatly in what is considered normative use of personal space (Hall, 1969). For example, the United States is a low-contact culture: Most Americans like to have a bubble of open space, a few feet in radius, surrounding them. Other cultures, such as those of South America and the Middle East, are high-contact ones: Strangers will think nothing of standing right next to each other, to the point of touching.

Gestures of the hands and arms are also a fascinating means of communication. We are very adept at understanding certain gestures, such as the OK sign, in which one forms a circle with the thumb and forefinger and the rest of the fingers

■ The rules for proxemic behavior vary across cultures. For example, in Japan strangers will stand so close to each other that they are touching, something that Americans would find extremely impolite if not abhorrent.

La barbe! Rasoir!: How dull. "Beard! Razor!" acquired the meaning "boring" in the nineteenth century.

Mon oeil!: "My eye!" You can't fool me!

Il est bourré!: He's stuffed; he's potted; he's drunk.

■ These photographs depict French nonverbal emblems. The gestures are clearly understood in France but might be difficult for an American to interpret. (Adapted from Wylie, 1977)

emblems: nonverbal gestures that have well-understood definitions within a given culture; they usually have direct verbal translations, such as the OK sign

curve above the circle, and "flipping the bird," in which one bends all the fingers down at the first knuckle except the longest, middle finger. Gestures like these, for which there are clear, well-understood definitions, are called **emblems** (Ekman & Friesen, 1975). The important point about emblems is that they are not universal; each culture has devised its own emblems, and these need not be understandable to people from other cultures. Thus, "flipping the bird" will be a clear communicative sign in American society, whereas in some parts of Europe you'd need to make a quick gesture with a cupped hand under your chin to convey the same message. The photos on this page illustrate some French emblems that are different from our American emblems.

Multichannel Nonverbal Communication

Except for certain specific situations (e.g., talking on the telephone), everyday life is made up of social interaction in a multichannel nonverbal sense (Rosenthal et al., 1979). Typically, many nonverbal cues are available to us when we talk to or observe other people. How do we use this information? And how accurately do we use it?

In order to study multichannel nonverbal decoding, Robin Akert and Dane Archer (Archer & Akert, 1991) have constructed a nonverbal communication decoding task that closely mirrors real-life interpretative situations. The Social Interpretations Task (SIT) videotape is composed of 20 scenes of naturally occurring nonverbal behavior (Archer & Akert, 1977a, 1977b, 1980, 1984). Real people, not actors, are seen and heard having real conversations, not scripted ones. The scenes last a minute or so, giving the viewer a slice of a real interaction. Following each scene, the viewer is asked a question about the people in the scene or their relationship to each other. For example, in one scene two women are seen playing with a baby. The viewer is asked, "Which woman is the mother of the baby?" A clear criterion for accuracy exists for each of the scenes; one of the

1. Which of these two women is the mother of the baby? a. The woman on the left. b. the woman on the right. c. neither woman.

2. Are these two people: a. Friends who have known each other for at least six months? b. Acquaintances who have had several conversations? c. Strangers who have never talked before?

3. All three of these men claim to have won the poker game. Who really won the game? a. The man on the left; b. The man in the center; c. The man on the right.

■ The above photographs provide examples of the Social Interpretations Task. The answers are printed below. (Adapted from Archer & Akert, 1977)

Answers: 1—b; 2—c; 3—c.

women really is the mother of the baby. However, neither of the women states this fact out loud; nor did the women realize this would be the interpretative question paired with their scene. In order to get this and the other scenes right, the viewer must pay attention to and interpret the nonverbal behavior of the people in the scenes. Akert and Archer found that 64 percent of the more than 1,400 people tested were able to decode this scene accurately, far above the chance level of accuracy of 33 percent.

Further research with the SIT videotape has shown that the important, or diagnostic, nonverbal information is actually diffused throughout each scene (Archer & Akert, 1980). In other words, it is not typically the case that only one significant clue signals the right answer. Instead, useful nonverbal information is present across many channels in each scene. This makes the decoder's job easier: If you fail to notice the eye gaze behavior, you may notice the tone of voice or the unusual gesture and still arrive at an accurate judgment. Research has also shown that some people are particularly talented at decoding nonverbal cues accurately, while others are dismally poor at this task. Robin Akert and Abigail Panter have explored various personality traits to see if these predict who the good decoders are; for example, there is some evidence that extraverts are more accurate decoders of nonverbal cues on a SIT-like task than introverts are (Akert & Panter, 1986).

Gender Differences in Nonverbal Communication

It may have occurred to you to wonder whether one sex is better than the other at understanding nonverbal communication. Who is better at decoding nonverbal cues—men or women? And who is better at encoding nonverbal information? A large number of studies have found that women are better at both decoding and encoding (Hall, 1979, 1984; Rosenthal & DePaulo, 1979).

As with most rules, however, there is an exception: Though women are superior to men at deciphering someone's nonverbal cues when that person is telling the truth, they lose their superiority when the person is lying. Robert Rosenthal and Bella DePaulo (1979) found that women were more likely to take deceptive communications at face value, believing the lie, while men were more likely to pick up on the nonverbal cues and correctly conclude the individual was lying. Given that women are generally superior decoders, why do they lose their advantage when faced with deceptive communications? Rosenthal and DePaulo (1979) suggest that it is because women are more polite than men. While women have the ability to decode nonverbal cues of lying, they tend to turn off this skill when faced with deception, in order to be polite to the speaker.

social-role theory: a theory that sex differences in social behavior are due to society's division of labor between the sexes; this division leads to differences in gender-role expectations and sex-typed skills, both of which are responsible for differences in men's and women's social behavior

This interpretation fits nicely with a theory of sex differences offered by Alice Eagly (1987). According to Eagly's **social-role theory,** in most societies there is a division of labor on the basis of gender. Typically, women are more likely than men to hold certain familial and occupational roles, such as being the primary caregiver to children. According to Eagly, this division of labor has two important consequences. First, gender-role expectations arise, wherein members of the society expect men and women to have attributes consistent with their role. Because of the social roles they occupy, women are expected to be more nurturing, friendly, expressive, and sensitive—and so they are. Second, men and women develop different sets of skills and attitudes, based on their gender roles. Because of their position in many societies, it is more important for women to learn skills such as sensitivity and communication. In addition, because women are less powerful in many societies and are less likely to occupy roles of higher status, it is more important for women to learn to be accommodating and polite (Deaux & Major, 1987; Henley, 1977). According to Eagly (1987), gender-role expectations and sex-typed skills combine to produce sex differences in social behavior, such as the differences in nonverbal behavior we just discussed.

One way to test this theory would be to examine sex differences in cultures that have different gender-role expectations and sex-typed skills. If women are more polite in reading nonverbal cues because of the social roles they occupy in society, then this tendency to be polite should be especially strong in those cultures where women are most oppressed. This is exactly what Judith Hall (1979) found in her cross-cultural study of nonverbal behavior. First, she classified each of 11 countries as to the level of oppression of women, based on such statistics as the number of women who go to college and the prevalence of women's groups in each country. She then examined how likely women in each country were to show the "politeness pattern" when reading other people's nonverbal behaviors—that is, to focus on nonverbal cues that convey what people want others to see and to ignore nonverbal cues that "leak" people's true feelings. Sure enough, the tendency of women to be nonverbally polite in this manner was especially strong in those cultures where women are most oppressed.

To summarize, we can learn quite a lot about people from their nonverbal behavior, including their attitudes, emotions, and personality traits. Nonverbal behavior gives us many bits of information, "data," as it were, that we then use to construct our overall impressions or theories about people. What is someone really like? What caused her to act as she did? In the next sections, we turn to the cognitive processes people use to form impressions of others.

Implicit Personality Theories: Filling in the Blanks

As we saw in Chapter 3, when people are unsure about the nature of the social world, they use their schemas to fill in the gaps. An excellent example of this use of schemas is the way in which we form impressions of other people. If we know someone is kind, we use an important type of schema called an **implicit personality theory** to determine what else the person is like. These theories consist of our ideas about what kinds of personality traits go together (Anderson & Sedikides, 1990; Schneider, 1973). If a person is kind, our implicit personality theory tells us he or she is probably generous as well; if a person is stingy, we believe he or she is probably irritable as well.

These implicit theories about personality serve the same function as any schema: As "cognitive misers," we can extrapolate from a small to a much larger amount of information (Fiske & Taylor, 1991; Markus & Zajonc, 1985). In this case, we can use just a few observations of a person as a starting point and then, using our schema, create a much fuller understanding of what that person is like (Kim & Rosenberg, 1980). This way, we can form impressions quickly, without having to spend weeks with people to figure out what they are like.

Implicit personality theories are interesting in that there are shared components to them—many of us have very similar theories—and there is also room for idiosyncratic variation—we have some theories that are very different (Hamilton, 1970; Kuusinen, 1969; Pedersen, 1965). These social theories are developed over time and with experience. Not surprisingly, they often have a strong cultural component: In a given society, most people will share some implicit personality theories because these are cultural beliefs passed on in that society. For example, Rosenberg, Nelson, and Vivekananthan (1968) asked college students to think of a number of people they knew who were quite different from each other. The researchers then asked the students to sort a stack of 60 personality traits into separate piles, each pile representing a student's personality description of a separate person. Though all of the participants were using the same 60 traits, they were each thinking about and describing different people. Would they group the personality traits into similar piles?

Rosenberg and colleagues (1968) found strong evidence for such similarity, or shared implicit personality theories. Figure 4.1 shows a kind of map of participants' responses. Personality traits that are close together on this map are the ones the students thought went together in the same person. For example, if someone was seen as helpful, they rated the person as sincere as well. The two axes, "Positive/Negative social traits" and "Positive/Negative intellectual traits," are a way of summarizing the implicit personality theories people used.

Cultural variation in implicit personality theories was demonstrated in an intriguing study by Curt Hoffman, Ivy Lau, and David Johnson (1986). They noted that different cultures have different ideas about personality types—that is, the kinds of people for whom there are simple, agreed-on verbal labels. For example, in Western cultures we agree that there is a kind of person who has an artistic personality: This is a person who is creative, intense, and temperamental and who has an unconventional lifestyle. The Chinese, however, do not have a schema or implicit personality theory for an artistic type. There are no labels in the Chinese language to describe someone with this collection of traits. Granted, there are words in Chinese to describe the individual characteristics of such people, such as the word for creative, but there are no labels like "an artistic type" or "a bohemian" that describe the whole constellation of traits implied by

implicit personality theory: a type of schema people use to group various kinds of personality traits together; for example, many people believe that if someone is kind, he or she is generous as well

> Others are to us like the "characters" in fiction, external and incorrigible; the surprises they give us turn out in the end to have been predictable—unexpected variations on the theme of being themselves.
>
> —Mary McCarthy

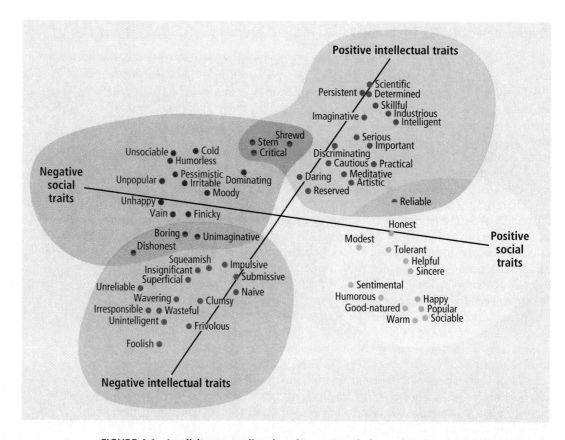

FIGURE 4.1   Implicit personality theories. ■ People have theories about which personality traits go together in a person. The traits that are close together in this figure are considered to be likely to exist in the same person. For example, if someone is known to be helpful, we assume he or she is sincere as well (see lower-right-hand corner of figure). (Adapted from Rosenberg, Nelson, & Vivekananthan, 1968)

the English term. Similarly, in China there are categories of personality that do not exist in Western cultures. For example, a *shi gú* person is someone who is worldly, devoted to his or her family, socially skillful, and somewhat reserved.

Hoffman and colleagues (1986) hypothesized that these cultural implicit personality theories influence the way people form impressions of others. To test this hypothesis, they wrote stories that described a person behaving like an artistic type of person or *shi gú* type of person, without using those labels to describe the person. These stories were written in both English and Chinese. The English versions were given to a group of native English speakers who did not speak any other language and to a group of Chinese-English bilinguals. Another group of Chinese-English bilinguals received the versions written in Chinese.

If people were using their cultural theories to understand the stories they read, what would we expect to happen? One measure of the use of theories (or schemas) is the tendency to fill in the blanks—that is, to believe that information fitting the schema was observed when in fact it was not. Hoffman and colleagues (1986) asked the participants to write down their impressions of the characters in the stories; they then looked to see whether the participants listed traits that were not used in the stories but did fit the artistic or *shi gú* personality type. For example, "unreliable" was not mentioned in the "artistic personality type" story but is consistent with that implicit personality theory.

As seen in Figure 4.2, when the native English speakers read about the characters in English, they were much more likely to form an impression that was consistent with the artistic type than with the *shi gú* type. Similarly, when the Chinese-English bilinguals read the descriptions of the characters in English, they too formed an impression that was consistent with the artistic type but not with the *shi gú* type, because English provides a convenient label for the artistic type. In comparison, Chinese-English bilinguals who read the descriptions in Chinese showed the opposite pattern of results. Their impression of the *shi gú* character was more consistent with the schema than their impression of the artist was, because the Chinese language provides a convenient label or implicit personality theory for this kind of person. These results are consistent with a well-known argument by Whorf (1956) that the language people speak influences the way they think about the world. Characters described identically were perceived differently by the bilingual research participants, depending on the language (and therefore the implicit personality theory) that was used. Thus, one's culture and one's language produce widely shared implicit personality theories, and these theories can influence the kinds of impressions people form of each other.

■ Implicit personality theories differ from culture to culture. Westerners assume there is an artistic type of person—someone who is creative, intense, temperamental, and unconventional. The Chinese have no such implicit personality theory. The Chinese have a category of a *shi gú* person—someone who is worldly, devoted to his or her family, socially skillful, and somewhat reserved. Westerners do not have this implicit personality theory.

FIGURE 4.2   Implicit personality theories: How our culture and language shape our impressions of other people. ■ People formed an impression of other people that was consistent with the implicit personality theory contained in their language. For example, when Chinese-English bilinguals read stories about people in English, they were likely to form impressions consistent with a Western implicit theory, the artistic personality. When Chinese-English bilinguals read the same stories in Chinese, they were likely to form impressions consistent with a Chinese implicit theory, the *shi gú* personality. (Adapted from Hoffman, 1986)

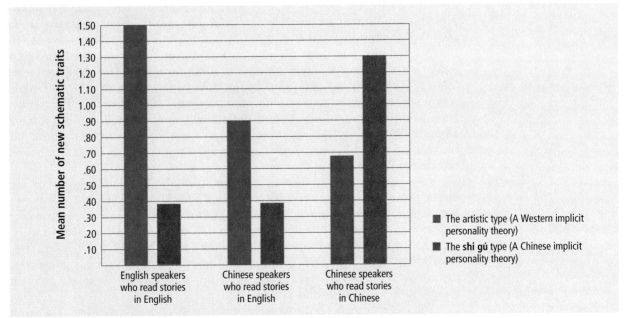

■ The artistic type (A Western implicit personality theory)

■ The **shi gú** type (A Chinese implicit personality theory)

Using Mental Shortcuts When Forming Impressions

Sometimes it is unclear which theory or trait applies to someone we meet. People's behavior can be ambiguous, making it difficult to decide what kind of person they are. Imagine, for example, that you are riding on a city bus and a man gets on and sits beside you. You can't help but notice that he's acting a little strangely. He mutters incoherently to himself, stares at everyone on the bus, and repeatedly rubs his face with one hand. How would you make sense out of his behavior? You have many implicit personality theories, and more than one could explain his ambiguous behavior. What dictates your choice?

The Role of Accessibility and Priming. Recent research indicates that your impression of the man on the bus can be affected by the **accessibility** of trait categories, defined as the extent to which thoughts, ideas, and traits are at the forefront of our minds and are therefore likely to be used when we are making judgments about the social world (Higgins, in press; Wyer & Srull, 1989).

accessibility: the ease with which different thoughts and ideas can be brought to mind; an idea that is accessible is already on our minds or can easily be brought to mind

Traits become accessible two ways. First, some traits can be chronically accessible due to past experience. For example, if in your family there is a history of alcoholism, traits describing an alcoholic are likely to be very accessible to you, increasing the likelihood that these traits will come to mind when you are thinking about the behavior of the man on the bus. On the other hand, if someone you know suffers from mental illness, then thoughts about how the mentally ill behave are more likely to be accessible than thoughts about alcoholics are, leading you to interpret the man's behavior very differently.

Second, several studies have shown that traits can also become accessible for more arbitrary reasons. Whatever we happen to have been thinking or doing prior to encountering an event can prime a trait, making it more accessible and thus more likely to be used to interpret that event. Suppose, for example, that right before the man on the bus sat down, you were reading Ken Kesey's *One Flew over the Cuckoo's Nest*, a novel about patients in a mental hospital. Given that thoughts about mental patients were accessible in your mind, you would probably assume that the man's strange behavior was due to mental illness. If, on the other hand, thoughts about alcoholism were fresh in your mind—for example, you had just looked out the window and seen an alcoholic leaning against a building drinking a bottle of wine—you would probably assume the man on the bus had had a few too many (see Figure 4.3). These are examples of **priming**, whereby a recent experience, such as reading Kesey's novel, increases the accessibility of certain traits, such as those describing the mentally ill, making it more likely that these traits will be used to interpret a new event—such as the behavior of the man on the bus—even though this new event is completely unrelated to the one that originally primed the traits.

priming: the process by which recent experiences increase a trait's accessibility

Tory Higgins, Stephen Rholes, and Carl Jones (1977) illustrated this priming effect in the following experiment. Research participants were told that they would take part in two unrelated studies. The first was a perception study, where they would be asked to identify different colors while at the same time memorizing a list of words. The second was a reading comprehension study, where they would be asked to read a paragraph about someone named Donald and then give their impressions of him. This paragraph is shown in Figure 4.4. Take a moment to read it. What do you think of Donald?

You might have noticed that many of Donald's actions are ambiguous, interpretable in either a positive or a negative manner. Take the fact that he piloted a

FIGURE 4.3 How we interpret an ambiguous situation: The role of accessibility and priming

boat without knowing much about it and wants to sail across the Atlantic. It is possible to put a positive spin on these acts, deciding that Donald has an admirable sense of adventure. It's just as easy, however, to put a negative spin on these acts, assuming that Donald is a rather reckless and foolhardy individual.

How did the participants interpret Donald's behavior? Higgins and his colleagues (1977) found, as expected, that it depended on whether positive or negative traits were primed and accessible. In the first study, the researchers divided people into two groups and gave them different words to memorize. People who had first memorized the words *adventurous, self-confident, independent,* and *persistent* later formed positive impressions of Donald, viewing him as a likable man who enjoyed new challenges. People who had first memorized *reckless, conceited, aloof,* and *stubborn* later formed negative impressions of Donald, viewing him as a stuck-up person who took needlessly dangerous chances.

We should note that it was not just memorizing any positive or negative words that influenced people's impressions of Donald. In other conditions, research participants memorized words that were also positive or negative, such

All thought is a feat of association: having what's in front of you bring up something in your mind that you almost didn't know you knew.

–Robert Frost, interview, *Writers at Work: Second Series,* 1963

Description of Donald

  Donald spent a great deal of time in his search of what he liked to call excitement. He had already climbed Mt. McKinley, shot the Colorado rapids in a kayak, driven in a demolition derby, and piloted a jet-powered boat—without knowing very much about boats. He had risked injury, and even death, a number of times. Now he was in search of new excitement. He was thinking, perhaps, he would do some skydiving or maybe cross the Atlantic in a sailboat. By the way he acted one could readily guess that Donald was well aware of his ability to do many things well. Other than business engagements, Donald's contacts with people were rather limited. He felt he didn't really need to rely on anyone. Once Donald made up his mind to do something it was as good as done no matter how long it might take or how difficult the going might be. Only rarely did he change his mind even when it might well have been better if he had.

FIGURE 4.4 Priming and accessibility. ■ People read the above paragraph about Donald and formed an impression of him. In a prior study, some people had memorized words that could be used to interpret Donald in a negative way (e.g., *reckless, conceited*), while others had memorized words that could be used to interpret Donald in a positive way (e.g., *adventurous, self-confident*). As seen in the graph, those who had memorized the negative words formed a much more negative impression of Donald than those who had memorized the positive words. (Adapted from Higgins, Rholes, & Jones, 1977)

as *neat* or *disrespectful*. However, these traits did not influence their impressions of Donald, because the words did not apply to Donald's actions. Thus, thoughts have to be both accessible and applicable before they will act as primes, exerting an influence on our impressions of the social world.

Causal Attribution: Answering the "Why" Question

We have seen that when we observe other people, we have a rich source of information—their nonverbal behavior—on which to base our impressions. From their nonverbal behavior, we can also make guesses about people's personalities, such as how friendly or outgoing they are. And once we get this far, we use our implicit personality theories to fill in the blanks: If a person is friendly, he or she must be sincere as well.

  However, nonverbal behavior is not a fail-safe indicator of what a person is really thinking or feeling. If you encounter an acquaintance and she says "It's great to see you!" with enthusiastic nonverbal cues, does she really mean it? Perhaps she is acting more thrilled than she really feels, out of politeness. Perhaps she is outright lying and really can't stand you. The point is that even though nonverbal communication is sometimes easy to decode, there is still substantial ambiguity as to what a person's behavior really means (DePaulo, 1992; DePaulo, Stone, & Lassiter, 1985; Schneider, Hastorf, & Ellsworth, 1979).

  To answer the "why" question, we need to go beyond the information given, inferring, from what we observe, what people are really like and what motivates

In the beginning was not the word, not the deed, not the silly serpent. In the beginning was *why*? Why did she pluck the apple? Was she bored? Was she inquisitive? Was she paid? Did Adam put her up to it? If not, who did?

–John le Carré,
The Russia House, 1989

them to act as they do. How we go about answering these questions is the focus of **attribution theory,** the study of how we infer the causes of other people's behavior

The Nature of the Attributional Process

Fritz Heider (1958) is frequently referred to as the father of attribution theory. His influential book defined the field of social perception, and his legacy is still very much evident in current research. Heider (1958) discussed what he called "naive" or "commonsense" psychology. In his view, people were like amateur scientists, trying to understand other people's behavior by piecing together information until they arrived at a reasonable explanation or cause. Heider (1958) was intrigued by what seemed reasonable to people and by how they arrived at their conclusions.

One of Heider's (1958) most valuable contributions is a simple dichotomy: When trying to decide why people behave as they do—for example, why a father has just yelled at his son—we can make either an **internal** (dispositional) **attribution** or an **external** (situational) **attribution.** We can decide that the cause of the father's observed behavior was something about him—his personality, attitudes, or character—an explanation that assigns the causality of his behavior *internally.* For example, we might decide that the father has poor parenting skills and disciplines his child in inappropriate ways. Conversely, we can decide that the cause of his behavior was something about the situation—such as the fact that his son had just stepped into the street without looking—an explanation that assigns the causality of his behavior *externally* (i.e., it was the child's actions that triggered the father's behavior, not something distinctive about the father's personality, attitudes, or character).

Notice that our impression of the father will be very different depending on the type of attribution we make. If we make an internal attribution, we'll have a negative impression of him. If we make an external attribution, we won't learn much about him—after all, most parents would have done the same thing if they were in that situation and their child had just disobeyed them by stepping into the street. Quite a difference!

Another of Heider's (1958) important contributions was his discussion of our preference for internal attributions over external ones. While either type of attribution is always possible, Heider (1958) noted that we tend to see the causes of a person's behavior as residing in that person. We are perceptually focused on people—they are who we notice—and the situation, which is often hard to see and hard to describe, can be overlooked. This observation of Heider's, that internal attributions are particularly attractive to perceivers, is the starting point for one of the basic theories of how people make attributions: correspondent inference theory (Jones & Davis, 1965).

Correspondent Inference Theory: From Acts to Dispositions

Edward Jones and Keith Davis developed **correspondent inference theory** to describe the process by which we arrive at an internal attribution: how we *infer dispositions,* or internal personality characteristics, from *corresponding behaviors* or actions (Jones, 1990; Jones & Davis, 1965; Jones & McGillis, 1976). Suppose, for example, we learn that Karen has accepted a job in an advertising

attribution theory: a description of the way in which people explain the causes of their own and other people's behavior

internal attribution: the inference that a person is behaving a certain way because of something about him or her, such as the person's attitudes, character, or personality

external attribution: the inference that a person is behaving a certain way because of something about the situation he or she is in; the assumption is that most people would respond the same way in that situation

correspondent inference theory: the theory that we make internal attributions about a person when there are (a) few noncommon effects of his or her behavior and (b) the behavior is unexpected agency in New York City. Why? Did Karen accept the job because she is interested in advertising? Because she wants to live in New York? Because the job pays well? Correspondent inference theory is concerned with how we narrow down these possibilities to a specific conclusion about why Karen did what she did.

The Role of Noncommon Effects.   The main way we make internal attributions, according to the theory, is by comparing what people could accomplish by the behavior they chose to perform with what they could have accomplished with alternative actions (comparing the effects of the different choices, in the words of the theory). For example, to determine why Karen accepted the advertising job, we would consider what Karen accomplished by accepting this job, compared to what she could have accomplished by making a different choice. An internal attribution is easier to the extent that there are few **noncommon effects** of these different choices—that is, if by accepting the job in New York Karen could accomplish only one or two things that she could not accomplish by accepting other jobs.

noncommon effects: effects produced by a particular course of action that could not be produced by alternative courses of action

For instance, suppose we knew that when Karen accepted the advertising job, she turned down an offer to teach history in a rural high school in Wyoming. Here it would be hard to know why she chose the advertising job, because by taking this job she could accomplish so many things that she could not accomplish by accepting the teaching job—starting a career in advertising, living in a large city, earning more money (see Figure 4.5). In this situation, there would be many noncommon (or unique) effects of the two options. Suppose, however, we knew that Karen had narrowed down her choices to two options: (a) a job with the Hook 'Em Agency, which specializes in cigarette ads, and (b) a job with the Help 'Em Agency, which specializes in public service ads. Suppose, further, that we knew the two jobs paid the same and had the same opportunities for advancement. If we learn that Karen accepted the job at the Help 'Em Agency, we would be more confident about why Karen made the choice she did, because there is

FIGURE 4.5   The role of noncommon effects. ■ When people can accomplish many things by one action that they cannot accomplish by an alternative action, it can be difficult to tell why they did what they did (see left side of figure). When there are few noncommon effects—when people can accomplish very few things by one action that they cannot accomplish by the other action—it is easier to make an internal attribution for why they did what they did (see right side of figure).

■ We learn more about people when they behave in unexpected ways than when they behave in expected ways.

only one noncommon effect between the two options: their areas of specialization. Clearly, Karen must have wanted to work on public service ads more than cigarette ads.

The Role of Expectations.   There is another type of information that people take into account when making attributions, according to Edward Jones (1990). A course of action may be uninformative even when it involves few noncommon effects, because everyone would have done the same thing. Think back to our example about Karen. Suppose we know she was deciding between two jobs that were nearly identical, except that one paid $50,000 a year and the other paid $10,000 a year. Since the only noncommon effect is the amount of pay, we should be able to make a confident, internal attribution about Karen when we learn that she chose the one that pays more. Or can we? Actually, we learn almost nothing about Karen, because anyone would have done the same thing. We learn more about people when the noncommon effects are something that not everyone would have chosen to accomplish. If Karen chose the $10,000 job, for example, this action would be so unexpected—and so unlike what most people would do—that we would learn a lot about her.

Two different types of expectations come into play here: category-based expectancies and target-based expectancies (Jones & McGillis, 1976). **Category-based expectancies** refer to expectations about people based on groups to which they belong. For example, you might be surprised to learn that Mick Jagger graduated from the London School of Economics, a very prestigious institution, for this is not the typical background or behavior of a rock-and-roll star. **Target-based expectancies** refer to how you expect a particular person to behave, based on his or her past actions. For example, many people were very surprised when, in 1995, former President George Bush publically withdrew his membership in the National Rifle Association, a group that he had supported and that had supported him in the past. In both examples, you would make a correspondent inference—the assumption that Mick Jagger's and George Bush's behaviors match their dispositions.

In sum, making attributions, according to correspondent inference theory, is kind of like being a detective. When we try to deduce why someone behaved the way he or she did, the culprits are the various things the person might have been

category-based expectancies: expectations about people based on the groups to which they belong, such as expecting someone to love going to parties because he or she belongs to a party-loving fraternity or sorority

target-based expectancies: expectations about a person based on his or her past actions, such as expecting someone to go to the beach on vacation because he or she has always gone to the beach in the past trying to accomplish (the effects of his or her actions). We reduce the number of possibilities by examining what the person could have accomplished by behaving in some alternative manner (Jones, 1990; Newtson, 1974). We also take into account how much we expected people to do what they did, for unexpected actions are much more diagnostic of what someone is really like than expected actions are.

The Covariation Model: Internal Versus External Attributions

Harold Kelley (1967) took a somewhat different approach when he developed his theory of attribution. Whereas Jones and Davis (1965) focused on the information people use to make a dispositional (internal) attribution, Kelley (1967) focused on the first step in the process of social perception—how people decide whether to make an internal or an external attribution. Another difference between the two theories is that correspondent inference theory applies to a single observation of a behavior (e.g., your friend refuses to lend you his car), whereas Kelley's (1967) **covariation model** applies to multiple instances of behavior, occurring across time and across different situations (e.g., Did your friend refuse to lend you his car in the past? Does he lend it to other people? Does he dislike lending you other possessions of his?).

covariation model: a theory which states that in order to form an attribution about what caused a person's behavior, we systematically note the pattern between the presence (or absence) of possible causal factors and whether or not the behavior occurs

Kelley (like Heider before him) assumes that when we are in the process of forming an attribution, we gather information, or data, that will help us reach a judgment. The data we use, according to Kelley, are how a person's behavior *covaries* across time, place, different actors, and different targets of the behavior. By discovering covariation in people's behavior (e.g., your friend refuses to lend you his car; he agrees to lend it to others), you are able to reach a judgment about what caused their behavior.

When we are forming an attribution, what kinds of information do we examine for covariation? Kelley (1967) states there are three important types of information: *consensus, distinctiveness,* and *consistency.* Let's describe these three through an example: You are working at your part-time job in a clothing store and you observe your boss yelling at another employee, Hannah, telling her in no uncertain terms that she's an idiot. Without any conscious effort on your part, you pose that attributional question: "Why is the boss yelling at Hannah and being so critical—is it something about the boss, or is it something about the situation that surrounds and affects him?"

consensus information: information about the extent to which other people behave the same way toward the same stimulus as the actor does

distinctiveness information: information about the extent to which one particular actor behaves in the same way to different stimuli

consistency information: information about the extent to which the behavior between one actor and one stimulus is the same across time and circumstances

Now let's look at how Kelley's (1967) model of covariation assessment answers this question. **Consensus information** refers to how other people behave toward the same stimulus—in this case, Hannah. Do other people at work also yell at Hannah and criticize her? **Distinctiveness information** refers to how the actor (the person whose behavior we are trying to explain) responds to other stimuli. Does the boss yell at and demean other employees in the store? **Consistency information** refers to the frequency with which the observed behavior between the same actor and the same stimulus occurs across time and circumstances. Does the boss yell at and criticize Hannah regularly and frequently, whether the store is busy with customers or empty?

According to Kelley's theory, when these three sources of information combine into one of two distinct patterns, a clear attribution can be made. People are most likely to make an *internal attribution* (deciding the behavior was due to something about the boss) when the consensus and distinctiveness of the act are

Why did the Boss yell at his employee, Hannah?			
People are likely to make an *internal attribution*—it was something about the Boss—if they see this behavior as	*low* in consensus: the Boss is the only person working in the store who yells at Hannah	*low* in distinctiveness: the Boss yells at all the employees	*high* in consistency: the Boss yells at Hannah almost every time he sees her
People are likely to make an *external attribution*—it was something about Hannah—if they see this behavior as	*high* in consensus: all of the employees yell at Hannah too	*high* in distinctiveness: the Boss doesn't yell at any of the other employees	*high* in consistency: the Boss yells at Hannah almost every time he sees her
People are likely to think it was something peculiar about the particular circumstances in which the Boss yelled at Hannah if they see this behavior as	*low or high* in consensus	*low or high* in distinctiveness	*low* in consistency: this is the first time that the Boss has yelled at Hannah

FIGURE 4.6   The covariation model. ■ Why did the Boss yell at his employee Hannah? To decide whether a behavior was caused by internal, or dispositional factors, or external, or situational factors, people use consensus, distinctiveness, and consistency information.

low but its consistency is high (see the example, Figure 4.6). We would be pretty confident that the boss yelled at Hannah because he is a mean and vindictive person if we knew that no one else yells at Hannah, that the boss yells at other employees, and that the boss yells at Hannah every chance he gets. People are likely to make an *external attribution* (in this case, about Hannah) if consensus, distinctiveness, and consistency are all high. Finally, when consistency is low we cannot make a clear internal or external attribution and so resort to a special kind of external or *situational attribution*, one that assumes something unusual or peculiar is going on in these circumstances—for example, the boss just received very upsetting news and lost his temper with the first person he saw.

Both correspondent inference theory and the covariation model assume that people make causal attributions in a rational, logical fashion. People observe the clues, such as the distinctiveness of the act, and then draw a logical inference about why the person did what he or she did. Several studies have confirmed that people often do make attributions the way that Jones and Davis's (1965) and Kelley's (1967) models say they should (Fosterling, 1989; Hazelwood & Olson, 1986; Hewstone & Jaspars, 1987; Major, 1980; Ruble & Feldman, 1976; Zuckerman, 1978)—with one exception. In research studies, people don't use consensus information as much as Kelley's theory predicted; they rely more on consistency and distinctiveness information when forming attributions (McArthur, 1972).

You can actually watch the attribution process in action. For example, when talking with your friends, pay special attention to the attributions they make about others. You could start the ball rolling by asking your friends why they think a mutual acquaintance did or said something you all know about. Are their spontaneous attributions external or internal? Are they using consistency, consensus, and distinctiveness information?

Taxonomy of Success and Failure Attributions

taxonomy of success and failure attributions: the types of internal and external attributions we can make about a person's performance—for example, success or failure

locus: information that indicates whether the cause of the success (or failure) is internal or external

stability: information that indicates whether the cause of the success (or failure) is an enduring characteristic or one that changes or disappears over time

controllability: information that indicates whether the cause of the success (or failure) is something the individual can control or cannot control

A final theory of attribution, developed by Bernard Weiner (1974, 1986), is very specific and looks at the attributions we make about someone's performance— how do we determine what caused a person's success or failure? Weiner's (1986) **taxonomy of success and failure attributions** examines the types of internal and external attributions we can make in this situation. He and his colleagues have found that three variables are particularly important when we are making success or failure attributions: locus, stability, and controllability (Weiner, 1986; Weiner et al., 1972, 1976). **Locus** refers to the most basic element: Is the cause of the observed behavior internal (something about the person) or external (something about the situation)? According to this theory, we follow Kelley's (1967) covariation model—using consistency, distinctiveness, and consensus information—to reach a decision as to whether an internal or external explanation is most feasible. **Stability** refers to whether the cause of the behavior is stable—an enduring characteristic that will be present in the future—or unstable—a characteristic that changes or disappears over time. **Controllability** refers to whether the cause of the behavior is something over which the individual can exert control or is something that is uncontrollable.

How do these three variables fit together? Imagine that an acquaintance tells you she has been accepted to Harvard Law School. What are all the attributions you could make to explain her success? (Some of these attributions might be quite mean, but go ahead!). Figure 4.7 demonstrates how these attributions fit the model's three variables—locus, stability, and controllability.

Clearly, the most flattering attribution about a person's success locates the cause internally and gives it stable and controllable properties. This means the individual deserved his or her success and can repeat it in the future. Conversely, the most flattering attribution about a person's failure locates causality externally and describes it as unstable and uncontrollable—it's not his or her fault, and it's not likely to happen again.

Weiner (1986) states that the *locus* variable affects people's self-esteem about their performance; an internal locus causes an individual or a perceiver to attribute feelings of pride after success and shame after failure. *Stability* affects perceptions of future performances; attributions to stable causes (e.g., intelligence) lead us to expect a similar performance in the future, while attributions to unstable causes (e.g., luck or an easy test) leave us unsure about how the person will do the next time. Finally, perceptions of *controllability* arouse what Weiner calls social emotions: When the cause was controllable but the person still fails, we feel irritated or even angry with him or her. If the cause is uncontrollable, we instead feel sorry for the individual (Lau & Russell, 1980; McAuley & Gross, 1983; Meyer, 1980; Schaufeli, 1988; Vallerand & Richer, 1988).

Internal attributions

Stable	Unstable
Controllable	
"She's always studied really hard, both in her classes and for the law school exam."	"She didn't always work hard in class, but she really studied for that law school exam."
Uncontrollable	
"She's really talented at the kinds of things that law schools are looking for."	"She got a lot of sleep the night before and worked on feeling confident before she took the exam."

External attributions

Stable	Unstable
Controllable	
"She took the Stanley Kaplan course, and that really helped her on the law school exam."	"She had some really smart friends she studied with in class, and they helped her prepare for the law school exam too."
Uncontrollable	
"She always took easy courses, and those law school exams aren't that hard either."	"Boy, is she lucky!"

FIGURE 4.7 "Monica got accepted into Harvard Law School. Why? What explains her success? ■ (Adapted from Weiner, 1972, 1986)

To summarize, correspondent inference theory, the covariation model, and the taxonomy for success and failure attributions all portray people as master detectives, deducing the causes of behavior as systematically and logically as Sherlock Holmes would. However, as we see in Chapters 3 and 6, people sometimes aren't that accurate or rational when forming judgments about others. Sometimes they distort information to satisfy their need for high self-esteem (see Chapter 6). Other times they use mental shortcuts that, while helpful, can lead to inaccurate judgments (see Chapter 3). Unfortunately, the attributions we make are sometimes just plain wrong. In the next section, we will discuss some specific errors or biases that plague the attribution process. One shortcut is very pervasive, at least in Western cultures: The idea that people do what they do because of the kind of people they are, not because of the situation they are in. This has been termed the fundamental attribution error.

The Fundamental Attribution Error: People as Personality Psychologists

As we are writing this chapter, an epic murder trial has just been concluded: Susan Smith was found guilty and sentenced to life in prison for drowning her two small sons. For nine emotional days, Smith claimed that her missing children had been carjacked; she then capitulated and confessed that she had rolled her car into a deep lake, with her sons strapped to their car seats inside (Bragg, 1995).

The attributional question demanded an answer: Why did she do it? Motives supplied by the prosecution described Smith as the personification of evil. Motives supplied by the defense, on the other hand, presented Smith as a pathetic victim (up to now, a good mother) who had suffered from mental illness and sexual abuse. Public opinion before and during the trial was almost unanimously

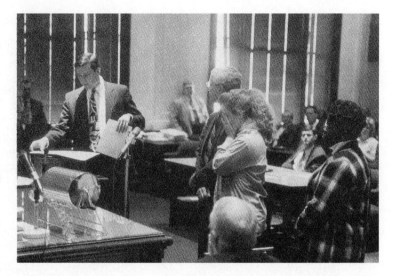

■ Susan Smith was sentenced to life in prison for drowning her two young sons in a car. Why did she do it? Dispositional attributions were the overwhelming preference of the media, the prosecution, and the public; situational attributions were rarely heard.

fundamental attribution error: the tendency to overestimate the extent to which people's behavior is due to internal, dispositional factors and to underestimate the role of situational factors

against Smith, holding that a woman who killed her children was inherently evil, and no circumstance or mitigating factor could cloud that view. In a national survey, 63 percent of respondents said Smith should receive the death penalty.

We mention this example neither to provide excuses for murder nor to pardon Smith's crime. Instead, we mention it as a real-life, subtle example of how perceivers see the individual as the sole cause of her or his behavior (in this case, a correspondent inference was made between Smith's evil actions and her evil character) and tend to ignore or underestimate the situational forces that act on and influence the individual.

The pervasive, fundamental theory or schema most of us have about human behavior is that people do what they do because of the kind of people they are, not because of the situation they are in. When thinking this way, we are more like personality psychologists, who see behavior as stemming from internal dispositions and traits, than social psychologists, who focus on the impact of social situations on behavior. This bias toward being personality psychologists is so pervasive that social psychologist Lee Ross (1977) termed it the **fundamental attribution error** (Heider, 1958; Jones, 1990).

There have been many empirical demonstrations of the tendency to see people's behavior as a reflection of their dispositions and beliefs, rather than as influenced by the situation. Jones and Harris (1967), for example, asked college students to read an essay written by a fellow student that either supported or opposed Fidel Castro's rule in Cuba and then to guess how the author of the essay really felt about Castro (see Figure 4.8). In one condition, the researchers told the students that the author freely chose which position to take in the essay, thereby making it easy to guess how he really felt. If he chose to write in favor of Castro, then clearly he must indeed be sympathetic to Castro. In another condition, however, the students learned that the author did not have any choice about which position to take—he had been assigned the position as a participant in a debate. Logically, if we know someone could not choose the topic, we should not assume the writer believes what he or she wrote. Yet the participants in this study, and in the dozens of others like it, assumed that the author really believed what he wrote, even when they knew he could not choose which position to take. As seen in Figure 4.8, people moderated their guesses a little bit—there was not as much difference in people's estimates of the author's attitude in the pro-Castro and anti-Castro conditions—but they still assumed that the content of the essay reflected the author's true feelings.

Why is the tendency to explain behavior in terms of people's dispositions called the fundamental attribution error? It is not always wrong to make an internal attribution; clearly, people often do what they do because of the kind of people they are. However, there is ample evidence that social situations can have a large impact on behavior; indeed, the major lesson of social psychology is that these influences can be extremely powerful. The point of the fundamental attribution error is that people tend to underestimate these influences when explaining other people's behavior. Even when a situational constraint on behavior is obvious, as in the Jones and Harris (1967) experiment, people persist in making internal attributions (Ross, 1977; Ross, Amabile, & Steinmetz; Ross & Nisbett, 1991).

The Role of Perceptual Salience.   Why do people commit the fundamental attribution error? One reason is that when we try to explain someone's behavior, our focus of attention is usually on the person, not on the surrounding situation (Heider, 1958; Jones & Nisbett, 1971). In fact, as Daniel Gilbert and Patrick Malone (1995) have pointed out, the situational causes of another person's behavior are practically invisible to us. If we don't know what happened to a person earlier in the day (e.g., she received an F on her midterm), we can't use that situational information to help us understand her current behavior. Even when we know "her situation," we still don't know how *she* interprets it—for example, the F may not have upset her, because she's planning to drop the course anyway. If we don't know the meaning of the situation for her, we can't accurately judge its effects on her behavior. Thus, information about the situational causes of behavior is frequently unavailable to us and/or difficult to interpret accurately (Gilbert & Malone, 1995).

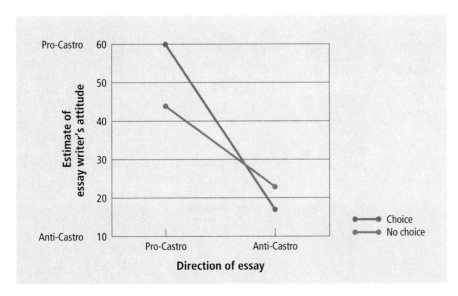

FIGURE 4.8   The fundamental attribution error. ■ Even when people knew that the author's choice of an essay topic was externally caused (i.e., in the no-choice condition), they assumed that what he wrote reflected how he really felt about Castro. That is, they made an internal attribution from his behavior. (Adapted from Jones & Harris, 1967)

What information does that leave us? While the situation may be close to invisible, the individual is extremely perceptually salient—people are what our eyes and ears notice. And as Heider (1958) pointed out, what we notice seems to be the reasonable and logical cause of the observed behavior.

Several studies have confirmed the importance of perceptual salience—in particular, an elegant one by Shelley Taylor and Susan Fiske (1975). In this study, two male students engaged in a "get acquainted" conversation. (They were actually both accomplices of the experimenters and were following a specific script during their conversation.) At each session, six actual research participants also took part. They sat in assigned seats, surrounding the two conversationalists (see Figure 4.9). Two of them sat on each side of the actors; they had a clear, profile view of both individuals. Two observers sat behind each actor; they could see the back of one actor's head but the face of the other. Thus, who was visually salient—that is, who the participants could see the best—was cleverly manipulated in this study.

After the conversation, the research participants were asked questions about the two men—for example, who had taken the lead in the conversation and who had chosen the topics to be discussed? As you can see in Figure 4.10, the person whom they could see the best was the person who they thought had the most impact on the conversation. Even though all the observers heard the same conversation, those who were facing student A thought he had taken the lead and chosen the topics, whereas those who were facing student B thought he had taken the lead and chosen the topics. In comparison, those who could see both students equally well thought both were equally influential. **Perceptual salience,** or our visual point of view, helps explain why the fundamental attribution error is so prevalent. We focus our attention more on people than on the surrounding situation because the situation is so hard to see or know; we underestimate (or even forget about) the influence of the situation when we are explaining human behavior. But this is only part of the story. Why should the simple fact that we are focused on a person make us exaggerate the extent to which that person is the cause of his or her actions?

> Be not swept off your feet by the vividness of the impression, but say "Impression, wait for me a little. Let me see what you are and what you represent."
>
> –Epictetus, *Discourses*

perceptual salience: information that is the focus of people's attention; people tend to overestimate the causal role of perceptually salient information

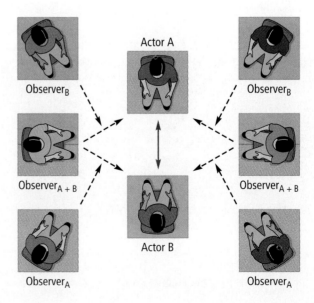

FIGURE 4.9   Manipulating perceptual salience. ▪ This is the seating arrangement for two actors and the six research participants in the Taylor and Fiske study. Participants rated each actor's impact on the conversation. Researchers found that people rated the actor they could see most clearly as having the largest role in the conversation. (Adapted from Taylor and Fiske, 1975)

Actor A

Observer_B   Observer_B

Observer_{A + B}   Observer_{A + B}

Observer_A   Observer_A

Actor B

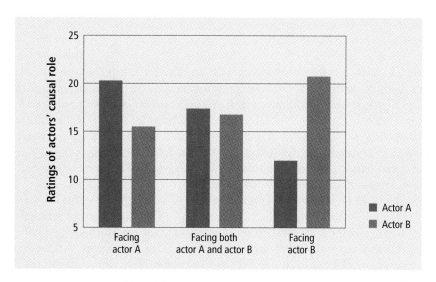

FIGURE 4.10   The effects of perceptual salience. ▪ These are the ratings of each actor's causal role in the conversation. People thought that the actor they could see the best had the most impact on the conversation. (Adapted from Taylor & Fiske, 1975)

The culprit is one of the mental shortcuts we discussed in Chapter 3: the *anchoring/adjustment heuristic.* We saw several examples in which people began with a reference point when making a judgment and then did not adjust sufficiently away from this point. The fundamental attribution error is another byproduct of this shortcut. When making attributions, people use the focus of their attention as a starting point. For example, when we hear someone argue strongly in favor of Castro's regime in Cuba, our first inclination is to explain this in dispositional terms: "This person must hold radical political views." We realize this explanation might not be the whole story, however. We might think, "On the other hand, I know he was assigned this position as part of a debate," and adjust our attributions more toward a situational explanation. However, the problem is that people often don't adjust their judgments enough. In the Jones and Harris (1967) experiment, participants who knew the essay writer did not have a choice of topics nevertheless thought he believed what he had written, at least to some extent. They adjusted insufficiently from their anchor, the position advocated in the essay.

In sum, people go through two steps when making attributions (Gilbert, 1989, 1991, 1993). They begin by making an internal attribution, assuming that a person's behavior was due to something about him or her. They then attempt to adjust this attribution by taking into account the situation the person was in. As we have seen, people often do not make enough of an adjustment in this second step. An interesting implication of this fact is that if people are distracted or preoccupied when explaining someone's behavior, they might not get to the second step, thereby making an even more extreme internal attribution. Why? Because the initial step (making the internal attribution) occurs quickly and spontaneously, whereas the second step (adjusting for the situation) requires more effort and conscious attention. Daniel Gilbert has performed several experiments that support this view. Subjects in his studies are asked to explain why someone did what he or she did, but are distracted by having to do something else at the same time, such as remembering an eight-digit number. These subjects make even more extreme internal attributions than subjects who are not distracted, because they are unable to mentally adjust their initial impression that the person's behavior emanated solely from within him or her, uninfluenced by the situation (Gilbert & Osborne, 1989; Gilbert, Pelham, & Krull, 1988).

The Role of Culture.   Recent research has suggested a second reason for why the fundamental attribution error occurs: Western culture, which emphasizes individual freedom and autonomy, socializes us to prefer dispositional attributions over situational ones. In comparison, collectivist (often Eastern) cultures emphasize group membership, interdependence, and conformity to group norms (Hsu, 1981; Triandis, 1990; Zebrowitz-McArthur, 1988). As a result of this very different socialization, do people in collectivist cultures make fewer fundamental attribution errors than Westerners do?

To find out, Joan Miller (1984) asked people of two cultures—Hindus living in India and Americans living in the United States—to think of various examples of behaviors performed by their friends and to explain why those behaviors occurred. Consistent with what we've said so far, the American participants preferred dispositional explanations for the behaviors. They were more likely to say that the causes of their friends' behaviors were the kind of people they were, rather than the situation or context in which the behaviors occurred. In contrast, Hindu participants preferred situational explanations for their friends' behaviors (Miller, 1984).

"But," you might be thinking, "perhaps the Americans and Hindus generated different kinds of examples. Perhaps the Hindus thought of behaviors that really were more situationally caused, whereas the Americans thought of behaviors that really were more dispositionally caused." To test this alternative hypothesis, Miller (1984) took some of the behaviors generated by the Hindu participants and gave them to Americans to explain. The difference in internal and external attributions was again observed: Americans preferred dispositional causes for the behaviors that the Hindus had thought were situationally caused.

The cultural explanation of the fundamental attribution error received further support from an elegant study that compared newspaper articles in Chinese- and English-language newspapers. Michael Morris and Kaiping Peng (1994) targeted two very similar crimes, both mass murders, one committed by a Chinese graduate student in Iowa, and one committed by a Caucasian postal worker in Michigan. The researchers coded all the news articles about the two crimes that appeared in the *New York Times* and the *World Journal*, a Chinese-language U.S. newspaper. As you can see in Figure 4.11, journalists writing in English made significantly more dispositional attributions about both mass

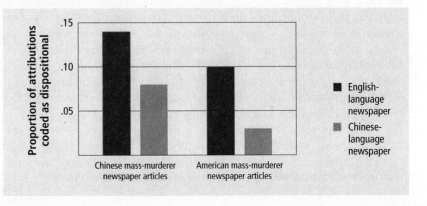

FIGURE 4.11   The role of culture in the fundamental attribution error. ■ Newspaper articles about two murderers, appearing in English and Chinese-language newspapers, were coded for the types of attributions made. Journalists writing in English made significantly more dispositional attributions about both the Chinese and Anglo-American murderer than did journalists writing in Chinese.

murderers than journalists writing in Chinese did. For example, American reporters described one murderer as a "darkly disturbed man" with a "sinister edge" to his personality. Chinese reporters, when describing the same murderer, emphasized more situational causes, such as "not getting along with his advisor" and his "isolation from the Chinese community."

Thus, people in Western cultures appear to be more like personality psychologists, viewing behavior in dispositional terms, whereas people in Eastern cultures seem to be more like social psychologists, viewing behavior in situational terms.

The Actor/Observer Difference

An interesting twist on the fundamental attribution error is that it does not apply to our attributions about ourselves to the same extent that it applies to our attributions about other people. While we tend to see others' behavior as dispositionally caused (the fundamental attribution error), we are less likely to rely so extensively on dispositional attributions when we are explaining our own behavior. Instead, we frequently make situational attributions about why we did what we did. Thus, an interesting attributional dilemma is created: The same action can trigger dispositional attributions in people observing the action and situational attributions in the person performing the action. This is called the **actor/observer difference** (Jones & Nisbett, 1972; Nisbett et al., 1973; Schoeneman & Rubanowitz, 1985; Watson, 1982; West, Gunn, & Chernicky, 1975). The letter to Ann Landers on this page is an interesting demonstration of the actor/observer difference. The writer is very aware of the external forces that are affecting her life and shaping her behavior. Ann Landers, however, will have none of it. Ann responds with a strong, internal attribution—the woman herself, not her situation, is the cause of her problems. As you might guess, the

actor/observer difference: the tendency to see other people's behavior as dispositionally caused, while focusing more on the role of situational factors when explaining one's own behavior

Dear Ann Landers:

I'm writing you in desperation, hoping you can help me with a problem I'm having with my mother.

A little over a year ago, I moved in with my boyfriend despite my mother's protests. She has never liked "Kevin." I'll admit he's far from perfect and we've had our problems. He's an alcoholic, has a bad temper, is mentally abusive, is a compulsive liar and cannot hold a job. I am in debt over my head because of him but my biggest problem is that my mother is obsessed with my situation. I understand her concern, but I can take only so much. . . .

OVER-MOTHERED IN MICHIGAN

Dear Over-Mothered:
Your mother didn't write to me. You did. So you're the one who is going to get the advice. Get into counseling at once and find out why you insist on hanging on to an alcoholic, abusive, unemployed liar. . . .

■ The letter and its response depict actor/observer differences in attribution. Schoeneman and Rubanowitz (1985) examined letters to the "Dear Ann Landers" and "Dear Abby" advice columns and found strong evidence for actor/observer differences. The letter writers tended to attribute their problems to external factors (e.g., this letter writer says her biggest problem is her mother), whereas the advice columnists tended to make dispositional attributions to the letter writers (e.g., "Get into counseling at once"). (From the *Boston Globe,* September 10, 1991) actor/observer difference can lead to some striking disagreements between people. Why, at times, do the attributions made by actors and observers diverge so sharply?

Perceptual Salience Revisited.   One reason for such divergence is our old friend perceptual salience (Jones & Nisbett, 1972). As we said earlier, just as we notice other people's behavior more than their situation, so too do we notice our own situation more than our own behavior. None of us is so egotistic or self-centered that we walk through life holding up a full-length mirror in order to observe ourselves constantly. We are looking outward; what is perceptually salient to us is other people, objects, the events that unfold, and so on. We don't (and can't) pay as much attention to ourselves. Thus, when the actor and the observer think about what caused a given behavior, they are swayed by the information that is most salient and noticeable to them: The actor for the observer and the situation for the actor.

Michael Storms (1973) conducted a fascinating experiment that demonstrates the role of perceptual salience in both the fundamental attribution error and the actor/observer difference. In a design reminiscent of the Taylor and Fiske (1975) study presented earlier, Storms (1973) seated groups of four research participants in a special way (see Figure 4.12). Two of them were going to chat with each other (actor A and actor B), and two of them would observe this conversation, focusing on one of the conversationalists (observer of A and observer of B). In addition, two video cameras were present; one filmed actor A's face, and the other filmed actor B's face.

Following the conversation, the four participants were asked to make attributions about themselves (for actors) or about the actor they were watching (for observers). For example, they were asked to what extent the actor's behavior was due to personal characteristics or to characteristics of the situation (the topic of conversation, the behavior of the conversational partner, etc.). Storms (1973) found that the observers attributed more *dispositional* characteristics to the actor they were watching (demonstrating the fundamental attribution error as in the Taylor & Fiske, 1975, study), whereas the actors made more *situational* attributions about the same behavior—their own (see the left-hand side of Figure 4.13).

> Resemblances are the shadows of differences. Different people see different similarities and similar differences.
> –Vladimir Nabokov, *Pale Fire*, 1962

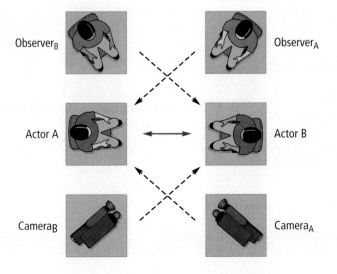

FIGURE 4.12   Seating arrangements in the Storms study. ■ People's behavior was videotaped, so that some of them could view it later from a different perspective. (Adapted from Storms, 1973)

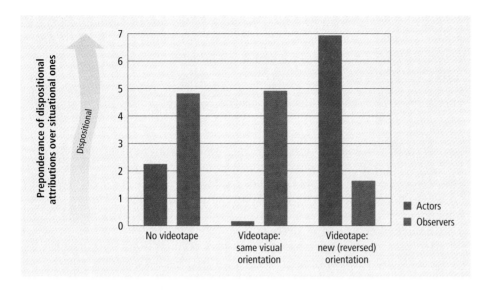

FIGURE 4.13   Effects of perceptual salience (visual orientation) on actors' and observers' attributions. ■ When people got to see their own or another person's behavior from a new orientation (see right-hand side of figure), they made attributions very different from those of people who did not see the behavior from a new orientation (see middle and left-hand side of figure). (Adapted from Storms, 1973)

In a particularly elegant addition to the study's design, Storms (1973) showed the videotapes to some of the participants before they made their ratings. Some of them saw on tape what they had experienced live—actor A saw a tape of actor B's face, and actor B saw the videotape of actor A's face; observer A saw a tape of actor A, and observer B saw a tape of actor B. When asked to make causal attributions, these participants showed the same actor/observer difference as before, although the actors made even stronger situational attributions about themselves when they had the chance to sit back and observe their situation again (see middle of Figure 4.13).

Another group of participants were placed in the most interesting position of all. After the conversation, they saw a videotape that had the opposite visual orientation to the one they had experienced in real life. Actor A and actor B each saw their own face; observer A saw the videotape of actor B; and observer B saw the tape of actor A. Now the object of perceptual salience was completely reversed. How did these participants assign causality? As can be seen on the far right of Figure 4.13, this change in perceptual salience erased the typical actor/observer difference. After looking at themselves, actors made more dispositional attributions. After looking at their actor's (the conversational partner's) situation, observers made more situational attributions about their actor.

The Role of Information Availability.   The actor/observer difference occurs for another reason as well. Actors have more information about themselves than observers do (Jones & Nisbett, 1972; Greenwald & Banaji, 1989). Actors know how they've behaved over the years; they know what happened to them that morning. They are far more aware than observers are of both the similarities and the differences in their behavior across time and across situations. In Kelley's (1967) terms, actors have far more consistency and distinctiveness information about themselves than observers do. For example, if you are behaving in a quiet, shy fashion at a party, an observer is likely to make a dispositional attribution about you—"Gee, that person is quite an introvert." In fact, you may know that this is not your typical way of responding to a party setting. Perhaps you are shy only at parties where you don't know anyone, or you might be tired, or depressed by some recent bad news. Thus, it is not surprising that actors' self-attributions often reflect situational factors, because they know more about how their behavior varies from one situation to the next than most observers, who see them in limited contexts, do.

The Role of Language.   Recent research by Klaus Fiedler and Gun Semin suggests a third reason for why the actor/observer difference occurs: Norms exist for how we use language, and these rules help to create the differing attributional patterns of actors and observers (Fiedler, Semin, Finkenauer, & Berkel, 1995). Fiedler and Semin have found that the language people use to discuss themselves is more "concrete," while the language they use to describe other people is more "abstract"—defined as moving from a reliance on verbs (concrete) to a reliance on adjectives (abstract; Fiedler et al., 1995).

Communicators tend to describe themselves in concrete terms, placing an emphasis on specific behaviors, and leave it up to their listeners to evaluate and interpret the information (Fiedler & Semin, 1992; Semin & Fiedler, 1989, 1991). This language style is considered polite and nonegotistic, as well as unbiased and objective—we simply present the information about ourselves and let others make sense of it (Grice, 1975). While language norms discourage talking about the self in very abstract, interpretative terms, these norms encourage such interpretation and evaluation when we discuss others. For example, Semin and Fiedler (1989) asked research participants, "Why do you like your boyfriend/girlfriend?" and "Why does your best friend like his or her boyfriend/girlfriend?" They found that the number of adjectives used—or dispositional attributions—differed depending on whom the participants were talking about. Observers used many more adjectives to describe another person than actors used to describe themselves.

Interestingly, this concrete-abstract difference in the language of actors and observers is apparent even when people are not making causal attributions but simply describing past events (Semin & Fiedler, 1989). In another study, the researchers asked participants to describe an experience from their past under several headings, such as "a successful party" or "bodily harm." They were instructed to relate an experience of their own or one that had occurred to somebody else. The participants' narratives were coded for the parts of speech used. Again, observers used more abstract language than actors did.

Thus, according to this theory, language habits or styles in and of themselves contribute to the actor/observer attributional difference. Our habitual ways of speaking about ourselves and other people influence our private thoughts about ourselves and others as well. We simply use language differently when we talk or think about ourselves as compared to when we talk or think about others—we become more dispositional when the topic is other people and less dispositional when the topic is ourselves.

So far, our discussion of the mental shortcuts people use when making attributions has covered the role of priming, accessibility, perceptual salience, information availability, culture, and language styles. But what about a person's needs, desires, hopes, and fears—do these more emotional factors also create biases in our attributions? Are you motivated to see the world in certain ways because these views make you feel better, about both yourself and life in general? The answer is yes. The shortcuts we will discuss below have a *motivational basis;* they are attributions that protect our self-esteem and our belief that the world is a safe and just place.

Self-Serving Attributions

Imagine that Bill goes to his chemistry class one day with some apprehension, because this is the day he will find out how he did on the midterm. The professor gives him his exam. Bill turns it over. He sees that he has received an A. What will Bill think is the reason for why he got such a good grade? It probably will come as no surprise that people tend to take personal credit for their successes but to explain away their failures as due to external events that were outside their control. Thus, Bill is likely to think that his success was due to him—he's good at chemistry and just plain smart.

How can we explain this departure from the typical actor/observer pattern of attributions? The answer is that when people's self-esteem is threatened, they often make **self-serving attributions.** Simply put, these attributions refer to our tendency to take credit for our successes (by making internal attributions) but to blame others (or the situation) for our failures (Miller & Ross, 1975). Many studies have shown that people make internal attributions when they do well on a task but make external attributions when they do poorly (Arkin & Maruyama, 1979; Carver, DeGregorio, & Gillis, 1980; Davis & Stephan, 1980; Elig & Frieze, 1979; Whitley & Frieze, 1985). Recall our earlier discussion of Bernard Weiner's (1986) taxonomy of success and failure attributions. We saw that there are many different attributions one can make about the outcome of a performance, enough to allow us to tailor-make a self-serving attribution.

Richard Lau and Dan Russell (1980) studied self-serving attributions in an interesting arena: professional sports. They examined the explanations made by professional athletes and coaches for why their team won or lost a game. When explaining their victories, the athletes and coaches overwhelmingly pointed to aspects of their own teams or players; in fact, 80 percent of the attributions for wins were to such internal factors. When explaining why the New York Yankees defeated the Los Angeles Dodgers in game 4 of the 1977 World Series, Yankees' manager Billy Martin attributed it to a player on his team: "Piniella has done it all" (Lau & Russell, 1980). Losses were more likely to be attributed to things external to one's own team. For example, members of the Dodgers attributed their loss not to their inferior ability or poor play but instead to bad luck or the superior play of the Yankees. In the words of Tommy Lasorda, the Dodgers' manager, "It took a great team to beat us, and the Yankees definitely are a great team" (Lau & Russell, 1980).

Why do people make self-serving attributions? As pointed out in our discussion of cognitive dissonance theory in Chapter 6, people try to maintain their self-esteem whenever possible, even if that means distorting reality by changing a cognition. Here we see a specific attributional strategy that can be used to maintain or raise self-esteem—just locate "causality" where it does you the most good (Greenberg, Pyszczynski, & Solomon, 1982; Ickes & Layden, 1978; Miller & Ross, 1975; Snyder & Higgins, 1988).

A second reason has to do with how we present ourselves to other people (Goffman, 1959). We want people to think well of us and to admire us. Telling others that our poor performance was due to some external cause is such a self-presentational strategy—in fact, we sometimes call it "making excuses"! (Greenberg et al., 1982; Tetlock, 1981; Weary & Arkin, 1981).

A third reason people make self-serving attributions has to do with our earlier discussion about the kind of information that is available to people. Let's imagine the attributional process of another student in the chemistry class,

self-serving attributions: explanations for one's successes that credit internal, dispositional factors and explanations for one's failures that blame external, situational factors

■ Self-serving attributions. People tend to take credit for their successes but to blame others for their failures. Baseball managers, such as Tommy Lasorda, are not immune from this tendency.

Dexter, who did poorly on the midterm. Dexter knows that he studied very hard for the midterm, that he typically does well on chemistry tests, and that in general he is a very good student. The D on the chemistry midterm comes as a surprise. The most logical attribution Dexter can make is that the test was unfair—the D grade wasn't due to a lack of ability or effort on his part. The professor, on the other hand, knows that some students did very well on the test; thus, given the information that is available to the professor, it is logical for him or her to conclude that Dexter, and not the fact that it was a difficult test, was responsible for the poor grade (Miller & Ross, 1975; Nisbett & Ross, 1980).

People also alter their attributions to deal with other kinds of threats to their self-esteem. One of the hardest things to understand in life is the occurrence of tragic events, such as rapes, terminal diseases, and fatal accidents. Even when they happen to strangers we have never met, they can be upsetting. They remind us that if such tragedies can happen to someone else, they can happen to us. Of all the kinds of self-knowledge that we have, the knowledge that we are mortal and that bad things can happen to us is perhaps the hardest to accept (Greenberg, Pyszczynski, & Solomon, 1986). We thus take steps to deny this fact. One way we do so is by making **defensive attributions,** which are explanations that defend us from feelings of vulnerability and mortality.

One form of defensive attribution is **unrealistic optimism** about the future. Suppose we asked you to estimate how likely it is that each of the following will happen to you, compared to how likely it is that they will happen to other students at your college or university: owning your own home, liking your post-graduate job, living past age 80, having a drinking problem, getting divorced, and being unable to have children. When Neil Weinstein (1980) asked college students these and similar questions, he found that people were too optimistic. Virtually everyone thought that the good things were more likely to happen to them than to their peers and that the bad things were less likely to happen to them than to their peers. Being overly optimistic is one way people try to protect themselves from unpleasant feelings of mortality.

Sometimes, of course, it's hard to deny that bad things happen in life. We have only to pick up a newspaper to see that people suffer terrible misfortunes every day. How do we deal with these unsettling reminders that bad things happen? One way is by explaining them in such a way as to make it seem like they could never happen to us. We do so by believing that bad things happen only to bad people. Melvin Lerner (1980) has called this a **belief in a just world**—the assumption that people get what they deserve. Because most of us view ourselves as decent, good human beings, then surely bad things won't happen to us.

The "just world" belief has some sad and even tragic consequences. For example, suppose a female student on your campus was the victim of a date rape by a male fellow student. How do you think you and your friends would react? Would you wonder if she'd done something to trigger the rape? Was she acting suggestively earlier in the evening? Had she invited the man into her room?

Research by Elaine Walster (1966) and others has focused on such attributions, which these investigators call "blaming the victim" (e.g., Burger, 1981; Lerner & Simmons, 1966; Shaver, 1970). In several experiments, they have found that the victims of crimes or accidents are often seen as causing their fate. For example, not only do people tend to believe that rape victims are to blame for the rape (Burt, 1980), but battered wives are often seen as responsible for their abusive husbands' behavior (Summers & Feldman, 1984). By using this attributional bias, the perceiver does not have to acknowledge that there is a certain

defensive attributions: explanations for behavior that avoid feelings of vulnerability and mortality

unrealistic optimism: a form of defensive attribution wherein people think that good things are more likely to happen to them than to their peers and that bad things are less likely to happen to them than to their peers

belief in a just world: a form of defensive attribution wherein people assume that bad things happen to bad people and that good things happen to good people randomness in life, that an accident or criminal may be waiting just around the corner for an innocent person—like oneself. The belief in a just world keeps anxious thoughts about one's own safety at bay.

The strategy of blaming the victim does not work, however, if misfortune befalls someone who is very similar to us. If something terrible happens to Sue, and we are similar to Sue, then blaming her for her misfortune is even more threatening: If it can happen to her, it can happen to us. Under these circumstances, people are likely to believe that the victim was not responsible and to attribute the cause of the event to chance factors. For example, in a study by Bill Thornton (1984) female college students read about a sexual assault that had supposedly happened to another student on their campus. Half the participants believed the victim was similar to them in terms of her attitudes and beliefs, whereas the others believed she was dissimilar. When the victim was viewed as dissimilar, people blamed her for the assault, saying she was relatively unintelligent, irresponsible, and poorly adjusted; that is, they blamed the victim. When the victim was viewed as similar, however, people were more likely to blame the assault on chance factors, rather than on the character of the victim.

How Accurate Are Our Attributions and Impressions?

When we make attributions, our goal is to be able to understand other people and predict what they will do. If we successfully sift through the complex layers of social behavior, accurately concluding that the reason Jake was mean to us at work is that he is insecure and aggressive at the office (but quite relaxed and kind at home), we are in a good position to know what to expect from Jake in the future—regardless of where we see him. To be able to predict how people will act toward us, it is obviously to our advantage to make attributions that are as accurate as possible. On balance, just how accurate are our attributions and impressions of other people?

The answer, in a nutshell, is that under many circumstances we are not very accurate, especially compared to how accurate we think we are. Consider first impressions, the quick, attributional snapshots we form when we first meet someone. Several studies have shown that first impressions are not very accurate (DePaulo et al., 1987; Funder & Colvin, 1988). What about when we get to know someone better, after spending hours or even years with her or him? Not surprisingly, our impressions of others become more accurate the more we get to know them. For example, David Funder and C. Randall Colvin (1988) compared the personality ratings that strangers gave to students they had observed for five minutes to ratings that close friends gave to the same students. As seen in Figure 4.14, the friends made more accurate assessments of the students than the strangers did.

It is not particularly earthshaking to conclude that the longer we know someone, the better we know that person. However, there are two interesting twists to this statement. First, in the Funder and Colvin (1988) study, the accuracy rate for close friends was not that high. As you can see in Figure 4.14, the correlation between the friends' impressions and the students' own impressions of their personalities was only .27; you'll recall from Chapter 2 that a perfect correlation is 1.00. Second, people are not as accurate as they think they are. David Dunning and colleagues (1990) found that while college roommates were fairly accurate at predicting each other's behavior, they were also overconfident,

> Things are seldom as they seem, skim milk masquerades as cream.
> –W. S. Gilbert,
> *H.M.S. Pinafore*, 1878

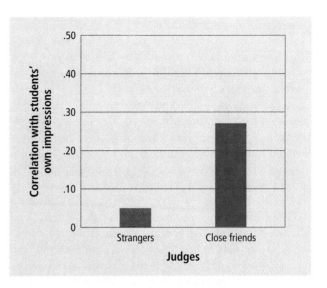

FIGURE 4.14   How accurate are our impressions of other people's personalities? ■ Strangers watched a videotape of a student and then rated his or her personality. The strangers' impressions corresponded very poorly to the student's impressions of his or her own personality. There was more agreement between a close friend's impressions of the student and the student's own impressions. (Adapted from Funder & Colvin, 1988)

believing their predictions to be more correct than they were. Whether we are thinking about close friends or strangers, why do we make attributional mistakes?

Why Are Our Impressions of Others Sometimes Wrong?

Our impressions are sometimes wrong because of the mental shortcuts we use when forming social judgments. The first culprit is our familiar friend the fundamental attribution error. People are too ready to attribute others' actions to their personalities rather than to the situation. For example, suppose you meet Andrea at a party and she is acting in an outgoing, sociable manner. If you are like most people, you will conclude that Andrea is outgoing and sociable. How accurate are you likely to be?

Not too accurate, if it is the social situation that is causing her to act extraverted. Maybe Andrea really isn't, as a rule, very outgoing or sociable. In fact, she may be rather shy and reserved but happens to be in a situation where most people act sociably—a fun party. Our conclusion that she is outgoing will be wrong, due to the fundamental attribution error: overestimating the extent to which Andrea's behavior reflects the way she always acts, rather than something about the situation.

We don't mean to imply that people are always wrong when making dispositional attributions. Even if people underestimate the power of social situations, their impressions can be correct because of the fact that actors' dispositions cause them to gravitate to certain situations and to avoid others. Suppose Andrea really is an outgoing person who chooses to attend parties on a frequent basis, spend her leisure time socializing with groups, and work in a job that requires a great deal of interaction and social contact. In this case, it is not so much the situation that is affecting her behavior as it is her disposition that is choosing her situations (Gilbert & Malone, 1995; Snyder & Ickes, 1985). In cases such as these, it really doesn't matter whether we say Andrea is outgoing because of the situation or her disposition, because both are true—her outgoing disposition caused her to be in a situation that encouraged her to act in an outgoing manner. Nonetheless, situations can be very powerful and sometimes override people's dispositions, and to the extent that we fail to take the situation into account, we will form inaccurate impressions.

Another reason our impressions can be wrong concerns our use of schemas. As we have seen, people use implicit personality theories to fill in the gaps in their knowledge about other people and use schemas or theories to decide why other people do what they do. Thus, our impressions are only as accurate as our theories. While many of our theories are likely to be correct, there are some dramatic illustrations of how they can lead us astray.

Consider what happened to David Rosenhan (1973). He and several other researchers went to the admissions departments of local mental hospitals and pretended they had been hearing voices. All were admitted to the hospitals, most with the diagnosis of schizophrenia. Despite the fact that from then on, all behaved in a perfectly normal manner, the psychiatric staff continued to treat them as if they were mentally ill. Not one of the researchers was identified as a fake by the staff, and all were kept in the hospitals for several days. (One person had to spend more than seven weeks in the hospital before being released.) Interestingly, the staff interpreted behavior that was perfectly normal as confirmation of their schema. For example, all of the fake patients kept diaries during their hospitalization, and the staff viewed this behavior as an indication that they were psychologically disturbed.

Why Does It Seem Like Our Impressions Are Accurate?

Why does it seem like our impressions are pretty accurate, when, as we have just reviewed, these impressions are often wrong? We can point to three reasons. First, we often see people in a limited number of situations and thus never have the opportunity to see that our impressions are wrong. For example, you probably interact with your social psychology professor only in an academic setting. Let's say you have formed attributions about her—she is stern and unyielding and not likely to give extensions on papers. Because you don't know her in other situations, you don't realize that she is also kind and fun-loving, a permissive parent, and a very giving friend. In fact, her behavior in your class is due to some bad experiences she has had with students and is not a reflection of her overall personality. Thus, you have committed the fundamental attribution error. But does it really matter? Your dispositional attribution may be overly harsh and, in a broad sense, inaccurate, but you are right about her behavior in the classroom, and that is what is most important and useful for you (Ross & Nisbett, 1991; Swann, 1984). In the narrow sphere where it matters, your attribution is accurate. However, you may never realize the wider inaccuracy of your attribution unless you happen to observe your professor in a completely different situation and see that she acts quite differently there.

Second, we will not realize that our impressions are wrong if we make them come true. This is the case with self-fulfilling prophecies, which we discussed in Chapter 3. Even if an initial impression is incorrect, we often make it come true by the way we treat a person. For example, suppose you ran into your social psychology professor at the mall and gave her a curt, unfriendly "Hello," because after all, she is a stern person who wouldn't give you an extension on your last paper. Your unfriendly greeting will probably cause your professor to respond in a less friendly manner than she normally would, thereby confirming your (in this case, inaccurate) impression of her.

Third, we might not realize we are wrong if a lot of people agree on what someone is like—even when everyone is wrong. David Kenny and colleagues have found that different observers often reach the same conclusion about what a person is like after a very brief time (Kenny, 1991; Kenny et al., 1992, 1994). This is particularly true for traits like extraversion, which people tend to "wear on their sleeves," in the sense that these traits translate into observable behaviors, such as how much a person talks or how animated she or he is. Thus, when everyone agrees with us that Sonya is extraverted but Barry is not, we feel confident that our impressions are correct—even if they are not.

In order to improve the accuracy of your attributions and impressions, remember that the fundamental attribution error and self-fulfilling prophecies exist, and try to counteract these biases. For example, the next time you hear about the victim of a crime or accident, stop yourself from immediately attributing responsibility to him or her. The world is not always a just place; bad things do happen to good people. Watch out for the other kinds of biases we have discussed as well, such as relying too much on implicit personality theories or falling prey to the actor/observer difference.

Now that we've delivered the sermon, let's cut to the chase. Yes, we are quite accurate perceivers of other people. We do very well indeed most of the time. We are adept at reading and interpreting nonverbal forms of communication; in fact, most of us are actually better at this than we realize. We become more accurate at perceiving others as we get to know them better, and since most of our truly important social interactions involve people we know well, this is good news. In short, we are capable of making both blindingly accurate assessments of people and horrific attributional mistakes—it's up to you to determine the difference in your life.

SUMMARY

Social perception is the study of how people form impressions and make inferences about other people. People constantly form such impressions, because doing so helps them understand and predict their social worlds. One source of information people use is the nonverbal behavior of others. **Nonverbal communication** is used to **encode** or express emotion, convey attitudes, communicate personality traits, and facilitate and regulate verbal speech. Many studies show that people can accurately **decode** subtle nonverbal cues. For example, the six major facial expressions of emotion are perceived accurately around the world. Other expressions vary according to culturally determined **display rules**. These rules dictate which expressions are appropriate to display. **Emblems**—nonverbal gestures that have specific meanings—are also culturally determined. In general, women are better at understanding and conveying emotion nonverbally. One exception,

though, is that women are less accurate at detecting deception when observing nonverbal behavior. According to the **social-role theory** of sex differences, this may be because in many societies women have learned different skills, one of which is to be polite in social interactions, overlooking the fact that someone is lying.

Often it is difficult to tell how someone feels, or what kind of person he or she is, solely from the person's nonverbal behavior. As a result, we go beyond the information given in people's behavior, making inferences about their feelings, traits, and motives. One way we do this is to rely on an **implicit personality theory** to fill in the blanks. Such a theory is composed of our general notions about which personality traits go together in one person. When people's behavior is ambiguous and we cannot rely on an implicit personality theory, our attributions about them may be affected by **priming**, a process whereby recent experiences increase a trait's **accessibility** or ready availability in our minds.

According to **attribution theory,** we try to determine why people do what they do, in order to uncover the feelings and traits that are behind their actions. **Correspondent inference theory** focuses on how we make **internal attributions,** or how we infer dispositions from corresponding behavior. We do so by observing how many **noncommon effects** are produced by a person's behavior and how much the behavior is inconsistent with our **category-based expectancies** and **target-based expectancies.** The **covariation model,** another theory of attribution, focuses on observations of behavior across time, place, different actors, and different targets of the behavior and examines how the perceiver chooses either an internal or an **external attribution.** We make such choices by using **consensus, distinctiveness,** and **consistency information.** A final attribution theory, the **taxonomy of success and failure attributions,** focuses on how we determine the cause of a person's performance; to reach an attribution, we rely on information that tells us the **locus, stability,** and **controllability** of the behavior.

People also use various mental shortcuts when making attributions, including the use of schemas and theories. One common shortcut is the **fundamental attribution error,** which is the tendency to overestimate the extent to which people do what they do because of internal, dispositional factors. A reason for this error is that a person's behavior often has greater **perceptual salience** than the surrounding situation does. The **actor/observer difference** is a qualification of the fundamental attribution error: We are more likely to commit this error when explaining other people's behavior than when explaining our own behavior. People's attributions are also influenced by their need to protect their self-esteem (**self-serving attributions**) and their need to avoid feelings of mortality (**defensive attributions**). One form of defensive attribution is **unrealistic optimism** about the future, whereby we think that good things are more likely to happen to us than to other people. Another is the **belief in a just world,** whereby we believe that bad things happen to bad people and good things happen to good people.

How accurate are people's attributions and impressions of others? Not surprisingly, the more we get to know someone, the more accurate we are. Even when judging people we know well, however, the shortcuts we use sometimes lead to mistaken impressions. For example, we tend to make more dispositional attributions about other people than are warranted. Often, however, we do not realize our impressions are wrong, because we see people in limited situations and because the way we treat people causes them to behave the way we expect them to (the self-fulfilling prophecy).

IF YOU ARE INTERESTED . . .

Dorris, Michael. *A Yellow Raft in Blue Water.* New York: Warner Books, 1988. Three generations of women—a daughter, a mother, and a grandmother—tell the stories of their lives on a Native American reservation, and in the telling, indicate how they have both understood and misunderstood each other.

Fiske, S. T., & Taylor, S. E. (1991). *Social cognition* (2nd ed.). New York: McGraw-Hill. A recent, encyclopedic review of the literature on social perception by two experts in the field.

Jones, E. E. (1990). *Interpersonal perception.* New York: Freeman. An up-to-date review of social perception (with an emphasis on attribution theory) by one of the pioneers in the field.

McArthur, L. Z. (1990). *Social perception.* Pacific Grove, CA: Brooks/Cole. A general review of social perception and impression formation.

Rashomon: A classic film set in medieval Japan, directed by Akira Kurosawa, and winner of the Academy Award for Best Foreign Film. A violent murder and rape occurs. In an exploration of truth, lies, and attributions, four people tell their own, very different versions of what happened.

Ross, L., & Nisbett, R. E. (1991). *The person and the situation: Perspectives of social psychology.* New York: McGraw-Hill. A lively, in-depth discussion of many of the aspects of social perception we have discussed, such as the fundamental attribution error.

Simpson, Mona. *Anywhere But Here.* New York: Vintage Books, 1988. A novel both comic and tragic, telling the story of a young girl and her mother, their confused, destructive, but often hilarious relationship, their relentless quest for the American dream, and how they make sense out of their lives and each other.

Chapter 5

Self-Understanding: How We Come to Understand Ourselves

Chapter Outline

There is one thing, and only one in the whole universe which we know more about than we could learn from external observation. That one thing is [ourselves]. We have, so to speak, inside information; we are in the know.

—C. S. Lewis, 1960

We are unknown, we knowers, ourselves to ourselves; this has its own good reason. We have never searched for ourselves—how should it then come to pass, that we should ever find ourselves?

—Friedrich Nietzsche, 1918

top for a moment and think about how you feel right now. Are you happy or sad? Tired or energetic? Calm or irritated? Questions like these are usually pretty easy to answer; as C. S. Lewis says, we are "in the know" about ourselves. Few of us, however, would claim to know ourselves perfectly. Sometimes our thoughts and feelings are a confused jumble of contradictory reactions. And even if we know how we feel, it is not always clear why we feel that way. A lot about ourselves is inscrutable and difficult to determine, as Nietzsche implies.

How do we gain self-knowledge? According to social psychologists, it is not a simple matter of looking inward. Because it is often difficult to know exactly how we feel or why we are doing what we are doing, we look outward to the social environment for clues. This is why self-knowledge is a key social psychological question: Our views of ourselves are shaped by the world around us. We learn a great deal by observing how people treat us and how we treat others.

Let's turn this question around for a moment: Not only do other people influence our self-views; we influence their self-views. The way in which we do so can have important consequences. Suppose, for example, that you are an elementary school teacher and want your students to develop a love of reading. In this case, you are deliberately trying to influence how your students view themselves—you want them to look in the mirror and see someone who loves books. How might you go about accomplishing this? If you are like many teachers and educators, you might arrive at the following solution: Reward the kids for reading. Maybe that would get them to love books.

Teachers have always rewarded kids with a smile or a pat on the head, of course, but recently they have used more powerful rewards. In some school districts, a national chain of pizza restaurants offers second-graders a certificate for a free pizza for every 22 books they read. A few years ago, Mel Steely, a professor at West Georgia College, decided to offer underprivileged children an even more lucrative reward. He started a program called Earning by Learning, in which low-income children were offered $2 for every book they read. The program was financed in part by a friend of Steely's, House Speaker Newt Gingrich, who donated some of his speaking fees to the program. Speaker Gingrich believed that the program was such a great success that it should be expanded nationwide (Buzbee, 1995).

Supporters of programs like these argue that kids are better off reading than watching television or playing video games and that whatever it takes to get them to read is well worth it. There is no doubt that rewards are powerful motivators and

Many programs try to get children to read more by rewarding them. Do such rewards influence a child's self-concept? Do they increase or decrease a child's love of reading?

that pizzas and money will get kids to read more. One of the oldest and most fundamental psychological principles is that behavior followed by rewards will increase in frequency. Whether it be a rat pressing a bar in order to obtain a food pellet or a child reading to get a free pizza, rewards can change behavior.

But people are not rats, and to understand the effects of rewards we have to look beyond the immediate effects of rewards on behavior. We have to consider how the social environment—including the rewards available in that environment—influences people's thoughts about themselves. Does getting money for reading, for example, change people's ideas about why they are reading? The danger of reward programs such as Earning for Learning is that the kids will begin to think they are reading to earn money, not because they find reading to be an enjoyable activity in its own right. Well-intentioned efforts to reward children might actually reduce their enjoyment of the activity, by encouraging them to think they are doing it for the money (or the pizzas). When the reward programs end and money or pizzas are no longer forthcoming, children may actually read less than they did before. In this chapter, on the self and self-knowledge, we will see why.

The Nature of the Self

Who are you? How did you come to be this person you call "myself"? The founder of American psychology, William James (1842–1910), described the basic duality that is the heart of our perception of self. First, the self is composed of our thoughts and beliefs about ourselves, or what James (1890) called the "known," or, more simply, the "me." Second, the self is also the active processor of information, the "knower," or "I." In modern terms, we refer to the known aspect of the self as the **self-concept,** or the definition of self, and to the knower aspect of the self as awareness, or consciousness. Together, these two psychological processes combine to create a coherent sense of identity: Your self is both a book (full of fascinating contents collected over time) and the reader of that book (who at any moment can access a specific chapter or add a new one).

James (1890) stressed the importance of social relationships in our definition of self, noting that we can have different "selves" that develop in response to different social situations. For example, when one of us is at the stable, training her horse and chatting with other riders and stablehands, she presents a different aspect of herself than when she is at a national psychology conference with her colleagues. Her "barn self" is more colloquial, less intellectual; she alters her vocabulary and topics of conversation. These multiple selves are all known, but it is up to the knower to recognize when it is appropriate to exhibit one self and not another.

The development of a sense of self requires the realization that one is a knower and that there is in fact something to be known. This feat is not so simple, as shown by research on different species of mammals (Povinelli, 1993). Do animals have a sense of self? Gordon Gallup (1977, 1993; Gallup & Suarez, 1986) addressed this question in a fascinating series of studies in which he placed

self-concept: the contents of the self; that is, our perception of our own thoughts, beliefs, and personality traits

"Steer clear of that group. They're all terribly self-aware."

■ Research by Gordon Gallup (1977) has found that the great apes (chimpanzees, gorillas, orangutans) have a sense of self, whereas other mammals do not.

different kinds of animals in front of a mirror. Most animals (e.g., dogs, rats) initially reacted to their reflected image with some curiosity and with "social displays"—the vocalizations, facial expressions, and postures each uses to communicate with another member of its species. However, the animals quickly tired of the mirror image and ignored it—except for the great apes. Gallup (1977) found that over the course of several days, the great apes began to use the mirror as an aid in grooming themselves (e.g., picking food out of their teeth) or for entertainment (e.g., making faces, blowing bubbles with their saliva).

But did the great apes really know that the image in the mirror was theirs? To find out, Gallup (1977) briefly anesthetized chimpanzees and painted an odorless red dye on one brow and one ear. When the chimps looked into the mirror, they immediately reached for their red brow and ear—proof not only that they realized the image in the mirror was themselves and not another ape but also that they knew they looked different from how they looked before. Researchers have used a variation of the red dye test with human infants and found that a sense of self-recognition develops at around two years of age in human beings (Bertenthal & Fischer, 1978; Lewis, 1986). Lewis and Brooks (1978), for example, found that 75 percent of 21- to 25-month-old infants touched their rouged noses, while only 25 percent of the 9- to 12-month-old infants did so.

It is a big step, however, from recognizing yourself in a mirror to having the type of multifaceted, complex definition of self that characterizes adult human beings. Psychologists have studied how people's self-concept changes from childhood to adulthood, by asking people of different ages to answer the simple question "Who am I?" Typically, our self-concepts start out being concrete, with references to clear-cut, easily observable characteristics like age, sex, neighborhood, and hobbies. In a study by Montemayor and Eisen (1977), for example, a 9-year-old answered the "Who am I?" question this way: "I have brown eyes. I have brown hair. I have brown eyebrows. . . . I'm a boy. I have an uncle that is almost 7 feet tall" (Montemayor & Eisen, 1977, p. 317). As we mature, we place less emphasis on physical characteristics and more emphasis on psychological states (e.g., our thoughts and feelings) and on considerations of how other people judge us (Hart & Damon, 1986; Livesley & Bromley, 1973; Montemayor & Eisen, 1977). Consider this twelfth-grade high school student's answer to the "Who am I" question:

> I am a human being . . . . I am a moody person. I am an indecisive person. I am an ambitious person. I am a very curious person. I am not an individual. I am a loner. I am an American (God help me). I am a Democrat. I am a liberal person. I am a radical. I am a conservative. I am a pseudoliberal. I am an atheist. I am not a classifiable person (i.e., I don't want to be). (Montemayor & Eisen, 1977, p. 318)

As you can see, this person has moved considerably beyond descriptions of her hobbies and physical appearance.

Definitions of Self in Different Cultures

In June, 1993, Masako Owada, a 29-year-old Japanese woman, married Crown Prince Naruhito of Japan. Masako was a very bright career diplomat in the foreign ministry, educated at Harvard and Oxford. She spoke five languages and was on the fast track to a prestigious diplomatic career. Her decision to marry the prince surprised some observers, because it meant she would have to give up her promising career. Indeed, she gave up any semblance of an independent life,

■ People had very different reactions to Masako Owada's decision to give up her promising career to marry Crown Prince Naruhito of Japan, due in part to cultural differences in the importance of independence versus interdependence.

becoming subservient to the prince and the rest of the royal family and spending much of her time participating in rigid royal ceremonies. Her primary role was to produce a male heir to the royal throne.

How do you feel about Masako's decision to marry the prince? Your answer may say something about the nature of your self-concept and the culture in which you grew up. In many Western cultures people have an **independent view of the self,** in which individualism is valued (Kitayama & Markus, 1994, in press; Markus & Kitayama, 1991, 1994; Triandis, 1989, 1995). Westerners learn to define themselves as quite separate from other people and to value independence and uniqueness. Consequently, many Western observers were mystified by Masako's decision to marry the crown prince. They assumed she was coerced into the marriage by a backward, sexist society that did not properly value her worth as an individual with an independent life of her own.

In contrast, many Asian and other non-Western cultures have an **interdependent view of the self,** in which the connectedness and interdependence between people is valued. Independence and uniqueness are frowned upon, whereas interdependence between people is stressed. For example, when asked to complete sentences beginning with "I am . . . ," people from Asian cultures are more likely to refer to social groups, such as one's family or religious group, than people from Western cultures are (Triandis, 1989). To many Japanese and other Asians, Masako's decision to give up her career was not at all surprising and was a positive, natural consequence of her view of herself as connected and obligated to others, such as her family and the royal family. What is viewed as positive and normal behavior by one culture might be viewed very differently by another, because of fundamental differences in the construction of the self-concept in the different cultures.

Recently, Ted Singelis (1994) has developed a questionnaire that measures the extent to which people view themselves as interdependent or independent. Sample items from this scale are shown in Figure 5.1. Singelis (1994) gave the questionnaire to students at the University of Hawaii at Manoa and found that

independent view of the self: a way of defining oneself in terms of one's own internal thoughts, feelings, and actions, and not in terms of the thoughts, feelings, and actions of other people.

interdependent view of the self: a way of defining oneself in terms of one's relationships to other people; recognizing that one's behavior is often determined by the thoughts, feelings, and actions of others.

MEASURE OF INDEPENDENCE AND INTERDEPENDENCE

	strongly disagree					strongly agree
1. My happiness depends on the happiness of those around me.	1 2 3 4 5 6 7
2. I will sacrifice my self-interest for the benefit of the group I am in.	1 2 3 4 5 6 7
3. It is important to me to respect decisions made by the group.	1 2 3 4 5 6 7
4. If my brother or sister fails, I feel responsible.	1 2 3 4 5 6 7
5. Even when I strongly disagree with group members, I avoid an argument.	1 2 3 4 5 6 7
6. I am comfortable with being singled out for praise or rewards.	1 2 3 4 5 6 7
7. Being able to take care of myself is a primary concern for me.	1 2 3 4 5 6 7
8. I prefer to be direct and forthright when dealing with people I've just met.	1 2 3 4 5 6 7
9. I enjoy being unique and different from others in many respects.	1 2 3 4 5 6 7
10. My personal identity independent of others, is very important to me.	1 2 3 4 5 6 7

FIGURE 5.1 A measure of independence and interdependence. ■ These questions are taken from a scale developed by Singelis (1994) to measure the strength of people's interdependent and independent views of themselves. The actual scale consists of 12 items that measure interdependence and 12 items that measure independence. We have reproduced 5 of each type of item here: The first 5 are designed to measure interdependence, and the last 5 are designed to measure independence. Singelis (1994) found that Asian Americans agreed more with the interdependence than the independence items, whereas Caucasian Americans agreed more with the independence than the interdependence items. (Adapted from Singelis, 1994)

> The squeaky wheel gets the grease.
> –American proverb

> The nail that stands out gets pounded down.
> –Japanese proverb

Asian Americans agreed more with the interdependence than the independence items, whereas Caucasian Americans agreed more with the independence than the interdependence items.

We do not mean to imply that every member of a Western culture has an independent view of the self and that every member of an Asian culture has an interdependent view of the self. Within cultures, there are differences in the self-concept, and these differences are likely to increase as contact between cultures increases. It is interesting to note, for example, that Masako's decision to marry the prince was unpopular among at least some young Japanese women, who felt that her choice was not a positive sign of interdependence but a betrayal to the feminist cause in Japan (Sanger, 1993).

Nonetheless, the differences between the Western and Eastern sense of self is real and has interesting consequences for communication between the cultures. Indeed, the differences in the sense of self are so fundamental that it is very difficult for people with independent selves to appreciate what it is like to have an interdependent self, and vice versa. Western readers might find it difficult to appreciate the Asian sense of interdependence; similarly, many Japanese find it difficult to comprehend that Americans could possibly know who they are separate from the social groups to which they belong. After giving a lecture on the Western view of the self to a group of Japanese students, one psychologist reported that the students "sighed deeply and said at the end, 'Could this really be true?'" (Kitayama & Markus, 1994, p. 18). To paraphrase William Shakespeare, in Western society the self is the measure of all things. However natural we consider this conception of the self to be, it is important to remember that it is only a construction and not an inherent reality.

Despite these cross-cultural differences, there are commonalities across cultures in the nature of the self-concept. For example, Mahzarin Banaji and Deborah Prentice (1994) identified two basic self-motives: self-knowledge and self-enhancement. Self-knowledge refers to our desire to form an accurate assessment of our traits, attitudes, and abilities, whereas self-enhancement refers to our desire to maintain and increase self-esteem. Though it may well be that the emphasis on these motives differs from culture to culture, most psychologists agree that they are fundamental human motives common to all people. We will discuss self-enhancement motives (i.e., self-esteem maintenance) in Chapter 6; in this chapter, we will discuss how the accuracy motive operates in the quest for self-knowledge. We will see that the way in which we come to know other people is often very similar to the way in which we come to know ourselves.

Knowing Ourselves Through Introspection

When we told you we were going to describe the sources of information you use to construct a self-concept, you may have thought, "Good grief! I don't need a social psychology textbook to tell me that! It's not exactly a surprise; I just think about myself. No big deal." In other words, you rely on **introspection,** where you look inward and examine the "inside information" that you, and you alone, have about your thoughts, feelings, and motives. And indeed, you do find some answers when you introspect. But there are two interesting things about introspection: (a) People do not rely on this source of information as often as you might think—surprisingly, people spend very little time thinking about themselves—and (b) even when people do introspect, the reasons for their feelings and behavior can be hidden from conscious awareness. In short, self-scrutiny isn't all it's cracked up to be, and if this were our only source of knowledge about ourselves, we would be in trouble.

How often do people think about themselves? To find out, Mihaly Csikszentmihalyi and Thomas Figurski (1982) asked 107 employees, who ranged in age from 19 to 63 and worked at five different companies, to wear beepers for one week. The beepers went off at random intervals between 7:30 A.M. and 10:30 P.M., for a total of seven to nine times a day. At the sound of the beeper, the participants answered a series of questions about their activities, thoughts, and moods at that time. The responses were content-analyzed into categories, including thoughts about oneself (e.g., "How lazy I've been all day," "It hurts," or "Why did I get this fat?"). As you can see in Figure 5.2, people thought about themselves surprisingly infrequently. Only 8 percent of the total thoughts recorded (4,721) were about the self; more often, the participants thought about work, chores, and time. In fact, the response of "no thoughts" was more frequent than that of thoughts about the self. Thus, while we certainly engage in introspection at times, it is not a frequent cognitive activity. Mundane thoughts about everyday life, and indeed thoughts about other people and our conversations with them, account for the vast majority of our daily thoughts (see Figure 5.2).

introspection: the process whereby people look inward and examine their own thoughts, feelings, and motives

> Introspection is difficult and fallible . . . [t]he difficulty is simply that of all observation of whatever kind.
> –William James, 1890

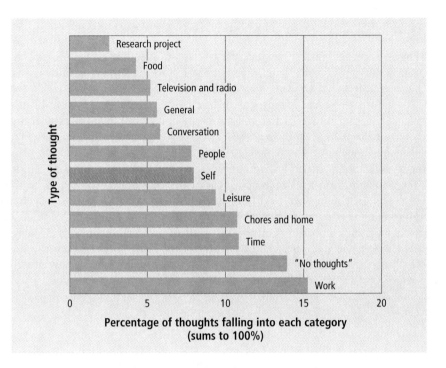

FIGURE 5.2   "What are you thinking about?" ■ For a week, people wore beepers that went off at random intervals several times a day. Each time the beepers went off, people described what they had just been thinking about. Thoughts about the self were surprisingly infrequent. (Adapted from Csikszentmihalyi & Figurski, 1982)

> But as I looked into the mirror, I screamed, and my heart shuddered: for I saw not myself but the mocking, leering, face of a devil.
> —Friedrich Nietzsche, *Thus Spake Zarathustra*

self-awareness theory: the idea that when people focus their attention on themselves, they evaluate and compare their behavior to their internal standards and values

Focusing on the Self: Self-Awareness Theory

When we are thinking about ourselves, what happens? What are the consequences of turning the spotlight of consciousness on ourselves, instead of focusing our attention on the world around us? As we just saw from the Csikszentmihalyi and Figurski (1982) study, we do not focus on ourselves very often. Sometimes, however, we encounter something in the environment that triggers self-awareness, such as knowing that people are watching us, hearing our tape-recorded voice, seeing ourselves on videotape, or staring at ourselves in a mirror. For example, if you are watching a home video taken by a friend with her new camcorder and you are the featured attraction, you will be in a state of self-awareness, where you become the focus of your attention.

According to **self-awareness theory,** when we focus on ourselves we evaluate and compare our current behavior against our internal standards and values (Carver & Scheier, 1981; Duval & Wicklund, 1972; Wicklund, 1975; Wicklund & Frey, 1980). In short, we literally become self-conscious, in the sense that we become objective, judgmental observers of ourselves. Are we behaving as we think we should? Let's say that you believe it is important for you to be honest with your friends. One day, while conversing with a friend, you lie to him. In the midst of this conversation, you catch sight of yourself in a large mirror. How do you think you will feel?

According to Shelley Duval and Robert Wicklund (1972), seeing yourself will make you aware of the disparity between your behavior and your moral standards. If you can change your behavior to match your internal guidelines (e.g., say something particularly nice to your friend or admit you lied and ask for forgiveness), you will do so. If you feel you can't change your behavior, then being in a state of self-awareness will be very uncomfortable, for you will be confronted with disagreeable feedback about yourself. In this situation, you will stop being self-aware as quickly as possible (e.g., by turning so that your back is to the mirror or by saying good-bye to your friend and leaving the room). Figure 5.3 illustrates this process: how self-awareness makes us conscious of our internal standards and directs our subsequent behavior.

Focusing on ourselves can thus be a very unpleasant state of mind. This dissatisfaction with ourselves can be painful, motivating us to escape self-scrutiny. Everyone avoids self-awareness at times, by engaging in such mundane, distracting activities as watching television or reading a book. Sometimes, however, people go even further in their attempt to escape the self. Roy Baumeister (1991) has pointed out that such diverse activities as alcohol abuse, binge eating, sexual masochism, and suicide have one thing in common: All are effective ways of turning off the internal spotlight on oneself. Getting drunk, for example, is one way of avoiding negative thoughts about oneself (at least temporarily). Suicide, of course, is the ultimate way of ending self-scrutiny. The fact that people regularly engage in such dangerous behaviors, despite their risks, is an indication of how aversive self-focus can be (Hull, 1981; Hull & Young, 1983).

Not all means of escaping the self, however, are so damaging. Baumeister (1991) points out that many forms of religious expression and spirituality are also an effective means of avoiding self-focus. Further, self-focus is not always

> I swear to you . . . that to be overly conscious is a sickness, a real, thorough sickness.
>
> –Dostoevsky,
> *Notes from Underground*

FIGURE 5.3 Self-awareness theory: The consequences of self-focused attention. (Adapted from Carver and Scheier, 1981)

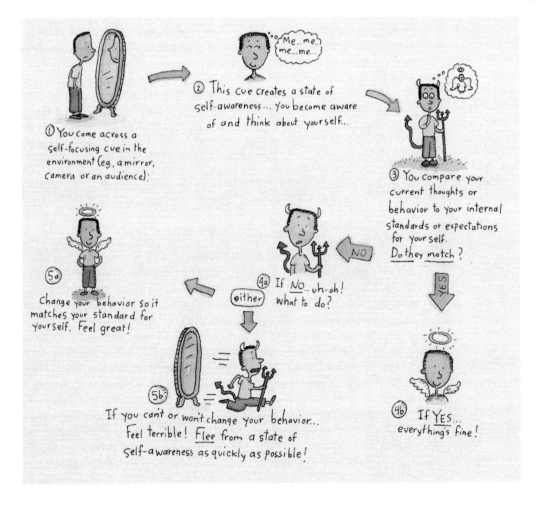

aversive. If you have just achieved a life goal or experienced a major success, then focusing on yourself can be pleasant indeed, because it highlights the match between your behavior and your ideals. Self-focus can also be a way of keeping you out of trouble, by reminding you of your sense of right and wrong. For example, several studies have found that when people are self-aware (e.g., in front of a mirror), they are more likely to follow their moral standards, such as avoiding the temptation to cheat on a test (e.g. Beaman, Klentz, Diener, & Svanum, 1979; Diener & Wallbom, 1976; Gibbons, 1978).

To summarize, self-awareness is particularly aversive when it reminds people of their shortcomings, and under these circumstances (e.g., right after failing a test) people try to avoid it. Other times, however—such as when that little devil is on your shoulder pushing you into temptation—a dose of self-awareness is not such a bad thing, because it makes us more aware of our morals and ideals.

Judging Why We Feel the Way We Do: Telling More Than We Can Know

Another kind of self-knowledge is more difficult to obtain, even when we are self-aware and introspect to our heart's content: knowing why we feel the way we do. Imagine trying to decide why you love someone. Being in love typically makes you feel giddy, euphoric, and preoccupied; in fact, the ancient Greeks thought love was a sickness. But why do you feel this way? Exactly what is it about your sweetheart that made you fall in love? Most of us would be tongue-tied when trying to answer this question. We know it is something about our loved one's looks, personality, values, and background. But precisely what? How can we possibly verbalize the special chemistry that exists between two people? A friend of ours once claimed he was in love with a woman because she played the saxophone. Was this really the only reason? Or even an important one? The heart works in such mysterious ways that it is difficult to tell.

Unfortunately, it's not just love that is difficult to explain. Many of our basic mental processes occur outside of awareness (Kihlstrom, 1987; Mandler, 1975; Neisser, 1976). This is not to say that we are thinkers without a clue—we are aware of the final result of our thought processes (e.g., that we are in love) but often unaware of the cognitive processing that led to the result. It's as if the magician pulled a rabbit out of a hat: You see the rabbit, but you don't know how it got there. How do we deal with this rabbit problem? Whereas we often don't know why we feel a certain way, it seems we are always able to come up with an explanation. We are the proud owners of the most powerful brain to evolve on this planet, and we certainly put it to use. Unfortunately, it didn't come with an owner's manual. Thus, introspection may not lead us to the true causes of our feelings and behavior, but we'll manage to convince ourselves that it did.

Richard Nisbett and Tim Wilson explored this phenomenon, or how we tell more than we know (Nisbett & Ross, 1980; Nisbett & Wilson, 1977; Wilson, 1985; Wilson & Stone, 1985). For example, Tim Wilson, Pat Laser, and Julie Stone (1982) asked college students to keep journals of their daily moods every day for five weeks. The students also kept track of other variables, such as what the weather was like and how much sleep they had gotten the night before. When asked, the participants reported that several things correlated with their moods. However, an analysis of the data indicated that in many cases people were wrong. For example, most people believed that the amount of sleep they got predicted how good a mood they were in the next day, when in fact this wasn't true:

> I have often wished I had time to cultivate modesty. . . . But I am too busy thinking about myself.
>
> –Dame Edith Sitwell

Amount of sleep was unrelated to people's moods. The participants had introspected and found or generated some logical-sounding theories that in fact weren't right (Bargh & Pietromonaco, 1982; Kihlstrom, 1987; Jacoby, Lindsay, & Toth, 1992; Niedenthal & Kitayama, 1994).

What these participants had relied on, at least in part, were their **causal theories.** People have many theories about what influences their feelings and behavior (e.g., "My mood should be affected by how much sleep I got last night") and often use these theories to help them explain why they feel the way they do (e.g., "I am in a bad mood; I bet the fact that I got only six hours of sleep last night has a lot to do with it"). We learn many of these theories from the culture in which we grow up, such as the idea that absence makes the heart grow fonder, that people are in bad moods on Mondays, or that people who have been divorced are a poor choice for a successful second marriage. The only problem is that, as discussed in Chapter 3, our schemas and theories are not always correct and thus can lead to incorrect judgments about the causes of our actions.

Consider this example of causal theories in action from the researchers who have studied them: One night, Nisbett and Wilson were meeting in an office at the University of Michigan. They were trying to think of ways to test the hypothesis that introspection often can't tell us why we feel the way we do and that we rely on causal theories when trying to uncover the reasons for our feelings, judgments, and actions. Brilliant insights were not forthcoming, and the researchers were frustrated by their lack of progress. Then they realized that a source of their frustration (or so they thought) was the annoying whine of a vacuum cleaner that a custodial worker was operating right outside their office. Because it took them a while to realize that the noise of the vacuum was disrupting their meeting, they experienced what seemed like an inspiration—maybe distracting background noises are more bothersome than people think. Maybe this was an example of the very kind of stimulus they were looking for—one that would influence people's judgments but, because their causal theories did not adequately cover this possibility, would be overlooked when people explained their behavior.

Nisbett and Wilson (1977) designed a study to test this possibility (after shutting the door). They asked people to rate how interesting a documentary film was. In one condition, a construction worker (actually, Dick Nisbett) ran a power saw right outside the door to the room in which the film was shown. The irritating burst of noise began about a minute into the film. It continued intermittently until Tim Wilson, the experimenter, went to the door and shouted to the worker to please stop sawing until the film was over. The participants rated how much they enjoyed the film, and then the experimenter asked them to indicate whether the noise had influenced their evaluations. To see if the noise really did have an effect, Nisbett and Wilson included a control condition in which participants viewed the film without any distracting noise. The hypothesis was that the noise would lower people's evaluation of the film but that people would not realize the noise was responsible for the negative evaluation.

As it happened, this hypothesis was completely wrong. The participants who watched the film with the annoying background noise did not like it any less than those who saw the film without the distracting noise did (in fact, they liked the film slightly more). When the participants were asked how much the noise had influenced their ratings, however, their hypothesis agreed with Nisbett and Wilson's. Even though the noise had no detectable effect on people's ratings, most people reported that it had lowered their ratings of the film. In this case, both the participants and the researchers had the same causal theory, but the theory wasn't

causal theories: theories about the causes of one's own feelings and behaviors; often we learn such theories from our culture (e.g., "absence makes the heart grow fonder")

> We can never, even by the strictest examination, get completely behind the secret springs of action.
> —Immanuel Kant

true—at least, not when it came to watching a documentary while hearing construction noise.

In further studies, other factors that seem like they should not influence people's judgments—that is, factors that are not part of people's causal theories—actually did have an effect. For example, in one study people evaluated the quality of items of clothing, such as pantyhose, in a shopping mall (Nisbett & Wilson, 1977). Much to the surprise of the researchers, the position of the items on the display table had a large effect on people's preferences. The more to the right an item was, the more people liked it. The researchers knew that it was the position and not something distinctive about the different pairs of pantyhose that influenced people's judgments, because in fact all four pairs were identical. However, the participants were completely in the dark about this effect of position on their judgments. Such an odd reason for their choice of pantyhose was not evident when they introspected about the reasons for their choice.

We do not mean to imply that people rely solely on their causal theories when introspecting about the reasons for their feelings and behaviors. In addition to culturally learned causal theories, we have a great deal of information about ourselves, such as how we have responded in the past and what we happen to have been thinking about before making a choice (Gavanski & Hoffman, 1987; Wilson & Stone, 1985). The fact remains, however, that introspecting about our past actions and current thoughts does not always yield the right answer about why we feel the way we do.

The Consequences of Introspecting About Reasons

Not only is it difficult to uncover all of our reasons by introspecting; it may not always be a good idea to try to do so. Have you ever, when faced with a difficult decision, spent time reflecting about why you felt the way you did about each alternative? Perhaps when you decided where to go to college, you were faced with two or more attractive alternatives and had trouble making up your mind. Maybe you couldn't decide which courses to take this year. In situations like these, people sometimes analyze the alternatives very carefully, maybe even making a list of the pluses and minuses of each choice. Benjamin Franklin argued that this is the best way to proceed:

> My way is to divide half a sheet of paper by a line into two columns, writing over the one Pro, and over the other Con. Then, during three or four days consideration, I put down under the different heads short hints of the different motives, that at different times occur to me, for or against each measure. . . . When each [reason] is thus considered, separately and comparatively, and the whole lies before me, I think I can judge better, and am less likely to make a rash step. (Quoted in Goodman, 1945, p. 746)

Tim Wilson has found, however, that analyzing the reasons for our feelings is not always the best strategy and in fact can make matters worse (Wilson, Dunn, Kraft, & Lisle, 1989; Wilson & Hodges, 1992; Wilson, Hodges, & LaFleur, 1995; Wilson & LaFleur, 1995). Because it is difficult to know exactly why we feel the way we do about something, we bring to mind reasons that sound plausible and come to mind easily. The reasons that sound plausible, however, may not be the correct reasons. Even worse, we might convince ourselves that these reasons are correct, thereby changing our minds about how we feel to match our reasons.

Suppose, for example, that we asked you to take out a piece of paper and write down exactly why you feel the way you do about a romantic partner. When people list reasons in this manner, **reasons-generated attitude change** tends to occur, whereby people change their attitudes toward their partners (Wilson, Dunn, Bybee, Hyman, & Rotondo, 1984; Wilson & Kraft, 1993). Why? It is difficult to know exactly why we love someone; thus, we latch onto reasons that sound good and that happen to be on our minds. In our studies, the reasons people report are such things as how well they communicate with their dating partner and how similar they are to him or her in their interests and backgrounds. Whereas these reasons may often be correct, people probably overlook other reasons that are not so easy to verbalize, such as the "special chemistry" that can exist between two people.

The trouble comes when the reasons that are accessible in people's memories and are easy to verbalize imply a different attitude from the one people had before. Suppose, for instance, that things are going well between you and your dating partner but you have trouble verbalizing exactly why this is so. What comes to mind is the fact that you have rather different backgrounds and interests. Consequently, you are likely to change your mind about how you feel, assuming that your feelings must match your reasons. "We really don't have much in common," you might say. "I guess this relationship doesn't have much of a future." Wilson and his colleagues have found just this sequence of events in a number of studies (e.g., Wilson & Kraft, 1993).

It's difficult to know, of course, which attitude is the right one—the positive feelings you had before analyzing reasons or the more negative ones you have afterward. Wilson and his colleagues have found, however, that the attitudes people express immediately after analyzing reasons should not be trusted too much. When people make decisions based on these attitudes, they come to regret what they have chosen (Wilson, Lisle, Schooler, Hodges, Klaaren, & LaFleur, 1993). Why? The determinants of your feelings that are hard to verbalize (e.g., that "something special" your sweetheart has) do not go away and are likely to shape your feelings in the future. Thus, if you focus only on the reasons that are easy to verbalize (e.g., the fact that you and your sweetheart have different backgrounds), you might behave in ways—such as breaking up with your sweetheart—that you later regret. Several studies, for example, have found that the attitudes people express after analyzing their reasons do not predict their future attitudes and behavior very well (Millar & Tesser, 1986; Wilson et al., 1984; Wilson & LaFleur, 1995).

reasons-generated attitude change: attitude change resulting from thinking about the reasons for one's attitudes; people assume their attitudes match the reasons that are plausible and easy to verbalize

Knowing Ourselves Through Observations of Our Own Behavior

As we have seen, it is often difficult to know exactly why we feel the way we do, and it can be dangerous to think too much about our reasons. If introspection has its limits, how else might we find out what sort of person we are and what our attitudes are? We turn now to another source of self-knowledge—observations of our own behavior.

Inferring Who We Are from How We Behave: Self-Perception Theory

If you aren't sure how you feel about something, there is another way you can find out: Observe your own behavior. If you want to know whether you like country music, for example, you might think, "Well, I always listen to the country

> I've always written poems . . . I never know what I think until I read it in one of my poems.
> –Virginia Hamilton Adair, 1995

self-perception theory: the theory that when our attitudes and feelings are uncertain or ambiguous, we infer these states by observing our behavior and the situation in which it occurs

music station on my car radio," concluding that you like country tunes. It might seem a little strange to say that you find out how you feel by observing what you do, but according to Daryl Bem's (1972) **self-perception theory,** such observations are an important source of self-knowledge.

Bem (1972) argues that we are especially likely to infer our feelings from our behavior when two conditions are met. First, our initial feelings must be weak or unclear. If you've always known that you are a country music lover, then you do not need to observe your behavior to figure out how you feel. Maybe, though, your feelings are murky; you've never really thought about how much you like country music. If so, you are especially likely to use your behavior as a guide to how you feel (Chaiken & Baldwin, 1981; Kunda, Fong, Sanitioso, & Reber, 1993; Wood, 1982).

Second, people think about why they behaved the way they did, to see if their behavior really reflects how they feel. If it is your spouse and not you who always tunes in the country station, or if your radio happens to be stuck on that station, you are unlikely to conclude that you listen to country music in your car because you love it. If you freely choose to listen to that station, however—no one makes you do it—you are especially likely to conclude that you listen to that station because you love country music.

Sound familiar? In Chapter 4 we discussed attribution theory—the way in which people infer someone else's attitudes and feelings by observing that person's behavior. Bem argues that people use the same attributional principles to infer their own attitudes and feelings. For example, if you were trying to decide whether a friend likes country music, you would observe her behavior and explain why she behaved that way. You might notice, for example, that your friend is always listening to country music in the absence of any situational pressures or constraints—no one makes her play those Garth Brooks CDs. You would make an internal attribution for her behavior and conclude that she loves those Nashville tunes. Bem's self-perception theory says we infer our own feelings in the same way: Observe our behavior and make an attribution about why we behaved that way.

Consider, for example, an experiment by James Olson (1992), in which participants read some jokes from a joke book while listening to canned laughter on a set of headphones. How funny did people think the jokes were? According to self-perception theory, people should decide this by observing their own behavior (in this case, how much they laughed) and making an attribution for why they laughed that much. To test this hypothesis, Olson (1992) had to accomplish two things: he had to make sure people laughed at the jokes and then provide them with different explanations for why they laughed as much as they did.

Here's how he did it: First, he gave people jokes to read that were moderately funny, ensuring that they laughed at least some of the time. For example, one joke was as follows:

> *Nurse:* Excuse me doctor, but that man you just gave a clean bill of health to walked out of the office and dropped dead. What should I do?

> *Doctor:* Turn him around so he looks like he was walking in.

Second, Olson supplied different explanations for people's laughter by telling them different things about the effects of the canned laughter. In one condition,

DENNIS THE MENACE

"MOM, WHAT DO I FEEL LIKE DOING?"

■ According to self-perception theory, people often do not know their own feelings and motives and must infer them from observing their behavior.

he told people that canned laughter is "contagious" and definitely increases how much people who listen to it laugh and smile. In a second condition, he told people that canned laughter has no effect on how much people laugh and smile. And in a third condition, he told people that canned laughter actually decreases how much people laugh and smile, because people feel manipulated by it. These instructions, he reasoned, would influence the kinds of attributions people made for why they were laughing, which should influence their conclusions about how funny the jokes were. To see how funny people thought the jokes were Olson left them alone for three minutes and observed how much additional time they spent reading jokes from the same book, with the assumption that if people thought the jokes were funny, they would spend time reading them during this "free time" period.

The results, as seen in Figure 5.4, were exactly as predicted by self-perception theory. When people were told that the laugh track increases laughter, they did not find the jokes to be very funny (i.e., they spent the least amount of time reading them in the free time period—see top of Figure 5.4). Why? In this condition, people assumed that they laughed because of the canned laughter, not because the jokes were funny. When people were told that canned laughter has no effect, they assumed that they laughed because the jokes were funny and thus spent more time reading the joke book during the free time period (see the middle of Figure 5.4). What about when people were told that the laugh track decreases laughter? In this condition, people ended up thinking that the jokes were the funniest of all (i.e., they spent the most time reading them in the free time period—see the bottom of Figure 5.4). They assumed that if they laughed at the jokes even when there was a manipulative laugh track that usually decreases laughter, then the jokes must *really* be funny. In short, just as self-perception theory suggests, people inferred how they felt about the jokes by observing their behavior (their laughter) and thinking about why they were behaving that way. Interestingly,

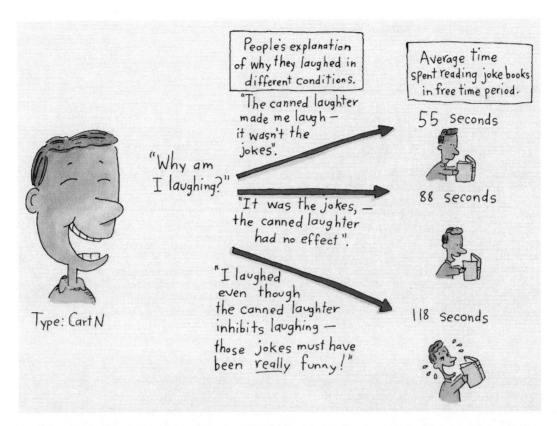

FIGURE 5.4   The self-perception of humor. ■ People read some jokes while listening to canned laughter. How funny did they think the jokes were? Consistent with self-perception theory, it depended on how they explained to themselves why they were laughing. In the top condition, people thought that the canned laughter, not the jokes, made them laugh; thus, they decided the jokes weren't very funny and spent relatively little time reading the joke book during a free time period. In the middle condition, people thought it was the jokes, not the canned laughter, that made them laugh; thus, they spent more time reading the joke book. In the bottom condition, people thought that the canned laughter made it hard for them to laugh. The fact that they still laughed, then, was taken as a sign that the jokes were *really* funny, and these people spent the most time reading the joke book. (Adapted from Olson, 1992)

such inferences are not always correct. In Olson's study, for example, the laugh track didn't really influence how much people laughed, but by believing that it did, people made assumptions about how funny the jokes were.

Being Rewarded Too Much: The Overjustification Effect

According to self-perception theory, when people realize their behavior is caused by an external factor, they do not assume it reflects their internal feelings. This is pretty logical; if you know the only reason you are waiting on tables over the summer is that the pay is good, you will not assume you are doing it because you just love standing on your feet all day. In other words, after looking at your behavior and the situation, you will make an external attribution ("I'm doing it for the money") and not an internal attribution ("I love doing this so much that I would do it for free"). The problem is that when external causes for our behavior are conspicuous, we go overboard, **discounting** the extent to which internal

discounting:
underestimating the effects of one cause of our behavior when another cause is conspicuous and salient

factors played a role (Kelley, 1972; Nisbett & Valins, 1972). We saw an example of discounting earlier: When people in Olson's (1992) experiment on humor thought they were laughing because of the canned laughter (an external factor), they underestimated how funny the jokes were (i.e., they discounted an internal reason for their laughter—the fact that they found the jokes to be funny). This process of discounting has important implications for a major area of life: our motivation to engage in activities and our subsequent interest in and enjoyment of those activities.

Let's say you love to play the piano. You spend many hours happily practicing, simply enjoying the act of making music and the feeling that you are getting better. We would say that your interest in playing the piano stems from **intrinsic motivation.** Your reasons for engaging in the activity have to do with you—the enjoyment and pleasure you feel when playing the piano. In other words, playing the piano is play, not work. According to Mihaly Csikszentmihalyi (1975, 1988), intrinsically motivated behavior creates an optimal experience called flow. When in a state of flow, the individual centers his or her attention on the task, blocks out other stimuli, and concentrates intently. The individual feels competent and is unconcerned about how well he or she is doing; feedback about performance is clear and unambiguous. Finally, the individual experiences a lack of self-awareness. Think about some recent activity of yours that you really enjoyed; you were probably experiencing this state of flow, as with our example of the piano player.

> **intrinsic motivation:** the desire to engage in an activity because we enjoy it or find it interesting, not because of external rewards or pressures

Now let's say your parents get the brilliant idea of rewarding you with money for playing the piano. They figure that this will make you practice even harder. After all, rewards work, don't they? However, your parents have now added an extrinsic reason for you to play the piano. Your playing, hitherto stemming from intrinsic motivation, now stems from **extrinsic motivation** as well: the desire to earn the money. Unfortunately, extrinsic rewards can undermine intrinsic motivation. Whereas before you played the piano because you loved it, now you're playing it so that you'll get the reward. What was once play is now work. The sad outcome is that replacing intrinsic motivation with extrinsic motivation (through the use of rewards) makes people lose interest in the activity they initially enjoyed. This result is called the **overjustification effect,** whereby people overjustify their behavior by focusing on its external causes (e.g., getting a reward) and underestimate their intrinsic interest in the behavior (e.g., Deci & Ryan, 1985; Harackiewicz, 1979; Kohn, 1993; Lepper, in press; Lepper & Greene, 1978; Lepper, Keavney, & Drake, in press; Tang & Hall, in press).

> **extrinsic motivation:** the desire to engage in an activity because of external rewards or pressures, not because we enjoy the task or find it interesting

> **overjustification effect:** the case whereby people view their behavior as caused by compelling extrinsic reasons, making them underestimate the extent to which their behavior was caused by intrinsic reasons

Sound familiar? The danger of programs such as Earning by Learning, described at the beginning of this chapter, now become clear: Giving children money or pizzas to read books may backfire, by lowering their intrinsic interest

■ Making children read for external reasons can lead to an overjustification effect, whereby they infer that they have no intrinsic interest in reading.

in reading. During the programs, children might well read more, in order to get the rewards. No one doubts that rewards are powerful motivators and can change what people do. It's the changes that occur inside people's heads that are often overlooked. Once the programs end, children might actually be *less* likely to read than they were before the programs began. Why? They might think, "I was reading to get money. Now that there is nothing in it for me, why should I read? I think I'll play a video game."

An overjustification effect similar to this has been found in dozens of laboratory and field experiments, with several kinds of rewards, activities, and age-groups. For example, David Greene, Betty Sternberg, and Mark Lepper (1976) conducted the following study with fourth- and fifth-grade students. The teachers introduced four new math games to the students, and during a 13-day baseline period they simply noted how long each child played with each math game. As seen in the first panel of Figure 5.5, the children had some intrinsic interest in the math games initially, in that they played with them for several minutes during this baseline period. For the next several days, a reward program was introduced, whereby the children could earn credits toward certificates and trophies by playing with the math games. The more time they spent playing with the games, the more credits they could earn. As seen in the middle panel of Figure 5.5 this program was effective in increasing the amount of time the kids spent on the math games, showing that the rewards were an effective motivator.

The key question, however, is what happened after the program was terminated and the kids could no longer earn rewards for playing with the games? According to the overjustification hypothesis, the children should conclude that they were playing with the math games only to earn prizes, thereby undermining any intrinsic interest they had at the outset; as a result, when the rewards were taken away, the children should spend significantly less time with the games than they had during the baseline period (e.g., "I can't earn prizes playing with these games anymore—why play with them at all?"). This is exactly what happened, as seen in the right-hand panel of Figure 5.5. After the reward program ended, the

FIGURE 5.5 The overjustification effect. ■ During the initial baseline phase, researchers measured how much time elementary school children played with math games. During the reward program, they rewarded the children with prizes for playing the games. When the rewards were taken away (during the follow-up), the children played with the games even less than they had during the baseline phase, indicating that the rewards had lowered their intrinsic interest in the games. (Adapted from Greene, Sternberg, & Lepper, 1976)

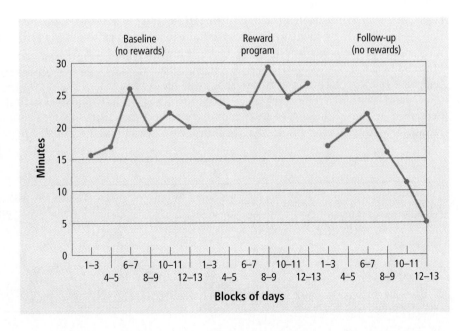

children spent significantly less time with the math games than they had initially, before the rewards were introduced. (The researchers determined, by comparing these results to those of a control condition, that it was the rewards that made people like the games less, and not the fact that everyone became bored with the games as time went by.) In short, the rewards destroyed the children's intrinsic interest in the games, such that by the end of the study they were hardly playing with the games at all.

The results of overjustification studies are distressing, given the wide use of rewards and incentives by parents, educators, and employers. In the workplace, for example, people sometimes find themselves doing things they used to do for the pure joy of it but for which they are now getting paid. Consider basketball great Bill Russell's description of how becoming a professional affected his love for the game:

> I remember that the game lost some of its magical qualities for me once I thought seriously about playing for a living. This first happened in 1955, in my junior year, after USF [the University of San Francisco] won the NCAA national championship. As a result, all through my senior year at USF I played with the idea of turning professional, and things began to change. Whenever I walked on the court I began to calculate how this particular game might affect my future. Thoughts of money and prestige crept into my head. Over the years the professional game would turn more and more into a business. (Russell & Branch, 1979, p. 98)

■ "I remember that the game lost some of its magical qualities for me once I thought seriously about playing for a living."—Basketball great Bill Russell (Russell & Branch, 1979, p.98)

What can we do to protect intrinsic motivation from the slings and arrows of our society's reward system? Fortunately, there is room for some optimism, as recent research has identified conditions under which overjustification effects can be avoided. First, rewards will undermine interest only if interest was high initially (Calder & Staw, 1975; Tang & Hall, in press). If you think a task is excruciatingly boring, rewards obviously can't reduce your interest any further. Similarly, if a child has no interest whatsoever in reading, then getting him or her to read by offering free pizzas is not a bad idea, because there is no initial interest to undermine. The danger arises when a child already likes to read, because then offering free pizzas is likely to convince the child that he or she is reading to earn pizzas, not because reading is interesting in its own right.

Second, the type of reward makes a difference. So far, we have discussed **task-contingent rewards**, meaning that people get them only for doing a task, regardless of how well they do it. Sometimes **performance-contingent rewards** are used, whereby the reward depends on how well people perform the task. For example, grades are performance-contingent, because you get a high reward (an A) only if you do well in the class. This type of reward is less likely to decrease interest in a task—and may even increase interest—because it conveys the message that you are good at the task (Deci & Ryan, 1985; Tang & Hall, in press). Thus, rather than giving kids a reward for playing with math games regardless of how well they do (task-contingent), it is better to reward them for doing *well* at math. Even performance-contingent rewards must be used with care, however, because they too can backfire. Though people like the positive feedback these rewards convey, they do not like the tension and apprehension that come with being evaluated (Harackiewicz, 1989; Harackiewicz, Manderlink, & Sansone, 1984). The trick is to convey positive feedback without making people feel nervous and apprehensive about being evaluated.

task-contingent rewards: rewards that are given for performing a task, regardless of how well we do that task

performance-contingent rewards: rewards that are based on how well we perform a task

Another hopeful sign is that children can be taught to avoid the damaging effects of rewards. Because rewards can never be eliminated from our society, Beth Hennessey and her colleagues focused on ways of helping children to operate within the system—that is, to maintain their intrinsic motivation even with rewards dangled all around them (Hennessey, Amabile, & Martinage, 1989; Hennessey & Zbikowski, 1993). They showed children a videotape in which a boy and girl noted that getting rewards was nice but that the real reason they did things, such as their schoolwork, was because of how much they enjoyed these activities. Did this videotape "immunize" the kids against the negative effects of rewards? To find out, the children came back the next day and took part in what they thought was another study. The researchers asked the kids to make up stories to accompany a series of pictures and offered half of them a reward for doing so.

Previous studies had found that when people are rewarded for activities such as these they lose interest and produce stories that are low in creativity (Amabile, Hennessey, & Grossman, 1986). Among the kids who did not see the videotape, the same thing happened here: The reward, looming before them, lessened their intrinsic motivation for what is typically an enjoyable task, and they produced stories that were less creative than those produced by the nonrewarded children (see the left-hand side of Figure 5.6). What about the kids who had watched the videotape? As seen in the right-hand side of Figure 5.6, the reward had little effect on the creativity of their stories (in fact, the kids who were rewarded made up stories that were slightly more creative than those who were not rewarded did). The information they learned in the video seems to have kept them focused on their intrinsic interest in the task, thereby "short-circuiting" the negative effects of rewards. This research suggests an encouraging solution to the dilemma posed by our society's use of rewards: Your intrinsic interest in an activity, as well as your creativity when engaged in that activity, can be maintained in the face of rewards, if you try to ignore the reward and remind yourself of how much you enjoy doing the task for its own sake.

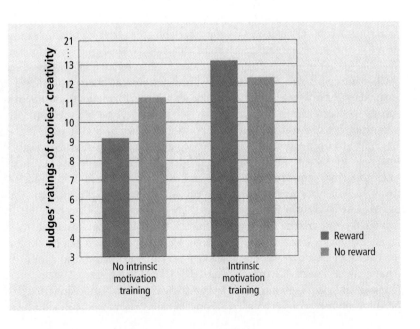

FIGURE 5.6 Avoiding the overjustification effect. ■ As seen on the left-hand side of the graph, children who were rewarded told stories that were less creative, demonstrating the standard overjustification effect. As seen on the right-hand side of the graph, children who were immunized—by watching a videotape that stressed the importance of intrinsic motivation—did not demonstrate the overjustification effect. That is, when they received a reward, they still wrote creative stories. (Adapted from Hennessey & Zbikowski, 1991)

Understanding Our Emotions: The Two-Factor Theory of Emotion

We have just seen that people often use observations of their behavior to determine what they think and what kind of person they are. You may have wondered whether the same is true of other kinds of views of yourself. For example, what about your emotions, such as how happy, angry, or afraid you feel at any given time—how do you know which emotion you are experiencing? Think about a time you felt angry—how did you know you felt that way? This question probably sounds kind of silly; it seems like we just know how we feel, without having to think about it or, as self-perception theory suggests, observing our behavior to see how we feel.

Though it may seem like we just know how we feel, the experience of emotion is not as simple as it appears. Stanley Schachter (1964) proposed a theory of emotion that says we infer what our emotions are in the same way that we infer what kind of person we are or how interested we are in math games: by observing our behavior and then explaining why we are behaving that way. The only difference is in the kind of behavior we observe. Schachter says we observe our internal behaviors—namely, how physiologically aroused we feel. If we feel aroused, we then try to figure out what is causing this arousal. For example, let's say your heart is pounding and your body feels tense. Is it because you just saw your professor—the one from whom you got a paper extension because supposedly you had to go to your grandmother's funeral that day—or is it because you just saw the person standing next to the professor—the one on whom you have the most amazing crush in the universe? Are you feeling unholy fear or stomach-churning love?

Schachter's theory is called the **two-factor theory of emotion,** because understanding our emotional states requires two steps: First, we must experience physiological arousal, and second, we must seek an appropriate explanation or label for it. Because our physical states are difficult to label on their own, we use information in the situation to help us make an attribution about why we feel aroused. Figure 5.7 illustrates the two-factor theory of emotion.

Stanley Schachter and Jerome Singer (1962) conducted an experiment to test this provocative theory; imagine you were a participant. Here's how the study was set up: When you arrive, the experimenter tells you he is studying the effects of a vitamin compound called Suproxin on people's vision. After a physician injects you with a small amount of Suproxin, the experimenter asks you to wait while the drug takes effect. He introduces you to another participant, who, he says, has also been given some Suproxin. The experimenter gives each of you a questionnaire to fill out, saying he will return in a little while to give you the vision tests. You look at the questionnaire and notice it contains some highly personal and insulting questions. For example, one question asks, "With how many men (other than your father) has your mother had extramarital relationships?" (Schachter & Singer, 1962, p. 385). The other participant reacts angrily to these offensive questions, becoming more and more furious, until he finally tears up his questionnaire, throws it on the floor, and stomps out of the room. How do you think you would feel? Would you feel angry as well?

As you have no doubt gathered, the real purpose of this experiment was not to test people's vision. The researchers set up a situation where the two crucial variables—arousal and an emotional explanation for that arousal—would be present or absent and then observed which, if any, emotions people experienced. The participants did not really receive an injection of a vitamin compound.

two-factor theory of emotion: the idea that emotional experience is the result of a two-step self-perception process in which people first experience physiological arousal and then seek an appropriate explanation for it; if they attribute the arousal to an emotional source, they experience that emotion (e.g., if people attribute their arousal to someone pointing a gun at them, they experience fear)

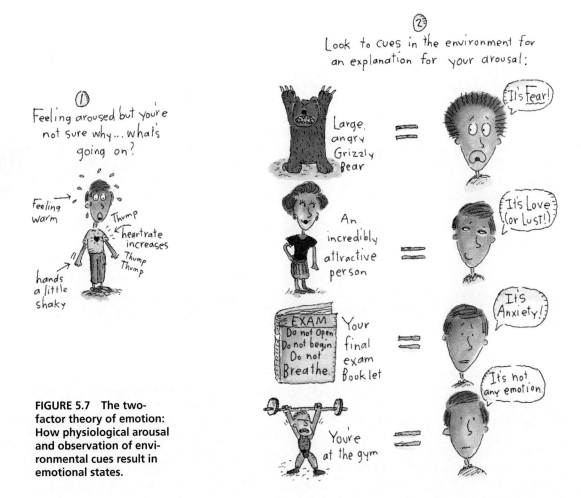

FIGURE 5.7   The two-factor theory of emotion: How physiological arousal and observation of environmental cues result in emotional states.

Instead, the arousal variable was manipulated in the following way: Some participants received epinephrine, a drug that causes arousal (body temperature and heart and breathing rates increase), and the other half received a placebo that had no physiological effects at all.

Imagine how you would have felt had you received the epinephrine: As you read the insulting questionnaire, you begin to feel aroused. (Remember, the experimenter didn't tell you the drug was epinephrine and so you don't realize that it's the drug that's making you aroused.) The other participant—who was actually an accomplice of the experimenter—reacts with rage. You are likely to infer that you are feeling flushed and aroused because you too are angry. You have met the conditions Schachter (1964) argues are necessary to experience an emotion—you are aroused, and you have sought out and found a reasonable explanation for your arousal in the situation that surrounds you. Ergo, you become furious. This is indeed what happened—participants who had been given epinephrine reacted much more angrily than participants who had been given the placebo did.

A fascinating implication of Schachter's theory is that people's emotions are somewhat arbitrary, depending on what the most plausible explanation for their arousal happens to be. Schachter and Singer (1962) demonstrated this idea in two ways. First, they showed that they could prevent people from becoming angry by providing a nonemotional explanation for why they felt aroused. They did this by informing some of the people who received epinephrine that the drug would increase their heart rate, make their face feel warm and flushed, and cause their hands to shake slightly. When people actually began to feel this way, they inferred that it was not because they were angry but because the drug was taking effect. As a result, these participants did not react angrily to the questionnaire.

Even more impressively, Schachter and Singer showed that they could make subjects experience a very different emotion by changing the most plausible explanation for their arousal. In other conditions, participants did not receive the insulting questionnaire and the other subject did not respond angrily. Instead, the other subject acted in a euphoric, devil-may-care fashion, playing basketball with rolled-up pieces of paper, making paper airplanes, and playing with a Hula-Hoop he found in the corner. How did the real participants respond? If they had received epinephrine but had not been told of its effects, they inferred that they must be feeling happy and euphoric and often joined the accomplice's impromptu games.

The Schachter and Singer (1962) experiment has become one of the most famous studies in social psychology, because it shows that emotions can be the result of a self-perception process whereby people look for the most plausible explanation for their arousal. Sometimes the most plausible explanation is not the right explanation, and so people end up experiencing a mistaken emotion. The people who became angry or euphoric in the Schachter and Singer (1962) study did so because they felt aroused and thought this arousal was due to the obnoxious questionnaire or to the infectious, happy-go-lucky behavior of the accomplice. The real cause of their arousal, the epinephrine, was hidden from them; all they had to go on were situational cues to explain their behavior.

> I could feel all the excitement of losing the big fish going through the transformer and coming out as anger at my brother-in-law.
> —Norman Maclean, *A River Runs Through It*

Finding the Wrong Cause: Misattribution of Arousal

To what extent do the results found by Schachter and Singer (1962) generalize to everyday life? Do people form mistaken emotions in the same way as participants in that study did? In everyday life, one might argue, people usually know why they are aroused. If a mugger points a gun at us and says "Stick 'em up!", we feel aroused and correctly label this arousal as fear. If our heart is thumping while we walk on a deserted moonlit beach with the man or woman of our dreams, we correctly label this arousal as love or sexual attraction.

Many everyday situations, however, present more than one plausible cause for our arousal, and it is difficult to identify how much of the arousal is due to one source versus another. Imagine that you go to see a scary movie with an extremely attractive date. As you are sitting there, you notice that your heart is thumping and you are a little short of breath. Is this because you are wildly attracted to your date, or because the movie is terrifying you? It is unlikely that you could say, "Fifty-seven percent of my arousal is due to the fact that my date is gorgeous, 32 percent is due to the scary movie, and 11 percent is due to indigestion from all the popcorn I ate." Because of this difficulty in pinpointing the precise causes of our arousal, we sometimes form mistaken emotions. You might think that most of your arousal is a sign of attraction to your date, when in fact a lot of it is due to the movie (or maybe even indigestion).

In recent years, many studies have demonstrated the occurrence of such **misattribution of arousal,** whereby people make mistaken inferences about what

misattribution of arousal: the attribution of one's arousal to the wrong source, resulting in a mistaken or exaggerated emotion is causing them to feel the way they do (Ross & Olson, 1981; Schachter, 1977; Storms & McCaul, 1976; Storms & Nisbett, 1970; Valins, 1966; Zillmann, 1978). Consider, for example, an intriguing field experiment by Donald Dutton and Arthur Aron (1974). Imagine you were one of the participants, who were all men. You are visiting a park in British Columbia. An attractive young woman approaches you and asks if you could fill out a questionnaire for her, as part of a psychology project on the effects of scenic attractions on people's creativity. You decide to help her out. After you complete the questionnaire, the woman thanks you and says she would be happy to explain her study in more detail when she has more time. She tears off a corner of the questionnaire, writes down her name and phone number, and tells you to give her a call if you want to talk with her some more. How attracted do you think you would be to this woman? Would you telephone her and ask for a date?

This is a hard question to answer. Undoubtedly, it depends on whether you are dating someone else, how busy you are, and so on. It might also depend, however, on how you interpret any bodily symptoms you are experiencing. If you are aroused for some extraneous reason, you might mistakenly think some of the arousal is the result of attraction to the young woman. To test this idea, Dutton and Aron (1974) had the woman (a confederate) approach males in the park under two very different circumstances. Again, imagine you were a participant. As you are walking in the park, you come to the edge of a deep canyon. Spanning the canyon is a narrow, 450-foot-long suspension bridge made of wooden planks attached to wire cables. You decide to walk across it. As you do, you have to stoop to hold onto the handrails, which are very low. When you get a little way across, the wind picks up and causes the bridge to sway from side to side. You feel like you are about to tumble over the edge, and you hold on for dear life. Then you make the mistake of looking down. You see nothing but a sheer 200-foot drop to a rocky, raging river. You become more than a little aroused—your heart is thumping, you breathe rapidly, and you begin to perspire. At this point, the attractive woman approaches and asks you to fill out her questionnaire. How attracted do you feel toward her?

■ Misattribution. When people are aroused for one reason, such as occurs when they cross a scary bridge, they often attribute this arousal to the wrong source—such as attraction to the person they are with.

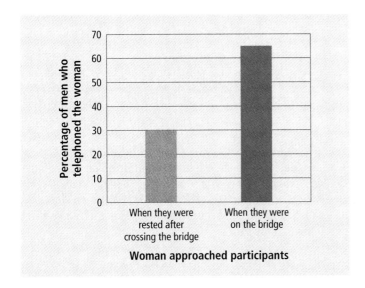

FIGURE 5.8   Misattribution of arousal.
■ When a woman approached men on a scary bridge and asked them to fill out a questionnaire, a high percentage of them were attracted to her and called her for a date. When the same woman approached men after they had crossed the bridge and were rested, relatively few called her for a date. (Adapted from Dutton & Aron, 1974)

Think about this for a moment, and now imagine that the woman approaches you under different circumstances. You make it across the bridge, and you have been resting awhile on a bench in the park. You have had a chance to calm down—your heart is no longer pounding against your chest, and your breathing rate has returned to normal. You are peaceably admiring the scenery when the woman asks you to fill out her questionnaire. How attracted do you feel toward her now? The prediction from Schachter's two-factor theory is clear: If you are on the bridge, you will be considerably aroused and will mistakenly think some of this arousal is the result of attraction to the beautiful woman. This is exactly what happened in the actual experiment. A large proportion of the men approached on the bridge telephoned the woman later to ask her for a date, whereas relatively few of the men approached on the bench telephoned the woman (see Figure 5.8). The moral is this: If you encounter an attractive man or woman and your heart is going thump-thump, think carefully about why you are aroused—you might fall in love for the wrong reasons!

Interpreting the Social World: Cognitive Appraisal Theories of Emotion

Though a great many studies have confirmed the idea that people can misattribute the cause of their arousal, ending up with a mistaken or exaggerated emotion (e.g., Sinclair, Hoffman, Mark, Martin, & Pickering, 1994), it has become clear that explaining why we are aroused is not the only way in which we determine our emotions. Sometimes our emotions result from an interpretation of a situation in the absence of any arousal. Suppose, for example, that your best friend tells you she was just admitted to the top medical school in the country. What emotion will you feel? A central idea of **cognitive appraisal theories of emotion** is that it depends on the way in which you interpret or appraise this event, even before any arousal occurs (Ellsworth, 1994; Frijda, 1986; Ortony, Clore, & Collins, 1988; Scherer, 1988). Two kinds of appraisals are especially important: (a) your view of whether the event has good or bad implications for you, and (b) your view of what caused the event.

cognitive appraisal theories of emotion: theories holding that emotions result from people's interpretations and explanations of events, in the absence of any physiological arousal

Virtually any event can be viewed in many different ways and people's emotional reaction will depend on whether they put a positive or negative spin on the event. If your life dream is to be a doctor but you haven't gotten into medical school yet, then you might feel threatened by your friend's success. Rather than feeling good about her acceptance to medical school, you might feel resentful and angry, due to your interpretation of her success as a threat to your own. Otherwise, you will probably interpret her success in quite positive terms and bask in her reflected glory (Tesser, 1988). The emotion people experience thus depends on whether they appraise an event as good or bad for themselves. It also depends on how they explain the cause of the event. If you think you contributed to your friend's success (she wouldn't have made it through that tough physics course without your help), you will probably feel pride; if you think she did it entirely on her own, you will probably feel admiration (assuming, of course, that you don't feel threatened by her success).

Cognitive appraisals are very much like one of the two factors in Schachter's two-factor theory: the part whereby people try to explain the causes of an event and their reactions to it (see the right-hand side of Figure 5.7). The main difference between Schachter's theory and cognitive appraisal theories concerns the role of arousal. According to cognitive appraisal theories, arousal does not always come first; the cognitive appraisals alone are a sufficient cause of emotional reactions. The two theories are not incompatible, however. When people are aroused and not certain where this arousal comes from, the way in which they explain the arousal determines their emotional reaction (Schachter's two-factor theory). When people are not aroused, the way in which they interpret and explain what happens to them determines their emotional reaction (cognitive appraisal theories). Both theories agree that one way people learn about themselves is by observing events—including their own behavior—and trying to explain those events.

People can thus learn a great deal about themselves through introspection and observations of their own behavior. What do people do with all of this information once they have it? Not surprisingly, we organize our self-knowledge in much the same way that we organize our knowledge about the external world: into schemas.

Knowing Ourselves Through Self-Schemas

In Chapter 3, we noted that people use *schemas*—knowledge structures about a person, topic, or object—to understand the social world. We do not have a random, helter-skelter collection of thoughts about the world; we organize our knowledge into schemas, which help us understand and interpret new experiences. It should come as no surprise that we form **self-schemas** as well: organized knowledge structures about ourselves, based on our past experiences, that help us understand, explain, and predict our own behavior (Cantor & Kihlstrom, 1987; Deaux, 1993; Linville & Carlston, 1994; Markus, 1977; Markus & Nurius, 1986). Thus, we do not have a random, helter-skelter collection of thoughts about ourselves either: We organize our self-views into coherent schemas, which influence how we interpret new things that happen to us. Suppose, for example, that you lose a close tennis match to your best friend. How will you react? In part, the answer depends on the nature of your self-schemas. If you define yourself as competitive and athletic, you are likely to feel bad and want a rematch as

self-schemas: organized knowledge structures about ourselves, based on our past experiences, that help us understand, explain, and predict our own behavior soon as possible, whereas if you define yourself as cooperative and nurturing, losing the match won't be such a big deal.

As children develop, their shallow, concrete self-concept progresses to a unique, complex one, based on the formation of increasingly sophisticated self-schemas. One line of research, conducted by William McGuire and his colleagues, suggests that people develop self-schemas for the aspects of self that make them distinct from other people (McGuire & McGuire, 1981; McGuire, McGuire, Child, & Fujioka, 1978; McGuire & Padawer-Singer, 1976). Thus, red-haired children are more likely to mention their hair color when asked to describe themselves, since this physical trait sets them apart from most other people. Similarly, an African American child in a predominantly white school is more likely to mention his or her ethnicity than the white children are, because this aspect of the individual is distinct in this setting.

> The sense of our own personal identity . . . is exactly like any of our other perceptions of sameness among phenomena.
> –William James, 1910

Autobiographical Memory

Self-schemas also help us organize our pasts, by influencing what we remember about ourselves, or our **autobiographical memories**. Whereas these memories define us, it is also the case that we define our memories. It is certainly not possible to remember everything that has happened in our lives or to remember it perfectly. Distortions, fabrications, and outright forgetting occur over time; as Anthony Greenwald (1980) has pointed out, if historians revised and distorted history to the same extent that we do with our own lives, they'd lose their jobs! Such distortion and revision of autobiographical memory are often not accidental—we rewrite our history. How? Just as self-schemas help us organize new information about ourselves, so too do they help us organize memories about our past actions. If being independent is part of your self-schema but being competitive is not, you will probably remember more times when you acted independently than competitively (Akert, 1993; Markus, 1977).

autobiographical memories: memories about one's own past thoughts, feelings, and behaviors

What about our memories for our past feelings and attitudes—do our theories and schemas color these memories as well? Michael Ross and his colleagues have found that the answer is yes (Conway & Ross, 1984; Ross, 1989; Ross & McFarland, 1988). People have many theories about the stability of their feelings. Some feelings, like our moods or how happy we are in a new romantic relationship, are expected to fluctuate over time. Other feelings, like our attitudes about social issues (e.g., the death penalty), are expected to be relatively stable—people assume that the way they feel now is how they felt in the past. Interestingly, Ross has found that these theories are not always correct, leading to distortions in memory. For example, attitudes toward social issues sometimes do change, but because people's theories are that these attitudes remain stable, they underestimate the amount of change that occurs. "I've always been against the death penalty," we might think, underestimating the extent to which our attitude has evolved over the years.

> Herein lies a difficulty in any autobiographical sketch. . . . It is a story of oneself in the past, read in light of one's present self. There is much supplementary inference—wherein "must have been" masquerades as "was so."
> –Lloyd Morgan

Recovered Memories: Real or Imagined?

Research by Ross and others, then, suggests that our memories can be reconstructive, whereby we invent our pasts in ways that were never so. Much of the research in this area, however, has concerned relatively benign memories, such as people's recollections about their past attitudes. What about much more important and jarring memories, such as the sudden recollection that one was sexually

■ In Olympia, Washington, in 1988, Paul Ingram was accused by his daughters of sexual abuse, satanic rituals, and murder. His daughters claimed to have suddenly recalled these events years after they occurred. According to experts who studied the case, Ingram's daughters genuinely believed the abuse and killing occurred, but in fact they were wrong: What they thought they remembered were actually false memories. Ingram eventually became convinced that he too must have repressed his past behavior and that he must have committed the crimes. Due to his "confession," he is currently serving a prison sentence.

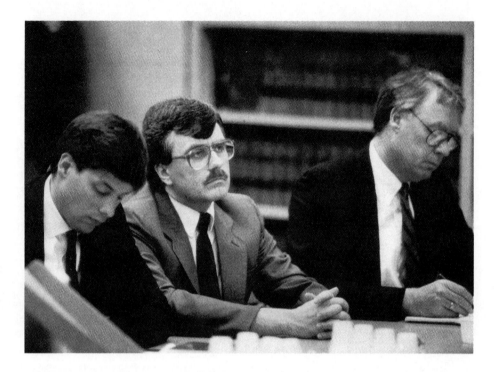

recovered memories: recollections of a past event, such as sexual abuse, that had been forgotten or repressed; a great deal of controversy surrounds the accuracy of such memories

abused as a child? How accurate are such **recovered memories**? For example, in 1988 in Olympia, Washington, Paul Ingram was accused of sexual abuse, satanic rituals, and murder by his daughters, who claimed to have suddenly recalled these events years after they occurred. The police could find no evidence for the crimes and Ingram initially denied that they had ever occurred. He eventually became convinced that he too must have repressed his past behavior and that he must have committed the crimes, even though he could not remember having done so. According to experts who have studied this case, Ingram's daughters genuinely believed the abuse and killing occurred, but they were in fact wrong. What they thought they remembered were actually false memories (Wright, 1994).

The question of the accuracy of recovered memories has become extremely controversial. On one side are writers such as Ellen Bass and Laura Davis (1994), who claim that it is not uncommon for women who were sexually abused to repress these traumas, so that they have absolutely no memory of them. The abuse and its subsequent repression, according to this view, are responsible for many psychological problems, such as depression and eating disorders. Later in life, often with the help of a psychotherapist, these events can be "recovered" and brought back into memory. On the other side of the controversy are academic psychologists and others, who argue that the accuracy of recovered memories cannot be accepted on faith (e.g., Loftus & Ketcham, 1994; Ofshe & Waters, 1994; Schacter, 1995; Wegner, Quillan, & Houston, 1995). These writers acknowledge that sexual abuse and other childhood traumas are a terrible problem and are more common than we would like to think. They further agree that claims of sexual abuse should be taken extremely seriously and investigated fully and that, when sufficient evidence of guilt exists, the person responsible for the abuse should be fully prosecuted.

But here's the problem: What is "sufficient evidence"? Is it enough that some-one remembers, years later, that she or he has been abused, in the absence of any other evidence of abuse? According to many researchers, the answer is no, because of what is called the **false memory syndrome**: People can recall a past traumatic experience that is objectively false but that they believe is true (Kihlstrom, in press). There is substantial evidence that people can acquire vivid memories of events that never occurred, especially if another person—such as a psychotherapist—suggests that the events occurred (Johnson & Raye, 1981; Loftus, 1993; for other evidence on the reconstructive nature of memory, see the section on eyewitness testimony in the applied module on law and social psychology). In addition to numerous laboratory demonstrations of false memories, there is evidence from everyday life that memories of abuse can be incorrect. Often these memories are contradicted by objective evidence (e.g., no evidence of satanic murders can be found); sometimes people who suddenly acquire such memories decide later that the events never occurred; and sometimes the memories are so bizarre (e.g., that people were abducted by aliens) as to strain credulity. Unfortunately, some psychotherapists do not sufficiently consider that, by suggesting past abuse, they may be implanting false memories rather than helping clients remember real events.

false memory syndrome: a memory of a past traumatic experience that is objectively false but that people believe occurred

This is not to say, however, that all recovered memories are inaccurate. Although scientific evidence for repression and recovery—the idea that something can be forgotten for years and then recalled with great accuracy—is sparse, there may be instances in which people do suddenly remember traumatic events that really did occur. Thus, any claim of abuse should be taken with the utmost seriousness. Unfortunately, however, it is very difficult to distinguish the accurate memories from the false ones, in the absence of any corroborating evidence. Thus, claims of abuse cannot be taken on faith, especially if they are the result of suggestions from other people.

Knowing Ourselves Through Social Interaction

So far, we have seen that people learn about themselves through introspection and observations of their own behavior and that they organize this information into self-schemas. As important as these sources of self-knowledge are, there is still something missing. We are not solitary seekers of self-knowledge but social beings who often see ourselves through the eyes of other people. In fact, much of what we learn about ourselves can, interestingly, be influenced by others. From early childhood onward, family, friends, and sometimes even strangers give you an appraisal of yourself. It's as if they've held up a mirror and reflected their image of you back at you to see. Sometimes this image is reassuring, reinforcing your own beliefs about yourself. Sometimes this image is a surprise, maybe even a jarring or unpleasant one. Have you ever had a friend make a comment about you that came as a surprise ("I'm like that?") and was all the more puzzling because your friend acted like it was obvious? Perhaps your friend said, "You get really angry at someone and talk like you're going to do something about it, but you never confront the person," whereupon you thought, "I do? Am I like that? Do I do that, really?" Maybe you said meekly, "What do you mean?" And after your friend explained at length, you perhaps admitted to yourself that there was truth in what she said—that here you'd always thought you had a big bark and a big bite, whereas your friends viewed you as a real softie at heart.

looking-glass self: the idea that we see ourselves through the eyes of other people and incorporate their views into our self-concept

The Looking-Glass Self

Basing our self-concept on how we appear to other people is called the **looking-glass self** (Cooley, 1902; Mead, 1934). The ability to look at ourselves through other people's eyes is crucial to developing a sense of self, because it allows us to understand that we may see the world differently from how others do. What would it be like to have no access to others' perspectives? Oddly, if we cannot see ourselves through the eyes of other people, our own image will be a blur, because we have no social looking glass in which to view ourselves. Remember the mirror and red dye test we discussed earlier, used to determine if animals and young children have a self-concept? You'll recall that children 9 to 12 months of age do not react to their red nose when they see it in a mirror, whereas 2-year-olds do. The younger children do not understand that this image is themselves. Why? One reason is that children at 1 year of age have far less experience with social interaction than 2-year-olds do.

Experiments conducted with great apes have indicated that social contact is indeed crucial to the development of a self-concept. For example, Gordon Gallup (1977) compared the behavior of chimpanzees raised in normal, family groupings with that of chimps who were raised alone, in complete social isolation. Both types of chimps were painted with the red dye, as described earlier, and placed alone in a room without a mirror. The frequency with which they touched their marked but unseen browridge and ear was noted; these are the pretest data shown in Figure 5.9. Then a mirror was brought into the room. Now the chimps could see themselves and their new "cosmetics." The socially experienced chimps showed the typical response of great apes (and human beings)—they immediately used their mirrored image to explore the red areas of their heads. However, the socially isolated chimps did not react to their reflections at all—they did not recognize themselves in the mirror (see Figure 5.9). In primates as well as human beings, social interaction is crucial for developing a sense of self.

Social Comparison Theory

We also come to know ourselves by comparison to other people (Brown, 1990; Kruglanski & Mayseless, 1990; McFarland & Miller, 1994; Suls & Wills, 1991;

FIGURE 5.9   Effects of social isolation on the development of the self-concept. ■ When in front of a mirror, chimps raised in social isolation touched the red-dyed parts of their bodies much less than chimps raised in social groups did. (Adapted from Gallup, 1977)

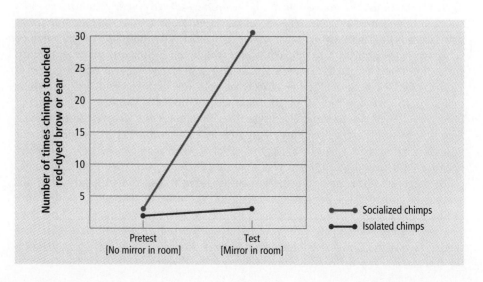

Wood, 1989). If you are trying to determine your feelings, traits, and abilities, other people and their feelings, traits, and abilities are a valuable source of information. Suppose, for example, we gave you a test that measured your social sensitivity, or how aware you are of other people's problems. The test involves reading excerpts from autobiographies and guessing the nature of the authors' personal problems, if any. After you've taken the test, we tell you that you achieved a score of 35. What have you learned about yourself? Not much, because you don't know what a score of 35 means. Is it a good score or a bad score? Suppose we told you that the test is scored on a scale from 0 to 50. Now what have you learned? A little more than you knew before, perhaps, because you know that although you did not achieve a perfect score, you did score above the middle of the scale. This is still pretty uninformative, however, without knowing how other people did on the test. If we told you that everyone else in your class scored between 0 and 20, you could pat yourself on the back, concluding that you are an extremely sensitive person. On the other hand, you might feel differently if we told you that everyone else scored between 45 and 50.

> Envy, like fire, soars upward.
>
> –Livy (59 B.C.–A.D. 17)

This example illustrates Leon Festinger's (1954) **social comparison theory.** The theory begins with the supposition that people have a need to evaluate their opinions and abilities, to figure out their strengths and weaknesses, so as to have an accurate view of themselves. Festinger (1954) stated that, when possible, people will rely on objective criteria, such as the reading on their stopwatch after they have run a mile. However, this kind of objective feedback is rather hard to come by in life. There are all sorts of interesting aspects of yourself that you would probably like to know more about, ones for which objective measurements do not exist. Are you physically attractive? How good a cello player are you? Are you a particularly empathic person? Are you calm and steady in the face of a crisis? Are you conservative in matters of private or political life? How much

social comparison theory: the idea that we learn about our own abilities and attitudes by comparing ourselves to other people

"Of course you're going to be depressed if you keep comparing yourself with successful people."

do you lie? Just how good at math are you? To answer such questions, you need to compare yourself to other people in these same areas—how do you stack up?

Social comparison theory revolves around two important questions (Goethals, 1986; Latané, 1966): (a) *When* do you engage in social comparison, and (b) *with whom* do you choose to compare yourself? As Festinger (1954) indicated, you socially compare when there is no objective standard for you to measure yourself against and when you experience some uncertainty about yourself in a particular area (Suls & Fletcher, 1983; Suls & Miller, 1977).

Thus, when you're not sure how well you're doing or what exactly you're feeling, you'll observe other people and compare yourself to them. For example, Jerry Suls and Barbara Fletcher (1983) examined the social comparison process in scientists, using the archival method of research. It is customary when preparing to publish a research article to ask esteemed colleagues for comments and feedback on the manuscript. When it is published, these readers are thanked in an acknowledgments section. Suls and Fletcher (1983) hypothesized that in sciences with more objective standards, scientists do not have as great a need to engage in social comparison as in those fields with fewer objective standards do. The natural sciences were defined as having more objective standards—in the sense of the research designs used and the highly defined areas of study—than the social sciences. Accordingly, the researchers predicted that natural scientists would thank fewer people in their paper, indicating that they had asked fewer people for feedback about their work prior to submitting it for publication. Content-analyzing several hundred articles, Suls and Fletcher (1983) found that physicists and chemists thanked, on average, 0.5 people per article, psychologists thanked 1.2 people, and sociologists thanked 2.0 people.

As to the second question—With whom should you compare yourself?—recent research by Daniel Gilbert and his colleagues suggests that we initially compare ourselves to everyone (Gilbert, Giesler, & Morris, 1995). After a quick assessment of how our performance compares to others', we then decide how appropriate that comparison is—realizing that not all comparisons are equally informative. If you're wondering about your artistic ability, is it most appropriate to compare yourself to Picasso, your 4-year-old sister, or your fellow students in a drawing class? Not surprisingly, people find it most informative to compare themselves to others who are similar to them on the important attribute, or dimension (Goethals & Darley, 1977; Miller, 1982; Wheeler, Koestner, & Driver, 1982). Observing the ability of your classmates in drawing class will give you an idea of how artistically talented you are. Comparing yourself to Picasso is aiming too high; you'll only become discouraged if, as a beginner, you compare yourself to one of the great artists of the twentieth century.

While research has shown that people sometimes engage in **upward social comparison** (i.e., comparing themselves to people more accomplished than they are), they do this only to determine what excellence or the best really is. It is more important to them, in terms of self-knowledge, to compare themselves to someone who is similar (Thornton & Arrowood, 1966; Wheeler et al., 1982; Zanna, Goethals, & Hill, 1975). Likewise, comparing your artistic talent to that of your little sister is aiming too low; her fingerpainting and scribbles tell you little about your abilities.

However, Festinger (1954) noted that constructing an accurate image of ourselves is only one reason, albeit the principal one, that we engage in social comparison. When we are trying to assess our standing on a trait that is very important to us, we also use social comparison in order to boost our egos. Is it

> There is little satisfaction in the contemplation of heaven for oneself if one cannot simultaneously contemplate the horrors of hell for others.
> –P. D. James, 1992, *The Children of Men*

upward social comparison: the process whereby we compare ourselves to people who are better than we are on a particular trait or ability, in order to determine the standard of excellence very important to you to believe that you are a fabulous artist-in-the-making? Then compare yourself to your little sister—you have her beat! This use of **downward social comparison** is a self-protective, self-enhancing strategy (Aspinwall & Taylor, 1993; Pyszczynski, Greenberg, & LaPrelle, 1985; Reis, Gerrard, & Gibbons, 1993; Wheeler & Kunitate, 1992). If you compare yourself to people who are less smart, talented, or kind than you are, you'll feel very good about yourself. Similarly, you can compare your health to that of people who are worse off than you, thereby bolstering your self-esteem. For example, Joanne Wood, Shelley Taylor, and Rosemary Lichtman (1985) found evidence of downward comparison in interviews with cancer patients. The vast majority of patients spontaneously compared themselves to other cancer patients who were more ill than they were, presumably as a way of making them feel more optimistic about the course of their own disease.

downward social comparison: the process whereby we compare ourselves to people who are worse than we on a particular trait or ability, in order to feel better about ourselves

In sum, to whom we compare ourselves depends on the nature of our goals. When we want an accurate assessment of our abilities and opinions, we compare ourselves to people who are similar to us. When we want information about what we can strive toward, we make upward social comparisons. Finally, when our goal is self-enhancement, we compare ourselves to those who are less fortunate; such downward comparisons make us look better by comparison.

Impression Management: All the World's a Stage

Now that you've come to know yourself, what do you do with all that knowledge? Being a member of a highly social species, you present yourself to others. You have many aspects to your self-concept; you can be many selves. Thus, a basic aspect of your social existence is **self-presentation**, whereby you present who you are (or who you want people to believe you are) through your words, nonverbal behavior, and actions (DePaulo, 1992; Goffman, 1959; Schlenker, 1980; Tedeschi, 1981). However, self-presentation is not always a simple, straightforward process; there are times when you want people to form a particular impression of you. At these times, you engage in **impression management**, consciously or unconsciously orchestrating a carefully designed presentation of self that will create a certain impression, one that fits your goals or needs in a social interaction (Goffman, 1959; Schlenker, 1980).

self-presentation: the attempt to present who we are, or who we want people to believe we are, through our words, nonverbal behaviors, and actions
impression management: our conscious or unconscious orchestration of a carefully designed presentation of self so as to create a certain impression that fits our goals or needs in a social interaction

The concepts of self-presentation and impression management were eloquently discussed by Erving Goffman (1955, 1959, 1967, 1971). His theory of social interaction was based on a dramaturgical model, which uses the theater as a metaphor for social life. On the stage, the actors present certain aspects of self (or their roles) to each other; Goffman says that in everyday life, we do the same thing in our social interactions. Further, just as in the theater, real life is made up of backstage and frontstage areas. Frontstage is when you're "on," when you are actively presenting a particular self to others so as to create or maintain a certain impression in their eyes. Thoroughly cleaning your room, apartment, or house before company arrives (and saying, "Oh, it's nothing," when they compliment you on how lovely it looks) is preparing for and being on frontstage. In contrast, backstage is when you are not actively managing or creating a particular impression. We become uncomfortable when people invade our backstage areas, for we are, by definition, unprepared. Witness how annoying and embarrassing it is when people you'd like to impress drop by to visit you unannounced and your place is a slovenly pigsty and you are looking your grungiest!

> Keep up appearances whatever you do.
> –Charles Dickens, 1843

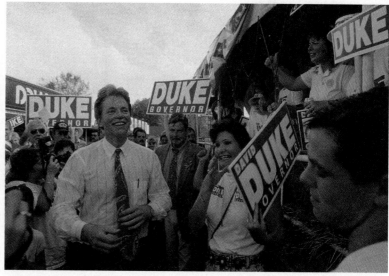

■ Impression management in action: In the 1970s, David Duke was a leader in the Ku Klux Klan; in 1991, he ran for governor of Louisiana as a mainstream conservative Republican. A remarkable change occurred in Duke's presentation of self during this time. Besides undergoing facial cosmetic surgery to improve his appearance, he claimed during his campaign that he no longer supported Nazi ideology or the Ku Klux Klan.

It is undoubtedly true that people in all cultures are concerned with impression management. The form in which this takes place, however, differs considerably from culture to culture. Earlier, we mentioned that people in Asian cultures tend to have a more interdependent view of themselves than people in Western cultures do. One consequence of this identity is that "saving face," or avoiding public embarrassment, is extremely important in Asian cultures. In Japan, for example, it is very important that people have the "right" guests at their weddings and enough mourners at the funerals of their loved ones—so important, in fact, that if not enough guests or mourners are available, you can go to a local "convenience agency" and rent some. These agencies (or *benriya*) keep a staff of employees ready to pretend that they are your closest friends. A woman named Hiroko, for example, was concerned that not enough guests would attend her second wedding. No problem—she spent $1,500 to rent a man to pose as her boss and five women to pose as her friends. Her "boss" even prepared a flattering speech about her that he delivered at the wedding (Jordan & Sullivan, 1995).

People from Western cultures are likely to chuckle at what to them seems like an extreme example of impression management. Sometimes, however, Westerners also go to great lengths to influence what others think of them. Consider this disturbing example of impression management from the 1991 gubernatorial campaign in Louisiana. David Duke, who for most of his adult life had been an open white supremacist and anti-Semite and who in 1989 had sold Nazi literature from his legislative office, was running for governor as a mainstream conservative Republican (*Duke*, 1991, p. 1). A remarkable change had occurred in Duke's presentation of self (see the photos on this page). Besides having undergone facial cosmetic surgery to improve his appearance, he claimed during the campaign that he no longer supported Nazi ideology or the Ku Klux Klan, of which he had been the leader (or Grand Wizard) in the 1970s. However, his

> To succeed in the world, we do everything we can to appear successful.
> –La Rochefoucauld, 1678

campaign rhetoric was correctly perceived by the majority of Louisiana voters as the same racist message disguised in new clothes, and he was defeated by the Democratic candidate, Edwin Edwards.

Most of us, of course, do not go to quite these lengths to manage the impressions we convey. All of us, however, attempt to manage our impressions to some extent. Edward Jones and Thane Pittman (1982) have described several strategic self-presentational techniques that people use in everyday life. One strategy is **ingratiation,** whereby you flatter, praise, and generally make yourself likable to another, often higher-status person (Jones & Wortman, 1973). One can ingratiate through compliments, by agreeing with another's ideas, by commiserating and offering sympathy, and so on. If your professor's 3-year-old spits on you and kicks you in the shin and you say "Oh, what an adorable child!" you are probably ingratiating. Ingratiation is a powerful technique, since we all enjoy having someone be nice to us—which is what the ingratiator is good at. However, such a ploy can backfire if the recipient of your ingratiation figures out what you're doing (Jones, 1964; Kauffman & Steiner, 1968).

Another self-presentational strategy, and the one that has attracted the most research attention, is **self-handicapping.** This strategy is a blend of self-serving attributions (which we discussed in Chapter 4) and impression management. Doing poorly or failing at a task is damaging to your self-esteem. In fact, just doing less well than you expected or than you have in the past can be upsetting, even if it is a good performance. How can you deal with this disappointment attributionally? Self-handicapping is the rather surprising solution: You can set up reasons, before the fact, for your failure. That is, before you even engage in the task, you can make sure that you have a ready-made excuse to explain your (potentially) poor performance (Arkin & Baumgardner, 1985; Jones & Berglas, 1978).

Let's say it's the night before the final exam in one of your courses. It's a difficult course, required for your major, and one in which you'd like to do well. A sensible strategy would be to eat a good dinner, study for a while, and then go to bed early and get a good night's sleep. The self-handicapping strategy would be to pull an all-nighter, studying (or partying), then wandering into the exam the next morning bleary-eyed and muddle-headed. If you don't do well on the exam, you have an excuse. In other words, you have an external attribution to offer to others to explain your performance, one that deflects the potential negative, internal attribution they might otherwise make (that you're not smart). And if you do ace the exam, well, all the better—you did it under adverse conditions (no sleep), which suggests that you really are smart and talented.

There are two major ways in which people self-handicap. In its most extreme form, people create obstacles that reduce the likelihood they will succeed on a task, so that if they do fail they can blame it on these obstacles rather than on their lack of ability. The obstacles people have been found to use include drugs, alcohol, reduced effort on the task, and failure to prepare for an important event (Berglas & Jones, 1978; Greenberg, 1983; Higgins & Harris, 1988; Koditz & Arkin, 1982; Rhodewalt & Davison, 1984; Tice & Baumeister, 1990).

The second type of self-handicapping is less extreme. People do not create obstacles to success but do devise ready-made excuses in case they fail (Baumgardner, Lake, & Arkin, 1985; Greenberg, Pyszczynski, & Paisley, 1984; Hirt, Deppe, & Gordon, 1991; Snyder, Smith, Augelli, & Ingram, 1985). Thus, we might not go so far as to pull an all-nighter the night before an important exam, but we might complain that we are sick. People have been found to arm

ingratiation: the process whereby people flatter, praise, and generally try to make themselves likable to another, often higher-status person

self-handicapping: creating obstacles and excuses for ourselves, so that if we do poorly on a task, we have ready-made excuses themselves with all kinds of excuses, such as blaming their shyness, test anxiety, bad moods, physical symptoms, and adverse events from their pasts. One problem with preparing ourselves with excuses in advance, however, is that we may come to believe these excuses and thus exert less effort on the task. Whereas self-handicapping may prevent unflattering attributions for our failures, it often has the adverse effect of causing the poor performance that is so feared.

SUMMARY

In this chapter, we have explored the nature of the self and how people come to know themselves. The "self" we come to know is made up of both awareness and consciousness (the "knower") and the **self-concept** (the "known"). There are interesting cross-cultural differences in the self-concept. In many Western cultures, people have an **independent view of the self**, whereby they define themselves mainly in terms of their own thoughts, feelings, and actions. In many Asian cultures, people have an **interdependent view of the self**, whereby they define themselves primarily in terms of their relationships with other people.

There are four basic ways in which we come to know ourselves: through (1) **introspection**, (2) observations of our own behavior, (3) self-schemas, and (4) social interaction. Research on **self-awareness theory** has found that introspecting about ourselves can be unpleasant, because it focuses our attention on how we fall short of our internal standards. A benefit of self-focus is that it can make us more aware of our own feelings and traits. Thinking about *why* we feel the way we do, however, is more difficult. Many studies show that people's judgments about the reasons for their feelings and actions are often incorrect, in part because people rely on **causal theories** when explaining their behavior. Further, the act of thinking about reasons can cause **reasons-generated attitude change**, convincing us that our feelings match the reasons that happen to come to mind.

Self-perception theory discusses how we come to know ourselves through observation of our own behavior, just as an outsider would. This occurs in particular when our internal states are unclear and there appears to be no external reason for our behavior. One interesting application of self-perception theory is the **overjustification effect**, which is the **discounting** of our **intrinsic motivation** in a task, as a result of inferring that we are engaging in the task because of **extrinsic motivation**. That is, rewards and other kinds of external influences can undermine our intrinsic interest; an activity we once liked will seem like work instead of play. The overjustification effect is especially likely to occur when **task-contingent rewards** are used. These rewards are given for completing a task, regardless of people's level of performance. **Performance-contingent rewards** are based on how well people perform a task. These rewards are less likely to decrease interest in a task and may even increase interest, if they convey the message that people are competent without making them feel nervous and apprehensive about being evaluated. Another example of self-perception is the **two-factor theory of emotion**, whereby we determine our emotions by observing how aroused we are and making inferences about the causes of that arousal. **Misattribution of arousal** can occur, whereby people attribute their arousal to the wrong source. Attributions about arousal are not the only source of emotions; **cognitive appraisal theories of emotion** argue that emotions can also result from our interpretations and explanations of events in the absence of any physiological arousal.

People also organize information about themselves into **self-schemas**, which are knowledge structures about the self that help people understand, explain, and predict their own behavior. Self-schemas also help us organize our pasts, by influencing what we remember about ourselves, or our **autobiographical memories**. There is evidence that our memories can be reconstructive, whereby we view the past not as it really was but in ways that are consistent with our current theories and schemas. A great deal of controversy exists over the validity of **recovered memories**, or the sudden recollection of an event, such as sexual abuse, that had been forgotten or repressed. Though recovered memories may be true in some instances, they can also be the result of a **false memory syndrome**, whereby people come to believe that memory is true when it actually is not. False memories are especially likely to occur when another person suggests to us that an event really occurred.

Another way we come to know ourselves is through social interaction. By interacting with other people, we develop a **looking-glass self**, whereby we determine who we are based on others' perceptions of us. We also know ourselves through comparison with others. **Social comparison theory** states that we will compare ourselves to others when we are unsure of our standing on some attribute and there is no objective criterion we can use. Typically, we choose to compare ourselves to similar others, for this is most diagnostic. When we want to find out what the best is, we engage in **upward social comparison,** comparing ourselves to those who are superior on the relevant attribute. When we want to feel better about ourselves, we engage in **downward social comparison,** comparing ourselves to those who are inferior on the relevant attribute.

Once we know ourselves, we often attempt to manage the self we present to others through the processes of self-presentation and **impression management.** Social life is much like the theater, where we present selves (or roles) to others. Two self-presentational strategies are **ingratiation** and **self-handicapping.** Self-handicapping involves lining up a behavior, trait, or situational event before a performance so that we can later use it as an excuse if we don't do well. One problem with preparing ourselves with excuses in advance, however, is that we may come to believe these excuses and thus exert less effort on the task. Whereas self-handicapping may prevent unflattering attributions for our failures, it often has the adverse effect of causing the poor performance that is so feared.

IF YOU ARE INTERESTED . . .

Baumeister, R. F. (1991). *Escaping the self: Alcoholism, spirituality, masochism, and other flights from the burden of selfhood.* New York: Basic Books. An intriguing look at the many different ways in which people try to escape too much self-focus.

Deci, E. L., & Ryan, R. M. (1985). *Intrinsic motivation and self-determination.* New York: Plenum. A review of research on intrinsic motivation and overjustification that presents an alternative to the attributional perspective we discussed in this chapter.

Fiske, S. T., & Taylor, S. E. (1991). *Social cognition* (2nd ed.). New York: McGraw-Hill. An encyclopedic review of the literature on social cognition by two experts in the field. Includes a chapter on social cognition and the self that covers in greater detail much of the same material we discussed in this chapter.

Hoop Dreams (1994). A fascinating documentary about two high school basketball stars from Chicago. In terms of research on the self and overjustification effects, it is fascinating to see what happens to these two players' love for the game as they are rewarded more and more for playing basketball.

Kitayama, S., & Markus, H. R. (Eds.) (1994). *Culture and emotion: Empirical investigations on mutual influences.* Washington, D. C.: American Psychological Association Press. A collection of chapters on culture and emotion by top researchers in the area. The topics include how emotions are experienced within a cultural context, the role of language in culture and emotion, and the relation between culture, emotion, and morality.

Mann, Thomas (1932). *The Magic Mountain.* This novel was reportedly the inspiration for Stanley Schacter's two-factor theory of emotion. While Hans Castorp is at a tuberculosis sanatorium high in the Swiss Alps, he experiences feelings of arousal and shortness of breath, due to the thin air. He interprets these feelings as signs of love for Clauvida Chauchat.

Olson, J., & Zanna, M. P. (Eds.). (1990). *Self-inference: The Ontario Symposium* (Vol. 6). Hillsdale, NJ: Erlbaum. A collection of chapters on self-perception theory and related formulations, by top researchers in the field.

Proust, Marcel (1934). *Remembrance of Things Past.* This classic novel is full of insights about how people gain self-knowledge.

Schlenker, B. R. (1980). *Impression management: The self-concept, social identity, and interpersonal relations.* Monterey, CA: Brooks/Cole. A classic look at research on impression management and self-presentation.

Tan, Amy (1989). *The Joy Luck Club.* A poignant novel about identity and growth within conflicting cultural contexts.

The Return of Martin Guerre (1984). A film about a young husband who disappears and then returns to his wife years later. But is it the same man or an imposter? The film raises interesting questions about the continuity of one's identity and how that identity is perceived by others. A 1993 remake of the film, starring Jodie Foster and Richard Gere, was called *Sommersby.*

Chapter 6

Self-Justification and the Need to Maintain Self-Esteem

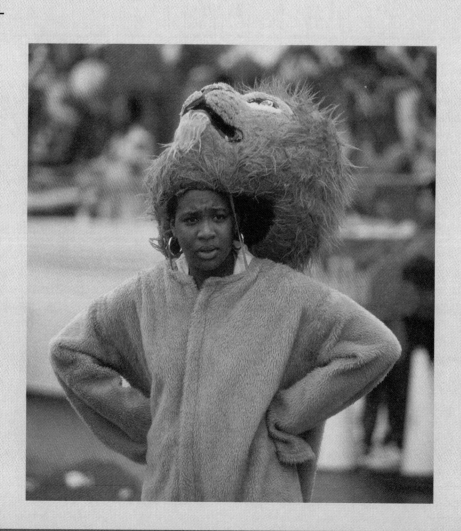

My memory tells me I did a very stupid thing. My heart tells me I'm too smart to have done such a thing. In the end, my memory yields.

–Hegel

everal years ago, *Dr. Bob Arnot, medical editor of* CBS Morning News, *appeared on the show to report some rather startling news: A group of medical researchers had just published the results of a study demonstrating that stretching before engaging in physical activity does not do athletes any good—and might even cause them harm. The data, based on thousands of cases, showed that people who always stretch a moderate amount suffer no fewer injuries than those who never stretch—while those who stretch deeply actually suffer more injuries than those who never stretch (*CBS Morning News, *March 9, 1990).*

While Dr. Arnot was reporting these data, the camera panned to New York's Central Park, where the roving reporter was interviewing several joggers. "How interesting!" exclaimed one jogger. "That's important information. Who, me? No, I almost never stretch—too much trouble." The reporter then went over to a fence that several joggers were using as a brace while they were dutifully stretching prior to their morning run and reported the latest finding. "I don't believe it," said one; "it can't be true." "That has to be wrong," said another; "after all, I've been stretching for over 15 years and I have had very few muscle injuries." "That's nothing but a pack of lies!" exclaimed a third stretcher. "Why would the scientists lie?" asked the roving reporter. "To keep their jobs," answered the stretcher. "They have to come up with new 'findings' every once in a while or else they'll get fired!"

We have not read the study reported by Dr. Arnot; we have no idea whether or not the findings have held up under attempts at replication. Our aim is neither to endorse nor to refute them but rather to focus on the responses generated by the findings, for the pattern of responses constitutes a provocative demonstration of an important phenomenon: Most of us have a readiness to believe or disbelieve information depending on how well it supports our own inclinations, past behavior, or prior commitments. Even to the casual viewer of Dr. Arnot's report, the contrast

was striking: Those people who almost never stretched didn't seem at all disturbed by the findings, while those who had spent a lot of time stretching over the years were obviously incredulous and annoyed, even to the point of concluding that scientists would intentionally falsify their data in order to keep their jobs. This phenomenon is not an isolated event—it seems to be a basic and pervasive aspect of being human. What are the underlying mechanisms of this phenomenon?

During the past half-century, social psychologists have discovered that one of the most powerful determinants of human behavior stems from the need to preserve a stable, positive self concept—that is, to maintain a relatively favorable view of ourselves, particularly when we encounter evidence that contradicts our typically rosy self-image (Aronson, 1969, 1992; Baumeister, 1993; Greenberg, Pyszcynski, & Solomon, 1986). Most of us try to believe that we are reasonable, decent folks who make wise decisions, do not behave immorally, and have integrity. In short, we try to believe that we do not do stupid, cruel, or absurd things. But as we go through life, we encounter a great many challenges to this belief. The topic of this chapter is how human beings deal with those challenges.

The Need to Justify our Actions

As we suggested in Chapter 1, we human beings have a strong need to maintain our self-concept and to think highly of ourselves. How does this get realized in our day-to-day lives? Let's take another look at the joggers in our opening example. Suppose you are a jogger, and out of sheer laziness, you've never stretched before jogging. You then learn that stretching does no good and might even do harm. For you, that is good news. You will feel exonerated. Indeed, even if your reason for not stretching in the past was not conviction but only laziness, somehow, in retrospect, you feel that you have behaved reasonably. The information provided by Dr. Arnot is not a challenge to your past behavior.

Now suppose you had spent a good deal of time, over the past few years, stretching prior to every run. In this case, the news conveyed by Dr. Arnot is not very welcome. It makes you feel uncomfortable. If you believe the data, then your past behavior is not sensible—indeed, in retrospect, it is even absurd. Therefore, you will be motivated to try to find a way to dismiss these new findings, even to the point of questioning the honesty of the scientists who conducted the research, as some of the interviewees did. The feeling of discomfort caused by information that is discrepant from your conception of yourself as a reasonable and sensible person is called **cognitive dissonance** (Aronson, 1992; Brehm & Cohen, 1962; Festinger, 1957; Festinger & Aronson, 1960).

> When the heart speaks, the mind finds it indecent to object.
> –Milan Kundera, 1989

cognitive dissonance: a drive or feeling of discomfort, originally defined as being caused by holding two or more inconsistent cognitions and subsequently defined as being caused by performing an action that is discrepant from one's customary, typically positive self-conception

■ Once we have committed a lot of time or energy to a cause, it is nearly impossible to convince us that the cause is unworthy.

cognitions: thoughts, feelings, beliefs, or pieces of knowledge

As originally conceived by Leon Festinger (1957), dissonance was defined as an inconsistency between any two **cognitions.** But not all cognitive inconsistencies are equally upsetting. Research has shown that dissonance is most powerful when we perform an action or learn something that threatens our image of ourselves. This creates an inconsistency between who we think we are and how we behave (Aronson, 1969; Greenwald & Ronis, 1978; Thibodeau & Aronson, 1992). Generally speaking, then, cognitive dissonance occurs whenever we do something that tends to make us feel absurd, stupid, or immoral.

Cognitive dissonance always produces discomfort and therefore motivates a person to try to reduce the discomfort, in much the same way as hunger and thirst produce discomfort that motivates a person to eat or drink. But unlike satisfying hunger or thirst by eating or drinking, the ways of reducing dissonance are not simple; rather, they often lead to fascinating changes in the way we think about the world and the way we behave. Many of these behaviors are powerful and nonobvious.

How can an individual reduce dissonance? There are three basic ways we do this:

- By changing our behavior to bring it in line with the dissonant cognition
- By attempting to justify our behavior through changing one of the cognitions to make it less dissonant (and therefore more consonant) with the behavior
- By attempting to justify our behavior by adding new cognitions that are consonant with the behavior and thus support it

The basic ways of reducing dissonance are displayed in Figure 6.1.

To illustrate, let's look at an absurd piece of behavior that a great many people engage in several times a day—smoking cigarettes. Suppose you are a smoker. You are likely to experience dissonance, because it is absurd to engage in behavior that might lead to a painful, early death. How can you reduce this dissonance? The most direct way is to change your behavior: to give up smoking. Your behavior would then be consistent with your knowledge of the link between smoking and cancer. While many people have succeeded in doing just that, it's not easy—many have tried to quit and failed. What do these people do? It would be erroneous to assume that they simply swallow hard and prepare to die. They don't. Instead, they try to reduce their dissonance by finding some justification for their behavior.

Some smokers will try to change one of the cognitions; for example, they might try to convince themselves that the data linking cigarette smoking to cancer are inconclusive. (This is similar to what some of the stretching joggers did in our opening example.) Others will try to add new cognitions—for example, the belief that filters trap most of the harmful chemicals and thus reduce the threat of cancer. Some will add a cognition that allows them to focus on the vivid exception: "Look at old Sam Carouthers—he's 97 years old and he's been smoking a pack a day since he was 12. That proves it's not always bad for you." Still others will add the cognition that smoking is an extremely enjoyable activity, one for which it is worth risking cancer. Others may even succeed in convincing themselves that, all things considered, smoking is worthwhile because it relaxes them, reduces nervous tension, and so on.

These justifications may sound silly to the nonsmoker, and that is precisely our point. People experiencing dissonance will often go to extreme lengths to reduce it. We did not make up the examples of denial, distortion, and justification listed above; they are based on actual examples generated by people who have

① Here you are, a reasonably happy, content person with a good amount of self-esteem.

② Then you do something that goes against your image of yourself... Something stupid, immoral or foolish.

③ You experience Dissonance! An unpleasant arousal state that you are motivated to reduce!

④ But How?

⑤ You could change your behavior...

⑥ You could change one of your cognitions...

⑦ Or, you could add consonant cognitions.

Ah...so relaxing.

⑧ Successfully doing any of these three will reduce your dissonance. You're a happy camper once again!

FIGURE 6.1 How we reduce cognitive dissonance.

tried and failed to quit smoking. Similar justifications have been generated by people who try and fail to lose weight, who refuse to practice safer sex, or who receive unwelcome information about their health (see Croyle & Jemmott, 1990; Goleman, 1982; Kassarjian & Cohen, 1965; Leishman, 1988). To escape from dissonance, people will engage in quite extraordinary rationalizing.

Rational Behavior Versus Rationalizing Behavior

Most people proudly believe that human beings are rational animals—and indeed, human beings are capable of rational behavior. But as the above examples illustrate, the need to maintain our self-esteem produces thinking that is not always rational; rather, it is rationalizing. The joggers who spent years stretching and refused to believe the antistretching research were not behaving rationally. Totally rational people would have read the report carefully, would have checked out the methodology to make sure it was sound, and, if there were no flaws, would have then ceased stretching. But people who are in the midst of reducing dissonance are so involved with convincing themselves that they are and always have been right that they frequently end up behaving irrationally and maladaptively. In this case, by continuing to justify their past behavior they would ultimately be persuading themselves to continue stretching. If the scientific methodology is sound, this would be a waste of time, at best. In the case of cigarette smoking, the end result could be tragic.

To demonstrate the irrationality of dissonance-reducing behavior, Edward E. Jones and Rika Kohler (1959) performed a simple experiment in a southern town in the late 1950s, before desegregation was widely accepted. First, they selected individuals who were deeply committed to a position on the issue of racial segregation—some of the participants were in favor of segregation, and others were opposed to it. Next, the researchers presented these individuals with a series of arguments on both sides of the issue. Some of the arguments, on each side, were plausible, and others, on each side, were rather silly. The question was, Which of the arguments would people remember best?

If Jones and Kohler's (1959) participants were behaving in a purely rational manner, we would expect them to remember the plausible arguments best and the implausible arguments the least—regardless of which side they were on. After all, why would anyone want to remember implausible arguments? What does dissonance theory predict? A silly argument in favor of one's own position arouses some dissonance, because it raises doubts about the wisdom of that position or the intelligence of the people who agree with it. Likewise, a sensible argument on the other side of the issue also arouses some dissonance, because it raises the possibility that the other side might be closer to the truth than the person had thought. Because these arguments arouse dissonance, one tries not to think about them; that is, one might not learn them very well, or one might simply forget about them. This is exactly what Jones and Kohler found. The participants in their experiment did not remember in a rational or functional manner. They tended to remember the plausible arguments agreeing with their own position and the implausible arguments agreeing with the opposing position. Other researchers have found similar results (e.g., Lord, Ross, & Lepper, 1979; Vallone, Ross, & Lepper, 1985), all of which indicate that we human beings do not process information in an unbiased manner. Rather, we distort it in a way that fits our preconceived notions. The major results of the Jones and Kohler experiment are presented in Figure 6.2.

This process probably accounts for the fact that, on issues like politics and religion, people who are deeply committed to a view different from our own will

FIGURE 6.2   The effects of plausibility on the learning of controversial statements. ■ People tend to remember plausible arguments that support their position and implausible arguments that support the opposing position. To remember either implausible arguments that support your position or plausible arguments that support the opposing position would arouse dissonance. (Adapted from Jones & Kohler, 1959)

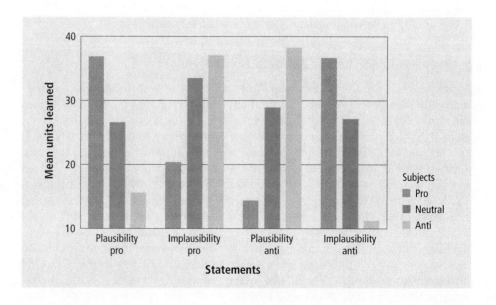

almost never come to see things our way (the proper way!), no matter how powerful and balanced our arguments might be. The next time you watch a presidential debate, check out each viewer's opinion of who won, depending on which candidate he or she favored before the debate began. If the outcome is at all close, chances are you will find little agreement across opposing camps about which candidate was the winner.

Decisions, Decisions, Decisions

What Happens After a Decision.   Based on our discussion thus far, you might guess that whenever we make an important decision, we will experience dissonance. This is called **postdecision dissonance.** An important decision can be defined as a decision that is costly, is difficult to change, is effortful, or causes harm to another person. Let us illustrate what we mean with a cogent example.

A few years ago, our friend Roger traded in his eight-year-old Honda Civic and bought a brand-new Mercedes. Soon after making the purchase, Roger, who tends to be shy and unassuming, began to engage in some uncharacteristic behaviors. He began to criticize his friends' cars, making statements like "Isn't it about time you traded in that wreck? Don't you think you deserve the pleasure of driving a well-engineered machine?" and "You know, it's really unsafe to drive little cars—if you got in an accident, it could kill you. Certainly, your life and the lives of your family members are worth an extra few thousand dollars. You have no idea how much peace of mind it brings me to know that my family is safe because I'm driving a solid, substantial automobile."

What's going on here? Why did our shy, unobtrusive friend suddenly begin imposing his views on anyone and everyone within earshot? Why did the cars we drive suddenly become so important to him? It could be that he simply got bitten by the safety or engineering bug and decided, coolly and rationally, that it would be wonderful if everyone drove a great car like the Mercedes. But there may be something else going on here. The Mercedes costs a lot of money. It is possible that after investing all that money in a new car, Roger might have felt foolish. His thinking might have gone like this: "Gee, was it really worth it? I'll be making payments on that car for the next five years. This will really strap me. If I had settled for a new Honda Civic, I would have had a lot of money left over for other things we need. What did I do? What kind of idiot am I?"

But then, in response to his self-doubt, Roger would have begun to marshal arguments in support of his action: "The Mercedes is a wonderful car; I've worked hard all my life; I deserve it. Besides, look at the safety factor. My family's well-being is worth the extra payments." Still feeling a bit uneasy, he would then have begun to tout the Mercedes to his friends. "After all," he might have reasoned, "if sensible folks like Elliot, Tim, and Robin can be convinced to go out and buy a Mercedes, how could I ever feel that I might have done a foolish thing?" In short, if Roger could persuade others, he would feel exonerated, his dissonance would be reduced, and his self-esteem would be intact.

When Prophecy Fails.   While our interpretation of what motivated Roger's behavior is purely speculative, a similar process of dissonance reduction through proselytizing, or trying to convince others to agree with your beliefs, has been studied closely (Festinger, Riecken, & Schachter, 1956). It all began with a newspaper article about an unusual woman and her small band of followers. Marian

postdecision dissonance: dissonance that is inevitably aroused after a person makes a decision; in this situation, dissonance is typically reduced by enhancing the attractiveness of the chosen alternative and devaluing the rejected alternatives

Keech was a charismatic, middle-aged woman living in a large midwestern city who, in the early 1950s, claimed to be receiving messages from outer space. One evening in September, she received a message from the planet Clarion informing her that on December 21 the world would be destroyed by a great flood. The message went on to say that a fleet of flying saucers would come from Clarion to rescue her and those close to her.

Keech attracted a small but loyal group of followers who fervently believed in her prophecy and who made a great many sacrifices consistent with this belief: They quit their jobs; gave away their money, houses, and possessions (who needs money and belongings on the planet Clarion?); and withdrew from their friends. A few even left their spouses.

Keech also attracted a small group of social psychologists: Leon Festinger, Henry Riecken, and Stanley Schachter. Using a participant-observation methodology, they infiltrated the movement, pretending to be believers. Their purpose was to get a precise, close-up view of what these people would do after December 21, when they discovered that their prophecy had (hopefully!) failed to come true. Festinger and his colleagues first noted that Keech and her followers constituted a gentle, benign, and reclusive group. One of the most interesting things about them was that they shunned publicity and discouraged converts; they were content to stick to themselves. They treated the newcomers politely, but they made it clear that it was of no consequence to them whether or not the newcomers chose to remain a part of the group. While the newspapers had picked up the story, Keech and her followers refused to grant interviews to reporters and declined to publicize their beliefs in any way.

On the morning of December 20, Marian Keech received a message from the planet Clarion instructing her group to be prepared to be picked up precisely at midnight. They were also told to remove all metal from their clothing. The group complied; zippers and clasps were dutifully removed from trousers, skirts, and blouses. When midnight passed, the members nervously checked the clock, thinking it must be running slow. As the minutes and hours dragged by, the group became increasingly engulfed by feelings of anxiety and despair. By 4:00, the group was sitting in stunned silence. Keech began to cry.

But then at 4:45, her face suddenly took on a radiant glow. She had just received a message from Clarion to the effect that there was no longer any need for the flying saucers to descend—the world had been spared a cataclysm because of the unflagging faith of this small group of believers. As you might imagine, the group was relieved and elated to hear this news. Keech's message added a new cognition that was consonant with the group members' beliefs and thus helped explain away the dissonance they were experiencing.

However, this rationalization was not enough to reduce their unease totally. Within 24 hours, they initiated a new rationalizing ploy. The true believers—a group of quiet, reclusive people—began calling newspapers and TV stations to talk about their prophecy. They made speeches at the drop of a hat and stood on street corners handing out leaflets, trying hard to attract new converts. The group suddenly found it of urgent importance to spread its message to as broad an audience as possible. Why? According to Festinger and his colleagues, the group, after its initial elation, experienced some doubts. Group members had given up a great deal because of their belief in the imminent end of the world. The world had not ended, and they were now devoid of their spouses, homes, jobs, and possessions. How could they be certain they had done the right thing? By convincing others, of course! In short, after their original prophecy failed to occur, the group felt

> Fanatics have their dreams, wherewith they weave a paradise for a sect.
>
> –John Keats

motivated to attract followers as a way of convincing themselves that the sacrifices they had made were not in vain. If they could somehow persuade others that their belief had saved the world, then they could allay their misgivings that perhaps they had behaved foolishly.

Distorting Our Likes and Dislikes.   In the two examples, both Roger and the followers of Mrs. Keech made an important decision and were in danger of feeling foolish. In short, they were experiencing the dissonance that comes from a threat to one's self-esteem. In these situations, the easiest way to reduce dissonance was to proselytize. But there are other ways to reduce dissonance following a decision. In most situations, we can do it all by ourselves, inside our own heads, by simply distorting our perceptions of how likable something is.

For example, in an early experiment Jack Brehm (1956) posed as a representative of a consumer testing service and asked women to rate the attractiveness and desirability of several kinds of appliances, such as a toaster and an electric coffee maker. Each woman was told that, as a reward for having participated in the survey, she could have one of the appliances as a gift. She was given a choice between two of the products she had rated as being equally attractive. After she made her decision, her appliance was wrapped up and given to her. Twenty minutes later, each woman was asked to rerate all the products. Brehm (1956) found that after receiving the appliance of their choice, the women rated its attractiveness somewhat higher than they had done the first time. Not only that, but they drastically lowered their rating of the appliance they might have chosen but decided to reject.

Making a decision produces dissonance. Cognitions about any negative aspects of the preferred object are dissonant with having chosen it, and cognitions about the positive aspects of the unchosen object are dissonant with not having chosen it. To reduce dissonance, people change the way they feel about both objects—cognitively spreading them apart in their own minds in order to make themselves feel better about the choice they made.

The Permanence of the Decision.   As we have seen, the more important the decision, the greater the dissonance. Deciding which person to marry is clearly a more important decision than deciding which car to own. Decisions also vary in terms of how permanent they are—that is, how difficult they are to revoke. It is usually a lot easier to go back to the car dealership and trade in your car for another one than it is to extricate yourself from an unhappy marriage. The more permanent and less revocable the decision, the greater the need to reduce dissonance.

An excellent place to investigate the significance of irrevocability is at the racetrack. Experienced bettors typically spend a great deal of time poring over the "dope sheets," trying to decide which horse to put their money on. When they make a decision, they head for the betting windows. While they are standing in line, they have already made their decision, but, we would hypothesize, because it is still revocable they have no urge to reduce dissonance. However, once they get to the window and place their bet—even if it's for only $2—it is absolutely irrevocable. Thirty seconds later, one cannot go back and tell the nice person behind the window that one has changed one's mind. Therefore, if irrevocability is an important factor, one would expect greater dissonance reduction among bettors a few minutes after placing the bet than a few minutes before placing the bet.

■ Once an individual makes a final and irrevocable decision, he or she has a greater need to reduce dissonance. For example, at the racetrack, once we've placed our bet, our certainty is greater than it is immediately before we've placed our bet.

In a simple but clever experiment, Knox and Inkster (1968) intercepted people who were on their way to place $2 bets and asked them how certain they were their horses would win. The investigators also intercepted other bettors just as they were leaving the $2 window, after having placed their bets, and asked them the same question. Almost invariably, people who had already placed their bets gave their horses a much better chance of winning than those who had yet to place their bets did. Since only a few minutes separated one group from another, nothing real had occurred to increase the probability of winning; the only thing that had changed was the finality of the decision—and thus the dissonance it produced.

The irrevocability of a decision always increases dissonance and the motivation to reduce it. Because of this, unscrupulous salespeople have developed techniques for creating the illusion that irrevocability exists. One such technique, called **lowballing,** is a successful ploy used by some car salespeople. The social psychologist Robert Cialdini temporarily joined the sales force of an automobile dealership to observe this technique closely. Here's how it works: You enter an automobile showroom, intent on buying a particular car. Having already priced it at several dealerships, you know you can purchase it for about $16,000. You are approached by a personable, middle-aged man who tells you he can sell you one for $15,679. Excited by the bargain, you agree to the deal and, at the salesperson's request, write out a check for the down payment so that he can take it to the sales manager as proof you are a serious customer.

Meanwhile, you rub your hands in glee as you imagine yourself driving home in your shiny new bargain. But alas, ten minutes later the salesperson returns, looking forlorn. He tells you that, in his zeal to give you a good deal, he made an error in calculation and the sales manager caught it. The price of the car actually comes to $16,178. You are disappointed. Moreover, you are pretty sure you can get it a bit cheaper elsewhere. The decision to buy is not irrevocable. And yet in this situation, research by Cialdini and his colleagues (1978) suggests that far more people will go ahead with the deal than if the original asking price had been

lowballing: an unscrupulous strategy whereby a salesperson induces a customer to agree to purchase a product at a very low cost, subsequently claims it was an error, and then raises the price; frequently the customer will agree to make the purchase at the inflated price

■ Car salespeople frequently use a high-pressure technique whereby they make the customer feel as if he or she had entered into an irrevocable agreement.

$16,178, even though the reason for purchasing the car from this particular dealer—the bargain price—no longer exists. How come?

There are at least three reasons that lowballing works. First, while the customer's decision to buy is certainly reversible, a commitment of sorts does exist, due to the act of signing a check for a down payment. This creates the illusion of irrevocability, even though, if the car buyer really thought about it, he or she would quickly realize it is a nonbinding contract. However, in the razzle-dazzle world of high-pressure sales, even temporary illusion can have powerful consequences. Second, this commitment triggered the anticipation of an exciting event: driving out with a new car. To have had the anticipated event thwarted (by not going ahead with the deal) would have produced dissonance and disappointment. Third, although the final price is substantially higher than the customer thought it would be, it is probably only slightly higher than the price at another dealership. Under these circumstances, the customer in effect says, "Oh, what the heck. I'm already here, I've already filled out the forms, I've already written out the check—why wait?" Thus, by using dissonance reduction and the illusion of irrevocability, high-pressure salespeople increase the probability that you will decide to buy their product at their price.

The Decision to Behave Immorally.   Life is made up of more than just decisions about cars, appliances, and racehorses. Often our decisions involve moral and ethical issues. When is it permissible to lie to a friend, and when is it not? When is an act stealing, and when is it borrowing? Resolving moral dilemmas is a particularly interesting area in which to study dissonance, because of the implications for one's self-esteem. Even more interesting is the fact that dissonance reduction following a difficult moral decision can cause people to behave either more or less ethically in the future (Mills, 1958).

Take the issue of cheating on an exam. Suppose you are a college sophomore taking the final exam in a physics course. Ever since you can remember, you have wanted to be a surgeon, and you know that your admission to medical school will depend heavily on how well you do in this physics course. The key question on the exam involves some material you know fairly well, but because so much is riding on this exam, you experience acute anxiety and draw a blank. The minutes tick away. You become increasingly anxious. You simply cannot think. You glance up and, lo and behold, you notice that you happen to be sitting behind the smartest person in the class.

You glance at her paper and notice she is just completing her answer to the crucial question. You know you could easily read her answer if you chose to. Time is running out. What do you do? Your conscience tells you it's wrong to cheat—and yet if you don't cheat, you are certain to get a poor grade. And if you get a poor grade, there goes medical school. You wrestle with your conscience.

Regardless of whether or not you decide to cheat, you are doomed to experience the kind of threat to your self-esteem that arouses dissonance. If you cheat, your cognition "I am a decent, moral person" is dissonant with your cognition "I have just committed an immoral act." If you decide to resist temptation, your cognition "I want to become a surgeon" is dissonant with your cognition "I could have acted in such a way that would have ensured a good grade and admission to medical school, but I chose not to. Wow, was that stupid!"

In this situation, some students—perhaps most—will decide to cheat; others will decide not to cheat. While that is interesting, we think an even more interesting question is, What happens to the students' attitudes about cheating after their decision? Suppose that after a difficult struggle, you decide to cheat. How do you reduce the dissonance? You can't very easily pretend you didn't cheat; that would constitute a complete denial of reality. What you could do is try to justify the action by finding a way to minimize the negative aspects of the action you chose. In this instance, an efficacious path of dissonance reduction would entail a change in your attitude about cheating. In short, you will adopt a more lenient attitude toward cheating, convincing yourself that it is a victimless crime that doesn't hurt anybody, that everybody does it and so it's not really that bad, and so on.

Suppose, on the other hand, that after a difficult struggle you decide not to cheat. How would you reduce your dissonance? Once again, you could change your attitude about the morality of the act—but this time in the opposite direction. That is, in order to justify giving up a good grade, you must convince yourself that cheating is a heinous sin, that it's one of the lowest things a person can do, and that cheaters should be rooted out and severely punished.

What has come about is not merely a rationalization of your own behavior but an actual change in your system of values; individuals faced with this kind of choice will undergo either a softening or a hardening of their attitudes toward cheating on exams, depending on whether or not they decided to cheat. The interesting and important thing to remember is that two people acting in the two different ways described above could have started out with almost identical attitudes toward cheating. Their decisions might have been a hair's breadth apart—one came within an inch of cheating but decided to resist, while the other came within an inch of resisting but decided to cheat. Once they made their decisions, however, their attitudes toward cheating will diverge sharply as a consequence of their actions.

These speculations were put to the test by Judson Mills (1958) in an experiment he performed in an elementary school. Mills first measured the attitudes of sixth-graders toward cheating. He then had them participate in a competitive exam, with prizes being offered to the winners. The situation was arranged so that it was almost impossible to win without cheating. Mills made it easy for the children to cheat and created the illusion that they could not be detected. Under these conditions, as one might expect, some of the students cheated and others did not. The next day, the sixth-graders were again asked to indicate how they felt about cheating. Those children who had cheated became more lenient toward cheating, and those who had resisted the temptation to cheat adopted a harsher attitude toward cheating.

The Justification of Effort

Most people are willing to put out a lot of effort in order to get something they really want. That's axiomatic. For example, if there's a particular job you want, you are likely to go the extra mile in order to get it. This might involve shopping for appropriate clothing, studying extra hard to meet entrance requirements, passing a battery of difficult exams, or putting up with a series of unpleasant interviews.

Let's turn that proposition inside out. Suppose you expend a great deal of effort in order to get into a particular club and it turns out to be a totally worthless organization, consisting of boring, pompous people engaged in trivial activities. You would feel pretty foolish, wouldn't you? A sensible person doesn't work hard in order to gain something trivial. Such a circumstance would produce a fair amount of dissonance; your cognition that you are a sensible, adept human being is dissonant with your cognition that you worked hard to get into a worthless club. How would you reduce this dissonance? How would you, after the fact, justify your behavior?

You could conceivably change your self-concept ("Perhaps I'm not a sensible, adept person, after all"), but as we shall see, the self-concept is a rather stable entity; it's the last thing a person will consider changing. A less drastic but equally effective way to reduce dissonance would be to convince yourself that the club and the people in it are nicer, more interesting, and more worthwhile than they at first glance appeared to be.

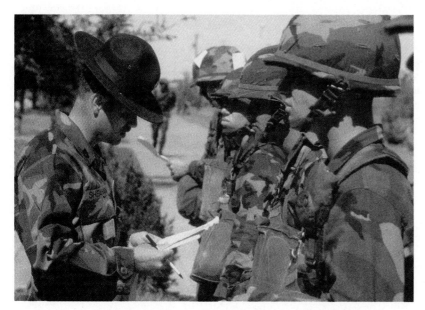

■ Going through a lot of effort to become a marine will increase the recruits' feelings of cohesiveness and their pride in the corps.

justification of effort: the tendency for individuals to increase their liking for something they have worked hard to attain

"But," you're probably thinking, "that would be crazy! How can one turn boring people into interesting people and a trivial club into a worthwhile one?" In actuality, it's not as crazy as it might appear. Even the most boring people and trivial clubs have some redeeming qualities. Activities and behaviors are also open to a variety of interpretations; if we are motivated to see the best in people and things, we will tend to interpret these ambiguities in a positive manner. In this type of situation, dissonance aroused by the need for **justification of effort** provides the necessary motivation for this kind of distortion.

The classic experiment that tested the effort-dissonance link was conducted by Elliot Aronson and Judson Mills (1959). In this experiment, college women volunteered to join a group that would be meeting regularly to discuss various aspects of the psychology of sex. The women were told that if they wanted to join, they would first have to go through a screening test designed to ensure that all people admitted to the group could discuss sex freely and openly. This instruction served to set the stage for the initiation procedure. One-third of the women were assigned to a severe initiation that required them to recite aloud, in the presence of the male experimenter, a list of obscene words and a few rather lurid sexual passages from contemporary novels. (It should be noted that this experiment was performed in the late 1950s, when this kind of procedure was far more embarrassing for most women than it would be today.) One-third of the students underwent a mild procedure, in which they recited a list of words that were sexual but not obscene. The final one-third of the participants were admitted to the group without undergoing any initiation.

Each participant was then allowed to listen in on a discussion being conducted by the members of the group she would be joining. Although the women were led to believe that the discussion was a live, ongoing one, what they actually heard was a prerecorded tape. The taped discussion was arranged so that it was as dull and bombastic as possible. After the discussion was over, each participant was asked to rate it in terms of how much she liked it, how interesting it was, how intelligent the participants were, and so forth. The major findings are shown in Figure 6.3.

FIGURE 6.3   The tougher the initiation, the more we like the group. ■ The more effort we put into gaining group membership, the more we like the group we have just joined. (Adapted from Aronson & Mills, 1959)

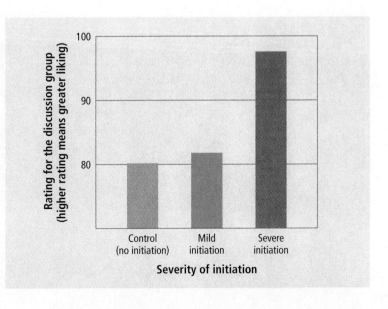

The results supported the predictions: Those participants who underwent little or no effort to get into the group did not enjoy the discussion very much. They were able to see it for what it was—a dull and boring waste of time. They regretted that they had agreed to participate. Those participants who went through a severe initiation, however, succeeded in convincing themselves that the same discussion, while not as scintillating as they had hoped, was dotted with interesting and provocative tidbits and therefore, in the main, was a worthwhile experience. In short, they justified their effortful initiation process by interpreting all the ambiguous aspects of the group discussion in the most positive manner possible (see also Gerard & Mathewson, 1966).

It should be clear that we are not suggesting that most people enjoy painful experiences—they do not. Nor are we suggesting that people enjoy things because they are associated with painful experiences. What we are asserting is that, if a person agrees to go through a difficult or a painful experience in order to attain some goal or object, that goal or object becomes more attractive. Thus, if you were walking to the discussion group and a passing car splashed mud all over you, you would not like that group any better. However, if you volunteered to jump into a mud puddle in order to be admitted to a group that turned out to be trivial and boring, you would like the group better.

It's the volunteering that motivates people to try to justify their behavior. The importance of volunteering was nicely demonstrated in an experiment by Joel Cooper (1980). The participants in this experiment were people who were suffering from serious snake phobias. Cooper first measured the extent of their fear of snakes by observing how closely they dared to approach a six-foot boa constrictor that was housed in a glass tank. He then put participants through an unpleasant set of experiences—for some, stressful; for others, effortful—that, they were informed, might have some therapeutic value in helping reduce their fear of snakes. But—and this is the crucial part—half of the participants were simply told about the procedure and then put through it. The other half were reminded of what they had all been told earlier: that they could leave the experiment at any time, that it was their choice to continue, and so on. In this manner, the sense of having volunteered for the next phase of the experiment was heightened and made salient for half of the participants. After going through the therapeutic procedure, each participant was then brought back into the presence of the boa constrictor and asked to approach it as closely as possible. Only those who had been induced to volunteer for the unpleasant therapeutic procedure showed improvement—they were able to come much closer to the boa constrictor than they had before. Those who were simply put through the unpleasant therapeutic procedure, without being strongly reminded that it was their choice and that they had volunteered, showed very little improvement (see also Axsom, 1989). The results of Cooper's experiment are shown in Figure 6.4.

The Psychology of Insufficient Justification

Saying Is Believing.   When we were little, we were taught never to tell a lie. Indeed, our elementary school history courses were full of mythical stories (disguised as truths) like that of George Washington and the cherry tree, apparently aimed at convincing us that we had better be truthful if we aspired to the presidency. Alas, the world is a complicated place. There may be some people in the world who have never told a lie, but most of us have yet to meet one. At

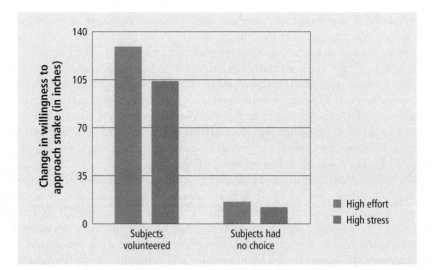

FIGURE 6.4   The act of volunteering to be subjected to a painful or traumatic experience in order to obtain a goal (in this case, to reduce one's fear of snakes) makes it more likely that we will carry through and obtain the goal. ■ (Adapted from Cooper, 1980)

external justification: a person's reason or explanation for his or her dissonant behavior that resides outside the individual (e.g., in order to receive a large reward or avoid a severe punishment)

internal justification: the reduction of dissonance by changing something about oneself (e.g., one's attitude or behavior)

times, most of us feel that, for good reason, we need to be less than perfectly truthful. One such reason involves something else that we were taught—namely, to be kind to one another. Occasionally, in order to be kind to someone, we find it necessary to tell a lie.

For example, suppose you walk into your friend Sam's house and notice an atrocious painting on the wall. You look at it, and it's so bad that you think it's a joke. You are about to burst into raucous laughter when Sam says, with considerable pleasure and excitement, "Do you like it? It cost a great deal. It's by a relatively unknown local artist named Carol Smear; I think she's very talented, so I went into hock to buy it from her. Don't you think it's beautiful?"

How do you respond? You hesitate. Chances are you go through something like the following thought process: "Sam seems so happy and excited. Why should I rain on his parade? If I were to tell him my true feelings, I would almost certainly cause him distress. He obviously likes the painting and paid a great deal for it. Telling him my honest opinion might make him annoyed with me or might make him feel he made a terrible mistake. Either way, it will be unpleasant. Even if I end up convincing Sam that it's a piece of garbage, he can't take it back. What's the sense in telling him the truth?"

So you tell Sam that you like the painting very much. Do you experience much dissonance? We doubt it. There are a great many thoughts that are consonant with having told this lie, as outlined in your reasoning in the above paragraph. In effect, your cognition that it is important not to cause pain to people you like provides ample **external justification** for having told a harmless lie.

But what happens if you say something you don't really believe and there is no ample external justification for doing so? What if your friend Sam was fabulously wealthy and bought paintings constantly? What if he sincerely needed to know your opinion of this purchase? What if in the past you'd told him he's bought a veritable eyesore and your friendship survived? Now the external justifications for lying to Sam about the painting are minimal. If you still refrain from giving your true opinion (saying instead, "Gee, Sam, uh, it's . . . interesting"), you will experience dissonance. When you can't find external justification for your behavior, you will attempt to find **internal justification,** by bringing the two cognitions (your attitude and your behavior) closer together. How can you do this? You begin looking for positive aspects of the painting—some evidence of creativity or sophistication that might have escaped you previously. Chances are that if you look hard enough, you will find something. Within a short time, your attitude toward the painting will have moved in the direction of the statement you made—and that is how "saying is believing." This phenomenon is generally referred to as **counterattitudinal advocacy,** a process by which individuals are induced to state publicly an opinion or attitude that runs counter to their own private attitudes. When this is accomplished with a minimum of external justification, it results in a change in the individual's private attitude in the direction of the public statement.

counterattitudinal advocacy: the process that occurs when a person states an opinion or attitude that runs counter to his or her private belief or attitude

This proposition was first tested in a classic experiment by Leon Festinger and J. Merrill Carlsmith (1959). In this experiment, male college students were induced to spend an hour performing a series of excruciatingly boring and repetitive tasks. The experimenter then told each student that the purpose of the study was to determine whether or not people would perform better if they were told in advance that the tasks were interesting. He went on to tell the subject that he had been randomly assigned to the control condition—that is, he had not been told anything in advance. However, he explained, the next participant, a young woman who was just arriving in the anteroom, was going to be in the experimental condition. The researcher said that he needed to convince her that the task was going to be interesting and enjoyable. Since it was much more convincing if a fellow student rather than the experimenter delivered this message, would the participant do so? Thus, with his request the experimenter induced the participants to lie about the task to another student (actually, a confederate).

Half of the students were offered $20 for telling the lie (a large external justification), while the others were offered only $1 for telling the lie (a very small external justification). After the experiment was over, an interviewer asked the lie-tellers how much they had enjoyed the tasks they had performed earlier in the experiment. The results validated the hypothesis: Those students who had been paid $20 for lying—that is, for saying the tasks had been enjoyable—rated the activities as the dull and boring experiences they were. But those who were paid only $1 for saying the task was enjoyable rated the task as significantly more enjoyable. In other words, people who had received an abundance of external justification for lying told the lie but didn't believe it, whereas those who told the lie without a great deal of external justification succeeded in convincing themselves that what they said was true.

■ Under specific conditions, saying is believing.

One might ask whether this phenomenon works when important attitudes are involved. Can you induce a person to change an attitude about things that matter? Subsequent research has shown that the Festinger-Carlsmith paradigm has wide ramifications in areas of great significance. Consider an experiment by A. R. Cohen (1962), for example. Cohen was a social psychologist at Yale University during a turbulent period, when the city police were often descending on the campus to control the overly exuberant behavior of the Yale students. Occasionally the police reacted with gleeful and excessive force. After one such altercation, Cohen visited a Yale dormitory, indicating he worked for a well-known research institute. He told the students that there were two sides to every issue and that the institute was interested in looking at both sides of the police-student issue. He then asked the students to write forceful essays supporting the behavior of the police. Moreover, he told them he was able to offer them an incentive for writing the essay. Depending on the condition to which the students were assigned, he offered them 50 cents, $1, $5, or $10. (None of the students was aware of what the others were being offered.) After the students wrote their essays, Cohen assessed their real attitude toward the actions of the city police.

The results were clear. The smaller the incentive, the more favorable people became toward the city police. In other words, when the students were given a great deal of external justification for writing the essay, they did not need to convince themselves that they really believed what they had written. However, when they were faced with the fact that they had written positive things about the police for 50 cents or $1, they needed to convince themselves that there may have been some truth in what they had written.

In a similar experiment, Elizabeth Nel, Robert Helmreich, and Elliot Aronson (1969) induced college students who were opposed to the use of marijuana to compose and recite a videotaped speech favoring its use and legalization. Some were offered large incentives; others were offered small incentives. Again the findings were clear: The smaller the incentive, the greater the softening of the attitude toward the use and legalization of marijuana.

As an additional wrinkle on this paradigm, these researchers also varied the audience to whom the videotape would supposedly be played. Nel and her colleagues hypothesized that if the audience consisted of high school students who had not yet made up their minds about the desirability of smoking marijuana, the college students making the tape would experience a great deal of dissonance. They would be in grave danger of convincing naive young people to engage in behavior they personally thought was bad. In order to reduce their dissonance, and in the absence of a large external justification for their act, they would have to persuade themselves that marijuana was not so bad after all.

On the other hand, Nel and her colleagues hypothesized, if the tape was going to be played to an audience that had already made up their minds about the use of marijuana, then it would have little or no effect on the audience's behavior and, consequently, much less dissonance would be aroused. If little dissonance was present, there would be little need to change one's attitude in the direction of the speech. The results of the experiment supported the predictions. The greatest shift in attitude toward the use and legalization of marijuana was in the condition where, for a very small incentive, people recorded a promarijuana message that

FIGURE 6.5 Students came to believe their own speech only if their audience was persuadable and the incentive was small. ■ (Adapted from Nel, Helmreich, & Aronson, 1969)

they believed would be shown to impressionable, persuadable young people. When the audience was believed to be strongly for or strongly against the use of marijuana, dissonance was minimal regardless of the size of the incentive. The results are illustrated in Figure 6.5.

Hypocrisy and AIDS Prevention.   In recent years, AIDS has become an epidemic of epic proportions. Hundreds of millions of dollars have been spent on AIDS information and prevention campaigns in the mass media. While these campaigns have been effective in conveying information, they have not been nearly so successful in preventing people from engaging in risky sexual behavior. For example, although college students are aware of AIDS as a serious problem, a surprisingly small percentage use condoms every time they have sex. The reason seems to be that condoms are inconvenient, are unromantic, and remind people of disease—the last thing they want to be reminded of when getting ready to make love. Rather, as researchers have consistently discovered, people have a strong tendency to experience denial where sexual behavior is involved—in this case, to believe that while AIDS is a problem for most people, they themselves are not at risk. If the mass media have been ineffective, is there anything else that can be done?

Recently Elliot Aronson, Carrie Fried, and Jeff Stone (1991) have had some success at convincing people to use condoms, by employing a variation of the saying is believing paradigm. They asked college students to compose a speech describing the dangers of AIDS and advocating the use of condoms every single time a person has sex. In one condition, the students merely composed the arguments. In another condition, the students composed the arguments and then recited them in front of a video camera, after being informed that the resulting videotape would be played to an audience of high school students. In addition, half the students in each condition were made mindful of their own failure to use condoms by making a list of the circumstances in which they had found it particularly difficult, awkward, or impossible to use them.

Essentially, then, the participants in one condition—those who made a video for high school students after having been made mindful of their own failure to use condoms—were in a state of high dissonance. This was caused by their being made aware of their own hypocrisy; they were fully aware of the fact that they were preaching behavior to high school students that they themselves were not practicing. In order to remove the hypocrisy and maintain their self-esteem, they would need to start practicing what they were preaching. And that is exactly what Aronson and his colleagues found: Students in the hypocrisy condition showed a greater willingness to increase their use of condoms, as compared to students in the control conditions. Moreover, in a follow-up experiment (Stone, Aronson, Crain, Winslow, & Fried, 1993) each student was given the opportunity to purchase condoms very cheaply. The results demonstrated that the students in the hypocrisy condition were far more likely to buy condoms than students in any of the other conditions were. Figure 6.6 illustrates the results of this experiment.

Insufficient Punishment.   Complex societies run, in part, on punishment or the threat of punishment. As members of society, we constantly find ourselves in situations where those who are charged with the duty of maintaining law and order are threatening to punish us if we do not comply with their rules and regulations. For example, while cruising down the highway at 70 miles an hour, we

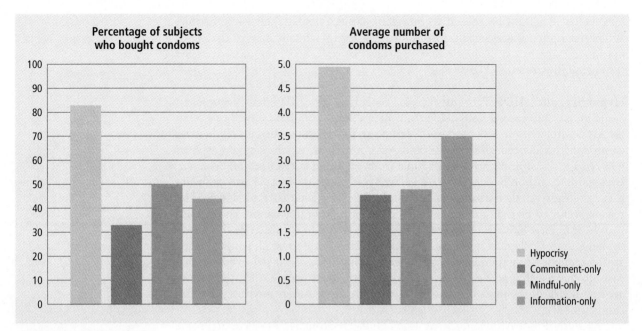

FIGURE 6.6 People who are made mindful of their hypocrisy begin to practice what they preach. ■ (Adapted from Stone, Aronson, Crain, Winslow, & Fried, 1993)

know that if we get caught, we will end up paying a substantial fine. If it happens often, we will lose our license. And so we learn to obey the speed limit when patrol cars are in the vicinity. By the same token, youngsters in school know that if they cheat on an exam and get caught, they could be humiliated by the teacher and severely punished. And so they learn not to cheat while the teacher is in the room watching them. But does harsh punishment teach adults to want to obey the speed limit? Does it teach youngsters to value honest behavior? We don't think so. Rather, we believe that all it teaches us is to try to avoid getting caught. In short, the use of threats of harsh punishment as a means of getting someone to refrain from doing something he or she enjoys doing requires constant vigilance and harassment.

Let's look at bullying behavior. It is extremely difficult to persuade children that it's not right or enjoyable to beat up smaller children. But theoretically, it is conceivable that under certain conditions they will persuade themselves that such behavior is unenjoyable. Imagine that you are the parent of a 6-year-old boy who often beats up his 4-year-old brother. You've tried to reason with him, but to no avail. Thus, in order to make him a nicer person (and in order to preserve the health and welfare of his little brother), you begin to punish him for his aggressiveness. As a parent, you have at your disposal a number of possible punishments, ranging from the extremely mild (a stern look) to the extremely severe (a hard spanking, forcing the child to stand in the corner for two hours, and depriving him of TV privileges for a month). The more severe the threat, the greater the likelihood the youngster will cease and desist—while you are watching him. But he may very well hit his brother again as soon as you are out of sight. In short, just as most drivers learn to be vigilant of the Highway Patrol while speeding, your 6-year-old has not lost his enjoyment of bullying his little brother; he has merely learned not to do it while you are around to punish him.

Suppose that you threaten him with a very mild punishment. In either case— under threat of severe punishment or of mild punishment—the child experiences dissonance. He is aware that he is not beating up his little brother, and he is also aware that he would very much like to beat him up. When he has the urge to hit his brother and doesn't, he implicitly asks himself, "How come I'm not beating up my little brother?" Under severe threat, he has a convincing answer in the form of a sufficient external justification: "I'm not beating him up because if I do, my parents are going to really punish me." This serves to reduce the dissonance.

The child in the mild threat situation experiences dissonance too. But when he asks himself, "How come I'm not beating up my little brother?" he doesn't have a very convincing answer, because the threat is so mild that it does not provide a superabundance of justification. In short, this is **insufficient punishment.** The child is refraining from doing something he wants to do, and while he does have a modicum of justification for not doing it, he lacks complete justification. In this situation, he continues to experience dissonance. Therefore, the child must find another way to justify the fact that he is not aggressing against his kid brother.

The less severe the threat, the less external justification; the less external justification, the greater the need for internal justification. The child can reduce his dissonance by convincing himself that he doesn't really want to beat up his brother. In time, he can go further in his quest for internal justification and decide that beating up little kids is not fun. Allowing children the leeway to construct their own internal justification is tantamount to enabling them to develop a permanent set of values.

Thus far, this has all been speculative. Will threats of mild punishment for performing any behavior diminish the attractiveness of that behavior to a greater extent than severe threats will? This proposition was first investigated in an experiment with preschoolers (Aronson & Carlsmith, 1963).

In this experiment, because the researchers were dealing with very young children, ethical concerns precluded their trying to affect important values, like those concerning aggressive behavior. Instead, they attempted to change something that was of no great importance to society but was of great importance to the children: their preference for different kinds of toys. The experimenter first asked each child to rate the attractiveness of several toys. He then pointed to a

insufficient punishment: the dissonance aroused when individuals lack sufficient external justification for having resisted a desired activity or object, usually resulting in individuals devaluing the forbidden activity or object

■ How can we induce this child to give up playing with an attractive toy?

toy that the child considered very attractive and told the child that he or she was not allowed to play with it. Half the children were threatened with mild punishment if they disobeyed; the other half were threatened with severe punishment. The experimenter then left the room and gave the children the opportunity to play with the other toys and to resist the temptation of playing with the forbidden toy. None of the children played with the forbidden toy.

After several minutes, the experimenter returned to the room and asked the child to rate how much he or she liked each of the toys. Initially, all of the children had wanted to play with the forbidden toy. During the temptation period, all of them had refrained from playing with it. Clearly, this disparity means that dissonance was aroused in the children. How did they respond? The children who had received a severe threat had ample justification for their restraint. They knew why they hadn't played with the attractive toy, and they thus had no reason to change their attitude about the toy. These children continued to rate the forbidden toy as highly desirable; indeed, some even found it more desirable than they had before the threat.

But what about the others? Lacking an abundance of external justification for refraining from playing with the toy, the children in the mild threat condition needed an internal justification to reduce their dissonance. They succeeded in convincing themselves that the reason they hadn't played with the toy was that they didn't really like it. They rated the forbidden toy as less attractive than they had at the beginning of the experiment. What we have here is a clear example of self-justification leading to self-persuasion in the behavior of very young children. The implications for child rearing are fascinating.

The Permanence of Self-Persuasion.   Let's say you've attended a lecture on the evils of cheating. It might have a temporary effect on your attitudes toward cheating. But if a week or two later you found yourself in a highly tempting situation, your recent change in attitude would probably lack the staying power to act as a deterrent. Social psychologists know that mere lectures do not usually result in permanent or long-lasting attitude change. In contrast, suppose you went through the kind of situation experienced by the children in Judson Mill's (1958) experiment on cheating, discussed earlier in this chapter. Here we would expect the attitude change to be far more deep-seated and permanent. Those children who were tempted to cheat but resisted the temptation came to believe that cheating is a dastardly thing to do, not because someone told them so but because they persuaded themselves of this belief as a means of justifying the fact that, by not cheating, they had given up an attractive prize.

self-persuasion: a long-lasting form of attitude change that results from attempts at self-justification

The long-lasting effects of attitudes generated by **self-persuasion** and self-justification have been clearly demonstrated in a number of contexts. To take one dramatic example, Jonathan Freedman (1965) performed a replication of Aronson and Carlsmith's (1963) forbidden toy experiment. In Freedman's version of the experiment, the forbidden toy was an attractive battery-powered robot; all the children in the experiment were eager to play with it. But Freedman forbade them from doing so, indicating that they could play with the other toys—which were pallid by comparison—if they wanted to. Just as in the original experiment, Freedman issued either a mild threat or a severe threat for breaking the rule. And just as in the original experiment, all of the children obeyed the rule. Freedman then left the school and never returned.

Now here is the interesting part. Several weeks later, a young woman came to the school, ostensibly to administer some paper-and-pencil tests to the children.

In actuality, she was working for Freedman; however, the children were totally unaware that her presence was in any way related to Freedman, the toys, or the threats that had occurred several weeks earlier. Coincidentally, she was administering her tests in the same room Freedman had used for his experiment—the room where the same toys were casually scattered about. After administering the test, she asked the children to wait for her while she went to the next room to score the test. She then casually suggested that the scoring might take a while and that—how lucky!—someone had left some toys around and the children could play with any of them they wanted to.

The results were striking: The overwhelming majority of the children whom Freedman had mildly threatened several weeks earlier decided, on their own, not to play with the robot; they played with the pallid toys instead. On the other hand, the great majority of the children who had been severely threatened did in fact play with the robot now that they had the opportunity to do so. Specifically, 78 percent of the children in the severe threat condition played with the toy, while only 33 percent of the children in the mild threat condition did so. Thus, a single mild threat was still very effective several weeks later, while a severe threat was not.

Again, the power of this phenomenon rests on the fact that the reason the children didn't play with the toy was not that some adult told them the toy was undesirable; such admonitions would not have persisted for very long after the admonishing adult had left the premises. The reason the mild threat persisted for at least several weeks was that the children were motivated to convince themselves the toy was undesirable. The results of Freedman's experiment are presented in Figure 6.7.

What Do We Mean by "Insufficient Justification"?   Throughout this chapter, we have talked about self-justification occurring in situations where there is insufficient external justification. For example, we showed how saying some-

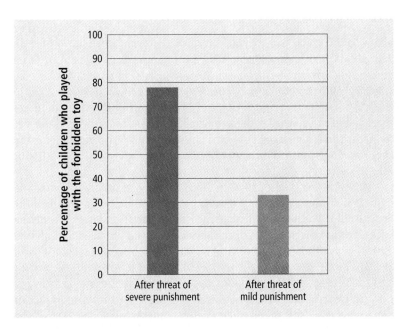

**FIGURE 6.7   Several weeks after-
ward, children who had received a
threat of mild punishment were far
less likely to play with the forbidden
toy than children who had received a
threat of severe punishment were.
Those given a mild threat had to
provide their own justification by
devaluing the attractiveness of the
toy.** ■ (Adapted from Freedman,
1965)

thing you don't believe will produce a shift in belief in the direction of what you said only if there is no adequate tangible reward for having said it. Similarly, we have shown that refraining from performing a particular activity will result in a derogation of that activity only if there is not fully adequate punishment to justify continued compliance.

The term *insufficient external justification* needs clarification. In one sense, it is sufficient—sufficient to produce the behavior. For example, the students in Festinger and Carlsmith's (1959) experiment did agree to lie about how interesting it was to perform the boring job. The experimenter's request was just sufficient to get them to do the behavior, but it wasn't sufficient, later, for them to explain to themselves how they could have done such a mean thing to another student. After all, nobody had held a gun to their heads; they agreed, of their own free will, to lie—at least, that's how these participants saw it.

In fact, this situation, like many others in life, is characterized by the "illusion of freedom." We think we're free to choose our response, but powerful social norms and rules often dictate what we will actually do. How could these participants say no to a politely worded, fairly innocuous request from an authority figure? The cards were stacked—indeed, close to 100 percent of participants in these types of studies agree to the experimenter's request; basically, no one says no. So how much real choice could there be? And yet the participants don't perceive the inherent restraints on their ability to truly choose between saying yes or no to the request. Later, when thinking about why they lied to an innocent person, they don't blame it on the experimenter and his or her request; they see it as their personal choice. And the best way to maintain their self-esteem is to decide that the task was sort of fun and interesting after all; hence, it wasn't such a lie.

Thus, while we like to think of ourselves as fully rational creatures, we frequently find ourselves doing things without entirely thinking them through— saying yes when we wanted to say no, and so on. Indeed, the irony is that precisely because we like to believe that we are rational, sensible, and moral creatures, we are vulnerable to dissonance-induced self-persuasion.

And It Isn't Just Rewards or Punishments.   As we have seen, a sizable reward or a severe punishment is an effective way of providing external justification for an action. Accordingly, if you want a person to do something or to refrain from doing something only once, the best strategy would be to promise a large reward or threaten a severe punishment. But if you want a person to develop a deep-seated attitude, the smaller the reward or punishment that will induce momentary compliance, the greater will be the eventual attitude change and therefore the more permanent the effect. Large rewards and severe punishments, because they are strong external justifications, militate against dissonance and thus prevent attitude change.

We should note that this phenomenon is not limited to tangible rewards and punishments; justifications can come in more subtle packages as well. Take friendship, for example. We like our friends; we trust our friends; we do favors for our friends. Suppose you are at a formal dinner party at the home of a close friend. Your friend is passing around a rather strange-looking appetizer. It's not quite a potato chip, but it looks like it's been fried. "What is it?" you ask warily. "Oh, it's a fried grasshopper; I'd really like you to try it," your friend answers. Because she's a good friend and you don't want to cause her any discomfort or embarrassment in front of the other guests, you gingerly pick one out of the bowl, place it in your mouth, chew it up, and swallow it. How much do you think you will like this new snack food?

Keep that in mind for a moment as we expand the example. Suppose you are a dinner guest at the home of a person you don't like very much, and he hands you, as an appetizer, a fried grasshopper and tells you that he'd really like you to try it. In much the same way, you put it in your mouth, chew it up, and swallow it.

Now the crucial question: In which of these two situations will you like the taste of the grasshopper better? Common sense might suggest that the grasshopper would taste better when recommended by a friend. But think about it for a moment; which condition involves less external justification? Common sense notwithstanding, dissonance theory makes the opposite prediction. In the first case, when you ask yourself "How come I ate that disgusting insect?" you have ample justification: You ate it because your good friend asked you to. In the second case, you lack this kind of justification for having eaten the grasshopper. Therefore, you must add some justification of your own; namely, you must convince yourself that it was tastier than you would have imagined, that as a matter of fact, it was quite good—"I'm thinking of laying in a supply myself."

While this may seem a rather bizarre example of dissonance-reducing behavior, it's not as far-fetched as you might think. Indeed, Philip Zimbardo and his colleagues (1965) conducted an experiment directly analogous to our example. In this experiment, army reservists were asked to eat fried grasshoppers as part of a research project on survival foods. Reservists who ate grasshoppers at the request of a stern, unpleasant officer increased their liking for grasshoppers far more than those who ate grasshoppers at the request of a well-liked, pleasant officer. Those who complied with the unfriendly officer's request had little external justification for their actions. As a result, they adopted more positive attitudes toward eating grasshoppers in order to justify their otherwise strange and dissonance-arousing behavior.

The Aftermath of Good and Bad Deeds

How We Come to Like Our Beneficiaries: The Ben Franklin Manipulation.   It is obvious that when we like people, we tend to treat them well, speak kindly to them, do them favors, and smile at them benevolently. If we don't like them, we treat them less kindly, avoid them, say bad things about them, and perhaps even go out of our way to snub them. But what happens when we do a person a favor? In particular, what happens when we are subtly induced to do a favor for a person we do not like—will we like them more? Or less? Dissonance theory predicts that we will like that person more after doing him or her the favor.

This phenomenon was hardly discovered by dissonance theorists; in fact, it is a part of folk wisdom. The great Russian novelist Leo Tolstoy wrote about it in 1869 (see quote in margin). And more than 100 years prior to Tolstoy's observation, Benjamin Franklin confessed to having utilized this bit of folk wisdom as a political strategy. While serving as a member of the Pennsylvania state legislature, Franklin was disturbed by the political opposition and apparent animosity of a fellow legislator. So he set out to win him over:

> We do not love people so much for the good they have done us as for the good we have done them.
>
> –Leo Tolstoy

> I did not . . . aim at gaining his favour by paying any servile respect to him but, after some time, took this other method. Having heard that he had in his library a certain very scarce and curious book I wrote a note to him expressing my desire of perusing that book and requesting he would do me the favour of lending it to

me for a few days. He sent it immediately and I returned it in about a week with another note expressing strongly my sense of the favour. When we next met in the House he spoke to me (which he had never done before), and with great civility; and he ever after manifested a readiness to serve me on all occasions, so that we became great friends and our friendship continued to his death. This is another instance of the truth of an old maxim I had learned, which says, "He that has once done you a kindness will be more ready to do you another than he whom you yourself have obliged." (Bigelow, pp. 216–217)

Benjamin Franklin was clearly pleased with the success of his blatantly manipulative strategy. As skeptical scientists, we should not be fully convinced by this anecdote. It is not entirely clear whether Franklin's success was due to this particular gambit or simply to his charm. In order to be certain, it is important to design and conduct an experiment that controls for such things as charm. Such a study was conducted by Jon Jecker and David Landy (1969), more than 240 years after Franklin's more casual experiment.

In the Jecker and Landy (1969) experiment, students participated in a concept-formation task that enabled them to win a substantial sum of money. After the experiment was over, one-third of the participants were approached by the experimenter, who explained that he was using his own funds for the experiment and was running short, which meant he might be forced to close down the experiment prematurely. He asked, "As a special favor to me, would you mind returning the money you won?" The same request was made to a different group of subjects—except this time, not by the experimenter but by the departmental secretary, who asked them if they would return the money as a special favor to the psychology department's research fund, which was running low. The remaining participants were not asked to return their winnings. Finally, all of the participants were asked to fill out a questionnaire that included an opportunity to rate the experimenter. Those participants who had been cajoled into doing a special favor for the experimenter found him the most attractive—they had convinced themselves he was a wonderful, deserving fellow. The others thought he was a pretty nice guy but not anywhere near as wonderful as the people who had been asked to do him a favor. Figure 6.8 shows the results of this experiment.

The Ben Franklin phenomenon has all kinds of interesting ramifications and applications. One of these was explored recently by Michael Leippe and Donna Eisenstadt (1994), who succeeded in applying the strategy to the rather sensitive area of race relations. In a well-controlled series of experiments, Leippe and Eisenstadt induced white college students to go out on a limb in behalf of African Americans; specifically, they got white students to endorse a pro-black policy that would have been costly to white students. After endorsing that policy, the attitudes of these white students became far more favorable to African Americans in general.

How We Come to Hate Our Victims.   Several years ago, during the height of the war in Vietnam, one of us hired a young man to help paint his house. Here are Elliot's reminiscences:

The painter was a gentle and sweet-natured person who had graduated from high school, joined the army, and fought in Vietnam. After leaving the army, he took up housepainting and was a good and reliable craftsman and an honest businessman. I enjoyed working with him. One day while we were taking a coffee break,

■ Without realizing it, Ben Franklin may have been the first dissonance theorist.

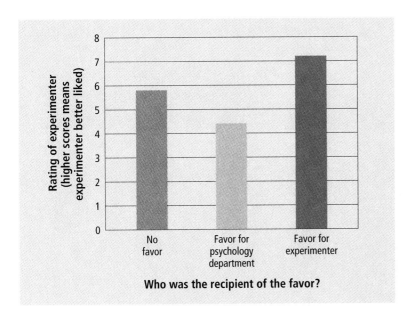

FIGURE 6.8 If we have done someone a favor, we are more likely to feel more positively toward that person. ■
(Adapted from Jecker & Landy, 1969)

we began to discuss the war and the intense opposition to it, especially at the local university. It soon became apparent that he and I were in sharp disagreement on this issue. He felt that the American intervention was reasonable and just and would "make the world safe for democracy." I argued that it was a terribly dirty war, that we were killing, maiming, and napalming thousands of innocent people: old people, women, children—people who had no interest in war or politics. He looked at me for a long time; then he smiled sweetly and said, "Hell, Doc, those aren't people; those are Vietnamese! They're gooks." He said it matter-of-factly, without obvious rancor or vehemence. I was astonished and chilled by his response. I wondered how it could be that this apparently good-natured, sane, and gentle young man could develop that kind of attitude. How could he dismiss an entire national group from the human race?

Over the next several days, as we continued our dialogue I got to know more about him. It turned out that during the war he had participated in actions in which Vietnamese civilians had been killed. What gradually emerged was that initially he had been wracked by guilt—and it dawned on me that he might have developed this attitude toward the Vietnamese people as a way of assuaging his guilt. That is, if he could convince himself that the Vietnamese were not fully human, it would make him feel less awful about having hurt them, and it would reduce the dissonance between his actions and his self-concept as a decent person.

It goes without saying that these speculations about the causes of the house-painter's attitude are far from conclusive. While it is conceivable that he derogated the Vietnamese people as a way of reducing dissonance, the situation is complex; for example, he might always have had a negative and prejudiced attitude toward the Vietnamese, and this might have made it easier for him to behave brutally toward them. To be certain that the justification of cruelty can occur in such situations, it is essential for the social psychologist to temporarily step back from the helter-skelter of the real world and test the proposition in the more controlled setting of the experimental laboratory.

■ During wartime, especially when defenseless civilians such as old people, women, and children are targets of military violence, the soldiers committing such acts of violence will become inclined to derogate or dehumanize their victims—after the fact—in order to reduce their own dissonance.

Ideally, if we want to measure attitude change as a result of dissonant cognitions, we should know what the attitudes were before the dissonance-arousing behavior occurred. Such a situation was produced in an early experiment performed by Keith Davis and Edward E. Jones (1960). Each student's participation consisted of watching a young man being interviewed and then, on the basis of this observation, providing him with an analysis of his shortcomings as a human being. Specifically, the participants were told to tell the young man (a confederate) that they believed him to be a shallow, untrustworthy, boring person. The participants succeeded in convincing themselves they didn't like the victim of their cruelty—after the fact. In short, after saying things they knew were certain to hurt him, they convinced themselves that he deserved it. They found him less attractive than they had prior to saying the hurtful things to him.

Let us return to our housepainter example. Suppose for a moment that all the people he killed and injured in Vietnam had been fully armed enemy soldiers, instead of a sizable number of noncombatants. Do you think he would have experienced as much dissonance? We think it is unlikely. When engaged in combat with an enemy soldier, it is a "you or me" situation; if the housepainter had not killed the enemy soldier, the enemy soldier might have killed him. Thus, while hurting or killing another person is probably never taken lightly, it is not nearly so heavy a burden as it would be if the victim was an unarmed civilian—a child, a woman, an old person.

These speculations are supported by the results of an experiment by Ellen Berscheid and her colleagues (Berscheid, Boye, & Walster, 1968). In this study, college students volunteered for an experiment in which each of them administered a (supposedly) painful electric shock to a fellow student. As one might expect, these students derogated their victim as a result of having administered the shock to him or her. However, half of the students were told there would be a turnabout: The other student would be given the opportunity to retaliate against them at a later time. Those who were led to believe their victim would be able to retaliate later did not derogate the victim. In short, because the victim was going

■ Dehumanizing their victims provides aggressors with justification for brutal acts that feeds into a horrifying, endless chain of escalating violence against their victims.

to be able to even the score, there was very little dissonance, and therefore the harm-doers had no need to belittle their victim in order to convince themselves that he or she deserved it.

The results of these laboratory experiments lend credence to our speculations about the behavior of the housepainter; the results suggest that during a war, military personnel have a greater need to derogate civilian victims (because these individuals can't retaliate) than military victims. Moreover, several years after Elliot's encounter with the housepainter, a similar set of events emerged during the court-martial of Lieutenant William Calley for his role in the slaughter of innocent civilians at My Lai in Vietnam. In a long and detailed testimony, Lieutenant Calley's psychiatrist made it clear that the lieutenant had come to regard the Vietnamese people as less than human.

As we have seen, systematic research in this area demonstrates that people do not perform acts of cruelty and come out unscathed. We can never be completely certain of how the housepainter, Lieutenant Calley, and thousands of other American military personnel came to regard the Vietnamese as subhuman, but it seems reasonable to assume that when people are engaged in a war where a great number of innocent people are being killed, they might try to derogate the victims in order to justify their complicity. They might poke fun at them, refer to them as "gooks," and dehumanize them. Ironically, success at dehumanizing the victim virtually guarantees a continuation or even an escalation of the cruelty. It becomes easier to hurt and kill subhumans than to hurt and kill fellow human beings. Thus, reducing dissonance in this way has sobering future consequences: It increases the likelihood that the atrocities people are willing to commit will become greater and greater through an endless chain of violence followed by self-justification (in the form of dehumanizing the victim), followed by greater violence and still more intense dehumanization. In this manner, unbelievable acts of human cruelty—such as the Nazi "Final Solution" that led to the murder of 6 million European Jews—can occur. Needless to say, atrocities are not a thing of the past but are as recent as today's newspaper.

> There's nothing people can't contrive to praise or condemn and find justification for doing so.
>
> –Molière,
> *The Misanthrope*

The Evidence for Motivational Arousal

The theory of cognitive dissonance is largely a motivational theory; in other words, the theorists maintain that discomfort and arousal are what drives the engine, what motivates the individual to change his or her attitude or behavior. How do we know this is in fact the case? Is there any independent evidence indicating that people who experience cognitive dissonance are in a state of discomfort or arousal? A fascinating experiment by Mark Zanna and Joel Cooper (1974) provides just such evidence. Participants in their study were given a placebo—a milk-powder pill having no physiological effect whatever. Some were told that the pill would arouse them and make them feel tense. Others were told that the pill would make them feel calm and relaxed. Participants in the control condition were told that the pill would not affect them in any way. After ingesting the pill, each person voluntarily wrote a counterattitudinal essay, thus creating dissonance.

Dissonance theory predicts that such participants will change their attitudes, bringing them in line with their essays in order to reduce their uncomfortable arousal state, only if they actually feel aroused. However, if some of the participants think the arousal they are experiencing is due to the pill, they won't need to alter their attitudes to feel better about themselves. At the opposite end of the spectrum, if some of the participants think they should be feeling relaxed due to the pill, any arousal they experience should be very salient to them and they should change their attitudes a great deal. Thus, the theory predicts that attitude change will come or go across conditions, depending on whether the arousal due to dissonance is masked by an alternative explanation ("Oh, right—I took a pill that's supposed to make me feel tense; that's why I'm feeling this way") or magnified by an alternative explanation ("Oh no—I took a pill that's supposed to make me feel relaxed and I feel tense").

Zanna and Cooper's (1974) results supported these predictions. Participants in the control condition underwent considerable attitude change, as would be expected in a typical dissonance experiment. Participants in the aroused condition, however, did not change their attitudes—they attributed their discomfort to the pill, not their counterattitudinal essay. Finally, participants in the relaxed condition changed their attitudes even more than the control participants did. They inferred that writing the counterattitudinal essay had made them very tense, since they were feeling aroused despite a relaxing drug. Thus, they inferred that their behavior was very inconsistent with their perception of themselves as decent and reasonable people, and they changed their attitude to bring it into line with their essay contents. These data are illustrated in Figure 6.9.

New Directions in Research on Self-Justification and Self-Esteem Maintenance

Throughout this chapter, we've indicated that human beings generally have a need to see themselves as intelligent, sensible, and decent folks who behave with integrity. Indeed, what triggers the attitude change and distortion that can take place in the process of dissonance reduction is precisely the need people have to maintain this picture of themselves. At first glance, much of the behavior described in this chapter may seem startling: people coming to dislike others

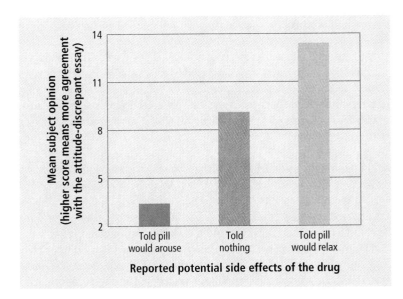

FIGURE 6.9 **If subjects can misattribute the arousal associated with the dissonance, they do not show the typical attitude change following a counterattitudinal essay. This is strong support for the notion that dissonance causes physiological arousal.** ■ (Adapted from Zanna & Cooper, 1974)

more after doing them harm, people liking others more after doing them a favor, people believing a lie they've told only if there is little or no reward for telling it, and so on. These behaviors would be difficult for us to understand if it weren't for the insights provided by the theory of cognitive dissonance.

In recent years, social psychologists have explored this basic premise—that people have a fundamental need to maintain a stable, positive sense of self—in greater depth and in new contexts. For example, most dissonance experiments have involved behavior that in some way falls short of people's standards of competence or morality, such as working hard for something of questionable value or lying to someone for no good reason. The work of E. Tory Higgins and his colleagues (Higgins, 1987, 1989; Higgins, Klein, & Strauman, 1987) is also concerned with understanding how such violations of personal standards influence people's emotional and motivational states. In particular, these researchers have taken a close look at the nature of the emotional distress that occurs when we perceive ourselves as not measuring up to our ideals and standards. It thus offers some support for the notion that dissonance involves specific patterns of psychological discomfort, in addition to physiological arousal.

Self-Discrepancy Theory

Self-discrepancy theory holds that people are motivated to maintain a sense of consistency among their various beliefs and perceptions about themselves. In particular, the theory posits that we become distressed when our sense of who we truly are—our *actual self*—is discrepant from our personal standards or desired self-conceptions. For Higgins and his colleagues, these standards are reflected most clearly in the various beliefs we hold about the type of person we aspire to be—our *ideal self*—and the type of person we believe we should be—or our *ought self*. Comparing our actual self with our ideal and ought selves provides us with an important means of self-evaluation—that is, of making judgments about our abilities, personal attributes, and behavior and the extent to which we are adhering to our goals.

What happens when we become aware that we have failed to measure up to our standards? Like dissonance theory, self-discrepancy theory also predicts that this blow to our self-esteem will generate psychological distress, along with the motivation to reduce the inconsistency associated with the self-discrepancy. In our efforts to do so, we strive to reduce dissonance by restoring harmony among our self-beliefs, particularly between our actual selves and our personal standards. Engaging in various forms of self-justification allows us to narrow the gap that sometimes exists between who we are, as implied by our self-discrepant actions, and who we aspire to be.

To illustrate, consider the predicament of Sarah, a first-year college student who has always had very high academic standards. In terms of self-discrepancy theory, academic competence is a central component of her ideal self. Moreover, she's become accustomed to living up to these high standards over the years: With only a modest level of effort, it was pretty much a breeze in high school to earn A's in most subjects and B's in the others. In her first semester at a competitive, prestigious college, however, Sarah has discovered those A's much harder to come by. It seems that the courses she has enrolled in are far more rigorous and demanding than she had anticipated. As a matter of fact, in her introductory chemistry course—a prerequisite for her major—she barely managed to earn a C. Given this scenario, how is Sarah likely to experience this discrepancy between her ideal and actual selves?

To begin with, we might imagine that the threat to her self-concept as a high achiever would almost certainly generate fairly strong levels of emotional discomfort—for example, disappointment in herself and perhaps an unaccustomed sense of uncertainty regarding her abilities. Self-discrepancy research supports this view. In a series of studies, Higgins and his colleagues (Higgins, 1989; Higgins, Bond, Klein, & Strauman, 1988) have found that when people are made mindful of a discrepancy between their actual and ideal selves, they tend to experience a pattern of feelings involving dejection, sadness, dissatisfaction, and other depression-related emotions.

On the other hand, what if Sarah had encountered a self-discrepancy involving her ought self—that is, not the ideal self she aspired to but the "should" self she felt obligated to uphold? Imagine that being a top-notch student was not enormously significant to Sarah as a means of satisfying her own ideal self-aspirations. Instead, suppose that her parents had always held this standard as highly important and that Sarah, out of respect for them, was very responsive to their expectations regarding academic excellence. How, then, would Sarah experience this discrepancy between her actual and ought selves, in the face of a mediocre performance in her first semester at college? Higgins and his colleagues have found that, unlike in the case of actual-ideal self-discrepancy described above, a different pattern of emotions would tend to occur. Specifically, their research indicates that Sarah would be likely to experience fear, worry, tension, and other anxiety-related emotions.

How might Sarah attempt to cope with the dissonance arousal and negative feelings generated by either of these two forms of self-discrepancy? According to the theory, self-discrepancies not only produce emotional discomfort but also provoke strivings to minimize the gap between the actual and the ideal, or ought, selves. As discussed throughout this chapter, self-justifying thoughts and behaviors provide a ready means of restoring a positive self-concept when it has been threatened by a self-discrepant experience. For example, recall the predicament of subjects in Festinger and Carlsmith's (1959) classic study who, for a paltry $1, told a "fellow student" that a tedious experimental task was actually quite fascinating. We could well imagine that the ideal or ought selves of these subjects included the notion of behaving with honesty and integrity. As a result, the act of lying would have produced a discrepancy between their actual selves and their standards. How did they reduce the dissonance associated with this self-discrepancy? By minimizing the extent of their dishonesty—that is, by expressing greater liking for the boring task.

In Sarah's case, reducing dissonance might involve construing her lackluster academic performance in a manner that protects her long-standing belief in herself as an excellent student. In fact, in several experiments undergraduate students who received a failing grade on an exam reacted in precisely this way: Failing students blamed their poor performance on the alleged unfairness of the test, rather than attributing it to personal factors such as poor ability or insufficient effort. In other words, when confronted with a discrepancy between their actual and desired selves, they reduced the discrepancy by eschewing personal responsibility for their dismal performance (Arkin & Maruyama, 1979; Davis & Stephan, 1980). Similarly, Sarah might convince herself that the grading was unfair, that her chemistry instructor was totally inept, or in some other way interpret her mediocre performance in the most positive light possible. Of course, as we've noted repeatedly in this chapter, self-justification—while a self-protective strategy in the short run—might not be the most adaptive approach Sarah could adopt in coming to terms with dissonance arousal. Rather, she would undoubtedly benefit far more from reassessing her situation—concluding, perhaps, that maintaining her high academic standards might require greater effort than she was accustomed to exerting in the past, when her courses were less challenging.

In sum, self-discrepancy theory offers an interesting framework for understanding dissonance arousal as a product of threats to one's self-concept, particularly when efforts to restore or maintain a positive self-image stem from violations of personal standards. In addition, the work of Higgins and his colleagues provides further insight into the specific patterns of emotional discomfort associated with dissonance arousal.

Self-Completion Theory

Other social psychologists have also taken in interesting new directions the need to protect a favorable self-image. For example, Robert Wicklund and Peter Gollwitzer (Gollwitzer & Wicklund, 1985; Wicklund & Gollwitzer, 1982) have investigated how the need for self-maintenance plays itself out in the realm of social relationships. Specifically, their work on self-completion theory indicates that when people experience a threat to a valued aspect of their self-concept, or identity, they become highly motivated to seek some sort of social recognition of that identity. Once achieved, this acknowledgment allows people to restore their valued self-conceptions—thereby serving as a means of reducing dissonance and maintaining the self.

Imagine, for example, that you are an aspiring poet. You think your work has a good deal of promise, and one of your poems has already been published in a small, regional poetry journal. Bolstered by this success, you have recently sent out a new batch of poems to a more prestigious journal with a larger circulation. You are also committed to developing your talents further, and so you sign up for a writing course offered by an up-and-coming poet whose work you greatly admire. As you're leaving the house on your way to the first class, you stop off at your mailbox to pick up the mail. Sorting through it, you discover a letter from the poetry journal to which you've submitted your work. With great excitement, you rip open the letter. To your dismay, however, you find an impersonal form letter from the editor, informing you that your poems have been deemed unacceptable for publication in the journal. Disappointed and annoyed, you tear up the letter, get into your car, and proceed to your writing class. After the classroom has filled, the instructor asks everyone to take out the samples of their work they had been asked to bring to the first meeting. She then announces that most of the class time will be spent listening to student poetry but that, given the unexpectedly large size of the group, only a few students will have the opportunity to read at the first meeting. She then asks for volunteers to read their work to the class.

Given the recent blow to your cherished identity as a poet, how do you think you would react to the instructor's request? Would you shrink back into your chair and let the others grab for the spotlight? Probably not. Rather, research on self-completion theory strongly suggests that even before the instructor had finished her sentence, your hand would have shot up into the air, vigorously vying for an opportunity to have your poems heard by the rest of the class. Why would this be the case? According to Wicklund and Gollwitzer, when we experience a threat to an identity to which we are committed, we become highly motivated to restore that aspect of our self-concept through social recognition. That is, we tend to look for ways to signal to others that we do in fact have a credible, legitimate claim to a particular identity that has been challenged. Through such *self-symbolizing activities*—in this case, reading poems to a group of strangers—we are able to reduce the dissonance stemming from the threat to our valued notions of self.

In an experiment very similar to this hypothetical scenario, subjects who were committed to their identities as promising dancers wrote essays about their training in dance (Gollwitzer, 1986). Half the subjects were asked to describe the very worst dance instructor they had ever trained with; the other half wrote essays about their most gifted instructor. In the former condition, then, subjects were made uncomfortably aware of an aspect about their training that undermined their identities as dancers, whereas in the latter condition subjects were asked to recall an aspect of their background that supported their identities as dancers. Later, in an entirely different setting, all of the subjects were invited to participate in a dance concert and were given an opportunity to select a date for their performance. As self-completion theory predicts, dancers whose identities had been threatened—those who had recently been asked to recall an inadequate aspect of their training—expressed the desire to perform in public nearly two weeks earlier than subjects whose self-concepts as dancers had not been challenged. Similar results have been found in research involving medical students whose identities as aspiring physicians were threatened (Gollwitzer, 1986), as well as individuals who were made to feel inadequate about their identities as athletes (Gollwitzer & Wicklund, 1985). Compared to subjects whose self-concepts had not been called into question, threatened subjects were especially eager to engage in self-symbolizing activities that bolstered their claim to an identity that had recently been challenged.

Research on self-completion theory thus adds a new dimension to previous work on dissonance as a process of maintaining a positive, stable self-concept. It provides evidence for the important role of the social world in sustaining our identities and indicates that efforts to reduce dissonance stemming from a threatened sense of self can assume a variety of forms, from the kinds of self-justification processes we have previously discussed to the self-symbolizing behaviors documented by Wicklund and Gollwitzer.

Self-Evaluation Maintenance Theory

Most dissonance research is concerned how our self-image is threatened by our own behavior, such as acting contrary to our attitudes or making a difficult decision. Abraham Tesser (1988) has explored how other people's behavior can threaten our self-concept in ways that have important implications for our interpersonal relationships.

Suppose you consider yourself to be a very good cook—in fact, the best cook of all your friends and acquaintances. You love nothing better than playing with a recipe, adding your own creative touches, until—voilà!—you have a wonderful, delectable new creation. Then you move to another town, make new friends, and—lo and behold!—your very favorite new friend turns out to be a superb cook, far better than you. How does that make you feel? We suspect you will agree that you might feel more than a little uneasy about the fact that your friend outdoes you in your area of expertise.

Now consider a slightly different scenario. Suppose your new best friend is, instead of a superb cook, a very talented artist. Are you likely to experience any discomfort in this situation? Undoubtedly not; in fact, you are likely to bask in the reflected glory of your friend's success. "Guess what?" you will probably tell everyone. "My new friend has sold some of her paintings in the most exclusive New York galleries."

The difference between these two scenarios is that in the first one, your friend is superior at an attribute that is very important to you and may even be a central part of how you define yourself. We all have abilities and traits that we treasure—we are especially proud of being good cooks, talented artists, gifted musicians, or inventive scientists. Whatever our most treasured ability, if we encounter someone who is better at it than we are, there is likely to be trouble—trouble of the dissonance variety. It is difficult to be proud of our ability to cook if our closest friend is a far better chef than we are.

This is the basic premise of Tesser's (1988) **self-evaluation maintenance theory,** which holds that there are three important predictors of dissonance in interpersonal relationships: how we perform on a task relative to another person, how close we are to this person, and how relevant the task is to our self-definition. As seen in Figure 6.10, there is no problem if a close friend outperforms us on a task that is not that relevant to us. In fact, we bask in the person's reflected glory and feel even better about ourselves. Dissonance occurs when a close friend outperforms us on a task that is relevant to our self-definition.

self-evaluation maintenance theory: the theory that one's self-concept can be threatened by another individual's behavior and that the level of threat is determined by both the closeness of the other individual and the personal relevance of the behavior

How Do We Reduce This Dissonance?   We can try to change any one of the three components that produced it. First, we can distance ourselves from the person who outperforms us, deciding that he or she is not such a close friend after all. Pleban and Tesser (1981) tested this possibility by having college students compete against another student, who was actually an accomplice of the experimenter, on general knowledge questions. They rigged it so that in some conditions, the questions were on topics that were highly relevant to people's self-definitions and the accomplice got many more of the questions correct. Just as predicted, this was the condition in which people distanced themselves the most from the accomplice, saying they would not want to work with him again.

FIGURE 6.10   Self-evaluation maintenance theory.

It is too dissonance-producing to be close to someone who is better than we in our treasured areas of expertise (Wegner, 1986).

A second way to reduce such threats to our self-esteem is to change how relevant the task is to our self-definition. If our new friend is a far better cook than we are, we might lose interest in cooking, deciding that auto mechanics is really our thing. To test this prediction, Tesser and Paulus (1983) gave people feedback about how well they and another student had done on a test of a newly discovered ability, cognitive-perceptual integration. When people learned that the other student was similar to them (high closeness) and had done better on the test, they were especially likely to say that this ability was not very important to them—just as the theory predicts.

Finally, people can deal with self-esteem threats by changing the third component in the equation: their performance relative to the other person's. If our new best friend is a superb cook, we can reduce the dissonance by trying to make ourselves an even better cook. This won't work, however, if we are already performing to the best of our abilities. If so, we can take a more diabolic route, wherein we try to undermine our friend's performance so that it is not as good as ours. If our friend asks for a recipe, we might leave out a critical ingredient, so that his or her salmon en brioche is not nearly so good as ours.

Why Might We Help a Stranger More Than a Friend?   Are people really so mean-spirited that they try to sabotage their friends' performance? Surely not always; there are many examples of times when we are extremely generous and helpful toward our friends. If our self-esteem is on the line, however, there is evidence that we are not as helpful as we would like to think. Tesser and Smith (1980) asked students to play a game of Password wherein one person gave clues to another to guess a word and to do so with both a friend and a stranger. The students could choose to give clues that were very helpful, making it easy for the other player to guess the word, or very obscure, making it hard for the other player to guess the word. The researchers set it up so that people first performed rather poorly themselves and then had the opportunity to help the other players by giving them easy or difficult clues. The question was, Who would they help more—the strangers or their friends?

By now, you can probably see what self-evaluation maintenance theory predicts. If the task is not very self-relevant to people, they should want their friends to do especially well, so that they can bask in the reflected glory. If the task is self-relevant, however, it would be threatening to people's self-esteem to have their friends outperform them. And so they might make it difficult for their friends, by giving them especially hard clues. This is exactly what Tesser and Smith found. They made the task very self-relevant for some participants, by telling them that performance on the game was highly correlated with their intelligence and leadership skills. Under these conditions, people gave more difficult clues to their friends than to the strangers, because they did not want their friends to shine on a task that was highly important to them. When the task was not self-relevant, people gave more difficult clues to the strangers than to their friends (see Figure 6.11).

In sum, research on self-evaluation maintenance theory has shown that threats to our self-concept have fascinating implications for our interpersonal relationships. Though much of the research has been with college students in

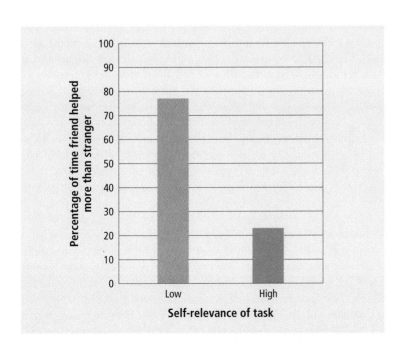

FIGURE 6.11   Self-relevance of task. ■ People are more inclined to be helpful to a friend if the friend's success does not pose a threat to their own self-esteem. (Adapted from Tesser & Smith, 1980)

laboratory settings, the theory has been confirmed in field and archival studies as well. Tesser (1980), for example, examined biographies of male scientists, noting how close these scientists were to their fathers. As the theory predicts, when the scientists' field of expertise was the same as their fathers', they had a more distant and strained relationship with their fathers. Similarly, the greatest amount of friction between siblings was found to occur when the siblings were close in age and one sibling was significantly better on key dimensions, such as popularity or intelligence. When performance and relevance are high, it can be difficult to avoid conflicts with family members. Consider how the novelist Norman Maclean (1983) describes his relationship with his brother in the story "A River Runs Through It": "One of the earliest things brothers try to find out is how they differ from each other. . . . Undoubtedly, our differences would not have seemed so great if we had not been such a close family."

Self-Affirmation Theory

As we have seen, people will go to great lengths to maintain a good image of themselves, by changing their attitudes, their behavior, or their relationships with other people. In each case, people try to restore a sense of integrity by warding off a specific threat to their self-concept. If we smoke cigarettes, we try to deal with the specific threat to our health by quitting or by convincing ourselves that smoking is not really bad for our health. Sometimes, however, threats to our self-concept can be so strong and difficult to avoid that the normal means of reducing dissonance do not work. It can be very difficult to stop smoking, as millions of people have discovered. It is also difficult to ignore all the evidence indicating that smoking is bad for us and might even kill us. So what can we do? Are smokers doomed to wallow in a constant state of dissonance?

self-affirmation theory: a theory suggesting that people will reduce the impact of a dissonance-arousing threat to their self-concept by focusing on and affirming their competence on some dimension unrelated to the threat

Research by Claude Steele (1988) on **self-affirmation theory** shows that people are creative and flexible when it comes to avoiding dissonance. Even if we cannot rationalize away a threat to our self-esteem, we can avoid dissonance by affirming our competence and integrity in some other area. "Yes, I smoke," you might say. "But I am a great cook" (or a terrific poet, or a wonderful friend, or a promising scientist). Self-affirmation occurs when our self-esteem is threatened; if possible, we will attempt to reduce the dissonance by reminding ourselves of some irrelevant aspect of our self-concept that we cherish, as a way of feeling good about ourselves in spite of some stupid or immoral action we have just committed.

In a series of fascinating experiments, Steele and his colleagues have demonstrated that if you provide people with an opportunity for self-affirmation, they will grab it and avoid reducing dissonance in more direct ways, such as by changing their attitudes (Steele, 1988; Steele, Hoppe, & Gonzales, 1986; Steele & Liu, 1981). For example, Steele, Hoppe, and Gonzales (1986) performed a replication of Jack Brehm's (1956) classic experiment on postdecision dissonance reduction. They asked students to rank-order ten record albums, ostensibly as part of a marketing survey. As a reward, the students were then told that they could keep either their fifth- or sixth-ranked album. Ten minutes after making their choice, they were asked to rate the albums again. You will recall that in Brehm's (1956) experiment, after selecting one of the kitchen appliances the participants spread apart their ratings of the appliances, rating the one they had chosen much higher than the one they had rejected. In this manner, they convinced themselves that they had made a smart decision. And that is exactly what most of the students did in Steele and his colleagues' (1986) record album experiment.

But Steele and his colleagues built an additional set of conditions into their experiment. Half of the students were science majors, and half were business majors. Half of the science majors and half of the business majors were asked to put on a white lab coat while participating in the experiment. Why the lab coat? As you know, a lab coat is associated with the idea of science. Steele and his colleagues suspected that the lab coat would serve a "self-affirmation function" for the science majors but not for the business majors. The results supported their predictions. Whether or not they were wearing a lab coat, business majors reduced dissonance just as the people in Brehm's (1956) experiment did: After their choice, they increased their evaluation of the chosen album and decreased their evaluation of the one they had rejected. Similarly, in the absence of a lab coat, science majors reduced their dissonance in the same way. However, science majors who were wearing the lab coat resisted the temptation to distort their perceptions; the lab coat reminded these students that they were promising scientists and thereby short-circuited the need to reduce dissonance by changing their attitudes toward the albums. In effect, they said, "I might have made a dumb choice in record albums, but I can live with that because I have other things going for me; at least I'm a promising scientist!" A simplified version of these findings is presented in Figure 6.12.

Abraham Tesser and David Cornell (1991) showed that self-affirmation can also short-circuit the need to reduce the kind of dissonance described by self-evaluation maintenance theory—that is, the kind produced when people feel threatened by another person's outstanding performance in their own area of expertise. Tesser and Cornell replicated the Tesser and Smith (1980) study we reviewed earlier, wherein people played Password with friends and strangers. As you recall, when people felt that Password was highly self-relevant, they tried to undermine their friends' performance by giving them difficult clues. Tesser and Cornell added a condition: People were first given the opportunity to affirm themselves in an area unrelated to the Password game. In this condition, people first completed a questionnaire that enabled them to express their most treasured values, such as how honest or religious they were. Once again, this opportunity to self-affirm

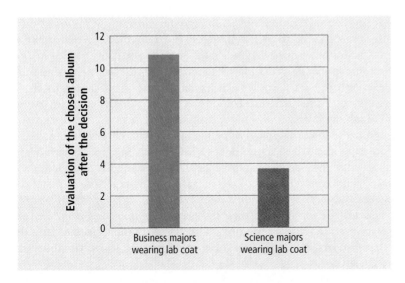

FIGURE 6.12 Dissonance and self-affirmation. ■ People who were allowed the opportunity to affirm their values (science majors wearing lab coats) were able to avoid the pressures to reduce dissonance by increasing the attractiveness of the chosen album. (Adapted from Steele, Hoppe, and Gonzales, 1986)

short-circuited the need to deal with the self-concept threats more directly: These participants did not try to undermine their friends' performance by giving them hard clues, even when the task was self-relevant. They seemed to have said to themselves, "It's OK if my friend does better than me on this test of intelligence, because I have a lot of other things in my favor, such as my overall honesty and integrity." In short, people are very flexible at maintaining their self-concepts. If we cannot ward off a threat directly, we can affirm ourselves in some unrelated domain if provided with the opportunity and the cues to do so.

Self-Justification Versus Self-Maintenance: The Role of Negative Self-Beliefs

We have said repeatedly that people will typically experience dissonance whenever their self-concepts are threatened—namely, whenever they do something that makes them feel absurd, stupid, or immoral. The astute reader may have noticed that this prediction becomes tricky when applied to people who have a poor opinion of themselves. To illustrate, let's reconsider our example of smokers who continue to smoke, knowing full well that smoking is a great danger to their health. As we've noted, smokers are likely to experience high levels of dissonance because knowingly jeopardizing one's health is inconsistent with maintaining a positive self-concept—that is, a view of oneself as a rational, competent person, rather than a fool. Note, however, that this conclusion rests on an important but implicit premise: It assumes that the smoker in question has a favorable self-image, one that would be inconsistent with foolish behavior. But what if we're dealing with smokers who have negative self-concepts, who already think of themselves as fairly incompetent and thus thoroughly capable of engaging in an absurdly self-destructive habit? In this case, dissonance reduction would not be required as a means of self-maintenance, since there is no need to reestablish a positive sense of self that is not present to begin with. While such individuals would almost certainly experience a blow to their self-esteem, the stability of their self-concepts would not be threatened by smoking, as would be the case for smokers who think highly of themselves.

It turns out that the vast majority of dissonance experiments have been conducted among college student populations who are known to have fairly high levels of self-esteem. For such individuals, acting in a foolish, immoral, or absurd manner not only is threatening to their self-esteem but also calls into question the stability of their self-conceptions. As a result, self-justification works in the service of self-maintenance: By reducing dissonance, people with favorable self-images are able to restore both a positive and a consistent, stable sense of self.

Research that has taken self-esteem into account reveals that, in some instances, individuals with negative self-concepts do not engage in the kinds of self-justifying behaviors that are typical of people with relatively high self-esteem. For example, an experiment by David Glass (1964) involved subjects who were induced to deliver what they believed to be painful electric shocks to an innocent "fellow student," who was actually a confederate of the experimenter. Before doing so, however, subjects were given bogus feedback on a personality test, designed to temporarily lower or raise their self-esteem. In one condition, the test results were esteem-enhancing, depicting subjects as compassionate, highly mature, and otherwise virtuous individuals. For other subjects, however, the feedback described them as fairly self-centered, insensitive to others' feelings, and so forth. Glass found that, after "shocking" the confederate, the two groups of subjects did not react in the same way to this potentially dissonance-arousing situation. Specifically, subjects in the high self-esteem condition reduced dissonance by justifying their immoral behavior. They rated the "fellow student" whom they believed they had injured as less attractive, less likable, and so forth. In contrast, subjects whose self-esteem had been temporarily lowered did not show this tendency to derogate the "victim." Why was this the case? For low self-esteem subjects, acting immorally was apparently consistent with their self-concepts. As a result, they had no need to derogate the "fellow student" as a means of restoring their self-concepts. Instead, they maintained their unfavorable self-concepts. High self-esteem subjects, on the other hand, engaged in self-justification in order to protect their threatened self-concepts as good and decent persons.

William Swann and his colleagues (Swann, 1984, 1990; Swann & Hill, 1982; Swann & Pelham, 1988; Swann & Schroeder, 1995) have further explored this tendency we have to preserve our customary self-beliefs, even when those beliefs are unfavorable. In particular, they have examined how the need for **self-verification**—or maintaining a consistent, stable sense of self—can lead people to reject positive information about themselves when it conflicts with their own self-beliefs. For example, consider Jason, who has always thought of himself as a lousy writer with poor verbal skills. One day he is working on a term paper with a friend, who remarks that she thinks his paper is skillfully crafted, beautifully written, and superbly articulate. How will Jason feel? He should feel pleased and gratified, we might predict, because the friend's praise gives Jason's self-esteem a boost.

self-verification theory: a theory suggesting that people have a need to seek confirmation of their self-concept, whether the self-concept is positive or negative; in some circumstances, this tendency can conflict with the desire to uphold a favorable view of oneself

On the other hand, Jason's friend has given him feedback that challenges a long-standing view of himself as a poor writer, and he might be motivated to maintain this negative view. Why? For two reasons. First, like dissonance theory (Aronson, 1968, 1969), self-verification theory also rests on the basic premise that it is unsettling and confusing to have our views of ourselves disconfirmed; if we changed our self-concept every time we encountered someone with a different opinion of us, it would be impossible to maintain a coherent, consistent self-concept. Second, self-verification theory holds that interacting with people who view us differently from the way we view ourselves can be embarrassing. People who don't know us might have unrealistic expectations, and we might be embarrassed when they find out that we are not as smart or as artistic or as creative as they think we are. Better to let them know our faults at the outset.

In short, when people with negative self-views receive positive feedback, opposing needs go head to head: the desire to feel good about themselves by believing the positive feedback (self-enhancement needs) versus the desire to maintain a consistent, coherent picture of themselves and avoid the embarrassment of being found out (self-verification needs). Which needs win out?

Throughout this chapter, we have been telling you that human beings have a powerful need to feel good about themselves—in short, that the need for **self-justification** is a major determinant of our attitudes and behaviors. We now have to qualify this statement. Along with the Glass (1964) experiment described above, several studies suggest that when the two motives are in conflict, our need to maintain a stable self-concept under certain conditions overpowers our compelling desire to view ourselves in a positive light (Aronson & Carlsmith,

self-justification: the tendency to justify one's actions in order to maintain one's self-esteem

1962; Brock et al., 1965; Marecek & Mettee, 1972; Swann, 1990). For example, Swann and his colleagues have found that people prefer to remain in close relationships with those friends, roommates, and romantic partners whose evaluations of their abilities are consistent with their own (sometimes negative) self-evaluations (Swann, Hixon, & De La Ronde, 1992; Swann & Pelham, 1988). In other words, people prefer to be close to someone whose evaluations of them are not more positive than their self-concept. In a close relationship, most people find it better to be known than to be overrated.

The need to self-verify, however, appears to dominate our behavior only under a limited set of circumstances. First, people generally strive to uphold their negative self-beliefs only when they are highly certain of those beliefs (Maracek & Mettee, 1972; Swann & Ely, 1984; Swann & Pelham, 1988). Thus, if Jason had been less thoroughly convinced of his poor talents as a writer, he almost certainly would have been more receptive to his friend's praise. Second, if the consequences of being improperly evaluated are not too great—for example, if our contact with these individuals is rare so that it is unlikely they will discover we are not who we appear to be—then even people with negative views prefer positive feedback (Aronson, 1992). Finally, if people feel there is nothing they can do to improve their abilities, then they generally prefer positive feedback to accurate feedback. Why remind ourselves that we are terrible if there is nothing we can do about it? If, however, people feel that a negative self-attribute can be changed with a little work, they prefer accurate feedback, because this information can help them figure out what they need to do to get better (Steele, Spencer, & Josephs, 1992).

Avoiding the Rationalization Trap

Dissonance-reducing behavior is ego-defensive behavior. It can be useful, because it keeps our egos from being continually battered; it provides us with a feeling of stability and high self-esteem. But as we have seen, dissonance-reducing behavior can be dangerous as well. The tendency to justify our past behavior can lead us into an escalation of rationalizations that can be disastrous. The irony, of course, is that in order to avoid thinking of ourselves as stupid or immoral, we set the stage for increasing our acts of stupidity or immorality. We call this phenomenon the **rationalization trap**: Through the reduction of dissonance, there is a tendency to trap ourselves in a web of distortion that prevents us from seeing things as they really are.

Human Beings Cannot Live by Consonance Alone

If we human beings did not learn from our mistakes, we would get stuck within the confines of our narrow minds and never grow or change. If we were to spend all of our time and energy defending our egos, we would never learn from our mistakes. Instead, we would sweep our mistakes under the rug or, worse still, would try to turn them into virtues. As we have seen throughout this chapter, this process frequently serves to perpetuate error and can lead to tragedy. For example, people who hurt others can derogate their victims to the point where their actions not only seem just but might even become heroic in their own eyes (we will elaborate on this phenomenon in our chapters on aggression and prejudice).

Similarly, we have seen how people who say something they don't really believe will come to believe the statement—and some of those beliefs might be

> The mind is a strange machine which can combine the materials offered to it in the most astonishing ways.
> –Bertrand Russell, *The Conquest of Happiness*, 1930

rationalization trap: the potential for dissonance reduction to produce a succession of self-justifications that ultimately result in a chain of stupid or immoral actions tragically erroneous. The memoirs of some of our most beleaguered former presidents are full of the kind of self-serving, self-justifying statements that can best be summarized as "If I had it all to do over again, I would not change anything important" (Johnson, 1971; Nixon, 1990; Reagan, 1990). An interesting and more complex example of this phenomenon comes from the recent memoirs of Robert McNamara (1995), who was secretary of defense and one of Lyndon Johnson's principal military advisers during the Vietnam War. In a painful revelation, McNamara admits he came to the realization that the war was unwinnable in 1967—several years prior to our eventual withdrawal from Vietnam. But he chose to remain silent on this issue after leaving office—while the war raged on, wasting several thousand additional American lives as well as countless Vietnamese lives. Most knowledgeable analysts believe that to have been a tragic and catastrophic error, arguing that if he had spoken out publicly, it could have shortened the war and saved thousands of lives. In his book, McNamara makes a spirited but unconvincing attempt to justify his public silence out of some sort of personal and professional loyalty to his commander in chief.

Dissonance Reduction and Culture

Occasionally, human beings in our culture do learn from their mistakes and do change. How does this come about? A clue comes from examining other cultures. For example, Harry Triandis (1995) has found that in less individualistic societies than ours, dissonance-reducing behavior often takes a backseat to behavior that promotes group harmony rather than individual consistency. In a similar vein, Gui-Young Hong (1992) argues that dissonance-reducing behavior is less extreme in Japan than it is in the Western world because the Japanese culture considers an individual's acceptance of inconsistency to be a sign of maturity and broad-mindedness. Accordingly, Japanese children are socialized to accept inconsistency and learn to live with it. Needless to say, this does not mean that dissonance-reducing behavior is unknown in collectively oriented countries like Japan—only that it appears to be far less extreme than in much of the rest of the world.

For the rest of us, the Japanese data suggest that, in order to learn from our mistakes, it would be helpful to learn to tolerate dissonance long enough to examine the situation critically and dispassionately. We then stand a chance of breaking out of the cycle of action, followed by self-justification, followed by more intense action. For example, suppose Mary has acted unkindly toward a fellow student. In order to learn from that experience, she must be able to resist the need to derogate her victim. Ideally, it would be effective if she were able to stay with the dissonance long enough to say, "OK, I blew it; I did a cruel thing. But that doesn't necessarily make me a cruel person. Let me think about why I did it."

We are well aware that this is easier said than done. But a clue as to how such behavior might come about is contained in some of the research on self-affirmation that we discussed previously (Steele, 1988). Suppose that, immediately after Mary acted cruelly but before she had an opportunity to derogate her victim, she was reminded of the fact that she had recently donated several pints of blood to the Red Cross to be used by earthquake victims, or that she had recently gotten a high score on her physics exam. This self-affirmation would be likely to provide her with the ability to resist engaging in typical dissonance-reducing behavior. In effect, Mary might be able to say, "It's true—I just did a cruel thing. But I am also capable of some really fine, intelligent, and generous behavior."

Indeed, self-affirmation can serve as a cognitive buffer, protecting a person from caving in to temptation and committing a cruel or immoral act. This was demonstrated in an early experiment on cheating (Aronson & Mettee, 1968). In this experiment, college students were first given a personality test and then given false feedback that was either positive (aimed at temporarily raising self-esteem) or negative (aimed at temporarily lowering self-esteem), or they received no information at all. Immediately afterward, they played a game of cards in which, to win a large pot, they could easily cheat without getting caught. The results were striking. Students in the high self-esteem condition were able to resist the temptation to cheat to a far greater extent than the students in the other conditions were. In short, a temporary boost in self-esteem served to inoculate these students against cheating, because the anticipation of doing something immoral was more dissonant than it would have been otherwise. Thus, when they were put in a tempting situation, they were able to say to themselves, "Terrific people like me don't cheat." And they didn't (see also Spencer, Josephs, & Steele, 1993; Steele, Spencer, & Lynch, in press). We find these results encouraging, inasmuch as they suggest a viable way of reversing the rationalization trap.

SUMMARY

One of the most powerful determinants of human behavior is the need to justify our actions so that we might maintain a high level of self-esteem. In this chapter, we have seen that this need has intriguing consequences for people's attitudes and behaviors. According to **cognitive dissonance** theory, people experience discomfort (dissonance) whenever they are confronted with **cognitions** about some aspect of their behavior that is inconsistent with their **self-concept.** People are motivated to reduce this dissonance by either changing their behavior or justifying their past behavior, bringing it into line with a positive view of themselves. The resulting change in attitude stems from a process of **self-persuasion.**

Dissonance inevitably occurs after important decisions (**postdecision dissonance**), because the thought that "I chose alternative X" is inconsistent with the thought that "I might have been a lot better off with alternative Y." People reduce this dissonance by increasing their liking for the chosen alternative and decreasing their liking for the negative alternative. Unscrupulous salespeople have been known to take advantage of this human tendency through the utilization of a strategy called **lowballing**, which creates the illusion in the customer's mind that a commitment has been made to purchase the product, when in fact no such commitment exists.

Dissonance also occurs after people choose to exert a lot of effort to attain something boring or onerous. A **justification of effort** occurs, whereby people increase their liking for what they attained.

A third source of dissonance occurs when people commit foolish, immoral, or absurd acts for insufficient justification. For example, when people say something against their attitudes (**counterattitudinal advocacy**) for low **external justification,** they find an **internal justification** for their behavior, coming to believe what they said. Similarly, if people avoid doing something desirable for insufficient punishment, they will come to believe that the activity wasn't really all that desirable. And if people find themselves doing someone a favor for insufficient justification, they assume that they did so because the person is likable. The flip side of this kind of dissonance reduction has sinister effects: If people find themselves acting cruelly toward someone for insufficient justification, they will derogate the victim, assuming he or she must have deserved it. Finally, consistent with the idea that dissonance is an uncomfortable state people are motivated to reduce, there is evidence that dissonance is accompanied by physiological arousal.

In recent years, social psychologists have taken in fascinating new directions the idea that people are motivated to maintain their self-esteem. **Self-evaluation maintenance theory** argues that dissonance is produced in interpersonal relationships, whenever someone close to us outperforms us on a task that is highly relevant to our self-definition. People can reduce this dissonance by distancing themselves from the person, improving their performance, lowering the other person's performance, or reducing the relevance of the task. **Self-affirmation theory** argues that people are very flexible at dealing with threats to their self-esteem. When dissonance cannot be reduced by dealing with a specific threat, people can feel better about themselves by affirming themselves in some other area. Research on **self-verification theory** suggests that the need to bolster our self-esteem sometimes conflicts with the need to verify our self-views. When people with negative self-views are concerned that other people will discover they are not who they appear to be, and when they think it's possible to change and improve the less desirable side of themselves, they will prefer feedback that confirms their low opinion of themselves to feedback that is self-enhancing.

The problem with reducing dissonance in ways that make us feel better about ourselves (**self justification**)is that it can result in a **rationalization trap,** whereby we set the stage for acts of increasing stupidity or immorality. As suggested by self-affirmation theory, we can avoid this trap by reminding ourselves that we are good and decent people, so that we do not have to justify and rationalize every stupid or immoral act we perform.

IF YOU ARE INTERESTED . . .

Aronson, E. (1969). The theory of cognitive dissonance: A current perspective. In L. Berkowitz (Ed.), *Advances in experimental social psychology* (Vol. 4, pp. 1–34). New York: Academic Press, 1969. A revision of the original theory in terms of self-esteem and the self-concept.

Aronson, E. (1992). The return of the repressed: Dissonance theory makes a comeback. *Psychological Inquiry, 3,* 303–311. A brief attempt to bring dissonance theory up to date by discussing the linkage between the theory of cognitive dissonance and recent developments in cognitive psychology.

Festinger, L. (1957). *A theory of cognitive dissonance.* Evanston, IL: Row, Peterson. The original presentation of dissonance theory. A classic in social psychology—clear, concise, and engagingly written.

Remains of the Day. Adapted from Ishiguru's classic novel, this stunning 1993 film explores self-justification from the perspective of a proper British butler, played by Sir Anthony Hopkins. Shying away from friendship and romance, the butler rationalizes his lonely lifestyle by reasserting his belief that such intimacy is improper for a man in his position

Swann, W. B. Jr., & Schroeder, D. G. (1995). The search for beauty and truth: A framework for understanding reactions to evaluations. *Personality and Social Psychology Bulletin, 21,* 1307–1318.

Wicklund, R., & Brehm, J. (1976). *Perspectives on cognitive dissonance.* Hillsdale, NJ: Earlbaum. A scholarly, readable presentation of dissonance theory some two decades after its inception. Contains a description of much of the early research as well as some of the more important conceptual modifications of the theory.

Chapter 7

Attitudes and Attitude Change: Influencing Thoughts and Feelings

Chapter Outline

H ow many times, in a given day, does someone attempt to change your attitudes? Be sure to count every advertisement you see or hear, because advertising is nothing less than an attempt to change your attitude toward a consumer product, be it a brand of laundry detergent, a type of automobile, or a political candidate. Don't forget to include ads you get in the mail, calls from telemarketers, and signs you see on the sides of buses, as well as those ever-present television commercials. How many did you come up with? You might be surprised at the answer, for on average Americans encounter 300 to 400 advertisements per day (Asker & Myers, 1987; Pratkanis & Aronson, 1991).

As if this were not enough, marketers are ever on the lookout for new ways to convince you to buy their products. Entire cable television channels are now devoted to pitching products, either through "home shopping networks" or "infomercials" designed to look like regular television programs. Yet ad agencies are still not satisfied. We can only imagine the conversation that must have occurred a few years ago between marketers trying to find new inroads for advertising. Maybe it went something like this:

227

Marketer 1: *You know, one of our best audiences is teenagers. They watch a lot of TV and thus see a lot of ads.*

Marketer 2: *Yeah, but doggone it, kids are out of reach for several hours a day—when they're in school. That's so unfair; if only we could figure out a way of reaching them during school hours.*

Marketer 1: *Wait a minute—maybe you're on to something. Why don't we show kids advertisements in their classrooms?*

Marketer 2: *Are you crazy? How are we going to show them ads during their English or math class? Teachers and principals would never stand for it.*

Marketer 1: *I think I've got a way . . .*

34 more cubic feet of nooks, niches, cubbyholes, crannies,

conveniences, comfort, cupholders and cargo room.

The New Dodge Caravan

Sound far-fetched? In 1990, "Channel One" was launched as a special news program broadcast via satellite to American schools. Whittle Communications offered hundreds of schools free video equipment if they agreed to show the 12-minute, daily news broadcasts to their students. The show consists of 10 minutes of news and 2 minutes of advertising. By 1992, nearly 40 percent of America's teenagers in school were watching Channel One—more than twice as many as watch popular television programs such as Beverly Hills, 90210 *(McGowan, 1993). Many companies jumped at the chance to pitch their products to captive audiences of teenagers, and by 1992 Whittle Communications was earning $100 million a year in advertising income.*

This might sound pretty harmless. After all, schools get much-needed equipment and kids see only a couple of advertisements a day. What are two more ads, on top of the hundreds people see already? One troubling finding is that advertisements shown in schools are especially powerful, because students believe that the schools endorse the advertised products (Toch, 1992). And as seen later in this chapter, there is evidence that advertising in general can be quite effective at shaping and changing people's attitudes.

How do advertisements try to change people's attitudes? Some go straight for the gut with the intent of manipulating your emotions, not your thoughts or beliefs. Many advertisements for perfume, soft drinks, and jeans, for example, tell you absolutely nothing about the product but try to associate it with good feelings—often sexual feelings. Other kinds of ads—such as those for mutual funds, CD players, or coffee makers—downplay emotions and instead throw lots of facts and figures at you. Often the same product can be advertised in either way. Consider the ad for the Dodge Caravan on this page. The ad is packed with facts and figures about cupholders, cubbyholes, and cargo room. At least for us, it evokes very little emotion. Compare it to other car ads you've seen that are just the opposite: They try hard to elicit feelings of freedom, autonomy, and sexual prowess. Meanwhile, they tell you nothing about the car.

Which type of ad works better? There seems to be little doubt that sex (and other emotions) sells. But surely facts and figures can be persuasive as well. More than likely, people's attitudes can be influenced in either way. Under some conditions, people are swayed by a logical consideration of the facts; under other conditions, people are swayed by appeals to their fears, hopes, and desires. What are these conditions? Exactly what is an attitude, and how is it changed? These questions, which are some of the oldest in social psychology, are the subject of this chapter.

The Nature and Origin of Attitudes

Though social psychologists do not completely concur on the precise definition of an **attitude**, most concur that it consists of an enduring evaluation—positive or negative—of people, objects, and ideas (Eagly & Chaiken, 1993; Olson & Zanna, 1993). Attitudes are enduring in the sense that they often persist over time. A momentary annoyance at something somebody says is not an attitude, but a lasting, negative impression of the person is. Attitudes are evaluative in the sense that they consist of a positive or negative reaction to something. People are not neutral observers of the world but constant evaluators of what they see (Bargh, Chaiken, Raymond, & Hymes, in press; Fazio, Sanbonmatsu, Powell, & Kardes, 1986). It would be very odd to hear someone say, "My feelings toward anchovies, snakes, chocolate cake, and my roommate are completely neutral."

attitude: an enduring evaluation—positive or negative—of people, objects, and ideas

Affective, Cognitive, and Behavioral Components

We can elaborate further on our definition of an attitude by stating more precisely what we mean by an "evaluation." Attitudes are made up of different components, or parts (Breckler, 1984; McGuire, 1985). Specifically, attitudes are made up of an affective component, consisting of your emotional reactions toward the attitude object (e.g., another person or a social issue); a cognitive component, consisting of your thoughts and beliefs about the attitude object; and a behavioral component, consisting of your actions or observable behavior toward the attitude object.

For example, consider your attitude toward a particular model of car. First, there is your affective reaction, or the emotions and feelings the car triggers. These feelings might be a sense of excitement and aesthetic pleasure when you see the car or feelings of anger and resentment (e.g., if you are a U.S. autoworker examining a new foreign-made model). Second, there is your cognitive reaction, or the beliefs you hold about the car's attributes. These might include your thoughts about the car's gas mileage, safety, steering and handling, and roominess. Third, there is your behavioral reaction, or how you act in regard to this type of car. For example, going to the dealership to test-drive the car and actually purchasing it are behaviors related to your attitude.

The Different Origins of Attitudes

Not all attitudes are created equally. Whereas attitudes have affective, cognitive, and behavioral components, any given attitude can be based more on one component than another (Zanna & Rempel, 1988). Sometimes our attitudes are based primarily on a perusal of the relevant facts, such as the objective merits of an automobile. How many miles to the gallon does it get? Does it have an air bag? To the extent that people's evaluation is based on beliefs such as these, we can say it is a **cognitively based attitude**. The function of such an attitude is "object appraisal," meaning that we classify objects according to the rewards and punishments they can provide (Katz, 1960; Smith, Bruner, & White, 1956). In other words, the purpose of this kind of attitude is to classify the pluses and minuses of an object so that we can quickly tell whether it is worth our while to have anything to do with it. Consider your attitude toward a utilitarian object like a vacuum cleaner. Your attitude is likely to be based on your beliefs about the

I only ask for information.

–Charles Dickens

We never desire passionately what we desire through reason alone.

–La Rochefoucauld, *Maxims*, 1678

cognitively based attitude: an attitude based primarily on people's beliefs about the properties of an attitude object affectively based attitude: an attitude based more on people's feelings and values than on their beliefs about the nature of an attitude object

objective merits of particular brands, such as how well they vacuum up dirt and how much they cost—not on how sexy they make you feel.

An attitude based more on emotions and values than on an objective appraisal of pluses and minuses is called an **affectively based attitude** (Breckler & Wiggins, 1989; Zanna & Rempel, 1988). Sometimes we simply like a certain brand of car, regardless of how many miles to the gallon it gets or whether it has an air bag. Occasionally we even feel very positively about something—such as another person—in spite of having negative beliefs. You have probably heard many songs about such feelings, such as Smokey Robinson's "You've Really Got a Hold on Me":

> That is the way we are made; we don't reason; where we feel, we just feel.
>
> –Mark Twain,
> *A Connecticut Yankee in King Arthur's Court*

> I don't like you, but I love you.
>
> Seems that I'm always, thinking of you.
>
> You treat me badly, I love you madly.
>
> You've really got a hold on me.

Interestingly, people's attitudes toward political candidates are often more affectively than cognitively based. People seem to vote more with their hearts than their minds, caring more about how they feel about a candidate than their beliefs about his or her specific policies (Abelson, Kinder, Peters, & Fiske, 1982; Granberg & Brown, 1989). In fact, Wattenberg (1987) estimates that one-third of the electorate knows virtually nothing about specific politicians but nonetheless has strong feelings about them!

If affectively based attitudes do not come from an examination of the facts, where do they come from? They have a variety of sources. First, they can stem from people's values, such as their basic religious and moral beliefs. People's feelings about such issues as abortion, the death penalty, and premarital sex are often based more on their values than on a logical examination of the facts. The function of such attitudes is not so much to paint an accurate picture of the world as

■ Prolife and prochoice activists argue in front of the U.S. Supreme Court. Some attitudes are based more on emotions and values than on facts and figures.

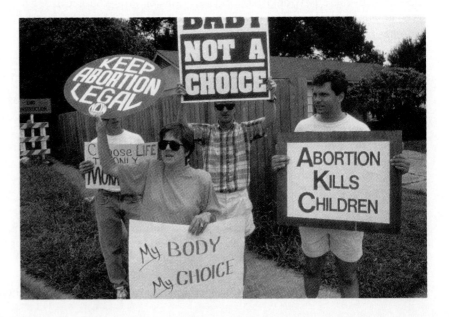

to express and validate one's basic value system (Katz, 1960; Maio & Olson, 1995; Schwartz, 1992; Smith, Bruner, & White, 1956; Snyder & DeBono, 1989).

Other affectively based attitudes can be the result of a sensory reaction, such as liking the taste of chocolate (despite how many calories it has!), or an aesthetic reaction, such as admiring a painting or the lines and color of a car. Still others can be the result of conditioning. **Classical conditioning** is the case in which a stimulus that elicits an emotional response is repeatedly experienced along with a neutral stimulus that does not, until the neutral stimulus takes on the emotional properties of the first stimulus. For example, suppose that when you were a child you experienced feelings of warmth and love when you visited your grandmother. Suppose also that there was always a faint smell of mothballs in the air at your grandmother's house. Eventually, the smell of mothballs themselves will trigger the emotions you experienced during your visits, through the process of classical conditioning.

In **instrumental conditioning**, behaviors that we freely choose to perform increase or decrease in frequency, depending on whether they are followed by positive reinforcement or punishment. How does this apply to attitudes? Imagine that a 4-year-old white girl goes to the playground with her father and chooses to play with an African American girl. Her father expresses strong disapproval, telling her, "We don't play with that kind of child." It won't take long before the child associates interacting with minorities with punishment, thereby adopting her father's racist attitudes. Attitudes can take on positive or negative affect through either classical or instrumental conditioning, as shown in Figure 7.1 (Cacioppo et al., 1992; Kuykendall & Keating, 1990).

Although affectively based attitudes can have varied sources, we can group them into one family, because they have certain key features in common: (a) They do not result from a rational examination of the issues; (b) they are not governed by logic (e.g., persuasive arguments about the issues seldom change an affectively based attitude); and (c) they are often linked to people's values, so that trying to change them challenges those values (Katz, 1960; Smith, et al., 1956).

classical conditioning: the case whereby a stimulus that elicits an emotional response is repeatedly experienced along with a neutral stimulus that does not, until the neutral stimulus takes on the emotional properties of the first stimulus

instrumental conditioning: the case whereby behaviors that people freely choose to perform increase or decrease in frequency, depending on whether they are followed by positive reinforcement or punishment

FIGURE 7.1   Classical and instrumental conditioning of attitudes. ■ Affectively based attitudes can result from either classical or instrumental conditioning.

behaviorally based attitude:
an attitude based on observations of how one behaves toward an attitude object

How can I know what I think till I see what I say?

–Graham Wallas,
The Art of Thought

attitude accessibility: the strength of the association between an object and a person's evaluation of that object; accessibility is measured by the speed with which people can report how they feel about an issue or object

Earlier we noted that attitudes have three components—cognitions, affect, and behavior. Just as an attitude can be based primarily on cognition or affect, so too can it be based primarily on behavior, resulting in a **behaviorally based attitude.** This may seem a little odd—how do we know how to behave if we don't already know how we feel? According to Daryl Bem's (1972) *self-perception theory*, under certain circumstances people don't know how they feel until they see how they behave. For example, suppose you asked a friend how much she enjoys exercising. If she replies, "Well, I guess I like it, because I always seem to be going for a run or heading over to the gym to work out," we would say she has a behaviorally based attitude. Her attitude is based more on an observation of her behavior than on her cognitions or affect.

As noted in Chapter 5, people infer their attitudes from their behavior only under certain conditions. First, their initial attitude has to be weak or ambiguous. If your friend already has a strong attitude toward exercising, she does not have to observe her behavior to infer how she feels about it. Second, people infer their attitudes from their behavior only when there are no other plausible explanations for their behavior. If your friend believes she exercises so as to lose weight or because her doctor has ordered her to, she is unlikely to assume that she runs and works out because she enjoys it.(See Chapter 5 for a more detailed description of self-perception theory.)

Attitude Strength and Accessibility

Not only do attitudes differ in their affective, cognitive, or behavioral origins; they also differ in their strength. This probably does not come as a surprise; for most of us, our attitude toward the current price of rutabagas is of much less importance, and held with much less conviction, than our religious views or our feelings toward a loved one. What might come as a surprise is that considerable disagreement exists among social psychologists about how best to define attitude strength. Some believe the key is how easily the attitude comes to mind (how accessible it is), whereas others believe the key is how important people think their attitude is, how knowledgeable they are about the attitude object, or how extreme their attitude is (Krosnick & Abelson, 1991; Petty & Krosnick, 1995; Pomerantz, Chaiken, & Tordesillas, 1995; Wood, 1982). Most definitions of attitude strength, however, agree that the stronger an attitude is, the more resistant to change it is. Let's see how this applies to attitude accessibility.

Consider this example: In a moment, we are going to give you the name of an object. When we do, simply think about that object for a few seconds. Ready? Here is the object: a mountain bike. What do you think? Did positive or negative feelings come to mind immediately, or did you think about a mountain bike without much feeling? These questions concern **attitude accessibility,** which Russell Fazio (1989, 1990, 1995) defines as the strength of the association between an object and your evaluation of it. If an attitude is highly accessible, then whenever you encounter the object your attitude comes to mind. For example, if your attitude toward mountain bikes is highly accessible, then as soon as you read the words, feelings of liking or disliking were triggered. If an attitude is relatively inaccessible, then feelings of liking or disliking came to mind more slowly.

Why is the accessibility of an attitude important? For one thing, as we will see toward the end of this chapter, it determines how likely people are to behave consistently with their attitude. Accessibility also influences how easily people change their attitudes. In general, the more accessible an attitude is—the more quickly it comes to mind—the harder that attitude is to change (Houston & Fazio, 1989).

How does an attitude become accessible? One way is through direct, repeated experience with the attitude object (Fazio & Zanna, 1981). The more times you have ridden a mountain bike, the more likely you are to associate positive or negative experiences with it, forming a strong association in your mind between "mountain bike" and these positive or negative feelings. Note that accessible attitudes can be positive or negative. After riding a bicycle down the side of a steep mountain, you might feel that it was the thrill of a lifetime, that it was only slightly preferable to visiting the dentist, or somewhere in between. The point is that when your attitude is behaviorally based, then whatever your feelings are, they will be accessible. In comparison, if you have only read about mountain bikes or watched other people ride them, you might have positive or negative reactions ("Gee, that looks like something I would enjoy") but these feelings will be much less accessible than those resulting from direct experience. In general, the more an attitude is behaviorally based, the more accessible and resistant to change it will be.

Attitude Change

Even though attitudes are more enduring than momentary whims or fancies, they do sometimes change. In America, for example, the popularity of the president often seems to rise and dip with surprising speed. Consider people's attitudes toward George Bush when he was president. In 1991, just after the Gulf War, nearly 90 percent of Americans approved of President Bush's performance. A mere one year later, as the country entered an economic recession, fewer than half

■ When an attitude is behaviorally based—such as this person's attitude toward mountain bikes—it is highly accessible and resistant to change.

of those polled approved of his performance. And in the presidential election of 1992, President Bush garnered only 38 percent of the vote.

When attitudes change, they often do so in response to social influence. Our attitudes toward everything from a presidential candidate to a brand of laundry detergent can be influenced by what other people do or say. This is why attitudes are of such interest to social psychologists—even something as personal and internal as an attitude is a highly social phenomenon, influenced by the imagined or actual behavior of other people. The entire premise of advertising, for example, is that your attitudes toward consumer products can be influenced by hearing someone say that new and improved Scrubadub detergent cleans clothes the best or by seeing a sexy model wearing a particular brand of jeans. Let's take a look at the conditions under which attitudes are most likely to change.

Changing Attitudes by Changing Behavior: Cognitive Dissonance Theory Revisited

We have already discussed one way that attitudes change: when people behave inconsistently with their attitudes and cannot find external justification for their behavior. We refer, of course, to *cognitive dissonance theory*. As we discussed in Chapter 6, people experience dissonance when they do something that threatens their image of themselves as decent, kind, and honest, particularly if there is no way they can explain away this behavior as due to external circumstances.

Consider an example we gave in Chapter 6. You walk into your friend Sam's house and notice an atrocious painting on the wall. You are about to burst into raucous laughter when Sam says, with a great deal of pleasure and excitement, "Do you like it? It's by a relatively unknown artist named Carol Smear; I think she is very talented, so I went into hock to buy it. Don't you think it's beautiful?"

How do you respond? You hesitate, your mind racing. "Sam seems so happy and excited. Why should I rain on his parade? If I tell him my honest opinion, I'll hurt his feelings; he might get mad. I might make him feel that he made a terrible mistake. Anyway, he can't take it back. What's the sense in telling him the truth?" So you tell Sam that you like the painting very much. Do you experience much dissonance? We doubt it. There are a great many thoughts that are consonant with having told this lie, as outlined in your reasoning in the above sentences. For example, your cognition that it is important not to cause pain to people you like provides ample *external justification* for having told a harmless lie.

But what happens if you say something you don't really believe and there is no ample external justification for doing so? What if your friend Sam was fabulously wealthy and bought paintings constantly? In addition, what if you were a noted art historian whose opinion Sam valued? What if, in the past, you'd told him he'd bought a veritable eyesore and your friendship had survived? Now the external justifications for lying to Sam about the painting are minimal. If you still refrain from giving your true opinion (saying instead, "Gee, Sam, it's, uh . . . interesting"), you will experience dissonance.

When you can't find external justification for your behavior, you will attempt to find *internal justification*—by bringing the two cognitions (your attitude and your behavior) closer together. How do you do this? You begin looking for positive aspects of the painting—some evidence of creativity or sophistication that might have escaped you previously. Chances are that if you look hard enough, you will find something. Within a short time, your attitude toward the painting will

> By persuading others, we convince ourselves.
> –Junius, 1769

have moved in the direction of the positive statement you have made, and that is how "saying is believing." This phenomenon is generally referred to as *counterattitudinal advocacy*: a process by which individuals are induced to state publicly an opinion or attitude that runs counter to their own private attitudes. When this is accomplished with a minimum of external justification, it results in a change in the individual's private attitude in the direction of the public statement.

As we saw in Chapter 6, there is substantial evidence that counterattitudinal advocacy is a powerful way to change someone's attitudes. If you wanted to change a friend's attitude toward smoking, you might succeed by getting him or her to give an antismoking speech, under conditions of low external justification. But what if your goal was to change attitudes on a mass scale? Suppose you were hired by the American Cancer Society to come up with an antismoking campaign that could be used nationwide. Though dissonance techniques are powerful, they are very difficult to carry out on a mass scale (e.g., it would be hard to have all American smokers make antismoking speeches under just the right conditions of low external justification). In order to change as many people's attitudes as possible, you would have to resort to other techniques of attitude change. You probably would construct some sort of **persuasive communication** or message that could be broadcast or published in the mass media. How should you construct your message so that it would really change people's attitudes?

> **persuasive communication:** communication (e.g., a speech or television ad) advocating a particular side of an issue

Persuasive Communications and Attitude Change

Suppose the American Cancer Society has given you a five-figure budget to develop your advertising campaign. You have a lot of decisions ahead of you. Should you pack your public service announcement with facts and figures? Or should you take a more emotional approach, including in your message frighten-

■ If you were buying a bass guitar, you would probably be more persuaded by Flea, bass player for the Red Hot Chili Peppers, than by a less credible source.

ing visual images of diseased lungs? Should you hire a famous movie star to deliver your message, or a Nobel Prize–winning medical researcher? Should you take a friendly tone and acknowledge that it is hard to quit smoking, or should you take a hard line and tell smokers to (as the Nike ads put it) "just do it"? You can see the point—it's not easy to figure out how to construct a truly persuasive communication.

Luckily, social psychologists have conducted many studies over the past 50 years on what makes a persuasive communication effective, beginning with Carl Hovland and his colleagues (Hovland, Janis, & Kelley, 1953). Because these researchers were at Yale University, this approach to the study of persuasive communications is known as the **Yale Attitude Change approach.** Drawing on their experiences during World War II, when they worked for the U.S. armed forces to increase the morale of U.S. soldiers (Stouffer et al., 1949), Hovland and his colleagues conducted many experiments on the conditions under which people are most likely to be influenced by persuasive communications. In essence, they studied "who says what to whom," looking at the *source of the communication* (e.g., how expert or attractive the speaker is), *the communication itself* (e.g., the quality of the arguments; whether the speaker presents both sides of the issue), and *the nature of the audience* (e.g., which kinds of appeals work with hostile versus friendly audiences).

The Yale Attitude Change approach yielded a great deal of useful information on how people change their attitudes in response to persuasive communications; some of this information is summarized in Figure 7.2. As the research mounted, however, a problem became apparent: Many aspects of persuasive communications turned out to be important, but it was not clear which were more important than others—that is, when one factor should be emphasized over another.

For example, let's return to that job you have with the American Cancer Society—they want to see their ad next month! If you were to read the many Yale Attitude Change studies, you might find lots of useful information about who should say what to whom in order to construct a persuasive communication. However, you might also find yourself saying, "Gee, there's an awful lot of information here, and I'm not sure where I should place the most emphasis: Should I worry most about who delivers the ads? Or should I worry more about the content of the message itself?"

The Central and Peripheral Routes to Persuasion. If you asked these questions, you would be in good company. Some well-known attitude researchers have wondered the same thing: When is it best to stress factors central to the communication—such as the strength of the arguments—and when is it best to stress factors peripheral to the logic of the arguments—such as the credibility or attractiveness of the person delivering the speech? This question has been answered by two influential theories of persuasive communication: Shelly Chaiken's (1987) *heuristic-systematic persuasion model* and Richard Petty and John Cacioppo's (1986) *elaboration likelihood model.* These theories specify when people will be influenced by what the speech says (i.e., the logic of the arguments) and when they will be influenced by more superficial characteristics (e.g., who gives the speech or how long it is). The theories have much in common; to avoid confusion, we will discuss here the ideas in the terminology of the **elaboration likelihood model,** and will return later to some of the specifics of the heuristic-systematic persuasion model.

Yale Attitude Change approach: the study of the conditions under which people are most likely to change their attitudes in response to persuasive messages; researchers in this tradition focus on "who said what to whom"—that is, on the source of the communication, the nature of the communication, and the nature of the audience

elaboration likelihood model: the theory that there are two ways in which persuasive communications can cause attitude change; the central route occurs when people are motivated and have the ability to pay attention to the arguments in the communication, and the peripheral route occurs when people do not pay attention to the arguments but are instead swayed by surface characteristics (e.g., who gave the speech)

THE YALE ATTITUDE CHANGE APPROACH

Who: The Source of the Communication

■ Credible speakers (e.g., those with obvious expertise) persuade people more than speakers lacking in credibility (Hovland & Weiss, 1951).

■ Attractive speakers (whether due to physical or personality attributes) persuade people more than unattractive speakers do (Eagly & Chaiken, 1975).

What: The Nature of the Communication

■ People are more persuaded by messages that do not seem to be designed to influence them (Walter & Festinger, 1962).

■ When the audience generally supports your position, it is best to present a one-sided communication (one that presents only arguments favoring your position). When the audience disagrees with your position, it is best to present a two-sided communication and then refute the arguments that are opposed to your position (Hovland, Lumsdaine, & Sheffield, 1949).

■ Is it best to give your speech before or after someone arguing for the other side? If the speeches are to be given back to back and there will be a delay before people have to make up their minds, it is best to go first. Under these conditions, there is likely to be a *primacy effect*, wherein people are more influenced by what they hear first. If there is a delay between the speeches and people will make up their minds right after hearing the second one, it is best to go last. Under these conditions, there is likely to be a *recency effect*, wherein people remember the second speech better than the first one (Miller & Campbell, 1959).

To Whom: The Nature of the Audience

■ An audience that is distracted during the persuasive communication will often be persuaded more than one that is not (Festinger & Maccoby, 1964).

■ People are particularly susceptible to attitude change during the impressionable ages of 18 to 25. Beyond those ages, people's attitudes are more stable and resistant to change (Krosnick & Alwin, 1989; Sears, 1981).

FIGURE 7.2   The Yale Attitude Change approach. ■ The effectiveness of persuasive communications depends on *who says what to whom.*

> Of the modes of persuasion furnished by the spoken word there are three kinds. The first kind depends on the personal character of the speaker; the second on putting the audience into a certain frame of mind; the third on the proof, or apparent proof, provided by the words of the speech itself.
> —Aristotle, *Rhetoric*

> Now, what I want is facts . . . Facts alone are wanted in life.
> —Charles Dickens, *Hard Times*

Both theories state that, under certain conditions, people are motivated to pay attention to the facts in a communication, thus they will be most persuaded when these facts are logically compelling. That is, sometimes people elaborate on what they hear, carefully thinking about and processing the content of the communication. Petty and Cacioppo (1986) call this the **central route to persuasion.** Under other conditions, people are not motivated to pay attention to the facts; instead, they notice only the surface characteristics of the message, such as how long it is and who is delivering it. Here people will not be swayed by the logic of the arguments, because they are not paying close attention to what the communicator says. Instead, they are persuaded if the surface characteristics of the message—such as the fact that it is long or is delivered by an expert or attractive communicator—make it seem like a reasonable one. Petty and Cacioppo (1986) call this the **peripheral route to persuasion,** because people are swayed by things peripheral to the message itself.

central route to persuasion: the case whereby people elaborate on a persuasive communication, listening carefully to and thinking about the arguments; this occurs when people have both the ability and the motivation to listen carefully to a communication

peripheral route to persuasion: the case whereby people do not elaborate on the arguments in a persuasive communication but are instead swayed by peripheral cues

FIGURE 7.3 ■ The elaboration likelihood model describes how people change their attitudes when they hear persuasive communications.

What are the conditions under which people take the central versus the peripheral route to persuasion? The key, according to Richard Petty, John Cacioppo, and Shelly Chaiken, is whether people have the motivation and ability to pay attention to the facts. To the extent that people are truly interested in the topic and thus motivated to pay close attention to the arguments, they are more likely to take the central route. Similarly, if people have the ability to pay attention—for example, if nothing is distracting them—they are more likely to take the central route (see Figure 7.3).

The Motivation to Pay Attention to the Arguments. A significant determinant of whether people are motivated to pay attention to a communication is the personal relevance of the topic, namely the extent to which a topic has important consequences for a person's well-being. For example, consider the issue of whether Social Security benefits should be reduced. How personally relevant is this to you? If you are a 72-year-old whose sole income is from Social Security, this issue is obviously extremely relevant; if you are a 20-year-old from a well-to-do family, the issue has little personal relevance.

The more personally relevant an issue is, the more willing people are to pay attention to the arguments in a speech, and thus the more likely people are to take the central route to persuasion. Richard Petty, John Cacioppo, and Rachel Goldman (1981) demonstrated this point by asking college students to listen to a speech arguing that all college seniors should be required to pass a comprehensive exam in their major before they graduate. Half of the participants were told that their university was currently giving serious thought to requiring comprehensive exams; thus, for these participants the issue was personally relevant. For the other half, the issue was of the "hohum" variety—the students were told that their university was considering requiring the exams but not for ten years.

The researchers then introduced two variables that might influence whether people would agree with the speech. The first was the strength of the arguments presented. Half the participants heard arguments that were strong and persuasive (e.g., "The quality of undergraduate teaching has improved at schools with the exams"), whereas the others heard arguments that were weak and unpersuasive (e.g., "The risk of failing the exam is a challenge most students would welcome"). The second variable concerned the prestige of the source of the speech: Half the participants were told that the author was an eminent professor at Princeton University, whereas the others were told that the author was a high school student.

Thus, when deciding how much to agree with the position advocated by the speaker, the participants could use one or both of these different kinds of information. They could listen carefully to the arguments and scrutinize how convincing they were, or they could simply go by who said them (i.e., how prestigious the source was). As predicted by the elaboration likelihood model, the way in which people were persuaded depended on the personal relevance of the issue. The left-hand panel of Figure 7.4 shows what happened when the issue was highly relevant to the listeners. These students were very much influenced by the quality of the arguments (i.e., persuasion occurred via the central route). Those who heard strong arguments agreed much more with the speech than those who heard weak arguments did. They were decidedly unimpressed by who presented the arguments (the Princeton professor or the high school student). A good argument was a good argument, even if it was written by someone who lacked prestige.

What happens when a topic is of low relevance to people? As seen in the right-hand panel of Figure 7.3, what mattered was not the strength of the arguments but who the speaker was. Those who heard the strong arguments agreed with the speech only slightly more than those who heard the weak arguments, whereas those who heard the Princeton professor were much more swayed than those who heard the high school student.

This finding reflects a general rule: When an issue is personally relevant, people will pay attention to the arguments in a speech and will be persuaded to the extent that the arguments are sound—the "proof" of the speech, in Aristotle's words. When an issue is of low personal relevance, people will not pay as close attention to the arguments. Instead, they will take a mental shortcut, following such peripheral rules as "Prestigious speakers can be trusted" or "Length implies strong arguments" (Chaiken, 1987; Chaiken, Liberman, & Eagly, 1989; Petty & Cacioppo, 1986).

In addition to the personal relevance of a topic, people's motivation to pay attention to a speech depends on their personality. People who enjoy carefully thinking things through more than others do are said to be high in the **need for cognition** (Cacioppo, Petty, Feinstein, & Jarvis, 1996). Such people are more

> The ability to kill or capture a man is a relatively simple task compared with changing his mind.
> –Richard Cohen, *Washington Post*, February 28, 1991

> I'm not convinced by proofs but signs.
> –Coventry Patmore

need for cognition: a personality variable reflecting the extent to which people desire to seek out and think about information in their social worlds

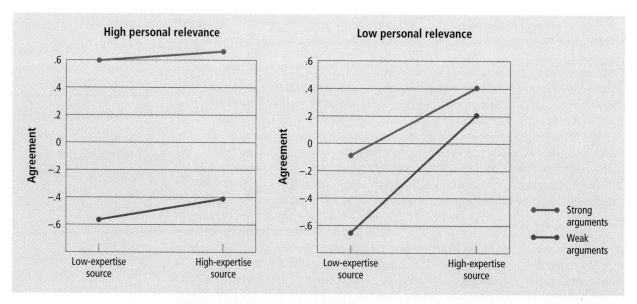

FIGURE 7.4   Effects of personal relevance on type of attitude change. ■ The higher the number, the more people agreed with the persuasive communication—namely, that their university should adopt comprehensive exams. *Left panel:* When the issue was highly relevant, people were swayed by the quality of the arguments more than the expertise of the speaker. This is the central route to persuasion. *Right panel:* When the issue was low in relevance, people were swayed by the expertise of the speaker more than the quality of the arguments. This is the peripheral route to persuasion. (Adapted from Petty & Cacioppo, 1986, based on a study by Petty, Cacioppo, & Goldman, 1981)

likely to form their attitudes by paying close attention to relevant arguments (i.e., via the central route), whereas people low in the need for cognition are more likely to rely on peripheral cues, such as how attractive or credible a speaker is.

The Ability to Pay Attention to the Arguments.   Sometimes even if we want to pay attention to a speech, it is difficult to do so. Maybe we're tired; maybe we're distracted by an annoying construction noise outside the window; maybe the issue is too complex and hard to evaluate. Under such circumstances, people are unable to pay close attention to the arguments and thus are swayed more by peripheral cues (Festinger & Maccoby, 1964; Petty & Brock, 1981; Petty, Wells, & Brock, 1976). For example, a few years ago an exchange of letters appeared in Ann Landers's advice column about whether drugs such as cocaine and marijuana should be legalized. Readers from across the country wrote in with all sorts of compelling arguments on both sides of the issue, and it was difficult to figure out which arguments had the most merit. One reader resolved this dilemma by relying less on the content of the arguments than on the prestige and expertise of the source of the arguments. The reader noted that several eminent people have supported the legalization of drugs, including a Princeton professor who wrote in the prestigious publication Science; the economist Milton Friedman; Kurt Schmoke, the former mayor of Baltimore; columnist William F. Buckley; and former Secretary of State George Schultz. The reader decided to support legalization as well, not because of the strength of pro-legalization arguments he or she had read, but because that's the way several experts felt—a clear case of the peripheral route to persuasion.

Thus, if you are worried that your message is rather weak, you might consider distracting your audience—maybe by arranging for some construction noise just outside the room in which you are speaking. If your arguments are strong and convincing, however, make sure you have your audience's full attention, so that they can listen to (and be swayed by) your arguments.

How to Achieve Long-Lasting Attitude Change.   Now that you know a persuasive communication can change people's attitudes in either of two ways— via the central or the peripheral route—you may be wondering what difference it makes. Does it really matter whether it was the logic of the arguments or the expertise of the source that changed students' minds about comprehensive exams in the Petty and colleagues (1981) study? Given the bottom line—they changed their attitudes—why should any of us care how they got to that point?

If we are interested in creating long-lasting attitude change, then we should care a lot. People who base their attitudes on a careful analysis of the arguments will be more likely to maintain this attitude over time, more likely to behave consistently with this attitude, and more resistant to counterpersuasion than people who base their attitudes on peripheral cues. For example, Shelly Chaiken (1980) conducted an experiment in which people changed their attitudes either by analyzing the logic of the arguments or by using peripheral cues. She accomplished this in the same way Petty, Cacioppo, and Goldman (1981) did—namely, by making the issue relevant to the former group but not to the latter. Chaiken telephoned the research participants ten days later to see if their attitude change had persisted. As predicted, people were more likely to have maintained their new attitude if they had formed it by analyzing the strength of the arguments in the communication—that is, if their attitude change had occurred via the central route.

Emotion and Attitude Change

If you are trying to create long-lasting attitude change, you should thus construct strong arguments and then get people to scrutinize and think about those arguments so that change occurs via the central route. Sounds pretty straightforward, doesn't it? You now know how to construct your ad for the American Cancer Society and will soon be able to pick up your check for your efforts. Right? Well, this approach can work, but there's a problem: Before people will consider your carefully constructed arguments, you will first have to get their attention. If you are going to show your antismoking ad on television, for example, how can you be sure people will watch the ad when it comes on, instead of changing the channel or heading for the refrigerator? One way is to grab people's attention by playing to their emotions. As we saw earlier, many advertisements do not simply present facts and figures—they go for the gut, evoking such feelings as fear, lust, or a general, fuzzy feeling of warmth and sentimentality. Does this approach work? As it turns out, there are several ways in which emotions can influence attitude change.

Emotion Influences the Route to Persuasion.   One interesting consequence of playing to people's emotions is that doing so can determine whether they pay close attention to the arguments in a speech (the central route) or take mental shortcuts (the peripheral route). For example, suppose things are really going your way one day, and you're feeling great. You pick up a copy of the student newspaper and glance at an editorial, written by the president of the student council, about a proposed increase in student fees. Are you likely to pore over every word in the editorial and carefully analyze the merits of each and every argument? Or will you give it a cursory glance and think, "Hey, whatever she says is cool with me." What if you are feeling kind of sad that day? Will you read the editorial carefully, or just take the author's word for it?

It turns out that when people are in good moods, they want to continue feeling that way; thus, they avoid activities—such as going to the effort to read an article very carefully—that are likely to spoil their moods (Isen, 1987). Good moods reduce people's motivation and ability to pay attention to arguments in a message, and, as we saw earlier, these are the exact conditions for the peripheral route to persuasion. Thus, if you are feeling great you are likely to glance at the newspaper editorial and take the author's word for it, without going to the effort to think carefully about all of her arguments. But if you are in a sad or a neutral mood, you are more likely to take the central route, analyzing each argument in detail.

To illustrate this point, let's consider a study by Herbert Bless, Gerd Bohner, Norbert Schwarz, and Fritz Strack (1990), who put college students in temporarily good or bad moods by having them write about happy or sad events in their lives. Then, as part of what was supposedly another study, the researchers had people listen to a speech arguing that student fees at their university should be increased. In one condition the speech contained strong, well-reasoned arguments, whereas in another condition the speech contained weak, poorly reasoned arguments. The results were clear: People in a sad mood paid close attention to the arguments and thus changed their attitudes when the arguments were strong but not when the arguments were weak (see left-hand side of Figure 7.5). People in a good mood paid relatively little attention to the strength of the arguments. They seemed to take the speaker's word for it regardless of how strong the arguments were, and thus they were no more convinced when the arguments were strong than when the arguments were weak (see right-hand side of Figure 7.5). Other studies have shown that people in good moods are more likely to rely on peripheral cues, such as agreeing with speakers who are experts (Sinclair, Mark, & Clore, 1994; Worth & Mackie, 1987). This is especially likely to be true when people think that paying attention to the message will ruin their good mood (Wegener, Petty, & Smith, 1995).

FIGURE 7.5 Effects of mood on attitude change. ■ People in a sad mood paid attention to a speech, and thus were more convinced when the arguments were strong (see left-hand side of figure). People in a happy mood paid less attention to the speech, and thus were equally convinced by weak and strong arguments (see right-hand side of figure). (Adapted from Bless, Bohner, Schwarz, & Strack, 1990)

■ How do people's moods influence the way in which their attitudes change? People who are in good moods often do not want to pay close attention to the content of persuasive communication, and thus they change their attitudes via the peripheral route.

In the study by Bless and colleagues (1990), people who were sad analyzed the message more carefully. What about other kinds of bad moods, such as being anxious, agitated, or afraid—what effect does this have on attitude change? By far the most research has examined the effects of fear on attitude change. Scaring people is one of the most common techniques for trying to change attitudes. When we asked you earlier how you would get people's attention when presenting your antismoking ad, it might have crossed your mind to use fear as your "hook." Public service ads often take this approach by trying to scare people into practicing safer sex, wearing their seatbelt, and staying away from drugs. We suspect that the use of fear to change attitudes has been around for as long as parents have been worried about their children ("Don't stray off the jungle path, Junior, or the tigers will tear you to pieces!").

Do **fear-arousing communications** work? The answer lies in the extent to which fear influences people's ability to pay attention to and process the arguments in a message. If a moderate amount of fear is created and people believe that listening to the message will teach them how to reduce this fear, then they will be motivated to analyze the message carefully, changing their attitudes via

fear-arousing communications: persuasive messages that attempt to change people's attitudes by arousing their fears

■ Here are two fear-arousing communications that differ in the extent to which they offer recommendations about how to change behavior. Which one is most likely to cause lasting changes in behavior?

the central route (Petty, 1995; Rogers, 1983). Consider a study by Howard Leventhal and his colleagues (Leventhal, Watts, & Pagano, 1967), who showed a group of smokers a graphic film depicting lung cancer and gave them pamphlets with specific instructions about how to quit smoking. As seen in the top line in Figure 7.6, the members of this group reduced their smoking significantly more than people who were shown only the film or only the pamphlet. Why? Seeing the film made people scared, and giving them the pamphlet reassured them that there was a way to reduce this fear—by following the instructions on how to quit. Seeing only the pamphlet didn't work very well, because little fear was motivating people to read it carefully. Seeing only the film didn't work very well either, for people are likely to tune out a message that raises fear but does not give information about how to allay it. This may explain why some attempts to frighten people into changing their attitudes and behaviors have not been very successful: They succeed in scaring people but do not provide specific recommendations for people to follow so that they can reduce their fear (Becker & Josephs, 1988; DeJong & Winsten, 1989; Job, 1988; Soames, 1988).

Fear-arousing appeals will also fail if they are too strong, such that people feel very threatened. If people are scared to death, they will become very defensive, will deny the importance of the threat, and will be unable to think very rationally about the issue (Janis & Feshbach, 1953; Jepson & Chaiken, 1990; Liberman & Chaiken, 1992). And so, if you have decided to arouse people's fear in your ad for the American Cancer Society, keep these points in mind: First, try to create enough fear to motivate people to pay attention to your arguments but

FIGURE 7.6   Effects of fear appeals on attitude change. ■ People were shown a scary film about the effects of smoking, instructions about how to stop smoking, or both. Those who were shown both reduced the number of cigarettes they smoked the most. (Adapted from Leventhal, Watts, & Pagano, 1967)

not so much fear that people will tune out or distort what you say. Second, include some specific recommendations about how to stop smoking, so that people will be reassured that paying close attention to your arguments will help them reduce their fear.

Emotions as a Heuristic.   Another way in which emotions can cause attitude change is by acting as a signal as to how we feel about an issue. According to Shelly Chaiken's (1987) **heuristic-systematic model of persuasion,** when people take the peripheral route to persuasion they often use heuristics. Recall that in Chapter 3 we defined heuristics as mental shortcuts people use to make judgments quickly and efficiently; in the present context, a heuristic can be viewed as a simple decision rule people use to decide what their attitude is, without having to spend a lot of time analyzing every little fact about the matter. Examples of such heuristics are "Length equals strength" (i.e., long messages are more persuasive than short ones) and "Experts are always right" (i.e., experts know what they are talking about).

Interestingly, our emotions and moods can themselves act as a heuristic to determine our attitudes. When trying to decide what our attitude is about something, we often rely on the "How do I feel about it?" heuristic (Forgas, 1995; Schwarz & Clore, 1988). If we feel good, we must have a positive attitude; if we feel bad, it's thumbs down. Now this probably sounds like a pretty good rule to follow, and, like most heuristics, it is—most of the time. Suppose you're at a Ford dealership checking out the new Taurus and trying to decide if you prefer it to the Toyota Corolla. If you use the "How do I feel about it?" heuristic, you do a quick check of your feelings and emotions. If you feel great while you're sitting in the driver's seat of the new Taurus, you decide that you like it a lot.

The only problem is that sometimes it is difficult to tell where our feelings come from. Is it really the Taurus that made you feel great, or is it something completely unrelated to cars? Maybe you were in a really good mood to begin with, or maybe on the way to the dealership you heard your favorite song on the radio. The problem with the "How do I feel about it" heuristic is that we can make mistakes about what is causing our mood. Sound familiar? In Chapter 5 we talked about *misattribution,* which is what happens when we think our feelings are coming from one source when they are really coming from another source. If people misattribute a prior good mood to something they are considering buying, they might get into trouble. Once they get the new car home, they might discover that the thrill is gone. From the point of view of advertisers, the goal is to create good feelings while they present their product (e.g., by playing appealing music or showing pleasant images), in the hope that people will attribute at least some of those feelings to the product the advertisers are trying to sell.

Emotion and Attitudes of Different Origins.   So far, we have been talking about the way in which persuasive communications and emotions influence attitude change in general. A question we have not considered is whether the success of different attitude change techniques depends on the type of attitude we are trying to change. For example, imagine you are about to listen to a speech, filled with facts and figures, that is opposed to one of your attitudes. Suppose you are at a college that does not require seniors to take comprehensive exams, and the speaker is going to try to convince you that it should—in time for you to take the exams before you graduate. Because this issue is of considerable personal

heuristic-systematic model of persuasion: the theory that there are two ways in which persuasive communications can cause attitude change; people either systematically process the merits of the arguments or use mental shortcuts (heuristics), such as "Length equals strength" relevance, you are likely to listen to the speech carefully. According to what we have seen so far, if the arguments are logically sound you are likely to change your attitude, becoming more favorable toward the idea of comprehensive exams. Indeed, this is what Petty, Cacioppo, and Goldman (1981) found (see Figure 7.3).

Now imagine the same scenario, except that the speech is concerned with a different topic: your choice of religion. The speech will challenge your religious beliefs and here again is filled with facts and figures. How likely do you think you are to change your religion after listening to the speech? Probably not very likely. But why? After all, this topic is certainly personally relevant. What exactly is it about your attitude toward religion that makes it more resistant to change than your attitude toward comprehensive exams? As we saw earlier not all attitudes are created equally; some are based more on beliefs about the attitude object (cognitively based attitudes) whereas others are based more on emotions and values (affectively based attitudes). Attitudes toward such things as religion are more likely to be based on emotion and values than on facts and arguments.

How can we change affectively based attitudes? This is an important question, because many consequential attitudes are affectively based. Prejudiced feelings toward minority groups are often based on values and emotions, as are people's views on such controversial issues as abortion, premarital sex, and politics. (As a guide to which attitudes are likely to be affectively based, consider the topics that etiquette manuals suggest should not be discussed at a dinner party: politics, sex, and religion.) If presenting people with logical arguments won't work, what will?

One approach that has been found to work is to fight fire with fire: If an attitude is based on rational arguments, try to change it with rational arguments. If it is based on affect, try to change it with affect (Edwards, 1990; Edwards & von

■ If people's attitudes are cognitively based (as they probably are for the printer), then persuasive communications should focus on cognitions. If the attitudes are affectively based (as they probably are for the perfume), then the persuasive communications should play on the viewer's emotions.

Hippel, 1995; Shavitt, 1989; Snyder & DeBono, 1989). Thus, if you want to use emotions to try to change attitudes, you should pay attention to the type of attitude you are trying to change.

Sharon Shavitt (1990) has demonstrated this point in a study of the effectiveness of different kinds of advertisements. Some ads, she notes, stress the objective merits of a product, such as an ad for an air conditioner or a vacuum cleaner that discusses its price, efficiency, and reliability. Other ads stress emotions and values, such as ones for perfume or designer jeans that try to associate their brands with sex, beauty, and youthfulness, rather than saying anything about the objective qualities of the product. Which kind of ad is most effective?

To find out, Shavitt gave people different kinds of advertisements for different kinds of consumer products. Some of the items were ones Shavitt called utilitarian products, such as air conditioners and coffee. People's attitudes toward such products tend to be based on an appraisal of the utilitarian aspects of the products (e.g., how energy-efficient an air conditioner is), and thus are cognitively based. The other items were ones Shavitt called social identity products, such as perfume and greeting cards. People's attitudes toward these types of products are based more on their values and concerns about their social identity, and so are more affectively based.

As seen in Figure 7.7, people reacted most favorably to the ads that matched the type of attitude they had. If people's attitudes were cognitively based (e.g., toward air conditioners or coffee), then the ads that focused on the utilitarian aspects of these products, such as the features of the air conditioner, were most

> It is useless to attempt to reason a man out of a thing he was never reasoned into.
> —Jonathan Swift

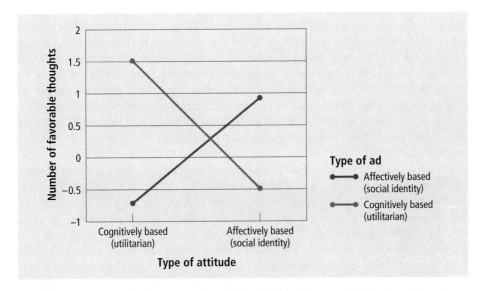

FIGURE 7.7   Effects of affective and cognitive information on affectively and cognitively based attitudes. ■ When people had cognitively based attitudes (e.g., toward air conditioners and coffee), then cognitively based advertisements that stressed the utilitarian aspects of the products worked best. When people had more affectively based attitudes (e.g., toward perfume and greeting cards), then affectively based advertisements that stressed values and social identity worked best. (The higher the number, the more favorable thoughts people listed about the products after reading the advertisements.) (Adapted from Shavitt, 1990)

successful. If people's attitudes were more affectively based (e.g., toward perfume or greeting cards), then the ads that focused on values and social identity concerns were most successful. The graph displayed in Figure 7.6 shows the number of favorable thoughts people had in response to the different kinds of ads. Similar results were found on a measure of how much people intended to buy the products. Thus, if you ever get a job in advertising, the moral is to know what type of attitude most people have toward your product and then tailor your advertising accordingly.

Culture and Different Types of Attitudes.   Shavitt (1990) found that people have different kinds of attitudes toward different kinds of consumer products (e.g., air conditioners versus perfume). Is it possible that there are differences across cultures in the kinds of attitudes people have toward the same products? As we discussed in Chapter 5, there are differences in people's self-concept across cultures; maybe these differences influence the kinds of attitudes people have and thus how those attitudes change. Recall that Western cultures tend to stress independence and individualism, whereas many Asian cultures stress interdependence and collectivism.

Sang-pil Han and Sharon Shavitt (1994) reasoned that these differences in self-concept might also reflect differences in the kinds of attitudes people have toward consumer products. Perhaps people in Western cultures base their attitudes more on concerns about individuality and self-improvement, whereas people in Asian cultures base their attitudes more on concerns about their standing in their social group, such as their families. If so, then advertisements that stress individuality and self-improvement might work better in Western cultures, whereas advertisements that stress one's social group might work better in Asian cultures. To test their hypothesis, Han and Shavitt (1994) created ads for the same product that stressed independence (e.g., an ad for shoes said, "It's easy when you have the right shoes") or interdependence (e.g., "The shoes for your family") and showed them to both Americans and Koreans. Americans were persuaded most by the ads stressing independence; Koreans were persuaded most by the ads stressing interdependence. The researchers also analyzed actual magazine advertisements in the United States and Korea and found that these ads were in fact different: American ads tended to emphasize individuality, self-improvement, and benefits of the product for the individual consumer, whereas Korean ads tended to emphasize the family, concerns about others, and benefits for one's social group.

In general, then, advertisements work best if they are tailored to the kind of attitude they are trying to change. Within a culture, some attitudes are more cognitively based, whereas others are more affectively based. There are differences across cultures as well, in that people in Western societies are more likely to base their attitudes on individualistic concerns, whereas people in Asian cultures are more likely to base their attitudes on collectivistic concerns.

How to Make People Resistant to Attitude Change

By now, you are no doubt getting nervous (and not just because the chapter hasn't ended yet): With all these clever methods available to change your attitudes, are you ever safe from persuasive communications? Indeed you are, or at least you can be, if you initiate some clever strategies of your own. Here's how to make sure all of those persuasive messages that bombard you don't turn you into a quivering mass of constantly changing opinion.

Attitude Inoculation

One approach is to get people to consider the arguments for and against their attitude before someone attacks it. The more people have thought about pro and con arguments beforehand, the better they can ward off attempts to change their minds using logical arguments. If people have not thought much about the issue—that is, if they formed their attitude via the peripheral route—they are particularly susceptible to an attack on that attitude using logical appeals.

William McGuire (1964) demonstrated this fact by using what he called **attitude inoculation**. His idea was that to prevent people from being influenced by a persuasive speech, they should be "inoculated" against the arguments they were likely to hear, by receiving a small dose of these arguments in advance. Having considered the arguments beforehand, people should thus be relatively immune to the effects of the communication, just as exposing people to a small amount of a virus can inoculate them against exposure to the full-blown viral disease.

In one study, for example, McGuire "inoculated" people by giving them brief arguments against cultural truisms, or beliefs that most members of a society believe uncritically, such as the idea that we should brush our teeth after every meal. Two days later, people came back and read a much stronger attack on the truism, one that contained a series of logical arguments about why brushing your teeth too frequently is a bad idea. The people who had been inoculated against these arguments were much less likely to change their attitudes than a control group who had not been. Why? Those inoculated with weak arguments had the opportunity to think about why these arguments were unfounded and therefore were in a better position to contradict the stronger attack they heard two days later. The control group, never having considered why people should or should not brush their teeth frequently, was particularly susceptible to the strong communication arguing that they should not.

As we have seen, many attacks on our attitudes consist not of logical arguments but of appeals to our emotions. Is there some way of warding off this kind of opinion change, just as we can ward off the effects of logical appeals? This is an important question, because many critical changes in attitudes and behaviors occur not in response to logic but via more emotional appeals. Consider the way in which many adolescents begin to smoke, drink, or take drugs. Often they do so in response to pressure from their peers, at an age when they are particularly susceptible to such pressure. For example, one study found that the best predictor of whether an adolescent smokes marijuana is whether he or she has a friend who does so (Yamaguchi & Kandel, 1984).

Think about how this occurs. It is not as if peers present a set of logical arguments ("Hey, Jake—did you know that recent studies show that moderate drinking may have health benefits?"). Instead, peer pressure is linked more to people's values and emotions, playing on their fear of rejection and their desire for freedom and autonomy. In adolescence, peers become an important source of social approval—perhaps the most important—and can dispense powerful rewards for holding certain attitudes or behaving in certain ways, such as using drugs or engaging in unprotected sex. What is needed is a technique that will make young

attitude inoculation: the process of making people immune to attempts to change their attitudes by initially exposing them to small doses of the arguments against their position

The chief effect of talk on any subject is to strengthen one's own opinions and, in fact, one never knows exactly what he does believe until he is warmed into conviction by the heat of the attack and defense.
–Charles Dudley Warner, *Backlog Studies*, 1873

■ Attitudes spread by peer pressure can be very persuasive, because they appeal to people's emotions—to their desire to be liked and accepted. By being inoculated against such appeals, young people may learn to resist persuasion via peer pressure.

> A companion's words of persuasion are effective.
>
> —Homer

people more resistant to attitude change attempts via peer pressure, so that they will be less likely to engage in dangerous behaviors.

One possibility is to extend the logic of McGuire's (1964) inoculation approach to more affectively based persuasion techniques, such as peer pressure. That is, besides inoculating people with doses of logical arguments that they might hear, we could also inoculate them with samples of the kinds of appeals to their emotions that they might encounter. Consider Jake, a 13-year-old who is hanging out with some classmates, many of whom are smoking cigarettes. The classmates begin to make fun of Jake for not smoking, calling him a wimp and a mama's boy. One of them even lights a cigarette and holds it in front of Jake, daring him to take a puff. Many 13-year-olds, faced with such pressure, would cave in. But suppose we immunized Jake to such social pressures by exposing him to mild versions of them and showing him ways to combat these pressures. We might have him role-play a situation where a friend calls him a chicken for not smoking a cigarette and teach him to respond by saying, "I'd be more of a chicken if I smoked it just to impress you." Would this help him to resist the more powerful pressures exerted by his classmates?

Several programs designed to prevent smoking in adolescents suggest that it would. For example, McAlister and his associates (1980) used a role-playing technique with seventh-graders, very much like the one described above. The researchers found that these students were significantly less likely to smoke three years after the study, compared to a control group that had not participated in the program. This result is encouraging and has been replicated in similar programs designed to reduce smoking (Chassin, Presson, & Sherman, 1990; Falck & Craig, 1988; Killen, 1985).

We should point out that it is sometimes difficult to determine precisely why programs such as these are effective. They usually involve several interventions, making it difficult to tell which of the interventions was most responsible for the program's success. For example, the McAlister and colleagues (1980) prevention program was multifaceted. In addition to the role-playing procedure to inoculate people against peer pressure, the participants made public commitments not to use tobacco, and they created antismoking skits and slogans (for which they received prizes). Thus, though the results are promising, it will take further research to illuminate which of these activities was most responsible for the success of the program.

When Persuasion Attempts Boomerang: Reactance Theory

It is important not to use too heavy a hand when trying to immunize people against assaults on their attitudes. Suppose you want to make sure that your child never smokes. "Might as well err on the side of giving too strong a message," you might think, absolutely forbidding your child to even look at a pack of cigarettes. "What's the harm?" you figure. "At least this way, my child will get the point about how serious a matter this is."

Actually, there is harm to administering strong prohibitions—the stronger they are, the more likely they will boomerang, causing an *increase* in interest in the prohibited activity. According to **reactance theory** (Brehm, 1966), people do not like to feel that their freedom to do or think whatever they want is being threatened. They will feel this way if an action is strongly prohibited, and they will respond by rebelling against the threat. This often involves an increased interest in performing the forbidden behavior, as well as anger and aggression toward the person who forbade it.

For example, James Pennebaker and Deborah Sanders (1976) placed one of two signs in the bathrooms on a college campus, in an attempt to get people to stop writing graffiti on the walls of restrooms. One sign read, "Do not write on these walls under any circumstances." The other gave a milder prohibition: "Please don't write on these walls." The researchers returned two weeks later and observed how much graffiti had been written since they posted the signs. What do you think they found? As they predicted, significantly more people wrote graffiti in the bathrooms with the "Do not write . . ." sign than with the "Please don't write . . ." sign. Similarly, people who receive strong admonitions against smoking, taking drugs, or dating the 17-year-old runaway from across the tracks become more likely to perform these behaviors, in order to restore their sense of personal freedom and choice.

reactance theory: the idea that when people feel their freedom to perform a certain behavior is threatened, an unpleasant state of reactance is aroused; people can reduce this reactance by performing the threatened behavior

When Will Attitudes Predict Behavior?

Now that we have seen how attitudes change, it is important to discuss the consequences of this change. Attitude change is a significant topic in part because of the relationship between attitudes and people's actual behavior. Many people bank on the fact that people act consistently with their attitudes. Advertisers assume that changing people's attitudes toward their products will result in increased sales. Politicians assume that positive feelings toward a candidate will result in a vote for that candidate on Election Day. And we all assume that people who like brussels sprouts will be more likely to eat them than people who do not, and that people who enjoy ballet will be more likely to go see the local company perform *Swan Lake* than people who do not. Sounds pretty straightforward, right?

Actually, the relationship between attitudes and behavior is not so straightforward, as indicated by a classic study by Richard LaPiere (1934). In the early 1930s, LaPiere embarked on a cross-country sightseeing trip with a young Chinese couple. Because prejudice against Asians was commonplace in the United States at this time, he was apprehensive about how his Chinese friends would be treated. At each hotel, campground, and restaurant they entered, LaPiere worried that anti-Asian prejudice would erupt and his friends would be refused service. Much to his surprise, this almost never happened. Of the 251 establishments he and his friends visited, only one refused to serve them.

Struck by this apparent lack of prejudice, LaPiere decided to explore people's attitudes toward Asians in a different way. After his trip, he wrote a letter to each establishment he and his friends had visited, asking if it would serve a Chinese visitor. Of the many establishments who replied, only one said it would. More than 90 percent said they definitely would not; the rest said they were undecided. People's attitudes—as expressed in their response to LaPiere's written inquiry—stood in stark contrast to their actual behavior toward LaPiere's Chinese friends.

> We give advice but we do not influence people's conduct.
>
> –La Rochefoucauld, *Maxims*, 1678

LaPiere's study was not, of course, a controlled experiment. As LaPiere acknowledged, there are several reasons why his results may not show an inconsistency between people's attitudes and behavior. For example, he had no way of knowing whether the proprietors who answered his letter were the same people who had served him and his friends. Further, people's attitudes may have changed in the months that passed between the time they served the Chinese couple and the time they received the letter. Nonetheless, the lack of correspondence between people's attitudes and what they actually did was so striking that we might question our earlier assumption that behavior routinely follows from attitudes. This is especially the case in light of research performed after LaPiere's study. Allan Wicker (1969) reviewed dozens of more methodologically sound studies and reached the same conclusion: People's attitudes are poor predictors of their behavior.

But how can this be? Does a person's attitude toward Asians, political candidates, or the ballet really tell us nothing about how he or she will behave? How can we reconcile the LaPiere findings—and other studies like it—with the obvious notion that many times people do act in accord with their attitudes? Fortunately, in recent years social psychologists have learned a great deal about when and how attitudes will predict behavior. It is now clear that Wicker's (1969) conclusions about attitude-behavior consistency were too pessimistic. Attitudes do predict behavior but only under certain specifiable conditions (DeBono & Snyder, 1995; Zanna & Fazio, 1982). One key factor is knowing whether the behavior we are trying to predict is spontaneous or is deliberative and planned (Fazio, 1990).

Predicting Spontaneous Behaviors

Sometimes we act spontaneously, giving little forethought to what we are about to do. When LaPiere and his Chinese friends entered a restaurant, the manager did not have a lot of time to reflect on whether to serve them; he or she had to make a snap decision. Similarly, when someone approaches us at a shopping mall and asks us to sign a petition in favor of a change in the local zoning laws, we usually don't stop to deliberate for ten minutes but instead decide whether to sign the petition on the spot.

■ It is commonly assumed that changing a person's attitude (e.g., an attitude toward a consumer product) will lead to a change in that person's behavior (e.g., buying the product in the store). But is this always true?

The extent to which attitudes predict spontaneous behaviors depends on a quality of the attitude we discussed earlier: its accessibility (Fazio, 1990, 1995). As you will recall, accessibility refers to the strength of the association between an object and your attitude toward that object. When accessibility is high, your attitude comes to mind whenever you see the object. When accessibility is low, your attitude comes to mind more slowly. It follows that highly accessible attitudes will be more likely to predict spontaneous behaviors, because people are more likely to be thinking about their attitude when they are called on to act.

Russell Fazio, Martha Powell, and Carol Williams (1989) demonstrated the role of accessibility in a study of people's attitudes and behaviors toward consumer items. People first rated their attitudes toward several products, such as different brands of gum and candy bars. The accessibility of these attitudes was assessed by measuring how long it took people to respond to the attitude questions. People's actual behavior was measured by placing ten of the products on a table (in two rows of five) and telling people they could choose five of them to take home as a reward for being in the study. To what extent did people's attitude toward the products determine which ones they chose?

As predicted, it depended on the accessibility of their attitudes. Attitude-behavior consistency was high among people with accessible attitudes and relatively low among people with inaccessible attitudes. That is, people acted in accord with their attitudes only if their attitudes came quickly to mind when they were making their choice. What about people with inaccessible attitudes—what determined which products they chose? Interestingly, they were more influenced by an arbitrary aspect of the situation—which products happened to be in the first row on the table in front of them. The closer an item was, the more likely they were to choose it. This is consistent with the idea that when attitudes are inaccessible, people are more influenced by situational variables—in this case, how noticeable and within reach the products were.

Predicting Deliberative Behaviors

Sometimes behavior is not spontaneous but deliberative and planned. Most of us give a good deal of thought about where to go to college, whether to accept a new job, or where to spend our vacation. Under these conditions, the immediate accessibility of our attitude is not as important. Given enough time to think about an issue, even people with inaccessible attitudes can bring to mind how they feel. It is only when we have to decide how to act on the spot—without time to think it over—that accessibility matters (Eagly & Chaiken, 1993; Fazio, 1990).

The best-known theory of how attitudes predict deliberative behaviors is Martin Fishbein and Icek Ajzen's **theory of reasoned action** (Ajzen & Fishbein, 1980; Fishbein & Ajzen, 1975). According to this theory, when people have time to contemplate how they are going to behave, the best predictor of their behavior is their intention: Does Sam intend to go to the concert? Does Sue intend to get a dog? Note that these are planned, deliberate actions, not the spontaneous kind covered by Fazio's notion of accessibility.

The Importance of Specific Attitudes. As seen in Figure 7.8, to know what a person's intentions are we need to know two things: (a) his or her attitude and (b) his or her beliefs about the subjective norms that operate in the situation. As you can see in the figure, what is important here is not people's general attitude about something but their specific attitude toward the behavior in question. According to the theory of reasoned action, only specific attitudes toward the behavior in question can be expected to predict that behavior.

For example, in a study of married women's use of birth control pills, Andrew Davidson and James Jaccard (1979) demonstrated that attitudes toward specific behaviors are better predictors of people's actions than more general attitudes are. A sample of women were asked a series of attitude questions, ranging from the general (their attitude toward birth control) to the specific (their attitude toward using birth control pills during the next two years; see Table 7.1). Two

theory of reasoned action: a theory holding that the best predictors of a person's planned, deliberate behaviors are that person's attitudes toward specific behaviors and his or her subjective norms

> If actions are to yield all the results they are capable of, there must be a certain consistency between them and one's intentions.
>
> –La Rochefoucauld, *Maxims*, 1678

FIGURE 7.8 The theory of reasoned action. ■ According to this theory, the best predictor of people's planned, deliberative behaviors are their behavioral intentions. The best predictors of their intentions are their attitudes toward the specific behavior and their subjective norms. (Adapted from Ajzen & Fishbein, 1980)

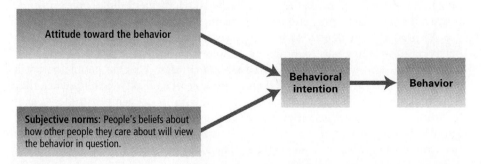

Table 7.1

Specific attitudes are better predictors of behavior.

Different groups of women were asked about their attitudes toward birth control. The more specific the question, the better it predicted their actual use of birth control. *Note:* If a correlation is close to 0, it means that there is no relationship between the two variables. The closer the correlation is to 1, the stronger the relationship between attitudes and behavior. (Adapted from Davidson & Jaccard, 1979)

Attitude Measure	Attitude-Behavior Correlation
Attitude toward birth control	.08
Attitude toward birth control pills	.32
Attitude toward using birth control pills	.53
Attitude toward using birth control pills during the next two years	.57

years later, they were asked whether they had used birth control pills at any time since the last interview. As seen in Table 7.1, the women's general attitude toward birth control did not predict their use of birth control at all. This general attitude did not take into account other factors that could have influenced their decision, such as the women's concern about the long-term effects of the pill and their attitude toward other forms of birth control. The more specific the question was about the act of using birth control pills, the better this attitude predicted their actual behavior.

This may be one reason LaPiere (1934) found such inconsistency between people's attitudes and behaviors in his study. His question to the proprietors—whether they would serve "members of the Chinese race"—was stated very generally. Had he asked a much more specific question—such as whether they would serve an educated, well-dressed, well-to-do Chinese couple accompanied by a white American college professor—they might have given an answer that was more in line with their behavior.

The Importance of Subjective Norms.   In addition to measuring attitudes toward the behavior, we also need to measure people's **subjective norms**: their beliefs about how people they care about will view the behavior in question (see Figure 7.7). To predict someone's intentions, knowing these beliefs can be as important as knowing her or his attitudes. For example, suppose we want to predict whether Kristen intends to go to a heavy-metal concert and we know that she has a negative attitude toward this behavior—she can't stand heavy-metal music. We would probably say she won't go. Suppose we also know, though, that Kristen's best friend, Malcolm, really wants her to go. Knowing this subjective norm—her belief about how a close friend views her behavior—we might make a different prediction. A considerable amount of research supports the idea that asking people about their subjective norms increases the ability to predict their planned, deliberative behaviors, such as the decision of what job to accept,

subjective norms: people's beliefs about how those they care about will view the behavior in question whether to wear a seatbelt, and whether to check oneself for disease (Sheppard, Hartwick, & Warshaw, 1988; Stasson & Fishbein, 1990; Steffen, 1990).

Advertising: How and Why Does It Work?

We began this chapter with a discussion of daily assaults on our attitudes, in the form of advertisements. The world of advertising is rich with examples of many of the principles of attitude and behavior change we have been discussing. But is there evidence that advertising really works? Most of the research we have discussed was conducted in the laboratory with college students. What about changes in attitudes and behavior out there in the real world? If we see an ad campaign for Scrubadub detergent, are we really more likely to buy Scrubadub when we go to the store? Or are companies wasting the billions of dollars a year they are spending on advertising?

A curious thing about advertising is that most people think it works on everyone but themselves (Wilson & Brekke, 1994). A typical comment is, "Sure, it influences most people but not me. Seeing those ads for Scrubadub doesn't influence me at all." Contrary to such beliefs, substantial evidence indicates that advertising works. It is not so powerful that we respond like robots, marching off to the store with images of Scrubadub dancing in our heads. When a product is advertised, however, sales increase. The best evidence that advertising works comes from studies using what are called **split cable market tests.** In this type of research, advertisers work in conjunction with cable television companies, showing a target commercial to a randomly selected group of people. They keep track of what people buy by giving potential consumers special ID cards that are scanned at checkout counters and can thus tell whether people who saw the commercial for Scrubadub actually buy more Scrubadub—the best measure of advertising effectiveness.

Magid Abraham and Leonard Lodish (1990) have conducted more than 300 split cable market tests. Their findings indicate that advertising does work, particularly for new products. About 60 percent of the advertisements for new products led to an increase in sales, compared to 46 percent of the advertisements for established brands. When an ad was effective, how much did it increase sales? The difference in sales between people who saw an effective ad for a new product and those who did not averaged 21 percent. Although this figure might seem modest, it translates into millions of dollars when applied to a national advertising campaign. Further, these effective ads worked quickly, increasing sales substantially within the first six months they were shown.

How does advertising work, and which types of ads work the best? The answer to this question follows from our earlier discussion of attitude change. By way of review, advertisers should consider the kind of attitude they are trying to change. If they are trying to change an affectively based attitude, then, as we have seen, it is best to fight emotions with emotions. Many advertisements take the emotional approach—for example, ads for different brands of soft drinks. Given that different brands of colas are not all that different, many people do not base their purchasing decisions on the objective qualities of the different brands. Consequently, soda advertisements do not stress facts and figures. As noted by one advertising executive, "The thing about soda commercials is that they actually have nothing to say" ("The Battle for Your Brain," *Consumer Reports*,

You can tell the ideals of a nation by its advertisements.
–George Norman Douglas, *South Wind*

split cable market tests: techniques used to test the effectiveness of advertising, whereby advertisers, in conjunction with cable television companies and grocery stores, show a commercial to a randomly selected group of people and then see whether these people are more likely to buy the product than those who did not see the commercial are

August 1991, p. 521). Instead of presenting facts, soda ads play to people's emotions, trying to associate feelings of excitement, youth, energy, and sexual attractiveness with their brand.

If people's attitudes are more cognitively based, then we need to ask an additional question: How personally relevant is the issue? Does it have important consequences for people's everyday lives, or is it a remote issue that does not directly affect them? Consider, for example, the problem of heartburn. This is not a topic that evokes strong emotions and values in most people. Thus, it is more cognitively based. To people who suffer from frequent heartburn, however, it clearly is of direct personal relevance. In this case, the best way to change people's attitudes is to use logical, fact-based arguments (Chaiken, 1987; Petty & Cacioppo, 1986).

What if you are dealing with a cognitively based attitude that is not of direct personal relevance to people? Here you have a problem, because people are unlikely to pay close attention to your advertisement. You might succeed in changing their attitudes via the peripheral route, such as having attractive movie stars endorse your product. The problem here, as we have seen, is that attitude change triggered by simple peripheral cues is not very long-lasting (Chaiken, 1987; Petty & Cacioppo, 1986). Thus, if you have a product that does not engage people's emotions and is not of direct relevance to people's everyday lives, you are in trouble.

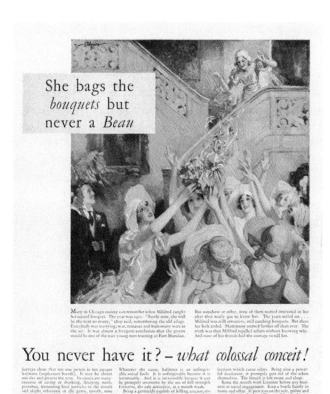

■ This ad is one of the most famous in the history of advertising. Although today it is easy to see how sexist and offensive it is, when it appeared in 1936 it succeeded in making a problem (bad breath) personally relevant, by playing to people's fears and insecurities about personal relationships. Can you think of any contemporary ads that try to raise similar fears?

But don't despair. The trick is to *make* your product personally relevant. Let's take a look at some actual ad campaigns to see how this is done. Consider the case of Gerald Lambert, who, in the early part of this century, inherited a company that made a surgical antiseptic used to treat throat infections—Listerine. Seeking a wider market for his product, Lambert decided to promote it as a mouthwash. The only problem was that no one at the time used a mouthwash or even knew what one was. And so, having invented the cure, Lambert invented the disease. Look at the ad on the previous page, which appeared in countless magazines over the years.

Even though today we would find this ad incredibly sexist, at the time most Americans did not find it offensive. Instead, the ad very successfully played on people's fears about social rejection and failure. The phrase "She was often a bridesmaid but never a bride" became one of the most famous in the history of advertising. In a few cleverly chosen, manipulative words, it succeeded in making a problem—*halitosis*—personally relevant to millions of people. Listerine became a best-selling product that has since earned a fortune. Incidentally, you might think halitosis is the official term of the American Medical Association for bad breath. In fact, it is nothing more than a fancy, medical-sounding term invented by Gerald Lambert and his advertising team to sound like a dreadful disease that we must avoid at all costs—by going to the nearest drugstore and stocking up on mouthwash.

Gerald Lambert's success at playing to people's fears and sense of shame was not lost on other advertisers. Similar ads have been designed to create new markets for many new products, most having to do with personal hygiene or health: underarm deodorants, deodorant soaps, vitamin supplements, oat bran, fish oil, and more. These campaigns work by convincing people they have problems of great personal relevance and that the advertised product can solve these problems.

Many advertisements also try to make people's attitudes more affectively based, by associating the product with important emotions and values (see our earlier discussion of classical conditioning). Consider, for example, advertisements for long-distance telephone service. This topic does not, for most of us, evoke deep-rooted emotional feelings—until, that is, we see an ad where a man calls his long-lost brother to tell him he loves and misses him, or an ad where a man calls his mother to tell her he has just bought her a plane ticket so that she can come visit him. There is nothing logically compelling about these ads. Logically, there is no reason to believe using AT&T service will magically make you closer to your family than using MCI or Sprint. However, by associating positive emotions with a product, an advertiser can turn a bland product into one that evokes feelings of nostalgia, love, warmth, and general goodwill.

Subliminal Advertising: A New Form of Mind Control?

We cannot leave the topic of advertising without discussing one of its most controversial topics—the use of **subliminal messages**, defined as words or pictures that, while not consciously perceived, may influence people's judgments, attitudes, and behaviors on an unconscious level. A majority of the public believe that these messages can shape their attitudes and behaviors, even though they do not know the messages have entered their minds (Zanot, Pincus, & Lamp, 1983). Given the near-hysterical claims that have been made about subliminal advertising, it is important to discuss whether it really works.

Profits can be obtained either by producing what consumers want or by making consumers want what is actually produced.
–Henry Simons

subliminal messages: words or pictures that are not consciously perceived but that supposedly influence people's judgments, attitudes, and behaviors

In the late 1950s, James Vicary convinced a movie theater in New Jersey to try a novel approach to selling drinks and popcorn. Imagine you happened to go to the theater that day to see *Picnic*, a popular movie at the time. Unbeknownst to you or the other patrons, you see more than the movie. Messages are flashed on the screen at speeds so quick that they are not consciously perceived, messages that urge you to "drink Coca-Cola" and "eat popcorn." Vicary claimed that these messages registered in the audience members' unconscious minds and caused them to develop a sudden hankering for a soda and a box of popcorn. Coca-Cola sales at the concession counter increased by 18 percent, he said, whereas popcorn sales increased by 58 percent.

When Vicary revealed what he had done, the public reaction was swift. Journalists blasted Vicary's sneaky attempt to boost sales. Minds have been "broken and entered," decried the *New Yorker* (1957, p. 33), and the *Nation* called it "the most alarming and outrageous discovery since Mr. Gatling invented his [machine] gun" ("Diddling the Subconscious," 1957, p. 206). The Federal Communications Commission banned the use of subliminal messages on radio and television, fearing a kind of mind control like that described in George Orwell's novel *1984*.

This was hardly, however, the last attempt to influence people with subliminal messages. According to Wilson Bryan Key (1973, 1989), who has written several best-selling books on hidden persuasion techniques, advertisers routinely implant sexual messages in print advertisements, such as the word *sex* in the ice cubes of an ad for gin, and male and female genitalia in everything from pats of

> In the field of marketing . . . the trend toward selling [has] reached something of a nadir with the unveiling of so called subliminal projection. That is the technique designed to flash messages past our conscious guard.
>
> –Vance Packard, 1958

PEOPLE HAVE BEEN TRYING TO FIND THE BREASTS IN THESE ICE CUBES SINCE 1957.

The advertising industry is sometimes charged with sneaking seductive little pictures into ads.

Supposedly, these pictures can get you to buy a product without your even seeing them.

Consider the photograph above. According to some people, there's a pair of female breasts

hidden in the patterns of light refracted by the ice cubes.

Well, if you really searched you probably *could* see the breasts. For that matter, you could also see Millard Fillmore, a stuffed pork chop and a 1946 Dodge.

The point is that so-called "subliminal advertising" simply

doesn't exist. Overactive imaginations, however, most certainly do.

So if anyone claims to see breasts in that drink up there, they aren't in the ice cubes.

They're in the eye of the beholder.

ADVERTISING
ANOTHER WORD FOR FREEDOM OF CHOICE.
American Association of Advertising Agencies

■ There is no scientific evidence that implanting sexual images in advertising boosts sales of the product. The public is very wary of this subliminal technique, however—so much so that some advertisers have begun to poke fun at subliminal messages in their ads.

butter to the icing in an ad for cake mix. Key (1973) argues that these images are not consciously perceived but put people in a good mood and make them pay more attention to the ad—all of which may increase sales of the product.

Subliminal messages are not just visual; they can be auditory as well. In the past decade, a large market has arisen for audiotapes containing subliminal messages to help people lose weight, stop smoking, improve their study habits, raise their self-esteem, and even shave a few strokes off their golf scores. In 1988 Americans bought more than 5 million of these self-help tapes, and 1990 sales were estimated to be $50 million (*Newsweek*, July 30, 1990). But are subliminal messages effective? Do they really make us more likely to buy consumer products, or help us to lose weight and stop smoking?

It is important to note that few of the proponents of subliminal advertising have conducted controlled studies to back up their claims. James Vicary did not have a control group who saw the same movie on the same day but with no subliminal messages about Coca-Cola and popcorn. In fact, Vicary reportedly later admitted that he had made up his claims to boost business (Weir, 1984). Similarly, Wilson Bryan Key did not conduct controlled studies comparing the impact of ads containing hidden sexual messages with the impact of the same ads containing no such messages. Fortunately, many controlled studies of subliminal perception have been conducted, allowing us to evaluate the sometimes hysterical claims that are made.

Simply stated, there is no evidence that the type of subliminal messages used in everyday life has any influence on people's behavior. Hidden commands to eat popcorn do not cause people to line up at the concession stand in greater numbers than they would normally do, and the subliminal commands on self-help tapes do not (unfortunately!) help us to quit smoking or lose a few pounds (Brannon & Brock, 1994; Merikle, 1988; Moore, 1982, 1992; Pratkanis, 1992). Anthony Greenwald and his colleagues (1991), for example, performed a careful test of the effectiveness of subliminal self-help tapes. Half the participants listened to tapes that, according to the manufacturer, contained subliminal messages designed to improve memory (e.g., "My ability to remember and recall is increasing daily"), whereas the others listened to tapes that had subliminal messages designed to raise self-esteem (e.g., "I have high self-worth and high self-esteem"). Neither of the tapes had any effect on people's memory or self-esteem. It would be nice if we could all improve ourselves simply by listening to music with subliminal messages, but alas, this study (and others) shows that subliminal tapes are no better at magically solving our problems than patent medicines or visits to an astrologist.

Interestingly, research participants in the Greenwald study *thought* the subliminal tapes were working, even though they were not. The researchers were a little devious, in that they correctly informed half the participants about which tape they listened to, but misinformed the others (i.e., half the people who got the memory tape were told it was designed to improve their memories, whereas the other half were told it was designed to improve their self-esteem). Those who thought they had listened to the memory tape believed their memories had improved, even if they had really heard the self-esteem tape. And people who thought they had listened to the self-esteem tape believed their self-esteem had improved, even if they had heard the memory tape. This finding explains why subliminal tapes are a $50 million business: Even though the tapes don't work, people think they do.

When we said that subliminal messages are ineffective, you may have noticed a qualification: They do not work when used in everyday life. There *is* some evidence for such effects in carefully controlled laboratory studies. For example, Sheila Murphy and Robert Zajonc (1993) showed participants a series of Chinese ideographs (characters used in the Chinese written language) and asked them to rate how much they liked the appearance of each one. Unbeknownst to the participants, the Chinese characters were preceded by another picture—a human face expressing happiness, a human face expressing anger, or a polygon conveying no emotion. These pictures were flashed for only four milliseconds, which is too fast for people to perceive consciously what is shown. Nonetheless, as seen in Figure 7.9, these subliminal flashes influenced people's evaluations of the Chinese

Shown for 4 milliseconds	→	Shown for 2 seconds	→	Ratings of how much people liked the Chinese ideograph*
(happy face)	→	菜	→	3.4
(polygon)	→	菜	→	3.1
(angry face)	→	菜	→	2.7

* On a scale that ranged from 1 ("did not like at all") to 5 ("liked quite a bit")

FIGURE 7.9   Effects of subliminal exposure to faces on liking for Chinese ideographs. ■ There is evidence from carefully controlled laboratory studies that subliminal exposures to words and faces can influence people's judgments and attitudes. In this study, people were shown pictures of Chinese ideographs (characters used in the Chinese written language) for two seconds, and asked how much they liked the appearance of each one. Unbeknownst to the participants, the ideographs were preceded by quick flashes of happy faces (top panel), unemotional polygons (middle panel), or angry faces (bottom panel). These flashes of pictures influenced how much people liked the ideographs, even though they could not be perceived consciously. All of the successful demonstrations of subliminal messages, however, have been done under carefully controlled laboratory conditions that would be difficult to duplicate in everyday life. Further, there is no evidence that subliminal messages can be used to get people to do things they prefer not to do. (Adapted from Murphy & Zajonc, 1993)

■ Advertising agencies are masters at linking emotional images and words to products.

"How about one of those sunny old grandpas who make things look honest?"

ideographs. People liked the ideographs the most when they were preceded by a happy face, second most when they were preceded by an unemotional polygon, and least when they were preceded by an angry face—even though people didn't know that these faces or polygraphs had been flashed. Several other researchers have found similar effects of pictures or words flashed at subliminal levels (e.g., Baldwin, Carrell, & Lopez 1990; Bargh & Pietromonaco, 1982; Bornstein, 1992; Bornstein, Leone, & Galley, 1987).

It is frightening to think that our behavior can be influenced by information we do not even know we have seen. Before a new wave of hysteria about mind control begins, however, we should mention some key qualifications. All of the successful demonstrations of subliminal stimuli have been conducted under carefully controlled laboratory conditions that are difficult to reproduce in everyday life. To get subliminal effects, researchers have to make sure that the illumination of the room is just right, that people are seated just the right distance from a viewing screen, and that nothing else is occurring to distract them as the subliminal words are flashed. Further, even in the laboratory there is no evidence that subliminal messages can get people to act counter to their wishes, values, or personalities (Neuberg, 1988). These messages might have subtle influences on people's liking for an ambiguous stimulus (e.g., a Chinese ideograph), but they cannot override people's wishes and desires, making them march off to the supermarket to buy products they don't want or vote for candidates they despise.

Ironically, the hoopla surrounding subliminal messages has obscured a significant fact about advertising: Ads are *more* powerful when we can consciously perceive them. As we have seen, ample evidence indicates that the ads we encounter in everyday life and perceive consciously can have substantial effects on our behavior—even though they do not contain subliminal messages. Further, such ads influence more than just our consumer behavior. Advertisements transmit cultural stereotypes in their words and images, subtly linking a product with a desired image (e.g., Marlboro ads linking cigarettes with the rugged, macho Marlboro Man; beer ads linking beer consumption with sex).

Advertisements can also reinforce and perpetuate stereotypical ways of thinking about social groups. Until recently, ads almost always showed groups of whites (token individuals of color are now mixed into the group); couples who are heterosexual; families that are traditional, with a mom, dad, and two kids (of each gender); and so on. You would think that divorced families, the elderly, people of color, lesbians and gay men, the physically disabled, and others just didn't exist. Gender stereotypes are particularly pervasive in advertising imagery. Men are doers; women are observers. Erving Goffman (1976), in his book *Gender Advertisements*, offers fascinating examples of how the models in ads are typically posed so that their nonverbal behavior (e.g., their gestures, body position, facial expressions, and eye gaze) is powerful, nonemotional, and active if they are male and passive, submissive, and highly expressive if they are female.

Even more disturbing is the recent trend in some ads, such as those for Newport cigarettes or Guess? clothing, that links the product with sexual hostility and violence (Leo, 1991). For example, a series of Newport cigarette ads depict women who are being pulled by a horse collar, are about to be slammed with a pair of cymbals, or are carried off on a pole like a dead animal. The violence toward women shown in such ads is in no way subliminal; such obvious and overt images are much more powerful than anything hidden in ice cubes or cake icing. Thus, even if effects of subliminal messages in advertisements are eventually documented, those effects are unlikely to be any stronger, or any harder to resist, than the effects of the more overt, consciously perceived kinds of advertising (Wilson & Brekke, 1994).

SUMMARY

An **attitude** is a person's enduring evaluation of people, objects, and ideas. All attitudes have affective, cognitive, and behavioral components. Attitudes can be based more on one component than another. A **cognitively based attitude** is based mostly on people's beliefs about the properties of the attitude object. An **affectively based attitude** is based more on people's emotions and values; it can be created through **classical conditioning** or **instrumental conditioning**. A **behaviorally based attitude** is based on people's actions toward the attitude object. For example, research on *self-perception theory* shows that when people's attitudes are weak or unclear, they infer how they feel by observing how they behave. Behaviorally based attitudes are likely to be high in **attitude accessibility**, or the strength of the association between an object and the person's attitude toward that object.

Attitudes can be changed in a number of ways. As shown by research on *cognitive dissonance theory*, attitudes change when people engage in *counterattitudinal advocacy* for low *external justification*. When this occurs, people find *internal justification* for their behavior, bringing their attitudes in line with their behavior.

Another way attitudes change is when people receive a **persuasive communication**. According to the **Yale Attitude Change approach**, the persuasiveness of a communication depends on aspects of the communicator, or source of the message; aspects of the message itself (e.g., its content); and aspects of the audience. The **elaboration likelihood model** specifies when people are persuaded more by the strength of the arguments in the communication and when they are persuaded more by surface characteristics, such as the attractiveness of the speaker. People will take the **central route to persuasion** when they have both the motivation and the ability to pay close attention to the arguments. This is likely to occur when the topic of the communication is high in **personal relevance** or when people are high in the **need for cognition**. People will take the **peripheral route to persuasion** when they either do not want to or cannot pay close attention to the arguments. Under these conditions, they are persuaded by such peripheral cues as the attractiveness of the speaker or the length of the speech. Attitude change is longer-lasting and more resistant to attack when it occurs via the central route.

Emotions influence attitude change in a number of ways. People in positive moods are less likely to analyze a message carefully than people in negative moods are. **Fear-arousing communications** can cause lasting attitude change if a moderate amount of fear is aroused and people believe they will be reassured by the content of the message. Consistent with the **heuristic-systematic model of persuasion,** emotions can also be used as heuristics to gauge one's attitude; if people feel good in the presence of an object, they often infer that they like it, even if those good feelings were caused by something else. Finally, the effectiveness of persuasive communications also depends on the type of attitude people have. Appeals to emotion and social identity work best if the attitude is based on emotion and social identity.

It is possible to make people resistant to attacks on their attitudes. **Attitude inoculation** is the technique whereby people are exposed to small doses of arguments against their position, making it easier for them to refute these arguments when they hear them later. This approach may also inoculate people against attacks that play on their emotions and values, if people are first given small doses of these kind of attacks. Attempts to manage people's attitudes, however, should not be used with too heavy a hand. Strongly prohibiting people from engaging in certain behaviors can actually cause an increase in liking for that activity. According to **reactance theory,** people experience an unpleasant state called reactance when their freedom of choice is threatened. One way people can reduce reactance is to perform the behavior that was threatened.

One reason that it is important to understand attitude change is that attitudes are presumed to influence behavior. The relation between attitudes and behavior, however, is not as straightforward as once thought. We need to distinguish between behaviors that are spontaneous versus those that are more planned and deliberative. Attitudes predict spontaneous behaviors only when they are relatively accessible. When attitudes are inaccessible, they are more likely to be influenced by situational and social factors. The **theory of reasoned action** specifies how we can predict people's planned and deliberative behaviors. Here it is necessary to know people's attitudes toward the specific act in question, as well as their **subjective norms—** people's beliefs about how others view the behavior in question. Knowing these two things allows us to predict well people's behavioral intentions, which are highly correlated with their planned behaviors.

We concluded with a discussion of advertising and why it works. Advertising has been found to be quite effective, as indicated by **split cable market tests.** It is most effective when the ad is tailored to the kind of attitude people have and when the product is made to appear to be personally relevant to people. One kind of advertising that has caused public concern is the use of words or pictures that are supposedly perceived unconsciously—that is, **subliminal messages.** Despite people's fears, this type of advertising has not been shown to influence consumer behavior. Under controlled laboratory conditions, subliminal messages can have subtle effects on people's preferences, but there is no evidence that subliminal messages have been used successfully in real-world marketing campaigns. Unfortunately, the use of such messages in self-help tapes is also ineffective.

IF YOU ARE INTERESTED . . .

Ajzen, I. (1988). *Attitudes, personality, and behavior.* Chicago, IL: Dorsey Press. An in-depth discussion of the relationship between attitudes and behaviors, with an emphasis on the theory of reasoned action.

Burgess, Anthony (1963). *A Clockwork Orange.* A nightmarish look at the future filled with out-of-control adolescents and harrowing techniques of mind control.

Eagly, A., & Chaiken, S. (1993). *The psychology of attitudes.* Fort Worth, TX: Harcourt Brace Jovanovich. An

extremely thorough, up-to-date, and insightful look at current social psychological research on attitudes.

Huxley, Aldous (1946). *Brave New World.* A classic portrayal of mind control in a futuristic society. It is interesting to draw parallels between Huxley's view of the future and modern techniques of attitude change.

Petty, R. E., & Cacioppo, J. T. (1986). *Communication and persuasion: Central and peripheral routes to attitude change.* New York: Springer-Verlag. A comprehensive discussion of the elaboration likelihood model of attitude change.

Pratkanis, A. R., & Aronson, E. (1991). *Age of propaganda: The everyday use and abuse of persuasion*. New York: Freeman. An engaging account of how our attitudes are shaped by the mass media.

The War Room (1994). A behind-the-scenes documentary of President Clinton's campaign in 1992. The film is an interesting portrayal of the day-to-day attempt to influence public opinion in a modern, presidential campaign.

Triumph of the Will (1934). A film commissioned by Adolph Hitler to disseminate Nazi propaganda. It is interesting to view this film in the light of research on attitude change and persuasion, to see how the film tries to change people's attitudes.

Chapter 8

Conformity: Influencing Behavior

Chapter Outline

> ## To swallow and follow, whether old doctrine or new propaganda, is a weakness still dominating the human mind.
>
> –Charlotte Perkins Gilman

I n the late 1960s, Jim Jones founded a church in northern California, the Peoples Temple, preaching racial tolerance and acceptance. In 1977, following the publication of an unfavorable magazine article about the church, Jones and his congregation immigrated to an isolated jungle in Guyana. There they constructed "Jonestown." Over the years, Jones had become a messiahlike figure to his followers. He demanded and received total loyalty, devotion, and obedience. Interviews with defectors from the church indicated that Jones had also implemented strong punishments, from public humiliation to severe beatings, for any adult or child who disagreed with him.

In November 1978, California congressman Leo Ryan flew to Jonestown and investigated charges that church members were being held there against their will. As Ryan and his entourage boarded their plane to leave, Temple gunmen ambushed them and killed five, including Congressman Ryan. While these murders were occurring, Jones gathered the community together and told them that their enemies were everywhere and that the time had come to commit "revolutionary suicide." While his most trusted followers armed themselves and stood guard, others passed out cyanide-laced Kool-Aid. Jones instructed parents to first give the poison to their children and then drink it themselves. A few people tried to argue with Jones against the mass suicide but were shouted down by the rest of the congregation. When authorities reached the scene, they found the members of the congregation dead, lying in each other's arms. More than 800 people died that day by their own hand (Osherow, 1988).

The world was shocked and horrified by the events at Jonestown. How could people so mindlessly follow such a leader, conforming to his

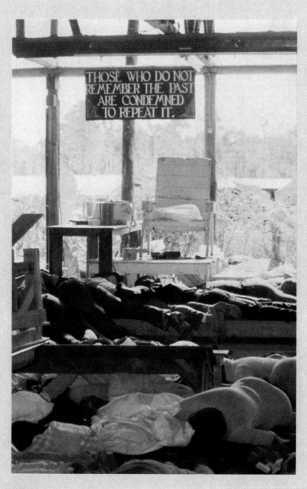

The mass suicide at Jonestown.

wishes and obeying his orders to the extent that they killed their children and committed suicide? Sadly, we saw history repeat itself in 1993, when David Koresh, the spiritual leader of the Branch Davidians, prompted an armed standoff for 51 days with government law enforcement officers at his compound in Waco, Texas. On April 20, a cataclysmic fire swept through the buildings and nearly all inside died. Government officials have stated that the Branch Davidians set fire to the compound themselves; in addition, several individuals, including Koresh, died from gunshot wounds to the head and not from fire or smoke inhalation. While we do not know all that happened in those final hours, it is clear that David Koresh had created such strong bonds of conformity and obedience among his followers that more than 80 adults and children remained inside the buildings and burned to death. How could such tragic conformity at Jonestown and Waco occur? Under what conditions and for what reasons do people fall under the influence of others?

Conformity: When and Why

Think for a moment about the word **conformity,** which we can define as a change in behavior due to the real or imagined influence of others (Kiesler & Kiesler, 1969). Which one of the two quotations on the right do you find more appealing? Which one best describes your immediate reaction to the word?

We wouldn't be surprised if you preferred the second quotation. American culture stresses the importance of not conforming (Hofstede, 1986). We think of ourselves as a nation of rugged individualists, people who think for themselves, who stand up for the underdog, who go against the tide for what they think is right. This cultural self-image has been shaped by the manner in which our nation was founded, by our very system of government, and by our society's historical experience with Western expansion—the "taming" of the Wild West (Turner, 1932).

American mythology has celebrated the rugged individualist in many ways. For example, one of the longest-running and most successful advertising campaigns in American history is the "Marlboro Man." Since 1955, the photograph of a cowboy alone on the range has been an archetypal image. It has also sold a lot of cigarettes. People who have never seen a horse, let alone the American West, have responded for more than 40 years to this simple, evocative image. Clearly, it tells us something about ourselves that we want and like to hear: that we make up our own minds; that we're not spineless, weak conformists; that we're not puppets but players.

But are we, in fact, nonconforming creatures? Are the decisions we make always based on what we think, or do we sometimes use other people's behavior to help us decide what to do? The mass suicide at Jonestown suggests that people sometimes conform in extreme and very surprising ways—even when making such a fundamental decision as whether or not to take their own lives. But, you might argue, this is an unusual case; surely most people do not conform to this extent. Perhaps the followers of Jim Jones and David Koresh were disturbed people who were somehow predisposed to do what a charismatic leader told them to do. There is, however, another, more chilling possibility: Maybe most of us would have acted the same way, had we been exposed to the same, long-standing conformity pressures as the Branch Davidians and the residents of Jonestown. According to this view, almost anyone would have conformed had she or he been put in these same extreme situations.

If this statement is true, we should be able to find other situations in which people, put under strong social pressures, conform to surprising degrees.

conformity: a change in behavior due to the real or imagined influence of other people

> Do as most do, and [people] will speak well of thee.
> —Thomas Fuller

> It were not best that we should all think alike; it is difference of opinion that makes horse races.
> —Mark Twain

© 1995, Washington Post Writers Group. Reprinted with permission.

Unfortunately, we do not have to look very far to find such instances. Consider the case of the My Lai massacre in Vietnam. On the morning of March 16, 1968, in the midst of the Vietnam War, a company of American soldiers boarded helicopters that would take them to the village of My Lai. The soldiers were very apprehensive, because they had never been in combat before and the village was rumored to be occupied by the Forty-Eighth Vietcong Battalion, one of the most feared units of the enemy. One of the helicopter pilots radioed that he saw Vietcong soldiers below, and so the American soldiers jumped off the helicopters, with rifles firing. They soon realized the pilot was wrong—there were no enemy soldiers. Instead, the Americans found several villagers, all women, children, and elderly men, cooking their breakfast over small fires. Inexplicably, the leader of the platoon, Lieutenant William Calley, ordered one of the soldiers to kill the villagers. Other soldiers began firing too, and the carnage spread. The Americans rounded up and systematically murdered all the villagers of My Lai. They shoved women and children into a ravine and shot them; they threw hand grenades into huts filled with cowering villagers. Though no one knows the exact number of deaths, the estimates range from 450 to 500 Vietnamese civilians (Hersch, 1970; *Time*, 1969).

The examples we have seen so far are all cases of "bad" conformity; human beings lost their lives as a result of people doing what others did. However, despite the American emphasis on rugged individualism, it is not always best to be a nonconformer. Would you rather be thought of as a team player or as someone who never cooperates? Conformity is not simply "good" or "bad" in and of itself. Rather than labeling conformity as good or bad, the social psychologist is interested in why people conform. Knowing why people are influenced by others, and when, will help us understand if a given act of conformity in our own lives is wise or foolish.

Some of the people at Jonestown and My Lai probably conformed because they did not know what to do in a confusing or unusual situation; the behavior of the people around them served as a cue as to how to respond, and so they decided

■ Victims of the My Lai massacre.

to act in a similar manner. Other people probably conformed because they did not wish to be ridiculed or punished for being different from everybody else; they chose to act the way the group expected them to so that they wouldn't be rejected or thought less of by group members. Let's see how each of these reasons for conforming operates.

Informational Social Influence: The Need to Know What's "Right"

One of the important things we get from interacting with other people is information. You won't be surprised to hear that sometimes people don't know what to do in a situation or even what is happening. Unfortunately, life, unlike our clothing, does not come with little labels attached, telling us what is going on and how we should respond. Instead, the social world is frequently ambiguous and ill-defined.

For example, how should you address your psychology professor—as Dr. Berman, Professor Berman, Ms. Berman, or Patricia? How should you vote in the upcoming college referendum that would raise your tuition in order to increase student services? What combination of physical features best describes a beautiful woman or a handsome man? Is the scream you just heard coming from a person joking with friends or from the victim of a mugging?

In these and many other everyday situations, we feel uncertain about what to think or how to act. We simply don't know enough to make a good or accurate choice. Luckily, we have a powerful and useful source of knowledge available to us—the behavior of other people. Asking others what they think or watching what they do helps us reach a definition of the situation (Deutsch & Gerard, 1955; Kelley, 1955; Thomas, 1928). When we subsequently act like everyone else, we are conforming, but not because we are weak, spineless individuals with no self-reliance. Instead, we act like others because their behavior is informative; it defines an ambiguous situation for us and helps us choose appropriate courses of action. This is called **informational social influence**.

As an illustration of how other people can be a source of information, imagine you are a participant in the following experiment by Muzafer Sherif (1936). In the first phase of the study, you are seated alone in a dark room and asked to focus your attention on a dot of light 15 feet away. The experimenter asks you to estimate in inches how far the light moves. You stare earnestly at the light, and yes, it moves a little. You say, "About two inches," though it is not easy to tell exactly. The light disappears and then comes back; you are asked to judge again. The light seems to move a little more, and you say, "Four inches." After several of these trials, the light seems to move about the same amount each time—about two to four inches.

Now, the interesting thing about this task is that the light was not actually moving at all. It looked like it was moving, because of a visual illusion called the *autokinetic effect*. If you stare at a bright light in a uniformly dark environment (e.g., a star on a dark night), the light will appear to waver back and forth. This occurs because you have no stable reference point to anchor the position of the light. The distance that the light appears to move varies from person to person but becomes consistent for each person over time. In Sherif's (1936) experiment, the subjects all arrived at their own, stable estimate during the first phase of the study, but these estimates differed from person to person. Some people thought

"It's always best on these occasions to do what the mob do."
"But suppose there are two mobs?" suggested Mr. Snodgrass.
"Shout with the largest," replied Mr. Pickwick.
—Charles Dickens, *Pickwick Papers*

informational social influence: the influence of other people that leads us to conform because we see them as a source of information to guide our behavior; we conform because we believe that others' interpretation of an ambiguous situation is more correct than ours the light was moving only an inch or so, whereas others thought it was moving as much as ten inches.

Sherif chose to use the autokinetic effect because he wanted a situation that would be ambiguous—where the correct definition of the situation would be unclear to his participants. In the second phase of the experiment, a few days later, the participants were paired with two other people, each of whom had had the same prior experience alone with the light. Now the situation became a truly social one, as all three made their judgments out loud. Remember, the autokinetic effect is experienced differently by different people; some see a lot of movement, some not much at all. After hearing their partners give judgments that were different from their own, what did people do?

Over the course of several trials, people reached a common estimate, and each member of the group conformed to that estimate. These results indicate that people were using each other as a source of information, coming to believe that the group estimate was the correct one (see Figure 8.1). An important feature of informational social influence is that it can lead to **private acceptance,** where people come to believe the definition of the situation they have learned from others.

It might seem equally plausible that people publicly conformed to the group but privately maintained the belief that the light was moving only a small amount. For example, maybe someone privately believed that the light was moving ten inches but announced that it had moved three inches, the group estimate, to avoid looking silly or foolish. (This would be a case of **public compliance** without *private acceptance*.) Sherif casted doubt on this interpretation, however, by asking people to judge the lights once more by themselves, after participating in groups. Even though they no longer had to worry about looking silly in front of other participants, they continued to give the answer the group had given earlier. One study even found that people still conformed to the group estimate when they participated by themselves a year later (Rohrer, Baron, Hoffman, & Swander, 1954). These results suggest that people were relying on each other to define reality and came to privately accept the group estimate.

In everyday life, of course, we are rarely asked to judge how much a stationary light is moving. It is thus important to note that there are many everyday situ-

private acceptance:
conforming to other people's behavior out of a genuine belief that what they are doing or saying is right

public compliance:
conforming to other people's behavior publicly, without necessarily believing in what we are doing or saying

FIGURE 8.1   One group's judgments in Sherif's (1936) autokinetic studies.
■ People estimated how far a point of light appeared to move in a dark room. When they saw the light by themselves, their estimates varied widely. When they were brought together in groups and heard other people announce their estimates, people conformed to the group's estimate of how much the light moved. (Adapted from Sherif, 1936)

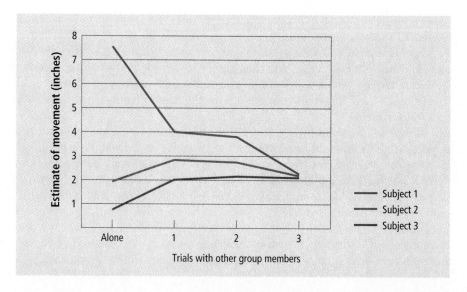

ations in which we rely on other people to help us define what is going on. Think about the first time you were at the symphony or ballet. You knew that applause was going to figure in sometime, but exactly when? What about standing ovations, or shouting "Encore!"? No doubt, you looked to others in the audience to help you interpret the appropriate way of showing approval in this quite formal setting. That the audience's behavior can be affected through conformity is not unknown in the performing arts. Davies (1988) describes the use of the claque (hired applause) in early nineteenth-century opera:

> An opera audience must contain people who know the work intimately. Nobody will dare to applaud if they don't know where, and when, and why. They might make an embarrassing mistake [and] look foolish. . . . [A] claque is a small body of experts . . . you must have your *bisseurs* who call out loud for encores; your *rieurs* who laugh at the right places . . . your *pleureurs* who sob when sobs are needed. . . . And all of this must be carefully organized—yes, orchestrated—by the *capo di claque*. (Davies, 1988, pp. 390–391)

Using other people to define social reality can also have a large impact on our emotions, as we saw in Chapter 5 (Schachter, 1959; Schachter & Singer, 1962). For example, you might be feeling quite calm about your upcoming midterm until you run into a group of acquaintances from the class, all of whom are extremely tense and stressed out about the exam. After talking with them, you feel a little disturbed too—are you being too complacent about this test? "Maybe they're right," you think. Like the research participants in Sherif's experiment, you may find yourself relying on other people to help you reach a definition of the situation: "Maybe I'm being way too calm about this midterm . . . I better study some more tonight."

Conversions and Crises

Informational social influence is certainly a part of everyday life. But this form of social influence also impinges on us in far more dramatic ways. For example, it comes into play when people experience a *conversion*—a sudden shift in the meaning of their lives based on new knowledge they have received from a group (Berger, 1963; Berger & Luckmann, 1967). People may experience conversion to a religion, to a political ideology, or to any one of the many cults that have arisen over recent decades. Often before the conversion experience, the individual feels indecisive and confused, dissatisfied with his or her life, and even despairing. On meeting members of the new group, the individual is exposed to a whole new definition of the situation, radically different from the one he or she knew before. These new beliefs are perceived by the individual to be more powerful and useful than his or her former convictions; conversion involves the individual conforming to the belief system of the new reference group. For example, Arthur Koestler (1959), a former Communist, describes his conversion to communism in the 1930s:

> To say that one had "seen the light" is a poor description of the mental rapture which only the convert knows (regardless of what faith he has been converted to). . . . [T]he whole universe falls into a pattern like the stray pieces of a jigsaw puzzle assembled by magic at one stroke. There is now an answer to every question; doubts and conflicts are a matter of the tortured past. (p. 19)

Another dramatic form of informational social influence occurs during crises. Here an individual is confronted with a frightening, potentially dangerous situation to which he or she is ill-equipped to respond (Killian, 1964). Literally, the person may have no idea of what is really happening or what he or she should do. When one's personal safety is involved, the need for information is acute—and the behavior of others is very informative.

Consider what happened on Halloween Night in 1938. Orson Welles, the gifted actor and film director, and the Mercury Theater broadcast a radio play based loosely on H. G. Wells's science fiction fantasy *The War of the Worlds*. (Remember, this was the era before television; radio was a source of entertainment, with music, comedy, and drama programs, and the only source for fast-breaking news.) That night, Welles and his fellow actors put on a radio drama of cataclysm—the invasion of Earth by hostile Martians—that was so realistic and effective that at least a million American listeners became frightened and several thousand were panic-stricken (Cantril, 1940).

Why were so many Americans convinced that what they heard was a real news report of an actual invasion by aliens? One reason is that the play parodied existing radio news shows very well, and many listeners missed the beginning of the broadcast (when it was clearly labeled as a play) because they had been listening to the nation's number-one-rated show, *Charlie McCarthy*. Another culprit, however, was informational social influence. Many people were listening with friends and family and naturally turned to each other, out of uncertainty, to see whether they should believe what they heard. Seeing looks of concern and worry on their loved ones' faces added to the panic people were beginning to feel. "We all kissed one another and felt we would all die," reported one listener (Cantril, 1940, p. 95).

In addition, many frightened listeners misinterpreted actual events so that they fit the news on the radio program: "We looked out the window and Wyoming Avenue was black with cars. People were rushing away, I figured," or

> Ninety-nine percent of the people in the world are fools and the rest of us are in great danger of contagion.
> –Thornton Wilder

■ The *New York Times* headlined the *War of the Worlds* incident. Partly because of informational social influences, many listeners believed that a fictional radio broadcast about an invasion by Martians was true.

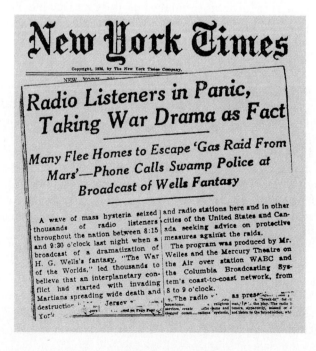

New York Times

Copyright, 1938, by The New York Times Company.

NEW YORK

Radio Listeners in Panic, Taking War Drama as Fact

Many Flee Homes to Escape 'Gas Raid From Mars'—Phone Calls Swamp Police at Broadcast of Wells Fantasy

A wave of mass hysteria seized thousands of radio listeners throughout the nation between 8:15 and 9:30 o'clock last night when a broadcast of a dramatization of H. G. Wells's fantasy, "The War of the Worlds," led thousands to believe that an interplanetary conflict had started with invading Martians spreading wide death and destruction ... Jersey ... York ...

and radio stations here and in other cities of the United States and Canada seeking advice on protective measures against the raids.

The program was produced by Mr. Welles and the Mercury Theatre on the Air over station WABC and the Columbia Broadcasting System's coast-to-coast network, from 8 to 9 o'clock.

The radio ... as prese...

"No cars came down my street. Traffic is jammed on account of the roads being destroyed, I thought" (Cantril, 1940, p. 93). When a situation is highly ambiguous and people begin to believe they know what is happening, they will even reinterpret potentially disconfirming evidence so that it fits their definition of the situation.

Gustav LeBon (1895) was the first researcher to document how emotions and behavior can spread, seemingly out of control, through a crowd—an effect he called **contagion**. As we have learned, anytime an individual is faced with a truly ambiguous situation, he or she will most likely rely on the interpretation of others. Unfortunately, in a truly ambiguous and confusing situation, other people may be no more knowledgeable or accurate than we are.

contagion: the rapid transmission of emotions or behaviors through a crowd

When Informational Conformity Backfires

The *War of the Worlds* incident reminds us that using other people as a source of information can be dangerous. If other people are misinformed, we will adopt their mistakes and misinterpretations. Depending on others to help us reach a definition of the situation can sometimes lead to an inaccurate definition indeed.

An example of extreme and misdirected informational social influence is **mass psychogenic illness** (Colligan, Pennebaker, & Murphy, 1982), the occurrence of similar physical symptoms, with no known physical cause, in a group of people. This form of contagion usually begins with just one person or a few people reporting physical symptoms; typically, these people are experiencing some kind of stress in their lives. Other people around them construct what seems to be a reasonable explanation for their illness. This explanation, a new definition of the situation, spreads, and more people begin to think that they too have symptoms. As the number of afflicted people grows, both the physical symptoms and their supposed explanation become more credible and thus more widespread (Kerckhoff & Back, 1968).

mass psychogenic illness: the occurrence, in a group of people, of similar physical symptoms with no known physical cause

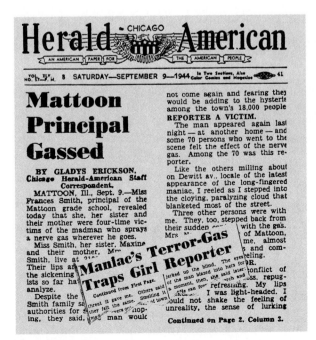

■ An example of mass psychogenic illness.

Several social psychologists have studied naturally occurring cases of mass psychogenic illness (e.g., Colligan & Murphy, 1979; Kerckhoff & Back, 1968; Schuler & Parenton, 1943; Singer, Baum, Baum, & Thew, 1982; Stahl & Lebedun, 1974). Donald Johnson (1945) examined a particularly fascinating case, that of the "phantom anesthetist" of Mattoon, Illinois. Here is Johnson's (1945) description of the panic:

> The story of the "phantom anesthetist" begins in Mattoon, Illinois, on the first night of September, 1944, when a woman reported to the police that someone had opened her bedroom window and sprayed her with a sickish sweet-smelling gas which partially paralyzed her legs and made her feel ill. Soon other cases with similar symptoms were reported, and the police organized a full-scale effort to catch the elusive "gasser." Some of the Mattoon citizens armed themselves with shotguns and sat on their doorsteps to wait for him; some even claimed that they caught a glimpse of him and heard him pumping his spray gun. As the number of cases increased—as many as seven in one night—and the facilities of the local police seemed inadequate to the size of the task, the state police . . . were called in, and scientific crime detection experts went to work, analyzing stray rags for gaseous chemicals and checking the records of patients recently released from state institutions. Before long the "phantom anesthetist" of Mattoon had appeared in newspapers all over the United States. . . . After ten days of such excitement, when all the victims had recovered and no substantial clues had been found, the police began to talk of "imagination" and some of the newspapers ran columns on "mass hysteria"; the episode of the "phantom anesthetist" was over. (p. 175)

How did the contagion spread? How did some people come to believe that their physical ailments were symptoms of a bizarre attack? Johnson (1945) determined that informational social influence had occurred primarily via newspaper articles. Few of the victims knew each other, and so they had not spread the information interpersonally. Instead, blaring headlines and sensationalist articles in the town newspapers were the means by which a new definition of the situation was communicated.

What is particularly interesting about modern cases of mass psychogenic illness (as well as other peculiar forms of conformity) is the powerful role that the mass media play in their dissemination. Through television, radio, newspapers, and magazines, information is spread quickly and efficiently to all segments of the population. While in the Middle Ages it took 200 years for the "dancing manias" (a kind of psychogenic illness) to crisscross Europe (Sirois, 1982), today it takes only minutes for most of the inhabitants of the planet to learn about a strange or even bizarre event. Luckily, the mass media also have the power to quickly squelch these uprisings of contagion by introducing more logical explanations for ambiguous events.

When Will People Conform to Informational Social Influence?

Let's review the situations that are the most likely to produce conformity because of informational social influence.

When the Situation Is Ambiguous.   This is the most crucial variable for determining if people use each other as a source of information. When you are unsure of the correct response, the appropriate behavior, or the right idea, you will be most open to influence from others. The more uncertain you are, the more you will rely on others (Allen, 1965). The situations we discussed at the beginning of this chapter were ambiguous ones for the people involved. While the conformity that occurred at Jonestown and My Lai was horrible and tragic in its consequences, informational social influence was at work. At Jonestown, for example, Reverend Jones had achieved such power that people allowed him to define reality for them. Over time, the residents of Jonestown came to entirely believe whatever Jones told them; they had no independent definition of the situation in any area of their lives. They believed him when he said that their situation was hopeless and that their enemies were closing in on them. They believed him when he said that suicide was the correct course of action. Instances of mind control or "brainwashing" can actually be extreme cases of informational social influence—so extreme that, in this case, Jones was able to convince nearly an entire village to commit suicide.

When the Situation Is a Crisis.   Another variable also promotes the use of others as a source of information and often co-occurs with ambiguous situations. When the situation is a crisis, we usually do not have time to stop and think about exactly which course of action we should take. We need to act, and act now. If we feel scared and panicky, and are uncertain what to do, it is only natural for us to look and see how other people are responding—and to do likewise. Unfortunately, the people we imitate may also feel scared and panicky and not be behaving rationally.

The soldiers at My Lai, for example, expected to experience combat for the first time and were undoubtedly scared and on edge. Further, it was not easy to tell who the enemy was. In the Vietnam War, Vietnamese civilians who were sympathizers of the Vietcong were known to have laid mines in the path of U.S. soldiers, fired guns from hidden locations, and thrown or planted grenades. In a guerrilla war like Vietnam, it was often difficult to tell if civilians were in fact civilians or combatants, allies or enemies. Thus, when one or two soldiers began firing on the villagers in My Lai, it is perhaps not surprising that others followed suit, believing this to be the proper course of action. Had the soldiers not been in a crisis situation and instead had more time to think about their actions, perhaps the tragedy would have been avoided.

When Other People Are Experts.   Typically, the more expertise or knowledge a person has, the more valuable he or she will be as a guide in an ambiguous situation (Bickman, 1974). For example, a passenger who sees smoke coming out of an airplane engine will probably look around for the flight attendants to check their reaction; they have more expertise than the vacationer in the next seat. However, experts are not always reliable sources of information. Imagine the fear felt by the young man who was listening to the *War of the Worlds*, called his local police department for an explanation—and discovered that the police too thought the events described on the radio were actually happening.

Resisting Informational Social Influence

As we have seen, relying on others to help us define what is happening can be an excellent idea or it can be a tragedy in the making. How can we tell when other people are a good source of information and when we should resist other people's definition of a situation?

First, it is important to remember that it *is* possible to resist illegitimate or inaccurate informational social influence. In all of our examples, some people resisted conforming to what they perceived to be incorrect information. At My Lai, not all the soldiers took part in the atrocity. One sergeant said he'd been ordered to "destroy the village," but he simply refused to follow the orders. Another soldier, watching as the others fired on civilians, purposefully shot himself in the foot so that he would have an excuse to be evacuated from the killing scene. One helicopter pilot, looking down on the grisly sight, landed and scooped up 15 Vietnamese children and ferried them off to safety deep in the forest. Thus, some soldiers rejected the behavior of others as a correct definition of what they should do. Instead, they relied on what they knew was right and moral; they refused to take part in the massacre of innocent people.

Similarly, during the *War of the Worlds* broadcast, not all of the listeners panicked (Cantril, 1940). Some engaged in rational problem solving; they checked other stations on the radio dial and discovered that no other station was broadcasting the same news. Instead of relying on others and being caught up in the contagion and mass panic, they searched for and found information on their own.

One reason that the decision about whether to conform is so important is that it influences how people define reality. If you decide to accept other people's definition of the situation, you will come to see the world as they do. If you decide to reject other people's definition of the situation, you will come to see the world very differently from the way they do. This basic fact was demonstrated in an interesting study by Roger Buehler and Dale Griffin (1994), who asked students to read newspaper reports of a real, highly controversial incident in which an African American teenager driving a stolen car was shot and killed by white police officers. Many of the details of the situation were ambiguous, such as how much the youth had threatened the officers and how much the officers feared for their lives.

Buehler and Griffin first asked participants how they interpreted the situation: How fast was the victim's car going? Was the victim trying to ram the police car? Did he realize that his pursuers were the police? What were the police officers thinking and feeling? Each participant was then told that other participants had agreed with the statement that the police were 75 percent responsible and the victim 25 percent responsible. After indicating whether they agreed with this assessment, the participants were asked how they interpreted the situation. The question was, Did people's interpretation of the situation change, depending on whether they agreed with other people's assessments?

The first result of interest was that not everyone conformed to other people's views. In fact, only 32 percent of the participants agreed that the police were 75 percent responsible for the incident. Thus, as we have discussed, it is possible to resist informational influence. Did people's decision about whether to conform influence their definition of the situation? The answer is yes: People who agreed with others that the police were responsible changed their interpretations to be consistent with the group; they now believed that the victim had not threatened the police and that police were not in fear of their lives. What about the people who did not conform? Interestingly, they also changed their interpretations, but in the opposite direction—they now believed that the victim's car was about to ram the police and that the police were in fear for their lives. In short, people changed their interpretations of reality to bolster their decision about whether to agree with the majority opinion.

> Yes, we must, indeed, all hang together or, most assuredly, we shall all hang separately.
>
> –Benjamin Franklin to John Hancock, at the signing of the Declaration of Independence

Your decision as to whether to conform to informational influence, then, will affect not only your behavior but also your interpretation of reality. It is thus important to consider carefully whether other people's reaction to a situation is any more legitimate than your own. Do other people know any more about what is going on than you do? Is there an expert handy, someone who should know more? Do the actions of other people or experts seem sensible? If you behave the way they do, will it go against your common sense, or against your internal moral compass that tells you what is right and wrong? By knowing how informational social influence works in daily life, you are in a better position to know when it is useful and when it is not.

Normative Social Influence: The Need to Be Accepted

In Rio de Janeiro, Brazil, teenage boys and girls engage in a highly dangerous, reckless game: They "surf" on the tops of trains, standing with arms outstretched as the trains speed along. Despite the fact that an average of 150 teenagers die each year from this activity and 400 more are injured by falling off the trains or hitting the 3,000-volt electric cable, the surfing continues (Arnett, 1995). In the United States, one teenager died and two more were critically injured when they responded to a dare to reenact a scene from the movie *The Program*. Like the movie's protagonist, they lay down in the middle of a highway at night. Unlike the movie's protagonist, they were run over (Hinds, 1993).

Why do these adolescents engage in such risky behavior? Why does anyone follow the group's lead when the resulting behavior is less than sensible and may even be dangerous? We doubt that the Brazilian or American teenagers risked their lives due to informational conformity—it is difficult to argue that a boy or girl staring at a train would say, "Gee, I don't know what to do. I guess standing on top of a train going 60 miles an hour makes a lot of sense; everybody else is doing it." This example tells us that there is another reason for why we conform, besides the need for information: We also conform so that we will be liked and accepted by other people. We conform to the group's **social norms,** which are implicit (and sometimes explicit) rules for acceptable behaviors, values, and beliefs (Deutsch & Gerard, 1955; Kelley, 1955). Groups have certain expectations about how the group members should behave, and members in good standing conform to these rules. Members who do not are perceived as different, difficult, and eventually deviant. Deviant members can be ridiculed, punished, or even rejected by other group members (Miller & Anderson, 1979; Schachter, 1951).

We human beings are by nature a social species. Few of us could live happily as hermits, never seeing or talking to another person. Through interactions with others, we receive emotional support, affection, and love, and we partake of enjoyable experiences. Other people are extraordinarily important to our sense of well-being. Research on individuals who have been isolated for long amounts of time indicates that being deprived of human contact is stressful and traumatic (Curtiss, 1977; Schachter, 1959; Zubek, 1969).

Given this fundamental human need for social companionship, it is not surprising that we often conform in order to be accepted by others. Conformity for normative reasons occurs in those situations where we do what other people are doing not because we are using them as a source of information but because we won't attract attention, be made fun of, get into trouble, or be rejected. We

social norms: the implicit or explicit rules a group has for the acceptable behaviors, values, and beliefs of its members

normative social influence: the influence of other people that leads us to conform in order to be liked and accepted by them; this type of conformity results in public compliance with but not necessarily private acceptance of the group's beliefs and behaviors

conform so that we can continue to belong and reap the benefits of group membership. This is called **normative social influence.**

You probably don't find it too surprising that people sometimes conform in order to be liked and accepted by others. After all, if the group is important to us and it is a matter of wearing the right kind of clothing or using the hip slang words, why not go along? But when it comes to more important kinds of behaviors, such as hurting another person, surely we will resist such conformity pressures. And surely we won't conform when we are certain of what the correct way of behaving is and the pressures are coming from a group that we don't care all that much about. Or will we? Remember that image of Americans as rugged individualists? Are we really like the Marlboro Man, setting trends instead of following them? How much will we conform to normative pressures?

To find out, Solomon Asch (1951, 1956) conducted a series of classic studies exploring the parameters of normative social influence. Asch initiated this program of research because he believed that there are limits to how much people will conform. Naturally, people conformed in the Sherif studies, he reasoned, given that the situation was highly ambiguous—trying to guess how much a light was moving. Asch believed, however, that when a situation was completely unambiguous, people would act like rational, objective problem-solvers. When the group said or did something that contradicted an obvious truth, surely people would reject social pressures and decide for themselves what was going on.

To test his hypothesis, Asch conducted the following study. Had you been a participant, you would have been told that this was an experiment on perceptual judgment and that you would be taking part with seven other students. Here's the scenario: The experimenter shows everyone two cards, one with a single line on it, the other with three lines labeled 1, 2, and 3. He asks each of you to judge and then announce aloud which of the three lines on the second card is closest in length to the line on the first card (see Figure 8.2).

It is crystal-clear that the correct answer is the second line. Not surprisingly, each participant says, "Line 2." Your turn comes next to last, and, of course, you say, "Line 2" as well. The last participant concurs. The experimenter then presents a new set of cards and asks the group to again make their judgments and

FIGURE 8.2 The judgment task in Asch's line studies.
■ Participants judged which of the three comparison lines on the right was closest in length to the standard line on the left. (Adapted from Asch, 1956)

Standard line   Comparison lines

■ Participants in an Asch line study. The real participant is seated in the middle. He is surrounded by accomplices of the experimenter, who have just given the wrong answer on the line task.

announce them out loud. Again, the answer is obvious, and everyone gives the correct answer. At this point, you are probably thinking to yourself, "What a boring experiment! How many times will we have to judge these silly lines? I wonder what they're serving for dinner in the dining hall tonight."

As your mind starts to wander, something surprising happens. The experimenter presents the third set of lines, and again the answer is obvious—line 3 is clearly the closest in length to the target line. But the first participant announces that the correct answer is line 1! "Geez, this guy must be so bored that he fell asleep," you think. Then the second person announces that he also believes that line 1 is the correct answer. The third, fourth, fifth, and sixth participants concur; then it is your turn to judge. By now startled, you are probably looking at the lines very closely to see if you missed something. But no, line 3 is clearly the correct answer. What will you do? Will you bravely blurt out, "Line 3," or will you go along with the group and give the obviously incorrect answer, "Line 1"?

As you can see, Asch set up a situation to see if people would conform even when the right answer was cut-and-dried. The other participants were actually accomplices of the experimenter, instructed to give the wrong answer on 12 of the 18 trials. Contrary to what Asch thought would happen, a surprising amount of conformity occurred: Seventy-six percent of the participants conformed on at least one trial. On average, people conformed on about a third of the 12 trials on which the accomplices gave the incorrect answer (see Figure 8.3).

Why did people conform so much of the time? One possibility is that people genuinely had a hard time with the task and thus assumed that other people were better judges of the length of lines than they were. If so, this would be another case of informational social influence, as we saw in the Sherif study. This interpretation doesn't make much sense, however, because the correct answers were obvious—so much so that when people in a control group made the judgments by themselves, they almost never made a mistake. Instead, normative pressures came into play. Even though the other participants were strangers, the fear of being the lone dissenter was very strong, causing people to conform, at least occasionally. One participant, for example, had this to say about why he conformed: "Here was a group; they had a definite idea; my idea disagreed; this might arouse anger. . . . I was standing out as a sore thumb. . . . I didn't want particularly to

> It isn't difficult to keep alive, friends—just don't make trouble—or if you must make trouble, make the sort of trouble that's expected.
> –Robert Bolt,
> *A Man for All Seasons,*
> 1962

40

Percentage of participants
showing each level of conformity

30

20

10

0

0   1–3   4–6   7–9   10–12

Number of trials on which participants conformed

FIGURE 8.3   Results of the Asch line study. ■ Seventy-six percent of the participants conformed on at least one trial. (Adapted from Asch, 1957)

make a fool of myself. . . . I felt I was definitely right. . . . [but] they might think I was peculiar" (Asch, 1955, p. 46).

These are classic normative reasons for conforming: People know that what they are doing is wrong but go along anyway so as not to feel peculiar or look like a fool. These reasons illustrate an important fact about normative pressures: In contrast to informational social influence, normative pressures usually result in public compliance without private acceptance—that is, people go along with the group even if they do not believe in what they are doing or think it is wrong.

What is especially surprising about Asch's results is that people were concerned about looking foolish in front of complete strangers. It is not as if the participants were in danger of being ostracized by a group that was important to them. Nor was there any risk of open punishment or disapproval for failing to conform, or of losing the esteem of people they really cared about, such as friends and family members. And yet decades of research indicate that conformity for normative reasons can occur simply because we do not want to risk social disapproval, even from complete strangers we will never see again (Crutchfield, 1955; Tanford & Penrod, 1984). As Moscovici (1985, p. 349) comments, the Asch studies are "one of the most dramatic illustrations of conformity, of blindly going along with the group, even when the individual realizes that by doing so he turns his back on reality and truth."

Asch (1957) did a variation of his study that demonstrates the power of social disapproval in shaping a person's behavior. The confederates gave the wrong answer 12 out of 18 times, as before, but this time the participants wrote their answers on a piece of paper, instead of saying them out loud. Now people did not have to worry about what the group thought of them, because the group would never find out what their answers were. Conformity dropped dramatically, occurring on an average of only 1.5 of the 12 trials.

Normative social influence most closely reflects the pejorative stereotype of conformity we referred to earlier. At times, conforming for normative reasons can be spineless and weak; it can have negative consequences. Even in a very dangerous situation, like that faced by the Brazilian teenagers, you might go ahead and conform because normative social pressures can be difficult to resist. The desire to be accepted is part of human nature, but it can have tragic consequences.

The Consequences of Resisting Normative Social Influence

One way to observe the power of normative social pressures is to see what happens when people manage to resist them (Milgram & Sabini, 1978). If a person refuses to do as the group asks and thereby violates its norms, what happens? Think for a moment about the norms that operate in your group of friends. Some friends have an egalitarian norm for making group decisions. For example, when choosing a movie such groups will make sure that everyone gets to state a preference; the choice is then discussed until agreement is reached on one movie. Think about what would happen if, in a group with this kind of norm, you stated at the outset that you only wanted to see *Rebel Without a Cause* and weren't going with them otherwise. Your friends would be surprised by your behavior; they would also be annoyed with you or even angry. If you continued to flout the friendship norms of the group by failing to conform to them, two things would most likely occur. First, the group members would attempt to bring you "back into the fold," chiefly through increased communication with you. Teasing comments and long discussions would ensue, as your friends tried to figure out why you were acting so strangely and also tried to get you to conform to their expectations (Garfinkle, 1967). If these discussions didn't work, your friends would most likely curtail communication with you (Festinger & Thibaut, 1951; Gerard, 1953). At this point, in effect you would have been rejected.

This process of monitoring, convincing, and eventually rejecting the deviant was demonstrated by the jury of the famous Los Angeles riot trial, in which two black assailants were tried for beating a white truck driver, Reginald Denny. The jury told the judge that they wanted one of the jurors removed. The jury fore-woman wrote, "On behalf of the 11 jurors, we are in agreement that Juror No. 373 cannot comprehend anything that we've been trying to accomplish. We tried patiently to talk and work with her, all to no avail! . . . She doesn't use common sense. Lastly, just when we've made progress in final decisions, she is totally oblivious to what we've discussed and decided" (Mydans, 1993, p. A16).

Stanley Schachter (1951) demonstrated how the group responds to an individual who is impervious to their normative influence. He asked groups of college students to read and discuss a case history of "Johnny Rocco," a juvenile delinquent. Most of the students took a middle-of-the-road position about the case, believing that Rocco should receive a judicious mixture of love and discipline. Unbeknownst to the participants, however, Schachter had planted an accomplice in the group, who was instructed to disagree with the group's recommendations. He consistently argued that Rocco should receive the harshest amount of punishment, regardless of what the other group members argued.

How was the deviant treated? He received the most comments and questions from the real participants throughout the discussion, until near the end, when communication with him dropped sharply. The group had tried to convince the deviant to agree with them; when it appeared that wouldn't work, they ignored him. In addition, they punished the deviant. After the discussion, they were asked to fill out questionnaires that supposedly pertained to future discussion meetings of their group. The participants were asked to nominate one group member who should be eliminated from further discussions if the size had to be reduced. They

> Customs do not concern themselves with right or wrong or reason. But they have to be obeyed; one reasons all around them until [one] is tired, but [one] must not transgress them, it is sternly forbidden.
> —Mark Twain

> Success or failure lies in conformity to the times.
> —Machiavelli

nominated the deviant. They were also asked to assign group members to various tasks in future discussions. They assigned the unimportant or boring jobs, such as taking notes, to the deviant. Social groups are very well versed in how to bring a nonconformist into line. No wonder we respond as often as we do to normative pressures!

A recent example of how a deviant is treated by the group is the case of Shannon Faulkner and her experiences as an entering cadet at the Citadel, a military college in Charleston, South Carolina. A federal court order allowed Faulkner to enroll in the 153-year-old, all-male institution; because the Citadel is a public institution supported by South Carolina taxpayers, the court ruled that all residents of the state, regardless of sex, should have the right to apply for admission.

The students and faculty of the Citadel were not pleased that a young woman was entering their ranks. Despite Faulkner's attempt to conform to all the rules and behaviors of the Citadel during the first week, her gender made her a deviant and she was punished. When she arrived the first day, for what the school calls "Hell Week," signs saying "Shannon go home" greeted her and she was heckled. "You should have heard the way they were talking to me, calling me names," Faulkner said. "I never looked in their direction. I did what the other guys were doing. I got in line and did what I was supposed to do" (Rogers, Dampier, & Sieder, 1995, p. 78). However, the stress of being different, of having no support, soon made her sick. After a few days in the school infirmary, Faulkner left permanently. As a male junior cadet said, "You just don't make it here on your own. You have to rely on each other [but] she had no one. No one spoke to her, and that wasn't going to change" (Rogers et al., 1995, p. 80). When news spread that Faulkner had left the campus, the cadets rejoiced boisterously and enthusiastically.

> I was . . . silenced solely because cadets did not want Blacks at West Point. Their only purpose was to freeze me out. What they did not realize was that I was stubborn enough to put up with their treatment to reach the goal I had come to attain.
>
> –Benjamin Davis, Jr.

■ Cadets celebrate after Shannon Faulkner, the first female cadet at the Citadel, drops out.

Normative Social Influence in Everyday Life

Normative social influence operates on many levels in our daily lives. The clothes we wear are but one example. While few of us are slaves of fashion, we nonetheless tend to wear what is considered appropriate and stylish at a given time. Men wore ties that were wide in the 1970s; then they wore ties that were narrow in the 1980s; and undoubtedly they'll be wearing wide ties again. Similarly, women's hemlines have gone up and down with alacrity over the past century. Normative social influence is at work whenever you notice a "look" shared by people in a certain group. The "bobby-soxer" teenage girls of the 1940s and 1950s had such a look; so did the "zoot-suiter" young men of the 1940s. No doubt 20 years from now our current fashions will look dated and silly and none of us will conform to them.

Another fairly frivolous example of normative social influence is fads. Certain activities or objects can suddenly become popular and sweep the country. College students in the 1930s ate goldfish; in the 1950s, crammed as many people as possible into telephone booths; and in the 1970s, "streaked" at (ran naked through) official gatherings.

Hula-Hoops were the toy you had to have in the 1950s or risk social ostracism. One of us, Robin Akert, remembers a Saturday afternoon with the family in 1958:

> We drove from store to store, trying to find Hula-Hoops. Everywhere we went, they were all sold out. My sister and I sat in the backseat, sobbing with disappointment. Much to our parents' chagrin, we were praying in little, high-pitched voices for help in finding Hula-Hoops before nightfall!

A more sinister form of normative social influence involves women's attempts to conform to cultural definitions of an attractive body. While many, if not most, world societies consider plumpness in females attractive (Ford &

■ The "zoot suiter" look in 1942. The jacket had six inches of shoulder pads, and the balloon trousers were hitched chest-high.

Beach, 1952; Rudofsky, 1972), Western culture and particularly American culture currently value thinness in the female form (Garner, Garfinkel, Schwartz, & Thompson, 1980).

For example, Silverstein, Perdue, Peterson, and Kelly (1986) analyzed photographs of women appearing in *Ladies' Home Journal* and *Vogue* magazines from 1901 to 1981, by measuring their busts and waists in centimeters and forming a bust-to-waist ratio. A high score indicates a heavier, more voluptuous body, while a lower score indicates a thin, lean body type. Their results show a startling series of changes in the cultural definition of female bodily attractiveness during the twentieth century (see Figure 8.4).

At the turn of the century, an attractive woman was voluptuous and heavy; by the "flapper" period of the 1920s, the correct look for women was rail-thin and flat-chested. The normative body changed again in the 1940s, when World War II "pinup girls" like Betty Grable exemplified a heavier standard. The curvaceous, heavier female body remained popular during the 1950s; witness, for example, Marilyn Monroe. However, the "swinging 1960s" fashion look, exemplified by the reed-thin British model Twiggy, introduced a very thin silhouette again. As Brett Silverstein and his colleagues (1986) point out, the average bust-to-waist ratio has been very low since 1963. This is the longest period of time in this century that women have been exposed to an extremely thin standard of feminine physical attractiveness.

FIGURE 8.4   The mean bust-to-waist ratios of models in *Vogue and Ladies' Home Journal* advertisements during this century. ■ What has been considered an attractive female body has changed dramatically over the past 100 years: from heavy women at the beginning of the century, to rail-thin women during the 1920s, to somewhat heavier, curvaceous women during the 1940s and 1950s, to a return to overly thin women in the 1960s and continuing. (Adapted from Silverstein, Perdue, Peterson, & Kelly, 1986)

■ Cultural standards for women's bodies change rapidly. While today most female models and movie stars are lean and athletic, the female icons of the 1940s and 1950s were curvaceous and heavy. Marilyn Monroe, pictured here in the film *Bus Stop*, would be considered over-weight by today's standards.

Whereas informational social influence is the mechanism by which women learn what kind of body is considered attractive at a given time in their culture, normative social influence helps to explain their attempts to create that body through dieting and, more disturbingly, through eating disorders like anorexia nervosa and bulimia (Bruch, 1973, 1978; Palazzoli, 1974). As early as 1966, researchers found that 70 percent of the high school girls surveyed were unhappy with their bodies and wanted to lose weight (Heunemann, Shapiro, Hampton, & Mitchell, 1966). In 1991, Elissa Koff and Jill Rierdan found that, when asked if they'd "ever felt overweight" in their lives, 72 percent of the 11- and 12-year-old girls surveyed answered yes (*Boston Globe*, 1992). The sociocultural pressure for thinness that is currently operating on women (and not to the same extent on men; see Silverstein et al., 1986) is a potentially fatal form of normative social influence. The last time that a very thin standard of bodily attractiveness for women existed—the mid–1920s—an epidemic of eating disorders appeared (Silverstein, Peterson, & Perdue, 1986).

Christian Crandall (1988) has conducted research on conformity pressures and eating disorders—in this case, bulimia, an eating pattern characterized by periodic episodes of uncontrolled "binge" eating, followed by periods of "purging" food through fasting, vomiting, or using laxatives. Crandall's research participants were women members of two college sororities. He found, first, that each sorority had its own social norm for binge eating. In one sorority, the group norm was that the more one binged, the more popular one was in the group. In the other sorority, popularity was associated with binging the right amount—the most popular women binged not too often and not too infrequently, compared to the others.

Did binge eating operate as a form of normative social influence? Yes, it did. Crandall tested the women throughout the school year and found that new members had conformed to the eating patterns of their friends. Probably, the initial conforming behavior was informational, as a new pledge learned from the

> You cannot make a man by standing a sheep on its hind-legs. But by standing a flock of sheep in that position you can make a crowd of men.
>
> –Sir Max Beerbohm

group how to manage her weight. However, normative conformity processes would then take over, as the woman matched her binging behavior to the sorority's standard and that of her friends. To not engage in the behavior or to do it differently from how the others did could easily have resulted in a loss of popularity and even ostracism.

When Will People Conform to Normative Social Influence?

People don't always cave in to peer pressure. Although conformity is commonplace, we are not lemmings who always do what everyone else is doing. And we certainly do not agree on all issues, as evidenced by the spirited public debates on such topics as abortion, family values, and affirmative action. (One need only tune in to a television or radio talk show to appreciate how much people disagree on topics such as these.) Exactly when are people most likely to conform to normative pressures?

social impact theory: the theory that conforming to social influence depends on the strength, immediacy, and number of other people in a group

The answer to this question is provided by Bibb Latané's (1981) **social impact theory**. According to this theory, the likelihood that you will respond to social influence from other people depends on three variables: (a) strength, referring to how important the group of people is to you; (b) immediacy, referring to how close the group is to you in space and time during the influence attempt; and (c) number, referring to how many people are in the group.

Social impact theory predicts that conformity will increase as strength and immediacy increase. Clearly, the more important a group is to us and the more we are in its presence, the more likely we will be to conform to its normative pressures. For example, the sorority sisters that Crandall (1988) studied experienced a high level of strength and immediacy in their groups, with tragic consequences.

Number, however, operates in a different manner. As the size of the group increases, each additional person has less of an influencing effect—going from 3 to 4 people makes more of a difference than going from 53 to 54 people. It is like the law of diminishing returns in economics, where increasing one's total wealth by $1 seems much greater if we have only $1 to start with than if we already have $1,000. Similarly, if we feel pressure from a group to conform, adding another person to the majority makes much more of a difference if the group consists of 3 rather than 15 people. Latané (1981) constructed a mathematical model that captures these hypothesized effects of strength, immediacy, and number and has applied this formula to the results of many conformity studies. It has done a good job of predicting the actual amount of conformity that occurred (Latané, 1981; Latané & Wolf, 1981; Tanford & Penrod, 1984).

Social impact theory covers conformity to all kinds of social influence. For present purposes, let's see in more detail what it says about the conditions under which people will conform to normative social pressures.

When the Group Size Is Three or More.   As we just saw, conformity increases as the number of people in the group increases—up to a point. Imagine you are a participant in Solomon Asch's study, where you judged the length of lines. If there are only you and 1 other participant and the latter gives a blatantly wrong answer about the length of the lines, will you be less likely to cave in and conform to the other participant's response than if there were 5 other participants all giving the wrong answer? What if there were 15 people in the majority? Asch (1955) studied this question, and as we can see in Figure 8.5,

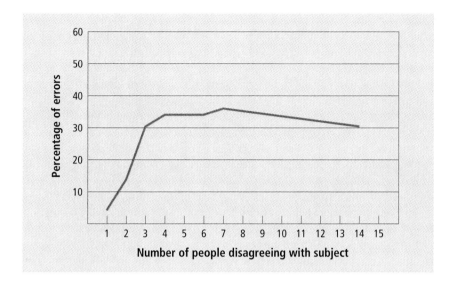

FIGURE 8.5   Effects of group size on conformity.
■ Asch varied the size of the unanimous majority and found that once the majority numbered four people, adding more people had little influence on conformity. (Adapted from Asch, 1955)

conformity increased as the number of people in the group increased, but only up to a point.

Asch's (1955) initial research and that of later researchers has established that in this kind of group situation, conformity does not increase much after the group size reaches 4 or 5 other people (Gerard, Wilhelmy, & Conolley, 1968; McGuire, 1968; Rosenberg, 1961)—just as social impact theory suggests. In short, it does not take an extremely large group to create normative social influence. As Mark Twain wrote in *The Adventures of Huckleberry Finn,* "Hain't we got all the fools in town on our side? And ain't that a big enough majority in any town?"

When the Group Is Important.   Another tenet of social impact theory is that the strength of the group—defined as how important the group is to us—makes a difference. Normative pressures are much stronger when they come from people whose friendship, love, and respect we cherish, because there is a large cost to losing this love and respect. Thus, groups to which we are highly attracted and with which we strongly identify will exert more normative influence on us than groups for which we have little or no attachment (Clark & Maass, 1988; Lott & Lott, 1961; Nowak, Szamrej, & Latané, 1990; Sakurai, 1975; Wolf, 1985). One consequence of this fact is that it can be dangerous to have policy decisions made by highly cohesive groups, because they care more about pleasing each other and avoiding conflict than arriving at the soundest, most logical decision. In Chapter 9, on group processes, we will see several examples of this phenomenon.

When the Group Is Unanimous.   Normative social influence is most powerfully felt when everyone in the group says or believes the same thing—for example, when your group of friends all believe that *101 Dalmatians* was the greatest movie ever made. Resisting such unanimous social influence is difficult or even impossible—unless you have an ally. If another person disagrees with the group—say, by nominating *Citizen Kane* as the best movie ever—this behavior will help you to buck the tide as well.

To illustrate the importance of having an ally, Asch (1955) conducted another version of his conformity experiment. In this variation, he had six of the seven confederates give the wrong answer, whereas one confederate gave the right answer on every trial. Now the subject was not alone. While he or she still disagreed with the majority of the group, having one ally helped him or her to resist normative pressures. People conformed on an average of only 6 percent of the trials in this study, compared to 32 percent in the version where all of the confederates gave the wrong answer. Several other studies have found that observing another person resist normative social influence emboldens the individual to do the same (Allen & Levine, 1969; Morris & Miller, 1975; Nemeth & Chiles, 1988).

This effect of allies produces some interesting anomalies in everyday life— people who hold unpopular beliefs are able to maintain them in the face of group pressure if they can convince at least a few others to agree with them. In Chapter 6, we saw the members of a small cult persevere in their belief that the world was going to end (even when it didn't). Clearly, the fact that the other cult members continued to believe helped every individual in the group to ignore the ridicule with which outsiders viewed them. Similarly, a man in Lancaster, California, believes that the earth is flat—despite proof from scientific experiments over a few centuries that it is not (see the newspaper article below). It is difficult to hold such an unpopular (and wrongheaded!) view; not surprisingly, this man has actively recruited followers and attempts to convince others of his views through his *Flat Earth Newsletter*.

When the Group is Affected by Culture.   "In America, the squeaky wheel gets the grease. In Japan, the nail that stands out gets pounded down" (Markus & Kitayama, 1991; p. 224). Is it the case, as this quote suggests, that the society in which one is raised affects the frequency of normative social influence? Perhaps not surprisingly, the answer is yes. Stanley Milgram (1961, 1977) replicated the

■ If you can get a few allies to agree with you, it's easier to buck the majority and believe some rather strange things. (*New York Times*, February 26, 1979)

Still a Hoax to Flat-Earth Group

Most people have come to accept the idea that the sun, the earth and the moon are all spheres, and that eclipses occur because of the rotation of the earth around the sun and of the moon around the earth. But one group of people, the International Flat Earth Research Society, contends that such an explanation is merely part of a gigantic hoax.

The president of the Flat Earth Society, Charles K. Johnson of Lancaster, Calif., believes that photographs taken from space, accounts of space travel and virtually everything else connected with modern science are all part of the hoax.

"Ever since Copernicus, the new religion — science, they call it — has been trying to fool the people with this notion that the earth is a ball," Mr. Johnson said in an interview.

"Starting around 1600, the facts were cast away by the priests of the new religion," he said, "and the vast, global con game began. They got most people to accept their hoax, but not us."

Nicolaus Copernicus was a Polish astronomer whose 1543 publication describing the motion of planets around the sun revolutionized astronomy. Formerly, the views of Ptolemy had prevailed, that the earth was the center of the universe around which everything else circled.

Mr. Johnson said that the society he heads, which was founded in 1888, now has about 1,600 formal members in the United States, in addition to some 2,000 believing outsiders. Members pay a $10 annual fee, for which they receive copies of the society's quarterly magazine, Flat Earth News.

The society president said he planned to "call President Carter's attention to the fact" that in 1959 a movie was made by the Three Stooges about a comic rocket trip to the planet Venus. "Purported photographs taken since then about space travel should be considered in the same category, as entertainment, rather than fact," he said.

"Only 10 or 20 percent of the people in the United States believe the hoax that men have traveled to the moon," Mr. Johnson said.

Asked how he would explain the eclipse of the sun, Mr. Johnson said, "We don't really go into all that. The Bible tells us that the heavens are a mystery."

Asch studies in Norway and France and found that the Norwegian participants conformed to a greater degree than the French participants did. Milgram (1961, p. 51) describes Norwegian society as "highly cohesive . . . [with] a deep feeling of group identification," while French society, in comparison, "show[s] far less consensus in both social and political life." In another cross-cultural study of normative social influence, James Whittaker and Robert Meade (1967) found that people in Lebanon, Hong Kong, and Brazil conformed to a similar extent (both to each other and to the American sample), while participants from the Bantu tribe of Zimbabwe conformed to a much greater degree. As the researchers point out, conformity has a very high social value in Bantu culture. While Japanese culture is more highly conforming than our own in many areas, an Asch-type study found that when the group unanimously gave the incorrect answer, Japanese students were less conformist in general than North Americans (Frager, 1970). In Japan, cooperation and loyalty are directed to the groups to which one belongs; there is little expectation that one should conform to the behavior of complete strangers, especially in such an artificial setting as a psychology experiment. Similarly, German research participants have shown less conformity in the Asch experiment than North Americans (Timaeus, 1968); in Germany, conformity to strangers is less valued than conformity to a few well-defined groups (Moghaddam, Taylor, & Sright, 1993.)

J. W. Berry (1967) explored the issue of conformity as a cultural value by comparing two cultures that had very different strategies for accumulating food. He hypothesized that societies that relied on hunting or fishing would value independence, assertiveness, and adventurousness in their members—traits that were needed to find and bring home food—whereas societies that were primarily agricultural would value cooperativeness, conformity, and acquiescence—traits that made close-living and interdependent farming more successful. Berry compared the Eskimo of Baffin Island in Canada, a hunting and fishing society, to the Temne of Sierra Leone in Africa, a farming society, on an Asch-type conformity task. The Temne showed a significant tendency to accept the suggestions of the group, while the Eskimo almost completely disregarded them. As one Temne put it, "When the Temne people choose a thing, we must all agree with the decision— this is what we call cooperation" (p. 417); in contrast, when the Eskimo did conform to the group's wrong answer, they did so with "a quiet, knowing smile" (p. 417).

Finally, some intriguing evidence indicates that conformity is actually decreasing. For example, replications of the Asch study conducted 25 to 30 years after the original, in Great Britain and the United States, have found lower percentages of conformity (Nicholson, Cole, & Rocklin, 1985; Perrin & Spencer, 1981).

When People Are a Certain Type.   Whereas the prior conditions under which normative conformity occurs involve the group, this last condition involves aspects of the individual. Is a certain sort of person more likely to conform to normative pressures than another? Research in this area has focused on two aspects of the individual: personality and gender.

It seems reasonable to propose that some people are just conforming types, while others' personalities make them highly resistant to normative pressures. Solomon Asch (1956) suggested that people who have low self-esteem may be particularly conforming, because they fear rejection or punishment by the group.

In the first study examining personality traits and conformity, Richard Crutchfield (1955) found evidence for this relationship between self-esteem and normative conformity; similarly, Mark Snyder and William Ickes (1985) found that people who perceived themselves as having a strong need for approval from others were more likely to demonstrate normative conformity.

Unfortunately, the relationship between personality traits and conforming behavior is not always so clear-cut. Some studies have found the relationship to be weak or nonexistent (Marlowe & Gergen, 1970). The reason is that, quite often, people are not very consistent in how they respond in different social situations (McGuire, 1968; Mischel, 1968). In other words, they don't always conform, across time and in different situations, the way they would if their personalities alone were affecting their behavior. Instead, the situation affects their behavior as well, so that in some situations they conform, and in other situations they don't, regardless of what type of person they are. You may recall from Chapter 1 that this is a fundamental principle of social psychology: Often the social situation is more important in understanding how someone behaves than his or her personality is.

The second person variable that has been studied is gender. Is it the case that women and men differ in how readily they conform to social pressures? For many years, the prevailing wisdom has been to answer this question in the affirmative: Women are more conforming than men (Crutchfield, 1955). When all three of your authors studied social psychology in college, this finding was presented as a fact. Recent reviews of the literature, however, have shown that matters are not so simple.

In the past few years, researchers have taken an objective look at this question by conducting *meta-analyses*. A meta-analysis is a statistical technique that allows you to combine results across a large number of studies and come up with a meaningful statistical summary. Alice Eagly and Linda Carli (1981), for example, performed a meta-analysis of 145 studies of influenceability that included more than 21,000 participants. Consistent with previous reviews of this literature, they found that, on average, men are less influenceable than women. But they found the size of the difference to be very small. A difference in influenceability shows up when one averages across thousands of participants, but that does not mean that every man you encounter will be less influenceable than every woman. In fact, Eagly and Carli (1981) found that only 56 percent of men are less influenceable than the average woman—which means, of course, that a sizable proportion of men are more influenceable than the average woman.

Not only are sex differences in influenceability small, but they depend on the type of conformity pressures impinging on people. Eagly (1987) and Becker (1986) report that gender differences are especially likely to be found in group-pressure situations, where an audience can directly observe how much you conform (e.g., the Asch study, where everyone can tell whether you give the same answer as the other participants). When faced with this kind of social pressure, women are especially more likely to conform than men are. In other situations, we are the only ones who know whether we conform, such as when we listen to someone give a speech against our views and then decide, privately, how much we agree with the speech. In this kind of situation, sex differences in influenceability virtually disappear. Eagly (1987) suggests that this pattern of results stems from the social roles men and women are taught in our society. Women are taught to be more agreeable and supportive, whereas men are taught to be more independent in the face of direct social pressures. And, Eagly suggests, both women and men are more likely to exhibit such gender-consistent behaviors in public situations, where everyone can see how they respond (e.g., the Asch-type conformity study). But remember, the size of these differences is relatively small.

One other finding in this area is surprising and controversial. Eagly and Carli (1981) took note of the gender of the researchers who conducted conformity studies and found that male authors were more likely than female authors to find that males were less influenceable. Though the reason for this finding is not yet clear, Eagly and Carli (1981) suggest one possibility: Researchers may be more likely to use experimental materials and situations that are familiar to their gender. Male authors, for example, may be more likely to see how people conform to persuasive messages about sports, whereas female authors may be more likely to see how people conform to persuasive messages about topics of greater familiarity to women. As we saw earlier, people are more likely to conform when confronted with an unfamiliar, ambiguous situation; thus, women may be more likely to conform in the unfamiliar situations designed by male experimenters.

To summarize, there appears to be a small tendency for women to be more influenceable, especially in group-pressure situations. Further, the already small magnitude of this difference may be exaggerated in studies conducted by male researchers, who are more likely than female researchers to find that women are more influenceable than men.

Resisting Normative Social Influence

Whereas normative social influence is often useful and appropriate, there are times when it is not. What can we do to resist inappropriate normative social influence? The best way to prevent ourselves from following the wrong social norm is to become more aware of what we are doing. If we stop and think carefully about whether the norm that seems to be operating is really the right one to follow, we will be more likely to recognize those times when it is not.

If becoming aware of normative influence is the first step to resistance, taking action is the second. Why do we fail to take action? Because of the possible ridicule, embarrassment, or rejection we may experience. However, we know that having an ally helps us resist normative pressures. Thus, if you are in a situation where you don't want to go along with the crowd but you fear the repercussions if you don't, try to find another person (or better yet, a group) who thinks like you do.

In addition, the very act of conforming to normative influence most of the time earns you the right to deviate occasionally without serious consequences. This interesting observation was made by Edwin Hollander (1958, 1960), who stated that conforming to a group over time earns you **idiosyncrasy credits,** much like putting money in the bank. Thus, your past conformity allows you, at some point in the future, to deviate from the group (or act idiosyncratically) without getting into too much trouble. If you refuse to lend your car, for example, your friends may not become upset with you if you have followed their friendship norms in other areas in the past, for you've earned the right to be different, to deviate from their normative rules in this area. Thus, resisting normative influence may not be as difficult (or scary) as you might think, if you have earned idiosyncrasy credits with the group.

> People create social conditions and people can change them.
> —Tess Onwueme

idiosyncrasy credits: the credits a person earns, over time, by conforming to group norms; if enough idiosyncrasy credits are earned, the person can, on occasion, behave deviantly without retribution from the group

Minority Influence: When the Few Influence the Many

We shouldn't leave our discussion of normative social influence with the impression that the individual never has an effect on the group. As Serge Moscovici (1985) says, if groups really did succeed in silencing nonconformists, rejecting deviants, and persuading everyone to go along with the majority point of view, then how could change ever be introduced into the system? We would all be like little robots, marching along with everyone else in monotonous synchrony, never able to adapt to changing reality.

Instead, Moscovici (1985) argues, the individual, or the minority, can affect change in the majority. This is called **minority influence**. The key is consistency: People with minority views must express the same view over time, and different members of the minority must agree with each other. If a person in the minority wavers between two different viewpoints or if two individuals express different minority views, then the majority will dismiss them as people who have peculiar and groundless opinions. If, however, the minority expresses a consistent, unwavering view, the majority is likely to take notice and may even adopt the minority view (Moscovici & Nemeth, 1974).

In a recent meta-analysis of nearly 100 studies, Wendy Wood and her colleagues describe how minority influence operates (Wood, Lundgren, Ouellette, Busceme, & Blackstone, 1994). People in the majority can cause other group members to conform through normative influence. As in the Asch experiments, the conformity that occurs may be a case of public compliance without private acceptance. People in the minority can rarely influence others through normative means—the majority has little concern for how the minority views them. In fact, majority group members may be loath to agree publicly with the minority; they don't want anyone to think that they agree with those unusual, strange views of the minority. Thus, minorities exert their influence on the group via the other principal method—informational social influence. The minority introduces new, unexpected information to the group and causes the group to examine the issues more carefully. Such careful examination may cause the majority to realize that the minority view has merit, leading the group to adopt all or part of the minority's view (Latané & Wolf, 1981; Levine & Russo, 1987; Maass & Clark, 1984; Moscovici, 1980; Nemeth, 1986; Nemeth, Mayseless, Sherman, & Brown, 1990). In short, majorities often cause public compliance because of normative social influence, whereas minorities often cause private acceptance because of informational social influence.

minority influence: the case where a minority of group members influence the behavior or beliefs of the majority

> Never let anyone keep you contained and never let anyone keep your voice silent.
> —Adam Clayton Powell

Compliance: Requests to Change Your Behavior

To summarize, we have discussed two main reasons why people conform: because other people serve as a useful source of information (informational social influence) and because of pressures to follow social norms (normative social influence). In the remainder of this chapter, we will see how these reasons for conformity apply to some familiar situations in which you might be asked to do something you really do not want to do. Some of these situations are quite common, such as a salesperson pressuring you into subscribing to some magazines or a charity trying to get you to donate money to their cause. Others are less common but more frightening, such as an authority figure asking you to do something that is against your morals. When and why will people conform in these situations?

We will begin with the case of **compliance**—that is, a change in behavior due to a direct request from another person. We can hardly make it through a day without someone asking us to do something we would rather not do, be it a letter from a charity asking for money, a telephone call (invariably during dinner) from someone selling vacation property, or a friend wanting to borrow $25. Social psychologists have studied when and why people are likely to comply with these kinds of requests (Cialdini, 1993).

compliance: a change in behavior due to a direct request from another person

Mindless Conformity: Operating on Automatic Pilot

We have a friend who recently drove to the center of a large city to attend a concert. He parked his car in an outdoor, commercial lot near the concert hall. As he got out of his car, a woman handed him a ticket to put on his dashboard and said that the parking fee was $5. Our friend gave the woman the money and went on his way, only to be stopped by the real parking attendant. It turned out that the woman did not work for the parking company at all but was a con artist who had found a way to make a quick buck: She made it look like she was the real parking attendant and quickly disappeared with people's money.

It is easy to shake our heads at such stories and think that we would never be so naive as to fall for such a scam. Few of us, however, stop and think carefully about every single social interaction we have; it is much more efficient to follow social norms quickly and automatically. There are many well-learned norms that we follow without thinking much about it, such as ones that say "Wear socks that are the same color," "Greet people by shaking their hands and not patting their heads," and "Give money to legitimate-looking salespeople or parking attendants." When people follow such norms automatically, we say they have engaged in **mindless conformity,** defined as following a norm without thinking about what they are doing or why—as if they were operating on automatic pilot.

mindless conformity: obeying internalized social norms without deliberating about one's actions

There is a great advantage to mindless conformity. If we had to stop and think about how to respond in every single social situation, it would be difficult to make it through the day. In most cases, the social norms we follow automatically lead to appropriate behavior. Most people who give us a ticket in a parking lot really are parking attendants, and most people would rather have us shake their hands than pat their heads. Imagine that every time you parked your car you had to ask the attendant for identification, or that every time you met someone new you had to figure out whether he or she preferred a handshake or a head pat. Not a very efficient way to live our lives.

As we discussed in Chapter 3, however, behaving and thinking automatically come with a cost: By putting ourselves on automatic pilot, without carefully monitoring what we are doing, we sometimes end up following the wrong social norm and behave inappropriately (Cialdini, 1993; Langer, 1989). For example, the atomic scientist Robert Oppenheimer is said to have been so engrossed in his newspaper at breakfast one morning that he put a tip down on the table when he got up, forgetting that he was eating at home and not at a restaurant (needless to say, his wife was not amused).

Ellen Langer and her colleagues have studied the conditions under which people engage in mindless conformity. To 40 secretaries at a New York university, they sent a memo that said, "This paper is to be returned immediately to Room

238 through interoffice mail." Like almost all other memos at this university, this one was unsigned. Note that this is a pretty silly request; if the person who sent the memo wanted it, why did he or she send it in the first place? Langer and her colleagues hypothesized that secretaries would go ahead and return the memo because they would mindlessly follow the norm that says "Do what memos tell you to do." They were right; 90 percent of the secretaries dutifully returned the memo to room 238.

When do people go off automatic pilot, realizing that they are following an inappropriate norm? Langer and her colleagues reasoned that anything that would make people stop and think about what they were doing would make them behave less mindlessly. One way of accomplishing this, they figured, was to make the memo look different from the hundreds of ones the secretaries normally received. They sent other secretaries the exact same memo except that it was signed, "Sincerely, John Lewis"—an aspect that was highly unusual at this university. Signing the memo in this way caused at least some of the secretaries to turn off their automatic pilot and think about what they were doing, thereby realizing that it was a silly request: In this condition, only 60 percent of the secretaries returned the memo.

The moral is, if you want people to do what you tell them, find a situation in which they normally comply with requests and do not give them much time to think about what they are doing—as in the case of the con artist in the parking lot. We turn now to another such situation that, though not illegal, is no less effective.

The Door-in-the-Face Technique

Suppose you have agreed to go door-to-door and ask people to donate money to the American Heart Association. Here is a good way to get people to give: First, ask people to donate a large amount of money, with the full expectation that they will refuse. When someone answers the door, you might say, "Hello, I'm asking for donations to the American Heart Association. Do you think you could donate $500?" Once people refuse, you immediately retreat to a more reasonable request: "Well, OK, but do you think you could donate $5?" This approach is called the **door-in-the-face technique,** because the first request is purposefully so large that people will want to slam the door shut. Several studies show that it works well in getting people to agree to the second, more reasonable request.

For example, Robert Cialdini and his colleagues (1975) decided to see if they could get students to volunteer to chaperon problem adolescents on a two-hour trip to the zoo. When they approached students on a college campus, only 17 percent agreed to this request. In another condition, before asking people to go on the zoo trip the experimenter made a very large request. "We're currently recruiting university students to work as volunteer, nonpaid counselors at the County Juvenile Detention Center," the experimenter said. "The position would require two hours of your time per week for a minimum of two years. Would you be interested in being considered for one of these positions?" (Cialdini et al., 1975, p. 208). Not surprisingly, no one agreed to such a large time commitment. When students refused, the experimenter said, "Well, we also have another program you might be interested in," and went on to ask if they would chaperon the zoo trip. These students were three times more likely to agree to go on the zoo trip than people asked this smaller request alone (see Figure 8.6).

door-in-the-face technique: a technique to get people to comply with a request, whereby people are presented first with a large request, which they are expected to refuse, and then with a smaller, more reasonable request, to which it is hoped they will acquiesce

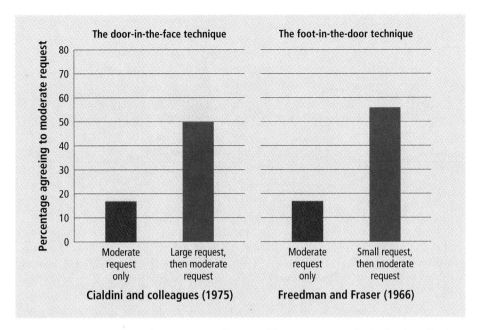

FIGURE 8.6   Two ways to increase compliance with a request. ■ Both the door-in-the-face technique and the foot-in-the-door technique increase compliance to a moderate request. But which technique is likely to lead to the most *long-term* compliance, whereby people agree to repeated moderate requests? See the text for the answer. (Adapted from Cialdini et al., 1975; Freedman & Fraser, 1966)

Why does the door-in-the-face technique work? The answer lies in the **reciprocity norm,** which says that if people do something nice for us, we should reciprocate by doing something nice for them. Salespeople and charities often capitalize on this tendency for people to follow the reciprocity norm mindlessly. They give us a small gift, such as greeting cards, personalized address labels, or free food to taste in the grocery store. Their plan is to make us feel obligated to reciprocate by buying their product or giving money to their cause. To illustrate how strong the reciprocity norm is—and how mindlessly people follow it—one researcher chose some names at random out of the telephone book and sent each person a Christmas card, signed with his name (Kunz & Woolcott, 1976). Most people sent a card back to him, even though he was a complete stranger!

In the case of the door-in-the-face technique, the reciprocity norm is invoked when the person backs down from an extreme request to a moderate one. This puts pressure on us to reciprocate by moderating our position too—from an outright "No" to a "Well, OK, I guess so." We feel as if the requester is doing us a favor by changing his or her position, trying to meet us halfway; because of the reciprocity norm, we then feel obligated to return the favor and appear reasonable too.

One disadvantage of the door-in-the-face technique is that it is likely to be short-lived. Once people have agreed to the smaller request, they have met their obligation by meeting the requester halfway; therefore, they will not be more likely to agree to subsequent requests. Suppose, for example, that your goal is to get people to donate money to the American Heart Association on a regular

reciprocity norm: a social norm stating that receiving anything positive from another person requires you to reciprocate (or behave similarly) in response

Calvin and Hobbes copyright © Watterson.

basis. Once you have retreated from your request for $500 to a more reasonable request for $5 and your neighbor has met you halfway by agreeing, his or her obligation is over. If you ask for another $5 next month, he or she may well feel exploited, thinking, "This person sure is pushy. You'd think I'd get a break after being so reasonable last time." If you want to get long-term compliance, it is better to use a different approach, called the **foot-in-the-door technique.**

The Foot-in-the-Door Technique

The expression *foot-in-the-door* comes from salespeople who discovered that they were more likely to make a sale if they could get the customer to agree to an initial, smaller request, such as letting them into his or her home to display their products. This technique is thus the opposite of the door-in-the-face method: You start with a very small request to which almost everyone will agree, and then follow that up with a larger request. Does this technique work? To find out, Jonathan Freedman and Scott Fraser (1966) tested whether homeowners would agree to put up a large, obtrusive sign in their front yards that said "Drive Carefully." When someone came to their door and asked the homeowners to do this, only 17 percent agreed. But what if they had agreed earlier to a smaller request? The researchers first asked a different group of homeowners to sign a petition indicating that they were in favor of safe driving. Just about everyone agreed to this innocuous request. Two weeks later, a different individual approached these homeowners and asked them to put the sign in their front yard. Though the sign was just as big and obtrusive to these people as to those in the control group, who had not been contacted earlier, they were more than three times more likely to agree to put it in their front yard (see Figure 8.6).

The foot-in-the-door technique works for a very different reason than the door-in-the-face technique. Instead of invoking a reciprocity norm, it triggers a kind of informational social influence, whereby people gain information by complying with the first request. In this case, the information people gain is about themselves: By agreeing to the small request, people come to view themselves as the kind of person who helps out on important community issues. Once this self-image is in place, it makes people more likely to agree to the second, larger request, even when it comes later. Thus, if you want to get long-term compliance, it is better to instill the relevant self-image in people with the foot-in-the-door technique. If you are collecting money for the American Heart Association and want your neighbors to donate on a long-term basis, first ask them for a small amount, such as 50 cents or $1. If they agree, they will come to view themselves as the kind of people who give to this worthy cause, increasing the likelihood that future donations will be forthcoming (Burger, 1986; Cialdini, 1993; DeJong, 1979; Dillard, Hunter, & Burgoon, 1984).

Obedience to Authority

The kinds of compliance we have just discussed can be annoying; a skillful salesperson, for example, can make us buy something we don't really need. Rarely, however, do such instances of everyday compliance have life-or-death consequences. Yet unfortunately, another kind of conformity can be extremely serious and even tragic: Obeying the orders of an authority figure to hurt or kill a fellow human being. Consider again the My Lai massacre. Why did the soldiers obey Lieutenant Calley's order to kill the innocent villagers? We suspect that all of the reasons that people conform combined to produce this atrocity: The behavior of the other soldiers made the killing seem like the right thing to do (informational influence); the soldiers wanted to avoid rejection and ridicule from their peers (normative influence); and the soldiers followed the obedience to authority social norm too readily, without questioning or taking personal responsibility for what they were doing (mindless conformity). It was the power of these conformity pressures that lead to the tragedy, not personality defects in the American soldiers. This makes the incident all the more frightening, because it implies that similar incidents can occur with any group of soldiers if similar conformity pressures are present.

■ Victims of the Holocaust, Nordhausen, April 1945. According to social psychologists, most of the German guards and citizens who participated in the Holocaust were not madmen but ordinary people exposed to extraordinary social influences.

The twentieth century has been marked by repeated atrocities and genocides—in Germany, Armenia, the Ukraine, Rwanda—and the list goes on. Thus, one of the most important questions facing the world's inhabitants is, where does obedience end and personal responsibility begin? The philosopher Hannah Arendt (1965) argues that most participants in the Holocaust were not sadists or psychopaths who enjoyed the mass murder of innocent people but ordinary citizens subjected to complex and powerful social pressures. She covered the trial of Adolf Eichmann, the Nazi official responsible for the transportation of Jews to the death camps, and concluded that he was not the monster that many people made him out to be but a commonplace bureaucrat like any other bureaucrat, who did what he was told without questioning his orders.

Our point is not that Eichmann or the soldiers at My Lai should be excused for the crimes they committed. The point is that it is too easy to explain their behavior as the acts of madmen. It is more fruitful—and indeed more frightening—to view their behavior as the acts of ordinary people exposed to extraordinary social influence. But how do we know whether this interpretation of the Holocaust and My Lai is correct? How can we be sure that it was social influence and not the work of evil people that produced these atrocities? The way to find out is to study social pressure in the laboratory under controlled conditions. We could take a sample of ordinary citizens, subject them to various kinds of social influence, and see to what extent they will conform and obey. Can an experimenter influence ordinary people to commit immoral acts, such as inflicting severe pain on an innocent bystander? Stanley Milgram (1963, 1974, 1976) decided to find out, in what has become the most famous series of studies in social psychology.

Imagine that you were a participant in one of Milgram's studies. You answer an ad in the paper asking for participants in a study on memory and learning. When you arrive at the laboratory, you meet another participant, a 47-year-old, somewhat overweight, pleasant-looking fellow. The experimenter explains that one of you will play the role of a teacher and the other a learner. You draw a slip of paper out of a hat and discover that you will be the teacher. It turns out that your job is to teach the other participant a list of word pairs (e.g., *blue-box, nice-day*) and then test him on the list. The experimenter instructs you to deliver an electric shock to the learner whenever he makes a mistake, because the purpose of the study is to examine the effects of punishment on learning.

■ Left: The shock generator used in the Milgram experiments. Right: The learner (an accomplice of the experimenter) is strapped into the chair, and electrodes are attached to his arm. (Adapted from Milgram, 1974)

You watch as the other participant—the learner—is strapped into a chair in an adjacent room and electrodes are attached to his arm. You are seated in front of a shock generator whose 30 switches deliver varying levels of shock in 15-volt increments, from 15 to 450 volts. There are labels accompanying these switches, from "Slight Shock," to "Danger: Severe Shock," to an ominous "XXX" next to the highest levels (see the photos on this page). The experimenter tells you that the first time the learner makes a mistake, you should give him a shock of 15 volts—the smallest amount—and then increase the amount by 15 volts for each subsequent mistake he makes. So that you will know what the shocks are like, the experimenter gives you a sample shock of 45 volts, which is rather painful.

You read the list of word pairs to the learner and then begin the testing phase. After announcing the first word of a pair, you give four possible answers; the learner responds by pressing one of four switches, which illuminates a light on the answer box in front of you. Everything begins smoothly, as the learner gets the first few right. Then he gets some wrong, and as instructed, you deliver the shocks. At this point, you are probably getting concerned about the number and severity of the shocks you will have to give. When you get to the 75-volt level, the learner, whom you can hear over an intercom, emits a painful "Ugh!" Perhaps you pause and ask the experimenter what you should do. "Please continue," he responds. As the learner continues to make mistakes, you deliver a few more shocks. The learner protests, shouting, "Ugh! Experimenter! That's all! Get me out of here!" You look at the experimenter with grave concern. He tells you, "It is absolutely essential that you continue." (See Figure 8.7.)

What would you do? How many people do you think would continue to obey the experimenter and increase the levels of shock until they had delivered the maximum amount—450 volts?

When this question was posed to psychology majors at Yale University, they estimated that only about 1 percent of the population would go to this extreme. A sample of middle-class adults and a panel of psychiatrists made similar predictions. However, from our discussion of conformity thus far, you are probably not so optimistic. Whereas no one would have believed that such travesties as the Holocaust or My Lai could have occurred, they did. Like the soldiers at My Lai, most of Milgram's participants succumbed to the pressure of an authority figure. The average maximum amount of shock delivered was 360 volts, and 62.5 percent of the participants delivered the 450-volt shock—the maximum amount. A full 80 percent of the participants continued giving the shocks even after the learner, who earlier had mentioned that he had a heart condition, screamed, "Let me out of here! Let me out of here! My heart's bothering me. Let me out of here! . . . Get me out of here! I've had enough. I won't be in the experiment any more" (Milgram, 1974, p. 56).

It is important to note that the learner was actually an accomplice of the experimenter and playacted his role; he did not receive any actual shocks. It is equally important to note that the study was very convincingly done, so that people believed they really were shocking the learner. Here is Milgram's description of one participant's response to the teacher role:

> I observed a mature and initially poised businessman enter the laboratory smiling and confident. Within 20 minutes he was reduced to a twitching, stuttering wreck, who was rapidly approaching a point of nervous collapse. He constantly pulled on his earlobe, and twisted his hands. At one point he pushed his fist into

TRANSCRIPT OF LEARNER'S PROTESTS IN MILGRAM'S OBEDIENCE EXPERIMENT

75 volts Ugh!

90 volts Ugh!

105 volts Ugh! (louder)

120 volts Ugh! Hey this really hurts.

135 volts Ugh!!

150 volts Ugh!!! Experimenter! That's all. Get me out of here. I told you I had heart trouble. My heart's starting to bother me now. Get me out of here, please. My heart's starting to bother me. I refuse to go on. Let me out.

165 volts Ugh! Let me out! (shouting)

180 volts Ugh! I can't stand the pain. Let me out of here! (shouting)

195 volts Ugh! Let me out of here. Let me out of here. My heart's bothering me. Let me out of here! You have no right to keep me here! Let me out! Let me out of here! Let me out! Let me out of here! My heart's bothering me. Let me out! Let me out!

210 volts Ugh!! Experimenter! Get me out of here. I've had enough. I won't be in the experiment any more.

225 volts Ugh!

240 volts Ugh!

255 volts Ugh! Get me out of here.

270 volts (Agonized scream) Let me out of here. Let me out of here. Let me out of here. Let me out. Do you hear? Let me out of here.

285 volts (Agonized scream)

300 volts (Agonized scream) I absolutely refuse to answer any more. Get me out of here. You can't hold me here. Get me out. Get me out of here.

315 volts (Intensely agonized scream) I told you I refuse to answer. I'm no longer part of this experiment.

330 volts (Intense and prolonged agonized scream) Let me out of here. Let me out of here. My heart's bothering me. Let me out, I tell you. (Hysterically) Let me out of here. Let me out of here. You have no right to hold me here. Let me out! Let me out! Let me out of here! Let me out!

Instructions used by Experimenter to Achieve Obedience

Prod 1: Please continue. *or* Please go on.
Prod 2: The experiment requires that you continue.
Prod 3: It is absolutely essential that you continue.
Prod 4: You have no other choice; you must go on.

The prods were always made in sequence: Only if prod 1 had been unsuccessful could prod 2 be used. If the subject refused to obey the experimenter after prod 4, the experiment was terminated. The experimenter's tone of voice was at all times firm, but not impolite. The sequence was begun anew on each occasion that the subject balked or showed reluctance to follow orders.

Special prods. If the subject asked whether the learner was likely to suffer permanent physical injury, the experimenter said:

Although the shocks may be painful, there is no permanent tissue damage, so please go on. [Followed by prods 2, 3, and 4 if necessary.]

If the subject said that the learner did not want to go on, the experimenter replied: Whether the learner likes it or not, you must go on until he has learned all the word pairs correctly. So please go on. [Followed by prods 2, 3, and 4 if necessary.]

FIGURE 8.7 ■ Transcript of the learner's protests in Milgram's obedience study (left). Transcript of the prods used by the experimenter to get people to continue giving shocks (right). (Adapted from Milgram, 1963, 1974)

his forehead and muttered, "Oh God, let's stop it." And yet he continued to respond to every word of the experimenter, and obeyed to the end. (Milgram, 1963, p. 377)

Why did so many research participants (who ranged in age from the twenties to the fifties and included blue-collar, white-collar, and professional workers) conform to the wishes of the experimenter, to the point where they (at least in their own minds) were inflicting great pain on another human being? And why were the college students, middle-class adults, and psychiatrists so wrong in their predictions about what people would do? Each of the reasons that people conform combined in an insidious way, causing Milgram's participants to obey—just as the soldiers did at My Lai. Let's take a close look at how this worked in the Milgram experiments.

The Role of Normative Influence

First, it is clear that normative pressures made it difficult for people to refuse to continue. As we have seen, if someone really wants us to do something, it can be difficult to say no. This is particularly true when the person is in a position of authority over us. Milgram's participants probably believed that if they refused to continue, the experimenter would be disappointed, hurt, or maybe even angry— all of which put pressure on them to continue. It is important to note that this study, unlike the Asch study, was set up so that the experimenter actively attempted to get people to conform, giving such stern commands as "It is absolutely essential that you continue." When an authority figure is so insistent that we obey, it is difficult to say no.

The fact that normative pressures were present in the Milgram experiments is clear from a variation of the study that he conducted. This time, there were three teachers, two of whom were confederates of the experimenter. One confederate was instructed to read the list of word pairs; the other, to tell the learner whether his response was correct. The (real) participant's job was to deliver the shocks, increasing their severity with each error, as in the original experiment. At 150 volts, when the learner gave his first vehement protest, the first confederate refused to continue, despite the experimenter's command that he do so. At 210 volts, the second confederate refused to continue. The result? Seeing their peers disobey made it much easier for the actual participant to disobey too. Only 10 percent of the participants gave the maximum level of shock in this experiment (see Figure 8.8). This result is similar to Asch's finding that people did not

FIGURE 8.8   The results of different versions of the Milgram experiment. ■ Obedience is highest in the standard version, where the participant is ordered to deliver increasing levels of shock to another person (left panel). Obedience drops when other participants model disobedience or when the authority figure is not present (two middle panels). Finally, when no orders are given to increase the shocks, almost no participants do so (right panel). The contrast in behavior between the far-left and -right panels indicates just how powerful the social norm of obedience is. (Adapted from Milgram, 1974)

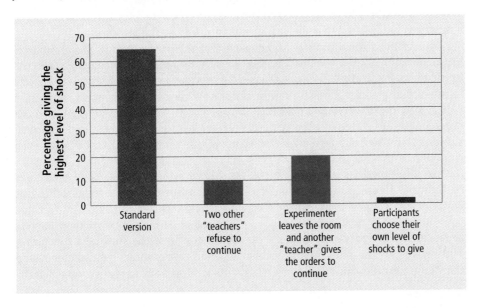

conform nearly so much when one accomplice bucked the majority and consistently gave the correct answer.

The Role of Informational Influence

Despite the power of the normative pressures in Milgram's original study, they are not the sole reason people complied. The experimenter was authoritative and insistent, but he was not pointing a gun at participants and telling them to "conform or else." The participants were free to get up and leave anytime they wanted to. Why didn't they, especially when the experimenter was a stranger they had never met before and probably would never see again?

As we saw earlier, when people are in a confusing situation and unsure of what they should do, they use other people to reach a definition of the situation. Informational social influence is especially powerful when the situation is ambiguous, when it is a crisis, and when the other people in the situation have some expertise. The situation faced by Milgram's participants was clearly confusing, unfamiliar, and upsetting. It all seemed straightforward enough when the experimenter explained it to them, but then it turned into something else altogether. The learner cried out in pain, but the experimenter told the participant that, while the shocks were painful, they did not cause any permanent tissue damage. The participant didn't want to hurt anyone, but he or she had agreed to be in the study and to follow the directions. When in such a state of conflict, it was only natural for the participants to use an expert—the experimenter—to help them decide what was the right thing to do.

Another version of the experiment that Milgram performed supports the idea that informational influence was operative. This version was identical to the original one except for three critical changes: First, the experimenter never said which shock levels were to be given, leaving this decision up to the teacher (the real participant). Second, before the study began the experimenter received a telephone call and had to leave the room. He told the participant to continue without him. Third, there was a confederate playing the role of an additional teacher, whose job was to record how long it took the learner to respond. When the experimenter left, this other teacher said that he had just thought of a good system: How about if they increased the level of shock each time the learner made a mistake? He insisted that the real participant follow this procedure.

Note that in this situation, the expertise of the person giving the commands has been removed: He was just a regular person, no more knowledgeable than the participants themselves. Because he lacked expertise, people were much less likely to use him as a source of information about how they should respond. As seen in Figure 8.8, in this version compliance dropped from 65 percent giving the maximum amount of shock to only 20 percent. (The fact that 20 percent still complied suggests that some people were so uncertain about what to do that they used even a nonexpert as a guide.)

An additional variation conducted by Milgram underscores the importance of authority-figures-as-experts in eliciting such conformity and obedience. In this variation, two experimenters gave the real participants their orders. At 150 volts, when the learner first cried out that he wanted to stop, the two experimenters began to disagree about whether they should continue the study. At this point, 100 percent of the participant-teachers stopped responding. Note that nothing the victim ever did caused all the participants to stop obeying; however, when the authorities' definition of the situation became unclear, the participants broke out of their conforming role.

Other Causes of Obedience

Both normative and informational social influences were very strong in Milgram's experiments. However, these reasons for complying still fall short of fully explaining why people acted so inhumanely. They seem to account for why people initially complied, but after it became increasingly obvious to people what they were doing to the learner, why didn't they realize that what they were doing was terribly wrong and stop? Just as the soldiers at My Lai persisted in killing the villagers long after it was obvious that they were unarmed and defenseless civilians, many of Milgram's participants pulled the shock levers time after time after time, despite the cries of anguish from a fellow human being.

To understand this continued compliance, we need to consider additional aspects of the situation. First, as we saw earlier, people sometimes follow the wrong social norm, such as the secretaries in Ellen Langer's study who followed the "do what memos tell you to do" norm, even when it was pretty pointless. Sometimes we are on automatic pilot and don't realize that the social norm we are following is inappropriate or nonapplicable to the situation we are in.

We don't mean to imply that Milgram's participants were completely mindless, or unaware of what they were doing. All were terribly concerned about the plight of the victim. The problem was that they were caught in a web of conflicting norms, and it was difficult to determine which one to follow. At the beginning of the experiment, it was perfectly reasonable to obey the norm that says, "Obey expert, legitimate authority figures." The experimenter was confident and knowledgeable, and the study seemed like it was a reasonable test of an interesting hypothesis. So why not cooperate and do as you are told?

But gradually the rules of the game changed, and this "obey authority" norm was no longer appropriate. The experimenter, who seemed so reasonable before, was now asking people to inflict great pain on their fellow participant. But once people are following one norm, it can be difficult to switch midstream, realizing that this norm is no longer appropriate and that another norm, "Do not inflict needless harm on a fellow human being," should be followed. For example, suppose the experimenter had explained, at the outset, that he would like people to deliver possibly fatal shocks to the other participant. How many people would have agreed? Very few, we suspect, because it would have been clear that this violated an important social and personal norm about inflicting harm on others. Instead, the experimenter pulled a kind of "bait-and-switch" routine, whereby he first made it look like an "obey authority" norm was appropriate and then gradually violated this norm.

It was particularly difficult for people to abandon the "obey authority" norm in the Milgram experiments, because of two key aspects of the situation. First, the experiment was fast-paced, preventing the participants from reflecting about what they were doing. They were busy recording the learner's responses, keeping track of which word pairs to test him on next, and determining whether his responses were right or wrong. Given that they had to attend carefully to these details and move along at a fast pace, it was difficult for them to realize that the norm that was guiding their behavior—cooperating with the authority figure—was, after a while, no longer appropriate. We suspect that if halfway through the

> When you think of the long and gloomy history of man, you will find more hideous crimes have been committed in the name of obedience than in the name of rebellion.
>
> –C. P. Snow

experiment, Milgram's participants had been told to take a 15-minute break and go sit in a room by themselves, many more would have successfully redefined the situation and refused to continue.

Second, it is important to remember that the experimenter asked people to increase the shocks in very small increments. The participants did not go from giving a small shock to giving a potentially lethal one. Instead, at any given point they were faced with the decision about whether to increase the amount of shock they had just given by 15 volts. As we saw in Chapter 6, every time a person makes an important or difficult decision, dissonance is produced, with resultant pressures to reduce it. An effective way of reducing dissonance produced by a difficult decision is to decide that the decision was fully justified. But because reducing dissonance provides a justification for the preceding action, in some situations it makes a person vulnerable to pressures leading to an escalation of the chosen activity.

Thus, in the Milgram study, once the participants agreed to administer the first shock, it created pressure on them to continue to obey. As the participants administered each successive level of shock, they had to justify it in their own minds. Once a particular shock level was justified, it became very difficult for them to find a place where they could draw the line and stop. How could they say, in effect, "OK, I gave him 200 volts, but not 215—never 215!"? Each succeeding justification laid the groundwork for the next shock and would have been dissonant with quitting; 215 volts is not that different from 200, and 230 is not that different from 215. Those who did break off the series did so against enormous internal pressure to continue.

Mika Haritos-Fatouros (1988) reports that this incremental approach was used by the Greek military dictatorship of the late 1960s to train torturers. In his interviews with former torturers, Haritos-Fatouros learned that their first contact with political prisoners was to bring them food and "occasionally" give them some blows. Next, they were put on guard while others conducted torture sessions. Next, they would take part in a few group floggings or beatings. The

■ These individuals are protesting the mayor of New York's proposed budget cuts to AIDS programs. The signs and masks silently reprimand bureaucrats for losing their sense of personal responsibility and hiding behind excuses of conformity and obedience.

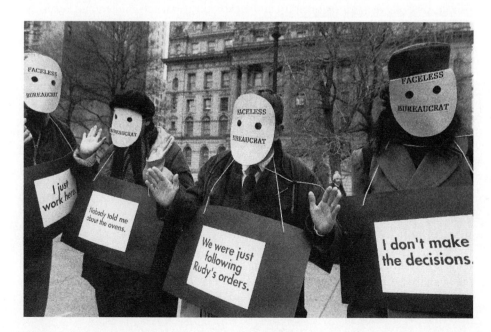

last step, being in charge of a torture session, "was announced suddenly to the [man] by the commander-in-chief without leaving him any time for reflection" (1988, p. 1117).

Before leaving our discussion of the Milgram studies, we should mention one other possible interpretation of his results: Did the participants act so inhumanely because there is an evil side to human nature, lurking just below the surface, ready to be expressed with the flimsiest excuse? After all, it was socially acceptable to inflict harm on another person in the Milgram experiment; in fact, subjects were ordered to do so. Perhaps this factor allowed the expression of a universal aggressive urge. To test this hypothesis, Milgram conducted another version of his study. Everything was the same except that the experimenter told the participants that they could choose any level of shock they wished to give the learner when he made a mistake. Milgram gave people permission to use the highest levels, telling them that there was a lot to be learned from all levels of shock. This instruction should have allowed any aggressive urges to be expressed unchecked. Instead, the participants chose to give very mild shocks (see Figure 8.8). Only 2.5 percent of the participants gave the maximum amount of shock. Thus, the Milgram studies do not show that people have an evil streak that shines through when the surface is scratched. Instead, these studies demonstrate that social pressures can combine in insidious ways to make humane people act in an inhumane manner. Let us conclude this chapter with the words of Stanley Milgram:

> Even Eichmann was sickened when he toured the concentration camps, but, in order to participate in mass murder he had only to sit at a desk and shuffle papers. At the same time the man in the camp who actually dropped Cyclon-B into the gas chambers is able to justify his behavior on the grounds that he is only following orders from above. Thus there is fragmentation of the total human act; no one man decides to carry out the evil act and is confronted with its consequences. The person who assumes full responsibility for the act has evaporated. Perhaps this is the most common characteristic of socially organized evil in modern society. (1976, pp. 183–184)

SUMMARY

In this chapter, we focused on **conformity,** or how people change their behavior due to the real (or imagined) influence of others. We found that there are two main reasons people conform: because of informational and normative social influences. **Informational social influence** occurs when people do not know what is the correct (or best) thing to do or say. This reaction typically occurs in new, confusing, or crisis situations, where the definition of the situation is unclear. People look to the behavior of others as an important source of information and use it to choose appropriate courses of action for themselves. Informational influence usually results in **private accep-**tance, wherein people genuinely believe in what other people are doing or saying.

People are most likely to use others as a source of information when the situation (and thus what they should do) is ambiguous; here a person is most open to the influence of others. Experts are powerful sources of influence, since they typically have the most information about appropriate responses. A special type of ambiguous situation is a crisis; fear, confusion, and panic increase our reliance on others to help us decide what to do.

Using others as a source of information can backfire, however, as when people panic because others are doing so. **Contagion** occurs when emotions and behaviors spread rapidly throughout a large group; one example is research on **mass psychogenic illness.** You can best resist the inappropriate use of others as a source of information by checking the information you are getting against your common sense and internal moral compass.

Normative social influence occurs for a different reason—we change our behavior to match that of others not because they seem to know better what is going on but because we want to remain a member of the group, continue to gain the advantages of group membership, and avoid the pain of ridicule and rejection. We conform to the group's **social norms,** implicit or explicit rules for acceptable behaviors, values, and beliefs. Normative social influence can occur even in unambiguous situations; people will conform to others for normative reasons even if they know that what they are doing is wrong. Normative social influence usually results in **public compliance** but not **private acceptance** of other people's ideas and behaviors.

Social impact theory specifies when normative social influence is most likely to occur, by referring to the strength, immediacy, and number of group members. We are more likely to conform when the group is one we care about, when the group members are unanimous in their thoughts or behaviors, and when the group size is three or more. Failure to respond to normative influences can be painful. Normative pressures operate on many levels in social life: They influence our eating habits, body image, hobbies, fashion, and so on; they promote correct (polite) behavior in society; and they can be an agent for social change. We can resist inappropriate normative pressures by gathering **idiosyncrasy credits,** over time, from a group whose membership we value. Further, **minority influence,** whereby a minority of group members influence the beliefs and behavior of the majority, can occur under certain conditions.

The reasons people conform can be applied to two kinds of everyday behavior: **compliance** and obedience. Sometimes people comply with inappropriate requests because of **mindless conformity,** whereby they operate as if on automatic pilot, never questioning or thinking about the social norms they are following. Another proven compliance method is the **door-in-the-face technique,** where a requester starts out with a big request in order to get people to agree to a second, smaller request. This technique works because of the **reciprocity norm;** when the requester retreats from the larger to the smaller request, it puts pressure on people to reciprocate by agreeing to the smaller request. The **foot-in-the-door technique** is also effective; here, the requester starts out with a very small request to get people to agree to a larger request.

In the most famous series of studies in social psychology, Stanley Milgram examined the limits of obedience to authority figures. Informational and normative pressures combined to cause chilling levels of obedience, to the point where a majority of the participants administered what they thought were near-lethal shocks to a fellow human being. In addition, the participants were caught in a web of conflicting social norms and were asked to increase the level of shocks in small increments. After justifying to themselves that they had delivered one level of shock, it was very difficult for people to decide that a slightly higher level of shock was wrong. Unfortunately, the conditions that produced such extreme antisocial behavior in Milgram's laboratory have been present in real-life tragedies, such as the Holocaust and the mass murders at My Lai in Vietnam.

IF YOU ARE INTERESTED . . .

Cialdini, R. B. (1993). *Influence: Science and practice* (3rd ed.). New York: HarperCollins. An extremely readable and entertaining account of research on conformity, with applications to everyday life.

Conroy, Pat. *The Lords of Discipline*. A story of conformity and disobedience set in a military academy (similar to the author's alma mater, The Citadel). The main character ultimately defies social norms, and puts his life on the line, to protect the lone African American cadet from the white students' violence.

Keneally, Thomas. *Schindler's List*. The compelling, true story of how one man protected and saved a thousand Polish Jews from certain death in Hitler's concentration camps. In particular, it traces his metamorphosis from a self-centered, opportunistic businessman to a compassionate humanitarian who bravely disobeys the Third Reich. The film based on this work won the Academy Award for Best Picture.

Milgram, S. (1974). *Obedience to authority: An experimental view*. New York: Harper & Row. A detailed description of the most famous studies in social psychology: those in which people were induced to deliver what they believed were lethal shocks to a fellow human being. Nearly 20 years after it was published, Milgram's book remains a poignant and insightful account of obedience to authority.

Priscilla, Queen of the Desert. A hilarious and heartwarming tale of three male transvestite entertainers who take their show on the road in the Australian outback. Needless to say, the townspeople have never seen such nonconformity. Remade in the United States as *To Wong Foo, with love, Julie Newmar,* starring Patrick Swayze and Wesley Snipes.

Salinger, J. D. *The Catcher in the Rye.* The classic "coming of age" novel, still a delight no matter how old you are. Follow teenager Holden Caulfield for a few days as he discourses on "the phonies" and other less than attractive aspects of adult conformity.

Sherif, M. (1936). *The psychology of social norms.* New York: Harper. An entertaining account of Sherif's study of informational social influence, wherein people judged how much a light was moving. It is still worth reading today.

The Age of Innocence. The tale of two star-crossed lovers (Daniel Day-Lewis and Michelle Pfeiffer), caught up in the constricting and unforgiving social norms of upper-class New York in the 1870s. Based on a novel by Edith Wharton.

Turner, J. C. (1991). *Social influence.* Pacific Grove, CA: Brooks/Cole. An up-to-date, in-depth account of social psychological research on social influence and conformity.

Twelve Angry Men. A gripping account of jury deliberations, this 1957 film stars Henry Fonda as the lone dissenter on the jury, desperately trying to convince his peers that their judgment of guilty in a murder case is wrong.

Wharton, Edith. *House of Mirth.* A huge bestseller upon its publication in 1905, this novel chronicles the elaborate and suffocating conformity of late nineteenth-century New York society, and how one young woman is destroyed by it.

Chapter 9

Group Processes: Influence in Social Groups

Chapter Outline

O n a cold January day in 1961, John F. Kennedy was inaugurated as the thirty-fifth president of the United States. The author of a romance novel could not have written a better script: Kennedy was young, bright, and handsome; he came from a wealthy, well-connected family; he was a war hero. He had an intelligent, beautiful wife and two adorable children. In his election victory over Richard Nixon, Kennedy proved to be a master political strategist whose dashing good looks, wit, and charm were perfect for the new medium of television. He surrounded himself with advisers and cabinet members who were so talented that one writer dubbed them "the best and the brightest" (Halberstam, 1972).

As Kennedy took the helm in these heady times, he was immediately faced with a major foreign policy decision. Should he go ahead with a plan, initiated by the Eisenhower administration, to invade Cuba? It might seem odd, from our current, 1990s perspective, that a small island off the coast of Florida was considered a major threat to U.S. security. This was in the midst of the cold war, however, and Fidel Castro, who had recently led a Communist revolution in Cuba (with the support of the Soviet Union), was definitely seen as a threat. The Eisenhower plan was to land a small force of CIA-trained Cuban exiles on the Cuban coast, who would then instigate and lead a mass uprising against Castro.

JFK and his advisers
in 1961.

Kennedy assembled his advisers to examine the pros and cons of such a plan. The group became a tightly knit, cohesive unit that brought a great deal of expertise to the topic. After a lengthy deliberation, they decided to go ahead, and on April 17, 1961, a force of 1,400 exiles invaded an area of Cuba known as the Bay of Pigs. The result was a complete disaster. Castro's forces captured or killed nearly all the invaders. Friendly Latin American countries were outraged that the United States had invaded one of their neighbors. Ironically, Cuba became even more closely allied with the Soviet Union as a result of the botched invasion. President Kennedy was later to ask, "How could we have been so stupid?" (Sorenson, 1966).

What went wrong? How could such a remarkably talented group of people, who met at great length to analyze the options, come up with such a disastrous plan? Most of us assume that groups make better decisions than individuals. However, in this case a committee of experts made an astonishing number of errors. Would President Kennedy have been better off making the decision by himself, without consulting his advisers?

Though you might think so, consider Kennedy's next foreign policy crisis, which also involved Cuba. The following October, the CIA discovered that the Soviet Union had placed nuclear missiles in Cuba, a scant 90 miles from the coast of Florida. The missiles were aimed toward U.S. cities, and the resulting crisis brought us the closest we have ever come to World War III (Rhodes, 1995). Kennedy and his advisers deftly avoided war with a brilliant strategy of threats, naval blockades, and conciliatory gestures that succeeded in getting Khrushchev, the leader of the Soviet Union, to back down and remove the missiles. What did Kennedy and his advisers do differently this time? Did they simply stumble onto a good strategy, or had they learned from their earlier mistakes at the Bay of Pigs? In this chapter, we will focus on how people interact in groups, which is one of the oldest topics in social psychology (Davis, 1992; Levine & Moreland, 1990; Levine, Resnick, & Higgins, 1993; Steiner, 1974; Zander, 1979).

Definitions: What Is a Group?

In its most basic form, a group can be defined as two or more people who are in the same place at the same time. According to this broad definition, people do not have to be interacting with each other to be considered a group; they simply need to be in each other's presence. Examples include students taking a test together, passengers on an airplane, and fans at a baseball game. In the first section of this chapter, we will consider how being in such a **nonsocial group**—where other people are around but we are not interacting with them—influences an individual's behavior. This is the most fundamental question concerning groups: What are the effects of the mere presence of other people?

Though the effects of nonsocial groups are interesting, most social psychologists, when defining groups, mean something more than a bunch of people who happen to be occupying the same space. We think of people who have assembled for some common purpose, such as Kennedy's advisers working together to reach a foreign policy decision, citizens meeting to solve a community problem, or people who have gathered to blow off steam at a party. **Social groups** are defined as a collection of two or more people who interact with each other and are interdependent, in the sense that their needs and goals lead them to rely on each other and to influence each other's behavior (Cartwright & Zander, 1968; Lewin, 1948). By this definition, Kennedy and his advisers were a social group, whereas a group of strangers waiting for a bus together are not. In the latter part of this chapter we will discuss the structure and composition of social groups, how they make decisions, and how they deal with conflict. For example, do social groups always make better decisions than individuals acting alone? Why did President Kennedy's advisers make so many errors when deciding to invade Cuba but plot a brilliant response to the Cuban missile crisis?

nonsocial group: a group in which two or more people are in the same place at the same time but are not interacting with each other (e.g., fans at a baseball game)

social groups: groups in which two or more people are interacting with each other and are interdependent, in the sense that to fulfill their needs and goals they must rely on each other

Nonsocial Groups: The Effects of the Mere Presence of Others

Do you act differently when other people are around? Simply being in the presence of other people can have a variety of interesting effects on our behavior. Let's begin by looking at how a group affects your performance on something with which you are very familiar: taking a test in a class.

Social Facilitation: When the Presence of Others Energizes Us

It is time for the final exam in your psychology class. You have spent countless hours studying the material, and you feel ready. When you arrive, you see that the exam is scheduled in a tiny, packed room. You squeeze into an empty desk, elbow to elbow with your classmates. The professor arrives and says that if any students are bothered by the close quarters, they can take the test by themselves in one of several smaller rooms down the hall. What should you do?

The answer concerns **social facilitation,** or how the mere presence of others affects individuals' performance (Geen, 1989; Guerin, 1993; Kent, 1994). The mere presence of other people can mean one of two things: (a) performing a task with coworkers who are doing the same thing you are or (b) performing a task in front of an audience who is not doing anything except observing you. The point is that in either case, you are not interacting with these other people—they're just present in the same room, constituting a nonsocial group. Does their presence

social facilitation: the arousal that results when other people are present and our performance can be evaluated; this arousal enhances our performance on simple tasks but impairs our performance on complex tasks make a difference? If you take your exam in the crowded room, will you feel nervous and have trouble recalling the material? Or will the presence of class-mates motivate you to do even better than if you took the test alone?

To answer this question, we need to talk about insects . . . cockroaches, in fact. Believe it or not, a classic study using cockroaches as research participants suggests an answer to the question of how you should take your psychology test. Robert Zajonc and his colleagues (1969) built a contraption to see how cock-roaches' behavior was influenced by the presence of their peers. The researchers placed a bright light, which is a noxious stimulus for cockroaches, at the end of a runway and timed how long it took a roach to escape the light by running to the other end, where it could scurry into a darkened box (see the left-hand side of Figure 9.1). The question was, Did roaches perform this simple feat faster when they were by themselves or when they were in the presence of other cockroaches?

You might be wondering how the researchers managed to persuade other cockroaches to be spectators. They did so by placing extra roaches in clear plas-tic boxes next to the runway. These roaches were in the bleachers, so to speak, observing the solitary cockroach do its thing (see Figure 9.1). As it happened, the individual cockroaches performed the task faster when they were in the presence of other roaches than when they were by themselves; their behavior was facili-tated (improved) by the mere presence of their peers.

Now, we would not give advice, based on one study that used cockroaches, on how you should take your psychology test. But the story does not end here. There have been dozens of studies on the topic of social facilitation, involving human beings as well as other species, such as ants and birds (e.g., Bond & Titus, 1983; Guerin, 1986; Rajecki, Kidd, & Ivins, 1976; Zajonc & Sales, 1966). There is a remarkable consistency to the findings of these studies. As long as the task is a relatively simple, well-learned one—as escaping a light is for cockroaches—the mere presence of others improves performance. For example, in one of the first social psychology experiments ever done, Norman Triplett (1898) asked children to wind up fishing line on a reel, either by themselves or in the presence of other children. They did so faster when in the presence of other children than when by themselves.

Mere social contact begets . . . a stimulation of the animal spirit that heightens the efficiency of each individual workman.

–Karl Marx (1818–1883)

■ Research on social facili-tation finds that people do better on a well-learned task when in the presence of others than when they are alone.

Simple maze **Complex maze**

FIGURE 9.1 Cockroaches and social facilitation. ▪ In the maze on the left, cockroaches had a simple task: to go from the starting point down the runway to the darkened box. They performed this feat faster when other roaches were watching than when they were alone. In the maze on the right, the cockroaches had a more difficult task. It took them longer to solve this maze when other roaches were watching than when they were alone. (Adapted from Zajonc, Heingartner, & Herman, 1969)

Simple Versus Difficult Tasks. Before concluding that you should stay in the crowded classroom to take your exam, we need to consider a different set of findings. Remember that we said the presence of others enhances performance on simple, well-learned tasks. Escaping a light is old hat for a cockroach, and winding fishing line on a reel is not difficult, even for a child. What happens when we give people a more difficult task to do and place them in the presence of others? To find out, Zajonc and his colleagues (1969) included another condition in the cockroach experiment. This time, the cockroaches had to solve a maze that had several runways, only one of which led to the darkened box (see the right-hand side of Figure 9.1). When working on this more difficult task, the opposite pattern of results occurred: The roaches took longer to solve it when other roaches were present than when they were alone. Many other studies have also found that people and animals do worse in the presence of others when the task is difficult (e.g., Bond & Titus, 1983; Geen, 1989).

Arousal and the Dominant Response. In an influential article published in 1965, Robert Zajonc offered an elegant theoretical explanation for why the presence of others facilitates a well-learned or dominant response but inhibits a less practiced or new response. His argument has two steps: First, the presence of others increases physiological arousal (i.e., our bodies become more energized), and second, when such arousal exists, it is easier to do things that are simple but harder to do something complex or learn something new. Consider, for example, something that is so easy that it is second nature to you, such as riding a bicycle or writing your name. Arousal, caused by the presence of other people watching you, should make it even easier to perform these well-learned behaviors. On the other hand, let's say you have to do something more complex, such as learning a new sport or working on a difficult math problem. Now arousal will lead you to feel flustered, make mistakes, and do less well than if you were alone (Schmitt, Gilovich, Goore, & Joseph, 1986).

Suppose, for example, that you decide to stop at a local pool hall and shoot a few racks. Will you perform better or worse if people are watching you wield your pool cue? As we have seen, it should depend on whether shooting pool is a simple or complex task for you. This is what James Michaels and his colleagues (1982) found in a field study conducted in the pool hall of a college student union. A team of four college students observed several different players from a distance, until they found ones who were experienced players (defined as those who made at least two-thirds of their shots) or novices (defined as those who made no more than one-third of their shots). The researchers then casually walked up to the table and watched people play. Imagine that you were one of the players. There you are, shooting a little pool, when suddenly you notice four strangers standing around watching you. What will happen to your performance? The prediction made by social facilitation theory is clear: If you have played so much pool that you would feel comfortable challenging Minnesota Fats, then the arousal caused by the presence of others should improve your game. If you are a novice and feel as if you have four thumbs, then the arousal caused by the presence of others should make your game go to pieces. This is exactly what Michaels and his colleagues (1982) found, as you can see in Figure 9.2. The experts made significantly more of their shots when they were observed, whereas the novices made significantly fewer shots.

Why the Presence of Others Causes Arousal.   We have seen that the mere presence of others leads to arousal and that our performance is facilitated by such arousal if the task is simple or well learned. But why should the presence of others lead to arousal? Researchers have developed three theories to explain the role of arousal in social facilitation: Arousal can cause us to become particularly alert and vigilant; it can make us apprehensive about how we're being evaluated; and it can distract us from the task at hand.

The first explanation suggests that the presence of other people makes us more alert. When we are by ourselves reading a book, we don't have to pay attention to anything but the book; we don't have to worry that the rug will start talk-

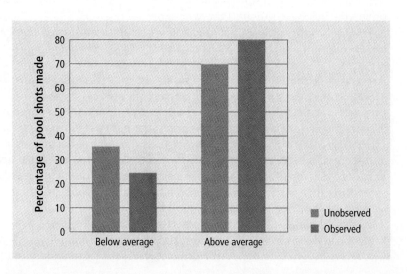

FIGURE 9.2 Social facilitation in a pool hall. ■ When four observers watched below-average players shoot pool, the players made fewer shots (left-hand bars). When the observers watched above-average players shoot pool, the players made more shots (right-hand bars). (Adapted from Michaels et al., 1982)

ing to us or that the sofa will offer us some tea. When someone else is in the room, however, we have to be alert to the possibility that he or she will do something that requires us to respond. Because other people are less predictable than rugs and sofas, we are in a state of greater alertness in their presence. This alertness, or vigilance, causes mild arousal. The beauty of this explanation (which is the one preferred by Robert Zajonc, 1980) is that it explains both the animal and the human studies. A solitary cockroach need not worry about what the cockroach in the next room is doing. However, it needs to be alert when in the presence of another cockroach—and the same goes for human beings.

The second explanation focuses on the fact that people are not cockroaches and often have other concerns about the presence of others. One concern involves what other people think of us. "Evaluation apprehension" refers to feeling worried and nervous (i.e., aroused) because you know that someone is making a judgment about how well you are doing. According to this explanation, what causes arousal is not the mere presence of others but the presence of others who are evaluating us.

The third explanation centers on how distracting other people can be (Baron, 1986; Sanders, 1983). It is similar to Robert Zajonc's (1980) notion that we need to be alert when in the presence of others, except that it focuses on the idea that any source of distraction—be it the presence of other people or noise from the party going on in the apartment upstairs—will put us in a state of conflict, because it is difficult to concentrate on what we are doing. Trying to pay attention to two things at once produces arousal, as anyone knows who has ever tried to read the newspaper while his or her 2-year-old clamors for attention. Consistent with this interpretation, Robert Baron (1986) found that nonsocial sources of distraction, such as a flashing light, cause the same kinds of social facilitation effects as the presence of other people.

We have summarized research on social facilitation in the top half of Figure 9.3 (we will discuss the bottom half in a moment). This figure illustrates that there is more than one reason that the presence of other people is arousing. The consequences of this arousal, however, are the same: When people are around other people, they do better on tasks that are simple and well learned, but they do worse on tasks that are complex and require them to learn something new.

We can now conclude that you should take your psychology exam in the presence of your classmates, assuming you know the material well, so that it is relatively simple for you to recall it. The arousal produced by being elbow to elbow with your classmates should improve your performance. We can also conclude, however, that when you study for an exam—that is, when you learn new material—you should do so by yourself, and not in the presence of others. In this situation, the arousal caused by others will make it more difficult to concentrate on the new material.

Social Loafing: When the Presence of Others Relaxes Us

When you take your psychology exam, your individual efforts will be evaluated (you will be graded on the test). This is typical of the research on social facilitation we have reviewed: People are doing their own thing (either alone or in the presence of others), and these individual efforts are easily observed and evaluated. Often when we are in the presence of others, however, we are working cooperatively on a joint project and our efforts cannot be distinguished from those of the other people in our group. Such is the case when we cook dinner with

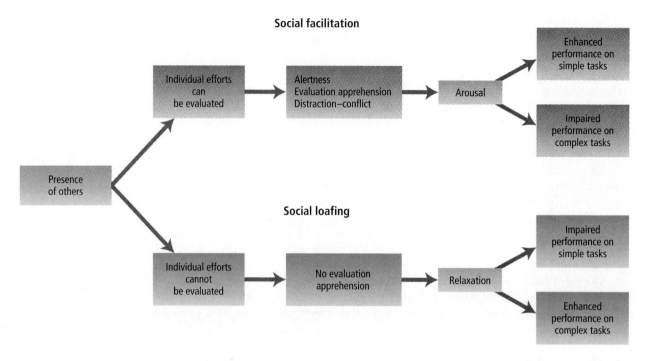

Social facilitation

Social loafing

FIGURE 9.3   Social facilitation and social loafing. ■ The presence of others can lead to social facilitation or social loafing. The important variables that distinguish the two are evaluation, arousal, and the complexity of the tasks. (Adapted from Cottrell et al., 1968)

a group of friends, work as a team on a class project, or help a group of neighbors push a car out of a ditch.

These situations are just the opposite of the kinds of social facilitation settings we have just considered. In social facilitation, the presence of others puts the spotlight on you, making you aroused. But if being with other people means we can merge into a group, becoming less noticeable than when we are alone, then we should become relaxed. Because no one can tell how well we are doing, we should feel less evaluation apprehension. What happens then? Will this relaxation produced by becoming lost in the crowd lead to better or worse performance? Once again, the answer depends on whether we are working on a simple or a complex task.

Let's first consider simple tasks, such as trying to pull as hard as we can on a rope. The question of how working with others would influence performance on such a task was first studied in the 1880s by a French agricultural engineer, Max Ringelmann (1913). He found that when a group of men pulled on a rope, each individual exerted less effort than when he did it alone. A hundred years later, social psychologists Bibb Latané, Kipling Williams, and Stephen Harkins (1979) called this reduction of individual effort in a group **social loafing.** "Many hands make light work," as the proverb says, and social loafing in groups has since been found for a variety of simple tasks, such as clapping your hands, cheering loudly, and thinking of as many uses for an object as you can (Ingham, Levinger, Graves, & Peckham, 1974; Karau & Williams, 1993; Shepperd, 1993; Williams, Karau, & Bourgeois, 1993).

social loafing: the relaxation that results when people are in a group and their individual performance cannot be evaluated; this relaxation impairs performance on simple tasks but enhances performance on complex tasks

To what extent is social loafing due to the relaxation that results from feeling that our performance cannot be evaluated? One way of finding out is to put people in a group but then arrange things so that each individual's performance can be evaluated. Evaluation apprehension should return under these conditions, eliminating social loafing. This is just what Kipling Williams, Stephen Harkins, and Bibb Latané (1981) found. They asked college students to shout as loudly as they could, supposedly to study the effects of sensory feedback on noise production in groups. In some conditions, the participants thought they were shouting alone; in others, they thought they were shouting along with five other people. (Because the participants were blindfolded and wore earphones, they could not tell whether or not other people were really shouting along with them.) Social loafing occurred when people thought they were one voice in a crowd; that is, their shouts weren't as loud as when they thought they were shouting by themselves. The researchers then told people that they would be shouting in groups again but that this time there would be a microphone in front of each person to measure the loudness of each person's shout. Under these conditions, no social loafing occurred. Because people believed the researchers were evaluating their individual performance, they shouted as loudly in the group as they did by themselves.

Pulling on a rope or shouting as loudly as we can is a pretty simple task. What happens on complex tasks when our performance is lost in the crowd? Recall that when our performance in a group cannot be identified, we become more relaxed. Recall also this chapter's earlier discussion of the effects of arousal on performance: Arousal enhances performance on simple tasks but impairs performance on complex tasks. By the same reasoning, becoming relaxed should impair performance on simple tasks—as we have just seen—but improve performance on complex tasks. The idea is that when people are not worried about being evaluated, they are more relaxed and should thus be less likely to "clam up" on a difficult task and do it better as a result.

To test this idea, Jeffrey Jackson and Kipling Williams (1985) asked participants to work on mazes that appeared on a computer screen. The mazes were either simple or complex. Another participant worked on identical mazes on another computer in the same room. The researchers either said that they would evaluate each person's individual performance (causing evaluation apprehension) or stated that a computer would average the two participants' scores and no one would ever know how well any one person performed (reducing evaluation apprehension). What should we expect to happen? When people think their score is being averaged with another person's, they should be more relaxed. This should lead to social loafing on the easy mazes, when the task is simple. When the task is difficult, however, being relaxed should be an advantage, leading to better performance. As seen in Figure 9.4, this is exactly the pattern of results the researchers found.

Gender and Cultural Differences in Social Loafing: Who Slacks Off the Most?
Jane and John are working with several classmates on a class project, and no one can assess their individual contributions. Who is more likely to slack off and let the others do most of the work—John or Jane? If you said John, you are probably right. Steven Karau and Kipling Williams (1993) recently reviewed more than 150 studies of social loafing and found that the tendency to loaf is stronger in men than women. Why? Women tend to focus more on the collective, caring more about the welfare of others in groups. Men, on the other

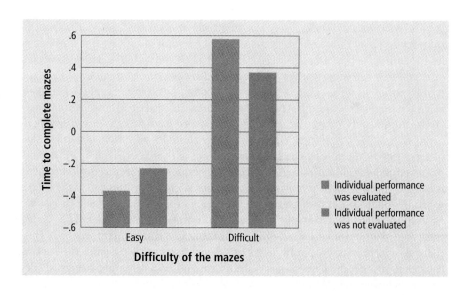

FIGURE 9.4   Social loafing. ■ When students worked on easy mazes, those who thought their individual performance would not be evaluated did worse (they took more time to complete them, as seen on the left-hand side of the graph). When students worked on difficult mazes, those who thought their individual performance would not be evaluated did better (they took less time to complete them, as seen on the right-hand side of the graph). (Adapted from Jackson & Williams, 1985)

> Which of us . . . is to do the hard and dirty work for the rest—and for what pay?
>
> –John Ruskin

hand, tend to be more individualistic, focusing more on their own performance and less on the group (Eagly, 1987; Wood, 1987). This different emphasis on collectivism versus individualism, as you may recall from Chapter 5, also exists across cultures. Many Asian societies stress collectivism, whereas many Western societies stress individualism. Consequently, there are also cultural differences in social loafing: Karau and Williams (1993) found that the tendency to loaf is stronger in Western cultures than Asian cultures. It is important not to exaggerate these differences; evidence for social loafing was found with both genders and in both Western and Asian cultures. Nonetheless, social loafing was stronger in men and members of Western cultures. Apparently, the good of the group is more important for women and members of collectivist societies than it is for men and members of individualistic societies.

Social Facilitation or Social Loafing: Which One When?

To summarize, to know whether the presence of others will help or hinder your performance, we need to know two things: whether your individual efforts can be evaluated and whether the task is simple or complex. If your performance can be evaluated, the presence of others will make you alert and aroused. This will lead to social facilitation effects, where people do better on simple tasks but worse on complex tasks (see Figure 9.3). If your efforts cannot be evaluated (i.e., you are one cog in a machine), you are likely to become more relaxed. This leads to social loafing effects, where people do worse on simple tasks but better on complex tasks (see Figure 9.3).

These findings have numerous implications for the way in which groups should be organized. If you are a manager who wants your employees to work on a relatively simple problem, a little evaluation apprehension is not such a bad thing—it should improve performance. You shouldn't place your employees in groups where their individual performance cannot be observed, because social loafing (lowered performance on simple tasks) is likely to result. On the other hand, if you want your employees to work on a difficult, complex task, then lowering their evaluation apprehension—by placing them in groups in which their individual performance cannot be observed—is likely to result in better performance.

Deindividuation: Getting Lost in the Crowd

If you are going to make people more anonymous, you should be aware of other consequences of being a nameless face in the crowd. So far, we have discussed the ways in which a group affects how hard people work and how successfully they learn new things. Being in a group can also cause **deindividuation**, defined as a feeling of anonymity and a reduced sense of ourselves as individuals. These feelings lead to the loosening of normal constraints on behavior, resulting in an increase in impulsive, atypical, and deviant acts. In other words, getting lost in a crowd can lead to an unleashing of behaviors that we would never dream of doing by ourselves.

Throughout history, there have been many examples of groups of people committing horrendous acts that no individual would do on his or her own. In Chapter 8, we discussed the My Lai incident in the Vietnam War, where a group of soldiers systematically murdered hundreds of defenseless women, children, and elderly men. In Europe, mobs of soccer fans sometimes attack and bludgeon each other, both before and after the game. In the United States, hysterical fans at rock concerts have trampled each other to death. And the United States has a shameful history of whites—often cloaked in the anonymity of white robes—lynching African Americans.

Brian Mullen (1986) content-analyzed newspaper accounts of 60 lynchings committed in the United States between 1899 and 1946 and discovered an interesting fact: The more people there were in the mob, the greater the savagery and

deindividuation: the loosening of normal constraints on behavior, leading to an increase in impulsive and deviant acts

■ The robes and hoods of the Ku Klux Klan cloak its members in anonymity; their violent and murderous behavior is consistent with research on deindividuation.

viciousness with which they killed their victims. Why do you think this was so? Here is a clue: Robert Watson (1973) studied 24 cultures and found that warriors who hid their identities before going into battle—for example, by using face and body paint—were significantly more likely to kill, torture, or mutilate captive prisoners than were warriors who did not hide their identities.

As you might guess, when a mob consists of a large number of people or when warriors disguise their identities, people feel more anonymous and feelings of deindividuation are likely to result. But exactly what is it about deindividuation that leads to impulsive (and often violent) acts? Research by Steven Prentice-Dunn and Ronald Rogers (1989) and Ed Diener (1980) points to two factors: First, the presence of others (or the wearing of disguises) makes people feel less accountable for their actions, because it reduces the likelihood that any individual will be singled out and blamed. In an experiment by Philip Zimbardo (1970), for example, female undergraduates participated in one of two conditions. In the deindividuated condition, the participants were asked to put on lab coats and hoods as soon as they arrived. No names were used, and the room was darkened to prevent identification of who was who. In the comparison condition, the participants wore their normal clothes, put on large name tags, were in a brightly lit room, and thus were easily identifiable. All the participants were then asked to deliver (supposed) electric shocks to another woman. Those in the anonymous, deindividuated condition were considerably more aggressive toward the woman, delivering more and longer shocks, than those who could easily be identified were.

In everyday life, of course, it is rare for us to be asked to put hoods over our heads and deliver shocks to another person. It is not so uncommon, however, to be asked to wear uniforms that make us look like everyone else in the vicinity, an arrangement that might also make us feel less accountable for our actions and hence more aggressive. Does wearing a uniform, such as one for a sports team, increase aggressiveness? A study by Jurgen Rehm, Michael Steinleitner, and Waldemar Lilli (1987) indicates that it does. They randomly assigned fifth-graders in German schools to various five-person teams and then watched the teams play handball against each other. In every game, all the members of one team wore orange shirts and all the members of the other team wore their normal street clothes. The children who wore the orange shirts (and were thus harder to tell apart) played the game significantly more aggressively than the children who wore their everyday clothing (and were thus easier to identify) did.

A second cause of deindividuation is that the presence of others lowers self-awareness, thereby shifting people's attention away from their moral standards. As discussed in Chapter 5, it is difficult to focus inward on ourselves and outward on the world around us at the same time; thus, at any given point we vary in how self-aware we are (Carver & Scheier, 1981; Duval & Wicklund, 1975). One consequence of focusing on ourselves is that we are reminded of our moral standards, making us less likely to behave in some deviant or antisocial manner (e.g., "I believe that hurting other people is wrong; I'm not going to hit this guy"). If we are focusing on our environment, self-awareness will be low and we will be more likely to forget our moral standards and act impulsively.

How self-aware do you think you would be if you found yourself in a mob of people who were screaming "Party on!"? The more stimulation there is in the environment to capture our attention, the less self-aware we will be, possibly leading to more deindividuation. Our attention is focused outward; we are not paying attention to ourselves or feeling self-conscious. Thus, being in large

Everyone looked at alone, is passably wise and discerning; when he is in a group, immediately there you'll find a dummy.
–Schiller

If you can keep your head when all about you are losing theirs . . .
–Rudyard Kipling

■ Exactly where, when, and by whom this photograph was taken is not known. It is a moving testament to the extraordinary evil of the deindividuated lynch mob.

groups can reduce self-awareness, thereby making us pay less attention to our moral standards and causing us to act in more antisocial and impulsive ways.

Deindividuation, then, is most likely to occur when people feel they are not accountable for their actions (i.e., when there is little chance they will be caught) and when they are in a state of reduced self-awareness (Harkins & Szymanski, 1987; Mullen & Baumeister, 1987; Prentice-Dunn & Rogers, 1989). The conditions that lower accountability and self-awareness are precisely those in which mob violence and other deviant acts tend to occur.

Before leaving this topic, we need to mention one important qualification. We said that deindividuation leads to impulsive, atypical, and deviant acts, and we have given several examples of deindividuation that results in violence and aggression. Not all impulsive acts, however, are negative or violent. Other examples include eating too much and dancing wildly at a party. Deindividuation increases these sorts of impulsive acts as well. But what determines whether deindividuation will lead to positive or negative behaviors? Being a good social psychologist, you can probably guess the answer: It depends on whether the context or situation encourages positive or negative behavior (Gergen, Gergen, & Barton, 1973; Johnson & Downing, 1979). If we feel angry toward someone, then being deindividuated will lower our inhibitions, making us more likely to act aggressively. If we are hungry and are at a party where there is lots of good food, then being deindividuated will increase the likelihood that we will scarf down large portions of it. In other words, if our inhibitions are preventing us from doing something nonaggressive (e.g., eating) or something pleasant (e.g., hugging someone), the more we are deindividuated, the more we will overcome these inhibitions.

Social Groups: Joining, Leading, Working, and Competing

So far, we have considered how the mere presence of others can influence an individual's behavior. When we are in a group, however, we are usually more than passive observers of each other—we socialize, mingle, hobnob, deliberate, and argue. In short, we interact with each other. We have already discussed many of the consequences of social interaction, such as attitude change (e.g., other people persuading us to change our attitudes—see Chapter 7) and conformity (e.g., other people pressuring us to change our behavior—see Chapter 8). We turn now to the situation in which people interact with and are interdependent on each other. Stop for a moment and think of the number of groups to which you belong. Don't forget to include your family; your roommates; campus groups such as fraternities, sororities, or political organizations; community groups such as churches or synagogues; sports teams; and more temporary groups such as your classmates in a small seminar. All of these count as social groups, because you interact with the other members and you are interdependent on them, in the sense that you influence them and they influence you.

Why do people join social groups? Forming relationships with other people fulfills a number of basic human needs. So basic, in fact, that there may be an innate need to belong to social groups. Roy Baumeister and Mark Leary (1995) argue that in our evolutionary past, there was a substantial survival advantage to establishing bonds with other people. People who bonded together were better able to hunt for and grow food, find mates, and care for children. Consequently, argue Baumeister and Leary, the need to belong has become innate and is present in all societies. Consistent with this view, people in all cultures are motivated to form relationships with other people and to resist the dissolution of these relationships.

Social groups have a number of other benefits. As we saw in Chapter 8, other people can be an important source of information, helping us to resolve ambiguity about the nature of the social world. Groups become an important part of our identity, helping us to define who we are—witness the number of times people wear shirts with the name of one of their groups (e.g., a fraternity or sorority) emblazoned on it. Groups also help establish social norms, which are explicit or implicit rules defining what is acceptable behavior. Given these significant functions, it is important to consider the nature of social groups and the ways in which they influence our behavior.

The Nature of Social Groups

What do the groups to which you belong have in common? They probably vary in size from 2 or 3 members to several dozen members. Most social groups, however, tend to have 20 or fewer members (McPherson, 1983). This is due in part to our definition of social groups as involving interaction between members. If groups become too large, you cannot interact with all the members; for example, the college or university that you attend is not a social group, because you are unlikely to meet and interact with every other student at that college or university.

Another important feature of social groups is that the members tend to be alike in age, sex, beliefs, and opinions (Levine & Moreland, 1995). There are two causes of homogeneity in groups: First, many groups tend to attract people who are already similar before they join. As we will see in Chapter 10, people are attracted to those who share their attitudes and thus are likely to recruit fellow group members who are similar to them. Second, groups tend to operate in ways that encourage similarity in the members. This can happen in a number of important ways, some of which we discussed in Chapter 8, on conformity.

For example, as we saw in Chapter 8, a powerful determinant of our behavior is social norms. All societies have norms about which behaviors are acceptable, some of which are shared by all members of the society (e.g., formal laws against stealing) and some of which vary from group to group (e.g., rules about what to wear). If you belong to a fraternity or sorority, you can probably think of social norms present in your group, such as whether alcoholic beverages are consumed and how you are supposed to feel about rival fraternities or sororities. It is unlikely that these norms are shared by other groups to which you belong, such as your church or synagogue. Social norms are powerful determinants of our behavior, as shown by what happens if people violate them too often: They are shunned by other group members and, in extreme cases, pressured to leave the group (Schachter, 1951; see Chapter 8).

Most groups also have well-defined **roles**, which are positions that come with a specified "script," or expected set of behaviors. Whereas norms specify how all group members should behave, roles specify how people who occupy certain positions in the group should behave. A boss and an employee in a business occupy different roles and are expected to act in different ways in that setting. Like social norms, roles facilitate social interaction, such that people know what to expect from each other.

There are, however, two potential costs to social roles. First, roles can shape people's behavior in powerful and frightening ways. Suppose, for example, that you agreed to take part in a two-week psychology experiment in which you were randomly assigned to play the role of a prison guard or a prisoner in a simulated prison. You might think that the role you were assigned to play would not be very important; after all, everyone knows that it is only an experiment and that people are just pretending to be guards or prisoners. Philip Zimbardo and his colleagues, however, had a different hypothesis. They believed that social roles can be so powerful that they "take over" our personal identities and we become the role we are playing. To see if this is true, Zimbardo and colleagues built a mock prison in the basement of the psychology department at Stanford University and paid students to play the role of guard or prisoner (Haney, Banks, & Zimbardo, 1973). The role students played was determined by a coin flip. The guards were outfitted with a uniform of khaki shirts and pants, a whistle, a police nightstick, and reflecting sunglasses, and the prisoners were outfitted with a loose-fitting smock with an identification number stamped on it, rubber sandals, a cap made from a nylon stocking, and a locked chain attached to one ankle.

roles: positions in a group that come with a specified "script," or expected set of behaviors

■ Philip Zimbardo and his colleagues randomly assigned students to play the role of prisoner or guard in a mock prison. The students assumed these roles all too well. Those playing the role of guard became quite aggressive, whereas those playing the role of prisoner became passive, helpless, and withdrawn. People got "into" their roles so much that their personal identities and sense of decency somehow got lost.

The researchers planned to observe the students for two weeks, to see whether they began to act like real prison guards and prisoners. As it turned out, the students very quickly assumed these roles—so much so that the researchers had to end the experiment after only six days. Many of the guards became quite aggressive, thinking of creative ways of verbally abusing and humiliating the "prisoners." The prisoners became passive, helpless, and withdrawn. Some prisoners, in fact, became so anxious and depressed that they had to be released from the study earlier than the others. Remember, everyone knew that they were in a psychology experiment and that the "prison" was only make-believe. The roles of guard and prisoner were so compelling and powerful, however, that this simple truth was often overlooked. People got "into" their roles so much that their personal identities and sense of decency somehow got lost.

If social roles are so powerful in make-believe prisons, imagine how powerful they are in real prisons and in other institutions with well-defined roles. The roles we assume can shape our behavior in powerful and unexpected ways. Parents of young children, for example, can often be heard exlaiming, "I swore I would never yell at my child in the way my parents yelled at me, and yet I just did!"

The second drawback of social roles is that there is a cost to acting inconsistently with the expectations associated with them. Try telling your boss, the next time you report to your job, that you would just as soon sit back and tell him or her what to do that day. Role expectations are especially problematic when they are arbitrary or unfair, such as societal expectations based on people's gender. All societies have expectations about how people who occupy the roles of women and men should behave. As we discuss in Chapter 13, these role expectations can constrain the way in which people behave and result in negative attitudes toward "uppity" people who decide to act inconsistently with how they are expected to behave. In many cultures, for example, women are expected to assume the role of wife and mother and have limited opportunities to pursue other careers. In the United States and other countries, these expectations are changing and women have more opportunities than ever before. Conflict can result, however, when expectations change for some roles but not for others occupied by the same person.

In India, for instance, women traditionally were permitted to occupy only the roles of wife, mother, agricultural laborer, and domestic worker. In recent years, the rights of women have improved and women have more opportunities in other professions. Many men, however, still expect their wives to assume the traditional role of child rearer and household manager, even if their wives have other careers. Conflict results, because many women are expected to "do it all"—maintain a career, raise the children, clean the house, and attend to their husband's needs (Brislin, 1993). Such role conflicts are not limited to India; we suspect that many American readers will find this kind of role conflict all too familiar.

Gender roles are not something we choose or are assigned by others; our gender is determined at conception. Most other roles in social groups are not so predetermined: They are positions that we choose or work for and earn. You choose to occupy the role of student in your social psychology class, for example, and with hard work you might someday occupy the role of teacher or lawyer or president of your own corporation. Perhaps the most important role in any social group is that of the leader. The performance of a group, and sometimes even its very survival, often depends on the abilities of the leader of the group. It is no surprise, then, that a considerable amount of research has been devoted to the topic of who makes the best leader.

Leadership

The question of what makes a great leader has intrigued psychologists, historians, and political scientists for ages. One of the best-known answers to this question is the **great person theory,** which maintains that certain key personality traits make a person a good leader, and if you don't have them, forget about it—you might as well go to the back of the line.

If the great person theory is true, then we ought to be able to isolate the key aspects of personality that make someone a great leader. Is it a combination of intelligence, charisma, and courage? Is it better to be introverted or extraverted? Should you add a measure of ruthlessness to the mix as well, as Niccoló Machiavelli described in 1513, in his famous treatise on leadership, *The Prince*? Or do highly moral people make the best leaders?

The relationships between personal characteristics and leadership that researchers have discovered are summarized in the text accompanying the photos on the next page. Some modest relationships have been found; for example, leaders tend to be slightly more intelligent than nonleaders, more driven by the desire for power, more charismatic (House, Spangler, & Woycke (1991), and more adaptive and flexible (Kenny & Zaccaro, 1983; Zaccaro, Foti, & Kenny, 1991). What is most telling from the summary, however, is the absence of strong relationships. Surprisingly few personality characteristics correlate with leadership effectiveness, and the relationships that have been found tend to be modest. For example, Simonton (1987, 1992) gathered information about 100 personal attributes of all U.S. presidents, such as their family backgrounds, educational experiences, occupations, and personalities. Only 3 of these variables—height, family size, and the number of books a president published before taking office—correlated with how effective the presidents were in office (as rated by historians). The other 97 characteristics, including personality traits, were not related to leadership effectiveness at all.

As you undoubtedly know by now, one of the most important tenets of social psychology is that to understand social behavior, it is not enough to consider personality traits alone—we must take the social situation into account as well. The inadequacy of the great person theory does not mean that personal characteristics are completely irrelevant to good leadership. Instead, being good social psychologists, we should consider both the nature of the leader and the situation in which he or she is leading. This view of leadership states that it is not enough to be a great person; you have to be the right person at the right time in the right situation.

A business leader, for example, can be highly successful in some situations but not in others. Consider Steve Jobs, who, at age 21, founded the Apple Computer company with Stephen Wozniak. Jobs was anything but an "MBA" type of corporate leader. A product of the 1960s counterculture, he turned to computers only after sampling LSD, traveling to India, and living on a communal fruit farm. In the days when there were no personal computers, Jobs's offbeat style was well suited to starting a new industry. Within five years, he was the leader of a billion-dollar company. Jobs's unorthodox style was ill-suited, however, to the fine points of managing a large corporation in a competitive market. Apple began to suffer in competition with other companies, and in 1985 Jobs was forced to leave Apple by John Sculley, a man who Jobs himself had hired to run the company (Patton, 1989). Interestingly, Jobs has recently resurfaced as the head of Pixar, another ground-breaking company that specializes in computer animation.

great person theory: the theory that certain key personality traits make a person a good leader, regardless of the nature of the situation facing the leader

> There is properly no history, only biography.
> –Ralph Waldo Emerson (1929)

	Intelligence	U.S. Supreme Court Justice Ruth Bader Ginsberg	There is a modest but positive relationship between intelligence and leadership effectiveness (Simonton, 1985; Stogdill, 1974).
	Morality	Queen Victoria of Great Britain	An examination of historical records showed that in a sample of 600 monarchs, the ones who became the most eminent were those who were either highly moral or highly immoral (Simonton, 1984). this suggests that there are two roads to eminence: having great moral virtue or having Machiavellian deviousness.
	Motivation	Colonel Mu'ammar al-Qaddafi of Libya	Leaders who have a strong power motive (self-direction, a concern for prestige, abundant energy) are somewhat more likely to be effective (McClelland, 1975; Sorrentino & Field, 1986; Winter, 1987).
	Family Size	Franklin Delano Roosevelt, thirty-second U.S. president	U.S. presidents who came form small families are more likely to have become great leaders, as rated by historians (Simonton, 1987).
	Height	Abraham Lincoln, sixteenth U. S. president	There is a modest correlation between a man's height and the likelihood that he will become the leader of a group (Stogdill, 1974). In the United States, the taller candidate has won every presidential election but two: Richard Nixon versus George McGovern in 1972 and Jimmy Carter versus Gerald Ford in 1976. (In 1992, Bill Clinton had a quarter-inch height advantage over George Bush). Once in office, tall presidents, such as Abraham Lincoln, are more likely to be great leaders, as rated by historians (Simonton, 1987; 1992).
	Personality Traits	Malcolm X, minister of the Nation of Islam	Surprisingly little evidence shows that such traits as dominance, charisma, and self-confidence will predict who will become leaders (Hollander, 1975; Stogdill, 1974).

> ■ Some modest relationships between characteristics and leadership performance have been found, but in general, it is difficult to predict how good a leader will be from his or her personal attributes alone.

Several recent theories of leadership focus on characteristics of the leader, his or her followers, and the situation (e.g. Dansereau, Graen, & Haga, 1975; Dienesch & Liden, 1986; Hollander, 1958). The best-known theory of this type is Fred Fiedler's (1967, 1978) **contingency theory of leadership.** Fiedler makes the assumption that there are two kinds of leaders, those who are task-oriented and those who are relationship-oriented. The **task-oriented leader** is primarily concerned with getting the job done, whereas the **relationship-oriented leader** is more concerned with the feelings of and relationships between the workers.

The crux of Fiedler's contingency theory is that neither type of leader is always more effective than the other; it depends on the nature of the situation—specifically, on the amount of control and influence a leader has over the group. In "high-control" work situations, the leader has excellent interpersonal relationships with subordinates, his or her position in the company is clearly perceived as powerful, and the work needing to be done by the group is structured and well defined. In "low-control" work situations, the opposite holds—the leader has poor relationships with subordinates and the work needing to be done is not clearly defined. As seen in Figure 9.5, task-oriented leaders are most effective in situations that are either very high or very low in control. When situational control is very high, people are happy, everything is running smoothly, and there is no need to worry about people's feelings and relationships. The leader who pays attention only to the task will get the most accomplished. When situational control is very low, the task-oriented leader is best at taking charge, imposing some order on a confusing, ill-defined work environment. Relationship-oriented leaders, on the other hand, are most effective in situations that are moderate in control. Under these conditions, the wheels are turning fairly smoothly but some attention to the squeakiness caused by poor relationships and hurt feelings is needed. The leader who can soothe such feelings will be most successful.

Fiedler's contingency theory has been tested with numerous groups of leaders, including business managers, college administrators, military commanders, and postmasters. Although the theory has been controversial (Hollander, 1985; Peters et al., 1985), the studies that have tested it have generally been supportive,

contingency theory of leadership: the theory that leadership effectiveness depends both on how task-oriented or relationship-oriented the leader is and on the amount of control and influence the leader has over the group

task-oriented leader: a leader who is concerned primarily with getting the job done and less so with the feelings of and relationships between the workers

relationship-oriented leader: a leader who is concerned primarily with the feelings of and relationships between the workers

> Leadership cannot really be taught, it can only be learned.
> –Harold Geneen, 1984

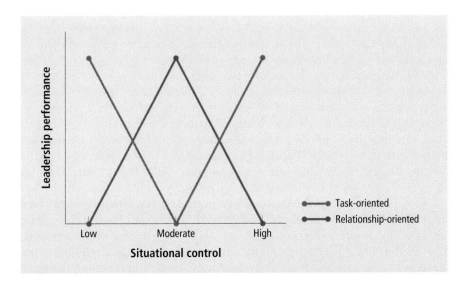

FIGURE 9.5 Fiedler's contingency theory of leadership. ■ According to Fiedler, task-oriented leaders perform best when situational control is high or low, whereas relationship-oriented leaders perform best when situational control is moderate.

conforming well to the pattern shown in Figure 9.5 (Chemers, Hays, Rhodewalt, & Wysocki, 1985; Peters, Hartke, and Pohlmann, 1985; Strube & Garcia, 1981).

Gender and Leadership. When we described the task-oriented and relationship-oriented types of leaders, did they remind you of anyone? Be honest: Did it seem like men are more likely to be task-oriented, whereas women are more likely to be relationship-oriented? If so, you have plenty of company: Stereotypes about the leadership styles of women and men abound. Women are thought to care more about the feelings of their coworkers, to be more interpersonally skilled than men, and thus to be more relationship-oriented. Men are often characterized as controlling, Machiavellian leaders who don't even notice what their coworkers are feeling, much less care about those feelings. Is there any truth to these stereotypes?

To find out, Alice Eagly and her colleagues examined hundreds of studies to answer questions about the leadership styles of women versus men (Eagly & Johnson, 1990; Eagly & Karau, 1991; Eagly, Karua, & Makhijani, 1995; Eagly, Makhijani, & Klonsky, 1992). She has found that, consistent with the stereotype, women do tend to lead more democratically than men, possibly because women tend to have better interpersonal skills, allowing them to seek input from group members when making a decision and to gracefully disregard this input when necessary (Eagly & Johnson, 1990).

Does this mean that women make better leaders than men? As we would expect from the contingency theory of leadership, it depends on the nature of the situation. Alice Eagly, Steven Karau, and Mona Makhijani (1995) found that women tend to be better leaders (as measured by both objective measures of performance and by ratings of coworkers) in jobs that require interpersonal skills, such as jobs in educational settings. Men tend to be better leaders in jobs that require the ability to direct and control people, such as jobs in the military.

Before we make too much of this finding, however, we must add some cautionary notes. First, the differences are not that large. Plenty of women are able to adopt the "masculine" leadership style, especially when the job requires it (Eagly & Johnson, 1990). And plenty of men have good interpersonal skills. Further, all studies of leadership effectiveness are plagued by the following problem: Do the findings reflect actual differences in ability, or people's stereotypes about the leader? If a woman is viewed as a less effective leader than a man, for example, is it because she really is a worse leader, or because her coworkers are using a different yardstick to measure her performance?

An old adage says that, because of sex discrimination, a woman has to be "twice as good as a man" in order to advance. Unfortunately, there do seem to be differences in the ways female and male leaders are evaluated. If a woman's style of leadership is stereotypically "masculine," in that she is autocratic, "bossy," and task-oriented, she is evaluated more negatively than men who have the same style are (Eagly et al., 1992). This is especially true if it is men who are doing the evaluating. For example, Doré Butler and Florence Geis (1990) instructed male and female accomplices to assume leadership roles in groups of students attempting to solve a business problem. Both the male and the female leaders were assertive but cordial, taking charge of the group discussion. How did the other members of the group react to these assertive leaders? The results were discouraging. When a man took charge of the group and acted assertively, the group members reacted favorably. When a woman acted in the same fashion, the group

> Old-fashioned ways which no longer apply to changed conditions are a snare in which the feet of women become entangled.
>
> –Jane Addams, 1907

members reacted much more negatively—especially the males. It appears that many men are uncomfortable with women who use the same leadership techniques that men typically use.

As in every aspect of life, these types of stereotypes and prejudice limit the ability of individuals to perform to their fullest abilities. Such a loss is experienced not only by the individual but by the business organization as well. As American business moves into the twenty-first century, it is imperative that attributes like gender, race, and religion no longer bar talented workers from contributing to the marketplace.

Group Performance: Are Two (or More) Heads Better Than One?

One of the main functions of groups is to solve problems and make decisions. In the American judicial system, many verdicts are determined by groups of individuals (juries), not single individuals (for a discussion of jury decision making, see Module 3, on Law and Social Psychology). The Supreme Court is made up of nine justices, not a single, sage member of the judiciary. Similarly, governmental and corporate decisions are often made by groups of people who meet to discuss the issues, and all U.S. presidents have a cabinet and the National Security Council to advise them.

Is it true that two (or more) heads are better than one? Most of us assume the answer is yes. A lone individual may be subject to all sorts of whims and biases, whereas several people together can exchange ideas and reach better decisions. Many common assumptions about the value of group decision making, however, turn out not to be true. Sometimes, two heads are not better than one, or at least no better than two heads working alone (Hackman & Morris, 1978; Littlepage, 1991; McGrath, 1984; Tindale, 1993). At the beginning of this chapter, for example, we saw that President Kennedy and his advisers, after deliberating at length, made a foolhardy decision to invade Cuba. Under what conditions will groups make good versus bad decisions?

Whether a group will outperform individuals depends on the type of task with which it is faced. One important question is whether a group is working on a **divisible versus a unitary task** (Steiner, 1972). Divisible tasks are those that can be broken down into different subtasks and assigned to individual members of a group, such as building a house: A carpenter builds the frame and walls, a plumber does the plumbing, and an electrician does the wiring. Obviously, the quality of the group performance will depend on how well individuals are assigned to the subtasks. If the electrician is assigned to do the plumbing and the plumber is assigned to do the wiring, problems will result.

Unitary tasks are those in which no division of labor is feasible, such as a group working together to push a car out of a ditch or deciding whether to invade Cuba. The key to problem solving on unitary tasks is how each member's outputs are combined to achieve the group's goal. How individual outputs are combined depends on a further distinction between types of unitary tasks: An **additive task** is one in which all group members perform basically the same job and the final product (or group performance) is a sum of all their contributions, such as the total amount of noise made by a group of cheerleaders. As we have seen, social loafing is likely to occur in this type of situation. Thus, a group of four people performing an additive task can be less successful than four individuals working alone, if some members of the group engage in social loafing (see Figure 9.6 on p. 332).

> Nor is the people's judgement always true: The most may err as grossly as the few.
> –John Dryden

divisible versus a unitary task: divisible tasks are those that can be broken down into different subtasks performed by individual members, whereas unitary tasks are those in which no division of labor is feasible; performance on unitary tasks depends on how group members' outputs are combined to reach a joint decision

additive task: a group task in which performance depends on the sum of each individual's effort (e.g., the total noise made by a group of cheerleaders)

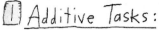

① Additive Tasks:

Group performance depends on the sum of each members contribution.
If <u>social loafing</u> occurs the group performance may not be better than that
of an individual working alone.

② Conjunctive Tasks:

Group performance depends on that of the weakest or least talented group member.
Groups usually do less well than individuals, since the weak member's performance
brings down that of the group.

3 Disjunctive Tasks:

Group performance depends on how well the best or most talented member does. Groups can outperform individuals if the group has a highly talented member, if that member can convince the others that he or she is right, and if that member (and others) presents to the group unique information only he or she knows.

Group Solving a Physics Problem:

Positive Outcome

Bob   Suzy   Albert Einstein   →   *WOW! Awesome Al!* (Bob)   *So you see it has to come out to $E=mc^2$* (Albert Einstein)   *Cool! Way to go Al!* (Suzy)   →   Group Solution: $E=mc^2$

Negative Outcome

Albert, I really don't think you know what you're talking about here... (Suzy)   *I agree with Suzy.* (Bob)   *They won't listen to me! I can't convince them!* (Albert)   →   Process Loss   →   Group Solution: $E=ABC^2$

Negative Outcome

I don't think this squiggle on the handout is a typo! I think it means something! (Bob)   *Yes! It clearly means we should take the square root of the denominator.* (Suzy)   *So if the clock is in the spaceship moving at the speed of light, then—* (Albert)   →   Failure to Share Unique Information   →   Group Solution: $E=mc^3 \sqrt{1/ABC}$

FIGURE 9.6 ■ (Opposite and above) Will groups perform better than lone individuals? It depends on the type of task.

On a **conjunctive task,** group performance is defined by the skills of the least capable member of the group, or "the weak link in the chain." A mountain-climbing team can climb only as fast as its slowest member, a chamber music group can produce a sound only as good as the least gifted musician, and a doubles tennis team can play only as well as the least proficient member of the pair. Groups typically do worse on conjunctive tasks than lone individuals do, since the weakest member brings the performance of the group down to his or her level (Steiner & Rajaratnam, 1961; see Figure 9.6, on p. 332). A more common type of group task is a **disjunctive task,** in which group performance is defined by how well the best member of the group does. Consider a group trying to solve a difficult math problem. If there is one mathematician in the group who knows how to solve the problem, he or she can provide the others with the answer; thus, one gifted individual can dominate the group, raising the performance of average and below-average individuals to his or her level.

In general, groups will do better if they are able to make it a disjunctive task, in which they can rely on the person with the most expertise. Clearly, this would be a better strategy than relying on people with little knowledge about how to solve the problem. As straightforward as this sounds, however, it is not always easy to accomplish. A group working on a disjunctive task will perform well only if the most talented member can convince the others that he or she is right—which is not always easy, given that many of us bear a strong resemblance to mules when it comes to admitting we are wrong (Laughlin, 1980; Maier &

conjunctive task: a group task in which performance depends on how well the least talented member does (e.g., how fast a team of roped-together mountain climbers can climb a mountain)

disjunctive task: a group task in which performance depends on how well the most talented member does (e.g., a group of people trying to solve a difficult math problem)

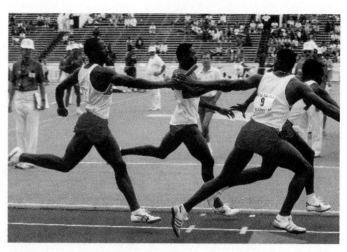

■ Additive tasks are those in which group members' contributions are each added together to create the group product.

■ In conjunctive tasks, group performance is defined by the skills of the least talented member of the group. A team of mountain climbers, for example, can go only as fast as its least proficient member.

process loss: any aspect of group interaction that inhibits good problem solving

Solem, 1952). Several factors, as we will see, can make groups actually do worse than individuals on disjunctive tasks.

Process Loss.   You undoubtedly know what it's like to try to convince a group to follow your idea, be faced with opposition and disbelief, and then have to sit there and watch the group make the wrong decision. Ivan Steiner (1972) called this phenomenon **process loss,** defined as any aspect of group interaction that inhibits good problem solving. Process loss can occur because groups do not try hard enough to find out who the most competent member is, because the most competent member has low status and nobody really takes his or her ideas seriously, or because the most competent member finds it difficult to break free from normative conformity pressures that discourage disagreement with the whole group (see our discussion of normative social pressures in Chapter 8). Other causes of process loss involve communication problems within the group— in some groups, people don't listen to each other (see Figure 9.6); in others, one person is allowed to dominate the discussion while the others tune out.

Failure to Share Unique Information.   Another reason groups can fail to outperform individuals is that group members sometimes fail to share unique information (that only they know) with each other. Frequently, no one member of a group is an expert on all aspects of the problem. Kennedy's advisers, for example, had different areas of expertise relevant to Cuba, the feasibility of an armed invasion, and the political repercussions of such an act. To reach the best decision, the group must pool their resources, so that each member shares his or her particular expertise with the rest of the group.

Interestingly, groups often fail to accomplish this rudimentary condition of good decision making. Garold Stasser and his colleagues have found that groups tend to discuss information that is shared by all the group members, instead of focusing on unique or unshared information (see Figure 9.7). In one study, for example, participants met in groups of four to discuss which candidate for student body president was the most qualified (Stasser & Titus, 1985). In the shared information condition, each participant was given the same packet of information to read, data indicating that candidate A was the best choice for office. As seen at the top of Figure 9.7, all participants in this condition knew that candidate A had eight positive qualities and four negative qualities, making him superior to the other candidates. Not surprisingly, when this group met to discuss the candidates, almost all of the members chose candidate A.

In the unshared information condition, each participant received a different packet of information. As seen at the bottom of Figure 9.7, each person knew that candidate A had two positive qualities and four negative qualities. However, the two positive qualities cited in each person's packet were unique—different from those listed in other participants' packets. Everyone learned that candidate A had the same four negative qualities; thus, if the participants shared with each other the information that was in their packets, they would learn that candidate A had a total of eight positive qualities and four negative qualities—just as people in the shared information condition knew.

Most of the groups in the unshared information condition never realized that candidate A had more good than bad qualities, because they focused on the information they shared, rather than on the information they did not share. As a result, few realized that candidate A was the most qualified. Thus, even on disjunctive tasks groups often do not outperform the most expert individual, because of process loss and the tendency to focus on information that everyone shares (Gigone & Hastie, 1993; Larson, Foster-Fishman, & Keys, 1994; Stasser, Taylor, & Hanna, 1989; Wittenbaum & Stasser, in press).

One way around the failure to share information is to make sure people know that different members of the group are responsible for different kinds of information (Stewart & Stasser, in press). Daniel Wegner and his colleagues, for

FIGURE 9.7   When people are in groups, do they share information that only they know?
■ Participants in a study met to discuss candidates for an election. In the shared information condition (top half of figure), each person was given the same positive and negative facts about the candidates. Candidate A was clearly the superior candidate, and most groups preferred him. In the unshared information condition (bottom half of figure), each person was given the same four negative facts about candidate A as well as two unique positive facts. In discussion, these people focused on the information they all shared and failed to mention their unique information; these groups no longer saw candidate A as superior. (Adapted from Stasser & Titus, 1985)

example, have found that married couples use this technique to remember things better; one member of a couple might be responsible for remembering the times of social engagements, whereas the other might be responsible for remembering when to pay the bills (Wegner, Erber, & Raymond, 1991). Similarly, Diane Liang, Richard Moreland, and Linda Argote (1995) found that if people know in advance that other group members know things they do not, they are more likely to focus on this unshared information. Liang and colleagues trained people alone or in groups of three to assemble transistor radios. A week later, everyone came back and tried to assemble a radio in groups of three: People who had been trained in groups took part with their same group members, whereas people who had been trained alone took part with two others who had also been trained alone. The people who had been trained in groups remembered significantly more about the task and made fewer errors than the people who had been trained alone. The reason for this superior performance was that the people trained in groups had learned who was best at remembering which details and had developed a system whereby different people were responsible for remembering different parts of the task; at the second session, these group members relied on each other to remember things they had forgotten. Thus, if groups know in advance who is responsible for remembering what, they are more likely to focus on unshared information.

Groupthink: Many Heads, One Mind.   A possible limitation of research on group problem solving is that most studies use people who have never met before and give people tasks that are unfamiliar and sometimes trivial. Would groups do better if their members were used to working with each other and if they were dealing with important, real-world problems? Our opening example of President Kennedy and his advisers deciding to invade Cuba at the Bay of Pigs suggests not. Let's see why.

Using real-world events, Irving Janis (1972, 1982) developed an influential theory of group decision making that he called **groupthink,** defined as a kind of thinking in which maintaining group cohesiveness and solidarity is more important than considering the facts in a realistic manner. According to Janis's theory, groupthink is most likely to occur when certain preconditions are met, such as when the group is highly cohesive, isolated from contrary opinions, and ruled by a directive leader who makes his or her wishes known. Kennedy and his advisers were riding high on their close victory in the 1960 election and were a very tight-knit, homogenous group. Since they had not yet made any major policy decisions, they lacked well-developed methods for discussing the issues. Moreover, Kennedy made it clear that he favored the invasion, and he asked the group to consider only details of how it should be executed, instead of questioning whether it should proceed at all.

When these preconditions of groupthink are met, several symptoms appear; these are outlined in Figure 9.8. The group begins to feel that it is invulnerable and can do no wrong. People do not voice contrary views (self-censorship), because they are afraid of ruining the high morale, or esprit de corps, of the group or because they are afraid of being criticized by the others. For example, Arthur Schlesinger, one of Kennedy's advisers, reported that he had severe doubts about the Bay of Pigs invasion but did not bring up any of these concerns during the discussions, out of a fear that "others would regard it as presumptuous of him, a college professor, to take issue with august heads of major government institutions" (Janis, 1982, p. 32). If anyone does voice a contrary viewpoint, the

> The only sin which we never forgive in each other is difference of opinion.
> –Ralph Waldo Emerson, *Society and Solitude*

groupthink: a kind of thinking in which maintaining group cohesiveness and solidarity is more important than considering the facts in a realistic manner rest of the group is quick to criticize that person, pressuring him or her to conform to the majority view. Schlesinger did voice some of his doubts to Dean Rusk, the secretary of state. When Robert Kennedy (the attorney general and the president's brother) got wind of this, he took Schlesinger aside at a party and told him that the president had made up his mind to go ahead with the invasion and that his friends should support him. This kind of behavior creates an illusion of unanimity, where it looks as if everyone agrees. On the day the group voted on whether to invade, President Kennedy asked all those present for their opinion except one: Arthur Schlesinger.

The pernicious state of groupthink causes people to implement an inferior decision-making process (see Figure 9.8). The group does not consider the full range of alternatives, does not develop contingency plans, and does not adequately consider the risks of its preferred choice. Can you think of other governmental decisions that were plagued by groupthink? Janis (1972, 1982) discusses several, such as the failure of the U.S. military commanders in Pearl Harbor to anticipate the Japanese attack in 1941; President Truman's decision to invade North Korea in 1950, despite explicit warnings from the Chinese that they would attack with massive force; President Johnson's decision to escalate the Vietnam War in the mid-1960s; and the Watergate cover-up by President Nixon and his advisers. Another, more recent example was the fateful decision by NASA to go ahead with the launching of the space shuttle *Challenger*, despite the objections of engineers who said that the freezing temperatures presented a severe

FIGURE 9.8 Groupthink: Antecedents, symptoms, and consequences. ■ Under some conditions, maintaining group cohesiveness and solidarity is more important to a group than considering the facts in a realistic manner (see antecedents). When this happens, certain symptoms of groupthink occur, such as the illusion of invulnerability (see symptoms). These symptoms lead to defective decision making. (Adapted from Janis, 1982)

Groupthink

Antecedents of groupthink	Symptoms of groupthink	Defective decision-making
The group is highly cohesive: The group is valued and attractive, and people very much want to be members.	**Illusion of invulnerability:** The group feels it is invincible and can do no wrong.	Incomplete survey of alternatives
Group isolation: The group is isolated, protected from hearing alternative viewpoints.	**Belief in the moral correctness of the group:** "God is on our side."	Failure to examine risks of the favored alternative
A directive leader: The leader controls the discussion and makes his or her wishes known.	**Stereotyped views of out-group:** Opposing sides are viewed in a simplistic, stereotyped manner.	Poor information search
High stress: The members perceive threats to the group.	**Self-censorship:** People decide themselves not to voice contrary opinions, in order to not "rock the boat."	Failure to develop contingency plans
Poor decision-making procedures: No standard methods to consider alternative viewpoints.	**Direct pressure on dissenters to conform:** If people do voice contrary opinions they are pressured by others to conform to the majority.	
	Illusion of unanimity: An illusion is created that everyone agrees, by, for example, not calling on people known to disagree.	
	Mindguards: Group members protect the leader from contrary viewpoints.	

■ The decision to launch the space shuttle *Challenger*, which tragically exploded due to defective O-ring seals, appears to have been the result of groupthink on the part of NASA officials, who disregarded engineers' concerns about the quality of the seals.

danger to the rubber O-ring seals (the ones that eventually failed during the launch, causing the rocket to explode and killing all aboard). All these decisions were plagued by many of the symptoms and consequences of groupthink, outlined in Figure 9.8 (Esser & Lindoerfer, 1989).

Since Janis proposed his theory, it has been put to the test by a number of other researchers. Some of these studies have been disappointing, in that group cohesiveness did not seem to be as related to groupthink as Janis had assumed (Aldag & Fuller, 1993; Tetlock, Peterson, McGuire, Chang, & Field, 1992). Janis's theory, however, suggests that group cohesiveness will increase groupthink only if other antecedent conditions are also met, such as the presence of a directive leader and high stress (see Figure 9.8). And indeed, the experimental evidence is consistent with this idea: Group cohesiveness does not increase groupthink by itself, only when it is accompanied by other risk factors (Mullen, Anthony, Salas, & Driskell, 1994; Turner, Pratkanis, Probasco, & Leve, 1992). Thus, support for the groupthink model has been found both in systematic analyses of historical events and in well-controlled laboratory experiments.

How can groupthink be avoided? A wise leader can take several steps to ensure that his or her group is immune to this style of decision making. The leader should not take a directive role but remain impartial. He or she should invite outside opinions from people who are not members of the group and who are thus less concerned with maintaining group cohesiveness. He or she should divide the group into subgroups that first meet separately and then meet together to discuss their different recommendations. The leader might also take a secret ballot or ask group members to write down their opinions anonymously; doing so would ensure that people give their true opinions, uncensored by a fear of recrimination from the group (Flowers, 1977; McCauley, 1989; Zimbardo & Andersen, 1993).

Fortunately, President Kennedy learned from his mistakes with the Bay of Pigs decision and, when faced with his next major foreign policy decision, the

Cuban missile crisis, took many of these steps to avoid groupthink. When his advisers met to decide what to do about the discovery of Soviet missiles in Cuba, Kennedy often absented himself from the group, so as not to inhibit their discussion. He also brought in outside experts (e.g., Adlai Stevenson) who were not members of the in-group. That Kennedy successfully negotiated the removal of the Soviet missiles was almost certainly due to the improved methods of group decision making he adopted.

Group Polarization: Going to Extremes.   Maybe you are willing to grant that groups sometimes make poor decisions. Surely, though, groups will usually make less *risky* decisions than a lone individual will—one individual might be willing to bet the ranch on a very risky proposition, but if others help make the decision, they will interject reason and moderation. Or will they? The question of whether groups or individuals make more risky decisions has been examined in numerous studies. Participants are typically given the Choice Dilemmas Questionnaire (CDQ), a series of stories that present a dilemma for the main character and ask the reader to choose how much probability of success there would have to be before the reader would recommend the risky alternative (Kogan & Wallach, 1964). An example of a CDQ item about a chess player appears in Figure 9.9. People choose their answers alone and then meet in a group to discuss the options, arriving at a unanimous group decision for each dilemma.

Many of the initial studies found, surprisingly, that groups make riskier decisions than individuals do. For example, when deciding alone, people said that the chess player should make the risky gambit only if there was at least a 30 percent chance of success. But after discussing the problem with others in a group, people said that the chess player should go for it even if there was only a 10 percent

> The bitter change of fierce extremes, extremes by change more fierce.
> –John Milton

THE CHOICE DILEMMAS QUESTIONAIRE

An example of an item from the Choice Dilemmas Questionnaire

A low-ranked participant in a national chess tournament, playing an early match against a highly favored opponent, has the choice of attempting or not trying a deceptive but risky maneuver that might lead to quick victory if it is successful or almost certain defeat if it fails.

Please indicate the lowest probability of success that you would accept before recommending that the chess player play the risky move:

____ 1 chance of success in 10

____ 3 chances of success in 10

____ 5 chances of success in 10

____ 7 chances of success in 10

____ 9 chances of success in 10

____ I would not recommend this alternative, no matter how high its likelihood of success

FIGURE 9.9   The Choice Dilemmas Questionnaire.
■ (Adapted from Wallach, Kogan, & Bem, 1962)

chance of success (Wallach, Kogan, & Bem, 1962). Findings such as these became known as the *risky shift*. Yet with increased research, it became clear that such shifts were not the full story. It turns out that groups tend to make decisions that are more extreme in the same direction as the individual's initial predispositions, which happened to be risky in the case of the chess problem. What would happen if people were initially inclined to be conservative? In cases such as these, groups tend to make even more conservative decisions than individuals do.

Consider this problem: Roger, a young married man with two children, has a secure but low-paying job and no savings. Someone gives him a tip about a stock that will triple in value if the company's new product is successful but that will plummet if the new product fails. Should Roger sell his life insurance policy and invest in the company? Most people recommend a safe course of action here: Roger should buy the stock only if the new product is very certain to succeed. When they talk it over in a group, they become even more conservative, deciding that the new product would have to have a nearly 100 percent chance of success before they would recommend that Roger buy stock in the company.

The finding that groups make more extreme decisions, in the direction of people's initial judgments, has become known as **group polarization.** This phrase captures the idea that a group pushes people's initial decisions to the extreme—toward greater risk if people's initial tendency is to be risky and toward greater caution if people's initial tendency is to be cautious (Brown, 1965; Myers & Arenson, 1972; Teger & Pruitt, 1967). Group polarization occurs for two main reasons: According to the persuasive arguments interpretation, all individuals bring to the group a set of arguments, some of which other individuals have not considered, supporting their initial recommendation. For example, one person might stress that cashing in the life insurance policy is an unfair risk to Roger's children, should he die prematurely. Another person might not have considered this possibility; thus, he or she becomes more conservative as well. A series of studies by Eugene Burnstein and Amiram Vinokur (1977) supports this interpretation of group polarization, whereby each member presents arguments that other members had not considered.

According to the social comparison interpretation, when people discuss an issue in a group they first check out how everyone else feels. What does the group value—being risky or being cautious? In order to be liked, many people then take a position that is similar to everyone else's but a little more extreme. In this way, the individual supports the group's values and also presents him- or herself in a positive light—a person in the vanguard, an impressive thinker. Both the persuasive arguments and the social comparison interpretations of group polarization have received support (Blaskovich, Ginsburg, & Veach, 1975; Brown, 1986; Isenberg, 1986; Zuber, Crott, & Werner, 1992).

group polarization: the tendency for groups to make decisions that are more extreme than the initial inclinations of its members

The Culture-Value Theory. While group polarization can go either way, Roger Brown (1965) has proposed that, relatively speaking, Americans value risk more than caution. In his culture-value theory, Brown discusses how American culture, based on the economic system of capitalism, requires a willingness to take risks and try new approaches. In comparison, other cultures operate under a dominant cultural value of caution—a relatively high level of wariness and conservatism. Hence, the hypothesis derived from culture-value theory is that some cultures should be more likely to evince risky shifts, while others should be more likely to evince cautious shifts.

In support of Brown's theory, research has indicated that Americans perceive people who take risks more positively than those who make cautious decisions (Madaras & Bem, 1968), find the riskier alternatives more admirable than the cautious ones (Lamm, Schaude, & Trommsdorff, 1971), and believe high-risk takers are more competent than those who choose cautious alternatives (Jellison & Riskind, 1970). Thus, it appears that risk does have value in the United States. In comparison, two cross-cultural studies have found evidence for a general cultural value of caution in African countries. In both Uganda and Liberia, groups made choices on the CDQ that were typically more cautious than those made by the individual members alone and that were more cautious than those made by Western research participants (Carlson & Davis, 1971; Gologor, 1977). Thus, when group discussion occurs, it reinforces whichever cultural value predominates in that society—for example, group polarization toward caution occurs when individuals learn they are not as cautious as others in the group and caution is valued in their culture.

Conflict and Cooperation

We have just examined how people work together to solve problems; in these situations, group members have a common goal. Often, however, people have incompatible goals, placing them in conflict with each other. This can be true of two individuals, such as romantic partners who disagree about who should clean the kitchen, or two groups, such as a labor union and company management who disagree over wages and working conditions. It can also be true of two nations, such as the long-standing conflict between Israel and its Arab neighbors or between the Serbians, Croatians, and Muslims in the former Yugoslavia. The opportunity for interpersonal conflict exists whenever two or more people interact. Freud (1930) went so far as to argue that conflict is an inevitable byproduct of civilization. The goals and needs of individuals often clash with the goals and needs of their fellow human beings.

Many conflicts are resolved peacefully, with little rancor. Couples can find a way to resolve their differences in a mutually acceptable manner, and labor disputes are sometimes settled with a friendly handshake. All too often, however, conflict erupts into open hostilities. The divorce rate in the United States is distressingly high. People are increasingly resorting to violence to resolve their differences, as shown by the skyrocketing murder rate in the United States, "the murder capital of the civilized world" (*Newsweek*, July 16, 1990). Warfare between nations remains an all-too-common solution to international disputes. In fact, when wars over the past five centuries are examined, the twentieth century ranks first in the severity of wars (defined as the number of deaths per war) and second in their frequency (Levy & Morgan, 1984). It is therefore of great importance to find ways of resolving conflicts peacefully. Given our capability to destroy ourselves many times over with nuclear weapons, humanity's need to study the causes and cures of interpersonal conflict is more pressing than ever.

Let's begin by defining our terms. Our concern is with interpersonal, not intrapersonal, conflict. **Intrapersonal conflict** is tension created by incompatible goals within one individual, such as a parent's desire to pursue a career but also to be the primary caregiver for his or her children. (We discussed intrapersonal conflict in Chapter 6). **Interpersonal conflict** is tension between two or more individuals or groups who have incompatible goals; this kind of conflict can be

> My own belief is that Russian and Chinese behavior is as much influenced by suspicion of our intentions as ours is by suspicion of theirs. This would mean that we have great influence over their behavior—that, by treating them as hostile, we assure their hostility.
>
> —J. William Fulbright

intrapersonal conflict: tension within one individual due to two or more incompatible goals (e.g., a parent's desires to stay home with his or her children and to pursue a career)

interpersonal conflict: tension between two or more individuals or groups who have incompatible goals

■ Intergroup conflict is clearly one of the most important problems confronting us today. For example, as we write this chapter, an uneasy peace has come to Bosnia, after years of conflict. In this photograph, refugees at a Bosnian checkpoint are seen hiding in a ditch during the shelling.

zero-sum conflict: conflict in which one side's gain is always the other side's loss, as in athletic contests

divided into two types. In **zero-sum conflict,** one party's gain is always the other person's loss. The two sides cannot both win or both lose in this kind of dispute. Examples include athletic contests in which there is always a clear winner and loser and games such as chess and poker. The reason for the term *zero-sum* is that if we think of people's rewards in numerical terms (e.g., the amount of money they win or lose in a poker game), then the sum of what one side wins and the other side loses always equals zero. If Janice is playing poker with Bob and she wins $5, then Bob has lost $5.

In everyday life, zero-sum conflicts are relatively rare. When people have conflicting goals, there are often solutions that are satisfactory to both parties, so that both come out ahead. Unfortunately, there are also solutions that are unattractive to both parties, so that nobody wins. Consider the arms race between the United States and the former Soviet Union. Both countries could win if they agreed to disarm, each reducing the number of costly, destructive missiles in their arsenal. Both could lose by continuing to spend a large proportion of their budgets on expensive weapons systems, neither achieving superiority over the other. Or one side could win by gaining so much military superiority that the other side was forced to capitulate to its demands.

mixed-motive conflict: conflict in which both parties can gain by cooperating but in which one side can gain even more by competing against its opponent

Social psychologists refer to this latter kind of dispute as a **mixed-motive conflict,** defined as any conflict in which both parties can gain by cooperating, but in which one side can gain even more by competing against its opponent. The term *mixed-motive* comes from the fact that people have two choices: They can compete (resulting in the most positive personal gain), or they can cooperate (maximizing the joint gain of both parties). Most social psychological research has examined mixed-motive conflicts (rather than zero-sum conflicts) for two reasons. First, mixed-motive conflicts are more common in everyday life than zero-sum conflicts are. Second, mixed-motive conflicts are more interesting, because it is not as obvious how each side should respond. Whereas in a zero-sum conflict people should compete with their adversary as hard as they can, because

■ Conflict often escalates so that neither side can win.

there is no way both sides can win, in a mixed-motive conflict it is not always clear whether one should adopt a cooperative or a competitive strategy.

There are many perspectives on how people respond to mixed-motive conflicts, including sociological studies of social movements and historical, economic, and political analyses of international relations. The social psychological approach is unique in its attempt to study conflict experimentally, testing both its causes and its resolutions in the laboratory. Researchers bring two or more people together and ask them to compete in some manner, studying how conflict develops. One of the most common techniques used is a game called the Prisoner's Dilemma. To illustrate this game, imagine that two men, Billy and Jesse, have been arrested for armed robbery but the police have only enough evidence to convict them of the lesser crime of breaking and entering. The police take the defendants to separate interrogation rooms and offer each of them a deal: If they agree to testify against their partner, they will be released with no jail time. What should they do? Should they confess or remain silent? The top of Figure 9.10 illustrates the consequences of each course of action. If both defendants remain silent, they will be convicted of breaking and entering and will each receive a sentence of 3 years. (The sentence Billy gets is listed first in each cell of the table, whereas the sentence Jesse gets is listed second.) Here both defendants are relatively well-off. If Billy confesses but Jesse remains silent, then Billy is released and Jesse gets a 30-year sentence. If both defendants confess, however, then there is no reason for the police to use one as a witness against the other, and both will receive sentences of 10 years.

This is a classic mixed-motive conflict, because it pits people's desire to look out for their own interests against their desire to look out for their partner as well. To find out how people resolve this conflict, social psychologists have asked participants to play this and similar games in hundreds of studies (Blumberg, 1994; Kelley & Thibaut, 1978; Pruitt & Kimmel, 1977; Rapoport & Chammah, 1965). Instead of using prison sentences, researchers typically use money or

> I wonder men dare trust themselves with men.
> —William Shakespeare

CONSEQUENCES OF DECISIONS IN MIXED-MOTIVE CONFLICTS

The Prisoner's Dilemma game

	Jesse doesn't confess		Jesse confesses	
BILLY:	Billy's sentence	Jesse's sentence	Billy's sentence	Jesse's sentence
DOESN'T CONFESS	3 years	3 years	30 years	Released
CONFESSES	Released	30 years	10 years	10 years

A mixed-motive game

	Student B chooses option X		Student B chooses option Y	
STUDENT A CHOOSES:	Student A's points	Student B's points	Student A's points	Student B's points
OPTION X	+3	+3	−6	+6
OPTION Y	+6	−6	−1	−1

FIGURE 9.10   Laboratory games used to study interpersonal conflict. ■ The top panel shows the Prisoner's Dilemma. The sentence each defendant receives depends both on whether he confesses and on whether the other person confesses. Billy's sentences are listed first in each cell of the table, followed by Jesse's sentences. For example, if Billy confesses but Jesse does not, Billy is released and Jesse receives a 30-year sentence. The bottom panel shows a similar mixed-motive game that is used in laboratory studies. The numbers represent the points that will be added or subtracted to a student's score on the final exam. Student A's points are listed first in each cell of the table, followed by student B's points. For example, if student A chooses option Y and student B chooses option X, student A receives 6 extra points and student B loses 6 points. (Adapted from Rapoport & Chammah, 1965)

points on an exam as payoffs and ask participants to play the game for several trials. Consider, for example, the payoff matrix shown at the bottom of Figure 9.10. Imagine that the numbers in this matrix represent points that will be added to or subtracted from your score on a final exam. You are playing against another student in the class, and you have to decide whether to choose option X or option Y, without knowing which option the other student will choose. Just as in the Prisoner's Dilemma, your payoff—the number of points you earn or lose—depends on the choices both you and your partner make. What would you do if you were playing?

If you are like most people, you will start out by choosing option Y. At worst you will lose only one point, and at best you will win the highest possible number—six points. Choosing option X raises the possibility that both sides will win some points, but this is also a very risky choice. If your partner chooses Y while you choose X, you stand to lose a great deal. Because people often do not know how much they can trust their partners, option Y frequently seems like the safest choice (Rapoport & Chammah, 1965). The rub is that both players will probably think this way, ensuring that both sides lose (see the lower right-hand corner of Figure 9.10).

People's actions in these games seem to mirror many conflicts in everyday life. To find a solution desirable to both parties, people must trust each other. Often they do not, and this lack of trust leads to an escalating series of competitive moves, so that in the end no one wins. Two countries locked in an arms race may feel they cannot afford to disarm, out of fear that the other side will take advantage of their weakened position. The result is that both sides add furiously to their stockpile of weapons, neither gaining superiority over the other and both spending money they could use to solve domestic problems (Deustch, 1973). Such an escalation of conflict is also seen all too often among couples who are divorcing. Sometimes the goal seems more to hurt the other person than to further one's own needs (or the children's). In the end, both suffer, because metaphorically speaking, they both choose option Y too often (see the bottom of Figure 9.10).

Such escalating conflict, though common, is not inevitable. Many studies have found that when people play a Prisoner's Dilemma game they will, under certain conditions, adopt the more cooperative response (option X), ensuring that both sides end up with a positive outcome. Not surprisingly, if people are playing the game with a friend or if they expect to interact with their partner in the future, they are more likely to adopt a cooperative strategy that maximizes both their and their partner's profits (Pruitt & Kimmel, 1977). In addition, growing up in some societies, such as Asian cultures, seems to foster a more cooperative orientation than growing up in the West does (Leung, 1987; Markus & Kitayama, 1991).

To increase cooperation, you can also try to communicate that you can be trusted not to exploit your opponent. You might do so by choosing option X and sticking with it as the game goes on, thereby showing your partner that you are not trying to exploit him or her. The problem is that you become an easy mark, and your partner knows he or she can nail you at any time by choosing option Y. A better strategy is known as the **tit-for-tat strategy:** Start out making the cooperative response (option X), then choose whichever option your partner chose on the last trial. If your partner chooses the competitive response (option Y), you respond in kind on the next trial. If your partner chooses the cooperative response (option X), then you respond cooperatively on the next trial. This strategy communicates a willingness to cooperate and an unwillingness to sit back and be exploited if the partner does not cooperate. The tit-for-tat strategy is usually successful in getting the other person to respond with the cooperative, trusting response (Axelrod, 1984; McClintock & Liebrand, 1988; Messick & Liebrand, 1995). The analogy to the arms race would be to match not only any military buildup made by an unfriendly nation but also any conciliatory gesture, such as a ban on nuclear testing.

tit-for-tat strategy: a means of encouraging cooperation by at first acting cooperatively but then always responding the way your opponent did (cooperatively or competitively) on the previous trial

The Use of Threats.   When caught in a conflict, many of us are tempted to use threats to get the other party to cave in to our wishes. Many people seem to endorse the strategy that we should "walk quietly and carry a big stick." Parents commonly use threats to get their children to behave, and teachers often threaten their students with demerits or a visit to the principal. More alarming is the increasing number of youths in the United States who carry guns and use them to resolve conflicts that used to be settled with a playground scuffle.

■ Would you say that Sally's boss is a task-oriented or relationship-oriented leader?

Threats are commonly used on an international scale as well, to further the interests of one nation over another.

A classic series of studies by Morton Deutsch and Robert Krauss (1960, 1962) indicates that threats are not an effective means of reducing conflict. These researchers developed a game in which two participants imagined they were in charge of trucking companies named Acme and Bolt. The goal of each company was to transport merchandise as quickly as possible to a destination. The participants were paid 60 cents for each "trip," but had 1 cent subtracted for every second it took them to make the trip. The most direct route for each company was over a one-lane road on which only one truck could travel at a time. This placed the two companies in direct conflict, as seen in Figure 9.11. If Acme and Bolt both tried to take the one-lane road, then neither truck could pass and both would lose money. Each company could take an alternate route, but this was much longer, guaranteeing they would lose at least 10 cents on each trial. The game lasted until each side had made 20 trips.

How did the participants respond to this dilemma? After a while, most of them worked out a solution that allowed both trucks to make a modest amount of money. They took turns waiting until the other person crossed the one-lane road; then they would take that route as well. They did so, that is, when neither had any weapons with which to threaten the other. In another version of the study, the researchers gave Acme a gate that could be lowered over the one-lane road, thereby blocking Bolt from using that route. You might think that using force—the gate—would increase Acme's profits, because all Acme had to do was to threaten Bolt, telling him or her to stay off the one-lane road or else. In fact, quite the opposite happened. When one side had the gate, both participants lost more than when neither side had the gate—as seen in the left-hand panel of Figure 9.12, on page 348. This figure shows the total amount earned or lost by both sides. (Acme won slightly more than Bolt when it had the gate but won substantially more when neither side had a gate.) Bolt did not like to be threatened and often retaliated by parking its truck on the one-lane road, blocking the other truck's progress. Meanwhile, the seconds ticked away and both sides lost money.

What would happen if the situation were more equitable, with both sides having gates? Surely they would learn to cooperate very quickly, recognizing the stalemate that would ensue if both of them used their gates—right? To the contrary (as you can see in the left-hand panel of Figure 9.12), both sides lost more money in the bilateral threat condition than in any of the others. The

The Deutsch and Krauss trucking game

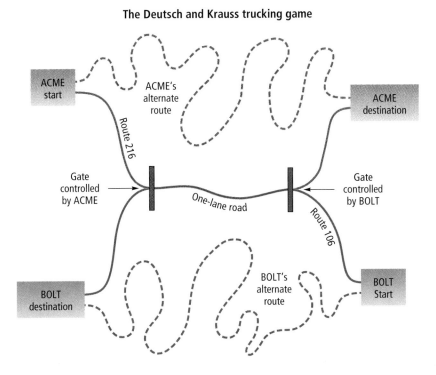

FIGURE 9.11   The trucking game. ■ Participants play the role of the head of either Acme or Bolt Trucking Company. In order to earn money, they have to drive their truck from the starting point to their destination as quickly as possible. The quickest route is the one-lane road, but both trucks cannot travel on this road at the same time. In some versions of the studies, participants were given gates they use to block the other's progress on the one-lane road. (Adapted from Deutsch & Krauss, 1960)

owners of the trucking companies both threatened to use their gates and did so with great frequency. Once Acme used the game to block Bolt, Bolt retaliated and blocked Acme the next time its truck came down the road—producing a stalemate that was in neither of their interests. Sound familiar? For the past few decades, the United States and the former Soviet Union were locked in an escalating nuclear arms race, each threatening the other with destruction.

Effects of Communication.   There is a way in which the Deutsch and Krauss (1960, 1962) trucking game does not approximate real life: The two sides could use behavioral threats (closing their gates) but were not allowed to communicate with each other. Would the two adversaries work out their differences if they could talk them over? To find out, Deutsch and Krauss allowed the participants to communicate over an intercom. In one condition, the participants were allowed to speak as often or as little as they liked. As seen in the middle of Figure 9.12, this communication had very little effect (compare the middle panel with the left-hand panel in the figure). Interestingly, people chose not to say much to each other in this condition, communicating on only about 5 of the 20 trials.

In another condition, the researchers decided to require the participants to communicate on every trial. Surely if people were forced to talk to each other

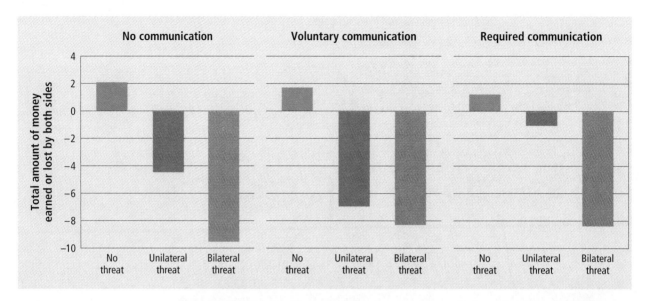

FIGURE 9.12 Results of the trucking game studies. ■ The left-hand panel shows the amount of money the participants made (summed over Acme and Bolt) when they could not communicate. When threats were introduced by giving one or both sides a gate, both sides lost more money. The middle panel shows the amount of money the participants made when they could communicate as little or as much as they wanted. Once again, giving them gates reduced the amount of money they won. The right-hand panel shows the amount of money the participants made when they were required to communicate on every trial. Once again, giving them gates reduced their winnings. (Adapted from Deutsch & Krauss, 1962)

they would cooperate more. As seen in the right-hand panel of Figure 9.12, however, no dramatic increase in profits occurred in the "required communication" condition. Requiring people to communicate reduced losses somewhat when Acme alone had the gate (the unilateral threat condition), but the required communication did not increase cooperation in either of the two other conditions (no threat; bilateral threat). Overall, requiring people to communicate did not raise profits dramatically. Why not?

The problem with the communication in the trucking studies is that it did not foster trust. To the contrary, people used the intercom to convey threats. Communication is helpful only when people learn to use it in such a way as to establish trust. Krauss and Deutsch demonstrated this fact in a later version of their trucking study, in which they specifically instructed people in how to communicate, telling them to work out a solution that was fair to both parties and that they would be willing to accept if they were in the other person's shoes. Under these conditions, verbal communication increased the amount of money both sides won, because it fostered trust, instead of adding fuel to the competitive fires (Deutsch, 1973, 1990; Krauss & Deutsch, 1966; Voissem & Sistrunk, 1971).

Negotiation and Bargaining. In the laboratory games we have discussed so far, people's options are limited. They have to choose option X or Y in the Prisoner's Dilemma, and they have only a couple of ways of getting their truck to its destination in the trucking game. In contrast, people often have a wide array of options in everyday conflicts. Consider two people haggling over the price of a car. Both the buyer and the seller can acquiesce to all of the other's demands, to some of them, or to none of them. Either party can walk away from the deal at any time. Given that there is considerable latitude in how people can resolve the conflict, communication between the parties is all the more important. By talking, bargaining, and negotiating, people can arrive at a satisfactory settlement. **Negotiation** is defined as a form of communication between opposing sides in a conflict, wherein the parties make offers and counteroffers and a solution occurs only when both parties agree (Bazerman & Neale, 1992; Pruitt & Carnevale, 1993; Rubin & Brown, 1975; Thompson, 1990). How successful are people at negotiating mutually beneficial solutions?

One limit to successful negotiation is that people often assume they are locked in a zero-sum conflict, in which only one party can come out ahead. They don't realize that, as in the mixed-motive conflicts we have reviewed, solutions favorable to both parties are available. Consider a labor union and a company who are negotiating a new contract. The company has proposed a 2 percent salary increase and no additional days of annual vacation, whereas the union has proposed a 6 percent salary increase and six additional days of annual vacation. After protracted negotiations, the two sides decide to compromise on both issues, agreeing to a 4 percent salary increase and three additional days of annual vacation. Sounds fair, doesn't it? The problem with such compromises is that they assume both issues (in this case, the salary increase and additional vacation days) are equally important to both parties, and often that is not the case. Suppose that the labor union cared much more about increasing salaries than getting additional vacation days, whereas the company cared much more about minimizing vacation days than keeping salaries in check. In this case, a better solution for both sides would be to trade off issues, such that the union got the 6 percent salary increase (which it cared about the most) in return for no increase in vacation days (which the company cared about the most). This type of compromise, whereby two parties trade off issues according to their relative importance to each side, is called an **integrative solution.**

It might seem like such integrative solutions would be relatively easy to find. After all, the two parties simply have to sit down and figure out which issues are the most important to each other. Leigh Thompson and her colleagues have found, however, that there are a number of barriers to identifying integrative solutions (Thompson, 1990, 1991; Thompson, Peterson, & Brodt, in press; Thompson, Peterson, & Kray, in press). For instance, the more people have at stake in a negotiation, the more biased their perceptions of their opponent. They will tend to distrust proposals made by the other side and to overlook interests they have in common (Ross & Ward, 1995, in press).

To illustrate this distrust, Thompson (1995) asked students to take a side in a hypothetical conflict between an employee and an employer. As in our example above, the employee had somewhat different interests than the employer; for example, obtaining a high salary was more important to the employee than the employer, whereas keeping medical benefits down was more important to the employer than the employee. The sides each knew how important the issues were to them but not to their opponent; the point was to see how well each side figured out what was most important to the other side, as they negotiated a solution.

It turned out that people were not very good at discovering their opponents' true interests. And, those who were directly involved in the negotiations were even worse at this task than those who were not. Other students watched video-

negotiation: a form of communication between opposing sides in a conflict in which offers and counteroffers are made and a solution occurs only when it is agreed on by both parties

integrative solution: a solution to a conflict whereby the parties make trade-offs on issues according to their different interests; each side concedes the most on issues that are unimportant to it but important to the other side

■ If the right strategies are used, negotiation can lead to successful resolutions of conflicts. Here Israeli prime minister Yitzhak Rabin and Palestinian Liberation Organization leader Yasser Arafat meet at the White House to sign a Middle East peace accord.

> Yet, there remains another wall. This wall constitutes a psychological barrier between us . . . [a] barrier of distorted and eroded interpretation of every event and statement. . . . I ask why don't we stretch out our hands with faith and sincerity so that together we might destroy this barrier?
>
> –Former Egyptian president Anwar al-Sadat, November 29, 1977, in a speech before the Israeli Knesset

tapes of the negotiations and were simply asked to estimate how important each issue was to each side. These uninvolved observers of the negotiations made more accurate judgments than the people actually involved in the negotiations. When negotiators are in the heat of the battle and care deeply about the outcome, they tend to distrust the other side, making it more difficult to realize that there is some common ground beneficial to both parties. This is one reason people often use neutral mediators to solve labor disputes, legal battles, and divorce proceedings: Mediators are often in a better position to recognize that there are mutually agreeable solutions to a conflict (Carnevale, 1986; Emery & Wyer, 1987; Kressel & Pruitt, 1989).

The bottom line? When you are negotiating with someone, it is important to keep in mind that integrative solutions are often available. Try to gain the other side's trust, and communicate your own interests in an open manner. Remember that the way you construe the situation is not necessarily the same as the way the other party construes the situation. You may well discover that the other side communicates its interests more freely as a result, increasing the likelihood that you will find a solution beneficial to both parties.

Conflict Between Individuals Versus Groups

Up to now, we have discussed conflict between two individuals as if it were similar to conflict between two social groups. As you might imagine, however, there are important differences between two individuals going at each other head-to-head and two groups doing so. Chet Insko and John Schopler and their colleagues, for example, have found that individuals act more cooperatively than groups do (Insko et al., 1994; McCallum et al., 1985; Schopler & Insko, 1992; Schopler et al., 1993). Individuals who play the Prisoner's Dilemma game against other individuals are more likely to act cooperatively than groups who play the Prisoner's Dilemma game against other groups. The reason for this is that we human beings are more likely to assume that a given individual is cooperative at heart and can be trusted but that most groups of individuals will, given the opportunity, stab us in the back. As we saw in our earlier discussion of deindividuation, there is some truth to this assumption—when in groups, people feel less accountable for their actions and are more likely to behave in an antisocial (e.g., competitive) manner. The implication is that two world leaders might be more cooperative when negotiating one-on-one than when groups of advisers from the two nations meet.

When people play the Prisoner's Dilemma game, however, they rarely have a chance to communicate with their adversary and never have a chance to negotiate compromise solutions. As we have just seen, in many types of real-world conflicts people can choose from a wide array of solutions, rather than having to choose a single competitive or cooperative response. Thompson and her colleagues have found that in such situations, in which many solutions are possible, groups of people make more accurate judgments and are better able to find integrative solutions than individual negotiators (Thompson, Peterson, & Brodt, in press). When people negotiate in teams, they have to reach consensus among themselves as well as with the other side. As a result, teams tend to share information with themselves and their opponents, increasing the likelihood that they will discover integrative solutions. In Thompson and colleagues' experiment, however, there was one exception to the rule that teams negotiated better than individuals: Groups of friends did less well than teams of strangers. Consistent with research on groupthink, friends focused more on maintaining cohesiveness and agreement, whereas strangers focused more on gathering objective information about their opponents. Thus, when communication and integrative solutions are available, a team of negotiators who are not too friendly with each other might do the best job.

SUMMARY

We began this chapter by examining the effects of being in a **nonsocial group**, in which there is no interaction between you and the people around you. We saw that when your individual efforts can be evaluated, the mere presence of others leads to **social facilitation:** Your performance is enhanced on simple tasks but impaired on complex tasks. When your individual efforts cannot be evaluated, the mere presence of others leads to **social loafing:** Your performance is impaired on simple tasks but enhanced on complex tasks. Finally, the mere presence of others can lead to **deindividuation**, or a sense of anonymity involving the loosening of normal constraints

on people's behavior. Prosocial and certainly antisocial group behavior occurs when people are deindividuated.

When other people are around, we often join them in **social groups**, which have a number of interesting properties. People often assume **roles** in groups, for example, and these roles can shape their behavior in powerful ways. Perhaps the most important role in a group is that of leader. Who makes the most effective leader? There is little support for the **great person theory**, which argues that good leadership is purely a matter of having the right personality traits. Leadership effectiveness is a function of both the kind of person a leader is and the nature of the work situation. Research on Fiedler's **contingency theory of leadership** has found that leadership performance depends both on whether a group has a **task-oriented leader** or a **relationship-oriented leader** and on whether the work environment is high or low in situational control. Women tend to lead more democratically than men, although women are able to adopt a "masculine" leadership style when the job requires it.

We examined whether social groups are better or worse than individuals at making decisions. The answer to this question depends on the type of task groups are working on, such as whether it is a **divisible versus a unitary task** (whether the task can be broken down into different subtasks). On unitary tasks, groups often do worse if people's outputs are combined in an **additive** or **conjunctive** manner. Groups will also do worse on a **disjunctive task** if **process loss** occurs—that is, if the most expert individual is unable to sway the rest of the group—and if groups fail to share unique information.

Tightly knit, cohesive groups are also prone to **groupthink,** a phenomenon in which maintaining group cohesiveness and solidarity is more important than considering the facts in a realistic manner. **Group polarization** indicates that groups are also prone to make more extreme decisions in the direction toward which its members were initially leaning; these group decisions can be more risky or more cautious, depending on which attitude is valued in the group.

When people interact, often the result is **interpersonal conflict**—tension between two or more individuals—as opposed to **intrapersonal conflict**—tension within one individual due to incompatible goals. There are two types of interpersonal conflict: **zero-sum conflict** and **mixed-motive conflict.** The most commonly studied form of mixed-motive conflict is the Prisoner's Dilemma, a game in which two people must decide whether to look out for only their own interests or for their partner's interests as well. The **tit-for-tat strategy** is a useful way of dealing with mixed-motive conflict, allowing one to respond cooperatively or competitively, given the other person's response. Creating trust is crucial in solving this kind of conflict. We examined the conditions under which hostilities are likely to increase or decrease, including how the use of threats and the inability to communicate can exacerbate a conflict. In **negotiation,** it is important to look for an **integrative solution**, whereby each side concedes the most on issues that are unimportant to it but very important to its adversary.

Much of the research discussed in this chapter points to ways to avoid the unpleasant consequences of group processes, making our associations with others more pleasant and fulfilling than they might otherwise be. Given the widespread incidence of conflict between individuals, groups, and nations, there is much to be learned from social psychological research on how to reduce hostilities.

IF YOU ARE INTERESTED . . .

Golding, William (1962). *Lord of the Flies*. After their plane crashes on a deserted island, a group of middle-class English boys must fend for themselves. The society they establish—with its norms, rules, and rejections of deviates—is thought-provoking and frightening.

Hendrick, C. (Ed.). (1987). *Group processes and inter-group relations*. Newbury Park, CA: Sage. Chapters by researchers in social psychology reviewing the current state of the field, including such topics as social loafing, groups in organizations, and the social psychology of terrorist groups.

Janis, I. (1982). *Groupthink: Psychological studies of policy decisions and fiascoes* (2nd ed.). Boston:

Houghton Mifflin. Janis argues persuasively that many important policy decisions, from the Bay of Pigs fiasco to the escalation of the Vietnam War, were flawed by groupthink, wherein maintaining group cohesiveness and solidarity was more important than considering the facts in a realistic manner.

Levine, J. M., & Moreland, R. L. (1990). Progress in small group research. *Annual Review of Psychology, 41,* 585–634. An up-to-date review of research on small groups by two of the best-known experts in the field.

Malcolm X, & Haley, Alex (1965). *The Autobiography of Malcolm X*. The autobiographical account of the life of Malcolm X, from his early days in Detroit to his electric leadership role in the Nation of Islam. Malcolm X's life raises many fascinating questions about the origins and causes of leadership. Made into a movie in 1992, directed by Spike Lee.

Paulus, P. B. (Ed.). (1989). *Psychology of group influence* (2nd ed.). Hillsdale, NJ: Erlbaum. Researchers in the area of group processes discuss the current theories and findings of their field; chapter topics include social facilitation, social loafing, and deindividuation.

Pruitt, D. G., & Rubin, J. Z. (1986). *Conflict*. New York: Random House. A review of research on conflict, including such topics as the sources of conflict, conflict resolution, bargaining, and mediation.

The Big Chill (1984). Seven college housemates meet again at the funeral of a close friend who has committed suicide. A poignant and often funny look at group dynamics.

Chapter 10

Interpersonal Attraction: From First Impressions to Close Relationships

Chapter Outline

*S*ometimes love blossoms at the most unexpected times. Consider Hilda Vogel and Nathan Serlin, who met on January 21, 1940—right after Hilda had fallen down an elevator shaft. Here is how columnist Andrew Malcolm describes it:

The whole thing started because Hilda Vogel got hungry. A 23-year-old medical secretary and recent German refugee, Miss Vogel was visiting her brother's sixth-floor photo studio on East 48th Street. He took forever to close. To save time en route to dinner, Miss Vogel summoned the elevator.

The elevator door opened. She stepped in to pull the string on the light bulb. Oops! There was no elevator. Just a black void. She began plummeting to her death.

Over at City Hospital, the duty intern was hungry too. The call came in: Woman falls down elevator shaft. The intern begged a colleague, Nathan Serlin, to take that ambulance run. "It's probably a D.O.A.," he said. "You'll be done in no time." . . .

[Because it was] 9 degrees that day, . . . Miss Vogel was wearing her thickest gloves. She grabbed the elevator cable. She slid down. She landed hard. But not as hard as a free fall.

It was the arriving Dr. Serlin who really fell. "She was sitting on those stairs," he recalls. "People hovered around. She was mortified. Her hands were greasy and burned. But all I could see were those blue eyes, the brightest blue I'd ever seen. They shined so in that dark hallway." (*New York Times*, September 29, 1992, p. B5)

After treating her hands, Dr. Serlin made careful note of Miss Vogel's address and phone number. Two days later, he called and asked her for a date. To his amazement, she said yes. Long walks and chats over coffee led to spaghetti dinners for 65 cents and, soon, to marriage. Now, more than 50 years later, they are still happily married, with two daughters and several grandchildren. "I still love that lady I met on those stairs," says Dr. Serlin.

Why were Nathan Serlin and Hilda Vogel initially attracted to each other? Why did they fall in love? And why has their marriage lasted so long, when so many other marriages fail? These questions are of great interest to the social psychologist, because of all the different twists and turns of social interaction, liking and loving are perhaps the most important.

At first glance, they might also seem the most incomprehensible. Falling in love (or making a friend) often feels like a magical process. As the old song says, "Just do it, just fall in love." Clearly, we become attracted to a person because of certain qualities that he or she has. But is that the whole story? In this chapter, you will learn that situational variables—aspects of your social world—also have an effect on your choice of friends and lovers.

As interesting as attraction is, the heart and soul of this experience is what comes next: We form an enduring bond with another person. You've probably noticed that your close relationships are made up of three entities, not just two: You, the other person, and "the relationship."

How do you make it work? How do you make love stay? In recent years, social psychologists have expanded their study of interpersonal attraction to include the relationship "process": the ways in which we negotiate and redefine our relationships with each other over time. Close relationships are not static, they change and evolve. If we asked Nathan Serlin and Hilda Vogel, they would undoubtedly tell us that their relationship has weathered bad times and good over the past fifty years. The theories and research presented in this chapter will give you a good idea about which variables promote commitment and satisfaction in long-term relationships.

Finally, the study of interpersonal attraction includes turmoil and sadness as well: some relationships end. Feelings of jealousy, perceptions of inequity, old behavior patterns that we learned in earlier relationships can all cause trouble with a current friend or lover. Why do our relationships end? And how do we go about ending them? In this chapter we will cover the full gamut of interpersonal attraction from how it begins to how it ends.

W hen Ellen Berscheid asked people of various ages what made them happy, at or near the top of their lists were making and maintaining friendships and having positive, warm relationships (Berscheid, 1985; Berscheid & Peplau, 1983). The feelings of loneliness that come from the absence of meaningful relationships with other people make people feel worthless, hopeless, helpless, powerless, and alienated (Gerstein & Tesser, 1987; Peplau & Perlman, 1982; Weiss, 1973).

We would all agree on the importance of finding close friends and companions. But what about our more casual acquaintances? Is it important to be well regarded by people we meet for the first time? It would seem so. In 1937, a successful businessman named Dale Carnegie wrote a simple little book called *How to Win Friends and Influence People*. This recipe book for quick and effective interpersonal relations was an instant success; indeed, it made publishing history by dominating the best-seller list, week in and week out, for a stupefying ten years. In addition, it was translated into 35 languages and read avidly by people in almost every corner of the globe.

The desire to be liked by others goes deeper, however, than simple recipes to help us succeed in the business world. As Ellen Berscheid (1985) has noted, we human beings, being the most social of social animals, have survived as a species largely because of our ability to know whether another creature or human being was good or bad for us. "Matters of interpersonal attraction," she argues, "are, quite literally, of life and death importance, not just to the individual but to all of humankind" (Berscheid, 1985, p. 414). In this chapter, we will discuss the antecedents of attraction, from the initial liking of two people meeting for the first time, to the attraction between two close friends, to the love that develops in close relationships.

Major Antecedents of Attraction

Every day, you cross paths with many strangers. Why have some of them become your acquaintances, friends, best friends, or romantic partners, while others have not? Before reading any further, stop for a moment and think about why you like certain people than others. What was it about them that first caught your interest? Think about your reasons as you read the next few sections, where we discuss the social psychological variables that predict who we will find interesting, appealing, and attractive.

The Person Next Door: The Propinquity Effect

There are approximately 5 billion people in the world. As hard as Dale Carnegie might try to win the friendship of all of them, he would be doomed to fail. In your lifetime, you have the opportunity to meet and interact with only a minuscule percentage of the people on this planet. Thus, it will not surprise you to learn that one of the simplest determinants of interpersonal attraction is proximity—sometimes called "propinquity." The people who, by chance, are the ones you see and interact with the most often are the most likely to become your friends and lovers (Newcomb, 1961; Priest & Sawyer, 1967; Segal, 1974).

> Contrary to popular belief, I do not believe that friends are necessarily the people you like best, they are merely the people who got there first.
> –Sir Peter Ustinov, 1977

■ Close friendships are often made in college, in part because of prolonged propinquity.

propinquity effect: the finding that the more we see and interact with people, the more likely they are to become our friends

Now, this might seem obvious; you are no doubt thinking, "Of course—how can I become best friends with someone I've never met who is currently residing 3,000 miles away?" But the striking thing about proximity and attraction, or the **propinquity effect,** as social psychologists call it, is that it works on a very micro level. For example, consider a classic study conducted in a housing complex for married students at MIT. Leon Festinger, Stanley Schachter, and Kurt Back (1950) tracked friendship formation among the couples in the various apartment buildings. For example, one section of the complex, Westgate West, was composed of 17 two-story buildings, each having ten apartments. The residents had been assigned to their apartments at random, as a vacancy opened up, and nearly all of them were strangers when they moved in. The researchers asked the residents to name their three closest friends in the entire housing project. Just as the propinquity effect would predict, 65 percent of the friends mentioned lived in the same building, even though the other buildings were not far away. Even more striking was the pattern of friendships within a building. Each Westgate West building was designed like the drawing in Figure 10.1; 19 feet separated the majority of the front doors, while the greatest distance between apartment doors was only 89 feet. The researchers found that 41 percent of the next-door neighbors indicated they were close friends, 22 percent of those who lived two doors apart did so, and only 10 percent of those who lived on opposite ends of the hall indicated they were close friends.

Festinger and his colleagues (1950) demonstrated that attraction and propinquity rely not only on actual physical distance but also on the more psychological, functional distance as well. Functional distance is defined as certain aspects of architectural design that make it more likely that some people will come into contact with each other more often than with others. For example, consider the friendship choices of the residents of apartments 1 and 5 (see Figure 10.1). Living at the foot of the stairs and in one case near the mailboxes meant that these couples saw a great deal of upstairs residents. Sure enough, apartment dwellers in apartments 1 and 5 throughout the complex had more friends upstairs than dwellers in the other first-floor apartments did.

FIGURE 10.1 The floor plan of a Westgate West building. ■ All the buildings in the housing complex had the same floor plan. (Adapted from Festinger, Schachter, & Back, 1950)

Even in a choice as important as a marriage partner, propinquity plays a major role. Researchers have found that most people marry someone who sits nearby in the same classroom, lives in the same neighborhood, or works in the same office or factory (Bossard, 1932; Burr, 1973; Clarke, 1952; Katz & Hill, 1958). You see the point: Had you just sat in the first row instead of the last, lived a few blocks over, or taken that other job at IBM, your whole life might have been different. Of course, if you are not happy with the relationships you have, the propinquity effect suggests a useful solution: Place yourself in a new locale, even if it's just down the hall in your dormitory or apartment building.

The propinquity effect works because of familiarity, or the **mere exposure** we have to individuals who are close by. We see them a lot, and the more familiar people become, the more friendship blooms. Of course, if the person in question is an obnoxious jerk then, not surprisingly, the more exposure you have to him or her, the greater your dislike (Swap, 1977). But in the absence of such negative qualities, familiarity breeds not contempt but attraction and liking (Bornstein & D'Agostino, 1992; Bornstein, Leone, & Galley, 1987; Moreland & Zajonc, 1982; Zajonc, 1968).

mere exposure: the finding that the more exposure we have to a stimulus, the more apt we are to like it

A good example of the propinquity and mere exposure effects is your college classroom. All semester long, you see the same people. Does this increase your liking for them? Richard Moreland and Scott Beach (1992) tested this hypothesis by planting female research confederates in a large college classroom. The women did not interact with the professor or the other students; they just walked in and sat quietly in the first row, where everyone could see them. The confederates differed in how many classes they attended, from 15 meetings down to the control condition of none. At the end of the semester, the students in the class were shown slides of the women, whom they rated on several measures of liking and attractiveness. As you can see in Figure 10.2, mere exposure had a definite effect on liking. Even though they had never interacted, the students liked the women more the more often they had seen them in class. Familiarity is indeed powerful stuff—and it almost always increases attractiveness.

The Effects of Physical Attractiveness on Liking

Of course, propinquity is not the only determinant of who we will come to like. For example, Nathan Serlin says that the moment he saw Hilda Vogel's blue eyes, he fell in love. Exactly how important is physical appearance to our first impres-

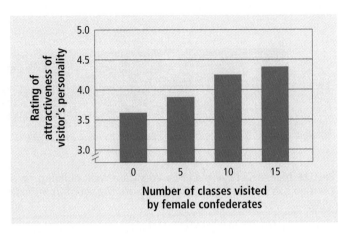

FIGURE 10.2 **The effects that mere exposure in the classroom has on attraction.** ■ The more often students saw a female confederate in their classroom, the more positively they rated her personality, even though they had never interacted with her. (Adapted from Moreland & Beach, 1992)

It is only the shallow people who do not judge by appearances.
–Oscar Wilde, 1891

sions of people? Do we fall for what is, after all, a pretty superficial characteristic? Or are we more likely to respond to "the beauty within"?In field experiments investigating people's actual behavior (rather than what they say they will do), people overwhelmingly go for physical attractiveness. For example, in a classic study Elaine Hatfield (Walster) and her colleagues (1966) randomly matched 752 incoming students at the University of Minnesota for a blind date at a computer dance during freshman orientation week. While the students had previously taken a battery of personality and aptitude tests, the researchers paired them up totally at random. On the night of the dance, the couples spent a few hours together dancing and chatting. They then evaluated their date and indicated the strength of their desire to date that person again. Of the many possible characteristics that could have determined whether they liked each other—such as their partner's intelligence, independence, sensitivity, or sincerity—the overriding determinant was physical attractiveness.

What's more, there was no great difference between men and women on this score. This is an interesting point, for while several studies have found that men and women pay equal attention to the physical attractiveness of others (Andersen & Bem, 1981; Crouse & Mehrabian, 1977; Stretch & Figley, 1980; Lynn & Shurgot, 1984; Woll, 1986), other studies have reported that men value attractiveness more than women do (Buss, 1989; Buss & Barnes, 1986; Howard, Blumstein, & Schwartz, 1987). In a recent meta-analysis of many studies, Alan Feingold (1990) reports that while both sexes value attractiveness, men do value it somewhat more than women do. In particular, Feingold (1990) found that this gender difference was much larger when men's and women's attitudes were being measured than when their actual behavior was being measured. Thus, it may be the case that men are more likely than women to say that physical attractiveness is important to them in a potential friend, date, or mate, but when it comes to actual behavior, the sexes are more similar in their response to the physical attractiveness of others.

The powerful role that physical appearance plays in attraction is not limited to heterosexual relationships. Paul Sergios and James Cody (1985) conducted a replication of the "computer blind date" study described above, with gay men as the research participants. The gay men responded just as the heterosexual men and women had in the earlier study: The physical attractiveness of their dates was the strongest predictor of their liking for them.

Cultural Standards of Beauty.   Is physical attractiveness totally in "the eye of the beholder," or do we all share some of the same notions of what is beautiful and handsome? From early childhood on, the media tell us what is beautiful and they tell us that this specific definition of beauty is associated with goodness. For example, illustrators of most traditional children's books, as well as the people who draw the characters in Disney movies, have taught us that gentle and charming heroines like Snow White, Cinderella, Belle (in *Beauty and the Beast*), and Sleeping Beauty—as well as the princes who woo and win them—all look alike. They all have regular features; small, pert noses; big eyes; shapely lips; blemish-free complexions; and slim, athletic bodies—pretty much like Barbie and Ken dolls.

Bombarded as we are with media depictions of attractiveness, it is probably not surprising to learn that we share a set of criteria for defining beauty. Look at the photographs on this page of models and actors who are considered very attractive in this culture. Can you label the facial characteristics that have earned them this label? Michael Cunningham designed a creative study to determine these standards of beauty. He asked college men to rate the attractiveness of 50 photographs of women, taken from a college yearbook and from an international beauty pageant program. The researchers then carefully measured the relative size of the facial features in each photograph. He found that high attractiveness ratings were associated with faces with large eyes, a small nose, a small chin, prominent cheekbones and narrow cheeks, high eyebrows, large pupils, and a big smile (Cunningham, 1986). Next, Michael Cunningham, Anita Barbee, and Carolyn Pike examined women's ratings of male beauty in the same manner. They found that higher attractiveness ratings were associated with men's faces with large eyes, prominent cheekbones, a large chin, and a big smile (Cunningham, Barbee, & Pike, 1995).

■ Research has found that we share some standards of beauty. In females, large eyes, prominent cheekbones and narrow cheeks, high eyebrows, and a small chin were associated with beauty; in males, large eyes, prominent cheekbones, and a large chin were rated as most beautiful. Today's popular models and film stars, such as Naomi Campbell and Brad Pitt, fit these criteria.

■ The desire to have a body that meets the current cultural standards of beauty has kept American plastic surgeons busy. Although most plastic surgery is performed on women, men often resort to it as well. The photos depict a man's chest before and after a silicon implant.

> Beauty is a greater recommendation than any letter of introduction.
>
> –Aristotle,
> fourth century B.C.

There is some overlap in the men's and women's ratings. Both sexes admire large eyes in the opposite sex, and these are considered a "babyface" feature, for newborn mammals have very large eyes for the size of their faces. Babyface features are thought to be attractive because they elicit feelings of warmth and nurturance in perceivers—for example, our response to babies, kittens, and puppies (e.g., McArthur & Berry, 1987; Zebrowitz & Montepare, 1992). Both sexes also admire prominent cheekbones in the opposite sex, an adult feature that is found only in the faces of those who are sexually mature. Note that the female face that is considered beautiful has more babyface features (small nose, small chin) than the handsome male face, suggesting that beauty in the female is associated more with childlike qualities than male beauty is.

Given these shared standards for beauty, is it any wonder that cosmetic surgery aimed at shortening or straightening noses, correcting thin lips, or changing the size of breasts is flourishing in this country? And such surgery is apparently effective. Michael Kalick (1977) asked students to rate photographs of several women either before or after cosmetic surgery; the "after" photos were rated as not only more beautiful but also more warm, sensitive, and sexually responsive.

Assumptions We Make About Attractive People.   One of the striking things about the physical attraction phenomenon is that most people assume that physical attractivenesss is highly correlated with other desirable traits. The results of many studies indicate that beauty constitutes a powerful *stereotype*—that is, we assume that an array of desirable traits go along with being beautiful. For example, men and women believe attractive people are more successful, more intelligent, better adjusted, more socially skilled, more interesting, more poised, more exciting, more independent, and more sexual than their less attractive counterparts (Brigham, 1980; Calvert, 1988; Dion et al., 1972; Hassebrauck, 1988; Hatfield & Sprecher, 1986; Moore, Graziano, and Millar, 1987). Karen Dion, Ellen Berscheid, and Elaine Walster (1972) have called this the "what is beautiful is good" stereotype (see Table 10.1).

Luckily for those of us who do not look like supermodels, the stereotype is relatively narrow, affecting people's judgments about an individual only in specific areas. Alice Eagly and her colleagues (1991) examined more than 70 studies and found that physical attractiveness has the largest effect on both men's and women's attributions when they are making judgments about social competence: The beautiful are thought to be more sociable, extraverted, and popular than the less attractive. In comparison, the "what is beautiful is good" stereotype is less powerful when people are judging intelligence, self-esteem, dominance, and

Table 10.1

The "what is beautiful is good" stereotype.

Male and female subjects judged that physically attractive people (males and females) were more likely than physically unattractive people to have the following characteristics:

Sexually warm and responsive	Sensitive
Kind	Interesting
Strong	Poised
Modest	Sociable
Outgoing	Exciting dates
Nurturant	Better character

These same subjects also believed that the future for physically attractive people would differ in the following ways from the future of physically unattractive individuals:

More prestige	Be more competent in marriage
Have a happier marriage	Have more fulfilling lives
Have more social and professional success	

(Adapted from Dion, Bersheid, & Walster, 1972)

career success. Finally, the stereotype does not operate in two areas: The beautiful are not thought to have any more integrity or empathy than the less attractive.

Interestingly, the stereotype that the beautiful are particularly gifted in the area of social competence has some research support; highly attractive people do develop good social interaction skills and report having more satisfying interactions with others than the less attractive do (Feingold, 1992; Reis, Nezlek, & Wheeler, 1980; Reis et al., 1982). Undoubtedly, this "kernel of truth" in the stereotype occurs because the beautiful, from a young age, receive a great deal of social attention that in turn helps them develop good social skills. You probably recognize our old friend, the *self-fulfilling prophecy* at work here, a concept we discussed earlier, in Chapter 3—the way we treat people affects how they behave and, ultimately, how they perceive themselves. Can a "regular" person be made to act like a "beautiful" one through the self-fulfilling prophecy? Mark Snyder, Elizabeth Decker Tanke, and Ellen Berscheid (1977) decided to find out. They gave college men a packet of information about another research participant, including her photograph. The photograph was rigged; it was either of an attractive woman or of an unattractive woman. The men were told that they would have a telephone conversation with this woman (in this experimental condition, only verbal communication—no gestures or facial expressions—were used). The experimental purpose of the photograph was to invoke the men's stereotype that "what is beautiful is good"—that the woman would be more warm, likable, poised, and fun to talk to if she was physically attractive than if she was unattractive. In fact, the photograph the men were given was not a photo of the woman with whom they spoke. Did the men's beliefs create reality?

Yes: The men who thought they were talking to an attractive woman responded to her in a warmer, more sociable manner than the men who thought

Oh, what a vileness human beauty is, corroding, corrupting everything it touches.
—Orestes, 408 B.C.

■ Research shows that our liking for a person can influence how physically attractive we think he or she is.

Drawing by Hamilton; © 1989 The New Yorker Magazine, Inc.

"When I fell in love with you, suddenly your eyes didn't seem close together. Now they seem close together again."

they were talking to an unattractive woman did. Not only that, but the men's behavior influenced how the women themselves responded. When independent observers listened to a tape recording of only the woman's half of the conversation (without looking at the photograph), they rated the women whose male partners thought they were physically attractive as more attractive, confident, animated, and warm than the women whose male partners thought they were unattractive. In short, because the male partner thought he was talking to an attractive woman, he spoke to her in a way that brought out her best and most sparkling qualities.

This study was later replicated with the roles switched: Susan Andersen and Sandra Bem (1981) showed women participants a photograph of an attractive or an unattractive man; the women then had a phone conversation with him. The men on the other end of the line were unaware of the women's belief about them. Just as in the Snyder, Tanke, and Berscheid (1977) study, the women acted on their "prophecy" and the unknowing men responded accordingly.

If you were not born looking like Naomi Campbell or Brad Pitt, take heart. While physical attractiveness does have a potent effect on initial attraction, how much we like someone also influences how physically attractive we think she or he is. In a study by Richard Nisbett and Timothy Wilson (1977), students watched a videotaped interview of a college instructor who conversed in a cold, critical, and aloof style in one version and in a warm, approachable, and caring style in the other version. Not surprisingly, students who saw the "warm" version liked the professor more than students who saw the "cold" version. But would the two groups of students differ in how physically attractive they thought the instructor was? As seen in Figure 10.3, those who saw the instructor being "cold" thought he was considerably less physically attractive than those who saw him being "warm." The researchers ruled out the possibility that the professor might have been less attractive in the cold version (because of frowns and grimaces), by showing a separate group of participants the tapes with the sound turned off. These participants liked him the same amount in both versions and, most importantly, did not find him any less physically attractive in the cold version than in the warm one. Thus, while there are objective qualities of a person that make him

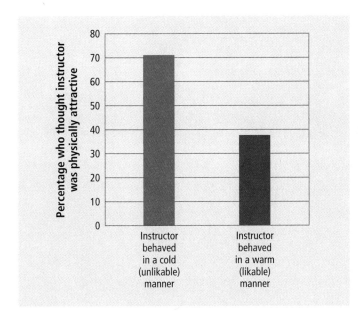

FIGURE 10.3   In the eye of the beholder. ■ People who saw a college instructor acting in a likable manner thought he was considerably more physically attractive than people who saw the same instructor acting in an unlikable manner did. This occurred not because the instructor was objectively more attractive when he was likable but because people's judgments of attractiveness are colored by how much they like someone. (Adapted from Nisbett & Wilson, 1977)

or her physically attractive to others, it is also true that beauty is in the eye of the beholder. The more we like someone, the more pleasing we will find his or her appearance.

Similarity: Birds of a Feather Flock Together

So far, we have seen that the more contact we have with people, the more apt we are to like them (propinquity and familiarity), and that physical attractiveness is a significant determinant of liking. The more we get to know individuals, however, the more other factors come into play. We learn much more about them, such as how kind, honest, and creative they are, their political preferences, and their favorite movies. To what extent do these qualities of a person influence how much we like him or her? One key is not what these exact qualities of the person are but how similar they are to our own qualities.

Consider Chia-Ann, an attorney who attends the office holiday party and finds herself chatting with Rebecca, a fellow attorney whom she barely knows. It turns out that they are in close agreement on several important issues: the death penalty, the fall television lineup, and the Red Sox's chance for the pennant. On returning home, Chia-Ann feels that even though she talked with Rebecca for only 15 minutes, she has made a new friend. What Chia-Ann has experienced is the strong pull of *similarity*—the sense that aspects of oneself are similar to aspects of the other person.

One way we perceive similarity is through shared attitudes or values, as Chia-Ann did with Rebecca. Literally dozens of tightly controlled experiments have shown that if all you know about a person are his or her opinions on several issues, the more similar those opinions are to yours, the more you will like the person. For example, in an experiment by Donn Byrne and Don Nelson (1965), research participants learned that another student agreed with their attitudes to varying degrees. When asked how much they liked this person (whom they had never met), participants indicated that the degree of liking was closely related to

■ Similarity is one of the major determinants of attraction.

the perceived similarity between their attitudes and those of the other student. As you can see in Figure 10.4, liking increased linearly with the percentage of attitudes shared.

Theodore Newcomb (1961) conducted a classic long-term study that examined the correlation between similarity and attraction. He randomly assigned male college students at the University of Michigan to be roommates in a particular dormitory at the start of the school year. Would similarity predict friendship formation? The answer was yes: Men became friends with those who were demographically similar (e.g., shared a rural background), as well as with those who were similar in attitudes and values (e.g., were also engineering majors or also held liberal political views).

FIGURE 10.4   Similarity and attraction. ■ The data in this figure summarize the results of eight studies conducted by Donn Byrne and his colleagues, who found that a strong, linear relationship exists between attraction and similarity in attitudes. The more the proportion of similar attitudes increased between research participants, the more those participants liked each other. (Adapted from Byrne & Nelson, 1965)

Why is similarity so important in attraction? There are at least two possibilities. First, people who are similar provide us with important social validation for our characteristics and beliefs—that is, they provide us with the feeling that we are right (Byrne & Clore, 1970). It simply feels good and reassuring to be validated; thus, we like those who agree with us. Second, it is likely that we make certain negative inferences about the character of someone who disagrees with us on important issues. We suspect the individual's opinion is indicative of the kind of person we have found in the past to be unpleasant, immoral, weak, or thoughtless. In short, disagreement on important attitudes leads to repulsion (Rosenbaum, 1986). Thus, the desire to be validated and the conclusions we draw about character both play a role in boosting the attractiveness of a like-minded person and diminishing the attractiveness of someone who is dissimilar (Byrne, Clore, & Smeaton, 1986; Condon & Crano, 1988; Griffitt & Veitch, 1974).

Complementarity: Don't Opposites Attract?

As we have seen, the venerable adage seems to be true: Birds of a feather do flock together. But where does this leave the equally venerable adage "Opposites attract"? There has been considerable speculation about the kinds of situations and characteristics where this potential rule of attraction might apply. For example, Winch (1958) suggests that a dependent person might be attracted to someone who loves to nurture others, a shy person might be attracted to someone who is outgoing and social, and a nonstop talker might be attracted to someone who is relatively quiet and loves to listen. The idea that opposites attract is the complementarity hypothesis, which states that we are attracted to people whose characteristics are not similar but opposite to ours. Research in this area has focused primarily on complementarity in personality characteristics, as when a shy person is paired with an extravert.

The research evidence for complementarity is mixed at best and is based on only a few studies. Whereas one researcher found that opposites in personality do indeed attract (Wagner, 1975), other researchers have found that similarity, not complementarity, describes the basis for relationship development (Felmlee,

■ Despite folklore about how "opposites attract," people are almost always more attracted to those who are similar to them.

1995; Cate & Lloyd, 1992; Levinger, 1964; Meyer & Pepper, 1977). Some researchers have argued that similarity is important early in a relationship, while complementarity becomes important later on, as the relationship lengthens (Campbell, 1980; Kerckhoff & Davis, 1962); however, other researchers have not found support for this role of complementarity over time (Levinger, Senn, & Jorgensen, 1970). In short, it's a muddle. While the idea of personality and need complementarity is appealing, the vast amount of research evidence strongly supports similarity over complementarity as the more significant predictor of attraction. For example, Tom Boyden and his colleagues (1984) found strong support for similarity in personality in gay men's relationships. Gay men who scored high on a test of stereotypical male traits desired a partner who was most of all logical—a stereotypical masculine trait. Gay men who scored high on a test of stereotypical female traits desired a partner who was most of all expressive—a stereotypical feminine trait.

Reciprocal Liking

We all like to be liked. This is a powerful feeling and one of the prime determinants of interpersonal attraction; indeed, it is so powerful that it can even make up for the absence of similarity. For example, in one experiment, when a young woman expressed interest in male subjects simply by maintaining eye contact, leaning toward them, and listening attentively, the men expressed great liking for her despite the fact that they knew she disagreed with them on important issues (Gold, Ryckman, & Mosley, 1984). Whether the clues are nonverbal or verbal, perhaps the most crucial determinant of whether we will like person A is the extent to which we believe person A likes us (Berscheid & Walster, 1978; Condon & Crano, 1988; Hays, 1984; Kenny & La Voie, 1982; Kenny & Nasby, 1980; Secord & Backman, 1964).

Of course, what we think influences what we do, and what we do influences how others respond to us. This is yet another example of the self-fulfilling prophecy. To illustrate this process, Rebecca Curtis and Kim Miller (1986) conducted the following experiment. College students took part in the study in pairs; they had not known each other prior to meeting at the study. One member of each pair was randomly chosen to receive special information. Curtis and Miller led some college students to believe that the other student liked them, and others to believe that the other student disliked them. The pairs of students were then allowed to meet and talk to each other again. Just as predicted, those individuals who thought they were liked behaved in more likable ways with their partner; they disclosed more about themselves, disagreed less about the topic under discussion, and generally behaved in a warmer, more pleasant manner toward the other student than those individuals who thought they were disliked. Moreover, those who believed they were liked came to be liked by the other student to a far greater extent than those who believed they were disliked. In short, the partner tended to mirror the behaviors of the person with whom he or she was paired (see Figure 10.5). These results suggest that if you behave as if you believe you are lovable and everyone will like you, you will increase the probability that the people around you will like you. "Smile, and the world smiles with you" has some truth to it.

The Role of Self-Esteem.   Most of the time, being liked by a person is a powerful determinant of our liking for them. But William Swann, Jr., has found that the

> Life is to be fortified by many friendships. To love, and to be loved, is the greatest happiness of existence.
> —Sydney Smith, 1855

FIGURE 10.5 Liking and being liked. ■ Research participants were given false feedback that their research partner either did or did not like them. They liked their partner more if they had been told before-hand that their partner liked them (see left-hand side of figure), and their partners responded in kind (see right-hand side of figure). Beliefs did indeed create reality. (Adapted from Curtis & Miller, 1986)

amount of self-esteem a person has mediates this process (Swann, 1992; Swann, Stein-Seroussi, & McNulty, 1992). People with a positive or moderate self-concept respond to other's liking with reciprocal liking, as we've discussed above. But people with a negative self-concept respond quite differently—in an experimental setting, such people indicate that they'd prefer to meet and talk to a person they know has criticized them earlier than meet and talk to a person they know has praised them earlier (Swann et al., 1992). If you think of yourself as not being worth very much or even as unlikable, other people's friendly behavior toward you will seem unwarranted and you may not respond.

Does self-esteem affect reciprocal liking in important, close relationships such as marriage? William Swann, Jr., and his colleagues (1992) have startling evidence that it does. They asked married couples to rate themselves and their partners on a series of traits and qualities. They also asked the spouses to rate several questions about how committed they were to their marriages. The researchers then compared the people's level of self-esteem, their commitment to their spouses, and their partner's appraisal of them. As you can see in Figure 10.6, there was little difference between participants when the spouse's appraisal of them was unfavorable or moderate. However, when the spouse's view of them was favorable, only those people whose self-concept was also positive or moderately so responded with reciprocal liking—they indicated a high level of commitment to the spouse. In comparison, people with a negative self-concept whose partner viewed them favorably were significantly less likely to respond in kind—they indicated the lowest level of commitment to their spouse. These data suggest a twist on the old adage that if you don't love yourself, no one else will: In fact, if you don't love yourself, someone else might, but you'll have trouble believing it and loving the person back.

Changes in Liking: The Gain-Loss Effect.   Does reciprocal liking simply mean that the more a person likes us, the more we like him or her? What if the person initially doesn't like us but then, over time, changes his or her mind and comes to like us more and more? Does one of these scenarios produce more attraction and liking than the other? To find out, Elliot Aronson and Darwyn Linder (1965) had college women research participants meet in pairs on several occa-

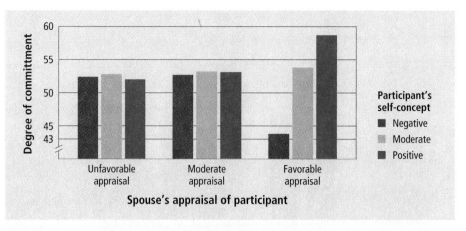

FIGURE 10.6   The effects of self-concept and spouse's appraisal on marital commitment. ■ Married couples rated themselves, their spouses, and their commitment to their marriage. As shown in the left and middle panels, the participants' self-concept had no effect on their commitment to their marriages when their spouse's appraisal of them was unfavorable or moderate. However, when their spouse's appraisal was unfavorable (see right panel), those with a negative self-concept indicated a significantly lower level of commitment than those with more positive self-concepts.

sions to discuss a variety of topics. After each meeting, the participants were allowed to eavesdrop on a conversation between the experimenter and the other student and overheard the other student evaluating them on a number of dimensions. In actuality, however, the student/evaluator was a confederate of the experimenters, instructed to evaluate each participant in one of four ways: (a) always positive, (b) always negative, (c) "gain" (beginning negative but gradually becoming positive), and (d) "loss" (beginning positive but gradually becoming negative). In which condition was the student/evaluator liked the most?

Surprisingly, participants in the "gain" condition liked the other student more than participants who had always received positive evaluations. Realizing that someone has had a change of heart and now sees us positively is very attractive; we believe the person is sincere in his or her current, positive view of us (Mettee et al., 1973). For the gain effect to occur, it is important that the change in attitude occur gradually (Mettee & Aronson, 1974). If someone goes from hating us one moment to liking us the next, our suspicions are likely to be aroused. Is this person after something? Is this an attempt at ingratiation (Jones, 1964)? On the other hand, participants in the "loss" condition disliked the other student more than participants who had always received negative feedback. While it is upsetting to be criticized, we can write it off when it's constant. But it is particularly galling to be criticized by someone who once praised us, and this event is not so easy to ignore. This pattern of results is called the **gain-loss effect:** We like people most if we feel we have won them over, and we dislike people the most if we feel we have lost their favor.

gain-loss effect: the finding that we like people the most if we feel we have gained in their estimation of us (i.e., if they initially disliked us but now like us) and that we dislike people the most if we feel we have lost their favor (i.e., if they initially liked us but now dislike us)

Recollections of Initial Attraction

We've now discussed several predictors of initial attraction and liking: propinquity, physical attractiveness, similarity, complementarity, and reciprocal liking. At the beginning of the chapter, we asked you to think about why you were first attracted to your friends and romantic partners. Arthur Aron, Donald Dutton, Elaine Aron, and Adrienne Iverson (1989) conducted a similar study, asking both college students and older adults to give accounts of how they fell into love or into friendship with specific people in their lives. The researchers then coded these accounts for the presence of the classic social psychological variables we have discussed. Do people spontaneously report such factors as the cause for their initial feelings of attraction?

Yes, they do. First, for the falling-in-love accounts, Aron and his colleagues found that reciprocal liking and attractiveness (involving both physical and personality qualities) were mentioned spontaneously with very high frequency. The power of these two variables together led the researchers to conclude, "Reading the actual accounts leads to the impression that people are just waiting for an attractive person to do something they can interpret as liking them" (1989, p. 251). Mentioned with moderate frequency was a set of variables that has received little attention in the literature: The researchers call these the "special falling-in-love processes," which include being ready for or looking for a romantic relationship, being unhappy in a current relationship, and finding oneself in an unusual situation that promotes romantic love. Finally, similarity and propinquity were mentioned with low to moderate frequency. The researchers suggest that these two variables may be underreported, because people do not remember or notice experiencing them or because they are seen as too mundane to explain something so exciting as falling in love. Aron and his colleagues also note that similarity and propinquity may play an important role before one falls in love, by narrowing the field to only those people who are "eligible."

Second, for the falling-into-friendship accounts, the researchers again found that reciprocal liking and attractiveness were the most frequently mentioned reasons, though they were mentioned less often than in the falling-in-love accounts. For friendship attraction, similarity and propinquity were mentioned very frequently, and more so than in the falling-in-love accounts. Thus, these attraction variables not only predict people's behavior in laboratory experiments but also are present in people's spontaneous recollections of their real-life experiences with attraction.

> Hatred which is completely vanquished by love passes into love, and love is thereupon greater than if hatred had not preceded it. For he who begins to love a thing which he was wont to hate or regard with pain, from the very fact of loving, feels pleasure.
>
> –Spinoza, 1663

Drawing by Hamilton; © June 10, 1991, The New Yorker Magazine, Inc.

■ The causes of initial attraction are not always the same as the causes of love and long-term intimacy.

"It's as though everything nice about you had been just some kind of introductory offer."

Steve Duck (1994) also wondered if the classic attraction variables operated when people were getting acquainted in real-life settings. He randomly paired college men and women and sent them off on a "get-acquainted date." When they returned, they filled out several questionnaires for him; specifically, they rated their date on physical attractiveness, on how similar he or she was to themselves, and on the quality of their conversation—a new variable, one that Duck hypothesized would be a powerful predictor of attraction. Duck found that for both men and women, the strongest predictor of romantic (dating) attraction was the perceived physical attractiveness of the other person. For both men and women, the second strongest predictor of romantic attraction was similarity. Quality of communication did not predict romantic attraction for men or women; it appears that after one date, what he or she looks like and how similar he or she is to you have far more of an effect than anything he or she says! In comparison, the pattern for opposite-sex friendship attraction was very different for men versus women. For men, perceived similarity was the strongest predictor of friendship attraction, followed by physical attractiveness. For women, the strongest predictor of friendship attraction was the quality of communication, followed by similarity. When experiencing friendship attraction, women appear to value conversation and respond positively to quality conversation to a greater extent than men do.

Theories of Interpersonal Attraction: Social Exchange and Equity

The determinants of attraction we have discussed so far concern aspects of the situation (propinquity, repeated exposure), the individual's attributes (physical attractiveness, similarity, complementarity, self-esteem), and the individual's behavior (conveying liking). We turn now to theories of interpersonal attraction that link these different phenomena together.

Social Exchange Theory. Many of the variables we have discussed can be thought of as examples of social rewards. It is pleasing to have our attitudes validated; thus, the more similar a person's attitudes are to ours, the more rewarded we feel. Likewise, it is rewarding to be around someone who likes us and is physically attractive. One way of summarizing much of our discussion so far is to say that the more social rewards a person provides us with (and the fewer costs), the more we will like him or her.

This point of view was expressed more than 300 years ago by the French essayist and social gadfly François La Rochefoucauld, who wryly defined friendship as "a scheme for the mutual exchange of personal advantages and favors." While La Rochefoucauld was perhaps overly cynical in this definition, there is certainly an element of truth in it. If a relationship costs (e.g., in terms of emotional turmoil) far more than it gives (e.g., in terms of validation or praise), chances are that it will not last very long.

This simple notion that relationships operate on an economic model of costs and benefits, much like the marketplace, has been expanded by psychologists and sociologists into complex theories of social exchange (Blau, 1964; Homans, 1961; Kelly & Thibaut, 1978; Thibaut & Kelley, 1959). **Social exchange theory** states that how people feel (positively or negatively) about their relationships will depend on their perception of the rewards they receive from the relationship and their perception of the costs they incur, as well as their perception of what kind of relationship they deserve and the probability that they could have a better rela-

> Love is often nothing but a favorable exchange between two people who get the most of what they can expect, considering their value on the personality market.
> –Erich Fromm, 1955

social exchange theory: the theory holding that how people feel about a relationship depends on their perceptions of the rewards and costs of the relationship, the kind of relationship they deserve, and their chances for having a better relationship with someone else tionship with someone else. In other words, we buy the best relationship we can get, one that gives us the most value for our emotional dollar. The basic concepts of social exchange theory are reward, cost, outcome, and comparison level (Secord & Backman, 1964).

Rewards are the positive, gratifying aspects of the relationship that make it worthwhile and reinforcing. They include the kinds of personal characteristics and behaviors of our relationship partner that we have already discussed and our ability to acquire external resources by virtue of knowing this person (e.g., gaining access to money, status, activities, or other interesting people; Lott & Lott, 1974). Costs are, obviously, the other side of the coin, and all friendships and romantic relationships have some costs attached to them (e.g., putting up with those annoying habits and characteristics of the other person). The outcome of the relationship is a direct comparison of its rewards and costs; you can think of it as a mathematical formula where outcome equals rewards minus costs. (If you come up with a negative number, your relationship is not in good shape.)

However, as Harold Kelley and John Thibaut (1978; Thibaut & Kelley, 1959) state, how satisfied you are with your relationship depends on another variable: your **comparison level,** or what you expect the outcome of your relationship to be in terms of costs and rewards. Over time, you have amassed a long history of relationships with other people, and this history has led you to have certain expectations as to what your current and future relationships should be like. Some people have a high comparison level, expecting to receive lots of rewards and few costs in their relationships. If a given relationship doesn't match this expected comparison level, they will be unhappy and unsatisfied. In contrast, people who have a low comparison level would be happy in the same relationship, because they expect relationships to be difficult and costly.

Finally, your satisfaction with a relationship also depends on your perception of the likelihood that you could replace it with a better one—or your **comparison level for alternatives.** There are a lot of people out there—could a relationship with a different person give you a better outcome, or greater rewards for fewer costs, than your current one? People who have a high comparison level for alternatives, either because they believe the world is full of fabulous people dying to meet them or because they know of a fabulous person dying to meet them, are more likely to get into circulation and make a new friend or find a new lover. People with a low comparison level for alternatives will be more likely to stay in a costly relationship, because to them, what they have is not great but is better than their expectation of what they could find elsewhere (Simpson, 1987).

Social exchange theory has received a great deal of empirical support; friends (and, as we shall see later, romantic couples) do pay attention to the costs and rewards in their relationships, and these affect how positively people feel about the status of the relationship (Jacobson, Waldron, & Moore, 1980; Rusbult, 1983; Wills, Weiss, & Patterson, 1974). However, we saw one exception to social exchange theory in Chapter 6, in the study finding that people like others for whom they have suffered. Specifically, college students who underwent an unpleasant initiation in order to become members of a group were more enamored of that group than those who became members without undergoing all that unpleasantness (Aronson & Mills, 1959). But where is the reward? Why would somebody who is associated with pain or unpleasantness be viewed as more attractive than someone who isn't? As we saw in Chapter 6, dissonance can be produced when we perform unpleasant behavior for low rewards, and we can reduce this dissonance by increasing our liking for the task (or person). Thus, in

> Don't threaten me with love, baby. Let's go walking in the rain.
> –Billie Holliday

comparison level: people's expectations about the level of rewards and punishments they are likely to receive in a particular relationship

comparison level for alternatives: people's expectations about the level of rewards and punishments they would receive in an alternative relationship the right situation, a person (or relationship) with high "costs" may be reinterpreted as giving high "rewards"—all to reduce the dissonance one feels for getting into this mess in the first place.

Equity Theory.   Some researchers have criticized social exchange theory for ignoring an essential variable in relationships: the notion of fairness, or *equity*. Those propounding **equity theory**, such as Elaine Walster, Ellen Berscheid, and George Homans, argue that people are not just out to get the most rewards for the least cost; they are also concerned about equity in their relationships, wherein the rewards and costs they experience and the contributions they make to the relationship are roughly equal to the rewards, costs, and contributions of the other person (Homans, 1961; Walster, Walster, & Berscheid, 1978). These theorists describe equitable relationships as the most happy and stable type. In comparison, inequitable relationships result in one person feeling overbenefited (getting a lot of rewards, incurring few costs, having to devote little time or energy to the relationship) or underbenefited (getting few rewards, incurring a lot of costs, having to devote a lot of time and energy to the relationship).

According to equity theory, both underbenefited and overbenefited partners should feel uneasy about this state of affairs, and both should be motivated to restore equity to the relationship. This makes sense for the underbenefited person (who wants to continue feeling miserable?), but why should the overbenefited individual want to give up what social exchange theory indicates is a cushy deal—lots of rewards for little cost and little work? Elaine Hatfield (Walster) and her colleagues argue that equity is a powerful social norm—people will eventually feel uncomfortable or even guilty if they get more than they deserve in a relationship. However, let's face facts—being overbenefited just doesn't seem as bad as being underbenefited, and research has borne out that inequity is perceived as more of a problem by the underbenefited individual (Hatfield, Greenberger, Traupmann, & Lambert, 1982; Traupmann, Petersen, Utne, & Hatfield, 1981).

When stripped to the bare bones, the rules of social exchange and equity may seem to be sterile and even crass ways to describe friendly and intimate relationships. Nevertheless, they operate—at least at some level of consciousness—in all relationships. But because they do seem crass, most people strive to avoid the appearance of a rigid tit-for-tat social exchange in their relationships. As we will see later, this avoidance is more likely to occur in long-term relationships, where people are less concerned with a daily tally of rewards and costs.

equity theory: the theory holding that people are happiest with relationships in which the rewards and costs a person experiences and the contributions he or she makes to the relationship are roughly equal to the rewards, costs, and contributions of the other person

"O.K., who *can* put a price on love? Jim?"

Drawing by Ziegler; © 1991 The New Yorker Magazine, Inc.

Close Relationships

After getting to this point in the chapter, you should be in a pretty good position to make a favorable first impression the next time you meet someone. Suppose you want Claudia to like you. You should hang around her so that you become familiar, act in ways that are rewarding to her, and emphasize your similarity to her. You should let her know you like her, though if you want to be especially clever, you should at first be a little critical, and then compliment her profusely. We make no guarantee that you and Claudia will become best friends, but all else being equal, these techniques work fairly well.

You may have noticed, however, that all of this advice concerns the first impressions we make on another person. A first impression can be extremely important; if we make a bad one, we may well not get a second chance to do better. On the other hand, we are frequently interested in more than just making a good first impression. We all want to develop relationships that go beyond the superficial, initial impressions we convey. Sometimes our goal is to become close friends or even lovers with another person, achieving lasting intimacy, love, and commitment. A valid question is whether the techniques we have discussed so far are as successful at developing close relationships as they are at winning new friends. Surely, you might ask, there is more to falling in love with someone and developing a lasting, intimate relationship with him or her (as did Hilda Vogel and Nathan Serlin, in our opening example) than such things as propinquity, similarity, and social rewards?

Until recently, social psychologists have had little to say in answer to this question; research on interpersonal attraction focused almost exclusively on first impressions. Why? Primarily because long-term, close relationships are much more difficult to study scientifically than first impressions. As we saw in Chapter 2, random assignment to different conditions is the hallmark of an experiment. When studying first impressions, a researcher can randomly assign you to a get-acquainted session with someone who is similar or dissimilar to you. But how could a researcher randomly assign you to the similar or dissimilar "lover" condition and make you have a relationship?

In addition, the feelings and intimacy associated with close relationships can be difficult to measure. As put so well by Beilby Porteus,

> Love is something so divine,
>
> Description would but make it less;
>
> 'Tis what I feel, but can't define,
>
> 'Tis what I know, but can't express.

Psychologists face a daunting task when trying to measure such inchoate feelings as love and passion.

Defining Love

Though the difficulties in studying close relationships are severe, they are not insurmountable. In the past decade, social psychologists have made significant strides in studying the nature of love, how it develops, and how it flourishes. Let's begin with perhaps the most difficult of these questions: Exactly what is love?

If you have ever been in love, think back to how you felt about your sweetheart when you first got to know him or her. You probably felt a combination of giddiness, longing, joy, and despair: "He noticed me tonight—I could barely catch my breath!" "When she kissed me, you could have knocked me over with a feather!" "I think he loves someone else—I could just curl up and die!" The ancient Greeks considered this strange, bewildering set of feelings to be a form of madness, causing all sorts of irrational and obsessional acts. Though times have changed, we are all familiar with the torment—and exhilaration—that comes with falling in love.

A number of psychologists have developed measures of love (Aron, Aron, & Smollan, 1990; Berscheid, 1988; Berscheid, Snyder, & Omoto, 1989; Henrick & Henrick, 1986; Kelley, 1983; Lee, 1977, 1988; Rubin, 1970, 1973; Shaver, Schwartz, Kirson, & O'Connor, 1987). Initial attempts tried to distinguish between liking and loving, showing that, as you might expect, love is something different from "lots of liking," and it isn't just sexual desire either (Rubin, 1970). Later attempts dived deeper into the phenomenon by addressing what we all know intuitively is true: There seem to be different kinds of love. Let's examine three of these conceptualizations of love.

Compassionate Versus Passionate Love. Consider the love between Herb and Mary, two septuagenarians who are celebrating their fiftieth wedding anniversary. They have deep feelings of devotion and intimacy, but their love is cooler than that of Jane and Frank, also in their seventies, who have just met and fallen in love. Herb and Mary would probably not say they are "giddy" about each other or that their feelings for each other are "like being on a roller coaster." But surely they can be every bit as much in love as Jane and Frank; in fact, we might even think they are more so. And what about the kind of nonsexual affection and warmth that close friends feel toward each other? We might want to use the word *love* to describe these feelings as well, though it seems to be a different kind of love than our two couples feel for each other.

Social psychologists have recognized that a good definition of love must encompass its myriad forms, including passionate, giddy feelings as well as deep, long-term devotion. One well-known distinction is between companionate love

> Try to reason about love and you will lose your reason.
>
> –French proverb

■ There are different forms of love, some "hotter" and more passionate than others.

and passionate love (Hatfield, 1988; Hatfield & Walster, 1978). **Companionate love** is defined as the feelings of intimacy and affection we feel toward someone that are not accompanied by passion or physiological arousal. People can experience companionate love in nonsexual relationships, such as close friendships, or in sexual relationships, where they experience great feelings of intimacy (companionate love) but not a great deal of the heat and passion they may once have felt.

Passionate love involves an intense longing for another person. When things are going well—the other person loves us too—we feel great fulfillment and ecstasy. When things are not going well—our love is unrequited—we feel great sadness and despair. This kind of love is characterized by the experience of physiological arousal, wherein we actually feel shortness of breath and a thumping heart in our loved one's presence. Elaine Hatfield and Susan Sprecher (1986) developed a questionnaire to measure passionate love (see Table 10.2). Passionate love, as measured by this scale, consists of strong, uncontrollable thoughts;

companionate love: the feelings of intimacy and affection we feel for another person when we care deeply for the person but do not necessarily experience passion or arousal in his or her presence

passionate love: the feelings of intense longing, accompanied by physiological arousal, we feel for another person; when our love is reciprocated, we feel great fulfillment and ecstasy, but when it is not, we feel sadness and despair

Table 10.2

The passionate love scale.

Please think of the person whom you love most passionately right now. If you are not in love right now, please think of the last person you loved passionately. If you have never been in love, think of the person whom you came closest to caring for in that way.

1. I would feel deep despair if _____ left me.
2. Sometimes I feel I can't control my thoughts; they are obsessively on _____ .
3. I feel happy when I am doing something to make _____ happy.
4. I would rather be with _____ than anyone else.
5. I'd get jealous if I thought _____ were falling in love with someone else.
6. I yearn to know all about _____ .
7. I want _____—physically, emotionally, mentally.
8. I have an endless appetite for affection from _____ .
9. For me, _____ is the perfect romantic partner.
10. I sense my body responding when _____ touches me.
11. _____ always seems to be on my mind.
12. I want _____ to know me—my thoughts, my fears, and my hopes.
13. I eagerly look for signs indicating _____ 's desire for me.
14. I possess a powerful attraction for _____ .
15. I get extremely depressed when things don't go right in my relationship with _____ .

Responses to each item are made along the following scale:

Not at all true	Moderately true	Definitely true
1 2 3	4 5 6	7 8 9

NOTE: These items are part of a questionnaire designed to measure passionate love. Note that the questions measure the extent to which people have strong, uncontrollable thoughts; intense feelings; and overt acts toward the target of their feelings. (Adapted from Hatfield & Sprecher, 1986) intense feelings; and overt acts toward the target of one's affection. Clearly, this kind of love is distinguishable from cooler, less passionate love, such as that between Herb and Mary.

triangular theory of love: the idea that different kinds of love consist of varying degrees of three components: intimacy, passion, and commitment

Triangular Theory of Love.   Other researchers are not satisfied with a simple dichotomy of two kinds of love. Robert Sternberg (1986, 1988; Sternberg & Beall, 1991), for example, presents a **triangular theory of love,** which depicts love as consisting of three basic ingredients: intimacy, passion, and commitment. Intimacy refers to feelings of being close to and bonded with a partner. Passion refers to the "hot" parts of a relationship—namely, the arousal you experience toward your partner, including sexual attraction. Commitment consists of two decisions—the short-term one that you love your partner, and the long-term one to maintain that love and stay with your partner. Sternberg (1988) developed a scale to measure the three components of love, including such questions as "I have a relationship of mutual understanding with _____" (intimacy), "I find myself thinking about _____ frequently during the day" (passion), and "I expect my love for _____ to last for the rest of my life" (commitment).

These three ingredients—intimacy, passion, and commitment—can be combined in varying degrees to form any of the different kinds of love (see Figure 10.7). Love can consist of one component alone or of any combination of these three parts. For example, a person may feel a great deal of passion or physical attraction for another (infatuation love) but not know the person well enough to experience intimacy and not be ready to make any kind of commitment. As the relationship develops, it might blossom into romantic love, characterized by passion and intimacy, and maybe even consummate love—the blending of all three components. Sternberg uses the term *companionate love* in the same way we depicted earlier, to describe love characterized by intimacy and commitment but not passion. Some of the heat may have gone out of Herb and Mary's relationship, for example, while their feelings of intimacy and commitment continued to grow.

FIGURE 10.7   The triangle of love. ■ According to the triangular theory of love, there are seven different forms of love, each made up of varying degrees of intimacy, passion, and commitment. (Adapted from Sternberg, 1988)

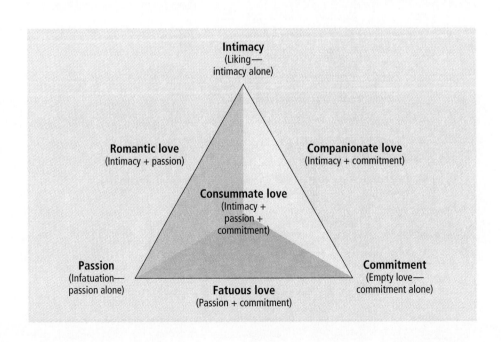

Intimacy
(Liking—
intimacy alone)

Romantic love
(Intimacy + passion)

Companionate love
(Intimacy + commitment)

Consummate love
(Intimacy +
passion +
commitment)

Passion
(Infatuation—
passion alone)

Commitment
(Empty love—
commitment alone)

Fatuous love
(Passion + commitment)

Love Styles. A third approach to defining love has focused on **love styles,** or the basic theories people have about love that guide their behavior in relationships (Hendrick & Hendrick, 1986,1992; Lee, 1973,1988). Clyde Hendrick and Susan Hendrick (1992) have identified six love styles. As you read each one, think about your own style and those of the people you know well. *Eros* is a passionate, physical love, where the partner's physical appearance is highly important. The Eros lover gets involved very quickly; "Eros is like being hit by a bolt of lightning" (1992; p. 65). *Ludus* is love played as a game, never taken too seriously. Very playful in their approach to love, ludic lovers don't mean to cause harm but they often do, with multiple partners at once. "Ludus likes all aspects of a rainstorm . . . but doesn't want to get wet" (p. 65). *Storge* is a slow-growing love, evolving out of affection and friendship. Similarity between partners is extremely important. Storgic lovers "would be likely to stay inside during the . . . thunder[storm] and go out when a . . . gentle rain began to fall" (p. 65). *Pragma* is pragmatic love—commonsensical, realistic, feet on the ground. Pragmic lovers know what they're looking for in a relationship and have "conditions" that must be met. In a rainstorm, "pragma will always have an umbrella" (p. 66). *Mania* is the highly emotional, roller-coaster ride of love. Manic lovers obsess about their partners, vascillate between elation and despair, and generally fit our culture's stereotype of "romantic love." Manic lovers "stand outside getting wet, self-destructively waiting for the . . . lightning" (p. 66). Finally, *Agape* is a totally selfless, giving, and altruistic love, and quite rare. Agapic lovers think not of themselves but of their partners and what they can do for them. Their love style is more spiritual than physical. The agapic lover "would give you his or her umbrella so that you won't get wet" (p. 65).

Research on the love styles is based on a questionnaire; examples of the items appear in Table 10.3. Clyde Hendrick and Susan Hendrick have found both similarities and differences between the sexes in their love styles. For Eros and Agape, men and women did not differ. However, men were more ludic, and women were more storgic and pragmatic (Hendrick & Hendrick, 1986; Dion & Dion, 1993b).

love styles: the basic theories people have about love that guide their behavior in relationships; six styles have been identified: Eros, Ludus, storge, pragma, mania, and Agape

> Love is or it ain't. Thin love ain't love at all.
> –Toni Morrison

Table 10.3

Sample items for the love attitudes scale.

Eros	My lover and I were attracted to each other immediately after we first met.
Ludus	I try to keep my lover a little uncertain about my commitment to him or her.
Storge	It is hard for me to say exactly when our friendship turned into love.
Pragma	I considered what my lover was going to become in life before I committed myself to him or her.
Mania	When things aren't right with my lover and me, my stomach gets upset.
Agape	I try to always help my lover through difficult times.

SOURCE: From Hendrick & Hendrick, 1992.
NOTE: These items are part of a questionnaire designed to measure one's love "style," or the approach one takes to romantic relationships.

The researchers have also found that real-life couples show considerable similarity in their love styles. In addition, couples whose romantic relationships lasted were more likely than those who broke up to be high on Eros—passionate—love and low on Ludus—game-playing—love (Hendrick, Hendrick & Adler, 1988).

The Role of Culture

Our discussion thus far has focused on how love is defined in American society. While love is certainly a human emotion experienced everywhere on the planet, culture does play a role in how people label their experiences and in what they expect (and tolerate) in close relationships. For example, the Japanese describe amae as an extremely positive emotional state in which one is a totally passive love object, indulged and taken care of by one's romantic partner, much like a mother-infant relationship. There is no equivalent word for amae in English or any other Western language; the closest in meaning is the word dependency, an emotional state which is considered by Western cultures to be unhealthy in adult relationships (Dion & Dion, 1993a; Doi, 1988).

Western and Eastern cultures vary in important ways in how the needs of the individual and the collective (or group) are defined. Western societies are individualistic, emphasizing that the individual is autonomous, self-sufficient, and defined by his or her personal qualities. Eastern cultures are collectivistic, emphasizing the individual's loyalty to the group and defining him or her through membership in the group (Hofstede, 1984; Hui & Triandis, 1986).

Karen Dion and Kenneth Dion (1988;1993a) have hypothesized that romantic love is an important, even crucial, basis for marriage in individualistic societies, while it has less value in collectivistic ones. In individualistic societies, romantic love is a heady, highly personal experience; one immerses oneself in the new partner and, if anything, virtually ignores friends and family for a while. The decision as to who to become involved with or marry is for the most part a personal one. In comparison, in collectivistic cultures the individual in love must take into account the wishes of family and other group members; in fact, marriages are often by arrangement, with the respective families matching up the

■ While all human beings experience love, culture plays a role in how it is labeled and experienced.

bride and groom (Levine, Sato, Hashimoto, & Verna, 1995). As Francis Hsu (1981) puts it, when in love, "an American asks, 'How does my heart feel?' A Chinese asks, 'What will other people say?'" (p. 50).

Karen Dion and Kenneth Dion (1993b) tested this hypothesis by giving the Love Attitudes Scale, which measures the love styles we discussed above, to a heterogeneous sample of Canadian college students. Their research participants fell into three groups by ethnocultural background: Asian (Chinese, Korean, Vietnamese, Indian, and Pakistani), Anglo-Celtic (English, Irish, and Scottish), and European (Scandinavian, Spanish, German, and Polish). The researchers found that the Asian respondents were significantly more likely to endorse the storgic love style than either of the two other groups. Thus, in comparison to their peers, the Asian students were more likely to identify with a companionable, friendship-based romantic love, a "style of love that would not disrupt a complex network of existing family relationships" (p. 465).

Additional cross-cultural research has supported this interpretation. For example, Carolyn Simmons, Alexander Vom Kolke, and Hideko Shimizu (1986) examined attitudes toward romantic love among single college students in West Germany, Japan, and the United States. They found that the West German sample had the most passionately romantic views of love, and the Japanese sample the least. The American sample's endorsement of romantic love fell between that of the other two cultures. Similarly, Robert Levine and his colleagues (1995) surveyed college students in 11 countries around the world, asking them, "If a man (woman) had all the qualities you desired, would you marry this person if you were not in love with him (her)?" These researchers found that marrying for love was most important to participants in Western and Westernized countries (e.g., the United States, Brazil, England, and Australia) and of least importance to participants in underdeveloped Eastern countries (i.e., India, Pakistan, and Thailand).

The results of these studies indicate that while "love makes the world go 'round," the concept of romantic love is to some extent culturally specific. Love can vary in definition and behavior in different societies. We all love, but we do not necessarily all love in the same way.

The Causes of Love

Now that scales have been developed to measure love, social psychologists have begun addressing the more important question of how love develops and how it is maintained. Are the causes of love similar to the causes of initial attraction? As you might imagine, some of the same principles apply, but additional variables come into play when one is developing and maintaining a close relationship. In our opening example, we saw that Nathan Serlin was initially attracted to Hilda Vogel by her blue eyes. It is doubtful, however, that beautiful eyes are enough to sustain a long-term relationship. We will review some of the factors we discussed in the beginning of the chapter as determinants of first impressions, to see how they play out in intimate relationships.

Social Exchange in Long-Term Relationships

We have seen that, in general, everyone likes rewarding relationships. When we meet new acquaintances, we are more attracted to those who reward us—that is, those who are nice to us, are friendly, and so on. And if we want other people to like us, it is important that we dole out social rewards to them as well (Blau, 1964; Homans, 1961). This is the rule of social exchange, which we discussed earlier in the chapter. But how does this play out in long-term relationships? Do people pay attention to rewards and costs in their most intimate relationships? Do they compare their current relationships to what they think they should be getting in a close relationship, which we defined earlier as their comparison level? And finally, are they keeping track of their options for other possible relationships, or their comparison level for alternatives?

Research has shown ample support for social exchange theory in intimate relationships. For example, Caryl Rusbult (1983) found that college-age dating couples focused much more on rewards during the first three months of their relationships. If the relationships were perceived as offering a lot of rewards, the people reported feeling happy and satisfied. The perception of rewards continued to be important over time. At seven months, couples who were still together, as compared to those who'd broken up, believed their rewards had increased over time. The perception and importance of costs came into play a few months into the relationships; this is when the glow created by all those rewards begins to be dimmed by the realization that costs too are involved. Not surprisingly, Rusbult found that satisfaction with the relationship decreased markedly over time for those who reported that costs were increasing in their relationships. Thus, rewards are always important to the outcome; costs become increasingly important over time.

Now, you may find this description of intimate relationships somewhat objectionable because it portrays people as coldhearted accountants who treat their relationships like they do their possessions. They tally the pros and cons of their partner and compare these to the pros and cons of alternative partners. If a relationship goes into the red—"Sorry, dear, but according to my latest tally, your negatives outweigh your positives, compared to what I can find down the street"—then that's it. The partner is gone. Not only is this portrayal distasteful, but it cannot explain the fact that many people do not leave their partners, even when they are dissatisfied and their other alternatives look bright.

Caryl Rusbult and her colleagues would agree, and go on to suggest that we need to consider at least one additional factor to understand close relationships: a person's level of investment in the relationship (Kelley, 1983; Rusbult, 1980, 1983, 1991). In her **investment model** of close relationships, Rusbult defines investments as anything people have put into a relationship that will be lost if they leave it. Examples include tangible things, such as financial resources and possessions (e.g., a house), as well as intangible things, such as the emotional welfare of one's children, the time and emotional energy spent building the relationship, and the sense of personal integrity that will be lost if one gets divorced. As seen in Figure 10.8, the greater the investment individuals have in a relationship, the less likely they are to leave, even if satisfaction is low and other alternatives look promising. In short, to predict whether people will stay in an intimate relationship, we need to know (a) how satisfied they are with the relationship, (b) what they think of the alternatives, and (c) how great their investment in the relationship is.

To test this model, Rusbult (1983) asked college students involved in heterosexual dating relationships to fill out questionnaires for seven months. Every three weeks or so, people answered questions about each of the components of the model shown in Figure 10.8. Rusbult also kept track of whether the students

> What, after all, is our life but a great dance in which we are all trying to fix the best going rate of exchange?
> –Malcolm Bradbury, 1992

investment model: the theory holding that people's commitment to a relationship depends on their satisfaction with the relationship in terms of rewards, costs, and comparison level; their comparison level for alternatives; and how much they have invested in the relationship that would be lost by leaving it

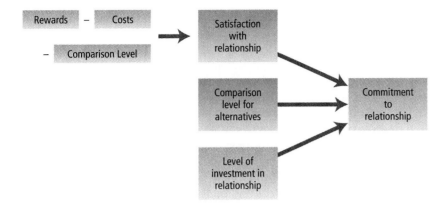

FIGURE 10.8   The investment model of commitment. ■ People's commitment to a relationship depends on their satisfaction with the relationship in terms of rewards, costs, and comparison level; their comparison level for alternatives; and how much they have invested in the relationship. (Adapted from Rusbult, 1983)

stayed in the relationships or broke up with their partner. As you can see in Figure 10.9, people's satisfaction, alternatives, and investments all predicted how committed they were to the relationship and whether it lasted. (The higher the number on the scale, the more each factor predicted the commitment to and length of the relationship.) Subsequent studies have found results similar to those shown in Figure 10.9 for married couples of diverse ages, for lesbian and gay couples, for close (nonsexual) friendships, and for residents of both the United States and Taiwan (Kurdek, 1992; Lin & Rusbult, 1995; Rusbult, 1991; Rusbult & Buunk, 1993).

FIGURE 10.9   A test of the investment model. ■ This study examined the extent to which college students' satisfaction with a relationship, their comparison level for alternatives, and their investment in the relationship predicted their commitment to the relationship and their decision about whether to break up with their partner. The higher the number, the more each variable predicted commitment and breakup, independently of the two other variables. All three variables were good predictors of how committed people were and whether or not they broke up. (Adapted from Rusbult, 1983)

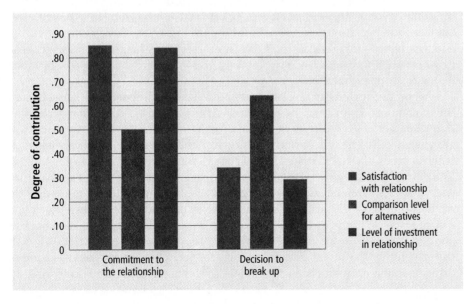

Recently, Rusbult has applied her investment model to the study of the "dark side of close relationships" (Duck, 1994). She and John Martz (1995) interviewed women who had sought refuge at a shelter for battered women about their abusive romantic relationships and marriages. Why had these women stayed in these relationships, even to the point that some of them returned to the abusive male partner when they left the shelter? As the theory would predict, the researchers found that feelings of commitment to the abusive relationship were greater among women who had poorer economic alternatives to the relationship, were more heavily invested in the relationship (e.g., were married; had children), and were less dissatisfied with the relationship (i.e., reported receiving less severe forms of abuse). Thus, when it comes to long-term relationships, commitment is more than just the amount of rewards and punishments people dole out.

Equity: Is It Always Tit-for-Tat?

Earlier we discussed equity theory, which argues that what matters in a relationship is not the total amount of rewards and costs but the fairness of how those rewards and costs are distributed. The argument here is that people strive for equity so that there is roughly an equal ratio of rewards to costs for each partner. Many early studies found that people use this rule and are dissatisfied if the ratio is imbalanced, tipped in the direction of one partner. For example, in research on college-age dating couples and on older married couples, those who felt their relationships were equitable were happy and content; by contrast, those who felt underbenefited reported feeling angry or depressed, and those who felt overbenefited reported feeling guilty or depressed (Schafer & Keith, 1980; Sprecher, 1986; Walster, Walster, & Traupmann, 1978).

> The friendships which last are those wherein each friend respects the other's dignity to the point of not really wanting anything from him.
>
> –Cyril Connolly

But does equity theory operate in long-term relationships the same way it does in new or less intimate relationships? The more we get to know someone, the more reluctant we are to believe that we are simply exchanging favors, and the less inclined we are to expect immediate compensation for a favor done. Elaine Hatfield and Richard Rapson (1993) note that in casual relationships we trade "in kind"—you loan someone your class notes, he buys you a beer. But in intimate relationships, we trade very different resources and it can be difficult to determine if equity has been achieved. As Hatfield and Rapson (1993) put it, does "dinner at an expensive restaurant on Monday balance out three nights of neglect due to a heavy work load"? (p. 130). In other words, long-term, intimate relationships seem to be governed by a looser, give-and-take notion of equity, rather than a rigid, tit-for-tat strategy.

exchange relationships: relationships governed by the need for equity (i.e., for an equal ratio of rewards and costs)

According to Margaret Clark and Judson Mills, interactions between new acquaintances are governed by equity concerns and are called **exchange relationships.** Interactions between close friends, family members, and romantic partners are governed less by a tit-for-tat equity norm and more by a desire to help each other in times of need (Clark, 1984, 1986; Clark & Mills, 1979, 1993; Mills & Clark, 1982). In exchange relationships, people keep track of who is contributing what and feel taken advantage of when they feel they are putting more into the relationship than they are getting out of it. In **communal relationships,** people give in response to the other's needs, regardless of whether they are paid back. A good example of a communal relationship is parenting. As a friend of ours recently put it, "You spend years catering to your child's every need—changing diapers, sitting up with her in the middle of the night when she is throwing up,

communal relationships: relationships in which people's primary concern is being responsive to the other person's needs

■ Which of these groups of people would you say have an exchange relationship, and which a communal relationship?

coaching her soccer team—knowing full well that sooner or later, she will reach an age when she will prefer to spend her time with anyone but you!"

In a series of clever experiments, Margaret Clark and her colleagues varied whether people desired an exchange or a communal relationship with another person, and then observed the extent to which people were concerned with equity in the relationship. In such experiments, the type of relationship is typically altered by having people interact with someone who is quite attractive and telling half of the participants that this person is new to the area and interested in making new friends—thereby increasing people's interest in establishing a communal relationship. The remaining participants are told that the other person is married and visiting the area for only a brief time—thereby making people more inclined to favor an exchange relationship with him or her. As predicted, people in the exchange condition operated according to the equity norm, as summarized in Figure 10.10. People in the communal condition, thinking there was a chance for a long-term relationship, were relatively unconcerned with a tit-for-tat accounting of who was contributing what (Clark, 1984; Clark & Mills, 1979; Clark & Waddell, 1985; Williamson & Clark, 1989). These results are not limited to exchange and communal relationships created in the laboratory. Other studies show that ongoing friendships are more communal than relationships between strangers are (Clark, Mills, & Corcoran, 1989).

Are people in communal relationships completely unconcerned with equity? No; as we saw earlier, people do feel distressed if they believe their intimate relationships are inequitable (Walster et al., 1978). However, equity takes on a somewhat different form in communal relationships than it does in less intimate ones. In communal relationships, the partners are more relaxed about what constitutes equity at any given time; they believe that things will eventually balance out and a rough kind of equity will be achieved. For any given day, week, or month, one partner might be feeling underbenefited, but in a good communal relationship, one can trust that this situation will change and even reverse itself. Thus, in the short run there are differences in how closely people adhere to the equity norm. In new acquaintanceships, people keep much more careful track of the debits and withdrawals of each partner. In communal relationships, people are much more relaxed and even resent a careful accounting of who is contributing what.

FIGURE 10.10 Exchange versus communal relationships.

Evolution and Sociobiology

When asked the question, "Why do I love thee? Let me count the ways," evolutionary theorists will give some rather startling answers. The basic tenet of evolutionary biology is that an animal's "fitness" is measured by its reproductive success—that is, its ability to pass on its genes to the next generation. Reproductive success is not just part of the game; it is the game. Has human behavior evolved in specific ways to maximize reproductive success? Sociobiologists say yes, and more controversially, they argue that males and females have very different agendas due to their differing roles in producing offspring.

For females, reproduction is costly in terms of time, energy, and effort, and this means they must consider carefully when and with whom to reproduce. In comparison, reproduction has few costs for males. The **sociobiological approach to love** concludes that reproductive success for the two sexes translates into two very different behavior patterns: male animals would do best to pursue frequent pairings with many females, and female animals would do best to pair infrequently and only with a carefully chosen male (Berkow, 1989; Symons, 1979).

Now, what does this have to do with falling in love? David Buss and his colleagues state that this evolutionary approach explains the different strategies of men and women in romantic relationships (1985; 1988a; Buss & Schmitt, 1993). Buss (1988b) explains that finding (and keeping) a mate requires one to display one's resources—the aspects of oneself that will appear attractive to potential mates. This approach argues that across millennia, human beings have been selected through evolution to respond to certain external cues in the oppo-

sociobiological approach to love: an approach derived from evolutionary biology, which states that men and women are attracted to different characteristics in each other (men are attracted by women's appearance; women are attracted by men's resources) because this maximizes their reproductive success site sex. Females, facing high reproductive costs, will look for a male who can supply the resources and support she needs to bear a child. Males will look for a female who appears capable of reproducing successfully. More specifically, men will respond to the physical appearance of women, since age and health denote reproductive fitness, and women will respond to the economic and career achievements of men, since these variables represent resources they and their offspring will need (Buss, 1986b).

Several recent studies have tested these predictions and found some support for them. For example, Buss and his colleagues (1990) asked more than 9,000 adults in 37 countries (representing 6 continents and 5 islands) how important and desirable various characteristics were in choosing a marriage partner. In general, the women participants valued ambition, industriousness, and good earning capacity in a potential mate more than the men did, and the men valued physical attractiveness in a mate more than the women did, a finding echoed in other research (Buss & Barnes, 1986; Buss & Schmitt, 1993; Feingold, 1992b). As we discussed earlier, men are more likely than women to say that physical attractiveness is important to them in a potential date (Feingold, 1990). Other survey studies have indicated that men prefer spouses who are younger than they are (youth indicating greater reproductive fitness), while women prefer spouses around their own age (Buss, 1989; Kenrick & Keefe, 1992). When college students were asked to imagine that their romantic partner had been sexually unfaithful or emotionally unfaithful, the men were more upset by the sexual infidelity scenario than the women were, while the women were relatively more upset by the emotional infidelity story (Buss, Larsen, Westen, & Semmelroth, 1992).

The sociobiological approach to love is a new addition to the field, and it has attracted its share of criticism. Some social psychologists argue that the theory is untestable: that because it is so flexible, it can be used to explain anything (Sternberg & Beall, 1991). Others suggest that it is an oversimplification of extremely complex human behavior (Travis & Yeager, 1991). Some note that the preference for different qualities in a male or female can be explained without sociobiology: Around the world, women have less power, status, wealth, and other resources than men do. If women need to rely on men to achieve economic security, they must consider this characteristic when choosing a mate. In comparison, men are free to choose a woman using more frivolous criteria like good looks. Thus, in the framework of equity theory, female youth and beauty are considered a fair exchange for male career and economic success. Finally, men may value physical attractiveness in a partner simply because they have been taught to value it; they have been conditioned by decades of advertising and media images to value beauty in women and to have a recreational approach to sex (Hatfield & Rapson, 1993). As a controversial theory, the sociobiological explanation of love is sure to generate more research and further theorizing.

> Men seek to propagate widely, whereas women seek to propagate wisely.
> –Robert Hinde

> She's beautiful and therefore to be woo'd.
> –William Shakespeare

Attachment Styles and Intimate Relationships

Most of the determinants of love and intimacy we have discussed so far have been in the here-and-now of a relationship: the attractiveness and similarity of the partners, how they treat each other, and so on. Sociobiology takes the long view—how people act today is based on behavior patterns that evolved from our species' hominid past. Another recent theory of love takes the middle ground, stating that our behavior in adult relationships is based on our experiences as a young infant with our parents or caregivers. This approach focuses on **attachment styles** and

attachment styles: the expectations people develop about relationships with others, based on the relationship they had with their primary caregiver when they were infants draws on the ground-breaking work of John Bowlby (1969, 1973, 1980) and Mary Ainsworth (Ainsworth, Blehar, Waters, & Wall, 1978) on how infants form bonds to their primary caregivers (e.g., their mothers or fathers). The theory of attachment styles states that the kinds of bonds we form early in life influence the kinds of relationships we form as adults.

Mary Ainsworth and her colleagues (1978) identified three types of relationships between infants and their mothers. Infants with a **secure attachment style** typically have caregivers who are responsive to their needs and who show positive emotions when interacting with them. These infants trust their caregivers, are not worried about being abandoned, and view themselves as worthy and well liked. Infants with an **avoidant attachment style** typically have caregivers who are aloof and distant, rebuffing the infant's attempts to establish intimacy. These infants desire to be close to their caregiver but learn to suppress this need, as if they know that attempts to be intimate will be rejected. Infants with an **anxious/ambivalent attachment style** typically have caregivers who are inconsistent and overbearing in their affections. These infants are unusually anxious, because they can never predict when and how their caregivers will respond to their needs.

The key assumption of attachment theory is that the particular attachment style we learn as infants and young children stays with us throughout life and generalizes to all of our relationships with other people: The securely attached person is able to develop mature, lasting relationships; people who have avoidant attachment styles are less able to trust others and find it difficult to develop close, intimate relationships; and people who have anxious/ambivalent attachment styles want to become close to their partners but worry that their partners will not return their affections. In short, the kinds of expectations about other people that we literally learned at our mother's or father's knee stay with us and influence our adult relationships throughout our lives.

We do not mean to imply that if you had an unhappy relationship with your parents, you are doomed to repeat this same kind of unhappy relationship with everyone you meet. People can change, and learn to have healthier and more fulfilling relationships than they had as a child. If you had an avoidant or anxious/ambivalent relationship with your parents, however, there is a greater likelihood that you will have these same kinds of relationships with romantic partners, as well as with your own children (Feeney & Noller, 1990; Hazan & Shaver, 1987; Main, Kaplan, & Cassidy, 1985). This has been shown in several studies that measure adults' attachment styles with questionnaires or interviews and then correlate these styles with the quality of their romantic relationships.

For example, Cindy Hazan and Philip Shaver (1987) asked adults to choose one of the three statements shown in Table 10.4, according to how they typically felt in romantic relationships. Each of these statements was designed to capture the three kinds of attachment styles we described above. The researchers also asked people questions about their current relationships. The results of this study—and several others like it—were consistent with an attachment theory perspective. Securely attached adults report that they easily become close to other people, readily trust others, and have satisfying romantic relationships. People with an avoidant style report that they are uncomfortable becoming close to others, find it hard to trust others, and have less satisfying romantic relationships. And people with an anxious/ambivalent style tend to have less satisfying relationships but of a different type: They are likely to be obsessive and preoccupied with their relationships, fearing that their partners do not want to be as intimate or

secure attachment style: an attachment style characterized by trust, a lack of concern with being abandoned, and the view that one is worthy and well liked

avoidant attachment style: an attachment style characterized by a suppression of attachment needs, because attempts to be intimate have been rebuffed; people with this style find it difficult to develop intimate relationships

anxious/ambivalent attachment style: an attachment style characterized by a concern that others will not reciprocate one's desire for intimacy, resulting in higher than average levels of anxiety

■ Attachment theory predicts that the attachment style we learn as infants and young children stays with us throughout life, and generalizes to all of our relationships with other people.

Table 10.4

Measuring attachment styles.

Secure style	56%	I find it relatively easy to get close to others and am comfortable depending on them and having them depend on me. I don't often worry about being abandoned or about someone getting too close.
Avoidant style	25%	I am somewhat uncomfortable being close; I find it difficult to trust them completely, difficult to allow myself to depend on them. I am nervous when anyone gets close, and often, love partners want me to be more intimate than I feel comfortable being.
Anxious style	19%	I find that others are reluctant to get as close as I would like. I often worry that my partner doesn't really love me or won't stay with me, I want to merge completely with another person, and this desire sometimes scares people away.

NOTE: As part of a survey of attitudes toward love published in a newspaper, people were asked to choose the statement that best described their romantic relationships. The attachment style each statement was designed to measure and the percentage of people who chose each alternative are listed after each statement. (Adapted from Hazan & Shaver, 1987)

close as they desire them to be (Collins & Read, 1990; Feeney & Noller, 1990; Kobak & Hazan, 1991; Shaver, Hazan, & Bradshaw, 1988; Simpson, 1990; Simpson, Rholes, & Nelligan, 1991).

Attachment styles have also been found to affect couples' behavior in an experimental setting. Jeffry Simpson, William Rholes, and Julia Nelligan (1992) brought heterosexual dating couples into the lab and measured their attachment styles by questionnaire. They then told the woman of each pair that, next, she would be taking part in an experimental procedure that aroused considerable anxiety and distress in most people but they couldn't tell her any more about it then. Each woman was asked to wait a few minutes before "the procedure" began, and did so with her boyfriend. Their interactions were recorded by the experimenters and later analyzed. Securely attached women turned to their boyfriends for support and comfort during the anxious waiting period, while avoidant women did not; they withdrew from their boyfriends. And what about the men? When the girlfriends of securely attached men began to signal their distress, the men responded with more comfort and reassurance. On the other hand, when the girlfriends of avoidant men began indicating they were upset, the men responded with less comfort and support.

Other investigators have asked research participants to describe (a) their childhood relationships with their parents, to determine their early attachment style, and (b) their current romantic relationships, to provide an even more exact test of the attachment hypothesis. For example, Judith Feeney and Patricia Noller (1990) found that securely attached individuals reported positive early family relationships, and as adults, had the most enduring, long-term romantic relationships in the sample. Anxious/ambivalently attached individuals reported that as children, they did not feel supported by their parents; their adult romantic rela-

> In my very own self, I am part of my family.
> –David Herbert Lawrence

tionships were the most short-lived of the sample. Finally, avoidant individuals stated that when young, they were distanced from and mistrustful of their parents; as adults, these individuals were the most likely to report never having been in love or not being in love at the time of the study, and the love relationships they had experienced were the least intense in the sample.

Using a similar approach, Nancy Collins and Stephen Read (1990) found that for heterosexual, college-age dating couples, childhood attachment styles are correlated with the type of romantic partner chosen and the outcome of the relationship. In particular, the participants' descriptions of their attachment history with their opposite-sex parent was related to their current choice of romantic partner. For example, men who felt their mothers were cold or inconsistent were more likely to be dating women who were anxious. Women who felt their fathers were warm and responsive were most likely to be dating men who were able to express intimacy.

At this point, we feel the need to issue a caveat. As interesting as the results in this section might be, we must remind you that they are often correlational rather than experimental. As we saw in Chapter 2, it is risky to infer causation from correlational data. Moreover, these studies rely in part on self-reports about recollections of the past—one's memories of one's childhood and how one's parents behaved. These recollections are subject to several alternative causal explanations, by dint of the fact that one's memories can be influenced by one's present situation. For example, consider the women who were currently dating men who were able to express intimacy. It may be that these women were made so happy by this situation that, when they thought about the past, it was primarily the most pleasant memories that were triggered. Accordingly, when asked to describe their fathers they might selectively have remembered more instances of warmth and responsiveness.

Taken as a whole, however, these studies are highly suggestive and do lend some support to the contention that the kind of relationship we had with our parents is likely to influence our relationships with others in adulthood. When you find yourself having problems in your close relationships, think about these research findings in attachment theory and see if they help you understand your behavior and that of your partner.

Relationships as an Interpersonal Process

What is the best visual metaphor for a close relationship? Are relationships like snapshots in a photo album—one photo per relationship? Or are they like home movies—showing the course of a relationship over time? A new approach to the study of intimate relationships takes the latter view, conceptualizing relationships as an interpersonal "process" and not a static, fixed entity (Duck, 1982; 1991; Duck & Sants, 1983). Relationships are always in a state of flux, continually going through stages of change and maintenance, growth and retreat (Acitelli & Duck, 1987; Baxter, 1988; Cate & Lloyd, 1988; Dindia & Canary, 1993; Duck, 1995; Montgomery, 1988). People engage in this process through communication—as they define and redefine their relationships, they share their understanding of the relationship with their partners. This ongoing communication about one's feelings and needs creates the sense of a mutually shared relationship (Acitelli, 1992; Duck, 1994; Fletcher & Fincham, 1991; Genero, Miller, Surrey & Baldwin, 1992). According to this view, many of the attraction variables we have

> Love, like electricity or revolution or becoming, is a process (not a thing).
>
> –Al Young

discussed, like similarity and physical appearance, are not only "magnets" that pull us into relationships but characteristics that shape how we behave and think once we are in relationships (Duck, 1991).

This approach is called **relational dialectics.** Close relationships are characterized by tension between opposite but interrelated forces: autonomy/connection, novelty/predictability, and openness/closedness. Leslie Baxter (1988; 1993) and Barbara Montgomery (1993) state that constant change results from the tension between these forces. For example, the tension within autonomy/connection means that as we become emotionally closer to our friend or partner, we feel the need to move away and regain our autonomy; as we become too emotionally distant, we feel the need to move back closer again. Novelty/predictability describes our desire for excitement and newness in the relationship, opposed by our desire for what is safe, secure, and understood. Openness/closedness refers to the tension partners experience when deciding what information they can share with each other and what information they cannot share—the tension between being revealing and being discrete. Any one or combination of these three forces can be operating in a relationship at any given time. Thus, because of these dialectical forces, relationships are constantly being "tweaked"—changed, modified, and redefined.

Because this is a new approach, there has not been a great deal of research on it, but what exists does offer support for the model and its emphasis on change and negotiation between partners. For example, a study of friends, dating partners, and spouses indicated that openness/closedness was a recurrent issue, with one or both members of the relationship periodically moving between the two states (VanLear, 1991). Relational dialectics has been found to predict what issues will be most intense at various developmental stages of a relationship. In the initial stages, issues of openness/closedness are at the forefront. How much should you reveal to your new friend or romantic partner, and when? Is he or she revealing the same amount? Once the relationship is established, issues of autonomy/connection and novelty/predictability become important. How close can you get to this person without losing your identity and independence? Is he or she becoming too distant? Is the relationship becoming boring, or is it too changeable

relational dialectics: a theory which states that close relationships are always in a state of change, due to opposing forces of autonomy/connection, novelty/predictability, and openness/closedness

■ Current research on close relationships stresses that they are continually changing, as partners respond to shifting needs and demands. According to this approach, communication plays an integral role in defining and maintaining the relationship.

and unpredictable (Baxter, 1990)? Finally, an inability to deal with autonomy/connection pressures can spell the end for some romantic relationships; for example, in people's accounts of why their relationships ended, themes of feeling trapped or suffocated are found, as are themes of too little commitment and sharing (Baxter, 1986).

As Julia Wood (1995) reminds us, research on close relationships must pay more attention to the uncertainty and change that characterize such intimate interactions, as well as to their "dark side," where "anger, resentment and meanness simmer, and violence, abuse and betrayal sometimes erupt" (p. 563). Let us turn now to this dark side.

Trouble in Paradise

As the old saying states, "What goes up must come down," and we all know what that means in intimate relationships: Oftentimes, they end. The current American divorce rate is holding at nearly 50 percent of the current marriage rate; in addition, many romantic relationships involving heterosexuals, lesbians, and gays are terminated every day. After several years of studying what love is and how it blooms, social psychologists are now beginning to explore the end of the story—how it dies. We will focus on research on the jealousy in romantic relationships and on how people experience the termination of their most intimate relationships.

Jealousy in Close Relationships.   Just about everyone has experienced what Shakespeare called the "green-eyed monster": that anxious, gnawing feeling of jealousy when we believe a romantic partner is interested in someone else. As much as we don't want to feel jealous, sometimes we just can't help it. But where does jealousy come from? It is commonly believed that the people who are most likely to be jealous are those who think least highly of themselves; after all, if people are secure and feel good about themselves, there is less reason to worry that they will lose a loved one to a rival (Mead, 1977). It turns out, however, that this conclusion is only partly true. The relationship between jealousy and a person's overall self-esteem has been found to be small, at best (Buunk, 1982; Pines & Aronson, 1983; Salovey & Rodin, 1989; White, 1981b). Instead, people are most likely to feel jealous when they feel threatened in areas that are especially relevant to their feelings of self-worth (Salovey & Rodin, 1989, 1991).

You may recall our discussion in Chapter 3 of self-evaluation maintenance theory, which holds that people are most likely to feel bad about a relationship if they are (a) very close to a person who (b) outperforms them (c) in an area central to their self-definitions (Tesser, 1978). For example, if it is important to us to become a doctor and our best friend is accepted at a top medical school, whereas we are rejected, we are likely to feel more than a little pang of discomfort. On the other hand, if becoming a doctor is unimportant to us, we are likely to be pleased for our friend and even to bask in his or her reflected glory.

Peter Salovey and Judith Rodin (1989) suggest that the same reasoning applies to romantic jealousy. People are most likely to feel jealous, they argue, when they experience competition from a rival in an area they especially value. Suppose, for example, that your lover likes to bowl. One night, he or she goes to the lanes with the local bowling champion, who has a 220-pin average. Are you likely to feel jealous? It depends on how central bowling is to your self-definition. If your life dream has been to turn professional and appear on *Bowling for*

Dollars, you are likely to feel pangs of jealousy. If, however, you couldn't care less about bowling, you are unlikely to feel jealous; you might even be pleased that your lover has found someone else to go bowling with so that you don't have to go yourself.

But what if your lover begins to show signs of a romantic interest in the local bowling champion? Virtually everyone will feel at least a little jealous in this situation, because for most of us, feeling desirable sexually is a central part of our self-definition. This is especially likely to be true if it is important to us to have an exclusive relationship with our lover (Bringle, 1981; Buunk, 1982; Salovey & Rodin, 1989).

It is perhaps obvious that people will feel the most threatened about things that are the most important to them. However, what people find important and thus are most likely to get jealous about is sometimes surprising, and differs across cultures. For example, college-age participants in the former Yugoslavia reported a strong jealousy reaction to the idea of their lover flirting with another person; in contrast, students in Hungary had a mild reaction to this jealousy scenario. Dutch students said they would experience strong feelings of jealousy if they knew their partner had sexual fantasies about someone else, but this scenario didn't bother the Yugoslav students at all (Buunk & Hupka, 1987). Thus, most of us are likely to feel jealous when we feel threatened in a domain that is important to us, but what that domain is differs from person to person and across cultures.

> Jealousy is . . . a tiger that tears not only its prey but also its own raging heart.
>
> –Michael Beer

Termination: Breaking Up Is Hard to Do.   Ending a romantic relationship is one of life's more painful experiences. How do people go about ending a relationship? During the past decade, researchers began to examine what makes people end their relationships and the disengagement strategies they use (Baxter, 1986; Felmlee, Sprecher, & Bassin, 1990; Frazier & Cook, 1993; Helgeson, 1994; Rusbult & Zembrodt, 1983; Simpson, 1987). For example, when asked to describe in detail how they had ended a romantic relationship, research participants' accounts revealed five basic categories: *positive tone* (e.g., telling the partner you care about him or her, but . . .), *verbal de-escalation* (e.g., telling the partner you no longer feel in love), *behavioral de-escalation* (e.g., avoiding contact with the partner), *negative identity management* (e.g., telling the partner you should both start dating other people), and *justification* (e.g., telling the partner that the relationship isn't meeting your needs; Cody, 1982).

At the same time, Steve Duck (1982) reminds us that relationship dissolution is not a single event but a process with many steps (see Figure 10.11). Duck theorizes that four stages of dissolution exist, ranging from the intrapersonal (the individual thinks a lot about how he or she is dissatisfied with the relationship), to the dyadic (the individual discusses the breakup with the partner), to the social (the breakup is announced to other people), and back to the intrapersonal (the individual recovers from the breakup and forms an account, or version, of how and why it happened). In terms of the last stage in the process, John Harvey and his colleagues (1986) have found that the version of "why the relationship ended" that we present to close friends can be very different from the official (i.e., cleaned-up) version that we present to coworkers or neighbors.

Why relationships end has been studied from several angles. A particularly profitable approach has used the investment model (e.g., Drigotas & Rusbult, 1992), which we discussed earlier. Diane Felmlee (1995) used the relational dialectics approach to study why relationships end. She asked 300 college men

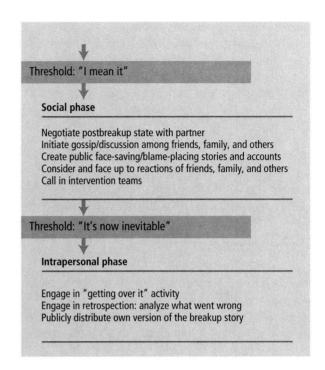

FIGURE 10.11 Steps in dissolving close relationships. ■ (Adapted from Duck, 1982)

> Love is like war; easy to begin but very hard to stop.
>
> –H. L. Mencken

and women to focus on a romantic relationship that had ended and to list the qualities that first attracted them to the person and the characteristics they ended up most disliking about the person. Felmlee found that 30 percent of these breakups were examples of "fatal attractions." The very qualities that were initially so attractive (e.g., "He's so unusual and different," "She's so exciting and unpredictable") became the very reasons why the relationship ended ("We have nothing in common," "I can never count on her"). According to relational dialectics, the tension between, for example, novelty and predictability suggests that relationships that begin with a heavy dose of novelty will soon need to be balanced by some predictability. If the partner can't supply it, the relationship is in big trouble. Note too that Felmlee's findings offer strong support for our old friend similarity, instead of complementarity, as a characteristic that promotes successful relationships.

If a romantic relationship is in bad shape, can we predict who will end it? Much has been made about the tendency in heterosexual relationships for one sex to end the relationship more than the other, for example, that women ended relationships more often than men (Rubin, Hill, & Peplau, 1981). Recent research has found, however, that one sex doesn't end romantic relationships any more frequently than the other (Akert, 1995; Hagestad & Smyer, 1982; Rusbult, Johnson, & Morrow, 1986).

Can we predict the different ways people will feel when their relationship ends? One key is the role people play in the decision to end the relationship (Akert, 1995; Helgeson, 1994; Lloyd & Cate, 1985). For example, Robin Akert asked 344 college-age men and women to focus on their most important romantic relationship that had ended and to respond to a questionnaire focusing on their experiences during the breakup. One question asked to what extent they, as compared to their partner, had been responsible for the decision to break up. Participants who indicated a high level of responsibility for the decision were labeled breakers; those who reported a low level or responsibility, breakees; and those who shared the decision making with their partners about equally, mutuals.

Akert found that the role people played in the decision to end the relationship was the single most powerful predictor of their breakup experiences. Not surprisingly, breakees were miserable—they reported high levels of loneliness, depression, unhappiness, and anger, and virtually all reported experiencing physical disorders in the weeks after the breakup as well. Breakers found the end of the relationship the least upsetting, the least painful, and the least stressful of the three. Although breakers did report feeling guilty and unhappy, they had the fewest negative physical symptoms (39 percent), such as head- and stomachaches, and eating and sleeping irregularities.

The mutual role, which carries with it a component of shared decision making, helped individuals evade some of the more negative emotional and physical reactions to breaking up. Mutuals were not as upset or hurt as breakees, but they were not as unaffected as breakers. Some 60 percent of the mutuals reported physical symptoms, indicating that a mutual conclusion to a romantic relationship is a more stressful experience than simply deciding to end it on one's own. Finally, gender played a role as well in the emotional and physical responses of the respondents, with women reporting somewhat more negative reactions to breaking up than men.

Do people want to stay friends when they break up? It depends on the role one plays in the breakup, as well as one's gender. Akert (1995) found that men are not very interested in remaining friends with their ex-girlfriends when they are in either the breaker or the breakee role, while women are more interested in remaining friends, especially when they are breakees (see Figure 10.12). Interestingly, the mutual role is the one where men's and women's interest in future friendship matches the most. These data suggest that when men experience either great control (breaker) or little control (breakee) over the ending of the relationship, they want to "cut their losses" and move on, severing ties with their ex-partner. In comparison, women wish to continue feeling connected to their

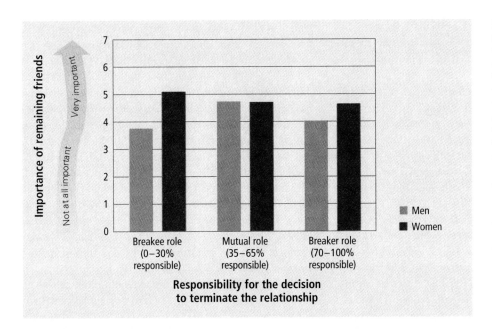

FIGURE 10.12   Importance of remaining friends after the breakup. ■ After ending a romantic relationship, do people want to remain friends with their ex-partner? It depends on both the role they played in the decision to break up and on their gender. Women are more interested than men in staying friends when they are in the breakee or breaker role; men and women are equally interested in staying friends when the relationship ends by mutual decision.

ex-partner and hope to reshape the intimate relationship into a platonic friend-ship. The mutual breakup is the one in which each effectively plays the breaker and breakee roles simultaneously, and this equality in roles appears to be impor-tant in producing an equivalent interest in future friendship for men and women (see Figure 10.12).

The breakup moral? If you find yourself in a romantic relationship and your partner seems inclined to break it off, try to end it mutually. Your experience will be less traumatic because you will share some control over the process (even if you don't want it to happen). Unfortunately for your partner, if you are about to be in the role of breaker, you will experience less pain and suffering if you continue to play that role; however, changing your role from the breaker to the mutual would be an act of kindness toward your soon-to-be ex-loved one.

SUMMARY

In the first part of this chapter, we discussed the variables that cause initial attraction between two people. One such variable is physical proximity, or the **propinquity effect:** People who, by chance, you come into contact with the most are the most likely to become your friends and lovers. This occurs because **mere exposure** to any stimulus, in general, produces liking for it. Though most people are reluctant to admit it, physical attractiveness also plays an important role in liking. The "what is beautiful is good" stereotype indicates that people assume physical attrac-tiveness is associated with all kinds of other desirable traits. On a happy note, research shows that how much we like people influences how physically attractive we think they are.

Similarity between people, whether in attitudes and values, personality traits, or demographic characteristics, is also a powerful cause of attraction and liking. Similarity appears to be a far stronger predictor of attraction than complementarity—the idea that opposites attract. How people behave toward us is also of obvious importance, as when we receive praise from another person. In general, we like others who behave as if they like us. One excep-tion, though, is the **gain-loss effect,** which indicates that we like people more if they initially are somewhat critical of us and then come to like us (we gain their esteem) than if they like us all along.

Many of these determinants of attractiveness can be explained by **social exchange theory,** which argues that how people feel about their relationships depends on their perception of the rewards they receive from the relation-ship (e.g., praise) and the costs they incur. In addition, in order to determine whether people will stay in a relation-ship, we also need to know their **comparison level**—their

expectations about the outcomes of their relationship—and their **comparison level for alternatives**—their expecta-tions about how happy they would be in other relationships. There are, however, exceptions to the rule of social exchange. Under some conditions, people do not prefer the person who is most rewarding. For example, some theorists argue that the most important determinant of satisfaction is the amount of equity in a relationship. **Equity theory** states that we are happiest when the ratio of rewards and punishments we receive is roughly equal to the ratio of rewards and punishments the other person experiences.

In the second part of this chapter, we examined the causes of attraction in long-term, intimate relationships. Social psychologists have offered several definitions of intimacy and love. One important distinction is between **companionate love**—feelings of intimacy that are not accompanied by intense longing and arousal—and **passionate love**—feelings of intimacy that are accompa-nied by intense longing and arousal. The **triangular theory of love** distinguishes among three components of love: intimacy, passion, and commitment. A third conceptual-ization of love focuses on six **love styles:** Eros, ludus, storge, pragma, mania, and agape. While love is universal, cultural variation does exist.

Many of the causes of love are similar to the causes of initial attraction, though there are differences in how these causes operate. Social exchange theories of close relation-ships, such as the **investment model,** say that to predict whether a couple will stay together, we need to know each person's level of investment in the relationship, as well as each person's comparison level and comparison level for alternatives. The notion of equity of rewards and costs is different in long-term versus short-term relationships. Short-term associations are usually **exchange relationships,** in which people are concerned about a fair distribution of rewards and costs. Long-term, intimate associations are usually **communal relationships,** in which people are less concerned with an immediate accounting of who is contributing what and are more concerned with helping their partner when he or she is in need.

The **sociobiological approach to love** derives from evolutionary biology theory and states that men and women are attracted to different characteristics in each other because this maximizes their reproductive success. This view maintains that when choosing a marriage partner, women care more about men's resources and men care more about women's appearance.

The theory of **attachment styles** points to people's past relationships with their parents as a significant determinant of the quality of their close relationships as adults. Infants can be classified as having one of three types of attachment relationships with their primary caregiver: **secure, avoidant,** and **anxious/ambivalent.** There is

evidence that people who as infants were securely attached have more intimate and satisfying romantic relationships than people with either of the other attachment styles.

Relational dialectics states that close relationships are always in a state of change, due to opposing forces of autonomy/connection, novelty/predictability, and openness/closeness that the two partners experience and respond to. Relationships are perceived as an ever-changing process, not a fixed entity.

Jealousy in intimate relationships occurs when people feel threatened that they will lose their loved one. People are most likely to be jealous when they feel threatened in areas especially relevant to their feelings of self-worth; the specific behaviors that meet these conditions differ across cultures. Unfortunately, intimate relationships end; the breaking-up process is composed of stages, not just a single event. A powerful variable that predicts how a person will weather the breakup is the role he or she plays in the decision to terminate the relationship; people differ in their behavior and reaction to breaking up, depending on whether they are in the breaker, breakee, or mutual role.

IF YOU ARE INTERESTED . . .

Annie Hall. Woody Allen's witty, wacky, and perceptive take on falling in love in New York City, with Diane Keaton. Winner of the 1977 Academy Award for best picture.

Brehm, S. S. (1992). *Intimate relationships* (2nd ed.). New York: McGraw-Hill. A comprehensive overview of the entire field of interpersonal attraction, from first impressions to intimate relationships.

Casablanca. "Play it again, Sam"—the all-time classic film, awarded the Oscar for best picture in 1943. Rick, Elsa, and Victor Laslo: the story of a love triangle set amid pre–World War II intrigue and treachery. It doesn't get any better than this.

Duck, S. (1991). *Understanding relationships.* New York: Guilford. An overview of the field of close relationships by an eminent researcher in this area.

Fried Green Tomatoes. A touching story of the meaning and power of friendship in three women's lives.

Hatfield, E., & Rapson, R. L. (1993). *Love, sex, and intimacy: Their psychology, biology, and history.* New York: HarperCollins. A fascinating look at love and intimacy, including both current scientific studies and

historical comparisons between concepts of love in other eras and cultures.

Hendrick, C. (Ed.). (1989). *Close relationships: Review of personality and social psychology* (Vol. 10). Newbury Park, CA: Sage. Chapters on close relationships by the leading researchers in the field, including many whose work we discussed in this chapter.

Márquez, Gabriel García. *Love in the Time of Cholera.* A magical tale of a man's unrequited but intrepid love, which, after 51 years of waiting, is richly rewarded.

McCauley, Stephen. *The Object of My Affection.* A romantic comedy about friends and lovers: a gay man, whose lover has dumped him, and his best friend, a single woman who's pregnant and wants him to be the surrogate dad.

Sternberg, R. J., & Barnes, M. L. (Eds.). (1988). *The psychology of love.* New Haven, CT: Yale University Press. Chapters on love by the leading researchers in the field, including many whose work we discussed in this chapter.

Tyler, Anne. *The Accidental Tourist.* A compassionate, compelling, and extremely funny tale of two apparently mismatched people who fall in love.

Chapter 11

Prosocial Behavior: Why Do People Help?

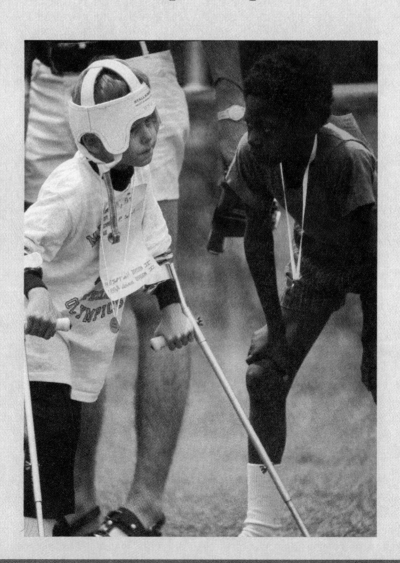

I am not interested in why man commits evil. I want to know why he does good (here and there), or at least feels that he ought to.

—Vaclav Havel, 1982

uman beings have an amazing capacity to act in selfish, uncaring ways. All too often, people resort to confrontation, violence, and force to resolve their differences, sometimes becoming locked in spiraling conflicts that harm everyone involved. Sometimes people appear simply not to care about their fellow human beings. In Chapter 2, on research methods, we discussed the tragic case of Kitty Genovese, who screamed in terror as she was assaulted, and eventually murdered, by an assailant outside an apartment building in the Queens section of New York City. Thirty-eight residents of the apartment building heard her cries, yet not one of them came to her aid. None of them even lifted a finger to dial the police. Unfortunately, such coldhearted acts are not uncommon. Recently six customers in a convenience store in Fredericksburg, Virginia, stood by while a 17-year-old youth grabbed the lone clerk and viciously beat her. The youth ran from the store, his arms raised in a victory salute, as the clerk lay bleeding from the attack. The customers' response? To do nothing. None of them called the police or offered aid to the clerk. "You just really can't trust anyone these days," said one resident of Fredericksburg (Hsu, 1995, p. A1).

Fortunately, there is also a brighter side to human nature. A recent survey revealed that 45 percent of Americans over the age of 18 engage in regular volunteer work (Wuthnow, 1991). Countless citizens reach out to others by volunteering in schools, helping a sick neighbor, giving money to charities, or donating blood. Many people, including social workers, nurses, firefighters, and teachers, devote their lives to serving others.

Sometimes people help in dramatic, selfless ways that capture the attention of the entire nation. Consider what happened in January 1982, when Air Florida Flight 90 crashed while attempting to take off in Washington, D.C. The plane lifted off the runway at National Airport during an icy, swirling snowstorm but was unable to gain altitude. It clipped a bridge spanning the Potomac River and slammed though the ice into the dark water, making a swishing sound as it sank. Most of the passengers and crew were killed by the impact, but a few survivors clung desperately to the tail section of the plane in the frigid waters of the Potomac. A helicopter from the National Park Service flew quickly to the scene. Every second counted, because no one could survive for long in the 30-degree water. The helicopter crew dropped a rescue line, hoping to tow the survivors to rescue workers waiting on the shore. But most of the survivors were in shock and failed to grab the line as it swung back and forth in the gale-force winds. One passenger, a balding man in his fifties, was more alert than the others and managed to catch the rope. Imagine

Lenny Skutnik saves Priscilla Triado after she drops the rescue line.

how strong his desire must have been to be saved from this terrible ordeal. But instead of letting the helicopter pull him to safety, he passed the line to another passenger. Each time the helicopter returned, he grabbed the line and passed it to someone else.

One survivor, Priscilla Triado, lost her grip as the helicopter towed her to shore. She dropped, semiconscious, into the icy water. Lenny Skutnik, a clerk at the Congressional Budget Office, was watching from the banks of the Potomac. Without hesitation, he tore off his coat and boots and dove into the freezing river, dragging Triado to waiting rescue workers. Doctors later found that Triado's body temperature was 81 degrees Fahrenheit, estimating that she was moments away from death when Skutnik reached her. Meanwhile, the helicopter continued to tow the other survivors to the shore. When it returned at last for the selfless man who had been passing the rope to the other passengers, he was nowhere to be found. He had succumbed to the freezing temperatures, slipping wordlessly beneath the black surface of the river.

The horror of the crash of Flight 90 was tempered by these extraordinary acts of self-sacrifice. Lenny Skutnik easily could have died in the freezing temperatures while trying to rescue Priscilla Triado. Instead, he thought, "Somebody had to go into the water," and decided without hesitation that that somebody would be him (Time, January 25, 1982). The entire country applauded his courageous, selfless act, as well as that of the unknown passenger who passed the rope to others, paying for his generosity with his life. The fact that he could not be identified added to his mystique. He seemed to represent the capacity in us all to act in selfless, altruistic, even heroic ways.

These strikingly different examples of human helpfulness—and the lack of it—raise some perplexing questions about human nature. Why is it that sometimes people perform acts of great self-sacrifice and heroism, whereas at other times they act in uncaring, heartless ways, ignoring the desperate pleas of those in need? In this chapter, we will consider the major determinants of **prosocial behavior,** which we define as any act performed with the goal of benefiting another person. We will be particularly concerned with the special kind of prosocial behavior called **altruism,** which is the attempt to help others with no regard to one's own safety or interests. Someone might act in a prosocial manner out of self-interest—he or she hopes to get something in return. Altruism is helping purely out of the desire to benefit someone else, with no benefit (and often a cost) to oneself. Lenny Skutnik, for example, dove into the river to save Priscilla Triado, even though he put himself in grave danger. We will begin by considering the basic origins of prosocial behavior and altruism: Why do people help others?

prosocial behavior: any act performed with the goal of benefiting another person

altruism: any act that benefits another person but does not benefit the helper and often involves some personal cost to the helper

Basic Motives Underlying Prosocial Behavior: Why Do People Help?

Few questions have intrigued observers of the human condition as much as why people help each other. Is the willingness to help a basic impulse with genetic roots? Is it something that must be taught and nurtured in childhood? Is there a pure motive for helping, such that people are willing to aid their fellow human beings even when they have nothing to gain? Or are people willing to help only when there is something in it for them? Let's see how psychologists have addressed these centuries-old questions.

Sociobiology: Instincts and Genes

According to Charles Darwin's (1859) theory of evolution, natural selection favors genes that promote the survival of the individual. Any gene that furthers our survival and increases the probability that we will produce offspring is likely to be passed on from generation to generation. Genes that lower our chances of survival, such as those causing life-threatening diseases, reduce the chances that we will produce offspring and thus are less likely to be passed on. In recent years, evolutionary biologists like E. O. Wilson (1975) and Richard Dawkins (1976) have used these principles of evolutionary theory to explain such social behaviors as aggression and altruism, spawning the field of **sociobiology.** Sociobiologists make two fundamental assumptions: (a) many social behaviors have genetic roots, so that people who have certain genes are more likely to perform these behaviors, and (b) evolutionary pressures have favored some of these social behaviors over others, so that they are now a fixed part of our genetic heritage.

sociobiology: the application of evolutionary theory to social behavior

Darwin realized early on that a potential problem exists with evolutionary theory: How can it explain altruism? If people's overriding goal is to ensure their own survival, why would they ever help others at a cost to themselves? It would seem that, over the centuries, altruistic behavior would be extinguished, because people who acted that way would, by putting themselves at risk, produce fewer offspring than people who acted selfishly. Genes promoting selfish behavior should be more likely to be passed on.

Modern sociobiologists attempt to resolve this dilemma, explaining the existence of altruistic behavior in three general ways. The first involves the notion of

kin selection: the idea that behaviors that help a genetic relative are favored by natural selection

kin selection (Hamilton, 1964). People can increase the chances that their genes will be passed along not only by having their own children but also by ensuring that their genetic relatives have children. Because a person's blood relatives share some of his or her genes, the more that person ensures their survival, the greater the chance that his or her genes will flourish in future generations. Thus, natural selection should favor altruistic acts directed toward genetic relatives. There is support for this notion in the animal kingdom, particularly among social insects. Les Greenberg (1979), for example, released bees near a nest protected by guard bees and observed which ones the guards admitted to the nest and which ones they rebuffed. He had bred the intruders to be of varying genetic similarity to the guards. Some were siblings, some were cousins, and some were more distant relatives. Consistent with the idea of kin selection, the guard bees were much more likely to admit bees that were close relatives. They could tell how related the bees were to them by their odors, and they essentially told their more distant relatives that there was no more room at the inn.

There is some evidence that kin selection operates in human beings as well. According to Gene Burnstein, Chris Crandall, and Shinobu Kitayama (1994), people's choice of whom to help is influenced by the "biological importance" of the outcome: People help others who are most closely related to them, especially when this help increases the likelihood that that person will have children. In one study, for example, people reported that they would be more likely to help genetic relatives than non-relatives in life-and-death situations, such as a house fire. People did not report that they would be more likely to help genetic relatives when the situation was non–life threatening. These results are consistent with the idea that people are most likely to help in ways that ensure the survival of their own genes, because saving someone's life will obviously have a big effect on the likelihood that he or she will have children. Interestingly, both males and females and American and Japanese participants followed this rule of kin selection in life-threatening situations.

Of course, in this study people only reported what they would do; this doesn't prove that in a real fire they would indeed be more likely to save their sibling than their cousin. There is some anecdotal evidence from real emergencies, however,

■ According to sociobiological theory, prosocial behavior occurs in part because of kin selection, as when a young woman helps her little brother.

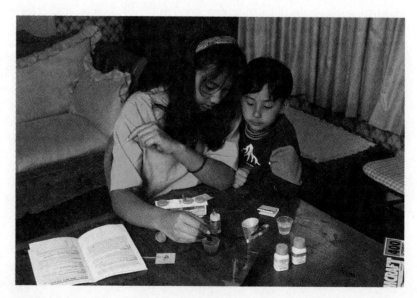

that is consistent with these results. Sime (1983) interviewed survivors of a fire at a vacation complex in 1973 and found that when people became aware there was a fire, they were much more likely to search for family members before exiting the building than they were to search for friends.

Burnstein and colleagues (1994) do not mean to imply that people consciously weigh the biological importance of their behavior before deciding whether to help. It is not as if people crassly compute the likelihood that their genes will be passed on before deciding whether to help someone push her or his car out of a ditch. According to evolutionary theory, however, the genes of people who follow this "biological importance" rule are more likely to survive than the genes of people who do not. Thus, over the millennia, kin selection became ingrained in human behavior.

J. Philippe Rushton (1989) goes so far as to suggest that conflict between different ethnic groups may have a genetic basis, stemming in part from evolutionary pressures to help only those who can pass along our genes. One problem with this explanation of prosocial behavior, however, is that it has difficulty explaining why complete strangers sometimes help each other, even when there is no reason for them to assume they share some of the same genes. For example, it seems absurd to say that the unknown hero of Air Florida Flight 90, who passed the rope to other passengers until he drowned, somehow calculated how genetically similar the other passengers were to him before deciding to save their lives.

To explain altruism, sociobiologists also point to the **norm of reciprocity**. This is the idea that people help others with the understanding that such behavior will be reciprocated at some point in the future. Sociobiologists suggest that as human beings were evolving, a group of completely selfish individuals, each living in his or her own cave, would have found it more difficult to survive than a group who had learned to cooperate with each other. Of course, if people cooperated too readily, they might have been exploited by an adversary who never helped in return. Those who were most likely to survive, the argument goes, were people who developed an understanding with their neighbors about reciprocity: "I will help you now, with the agreement that when I need help, you will return the favor." Because of its survival value, such a norm of reciprocity may have become genetically based (Cosmides & Tooby, 1992).

A third way in which evolutionary theory can explain altruism has been offered by Nobel laureate Herbert Simon (1990). He argues that it is highly adaptive for individuals to learn social norms from other members of a society. People who are the best learners of the norms and customs of a society have a survival advantage, Simon argues, because many of these norms and customs are beneficial. Over the centuries, a culture learns such things as which foods are poisonous and how best to cooperate with each other, and the person who learns these rules is more likely to survive than the person who does not. Consequently, through natural selection the ability to learn social norms has become part of our genetic makeup. One norm that people learn is the value of helping others; this is considered to be a valuable norm in virtually all societies. In short, people are genetically programmed to learn social norms, and one of these norms is altruism.

In sum, sociobiologists believe that people help others because of three factors that have become ingrained in our genes: kin selection, the norm of reciprocity, and the ability to learn and follow social norms. Sociobiology is a challenging and creative approach to understanding prosocial behavior, though it is important to note that not all psychologists accept its claims. Many are skeptical of the idea that all social behaviors can be traced back to our ancestral roots,

> Altruism based on kin selection is the enemy of civilization. If human beings are to a large extent guided to favor their own relatives and tribe, only a limited amount of global harmony is possible.
>
> –E. O. Wilson, 1978

norm of reciprocity: the assumption that others will treat us the way we treat them (e.g., if we help someone, he or she will help us) becoming instilled in our genes because of their survival value (Economos, 1969; Gangestad, 1989). For example, just because people are more likely to save family members than strangers from a fire does not necessarily mean that they are genetically programmed to help genetic relatives. It may simply be that they cannot bear the thought of losing a loved one and so go to greater lengths to save the ones they love over people they have never met. We turn now to other possible motives behind prosocial behavior that do not necessarily originate in people's genes.

Social Exchange: The Costs and Rewards of Helping

Though some social psychologists disagree with sociobiological approaches to prosocial behavior, they share the view that altruistic behavior can be based on self-interest. In fact, a principal theory in social psychology, *social exchange theory,* argues that much of what we do stems from the desire to maximize our rewards and minimize our costs (Homans, 1961; Thibaut & Kelley, 1959). The difference from sociobiological approaches is that there is neither an attempt to trace this desire back to our evolutionary roots nor an assumption that the desire is genetically based. We reviewed this theory in some depth in Chapter 10, on interpersonal attraction, and thus will only summarize it here. Social exchange theorists assume that just as people in an economic marketplace try to maximize the ratio of their monetary profits to their monetary losses, so too do people in their relationships with others try to maximize the ratio of social rewards to social costs.

> Let him who neglects to raise the fallen, fear lest, when he falls, no one will stretch out his hand to lift him up.
> –Saadi (1184–1291)

This does not mean that we keep a little notebook handy, entering a plus or minus every time our friends are nice or mean to us. Social exchange theory does argue, however, that we keep track, at a more implicit level, of the rewards and costs in social relationships. Helping can be rewarding in a number of ways. As we saw with the norm of reciprocity, it can increase the likelihood that someone will help us in return. Helping someone is an investment in the future, the social exchange being that someday, someone will help you when you need it. If this sounds a bit far-fetched or even naive, think about how deeply this idea permeates our society on both a secular and a religious level. Being a good person and treating others with compassion (and receiving such treatment in return) are the hallmark of a civilized society, part of what early philosophers called the social contract. Few of us would want to live in a "dog-eat-dog" world; we need to believe that kindness will be reciprocated, at least some of the time.

Helping can be rewarding in a number of other ways, such as relieving the personal distress of the bystander. Considerable evidence indicates that people are aroused and disturbed when they see another person suffer and that they help at least in part to relieve their distress (Dovidio, 1984; Dovidio, Piliavin, Gaertner, Schroeder, & Clark, 1991; Eisenberg & Fabes, 1991). By helping others, we can also gain such rewards as social approval from others and increased feelings of self-worth.

The other side of the coin, of course, is that helping can be costly. Helping decreases when the costs are high, as when it would put us in physical danger, result in pain or embarrassment, or simply take too much time (Piliavin, Dovidio, Gaertner, & Clark, 1982; Piliavin, Piliavin, & Rodin, 1975). The basic assumption of social exchange theory is that people help only when the benefits outweigh the costs. Perhaps for Lenny Skutnik, the rewards of helping Priscilla Triado (e.g., relieving his distress at seeing her drown) were greater than the costs

■ In 1992, a white truck driver named Reginald Denny was driving his 18-wheeler through South Central Los Angeles just as riots broke out over the acquittal of the police officers who had beaten Rodney King. Two black males pulled Denny from his truck; they beat him, kicked him, and hit him in the head repeatedly with a fire extinguisher. A news crew flying overhead in a helicopter filmed the entire attack—but did nothing to stop it or to aid the victim. Left for dead in the street, Denny was saved by five African Americans who went to extraordinary lengths to help him. After seeing Denny's beating on television, Lei Yuille and her brother got in their car and drove to the intersection to offer their aid. Titus Murphy and Terri Barnett also rushed to the scene from their nearby home, thinking someone had to help Denny. A truck driver named Bobby Green figured he could help by driving Denny's truck away from the riots, and so he rushed to the intersection as well. Based on the different theories of prosocial behavior we have discussed, why do you think these five people went to such lengths to help Denny?

(placing himself in direct physical danger). Basically, social exchange theory argues that true altruism, in which people help even when doing so is costly to themselves, does not exist. People help when it is in their interests to do so, but not when the costs outweigh the benefits.

If you are like many of our students, you may be experiencing discomfort over this view of helping behavior, finding it to be a rather cynical portrayal of human nature. Is true altruism, motivated only by the desire to help someone else, really such a mythical act? Must we trace all prosocial behavior back to the self-interest of the helper? Such a view seems to demean prosocial behavior. When someone behaves generously, as by saving another person's life or donating a huge sum to charity, should we view it as a mere act of self-interest that deserves no plaudits or praise?

Well, a social exchange theorist might reply, there are many ways in which people can obtain gratification and we should be thankful that one way is by helping others. After all, wealthy people could decide to get their pleasure only from lavish vacations, expensive cars, and gourmet meals at fancy restaurants. We should applaud their decision to give money to the disadvantaged, even if, ultimately, it is just another way for them to obtain gratification. Prosocial acts

> I once saw a man out of courtesy help a lame dog over a stile, and [the dog] for requital bit his fingers.
> —William Chillingworth

> What seems to be generosity is often no more than disguised ambition.
> —La Rochefoucauld, 1678

> I expect to pass through this world only but once. Any good therefore that I can do, or any kindness that I can show to any fellow creature, let me do it now. Let me not deter or neglect it, for I shall not pass this way again.
>
> –Stephen Grelle

empathy: the ability to put oneself in the shoes of another person—to experience events and emotions (e.g., joy and sadness) the way that person experiences them

empathy-altruism hypothesis: the idea that when we feel empathy for a person, we will attempt to help him or her purely for altruistic reasons—that is, regardless of what we have to gain

> It is a feeling common to all mankind that they cannot bear to see others suffer. . . . This feeling of distress (at the suffering of others) is the first sign of humanity.
>
> –Mencius, fourth century B.C.

are doubly rewarding, in that they help both the giver and the recipient of the aid. Thus, it is to everyone's advantage to promote and praise such acts. Still, many people are dissatisfied with the argument that all helping stems from self-interest. How can it explain why people give up their lives for others, as in the passing of the rope by the unknown hero of Air Florida Flight 90? According to some social psychologists, people do have hearts of gold and sometimes help only for the sake of helping—as we will see now.

Empathy and Altruism: The Pure Motive for Helping

Daniel Batson (1991) is the strongest proponent of the idea that people often help purely out of the goodness of their hearts. Batson acknowledges that people sometimes help others for selfish reasons, such as to relieve their own distress at seeing another person suffer, but argues that at other times people's motives are purely altruistic, in that their only goal is to help the other person, even if doing so involves some cost to themselves. Pure altruism is likely to come into play, he maintains, when we feel **empathy** for the person in need of help—that is, when we experience some of the pain and suffering the needy person is experiencing. Suppose, for example, that you are grocery-shopping one day. As you walk down the cereal aisle, you see a man holding a baby and a bag full of diapers, toys, and rattles. As the man reaches for a box of Wheaties, he loses his grip on the bag and all of its contents spill on the floor. Will you stop and help him pick up his things? According to Batson's **empathy-altruism hypothesis,** it depends first on whether you feel empathy for him. If you do—if you can "feel his pain," in Bill Clinton's words—you will help, regardless of what you have to gain. Your goal will be to relieve the other person's distress, not to gain something for yourself.

What if you do not feel empathy? If, for whatever reason, you do not share the man's distress, then, Batson says, social exchange concerns come into play. What's in it for you? If there is something to be gained, such as obtaining approval from the man or from onlookers, then you will help the man pick up his things. If you will not profit from helping, you will go on your way without stopping. Batson's empathy-altruism hypothesis is summarized in Figure 11.1.

Batson and his colleagues would be the first to acknowledge that it can be very difficult to disentangle the causes of complex social behavior. If you saw someone help the man pick up his possessions, how could you tell whether he or she was acting out of empathic concern or to gain some sort of social reward? Consider a famous story about Abraham Lincoln. One day, while riding in a coach, Lincoln and a fellow passenger were debating the very question we are considering: Is helping ever truly altruistic? Lincoln argued that helping always stems from self-interest, whereas the other passenger took the view that true altruism exists. Suddenly the men were interrupted by the screeching whine of a sow, who was trying to save her piglets from drowning in a creek. Lincoln promptly called out, "Driver, can't you stop for just a moment?" He jumped out of the coach, ran down to the creek, and lifted the piglets to the safety of the bank. When he returned, his companion said, "Now, Abe, where does selfishness come in on this little episode?" "Why, bless your soul, Ed," Lincoln replied. "That was the very essence of selfishness. I should have had no peace of mind all day had I gone on and left that suffering old sow worrying over those pigs. I did it to get peace of mind, don't you see?" (Sharp, 1928, p. 75).

As this example shows, an act that seems truly altruistic is sometimes motivated by self-interest. How, then, can we tell which is which? Batson and his

FIGURE 11.1   Batson's (1991) empathy-altruism theory.

colleagues have devised a series of clever experiments to unravel people's motives (e.g., Batson, Duncan, Ackerman, Buckley, & Birch, 1981; Batson & Shaw, 1991; Batson et al., in press; Batson & Weeks, in press; Toi & Batson, 1982). Imagine you were one of the participants (who were introductory psychology students) in a study by Miho Toi and Daniel Batson (1982). You are asked to evaluate some tapes of new programs for the university radio station, one of which is called *News from the Personal Side*. There are lots of different pilot tapes for this program, and you are told that only one person will be listening to each tape. The one you hear is an interview with a student named Carol Marcy. She describes a bad automobile accident in which both of her legs were broken and talks about how hard it has been to keep up with her class work as a result of the accident, especially because she is still in a wheelchair. Carol says she is especially concerned with how far she has fallen behind in her introductory psychology class. She mentions that she will have to drop the class unless she can find another student to tell her what she missed in the lectures.

After you listen to the tape, the experimenter hands you an envelope marked "To the student listening to the Carol Marcy pilot tape." The experimenter says she doesn't know what's in the envelope but was asked by the professor supervising the research to hand it out. You open the envelope and find a note from the

Calvin and Hobbes

by Bill Watterson

■ Calvin seems to be an advocate of social exchange theory.

professor in charge. In it he says he was wondering if the student who listened to Carol's tape might be willing to help her out with her psychology class. He says he contacted Carol and asked if she would write a letter to the student listening to her tape, asking for help. She was reluctant to do so, but since she really needs help in the class, she agreed. You then read a handwritten note from Carol, asking if you could go over your introductory psychology lecture notes with her.

As you have no doubt gathered, the point of the study was to look at the conditions under which people agreed to help Carol. Toi and Batson (1982) pitted two motives against each other—self-interest and empathy. First, they varied how much empathy people felt toward Carol by telling different participants to adopt different perspectives when listening to the tape. In the high-empathy condition, people were told to try to imagine how Carol felt about what happened to her and how it changed her life. In the low-empathy condition,

■ This touching story of early hominid prosocial behavior is intriguing to think about in terms of different theories of prosocial behavior. Sociobiologists might argue that the caregivers helped the dwarf because he was a relative and that people are programmed to help those who share their genes (kin selection). Social exchange theory would maintain that the dwarf's caregivers received sufficient rewards from their actions so as to outweigh the costs of caring for him. The empathy-altruism hypothesis would hold that the caregivers helped out of strong feelings of empathy and compassion for him—an interpretation supported by the article's final paragraph.

Study: Cavemen helped disabled

United Press International
NEW YORK—The skeleton of a dwarf who died about 12,000 years ago indicates that cave people cared for physically disabled members of their communities, a researcher said yesterday.

The skeleton of the 3-foot-high youth was initially discovered in 1963 in a cave in southern Italy but was lost to anthropologists until American researcher David W. Frayer reexamined the remains and reported his findings in the British journal Nature.

Frayer, a professor of anthropology at the University of Kansas at Lawrence, said in a telephone interview that the youth "couldn't have taken part in normal hunting of food or gathering activities so

he was obviously cared for by others."

Archaeologists have found the remains of other handicapped individuals who lived during the same time period, but their disabilities occurred when they were adults, Frayer said.

"This is the first time we've found someone who was disabled since birth . . . .", Frayer said. He said there was no indication that the dwarf, who was about 17 at the time of his death, had suffered from malnutrition or neglect.

He was one of six individuals buried in the floor of a cave and was found in a dual grave in the arms of a woman, about 40 years old.

people were told to try to be objective and to not be concerned with how Carol felt. These instructions had the expected effect on people's feelings—those in the high-empathy condition reported feeling more sympathy with Carol than people in the low-empathy condition did.

Second, Toi and Batson varied how costly it would be not to help Carol. In one condition, participants learned that Carol would start coming back to class the following week and happened to be in the same psychology section as they were; thus, they would see her every time they went to class and would be reminded of her need for help. This was the high-cost condition, because it would be unpleasant not to help Carol and then have to see her in her wheelchair every week in class. In the low-cost condition, people learned that Carol would be studying at home and would not be coming to class; thus, they would never have to face her in her wheelchair and feel guilty about not helping her out.

When deciding whether to help Carol, did people take into account the costs involved? According to the empathy-altruism hypothesis, people should have been be motivated by genuine altruistic concern, and helped regardless of the costs—if empathy was high (see Figure 11.1). As you can see in the right-hand side of Figure 11.2, this prediction was confirmed: In the high-empathy condition, about as many people agreed to help when they thought they would see Carol in class as when they thought they would not see her in class. This suggests that people had Carol's interests in mind, and not their own. In the low-empathy condition, however, many more people agreed to help when they thought they would see Carol in class than when they thought they would not see her in class. This suggests that when empathy was low, social exchange concerns came into play, in that people based their decision to help on the costs and benefits to themselves. They helped when it was in their interests to do so (i.e., when they would see Carol in her wheelchair and feel guilty for not helping) but not otherwise (i.e., when they thought they would never see her again).

The Toi and Batson (1982) study suggests that true altruism exists when people experience empathy toward the suffering of another. But as illustrated by

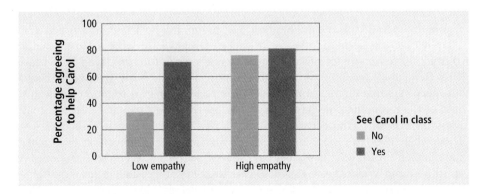

FIGURE 11.2 Altruism Versus Self-Interest. ■ Under what conditions did people agree to help Carol with the work she missed in her introductory psychology class? When empathy was high, people helped regardless of the costs and rewards (i.e., regardless of whether they would encounter her in their psychology class). When empathy was low, people were more concerned with the rewards and costs for them—they helped only if they would encounter Carol in their psychology class and thus feel guilty about not helping. (Adapted from Toi & Batson, 1982)

our example of Abraham Lincoln and the pigs, it can be exceedingly difficult to disentangle people's exact motives when they help someone, and a lively debate over the empathy-altruism hypothesis has arisen (e.g. Cialdini, 1991; Hornstein, 1991; Martz, 1991; Smith, Keating, & Stotland, 1989; Sorrentino, 1991). Some researchers question whether people who experience empathy help purely out of concern for the person in need or, like Abe Lincoln, help in order to lower their own distress at seeing someone they care about suffer. The purity of our motives when we help others is a fascinating question that social psychologists continue to address.

In summary, we have discussed three basic motives underlying prosocial behavior: the idea that helping is an instinctive reaction to promote the welfare of those genetically similar to us (sociobiology); that the rewards of helping often outweigh the costs, making it in people's self-interest to help (social exchange theory); and that under some conditions, powerful feelings of empathy and compassion for the victim prompt selfless giving (the empathy-altruism hypothesis). Each of these approaches has vocal proponents and vociferous critics.

Personal Determinants of Prosocial Behavior: Why Do Some People Help More Than Others?

Whatever the nature of people's basic motives, these motives are not the sole determinants of whether people help, for many personal and situational factors can suppress or trigger these motives. If basic human motives were all there was to it, how could we explain the fact that some people are much more helpful than others? Clearly, we need to consider the personal determinants of prosocial behavior that distinguish the helpful person from the selfish one.

Individual Differences: The Altruistic Personality

When you read the examples at the beginning of this chapter, did you think about the different personalities of the people involved? It is natural to assume that Kitty Genovese's neighbors happened to be particularly uncaring, heartless people. In comparison, Lenny Skutnik and the man who passed the rope to his fellow passengers seemed to be cut from a different cloth: selfless, caring people who would never dream of ignoring someone's pleas for help. Had they heard Kitty Genovese's screams, she might be alive today. Had Kitty Genovese's neighbors been standing on the shore of the Potomac watching the flight attendant lose hold of the rescue line, perhaps they would have stood there and done nothing, allowing Priscilla Triado to perish. Similarly, there are Mother Teresas who devote their lives to others and Saddam Husseins who are bent on destruction and mayhem. And, of course, there are lots of people between these extremes of sainthood and wickedness. Psychologists are very interested in how prosocial behavior develops, as well as the extent to which individual differences in altruism determine prosocial behavior.

Instilling Helpfulness with Rewards and Models. Developmental psychologists have discovered that prosocial behavior occurs early in life. Even children as young as 18 months frequently help others, such as assisting a parent with

■ Adult approval serves as a powerful reward for children when they behave prosocially.

household tasks or trying to make a crying infant feel better (Rheingold, 1982; Zahn-Waxler, Radke-Yarrow, & King, 1979). One powerful way to encourage prosocial behavior is for parents and others to reward such acts with praise, smiles, and hugs. Several studies suggest that these kinds of rewards do increase prosocial behavior in children (Grusec, 1991). Rewards should not, however, be emphasized too much. If children decide to help others only to obtain praise from their parents, they will not come to view themselves as helpful, altruistic people; instead, they will believe it is valuable to help others only when they get rewarded for it. The same is true for adults—believing we are helping someone in order to get a reward diminishes our view of ourselves as altruistic, selfless people (Batson, Coke, Jasnoski, & Hanson, 1978; Uranowitz, 1975).

This undermining effect of rewards is identical to the *overjustification effect* we discussed in Chapter 5: Rewarding people too strongly for performing a behavior can lower their intrinsic interest in it, because they come to believe they are doing it only to get the reward. The trick is to encourage children to act prosocially but not to be too heavy-handed with rewards. One way of accomplishing this is to tell children, after they have helped, that they did so because they are kind and helpful people. Such comments encourage children to perceive themselves as altruistic people, so that they will help in future situations even when no rewards are forthcoming (Grusec, Kuczynski, Rushton, & Simutis, 1979).

Another way for parents to increase prosocial behavior in their children is to behave prosocially themselves. Children often model behaviors they observe in others, including prosocial behaviors (Dodge, 1984; Mussen & Eisenberg-Berg, 1977). Children who observe their parents helping others (e.g., volunteering time to help the homeless) learn that helping others is a valued act. Interviews with people who have gone to great lengths to help others—such as Christians who helped Jews escape from Nazi Germany during World War II and civil rights activists in this country—indicate that their parents too were dedicated helpers (London, 1970; Rosenhan, 1970).

Children imitate other adults, besides their parents. Teachers, relatives, and even television characters can serve as models for children. J. Philippe Rushton (1975) demonstrated this fact in an interesting study of elementary school children. He asked the children to play a bowling game in which they could win tokens. The tokens could be either exchanged for prizes or donated to a needy child named Bobby as part of a "Save the Children" fund. Before playing the game, the children watched an adult—who was said to be a future teacher at the school—play the game. In one condition, the adult kept all the tokens, refusing to donate any to Bobby. In another condition, the adult put half of her tokens in a jar for Bobby. All the children then played the game by themselves, and the researchers kept track of how many tokens the kids donated to Bobby.

The children who watched the generous adult were much more likely to follow suit, donating some of their tokens. Does this finding surprise you? Probably not. The children who saw the generous adult may have felt some pressure to donate, even if they didn't want to. Instead of teaching the kids to be more altruistic, perhaps the generous adult simply made it more difficult for them to act selfishly in that one situation. For example, has someone ever asked you to donate money—say, to buy a collective birthday present for an acquaintance? You might not have really wanted to chip in, but if everyone else was donating, you probably felt pressured to throw in a few dollars too.

Rushton (1975) conducted a second phase of his experiment to demonstrate that the children who saw the generous adult became genuinely altruistic themselves. Two months after the first session, a different experimenter took the children to a room and left them to play the bowling game again. This time, they could choose to donate some of their tokens to a different charity—namely, a fund for starving Asian children. The kids who had seen the adult give tokens to Bobby two months earlier gave more of their tokens to the fund for Asian children than the kids who had seen the adult keep all the tokens did. These children came to value altruism for its own sake, causing them to act generously several weeks later in a new situation, where no models were present.

> If an accident happens on the highway, everyone hastens to help the sufferer. If some great and sudden calamity befalls a family, the purses of a thousand strangers are at once willingly opened and small but numerous donations pour in to relieve their distress.
>
> –Alexis de Tocqueville, *Democracy in America* (1835)

■ Children are good imitators and learn prosocial behavior from observing other people (e.g., their parents) behaving prosocially.

Thus, children are good imitators and from observing other people learn what is a valued and desired act. Is this kind of modeling limited to prosocial behavior? You may be wondering if children also imitate people they see acting aggressively and violently, such as their favorite characters on television. We will see in the next chapter, on aggression, that such antisocial modeling can occur as well.

Is Personality the Whole Story?   As we have just seen, parents and other adults can influence how altruistic a child becomes. We should be careful, however, about the kinds of conclusions we draw from this fact. True, some people have learned to be more altruistic than others. We can all think of people who are consistently helpful, such as our saintly Aunt Sarah, who always puts other people's needs ahead of her own, or our cousin Tom, who has just joined the Peace Corps. But this does not mean that when we want to predict how helpful someone will be, all we need to know is how much of an altruistic personality he or she has. If this were all there is to it, then we should be able to divide the world into different types of people: helpers, who regularly come to the aid of their fellow human beings, regardless of the situation, and selfish people, who consistently sit on their duffs when others need help.

As we saw in Chapter 1, however, people's personalities are not the sole determinant of how they behave. According to social psychologists, to understand human behavior—such as how helpful people will behave in a given situation—we need to consider the situational pressures impinging on them. Predicting how helpful people will be is no exception to the rule. Consider, for example, a classic study by Hugh Hartshorne and Mark May (1929). They observed how helpful 10,000 elementary and high school students were in a variety of situations, including the students' willingness to find stories and pictures to give to hospitalized children, donate money to charity, and give small gifts to needy children. If personality differences were all there is to it, then we should expect to see a good deal of consistency in how each child acted in these different situations. If Nicole is one of those people with an **altruistic personality**, she should be more likely than the others to be altruistic in all the situations. If Philip tends to be self-centered, then he should be less willing than the others to do any of the prosocial acts. Makes sense, doesn't it?

Surprisingly, the extent to which the children were prosocial in one situation (e.g., finding many stories and pictures for the hospitalized children) was not highly related to how prosocial they were in another. The average correlation between helping in one situation and helping in another was only .23. This means that if you knew how helpful a child was in one situation, you could not predict with much confidence how helpful he or she would be in another. Moreover, researchers who have studied both children and adults have not found much evidence that people with high scores on personality tests of altruism are more likely to help than those with lower scores (Piliavin & Charng, 1990). Magoo and Khanna (1991), for example, found that students at Indian universities who scored high on a measure of altruism were no more likely to volunteer to give blood than students who scored low on a measure of altruism. Clearly, people's personality is not the only (or even the most important) determinant of whether they will help, at least in many situations.

Does this mean that any two people we pick off the street—be they Mother Teresa or Saddam Hussein—are equally likely to help the survivors of a plane crash or a neighbor who is seriously ill? Of course not. It's just that individual

altruistic personality: the aspects of a person's makeup that are said to make him or her likely to help others in a wide variety of situations differences in personality are not all we need to know when trying to predict how helpful someone will act. We need also to know several other critical factors, such as what mood the person is in and what kinds of situational pressures are impinging on the person. Even Mother Teresa is probably more likely to help in some situations than in others. And surely Saddam Hussein is not always evil—perhaps some situations are more likely to bring out his diabolic nature than others.

In short, to predict how helpful someone will be, it is most useful to know a lot about his or her personality and the nature of the situation he or she is in. Several studies have demonstrated that certain kinds of people are more likely to help in one situation, whereas other kinds of people are more likely to help in different situations (e.g., Batson, Bolen, Cross, & Neuringer-Benefiel, 1986; Clark, Ouellette, Powell, & Milberg, 1987; Deutsch & Lamberti, 1986). Consider, for example, how helpful you think people would be in these two situations: (a) People are standing on the shores of the Potomac, watching the rescue of Flight 90, and see Priscilla Triado lose hold of the rescue line, and (b) a retarded boy befriends a neighbor and asks the neighbor to take him to the movies. Who is most likely to help in the first situation, and who is most likely to help in the second situation?

Gender Differences in Prosocial Behavior

According to a recent review by Alice Eagly and Maureen Crowley (1986; Eagly, 1987), who focused on differences in helping between males and females, the answer is males in the first situation and females in the second situation. In virtually all cultures, there are different norms for males and females, so that men and women learn to value different traits and behaviors. In Western cultures, part of the male sex role is to be chivalrous and heroic, whereas part of the female sex role is to be nurturant and caring, valuing close, long-term relationships. As a result, we might expect men to help more in situations that call for brief chivalrous and heroic acts, such as Lenny Skutnik's decision to dive into the Potomac and save Priscilla Triado, and women to help more in long-term relationships that involve less danger but more commitment, such as volunteering at a nursing home.

■ Whereas men are more likely to perform chivalrous and heroic acts, women are more likely to be helpful in long-term relationships that involve greater commitment.

In a review of more than 170 studies on helping behavior, Eagly and Crowley (1986) found that men are indeed more likely to help in chivalrous, heroic ways. For example, of the 7,000 people who received medals from the Carnegie Hero Fund Commission, for risking their lives to save a stranger, 91 percent of them have been men. What about helping that involves more nurturance and commitment? Not nearly so many studies have addressed this issue, because social psychologists have focused primarily on helping of the chivalrous, heroic kind. The few studies that have examined gender differences in long-term, nurturant relationships are consistent with Eagly and Crowley's (1986) speculations: Women help more on these tasks than men do (Belansky & Boggiano, 1994; Otten et al., 1988; Smith, Wheeler, & Diener, 1975). For example, when Anne McGuire (1994) asked students to describe times they had helped friends versus strangers, men reported helping strangers more than women did, but women reported helping friends more than men did.

> Both men and women belie their nature when they are not kind.
> –Gamaliel Bailey
> (1807–59)

The Effects of Mood on Helping: Feel Good, Do Good

Another reason personality alone is an insufficient predictor of people's helping behavior is that helping depends on a person's current mood. Sometimes we're in a great mood, sometimes a lousy one, and these transitory emotional states are another key determinant of prosocial behavior. For example, imagine you are at your local shopping mall. As you walk from one store to another, a fellow in front of you suddenly drops a manila folder, and papers go fluttering in all directions. He looks around in dismay, then bends down and starts picking up the papers. Would you stop and help him? What do you think the average shopper would do? One way to answer this question is to think about how many altruistic people there are in the world (or at least in shopping malls). But as we have just seen, it is not enough to consider only differences in personality. The mood people happen to be in at the time can strongly affect their behavior—in this case, whether or not they will offer help.

Alice Isen and Paul Levin (1972) explored the effect of mood on prosocial behavior in shopping malls in San Francisco and Philadelphia. They boosted the mood of shoppers in a clever way—namely, by leaving dimes in the coin-return slot of a pay telephone at the mall and waiting for someone to find them. (Remember the year this study was done—it would be like finding a quarter today.) As the lucky shoppers left the phone with their newly found dime, an assistant of Isen and Levine played the role of the man with the manila folder. He purposefully dropped the folder a few feet in front of the shopper, to see whether he or she would stop and help him pick up his papers. It turned out that finding the dime had a dramatic effect on helping. Only 4 percent of the people who did not find a dime helped the man pick up his papers. In comparison, 84 percent of the people who found a dime helped.

Researchers have found this "feel good, do good" effect in diverse situations and have shown that it is not limited to the little boost we get when we find some money. People are more likely to help others when they are in a good mood for a number of reasons, including doing well on a test, receiving a gift, thinking happy thoughts, and listening to pleasant music. And when people are in a good mood, they are more helpful in many ways, including contributing money to charity, helping someone find a lost contact lens, tutoring another student, donating blood, and helping coworkers on the job (Carlson, Charlin, & Miller, 1988; George & Brief, 1992; Salovey, Mayer, & Rosenhan, 1991).

What is it about being in a good mood that makes people more altruistic? It turns out that good moods can increase helping for three reasons. First, good moods make us look on the bright side of life. If you saw the man drop his manila folder full of papers, you could view this incident in at least two ways. "What an idiot," you might think. "This guy is really clumsy. Let him clean up his own mess." Or you might have more sympathy for him, thinking, "Oh, that's too bad. I bet he's really in a hurry—the poor guy, he probably feels really frustrated." When we are in a good mood, we tend to see the good side of other people, giving them the benefit of the doubt. A victim who might normally seem clumsy or annoying will, when we are feeling cheerful, seem like a decent, needy person who is worthy of our help (Carlson, Charlin, & Miller, 1988; Forgas & Bower, 1987).

Second, "feel good, do good" occurs because it is an excellent way of prolonging our good mood. If we see someone in need of help, then being a Good Samaritan will spawn even more good feelings, and we can walk away continuing to feel like a million bucks. In comparison, not helping when we know we should is a surefire "downer," deflating our good mood (Clark & Isen, 1982; Isen, 1987; Williamson & Clark, 1989).

Finally, good moods increase self-attention. As we noted in Chapters 5 and 9, at any given time people vary in how much attention they pay to their feelings and values versus the world around them. Sometimes we are particularly attuned to our internal worlds, and sometimes we are not. Good moods increase the amount of attention we pay to ourselves, and this factor in turn makes us more likely to behave according to our values and ideals. Because most of us value altruism and because good moods increase our attention to this value, good moods increase helping behavior (Berkowitz, 1987; Carlson, Charlin, & Miller, 1988; Salovey & Rodin, 1985).

Negative-State Relief: Feel Bad, Do Good. What about when we are in a bad mood? Suppose that when you saw the fellow in the mall drop his folder, you were feeling down in the dumps—would this influence the likelihood that you would help the man pick up his papers? One kind of bad mood clearly leads to an increase in helping: feeling guilty. People often act on the idea that good deeds cancel out bad deeds. When they have done something that has made them feel guilty, helping another person balances things out, reducing their guilty feelings. For example, Mary Harris and her colleagues found that churchgoers were more likely to donate money to charities before attending confession than afterward, presumably because confessing to a priest reduced their guilt (Harris, Benson, & Hall, 1975). Thus, if you just realized you had forgotten your best friend's birthday and you felt guilty about it, you would be more likely to help the fellow in the mall, to repair your guilty feelings.

But suppose you just had a fight with a friend or just found out you did poorly on a test and you were feeling sad and blue. Given that feeling happy leads to greater helping, it might seem that feeling sad will decrease helping. Surprisingly, however, sadness can also lead to an increase in helping, at least under certain conditions (Carlson & Miller, 1987; Salovey et al., 1991). When people are sad, they are motivated to engage in activities that make them feel better (Wegener & Petty, 1994). To the extent that helping is rewarding, it can lift us out of the doldrums.

This view, called the **negative-state relief hypothesis** by Robert Cialdini (Cialdini, Darby, & Vincent, 1973; Cialdini & Fultz, 1990; Cialdini, Schaller,

negative-state relief hypothesis: the idea that people help in order to alleviate their own sadness and distress

Houlihan, Arps, Fultz, & Beaman, 1987), is an example of the social exchange theory approach to helping that we discussed earlier. People help someone else with the goal of helping themselves—namely, to relieve their own sadness and distress. This is pretty obvious if we help in a way that deals with the cause of our sadness. If our best friend is depressed, we might feel a little depressed as well. As a result, we might bake our friend a batch of cookies. If this cheers up our friend, we have alleviated the cause of our own sadness. Cialdini argues, however, that when we feel blue we are also more likely to help in some totally unrelated way. If we are feeling down because our best friend is unhappy, we are more likely to donate money to a charity. The warm glow of helping the charity reduces our gloom, even though the charity and our friend's unhappiness are unrelated.

> If you want others to be happy, practice compassion. If you want to be happy, practice compassion.
> –The Dalai Lama

If the negative-state relief hypothesis is true, then people in a bad mood should be particularly helpful when there is no other way they can repair their mood. Imagine, for example, that you were a participant in a study by Robert Cialdini, Betty Lee Darby, and Joyce Vincent (1973). The experimenter greets you and takes you to a graduate student's office. When she pulls out a chair for you, three boxes of computer cards come crashing down, spilling all over the floor. "Oh no!" she says. "I think it's the data from Tom's master's thesis! And I know he doesn't have time to put the cards back in order because he's studying for his qualifying exams" (Cialdini et al., 1973, p. 507).

At this point, you are probably feeling a bit distressed. Even though it wasn't your fault that the cards spilled onto the floor, you probably feel bad for this guy Tom. You and the experimenter pick up the cards as best you can, but it is clear they are hopelessly out of order. The experimenter then goes on with the study, asking you to rate some photographs. When she leaves to get your research participation credit slip, another experimenter enters the room. "Oh," she says. "Isn't Betty here? I'm in the same class she's in and she said it would be all right if I asked her subjects to help me out with my class project." She explains that she needs people to help her do a telephone survey. "I can't give you any experimental credit for doing this," she says, "but I would appreciate your help. Would you make some interview calls for me? Any number of calls up to 15 would help" (Cialdini et al., 1973, p. 507). What would you say?

As you have probably gathered, Cialdini and his colleagues were interested in how much people would help the second experimenter after experiencing the distress of seeing Tom's computer cards spilled all over the floor. To find out, they also included a condition where the experimenter did not spill the cards. In this condition, people agreed to make an average of about three calls for the second experimenter. As predicted by the negative-state relief hypothesis, those who saw the cards spill (and were thus feeling a little bad) helped even more, agreeing to make more than twice as many calls (see Figure 11.3). But how can we be sure they did so to repair their distress at seeing Tom's cards spilled on the floor? The researchers reasoned that if people could repair their mood in some other way, they would not have to repair it by helping the second experimenter. To test this hypothesis, they included a third condition, where people saw Tom's cards spilled but then were rewarded for doing the first experiment: Unexpectedly, the first experimenter gave them $1, in appreciation for completing her study. Then the second experimenter came in and asked them to help her make the phone calls. As Cialdini and his colleagues predicted, getting $1 eliminated participants' need to feel better by helping the second experimenter. Because people's moods were already repaired by getting a surprise payment of money, they didn't need the mood boost they would get from helping (see Figure 11.3).

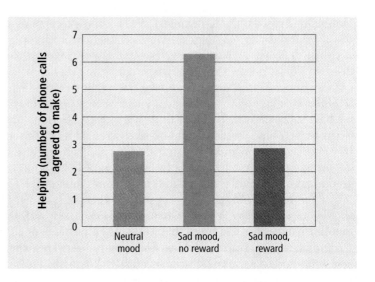

FIGURE 11.3   The negative-state relief hypothesis. ■ Does sadness lead to an increase in helping? In this study, it did so only when people's moods were not already repaired by receiving a reward. When people had received no reward, those in a sad mood (middle bar) helped substantially more than those in a neutral mood (left-hand bar). When sad people had received a reward, however, they did not help any more than people in a neutral mood (right-hand bar). (Adapted from Cialdini et al., 1973)

Situational Determinants of Prosocial Behavior: When Will People Help?

In the previous section, we considered three personal determinants of prosocial behavior: personality differences, gender differences, and people's moods. People differ in how altruistic they are and the way in which they are altruistic, depending on their upbringing, their gender, and their mood. This does not mean, however, that to predict how altruistically people will act, all you need to know is their standing on these three variables. While each contributes a piece to the puzzle of why people help others, they do not complete the picture. To understand more fully why people help, we need to consider the social situation in which they find themselves.

Rural Versus Urban Environments

Suppose you are riding your bike one day and, as you turn a corner, your front wheel suddenly drops into a pothole, sending you tumbling over the handlebars. You sit there stunned for a moment, then notice a sharp pain in your shin. Sure enough, you have broken your leg and there is no way you can get up and get help by yourself. You look around, hoping to see someone who will give you a hand. Now consider this question: Where would you rather have this accident—on the main street of a small, rural town, or in the downtown area of a large city? In which place would passersby be more likely to offer you help?

If you said the small town, you are right. Several researchers have compared the likelihood that people will help in rural versus urban areas and have consistently found that people in rural areas help more (Korte, 1980; Steblay, 1987). Paul Amato (1983), for example, staged an incident where a man limped down the street and then suddenly fell down with a cry of pain. The man lifted the leg of his pants, revealing a heavily bandaged shin that was bleeding profusely (with theatrical blood that looked real). In small towns, about half the pedestrians who

Do not wait for extraordinary circumstances to do good actions; try to use ordinary situations.

–John Paul Richter
(1763–1826)

witnessed this incident stopped and offered the man help. In large cities, however, only 15 percent of pedestrians stopped and helped. People in small towns have been found to help more in a multitude of ways, including helping a stranger who has had an accident, helping a lost child, giving directions, participating in a survey, and returning a lost letter. The same relationship between size of town and helping has been found in several countries, including the United States, Canada, Israel, Australia, Turkey, Great Britain, and the Sudan (Hedge & Yousif, 1992; Steblay, 1987).

Why are our chances of being helped greater in small towns? One possibility is that people who grow up in small towns learn to be more neighborly and that this neighborliness makes them more trusting and altruistic. In comparison, people who grow up in large cities might learn that you can't trust strangers, and that it is often best to mind your own business. Alternatively, it might be something about the urban environment and not the kinds of values people learned while they were growing up that causes people to be less likely to help in large cities. Stanley Milgram (1970), for example, argued in his **urban-overload hypothesis** that people living in cities are constantly being bombarded with stimulation, with the result that they keep to themselves so as to avoid being overloaded by it. If you put urban dwellers in a calmer, less stimulating environment, they should be as likely as anyone else to reach out to others.

Interestingly, the evidence supports the view that people's unwillingness to help stems from the urban environment, not from the upbringing people in cities receive. If such unwillingness could be explained by the values people learn when growing up, then the key to whether or not people will help should be their birthplace, not the location of the incident providing an opportunity for helping.

urban-overload hypothesis: the theory suggesting that people living in cities are likely to keep to themselves in order to avoid being overloaded by all the stimulation they receive

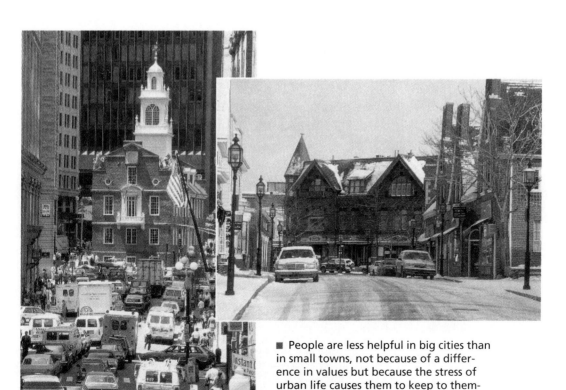

■ People are less helpful in big cities than in small towns, not because of a difference in values but because the stress of urban life causes them to keep to themselves.

However, Nancy Steblay (1987), in a review of dozens of studies, found that this explanation did not hold up. When an opportunity for helping arises, it matters more whether the incident occurs in a rural or urban area than which kind of person happens to be there. Further, Robert Levine and his colleagues found, in field studies conducted in 36 cities in the United States, that population density (the number of people per square mile) was more related to helping than population size was (Levine, Martinez, Brase, & Sorenson, 1994). The greater the density of people, the less likely people were to help. This makes sense, according to the urban overload hypothesis: There should be more stimulation in a small area packed with a lot of people than in a large area where the same number of people are spread out. In short, it would be better to have a city slicker witness your bicycle accident in a small town than to have a small-town person witness it in an urban area packed with people. The hustle and bustle in cities can be so overwhelming that even caring, altruistic people turn inward, responding less to the people around them.

The Number of Bystanders: The Bystander Effect

Remember Kitty Genovese? We have just seen one reason that her neighbors turned a deaf ear to her cries for help: The murder took place in New York City, one of the most populated areas in the world. Perhaps her neighbors were so overloaded with urban stimulation that they dismissed Genovese's cries as one small addition to the surrounding din. While it is true that people help less in urban environments, this explanation is not the only reason Genovese's neighbors failed to help. Her desperate cries surely must have risen above the everyday noises of garbage trucks and car horns. And there have been cases where people ignored the pleas of their neighbors in small towns: Fredericksburg, Virginia, where the convenience store clerk was beaten in front of customers who did nothing to help, has only 20,000 residents.

■ Kitty Genovese and the alley in which she was murdered. Ironically, she would probably be alive today had fewer people heard her cries for help.

Bibb Latané and John Darley (1970) are two social psychologists who taught at universities in New York at the time of the Genovese murder. As we discussed in Chapter 2, they too were unconvinced that the only reason her neighbors failed to help was the stresses and stimulation of urban life. They focused on the fact that so many people heard her cries. Paradoxically, they thought, it might be that the greater the number of bystanders who observe an emergency, the less likely any one of them is to help. As Bibb Latané put it, "We came up with the insight that perhaps what made the Genovese case so fascinating was itself what made it happen—namely, that not just one or two, but thirty-eight people had watched and done nothing" (1987, p. 78).

How can this be? Surely, the more people who witness an emergency—such as your hypothetical bicycle accident—the greater one's chance of receiving help. In a series of now classic experiments, Latané and Darley (1970) found that just the opposite was true: In terms of receiving help, there is no safety in numbers. Think back to the seizure experiment we discussed in Chapter 2. In this study, people sat in individual cubicles, participating in a group discussion of college life (over an intercom system) with students in other cubicles. One of the other students suddenly had a seizure, crying out, "I could really—er—use some help so if somebody would—er—give me a little h—help—uh—er—er—er—er— c— could somebody—er—er—help—er—uh—uh—uh (choking sounds) . . . I'm gonna die—er—er—I'm . . . gonna die—er—help—er—er—seizure—er (chokes, then quiet)" (Darley & Latané, 1968, p. 379). There was actually only one real participant in the study. The other "participants," including the one who had the seizure, were prerecorded voices. The point of the study was to see whether the real participant tried to help the seizure victim, by trying to find him or by summoning the experimenter, or whether, like Kitty Genovese's neighbors, he or she simply sat there and did nothing.

As Latané and Darley anticipated, the answer depended on how many people the participant thought witnessed the emergency. When people believed they were the only ones listening to the student have the seizure, nearly all of them (85 percent) helped within 60 seconds. By two and a half minutes, 100 percent of the people who thought they were the only bystander had offered assistance (see Figure 11.4). In comparison, when the research participants believed there was one other student listening, fewer people helped: only 62 percent within 60 seconds. As you can see in Figure 11.4, helping occurred more slowly when there were two bystanders and never reached 100 percent, even after six minutes, when the experiment was terminated. Finally, when the participants believed there were four other students listening in addition to themselves, the percentage of people who helped dropped even more dramatically. Only 31 percent helped in the first 60 seconds, and after six minutes only 62 percent had offered help. Dozens of other studies, conducted in the laboratory and in the field, have found the same thing: The greater the number of bystanders who witness an emergency, the less likely any one of them is to help the victim—a phenomenon called the **bystander effect.**

Why is it that people are less likely to help when other bystanders are present? Latané and Darley (1970) developed a step-by-step description of how people decide whether to intervene in an emergency (see Figure 11.5). Part of this description, as we will see, is an explanation of how the number of bystanders can make a difference. But let's begin with the first step—whether people notice that someone needs help.

bystander effect: the finding that the greater the number of bystanders who witness an emergency, the less likely any one of them is to help

FIGURE 11.4   Bystander intervention: The presence of bystanders reduces helping. ■
When people believed they were the only one witnessing a student having a seizure—
when they were the lone bystander—most of them helped him immediately, and all did
within a few minutes. When they believed someone else was listening as well—that
there were two bystanders—they were less likely to help and did so more slowly. And
when they believed four others were listening—that there were five bystanders—they
were even less likely to help. (Adapted from Darley & Latané, 1968)

Noticing an Event.   Sometimes it is very clear that an emergency has occurred,
as in the seizure experiment, where it was obvious that the other student was in
danger. Other times, however, it is not so clear. If you are late for an
appointment and are hurrying down a crowded street, you might not notice that
someone has collapsed in the doorway of a nearby building. Obviously, if people
don't notice that an emergency has occurred, they will not intervene and offer to
help.

What determines whether people notice an emergency? John Darley and
Daniel Batson (1973) demonstrated that something as seemingly trivial as how
much of a hurry people are in can make more of a difference than what kind of
person they are. These researchers conducted a study that mirrored the parable of
the Good Samaritan, wherein many passersby failed to stop to help a man lying
unconscious on the side of the road. The research participants were people we
might think would be extremely altruistic: seminary students preparing to devote
their lives to the ministry. The students were asked to walk to another building,
where the researchers would record them making a brief speech. Some were told
that they were late and should hurry to keep their appointment. Others were told
that there was no rush, because the assistant in the other building was a few
minutes behind schedule. As they walked to the other building, each of the
students passed a man who was slumped in a doorway. The man (an accomplice

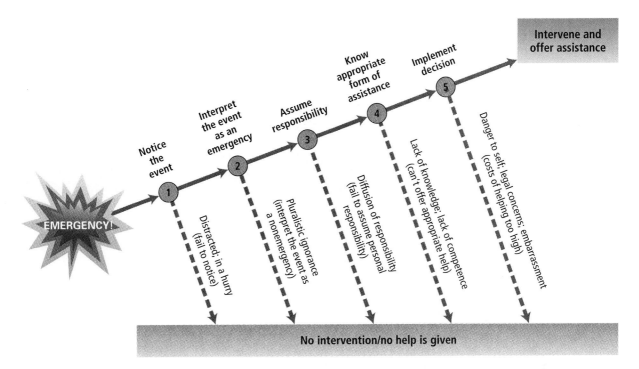

FIGURE 11.5   Bystander intervention decision tree: Five steps to helping in an emergency. ■ Latané and Darley (1970) showed that people go through five decision-making steps before they help someone in an emergency. If bystanders fail to take any one of the five steps, they will not help. Each step, as well as the possible reasons for why people decide not to intervene, is outlined above. (Adapted from Latané & Darley, 1970)

of the experimenters) coughed and groaned as the students each walked by. Did the seminary students stop and offer to help him? If they were not in a hurry, most of them (63 percent) did. If they were hurrying to keep their appointment, however, very few of them (10 percent) did. Many of the students who were in a hurry did not even notice the man.

It is perhaps unsurprising that when people are in a rush, they pay less attention to what's going on around them, making them less likely to help someone in need. What is surprising is that such a seemingly trivial matter as how much of a hurry we are in can overpower the kind of people we are. Darley and Batson (1973) tested the seminary students on a variety of personality measures that assessed how religious they were and found that people who scored high on these measures were no more likely to help than those who scored low. The researchers also varied the topic of the speech they asked the students to give. Whereas some students were asked to discuss the kinds of jobs seminary students would like to have, others were asked to discuss the parable of the Good Samaritan. It might seem that seminary students who were thinking about the parable of the Good Samaritan would be especially likely to stop and help a man slumped in a doorway, given the similarity of this incident to the parable. However, the topic of the speech made little difference in whether they helped. If the students were in a hurry, they were unlikely to help, even if they were very religious individuals about to give a speech about the Good Samaritan.

■ Emergency situations can be confusing. Does this man need help? Have the bystanders failed to notice him, or has the behavior of the others led each of them to interpret the situation as a nonemergency—an example of pluralistic ignorance?

Interpreting the Event as an Emergency.   Just because people notice someone slumped in a doorway does not mean they will help him or her. The next determinant of helping is whether the bystander interprets the event as an emergency—in other words, as a situation where help is needed (see Figure 11.5). Is the person in the doorway drunk, or seriously ill? If we see white smoke coming out of a vent, is it something innocuous, such as mist from an air conditioner, or a sign that the building is on fire? Is that couple having a particularly loud argument, or is one partner about to beat up the other? If people assume nothing is wrong when an emergency is taking place, obviously they will not help.

Interestingly, when other bystanders are present, people are more likely to assume an emergency is something innocuous. To understand why, think back to our discussion of *informational social influence* in Chapter 8. This type of social influence occurs when we use other people to help us define reality. When we are uncertain about what's going on, such as whether the smoke we see is a sign of a fire, one of the first things we do is look around to see how other people are responding. If other people look up, shrug, and go about their business, we are likely to assume there is nothing to worry about. If other people look panic-stricken and yell "Fire!" we immediately assume the building is indeed on fire. As we saw in Chapter 8, it's often a good strategy to use other people as a source of information when we are uncertain about what's going on. The danger in doing so, however, is that sometimes no one is sure what is happening. Since an emergency is often a sudden and confusing event, bystanders tend to freeze, watching and listening with blank expressions as they try to figure out what's going on. When they glance at each other, they see an apparent lack of concern on the part of everyone else. This state of **pluralistic ignorance,** in which bystanders mislead each other by their blank response, leads to the assumption that there must not be any danger, since no one else looks panic-stricken.

Pluralistic ignorance was demonstrated in another classic experiment by Latané and Darley (1970). Imagine that you have agreed to take part in a study of people's attitudes toward the problems of urban life, and you arrive at the appointed time. A sign instructs you to fill out a questionnaire while you are waiting for the study to begin. You take a copy of the questionnaire, sit down,

pluralistic ignorance: the phenomenon whereby bystanders assume that nothing is wrong in an emergency, because no one else looks concerned and work on it for a few minutes. Then something odd happens: White smoke starts coming into the room through a small vent in the wall. Before long, the room is so filled with smoke that you can barely see the questionnaire. What will you do?

In fact, there was no real danger—the experimenters were pumping smoke into the room to see how people would respond to this potential emergency. Not surprisingly, when people were by themselves, most of them took action. Within two minutes, 50 percent of the participants left the room and found the experimenter down the hall, reporting that there was a potential fire in the building; by 6 minutes, 75 percent of the participants left the room to alert the experimenter. But what would happen if people were not alone? Given that 75 percent of the participants who were by themselves reported the smoke, it would seem that the larger the group, the greater the likelihood that someone would report the smoke. In fact, this can be figured mathematically: If there is a 75 percent chance that any one person will report the smoke, then there is a 98 percent chance that at least one person in a three-person group will do so.

To find out if there really is safety in numbers, Latané and Darley (1970) included a condition in which three participants took part at the same time. Everything was identical except that three people sat in the room as the smoke began to seep in. Surprisingly, in only 12 percent of the three-person groups did someone report the smoke within two minutes, and in only 38 percent of the groups did someone report the smoke within six minutes. In the remaining groups, the participants sat there filling out questionnaires even when they had to wave away the smoke with their hands to see what they were writing. What went wrong?

Because it was not clear that the smoke constituted an emergency, the participants used each other as a source of information. If the people next to you glance at the smoke and then go on filling out their questionnaires, you will feel reassured that nothing is wrong; otherwise, why would they be acting so unconcerned? The problem is that they are probably looking at you out of the corner of their eyes, and seeing that you appear to be not overly concerned, they too are reassured that everything is OK. Group members gain false reassurance from each other whenever each person assumes the others know more about what's going on than he or she does. This is particularly likely to happen when the event is ambiguous. If an event is clearly an emergency, as in the case of Kitty Genovese's cries for help, then we do not need to rely on other people to interpret it for us; however, the more ambiguous an event is, the more likely people are to look to each other to define what's going on. As a result, it is in ambiguous situations—such as seeing smoke coming from a vent—that people in groups will be in a state of pluralistic ignorance, convincing each other that nothing is wrong (Clark & Word, 1972; Solomon, Solomon, & Stone, 1978).

Assuming Responsibility.   Let's say that as a potential help-giver, you have successfully navigated the first two steps in the decision tree (see Figure 11.5): You have noticed something odd, and you have correctly interpreted it as an emergency where help is needed. What's next? Now you must decide that you will help. After hearing Kitty Genovese cry out, "Oh my God, he stabbed me! Please help me! Please help me!" (Rosenthal, 1964, p. 33), Genovese's neighbors must have believed that something terrible was happening and that she was desperately in need of assistance. That they did nothing indicates that even if we interpret an event as an emergency, we have to decide that it is our responsibility—not someone else's—to do something about it. When dealing with issues of personal responsibility, the number of bystanders is again a crucial variable, but for different reasons. Consider the condition in the Latané and Darley (1968) seizure experiment where participants believed they were the only one listening to the student while he had a seizure. The responsibility was totally on their shoulders. If they didn't help, no one would, and the student might die. As a result, in this condition most people helped almost immediately, and all helped within a few minutes.

diffusion of responsibility: the phenomenon whereby each bystander's sense of responsibility to help decreases as the number of witnesses increases

But what happens when there are many witnesses? Here a **diffusion of responsibility** occurs: Because other bystanders are present, no individual bystander feels a strong sense that it is his or her personal responsibility to take action. Recall from our earlier discussion that helping often entails costs—we can place ourselves in danger; we can risk looking foolish by overreacting or doing the wrong thing; and so on. Why should we risk these costs when many other people who can help are present? The problem is that everyone is likely to feel this way, making all the bystanders less likely to help. This is particularly true if people cannot tell whether someone else has already intervened. When participants in the seizure experiment believed that other students were witnesses as well, they couldn't tell whether another student had already helped, because the intercom system allowed only the voice of the student having the seizure to be transmitted. Each student probably assumed he or she did not have to help, because surely someone else had already done so. Similarly, Kitty Genovese's neighbors had no way of knowing whether someone else had called the police. Most likely, they assumed there was no need to do so, because someone else had already made the call. Tragically, everyone assumed it was somebody else's responsibility to take action, thereby leaving Kitty Genovese to fight her assailant alone. The sad irony of Kitty Genovese's murder is that she probably would be alive today had fewer people heard her cries for help.

Knowing How to Help.   Even if a person has made it this far in the helping sequence—noticing an event has occurred, interpreting it as an emergency, and taking responsibility—an additional condition must still be met: The person must decide what form of help is appropriate. Suppose, for example, that you see a woman collapse in the street and you decide she is gravely ill. No one else seems to be helping, and so you decide it is up to you. But what should you do? Has the woman had a heart attack? Or did she faint for some other reason? If people don't know what form of assistance to give, obviously they will be unable to help.

Deciding to Implement the Help.   Finally, even if you know exactly what kind of help is appropriate, there are reasons why you might decide not to intervene. For one thing, you might not be qualified to deliver the right kind of help. It may be clear, for instance, that the woman has had a heart attack and is in desperate need of CPR, but if you don't know how to administer CPR, you'll be unable to help her. Or you might be afraid of making a fool of yourself, of doing the wrong thing and making matters worse, or even of placing yourself in danger by trying to help. Consider, for example, the fate of three CBS technicians who, in 1982, encountered a man beating a woman in a parking lot on the west side of Manhattan, tried to intervene, and were shot and killed by the assailant. Even when we know what kind of intervention is needed, we have to weigh the costs of trying to help.

In sum, five steps have to be taken before people will intervene in an emergency: They have to notice the event, interpret it as an emergency, decide it is their responsibility to help, know how to help, and decide to act. If people fail to take any one of these steps, they will not intervene. Given how difficult it can be to take all five steps, it is not surprising that incidents like the Kitty Genovese murder are all too common.

The Nature of the Relationship: Communal Versus Exchange Relationships

A great deal of research on prosocial behavior has looked at helping between strangers, such as Latané and Darley's research on bystander intervention. Whereas this research is very important, most helping in everyday life occurs between people who know each other well: family members, lovers, close friends. What determines whether people help in these kinds of relationships?

As we saw earlier, the negative-relief state hypothesis holds that people will help only if there are immediate, short-term benefits for doing so. It is important to point out, however, that when people know each other well, they are often more concerned with the long-term benefits of helping than with the immediate effects (Salovey et al., 1991). Consider the mother of a 4-year-old. One Saturday morning, she sits down with a cup of coffee to read the newspaper. She wants nothing more than a moment's peace while she catches up on the news. Her daughter, however, has other ideas: She asks her mother to read her *The Berenstain Bears Visit the Dentist*, for the fiftieth time. Reading to the child has few short-term benefits in this situation. The coffee gets cold, the newspaper goes unread, and the moment's peace disappears. Even when there are no short-term benefits, however, helping can reap large long-term rewards. Parents who sit around sipping coffee and reading the newspaper while ignoring their children are less likely to obtain the long-term satisfaction of having a good relationship

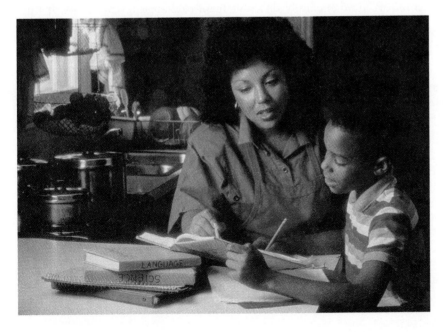

■ In communal relationships, such as those between parents and their children, people are concerned less with who gets what and more with how much help the other person needs.

with their kids and seeing their kids flourish. Thus, parents might read to their children with this long-term goal in mind, enduring the short-term annoyance of being interrupted and having to read about Brother and Sister Bear's cavities for the fiftieth time.

Even more fundamentally, in some types of relationships people may not be concerned at all with the rewards they receive. In Chapter 10, we distinguished between *communal* and *exchange relationships*. Communal relationships are those in which people's primary concern is with the welfare of the other person (e.g., a child), whereas exchange relationships are those that are governed by concerns about equity: that what you put into the relationship equals what you get out of it. Most of the research we have reviewed so far has looked at helping in exchange relationships—namely, ones in which people do not know each other very well and in which people who help expect to be helped in return. What about helping in communal relationships, such as our example of the parent whose child is clamoring for attention?

One possibility is that the rewards for helping are as important in communal as exchange relationships—it's just that the nature of the rewards differ (Batson, 1993). In exchange relationships, we expect our favors to be repaid pretty quickly. If we invite our new friend Sam to a party, we expect that he will invite us to his next party. If we help a coworker learn how to use the Internet on Monday, we expect that the coworker will help us learn how to use the new Xerox machine next week. Maybe people in communal relationships also expect an equal exchange of benefits, but the benefits are different from those in exchange relationships. When parents are deciding whether to help their children, for example, they seldom think, "Well, what have they done for me lately?" Nonetheless, they might help with the expectation that they will eventually be rewarded for their help. In our example of the mother and her 4-year-old, for instance, perhaps the mother was motivated by the rewards of seeing her daughter become a healthy, well-adjusted adult. Maybe this relationship involves an exchange of long-term instead of short-term benefits.

Margaret Clark and Judson Mills (1993), however, argue that communal relationships are fundamentally different from exchange relationships: It's not just that different kinds of rewards govern the relationship; people in communal relationships are less concerned with the benefits they will receive by helping, these researchers argue, and more with simply satisfying the needs of the other person. In support of this argument, Clark and her colleagues have found that people in communal relationships pay less attention to who is getting what than people in exchange relationships do (Clark, 1984; Clark, Mills, & Corcoran, 1989). Consider a study in which the researchers measured how often people in different relationships looked at some lights, which meant different things in different conditions. In one condition, people thought that the lights would change when their partner in another room needed help on a task. Participants were not in a position to help their partner on the task, but the idea was that the more concerned they were with their partner's needs, the more they would look at the lights. In another condition, people thought that the lights would change whenever their partner in the other room did especially well on a task they were both working on and would be rewarded for. The idea here was that people who were concerned about exchange and equity should be especially likely to look at the lights, to keep track of what they "owed" their partner for helping them to get the reward.

As seen in Figure 11.6, the number of times people looked at the lights in each condition depended on whether they were in a communal relationship (their partner was a friend) or an exchange relationship (their partner was a stranger). In communal relationships, people were much more concerned with the needs of their partner (whether this person needed help on the task) than with whether they "owed" their partner (whether this person did well on the task). Keep in mind that people did not think they could go help their partner; they simply seemed concerned with whether the person was in need. In exchange relationships, people were relatively unconcerned with whether their partner needed help. Instead, they were concerned with how well their partner was doing on the task, presumably to keep track of what they owed their partner in return.

In short, helping in exchange relationships appears to be governed by rules and norms that differ from those governing helping in communal relationships. In exchange relationships, people are concerned more with who is getting what, and they get upset if the scales are tipped too far toward one person ("It seems like I'm always doing favors for Bob, but he never helps me in return"). In communal relationships, people are concerned less with who gets what and more with how much help the other person needs ("My daughter really needs my help right now").

Does this mean that people are more helpful toward friends than strangers? Yes—at least under most circumstances. We are more likely to have communal relationships with friends and thus are more likely to help even when there is nothing in it for us. In fact, we *like* to help a partner in a communal relationship more than a partner in an exchange relationship (Williamson, Clark, Pegalis, & Behan, in press). There is, however, an interesting exception to this rule. Research by Abraham Tesser (1988) on self-esteem maintenance (see Chapter 6) shows that when a task is of little relevance to us, we do indeed help friends more than strangers. But suppose that the most important thing in the world for you is to be a doctor, that you are struggling to pass a difficult premed physics course, and that two other people in the class—your best friend and a complete stranger—ask you to lend them your notes from a class they missed. According to Tesser's

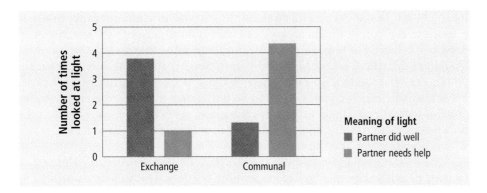

FIGURE 11.6   Keeping track in relationships. ■ In communal relationships, people looked at the light the most when it signified how much help their partner needed. In exchange relationships, people looked at the light the most when it signified how well their partner did on a joint task, presumably to keep track of what they "owed" their partner in return. (Adapted from Clark et al., 1989)

research, you will be more inclined to help the stranger than your friend (Tesser, 1991; Tesser & Smith, 1980). Why? Because it hurts to see a close friend do better than we do in an area of great importance to our self-esteem. Consequently, we are less likely to help a friend in these important areas than in those areas we don't care as much about.

How Can Helping Be Increased?

Most religions stress some version of the Golden Rule, urging us to do unto others as we would have others do unto us. There are many saintly people in the world who succeed in following this rule, devoting their lives to the welfare of others. We would all be better off, however, if prosocial behavior was more common that it is. How can we get people, when faced with an emergency, to act more like Lenny Skutnik and less like Kitty Genovese's neighbors?

Before addressing this question, we should point out that people do not always *want* to be helped. Imagine that you are sitting at a computer terminal at the library and are struggling to learn a new E-mail system. You can't figure out how to send and receive mail and are becoming increasingly frustrated as the computer responds with messages like "Command not understood." A confident-looking guy strides into the room and looks over your shoulder for a few minutes. "Boy," he says. "You sure have a lot to learn. Let me show you how this baby works." How will you feel? You might feel some gratitude at receiving this guy's help; after all, you will now learn how to send E-mail. More than likely, however, you will also feel some resentment. His offer of help comes with a message: "You are too stupid to figure this out for yourself." Receiving help can make us feel inadequate and dependent. As a result, people do not always react positively when someone offers them aid. People do not want to appear incompetent, and so they often decide to suffer in silence—even if doing so lowers their chances of successfully completing a task (DePaulo, 1983; Nadler, 1991; Nadler & Fisher, 1986).

Nonetheless, it seems clear that the world would be a better place if more people would help their fellow human beings. How can we increase everyday acts of kindness, such as looking out for an elderly neighbor or volunteering at the local school? The answer to this question lies in our discussion of the causes of prosocial behavior. For example, we saw that several personal characteristics of potential helpers are important, and promoting those factors can increase the likelihood that these people will help (Clary, Snyder, Ridge, Miene, & Haugen, 1994). Personal factors, however, are not the sole cause of prosocial behavior. Even kind, altruistic people will fail to help if certain situational constraints are present, such as being in an urban environment or witnessing an emergency in the presence of numerous bystanders. Another important factor is the nature of the relationship between the helper and the person in need.

There is evidence that simply being aware of the barriers to helping can increase people's chances of overcoming those barriers. This was demonstrated in a striking experiment by Arthur Beaman and his colleagues (1978), who randomly assigned students to listen to a lecture on Latané and Darley's (1970) bystander intervention research or a lecture on an unrelated topic. Two weeks later, all the students participated in what they thought was a completely unre-

> When death, the great reconciler, has come, it is never our tenderness that we repent of, but our severity.
> —George Eliot (Marian Evans Cross)

■ Becoming aware of the barriers to helping can actually make people more likely to overcome those barriers. People who learned about Latané and Darley's (1970) research on bystander intervention, for example, were more likely to help in an emergency.

lated sociology study, during which they encountered a student lying on the floor. Was he in need of help? Had he fallen and injured himself, or was he simply a student who had fallen asleep after pulling an all-nighter? As we have seen, when in an ambiguous situation such as this people look and see how other people are reacting. Because an accomplice of the experimenter (posing as another participant) purposefully acted unconcerned, the natural thing to do was to assume nothing was wrong. This is exactly what most of Beaman's participants did, if they had not heard the lecture about bystander intervention research; in this condition, only 25 percent of them stopped to help the student. However, if the participants had heard the lecture about bystander intervention, 43 percent stopped to help the student. Thus, knowing how we can be unwittingly influenced by others can by itself help us overcome this type of social influence. We can only hope that knowing about other barriers to prosocial behavior will make them easier to overcome as well.

We conclude with the reminder that we should not impose help on everyone we meet, whether the person wants it or not. Research on reactions to help indicates that under certain conditions, receiving help can have damaging effects on a person's self-esteem. The goal is to make the help supportive, highlighting your concern for the recipient, rather than using the helping encounter to communicate your superior knowledge and skill.

SUMMARY

For centuries people have debated the determinants of **prosocial behavior**—that is, acts performed with the goal of benefiting another person. People have been particularly intrigued with the causes of **altruism,** or the attempt to help others with no regard to one's own safety or interests. According to **sociobiology,** prosocial behavior has genetic roots because it has been selected for in three ways: People further the survival of their genes by helping genetic relatives (**kin selection**); there is a survival advantage to following the **norm of reciprocity,** whereby people help strangers in the hope that they will receive help when they need it; and there is a survival advantage to the ability to learn and follow social norms of all kinds, including altruism. **Social exchange theory** views helping behavior as a weighing of rewards and costs; helping occurs due to self-interest—that is, in situations where the rewards of helping are greater than the costs. Rewards include recognition, praise, and the relief of personal distress. Neither of these theories sees helping behavior as a form of altruism; self-gain is always involved. In comparison, the **empathy-altruism hypothesis** sees prosocial behavior as motivated only by **empathy** and compassion for those in need.

Prosocial behavior is multidetermined, and both personal and situational factors can override or facilitate basic motives to help. Personal determinants of helping include the **altruistic personality,** the idea that some people are more helpful than others. Children can develop this personality by being rewarded for helping by their parents and by modeling people they observe helping. Rewards must be used carefully, however, or they will undermine the child's intrinsic interest in helping—causing an *overjustification effect*. Gender is another personal factor that comes into play. Though one sex is not more altruistic than the other, the ways in which men and women help often differs, with men more likely to help in heroic, chivalrous ways and women more likely to help in ways that involve a long-term commitment.

Mood also affects helping. Interestingly, being in either a good or a bad mood—compared to being in a neutral mood—can increase helping. Good moods increase helping for several reasons, including the fact that they make us see the good side of other people, making us more willing to help them. Bad moods increase helping because of the **negative-state relief hypothesis,** which maintains that helping someone makes us feel good, lifting us out of the doldrums.

Social determinants of prosocial behavior include rural versus urban environments, with helping behavior more likely to occur in rural settings. One reason for this is the **urban-overload hypothesis,** which says that cities bombard people with so much stimulation that they keep to themselves to avoid being overloaded. The **bystander effect** points out the impact of the number of bystanders on whether help is given—the fewer the bystanders, the better. The bystander decision tree indicates that a potential helper must make five decisions before providing help: notice the event, interpret the event as an emergency (here **pluralistic ignorance** can occur, whereby everyone assumes nothing is wrong, because no one else looks concerned; pluralistic ignorance is an example of *informational social influence*), assume personal responsibility (here **diffusion of responsibility** created by several bystanders may lead us to think it's not our responsibility to act), know how to help, and implement the help. In addition, the nature of the relationship between the helper and the person in need is important. In **exchange relationships,** people are concerned with equity and keep track of who is contributing what to the relationship. In **communal relationships,** people are concerned less with who gets what and more with how much help the other person needs.

How can helping be increased? Research has indicated that teaching people about the determinants of prosocial behavior makes them more aware of why they sometimes don't help, with the happy result that they help more in the future.

IF YOU ARE INTERESTED . . .

Clark, M. S. (1991). *Prosocial behavior: Review of personality and social psychology* (Vol. 12). Newbury Park, CA: Sage. A resource containing up-to-date chapters by top researchers in the field of prosocial behavior, many of whom were cited in this chapter. Topics include the development of altruism, the debate about whether people are ever truly altruistic or are always concerned with their self-interest, the effects of mood on helping, and the consequences of helping.

DePaulo, B. M., Nadler, A., & Fisher, J. D. (1983). *New directions in helping: Help seeking* (Vol. 2). New York: Academic Press. Chapters address the conditions under which people are likely to seek out help from others and the consequences of receiving help.

Gandhi (1982). An award-winning film about the life of Mahatma Gandhi, the Indian leader who captured the minds and hearts of the world by leading a persistent, peaceful revolt against the British Empire. He became an international symbol of selflessness and nonviolence. His life raises many interesting questions about the causes of altruism.

Latané, B., & Darley, J. M. (1970). *The unresponsive bystander: Why doesn't he help?* Englewood Cliffs, NJ: Prentice Hall. A classic look at why bystanders often fail to help victims in emergencies, including an in-depth discussion of the "seizure" and "smoke" studies described in this chapter.

Rushton, J. P., & Sorrentino, R. M. (1981). *Altruism and helping behavior: Social, personality, and developmental perspectives*. Hillsdale, NJ: Erlbaum. The chapters present many perspectives on prosocial behavior, including how prosocial behavior develops, personality differences in altruism, and social determinants of altruism.

Schindler's List (1994, Stephen Spielberg). The true story of how a German profiteer saved the lives of hundreds of Jews during World War II. Whereas Oscar Schindler's original motivation stemmed from capitalistic need for cheap labor, his actions went far beyond his original intentions—raising intriguing questions about the origins of altruism.

Spacapan, S., & Oskamp, S. (1992). *Helping and being helped: Naturalistic studies*. Newbury Park, CA: Sage. This book contains chapters by researchers investigating helping in everyday life, including self-help groups, spousal caregiving, organ donation, and AIDS volunteerism.

Wolpert, Stanley (1962). *Nine Hours to Rama*. A fictionalized account of the life of Mahatma Gandhi.

Chapter 12

Aggression:
Why We Hurt Other People

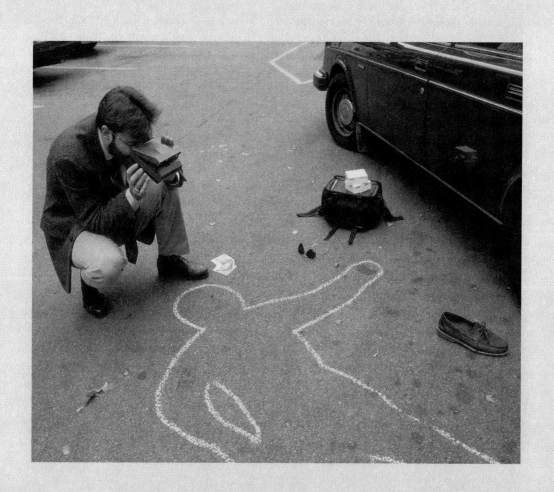

Chapter Outline

It don't matter what you say about gangbangin', you know, don't matter if anybody understand it or not. We just bringin' home the hate.

—A Los Angeles gang member, 1992

The 1990s in America have proved to be a time of particularly devastating violence. Just to take a couple of examples: In the spring of 1992, following the acquittal of several members of the Los Angeles Police Department on charges of savagely beating an African American motorist named Rodney King, hundreds of minorities in the inner city went on a rampage of rioting, arson, and looting. When the smoke cleared, 55 people had been killed, some 2,000 were seriously injured, and entire city blocks in South Central Los Angeles were in flames, resulting in more than $1 billion in property damage.

And just a few years later, a handful of disgruntled citizens, angry at various government agencies, loaded a large truck with a volatile mixture of chemical fertilizer and fuel oil, parked it in front of a federal office building in downtown Oklahoma City, and detonated it. The resulting explosion caused the structure to collapse on itself, killing 168 innocent people—including a roomful of young children at play in a day-care center housed on the second floor of the building.

In the aftermath of each of these tragic events, there was no shortage of explanations. Some members of Congress attributed the rioting to simple lawlessness. Others blamed it on grinding poverty. Former Vice-President Dan Quayle blamed it on a breakdown in "family values." Presidential spokesman Marlin Fitzwater laid the blame on frustration caused by the failure of the antipoverty programs initiated during a Democratic presidency some 25 years earlier. Democrats attributed it to 12 years of the neglect of inner cities and their residents by the Reagan and Bush administrations. After the Oklahoma City bombing, several commentators, including President Clinton, felt that part of the blame should be laid at the doorstep of certain talk-radio hosts who seemed to feed the anger and frustration of many citizens and direct it at a faceless government. Indeed, shortly before the tragedy in Oklahoma City, one popular talk-radio host, G. Gordon Liddy, had actually provided his listeners with detailed instructions for shooting federal employees.

What is aggression? What causes it? Are human beings instinctively aggressive? Can normal people be inspired to commit violence by the exhortations of a talk-radio host or by the example of violent characters on TV or in films? Can aggression be prevented or reduced? These are social psychological questions of the utmost importance.

Violence is certainly not a recent phenomenon. Indeed, it seems as though human beings have always been aggressive. When we reach back into ancient times, even to an era referred to as "the golden age of antiquity," when ancient Greece was graced by such humane and exciting thinkers as Socrates, Plato, Aristotle, Sophocles, and Aristophanes, there were nevertheless a great many barbarous wars in which tens of thousands were killed, cities were sacked, and noncombatant women and children were slaughtered, raped, or forced into slavery. Needless to say, human beings have progressed since then—but progress isn't always for the better. Along with our astonishing creativity has come the propensity to invent ever more efficient weapons of destruction; thus, the bloodiest war in history was fought just over five decades ago, when in the course of about seven years, an estimated 55 million human beings were killed. Current news broadcasts reverberate with stories of atrocities in Bosnia, Africa, and the Middle East. Moreover, these events are not confined to wars or riots. It is difficult to pick up a newspaper without learning of some dramatic example of aggressiveness, some gruesome event: A mass murderer in Tasmania or a mild-mannered loner in Milwaukee who habitually killed and devoured his acquaintances.

Most of us know that the majority of our fellow human beings are unlikely to engage in such extreme acts of cruelty. But putting aside extreme acts of cruelty, we are constantly bombarded by evidence of minor league aggressiveness even among the very young—for example, when we observe toddlers fighting over who owns which toys or when we notice the taunting that takes place in a typical school yard, as well as the fact that most children tend to settle their disputes by fighting rather than by reasoning. In a moment, we will examine the important questions of what causes aggression and how it might be reduced. But first, let's be sure we know what we mean by the term.

What Is Aggression?

Defining aggression is not as simple as it might seem, because in the vernacular, most people use the term very loosely. Social psychologists define **aggressive action** as behavior aimed at causing either physical or psychological pain. It is not to be confused with assertiveness—even though people sometimes loosely refer to others as "aggressive" if they stand up for their rights, write letters to the editor complaining about real or imagined injustices, work extra hard, display a great deal of ambition, or are real "go-getters." Similarly, in a sexist society a woman who simply speaks her mind or picks up the phone and makes the first move by inviting a male acquaintance to dinner might be called aggressive by some—but not by the authors of this book. Our definition is clear—aggression is an intentional action aimed at doing harm or causing pain. The action might be physical or verbal; it might succeed in its goal or not. It is still aggression. Thus, if someone throws a beer bottle at your head and you duck, so that the bottle misses your head, it is still an aggressive act. The important thing is the intention. By the same token, if someone is a careless driver and unintentionally runs you down while you're attempting to cross the street, that is not an act of aggression, even though the damage would be far greater than that caused by the beer bottle that missed.

It is also useful to distinguish between **hostile aggression** and **instrumental aggression.** Hostile aggression is the result of anger; the goal is solely to inflict pain or injury. In instrumental aggression, there is an intention to hurt the other person but this is done as a means to some other end. For example, in a professional football game, a defensive lineman will usually do whatever it takes to thwart his opponent (the offensive lineman) and ultimately tackle the ball carrier. This typically includes intentionally inflicting pain on his opponent if doing so is useful in helping him get the blocker out of the way so that he can get to the ball carrier. This is instrumental aggression. On the other hand, if he feels that his opponent has been playing dirty, he might become angry and go out of his way to hurt his opponent, even if doing so does not increase his opportunity to tackle the ball carrier. This is hostile aggression.

Is Aggression Inborn, or Is It Learned?

Scientists, philosophers, and other serious thinkers are not in complete agreement with one another about whether aggression is an innate, instinctive phenomenon or whether such behavior must be learned. This controversy is not new; it has been raging for centuries. For example, Thomas Hobbes, in his classic work *Leviathan* (first published in 1651), took the view that we human beings, in our natural state, are brutes and that only by enforcing the law and order of society could we curb what to Hobbes was a natural instinct toward aggression. On the other hand, Jean-Jacques Rousseau's concept of the noble savage (a theory he developed in 1762) suggested that we human beings, in our natural state, are benign, happy, and good creatures and that it is a restrictive society that forces aggression and depravity on us.

Hobbes's more pessimistic view was elaborated in the twentieth century by Sigmund Freud (1930), who theorized that human beings are born with an instinct toward life, which he called **Eros,** and an equally powerful death instinct, **Thanatos.** About the death instinct, Freud wrote: "It is at work in every living

aggressive action: a behavior aimed at causing either physical or psychological pain

hostile aggression: an act of aggression stemming from feelings of anger and aimed at inflicting pain

instrumental aggression: aggression as a means to some goal other than causing pain

Eros: the instinct toward life, posited by Freud

Thanatos: according to Freud, an instinctual drive toward death, leading to aggressive actions

hydraulic theory: the theory that unexpressed emotions build up pressure and must be expressed to relieve that pressure

being and is striving to bring it to ruin and to reduce life to its original condition of inanimate matter" (p. 67). Freud believed this aggressive energy must come out somehow, lest it continue to build up and produce illness. Freud's notion can best be characterized as a **hydraulic theory**—that is, the analogy is one of water pressure building up in a container: Unless aggression is allowed to drain off, it will produce some sort of explosion. According to Freud, society performs an essential function in regulating this instinct and in helping people to sublimate it—that is, to turn the destructive energy into acceptable or useful behavior.

Breeding Organisms for Aggression.   Much of the evidence on whether or not aggression is instinctive in human beings is based on the observation of and experimentation with species other than the human race. The idea behind this research is that if one can succeed in demonstrating that certain so-called instinctive aggressive behaviors in the lower animals are not rigidly preprogrammed, then surely aggression is not rigidly preprogrammed in human beings. For example, consider the prevalent belief about cats and rats. Among the general public, it is considered axiomatic that cats will instinctively stalk and kill rats. After all, don't all cats go after rats? Biologist Zing Yang Kuo (1961) attempted to demonstrate that this was a myth. And so he performed a simple little experiment: He raised a kitten in the same cage with a rat. What did he find? Not only did the cat refrain from attacking the rat, but the two became close companions. Moreover, when given the opportunity the cat refused either to chase or to kill other rats; thus, the benign behavior was not confined to his buddy but generalized to rats the cat had never met before.

While this experiment is charming, it fails to prove that aggressive behavior is not instinctive; it merely demonstrates that the aggressive instinct can be inhibited by early experience. What if an organism grows up without any experience with other organisms? Will it or won't it show normal aggressive tendencies?

> Man's inhumanity to man / Makes countless thousands mourn.
>
> –Robert Burns, *Man Was Made to Mourn*

Drawing by D. Reilly; © 1994 The New Yorker Magazine, Inc.

"What are you, anyway—an only child?"

Irenaus Eibl-Eibesfeldt (1963) showed that rats raised in isolation (i.e., without any experience in fighting other rats) will attack a fellow rat when one is introduced into the cage; moreover, the isolated rat uses the same pattern of threat and attack that experienced rats use. Thus, although aggressive behavior can be modified by experience (as shown by Kuo's experiment), Eibl-Eibesfeldt showed that aggression apparently does not need to be learned. On the other hand, one should not conclude from this study that aggression is necessarily instinctive, for, as John Paul Scott (1958) pointed out, in order to draw this conclusion there must be physiological evidence of a spontaneous stimulation for fighting that arises from within the body alone. The stimulus in Eibl-Eibesfeldt's experiment came from the outside—that is, the sight of a new rat stimulated the isolated rat to fight. Scott concluded from his survey of the evidence that there is no inborn need for fighting: If an organism can arrange its life so there is no outside stimulation to fight, then it will experience no physiological or mental damage as a result of not expressing aggression. This view contradicts Freud's contention and in effect asserts that there is no instinct of aggression.

The argument continues to go back and forth. Scott's conclusion was called into question by the Nobel Prize–winning ethologist Konrad Lorenz (1966), who observed the behavior of cichlids—highly aggressive tropical fish. Male cichlids will attack other males of the same species to establish and defend their territory. In its natural environment, the male cichlid does not attack female cichlids; nor does it attack males of a different species—it attacks only males of its own species. What happens if all other male cichlids are removed from an aquarium, leaving only one male alone with no appropriate target? According to the hydraulic theory of instinctive aggression (mentioned above), the need to aggress will build up to the point where the cichlid will attack a fish that doesn't usually serve as an appropriate stimulus for attack. And that is exactly what happens. In the absence of other males, the cichlid will attack males of other species—males it previously ignored. Moreover, if all other males are removed, the male cichlid will eventually attack and kill females.

More recently, Richard Lore and Lori Schultz (1993) have reported that the apparent universality of aggression among vertebrates strongly suggests that aggressiveness has evolved and been maintained because it has survival value. At the same time, these researchers are quick to point out that nearly all organisms also seem to have evolved strong inhibitory mechanisms that enable them to suppress aggression when it is in their best interests to do so. Thus, even in the most violence-prone species, aggression is an optional strategy—whether or not it is expressed is determined by the animal's previous social experiences, as well as by the specific social context in which the animal finds itself.

Aggressiveness Across Cultures

Social psychologists are in general agreement with the interpretation of the animal research offered by Lore and Schultz. And where humans are concerned, the social situation becomes even more important (Bandura, 1973; Lysak, Rule, & Dobbs, 1989; Baron & Richardson, 1992; Berkowitz, 1968, 1993). As Berkowitz (1993) has suggested, we human beings seem to have an inborn tendency to respond to certain provocative stimuli by striking out against the perpetrator. Whether or not the aggressive action is actually expressed is a function of a complex interplay between these innate propensities, a variety of learned inhibitory responses, and the precise nature of the social situation. For example, although it is true that many animals, from insects to apes, will usually attack another animal that invades their territory, it is a gross oversimplification to imply, as some popular writers have, that human beings are likewise programmed to protect their territory and behave aggressively in response to highly specific stimuli. Rather, much evidence supports the contention held by most social psychologists that, for humankind, innate patterns of behavior are infinitely modifiable and flexible. This is illustrated by the fact that human cultures vary widely in their degree of aggressiveness. For example, certain primitive tribes, such as the Lepchas of Sikkim, the Pygmies of Central Africa, and the Arapesh of New Guinea, live in apparent peace and harmony, wherein acts of aggression are extremely rare (see Baron & Richardson, 1992). Meanwhile, a few years ago in a more "civilized" society, our own government, already heavily in debt, spent billions of dollars on a brief military encounter against a relatively small and impoverished country in the Persian Gulf—killing tens of thousands in the process. In the aftermath of that brief war, the overwhelming majority of the citizens of the victorious country were pleased and proud of that accomplishment.

Aggression Among the Iroquois and in the South.   Within a given culture, changing social conditions frequently lead to striking changes in aggressive behavior. For example, for hundreds of years the Iroquois Indians lived in benign peacefulness as a hunting nation; they simply did not engage in aggressive behavior. But in the seventeenth century, barter with the newly arrived Europeans brought the Iroquois into direct competition with the neighboring Hurons over furs, which dramatically increased in value, because they could now be traded for manufactured goods. A series of skirmishes with the Hurons ensued, and within a short time the Iroquois developed into ferocious warriors. It would be hard to argue that they were spectacular warriors because of uncontrollable aggressive instincts; rather, their aggressiveness almost certainly came about because a social change produced increases in competition (Hunt, 1940).

In our own society, there are a great many regional differences in aggressive behavior and in the kinds of events that trigger violence. For example, Richard Nisbett and his colleagues have shown that homicide rates for white southern males are substantially higher than those for white northern males, especially in rural areas (Nisbett, 1993). But this is true only for "argument-related" homicides. Their surveys show that southerners do not endorse violence more than northerners do when survey questions are expressed in general terms but that southerners are more inclined to endorse violence for protection and in response to insults. This pattern suggests that the "culture of honor" may be characteristic of particular economic and occupational circumstances, including the herding society of the early South where protection of the herd is vital. Indeed, those areas of the South where herding is still pervasive continue to be the most violent.

To sum up, after reviewing all of these finding we believe that one cannot draw a firm conclusion—aggression may or may not have an instinctual component in human beings. But whether or not aggression has an instinctual component, we know that, in human beings as well as in the lower animals, aggression is not caused entirely by instinct—that there are important situational and social events that frequently lead to aggressive behavior. And even more importantly, we know that, in human beings, such behavior is infinitely modifiable by situational and social factors. In short, aggressive behavior can be changed. This makes the study of aggression a prime interest for social psychologists.

■ Although the Iroquois Indians have a reputation for being fierce warriors, they developed aggressive tendencies only after a change in their social situation was induced by increasing competition with another tribe.

Situational Causes of Aggression

Neural and Chemical Causes of Aggression

Some of the so-called situational causes of aggression result from situations inside the body. For example, an area in the core of the brain called the **amygdala** seems to control aggression, in human beings as well as in the lower animals. When that area is stimulated, docile organisms become violent; similarly, when neural activity in that area is blocked, violent organisms become docile (Moyer, 1976). But it should be noted that there is flexibility here also: The impact of neural mechanisms can be modified by social factors, even in subhumans. For example, if a male monkey is in the presence of other, less dominant monkeys, he will indeed attack the other monkeys when the appropriate area of his brain is stimulated. But if the same area is stimulated while the monkey is in the presence of more dominant monkeys, then he will not attack but will instead run away.

amygdala: an area in the core of the brain that is associated with aggressive behaviors

Testosterone.   Certain chemicals have been shown to influence aggression. For example, the injection of **testosterone,** a male sex hormone, will increase aggression in animals (Moyer, 1983). Among human beings, there is a parallel finding: Naturally occurring testosterone levels are significantly higher among prisoners convicted of violent crimes than among those convicted of nonviolent crimes. Interestingly enough, this is true for both male and female prisoners (Dabbs et al., 1988; Dabbs et al., 1995).

testosterone: a hormone associated with aggression

If testosterone level affects aggressiveness, does that mean men are more aggressive than women? Apparently so; in their exhaustive survey of research on children, Eleanor Maccoby and Carol Jacklin (1974) demonstrate convincingly—in dozens of laboratory experiments and field observations and in several cultures and across social classes—that boys are consistently more aggressive than girls. For example, in one study the investigators closely observed children at play in a variety of different cultures, including the United States, Switzerland, and Ethiopia. Among boys, there was far more "nonplayful" pushing, shoving, and hitting than among girls.

Similarly, among adults worldwide, the great majority of persons arrested for criminal offenses of all kinds are men. Further, when women are arrested, it is usually for property crimes (forgery, fraud, larceny), rather than for violent crimes (murder, aggravated assault). Are these differences due to biological differences or to social differences? We cannot be sure, but there is some evidence of a biological difference. Specifically, in our own country the enormous social changes affecting women during the past 35 years have not produced concomitant increases in the incidence of violent crimes committed by women relative to those committed by men. Women do commit non-violent crimes; when one looks at the comparative data between men and women involving nonviolent crimes, women have shown a far greater increase relative to that shown by men (Wilson & Herrnstein, 1985).

Needless to say, this should not be construed to mean that aggressiveness among women is unknown or even that it is rare but aggressiveness does appear to be less common among women than among men (Eagly & Steffen, 1986). Eagly and Steffen also found that when women do commit acts of aggression, they tend to feel more guilt or anxiety about such acts than men do. These investigators suggest that the actual differences between men and women, while consistent, are not great in an absolute sense. Nevertheless, it is the clarity and consistency of these gender differences that stand out—and should not be underestimated. The near universality of gender differences is bolstered by the results of a cross-cultural study recently reported by Dane Archer and Patricia McDaniel (1995). Archer and McDaniel asked teenagers from 11 countries to read stories involving conflict among people. The stories were interrupted prior to their resolution, and the teenagers were instructed to complete the story on their own. Archer and McDaniel found that, within each of the 11 countries, young men showed a greater tendency toward violent solutions to conflict than young women did. It is reasonably clear that biochemical differences between men and women are involved in these findings; it is also apparent that these findings are not due solely to biochemical differences. This point is nicely illustrated in the Archer and McDaniel study. While within a given culture men showed evidence of consistently higher levels of aggression than women, culture also played a major role. For example, women from Australia and New Zealand showed greater evidence of aggressiveness than men from Sweden and Korea did.

Alcohol. As most socially active college students know, alcohol tends to lower our inhibitions against committing behaviors frowned on by society, including acts of aggression (see Desmond, 1987; Taylor & Leonard, 1983). The linkage between the consumption of alcoholic beverages and aggressive behavior is a common observation. For example, we are well aware of the fact that fistfights frequently break out in bars and nightclubs and that family violence is often associated with the abuse of alcohol; in addition, the "belligerent drunk" is a cliché in films and on TV. A wealth of hard data support these casual observations and cultural clichés. For example, crime statistics reveal that 75 percent of those individuals arrested for murder, assault, and other crimes of violence were legally drunk at the time of their arrest (Shupe, 1954). In addition, controlled laboratory experiments demonstrate that when individuals ingest enough alcohol to make them legally drunk, they tend to respond more violently to provocations than those who have ingested little or no alcohol (Taylor & Leonard, 1983).

This does not mean that alcohol automatically increases aggression; people who have ingested alcohol are not necessarily driven to go around picking fights. Rather, the results of well-controlled laboratory experiments indicate that alcohol

"Oh, that wasn't me talking. It was the alcohol talking."

Drawing by Dana Fradon; ©1985 The New Yorker Magazine, Inc.

serves as a disinhibitor—that is, our social inhibitions are reduced; thus, under the influence of alcohol, a person's primary tendencies will be evoked, so that people prone to affection will become more affectionate and people prone to violence will become more aggressive. By the same token, after ingesting alcohol people who are subjected to social pressure to aggress or who are frustrated or provoked will experience fewer restraints or inhibitions to commit violent acts (Jeavons & Taylor, 1985; Steele & Josephs, 1990; Steele & Southwick, 1985; Taylor & Sears, 1988).

Pain and Discomfort as a Cause of Aggression

If an animal experiences pain and cannot flee the scene, it will almost invariably attack; this is true of rats, mice, hamsters, foxes, monkeys, crayfish, snakes, raccoons, alligators, and a host of others (Azrin, 1967; Hutchinson, 1983). Such animals will attack members of their own species, members of different species, or anything else in sight, including stuffed dolls and tennis balls. Do you think this is true of human beings as well? A moment's reflection might help you guess that it may very well be. Most of us have experienced becoming irritable when subjected to a sharp, unexpected pain (e.g., when we stub our toe) and hence being prone to lash out at the nearest available target. In a well-designed experiment, Leonard Berkowitz (1983, 1988) showed that students who underwent the pain of having their hand immersed in very cold water showed a sharp increase in their likelihood to aggress against another student.

By the same token, it has long been speculated that other forms of bodily discomfort, such as heat, humidity, air pollution, and offensive odors, might act to lower the threshold for aggressive behavior. During the late 1960s and early 1970s, when a great deal of tension existed in the United States concerning issues of national policy involving the war in Vietnam, racial injustice, and the like, national leaders worried a lot about a phenomenon they referred to as "the long, hot summer"—that is, the assumed tendency for riots and other forms of civic unrest to occur with greater frequency in the heat of summer than in the fall, winter, or spring. Was this actually true, or mere speculation? It turns out to be true. In a systematic analysis of disturbances occurring in 79 cities between 1967 and 1971, J. Merrill Carlsmith and Craig Anderson (1979) found that riots were far more likely to occur during hot days than during cool days. This is nicely illustrated in Figure 12.1, on the next page. Similarly, in major American cities, from Houston, Texas, to Des Moines, Iowa, the hotter it is on a given day, the greater the likelihood that violent crimes will occur (Anderson & Anderson, 1984; Cotton, 1981, 1986; Harries & Stadler, 1988; Rotton & Frey, 1985).

As the reader knows by this time, one has to be cautious about interpreting events that take place in natural settings. For example, the scientist in you might be tempted to ask whether increases in aggression are due to the temperature itself or merely to the fact that more people are apt to be outside (getting in one another's way!) on hot days than on cool or rainy days. And so how might we determine that it's the heat itself that caused the aggression, and not merely the greater opportunity for contact? We can bring the phenomenon into the laboratory. This is remarkably easy to do. For example, in one such experiment William Griffitt and Roberta Veitch (1971) simply administered a test to students, some of whom took it in a room with normal temperature, while others took it in a room where the temperature was allowed to soar to 90 degrees. The students in the hot room not only reported feeling more aggressive but also expressed more

FIGURE 12.1   The long, hot summer. ■ Warm temperatures increase the likelihood that violent riots and other aggressive acts will occur. (Adapted from Carlsmith & Anderson, 1979)

hostility to a stranger whom they were asked to describe and rate. Similar results have been reported by a number of investigators (Bell, 1980; Rule et al., 1987). Additional evidence from the natural world helps bolster our belief in the cause of this phenomenon. For example, it has been shown that in major league baseball games, significantly more batters are hit by pitched balls when the temperature is above 90 than when it is below 90 (Reifman, Larrick, & Fein, 1988). And in the desert city of Phoenix, Arizona, drivers without air-conditioned cars are more likely to honk their horns in traffic jams than drivers with air-conditioned cars are (Kenrick & MacFarlane, 1986).

Social Situations Leading to Aggression

Frustration as a Cause of Aggression.   Imagine your friend Sam is driving you to the airport so that you can take a plane home for the Christmas holidays. Sam is starting out a bit later than you feel comfortable with, but when you mention it, he accuses you of being overly anxious and assures you that he knows the route well and that you will arrive there with a good 30 minutes to spare. Halfway to your destination, Sam's car grinds to a halt in bumper-to-bumper traffic. You glance at your watch. Once again, Sam assures you that there is plenty of time—but this time you detect less confidence in his tone. After a few minutes, you notice that your palms are sweating and you are beginning to wring your hands. A few minutes later, you open the car door and survey the road ahead: nothing but gridlock as far as the eye can see. You get back in the car, slam the door, and glare at your friend. Sam smiles lamely and says, "How was I supposed to know there would be so much traffic?" Should he be prepared to duck?

Frustration occurs when a person is thwarted on the way to an expected goal or gratification. All of us have experienced some degree of frustration from time to time; indeed, it's unlikely we can get through a week without experiencing it. Research has shown that the experience of frustration can increase the probability of an aggressive response. This tendency is referred to as the **frustration-aggression theory.** As we shall see in a moment, this is not meant to imply that frustration always leads to aggression—but it frequently does, especially when the frustration is a decidedly unpleasant experience. In a classic experiment by Roger Barker, Tamara Dembo, and Kurt Lewin (1941), young children were shown a roomful of very attractive toys that were kept out of their reach. The children stood outside a wire screen looking at the toys—fully expecting to play with them—but were unable to reach them. After a painfully long wait, the children were finally allowed to play with the toys. In a control condition, a different group of children were allowed to play with the toys directly, without first being frustrated. This second group of children played joyfully with the toys. But the frustrated group, when finally given access to the toys, were extremely destructive: They tended to smash the toys, throw them against the wall, step on them, and so forth.

Several factors can accentuate this frustration and, accordingly, increase the probability that some form of aggression will occur. One such factor involves your closeness to the goal or the object of your desire. The greater the closeness, the greater the expectation of pleasure that is thwarted; the greater the expectation, the more likely the aggression. This was demonstrated in a field experiment by Mary Harris (1974), who instructed her confederate to cut in front of people who were waiting in line in a variety of places—for movie tickets, outside crowded restaurants, or at the checkout counter of a grocery store. On some occasions, the confederates were instructed to cut in front of the second person in line; on other occasions, they cut in front of the twelfth person in line. The results were clear: The responses of the people standing behind the intruder were much more aggressive when the confederate cut into the second place in line.

frustration-aggression theory: the theory that frustration—the perception that you are being prevented from obtaining a goal—will increase the probability of an aggressive response

■ Feelings of frustration can occur when we are blocked or delayed as we strive to reach a goal. For example, being stuck in a bad traffic jam can elicit aggressive responses, ranging from honking pointlessly to precipitating fistfights or even shootings.

Aggression also increases when the frustration is unexpected. James Kulik and Roger Brown (1979) hired students to telephone strangers and ask for donations to a charity. The students were hired on a commission basis—that is, they received a small fraction of each dollar pledged. Some of the students were led to expect a high rate of contributions; others, to expect far less success. The experiment was rigged so that none of the potential donors agreed to make a contribution. The experimenters found that the callers with high expectations directed more verbal aggression toward the nondonors, speaking more harshly and slamming down the phone with more force than the callers with low expectations.

As mentioned above, frustration does not always produce aggression. Rather, it seems to produce anger or annoyance and a readiness to aggress if other things about the situation are conducive to aggressive behavior (see Berkowitz, 1978, 1988, 1989, 1993; Gustafson, 1989). What are those other things? Well, one obvious other thing would be the size and strength of the person responsible for your frustration—as well as that person's ability to retaliate. It is undoubtedly easier to slam the phone down on a reluctant donor who is miles away and has no idea who you are than to take out your anger against your frustrator if he turned out to be the middle linebacker of the Chicago Bears and was staring you right in the face. Similarly, if the frustration is understandable, legitimate, and unintentional, it usually does not lead to aggression. For example, in an experiment by Eugene Burnstein and Philip Worchel (1962), when a confederate "unwittingly" sabotaged the problem solving of his groupmates because his hearing aid stopped working, the resulting frustration did not lead to aggression. In other words, most people, when frustrated, are better able to control their aggressive responses if the source of the frustration is a person trying to do his or her best.

We should also point out that frustration is not the same as deprivation. Children who simply don't have toys do not necessarily aggress. In the experiment by Barker and his colleagues, discussed above, frustration and aggression occurred because the children had every reason to expect to play with the toys, and that reasonable expectation was thwarted; this thwarting was what caused the children to behave destructively. In accord with this distinction, the Reverend Jesse Jackson (1981), with great insight, pointed out that the race riots of 1967 and 1968 occurred "in the middle of rising expectations and the increased, though inadequate, social spending." In short, Jackson was suggesting that thwarted expectations were largely responsible for the frustration and aggression. This is consistent with the earlier observations of psychiatrist Jerome Frank (1978), who pointed out that the most serious riots in this era occurred not in the geographic areas of greatest poverty but in Watts and Detroit, where things were not nearly so bad for blacks as they were in some other sections of the country. The point is that things were bad, relative to the blacks' perception of how white people were doing and relative to the positive changes many of the blacks had a right to expect. Thus, what causes aggression is not deprivation but **relative deprivation:** the feeling that comes from knowing that you have less than what you deserve, what you have been led to expect, or what people similar to you have.

A similar phenomenon occurred in Eastern Europe in 1991, when serious rebellion against the Soviet monolith took place only after the chains had been loosened somewhat. In the same vein, Primo Levi (1985, p. 203), a survivor of Auschwitz, contends that even in concentration camps the few instances of rebellion were performed not by the inmates at the very bottom of the camp totem

relative deprivation: the perception that you (or your group) have less than you deserve, less than you have been led to expect, or less than people similar to you have pole—the suffering victims of unrelenting horror—but "by prisoners who were privileged in some way."

To sum up this section, frustration does not automatically lead to aggression. And frustration is not simply the result of deprivation; it is the result of relative deprivation. It is reasonable to speculate that, as bad as things were, the citizens of Romania, Latvia, Estonia, and what was once Yugoslavia did not fully experience frustration until after they'd found reason to begin to hope for something better.

Direct Provocation and Reciprocation. There you are, at your part-time job behind the counter, flipping hamburgers in a crowded fast-food restaurant. You are working harder than usual, because the other short-order cook went home ill, and the customers are lining up at the counter, clamoring for their burgers. In your eagerness to speed up the process, you spin around too fast and knock over a large jar of pickles, which smashes on the floor just as the boss sticks his head in. "Boy, are you clumsy!" he yells at you. "I'm gonna dock your pay $10 for that one; grab a broom and clean that up! I'll take over here!" You glare at him. If looks could kill! You feel like throwing something at him or at least telling him what he can do with this lousy job!

One obvious cause of aggression stems from the need to reciprocate after being provoked by aggressive behavior from another person. While the Christian plea to "turn the other cheek" is wonderful advice, it is not an apt description of what most human beings in the world do. This has been illustrated in countless experiments in and out of the laboratory. Typical of this line of research is an experiment by Robert Baron (1988) in which subjects prepared an advertisement for a new product; their ad was then evaluated and criticized by an accomplice of the experimenter. In one condition, the criticism, while strong, was done in a gentle and considerate manner ("I think there's a lot of room for improvement"); in the other condition, the criticism was given in an insulting manner ("I don't think you could be original if you tried"). When provided with an opportunity to retaliate, subjects who were treated harshly were far more likely to do so than those in the "gentle" condition.

Just as occurs in our responses to frustration, we do not always reciprocate when provoked. One determinant of reciprocation is the intentionality of the provocation; if we think it was unintentional, most of us will not reciprocate (Kremer & Stephens, 1983). Similarly, if there are mitigating circumstances, counteraggression will not occur. But in order to be effective at curtailing an aggressive response, these mitigating circumstances must be known at the time of the provocation. This was neatly demonstrated in an experiment by Johnson and Rule (1986). Students were insulted by the experimenters' assistant, but half of them were first told that the assistant was upset after receiving an unfairly low grade on a chemistry exam, whereas the other students were given this information only after the insult was delivered. All subjects later had an opportunity to retaliate by choosing the level of unpleasant noise to zap the assistant with. Those students who knew about the mitigating circumstances before being insulted delivered less intense bursts of noise. How can we account for this difference? Apparently, at the time of the insult the informed students simply did not take it personally and therefore had no strong need to retaliate. This interpretation is bolstered by evidence of their physiological arousal: At the time of the insult, the heartbeat of the insulted students did not increase as rapidly if they knew about the assistant's unhappy state of mind beforehand.

> Nothing is more costly, nothing is more sterile, than revenge.
> –Winston Churchill (1874–1965)

Drawing by Peter Arno; © 1940 The New Yorker Magazine, Inc.

■ Does the finger pull the trigger, or does the trigger pull the finger?

"There's a burglar prowling in the Blue Room, sir. Would you care to have a crack at him before I notify the police?"

aggressive stimulus: an object that is associated with aggressive responses (e.g., a gun) and whose mere presence can increase the probability of aggression

Aggressive Objects as a Cause of Aggressive Behavior. As we have seen, we human beings are complex creatures. Our cognitive ability is awesome, enabling us to solve difficult problems by allowing us to make creative leaps. This same cognitive ability can, however, get us into trouble. In the realm of aggression, the mere presence of an **aggressive stimulus**—an object usually associated with aggression—can act in a way that increases the probability of an aggressive response. Our guess is that this would occur as a result of "priming" (discussed in Chapter 5), a process by which recent experiences tend to increase the availability of a schema or course of action.

In a classic experiment by Berkowitz and LePage (1967), college students were made angry. Some of them were made angry in a room in which a gun was left lying around (ostensibly from a previous experiment), and others were made angry in a room in which a neutral object (a badminton racket) was substituted for the gun. Subjects were then given the opportunity to administer some electric shocks to a fellow college student. Those individuals who had been made angry in the presence of the gun administered more intense electric shocks than those made angry in the presence of the badminton racket. The results are illustrated in Figure 12.2. This experiment is indeed provocative; it points to an opposite conclusion from the slogan often seen on bumper stickers—"Guns don't kill; people do." As Leonard Berkowitz (1981) puts it, "An angry person can pull the trigger of his gun if he wants to commit violence; but the trigger can also pull the finger or otherwise elicit aggressive reactions from him, if he is ready to aggress and does not have strong inhibitions against such behavior" (p. 12).

Does the presence of guns increase the aggressive behavior of people in the real world? We think so. Consider this tale of two cities: Seattle, Washington, and Vancouver, British Columbia, are virtually twin cities in a lot of ways; they have very similar climates, populations, economies, general crime rates, and rates of

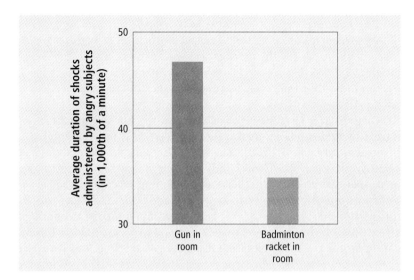

FIGURE 12.2   The trigger can pull the finger. ■ Aggressive cues, such as weapons, tend to increase levels of aggression. (Adapted from Berkowitz & LePage, 1967)

physical assault. They differ in two respects: (a) Vancouver severely restricts handgun ownership, while Seattle does not, and (b) the murder rate in Seattle is more than twice as high as that in Vancouver (Sloan et al., 1988). Is the one the cause of the other? We cannot be sure. But laboratory experiments by Berkowitz and his colleagues strongly suggest that the ubiquitous presence of that aggressive stimulus in the United States might be a factor. This is consistent with the findings of Dane Archer and Rosemary Gartner (1984), who, in a cross-national study of violence, found that the homicide rate in countries all over the world is highly correlated with the availability of handguns; Britain, for example, where hand-guns are banned, has one-fourth the population of the United States and one-sixteenth as many homicides.

In a large-scale follow-up study (discussed earlier in this chapter), Archer and his colleagues (Archer, 1994; Archer & McDaniel, 1995) asked teenagers from the United States and ten other countries to read stories involving conflict among people and to supply their own guess as to the outcome of the conflict. The data show that American teenagers were more likely to anticipate a violent conclusion to the conflict than teenagers from other countries were. Moreover, the violent conclusions drawn by American teenagers were far more likely to be "lethal, gun-laden and merciless" than those by teenagers in any of the other countries were (Archer, 1994, p. 19). The conclusions are undeniable: Lethal violence, especially involving guns, is simply a major part of American society—and therefore plays a major role in the expectations and fantasies of American youngsters.

Social Learning Theory: Imitation and Aggression.   A major cause of aggression is social learning. Children frequently learn to solve conflicts aggressively by imitating adults and their peers, especially when they see that the aggression is rewarded. For example, in most high-contact sports (e.g., football and hockey) it is frequently the case that the more aggressive players achieve the greatest fame (and the highest salaries) and the more aggressive teams win more games. In these sports, it usually doesn't pay to be a gentle soul—or, as famed baseball manager Leo Durocher once said, "Nice guys finish last!" The data

> Children have never been very good at listening to their elders, but they have never failed to imitate them.
> –James Baldwin, *Nobody Knows My Name*, 1961

bear him out. For instance, in one study it was found that among hockey players, those most frequently sent to the penalty box for overly aggressive play tended to be the ones who scored the most goals (McCarthy & Kelley, 1978). To the extent that athletes serve as role models for children and adolescents, what is being modeled might be that fame and fortune go hand in hand with excessive aggressiveness.

It is also the case that a large percentage of physically abusive parents were themselves abused by their own parents when they were kids (Silver, Dublin, & Lourie, 1969; Strauss & Gelles, 1980). The speculation is that when children experience aggressive treatment at the hands of their parents, they learn that violence is the proper way to socialize their own kids. But, of course, that is not the only conclusion one might draw from these family data. As mentioned earlier, aggressiveness may have a strong genetic component; if so, perhaps aggressive parents simply breed aggressive children. How can one determine whether or not imitation might be operating here? As you might guess, we could examine the phenomenon in the laboratory. In a classic series of experiments, Albert Bandura and his associates (1961, 1963) demonstrated the power of **social learning theory:** Simply seeing another person behave aggressively serves to increase the aggressive behavior of young children. The basic procedure in these studies was to have an adult knock around a plastic, air-filled "Bobo" doll (the kind that bounces back after it's been knocked down). The adult would smack the doll around with the palm of his or her hand, strike it with a mallet, kick it, and yell aggressive things at it. The kids were then allowed to play with the doll. In these experiments, the children imitated the aggressive models and treated the doll in a very abusive manner. Children in a control condition, who did not see the aggressive adult in action, almost never unleashed any aggression against the hapless doll. Moreover, the children who watched the aggressive adult used the same actions and the same aggressive words as the adult. In addition, many went beyond mere imitation—they also engaged in novel forms of aggressive behavior.

social learning theory: the theory that we learn social behavior (e.g., aggression) by observing others and imitating them

■ It is clear from the studies of Bandura and colleagues (1961, 1963) that children learn aggressive behavior through imitation and modeling.

The Effects of Watching Violence in the Media

Effects on Children.   If children can be influenced to imitate adult violence against a doll, what does this say about the effects of TV and movie violence on their behavior? This is an interesting question, with important societal implications. A number of long-term studies indicate that the more violence individuals watch on TV as children, the more violence they exhibit years later as teenagers and young adults (Eron, 1982, 1987; Huesmann, 1982; Turner et al., 1986). In a typical study of this kind, teenagers are asked to recall which shows they watched on TV when they were kids and how frequently they watched them; the shows are independently rated by judges as to how violent they are; and the general aggressiveness of the teenagers is independently rated by their teachers and classmates. Not only is there a high correlation between the amount of violent TV watched and the viewer's subsequent aggressiveness, but the impact also accumulates over time—that is, the strength of the correlation increases with age. While these are fairly powerful data, they do not definitively prove that watching a lot of violence on TV causes children to become violent teenagers. After all, it is at least conceivable that the aggressive kids were born with a tendency to enjoy violence and that this enjoyment manifests itself in both their aggressive behavior and their liking for watching violence on TV. Once again, we see the value of the controlled experiment in helping us to understand what causes what. In order to demonstrate conclusively that watching violence on TV actually causes violent behavior, the relationship must be shown experimentally.

Because this is an area of great importance to society, it goes without saying that it has been well researched. While not all of the research is consistent, the overwhelming thrust of the experimental evidence demonstrates that watching violence does indeed cause aggressive behavior in children (for a review, see Hearold, 1986; Wood et al., 1991). For example, in an early experiment on this issue, Robert Liebert and Robert Baron (1972) exposed a group of children to a television production of *The Untouchables*, an extremely violent cops-and-robbers type of program that was popular in the 1960s and 1970s. In a control

> Television has brought back murder into the home—where it belongs.
> –Alfred Hitchcock,
> *Observer*,
> December 19, 1965

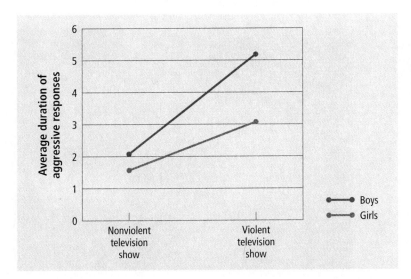

FIGURE 12.3   TV violence and aggression. ■ Being exposed to violence on TV increases aggressive behavior in children. (Adapted from Liebert & Baron, 1972)

condition, a similar group of children were exposed to a television production of an exciting but nonviolent sporting event for the same length of time. Each child was then allowed to play in another room with a group of other children. Those who had watched the violent television program showed far more aggression against their playmates than those who had watched the sporting event. The results of this experiment are depicted in Figure 12.3.

A subsequent experiment (Josephson, 1987) showed, as one might expect, that watching TV violence has the greatest impact on youngsters who are somewhat prone to violence to begin with. In this experiment, youngsters were exposed to either a film depicting a great deal of police violence or an exciting, nonviolent film about bike racing. The youngsters then played a game of floor hockey. Watching the violent film had the effect of increasing the number of aggressive acts committed during the hockey game—primarily by those youngsters who had previously been rated as highly aggressive by their teachers. These kids hit others with their sticks, threw elbows, and yelled aggressive things at their opponents to a much greater extent than either the kids rated as nonaggressive who had also watched the violent film or the kids rated as aggressive who had watched the nonviolent film. Thus, it may be that watching media violence in effect serves to give aggressive kids permission to express their aggression. Josephson's experiment suggests that youngsters who do not have aggressive tendencies to begin with do not necessarily act aggressively—at least, not on the basis of seeing only one violent film.

And that last phrase is an important one, because it may be that even youngsters who are not prone toward aggression will become more aggressive if exposed to a steady diet of violent film fare over a long period. And that is exactly what was found in a set of field experiments performed in Belgium by Phillippe Leyens and his colleagues (Leyens et al., 1975; Parke et al., 1977). In these experiments, different groups of children were exposed to differing amounts of media violence over a longer period than typically happens in the "one-shot" laboratory experiments described above. In these field experiments, the great majority of the kids (even those without strong aggressive tendencies) who were exposed to a high degree of media violence over a long period were shown to have a strong tendency to be more aggressive than those who watched more benign shows.

■ Does watching violence on TV promote violence and aggression in children? What about in adults?

■ Do violent sports events
increase homicide rates?

We might mention, in passing, that at a congressional hearing on TV violence
conducted in the summer of 1993, it was estimated that the average 12-year-old
has witnessed more than 100,000 acts of violence on television. We mention this
because we believe that one of the crucial factors involved in these findings (in
addition to social learning and imitation) is the simple phenomenon of priming.
That is, just as exposing children to rifles, knives, and other weapons left lying
around the house or the laboratory has a tendency to increase the probability of
an aggressive response when children subsequently experience pain or frustration, so too might exposing children to an endless supply of violence in films and
on TV have a similar tendency to prime an aggressive response.

What About Adults?   Thus far, in discussing the effects of media violence we
have focused much of our attention on children—and for good reason.
Youngsters are by definition much more malleable than adults—that is, it is
generally assumed that their attitudes and behaviors can be more deeply
influenced by the things they view. But the effect of media violence on violent
behavior may not be limited to children. On numerous occasions, adult violence
seems to be a case of life imitating art. For example, a few years ago a man drove
his truck through the window of a crowded cafeteria in Killeen, Texas, emerged
from the cab, and began shooting people at random. By the time the police
arrived, he had killed 22 people, making this the most destructive shooting spree
in American history. He then turned the gun on himself. In his pocket, police
found a ticket stub to *Fisher King,* a film depicting a deranged man firing a
shotgun into a crowded bar, killing several people.
    Did seeing the film cause the violent act? We cannot be sure. But we do know
that violence in the media can and does have a profound impact on the behavior
of adults. Several years ago, David Phillips (1983, 1986) performed an interesting
analysis of homicides in the United States. He simply scrutinized the daily homicide rates and found that they almost always increased during the week following
a heavyweight boxing match. Moreover, the more publicity surrounding the
fight, the greater the subsequent increase in homicides. Still more striking is that

the race of prizefight losers was related to the race of victims of murders after the fights. After white boxers lost fights, there was a corresponding increase in murders of white men but not of black men; conversely, after black boxers lost fights, there was a corresponding increase in murders of black men but not of white men. Phillips's results are convincing; they are far too consistent to be dismissed as merely a fluke. Again, this should not be construed as indicating that all people or even a sizable percentage of people are motivated to commit violence through watching media violence. But the fact that some people are influenced—and that the results can be tragic—cannot be denied.

The Numbing Effect of TV Violence.   It seems to be the case that repeated exposure to horrifying events has a numbing effect on our sensitivity to those events. One of the authors of this book, Elliot Aronson, offers the following personal example:

> Several years ago, I moved to Manhattan for a few months. Soon after my arrival, I was walking down Fifth Avenue with a friend who is a native New Yorker. I was struck and touched by the great number of obviously homeless people, living in cardboard boxes, carrying their meager possessions in paper bags or wheeling them around in broken-down supermarket shopping carts. I was both deeply moved and appalled. All during our walk, I kept reaching into my pockets and dropping coins into the hands of those unfortunate souls. My friend was appalled at my behavior. "You'll have to learn to ignore these people," my friend said. "Never," I replied, indignantly and self-righteously. Yet sure enough, within a few weeks I found myself walking down the streets of Manhattan staring straight ahead and keeping my hands out of my pockets. Amazingly, I had gotten so accustomed to the sight that, for all intents and purposes, I had become virtually indifferent to it.

Is it possible that, by a similar process, being constantly exposed to violence on TV tends to make people more tolerant of real violence? There is good evidence that this is so. In one experiment, Victor Cline and his associates (1973) measured the physiological responses of several young men while they were watching a rather brutal and bloody boxing match. Those who watched a lot of TV in their daily lives seemed relatively indifferent to the mayhem in the ring—that is, they showed little physiological evidence of excitement, anxiety, or the like. They treated the violence in a lackadaisical manner. On the other hand, those who typically watched relatively little TV underwent major physiological arousal. The violence really got to them. In a related vein, Margaret Hanratty Thomas and her colleagues (1977) demonstrated that viewing television violence can subsequently numb people's reactions when they are faced with real-life aggression. Thomas had her subjects watch either a violent police drama or an exciting but nonviolent volleyball game. After a short break, they were allowed to observe a verbally and physically aggressive interaction between two preschoolers. Those who had watched the police show responded less emotionally than those who had watched the volleyball game. It seems that viewing the initial violence served to desensitize them to further acts of violence—they were not upset by an incident that by all rights should have upset them. While such a reaction may psychologically protect us from upset, it may also have the unintended effect of increasing our indifference to victims of violence and perhaps render us more accepting of violence as a necessary aspect of life in the modern era.

Death has been tidied up, cleansed of harmful ingredients, and repackaged in prime-time segments that pander to baser appetites but leave no unpleasant aftertaste. The Caesars of network television permit no mess on the living room floor.

–Donald Goddard,
New York Times,
February 27, 1977

Why Does Media Violence Affect Viewers' Tendencies to Aggress?   As suggested throughout this section, there are four distinct reasons that exposure to violence via the media might increase aggression:

1. **"If they can do it, so can I."** When people watch characters on TV expressing violence, it might simply weaken their previously learned inhibitions against violent behavior.

2. **"Oh, so that's how you do it!"** When people watch characters on TV expressing violence, it might trigger imitation, providing them with ideas as to how they might go about it.

3. **"I think it must be aggressive feelings that I'm experiencing."** There is a sense in which watching violence makes feelings of anger more easily available and makes an aggressive response more likely simply through priming. Thus, an individual might erroneously construe his or her own feelings of mild irritation as anger—and might be more likely to lash out.

4. **"Ho-hum, another brutal beating; what's on the other channel?"** Watching a lot of mayhem seems to reduce both our sense of horror about violence and our sympathy for the victims, thereby making it easier for us to live with violence and perhaps easier for us to act aggressively.

Violent Pornography and Violence Against Women

A particularly troubling aspect of aggression in this country is the staggering increase in reports of violence expressed by some men against women—especially in the form of rape. In 1990, approximately 103,000 American women were known to have been raped. This is more than one rape every five minutes. According to the FBI, the number of reported rapes has increased fourfold since the mid–1960s. The actual occurrences are obviously much higher, since a great many rapes go unreported, particularly those involving "date rape," in which the victim is acquainted with the assailant.

Coincidental with the increase in rape during the past few decades has been an increase in the availability of magazines, films, and videocassettes depicting vivid, explicit sexual behavior. For better or worse, in recent years our society has become increasingly freer and more tolerant of pornography. If viewing violence in films and on television contributes to violence, doesn't it follow that viewing pornographic material could increase the incidence of rape? Although this possibility has been presented as an undeniable fact by some of our nation's self-appointed guardians of our morality, it turns out to be incorrect. In 1970, after carefully studying all the evidence, the Presidential Commission on Obscenity and Pornography concluded that explicit sexual material, in and of itself, does not contribute to sexual crimes, violence against women, or other antisocial acts. But as you will recall, in Chapter 2 we discussed the fact that in 1985, Edwin Meese, while serving as Ronald Reagan's attorney general, convened a commission that disagreed with the findings of the earlier report and concluded that pornography does indeed contribute to violent crimes against women. Which commission was right? Or were both right—that is, was new evidence uncovered during the intervening 15 years that led the Meese Commission to a different conclusion?

After carefully analyzing the available evidence, we can find no foundation for the conclusions drawn by the Meese Commission. Rather, those conclusions appear to have been politically and ideologically motivated, rather than the result of dispassionate scientific inquiry. This is not to say that the issue is simple, for it

7/18/73

AN ORGY OF BLOOD! EXPLICIT TORTURE HORROR

TERROR

THE DISEMBOWELED CORPSE OF SCREAMING MANOR

EXQUISITE MAIMING!

NOW SHOWING

SHOWS AT

RATED G

I PITY THE CAT WHEN HE GETS HOME!

"AT LAST, A MOVIE WITHOUT ALL THOSE FILTHY SEX SCENES!"

■ In the United States, we try to protect children from erotic films. But research shows that violent films are much more harmful.

is not. Indeed, the reader should note that the key phrase in our description of the findings of the 1970 report is "in and of itself." That is, now as in 1970, we would conclude that viewing explicit sexual material, in and of itself, is harmless. But we would also conclude that there are clearly undesirable effects caused by viewing materials that combine sex with violence. During the past several years, Neil Malamuth, Edward Donnerstein, and their colleagues have conducted careful studies, both in naturalistic and laboratory settings, to determine the effects of violent pornography. Taken as a whole, these studies indicate that exposure to violent pornography promotes greater acceptance of sexual violence toward women and is almost certainly a factor associated with actual aggressive behavior toward women (Donnerstein, 1980; Donnerstein & Berkowitz, 1981; Malamuth, 1981, 1986; Malamuth & Briere, 1986). In one experiment (Donnerstein & Berkowitz, 1981), male subjects were angered by a female accomplice. They were then shown one of three films—an aggressive-erotic one involving rape, a purely erotic one without violence, or a film depicting nonerotic violence against women. After viewing one of these films, the men took part in a supposedly unrelated experiment that involved teaching the female accomplice by means of administering electric shocks to her whenever she gave incorrect answers. They were also allowed to choose whatever level of shock they wished to use. (Needless to say, no shocks were actually received.) Those men who had earlier seen the violent pornographic film subsequently administered the most intense shocks; those who had seen the pornographic but nonviolent film administered the lowest level of shocks. There is also evidence showing that, under these conditions, subjects who view violent pornographic films will administer more intense shocks to a female confederate than to a male confederate (Donnerstein, 1980).

Similarly, Neil Malamuth (1981) conducted an experiment in which male college students viewed one of two erotic films. One version portrayed two mutually consenting adults engaged in lovemaking; the other version portrayed a rape incident. After viewing the film, the men were asked to engage in sexual fantasy. Those men who had watched the rape version of the film created more violent sexual fantasies than those who had watched the mutual consent version.

Further, just as we saw with violence, prolonged exposure to depictions of sexual violence against women (so-called slasher films) makes viewers more accepting of this kind of violence and less sympathetic toward the victim (Linz, Donnerstein, & Penrod, 1984, 1988; Zillmann & Bryant, 1984). Interestingly, this applies to female viewers as well as male viewers. Again, it should be underscored that these experiments do not support the conclusion of the Meese Commission. That is, there is no evidence indicating that scenes depicting sexual behavior between consenting adults cause any harm. These experiments make it clear that it is only the films depicting explicit sexual violence against women that produce measurable harmful effects.

How to Reduce Aggression

Does Punishing Aggression Reduce Aggressive Behavior?

Much folk wisdom is aimed at the curbing of overly aggressive behavior. It is important to scrutinize this wisdom and, where possible, subject it to objective scientific inquiry. For example, "Spare the rod, and spoil the child," the old saying goes. Following on that advice, if your little boy tends to aggress—especially against younger, smaller children—then give him a sound spanking and he will soon learn not to aggress. By the same token, if we increase the penalties for aggression in this society—say, by adding decades to the aggressor's prison term or even by invoking the death penalty—this might be a great way to reduce aggression. Or would it?

Punishment is a complex event, especially as it relates to aggression. On the one hand, one might guess that punishing any behavior, including aggression, might reduce its frequency. On the other hand, since severe punishment itself usually takes the form of an aggressive act, then the punisher is actually modeling aggressive behavior for the person whose aggressive behavior he or she is trying to stamp out and might induce that person to imitate the action. This seems to be true—for children. As we have seen earlier in this chapter, children who grow up with punitive, aggressive parents tend to be prone toward violence when they grow up.

> All punishment is mischief; all punishment itself is evil.
> –Jeremy Bentham,
> *Principles of Morals and Legislation*

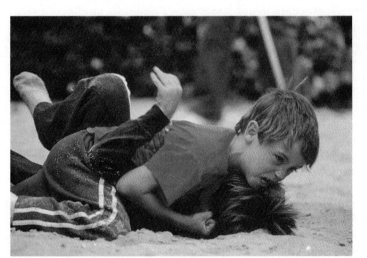

■ If a parent wants to curb the aggression of his or her child, threats of severe punishment will have only a temporary effect.

Moreover, as we saw in Chapter 3, several experiments with children in kindergarten have demonstrated that the threat of relatively severe punishment for committing a transgression has little impact on diminishing the attractiveness of the transgression. On the other hand, the threat of mild punishment—of a degree just powerful enough to get the child to cease the undesired activity temporarily—serves to induce the child to try to justify his or her restraint and, as a result, can produce a diminution in the attractiveness of the action (Aronson & Carlsmith, 1963; Freedman, 1965). Recently, David Olweus (1991), working in the Norwegian school system, was able to sharply curtail the prevalence of bullying behavior by as much as 50 percent by training teachers and administrators to be vigilant to the problem and to make reasonable and swift interventions. This research indicates that children, who have not yet formed their values, are more apt to develop a distaste for aggression if the punishment for aggressive actions is swift and not severe.

But what about adults, especially those who already manifest a tendency to commit aggressive acts? Here a slightly different picture emerges. On a societal level, the criminal justice system of most cultures administers harsh punishments as a means of deterring violent crimes. Does the implicit threat of harsh punishments for crimes like murder, manslaughter, and rape diminish the occurrence of such crimes? Do people who are about to commit such crimes say to themselves, "I'd better think twice about this, because if I get caught, I'll be severely punished"? Here the scientific evidence is mixed. Under ideal conditions, laboratory experiments indicate that punishment can act as a deterrent (Bower & Hilgard, 1981). By "ideal conditions," we mean that the punishment must be both very prompt and virtually certain; that is, it must come close on the heels of the commission of the violent act, and the chances of escaping punishment must be very remote. Alas, these ideal conditions are almost never met in the real world, especially in a complex society with a high crime rate like our own. In most American cities, the probability of a person committing a violent crime and being apprehended, charged, tried, and convicted is not high. Moreover, given the clogged calendars that exist in our courts, as well as the necessary care and caution with which the criminal justice system must operate, promptness is rarely possible—punishment is typically delayed by months or even years. Consequently, in the real world of the criminal justice system, severe punishment is unlikely to have the kind of deterrent effect that it does in the laboratory.

And indeed, the societal data indicate that severe punishment does not seem to deter violent crimes. For example, countries that invoke the death penalty for murder do not have fewer murders per capita than those that do not invoke the death penalty; similarly, within our own country, states that have abolished the death penalty have not experienced the increase in capital crimes that some experts predicted (Archer & Gartner, 1984; Nathanson, 1987). In a similar vein, Ruth Peterson and William Bailey (1988) examined a period in our nation just after a national hiatus on the death penalty, resulting from a Supreme Court ruling that found it to constitute cruel and unusual punishment; when the Court reversed itself in 1976, there was no indication that the return to capital punishment produced a decrease in homicides. Some representative homicide data, comparing the United States with other countries, are shown in Figure 12.4.

Similarly, a recent study by the National Academy of Sciences (quoted in Berkowitz, 1993) demonstrates that consistency and certainty of punishment are far more effective deterrents of violent behavior than severe punishment and do have a deterrent effect on violent crime. Similarly, in the realm of domestic

> Something of vengeance I had tasted for the first time; an aromatic wine it seemed, on swallowing, warm and racy; its after-flavour, metallic and corroding, gave me a sensation as if I had been poisoned.
> —Charlotte Brontë, *Jane Eyre*, 1847

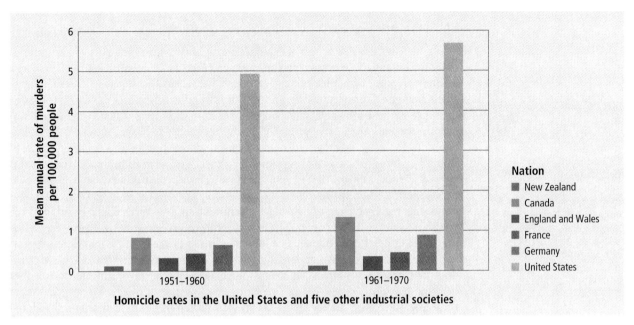

FIGURE 12.4   America leads the way. ■ The homicide rate in the United States far outstrips that of other industrial countries. (Adapted from Archer & Gartner, 1984)

violence, or, more specifically, wife-battering, mild punishment, consistently meted out, has been effective, at least in the short term. Domestic violence has been a thorny problem for the police, who traditionally have been reluctant to intervene in family disputes. In the past, when the police have intervened in a wife-battering situation, they would almost never arrest the husband but instead would either give him on-the-spot counseling or ask him to leave the scene for a few hours until he cooled off.

How effective is this kind of intervention? Would arresting the violent husband be more effective? To find out, the Minneapolis Police Department conducted a simple but powerful field experiment (Sherman & Berk, 1984). In this experiment, police officers were randomly assigned to one of three conditions: In the first condition, they performed brief, on-the-spot counseling; in the second condition, they asked the perpetrator to leave the scene for eight hours; and in the third condition, they placed the perpetrator under arrest. Police reports were then carefully monitored over the next six months. The results indicated that, during those months, 19 percent of the perpetrators given counseling and 24 percent of those asked to leave the premises repeated their aggressive actions, whereas only 10 percent of those placed under arrest (and made to spend a night or two in jail) repeated their actions. These data show that when law enforcement officers demonstrate they are taking the offense seriously by hauling the perpetrator off to jail, domestic violence is diminished. The findings led the Minneapolis Police Department to revamp its policies regarding the arrest of perpetrators of domestic violence and have attracted national attention. Unfortunately, subsequent research reported by Langer (1986) and Sherman (1992) suggests that the deterrent effects of this procedure tend to diminish over time. More detailed research is needed to determine the ideal conditions for long-term results.

Catharsis and Aggression

It is generally believed that one way for an individual to reduce his or her feelings of aggression is to do something aggressive. "Get it out of your system" has been a common piece of advice for a great many years. And so if you are feeling angry (the belief goes), don't try to ignore it, but instead yell, scream, curse, throw some crockery at the wall—and then you'll be rid of it and it won't fester and grow into something truly uncontrollable. This common belief is based on an oversimplification of the psychoanalytic notion of **catharsis** (see Freud, 1933; Dollard, 1939) that has filtered down to the popular culture. As we mentioned earlier in this chapter, Freud held a "hydraulic" idea of aggressive impulses; he believed that unless people were allowed to express their aggression in relatively harmless ways, the aggressive energy would be dammed up, pressure would build, and the energy would seek an outlet, either exploding into acts of extreme violence or manifesting itself as symptoms of mental illness. There is some evidence suggesting that stifled feelings can produce illness (Pennebaker, 1990). However, this does not necessarily mean that venting those feelings indiscriminately is either healthy or useful. Freud was a brilliant and complex thinker who stopped short of giving simplistic advice. Alas, as the simplified version of his theory filtered down to the popular culture, it took on the mantle of established fact; thus, by the time catharsis theory found its way to famed advice columnist Ann Landers (1969), it translated itself into the pronouncement that "Youngsters should be taught to vent their anger." The idea behind this advice is that blowing off steam will not only make angry people feel better but also serve to make them less likely to engage in subsequent acts of destructive violence.

On a superficial level, this seems to square with our own experience. Many of us, when frustrated or angry, have felt less tense when we have "blown off steam" by yelling, cursing, or perhaps even hitting someone. But does an act of aggression reduce the need for further aggression? Before we try to answer that question, let's first consider some of the ways in which aggressive energy could

catharsis: the notion that "blowing off steam"—by performing an aggressive act, watching others engage in aggressive behaviors, or engaging in a fantasy of aggression—relieves built-up aggressive energies and hence reduces the likelihood of further aggressive behavior

■ Fans watching aggressive sports do not become less aggressive.

conceivably be discharged: (a) by expending it in the form of physical activity (e.g., playing competitive games), (b) by watching other people engage in aggressive play and thus vicariously discharging aggressive energy, and (c) by engaging in direct aggression (e.g., lashing out at someone, hurting the person, getting the person into trouble, saying nasty things about him or her).

Let's take the first one: engaging in socially acceptable aggressive behavior like football or boxing. There is widespread belief—even among professional psychologists—that this procedure is effective. For example, William Menninger (1948), the distinguished therapist and cofounder of the justly famous Menninger Clinic, tells us that "competitive games provide an unusually satisfactory outlet for the instinctive aggressive drive" (p. 344). It would be great if it were that simple. Alas, we can find no evidence to support this contention. In fact, a field study by Arthur Patterson (1974) leads to quite the opposite conclusion. He measured the hostility of high school football players, rating them both one week before and one week after the football season. If it is true that the intense competitiveness and aggressive behavior that are part of playing football serve to reduce the tension caused by pent-up aggression, then the players could be expected to exhibit a decline in hostility over the course of the season. Instead, the results of the measures showed a significant increase in feelings of hostility. Similarly, in a detailed study of college athletes Warren Johnson (1970) found no evidence to support the notion of catharsis. This is not to say that people do not get pleasure out of these games; they do. But engaging in these games does not decrease participants' aggressive feelings—if anything, it increases them.

Even though engaging in competitive and aggressive games does not result in less aggression, perhaps watching these kinds of games does. Gordon Russell (1983), a Canadian sports psychologist, tested this proposition by measuring the hostility of spectators at an especially violent hockey game. As the game progressed, the spectators became increasingly belligerent; toward the end of the final period, their level of hostility was enormous and did not return to the pregame level until several hours after the game was over. Similar results have been found among spectators at football games and wrestling matches (Arms, Russell, & Sandilands, 1979; Goldstein & Arms, 1971). Thus, as with participating in an aggressive sport, watching one serves to increase aggressive behavior.

Now let's take a look at research on acts of direct aggression against the source of your anger. Do such actions reduce the need for further aggression? The overwhelming majority of experiments on the topic have failed to find such effects (see Geen & Quanty, 1977). In fact, by far the most common finding resembles the research on watching violence, as cited above—namely, when people commit acts of aggression, such acts increase the tendency toward future aggression. For example, in an experiment by Russell Geen and his associates (1975), each of the subjects in their experiment (male college students) was paired with another student, who was actually a confederate of the experimenters. First, the subject was angered by the confederate; during this phase, which involved the exchanging of opinions on various issues, the subject was given electric shocks when his partner disagreed with his opinion. Next, during a bogus study of "the effects of punishment on learning," the subject acted as a teacher, while the confederate served as learner. On the first learning task, some of the subjects were required to deliver electric shocks to the confederate each time he made a mistake; other subjects merely recorded his errors. On the next task, all the subjects were given the opportunity to deliver shocks. If a cathartic effect were operating, we would expect the subjects who had previously given shocks to the confederate to administer fewer and less intense shocks the second time. This didn't happen; in fact, the subjects who had previously delivered shocks to the confederate expressed even greater aggression when given the subsequent opportunity to attack him. This phenomenon is not limited to the laboratory; the same tendency has also been systematically observed in naturally occurring events in the real world, where verbal acts of aggression served to facilitate further attacks. In one such "natural experiment," several technicians who had recently been laid off were given a chance to verbalize their hostility against their ex-bosses; later, when asked to describe that person, these technicians were much more punitive in their descriptions than those technicians who had not previously voiced their feelings (Ebbesen, Duncan, & Konecni, 1975). In summary, the weight of the evidence does not support the catharsis hypothesis.

Again, on the surface, it appears to be a reasonable idea, in a limited way. That is, when somebody angers us, venting our hostility against that person does indeed seem to relieve tension and make us feel better. But "feeling better" should not be confused with a reduction in our hostility. With human beings, aggression is dependent not merely on tensions—what a person feels—but also on what a person thinks. Put yourself in the place of a subject in the previous experiments: After once administering shocks to another person or expressing hostility against your old boss, it becomes easier to do so a second time. Aggressing the first time can reduce your inhibitions against committing other such actions; in a sense, the aggression is legitimized, making it easier to carry out such assaults. Further, and more importantly, the main thrust of the research on this issue indicates that committing an overt act of aggression against a person changes one's feelings about that person, increasing one's negative feelings toward the target and therefore increasing the probability of future aggression against that person.

Does this material begin to sound familiar? It should. As we have seen in Chapter 6, when one person does harm to another person, it sets in motion cognitive processes aimed at justifying the act of cruelty. Specifically, when you hurt another person, you experience cognitive dissonance. The cognition "I have hurt Charlie" is dissonant with the cognition "I am a decent, reasonable person." A good way for you to reduce dissonance is somehow to convince yourself that hurting Charlie was not an indecent, unreasonable, bad thing to do. You can accomplish this by blinding yourself to Charlie's virtues and emphasizing his faults, by convincing yourself that Charlie is a terrible human being who deserved to be hurt. This would especially hold if the target was an innocent victim of your aggression. Thus, as discussed in Chapter 6, in experiments by David Glass (1964) and by Keith Davis and Edward E. Jones (1960) the subjects inflicted either psychological or physical harm on an innocent person who had done them no prior harm. The subjects then proceeded to derogate their victims, convincing themselves they were not very nice people and therefore deserved what they got. This reduces dissonance, all right—and it also sets the stage for further aggression, for once a person has succeeded in derogating someone, it makes it easier for him or her to do further harm to the victim in the future.

What happens if the victim isn't totally innocent? That is, imagine the victim has done something that hurts or disturbs you and is therefore deserving of your retaliation. Here the situation becomes more complex and more interesting. One of several experiments to test this idea was performed several years ago by

> In war, the state is sanctioning murder. Even when the war is over, this moral corruption is bound to linger for many years.
>
> –Erasmus, 1514

Michael Kahn (1966). In Kahn's experiment, a young man posing as a medical technician, taking some physiological measurements from college students, made derogatory remarks about the students. In one experimental condition, the subjects were allowed to vent their hostility by expressing their feelings about the technician to his employer—an action that looked as though it would get the technician into serious trouble, perhaps even cost him his job. In another condition, the subjects were not given the opportunity to express any aggression against the person who had aroused their anger. Those who were allowed to express their aggression subsequently felt greater dislike and hostility for the technician than those who were inhibited from expressing their aggression did. In other words, expressing aggression did not inhibit the tendency to aggress; rather, it tended to increase it—even when the target was not simply an innocent victim.

These results suggest that when people are made angry, they frequently engage in overkill. In this case, costing the technician his job is much more devastating than the minor insult delivered by the technician. The overkill produces dissonance in much the same way hurting an innocent person produces dissonance. That is, if there is a major discrepancy between what the person did to you and the force of your retaliation, you must justify that discrepancy by derogating the object of your wrath.

If our reasoning is correct, it might help to explain why it is that when two nations are at war, a relatively small percentage of the members of the victorious nation feel much sympathy for the innocent victims of the nation's actions. For example, near the end of World War II, American planes dropped atom bombs on Hiroshima and Nagasaki. More than 100,000 civilians—including a great many

■ During World War II, we derogated the Japanese by depicting them as less than human. This helped to justify our own destructiveness—as in the bombing of Nagasaki.

children—were killed, and countless thousands suffered severe injuries. Shortly thereafter, a poll taken of the American people indicated that less than 5 percent felt we should not have used those weapons, whereas 23 percent felt we should have used many more of them before giving Japan the opportunity to surrender. Why would so many Americans favor the wanton death and destruction of innocent victims? Our guess is that, in the course of the war, a sizable proportion of Americans gradually adopted increasingly derogatory attitudes toward the Japanese that made it increasingly easy to accept the fact that we were causing them a great deal of misery. And the more misery we inflicted on them, the more these Americans derogated them—leading to an endless spiral of aggression and the justification of aggression, even to the point of favoring a delay in the ending of the war so that still more destruction might be inflicted.

Does this sound like ancient history? We hasten to remind you that, in this decade, our nation won a swift and stunning victory over Iraq in a lopsided war in which American casualties were few but tens of thousands of Iraqis—including numerous civilians—lost their lives. The vast majority of U.S. citizens were elated by the outcome of the war; there were celebrations, parades, and a huge—if temporary—increase in the popularity of former President George Bush. Please note that we are not raising the question of whether or not the war was just or necessary. The only question we are raising is this: What percentage of the American population do you suppose paused for a few moments to feel sadness or regret about the Iraqi civilians who were killed in that war? The polls indicate very little sympathy for the innocent victims. How come? Are we a particularly callous, unsympathetic nation? We don't believe so. You now have the tools to begin to understand the mechanics of how that phenomenon comes about.

Interestingly, when a nation is at war the impact of that situation extends even beyond feelings of hostility toward the enemy. Specifically, being at war makes the population—even the noncombatants—more prone to commit aggressive actions against one another. Dane Archer and Rosemary Gartner (1976, 1984) compared the crime rates for 110 countries since 1900 (see Figure 12.5). They found that, compared with similar nations that remained at peace, countries that fought wars exhibited substantial postwar increases in their homicide rates. This should not be surprising; it is consistent with everything we have been

> **To jaw-jaw is better than to war-war.**
> –Winston Churchill, 1954

FIGURE 12.5   The effects of war on combatants versus noncombatants. ■ Immediately after a war, combatant countries are more likely to show an increase in violent crimes than countries not involved in a war. How would you explain this? (Adapted from Archer & Gartner, 1976)

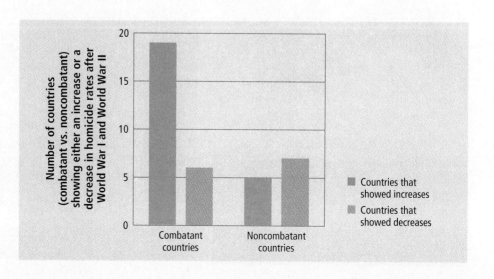

saying about the social causes of aggression. In a sense, when a nation is at war it's like one big, all-pervasive, violent TV drama. Thus, just as with overexposure to TV violence, the fact that a nation is at war (a) weakens the population's inhibitions against aggression, (b) leads to imitation of aggression, (c) makes aggressive responses more available, and (d) numbs our senses to the horror of cruelty and destruction, making us less sympathetic toward the victims. In addition, being at war serves to legitimize to the population the use of violent solutions to address difficult problems.

What Are We Supposed to Do with Our Anger?

Venting Versus Self-Awareness. If violence leads to self-justification, which in turn breeds more violence, then if we are feeling angry at someone, what are we to do with our angry feelings—stifle them? Surely, Sigmund Freud and Ann Landers were not totally wrong when they indicated that stifled anger might be harmful to the individual. Indeed, as mentioned earlier, recent research suggests that stifling powerful emotions can lead to physical illness (Pennebaker, 1990). But if it is harmful to keep our feelings bottled up and harmful to express them, what are we supposed to do with them? This dilemma isn't as difficult as it might seem. We would suggest that there is an important difference between being angry and expressing that anger in a violent and destructive manner. To experience anger in appropriate circumstances is normal and almost invariably harmless. It is certainly possible to express that anger in a nonviolent manner— for example, by making a clear and simple statement indicating that you are feeling angry and why. Indeed, such a statement in itself is a vehicle for self-assertion and probably serves to relieve tension and to make the angered person feel better. At the same time, because no actual harm befalls the target of your anger, such a response does not set in motion the cognitive processes that would lead you to justify your behavior by ridiculing or derogating the target person. Moreover, when such feelings are expressed among friends or acquaintances in a clear, open, nonpunitive manner, greater mutual understanding and a strengthening of the friendship can result. It almost seems too simple. Yet we have found such behavior to be a reasonable option that will have more beneficial effects than shouting, name-calling, and throwing crockery, on the one hand, or suffering in silence as you grin and bear it, on the other.

> I was angry with my friend: I told my wrath, my wrath did end.
> –William Blake
> (1757–1827)

While it is probably best to reveal your anger to the friend who caused it, you may also derive some benefit from sharing your anger with a third party. Although he did not work specifically with anger, the research of James Pennebaker (1990) indicates that when we are experiencing emotional stress, it is helpful to reveal that emotion to another person. In Pennebaker's experiments with people undergoing a wide range of traumatic events, those who were induced to reveal the details of the event, as well as their feelings at the time they were experiencing the event, felt healthier and suffered fewer physical illnesses six months later than either people who were allowed to suffer in silence or those who were induced to talk about the details of the events but not the underlying feelings.

Pennebaker suggests that the beneficial effects of "opening up" are due not simply to the venting of feeling but at least in part to the insights and self-awareness that usually accompany such self-disclosure. Some independent corroboration of this suggestion comes from a rather different experiment by Leonard Berkowitz and Bartholmeu Troccoli (1990). In this experiment, young women listened to another woman talk about herself as part of a job interview. Half of the listeners did so while extending their nondominant arm, unsupported (causing discomfort and mild pain), while the others listened with their arms resting comfortably on the table. In each condition, half of the subjects were asked to rate their feelings while they were listening to the job interview; according to the researchers, this procedure provided those subjects with a vehicle for understanding their discomfort and a way to gain insight into it. The results were striking: Those subjects who experienced pain and discomfort during the interview but were not given the opportunity to process it experienced the most negative feelings toward the interviewee—and the more unpleasant it was for them, the more negative they felt toward the interviewee. On the other hand, those subjects who were given the opportunity to process their pain were able to avoid being unfairly harsh to the interviewee.

Defusing Anger Through Apology.   An effective way to reduce aggression in another person is to take some action aimed at diminishing the anger and annoyance that cause it. For example, earlier in this chapter we learned that when people had been frustrated by someone and then learned that he or she simply couldn't do any better, that frustration did not bubble over into anger or aggression. This suggests that one way to reduce aggression is for the individual who caused the frustration to take responsibility for the action, apologize for it, and indicate that it is unlikely to happen again. Suppose you are scheduled to be at your friend's house at 7:30 P.M. in order to drive her to a concert scheduled to start at 8:00. The concert is an exciting one for her—it involves one of her favorite soloists—and she has been looking forward to it for several weeks. You rush out of your house with just barely enough time to get there, but after driving for a few minutes, you discover that you have a flat tire. By the time you change the tire and get to her house, you are already twenty minutes late for the concert. Imagine her response if you (a) casually walk in, grin at her, and say, "Oh well, it probably wouldn't have been an interesting concert anyway. Don't take it so seriously; it's not such a big deal. Where's your sense of humor?" or (b) run in with a sad and anguished look on your face, show her your greasy and dirty hands, tell her you left your house in time to make it but unaccountably got this flat, apologize sincerely and profusely, and vow to find a way to make it up to her.

Our guess is that your friend would be prone toward aggression in the first instance but not in the second. This guess is supported by the results of several experiments (Baron, 1988, 1990; Weiner, Amirkhan, Folkes, & Verette, 1987). Typical of these experiments is one by Ohbuchi, Kameda, and Agarie (1989), in which college students performed poorly on a complex task because of errors made by the experimenter's assistant while presenting the materials. In three conditions, the assistant apologized publicly, apologized privately, or did not apologize at all. In a fourth condition, the senior experimenter removed the harm by indicating that he surmised there was an administrative blunder and therefore did not hold the students responsible for their poor performance. The results were clear: The students liked the assistant better and showed far less tendency to aggress against him if he apologized than if he didn't apologize, even if the harm was subsequently removed by the experimenter. Moreover, whether the apology was public or private made little difference; any apology—sincerely given, and in which the perpetrator took full responsibility—proved to be an effective way to reduce aggression.

With this in mind, one of the authors of this book (Elliot Aronson) has occasionally speculated about the great advantages that might be gained by equipping automobiles with "apology" signals. Picture the scene: You stop at a stop sign and then proceed, but too late you realize you have taken the right of way that wasn't really yours. What happens? In most urban centers, the offended driver will honk his or her horn angrily at you, or open the window and give you that near-universal symbol of anger and contempt that consists of the middle finger pointed skyward. Because nobody likes to be the recipient of such abuse, you might be tempted to honk back—and the escalating anger and aggression could be very unpleasant. Such escalation might be avoided, though, if in addition to the horn (which throughout the world is most often used as an instrument of aggression), every car were equipped with an apology signal—perhaps at the push of a button, a little flag could pop up, saying, "Whoops! Sorry!" In the foregoing scenario, had you pushed such a button as soon as you became aware of your transgression, doing so might well have defused the cycle of anger and retaliation that is all too frequently a part of the driving experience.

> Man must evolve for all human conflict a method which rejects revenge, aggression and retaliation.
> –Martin Luther King, Jr., *Nobel Prize Acceptance Speech,* December 11, 1964

The Modeling of Nonaggressive Behavior.   We have seen that children will be more aggressive (toward dolls as well as other children) if they witness examples of aggressive behavior in similar situations. What if we were to turn that inside out and expose children to nonaggressive models—to people who, when provoked, expressed themselves in a restrained, rational, pleasant manner? This has been tested in several experiments (Baron, 1972; Donnerstein & Donnerstein, 1976) and found to work. In those experiments, children were first allowed to witness the behavior of youngsters who behaved nonaggressively when provoked; when the children were subsequently placed in a situation in which they themselves were provoked, they showed a much lower frequency of aggressive responses than children who were not exposed to the nonaggressive models.

■ Martin Luther King, Jr., was effective in reducing and preventing violence by using and modeling nonviolence. Being nonviolent in the face of violence is difficult but effective.

Training in Communication and Problem-Solving Skills.   It is impossible to go through life—or, in some circumstances, to get through the day—without experiencing frustration, annoyance, anger, or conflict. As we have indicated earlier, there is nothing wrong with anger—it is part of being human. What causes the problem is the expression of anger in violent ways. Yet we are not born with the knowledge of how to express anger or annoyance in constructive, nonviolent, nondisruptive ways. Indeed, as we have seen, it seems almost natural to lash out when we are angry. As Hans Toch (1980) has indicated, in most societies it is precisely the people who lack proper social skills who are most prone to violent solutions to interpersonal problems. Thus, one way to reduce violence is to teach people how to communicate anger or criticism in constructive ways, how to negotiate and compromise when conflicts arise, how to be more sensitive to the needs and desires of others, and so on. There is some evidence that such formal training can be an effective means of reducing aggression (see Aronson, 1992; Davitz, 1952). In Joel Davitz's experiment, children were allowed to play in groups of four. Some of these groups were taught constructive ways to relate to one another and were rewarded for such behavior; others were not so instructed but were rewarded for aggressive or competitive behavior. Next, the youngsters were deliberately frustrated. This was accomplished by building up the expectation that they would be shown a series of entertaining movies and be allowed to have fun. The experimenter began to show a movie and to hand out candy bars, but then he abruptly terminated the movie at the point of highest interest and took the candy bars away. Now the children were allowed to play freely. As you have learned, this was a setup for the occurrence of aggressive behavior. But those children who had been trained for constructive behavior displayed far more constructive activity and far less aggressive behavior than those in the other group.

Building Empathy.   Let's look at horn-blowing again. Picture the following scene: A long line of cars is stopped at a traffic light at a busy intersection; the light turns green; the lead car hesitates for ten seconds. What happens? Almost inevitably, there will be an eruption of horn-honking. We're talking not about one little jab of the horn (which might be a way of informing the lead car that the light has changed) but about loud and persistent honking. In a controlled experiment, Robert Baron (1976) found that when the lead car failed to move after the light turned green, almost 90 percent of the drivers of the second car honked their horn in an aggressive manner. As part of the same experiment, a pedestrian crossed the street between the first and the second car while the light was still red and was out of the intersection by the time the light turned green. As you might imagine, this did not have an effect on the behavior of the drivers of the next car in line—almost 90 percent honked their horn when the light turned green. But in another condition, the pedestrian was on crutches. Even though he was on crutches, he was able to hobble across the street before the light turned green. Interestingly, however, in this condition only 57 percent of the drivers honked their horn. How come? Apparently, seeing a person on crutches evoked an empathic response, and the feeling of empathy overwhelmed the desire to be aggressive. The results of this experiment are shown in Figure 12.6.

Empathy is an important phenomenon. As Seymour Feshbach and Norma Feshbach (1969, 1971, 1978) have observed, most people find it difficult to inflict pain purposely on another human being unless they can find some way of dehumanizing their victim. Thus, when our nation was fighting wars against

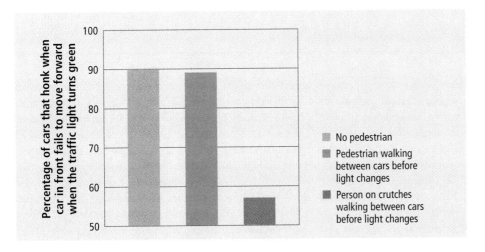

FIGURE 12.6   The effects of empathy on aggression.
■ When we are feeling empathy, in this case brought on by seeing a person on crutches, we are less likely to behave aggressively. (Adapted from Baron, 1976)

Asians (Japanese in the 1940s, Koreans in the 1950s, Vietnamese in the 1960s), our military personnel frequently referred to them as "gooks." We see this as a dehumanizing rationalization for acts of cruelty; it's easier to commit violent acts against a gook than against a fellow human being. But as you know from reading this book, this kind of rationalization not only makes it possible for us to aggress against another person but also guarantees we will continue to aggress against him or her. Why? Because once we succeed in convincing ourselves that our enemy is not really a human being at all but just a gook, it lowers our inhibitions for committing all kinds of atrocities. The photos on page 463 illustrate this point.

Dehumanization is not a rare phenomenon. Indeed, almost every week we read something in the newspapers or magazines illustrating dehumanization in action. For example, as we were writing an early draft of this chapter, one of us read the following item in the *New Yorker* magazine.

> In a two-day period in New York City recently, a homeless man, a train maintenance worker and a dog were killed on the subway tracks. Ninety people telephoned the Transit Authority to express concern about the dog, but only three called about the worker and no one about the homeless man. (*New Yorker*, November 4, 1991, p. 106)

An understanding of the process of dehumanization is the first step toward reversing it. Specifically, if it is true that most individuals must dehumanize their victims in order to commit an extreme act of aggression, then by building empathy among people, aggressive acts will become more difficult to commit. Feshbach and Feshbach (1969) have demonstrated a negative correlation between empathy and aggression in children: The more empathy a child has, the less he or she resorts to aggressive actions. They have also developed a successful method of teaching children to take the perspective of others. In particular, they taught children to be able to identify different emotions in people by having them act out roles in various emotionally laden situations, and these "empathy training activities" led to significant decreases in these children's aggressive behaviors. This kind of process will be discussed in greater detail in the next chapter, on prejudice.

dehumanization: the act of seeing victims as nonhumans (e.g., "gooks" instead of fellow human beings); dehumanization lowers inhibitions against aggressive actions and makes continued aggression easier and more likely

SUMMARY

We define an **aggressive action** as an intentional act aimed at doing harm or causing physical or psychological pain to another person. **Hostile aggression** involves having the goal of inflicting pain; **instrumental aggression** involves inflicting pain on the way to some other goal. Aggression has become an increasingly serious concern to Americans because of the rapid increase in violent crimes, especially in major urban centers.

Over the centuries, there has been a great deal of disagreement among scholars over whether aggressiveness is primarily instinctive or learned. Sigmund Freud theorized that human beings are born with an instinct toward life, called **Eros,** and a death instinct, **Thanatos.** The death instinct, when turned inward, manifests itself as suicide and, when turned outward, as hostility, destructiveness, and murder. Freud's **hydraulic theory** states that aggressive energy must be released to avoid buildup resulting in an explosion.

Because aggressiveness has had survival value, most contemporary social psychologists accept the proposition that it is part of our evolutionary heritage. At the same time, we know that human beings have developed exquisite mechanisms for controlling their aggressive impulses and that human behavior is flexible and adaptable to changes in the environment. Thus, whether or not aggression is actually expressed depends on a complex interplay between our biological propensities, our innate and learned inhibitory responses, and the precise nature of the social situation.

There are many situational causes of aggression, ranging from the neurological and chemical to the social. The area in the core of the brain called the **amygdala** is thought to control aggression. It is reasonably clear that the hormone **testosterone** is correlated with aggressive behavior—for example, prisoners convicted of violent crimes tend to have higher levels of testosterone than those convicted of nonviolent crimes. This is consistent with the more general finding that men are more aggressive than women. At least one other chemical, alcohol, is associated with increases in aggression, due to the fact that alcohol acts as a general disinhibitor, lowering a person's inhibitions against violent behavior, as well as a variety of other behaviors frowned on by society. It has also been shown that pain and other physical discomforts (e.g., the proverbial "long, hot summer") will increase aggressive behavior.

There are also many social causes of aggression. Among these, frustration is prominent. The **frustration-aggression theory** states that the experience of frustration can increase the probability of an aggressive response. However, frustration alone does not automatically lead to aggression; it is more likely to produce aggression if one is thwarted on the way to a goal in a manner that is either illegitimate or unexpected. In addition, frustration is the result not simply of deprivation, but of **relative deprivation**—the feeling that comes from knowing that you have less than what you deserve, less than what you have been led to expect, or less than what people similar to you have.

Aggression can also be produced by social provocation or the mere presence of an **aggressive stimulus,** or an object associated with aggressive responses, such as a gun. **Social learning theory** states that aggression can also be produced through the imitation of aggressive models, either in face-to-face situations or by viewing violence in films or on TV. The possible effects of viewing violence in the media are of particular interest to social psychologists in our country because of the pervasiveness of violent programming. Violence in the media has been shown not only to lead to greater aggressiveness in the viewer but also to create a numbing effect, making us more accepting of violence in society. The viewing of pornographic material appears to be relatively harmless; however, if the pornographic material is of a violent nature, it promotes greater acceptance of sexual violence toward women and is almost certainly a factor associated with actual aggressive behavior toward women.

Aggression can be reduced in a number of ways. These include discussing the reasons for anger and hostility, modeling nonaggressive behavior, training people in the use of nonviolent solutions to conflict and in communication and negotiation skills, and building people's empathy toward others. Building empathy is particularly useful as a means of thwarting the human tendency to **dehumanize** one's victim.

Punishing aggressive behavior in order to reduce it is tricky; punishment can be effective if it is not too severe and if it follows closely on the heels of the aggressive act. But severe or delayed punishment is not an effective way to reduce aggression. Similarly, there is no evidence to support the notion of **catharsis**—the idea that committing an aggressive action or watching others behave aggressively is a good way to get the impulse toward aggression out of one's system. On the contrary, careful research has shown that committing an act of aggression can trigger the tendency to justify that action and might thus eventually produce an increase in aggressive behavior.

IF YOU ARE INTERESTED . . .

Baron, R. A. (1992). *Human aggression*. New York: Plenum. A penetrating analysis of the social psychology of aggression.

Berkowitz, L. (1993). *Aggression: Its causes, consequences, and control*. New York: McGraw-Hill. One of the greatest living experts on aggression summarizes his thinking in this up-to-date revision of his classic work.

Tavris, C. (1989). *Anger: The misunderstood emotion*. New York: Touchstone/Simon & Schuster. An interesting and well-written analysis of anger.

Chapter 13

Prejudice:
Causes and Cures

Chapter Outline

"AIDS is a disease transmitted by people deliberately engaging in unnatural acts."

—Senator Jesse Helms of North Carolina

I wonder if Senator Helms feels the same about Americans dying of cancer because they smoke?"

—Mrs. Jeanne White-Ginder, whose young son died of AIDS,
after acquiring the disease from a blood transfusion

O f all the social behaviors we discuss in this book, prejudice is probably the most widespread and certainly among the most dangerous. Prejudice touches nearly everyone's life. Many of us are victims of stereotyping and even violence, all because of a particular group to which we belong—whether it is ethnic, religious, gender, national origin, sexual preference, or what have you. Those who hold the prejudiced beliefs are affected negatively as well; living a life punctuated by active dislike or hatred for other groups of people is surely not a life-affirming, positive experience. Consider one of Thurgood Marshall's favorite stories:

When he was a young lawyer working for the NAACP, Mr. Marshall recalls, he journeyed to a small town in the South to defend a black man who was accused of a serious crime. When he arrived, he was shocked and dismayed to learn that the defendant was dead—lynched by an angry white mob. With a heavy heart, Mr. Marshall returned to the railroad station to wait for a train back to New York. Not having eaten for several hours, he realized that he was very hungry; luckily, there was a small food stand on the platform. As he walked toward the stand, he debated with himself whether to go right up to the front and order a sandwich (as was his legal right) or to go around to the back of the stand (as was the common practice for African Americans in the South at that time). However, before he reached the stand, he was approached by a large, bulky man, who looked at him suspiciously. Mr. Marshall took him to be a lawman of some sort; he walked with an air of authority and had a bulge in his pants pocket that could only have been made by a handgun.

Thurgood Marshall, NAACP chief counsel, in front of the Supreme Court in 1954.

"Hey, boy," the man shouted at Marshall, "What are you doing here?" "I'm just waiting for a train," Marshall replied.

The man scowled, took a few steps closer, glared at him menacingly, and said, "I didn't hear you. What did you say, boy?"

Marshall realized that his initial reply had not been sufficiently obsequious. "I beg your pardon, sir, but I'm waiting for a train."

There was a long silence, during which the man slowly looked Marshall up and down, and then said, "You'd better catch that train, boy—and soon, because in this town, the sun has never set on a live nigger."

As Marshall recalls, at that point his internal debate about how to get the sandwich proved academic. He decided not to get a sandwich at all but to catch the very next train out—no matter where it was headed. Besides, somehow he didn't feel hungry anymore. (NPR, June 28, 1991)

Thurgood Marshall went on to become chief counsel for the NAACP; in 1954, he argued the Supreme Court case of Brown v. Board of Education *that put an end to legalized racial segregation in public schools. Subsequently, Marshall was appointed to the Supreme Court, where he served with distinction until his retirement in 1991. We are not sure what became of the man with the bulge in his pocket.*

A great many years have passed since the incident recounted by Justice Marshall. There hasn't been a lynching in the South for a long time, and the civil rights movement has made enormous progress in the second half of the twentieth century. However, while contemporary manifestations of prejudice tend to be less flagrant than they used to be, they continue to exact a heavy toll on their victims—in terms of extreme anxiety, diminished self-esteem, curtailed opportunities, and sometimes physical violence.

Moreover, on a wide variety of important social issues and social institutions, there is a huge racial divide in this country in terms of attitude and experience. While sophisticated observers have long been aware of this divide, it came home with stunning force in the mid-1990s during the trial of O. J. Simpson for the murders of Nicole Brown Simpson and Ronald Goldman. The trial was powerful, dramatic, and, alas, entertaining—capturing the rapt attention of millions of Americans. From the outset, it seemed as if white Americans and black Americans were watching two different trials. The overwhelming majority of whites firmly believed that Simpson was guilty of murder; the overwhelming majority of blacks believed that the evidence was unconvincing.

Social critics will be pondering this "racial divide" for many years to come. Among other things, they will try to decide whether this huge difference was due to differences among the racial groups in their respective experiences with the criminal justice system, or differences in the degree to which they found the defendant to be attractive and sympathetic (Gates, 1995; Toobin, 1995). In order to understand this phenomenon and others like it, we must take a long look at prejudice as a social psychological phenomenon.

Prejudice: The Ubiquitous Social Phenomenon

In the above paragraphs is an unintended implication that only minority groups are the targets of prejudice at the hands of the dominant majority. Needless to say, this aspect of prejudice is extremely powerful and poignant. But the truth is that prejudice is ubiquitous; in one form or another, it affects all of us. For one thing, prejudice is a two-way street; it frequently flows from the minority group to the majority group as well as from the majority to the minority. In addition, any group can be a target of prejudice for someone. Let us take one of the most superordinate groups to which you belong—your nationality. As you well know, Americans are not universally loved, respected and admired; at one time or another, we Americans have been the target of prejudice around the world. To take some recent examples, in the 1960s and 1970s North Vietnamese Communists referred to Americans as the "running dogs of capitalist imperialism." In the 1980s, the Iranian regime under the Ayatollah Khomeini depicted America as a ruthless, power-hungry, amoral nation—referring to us as "the great Satan." In many parts of our own hemisphere, many of our neighbors to the south look upon Americans (or, strictly speaking, *North* Americans) as overfed economic and military bullies.

On a more subtle level, even our political allies see us as stereotypically American. For example, in research on stereotyping it turns out that British citizens tend to label Americans as intrusive, forward, and pushy. Needless to say, stereotyping cuts both ways: Americans tend to label the British as cold and unfriendly (Campbell, 1967).

Your nationality is only one of a number of aspects of your identity that can cause you to be labeled and discriminated against. Racial and ethnic identity is a major focal point for prejudiced attitudes. As you know, Americans who are African American, Asian, Hispanic, or Native American are targets of prejudice. So are some groups of Anglo or white Americans: Note the long-standing popularity of Polish jokes, or the negative stereotypes used throughout this century to describe Italian and Irish Americans. Other aspects of your identity also leave you vulnerable to prejudice—for example, your gender, your sexual preference, and your religion. Your appearance or physical state can arouse prejudice as well; obesity, disabilities, and diseases like AIDS, for instance, cause people to be treated unfairly by others. In recent years, a new type of joke has been sweeping the country: "dumb blond" jokes. The old stereotype that blonds are ditzy bimbos has been given a new life. Finally, even your profession or hobbies can lead to your being stereotyped. We all know the "dumb jock" and the "computer nerd" stereotypes. Some people have negative attitudes about blue-collar workers; others, about Fortune 500 CEOs. The point is that none of us emerges completely unscathed from the effects of prejudice; it is a problem of and for all humankind.

In addition to being widespread, prejudice is dangerous. Simple dislike of a group can be relentless and can lead to extreme hatred, to thinking of its members as less than human, and to torture, murder, and even genocide.

But even when murder or genocide is not the culmination of prejudiced beliefs, the targets of prejudice will suffer in less dramatic ways. One nearly inevitable consequence of being the target of relentless prejudice is a diminution of one's self-esteem. As we discussed in Chapter 6, self-esteem is a vital aspect of a person's life. Who we think we are is a key determinant of how we behave and

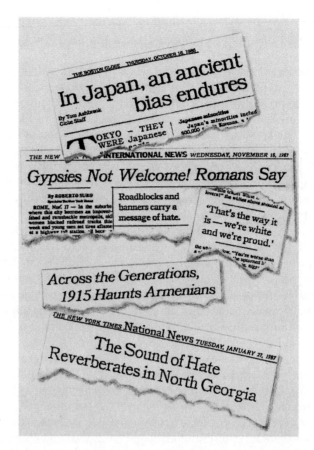

■ Anyone can be the target of prejudice.

who we become. A person with low self-esteem will, by definition, conclude that he or she is unworthy of a good education, a decent job, an exciting romantic partner, and so on. Thus, a person with low self-esteem is more likely to be unhappy and unsuccessful than a person with high self-esteem. In a democracy, such a person is also less likely to take advantage of available opportunities.

For those who are the targets of relentless prejudice, the seeds of low self-esteem are sown early in life. In a classic experiment conducted in the late 1940s, social psychologists Kenneth Clark and Mamie Clark (1947) demonstrated that African American children—some of them only 3 years old—were already convinced that it was not particularly desirable to be black. In this experiment, the children were offered a choice between playing with a white or a black doll. The great majority of them rejected the black doll, feeling that the white doll was prettier and generally superior.

In his argument before the Supreme Court in 1954, Thurgood Marshall cited this experiment as evidence that, psychologically, segregation did irreparable harm to the self-esteem of African American children. Taking this evidence into consideration, the Court ruled that separating black children from white children on the basis of race alone "generates a feeling of inferiority as to their status in the community that may affect their hearts and minds in a way unlikely ever to be undone . . . . [S]eparate educational facilities are therefore inherently unequal" (Justice Earl Warren, speaking for the majority in the case of *Brown v. Board of Education*, 1954, quoted in Stephan, 1978).

> A little black girl yearns for the blue eyes of a little white girl, and the horror at the heart of her yearning is exceeded only by the evil of fulfillment.
>
> –Toni Morrison,
> *The Bluest Eye*, 1970

This diminution of self-esteem affects other oppressed groups as well. For example, Philip Goldberg (1968) demonstrated that, like African Americans, women in this culture have learned to consider themselves intellectually inferior to men. In his experiment, Goldberg asked female college students to read scholarly articles and to evaluate them in terms of their competence and writing style. For some students, specific articles were signed by male authors (e.g., "John T. McKay"), while for others, the same articles were signed by female authors (e.g., "Joan T. McKay"). The female students rated the articles much higher if they were attributed to a male author than if the same articles were attributed to a female author. In other words, these women had learned their place; they regarded the output of other women as necessarily inferior to that of men, just as the African American youngsters learned to regard black dolls as inferior to white dolls. This is the legacy of a prejudiced society.

Clark and Clark's experiment was conducted some 50 years ago; Goldberg's was conducted some 30 years ago. As we have indicated, significant changes have taken place in American society since then. For example, the number of blatant acts of overt prejudice and discrimination has decreased sharply, legislation on affirmative action has opened the door to greater opportunities for women and minorities, and the media have increased our exposure to women and minorities doing important work in positions of power and influence. And as one might expect, these changes are reflected in the gradual increase in self-esteem of people in these groups, an increase underscored by the fact that most recent research has failed to replicate the results of those earlier experiments. African American children are now more content with black dolls than they were in 1947 (Porter,

■ Fifty years ago, African American children considered black dolls to be undesirable. This is no longer the case. Why?

1971; Porter & Washington, 1979), and people no longer discriminate against a piece of writing attributed to a woman (Swim et al., 1989). Similarly, recent research suggests that there might not be any major differences in global self-esteem between blacks and whites or between men and women (Crocker & Major, 1989; Steele, 1992).

While this progress is real, it would be a mistake to conclude that prejudice has ceased to be a serious problem in our country. Prejudice exists in countless subtle and not-so-subtle ways. For the most part, here in America at the close of the twentieth century prejudice has gone underground and become less overt (Pettigrew, 1985). But occasionally it is flagrant enough to capture national head-lines—as when Yusuf Hawkins, a young African American, was brutally beaten and murdered by a gang of youths while peacefully going about his business in Bensonhurst, a largely Italian American section of Brooklyn. The reason? He was mistakenly identified as someone who was dating a white woman.

During the past half-century, social psychologists have contributed greatly to our understanding of the psychological processes underlying prejudice and have begun to identify and demonstrate some possible solutions. What is prejudice? How does it come about? And why is it so difficult to change?

Prejudice, Stereotyping, and Discrimination Defined

Prejudice is an attitude. As we discussed in Chapter 8, attitudes are made up of three components: an affective or emotional component, representing both the type of emotion linked with the attitude (e.g., anger, warmth) and the extremity of the attitude (e.g., mild uneasiness, outright hostility); a cognitive component, involving the beliefs or thoughts (cognitions) that make up the attitude; and a behavioral component, relating to one's actions—people don't simply have attitudes; they also act on them.

Prejudice: The Affective Component

The term *prejudice* refers to the general attitude structure and its affective component. Technically, there are positive and negative prejudices. For example, you could be prejudiced against Texans or prejudiced in favor of Texans. In one case, your emotional reaction is negative; when a person is introduced to you as "This is Bob from Texas," you will expect him to act in particular ways that you associate with "those obnoxious Texans." Conversely, if your emotional reaction is positive, you will be delighted to meet another one of "those wonderful Texans," and you'll expect Bob to demonstrate many positive qualities, such as warmth and friendliness. While prejudice can involve either positive or negative affect, social psychologists (and people in general) reserve the word *prejudice* for use only when it refers to negative attitudes about others. Specifically, **prejudice** is defined as a hostile or negative attitude toward people in a distinguishable group, based solely on their membership in that group. For example, when we say an individual is prejudiced against blacks, we mean that he or she is primed to behave coolly or with hostility toward blacks and that he or she feels that all blacks are pretty much the same. Thus, the characteristics this individual assigns to blacks are negative and zealously applied to the group as a whole—the individual traits or behaviors of the target of prejudice will either go unnoticed or be dismissed.

prejudice: a hostile or negative attitude toward a distinguishable group of people, based solely on their membership in that group

Drawing by Ziegler; © 1994 The New Yorker Magazine, Inc.

"It's a cat calendar, so it may not be all that accurate."

Stereotypes: The Cognitive Component

Close your eyes for a moment and imagine the looks and characteristics of the following people: a high school cheerleader, a New York cab driver, a Jewish doctor, a black musician. Our guess is that this task was not difficult. We all walk around with pictures in our heads. The distinguished journalist Walter Lippman, who introduced the term *stereotype* more than 70 years ago in his book *Public Opinion* (1922), wrote about the distinction between the world out there and stereotypes—"the little pictures we carry around inside our heads." Within a given culture, these pictures tend to be remarkably similar. For example, we would be surprised if your image of the high school cheerleader was anything but bouncy, full of pep, pretty, nonintellectual, and (of course!) female. We would also be surprised if the Jewish doctor or the New York cab driver in your head was female—or if the black musician was playing classical music.

It goes without saying that there are male cheerleaders, female doctors, and black classical musicians, and it goes without saying that New York cab drivers come in every size, shape, race, and gender. But we tend to categorize according to what we regard as normative. And within a given culture, what people regard as normative is very similar, in part because these images are perpetuated and broadcast widely by the media of that culture. Stereotyping, however, goes a step beyond simple categorization. A **stereotype** is a generalization about a group of people in which identical characteristics are assigned to virtually all members of the group, regardless of actual variation among the members. Once formed, stereotypes are resistant to change on the basis of new information.

It is important to point out that stereotyping is not necessarily emotional and does not necessarily lead to intentional acts of abuse. Frequently, stereotyping is merely a way we have of simplifying how we look at the world—and we all do it

stereotype: a generalization about a group of people in which identical characteristics are assigned to virtually all members of the group, regardless of actual variation among the members to some extent. For example, Gordon Allport (1954) described stereotyping as "the law of least effort." According to Allport, the world is just too complicated for us to have a highly differentiated attitude about everything. Instead, we maximize our cognitive time and energy by developing elegant, accurate attitudes about some topics, while relying on simple, sketchy beliefs for others. (This should remind you of the many facets of social cognition that we discussed in Chapter 4.) Given our limited information-processing capacity, it is reasonable for human beings to behave like "cognitive misers"—to take shortcuts and adopt certain rules of thumb in our attempt to understand other people (Fiske, 1989; Jones, 1990; Taylor, 1981). To the extent that the resulting stereotype is based on experience and is at all accurate, it can be an adaptive, shorthand way of dealing with complex events. On the other hand, if the stereotype blinds us to individual differences within a class of people, it is maladaptive, harmful, and potentially abusive.

Stereotypes, Attribution, and Gender.   A particularly ubiquitous manifestation of stereotyping takes place as a function of gender roles. For example, it is almost universal for women to be seen as genetically more nurturant and less assertive than men. As Alice Eagly and Valerie Steffen (1984) suggest, this perception may be role-related—that is, traditionally women have been assigned the role of homemaker.

The phenomenon cuts deeper still. In one experiment, when confronted with a highly successful female physician, male undergraduates perceived her as being

■ In this cartoon, while the teacher may not intend to be hurtful, his sexism is damaging nonetheless.

less competent and having had an easier path toward success than a successful male physician (Feldman-Summers & Kiesler, 1974). Female undergraduates saw things differently: Although they saw the male physician and the female physician as being equally competent, they saw the male as having had an easier time of it. Both males and females attributed higher motivation to the female physician. It should be noted that attributing a high degree of motivation to a woman can be one way of implying that she has less skill than her male counterpart (i.e., "She's not very smart, but she tries hard"). This possibility comes into clear focus when we examine a similar study by Kay Deaux and Tim Emsweiler (1974), in which they found that if the sexual stereotype is strong enough, even members of the stereotyped group tend to buy it. Specifically, male and female students were shown a highly successful performance on a complex task by a fellow student and were asked how it came about. When it was a man who succeeded, both male and female students attributed his achievement almost entirely to his ability; when it was a woman who succeeded, students of both genders thought the achievement was largely a matter of luck.

In subsequent research, it has been shown that young girls have a tendency to downplay their own ability; specifically, while fourth-grade boys attributed their own successful outcomes on a difficult intellectual task to their ability, girls tended to derogate their own successful performance. Moreover, this experiment also showed that while boys had learned to protect their egos by attributing their own failures to bad luck, girls took more of the blame for failures on themselves (Nichols, 1975).

Gender-related attributions can cut both ways—that is, men are expected to succeed, but if they fail, they are treated more harshly than women who fail. This was demonstrated in an experiment by Kay Deaux and Janet Taynor (1973), who had participants listen to a taped interview with a college student, a candidate for a prestigious scholarship. If the candidate did well in the interview and was male, participants rated him as being more competent than a female who had done just as well. However, if the male candidate did poorly in the interview, they rated him as considerably less competent than a female candidate who had done as poorly.

To summarize the research on gender-related stereotypes, we would conclude that society is particularly tough on men when they fail and particularly ungenerous toward women when they succeed. More specifically, because men are expected to succeed in our society, they are treated harshly when they do not do so. Because women are not expected to succeed, when they do succeed they are seen by others (and by themselves) either as the rare person with an extraordinarily high degree of motivation or as simply lucky. When women fail, they are treated more leniently; after all, if you don't expect much from a person, how can you judge the person's failure harshly?

Discrimination: The Behavioral Component

This brings us to the final component of prejudice: when beliefs are translated into behavior. In this case, stereotyped beliefs, combined with a negative emotional reaction, translate into unfair treatment or even violence—in other words, into **discrimination,** defined as unjustified negative or harmful action toward the members of a group, simply because of their membership in it.

An excellent example of discrimination is contained in a study conducted by Charles Bond and his colleagues (1988), who departed from the friendly confines

discrimination: unjustified negative or harmful action toward a member of a group, simply because of his or her membership in that group

FIGURE 13.1   Use of Extreme Measures Against Black Mental Patients. ■ During the first 30 days of confinement, there appeared to be an assumption that blacks would be more violent than whites. (Adapted from Bond et al., 1988)

> Prejudices are the props of civilization.
>
> —André Gide, 1939

of the college campus to compare the treatment of black versus white patients in a psychiatric hospital run by an all-white professional staff. The results of the study are illustrated in Figure 13.1. The researchers examined the two most common methods used by staff members to handle patients' violent behavior: (a) secluding the individual in a time-out room and (b) restraining the individual in a straitjacket and administering tranquilizing drugs. An examination of hospital records over 85 days revealed that the harsher method—physical and chemical restraint—was used against black patients nearly four times as often as against white patients. This was the case despite the virtual lack of differences in the number of violent incidents committed by the black and the white patients. Moreover, this discriminatory treatment occurred even though the black patients, on being admitted to the hospital, had on average been diagnosed as less violent than the white patients.

This study did uncover an important positive finding: After several weeks, reality managed to overcome the effects of the existing stereotype. The staff eventually noticed that the black and the white patients did not differ in their degree of violent behavior, and they began to treat black and white patients equally. While this is encouraging, the overall meaning of the study is both clear and disconcerting: The existing stereotype resulted in undeserved, harsher initial treatment of black patients by trained professionals. At the same time, the fact that reality overcame the stereotype is a tribute to the professionalism of the staff, because, as we shall see, in most cases deeply rooted prejudice, stereotypes, and discrimination are not easy to change.

What Causes Prejudice?

What makes people prejudiced? Is it part of our biological survival mechanism to favor our own family, tribe, and race and to express hostility to outsiders? As noted in Chapter 11, sociobiologists have suggested that all organisms have a tendency to feel more favorably toward genetically similar others and to express fear and loathing toward genetically dissimilar organisms, even if the latter have never done them any harm (Rushton, 1989; Trivers, 1985). Conversely, are we taught by our culture (i.e., by our parents, peers, the local community, and the media) to assign negative qualities and attributes to people who are different from us? Psychologists and sociologists know that prejudice is easy to learn and that young children tend to hold the same prejudiced attitudes as their parents. While we human beings might have inherited biological tendencies that predispose us toward prejudicial behavior, no one knows for sure whether or not prejudice is a part of our biological makeup. We do know that prejudice is not confined to such biologically obvious aspects of human difference as race and gender; it also exists among biologically similar people who happen to hold slightly different beliefs—for example, in religion, as with Protestant and Catholic Northern Irish. Indeed, prejudice can even be fostered in schoolchildren over such trivial differences as eye color, length of hair, and style of dress. Let's take a close look at some of the known causes of prejudice.

In the late 1960s, a third-grade teacher in Riceville, Iowa, Jane Elliot, grew concerned that her young students had no real idea of what racism or prejudice was. The children all lived in rural Iowa, they were all white, and they were all Christian. How could Elliot teach them what stereotyping and discrimination felt like?

> The world is full of pots jeering at kettles.
> –La Rochefoucauld, 1678

One day, Elliot divided her class by eye color. She told her students that blue-eyed people were better than brown-eyed people—smarter, nicer, more trustworthy, and so on. The brown-eyed kids had to wear cloth collars around their necks so that they would be instantly recognizable as one of the inferior group. The blue-eyed kids got to play longer at recess, could have second helpings at the cafeteria, were praised in the classroom, and so on. How did the children respond?

In less than a half-hour, Elliot had created a microcosm of society in her classroom: a prejudiced society. While before, the children had been a cooperative, cohesive group, now they were indeed divided. The superior kids, the blue-eyed ones, made fun of the brown-eyed kids, refused to play with them, tattled on them to the teacher, thought up new restrictions and punishments for them, and even started a fistfight with them in the school yard. The inferior kids, the brown-eyed ones, were depressed and demoralized. They did significantly less well on classroom tests that day. They became shadows of their formerly happy selves.

The next day, Elliot switched the stereotypes about eye color. She said she'd made a mistake—that brown-eyed people were really the better ones. She told the brown-eyed kids to put their collars on the blue-eyed kids. They gleefully did so. The tables had turned—and the brown-eyed kids exacted their revenge.

On the morning of the third day, Elliot explained to her students that they had been learning about prejudice and discrimination and how it feels to be a person of color in this society. The children discussed the two-day experience and clearly understood its message. In a follow-up, Elliot met with these students at a class reunion, when they were in their midtwenties. Their memories of the exercise were startlingly clear—they each said it had had an amazing effect on their lives. They felt that they were less prejudiced and more aware of discrimination against others because of this childhood experience. They said they thought every child in America should experience the eye-color exercise.

The Way We Think: Social Cognition

Our first explanation for what causes prejudice is that it is the inevitable byproduct of the way we process and organize information—in other words, it is the dark side of human *social cognition* (as discussed in Chapter 4). Our tendency to categorize and group information together, to form schemas and to use these to interpret new or unusual information, to rely on potentially inaccurate *heuristics* (shortcuts in mental reasoning), and to depend on what are often faulty memory processes—all of these aspects of social cognition can lead us to form negative stereotypes and to apply them in a discriminatory fashion. Let's examine this dark side of social cognition more closely.

Social Categorization: Us Versus Them.   The first step in prejudice is the creation of groups—that is, the categorization of some people into one group based on certain characteristics and of others into another group based on their different characteristics. The underlying theme of human social cognition is such categorization—grouping stimuli according to their similarities and contrasting stimuli according to their disparities (Rosch & Lloyd, 1978; Taylor, 1981; Wilder, 1986). For example, we make sense out of the physical world by grouping animals and plants into taxonomies; we make sense out of our social world by grouping people by gender, nationality, ethnicity, and so on. We do not react to each stimulus we encounter as new and completely unknown. Instead, we rely on our perceptions of what similar stimuli have been like in the past to help us determine how to react to this particular stimulus (Andersen & Klatzky, 1987). Thus, social categorization is both useful and necessary; however, this simple cognitive process has profound implications.

For example, in Jane Elliot's third-grade classroom, children grouped according to eye color began to act differently based on that social categorization. Blue-eyed children, the superior group, stuck together and actively promoted and used their higher status and power in the classroom. They formed an **in-group,** defined as the group with which an individual identifies and of which he or she feels a member. The blue-eyed kids saw the brown-eyed ones as outsiders—different and inferior. To the blue-eyed children, the brown-eyed kids were the **out-group,** defined as the group with which the individual does not identify.

Kurt Vonnegut captures this concept beautifully in his novel *Cat's Cradle.* A woman discovers that a person she has just met, casually, on a plane, is from Indiana. Immediately, a bond is formed between them:

> "My God," she said, "are you a Hoosier?"
>
> I admitted I was.
>
> "I'm a Hoosier too," she crowed. "Nobody has to be ashamed of being a Hoosier."
>
> "I'm not," I said. "I never knew anybody who was."

What is the mechanism that produces this **in-group bias**—that is, positive feelings and special treatment for people we have defined as being part of our in-group, and negative feelings and unfair treatment for others simply because we have defined them as being in the out-group? The British social psychologist Henri Tajfel (1982) believed that the major underlying motive is self-esteem: Individuals seek to enhance their self-esteem by identifying with specific social groups. Yet self-esteem will be enhanced only if the individual sees these groups as superior to other groups. Thus, for members of the Ku Klux Klan it is not enough to believe the races should be kept separate; they must convince themselves of the supremacy of the white race in order to feel good about themselves.

---

in-group: the group with which an individual identifies and feels he or she is a member

out-group: a group with which an individual does not identify

in-group bias: especially positive feelings and special treatment for people we have defined as being part of our in-group, and negative feelings and unfair treatment for others simply because we have defined them as being in the out-group

To get at the pure, unvarnished mechanisms behind this phenomenon, Tajfel and his colleagues have created entities that they refer to as **minimal groups** (Tajfel, 1982; Tajfel & Billig, 1974; Tajfel & Turner, 1979). In these experiments, complete strangers are formed into groups using the most trivial criteria imaginable. For example, in one experiment participants watched a coin toss that randomly assigned them to either group X or group W. In another experiment, participants were first asked to express their opinions about artists they had never heard of and were then randomly assigned to a group that appreciated either the "Klee style" or the "Kandinsky style," ostensibly due to their picture preferences. The striking thing about the Tajfel research is that despite the fact that the participants were strangers prior to the experiment and didn't interact with one another during it, they behaved as if those who shared the same meaningless label were their dear friends or close kin. They liked the members of their own group better; they rated the members of their in-group as more likely to have pleasant personalities and to have done better work than out-group members. Most striking, the participants allocated more money and other rewards to those who shared their label and did so in a rather hostile, cutthroat manner—that is, when given a clear choice, they preferred to give themselves only $2, if it meant giving the out-group person $1, over giving themselves $3, if that meant the out-group member received $4 (Brewer, 1979; Hogg & Abrams, 1988; Oakes & Turner, 1980; Wilder, 1981).

In short, even when the reasons for differentiation are minimal, being in the in-group makes you want to win against members of the out-group and leads you to treat the latter unfairly, because such tactics serve to build your self-esteem. And when your group does win, it strengthens your feelings of pride and identification with that group. For example, our casual observation suggests that there was much more flag-waving and many more parades and patriotic speeches by

minimal groups:
meaningless groups formed by grouping strangers on the basis of trivial criteria; minimal group members still display in-group biases, however

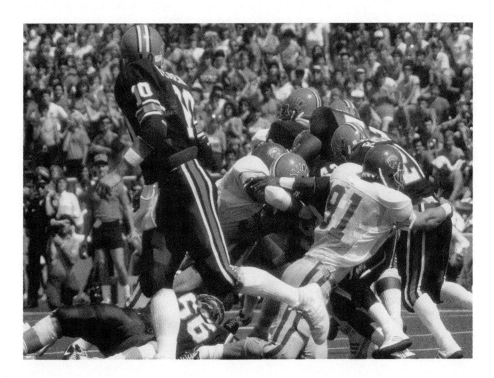

■ Wearing our school colors is a way of demonstrating that we are a member of the in-group.

politicians following the victorious Desert Storm war against Iraq than there was following the less than victorious war in Vietnam. In a more systematic observation, Robert Cialdini and his colleagues (1976) simply counted the number of college insignia T-shirts and sweatshirts worn on the Monday following a football game at seven universities that take football very seriously: Arizona State, Louisiana State, Notre Dame, Michigan, Ohio State, Pittsburgh, and the University of Southern California. The results? You guessed it: Students were more likely to wear their university's insignia after victory than after defeat.

Besides the in-group bias, there is another consequence of social categorization: the perception of **out-group homogeneity** (Linville, Fischer, & Salovey, 1989; Quattrone, 1986). This is the familiar "They're all alike" belief, which you've undoubtedly encountered before. In-group members tend to perceive those in the out-group as being more homogeneous than they really are, as well as more homogeneous than the in-group members are.

Does your college have a traditional rival, whether in athletics or academics? If so, as an in-group member, you probably value your institution more highly than this rival (thereby raising and protecting your self-esteem) and you probably perceive students at this rival school to be more similar to each other (e.g., as a given type) than you perceive students at your own institution to be. George Quattrone and Edward E. Jones (1980) studied this phenomenon using rival universities: Princeton and Rutgers. The rivalry between these colleges is based on athletics, academics, and even class-consciousness, with Princeton being private and Rutgers public. Male research participants at the two schools watched videotaped scenes in which three different young men were asked to make a decision—for example, in one videotape an experimenter asked a man whether he wanted to listen to rock music or classical music while he participated in an experiment on auditory perception. The participants were told that the man was either a Princeton or a Rutgers student; thus, for some of them the student in the videotape was an in-group member, and for others, an out-group member. The participants' job was to predict what the man in the videotape would choose. After they saw the man make his choice (e.g., rock or classical music), they were asked to predict what percentage of male students at that institution would make the same choice. Did the predictions vary due to the in- or out-group status of the

out-group homogeneity: the perception that those in the out-group are more similar (homogeneous) to each other than they really are, as well as more similar than the members of the in-group are

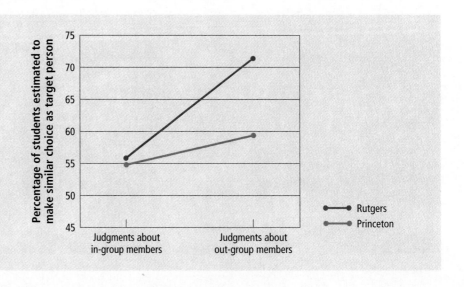

FIGURE 13.2 Judgments about in-group and out-group members. ■ After watching the target person make a choice between two alternatives, participants were asked to estimate what percentage of students at their school (in-group) and their rival school (out-group) would make the same choice. An out-group homogeneity bias was found: Students' estimates for out-group members were higher (greater similarity) than for in-group members. (Adapted from Quattrone & Jones, 1980)

target men? As you can see in Figure 13.2, the results support the out-group homogeneity hypothesis: When the target person was an out-group member, the participants believed his choice was more predictive of what his peers would choose than when he was an in-group member (a student at their own school). In other words, if you know something about one out-group member, you are more likely to feel you know something about all of them. Knowing something about an in-group member is not so diagnostic; after all, you know how different and unique your in-group members are (Judd & Park, 1988; Park & Rothbart, 1982).

The Failure of Logic.   Anyone who has ever tried to argue with people who hold a deep-seated prejudice against some group knows it is difficult to get them to change their minds. Even people who are usually sensible and reasonable about most topics become relatively immune to rational, logical arguments when it comes to the topic of their prejudice. Why is this so? There are two reasons, involving the affective and cognitive aspects of an attitude. First, it is primarily the emotional aspect of attitudes that makes a prejudiced person so hard to argue with; as you well know, logical arguments are not effective in countering emotions. The difficulty of using reason to change prejudiced attitudes is beautifully illustrated by Gordon Allport in his landmark book *The Nature of Prejudice* (1954). Allport reports a dialogue between Mr. X and Mr. Y:

> Mr. X: The trouble with the Jews is that they only take care of their own group.
>
> Mr. Y: But the record of the Community Chest campaign shows that they gave more generously, in proportion to their numbers, to the general charities of the community than did non-Jews.
>
> Mr. X: That shows they are always trying to buy favor and intrude into Christian affairs. They think of nothing but money; that is why there are so many Jewish bankers.
>
> Mr. Y: But a recent study shows that the percentage of Jews in the banking business is negligible, far smaller than the percentage of non-Jews.
>
> Mr. X: That's just it; they don't go in for respectable business; they are only in the movie business or run night clubs. (Allport, 1954, pp. 13–14)

Because Mr. X is emotionally involved in his beliefs about Jews, he does not feel particularly bound by the usual confines of a logical discussion. In effect, the prejudiced Mr. X is saying, "Don't trouble me with facts; my mind is made up." He makes no attempt to refute the powerful data presented by Mr. Y. Either he proceeds to distort the facts in order to make them support his hatred of Jews or he ignores them and simply initiates a new area of attack. The prejudiced attitude remains intact, despite the fact that the specific arguments Mr. X began with are now lying in tatters at his feet.

Second, the cognitive component of a prejudiced attitude in and of itself presents difficulties for the person trying to reduce a friend's prejudice, because, as we discussed in earlier chapters, an attitude tends to organize the way we process relevant information about the targets of that attitude. None of us is a 100 percent reliable accountant when it comes to processing social information we care about; the way the human mind works, we simply do not tally events

> Our minds thus grow in spots; and like grease spots, the spots spread. But we let them spread as little as possible; we keep unaltered as much of our old knowledge, as many of our old prejudices and beliefs, as we can.
> —William James, 1907

> The mind of a bigot is like the pupil of the eye; the more light you pour upon it the more it will contract.
> —Oliver Wendell Holmes, Jr., 1901

objectively. Accordingly, individuals who hold specific opinions (or schemas) about certain groups will process information about those groups differently from the way they process information about other groups. Specifically, information consistent with their notions about these target groups will be given more attention, will be rehearsed (or recalled) more often, and therefore will be remembered better than information that is not consistent with these notions (Bodenhausen, 1988; Bodenhausen & Lichtenstein, 1987; Dovidio, Evans, & Tyler, 1986; O'Sullivan & Durso, 1984; Wyer, 1988). These are the familiar effects of schematic processing that we discussed in Chapter 4. Applying these effects to the topic of prejudice, we can see that whenever a member of a group behaves as we expect him or her to, the behavior confirms and even strengthens our stereotype. Thus, stereotypes become relatively impervious to change; after all, proof that they are accurate is always out there—that is, when our beliefs guide us to see it.

Table 13.1

Some common stereotypes held by Princeton students over the years.

GROUP	1933	1951	1969
Americans	industrious	materialistic	materialistic
	intelligent	intelligent	ambitious
	materialistic	industrious	pleasure-loving
	ambitious	pleasure-loving	industrious
	progressive	individualistic	nonventional
Japanese	intelligent	imitative	industrious
	industrious	sly	ambitious
	progressive	extremely	efficient
	shrewd	nationalistic	intelligent
	sly	treacherous	progressive
Jews	shrewd	shrewd	ambitious
	mercenary	intelligent	materialistic
	industrious	industrious	intelligent
	grasping	mercenary	industrious
	intelligent	ambitious	shrewd
Negroes (African Americans)	superstitious	superstitious	musical
	lazy	musical	happy-go-lucky
	happy-go-lucky	lazy	lazy
	ignorant	ignorant	pleasure-loving
	musical	pleasure-loving	ostentatious

Source: Adapted from Gilbert, 1951; Karlins, Coffman, & Walters, 1969; Katz & Braly, 1933.
Note: The general stability as well as changes in these stereotypes.

The Activation of Stereotypes.   Stereotypes reflect cultural beliefs—that is, within a given society, they are easily recognized descriptions of members of a particular group. For example, we all know the stereotype of the woman driver or the overemotional female. Even if we don't believe these stereotypes, we can easily recognize them as common beliefs held by others. For instance, in a series of studies conducted at Princeton University over 36 years, students were asked to assign traits to members of various ethnic and national groups (Gilbert, 1951; Karlins, Coffman, & Walters, 1969; Katz & Braly, 1933). The participants could do so easily, and to a large extent they agreed with each other. They knew the stereotypes, even for groups about whom they had little real knowledge, such as Turks. Table 13.1 shows some of the results of these studies, which were conducted in 1933, 1951, and 1969. Note how negative the early stereotypes were in 1933 and how they became somewhat less negative over time. What is particularly interesting about these studies is that participants in 1951 began to voice discomfort with the task (such discomfort, by the way, didn't exist in 1933). By 1969, many participants not only felt discomfort but they also were reluctant to label the various groups, because they did not believe the stereotypes; they performed the task only after making clear that their choice of labels reflected the stereotypes present in society (and thus were known to them) but did not reflect their own beliefs (Karlins et al., 1969).

This brings us to an intriguing social cognition puzzle: If you know a stereotype, will it affect your cognitive processing about a target person, even if you neither believe the stereotype nor consider yourself prejudiced against this group? Imagine this scenario: You are a member of a group, judging another person's performance. Someone in your group makes an ugly, stereotypical comment about the individual. Will the comment affect your judgment of his or her performance? "No," you are probably thinking; "I'd disregard it completely." But would you be able to do so? Is it possible that the comment would trigger in your mind all the other negative stereotypes and beliefs about people in that group and affect your judgment about this particular individual?

Jeff Greenberg and Tom Pyszczynski (1985) decided to find out. They had two confederates, one African American and one white, stage a debate about nuclear energy for groups of research participants. For half the groups, the African American debater presented far better arguments and clearly won the debate; for the other half, the white debater performed far better and won the debate. The participants were asked to rate both debaters' skill. However, right beforehand the critical experimental manipulation occurred. A confederate planted in the group did one of three things: (a) He made a highly racist remark about the African American debater—"There's no way that nigger won the debate"; (b) he made a nonracist remark about the African American debater—"There's no way the pro [or con] debater won the debate"; or (c) he made no comment at all.

The researchers reasoned that if those participants who heard the racist comment were able to disregard it completely, they would not rate the African American debater any differently from the way participants in the other conditions, who had not heard such a comment, rated him. Was that the case? The data presented in Figure 13.3 clearly show that the answer is no. The data compared the ratings of skill given to the African American and white debaters when they were each in the losing role. As you can see, the participants rated the African American and white debaters as being equally skillful when no comment

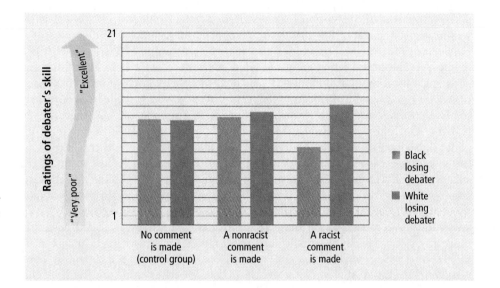

FIGURE 13.3 The activation of a stereotypical belief. ■ When a derogatory comment was made about the black debater, it activated the latent stereotype held by the observers, causing them to lower their rating of his performance. (Adapted from Greenberg & Pyszczynski, 1985)

was made; similarly, when a nonracist, nonstereotypical comment was made about the African American debater, he was rated as being just as skillful as the white debater. However, after the racial stereotype was activated in participants' minds by the racist comment, they rated the African American debater significantly lower than participants in the other groups did. In other words, this derogatory comment activated other negative, stereotypical beliefs about African Americans, so that the participants who heard it rated the same performance by the debater as less skilled than those who had not heard the racist remark.

These results suggest that anything that activates a stereotype can have dire consequences for how a particular member of that out-group is perceived. How does this activation process work? Patricia Devine (1989) has done some fascinating work on how stereotypical and prejudiced beliefs affect cognitive processing. Devine differentiates between *automatic processing* of information and *controlled processing* of information. An automatic process is one over which we have no control. For example, even if you score very low on a prejudice scale, you are certainly familiar with certain stereotypes that exist in the culture, such as "African Americans are hostile," "Jews are materialistic," or "Homosexual men are effeminate." These stereotypes are automatically triggered under certain conditions—they just pop into one's mind. Since the process is automatic, you can't control it or stop it from occurring. You know the stereotypes, and thus they come to mind—say, when you are meeting someone or rating a person's performance. However, for people who are not deeply prejudiced, their controlled processes can suppress or override these stereotypes. For example, such a person can say to him- or herself, "Hey, that stereotype isn't fair and it isn't right—African Americans are no more hostile than whites. Ignore the stereotype about this person's ethnicity."

What Devine's theory suggests, therefore, is a two-step model of cognitive processing: The automatic processing brings up information—in this case, stereotypes—but the controlled (or conscious) processing can refute or ignore it. But what happens if you are busy, overwhelmed, distracted, or not paying much attention? You may not initiate that controlled level of processing, meaning that the information supplied by the automatic process—the stereotype—is still present in your mind and unrefuted. Devine (1989) set out to study exactly this process: that a stereotype is automatically activated when a member of an out-group is encountered, and the stereotype can be ignored through conscious processing—for example, by people who are not prejudiced (see Figure 13.4).

First, Devine administered a test of prejudice to a large number of students and, according to their scores, divided them into high-prejudice and low-prejudice groups. Next, she demonstrated that both high- and low-prejudice people possessed equal knowledge of racial stereotypes. Next came the test of automatic and conscious processing: She flashed stereotyped words (e.g., *black, hostile, lazy, welfare*) and neutral words (e.g., *however, what, said*) on a screen so quickly that the words were just below the participants' perceptual (conscious) awareness. They saw something, but they weren't sure what—that is, their conscious processing couldn't identify the words. However, their automatic processing could recognize the words. How could Devine be sure?

FIGURE 13.4   A two-step model of the cognitive processing of stereotypes.

A TWO-STEP MODEL OF THE COGNITIVE PROCESSING OF STEREOTYPES

AUTOMATIC PROCESSING occurs whenever an appropriate stimulus is encountered--either a member of a stereotyped group or contact with a stereotypical statement--causing the stereotypes for that group to be accessed from memory.
Automatic processing occurs without your awareness. You don't purposefully think these thoughts; they just "happen"--triggered by the presence of the stimulus.

Controlled Processing occurs with your awareness--as when you choose to disregard or ignore the stereotyped information that has been brought to mind.

After flashing the words, she asked the participants to read a story about "Donald" (his ethnicity was not mentioned) and to rate their impressions of him. Donald was described somewhat ambiguously; he did some things in the story that could be interpreted either positively or negatively. The participants who had seen the words reflecting the stereotype of black Americans interpreted Donald significantly more negatively than those who had seen the neutral words did. Thus, for one group the negative stereotype had been primed (activated unconsciously through automatic processing); without their awareness, the participants were affected by these hostile and negative words, as indicated in their ratings of the Donald character. Because these stereotypes were operating outside their conscious cognitive control, white students who were low in prejudice were just as influenced by the cultural stereotype (e.g., that blacks are hostile) as the prejudiced students.

In her final experiment, Devine gave the students a task that involved their conscious processing: She asked them to list all the words they could think of that are used to describe black Americans. The high-prejudice students listed significantly more negative words than the low-prejudice students did. In other words, the less prejudiced participants used their conscious processing to edit out the negative stereotype and therefore were able to respond in a manner that was free of its influence.

While Devine's work is of great interest, recent research has suggested some important correctives—primarily, that the phenomenon is not as universal as she believed. Let us explain: According to Devine, pretty much everyone in American society has learned the negative stereotype of African Americans; thus, this negative stereotype is activated automatically in everyone. Accordingly, to be nonprejudiced we must learn to suppress or overcome this automatic response. But Russell Fazio and his colleagues have shown that considerable variability exists in people's automatic processing of negative stereotypes (Fazio, Jackson, Dunton, & Williams, in press).

The Fazio team developed a clever way of measuring people's automatic processing of stereotypes. They presented people with words on a computer screen and asked them to judge whether the meaning of the words was good or bad. For example, when people saw the word *attractive* they pressed a key to indicate that this word has a good meaning, and when they saw the word *disgusting* they pressed a key to indicate that this word has a bad meaning.

On some trials, the words were preceded by a quick flash of a picture of a human face. People were told to look at the faces but to respond only to the meaning of the word that subsequently appeared on the screen. Thus, if you were a participant you would have seen a quick flash of a face, then a word such as *attractive*, and pressed a key to indicate that this was a "good" word. Now here's the interesting part: It just so happened that some of the faces were of African Americans and some were of whites. Remember, these faces were flashed very quickly (for about a third of a second). This was long enough for people to see the faces and have an automatic emotional reaction to them but too brief for people to control or suppress this reaction. As soon as they had a positive or negative reaction to the face, the word appeared on the screen and they had to decide whether the word was good or bad.

The point of the study was to see whether or not the presentation of the faces influenced how long it took people to respond to positive and negative words. Think about how this would work: If a participant is prejudiced against African Americans and this prejudice is ingrained and automatic, then negative feelings will be triggered automatically when the person sees a picture of an African American. This negative reaction should make it easier to respond "bad" to a negative word such as *disgusting*, because negative feelings are already present when the word appears. A negative reaction should make it harder to respond "good" to a positive word such as *attractive*, because this feeling is opposite to the meaning of the word.

The researchers constructed an index of automatic prejudice by computing the extent to which faces of African Americans slowed down responses to positive words and sped up responses to negative words. Fazio and his colleagues found considerable variability in people's level of automatic prejudice. Some people appeared to have automatic negative reactions to African Americans, whereas others did not. Further, this amount of automatic prejudice was found to predict people's behavior. At the end of the study, all participants were debriefed by an experimenter who "happened" to be an African American woman. This experimenter rated how friendly the participants treated her. Those who had shown the highest level of automatic prejudice on the word judgment task tended to act in a cold and disinterested manner toward the experimenter, whereas those who had shown the lowest amount of prejudice were far more likely to act in a warm and friendly manner.

Fazio and his colleagues suggest that, regarding attitudes toward African Americans, there are three kinds of people: (a) those who do not have an automatic negative reaction to African Americans, (b) those who do have an automatic negative reaction but have no qualms about expressing these feelings (i.e., are willing to be prejudiced), and (c) those who have an automatic negative reaction but want to suppress this reaction.

John Bargh has taken the idea of automatic prejudice a step further, showing that it can be triggered when certain ideas about the target group come to mind. Bargh and his colleagues examined negative reactions of men toward women (Bargh, Raymond, Pryor, & Strack, 1995). As you know, some men are prone to use sexual violence against women. Bargh and his colleagues investigated the possibility that in these men's minds there may be an automatic link between power and sex, such that thinking about power automatically triggers sexual attraction, without the men even recognizing this link. Just as some people have negative feelings toward African Americans that are expressed quickly and automatically, so too may some men have aggressive, sexual reactions to women that are expressed automatically, especially when power is on their minds.

To illustrate this idea, Bargh and his colleagues gave men a questionnaire that measured how prone they were toward sexual aggression (e.g., how much of a "turn-on" they found rape fantasies to be). The men also participated in a laboratory study in which the concept of power was primed in some men but not in others. (Recall that priming is a technique designed to activate a concept and make it salient.)

In the experiment, the men participated in the company of a young woman who they believed was another participant but who was really a confederate of the experimenter. After the priming procedure, the men were asked to rate how attractive they thought this woman was. Did priming the concept of power increase their attraction to the woman? The answer was yes for men who scored high on the sexual aggression questionnaire but no for the men who scored low on that questionnaire. In other words, for some men (but not for others) there is an automatic link in their minds between power and sexual attractiveness; priming or activating the concept of power increases the extent to which they find women attractive. The disturbing implication of this research is that these men are not aware of the link between power and sex in their minds and thus may not know that their attraction to women is influenced by feelings of power. They may simply "not get it," due to the fact that these feelings are triggered automatically, with no conscious awareness of where they came from (Bargh & Raymond, 1995).

illusory correlation: the tendency to see relationships, or correlations, between events that are actually unrelated

The Illusory Correlation. Another way that our cognitive processing perpetuates stereotypical thinking is through the phenomenon of **illusory correlation** (Chapman, 1967). When we expect two things to be related, we fool ourselves into believing that they are—even when they are actually unrelated. Many illusory correlations exist in our society. For example, there is a common belief that couples who haven't been able to have children will conceive a child after they adopt a child—apparently because after the adoption, they feel less anxious and stressed. Guess what? This correlation is entirely illusory. Occasionally, an apparently infertile couple does conceive after adopting a child, but this occurs with no greater frequency than for apparently infertile couples who do not adopt. The former event, because it is so charmingly vivid, simply makes more of an impression on us when it happens, creating the illusory correlation (Gilovich, 1991).

What does all this have to do with prejudice and stereotypes? Illusory correlations are most likely to occur when the events or people are distinctive or conspicuous—that is, when they are different from the run-of-the-mill, typical social scene we are accustomed to (Hamilton, 1981; Hamilton & Gifford, 1976). Minority group members—for example, as defined by race—are by definition distinctive, since fewer of them than of majority group members—in this case, whites—are present in the society. Other groups, who are not distinctive in terms of numbers—such as women, who make up 50 percent of the species—may nonetheless become distinctive or conspicuous because of a nonstereotypical profession or talent—for example, a woman member of the U.S. Senate.

David Hamilton and Robert Gifford (1976) have shown that such distinctiveness leads to the creation of and belief in an illusory correlation—that is, a relationship between the distinctive target person and the behavior he or she displays. This illusory correlation is then applied to all members of the target group. Hamilton and Gifford (1976) presented information to research participants about two hypothetical groups of people: the A's and the B's. Of the information presented, two-thirds was positive about both groups, and one-third was negative about both groups. However, more information in general was presented about group A than about group B. Thus, while the ratio of desirable to undesirable information was the same for both groups, more than twice as much information of both types was given about the A's than about the B's. When asked to estimate how much information of both types was presented about each group, the participants overestimated the number of times the two most distinctive (less frequent) variables were paired—group B and undesirable behavior. Figure 13.5 depicts this finding. B's were more distinctive because there were fewer of them; undesirable behavior was more distinctive because there was less of it; and—voilà!—an illusory correlation was perceived between the two.

How does this work in everyday life? Let's say you don't know many Jews, so that for you, interacting with a Jew is a distinctive event and for you, Jews in general are distinctive people. Let's say you meet a Jewish individual who is an investment broker. Let's say you meet a second Jew who is a bond trader. An illu-

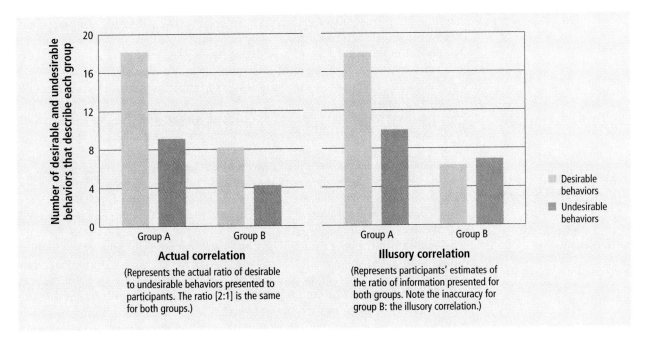

FIGURE 13.5   The illusory correlation. ■ The less information you have about a group, the more likely it is that you will fall victim to the illusory correlation. (Adapted from Hamilton & Gifford, 1976)

sory correlation between Jews and money is created. If you also know the stereotype that Jews are materialistic, the correlation you perceived based on your personal experiences seems all the more sound. The result is that, in the future, you will be more likely to notice situations in which Jews are behaving materialistically; you will be less likely to notice situations in which Jews are not behaving materialistically; and you will be less likely to notice situations in which non-Jews are behaving materialistically. You will have processed new information guided by your illusory correlation, seeing what you expect to see. You will also have strengthened your illusory correlation, confirming in your mind that your stereotype is right (Hamilton & Gifford, 1976; Hamilton & Sherman, 1989; Mullen & Johnson, 1988).

We should note that illusory correlations are created in a far more passive fashion too. It is not necessary to have personal experience with people in a distinctive group—television, newspapers, and other forms of media create illusory correlations when they portray women, minorities, and other groups in stereotypical roles (Busby, 1975; Friedman, 1977; McArthur & Resko, 1975).

Revising Stereotypical Beliefs.   All this discussion of the perils of information processing has probably left you quite depressed. How do you get people to change their stereotypical beliefs? Is it possible to override these social cognition processes? What sort of information would refute a stereotype? Let's say our next-door neighbor harbors two pet stereotypes that we find particularly annoying: He thinks that professors are lazy and that African Americans and Asian Americans are unpatriotic. What would happen if we provided him with evidence that his stereotypes are incorrect? For example, what if we showed him data, based on the random observation of 27,000 professors across the country,

> A fanatic is one who can't change his mind and won't change the subject.
> –Winston Churchill, 1944

demonstrating that professors work a 50-hour week? What if we pointed out that General Colin Powell, former chairman of the Joint Chiefs of Staff and the most influential military figure in the country, happens to be African American? What if we told him that the most highly decorated combat unit in World War II was composed solely of Asian Americans? Would this information affect our neighbor's stereotypes?

bookkeeping model: information inconsistent with a stereotype that leads to a modification of the stereotype

conversion model: information inconsistent with a stereotype that leads to a radical change in the stereotype

subtyping model: information inconsistent with a stereotype that leads to the creation of a new substereotype to accommodate the information without changing the initial stereotype

According to Renée Webber and Jennifer Crocker (1983), it depends on how the disconfirming information is presented. Webber and Crocker proposed three possible theories, or models, for revising stereotypical beliefs: (a) the **bookkeeping model,** wherein each piece of disconfirming information modifies the stereotype; (b) the **conversion model,** wherein the stereotype radically changes in response to a powerful, salient piece of information; and (c) the **subtyping model,** wherein new subtype or subcategory stereotypes are created to accommodate the disconfirming information.

Webber and Crocker (1983) then conducted several experiments to see which model(s) might be right. They presented participants with information that disconfirmed their stereotypes about two occupational groups: librarians and corporate lawyers. In one condition, the participants received information in the bookkeeping style, one disconfirming fact after another. In another condition, the participants received conversion information, a fact that strongly disconfirmed their stereotype. In the final condition, the participants received information that could lead them to create a subtype of their stereotype. Did these three styles of disconfirming information change people's minds about their stereotypes?

Webber and Crocker (1983) found that the bookkeeping information and the subtyping information did weaken the participants' stereotypes but that the conversion information did not. Why? Here is what occurred. When the information inconsistent with the stereotype was dispersed, with many members of the categorized group exhibiting the disconfirming traits, participants employed a bookkeeping strategy and gradually modified their beliefs. In other words, if our neighbor found out, on many occasions, that numerous professors worked a 50-hour week, this would slowly but eventually lead him to abandon the notion that

■ General Colin Powell (photographed here while serving as chairman of the Joint Chiefs of Staff) is a popular hero and the first African American to have received serious popular consideration for the presidency. Might a bigoted person vote for him? Perhaps—if the bigot characterized General Powell as "the exception that proves the rule."

professors are lazy. In contrast, when the disconfirming traits were concentrated among only a few individuals of the group, participants used a subtyping model. In other words, if our neighbor was confronted with the undeniable patriotism of General Powell, this would lead to the persistence of the old stereotype about African Americans, plus the creation of a new substereotype to the effect that "There may be a few exceptions, like Colin Powell"; thus, General Powell becomes the well-known exception that proves the rule, leaving the original stereotype pretty much intact. Finally, the conversion approach just didn't work: One fact about an out-group that is evidence against the stereotype was just not powerful enough to change people's minds—which shouldn't surprise you, given our discussion of social cognition processes.

Two points need to be emphasized: (a) We all stereotype others to some extent—it is part of being a cognitive miser—and (b) emotional attitudes are harder to change than nonemotional ones. Thus, a strongly prejudiced person engages in stereotyping in a deeper, more thorough manner than the rest of us. Through this process, prejudiced attitudes become like a fortress—a closed circuit of cognitions, if you will—and this fortress drastically reduces the effectiveness of logical argument or disconfirming information.

The Way We Assign Meaning: Attributional Biases

As we discussed in Chapter 5, the people and situations we encounter in our social world are not labeled with neon signs telling us everything we need to know about them. Instead, we must rely on one aspect of social cognition—*attributional processes*—to determine why people behave as they do. Just as we form attributions to make sense out of one person's behavior, so too do we make attributions about whole groups of people. As you shall see, the attributional biases we discussed in Chapter 5 come back to haunt us now in a far more damaging and dangerous form: prejudice and discrimination.

Dispositional Versus Situational Explanations.   One reason stereotypes are so insidious and persistent is the human tendency to make dispositional attributions—that is, to leap to the conclusion that a person's behavior is due to some aspect of his or her personality rather than to some aspect of the situation. This is the familiar *fundamental attribution error* we discussed in Chapter 5. Although attributing people's behavior to their dispositions is often accurate, human behavior is also shaped by situational forces. Thus, an overreliance on dispositional attributions frequently leads us to make attributional mistakes. We hear Dawn make an insulting remark to Kristen and we form a dispositional attribution about Dawn: that she's a rude, arrogant person. In doing so, we haven't taken into account what else might have been going on in the situation to have caused Dawn's behavior. (What did Kristen say to her first? Did something terrible happen to Dawn today, so that she's in a tense, upset mood?) Making dispositional attributions when they are not warranted can get us into trouble. Your opinion of Dawn will certainly be different after making that dispositional attribution than if you had made a situational one. Seeing her behavior as dispositionally caused will lead you to expect her to be mean-spirited in the future; you may suspect you can't trust her. Given that this sort of process operates on an individual level, you can only imagine the problems and complications that arise when we overzealously act out the fundamental attribution error for a whole group of people—an out-group.

> The cause is hidden, but the result is known.
> –Ovid

■ Unfortunately, classic works such as *Oliver Twist* may have helped perpetrate negative stereotypes of Jews.

ultimate attribution error: our tendency to make dispositional attributions about an entire group of people

Stereotypes are dispositional attributions—negative ones. Thomas Pettigrew (1979) has called our making dispositional attributions about a whole group of people (as occurs when we stereotype them) the **ultimate attribution error.** For example, some of the stereotypes that characterize anti-Semitism are the result of Christians committing the fundamental attribution error when interpreting the behavior of Jews. These stereotypes have a long history, extending over several centuries. When the Jews were first forced to flee their homeland during the third Diaspora, some 2,500 years ago, they were not allowed to own land or become artisans in the new regions in which they settled. Needing a livelihood, some took to lending money—a profession they were allowed to have. Although this choice of occupation was an accidental byproduct of restrictive laws, it led to a dispositional attribution about Jews: that they were interested only in dealing with money and not in honest work, like farming. As this attribution became an ultimate error, Jews were labeled conniving, vicious parasites of the kind dramatized and immortalized by Shakespeare in the character of Shylock in *The Merchant of Venice* or of Fagin in Dickens's *Oliver Twist*. This dispositional stereotype contributed greatly to the barbarous consequences of anti-Semitism in Europe during the 1930s and 1940s and has persisted even in the face of clear, disconfirming evidence—such as that produced by the birth of the State of Israel, where Jews tilled the soil and made the desert bloom.

Dispositional attributions are easy to see in action. As mentioned earlier, Alice Eagley and Valerie Steffen (1984) suggest that women are thought of as genetically more nurturant and less assertive than men because women have traditionally been assigned the role of homemaker. Thus, the attributions about what women are like become dispositional (e.g., nurturant, submissive), while the situational causes for their behavior (the demands and constraints of the homemaker role) are ignored or simply not noticed.

Similarly, many Americans have a stereotype about African American and Hispanic men that involves aggression and the potential for violence—a very powerful dispositional attribution. Galen Bodenhausen (1988) found that college students, playing the role of jurors in a mock trail, were more likely to find a defendant guilty of a given crime simply if his name was Carlos Ramirez rather than Robert Johnson. Thus, any situational information or extenuating circumstances that might have explained the defendant's actions were ignored when the powerful dispositional attribution was stereotypically triggered—in this case, by the Hispanic name.

In a further study, Galen Bodenhausen and Robert Wyer (1985) set up another dispositional versus situational possibility, wherein college students read fictionalized files on prisoners who were being considered for parole, and used the information contained in the files to make a parole decision. Sometimes the crime matched the common stereotype of the offender—for example, when a Hispanic male, Carlos Ramirez, committed assault and battery, or when an upper-class Anglo-Saxon, Ashley Chamberlaine, committed embezzlement. In other instances, the crimes were inconsistent with the stereotypes. When the prisoners' crimes were consistent with participants' stereotypes, the students were harsher in their recommendations for parole. In addition, they tended to ignore other information that was relevant to a parole decision but was inconsistent with the stereotype, such as evidence of good behavior in prison. Thus, when people behave in a way that conforms to our stereotype, we tend to blind ourselves to information that would provide clues about why they might have behaved as they did. Instead, we assume that something about their character or disposition, and not their situation or life circumstances, caused their behavior. In other words, when the fundamental attribution error raises its ugly head, we make dispositional attributions (based on our stereotypical beliefs about an ethnic or racial group) and not situational ones.

***The Bell Curve* Revisited.**   This decade bore witness to the reemergence of an angry and vituperative debate that has raged in our society for almost two centuries. The recent flare-up occurred when a scholarly book, *The Bell Curve* (Herrnstein & Murray, 1995), suggested that the statistically significant difference in academic performance between African Americans and Anglo Americans might have a genetic component.

Let us look at the facts. There is a statistical difference in academic test performance among various cultural groups in this country. In general, although there is considerable overlap, as a group Asian Americans perform slightly better than Anglo Americans, who in turn perform better than African Americans. This difference is undeniably true. The key question is, why does it occur? Is the reason for the difference dispositional or situational? In a striking series of experiments, Claude Steele and Joshua Aronson (1995) demonstrated that at least one major contributing factor is clearly situational and is based on a phenomenon they call **stereotype vulnerability**. Specifically, when African American students find themselves in highly evaluative educational situations, most tend to experience apprehension about confirming the existing negative cultural stereotype of "intellectual inferiority." In effect, they are saying, "If I perform poorly on this test, it will reflect poorly on me and on my race." This extra burden of apprehension in turn interferes with their ability to perform well in these situations. For example, in one of their experiments Steele and Aronson administered a difficult verbal test, the GRE, individually to African American and white students at

stereotype vulnerability: the apprehension experienced by members of a minority group that they might behave in a manner that confirms an existing cultural stereotype

Stanford University. Half the students of each race were led to believe that the investigator was interested in measuring their intellectual ability; the other half were led to believe that the investigator was merely trying to develop the test itself—and, because the test was not yet valid or reliable, they were assured that their performance would mean nothing in terms of their actual ability.

The results confirmed the researchers' speculations. White students performed equally well regardless of whether or not they believed the test was being used as a diagnostic tool. Those African American students who believed the test was nondiagnostic of their abilities performed as well as white students; in contrast, those African American students who were led to believe that the test was measuring their abilities performed less well than white students. In subsequent experiments in the same series, Steele and Aronson also found that, if race is made more salient, the decrement in performance among African Americans is even more pronounced.

The phenomenon of stereotype vulnerability is not limited to race but applies to gender as well. Thus, a similar pattern of results was found for women (compared to men) when taking math tests (Spencer & Steele, 1996). That is, as you know, a common stereotype of women: that compared to men, they are not very good at math. In this experiment, when women were led to believe that a particular test was gender-relevant, they did not perform as well as men; however, in another condition, when women were led to believe that the same test was *not* gender-relevant, they performed as well as men.

Expectations and Distortions.   As we noted above, when a member of an out-group behaves as we expected him or her to behave, it confirms and even strengthens our stereotype. But what happens when an out-group member behaves in an unexpected, nonstereotypical fashion? Attribution theory provides

■ This cartoon depicts a common stereotype of the Mexican as lazy. Note how your eye focuses on the one sleeping person but tends to ignore the ten hardworking persons. Without intending to, the cartoonist is showing us how powerfully distorting a stereotype can be.

Drawing by Alain; © 1951 The New Yorker: 25th Annual Album: Harper & Bros.

the answer: We can simply engage in some attributional fancy footwork and emerge with our dispositional stereotype intact. Principally, we can make situational attributions about the exception—for example, that the person really is like that but it just isn't apparent in this situation.

This phenomenon was beautifully captured in the laboratory by William Ickes and his colleagues (1982). Here college men were scheduled, in pairs, to participate in the experiment. In one condition, the experimenter casually informed one participant that his partner was extremely unfriendly; in the other condition, the experimenter told one participant that his partner was extremely friendly. In both conditions, the participants went out of their way to be nice to their partner, and their partner returned their friendliness—that is, he behaved warmly and smiled a lot, as college men tend to do when they are treated nicely. The difference was that those participants who expected their partner to be unfriendly interpreted his friendly behavior as phony—as a temporary, fake response to their own nice behavior. They were convinced that underneath it all, he really was an unfriendly person. Accordingly, when the observed behavior—friendliness—was unexpected and contrary to their dispositional attribution, participants attributed it to the situation: "He's just pretending to be friendly." The dispositional attribution emerged unscathed.

The cartoon on the previous page demonstrates this ability to explain away disconfirming situational evidence and maintain a dispositional stereotype. This cartoon, from 1951, is a racist depiction using the stereotype of Mexicans as lazy. While ten Mexicans are seen in the background working hard, the cartoon focuses on the stereotypical image in the foreground. The cartoon's message is that the lazy individual is the true exemplar of his ethnic group. No matter how many others refute the stereotype, the cartoon is implying, it is still true. (Note that some 40 years ago, not only was this message considered acceptable, but this cartoon was chosen as one of the best of the year.)

> I will look at any additional evidence to confirm the opinion to which I have already come.
>
> –Lord Molson, British politician

Blaming the Victim.   Try as they might, it is not always easy for people who have rarely been discriminated against to fully understand what it's like to be a target of prejudice. Well-intentioned members of the dominant majority will sympathize with the plight of African Americans, Hispanic Americans, Asian Americans, Jews, women, homosexuals, and other groups who are oppressed in our society, but true empathy does not come easily to those who are accustomed to being judged on the basis of their own merit and not their racial, ethnic, religious, or other group membership. And when empathy is absent, it is sometimes hard to avoid falling into the trap of **blaming the victim** for his or her plight. This may take the form of the "well-deserved reputation." It goes something like this: "If the Jews have been victimized throughout their history, they must have been doing something to deserve it," or "That woman who got herself raped should have been more suspicious of her date." Such suggestions constitute a demand that members of the out-group conform to more stringent standards of behavior than those set for the majority.

blaming the victim: our tendency to blame individuals (make dispositional attributions) for their victimization, typically motivated by a desire to see the world as a fair place

Ironically, as we discussed in Chapter 5, this tendency to blame victims for their victimization—attributing their predicaments to deficits in their abilities and character—is typically motivated by an understandable desire to see the world as a fair and just place, one where people get what they deserve and deserve what they get. As Melvin Lerner (1980) has shown, most people, when confronted with evidence of an inequitable outcome that is otherwise difficult to explain, find a way to blame the victim. For example, in one experiment Lerner and his colleagues found that if two people worked equally hard on the same task and, by the flip of a coin, one received a sizable reward and the other received nothing, observers—after the fact—tended to reconstruct what happened and convince themselves that the unlucky person must have worked less hard. Similarly, negative attitudes toward the poor and the homeless—including blaming them for their own plight—are more prevalent among individuals who display a strong belief in a just world (Furnham & Gunter, 1984).

How does the belief in a just world lead to derogation of a victim? When something bad happens to another person (e.g., the person is mugged or raped), we will undoubtedly feel sorry for him or her but at the same time will also feel relieved that this horrible thing didn't happen to us. In addition, we will also feel scared that such a thing might happen to us in the future. How can we cope with these fears and worries? The best way to protect ourselves from the fear we feel when we hear about someone else's tragedy is to convince ourselves that the person must have done something to bring it on him- or herself. Therefore, in our own minds we are safe, because we would have behaved more cautiously (Jones & Aronson, 1973).

Most of us are quite adept at reconstructing situations after the fact, in order to support our belief in a just world. It simply requires making a dispositional attribution—to the victim—and not a situational one—to the scary, random events that can happen to anyone at any time. In a fascinating experiment by Ronnie Janoff-Bulman and her colleagues (1985), college students who were provided with a description of a young woman's friendly behavior toward a man judged that behavior as completely appropriate. Yet in another condition of the experiment, students were given the same description, plus the information that the encounter ended with the young woman being raped by the man. In this condition, the students rated her behavior as inappropriate, as her having brought the rape on herself. Such findings are not limited to American college students reading hypothetical cases. For example, in a survey conducted in England, a striking 33 percent of the population were found to believe that victims of rape are almost always to blame for it (Wagstaff, 1982). How can we account for such harsh attributions? Most of us find it frightening to think that we live in a world where people, through no fault of their own, can be raped, discriminated against, deprived of equal pay for equal work, or denied the basic necessities of life. By the same token, if 6 million Jews are exterminated for no apparent reason, it is, in some strange way, comforting to believe they must have done something to bring those events on themselves. The irony is overwhelming: Such thinking makes the world seem safer to us.

Self-Fulfilling Prophecies.   All other things being equal, if you believe that Amy is stupid and treat her accordingly, chances are that she will not say a lot of clever things in your presence. This is the well-known **self-fulfilling prophecy**, discussed in Chapter 4. How does this come about? If you believe Amy is stupid, you probably will not ask her interesting questions and you will not listen intently while she is talking; indeed, you might even look out the window or yawn. You behave this way because of a simple expectation: Why waste energy paying attention to Amy if she is unlikely to say anything smart or interesting? This is bound to have an important impact on Amy's behavior, for if the people she is talking to aren't paying much attention, she will feel uneasy and will probably clam up and not come out with all the poetry and wisdom within her. This serves to confirm the belief you had about her in the first place. The circle is closed; the self-fulfilling prophecy is complete.

The relevance of this phenomenon to stereotyping and discrimination was elegantly demonstrated in an experiment by Carl Word, Mark Zanna, and Joel Cooper (1974). They asked white college undergraduates to interview several job applicants; some of the applicants were white, and others were African American. Unwittingly, the college students displayed discomfort and lack of interest when interviewing African American applicants. For example, they sat farther away, they tended to stammer when talking, and they terminated the interview far sooner than was the case when they were interviewing white applicants. Can you guess how this behavior might have affected the African American applicants? To find out, the researchers, in a second experiment, systematically varied the behavior of the interviewers (actually confederates) so that it coincided with the way the real interviewers had treated the African American or white interviewees in the first experiment. But in the second experiment, all of the interviewees were white. The researchers videotaped the proceedings and had the applicants rated by independent judges. They found that those applicants who were interviewed the way African Americans had been interviewed in the first experiment were judged to be far more nervous and far less effective than those who were interviewed the way whites had been interviewed in the first experiment. In sum, these experiments demonstrate clearly that when African Americans are interviewed by whites, they are unintentionally placed at a disadvantage and are likely to perform less well than their white counterparts (see Figure 13.6).

On a societal level, the insidiousness of the self-fulfilling prophecy goes even further. Suppose there is a general belief that a particular group is irredeemably stupid, uneducable, and fit only for menial jobs. Why waste educational

FIGURE 13.6 An experiment demonstrating self-fulfilling prophecies.

STUDY #1:

Interviewer sits far away and has short interview.

Applicant's judged nervous, ineffective, and less competent.

Interviewer sits closer and has longer interview.

Applicant's judged poised, effective, and competent.

White interviewer treats job applicants differently during interview, based on their race. Independent judges later rate black applicants as performing more poorly than white applicants.

STUDY #2:

Sits far away and has short interview.

Applicant's judged nervous, ineffective, and less competent.

Sits closer and has longer interview.

Applicant's judged poised, effective, and competent.

When white interviewers were trained to use one of the two interviewing "styles" from study #1, white applicants were judged as performing more poorly when they received the style previously used for Blacks than when they received the style previously used for whites.

resources on them? Hence, they are given inadequate schooling. Thirty years later, what do you find? An entire group that, with few exceptions, is fit only for menial jobs. "See? I was right all the time," says the bigot. "How fortunate that we didn't waste our precious educational resources on such people!" The self-fulfilling prophecy strikes again.

The Way We Allocate Resources: Realistic Conflict Theory

One of the most obvious sources of conflict and prejudice is competition—for scarce resources, for political power, and for social status. Indeed, it can be said that whatever problems result from the simple in-group versus out-group phenomenon, they will be magnified by real economic, political, or status competition. **Realistic conflict theory** states that when resources are limited, a real conflict between groups exists; there simply isn't enough of the valuable commodity to go around. Competition results, and not surprisingly, negative feelings develop toward the group against which one is competing. From there, it's a short step to derogatory attributions, ugly stereotypes, and outright discrimination against members of the out-group (Levine & Campbell, 1972; Olzak & Nagel, 1986; Sherif, 1966; White, 1977). Thus, prejudiced attitudes tend to increase when times are tense and conflict exists over mutually exclusive goals. For example, prejudice has existed between Anglos and Mexican American migrant workers over a limited number of jobs, between Arabs and Israelis over disputed territory, and between northerners and southerners over the abolition of slavery. At the present time, such realistic conflict in Germany is erupting in violence against residents of Turkish origin at the hands of the German neo-Nazis.

realistic conflict theory: the theory that limited resources lead to conflict between groups and result in increased prejudice and discrimination

Economic and Political Competition.   In his classic study of prejudice in a small industrial town, John Dollard (1938) was among the first to document the relationship between discrimination and economic competition. While initially there was no discernible prejudice against the new German immigrants to this American town, prejudice flourished as jobs grew scarce:

> Local whites largely drawn from the surrounding farms manifested considerable direct aggression toward the newcomers. Scornful and derogatory opinions were expressed about these Germans, and the native whites had a satisfying sense of superiority toward them. . . . The chief element in the permission to be aggressive against the Germans was rivalry for jobs and status in the local woodenware plants. The native whites felt definitely crowded for their jobs by the entering German groups and in case of bad times had a chance to blame the Germans, who by their presence provided more competitors for the scarcer jobs. There seemed to be no traditional pattern of prejudice against Germans unless the skeletal suspicion against all out-groupers (always present) can be invoked in its place. (Dollard, 1938)

In a similar fashion, the prejudice, violence, and negative stereotyping directed against Chinese immigrants in the United States fluctuated wildly throughout the nineteenth century, as a result of changes in economic competition. For example, when the Chinese joined the gold rush in California, in direct competition with miners of Anglo-Saxon origin, they were described as "depraved and vicious . . . gross gluttons, . . . bloodthirsty and inhuman" (Jacobs & Landau, 1971, p. 71). However, only a few years later, when they were willing to accept backbreaking work as laborers on the transcontinental railroad—work

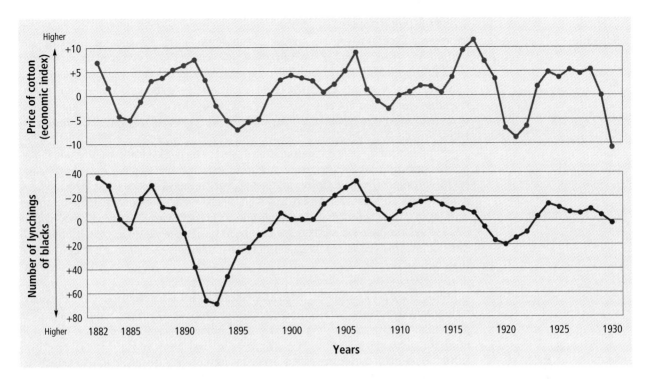

FIGURE 13.7   Relation of total lynchings to the price of cotton. ■ Note that the lynching scale shows greatest frequency at the bottom of the graph. (Adapted from Hovland & Sears, 1940)

few white Americans were willing to do—they were regarded as sober, industrious, and law-abiding. They were so highly regarded, in fact, that Charles Crocker, one of the great tycoons financing the railroad, wrote, "They are equal to the best white men. . . . They are very trusty, very intelligent and they live up to their contracts" (Jacobs & Landau, 1971, p. 81). With the end of the Civil War came an influx of former soldiers into an already tight job market. This was immediately followed by a dramatic increase in negative attitudes toward the Chinese: The stereotype changed to criminal, conniving, crafty, and stupid (Jacobs & Landau, 1971).

These changes suggest that when times are tough and resources are scarce, members of the in-group will feel more threatened by members of the out-group and will therefore show more of an inclination toward prejudice, discrimination, and violence toward the latter. How might the hypothesis be tested? We might look for increases in violent acts directed at minority group members during times of economic hardship. Carl Hovland and Robert Sears (1940) did just that, by correlating two sets of very different data: (a) the price of cotton in the southern states from 1882 to 1930 and (b) the number of lynchings of southern African Americans during that same period. During this period, cotton was by far the most important crop in the South; as cotton went, so went the economy. Hovland & Sears (1940) found that a significant correlation existed between the two variables, $r = -72$. As you'll recall from Chapter 2, this is both a large correlation, meaning that the two variables are highly related, and a negative correlation, meaning that increases in one variable are related to decreases in the other variable. In other words, as the price of cotton dropped the number of lynchings increased (see Figure 13.7, on this page). In short, as members of the in-group experienced the hardships of an economic depression, they became more hostile toward out-group members, whom they almost certainly perceived as a threat to their livelihood. This hostility led to an increase in the number of violent acts. (Although these data were gathered more than 50 years ago, we hasten to add that they are extremely reliable; modern investigators, using more sophisticated statistical techniques, have confirmed the accuracy of the original research; Hepworth & West, 1988.)

Similarly, in a survey conducted in the 1970s, most antiblack prejudice was found among people who were just one rung above the African Americans socioeconomically. And as we might expect, prejudice was most pronounced when whites and African Americans were in close competition for jobs (Simpson & Yinger, 1985; Vanneman & Pettigrew, 1972). We should note, however, that this research is correlational; as we discussed in Chapter 2, experimental research designs allow us to make cause-and-effect statements with far more confidence than we can on the basis of correlational research. How might we study the relationship between competition and prejudice experimentally?

In a classic experiment, Muzafer Sherif and his colleagues (1961) tested group conflict theory using the natural environment of a Boy Scout camp. The participants in the camp were normal, well-adjusted 12-year-old boys who were randomly assigned to one of two groups, the Eagles or the Rattlers. Each group stayed in its own cabin; the cabins were located quite a distance apart in order to reduce contact between the two groups. The youngsters were placed in situations designed to increase the cohesiveness of their own group. This was done by arranging enjoyable activities like hiking and swimming and by having the campers work with their group on various building projects, preparing group meals, and so on.

After feelings of cohesiveness developed within each group, the researchers set up a series of competitive activities in which the two groups were pitted against each other—for example, in games like football, baseball, and tug-of-war, where prizes were awarded to the winning team. These competitive games aroused feelings of conflict and tension between the two groups. In addition, the investigators created other situations to further intensify the conflict. For example, a camp party was arranged, but each group was told it started at a different time, thereby ensuring that the Eagles would arrive well before the Rattlers. The refreshments at the party consisted of two different kinds of food: Half the food was fresh, appealing, and appetizing, while the other half was squashed, ugly, and unappetizing. As one might expect, the early arriving Eagles grabbed most of the appealing refreshments, leaving only the less interesting, less appetizing, squashed, and damaged food for their adversaries. When the Rattlers finally arrived and saw what had happened, they became angry—so angry, in fact, they began to call the exploitive group rather uncomplimentary names. Because the Eagles believed they deserved what they got (first come, first served), they resented the name-calling and responded in kind. Name-calling escalated into food-throwing, and within a short time, punches were thrown and a full-scale riot ensued.

Following this incident, the investigators tried to reverse the hostility they had promoted. Competitive games were eliminated, and a great deal of nonconflictual social contact was initiated. Once hostility had been aroused, however, simply eliminating the competition did not eliminate the hostility. Indeed, hostility continued to escalate, even when the two groups were engaged in such benign activities as watching movies together. Eventually, the investigators did manage to reduce the hostility between the two groups; exactly how this was accomplished will be discussed at the end of this chapter.

The Role of the Scapegoat.   A special case of the conflict-competition theory is the scapegoat theory (Allport, 1954; Berkowitz & Green, 1962; Miller & Bugelski, 1948). As indicated above, if times are tough and things are going poorly, individuals have a tendency to lash out at members of an out-group with whom they are in direct competition for scarce resources. But there are situations in which a logical competitor does not exist. For example, in Germany following World War I, inflation was out of control and people were extremely poor, demoralized, and frustrated. When the Nazis gained power in the 1930s, they managed to focus the frustration of the German population on the Jews, an easily identifiable, powerless out-group. The Jews were not the reason the German economy was in such bad shape, but who was? It's hard to fight back against world events, or one's government—particularly when one's government is evading responsibility by blaming someone else. Thus, the Nazis created the illusion that if the Jews could be punished, deprived of their civil rights, and ultimately eliminated, all of the problems then plaguing Germany would disappear. The Jews served as a convenient scapegoat because they were easily identifiable and were not in a position to defend themselves or strike back (Berkowitz, 1962).

It is not always easy to separate prejudice due entirely and directly to economic competition from prejudice due to general scapegoating. For example, the correlation we discussed between the price of cotton and the number of lynchings in the South probably had elements of both. Another example of the combination of these two elements is the tragic case of a young Asian American who was beaten to death by several white Americans in Detroit several years ago. The murderers were unemployed autoworkers, angry at the Japanese auto industry because they felt that competition from this industry was the main reason for their unemployment. And so in their frustration, their irrational hostility toward all people of Japanese origin erupted, and they took it out on this unfortunate young man (who, ironically, was Chinese American).

Does scapegoating occur whenever people are feeling frustrated and angry, even in the absence of direct competition or conflict? In an experiment by Ronald Rogers and Steven Prentice-Dunn (1981), white students at the University of Alabama were instructed to administer a series of electric shocks to another student as part of a learning experiment. The students were free to adjust the level of intensity of the shocks. In actuality, the learner was a confederate who was not really connected to the shock apparatus. There was no conflict or competition involved in this study; however, for some participants, feelings of frustration and anger were aroused. The confederate was trained to be either friendly or insulting to the participant. In addition, the confederate was either black or white. Would angry white students respond more aggressively toward a black peer than a white one? The answer is yes. When the confederate insulted them, the students administered far more intense shocks to the black student than to the white student; when the confederate was friendly, the students administered slightly less intense shocks to the black student. The results of this experiment are shown in Figure 13.8.

This experiment produced findings almost identical with those of an earlier experiment performed by Donald Weatherly (1961). In Weatherly's experiment,

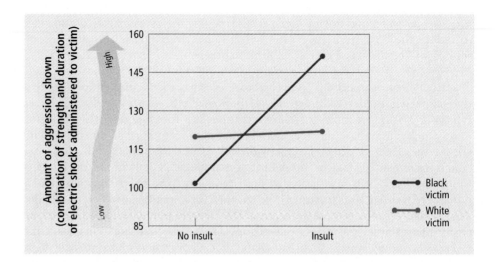

**FIGURE 13.8
Scapegoating.** ■ When insulted, people are more prone to aggress against minorities. (Adapted from Rogers & Prentice-Dunn, 1981)

scapegoating: the tendency for individuals, when frustrated or unhappy, to displace aggression onto groups that are disliked, visible, and relatively powerless

college students were subjected to a great deal of frustration. Some of these students were highly anti-Semitic; others were not. The subjects were then asked to write stories based on pictures they were shown. For some subjects, the characters in these pictures were assigned Jewish names; for others, they were not. Two major findings emerged: (a) After being frustrated, anti-Semitic subjects wrote stories that directed more aggression toward the Jewish characters than people who were not anti-Semitic did, and (b) no difference between the anti-Semitic students and the others was found when the characters they were writing about were not identified as Jewish. In a conceptually similar experiment performed in Canada, English-speaking Canadians, after undergoing a frustrating failure experience, rated members of the out-group (French-speaking Canadians) more negatively than those who had not undergone the frustrating experience (Meindl & Lerner, 1985).

Once again, the laboratory experiments help to clarify the dynamics that underlie real-world events. What all three of the above experiments have in common is **scapegoating.** The general picture emerges that individuals, when frustrated or unhappy, tend to displace aggression onto groups that are disliked, are visible, and are relatively powerless. Moreover, the form the aggression takes depends on what is allowed or approved by the in-group in question. In the past 40 years, lynchings of African Americans and pogroms against Jews have diminished dramatically, because these are now deemed illegal by the dominant subculture. But not all progress is linear. In the past few years, we have seen the former Soviet Union lose its grip on several Eastern European countries and indeed on its own Soviet republics. Although we are cheered by the new freedom that exists in this region, that freedom has been accompanied by increased feelings of nationalism ("us versus them") that in turn have produced intensified feelings of rancor and prejudice against out-groups. Thus, in the Baltics and Balkans the rise in nationalistic feelings has been accompanied by eruptions of hostility (and war) among Serbs, Muslims, and Croats, between Azerbaijanis and Armenians, and so on. And, of course, over the past several years we have also seen increases in the inevitable hostility toward the world's favorite scapegoat, with anti-Semitism on the rise throughout Eastern Europe (Singer, 1990).

The Way We Conform: Normative Rules

As we have seen, prejudice is created and maintained by many forces in the social world. Some we can observe operating within the individual, such as the ways we process information and assign meaning to observed events. Some we can observe operating on whole groups of people, such as the effects of competition, conflict, and frustration. Our final explanation for what causes prejudice is also observed on the group level: conformity to normative standards or rules in the society. As we discussed in Chapter 7, conformity is a frequent part of social life, whether we conform to gain information (informational conformity) or to fit in and be accepted (normative conformity). Again, a relatively innocuous social behavior—in this case, conformity—becomes particularly dangerous and debilitating when we enter the realm of prejudice.

Social Learning Theory.   Norms are beliefs held by a society as to what is correct, acceptable, and permissible. Obviously, norms vary widely across cultures; they are socially constructed standards or rules attached to certain aspects of human behavior (Berger & Luckman, 1967). For example, in the United States pregnancies outside of marriage are frowned on and avoided when possible, whereas in Sweden about 50 percent of all births occur outside of marriage and being an unwed parent is socially acceptable—no one even raises an eyebrow. Important regional differences in norms also occur within the same country. For example, until recently, the racial segregation of hotels, eating places, motion picture theaters, drinking fountains, and toilet facilities was normative in the American South but not in the North. Indeed, it can be said that, prior to 1954, segregation controlled most aspects of social life in the South.

How do we learn the norms of our culture? It's very simple, really. As social learning theory explains, everyone teaches us, beginning in our earliest childhood. For example, parents, the school system, peers, and the media both subtly and openly instruct us in how to behave and what to think (Kelly, Ferson, & Holtzman, 1958). Norms are then passed on, generation to generation. Clearly, stereotypes and prejudiced attitudes are part of this normative package (Ashmore & DelBoca, 1976). A newborn does not know who the out-groups are; he or she must be taught—who to distrust, who to dislike, who to hate.

Normative prejudice need not be as blatant as that depicted in the photograph of the young neo-Nazi mother, who presumably is teaching her children to hate African Americans, Jews, and other groups. Simply by living in a society where stereotypical information abounds and where discriminatory behavior is the norm, the vast majority of us will develop prejudiced attitudes and discriminatory behavior to some extent. We can refer to this as institutional discrimination, or, more specifically, as **institutionalized racism** and **institutionalized sexism**. For example, if you grow up in a society where minority and female professors, business executives, or physicians are few but where most people in these groups tend to hold menial jobs, then simply living in that society will increase your likelihood of developing certain (negative) attitudes about the native abilities of minorities and women. This state of affairs can come about without anyone actively teaching you that minorities and women are inferior and without any law or decree banning minorities and women from college faculties, boardrooms, or medical schools. Instead, societal barriers have created a lack of opportunity for these groups that makes their success extremely unlikely.

institutionalized racism: racist attitudes that are held by the vast majority of us because we are living in a society where stereotypes and discrimination are the norm

institutionalized sexism: sexist attitudes that are held by the vast majority of us because we are living in a society where stereotypes and discrimination are the norm

normative conformity: the tendency to go along with the group in order to fulfill their expectations and gain acceptance

How does normative prejudice work? As you'll recall from our discussion of **normative conformity** in Chapter 7, being accepted and feeling part of the group are important to us; in contrast, being the deviant or nonconformist can be painful. Thus, as Thomas Pettigrew (1958, 1985) has noted, many people hold prejudiced attitudes and engage in discriminatory behaviors in order to conform to, or fit in with, the prevailing majority view of their culture. It's as if people say, "Hey, everybody else thinks X's are inferior; if I behave cordially toward X's, people will think I'm crazy. They won't like me. They'll say bad things about me. I don't need the hassle. I'll just go along with everybody else." Pettigrew (1958) argues convincingly that while economic competition, frustration, and social cognition processes do account for some prejudice, by far the greatest determinant of prejudice is slavish conformity to social norms.

For example, Ernest Campbell and Thomas Pettigrew (1959) studied the ministers of Little Rock, Arkansas, after the 1954 Supreme Court decision ushered in desegregation. As religious people, the ministers favored integration and equality for all American citizens. However, they kept these views to themselves. They were afraid to support desegregation from their pulpits, because they knew that their white congregations were violently opposed to it. Going against the prevailing norm would have meant losing church members and contributions, and under such normative pressure, even ministers found it difficult to do the right thing.

Another way to determine the role of normative conformity is to track changes in prejudice and discrimination over time. As social norms change, so too should the strength of prejudiced attitudes and the amount of discriminatory behavior. For example, what happens when people move from one part of the country to another? If conformity is a factor in prejudice, we would expect individuals to show dramatic increases in their prejudice when they move to an area in which the norm is more prejudicial and to show dramatic decreases when they move to an area in which the norm is less prejudicial. And that is just what happens. In one study, Jeanne Watson (1950) found that people who had recently moved to New York City and had come into direct contact with an anti-Semitic norm became more anti-Semitic themselves. In another study, Pettigrew (1958) found that when southerners entered the army and came into contact with a less prejudiced set of social norms, their prejudice against African Americans gradually decreased. A somewhat different example of shifting norms was found by researchers in a small mining town in West Virginia: African American miners and white miners developed a pattern of living that consisted of total integration while they were under the ground and total segregation while they were above the ground (Minard, 1952; Reitzes, 1952).

Moreover, surveys conducted over the past 50 years make it clear that what is going on inside the minds of Americans has changed a great deal. For example, in 1942 the overwhelming majority of white Americans believed that it was a good idea to have separate sections for African American and white people on buses. Two out of every three white Americans surveyed believed that schools should be segregated. In the South, the numbers were even more striking: In 1942, fully 98 percent of the white population was opposed to desegregating schools (Hyman & Sheatsley, 1956). In contrast, by 1988 only 3 percent of white Americans said they wouldn't want their child to attend school with black children. That is a dramatic change indeed!

Shifting cultural norms are well illustrated by the two photographs on this page, each depicting Governor George Wallace of Alabama. In one, the governor,

■ What a difference a decade makes! On the left, in 1963, Governor George Wallace defies a federal order by physically blocking the entrance of the first black student to the University of Alabama. On the right, ten years later, Governor Wallace happily congratulates the University of Alabama homecoming queen.

along with his state militia, is attempting to block the doors of the University of Alabama as the first African American students seek to register for college. Only the presence of federal troops and telephone intervention by President John Kennedy caused Governor Wallace to back down. And yet just a decade later, the normative climate of Alabama had changed to the extent that Governor Wallace could be seen—as in the second photograph—congratulating the young African American woman whom the University of Alabama student body had chosen to be homecoming queen.

Modern Racism.   While normative changes in our own country have led to decreases in discrimination over the past 50 years, prejudice is in no way eradicated. Instead, it has become more subtle. As the norm changes to become one of tolerance for out-groups, many people simply become more careful— outwardly acting unprejudiced, yet inwardly maintaining their stereotyped views. This phenomenon is called **modern racism.** Here people's prejudice is typically revealed in subtle, indirect ways, for they have learned to hide their prejudice in situations where it would cause them to be labeled as racists. When the situation becomes safe, however, their prejudice will be revealed (Gaertner & Dovidio, 1986; Kinder & Sears, 1981; McConahay, 1986).

For example, while it is true that few Americans say they are generally opposed to school desegregation, it is interesting that most white parents oppose busing their own children to achieve racial balance. When questioned, these parents insist that their opposition has nothing to do with prejudice; they simply don't want their kids to waste a lot of time on a bus. But as John McConahay (1982) has shown, most white parents are quite tranquil about busing when their kids simply are being bused from one white school to another—most show vigorous opposition only when the busing is interracial in nature.

Given the properties of modern prejudice, racism and sexism can best be studied with subtle or unobtrusive measures (Crosby, Bromley, & Saxe, 1980). For example, Edward E. Jones and Harold Sigall (1971) created an ingenious

modern racism: prejudice revealed in subtle, indirect ways because people have learned to hide prejudiced attitudes in order to avoid being labeled as racist contraption, the bogus pipeline, to get at the real attitudes—not the socially desirable ones—of their research participants. The bogus pipeline is an impressive-looking machine that is described to research participants as a kind of lie detector. In fact, it is just a pile of electronic hardware whose dials the experimenter can secretly manipulate. Here's how researchers use the pipeline: Participants are randomly assigned to one of two conditions, in which they indicate their attitudes either on a paper-and-pencil questionnaire (where it is easy to give socially correct responses) or by using the bogus pipeline (where they believe the machine will reveal their true attitudes if they lie). Sigall and Richard Page (1971) found that more racial prejudice was present in students' responses when the bogus pipeline was used. In a similar experiment, college men and women expressed almost identical positive attitudes about women's rights and women's roles in society on a paper-and-pencil measure. However, when the bogus pipeline was used, most of the men displayed far less sympathy to women's issues than the women did.

We can also find examples of racism and sexism in overt behavior—although it is often subtle. For example, Ian Ayers and his colleagues (1991) visited 90 automobile dealerships in the Chicago area and, using a carefully rehearsed, uniform strategy to negotiate the lowest possible price on a new car (one that cost the dealer approximately $11,000), found that white males were given a final price that averaged $11,362; white females, $11,504; African American males, $11,783; and African American females, $12,237. Thus, all other things being equal, when it comes to buying a new car, being African American or female puts a person at a disadvantage. This also seems to be the case in a great many economic endeavors, even though such discrimination is technically illegal.

Subtle and Blatant Prejudice in Western Europe. Although this chapter has dealt primarily with prejudice and stereotyping in the United States, it goes without saying that prejudice exists throughout the world. Examples of blatant prejudice abound in daily newspaper headlines: ethnic cleansing in Bosnia, violent conflict between Arabs and Jews in the Middle East, mass murder between warring tribes in Rwanda. This prejudice exists in "modern" forms as well. For example, in a recent transnational study, Thomas Pettigrew and R. W. Meertens (1995) demonstrated the existence of blatant as well as more "modern," subtle racism in three major Western European countries: France, the Netherlands, and Great Britain. These researchers showed that the difference between blatant and subtle racism is important and has interesting consequences. One of their major findings is that, while the targets of prejudice differ in the three countries, the behavior of the native population toward recent immigrants can be predicted from a knowledge of how the natives score on both blatant and subtle measures of prejudice. For example, in all three countries those people who score high on the blatant prejudice scale want to send immigrants back to their home country and wish to restrict their meager rights even further. In contrast, those who score low on both scales want to improve the rights of immigrants, are prepared to take action to help them remain in the country, and are willing to act forcefully to improve the relations between immigrants and natives. Those who score high on the subtle racism scale but low on the blatant scale tend to reject immigrants in ways that are more covert and socially acceptable. Specifically, while they will not take action to send

> We all decry prejudice, yet are all prejudiced.
> –Herbert Spencer, 1873

immigrants back to their home country, they are willing neither to do anything to help improve their relations with the immigrant population nor to go along with any attempt to increase that population's civil rights.

How Can Prejudice Be Reduced?

Sometimes subtle, sometimes brutally overt—prejudice is indeed ubiquitous. Does this mean that prejudice is an essential aspect of human social interaction and will therefore always be with us? We social psychologists do not take such a pessimistic view. We tend to agree with Thoreau (see his statement in the margin). People can change. But how? What can we do to eliminate or at least reduce this noxious aspect of human social behavior?

> It is never too late to give up our prejudices.
> –Henry David Thoreau, 1854

Because stereotypes and prejudice are based on erroneous information, for many years social observers believed that all one needed to do was educate people—expose them to accurate information—and their prejudice would disappear. But this has proved to be a naive hope (Lazarsfeld, 1940). After reading this chapter thus far, you can see why this might be the case. Because of the underlying emotional aspects of prejudice, as well as some of the cognitive ruts we get into (e.g., attributional biases, biased expectations, and illusory correlations), stereotypes based on misinformation are difficult to modify simply by providing people with correct information. On the other hand, there is hope. As you have perhaps experienced in your own life, repeated contact with members of an outgroup can have a positive effect on stereotypes and prejudice. But as we shall see, mere contact is not enough; it must be a special kind of contact (Pettigrew, 1958).

The Contact Hypothesis

In 1954, when the U. S. Supreme Court ordered an end to segregated schools, there was widespread excitement among social psychologists. Because segregation lowered the self-esteem of minority children, most social psychologists believed that desegregating the schools would lead to increases in these youngsters' self-esteem. In addition, social psychologists hoped that the desegregation of schools would be the beginning of the end of prejudice. The idea was that by bringing children of different races and ethnicities together, this contact would eventually erode prejudice.

There was good reason for this optimism, for not only did it make sense theoretically, but empirical evidence supported the power of contact among races. For example, as early as 1951 Morton Deutsch and Mary Ellen Collins examined the attitudes of whites toward blacks in two public housing projects that differed in their degree of racial integration. Specifically, in one housing situation, black and white families had been randomly assigned to buildings in a segregated manner—that is, they were assigned to separate buildings in the same project. In another situation, their assignment was to integrated buildings—black and white families were placed in the same building. After several months, residents in the integrated project reported a greater positive change in their attitudes toward blacks than residents of the segregated project did, even though the former had not chosen to live in an integrated building initially.

But the desegregation of schools did not work as smoothly as most knowledgeable people had expected. Indeed, far from producing the hoped-for harmony, school desegregation frequently led to tension and turmoil within the classroom. In his careful analysis of the research on desegregated schools, Walter Stephan (1978) was unable to find a single study demonstrating a significant increase in self-esteem among African American children, whereas 25 percent of the studies showed a significant decrease in the self-esteem of African American children following desegregation. In addition, prejudice was not reduced. Stephan (1978) found that in 53 percent of the studies, prejudice actually increased; in 34 percent of the studies, no change in prejudice occurred. And if one had taken an aerial photograph of the school yards of most desegregated schools, one would have found that there was very little true integration: White kids tended to cluster with white kids, African American kids tended to cluster with African American kids, Hispanic kids tended to cluster with Hispanic kids, and so on (Aronson, 1978; Aronson & Gonzalez, 1988; Schofield, 1986). Clearly, mere contact did not work.

What went wrong? Why did desegregated housing work better than desegregated schools? Let's take a closer look at the contact hypothesis. A moment's reflection will make it obvious that not all kinds of contact will reduce prejudice and raise self-esteem. For example, in the South, African Americans and whites have had a great deal of contact, dating back to the time when African Americans first arrived on slave ships; however, prejudice flourished nonetheless. Obviously, the kind of contact they were having was not the kind that would lead to pleasant outcomes. In his strikingly prescient masterwork *The Nature of Prejudice*, Gordon Allport (1954) stated the contact hypothesis this way:

> Prejudice may be reduced by equal status contact between majority and minority groups in the pursuit of common goals. The effect is greatly enhanced if this contact is sanctioned by institutional supports (i.e., by law, custom or local atmosphere), and provided it is of a sort that leads to the perception of common interests and common humanity between members of the two groups. (1954, p. 281)

In other words, Allport is not talking about mere contact; he is clear that contact must be between people who are of equal status and in pursuit of common goals. Note that implicit in the Deutsch & Collins (1951) housing study was the fact that the two groups were of equal status within the project and that no obvious issues of conflict existed between them. A few decades of research have substantiated Allport's early claim that these conditions must be met before contact will lead to a decrease in prejudice between groups (Cook, 1985). Let's now turn to a discussion of these conditions.

When Contact Reduces Prejudice: Six Conditions

Remember Muzafer Sherif's (1961) study at the boys' camp—the "Eagles" and the "Rattlers"? Stereotyping and prejudice were created by instigating conflict and competition between the boys. As part of the study, Sherif and his colleagues also staged several events to reduce the prejudice they had created. Their findings at the boys' camp tell us a great deal about what contact can and cannot do.

First, the researchers found that once hostility and distrust were established, harmony between the boys could not be restored simply by removing the conflict and the competition. As a matter of fact, all attempts to bring the two groups together in neutral situations served only to increase the hostility and distrust.

For example, the children in these groups had trouble with each other even when they were simply watching a movie together.

How did Sherif succeed in reducing their hostility? By placing the two groups of boys in situations where they were **mutually interdependent**—situations in which they were forced to cooperate with each other in order to accomplish their goal. For example, the investigators set up an emergency situation by damaging the water supply system. The only way the system could be repaired was if all the Rattlers and Eagles cooperated immediately. On another occasion, the camp truck broke down while the boys were on a camping trip. In order to get the truck going again, it was necessary to pull it up a rather steep hill. This could be accomplished only if all the youngsters pulled together, regardless of whether they were Eagles or Rattlers. Eventually, these sorts of situations brought about a diminution of hostile feelings and negative stereotyping among the campers. In fact, after these cooperative situations were introduced, the number of boys who said their closest friend was in the other group increased dramatically (see Figure 13.9). Thus, two of the key factors in the success of contact are mutual interdependence and a common goal—a situation where two or more groups need each other and must depend on each other in order to accomplish a goal that is important to each of them (Amir, 1969, 1976).

The third condition is equal status. At the boys' camp (Sherif et al., 1961) and in the public housing project (Duetsch & Collins, 1951), the group members were very much the same in terms of status and power. For example, no one was the boss, and no one was the less powerful employee. When status is unequal, interactions can easily follow stereotypical patterns. The whole point of contact is to allow people to learn that their stereotypes are inaccurate; contact and interaction should lead to disconfirmation of negative, stereotyped beliefs. However, if status is unequal between the groups, their interactions will be shaped by that status difference—the bosses will act like stereotypical bosses, the employees like stereotypical subordinates—and no one will learn new, disconfirming information about the other group (Pettigrew, 1969; Wilder, 1984).

Fourth, contact must occur in a friendly, informal setting, where in-group members can interact with out-group members on a one-to-one basis (Brewer &

mutual interdependence: a situation where two or more groups need each other and must depend on each other in order to accomplish a goal that is important to each of them

> We must recognize that beneath the superficial classification of sex and race the same potentialities exist, recurring generation after generation only to perish because society has no place for them.
>
> –Margaret Mead,
> *Male and Female,* 1943

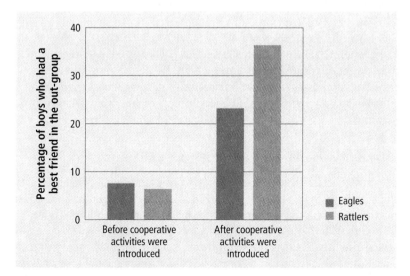

FIGURE 13.9 Intergroup relations. ■ Intergroup tensions were eased only after members engaged in cooperative activities. (Adapted from Sherif et al., 1961)

"I WISH WE COULD HAVE MET
UNDER DIFFERENT CIRCUMSTANCES . . ."

Drawing by Oliphant, An Informal Gathering. ©1978, Simon & Schuster.

■ The caption is amusing, but in actuality, a cooperative effort enhances liking; thus, the circumstances are ideal.

Miller, 1984; Cook, 1984; Wilder, 1986). Simply placing two groups in contact in a room where they can remain segregated will do little to promote their understanding or knowledge of each other.

Fifth, through friendly, informal interactions with multiple members of the out-group, an individual will learn that his or her beliefs about the out-group are wrong. It is crucial for the individual to believe that the out-group members he or she comes to know are typical of their group; otherwise, the stereotype can be maintained by labeling one out-group member as the exception (Wilder, 1984). For example, a study of male police officers assigned female partners in Washington, D.C., found that although the men were satisfied with their female partner's performance, they still felt strongly that more women should not be hired as police officers. They perceived their partner as an exception; their stereotypes about women's ability to do police work remained unchanged and in fact were identical with those of male officers with male partners (Milton, 1972).

Sixth and last, contact is most likely to lead to reduced prejudice when social norms that promote and support equality among groups are operating in the situation (Amir, 1969; Wilder, 1984). We know the power of social norms; here they can be harnessed to motivate people to reach out to members of the out-group. For example, if the boss in a work setting or the professor in a classroom creates and reinforces a norm of acceptance and tolerance, group members will modify their own behavior to fit the norm.

To conclude, when these six conditions of contact—mutual interdependence; a common goal; equal status; informal, interpersonal contact; multiple contacts; and social norms of equality—are met, suspicious or even hostile groups will reduce their stereotyping, prejudice, and discriminatory behavior (Aronson & Bridgeman, 1979; Cook, 1984; Riordan, 1978).

Cooperation and Interdependence: The Jigsaw Classroom

Now that we know what conditions must exist for contact to work, we can better understand the problems that occurred when schools were integrated. Let's paint a typical scenario. Imagine a sixth-grader of Mexican American origin, whom we will call Carlos. Carlos has been attending schools in an underprivileged neighborhood for his entire life. Because the schools in his neighborhood were not well equipped or well staffed, his first five years of education were somewhat deficient. Suddenly, without much warning or preparation, he is bused to a school in a predominantly white middle-class neighborhood.

As you know from experience, the traditional classroom is a highly competitive, factorylike environment. The typical scene involves the teacher asking a question; immediately, several hands go into the air as the children strive to show the teacher that they know the answer. When a teacher calls on one child, several others groan, because they've missed an opportunity to show the teacher how smart they are. If the child who is called on hesitates or comes up with the wrong answer, there is a renewed and intensified flurry of hands in the air, perhaps even accompanied by whispered, derisive comments directed at the student who failed. Thus, Carlos finds he must compete against white middle-class students who have had better preparation than he and who have been reared to hold white middle-class values, which include working hard in pursuit of good grades, raising one's hand enthusiastically whenever the teacher asks a question, and so on. In effect, Carlos has been thrust into a highly competitive situation for which he is unprepared and in which payoffs are made for abilities he has not yet developed. He is virtually guaranteed to lose. After a few failures, Carlos, feeling defeated, humiliated, and dispirited, stops raising his hand and can hardly wait for the bell to ring to signal the end of the school day.

In the typical desegregated classroom, to use Allport's (1954) terms, the students were not of equal status and were not pursuing common goals. Indeed, one might say that they were in a tug-of-war on an uneven playing field. When one examines the situation closely, it is easy to see why Stephan (1978) found a general decrease in the self-esteem of minority youngsters following desegregation. Moreover, given the competitive atmosphere of the classroom, it is likely that the situation would have exacerbated whatever stereotypes were present in the youngsters' minds prior to desegregation. Specifically, given that the minority kids were ill-prepared for the competitiveness of the classroom, it is not surprising that some of the white kids quickly concluded that the minority kids were stupid, unmotivated, and sullen—just as they had suspected (Wilder & Shapiro, 1989). Moreover, it is likely that the minority kids might conclude that the white kids were arrogant show-offs. This is an example of the self-fulfilling prophecy we discussed earlier.

How could we change the atmosphere of the classroom so that it comes closer to Gordon Allport's prescription for the effectiveness of contact? Specifically, how could we get white students and minority students to be of equal status, mutually dependent, and in pursuit of common goals? One of the authors of this textbook got to find out. In 1971, the school system of Austin, Texas, was desegregated. Within a few weeks, the schools were in turmoil. African American, white, and Mexican American children were in open conflict; fistfights broke out between the various racial groups in the corridors and school yards. The school superintendent invited Elliot Aronson, who was then a professor at the University of Texas, to enter the system with the mandate to do anything within reason to create a more harmonious environment. After spending a few days observing the dynamics of several classrooms, Aronson and his graduate students were strongly reminded of the situation that existed in the Sherif (1961) camp experiment. With the findings of that study in mind, they developed a technique that created an interdependent classroom atmosphere, designed to place the students of various racial and ethnic groups in pursuit of common goals. They called it the **jigsaw classroom,** because it resembled the assembling of a jigsaw puzzle (Aronson & Bridgeman, 1979; Aronson &

jigsaw classroom: a classroom setting designed to reduce prejudice and raise the self-esteem of children by placing them in small, desegregated groups and making each child dependent on the other children in his or her group to learn the course material and do well in the class

Gonzalez, 1988; Aronson, Stephan, Sikes, Blaney, & Snapp, 1978; Aronson & Thibodeau, 1992).

Here is how the jigsaw classroom works: Students are placed in six-person learning groups. The day's lesson is divided into six paragraphs, so that each student has one segment of the written material. For example, if the students are to learn the life of Eleanor Roosevelt, her biography is arranged in six parts. Each student has possession of a unique and vital part of the information, which, like the pieces of a jigsaw puzzle, must be put together before anyone can learn the whole picture. The individual must learn his or her own section and teach it to the other members of the group—who do not have any other access to that material. Thus, if Debbie wants to do well on the ensuing exam about the life of Eleanor Roosevelt, she must pay close attention to Carlos (who is reciting on Roosevelt's girlhood years), to Natalie (who is reciting on Roosevelt's years in the White House), and so on.

Unlike the traditional classroom, where students are competing against each other, the jigsaw classroom has students depending on each other. In the traditional classroom, if Carlos, because of anxiety and discomfort, is having difficulty reciting, the other students can easily ignore him (or even put him down) in their zeal to show the teacher how smart they are. But in the jigsaw classroom, if Carlos is having difficulty reciting, it is now in the best interests of the other students to be patient, make encouraging comments, and even ask friendly, probing questions to make it easier for Carlos to bring forth the knowledge within him.

Through the jigsaw process, the children begin to pay more attention to each other and to show respect for each other. As you might expect, a child like Carlos would respond to this treatment by simultaneously becoming more relaxed and more engaged; this would inevitably produce an improvement in his ability to communicate. In fact, after a couple of weeks the other students were struck by their realization that Carlos was a lot smarter than they had thought he was. They began to like him. Carlos began to enjoy school more and began to see the Anglo students in his group not as tormentors but as helpful and responsible teammates. Moreover, as he began to feel increasingly comfortable in class and started to gain more confidence in himself, Carlos's academic performance began to improve. As his academic performance improved, so did his self-esteem. The vicious circle had been broken; the elements that had been causing a downward spiral were changed—the spiral moved dramatically upward.

The formal data that Aronson and his colleagues gathered from the jigsaw experiments were clear and striking. Compared to students in traditional classrooms, students in jigsaw groups showed a decrease in prejudice and stereotyping, as well as an increase in their liking for their groupmates, both within and across ethnic boundaries. In addition, children in the jigsaw classrooms performed better on objective exams and showed a significantly greater increase in self-esteem than children in traditional classrooms. Children in the jigsaw classrooms also showed far greater liking for school than those in traditional classrooms. Moreover, children in schools where the jigsaw technique was practiced showed substantial evidence of true integration—that is, in the school yard there was far more intermingling among the various races and ethnic groups than in the yards of schools using more traditional classroom techniques. Finally, children in the jigsaw classrooms developed a greater ability to empathize with others and to see the world through the perspective of others than children in traditional classrooms did (Aronson & Bridgeman (1979).

> Two are better than one because they have a good reward for their toil. For if they fail, one will lift up his fellow, but woe to him who is alone when he falls and has not another to lift him up. Again, if two lie together, they are warm; but how can one be warm alone?
>
> –Ecclesiastes 4:9–12

The jigsaw approach was first tested in 1971; since then, several similar cooperative techniques have been developed (see Cook, 1985; Johnson & Johnson, 1987, 1989; Sharan, 1980; Slavin, 1980). The striking results described above have been successfully replicated in thousands of classrooms in all regions of the country and abroad. The cooperative movement in education, as a way of achieving the goals of school desegregation, has grown by leaps and bounds and now constitutes something of a revolution within the field of public education. Alfie Kohn (1986) estimated that by the mid-1980s more than 25,000 teachers were using some form of cooperative learning in the United States alone—and hundreds more have been adopting it every year. John McConahay (1981), one of our nation's foremost experts on race relations, has called the cooperative learning revolution the single most effective practice for improving race relations in desegregated schools. According to Samuel Gaertner and his colleagues (1990), the process of cooperation is effective in part because the mere act of participating in a cooperative group succeeds in breaking down in-group versus out-group perceptions and allows the individual to develop the cognitive category of "one group."

In recent years, cooperative strategies have been extended from students in the classroom to teachers working together to sharpen their teaching abilities (Hammerman, 1995). And an even more radical departure from the factorylike competitiveness of the traditional classroom to a more cooperative, nonbureaucratic, student-centered approach is beautifully documented by Deborah Meier (1995) in her recent book *The Power of Their Ideas*. Meier, as founder and director of a cluster of cooperatively run public schools in East Harlem, has succeeded, over the years, in dramatically raising the performance and lowering the dropout rate of her students.

In sum, although the initial optimism about eliminating prejudice that occurred after the 1954 Supreme Court decision was a bit premature, we now have good evidence that we are on the right track. Research on cooperative learning groups is extremely encouraging and demonstrates beyond a doubt that, with proper care and in a sensible environment, integrated contact can produce a significant decrease in prejudice and marked improvements in students' self-esteem and classroom performance. The jigsaw experiments have taught us that under the proper conditions, contact is a viable and powerful tool in the battle against prejudice.

SUMMARY

Prejudice is a widespread phenomenon, present in all societies of the world. Social psychologists define **prejudice** as a hostile or negative attitude toward a distinguishable group of people based solely on their group membership. A **stereotype** is the cognitive component of the prejudiced attitude; it is defined as a generalization about a group whereby identical characteristics are assigned to virtually all members, regardless of actual variation among the members. **Discrimination,** the behavioral component of the prejudiced attitude, is defined as unjustified negative or harmful action toward members of a group based on their membership in that group.

As a broad-based and powerful attitude, prejudice has many causes. We discussed four aspects of social life that bring about prejudice: the way we think, the way we assign meaning or make attributions, the way we allocate resources, and the way we conform to social rules.

Social cognition processes are an important element in the creation and maintenance of stereotypes and prejudice. Categorization of people into groups leads to the formation of **in-groups** and **out-groups**. The **in-group bias** means that we will treat members of our own group more positively than members of the out-group, as demonstrated by the research on **minimal groups**. The perception of **out-group homogeneity** is another consequence of categorization: In-group members perceive out-group members as being more similar to each other than the in-group members are. Stereotypes are widely known in a culture; even if you do not believe in them, they can affect your cognitive processing of information about an out-group member. For example, recent research has shown that stereotypes are activated by automatic processing; they must be ignored or suppressed by conscious, controlled processing. The **illusory correlation** is another way that cognitive processing perpetuates stereotypical thinking; we tend to see correlations where they don't exist, particularly if the events or people are distinctive. Social cognitive research has indicated that stereotypes can be revised; the **bookkeeping model** and the **subtyping model** (but not the **conversion model**) describe such a process.

The fundamental attribution error applies to prejudice—we tend to overestimate the role of dispositional forces when making sense out of others' behavior. Stereotypes can be described as the **ultimate attribution error**—making negative dispositional attributions about an entire out-group. When out-group members act nonstereotypically, we tend to make situational attributions about them, thereby maintaining our stereotypes. For their part, members of an out-group experience **stereotype vulnerability**—a fear they might behave in a manner that confirms an existing stereotype about their group. Our belief in a just world leads us to derogate victims as well as members of out-groups—we see them as causing their fate and circumstances, a phenomenon known as **blaming the victim**. Finally, **self-fulfilling prophecies** are an attributional process by which we find confirmation and proof for our stereotypes by unknowingly creating stereotypical behavior in out-group members through our treatment of them.

Realistic conflict theory states that prejudice is the inevitable byproduct of real conflict between groups for limited resources—whether involving economics, power, or status. Competition for resources leads to derogation of and discrimination against the competing out-group. **Scapegoating** is a process whereby frustrated and angry people tend to displace their aggression from its real source to a convenient target—an out-group that is disliked, visible, and relatively powerless. Social learning theory states that we learn the appropriate norms of our culture—including stereotypes and prejudiced attitudes—from adults, peers, the media, and so on.

Institutionalized racism and **institutionalized sexism** are norms operating throughout the society's structure. **Normative conformity,** or the desire to be accepted and "fit in," leads us to go along with stereotyped beliefs and not challenge them. **Modern racism** is an example of a shift in normative rules about prejudice: Nowadays, many people reveal their prejudice in subtle, indirect ways, for they have learned to hide their prejudice in situations where it would lead them to be labeled as racist. Given the more hidden nature of prejudice today, techniques like the bogus pipeline are used to study people's real attitudes about out-groups.

How can prejudice be reduced? The most important way to reduce prejudice is through contact—bringing in- and out-group members together. However, mere contact, as occurred when public schools were first desegregated, is not enough and can even exacerbate the existing negative attitudes. Instead, contact situations must include the following conditions: **mutual interdependence;** a common goal; equal status; informal, interpersonal contact; multiple contacts; and social norms of equality. The **jigsaw classroom,** a learning atmosphere in which children must depend on each other and work together to learn and to reach a common goal, has been found to be a powerful way to reduce stereotyping and prejudice among children of different ethnicities.

IF YOU ARE INTERESTED . . .

Allport, G. (1954). *The nature of prejudice*. Reading MA: Addison-Wesley. Written the same year as the landmark Supreme Court decision on desegregation, this classic work remains an exciting and penetrating analysis of the social psychology of prejudice.

Aronson, E., Stephan, C., Sikes, J., Blaney, N., & Snapp, M. (1978). *The jigsaw classroom*. Beverly Hills, CA: Sage. The story of the classroom experiment that helped make school desegregation work—and that contributed to the launching of the trend toward cooperative education.

Meier, D. (1995). *The power of their ideas*. New York: Beacon. An outstanding educator demonstrates how the motivation and academic performance of minority students can be dramatically improved by abandoning the "factory" model of traditional education and moving toward a more cooperative, student-centered atmosphere.

Pettigrew, T. F., & Meertens, R. W. (1995). Subtle and blatant prejudice in Western Europe. *European Journal of Social Psychology, 25,* 57–75. An excellent analysis of the distinctive difference between blatant and subtle forms of prejudice and how they affect behavior in different ways.

Stephan, W. G. (1985). Intergroup relations. In G. Lindzey & E. Aronson (Eds.), *Handbook of social psychology* (Vol. 3, pp. 599–658). Reading, MA: Addison-Wesley. Perhaps the most accessible brief introduction to the areas of prejudice and prejudice reduction; both scholarly and engagingly written.

Part V
Social Psychology
in Action

Applied Module 1: Social Psychology and Health

Applied Module 2: Social Psychology and the Environment

Applied Module 3: Social Psychology and the Law

There is not one big cosmic meaning for all,
there is only the meaning we each give to our life.

–Anaïs Nin, 1967

Throughout this book, we have discussed the ways in which social psychological research can be applied to solve real-world problems. Examples include preventing errors in reasoning (Chapter 3), changing undesirable attitudes (Chapter 7), improving group decision making (Chapter 9), increasing prosocial behavior (Chapter 11), reducing aggression (Chapter 12), and eliminating prejudice (Chapter 13). In the following three modules, we discuss more specifically additional applied topics that touch all our lives: health, the environment, and the law. Each of these applied areas involves a number of interesting psychological issues. For example, few would deny that our minds and bodies are intricately linked and that the way in which we perceive and interpret the world has important implications for our physical health.

Psychological research in the areas of health, the environment, and the law has blossomed in recent years, growing into separate subareas within psychology. These subareas are called health psychology (Cohen & Herbert, in press; Pennebaker, 1982; Taylor, 1985), environmental psychology (Darley & Gilbert, 1985; Stokols & Altman, 1987), and law and psychology (Wrightsman, 1987). Each of these fields draws on many subdisciplines of psychology, including clinical, social, personality, developmental, cognitive, and physiological psychology.

What do social psychologists have to offer to such applied fields? First, social psychologists believe that, when trying to understand social behavior, it is often more important to examine the nature of the social situation than the nature of the person. Thus, social psychologists believe, in the words of Judith Rodin, that "it is not bad people but . . . bad situations that create social problems" (Rodin, 1985, p. 808). Second, as we emphasized in Chapter 1, it is not objective but subjective situations that cause behavior. That is, to understand why people behave the way they do in a particular situation, we must view that situation through their eyes, understanding how they interpret and define it. This principle will be important in understanding many of the applications of social psychology we will examine in our three applied modules.

Each module will touch upon issues we have discussed in previous chapters. The modules can be understood without having read the previous chapters, however. Our intention is that they can be read at any point in a course in social psychology. The module on health, for example, could be read after finishing Chapter 3 (on social cognition), because many of the principles of social cognition have been used to understand human health. Or it could be read after finishing Chapter 6 (on self-justification), because some of the techniques that have been used to get people to improve their health habits are based on research described in this chapter. Regardless of when they are read, the modules should reveal a great deal about how social psychology has addressed important, real-world problems.

Social Psychology
and Health

Chapter Outline

It is the mind that makes the body.

–Sojourner Truth, c. 1877

Ay, there's the thing! The body pays for the mind.

–Maria Edgeworth, 1812

Let us introduce you to a woman named Beatrice Cole. Ms. Cole has very much enjoyed the past ten years of her life—those between ages 80 and 90, that is. Ms. Cole, now in her nineties, greets each day "as a gift that I unwrap with anticipation, and live each day as if it were the last" (Cole, 1991, p. 20). She keeps a busy schedule, rising early every morning to take her dog, Pierre, for a long walk. After returning to her Manhattan apartment, she eats a large breakfast, reads the newspaper, and does some housecleaning; when the mood strikes her she ties Pierre to a shopping cart and goes to the market. She spends one day a week doing volunteer work at a local synagogue, and another in the public relations department of a museum. Every night she prepares a four-course dinner, serving herself as if she were a guest. She entertains regularly, treating her friends to a fancy dinner and a game of Scrabble.

Ms. Cole's life is not free of misfortune. Recently she found herself asking people to repeat what they had said, and realized that her hearing was failing. When she was 88, she kept turning her ankle and falling, due to nerve damage in her spine. Characteristically, however, she treats these hardships as minor inconveniences. "Deafness is not a bad handicap," she says. "At night when I remove my hearing aids . . . the silence is delicious" (p. 21). She obtained a brace for her leg and now, with the help of a cane, is as mobile as ever. She regularly takes buses around Manhattan, and she frequently travels outside the city to visit friends and family. Her personal philosophy is that you should always look on the bright side and never brood about anything for more than 20 minutes.

How does Ms. Cole feel about the fact that her life is drawing to a close? Far from feeling depressed or apprehensive, she approaches her impending death with characteristic optimism:

> There is still one adventure ahead of me that is the greatest experience of all—the only perfect happenstance in life, with no strings attached, no loose ends. Absolute perfection. That is death. I think of it as the perfect end to a long, happy life. (p. 21)

■ Beatrice Cole relaxes with her dog, Pierre.

Why has Beatrice Cole lived such a long and satisfying life? Is it a coincidence that her life seems to be remarkably free of stress, or is this related to her good health? How about her positive outlook on life—is this related to her longevity, or is she simply blessed with good genes and good luck? We do not know Ms. Cole personally, and even if we did, it would be hard to answer these questions definitively. It is difficult to tell, in any single case, the extent to which stress or a person's outlook on life affects her or his health. Fortunately, with careful research, it is possible to find some answers on a broader scale. Looking at people in general, what are the effects of stress on the human body? Do people's outlooks on life influence their physical health? Questions such as these about the relation between the mind and the body have intrigued human beings for centuries, and recent research suggests some fascinating answers. As we will see, it may be more than a coincidence that Ms. Cole is so upbeat and in control of her life and in such good health in her nineties.

We will spend most of this module discussing how people cope with stress in their lives and the relationship between their coping styles and their physical and mental health. We will then turn to another important question related to health: How can social psychological techniques be used to change behaviors that are bad for people's health? Getting people to behave in healthier ways, such as not smoking, is of obvious benefit. When it comes to influencing attitudes and behaviors, social psychologists are the experts (see Chapters 7–10). In the latter part of this module, we will see how social psychologists have succeeded in getting people to change health-related behaviors.

Stress and Human Health

A great deal of anecdotal evidence indicates that stress can affect the body in dramatic ways. Consider these examples, reported by the psychologist W. B. Cannon (1942):

- After eating some fruit, a New Zealand woman learns that it came from a forbidden supply reserved for the chief. Horrified, her health deteriorates, and the next day she dies—even though it was a perfectly fine piece of fruit.
- A man in Africa has breakfast with a friend, eats heartily, and goes on his way. A year later, he learns that his friend made the breakfast from a wild hen, a food strictly forbidden in his culture. The man immediately begins to tremble, and is dead within 24 hours.
- After a witch doctor in Australia casts a spell on a man, the man's health deteriorates, and he recovers only when the witch doctor removes the spell.

These examples may seem like bizarre tales, on a par with something you would read in the "Ripley's Believe It or Not" column in the Sunday paper. But let's fast-forward to the end of the twentieth century in the United States, where many similar cases of sudden death occur following a psychological trauma. When people undergo a major upheaval in their lives, such as losing a spouse, declaring bankruptcy, or being forced to resettle in a new culture, their chance of dying increases (Morse, Martin, & Moshonov, 1991). There have been many cases of sudden, unexplained death, for example, among refugees who escaped Southeast Asia and settled in the United States (Kirschner, Eckner, & Baron, 1986). Or

> Reality is the leading cause of stress amongst those in touch with it. I can take it in small doses, but as a life style I find it too confining.
> –Jane Wagner;
> *The Search for Signs of Intelligent Life in the Universe, 1986*
> (performed by Lily Tomlin)

consider the plight of an older person who is institutionalized in a long-term health care facility in the United States. In many such institutions, the residents have little responsibility for or control over their own lives. They cannot choose what to eat, what to wear, or even when to go to the bathroom. Residents in such institutions often become passive and withdrawn and fade into death as if they have simply given up. Quite a contrast to the zest shown by Beatrice Cole in her tenth decade of life! These examples suggest that there is more to our physical health than germs and disease—we also need to consider the amount of stress in our lives and how we deal with that stress.

Effects of Negative Life Events

Among the pioneers in research on stress was Hans Selye (1956, 1976), who defined stress as the body's physiological response to threatening events. He focused on how the human body adapts to threats from the environment, regardless of the source of a threat—be it a psychological or physiological trauma. Later researchers have focused on exactly what it is about a life event that makes it threatening. Holmes and Rahe (1967), for example, suggested that stress is the degree to which people have to change and readjust their lives in response to an external event. The more change that is required, the more stress that occurs. For

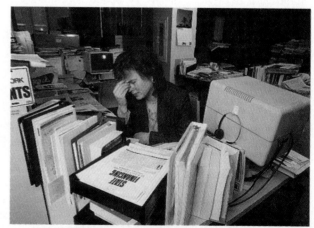

■ Some of these events are happy, yet they cause stress. Which of these situations might make you experience stress?

example, if a spouse or partner dies, just about every aspect of a person's life is disrupted, leading to a great deal of stress. This definition of stress applies to happy events in one's life as well, if the event causes a person to change his or her daily routine. Graduating from college is a happy occasion, but it can be stressful because of the major changes it creates in one's life.

To assess such life changes, Holmes and Rahe (1967) developed a measure called the Social Readjustment Rating Scale (see Table M1.1). Some events, such as the death of a spouse or partner, have many "life change units," because they involve the most change in people's daily routines. Other events, such as getting a traffic ticket, have relatively few life change units. Here's how the scale works: Participants check all the events that have occurred to them in the preceding year and then get a score for the total number of life change units caused by those events. The scores are then correlated with the frequency with which the participants become sick or have physical complaints. Several studies have found that the more life changes people report, the more anxiety they feel and the more likely they are to have been sick (Elliot & Eisdorfer, 1982; Seta, Seta, & Wang, 1990).

These findings probably don't come as much of a surprise; it seems pretty obvious that people who are experiencing a lot of change and upheaval in their lives are more likely to get sick and are more likely to feel anxious. A closer look, however, reveals that these findings aren't all that straightforward. One problem, as you may have recognized, is that most studies in this area use correlational designs, not experimental designs. Just because life changes are correlated with health problems does not mean that the life changes caused the health problems (see our discussion in Chapter 2 of correlation and causality). Can you think of any other interpretations of these findings? Some researchers have argued persuasively for the role of "third variables," such that certain kinds of people are more likely to be experiencing difficult life changes and to report that they are ill (Schroeder & Costa, 1984; Watson & Pennebaker, 1989). According to these researchers, it is not life changes that cause health problems. Instead, people with certain personality traits, such as the tendency to experience negative moods, are more likely to experience life difficulties and to have health problems.

Perceived Stress and Its Determinants

Another limitation of simply counting the number of negative life events that people experience—such as whether people have gotten married or lost their job—is that it violates a basic principle of social psychology: Subjective situations have more of an impact on people than objective situations do (Griffin & Ross, 1991). It is important to consider how people perceive and interpret an event. Some people view getting a traffic ticket as a major hassle, whereas others view it as a minor inconvenience. Some people view a major life change such as getting divorced as a liberating escape from an abusive relationship, whereas others view it as a devastating personal failure. As recognized by Richard Lazarus (1966, 1993) in his pioneering work on **stress,** it is subjective, not objective, stress that causes problems. An event is stressful for people only if they interpret it as stressful—which occurs whenever people feel unable to cope with demands from their environment (Lazarus & Folkman, 1984).

stress: the negative feelings and beliefs that occur whenever people feel they cannot cope with demands from their environment

Consider, for instance, our opening example of Beatrice Cole. If she were filling out the Social Readjustment Rating Scale, she would check item 6, "personal injury or illness," given that she was experiencing a number of health problems.

Table M1.1

The social readjustment scale

Rank	Life Event	Life Change Units
1	Death of spouse	100
2	Divorce	73
3	Marital separation	65
4	Jail term	63
5	Death of close family member	63
6	Personal injury or illness	53
7	Marriage	50
8	Fired at work	47
9	Marital reconciliation	45
10	Retirement	45
11	Change in health of family member	44
12	Pregnancy	40
13	Sex difficulties	39
14	Gain of new family member	39
15	Business readjustment	39
16	Change in financial state	38
17	Death of close friend	37
18	Change to different line of work	36
19	Change in number of arguments with spouse	35
20	Mortgage over $10,000	31
21	Foreclosure of mortgage or loan	30
22	Change in responsibilities at work	29
23	Son or daughter leaving home	29
24	Trouble with in-laws	29
25	Outstanding personal achievement	28
26	Wife begins or stops work	26
27	Begin or end school	26
28	Change in living conditions	25
29	Revision of personal habits	24
30	Trouble with boss	23
31	Change in work hours or conditions	20
32	Change in residence	20
33	Change in schools	20
34	Change in recreation	19
35	Change in church activities	19
36	Change in social activities	18
37	Mortgage or loan less than $10,000	17
38	Change in sleeping habits	16
39	Change in number of family get-togethers	15
40	Change in eating habits	15
41	Vacation	13
42	Christmas	12
43	Minor violations of the law	11

Note: According to Holmes and Rahe (1967), the greater the number of "life change units" you are experiencing right now, the greater the likelihood that you will become physically ill. (Adapted from Holmes & Rahe, 1967)

She would thus receive a large number of life change units. According to the theory, she should be at high risk for further physical problems, due to the stress caused by her hearing loss and problems with her spine. But as we saw, Ms. Cole is not particularly bothered by these problems. With her characteristic optimism, she looks on the bright side, welcoming the fact that her deafness blocks out annoying sounds at night. Because she finds these events relatively easy to cope with, they do not fit our definition of stress.

In a series of classic studies, Richard Lazarus (1966) showed that it is people's interpretation of an event that influences how stressful they find it. In one study, for example, he asked people to watch a film of gory industrial accidents, such as a scene in which a worker operating a power saw accidentally cuts off his finger. How upsetting was this film? It depended on how people interpreted it. Lazarus instructed some participants to adopt an intellectual stance while watching the film, concentrating less on the accident and more on the relationships between the workers. Compared to people who were given no special instructions, this group was relatively unaffected by the film. Just as a physician reacts to blood and gore differently from how most other people do, these participants succeeded in adopting a detached, clinical view of the accidents, turning a stressful experience into a relatively neutral one.

Studies using this subjective definition of stress confirm the idea that negative life experiences are bad for our health. In fact, stress caused by negative interpretations of events can directly affect our immune systems, making us more susceptible to disease. Consider, for example, the common cold. When people are exposed to the virus that causes a cold, only 20 to 60 percent of them become sick. Is it possible that stress is one determinant of who this 20 to 60 percent will be? To find out, Sheldon Cohen, David Tyrrell, and Andrew Smith (1991, 1993) asked volunteers to spend a week at a research institute in southern England. As a measure of stress the participants listed recent events that had had a negative impact on their lives. That is, consistent with our definition of stress, the participants listed only those events they perceived to be negative.

The researchers then gave participants nasal drops that contained either the virus that causes the common cold or saline (salt water). The participants were subsequently quarantined for several days, so that they had no contact with other people. As you can see in Figure M1.1, the people who were experiencing a great deal of stress in their lives were more likely to catch a cold from the virus. Among people who reported the least amount of stress, about 27 percent came down with a cold. This rate increased steadily the more stress people reported, topping out at a rate of nearly 50 percent in the group that was experiencing the most stress. This effect of stress was found even when several other factors that influence catching a cold were taken into account, such as the time of year people participated and the participants' age, weight, and gender. This study, along with others like it, shows that the more stress people experience, the lower their immunity to disease (Cohen & Williamson, 1991; Herbert & Cohen, 1993; Krantz, Grunberg, & Baum, 1985; O'Leary, 1990).

The careful reader will have noted that the Cohen and colleagues study used a correlational design and that this must make us cautious about its interpretation. The amount of stress people were experiencing was measured and correlated with the likelihood that people caught a cold. It is possible that stress per se did not lower people's immunity but rather that some variable correlated with stress did. A better design would have been to conduct an experiment in which people were randomly assigned to conditions in which they experienced a great

> The greatest griefs are those we cause ourselves.
> –Sophocles (c. 496–406 B.C.), *Oedipus Rex*

FIGURE M1.1 Stress and the likelihood of catching a cold. ■ People were first exposed to the virus that causes the common cold and then isolated. The greater the amount of stress they were experiencing, the greater the likelihood that they caught a cold from this virus. (Adapted from Cohen et al., 1991)

deal of prolonged stress or no stress. Such a study is impossible to do, however, for ethical reasons. Who among us would want to participate in a study in which we were tormented by the researchers for a long period of time, to see if we caught all sorts of diseases? To address this problem, experiments have been conducted with animals that have immune systems similar to those of human beings, and similar results have been found. Cohen, Kaplan, Cunnick, Manuck, and Rabin (1992), for example, found that monkeys randomly assigned to live in social groups that were constantly changing—a situation quite stressful for monkeys—had less efficient immune systems than a control group of monkeys living in stable social groups.

The finding that stress has negative effects on people's health raises two important questions: What exactly is it that makes people perceive a situation as stressful? And how do people cope with this perceived stress? We will begin with the first question, considering two key determinants of whether an event will be stressful: (a) how much control people believe they have over the event and (b) how people explain the causes of the event.

The Importance of Perceived Control

Compared to many other people in their nineties, Beatrice Cole has a great deal of control over her life: She lives alone and can decide what to do with each day; she is responsible for taking care of her dog, Pierre; she decides when to entertain guests and when to take out-of-town trips to visit friends and family; and so on. Is it possible that the control she has over her life is related to her good health?

Studies with the chronically ill suggest that it is. Shelley Taylor and her colleagues (1984), for example, interviewed women with breast cancer and found that many of them believed they could control whether their cancer returned. Here is how one man described his wife: "She got books, she got pamphlets, she studied, she talked to cancer patients. She found out everything that was happening to her and she fought it. She went to war with it. She calls it 'taking in her covered wagons and surrounding it'" (quoted in Taylor, 1989, p. 178). The researchers found that women like this, who believed their cancer was control-

> The knowledge that one has a remedy within reach is often as effectual as the remedy itself.
>
> –F. Anstey, 1900

lable, were better adjusted psychologically than women who felt their cancer was uncontrollable. And there is some evidence that people who try to control their cancer and its treatment live slightly longer than those who do not (Taylor, 1989).

It is important to note that the beliefs of at least some of the women about their control over their cancer were probably incorrect. One woman, who worked in a dress shop, said that for years she carried dresses from the racks to the fitting room over her left arm, so that the hangers banged against her left breast. When she developed a tumor in her left breast, she assumed these repeated blows had caused it. From that point on, she put the dresses on a rack and rolled them to the fitting room. According to the experts, blows to the breast are not a cause of cancer. Nonetheless, this woman gained a sense of control by believing she knew the cause of her tumor and by doing something she believed helped— which suggests that **perceived control** can be as important as real control.

It should be noted that studies of perceived control in the chronically ill by necessity use correlational rather than experimental designs. Researchers measure the amount of control people are experiencing and correlate this with their psychological and physical adjustment to the disease. These studies cannot prove that feelings of control cause one's health to improve; for example, it is possible that improving health causes one to feel more in control. To address the question of whether feelings of control have beneficial and causal effects, we need to conduct experimental studies in which people are randomly assigned to conditions of "high" versus "low" perceived control.

Fortunately, a number of such experimental studies have been conducted. Interestingly, this line of research began not with human beings but with animals. Martin Seligman and his colleagues, for example, conducted a series of classic studies on perceived control in dogs (Overmeier & Seligman, 1967; Seligman & Maier, 1967). In one condition, the researchers placed dogs in a harness and observed how long it took them to discover that pressing a button with their noses turned off a mild electric shock. Most dogs learned this very quickly. Dogs in a second condition received the same number and duration of shocks, except that nothing happened when they pressed the button. Thus, the objective event— the number and duration of shocks—was identical in the two groups of dogs. Psychologically, however, the experience was quite different, because the first group could control the shocks (the shocks ended when the dogs pressed the button), whereas the second group could not (the shocks just came and went, outside of their control).

The researchers then put all of the dogs in a new situation, where they could all learn to escape the shocks. The dogs were placed in a large box with a shoulder-high wall down the middle. When a signal was given, shocks were delivered ten seconds later unless the dog jumped over the barrier to the other side of the box. The dogs who could control the earlier shocks learned to avoid the new ones quite well. In fact, performance in this group was slightly better than the performance of a group of dogs who had never been shocked (see Figure M1.2). However, the dogs who could not control the earlier shocks reacted quite differently: They seemed to assume they could not control the new ones either, and most of them helplessly endured the shocks without trying to find a way to escape them; they simply seemed to give up (see Figure M1.2). Similar reactions to the loss of control have been documented in other species, including rats, cats, and fish (Richter, 1957; Seligman, 1975).

Several experiments have shown that having a sense of control is beneficial for people as well (e.g., Wiedenfeld, O'Leary, Bandura, Brown, Levine, & Raska,

perceived control: the belief that we can influence our environment in ways that determine whether we experience positive or negative outcomes

FIGURE M1.2 Debilitating effects of the lack of control on learning. ■ After experiencing no shocks, controllable shocks, or uncontrollable shocks, dogs were placed in a situation in which they had to learn a new way of avoiding shocks. Fewer of those who had experienced uncontrollable shocks learned how to escape the new shocks. (Adapted from Seligman & Maier, 1967)

1990). Some of the most dramatic effects have been found in studies of older people in nursing homes. Many people who end up in nursing homes and hospitals feel they have lost control of their lives (Raps, Peterson, Jonas, & Seligman, 1982). People are often placed in long-term care facilities against their wishes and, once there, have little say in what they do, whom they see, or what they eat. Ellen Langer and Judith Rodin (1976) reasoned that it would be beneficial to such residents to boost their feelings of control. In these researchers' study, the director of a nursing home in Connecticut gathered some of the residents together and told them that, contrary to what they might think, they had a lot of responsibility for their own lives. Here is an excerpt of his speech:

> Take a minute to think of the decisions you can and should be making. For example, you have the responsibility of caring for yourselves, of deciding whether or not you want to make this a home you can be proud of and happy in. You should be deciding how you want your rooms to be arranged—whether you want it to be as it is or whether you want the staff to help you rearrange the furniture. You should be deciding how you want to spend your time. . . . If you are unsatisfied with anything here, you have the influence to change it. . . . These are just a few of the things you could and should be deciding and thinking about now and from time to time every day. (Langer & Rodin, 1976, pp. 194–195)

The director went on to say that a movie would be shown on two nights the next week and that the residents should decide which night they wanted to attend. Finally, he gave each resident a gift of a house plant, emphasizing that it was up to him or her to take care of it.

The director also gave a speech to residents assigned to a comparison group. This speech was different in one crucial way—all references to making decisions and being responsible for oneself were deleted. The director emphasized that he wanted the residents to be happy, but he did not say anything about the control they had over their lives. He said that a movie would be shown on two nights the next week but that the residents would be assigned to see it on one night or the other. He gave plants to these residents as well but said that the nurses would take care of the plants.

This may not seem like a major intervention in the lives of the residents. The people in the induced control group heard one speech about the responsibility they had for their lives and were given one plant to water. That doesn't seem like very strong stuff, does it? The important point to keep in mind is that to an institutionalized person, who feels helpless and constrained, even a small boost in control can have a dramatic effect. Langer and Rodin (1976) found that the residents in the induced control group became happier and more active than residents in the comparison group. Most dramatically of all, the induced control intervention affected the residents' health and mortality (Rodin & Langer, 1977). Eighteen months after the director's speech, 15 percent of the residents in the induced control group had died, compared to 30 percent in the comparison condition (see the left-hand side of Figure M1.3).

Richard Schulz (1976) also examined the link between control and health in the elderly; he increased feelings of control in residents of nursing homes in a different way. Schulz started a program in a North Carolina nursing home wherein undergraduates visited the residents once a week for two months. In the induced control condition, the residents decided when the visits would occur and how long they would last. In a randomly assigned comparison condition, it was the students, not the residents, who decided when the visits would occur and how long they would last. Thus, the residents received visits in both conditions, but in only one could they control the visits' frequency and duration. This may seem like a minor difference, but again, giving the residents some semblance of control over their lives had dramatic effects. After two months, those in the induced control condition were happier, healthier, more active, and taking fewer medications than those in the comparison group.

> To be discouraged is to yield to misfortune.
> –Daniel Defoe,
> *Moll Flanders*, 1722

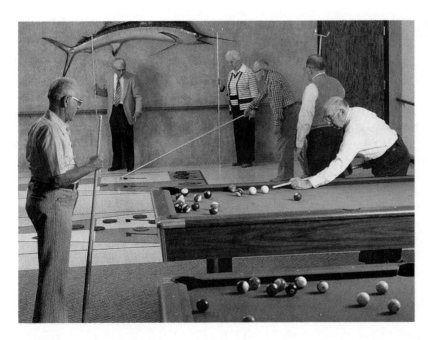

■ Giving senior citizens a sense of control over their lives has been found to have positive benefits, both physically and psychologically.

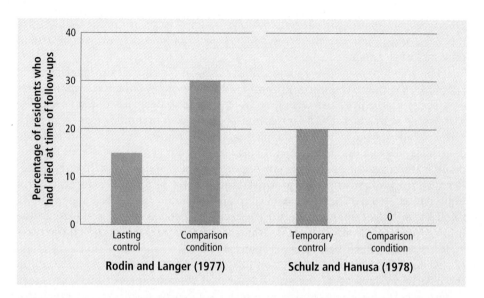

FIGURE M1.3 Perceived control and mortality. ■ In two studies, elderly residents in nursing homes were made to feel more in control of their lives. In one (Rodin & Langer, 1977), the intervention endured over time, so that people continued to feel in control. As seen in the left-hand side of the figure, this intervention had positive effects on mortality rates. Those who received it were more likely to be alive 18 months later than those who did not. In the other study (Schulz & Hanusa, 1978), the intervention was temporary. Being given control and then having it taken away had negative effects on mortality rates, as seen in the right-hand side of the figure. (Adapted from Rodin & Langer, 1977, and Schulz & Hanusa, 1978)

Schulz returned to the nursing home several months later to assess the long-term effects of his intervention, including its effect on mortality rates. Based on the results of the Langer and Rodin (1976) study, we might expect that those residents who could control the students' visits would be healthier and more likely to still be alive than those residents who could not. But there is a crucial difference between the two studies that should affect how durable the interventions were. The residents in the Langer and Rodin study were given an enduring sense of control. They could continue to choose which days to participate in different activities, continue to take care of their plant, and continue to feel they could make a difference in what happened to them—even after the study ended. By contrast, when Schulz's study was over the student visits ended. The residents who could control the visits suddenly had that control taken away. The question is, What happens when people are given a sense of control, only to have it eliminated?

Unfortunately, Schulz's intervention had an unintended effect: Over time, the people in the induced control group did worse (Schulz & Hanusa, 1978). Compared to people in the comparison group, they were more likely to have experienced deteriorating health and zest for life, and they were more likely to have died (see the right-hand side of Figure M1.3). This study has sobering implications for the many college-based volunteer programs in which students visit residents of nursing homes, prisons, and mental hospitals. These programs might be beneficial in the short run but do more harm than good after they end.

In sum, we have seen that having a sense of control over what happens to us is beneficial, helping us cope with a world that is often uncontrollable and harsh.

Perceived control is associated with better adjustment to chronic illnesses, greater immunity to disease, and, among residents of nursing homes, better health and adjustment (Heckhausen & Schulz, 1995; Rodin, 1986; Taylor & Brown, 1988). The Schulz (1976) study suggests that the effects of perceived control are so powerful that we should be very careful not to introduce it and then take it away. It is not better to have controlled and lost than never to have controlled at all.

We end this section with a word of caution. Though there is evidence for a relationship between perceived control and physical health, it can be dangerous to exaggerate that relationship. As noted by Susan Sontag (1978, 1988), when a society is plagued by a deadly but poorly understood disease, such as tuberculosis in the nineteenth century and AIDS today, the illness is often blamed on some kind of human frailty, such as a lack of faith, a moral weakness, or a broken heart. As a result, people sometimes blame themselves for their illnesses, even to the point where they do not seek out effective treatment.

The extent to which feelings of control determine physical health is therefore somewhat paradoxical. On the one hand, it is beneficial for people to feel that they are in control of their illnesses, like the cancer patient we described earlier. But the downside of this strategy is that if a person does not get better, he or she may feel a sense of self-blame and failure. Tragically, diseases such as cancer can be fatal no matter how much control a person feels. It only adds to the tragedy if people with serious diseases feel a sense of moral failure, blaming themselves for a disease that was unavoidable.

Fortunately, there are ways to maintain a sense of control even when one's health fails. Suzanne Thompson and her colleagues studied people with serious illnesses such as cancer and AIDS and found that even if they felt no control over the disease, many of them believed they could control the *consequences* of the disease (e.g., their emotional reactions and the nature of the physical symptoms related to the disease). These perceptions of control over the consequences were highly related to people's psychological adjustment: The more people felt they could control the consequences, the better adjusted they were, even if they knew they could not control the course the disease took (Thompson, Nanni, & Levine, 1994; Thompson, Sobolew-Shubin, Galbraith, Schwankovsky, & Cruzen, 1993). In short, it is important to feel in control of *something*—even if it is not the disease itself.

Explaining Negative Events: Learned Helplessness

We have just seen that life events are perceived as more stressful when the individual feels he or she has little or no control over them. The second important determinant of stress is how people explain to themselves why a negative event occurred. For example, consider two college sophomores who both got poor grades on their first calculus test. Student 1 says to herself, "I bet the professor deliberately made the test difficult, to motivate us to do better. I'll just have to study harder. If I really buckle down for the next test, I'll do better." Student 2 says to himself, "Wow—I guess I can't really cut it here at State U! I was worried that I wasn't smart enough to make it in college, and boy, was I ever right." Which student do you think will do better on the next test? Clearly the first one, because she has explained her poor performance in a way that is more flattering to herself and makes her feel more in control. In contrast, the second student is likely to settle into a state of **learned helplessness**, believing there is nothing he can do to improve his performance.

learned helplessness: the state of pessimism that results from explaining a negative event as due to stable, internal, and global factors; learned helplessness causes depression, reduced effort, and difficulty in learning new material

Learned helplessness is a pessimistic, maladaptive way of explaining negative events (Abramson, Seligman, & Teasdale, 1978). There are three ways in which an explanation can be pessimistic: viewing the cause of a bad event as stable (long-lived), as opposed to unstable (short-lived); viewing it as internal (something about you), as opposed to external (something not about you); and viewing it as global (something that will affect you in a wide variety of situations), as opposed to specific (something that will affect you in only one situation). According to learned helplessness theory, making **stable, internal,** and **global attributions** for negative events leads to depression, reduced effort, and difficulty in learning (see Figure M1.4).

Student 2, for example, believes that the cause of his poor grade is stable (being unintelligent will last forever), internal (something about him is to blame), and global (being unintelligent will affect him in many situations other than calculus classes). This kind of explanation will lead to learned helplessness, thereby producing depression, reduced effort, and the inability to learn new things. Student 1, on the other hand, believes that the cause of her poor grade is unstable (the professor will make the tests easier, and she can study harder next time), external (the professor purposefully made the test hard), and specific (the things that caused her poor calculus grade are unlikely to affect anything else, e.g., her grade in English). People who explain bad events in this more optimistic way are less likely to be depressed and more likely to do better on a broad range of tasks (Peterson & Seligman, 1984; Sweeney, Anderson, & Bailey, 1986).

Learned helplessness theory is intimately related to attribution theory, which we discuss in Chapter 4. Attribution theorists assume that your attitudes and behaviors depend on how you interpret the causes of events, an assumption that learned helplessness shares. Note that we do not know the real reason our hypothetical students did poorly on their calculus test. Instead, learned helplessness theory states that it is more important to consider people's *perceptions* of these causes. The real causes, of course, are not irrelevant. If the students lack ability in calculus, they are likely to do poorly on future calculus tests. However, often in life what actually causes our behavior is not so clear-cut or so fixed. In such situations, people's attributions about the causes of their problems can be very important.

To explore this link between learned helplessness and academic performance, Tim Wilson and Patricia Linville (1982, 1985) conducted a study with first-year college students. They assumed that many first-year students experience academic difficulties because of a damaging pattern of attributions. Due to the difficulty of adjusting to a new academic and social environment, the first year of college has its rough spots for nearly everyone. The problem is, many first-year students do not realize how common such adjustment problems are and assume that their problems are due to personal predicaments that are unlikely to change—just the kind of attribution that leads to learned helplessness.

Wilson and Linville tried to combat this pessimism by convincing students that the causes of poor performance are often temporary. At Duke University, first-year students who were concerned about their academic performance took part in what they thought was a survey of college experiences. In the treatment condition the students watched videotaped interviews of four upper-class students, each of whom, during the interviews, mentioned that his or her grades were poor or mediocre during the first year but had improved significantly since then. The students were also given statistics indicating that academic perfor-

stable attribution: the belief that the cause of an event is due to factors that will not change over time (e.g., your intelligence), as opposed to unstable factors that will change over time (e.g., the amount of effort you put into a task)

internal attribution: the belief that the cause of an event is due to things about you (e.g., your own ability or effort), as opposed to factors that are external to you (e.g., the difficulty of a test)

global attribution: the belief that the cause of an event is due to factors that apply in a large number of situations (e.g., your intelligence, which will influence your performance in many areas), as opposed to the belief that the cause is specific and applies in only a limited number of situations (e.g., your music ability, which will affect your performance in music courses but not in other courses)

> If the human mind will busy itself to make the worst of every disagreeable occurrence, it will never want woe.
> –Samuel Richardson, 1747

FIGURE M1.4   The theory of learned helplessness.

mance is often poor in the first year of college but improves thereafter. The researchers hypothesized that this simple message would help prevent learned helplessness, increasing the students' motivation to try harder and removing needless worries about their abilities. Judging by the students' future performance, this is just what happened. Compared to students in a control group who participated in the study but did not watch the videotaped interviews or see the statistics, students in the treatment condition improved their grades more in the following year and were less likely to drop out of college (see Figure M1.5). Similar results have been found in studies in other countries, such as Canada and Belgium (Menec et al., 1994; Van Overwalle & De Metsenaere, 1990).

Because people's attributions were not directly measured in the Wilson and Linville (1982) study, we can only infer that the students improved their academic performance because of a beneficial change in their attributions. However, several other studies have directly measured people's attributions and found that people who explain bad events in optimistic ways are in better health and do better in school and in their careers (Nolen-Hoeksema, Girgus, & Seligman, 1986; Peterson, Seligman, & Vaillant, 1988; Seligman & Schulman, 1986; Snyder, Irving, & Anderson, 1991).

Twixt the optimist and the pessimist the difference is droll:

The optimist sees the doughnut

But the pessimist sees the hole.

–McLandburgh Wilson, 1915

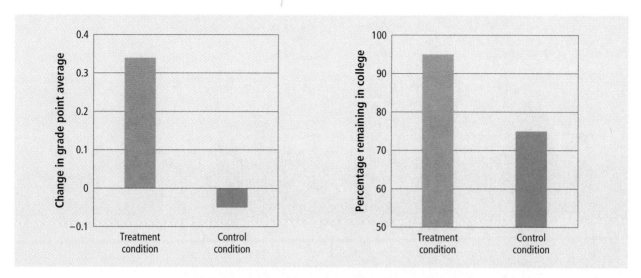

FIGURE M1.5 Combating learned helplessness in first-year college students. ■ In the treatment condition, first-year college students learned that the causes of poor academic performance in the first year can be temporary. This knowledge led to improvements in their grade point average and made them less likely to drop out of college. (Adapted from Wilson & Linville, 1982)

Thus, explaining a negative event in a pessimistic, hopeless way can be damaging. But what determines whether people will explain their setbacks in a pessimistic or optimistic manner? Interestingly, the culture in which we grow up can be very powerful in providing such explanations. Cultural wisdom about why people do what they do abounds, some of it quite insidious and damaging. For example, in the United States there is a cultural stereotype that African Americans are less intelligent than whites. What effect might this stereotype have on attributions for one's own performance? Suppose an African American and a white college student are taking the same test and are having difficulty solving the same problem. Both students are likely to be worried about their performance, but the African American has a worry the white student does not: the fear of confirming the cultural stereotype that African Americans are unintelligent. If the white student does poorly, it reflects badly only on him- or herself. If the African American does poorly, it not only reflects badly on him- or herself but also confirms the negative stereotype about African Americans.

Claude Steele and Joshua Aronson (1996) called this worry *stereotype vulnerability*—that is, apprehension about confirming a negative stereotype of one's group. As we saw in Chapter 13, Steele and Aronson (1996) reasoned that preventing such negative explanations might improve academic performance, by short-circuiting the worry and apprehension associated with stereotype vulnerability. They administered a difficult verbal test to African American and white students at Stanford University. Half of the students of each race were led to believe that the investigator was measuring their intellectual ability—which was likely to raise concerns about stereotype vulnerability among the African Americans. The other half were led to believe that the investigator was merely trying to develop a new test and that, because the test was not yet valid or reliable, their performance would mean nothing in terms of their actual ability. The results were striking: White students performed equally well regardless of

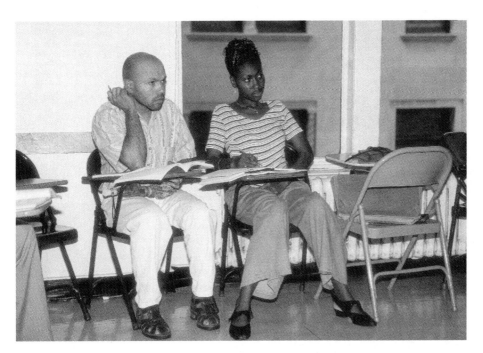

■ Stereotype vulnerability occurs when people are apprehensive about confirming a negative stereotype concerning their group. African Americans taking academic tests, for example, might worry that a bad performance will confirm the negative cultural stereotype that African Americans are unintelligent. This worry can, paradoxically, make it more difficult to do well. Studies have shown that when African American college students think a test is a measure of intelligence, they do less well than whites. When they think the same test is not a measure of intelligence—thereby removing concerns about stereotype confirmation—they do as well as whites (Steele & Aronson, 1996).

whether they believed the test was a measure of their intelligence. African American students who believed they were taking a test of intellectual ability performed less well than the whites; in contrast, African Americans who believed the test was not measuring their ability performed as well as whites.

Similar results were found by Steven Spencer and Claude Steele (1996) in a study of women's and men's performance on difficult math tests. Women performed as well as men when they were told that there were no gender differences on the test. When told that men and women tended to do differently on the test, however, women did significantly worse—presumably because of their anxiety over confirming the cultural stereotype that men are better at math than women are (see Figure M1.6). These studies, along with Wilson and Linville's (1982), show that the way in which people explain their academic performance can have considerable effects on how well they do. Finding ways of preventing negative, unflattering explanations can be quite beneficial, by preventing the anxiety and worry such explanations trigger.

In conclusion, we have seen that when people initially experience a negative event, such as failing a test, two psychological factors determine how stressful that event will be: (a) the amount of control they feel they have over the event and (b) how they explain the causes of the event. Feelings of control and optimistic attributions are associated with better psychological and physical adjustment. People who feel a lack of control or explain events in pessimistic terms (i.e., who

FIGURE M1.6   Stereotype vulnerability and performance on math tests. ■ When female college students believed there were gender differences on the difficult math test they were taking, they did worse than male college students. When they took the same test but believed there were no gender differences, they did as well as men. (Adapted from Spencer & Steele, 1996)

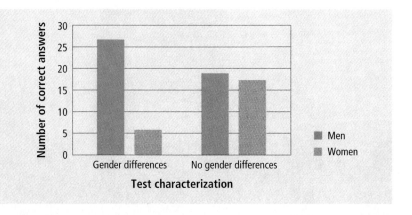

experience learned helplessness or stereotype vulnerability) are more likely to be in poor health and experience academic and professional problems. The power of our minds over our bodies is, of course, limited. But research shows that both perceived control and the absence of learned helplessness are beneficial, making it easier for us to cope with the hardships life deals us.

Coping with Stress

coping styles: the ways in which people react to stressful events

Now that we know what the causes of perceived stress are, it is important to consider how people deal with stress. There has been a great deal of research on the kinds of **coping styles** that are most successful at dealing with perceived threats from the environment (e.g., Lazarus & Folkman, 1984; Lehman, Davis, DeLongis, & Wortman, 1993; Moos & Schaefer, 1993; Pennebaker & Harber, 1993; Taylor & Aspinwall, 1993). We will examine a few of these styles here, beginning with research on personality traits that are related to coping.

Personality and Coping Styles

Type A versus B personality: a personality typology based on how people typically confront challenges in their lives; the Type A person is typically competitive, impatient, hostile, and control-oriented, whereas the Type B person is typically more patient, relaxed, and noncompetitive; numerous studies show that Type A people are more successful in life but also more prone to coronary heart disease

What is it about some people that seems to make them more resistant to stress? A number of personality variables have been studied, such as optimism. As we have just seen, explaining events in an optimistic fashion has some definite advantages. Michael Scheier and Charles Carver (1987) have looked at this from the vantage point of personality: It seems that some people are by nature optimistic, generally expecting the best out of life, whereas others are sourpusses who always see the dark underside of life. Consistent with research on learned helplessness, there is evidence that optimistic people react better to stress and are healthier than their pessimistic counterparts (Scheier & Carver, 1987; Scheier et al., 1990; Scheier, Weintraub, & Carver, 1986).

Another personality variable that has received a great deal of attention is the **Type A versus B personality**—that is, the way in which people typically confront challenges in their environment (Rosenman, 1993). The Type A individual is hard-driving, competitive, impatient, hostile, aggressive, control-oriented, and fast-paced; this is the type of person who honks and yells at other drivers when they don't drive to his or her satisfaction. People with this personality trait appear to deal with stress efficiently and aggressively. Their hard-driving, competitive approach to life often pays off, in that Type A individuals tend to get good grades in college and to be very successful in their careers (Ovcharchyn, Johnson, & Petzel, 1981). However, this success comes with a cost: Numerous studies show that Type A individuals are more prone to getting coronary heart disease, as compared to Type B people, who are more laid-back, patient, relaxed, and noncompetitive (Matthews, 1988). Subsequent studies have tried to narrow down what it is about the Type A personality that is most related to heart disease, with some researchers suggesting that the main culprit is hostility (Williams, 1987).

What determines whether people have Type A or Type B personalities? A number of factors have been found to be related to which type you are. You are more likely to be a Type A if you are male, your parents are Type A, and you live in an urban rather than a rural area (Rosenman, 1993). The culture in which you grow up may also play a role. It is well known that a higher incidence of coronary disease exists in many Western cultures than in many Asian cultures, such as Japan. Triandis (1995) suggests that one reason for this disparity is the emphasis on independence and individualism in Western cultures and on interdependence and collectivism in Asian cultures. He points to two ways in which these emphases might be related to heart disease: First, cultures that stress individualism emphasize competitiveness more and thus might encourage personality types more like Type A. Second, people who live in cultures that stress collectivism might have more support from other people when they experience stress, and as we will see shortly, such social support is a valuable way of making stress more manageable.

Investigations such as these are in the domain of personality psychology, in that they focus on traits that set people apart: What is it about one person that makes her or him more resistant to health problems than another person? The social psychologist takes a different tack: Rather than pigeonholing people into categories of optimists versus pessimists or Type A versus Type B, can we identify ways of coping with stress that everyone can adopt to make it easier to deal with the blows life deals us?

■ People with a Type A personality—those who are impatient, competitive, and hostile—are more likely to get coronary disease than people with a Type B personality—those who are relaxed, patient, and nonhostile. Recent research suggests that it is hostility in particular that is most related to coronary disease.

"Opening Up"

When something traumatic happens to you, is it best to try to bury it as deep as you can and never talk about it, or is it best to open up and discuss your problems with others? Although folk wisdom has long held that it is best to open up, only recently has this assumption been put to the test. James Pennebaker (1990) and his colleagues have conducted a number of interesting experiments on the value of confiding in others. Pennebaker and Beale (1986), for example, asked college students to write, for 15 minutes on each of four consecutive nights, about a traumatic event that had happened to them. Students in a control condition wrote for the same amount of time about a trivial event. The traumas that people chose to write about were highly personal and in many cases quite tragic, including such events as rape and the death of a sibling. Writing about these events was upsetting in the short run: People who wrote about traumatic events reported more negative moods and showed greater increases in blood pressure. However, there were long-term benefits: The people who wrote about traumatic events were less likely to visit the student health center during the next six months and they reported having fewer illnesses. Similarly, Pennebaker and his colleagues found that first-year college students who wrote about the problems of entering college improved their health over the next several months (Pennebaker, Colder, & Sharp, 1990) and that survivors of the Holocaust who disclosed the most about their experiences during World War II showed the largest improvements in health over the next several months (Pennebaker, Barger, & Tiebout, 1989).

What is it about "opening up" that leads to better health? Pennebaker argues that actively trying to inhibit or not think about a traumatic event takes a lot of mental and physical energy and is thus itself stressful. Having to constantly fight

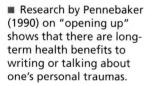

■ Research by Pennebaker (1990) on "opening up" shows that there are long-term health benefits to writing or talking about one's personal traumas.

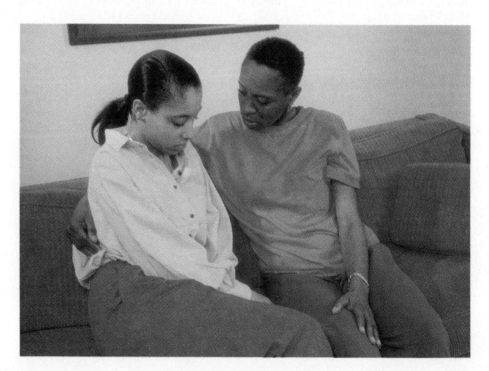

back thoughts about a trauma exerts a toll on our bodies that might lead to health problems. Further, trying to suppress negative thoughts can lead to an obsession with those very thoughts, such that people think about them more and more (Wegner, 1994). Writing about or confiding in others about a traumatic event may help people to gain a better understanding of the event, helping them to put it behind them. It might also elicit emotional support from others—which, as we will now see, can be an important part of the coping process.

Social Support

A final coping strategy is to get help from other people. A number of studies find that **social support,** defined as the perception that others are responsive and receptive to one's needs, is an important aid in dealing with stress (Hobfoll & Vaux, 1993; Sarason, Sarason, & Pierce, 1990). Clearly, when we have someone to lean on, we can better deal with life's problems. As we saw, there is evidence that people who live in cultures that stress interdependence and collectivism suffer less from stress-related diseases, possibly because it is easier for people in these cultures to obtain social support. People who live in cultures that stress individualism are expected more to "go it alone" (Bond, 1991; Brislin, 1993).

social support: the perception that others are responsive and receptive to one's needs

One of the most dramatic studies of social support was conducted by David Spiegel and his colleagues (Spiegel, Bloom, Kraemer, & Gottheil, 1989), who randomly assigned women with advanced breast cancer to a social support condition or a control condition. People in the social support condition met weekly with other patients and doctors to discuss their problems and fears, whereas people in the control group did not have access to this support system. Not only did the social support improve women's moods and reduce their fears; it lengthened their lives by an average of 18 months.

Social support can be helpful in a number of ways. Other people can offer emotional support, whereby they listen to us and sympathize with what we are going though. They can offer direct aid, by, for example, offering advice about how to deal with a specific problem. Discussing our problems with others can also help us understand those problems better, as indicated by Pennebaker's research on opening up. Exactly when and how social support is beneficial is the topic of a good deal of research and controversy (Helgeson & Cohen, in press; Hobfoll & Vaux, 1993). One interesting viewpoint is that we do not require the same amount of social support all of the time. When times are tough, we need other people; when things are going swimmingly, we can go it alone. In this way, social support acts like a "buffer," protecting us from the hard times in life (Cohen & Wills, 1985).

Using Social Psychology to Improve Health Habits

In addition to reducing stress, it would be beneficial to get people to change their health habits more directly—to stop smoking, lose weight, eat a healthier diet, and not abuse alcohol or other drugs. This is an area in which social psychology can be especially helpful, given what we know about social influence and social interaction.

Americans are doing a pretty good job of improving some of their health habits. A 1993 Harris poll found that only 24 percent of adults smoked cigarettes, the lowest smoking rate ever recorded (*USA Today*, March 12, 1993).

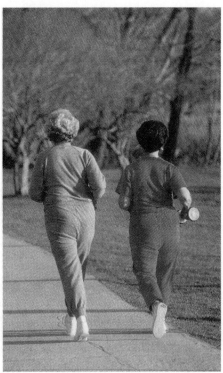

■ Americans are making progress in improving some areas of health. Smoking is becoming so unpopular that in many areas people must go outside to smoke. Americans are not doing very well in other areas. Many people find it difficult to lose weight and maintain a regular exercise program. How can social psychology help people act in healthier ways?

> Public smoking, like public spitting, is becoming a socially unacceptable habit.
> –Ellen Goodman, 1988

People are more likely today to avoid high-cholesterol and fatty foods than they were a few years ago, and more women are getting Pap smears to detect cancer. In many other important health areas, however, people are not doing nearly so well. The same Harris poll found that 66 percent of Americans are overweight—more than ever before. Other polls have found that people drink more alcohol, exercise less, and get fewer hours of sleep than they did five years earlier (*Scientific American*, September, 1986; *Washington Post Health*, January 9, 1996). Finally, a national survey found that people who are at risk for getting AIDS are not taking as many precautions as they should. Of those who said they had had more than one sex partner in the prior year, the vast majority had not used condoms at least some of the time. Only 17 percent said they had used condoms in all their sexual encounters (*Science News*, August 31, 1991).

How can we persuade people to change their health habits? Think for a moment, based on what you have already learned, about how you would go about trying to do this. One approach, as we discussed in Chapter 7, on attitude change, would be to try to scare people into adopting better health habits. For example, we could show people vivid pictures of someone dying of AIDS, sending the message that if they don't practice safer sex, this could happen to them. As we saw in Chapter 7, fear appeals can work, if they are not too strong and are accompanied by specific information about how best to deal with the problem.

For example, Cindy Struckman-Johnson and her colleagues (1994) showed college students a variety of public service messages urging people to use condoms and asked them to rate how much the commercials increased the likelihood that they would use condoms with a new sexual partner. The most effective ads were those evoking a fear of AIDS, such as one in which a woman receives the results of a blood test indicating she is HIV-positive.

Saying that you will use condoms is one thing, however; actually doing so is another. When it comes to changing intractable, ingrained health habits, fear appeals may be of limited success. The problem is that with many health problems, there are overwhelming barriers to change. Consider the use of condoms. Most people are aware that AIDS is a serious problem and that using condoms provides some protection against AIDS. Still, a surprisingly small percentage of people use condoms. One reason is that many people find condoms to be inconvenient and unromantic, as well as a reminder of disease—something they don't want to be reminded of when they are having sex. Where sexual behavior is involved, there is a strong tendency to go into denial—in this case, to decide that whereas AIDS is a problem, we are not at risk. What can be done to change this potentially fatal attitude?

One of the most important messages of social psychology is that to change people's behavior, you need to challenge their self-esteem in such a way that it becomes to their advantage—psychologically—to change their behavior. By doing so, they feel good about themselves, maintaining their self-esteem. Sound familiar? This is a basic tenet of dissonance theory. As we discussed in Chapter 6, Elliot Aronson and his colleagues have recently shown that the principles of dissonance theory can be used to get people to behave in healthier ways, including using condoms more. To review briefly, Aronson, Fried, and Stone (1991; Stone, Aronson, Crain, Winslow, & Fried, 1994) asked college students to compose a speech describing the dangers of AIDS and advocating the use of condoms "every single time you have sex." The students gave their speech in front of a video camera, after being informed that the resulting videotape would be played to an audience of high school students. Was giving this speech sufficient to change their own behavior, making the students more likely to use condoms themselves?

The answer is, Only when the students were also made mindful of their own failures to use condoms by making a list of the circumstances in their own lives when they found it particularly difficult, awkward, or "impossible" to use condoms. These students were most aware of their own hypocrisy—namely, that they were preaching behavior to high school students that they themselves were not practicing. Because no one likes to feel like a hypocrite, these participants needed to take steps to fix their damaged self-esteem. A clear way of doing this would be to start practicing what they were preaching. This is exactly what Aronson and his colleagues found: Students in the hypocrisy condition showed the greatest willingness to use condoms in the future and, when given the opportunity, purchased significantly more condoms for their own use than students in the nonhypocrisy conditions did.

The Aronson and colleagues (1991) condom study is yet another illustration of a familiar point: Sometimes the best way to change people's behavior is to change their interpretation of themselves and the social situation. No attempt was made to modify the research participants' behavior (their use of condoms) directly. They were not rewarded for using condoms; nor were they given any

> Future shock . . . the shattering stress and disorientation that we induce in individuals by subjecting them to too much change in too short a time.
> –Alvin Toffler,
> *Future Shock,* 1970

information about what would happen if they didn't. Instead, the researchers altered the way in which the participants interpreted their failure to use condoms. In the hypocrisy condition, the failure to use condoms took on a new meaning. Before the study, the students probably viewed failing to use a condom as no big deal; after all, surely they would never contract AIDS. After creating a speech for high school students and thinking about their own past actions, not using a condom took on a very different meaning: It became an unprincipled, hypocritical act, and—presto!—the students now wanted to use condoms more. We cannot overemphasize this important social psychological message: One of the best ways to solve applied problems is often to change people's interpretation of the situation.

SUMMARY

In this module, we examined the effects of stress on human health, the causes of stress, and how people cope with stress. Stress has been found to have a number of negative effects, such as an impairment of the immune system. **Stress** is best defined as the negative feelings that occur when people feel they cannot cope with the environment and is thus related to the way in which people perceive the objective world. One key determinant of stress is how much **perceived control** people have over their environment. The less control people believe they have, the more likely it is that the event will cause them physical and psychological problems. For example, the loss of control experienced by many older people in nursing homes can have negative effects on their health. In addition, the way in which people explain the causes of negative events is critical to how stressful those events will be. When bad things happen, **learned helplessness** results if people make **stable, internal,** and **global attributions** for those events. Learned helplessness leads to depression, reduced effort, and difficulty in learning new material.

We also examined people's **coping styles**, or the way in which they react to stressful events. Research on personality traits, such as the **Type A versus B personality**, focuses on how people typically deal with stress and how these styles are related to their physical health. Other researchers focus on ways of coping with stress that everyone can adopt. Several studies show that "opening up," which involves writing or talking about one's problems, has long-term health benefits. **Social support**—the perception that other people are responsive to one's needs—is also beneficial.

We also addressed some of the ways in which social influence techniques have been used to change people's behavior so that it is healthier (e.g., practicing safer sex). Using proven techniques to change people's attitudes and behaviors, social psychologists have had some success in getting people to act in healthier ways.

IF YOU ARE INTERESTED . . .

Goldberger, L., & Breznitz, S. (Eds.) (1993). *Handbook of stress: Theoretical and clinical aspects* (2nd ed.). New York: Free Press. A large collection of chapters on all aspects of stress, written by experts in the field. The topics include basic psychological and biological aspects of stress, the measurement of stress and coping, sociocultural and developmental sources of stress, and treatment for stress.

Rodin, J. , & Salovey, P. (1989). Health psychology. *Annual Review of Psychology, 40,* 533–579. A broad, insightful review of the emerging field of health psychology.

Seligman, M. E. P. (1990). *Learned optimism*. New York: Springer-Verlag. An interesting book on optimism and learned helplessness theory, by one of its originators.

Taylor, S. E. (1989). *Positive illusions: Creative self-deception and the healthy mind*. New York: Basic Books. A readable book that examines the relationship between people's illusions about themselves and the social world and their physical and mental health. Includes an in-depth discussion of many of the issues covered in this module, including perceived control and learned helplessness.

The Doctor (1991). A surgeon discovers what it is like to be on the other side of the health system when he develops throat cancer. The surgeon develops a close relationship with a terminally ill patient as he struggles with his own mortality. An interesting look at issues of learned helplessness and perceived control and health.

Applied Module 2

Social Psychology
and the Environment

Chapter Outline

> ## To waste, to destroy, our natural resources, to skin and exhaust the land . . . will result in undermining in the days of our children the very prosperity which we ought by right to hand down to them amplified and developed.
>
> –Theodore Roosevelt, *Message to Congress*, 1907

> ## We abuse land because we regard it as a commodity belonging to us. When we see land as a community to which we belong, we may begin to use it with love and respect.
>
> –Aldo Leopold, 1949

here is no better symbol of current environmental problems than the barge full of trash that nobody wanted. In 1987, a load of trash from New York City was rejected by a landfill in Islip, New York, because the landfill was already overflowing. The company hauling the trash hired some entrepreneurs to take it somewhere else. These unlucky transporters filled a barge called the Mobro 4000 with the trash and departed for a dump in Morehead City, North Carolina. Their idea was to dump it at a gas conversion project there, profiting from the methane gas that would be released as the trash decayed. This plan was quickly rejected by North Carolina authorities, who would not even allow the barge to dock. You see, these days trash is not simply trash. Many of the things we throw away contain toxic chemicals and dangerous metals, and the North Carolinians did not want their backyard poisoned with the decay from New York's toxic waste.

■ It is becoming increasingly difficult to find a place to dump the trash human beings create.

Thus began the lonely, meandering, 6,000-mile voyage of the Mobro 4000. For six months, the barge owners searched for someone to take the trash, making ports of call in Florida, Alabama, Mississippi, Louisiana, Mexico, Belize, and the Bahamas. But there were no takers. Finally, the barge returned home. After considerable wrangling by local and state officials, the trash was incinerated and buried in—you guessed it—the landfill in Islip, New York.

The circuitous voyage of the Mobro 4000 is symbolic of many of the environmental problems we face today. As the number of human beings on the planet has exploded, so have the environmental problems human beings cause. We are running out of room to dispose of the waste we create and we are depleting many crucial natural resources. The presence of so many people can also be a source of stress, as evidenced by overcrowding in many urban areas. Can social psychology offer any solutions to these environmental problems?

Few problems are as pressing as the damage we are doing to the environment, including toxic waste, overflowing landfills, pollution, global warming, and the destruction of rain forests. In this module, we will consider two questions about environment problems that are of particular interest to social psychologists. First, to what extent and under what conditions is the environment a source of stress? And second, how can social influence techniques be used to get people to behave in more environmentally sound ways?

The Environment as a Source of Stress

In Module 1, on health, we discussed the effects of stress on people's health. A major source of stress is the environment in which we live. As we human beings continue to populate the earth at an alarming rate, our physical world is becoming an increasingly difficult place in which to live.

Have you ever been stuck in rush-hour traffic, venting your anger and frustration by leaning on your car horn? Or been bothered by the noise we human beings generate from cars, planes, and loud parties? If so, you have found your environment to be a source of stress. But what makes our environments stressful? Why is it that the identical event—such as loud music—can be enjoyable on some occasions but highly stressful on others? The answer has to do with a basic assumption of social psychology: It is not objective but subjective situations that influence people. The same stimulus, such as loud music, is interpreted as a source of pleasure on some occasions and as an annoying interruption on others. To understand when our environment will be stressful, then, we have to understand how and why people construe that environment as a threat to their well-being.

> The earth we abuse and the living things we kill, in the end, take their revenge; for in exploiting their presences we are diminishing our future.
> –Marys Mannes, 1958

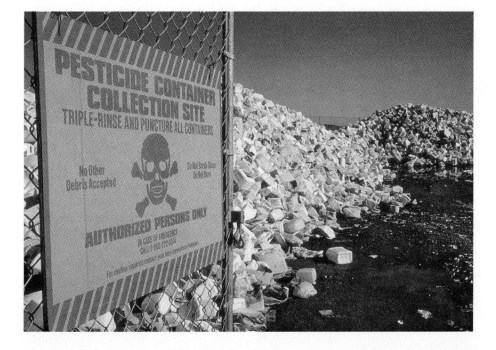

■ Just as our environment can exert stress on us, so too can we exert stress on our environment.

In one sense, the environment has always been a source of stress to human beings. We sometimes forget, as we sit in our comfortable, well-heated homes, eating food we purchased at the grocery store, how tenuous our existence has been throughout most of our history. Starvation was no stranger to our ancestors, no further away than one bad harvest or unlucky hunting season. Severe winters claimed many victims, as did diseases that spread unchecked due to contaminated drinking water, poor sanitation, and close living quarters.

As we approach the twenty-first century, we have learned to master most of the harsh environmental hazards that plagued our ancestors (though tragically, in many areas of the world starvation and preventable diseases are still a major cause of death). But the irony is that, as human beings have learned how to master the environment, they have also learned how to destroy it. As the human race expands, more and more wildlife areas are being destroyed and more and more pollution is being produced. Some of this pollution, in the form of nuclear waste, will still be around centuries from now. There is an urgent need to find ways of halting this destruction.

Further, as civilization has progressed we have created new environmental stressors that our ancestors did not have to face. Consider, for example, the lives of a group of people called the Mabaan, who live in the Republic of Sudan in Africa, near the equator. When studied by Samuel Rosen and his colleagues in 1962, this culture was relatively untouched by modern civilization. The Mabaan lived in bamboo huts, wore little clothing, and thrived on a diet of grains, fish, and small game. Their environment was quiet and uncrowded, free of many of the stressors associated with modern urban life. There were no sleep-jarring noises from sirens and trucks, no traffic jams to endure at the end of the day, and little fear of crime. Rosen and his colleagues found that, compared to adults in the United States, the Mabaan had less hypertension (high blood pressure), less obesity, and superior hearing.

We cannot be sure, of course, that the absence of modern environmental stressors, such as the problems with urban life, was responsible for the excellent health of the Mabaan. Even if it was, we might not want to conclude that living in modern, urban areas is always stressful, inevitably causing health problems. As we mentioned, the same objective event, such as loud noise, is experienced as stressful under some conditions and pleasurable under others. When will modern environmental conditions like noise and crowding be stressful? Social psychologists have conducted numerous studies to find out.

Noise as a Source of Stress

Michael and Jeanne Schatzki longed to escape the hustle and bustle of urban life. After a long search, they finally found what seemed like an idyllic spot—a house at the end of a cul-de-sac in a peaceful, secluded neighborhood in Far Hills, New Jersey. "Then spring came," says Mr. Schatzki, "and we were sitting on the porch out back. And I said to Jeannie, 'You know, there are an awful lot of airplanes overhead.' And I looked up, and it was one after another" (*New Yorker*, October 21, 1991, p. 31). It turned out that the Federal Aviation Administration (FAA) had just changed the landing patterns at Newark Airport, 35 miles away. Whereas the planes landing and taking off at Newark Airport used to fly some distance from Far Hills, as many as 300 jets a day now roared directly over the Schatzkis' house.

Noise, n. A stench in the ear. . . . The chief product and authenticating sign of civilization.

—Ambrose Bierce,
Devil's Dictionary, 1911

It is well known that repeated exposure to loud noises eventually causes hearing loss. Samuel Rosen and his colleagues (1962), for example, attributed the superior hearing of the Mabaan in part to the fact that the environment in which they lived was, compared to modern, urban areas, extremely quiet. Are loud noises always psychologically stressful? The answer is that it depends on how people interpret the noise and how much control they feel they have over it. Many people voluntarily go to rock concerts where the music is extremely loud, louder than the sounds of jets flying overhead. Many people thrive on the hustle, bustle, and noise of urban life, as long as they can escape to a quiet corner of their apartment when they choose to do so. In contrast, Michael and Jeanne Schatzki did not choose to hear the jets screaming over their house and could not escape this noise.

As compelling as our examples may be, we cannot be sure that perceived control eliminates the stressful effects of noise without conducting well-controlled experiments. Fortunately, David Glass and Jerome Singer (1972) have performed just such a series of studies. A typical experiment went like this: Participants were given several problems to solve, such as complex addition problems and a proofreading task. While they worked on these problems, they heard very loud bursts of noise. The noise was of such things as a mimeograph machine, a typewriter, and two people speaking in Spanish. It was played at 108 decibels, about what you would hear if you were operating a riveting machine or were standing near the runway when a large commercial jet took off.

In one condition, the bursts of noise occurred at unpredictable lengths and at unpredictable intervals over the course of the 25-minute session. In a second condition, people heard the same sequence of noises but were given a sense of control over them. The experimenter told participants that they could stop the noise at any point by pressing a button. "Whether or not you press the button is up to you," explained the experimenter. "We'd prefer that you do not, but that's entirely up to you" (Glass & Singer, 1972, p. 64). A key fact to remember is that no one actually pressed the button. Thus, people in this condition heard the same amount of noise as people in the uncontrollable noise condition; the only difference was that they believed they could stop the noise whenever they wanted. Finally, a third condition was included wherein people worked on the problem in peace and quiet. After the 25-minute session was over, people in all conditions worked on new problems without any noise being played.

Interestingly, the noise had little effect on people during the initial 25-minute session. As long as a task was not too complex, people could bear down and ignore unpleasant noises, doing just as well on the problems as people who worked on them in quiet surroundings. A different picture emerged, however, when people worked on problems in the next session, in which everyone could work in peace and quiet. As you can see in Figure M2.1, those who had endured the uncontrollable noises made significantly more errors during this session than people who had not heard noises during the first session did. And what about the people who heard the noises but believed they could control them? As Figure M2.1 shows, these people did almost as well on the subsequent problems as the people who heard no noise at all. When people knew they could turn off the noise at any point, the noise was much easier to tolerate and did not impair later performance—even though people never actually turned it off.

Why did noise lower performance after it ended, and why did this occur only in the condition where the noise couldn't be controlled? When people are initially exposed to uncontrollable, negative events, they often attempt to overcome them as best they can. Many of the people who lived under the new landing pattern at Newark Airport initially fought back, repeatedly contacting officials at the FAA to protest the din of the jets. As long as they felt progress was being made, the noise was probably bearable. Similarly, in Glass and Singer's (1972) study, people initially were able to overcome the noxious effects of the noise by bearing down and concentrating as best they could.

However, if negative, uncontrollable events continue despite our best efforts to overcome them, *learned helplessness* sets in (Abramson et al., 1978; Wortman & Brehm, 1975). As discussed in Module 1, on health, learned helplessness occurs when people explain a negative event in a pessimistic way, by, for example, assuming that the event is caused by things that can't be changed. One consequence of learned helplessness is reduced effort and difficulty in learning new material. Thus, those participants who could not control the noise in the Glass and Singer (1972) experiment were able to deal with it and do well on the problems initially, but the lack of control they experienced eventually took its toll, causing them to do poorly on the second task. In contrast, those participants who believed they could control the noise never experienced learned helplessness and thus were able to do well on the second set of problems.

Unfortunately, in modern, urban life loud noises are often not controllable, and they last a lot longer than the 25-minute sessions in the Glass and Singer (1972) study. Sheldon Cohen and his colleagues have shown that people who are exposed to such real-life noises respond like the participants in the uncontrollable noise condition of Glass and Singer's (1972) studies. For example, these researchers studied children living in a New York City high-rise apartment building located right next to a busy highway (Cohen, Glass, & Singer, 1973). The children who lived on the lower floors and thus were subjected to the most traffic noise did poorer on reading tests than children living on the upper floors did.

In a later study, Cohen and his colleagues (1980, 1981) studied children who attended schools in the air corridor of Los Angeles Airport. More than 300 jets roared over these schools every day, causing an extremely high level of noise. Compared to children who attended quiet schools (matched on the basis of their

FIGURE M2.1 Noise and perceived control. ■ People who believed they could control the noxious noise did about as well on a subsequent task as people who heard no noise at all. (Adapted from Glass & Singer, 1972)

■ Frequent, loud noise is an unavoidable fact of urban life. Studies have shown that children who are exposed to constant noise from airplanes have higher blood pressure, are more easily distracted, and are more likely to give up when working on difficult puzzles than other children are.

race, ethnic group, economic background, and social class), the children at the noisy schools had higher blood pressure, were more easily distracted, and were more likely to give up when working on difficult puzzles. These deficits are classic signs of learned helplessness. Many of these problems were still there when the researchers tested the kids again a year later, suggesting that long-term exposure to loud, uncontrollable noise can cause serious problems in children. More recent studies have also found detrimental effects of noise (Nivison & Endresen, 1993; Topf, 1992). Due in part to studies such as these, attempts have recently been made to reduce the amount of noise to which people are subjected—for example, by adding soundproofing materials to schools and devices to jet engines to make them less noisy.

Crowding as a Source of Stress

As we write, more than 5 billion human beings inhabit the earth—more people than the total number of all human beings who have ever lived before. The world's population is increasing at the rate of 250,000 people every day. At our current rate of growth, the world population will double by the year 2025, and double again at increasingly shorter intervals. Two hundred years ago, the English clergyman Thomas Malthus warned that the human population was expanding so rapidly that soon there would not be enough food to feed everyone. He was wrong about when such a calamity would occur, largely because of technological advances in agriculture that have vastly improved grain yields. The food supply is dwindling, however, and the number of malnourished people in the world is increasing (Sadik, 1991). Malthus's timing may have been a little off, but many scientists fear his predictions are becoming truer every day.

Even when there is enough food to feed everyone, overcrowding can be a source of considerable stress, to both animals and human beings. When animals are crowded together, in either their natural environments or the laboratory, they reproduce more slowly, take inadequate care of their young, and become more susceptible to disease (Calhoun, 1973; Christian, 1963). Studies of crowding in

[Describing London]
Crowds without company and dissipation without pleasure.
–Edward Gibbon,
Memoirs, 1796

■ As the human population explodes, our planet is becoming more and more crowded. Under what conditions will crowding be stressful?

density: the number of people who occupy a given space

crowding: the subjective feeling of unpleasantness due to the presence of other people

human beings show similar negative effects. As crowding increases in prisons, for example, disciplinary problems, suicides, and overall death rates increase as well (Paulus et al., 1981). Studies at universities find that students living in crowded dorms (e.g., ones that have long corridors with common bathroom and lounge facilities) are more withdrawn socially and are more likely to show signs of learned helplessness than students living in less crowded dorms (e.g., ones with smaller suites that have their own bathrooms; Baum & Valins, 1977, 1979).

What is it about crowding that is so aversive? To answer this question, we must first recognize that the presence of other people is not always unpleasant. Many people love living in large cities. And when Saturday night arrives, many of us are ready to join our friends for an evening of fun, feeling that the more people we round up, the merrier. This fact has led researchers to distinguish between two terms: **Density** is a neutral term that refers to the number of people in a given space. A classroom with 20 students has a lower density of people than the same classroom with 50 students. **Crowding** is defined as the subjective feeling that there are too many people in a given space; it is the stress we feel when density becomes unpleasant. Under some circumstances, the class with 20 students might be experienced as more crowded than the class with 50 students.

When will density turn into crowding? One factor, as you might expect, pertains to how people interpret the presence of others, including how much control they feel they have over the crowded conditions (Baron & Rodin, 1978; Schmidt & Keating, 1979; Sherrod & Cohen, 1979). If the presence of others lowers our feelings of control—for example, making us feel it is harder to move around as freely as we would like, or harder to avoid running into people we would just as soon avoid—then we are likely to experience a crowd as stressful. If we feel we have control over the situation—for example, if we know we can leave the crowd at any point and find solace in a quiet spot—then we are unlikely to experience it as stressful.

To test this hypothesis, Drury Sherrod (1974) performed a study that was very much like the one Glass and Singer (1972) conducted on the effects of noise. He asked high school students to work on some problems in a room that was jam-packed with other people. In one condition, he told the students that they were free to leave at any point. "In the past, some people who have been in the experiment have chosen to leave," he said. "Others have not. We would prefer that you do not, but that's entirely up to you" (Sherrod, 1974, p. 176). Students in a second condition worked under identical crowded conditions but were not given the choice to leave at any point. Finally, students in a third condition worked in uncrowded conditions. After working on the initial set of problems, the participants were moved to uncrowded quarters, where they worked on a series of difficult puzzles.

The results mirrored those of Glass and Singer (1972). First, students who were crowded—regardless of whether or not they had a sense of control—solved as many problems as students who were not crowded. Initially, they were able to concentrate, ignoring the fact that they were shoulder to shoulder with other people. However, in the condition where the students thought they could not escape, the lack of control eventually took its toll. As seen in Figure M2.2, those students who had no control over the crowded conditions in the first session tried to solve significantly fewer puzzles in the second session, as compared to students in the other conditions. The students who had a sense of perceived control over the crowded conditions worked on almost as many difficult puzzles as the students who had not been crowded at all.

Thus, the effects of noise and crowding appear to be similar. If we feel we have control over these environmental conditions, they do not bother us very much. If we feel we do not have control over them, we can, in the short run, concentrate on our tasks and ignore the unpleasant effects of these stressors. Eventually, however, they take their toll, impairing our ability to cope.

> The thing which in the subway is called congestion is highly esteemed in the night spots as intimacy.
> –Simeon Strunsky, 1954

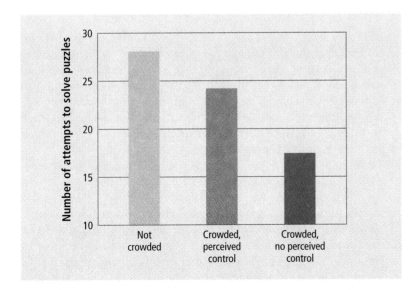

FIGURE M2.2 Crowding and perceived control. ■ People who believed they had control over the crowded conditions tried almost as hard on a subsequent task as people who were not crowded at all. (Adapted from Sherrod, 1974)

Consequently, it is important for people to feel they can control how crowded and noisy their environments are. It might seem like this is much easier in some parts of the world than others. If you live in a high-rise in New York City, for example, it would seem to be more difficult to avoid crowded conditions than if you live on a farm in Iowa. Similarly, homes and apartments are much smaller in Japan than in the United States, and to Americans, at least, it might seem that it is more difficult to escape crowded conditions in Japan than in the United States. Yet even in areas where the density of people is quite high, norms develop to protect people's privacy and to allow an escape from feeling overcrowded. Richard Brislin (1993) notes, for instance, that in both Japan and the slums of Mexico, both of which have a very high density of people, norms about visiting people in their homes are different from those in the United States. In Mexico, people's homes are respected as a sacrosanct place where people can be by them-selves and escape the stress of crowded conditions; it is virtually unheard of for people to "drop in" at someone else's house (Pandey, 1990). Similarly, the Japanese entertain in their homes much less than Americans do; they are more likely to invite guests for a meal in a restaurant. The way in which people in different cultures gain control over crowding differs, then, but the need for control appears to be universal.

In addition to perceived control, other factors determine how aversive people will find crowded conditions. It is well known, for example, that the presence of others makes people physiologically aroused (Zajonc, 1965). As we have seen elsewhere in this book, arousal can have intriguing consequences. It can lead to quite different emotions, depending on the attributions people make about the source of their arousal (Schachter & Singer, 1962). Thus, as we might expect, an important determinant of how aversive crowding will be is the nature of the attri-butions people make for the arousal caused by crowding. If people attribute their arousal to the presence of the other people, they will interpret it as a sign that the setting is too crowded and will feel uncomfortable, cramped, and irritated. If they attribute the arousal to another source, they will not feel crowded (Aiello, Thompson, & Brodzinsky, 1983; Schmidt & Keating, 1979). For example, if a student in a class of 300 people attributes her arousal to the stimulating and fascinating lecture she is hearing, she will feel less crowded than if she attributes her arousal to the fact that she feels like a sardine in a can.

sensory overload: the situation in which we receive more stimulation from the environment than we can pay attention to or process

Finally, crowding will be aversive if it leads to **sensory overload** (Cohen, 1978; Milgram, 1970), a term referring to our being bombarded by more stimu-lation from the environment than we can reasonably pay attention to. Since other people are a key source of stimulation, one instance in which sensory overload can occur is when so many people are around that we cannot pay attention to everyone. For example, if you were being interviewed for a job by a committee of ten persons, you'd feel that you had to pay close attention to everything each interviewer said and did. The result? A severe demand placed on your attentional system—and most likely negative consequences for you.

In sum, as the human race has evolved, it has learned to master many envi-ronmental hazards but in the process has produced new ones, such as noise and crowding. We turn now to another consequence of having become a crowded and technologically advanced society: People are harming the physical environment in multiple ways. Changes in attitudes and behaviors are urgently needed in order to avert environmental catastrophe. Social psychologists have studied a number of techniques involving social influence and social interaction that encourage people to behave in more environmentally sound ways.

"Help!"

Using Social Psychology to Change Environmentally Damaging Behaviors

Human beings have been treating the planet as a humongous garbage can, rapidly filling up the ground, water, and atmosphere with all sorts of pollutants. Pollution in the Los Angeles area, for example, is so bad that children who grow up there have lungs that function 10 to 15 percent less efficiently than the lungs of children who grow up in less polluted areas (Basu, 1989). When human beings lived in small groups of hunters and gatherers, they could get away with discarding their trash wherever they pleased; now that there are more than 5 billion of us (and counting), and we have developed toxic wastes that will remain poisonous for centuries, we have to change our ways (Gilbert, 1990).

How can we get people to treat the environment better? Naturally, you will recognize this as a classic social psychological question, in that it concerns how we can change people's attitudes and behaviors. Let's see what solutions social psychologists have come up with for the planet's pressing environmental problems.

Resolving Social Dilemmas

The first step is to realize that we are dealing with a special kind of mixed-motive conflict (see Chapter 9) called a **social dilemma.** A social dilemma exists when it is to an individual's benefit to act in a certain way but if most people act that way, everyone suffers. Consider the case of water conservation in states that often experience severe water shortages, such as California. A few years ago, water became so scarce in some areas that residents were urged to take very brief showers, shutting off the water while they lathered their hair with shampoo. Watering the lawn was viewed as an outdated, even obscene waste of a precious resource. Many communities employed "water police," who patrolled the neighborhoods, ready to pounce on residents who dared to turn on a garden hose.

social dilemma: a situation in which the most beneficial action for an individual will, if chosen by most people, have harmful effects on everyone

Suppose you lived in California at this time. You come home from a hard day at work and want nothing more than to take a long hot shower. What would you do? You might figure that a 20-minute shower will have only a minuscule effect on the total water supply. What's a few gallons here or there? And so you go ahead. Clearly, however, if everyone adopted this attitude, much more than a few gallons of water would be wasted—the total supply would drop precipitously and everyone would suffer. This is a classic social dilemma, because what is good for the individual is bad for the group as a whole (Dawes, 1980; Hardin, 1968; Komorita, 1995; Liebrand, Messick, & Wilke, 1992). As natural resources become scarcer and scarcer, people are faced with increasingly important environmental social dilemmas, wherein the needs and desires of the individual conflict with the needs and desires of human beings in general. How can we resolve social dilemmas? How can we convince people to act for the greater good of everyone, rather than purely out of self-interest?

Social psychologists have devised some fascinating laboratory games to try to answer this question. For example, imagine you were a participant in a game developed by John Orbell, Alphons van de Kragt, and Robin Dawes (1988). You arrive for the study and discover that there are six other participants you have never met before. The experimenter gives you and the other participants $6 and says each of you can keep the money. There is, however, another option. Each person can donate his or her money to the rest of the group, to be divided equally among the six other members. If anyone does so, the experimenter will double the contribution. For example, if you donate your money, it will be doubled to $12 and divided evenly among the six other participants. If other group members donate their money to the pot, it will be doubled and you will get a share.

Think about the dilemma with which you are faced. If everyone (including you) cooperates by donating his or her money to the group, once it is doubled and divided up, your share will be $12—double what you started with. Donating your money is risky, however; if you are the only one who does so, you will end up with nothing, while having increased everyone else's winnings (see Table M2.1). Clearly, the most selfish (and safest) course of action is to keep your money, hoping everyone else donates theirs. That way, you would make up to $18—your $6, plus your share of the money everyone else threw into the pot. Of course, if everyone thinks this way, you'll make only $6, because no one will donate any money to the group. Note that this dilemma is similar to the one faced by Californians over water usage: Individuals gain by hoarding water for their own use, but if everyone hoards water, everyone suffers.

What would you do if you were in the Orbell and colleagues (1988) study? If you are like most of the actual participants, you would keep your six bucks. After all, as you can see in Table M2.1, you will always earn more money by keeping your $6 than by giving it away (i.e., the winnings in the top row of Table M2.1 are always higher than the winnings in the bottom row). The only problem with this strategy is that because most people adopted it, everyone suffered. That is, the total pool of money to be divided remained low, because few people allowed the experimenter to double the money by donating it to the group. As with many social dilemmas, most people looked out for themselves, and as a result, everyone lost.

How can people be convinced to trust their fellow group members, cooperating in such a way that everyone benefits? It is notoriously difficult to resolve social dilemmas, as indicated by the difficulty of getting people to conserve water

Table M2.1

Your Decision	Other People's Decision						
	6 Keep 0 Give	5 Keep 1 Give	4 Keep 2 Give	3 Keep 3 Give	2 Keep 4 Give	1 Keep 5 Give	0 Keep 6 Give
Keep Your $6	$6	$8	$10	$12	$14	$16	$18
Give Your $6	$0	$2	$4	$6	$8	$10	$12

NOTE: Amount of money you stand to win in the Orbell, van de Kragt, and Dawes experiment. You can either keep your $6 or donate it to the six other group members. If you donate it, the money will be doubled, so that each group member will receive $2. Most people who play this game want to keep their money, to maximize their own gains. The more people who keep their money, however, the more everyone loses. (Adapted from Orbell et al., 1988)

when there are droughts, recycle their waste goods, and clean up a common area in a dormitory or apartment. In another condition of their experiment, however, John Orbell and his colleagues (1988) found an intriguing result: Simply allowing the group to talk with each other for ten minutes dramatically increased the number of people who donated money to the group, from 38 to 79 percent. The increase in the number of donators led to a larger pool of money to be divided, from an average of $32 to $66. Communication works because it allows each person to find out whether the others are planning to act cooperatively or competitively, as well as to persuade others to act for the common good (e.g., "I'll donate my money if you donate yours").

This finding is encouraging, but it may be limited to small groups that are able to communicate face to face. What happens when an entire community is caught in a social dilemma? It would be impossible for all the residents of California to gather together and talk about water conservation, or even for all the residents of one city to communicate in this way. When large groups are involved, alternative approaches are needed. One approach is to make people's behavior as public as possible. If people can take the selfish route privately, undiscovered by their peers, they will often do so. But if their actions are public, then the kinds of normative pressures we discussed in Chapter 7 come into play, making people's behavior more consistent with group norms. For example, some Californians might be tempted to water their gardens on the sly, but if they believe they will become the object of derision and scorn from their neighbors, they will most likely refrain from doing so.

Another proven technique is to change the way in which people perceive themselves and their social behavior. In Module 1, we saw that Aronson, Fried, and Stone (1991) succeeded in getting people to behave in healthier and more socially responsible ways—purchasing (and presumably using) more condoms—by making them see their own past actions as hypocritical. Could similar techniques be used to convince people to behave in more environmentally sound ways?

> In an age where man has forgotten his origins and is blind even to his most essential needs for survival, water along with other resources has become the victim of his indifference.
>
> –Rachel Carson,
> *The Silent Spring*, 1962

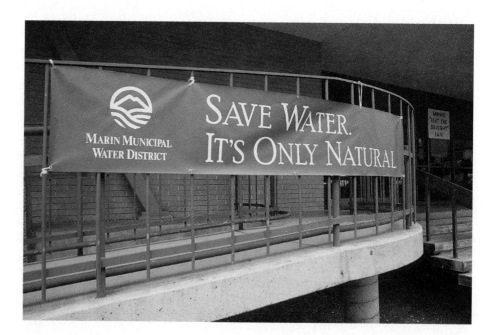

■ According to social psychological research, what is the best way to get people to change behaviors that damage the environment?

God gave Noah the rainbow sign,

No more water, the fire next time.

—"Home in the Rock," Negro spiritual

Conserving Water

Several years ago, the administrators at one campus of the University of California realized that an enormous amount of water was being wasted by students utilizing the university athletic facilities. The administrators posted signs in the shower rooms of the gymnasiums, exhorting students to conserve water by taking briefer, more efficient showers. The signs appealed to the students' conscience by urging them to take brief showers and to turn off the water while soaping up. The administrators were confident the signs would be effective because the vast majority of students at this campus were ecology-minded and believed in preserving natural resources. However, systematic observation revealed that less than 15 percent of the students complied with the conservation message on the posted signs.

The administrators were puzzled—perhaps the majority of the students hadn't paid attention to the sign? After all, a sign on the wall is easy to ignore. And so administrators made each sign more obtrusive, putting it on a tripod at the entrance to the showers so that the students needed to walk around the sign in order to get into the shower room. While this increased compliance slightly (19 percent turned off the shower while soaping up), it apparently made a great many students angry—the sign was continually being knocked over and kicked around, and a large percentage of students took inordinately long showers, apparently as a reaction against being told what to do. The sign was doing more harm than good—time to call in the social psychologists.

Elliot Aronson and his students (Dickerson, Thibodeau, Aronson, & Miller, 1992) decided to apply the hypocrisy technique they had used in the condom study to this new situation. The procedure involved intercepting female students who were on their way from the swimming pool to the women's shower room, introducing the experimental manipulations, then having a research assistant casually follow them into the shower room, where she unobtrusively timed their showers. Research participants in one condition were asked to respond to a brief questionnaire about their water use, a task designed to make them mindful of how they sometimes wasted water while showering. In another condition, research participants made a public commitment, exhorting others to take steps to conserve water. Specifically, these participants were asked to sign their names to a public poster that read, "Take Shorter Showers. Turn Shower Off While Soaping Up. If I Can Do It, So Can YOU!" In the crucial condition—the "hypocrisy" condition—the participants did both; that is, they were made mindful of their own wasteful behavior and they indicated publicly (on the poster) that they were practicing water conservation. In short, they were made aware that they were preaching behavior they themselves were not practicing. Just as in the condom study described earlier, those participants who were made to feel like hypocrites changed their behavior so that they could feel good about themselves. In this case, they took very brief showers. Indeed, the procedure was so effective that the average time students in this condition spent showering was reduced to three and a half minutes. The hypocrisy procedure has been found to increase other environmentally sound practices as well, such as recycling (Fried & Aronson, 1995).

Conserving Energy

It may be possible to draw on other social psychological techniques to increase environmentally sound behaviors. Consider the case of energy conservation. As a nation, the United States consumes far more energy, per capita, than any other nation on earth. Historically, we have felt perfectly content using as much energy as we needed, assuming that the planet had an infinite supply of oil, natural gas, and electric power. But this is not true. We have already depleted many of our national oil reserves, and we must import much of our oil from other countries.

It's imperative that we conserve energy. Let's take private homes as an example. By taking such simple measures as increasing ceiling, wall, and floor insulation, plugging air leaks, using more efficient light bulbs, and maintaining furnaces properly, the typical American energy consumer could reduce the amount of energy used to heat, light, and cool his or her home by 50 to 75 percent (Williams & Ross, 1980). The technology needed to increase energy efficiency currently exists and is well within the financial means of most homeowners. Not only would this technology save energy, but it would also save the individual homeowner a great deal of money. Yet despite the fact that the societal and financial advantages of conservation have been well publicized, the vast majority of homeowners have not taken action. How come? Why have Americans been slow to act in a manner that is in their economic self-interest? This lack of compliance has puzzled economists and policymakers, because they have failed to see that the issue is partly a social psychological one.

In Chapter 5, we noted that people's attention is typically directed to the aspects of their environment that are most salient and vivid (i.e., the aspects that are particularly noticeable). Elliot Aronson and his colleagues (Aronson, 1990; Aronson & Yates, 1985; Coltrane, Archer, & Aronson, 1986; Stern & Aronson, 1984) reasoned that energy conservation in the home is not a particularly vivid problem and so people do not spend much time thinking about it. The bill for natural gas and electricity comes only once a month and is spread out over dozens of appliances; thus, the homeowner has no clear idea which of the many appliances are using the most energy. It is as if you were buying food in a supermarket where the prices of individual items were unmarked and you were billed only at the end of the month. How would you know what to do to save money on your purchases? Perhaps if the sources of home energy consumption were made more vivid, people would take action.

To test this hypothesis, Elliot Aronson and his colleagues (Aronson & Gonzales, 1990; Gonzales, Aronson, & Costanzo, 1988) worked with several energy auditors in California. As in many states, California utility companies offer a free service wherein an auditor will come to people's homes and give them a customized assessment of what needs to be done to make their homes more energy efficient. What a deal! The problem was that less than 20 percent of the individuals requesting audits were actually following the auditors' recommendations.

To increase compliance, the Aronson research team trained the auditors to present their findings in a more vivid manner. For example, let's consider weather stripping: For most people, a small crack under the door didn't seem like a huge drain of energy, so when an auditor told them they should put in some weather stripping, they thought, "Yeah, big deal." Aronson and his colleagues told the auditors to make this statement more vivid:

> If you were to add up all the cracks around and under the doors of your home, you'd have the equivalent of a hole the size of a football in your living room wall. Think for a moment about all the heat that would escape from a hole that size. That's precisely why I'm recommending that you install weather stripping. (Gonzales et al., 1988, p. 1052)

Similar attempts were made to make other problems more vivid—for example, referring to an attic that lacks insulation as a "naked attic" that is like "facing winter not just without an overcoat, but without any clothing at all." (Gonzales et al., 1988, p. 1052)

The results were striking. The percentage of homeowners who followed the vivid recommendations jumped to 61 percent. This study demonstrates that people will act in a manner that is sensible in terms of national goals and their own economic self-interest, but if old habits are involved, the communication must be one that is vivid enough to break through those established habits.

Reducing Litter

Compared to other environmental problems, littering may not seem to be all that serious a matter. Although billboards implore us to "Keep America Beautiful," most people seem to think it isn't a big deal to leave their paper cup at the side of the road instead of in a trash barrel. Unfortunately, those paper cups add up. In California, for example, littering has increased steadily over the past 15 years, to the point where $100 million of tax money is spent cleaning it up—every year (Cialdini, Kallgren, & Reno, 1991). The stuff we discard is polluting our water systems, endangering wildlife, and costing us millions of dollars.

Littering is another classic social dilemma. Sometimes it's a pain to find a trash can, and from an individual's point of view, the addition of one more paper cup to the side of the road is not going to make much difference. As with all social dilemmas, the problem is that if everyone thinks this way, everyone suffers. How can we get people to act less selfishly when they have that paper cup in hand?

According to Robert Cialdini, Raymond Reno, and Carl Kallgren, the answer is to remind people of the social norms against littering (Cialdini, Kallgren, & Reno, 1991; Cialdini, Reno, & Kallgren, 1990; Reno, Cialdini, & Kallgren, 1993). The phrase "social norm," which has a long history in social

■ Besides being unsightly, litter can cost millions of dollars to clean up. Social psychologists have found that emphasizing different kinds of social norms against littering is an effective way to prevent it.

psychology and sociology, actually has several meanings. Cialdini and his colleagues (1991) suggest that two of these meanings are critical to understanding when people will litter. First, there are **injunctive norms,** referring to our perceptions of what other people approve of. Regardless of what other people really are doing, injunctive norms pertain to the kinds of things that are socially sanctioned by others. For example, we may be in an environment where many people are littering but know there is an injunctive norm against littering—most people disapprove of it.

Second, there are **descriptive norms,** referring to people's perceptions of what most people are actually doing, regardless of what they ought to be doing. Even if there were no injunctive norms against littering, people might be reluctant to litter if they saw that no one else was doing so. As we saw in Chapter 8, we often use observations of other people's behavior to decide on the proper course of action in a particular situation.

Focusing people's attention on either of these norms reduces littering. For example, Raymond Reno and his colleagues (1993) conducted a field experiment to investigate the power of injunctive norms. As people left a local library and approached their cars in the parking lot, an accomplice walked by them, picked up a fast-food bag that had been discarded on the ground, and put the bag in the trash. In a control condition, no bag was on the ground, and the accomplice simply walked by the library patrons. When the patrons got to their car, they found a handbill on their windshield. The question was, How many of these people would litter by throwing the handbill on the ground? Reno and colleagues hypothesized that seeing the accomplice pick up the fast-food bag would be a vivid reminder of the injunctive norm—littering is bad, and other people disapprove of it—and hence would lower their own inclination to litter. They were right: In this condition, only 7 percent of the people tossed the handbill on the ground, compared to 37 percent in the control condition.

What is the best way to communicate descriptive norms against littering? The most straightforward way, it would seem, would be to clean up all the litter in an environment, to illustrate that "no one litters here." In general, this is true: The less litter there is in an environment, the less likely people are to litter (Krauss, Freedman, & Whitcup, 1978; Reiter & Samuel, 1980). There is, however, an

injunctive norms: socially sanctioned behaviors—that is, people's perceptions of what behaviors are approved of by others

descriptive norms: people's perceptions of how other people are actually behaving in a given situation, regardless of what behaviors are socially sanctioned interesting exception to this finding. Cialdini and colleagues (1990) figured that seeing one piece of litter on the ground, spoiling an otherwise clean environment, would be a better reminder of descriptive norms than seeing a completely clean environment. The single piece of trash sticks out like a sore thumb, reminding people that no one has littered here—except one thoughtless person. In comparison, if there is no litter on the ground, people might not even think about what the descriptive norm is. Ironically, then, littering may be more likely to occur in a totally clean environment than in one containing a single piece of litter.

To test this hypothesis, the researchers stuffed students' mailboxes with handbills and then observed, from a hidden vantage point, how many of the students dropped the handbills on the floor (Cialdini et al., 1990). In the first condition, the researchers cleaned up the mailroom so that there were no other pieces of litter to be seen. In the second condition, they placed one very noticeable piece of litter on the floor: a hollowed-out heel of a watermelon. In the third condition, they not only put the watermelon rind on the floor but also spread out dozens of discarded handbills. As predicted, the lowest rate of littering occurred in the condition where there was a single piece of trash on the floor (see Figure M2.3). A single violation of a descriptive norm—the watermelon rind—highlighted the fact that most people had not littered. Now that people's attention was focused on the descriptive norm against littering, virtually none of the students littered. The highest percentage of littering occurred when the floor was littered with lots of handbills; here it was clear that there was a descriptive norm in favor of littering, and many of the students followed suit.

Thus, drawing people's attention to both injunctive and descriptive norms can reduce littering. Of the two kinds of norms, Robert Cialdini and his colleagues suggest that injunctive norms work better. Descriptive norms work only if everyone cooperates—for example, by keeping an environment relatively free of litter. This method is not perfect, however; if trash starts accumulating, then the descriptive norm becomes "See, lots of people litter here!" and littering will increase. In contrast, Raymond Reno and his colleagues (1993) found that reminding people of the injunctive norm works in a wide variety of situations, regardless of how clean the environment is. Once we are reminded that "people disapprove of littering," we are less likely to litter in virtually all circumstances.

We live in an environment whose principal product is garbage.
–Russell Baker, 1968

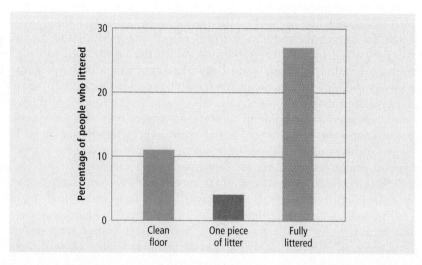

FIGURE M2.3 Descriptive norms and littering. ■ Who littered the least—people who saw that no one else had littered, people who saw one piece of litter on the floor, or people who saw several pieces of litter? As shown in the figure, it was people who saw one piece of litter. Seeing the single piece of litter was most likely to draw people's attention to the fact that most people had not littered, making people less likely themselves to litter. (Adapted from Cialdini et al., 1990)

SUMMARY

In the first part of this module, we discussed the environment as a source of stress on people. As we human beings continue to populate the earth at an alarming rate, our physical world is becoming a crowded and noisy place to live. Social psychologists have focused on how people interpret and explain crowded conditions and noise. One key interpretation is how much perceived control people have over the event. The less control people believe they have, the more likely it is that the event will cause them physical and psychological problems. For example, if people in high **density** settings feel they have a low level of control (i.e., they believe it is difficult to escape to a less dense setting), they will experience **crowding,** with negative consequences. Crowding can also be aversive if it leads to **sensory overload,** which occurs when other people place a severe demand on our attentional system. In addition, the way in which people explain the causes of negative events is critical to how an event is interpreted and thus to how stressful it will be.

We also discussed the effects people are having on the environment and the ways in which social influence techniques can be used to get people to behave in more environmentally sound ways. This is not easy, because many environmental problems represent a **social dilemma,** wherein actions that are beneficial for individuals are, if performed by most people, harmful to everyone. Using proven techniques to change people's attitudes and behaviors, however, social psychologists have had some success in getting people to act in more environmentally sound ways. One technique is to arouse dissonance in people by making them feel that they are not practicing what they are preaching—for example, that even though they believe in water conservation, they are taking long showers. Another is to remind people of both **injunctive** and **descriptive norms** against environmentally damaging acts, such as littering. Focusing people's attention on injunctive norms against littering—the idea that throwing trash on the ground is not a socially accepted behavior—was found to be especially effective.

IF YOU ARE INTERESTED . . .

Cohen, S., Evans, G. W., Stokols, D. S., & Krantz, D. S. (1986). *Behavior, health, and environmental stress.* New York: Plenum. An in-depth discussion of stress and human health, with a focus on studies the authors conducted on the effects of aircraft noise on children.

Gore, Al (1992, Houghton Mifflin). *Earth in the Balance: Ecology and the Human Spirit.* A sobering look at the relationship between human beings and the environment.

Ecological Psychology: Healing the Split Between Planet and Self (1966, HarperCollins). Deborah Du Nann Winter argues that because environmental problems have been caused by human behaviors, beliefs, and values, they are directly related to psychology and it is in psychology that the solutions will be found.

Komorita, S. S., & Parks, C. D. (1994). *Social dilemmas.* Dubuque, IA: Brown & Benchmark. A readable introduction to research on social dilemmas. Several examples relevant to environmental issues are used.

Liebrand, W. B. G., Messick, D. M., & Wilke, H. A. M. (1992). *Social dilemmas: Theoretical issues and research findings.* Oxford, England: Pergamon Press. A collection of state-of-the-art chapters by researchers investigating the causes and cures of social dilemmas.

Woodstock (1970). A documentary about the definitive rock festival; in addition to vintage rock-and-roll, the movie shows some interesting crowd scenes. An interesting application of research on crowding: When is a dense crowd of people pleasing and when is it stressful?

Social Psychology
and the Law

Eyewitness identifications are not very reliable, and when an eyewitness who is sincere but mistaken takes the stand and says, "I'll never forget that face," that leads to more unjust convictions than any other factor.

–Peter Neufeld (1994), director of the Innocence Project,
which helps free falsely convicted felons

You be the jury: How would you vote, after hearing the following testimony, taken from an actual case in Texas?

On a cold, dark night in November 1976, police officer Robert Wood and his partner noticed a car driving with its headlights off. Wood signaled the car to pull over, got out, and walked up to the driver's side. He intended only to tell the driver to turn on his lights, but he never got the chance. Before Wood could even speak, the driver pulled out a gun and shot Wood, killing him instantly. Wood's partner emptied her revolver at the car as it sped away, but the killer escaped.

A month later, the police picked up a suspect, 16-year-old David Harris. Harris admitted that he had stolen a neighbor's car and revolver the day before the murder, that this was the car Officer Wood had pulled over that night, and that he was in the car when the murder occurred. Harris denied, however, that he was the one who shot Wood. He said he had picked up a hitchhiker by the name of Randall Adams and had let Adams drive. It was Adams, he claimed, who reached under the seat, grabbed the revolver, and shot the officer.

When the police questioned Randall Adams, he admitted he had gotten a ride from David Harris but said Harris had dropped him off at his motel three hours before the murder occurred. It was Harris, he claimed, who was the murderer. Who was telling the truth? It was Harris's word against Adams's—until the police found three eyewitnesses who corroborated Harris's story. Emily and Robert Miller testified that they were driving by just before Officer Wood was shot. Though it was very dark, they said they got a good look at the driver of the car, and both identified him as Randall Adams. "When he rolled down the window that's what made his face stand out," said Robert Miller. "He had a beard, mustache, kind of dishwater blond hair" (Morris, 1988). David Harris was clean-shaven, and at the time of the murder, Randall Adams did indeed fit Miller's description, as seen in the photo on this page. Michael Randell, a salesman, also happened to be driving by right before the murder and claimed to have seen two people in the car. He too said the driver had long hair and a mustache.

Who do you think committed the murder? The real jury believed the eyewitnesses and convicted Adams, sentencing him to death. However, as Adams languished in jail, waiting for the courts to hear his appeals, several experts began to doubt he was guilty. New evidence came to light (largely because of a documentary film made about the case, Errol Morris's The Thin Blue Line), and it is now almost certain that David Harris was the murderer. Harris was later convicted of another murder and, while on death row, strongly implied that he, not Randall Adams, had shot Officer Wood. An appeals court overturned Adams's conviction. He was a free man—after spending 12 years in prison for a crime he did not commit.

If Adams was innocent, why did the eyewitnesses say that the driver of the car had long hair and a mustache? And why did the jury believe them? How common are such miscarriages of justice? In this module, we will discuss the answers to these questions, focusing on the role social psychological processes play in the legal system.

■ Randall Adams (left) and David Harris (right). The fact that eyewitnesses said the murderer had long hair and a mustache was the main reason Adams was convicted of murdering Officer Wood.

Let's begin with a brief review of the American justice system. When someone commits a crime and the police arrest a suspect, a judge or a grand jury decides whether there is enough evidence to press formal charges. If there is, lawyers for the defense and the prosecution gather evidence and negotiate with each other. As a result of these negotiations, the defendant often pleads guilty, to a lesser charge. About a quarter of the cases go to trial, in which a jury or a judge decides the defendant's fate. There are also civil trials, where one party (the plaintiff) brings a complaint against another (the defendant) for violating the former's rights in some way.

All of these steps in the legal process are intensely social psychological. For example, first impressions of the accused and of the witnesses have a powerful effect on police investigators and the jury; attributions about what caused the criminal behavior are made by police, lawyers, jurors, and the judge; prejudiced beliefs and stereotypical ways of thinking affect those attributions; attitude change and persuasion techniques abound in the courtroom, as lawyers for each side argue their case and jurors later debate with one another; and the processes of social cognition affect the jurors' decision making when deciding guilt or innocence. Social psychologists have studied the legal system a great deal in recent years, both because it offers an excellent applied setting in which to study basic psychological processes and because of its immense importance in daily life. If you, through no fault of your own, become the accused in a court trial, what do you need to know to convince the system of your innocence?

We will begin our discussion with eyewitness testimony, the most troubling aspect of the Randall Adams case we just presented. In Chapter 4, we saw that whereas people do form accurate impressions of others, systematic biases can come into play, leading to serious misunderstandings. A closely related question is, How accurate are people at identifying someone who has committed a crime?

Eyewitness Testimony

The American legal system assigns a great deal of significance to eyewitness testimony. If an eyewitness fingers you as the culprit, you are quite likely to be convicted, even if considerable circumstantial evidence indicates you are innocent. Randall Adams was convicted largely because of the eyewitnesses who identified him, even though in other ways the case against him was weak: He had no criminal record; he had just found steady employment; and he had no reason to be concerned about being pulled over by the police—he was only a hitchhiker (if, indeed, he really was in the car at the time of the shooting). In comparison, David Harris did have reason to fear the police: He had stolen the car and was in possession of a stolen, loaded handgun. Given these facts, why would Randall Adams murder a police officer? Doesn't David Harris seem a more logical suspect? Despite the implausibility of the Adams-as-murderer scenario and despite the lack of physical evidence linking Adams to the scene of the crime, the eyewitness testimony that Adams was driving the car was enough to convict him.

Systematic experiments have confirmed that jurors rely heavily on eyewitness testimony when they are deciding whether someone is guilty. Unfortunately, jurors also tend to overestimate the accuracy of eyewitnesses (Leippe, Manion, &

Romanczyk, 1992; R. Lindsay, 1994; Loftus, 1979; Wells, Lindsay, & Ferguson, 1979). Rod Lindsay and his colleagues (1981) conducted a clever experiment that illustrates both of these points. The researchers first staged the theft of a calculator in front of unsuspecting students and then saw how accurately the students could pick out the "thief" from a set of six photographs. In one condition, it was difficult to identify the thief because he had worn a knit cap pulled over his ears and was in the room for only 12 seconds. In the second condition, the thief had worn the knit cap higher on his head, revealing some of his hair, so that it was moderately difficult to identify him. In the third condition, the thief had worn no hat and stayed in the room for 20 seconds, making it relatively easy to identify him.

The first set of results is as we'd expect: The more visual information available about the thief, the higher the percentage of students who correctly identified him in the photo lineup (see the bottom line in Figure M3.1). In the next stage of the experiment, a researcher playing the role of lawyer questioned the students about their eyewitness identifications, just as a real lawyer would cross-examine witnesses in a trial. These question-and-answer sessions were videotaped. A new group of participants, playing the role of jurors, watched the videotapes of these cross-examinations and rated the extent to which they believed the witnesses had correctly identified the thief. As seen by the top line in Figure M3.1, these jurors overestimated the accuracy of the witnesses, especially in the condition where the thief was difficult to identify.

How accurate are eyewitnesses to real crimes? Although it is impossible to say exactly what percentage of the time eyewitnesses are accurate, there is reason to believe that they often make mistakes. Researchers have documented more than 1,000 cases of wrongful arrests and in a remarkably high proportion of these cases the wrong person was convicted because an eyewitness mistakenly identified him or her as the criminal (Brandon & Davies, 1973; Span, 1994; Wells, 1993).

Biases in Memory Processing That Reduce Eyewitness Accuracy

The problem is that our minds are not like video cameras that can record an event, store it over time, and play it back later, all with perfect accuracy. Think back to our discussion of social perception in Chapters 3 and 4, where we saw

FIGURE M3.1   The accuracy of eyewitness identification. ■ The accuracy of eyewitness identification depends on the viewing conditions at the time the crime was committed. As in this study, however, most jurors believe that witnesses can correctly identify the criminal even when viewing conditions are poor. (Adapted from R. Lindsay et al., 1981)

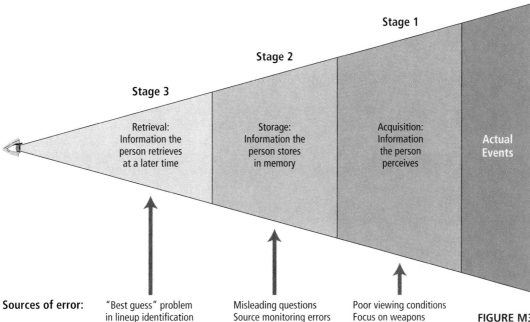

Sources of error:

"Best guess" problem in lineup identification	Misleading questions Source monitoring errors	Poor viewing conditions Focus on weapons Effects of expectations

FIGURE M3.2   Acquisition, storage, and retrieval.

that a number of distortions in social cognition and attribution can occur. Because eyewitness identification is a form of social perception, it is subject to similar problems, particularly ones involving memory. In order for someone to be an accurate eyewitness, he or she must successfully complete three stages of memory processing: **acquisition, storage,** and **retrieval** of the events witnessed. At any given time, people notice and pay attention to only a fraction of the information in the surrounding environment, and acquisition refers to the subset of information that is perceived. Of this information, a still smaller subset is actually stored in memory. Of the information that is stored in memory, only a subset can be retrieved at a later time (see Figure M3.2). Eyewitnesses can be inaccurate because of problems at any of these three stages.

Acquisition.   No one doubts that people accurately perceive a great deal of information about the world around them. Nonetheless, our ability to take in information is limited, particularly when we observe unexpected, complex events. The psychologist Hugo Münsterberg (1908), for example, described the following event, which occurred at a scientific meeting attended by psychologists, lawyers, and physicians: In the middle of the meeting, a clown burst into the room, followed closely by a man with a revolver. The two men shouted wildly, grabbed each other, then fell to the ground in a fierce struggle. One of them fired a shot; then both men ran out of the room.

All the witnesses were asked to write down an exact account of what they had just seen (which was actually an event staged by two actors). The eyewitness accounts were surprisingly inaccurate—most of the witnesses omitted or wrote mistaken accounts of about half the actions they had observed. Nor were they very accurate about the duration of the incident—though the two men were in the room for about 20 seconds, the witnesses' estimates ranged from a few seconds to several minutes.

acquisition: the process by which people notice and pay attention to information in the environment; because people cannot perceive everything that is happening around them, they acquire only a subset of the information available in the environment

storage: the process by which people store in memory information they have acquired from the environment

retrieval: the process by which people recall information stored in their memories

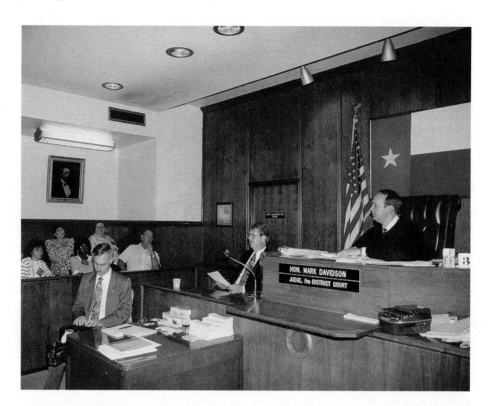

■ Eyewitness testimony has a far greater effect on jurors than it should, given that it is often inaccurate. Many cases of wrongful arrests and convictions are due to mistaken identifications made by eyewitnesses.

Patricia Tollestrup, John Turtle, and John Yuille (1994) found many similar eyewitness errors in a study of actual criminal cases. They examined police records of robbery and fraud cases in which a suspect was caught and confessed to the crime. They then assessed the accuracy of both victims' and bystanders' descriptions of the criminal, by comparing the witness's initial descriptions of the criminal to the criminal's actual physical characteristics (e.g., were witnesses correct that a witness had blond hair and a mustache?). Eyewitnesses weren't too bad at remembering some details; 100 percent of bystanders correctly remembered whether or not the criminal had facial hair (although crime victims correctly remembered this only 60 percent of the time). Only 48 percent of the bystanders and 38 percent of the victims correctly remembered the suspect's hair color, however. Most importantly, neither bystanders nor victims did a very good job of picking the criminal out of a lineup; overall, they correctly identified the criminal only 48 percent of the time.

A number of factors limit the amount of information about a crime that people take in, such as how much time they have to watch an event and the nature of the viewing conditions. As obvious as this sounds, people sometimes forget how these factors limit eyewitness reports of crimes. Crimes usually occur under the very conditions that make acquisition difficult: quickly, unexpectedly, and under poor viewing conditions, such as at night. These conditions certainly describe the scene of the murder of Officer Wood. Eyewitnesses were driving down a dimly lit road, past a pulled-over car, when the unexpected happened—shots rang out and a policeman crumpled to the ground. How well could they see? How much information could they take in, in the few seconds it took to drive by?

We should also remember that eyewitnesses who are the victims of a crime will be terribly afraid, and this factor can make it difficult to take in everything that is happening. As we saw, Patricia Tollestrup and her colleagues (1994) found that robbery victims tended to make more mistakes than bystanders. One reason victims of crimes have a poor memory for a suspect is that they focus their attention mostly on any weapon they see and less on the suspect's features (Christianson, 1992; Deffenbacher, 1983; Kramer, Buckhout, & Eugenio, 1990; Loftus, Loftus, & Messo, 1987). If someone points a gun at you and demands your money, your attention is likely to be more on the gun than on whether the robber has blue or brown eyes.

The information people notice and pay attention to is also influenced by what they expect to see. Consider our friend Alan, a social psychologist who is an expert on social perception. One Sunday, Alan became concerned when his neighbor, a frail woman in her eighties, did not appear for church. After knocking on her door repeatedly and receiving no response, Alan jimmied open a window and searched her house. Soon his worst fears were realized: The woman was lying dead on the floor of her bedroom.

Shaken, Alan went back to his house and telephoned the authorities. The police spent a great deal of time in the woman's house, and afterward a detective came over and asked Alan increasingly detailed questions, centering on whether he had noticed any suspicious activity around his neighbor's house. Alan was confused by this line of questioning and finally burst out, "Why are you asking me these questions? Isn't it obvious that my neighbor died of old age? Shouldn't we be notifying her family?" Now it was the detective's turn to look puzzled. "Aren't you the one who discovered the body?" he asked. Alan said he was. "Well," said the detective, "didn't you notice that her bedroom had been ransacked, that there was broken glass everywhere, and that there was a belt tied around her neck?"

> When an actual perceptual fact is in conflict with expectation, expectation may prove a stronger determinant of perception and memory than the situation itself.
>
> –Gordon Allport and Leo Postman, 1947

■ Imagine you are on this street corner and suddenly witness a holdup across the street. A thief robs a man of his wallet and is gone in a matter of seconds. How accurate do you think your description of the thief will be?

It turned out that Alan's neighbor had been strangled by a man who had come to spray her house for insects. There had been a fierce struggle, and the fact that the woman was murdered could not have been more obvious. But Alan saw none of the signs. He was worried that his elderly neighbor had passed away. When he discovered that she had in fact died, the farthest thing from his mind was that she had been murdered. As a result, he saw what he expected and failed to see what he did not expect. When the police later showed him photographs of the crime scene, he felt as though he had never been there. He recognized almost nothing. Alan's experiences are consistent with our discussion in Chapter 3 of how people use theories and schemas. We have many theories about the world and the people in it, and these theories influence what we notice and remember.

Similarly, the information we take in is influenced by how familiar we are with it: Unfamiliar things are more difficult to remember than familiar things. For example, people are better at recognizing faces that are of the same race as they are. Several studies have documented this **own-race bias**. Whites are better at recognizing white faces than black or Asian faces, blacks are better at recognizing black than white faces, and Asians are better at recognizing Asian than white faces (Bothwell, Brigham, & Malpass, 1989; Ng & R. Lindsay, 1994). Though the reasons for this finding are not entirely clear, something about our increased familiarity with our own race appears to make it easier for us to identify faces of that same race.

own-race bias: the finding that people are better at recognizing faces of their own race than of other races

Storage. We have just seen that several variables limit what people perceive and thus what they are able to store in their memories. Once a piece of information is in memory, it might seem like it stays there, unaltered, until we recall it at a later time. Many people think memory is like a photograph album. We record a picture of an event, such as the face of a robber, and place it in the memory "album." The picture may not be perfect—after all, few of us have photographic memories. Further, it might fade a bit over time, because memories, like real photographs, fade with age. It seems unlikely, however, that the picture can be altered or retouched, such that things are added to or subtracted from the image. If the robber we saw was clean-shaven, surely we will not pencil in a mustache at some later time. Thus, the fact that the witnesses who testified at the Randall Adams trial remembered that the driver of the car had long hair and a mustache seems like pretty incriminating evidence for Randall Adams.

Unfortunately, the way in which our memories actually work is not so simple. People can get mixed up about where they heard or saw something, so that memories in one "album" get confused with memories in another. As a result, people can have quite inaccurate recall about what they saw. This is the conclusion reached by Elizabeth Loftus and her colleagues after years of research on **reconstructive memory,** defined as a cognitive process whereby memories for an event become distorted by information encountered after the event has occurred (Loftus, 1979; Loftus & Hoffman, 1989; Weingardt, Toland, & Loftus, 1994). According to Loftus, information we obtain after witnessing an event can change our memories of the event.

reconstructive memory: the process whereby memories for an event become distorted by information encountered after the event has occurred

In one of her studies, she showed students 30 slides depicting different stages of an automobile accident. The contents of one slide varied; some students saw a car stopped at a stop sign, whereas others saw the same car stopped at a yield sign (see the photos on page 579). After the slide show, the students were asked several questions about the car accident they had "witnessed." The key question varied how the traffic sign was described. In one version, the question asked, "Did another car pass the red Datsun while it was stopped at the stop sign?" In the other version, the question asked, "Did another car pass the red Datsun while it was stopped at the yield sign?" Thus, for half the participants the question described the traffic sign as they had in fact seen it. But for the other half, the wording of the question subtly introduced new information—for example, if they had seen a stop sign, the question described it as a yield sign. Would this small change (akin to what might occur when witnesses are being questioned by police investigators or attorneys) have an effect on people's memories of the actual event?

All the students were shown the two pictures reproduced on this page and asked which one they had originally seen. Most people (75 percent) who were asked about the sign they had actually seen chose the correct picture; that is, if they had seen a stop sign and were asked about a stop sign, most of them correctly identified the stop-sign photograph (note that 25 percent made a crucial mistake on what would seem to be an easy question). However, of those who got the misleading question, only 41 percent chose the correct photograph (Loftus, Miller, & Burns, 1978).

In subsequent experiments, Loftus and her colleagues have found that misleading questions can change people's minds about how fast a car was going, whether broken glass was at the scene of an accident, whether a traffic light was green or red, and—of relevance to the Randall Adams trial—whether a robber

■ Students saw one of these pictures and then tried to remember whether they had seen a stop sign or a yield sign. Many of those who heard leading questions about the street sign made mistaken reports about which sign they had seen. (From Loftus, Miller, & Burns, 1978)

had a mustache (Loftus, 1979). Her studies show that the way in which the police and lawyers question witnesses can change the witnesses' reports about what they saw. (There is some suspicion that in the Randall Adams case, the police may have led the witnesses by asking questions that implicated Adams and not Harris. At the time of the murder, Harris was a juvenile and could not receive the death penalty for killing a police officer; Adams was in his thirties and could do so. According to this reasoning, Adams was a "better" suspect in the eyes of the police). But, we might ask, do misleading questions alter what is stored in eyewitnesses' memories, or do the questions change only what these people are willing to report, without retouching their memories?

Though some controversy exists over the answer to this question (Belli, 1989; Loftus & Hoffman, 1989; McCloskey & Zaragoza, 1985; Smith & Ellsworth, 1987; Tversky & Tuchin, 1989), most researchers endorse the following position: Misleading questions cause a problem with **source monitoring**, the process by which people try to identify the source of their recollections (Johnson, Hashtroudi, & D. Lindsay, 1993; D. Lindsay, 1994; D. Lindsay & Johnson, 1989). People who saw a stop sign but received the misleading question about a yield sign now have two pieces of information in memory, the stop sign and the yield sign. This is all well and good, as long as they remember where these memories came from: the stop sign from the accident they saw earlier, and the yield sign from the question they were asked subsequently. The problem is that people often get mixed up about where they heard or saw something, mistakenly believing that the yield sign looks familiar, because they saw it during the slide show. This process is similar to the misattribution effects we discussed in Chapter 5, wherein people are unsure about what has caused their arousal. It's easy to get confused about the source of our memories as well. When information gets stored in memory, it is not always well "tagged" as to where it came from.

The implications for legal testimony are sobering. Eyewitnesses who are asked misleading questions often report seeing things that were not really there. In addition, eyewitnesses might be confused as to why a suspect looks familiar. It is likely, for example, that the eyewitnesses in the Randall Adams trial saw pictures of Adams in the newspaper before they testified about what they saw the night of the murder. When asked to remember what they saw that night, they might have become confused because of a source-monitoring error. They remembered seeing a man with long hair and a mustache, but they may have gotten mixed up about where they had seen his face before.

Retrieval.   Suppose the police have arrested a suspect and want to see if you, the eyewitness, can identify the person. It is common practice for the police to arrange a lineup at the police station, where you will be asked whether one of several people is the perpetrator. Sometimes you will be asked to look through a one-way mirror at an actual lineup of the suspect and some foils (people known not to have committed the crime). Other times you will be asked to examine videotapes of a lineup or photographs of the suspect and the foils. In each case, if a witness identifies a suspect as the culprit, the suspect is likely to be charged and convicted of the crime. After all, the argument goes, if an eyewitness saw the suspect commit the crime and then picked the suspect out of a lineup later, that's pretty good evidence the suspect is the guilty party.

Just as there are problems with acquisition and storage of information, so too can there be problems with how people retrieve information from their memories. A number of things other than the image of a person that is stored in

---

source monitoring: trying to identify the source of one's recollections; sometimes people make errors about the source of their memories (e.g., believing a man looks familiar because they saw him at the scene of a crime, when in fact he looks familiar because they saw his picture in the newspaper)

Give us a dozen healthy memories, well-formed, and . . . we'll guarantee to take any one at random and train it to become any type of memory we might select—hammer, screwdriver, wrench, stop sign, yield sign, Indian chief—regardless of its origin or the brain that holds it.

–Elizabeth Loftus and Hunter Hoffman, 1989

memory can influence whether eyewitnesses will pick someone out of a lineup. Witnesses often choose the person in a lineup who most resembles the criminal, even if the resemblance is not very strong. Suppose, for example, that a 19-year-old woman committed a robbery and the police mistakenly arrest you, a 19-year-old woman, for the crime. They put you in a lineup and ask witnesses to pick out the criminal. Which do you think would be more fair: if the other people in the lineup were a 20-year-old man, a 3-year old child, and an 80-year-old woman, or if the other people were all 19-year-old women? In the former case, the witnesses might pick you out only because you are the one who most resembles the actual criminal (Buckhout, 1974). In the latter case, it is much less likely that the witnesses will mistake you for the criminal, because everyone in the lineup is the same age and sex as the culprit (Wells, 1993; Wells & Luus, 1990).

To avoid this "best guess" problem wherein witnesses pick the person who looks most like the suspect, social psychologists recommend that police follow these five steps:

1. Make sure everyone in the lineup resembles the witness's description of the suspect. Doing so will minimize the possibility that the witness will simply choose the person who looks most like the culprit (Wells, Seelau, Rydell, & Luus, 1994).
2. Tell the witnesses that the person suspected of the crime may or may not be in the lineup. If witnesses believe the culprit is present, they are much more likely to choose the person who looks most like the culprit, rather than saying that they aren't sure or that the culprit is not present. As a result, false identifications are more likely to occur when people believe the culprit is in the lineup (Gonzalez, Ellsworth, & Pembroke, 1993; Malpass & Devine, 1981; Wells et al., 1994).
3. Do not always include the suspect in an initial lineup. If a witness picks out someone as the culprit from a lineup that includes only foils, then you will know the witness is not reliable (Wells, 1984).

"That's him! That's the one! ... I'd recognize that silly little hat anywhere!"

4. Present pictures of people sequentially instead of simultaneously, because doing so makes it more difficult for witnesses to compare all the pictures, choosing the one that most resembles the criminal, even when the criminal is not actually in the lineup (R. Lindsay & Wells, 1985; Sporer, 1994).

5. Present witnesses with both photographs of people and sound recordings of their voices. Witnesses who both see and hear members of a lineup are much more likely to identify the person they saw commit a crime than people who only see the pictures or only hear the voice recordings are (Melara, DeWitt-Rikards, & O'Brien, 1989).

How Can We Tell if Eyewitness Testimony Is Accurate?

Suppose you are a police detective or a member of a jury who is listening to a witness describe a suspect. How can you tell whether the witness's memory is accurate or whether he or she is making one of the many mistakes in memory we have just documented? It might seem like the answer to this question is pretty straightforward: Pay careful attention to how confident the witness is. Suppose the witness stands up in the courtroom, points her finger at the defendant, and says, "That's the man I saw commit the crime. There's absolutely no doubt in my mind—I'd recognize him anywhere." Sounds pretty convincing, doesn't it? Compare this testimony to a witness who says, "Well, gee, I'm really not sure, because it all happened so quickly. If I had to guess, I'd say it was the defendant, but I'm not really sure." Which witness would you be more likely to believe? The eyewitness who was more confident, of course! The U.S. Supreme Court concurs with this reasoning, ruling that the amount of confidence witnesses express is a good indicator of their accuracy (*Neil v. Biggers,* 1972).

The only problem—and it is a big one—is that numerous studies have shown that a witness's confidence is not strongly related to how accurate he or she is (Bothwell, Deffenbacher, & Brigham, 1987; Luus & Wells, 1994a; Smith, Kassin, & Ellsworth, 1989). We don't mean to say there is no relation between confidence and accuracy; if witnesses pick a suspect out of a lineup, there is a modest relationship between how confident they are and whether their identification is correct (Sporer, Penrod, Read, & Cutler, 1995). Surprisingly, however, this relationship is not very strong, and it is dangerous to assume that because a witness is very confident he or she must be correct. For example, in the Lindsay and colleagues (1981) experiment we discussed earlier, witnesses who saw the crime under poor viewing conditions (in which the thief wore the cap over his ears) had as much confidence in their identifications as witnesses who saw the crime under moderate or good viewing conditions, even though they were considerably less accurate (See Figure M3.1).

The reason confidence is not always a sign of accuracy is that the things that influence people's confidence are not necessarily the same things that influence their accuracy. After identifying a suspect, for example, people's confidence increases if they find out that other witnesses identified the same suspect and decreases if they find out that other witnesses identified a different suspect (Luus & Wells, 1994b). This change in confidence cannot influence the accuracy of the identification people made earlier. Thus, just because a witness is confident does not mean he or she is accurate.

Well, then, how can we tell whether a witness's testimony is accurate? It is by no means easy, but research by David Dunning and Lisa Beth Stern (1994; Stern

> Take nothing on its looks; take everything on evidence. There's no better rule.
> –Charles Dickens, *Great Expectations*, 1861.

> No subjective feeling of certainty can be an objective criterion for the desired truth.
> –Hugo Münsterberg, 1908

& Dunning, 1994) suggests some answers. They showed participants a film in which a man stole some money from a woman's wallet, asked participants to pick the man out of a photo lineup, and then asked participants to describe how they had made up their minds. Dunning and Stern found some interesting differences between the reports of people who accurately identified the man and the reports of people who did not. Accurate witnesses tended to say that they didn't really know how they recognized the man, that his face just "popped out" at them. Inaccurate witnesses tended to say that they used a process of elimination whereby they deliberately compared one face to another. Ironically, taking more time and thinking more carefully about the pictures were associated with making more mistakes. We should thus be more willing to believe a witness who says "I knew it was the defendant as soon as I saw him in the lineup" than one who says "I compared everyone in the lineup to each other, thought about it, and decided it was the defendant."

The research by Dunning and Stern, while intriguing, leaves unanswered an important question: Did taking more time on the identification task make people less accurate, or did people who were less accurate to begin with simply take more time? Maybe some people did not pay close attention to the film of the robbery and thus had difficulty recognizing the robber in the lineup. Consequently, they had to spend more time thinking about it and comparing the faces, such that inaccuracy caused a longer decision time. Alternatively, there might have been something about making identifications thoughtfully and deliberately that impaired accuracy. Maybe there was something about making an identification slowly and deliberately that made people less accurate.

Some fascinating studies by Jonathan Schooler and Tonya Engstler-Schooler (1990) support this second possibility and suggest one aspect of making an identification slowly and deliberately that can cause problems: trying to put an image of a face into words. They showed students a film of a bank robbery and asked some of the students to write detailed descriptions of the robber's face (the verbalization condition). The others spent the same amount of time completing an unrelated task (the no verbalization condition). All students then tried to pick out the robber from a photo lineup of eight faces. It might seem that writing a description of the robber would be a good memory aid and make people more accurate. In fact, the reverse was true: Only 38 percent of the people in the verbalization condition correctly identified the robber, compared to 64 percent of the people in the no verbalization condition.

Schooler and Engstler-Schooler (1990) suggest that trying to put a face into words is difficult and impairs memory for that face. Using the word *squinty* to describe a robber's eyes, for example, might be a general description of what his eyes looked like, but probably does not capture the subtle contours of his eyes, eyelids, eyelashes, eyebrows, and upper cheeks. When you see the photo lineup, you look for eyes that are squinty, and doing so interferes with your attention to the finer details of the faces. If you ever witness a crime, then, you should not try to put into words what the criminal looked like. And if you hear someone say she or he wrote down a description of the criminal and then took a long time deciding whether the person was present at a lineup, you might doubt the accuracy of the witness's identification.

By now we have seen several factors that make eyewitness testimony inaccurate, leading to all too many false identifications. Perhaps the legal system in the United States should rely less on eyewitness testimony than it now does. In the legal systems of some countries, a suspect cannot be convicted on the basis of a

FIGURE M3.3   Does experience in law enforcement improve the ability to detect deception? ■ Experienced law enforcement officers were no better at telling who was lying than inexperienced law enforcement officers or college students were. (Adapted from DePaulo & Pfeiffer, 1986)

sole eyewitness; at least two independent witnesses are needed. Adopting this more stringent standard in the United States might mean that some guilty people go free, but it would avoid many false convictions.

Detecting Deception

There is yet another reason eyewitness testimony can be inaccurate: Even if witnesses have very accurate memories for what they saw, they might deliberately lie when on the witness stand. After Randall Adams was tried and convicted, evidence came to light suggesting that some of the eyewitnesses who testified against him had lied. For example, one witness may have struck a deal with the police, agreeing to say what they wanted her to say, in return for lenient treatment of her daughter (who had been arrested for armed robbery). If so, why couldn't the jurors tell she was lying when she said she saw Randall Adams at the wheel of the car right before the murder?

Consider the controversy over the guilt or innocence of O. J. Simpson. Was he lying when he denied murdering Nicole Simpson and Ronald Goldman? What about the testimony of Mark Fuhrman, the police detective who discovered the bloody glove at O. J. Simpson's house? Some people believe that Fuhrman was lying and that he planted the glove at the estate. Others believe that while he may well be a racist, he was telling the truth about finding the glove. How can we tell whether witnesses such as these are lying or telling the truth?

Several studies have tested people's ability to detect deception. When people watch videotapes of actors who are either lying or telling the truth, their ability to tell who is lying is only slightly better than chance, (i.e., only slightly better than pure guessing; DePaulo, 1994; DePaulo, Stone, & Lassiter, 1985). But surely some people must be very good at detecting deception; after all, some jobs require exactly that skill. For example, law enforcement officials, most of whom have

> If falsehood, like truth, had only one face, we would be in better shape. For we would take as certain the opposite of what the liar said. But the reverse of truth has a hundred thousand shapes.
>
> –Montaigne, *Essays*, 1595

spent years with suspects who concoct stories professing their innocence, may be much more skilled than the average person at seeing through these stories to the underlying truth. Unfortunately, research by Bella DePaulo and Roger Pfeiffer (1986) and Paul Ekman and Maureen O'Sullivan (1991) suggests otherwise. These researchers tested the ability of experienced law enforcement officers—including members of the U.S. Customs Service, the Secret Service, the armed forces, police detectives, and judges—to detect deception. In general, these officials were no better at telling whether someone was lying than untrained college students were (see Figure M3.3). The moral is this: If someone is motivated to tell a lie, he or she can usually get away with it. Even the experts will have trouble telling who is lying and who is telling the truth.

The Lie-Detector Test.   If people are poor lie detectors, perhaps machines can do the job for them. The lie-detector machine, called a **polygraph**, monitors people's physiological responses, such as their heart rate, breathing rate, and amount of perspiration. The assumption is that when people lie, they become anxious and this anxiety can be detected by increases in heart rate, breathing rate, and so on. But do polygraphs really work? Many employers, including the federal government, require people to take lie-detector tests before being hired. At some federal agencies, such as the CIA, employees must take periodic lie-detector tests to see if they have committed any crimes. In at least one well-known case,

polygraph: a machine that measures people's physiological responses (e.g., their heart rate); when these machines are used in lie detection, polygraph operators attempt to tell if someone is lying by observing how that person responds physiologically while answering questions

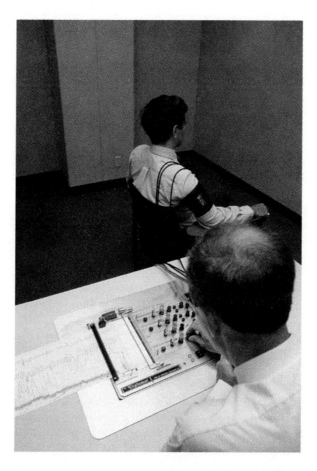

■ Though polygraphs can detect whether someone is lying at levels better than chance, they are by no means infallible.

however, the test failed to do its job. Aldrich Ames is a former CIA official who was recently convicted of spying for the Soviet Union for many years. He revealed a great deal of damaging information to the Soviets, reportedly passing along secrets that led to the death of several American agents. Apparently, at the time he was spying he passed at least two polygraph tests, during which he was specifically asked questions about espionage.

A great deal of controversy over the accuracy of polygraph tests exists among psychological researchers, and the test has both strong supporters (e.g., Raskin, 1986) and steadfast critics (e.g., Lykken, 1984). Given this disagreement and given how widespread polygraph tests have become, the U.S. Congress asked the Office of Technology and Assessment in 1983 to write a review of the scientific evidence regarding the polygraph's validity. Several social psychologists have also reviewed this evidence (Ekman, 1992; Saxe, 1994; Saxe, Dougherty, & Cross, 1985) and reached similar conclusions. First, under optimal conditions (e.g., the test is given by an experienced examiner), the polygraph can reveal whether someone is lying or telling the truth at levels better than chance. But that doesn't mean the machine is perfect. Even under optimal conditions, the test can be inaccurate, and it often has high error rates. The error rates vary somewhat, depending on the technique used to administer the test. A recent review by Paul Ekman (1992), averaging across all the different techniques, estimates that the polygraph typically misidentifies about 15 percent of liars as truth-tellers (false negatives) and about 15 percent of truth-tellers as liars (false positives). Other reviewers suggest that false negatives, in which liars are found to be telling the truth, are the most common kind of error—as in the Aldrich Ames case (Honts, 1994).

Thus, failing a lie-detector test is not, like Pinocchio's nose, an infallible sign of deceit. Suppose, for example, you are an honest employee working in a convenience store. The owners tell you that someone has been stealing money from the cash register, and they want you to take a lie-detector test to prove your innocence. "If you are innocent," they say, "what do you have to fear?" What you have to fear is the 15 percent chance that the machine will say you are guilty when you are not (this chance is even higher with inexperienced examiners). Would you be willing to take a 15 percent chance of losing your job and being arrested for a crime you did not commit? Because of this high rate of error, most states do not allow the results of polygraph tests to be used in court. And in 1988, Congress passed the Employee Polygraph Protection Act, which bars the use of lie-detector machines by private employers, except under special circumstances (e.g., employees who have direct access to drugs can be tested).

It would be nice if there were a foolproof method of telling whether or not someone is lying. Controversies like the O. J. Simpson case could be easily resolved, and Randall Adams would never have had to endure 12 long years in prison for a crime he did not commit. Many psychologists doubt, though, that such a test will ever be developed; the nuances of human behavior are too rich and complex to allow foolproof tests of honesty.

Juries: Group Processes in Action

Ultimately, it is not a polygraph that decides whether witnesses are telling the truth but a judge or jury. Juries are of particular interest to social psychologists, because the way they reach verdicts is directly relevant to social psychological research on group processes and social interaction. The right to be tried by a jury of one's peers has a long tradition in English and American law. Trial by jury was an established institution in England at the beginning of the seventeenth century, and the people who founded the first permanent English settlement in North America, at Jamestown, Virginia, carried this tradition with them (though this right was not accorded to Native Americans or other nonwhites or to a few rebellious English settlers who were summarily hanged). In the United States today, everyone has the right, under most circumstances, to be tried by a jury.

Despite this tradition, the jury system has often come under attack. Many television viewers placed themselves in the role of a juror in the O. J. Simpson trial and formed strong opinions about whether the real jurors reached the correct verdict. Sometimes it is clear that juries made the wrong decision, as did the one that convicted Randall Adams of murdering Officer Wood. Harry Kalven, Jr., and Hans Zeisel (1966) found that judges who presided over criminal jury trials disagreed with the verdict rendered by the jury a full 25 percent of the time. Such findings have led some experts to doubt the wisdom of leaving such important decisions up to juries of ordinary citizens. A former dean of the Harvard Law School, for example, wondered, "Why should anyone think that 12 persons brought in from the street, selected in various ways, for their lack of general ability, should have any special capacity for deciding controversies between persons?" (Kalven & Zeisel, 1966, p. 5).

The jury system has its staunch supporters, of course, and few people argue that it should be abolished. The point is that it is not a perfect system and that, based on research in social psychology, there are ways we might expect it to go wrong. Problems can arise at each of three phases of a jury trial: the way in which jurors use information they obtain before the trial begins (pretrial publicity), the way in which they process information during the trial, and the way in which they deliberate in the jury room, after all the evidence has been presented.

Effects of Pretrial Publicity

Because the murder of Officer Wood in Texas received considerable attention in the media, it is possible that the jury, before the trial began, was biased by what they had read in the newspapers. The press reported that a key eyewitness had picked Randall Adams out of a police lineup, but this information was untrue and was never presented to the jury during the trial. Nonetheless, two jurors mentioned during the deliberations that they believed the eyewitness had picked Adams out of the lineup (*Dallas Morning News*, May 4, 1987).

Even when the information reported by the media is accurate, it is often stacked against a suspect for a simple reason—the press gets much of its information from the police and the district attorney, who are interested in presenting as strong a case as they can against the suspect. Thus, it's not surprising that the more people hear about a case in the media, the more they believe the suspect is guilty (Otto, Penrod, & Dexter, 1994).

Geoffrey Kramer, Norbert Kerr, and John Carroll (1990) showed that emotional publicity that arouses public passions, such as lurid details about a murder, is particularly biasing. They contacted people who had just finished serving on juries in Michigan and asked them to watch a videotaped trial of a man accused of robbing a supermarket. Before the jurors viewed the trial, the researchers exposed them to emotional publicity (reports that a car matching the one used in the robbery struck and killed a 7-year-old girl after the robbery), factual publicity (a report that the suspect had an extensive prior criminal

> 'Tis with our judgements as our watches, none go just alike, yet each believes his own.
> —Alexander Pope (1688–1744)

> A court is no better than each . . . of you sitting before me on this jury. A court is only as sound as its jury, and a jury is only as sound as the [people] who make it up.
> —Harper Lee, *To Kill a Mockingbird*, 1960

"Since you have already been convicted by the media, I imagine we can wrap this up pretty quickly."

record), or no publicity. After watching the trial and deliberating in 12-member mock juries, the participants rated whether they would vote to convict the suspect. The emotional publicity biased jurors the most, significantly increasing the percentage of jurors who gave guilty verdicts—even though the jurors knew they were not supposed to be influenced by any information they learned before viewing the trial.

Judges and lawyers have a variety of options to try to remedy this problem. First, lawyers are allowed to question prospective jurors before the trial (a process called *voir dire*). The lawyers ask people whether they have heard anything about the case, and if so, whether they feel they can render an unbiased verdict. One problem with this approach, however, is that people are often unaware they have been biased by pretrial publicity (Ogloff & Vidmar, 1994). In the Kramer and colleagues (1990) study we just reviewed, for example, the researchers put the jurors through a *voir dire* process, removing from the study any jurors who said that because of the pretrial publicity they could not form an unbiased opinion. Nonetheless, the emotional publicity still influenced the verdicts given by the remaining jurors.

Second, judges can instruct jurors to disregard what they have heard in the media. Several studies have shown, however, that these instructions do little to erase the effects of pretrial publicity and may even increase the likelihood that jurors use it (Kramer et al., 1990). One reason this can happen is that it's very difficult to erase something from our minds once we have heard it. In fact, as mentioned in Chapter 3, the more we try not to think about something, the more that very thing keeps popping into consciousness (Wegner, 1989, 1992, 1994).

Another problem with pretrial publicity is that linking a person's name with incriminating events can cause negative impressions of the person, even if the media explicitly deny any such connection. Daniel Wegner, Richard Wenzlaff, Michael Kerker, and Ann Beattie (1981), for example, found that when research participants read a headline denying any wrongdoing on someone's part—such as "Bob Talbert Not Linked with Mafia"—they had a more negative impression of the person than participants who read an innocuous headline—such as "Bob Talbert Arrives in City." The mere mention of Bob Talbert and the Mafia in the same headline was enough to plant seeds of doubt in readers, despite the head-line's explicit denial of a connection. Thus, media reports can have unintended negative effects, and once there, those effects are hard to erase. The best solution is to include in a trial only those jurors who have heard nothing about the case. In highly publicized cases such as the O. J. Simpson trial, finding such jurors can be difficult. Sometimes a trial is moved to a new location where there has been less publicity.

Information Processing During the Trial

How do individual jurors think about the evidence they hear during a trial? As we saw in Chapter 3, people often construct theories and schemas to interpret the world around them, and the same is true of jurors (Hart, 1995; Kuhn, Weinstock, & Flaton, 1994; Smith, 1991). Nancy Pennington and Reid Hastie (1990, 1992, 1993) suggest that jurors decide on one story that best explains all the evidence; they then try to fit this story to the possible verdicts they are allowed to render, and if one of those verdicts fits well with their preferred story, they are likely to vote to convict on that charge.

This explanation has important implications for how lawyers present their cases. Lawyers typically present the evidence in one of two ways. In the first, called the story order, they present the evidence in the sequence events occurred, corresponding as closely as possible to the story they want the jurors to believe. In the second, called the witness order, they present witnesses in the sequence they think will have the greatest impact, even if this means that events are described out of order. For example, a lawyer might save his or her best witness for last, so that the trial ends on a dramatic, memorable note, even if this witness describes events that occurred early in the alleged crime.

If you were a lawyer, in which order would you present the evidence? You probably can guess which order Pennington and Hastie hypothesized would be the most successful. If jurors are ultimately swayed by the story or schema they think best explains the sequence of events, then the best strategy should be to present the evidence in the story order and not the witness order. To test their hypothesis, Pennington and Hastie (1988) asked mock jurors to listen to a simu-lated murder trial. The researchers varied the order in which the defense attorney and the prosecuting attorney presented their cases. In one condition, both used the story order, whereas in another condition, both used the witness order. In

Table M3.1

How should lawyers present their cases?

Percentage of people voting to convict the defendant

	Defense evidence	
	Story order	Witness order
Prosecution evidence		
Story order	59%	78%
Witness order	31%	63%

NOTE: Lawyers can present their cases in a variety of ways. This study found that the story, in which lawyers present the evidence in the order that corresponds most closely to the "story" they want the jurors to believe, works the best. (Adapted from Pennington & Hastie, 1988)

other conditions, one attorney used the story order, whereas the other used the witness order.

The results provided clear and dramatic support for the story order strategy. As seen in Table M3.1, when the prosecutor used the story order and the defense used the witness order, the jurors were most likely to believe the prosecutor—78 percent voted to convict the defendant. When the prosecutor used the witness order and the defense used the story order, the tables were turned—only 31 percent voted to convict. Pennington and Hastie (1990) speculate that one reason the conviction rate in felony trials in America is so high—approximately 80 percent—is that in real trials, prosecutors usually present evidence in the story order, whereas defense attorneys usually use the witness order. To those of our readers who are budding lawyers, remember this when you are preparing for your first trial!

Deliberations in the Jury Room

You may have noticed that our discussion so far has left out a crucial part of the jury process: the part where the jury retires to the jury room and deliberates before deciding on the verdict. Even if most jurors are inclined to vote to convict, there might be a persuasive minority who change their fellow jurors' minds. Sometimes this can be a minority of one, as in the classic movie *Twelve Angry Men*. When this film begins, a jury has just finished listening to the evidence in a murder case and all the jurors except one vote to convict the defendant. But over the course of the next 90 minutes, the lone holdout, played by Henry Fonda, persuades his peers that there is reason to doubt that the young Hispanic defendant is guilty. At first, the other jurors pressure Fonda to change his mind (using techniques of normative and informational conformity, as discussed in Chapter 8), but in the end, reason triumphs and the other jurors come to see that Fonda is right.

As compelling as this movie is, research indicates that it does not reflect the reality of jury deliberations (Kalven & Zeisel, 1966; MacCoun, 1989; Stasser,

Stella, Hanna, & Colella, 1984). In the Randall Adams trial, for example, a majority of the 12-person jury (7 men and 5 women) initially voted to convict Adams. After eight hours of deliberations, the majority prevailed: The holdouts changed their minds, and the jury voted unanimously to convict. In the O. J. Simpson trial, 1 juror initially voted guilty, but quickly changed her mind. This tendency for juries to go with the initial majority is common. Harry Kalven, Jr., and Hans Zeisel (1966) interviewed the members of more than 200 juries in actual criminal trials. In the vast majority of the cases (97 percent), the jury's final decision was the same as the one favored by a majority of the jurors on the initial vote. Thus, just as we saw in Chapter 8, on conformity, majority opinion usually carries the day, bringing dissenting jurors into line.

If jury deliberation is stacked toward the initial, majority opinion, should we just abandon the deliberation process, letting the jury's initial vote determine a defendant's guilt or innocence? For two reasons, this would not be a good idea. First, forcing juries to reach a unanimous verdict makes them consider the evidence more carefully, rather than simply assuming their initial impressions of the case were correct (Hastie, Penrod, & Pennington, 1983). Second, even if minorities seldom succeed in persuading the majority to change their minds about guilt or innocence, minorities often do change people's minds about how guilty a person is. In criminal trials, juries usually have some discretion about the type of guilty verdict they can reach. In a murder trial, for example, they often can decide whether to convict the defendant of first-degree murder, second-degree murder, or manslaughter. Pennington and Hastie (1990) found that people on a jury who have a minority point of view often do convince the majority to change their minds about the specific verdict to render. Thus, while a minority are unlikely to convince a majority to change their verdict from first-degree murder

■ In the classic movie *Twelve Angry Men*, Henry Fonda convinces all of his fellow jurors to change their minds about a defendant's guilt. In real life, however, such cases of a minority in a jury convincing the majority to change its mind are rare.

to not guilty, they might be able to convince the majority to change the verdict to second-degree murder.

In sum, social psychological research indicates that the American legal system can go wrong in a number of ways: Juries rely heavily on eyewitness testimony, when in fact such testimony is often in error; determining when witnesses are telling the truth is very difficult, even with the use of polygraphs; and since juries are groups of people who try to reach consensus by discussing, arguing, and bargaining, the kinds of conformity pressures and group processes we discussed in Chapters 8 and 9 can lead to faulty decisions. By illuminating these problems in their research, however, social psychologists can help to initiate change in the legal system—change that will lead to greater fairness and equity for all participants.

SUMMARY

Many social psychological principles predict how people will respond in the legal arena. Because of the limitations of people's memory, eyewitness testimony is often inaccurate. A number of factors bias the **acquisition, storage,** and **retrieval** of what people observe, sometimes leading to the false identification of criminals. For example, research on the **own-race bias** shows that people find it more difficult to recognize members of other races than members of their own race. Research on **reconstructive memory** indicates that errors in **source monitoring** can occur, whereby people become confused about where they saw or heard something. Jurors often place a great deal of faith in eyewitness testimony, even though jurors are not very good at telling when someone is lying. Because the **poly-graph** is also an imperfect measure of lie detection, false testimony by eyewitnesses and others sometimes goes undetected. Jurors are susceptible to the same kinds of biases and social pressures we documented in earlier chapters. They are sometimes biased by pretrial publicity, even when trying to put it out of their minds. During a trial, jurors attempt to make sense out of the testimony and often decide on one story that explains all of the evidence. Juries are thus most swayed by lawyers who present the evidence in a way that tells a consistent story. During deliberations, jurors with minority views are often pressured into conforming to the view of the majority; thus, verdicts usually correspond to the initial feelings of the majority of jurors.

IF YOU ARE INTERESTED . . .

Abramson, J. (1995). *We, the Jury: The Jury System and the Ideal of Democracy.* New York: Basic Books. An analysis of the jury system in the United States, with a discussion of such topics as whether juries should be required to reach unanimous verdicts and when an individual juror will conform to the opinion of the rest of the jury.

Kassin, S. M., & Wrightsman, L. S. (1988). *The American jury on trial: Psychological perspectives.* New York: Hemisphere. A comprehensive look at the psychological issues involved at all levels of jury trials, from jury selection to jury verdicts.

Loftus, E., & Ketcham, K. (1991). *Witness for the defense: The accused, the eyewitness, and the expert who puts memory on trial.* New York: St. Martin's. An account of the role of memory biases in eyewitness identification, by one of the leading researchers in this area.

Ross, D. F., Read, D. J., & Toiglia, M. P. (Eds.). (1994). *Adult eyewitness testimony: Current trends and developments.* New York: Cambridge University Press. A collection of chapters about eyewitness testimony from leading researchers in the field. They cover such topics as what factors influence the accuracy of eyewitness testimony, how to construct unbiased lineups, and how to tell whether an eyewitness is accurate.

Thin Blue Line (1988). Errol Morris's documentary portrays the Randall Adams case discussed in this module. It is a fascinating portrayal of the way in which the American justice system can go wrong.

Turow, Scott (1987). *Presumed Innocent.* An engrossing story of a trial in which an innocent man is accused of murder. It is an interesting portrayal of the intricacies of the American justice system.

Twelve Angry Men (1957). A classic film in which a character played by Henry Fonda convinces all of his fellow jurors that a defendant accused of murder is innocent. As discussed in the module the film is an interesting depiction of jury decision making, but is not one that reflects everyday life. In real life, a lone juror seldom succeeds in changing the minds of the other 11 jurors.

GLOSSARY

accessibility: the ease with which different thoughts and ideas can be brought to mind; an idea that is accessible is already on our minds or can easily be brought to mind [4]

acquisition: the process by which people notice and pay attention to information in the environment; because people cannot perceive everything that is happening around them, they acquire only a subset of the information available in the environment [M–3]

actor/observer difference: the tendency to see other people's behavior as dispositionally caused, while focusing more on the role of situational factors when explaining one's own behavior [4]

additive task: a group task in which performance depends on the sum of each individual's effort (e.g., the total noise made by a group of cheerleaders) [9]

affectively based attitude: an attitude based more on people's feelings and values than on their beliefs about the nature of an attitude object [7]

aggressive action: a behavior aimed at causing either physical or psychological pain [12]

aggressive stimulus: an object that is associated with aggressive responses (e.g., a gun) and whose mere presence can increase the probability of aggression [12]

altruism: any act that benefits another person but does not benefit the helper and often involves some personal cost to the helper [11]

altruistic personality: the aspects of a person's makeup that are said to make him or her likely to help others in a wide variety of situations [11]

amygdala: an area in the core of the brain that is associated with aggressive behaviors [12]

anchoring and adjustment heuristic: a mental shortcut that involves using a number or value as a starting point, and then adjusting one's answer away from this anchor; people often do not adjust their answer sufficiently [3]

anxious/ambivalent attachment style: an attachment style characterized by a concern that others will not reciprocate one's desire for intimacy, resulting in higher than average levels of anxiety [10]

applied research: studies designed specifically to solve a particular social problem; building a theory of behavior is usually secondary to solving a specific problem [2]

archival analysis: a form of systematic observation whereby the researcher observes social behavior by examining the accumulated documents, or archives, of a culture (e.g., diaries, novels, magazines, and newspapers) [2]

attachment styles: the expectations people develop about relationships with others, based on the relationship they had with their primary caregiver when they were infants [10]

attitude accessibility: the strength of the association between an object and a person's evaluation of that object; accessibility is measured by the speed with which people can report how they feel about an issue or object [7]

attitude inoculation: the process of making people immune to attempts to change their attitudes by initially exposing them to small doses of the arguments against their position [7]

attitude: an enduring evaluation—positive or negative—of people, objects, and ideas [7]

attribution theory: a description of the way in which people explain the causes of their own and other people's behavior [4]

autobiographical memories: memories about one's own past thoughts, feelings, and behaviors [5]

automatic processing: thinking that is nonconscious, unintentional, involuntary, and effortless [3]

availability heuristic: a mental rule of thumb whereby people base a judgment on the ease with which they can bring something to mind [3]

avoidant attachment style: an attachment style characterized by a suppression of attachment needs, because attempts to be intimate have been rebuffed; people with this style find it difficult to develop intimate relationships [10]

base rate information: information about the frequency of members of different categories in the population [3]

basic research: studies that are designed to find the best answer to the question of why people behave the way they do and that are conducted purely for reasons of intellectual curiosity [2]

behaviorally based attitude: an attitude based on observations of how one behaves toward an attitude object [7]

behaviorism: a school of psychology maintaining that to understand human behavior, one need only consider the reinforcing properties of the environment—that is, how positive and negative events in the environment are associated with specific behaviors [1]

belief in a just world: a form of defensive attribution wherein people assume that bad things happen to bad people and that good things happen to good people [4]

biased sampling: making generalizations from samples of information that are known to be biased or atypical [3]

blaming the victim: our tendency to blame individuals (make dispositional attributions) for their victimization, typically motivated by a desire to see the world as a fair place [13]

bookkeeping model: information inconsistent with a stereotype that leads to a modification of the stereotype [13]

bystander effect: the finding that the greater the number of bystanders who witness an emergency, the less likely any one of them is to help. [11]

category-based expectancies: expectations about people based on the groups to which they belong, such as expecting someone to love going to parties because he or she belongs to a party-loving fraternity or sorority [4]

catharsis: the notion that "blowing off steam"—by performing an aggressive act, watching others engage in aggressive behaviors, or engaging in a fantasy of aggression—relieves built-up aggressive energies and hence reduces the likelihood of further aggressive behavior [12]

causal theories: theories about the causes of one's own feelings and behaviors; often we learn such theories from our culture (e.g., "absence makes the heart grow fonder") [5]

central route to persuasion: the case whereby people elaborate on a persuasive communication, listening carefully to and thinking about the arguments; this occurs when people have both the ability and the motivation to listen carefully to a communication [7]

classical conditioning: the case whereby a stimulus that elicits an emotional response is repeatedly experienced along with a neutral stimulus that does not, until the neutral stimulus takes on the emotional properties of the first stimulus [7]

cognitions: thoughts, feelings, beliefs, or pieces of knowledge [6]

cognitive appraisal theories of emotion: theories holding that emotions result from people's interpretations and explanations of events, in the absence of any physiological arousal [5]

cognitive dissonance: a drive or feeling of discomfort, originally defined as being caused by holding two or more inconsistent cognitions and subsequently defined as being caused by performing an action that is discrepent from one's customary, typically positive self-conception [6]

cognitive misers: The idea that people are so limited in their ability to think and make inferences that they take mental shortcuts whenever they can [3]

cognitively based attitude: an attitude based primarily on people's beliefs about the properties of an attitude object [7]

communal relationships: relationships in which people's primary concern is being responsive to the other person's needs [10]

companionate love: the feelings of intimacy and affection we feel for another person when we care deeply for the person but do not necessarily experience passion or arousal in his or her presence [10]

comparison level for alternatives: people's expectations about the level of rewards and punishments they would receive in an alternative relationship [10]

comparison level: people's expectations about the level of rewards and punishments they are likely to receive in a particular relationship [10]

compliance: a change in behavior due to a direct request from another person [8]

conformity: a change in behavior due to the real or imagined influence of other people [8]

conjunctive task: a group task in which performance depends on how well the least talented member does (e.g., how fast a team of roped-together mountain climbers can climb a mountain) [9]

consensus information: information about the extent to which other people behave the same way toward the same stimulus as the actor does [4]

consistency information: information about the extent to which the behavior between one actor and one stimulus is the same across time and circumstances [4]

construal: the way in which people perceive, comprehend, and interpret the social world. [1]

contagion: the rapid transmission of emotions or behaviors through a crowd [8]

contingency theory of leadership: the theory that leadership effectiveness depends both on how task-oriented or relationship-oriented the leader is and on the amount of control and influence the leader has over the group [9]

controllability: information that indicates whether the cause of the success (or failure) is something the individual can control or cannot control [4]

controlled processing: thinking that is conscious, intentional, voluntary, and effortful [3]

conversion model: information inconsistent with a stereotype that leads to a radical change in the stereotype [13]

coping styles: the ways in which people react to stressful events [M-1]

correlational method: the method whereby two or more variables are systematically measured and the relationship between them (i.e., how much one can be predicted from the other) is assessed [2]

correspondent inference theory: the theory that we make internal attributions about a person when there are (a) few noncommon effects of his or her behavior and (b) the behavior is unexpected [4]

counterattitudinal advocacy: the process that occurs when a person states an opinion or attitude that runs counter to his or her private belief or attitude [6]

counterfactual thinking: mentally changing some aspect of the past as a way of imagined what might have been [3]

covariation model: a theory which states that in order to form an attribution about what caused a person's behavior, we systematically note the pattern between the presence (or absence) of possible causal factors and whether or not the behavior occurs [4]

cover story: a description of the purpose of a study, given to participants, that is different from its true purpose; cover stories are used to maintain psychological realism [2]

crowding: the subjective feeling of unpleasantness due to the presence of other people [M-2]

debriefing: the procedure whereby the purpose of the study and exactly what transpired is explained to participants at the end of an experiment [2]

deception: the procedure whereby participants are misled about the true purpose of a study or the events that will actually transpire [2]

decode: to interpret the meaning of the nonverbal behavior other people express, such as deciding that a pat on the back was an expression of condescension and not kindness [4]

defensive attributions: explanations for behavior that avoid feelings of vulnerability and mortality [4]

dehumanization: the act of seeing victims as nonhumans (e.g., "gooks" instead of fellow human beings); dehumanization lowers inhibitions against aggressive actions and makes continued aggression easier and more likely [12]

deindividuation: the loosening of normal constraints on behavior, leading to an increase in impulsive and deviant acts [9]

density: the number of people who occupy a given space [M-2]

dependent variable: the variable a researcher measures to see if it is influenced by the independent variable; the researcher hypothesizes that the dependent variable will depend on the level of the independent variable [2]

descriptive norms: people's perceptions of how other people are actually behaving in a given situation, regardless of what behaviors are socially sanctioned [M-2]

diffusion of responsibility: the phenomenon whereby each bystander's sense of responsibility to help decreases as the number of witnesses increases [11]

discounting: underestimating the effects of one cause of our behavior when another cause is conspicuous and salient [5]

discrimination: unjustified negative or harmful action toward a member of a group, simply because of his or her membership in that group [13]

disjunctive task: a group task in which performance depends on how well the most talented member does (e.g., a group of people trying to solve a difficult math problem) [9]

display rules: culturally determined rules about which nonverbal behaviors are appropriate to display [4]

distinctiveness information: information about the extent to which one particular actor behaves in the same way to different stimuli [4]

divisible versus a unitary task: divisible tasks are those that can be broken down into different subtasks performed by individual members, whereas unitary tasks are those in which no division of labor is feasible; performance on unitary tasks depends on how group members' outputs are combined to reach a joint decision [9]

door-in-the-face technique: a technique to get people to comply with a request, whereby people are presented first with a large request, which they are expected to refuse, and then with a smaller, more reasonable request, to which it is hoped they will acquiesce [8]

downward social comparison: the process whereby we compare ourselves to people who are worse than we on a particular trait or ability, in order to feel better about ourselves [5]

elaboration likelihood model: the theory that there are two ways in which persuasive communications can cause attitude change; the central route occurs when people are motivated and have the ability to pay attention to the arguments in the communication, and the peripheral route occurs when people do not pay attention to the arguments but are instead swayed by surface characteristics (e.g., who gave the speech) [7]

emblems: nonverbal gestures that have well-understood definitions within a given culture; they usually have direct verbal translations, such as the OK sign [4]

empathy: the ability to put oneself in the shoes of another person—to experience events and emotions (e.g., joy and sadness) the way that person experiences them [11]

emphathy-altruism hypothesis: the idea that when we feel empathy for a person, we will attempt to help him or her purely for altruistic reasons—that is, regardless of what we have to gain [11]

encode: to express or emit nonverbal behavior, such as smiling or patting someone on the back [4]

equity theory: the theory holding that people are happiest with relationships in which the rewards and costs a person experiences and the contributions he or she makes to the relationship are roughly equal to the rewards, costs, and contributions of the other person [10]

Eros: the instinct toward life, posited by Freud [12]

exchange relationships: relationships governed by the need for equity (i.e., for an equal ratio of rewards and costs) [10]

experimental method: the method of choice to study cause-and-effect relationships; the researcher randomly assigns participants to different conditions and ensures that these conditions are identical except for the independent variable (the one thought to have a causal effect on people's responses) [2]

external attribution: the inference that a person is behaving a certain way because of something about the situation he or she is in; the assumption is that most people would respond the same way in that situation [4]

external justification: a person's reason or explanation for his or her dissonant behavior that resides outside the individual (e.g., in order to receive a large reward or avoid a severe punishment) [6]

external validity: the extent to which the results of a study can be generalized to other situations and other people [2]

extrinsic motivation: the desire to engage in an activity because of external rewards or pressures, not because we enjoy the task or find it interesting [5]

factorial design: an experimental design in which there is more than one independent variable; each independent variable has more than one version, or level; and all possible combinations of these levels occur in one study [2]

false memory syndrome: a memory of a past traumatic experience that is objectively false but that people believe occurred [5]

fear-arousing communications: persuasive messages that attempt to change people's attitudes by arousing their fears [7]

field experiments: experiments conducted in real-life settings, rather than in the laboratory [2]

foot-in-the-door technique: a technique to get people to comply with a request, whereby people are presented first with a small request, to which they are expected to acquiesce, followed by a larger request, to which it is hoped they also acquiesce [8]

frustration-aggression theory: the theory that frustration—the perception that you are being prevented from obtaining a goal—will increase the probability of an aggressive response [12]

fundamental attribution error: the tendency to overestimate the extent to which people's behavior is due to internal, dispositional factors, and to underestimate the role of situational factors [1]

gain-loss effect: the finding that we like people the most if we feel we have gained in their estimation of us (i.e., if they initially disliked us but now like us) and that we dislike people the most if we feel we have lost their favor (i.e., if they initially liked us but now dislike us) [10]

Gestalt psychology: a school of psychology stressing the importance of studying the subjective way in which an object appears in people's minds, rather than the objective, physical attributes of the object [1]

global attribution: the belief that the cause of an event is due to factors that apply in a large number of situations (e.g., your intelligence, which will influence your performance in many areas), as opposed to the belief that the cause is specific and applies in only a limited number of situations (e.g., your music ability, which will affect your performance in music courses but not in other courses) [M-1]

great person theory: the theory that certain key personality traits make a person a good leader, regardless of the nature of the situation facing the leader [9]

group polarization: the tendency for groups to make decisions that are more extreme than the initial inclinations of its members [9]

groupthink: a kind of thinking in which maintaining group cohesiveness and solidarity is more important than considering the facts in a realistic manner [9]

heuristic-systematic model of persuasion: the theory that there are two ways in which persuasive communications can cause attitude change; people either systematically process the merits of the arguments or use mental shortcuts (heuristics), such as "Length equals strength" [7]

hostile aggression: an act of aggression stemming from feelings of anger and aimed at inflicting pain [12]

hostile media phenomenon: the finding that opposing partisan groups both perceive neutral, balanced media presentations as hostile to their side, because the media have not presented the facts in the one-sided fashion the partisans "know" to be true [3]

hydraulic theory: the theory that unexpressed emotions build up pressure and must be expressed to relieve that pressure [12]

idiosyncrasy credits: the credits a person earns, over time, by conforming to group norms; if enough idiosyncrasy credits are earned, the person can, on occasion, behave deviantly without retribution from the group [8]

illusory correlation: the tendency to see relationships, or correlations, between events that are actually unrelated [13]

implicit personality theory: a type of schema people use to group various kinds of personality traits together; for example, many people believe that if someone is kind, he or she is generous as well [4]

impression management: our conscious or unconscious orchestration of a carefully designed presentation of self so as to create a certain impression that fits our goals or needs in a social interaction [5]

in-group bias: especially positive feelings and special treatment for people we have defined as being part of our in-group, and negative feelings and unfair treatment for others simply because we have defined them as being in the out-group [13]

in-group: the group with which an individual identifies and feels he or she is a member of [13]

independent variable: the variable a researcher changes or varies to see if it has an effect on some other variable; this is the variable the researcher thinks will cause a change in some other variable [2]

independent view of the self: a way of defining oneself in terms of one's own internal thoughts, feelings, and actions, and not in terms of the thoughts, feelings, and actions of other people [5]

individual differences: the aspects of people's personalities that make them different from other people [1]

informational social influence: the influence of other people that leads us to conform because we see them as a source of information to guide our behavior; we conform because we believe that others' interpretation of an ambiguous situation is more correct than ours [8]

informed consent: the procedure whereby the nature of the experiment is explained to participants before it begins and their consent to participate in the experiment is obtained [2]

ingratiation: the process whereby people flatter, praise, and generally try to make themselves likable to another, often higher-status person [5]

injunctive norms: socially sanctioned behaviors—that is, people's perceptions of what behaviors are approved of by others [M-2]

institutionalized racism: racist attitudes that are held by the vast majority of us because we are living in a society where stereotypes and discrimination are the norm [13]

institutionalized sexism: sexist attitudes that are held by the vast majority of us because we are living in a society where stereotypes and discrimination are the norm [13]

instrumental aggression: aggression as a means to some goal other than causing pain [12]

instrumental conditioning: the case whereby behaviors that people freely choose to perform increase or decrease in frequency, depending on whether they are followed by positive reinforcement or punishment [7]

insufficient punishment: the dissonance aroused when individuals lack sufficient external justification for having resisted a desired activity or object, usually resulting in individuals devaluing the forbidden activity or object [6]

integrative solution: a solution to a conflict whereby the parties make trade-offs on issues according to their different interests; each side concedes the most on issues that are unimportant to it but important to the other side [9]

interdependent view of the self: a way of defining oneself in terms of one's relationships to other people; recognizing that one's behavior is often determined by the thoughts, feelings, and actions of others [5]

interjudge reliability: the level of agreement between two or more people who independently observe and code a set of data; by showing that two or more judges independently come up with the same observations, researchers ensure that the observations are not the subjective, distorted impressions of one individual [2]

internal attribution: the inference that a person is behaving in a certain way because of something about him or her, such as the person's attitudes, character, or personality [4]

internal justification: the reduction of dissonance by changing something about oneself (e.g., one's attitude or behavior) [6]

internal validity: making sure that nothing else besides the independent variable can affect the dependent variable; this is accomplished by controlling all extraneous variables and by randomly assigning people to different experimental conditions [2]

intrapersonal conflict: tension within one individual due to two or more incompatible goals (e.g., a parent's desires to stay home with his or her children and to pursue a career) [9]

intrinsic motivation: the desire to engage in an activity because we enjoy it or find it interesting, not because of external rewards or pressures [5]

introspection: the process whereby people look inward and examine their own thoughts, feelings, and motives [5]

investment model: the theory holding that people's commitment to a relationship depends on their satisfaction with the relationship in terms of rewards, costs, and comparison level; their comparison level for alternatives; and how much they have invested in the relationship that would be lost by leaving it [10]

jigsaw classroom: a classroom setting designed to reduce prejudice and raise the self-esteem of children by placing them in small, desegregated groups and making each child dependent on the other children in his or her group to learn the course material and do well in the class [13]

judgmental heuristics: mental shortcuts people use to make judgments quickly and efficiently [3]

justification of effort: the tendency for individuals to increase their liking for something they have worked hard to attain [6]

kin selection: the idea that behaviors that help a genetic relative are favored by natural selection [11]

learned helplessness: the state of pessimism that results from explaining a negative event as due to stable, internal, and global factors; learned helplessness causes depression, reduced effort, and difficulty in learning new material [M-1]

locus: information that indicates whether the cause of the success (or failure) is internal or external [4]

looking-glass self: the idea that we see ourselves through the eyes of other people and incorporate their views into our self-concept [5]

love styles: the basic theories people have about love that guide their behavior in relationships; six styles have been identified: Eros, ludus, storge, pragma, mania, and agape [10]

lowballing: an unscrupulous strategy whereby a salesperson induces a customer to agree to purchase a product at a very low cost, subsequently claims it was an error, and then raises the price; frequently the customer will agree to make the purchase at the inflated price [6]

mass psychogenic illness: the occurrence, in a group of people, of similar physical symptoms with no known physical cause [8]

mere exposure: the finding that the more exposure we have to a stimulus, the more apt we are to like it [10]

mindless conformity: obeying internalized social norms without deliberating about one's actions [8]

minimal groups: meaningless groups formed by grouping strangers on the basis of trivial criteria; minimal group members still display in-group biases, however [13]

minority influence: the case where a minority of group members influence the behavior or beliefs of the majority [8]

misattribution of arousal: the attribution of one's arousal to the wrong source, resulting in a mistaken or exaggerated emotion [5]

mixed-motive conflict: conflict in which both parties can gain by cooperating but in which one side can gain even more by competing against its opponent [9]

modern racism: prejudice revealed in subtle, indirect ways because people have learned to hide prejudiced attitudes in order to avoid being labeled as racist [13]

motivated tacticians: The idea that people have a large arsenal of mental rules and strategies, and choose wisely among these strategies depending on their particular needs and goals [3]

mundane realism: the extent to which an experiment is similar to situations encountered in everyday life [2]

mutual interdependence: a situation where two or more groups need each other and must depend on each other in order to accomplish a goal that is important to each of them [13]

need for cognition: a personality variable reflecting the extent to which people desire to seek out and think about information in their social worlds [7]

negative correlation: a relationship between two variables wherein increases in the value of one variable are associated with decreases in the value of the other variable [2]

negative-state relief hypothesis: the idea that people help in order to alleviate their own sadness and distress [11]

negotiation: a form of communication between opposing sides in a conflict in which offers and counteroffers are made and a solution occurs only when it is agreed on by both parties [9]

noncommon effects: effects produced by a particular course of action that could not be produced by alternative courses of action [4]

nonsocial group: a group in which two or more people are in the same place at the same time but are not interacting with each other (e.g., fans at a baseball game) [9]

nonverbal communication: the way in which people communicate, intentionally or unintentionally, without words; nonverbal cues include facial expressions, tone of voice, gestures, body position and movement, the use of touch, and eye gaze [4]

norm of reciprocity: the assumption that others will treat us the way we treat them (e.g., if we help someone, he or she will help us) [11]

normative conformity: the tendency to go along with the group in order to fulfill their expectations and gain acceptance [13]

normative social influence: the influence of other people that leads us to conform in order to be liked and accepted by them; this type of conformity results in public compliance with but not necessarily private acceptance of the group's beliefs and behaviors [8]

observational method: the technique whereby a researcher observes people and systematically records measurements of their behavior [2]

out-group homogeneity: the perception that those in the out-group are more similar (homogeneous) to each other than they really are, as well as more similar than the members of the in-group are [13]

out-group: a group with which an individual does not identify [13]

overconfidence barrier: the finding that people usually have too much confidence in the accuracy of their judgments; people's judgments are usually not as correct as they think they are [3]

overjustification effect: the case whereby people view their behavior as caused by compelling extrinsic reasons, making them underestimate the extent to which their behavior was caused by intrinsic reasons [5]

own-race bias: the finding that people are better at recognizing faces of their own race than of other races [M–3]

participant observation: a form of systematic observation whereby the observer interacts with the people being observed, but tries not to alter the situation in any way [2]

passionate love: the feelings of intense longing, accompanied by physiological arousal, we feel for another person; when our love is reciprocated, we feel great fulfillment and ecstacy, but when it is not, we feel sadness and despair [10]

perceived control: the belief that we can influence our environment in ways that determine whether we experience positive or negative outcomes [M-1]

perceptual salience: information that is the focus of people's attention; people tend to overestimate the causal role of perceptually salient information [4]

performance-contingent rewards: rewards that are based on how well we perform a task [5]

peripheral route to persuasion: the case whereby people do not elaborate on the arguments in a persuasive communication but are instead swayed by peripheral cues [7]

perseverance effect: the finding that people's beliefs about themselves and the social world persist even after the evidence supporting these beliefs is discredited [3]

persuasive communication: communication (e.g., a speech or television ad) advocating a particular side of an issue [7]

pluralistic ignorance: the phenomenon whereby bystanders assume that nothing is wrong in an emergency, because no one else looks concerned [11]

polygraph: a machine that measures people's physiological responses (e.g., their heart rate); when these machines are used in lie detection, polygraph operators attempt to tell if someone is lying by observing how that person responds physiologically while answering questions [M–3]

positive correlation: a relationship between two variables wherein increases in the value of one variable are associated with increases in the value of the other variable [2]

postdecision dissonance: dissonance that is inevitably aroused after a person makes a decision; in this situation, dissonance is typically reduced by enhancing the attractiveness of the chosen alternative and devaluing the rejected alternatives [6]

prejudice: a hostile or negative attitude toward a distinguishable group of people, based solely on their membership in that group [13]

primacy effect: the process whereby our first impression of another person causes us to interpret his or her subsequent behavior in a manner consistent with the first impression [3]

priming: the process by which recent experiences increase a trait's accessibility [4]

private acceptance: conforming to other people's behavior out of a genuine belief that what they are doing or saying is right [8]

probability level (*p*-value): a number, calculated with statistical techniques, that tells researchers how likely it is that the results of their experiment occurred by chance (due to the failure of random assignment) and not because of the independent variable(s); the convention in science, including social psychology, is to consider results significant if the probability level is less than 5 in 100 that the results might be due to chance factors and not the independent variable(s) studied [2]

process loss: any aspect of group interaction that inhibits good problem solving [9]

propinquity effect: the finding that the more we see and interact with people, the more likely they are to become our friends [10]

prosocial behavior: any act performed with the goal of benefiting another person [11]

psychological realism: the extent to which the psychological processes triggered in an experiment are similar to psychological processes occurring in everyday life; psychological realism can be high in an experiment, even if mundane realism is low [2]

public compliance: conforming to other people's behavior publicly, without necessarily believing in what we are doing or saying [8]

random assignment to condition: the process whereby all participants have an equal chance of taking part in any condition of an experiment; through random assignment, researchers can be relatively certain that differences in their participants' personalities or backgrounds are distributed evenly across conditions [2]

random selection: a way of ensuring that a sample of people is representative of a population, by making sure that everyone in the population has an equal chance of being selected for the sample [2]

rationalization trap: the potential for dissonance reduction to produce a succession of self-justifications that ultimately result in a chain of stupid or immoral actions [6]

reactance theory: the idea that when people feel their freedom to perform a certain behavior is threatened, an unpleasant state of reactance is aroused; people can reduce this reactance by performing the threatened behavior [7]

realistic conflict theory: the theory that limited resources lead to conflict between groups and result in increased prejudice and discrimination [13]

reasons-generated attitude change: attitude change resulting from thinking about the reasons for one's attitudes; people assume their attitudes match the reasons that are plausible and easy to verbalize [5]

reciprocity norm: a social norm stating that receiving anything positive from another person requires you to reciprocate (or behave similarly) in response [8]

reconstructive memory: the process whereby memories for an event become distorted by information encountered after the event has occurred encountered after the event has occurred [M–3]

recovered memories: recollections of a past event, such as sexual abuse, that had been forgotten or repressed; a great deal of controversy surrounds the accuracy of such memories [5]

relational dialectics: a theory which states that close relationships are always in a state of change, due to opposing forces of autonomy/connection, novelty/predictability, and openness/closedness [10]

relationship-oriented leader: a leader who is concerned primarily with the feelings of and relationships between the workers [9]

relative deprivation: the perception that you (or your group) have less than you deserve, less than you have been led to expect, or less than people similar to you have [12]

replication: repetition of a study, often with different subject populations or in different settings [2]

representativeness heuristic: a mental shortcut whereby people classify something according to how similar it is to a typical case [3]

retrieval: the process by which people recall information stored in their memories [M–3]

roles: positions in a group that come with a specified "script," or expected set of behaviors [9]

scapegoating: the tendency for individuals, when frustrated or unhappy, to displace aggression onto groups that are disliked, visible, and relatively powerless [13]

schemas: cognitive structures people have to organize their knowledge about the social world by themes or subjects; schemas powerfully affect what information we notice, think about, and remember [3]

secure attachment style: an attachment style characterized by trust, a lack of concern with being abandoned, and the view that one is worthy and well liked [10]

self-affirmation theory: a theory suggesting that people will reduce the impact of a dissonance-arousing threat to their self-concept by focusing on and affirming their competence on some dimension unrelated to the threat [6]

self-awareness theory: the idea that when people focus their attention on themselves, they evaluate and compare their behavior to their internal standards and values [5]

self-concept: the contents of the self; that is, our perception of our own thoughts, beliefs, and personality traits [5]

self-esteem: people's evaluations of their own self-worth—that is, the extent to which they view themselves as good, competent, and decent [1]

self-evaluation maintenance theory: the theory that one's self-concept can be threatened by another individual's behavior and that the level of threat is determined by both the closeness of the other individual and the personal relevance of the behavior [6]

self-fulfilling prophecy: the case whereby people (a) have an expectation about what another person is like, which (b) influences how they act toward that person, which (c) causes that person to behave in a way consistent with people's original expectations [3]

self-handicapping: creating obstacles and excuses for ourselves, so that if we do poorly on a task, we have ready-made excuses [5]

self-justification: the tendency to justify one's actions in order to maintain one's self-esteem [6]

self-perception theory: the theory that when our attitudes and feelings are uncertain or ambiguous, we infer these states by observing our behavior and the situation in which it occurs [5]

self-persuasion: a long-lasting form of attitude change that results from attempts at self-justification [6]

self-presentation: the attempt to present who we are, or who we want people to believe we are, through our words, nonverbal behaviors, and actions [5]

self-schemas: organized knowledge structures about ourselves, based on our past experiences, that help us understand, explain, and predict our own behavior [5]

self-serving attributions: explanations for one's successes that credit internal, dispositional factors and explanations for one's failures that blame external, situational factors [4]

self-verification theory: a theory suggesting that people have a need to seek confirmation of their self-concept, whether the self-concept is positive or negative; in some circumstances, this tendency can conflict with the desire to uphold a favorable view of oneself [6]

sensory overload: the situation in which we receive more stimulation from the environment than we can pay attention to or process [M-2]

social cognition: how people think about themselves and the social world; more specifically, how people select, interpret, remember, and use social information to make judgments and decisions [1]

social comparison theory: the idea that we learn about our own abilities and attitudes by comparing ourselves to other people [5]

social dilemma: a situation in which the most beneficial action for an individual will, if chosen by most people, have harmful effects on everyone [M-2]

social exchange theory: the theory holding that how people feel about a relationship depends on their perceptions of the rewards and costs of the relationship, the kind of relationship they deserve, and their chances for having a better relationship with someone else [10]

social facilitation: the arousal that results when other people are present and our performance can be evaluated; this arousal enhances our performance on simple tasks but impairs our performance on complex tasks [9]

social groups: groups in which two or more people are interacting with each other and are interdependent, in the sense that to fulfill their needs and goals they must rely on each other [9]

social impact theory: the theory that conforming to social influence depends on the strength, immediacy, and number of other people in a group [8]

social learning theory: the theory that we learn social behavior (e.g., aggression) by observing others and imitating them [12]

social loafing: the relaxation that results when people are in a group and their individual performance cannot be evaluated; this relaxation impairs performance on simple tasks but enhances performance on complex tasks [9]

social norms: the implicit or explicit rules a group has for the acceptable behaviors, values, and beliefs of its members [8]

social perception: the study of how we form impressions of and make inferences about other people [4]

social psychology: the scientific study of the way in which people's thoughts, feelings, and behaviors are influenced by the real or imagined presence of other people. [1]

social support: the perception that others are responsive and receptive to one's needs [M-1]

social-role theory: the theory that sex differences in social behavior are due to society's division of labor between the sexes; this division leads to differences in gender-role expectations and sex-typed skills, both of which are responsible for differences in men's and women's social behavior [4]

sociobiological approach to love: an approach derived form evolutionary biology, which states that men and women are attracted to different characteristics in each other (men are attracted by women's appearance; women are attracted by men's resources) because this maximizes their reproductive success [10]

sociobiology: the application of evolutionary theory to social behavior [11]

source monitoring: trying to identify the source of one's recollections; sometimes people make errors about the source of their memories (e.g., believing a man looks familiar because they saw him at the scene of a crime, when in fact he looks familiar because they saw his picture in the newspaper) [M–3]

split cable market tests: techniques used to test the effectiveness of advertising, whereby advertisers, in conjunction with cable television companies and grocery stores, show a commercial to a randomly selected group of people and then see whether these people are more likely to buy the product than those who did not see the commercial are [7]

stability: information that indicates whether the cause of the success (or failure) is an enduring characteristic or one that changes or disappears over time [4]

stable attribution: the belief that the cause of an event is due to factors that will not change over time (e.g., your intelligence), as opposed to unstable factors that will change over time (e.g., the amount of effort you put into a task) [M-1]

stereotype vulnerability: the apprehension experienced by members of a minority group that they might behave in a manner that confirms an existing cultural stereotype [13]

stereotype: a generalization about a group of people in which identical characteristics are assigned to virtually all members of the group, regardless of actual variation among the members [13]

storage: the process by which people store in memory information they have acquired from the environment [M–3]

stress: the negative feelings and beliefs that occur whenever people feel they cannot cope with demands from their environment [M-1]

subjective norms: people's beliefs about how those they care about will view the behavior in question [7]

subliminal messages: words or pictures that are not consciously perceived but that supposedly influence people's judgments, attitudes, and behaviors [7]

subtyping model: information inconsistent with a stereotype that leads to the creation of a new substereotype to accommodate the information without changing the initial stereotype [13]

systematic observation: a form of the observational method whereby the observer is a trained social scientist who sets out to answer questions about a particular social phenomenon by observing and coding it according to a prearranged set of criteria [2]

target-based expectancies: expectations about a person based on his or her past actions, such as expecting someone to go to the beach on vacation because he or she has always gone to the beach in the past [4]

task-contingent rewards: rewards that are given for performing a task, regardless of how well we do that task [5]

task-oriented leader: a leader who is concerned primarily with getting the job done and less so with the feelings of and relationships between the workers [9]

taxonomy of success and failure attributions: the types of internal and external attributions we can make about a person's performanceÑfor example, success or failure [4]

testosterone: a hormone associated with aggression [12]

Thanatos: according to Freud, an instinctual drive toward death, leading to aggressive actions [12]

theory of reasoned action: a theory holding that the best predictors of a person's planned, deliberate behaviors are that person's attitudes toward specific behaviors and his or her subjective norms [7]

thought suppression: the attempt to avoid thinking about something we would just as soon forget [3]

tit-for-tat strategy: a means of encouraging cooperation by at first acting cooperatively but then always responding the way your opponent did (cooperatively or competitively) on the previous trial [9]

triangular theory of love: the idea that different kinds of love consist of varying degrees of three components: intimacy, passion, and commitment [10]

two-factor theory of emotion: the idea that emotional experience is the result of a two-step self-perception process in which people first experience physiological arousal and then seek an appropriate explanation for it; if they attribute the arousal to an emotional source, they experience that emotion (e.g., if people attribute their arousal to someone pointing a gun at them, they experience fear) [5]

Type A versus B personality: a personality typology based on how people typically confront challenges in their lives; the Type A person is typically competitive, impatient, hostile, and control-oriented, whereas the Type B person is typically more patient, relaxed, and noncompetitive; numerous studies show that Type A people are more successful in life but also more prone to coronary heart disease [M-1]

ultimate attribution error: our tendency to make dispositional attributions about an entire group of people [13]

unrealistic optimism: a form of defensive attribution wherein people think that good things are more likely to happen to them than to their peers and that bad things are less likely to happen to them than to their peers [4]

upward social comparison: the process whereby we compare ourselves to people who are better than we are on a particular trait or ability, in order to determine the standard of excellence [5]

urban-overload hypothesis: the theory suggesting that people living in cities are likely to keep to themselves in order to avoid being overloaded by all the stimulation they receive [11]

Yale Attitude Change approach: the study of the conditions under which people are most likely to change their attitudes in response to persuasive messages; researchers in this tradition focus on "who said what to whom"—that is, on the source of the communication, the nature of the communication, and the nature of the audience [7]

zero-sum conflict: conflict in which one side's gain is always the other side's loss, as in athletic contests [9]

REFERENCES

Aaker, D. A., & Myers, J. G. (1987). *Advertising management.* Englewood Cliffs, NJ: Prentice Hall.

Abelson, R. P. (1976). Script processing in attitude formation and decision making. In J. S. Carroll & J. W. Payne (Eds.), *Cognition and social behavior* (pp. 13–32). Hillsdale, NJ: Erlbaum.

Abelson, R. P., Kinder, D. R., Peters, M. D., & Fiske, S. T. (1982). Affective and semantic components in political person perception. *Journal of Personality and Social Psychology, 42,* 619–630.

Abraham, M. M., & Lodish, L. M. (1990). Getting the most out of advertising and promotion. *Harvard Business Review, 68,* 50–60.

Abramson, L. Y., Seligman, M. E. P., & Teasdale, J. D. (1978). Learned helplessness in humans: Critique and reformulation. *Journal of Abnormal Psychology, 87,* 49–74.

Acitelli, L. K. (1992). Gender differences in relationship awareness and marital satisfaction among young married couples. *Personality and Social Psychology Bulletin, 18,* 102–110.

Acitelli, L. K., & Duck, S. W. (1987). Intimacy as the proverbial elephant. In D. Perlman and S. W. Duck (Eds.), *Intimate relationships: Development, dynamics, and deterioration* (pp. 297–308). Beverly Hills, CA: Sage.

Adorno, T. W., Frenkel-Brunswick, E., Levinson, D. J., & Sanford, R. N. (1950). *The authoritarian personality.* New York: Harper & Row.

Aiello, J. R., Thompson, D. E., & Brodzinsky, D. M. (1983). How funny is crowding anyway? Effects of room size, group size, and the introduction of humor. *Basic and Applied Social Psychology, 4,* 193–207.

Ainsworth, M. D. S., Blehar, M. C., Waters, E., & Wall, S. (1978). *Patterns of attachment: A psychological study of the strange situation.* Hillsdale, NJ: Erlbaum.

Ajzen, I., & Fishbein, M. (1980). *Understanding attitudes and predicting social behavior.* Englewood Cliffs, NJ: Prentice Hall.

Akert, R. M. (1992). *Terminating romantic relationships: The role of personal responsibility and gender.* Unpublished manuscript, Wellesley College.

Akert, R. M. (1993). *The effect of autobiographical memories on the current definition of self.* Unpublished manuscript, Wellesley College.

Akert, R. M., & Panter, A. T. (1988). Extraversion and the ability to decode nonverbal communication. *Personality and Individual Differences, 9,* 965–972.

Akert, R. M., Chen, J., & Panter, A. T. (1991). *Facial prominence and stereotypes: The incidence and meaning of faceism in print and television media.* Unpublished manuscript, Wellesley College.

Aldag, R. J., & Fuller, S. R. (1993). Beyond fiasco: A reappraisal of the groupthink phenomenon and a new model of group decision processes. *Psychological Bulletin, 113,* 533–552.

Allen V. L. (1965). Situational factors in conformity. In L. Berkowitz (Ed.), *Advances in experimental social psychology* (Vol. 2, pp. 133–175). New York: Academic Press.

Allen, V. L., & Levine, J. M. (1969). Consensus and conformity. *Journal of Personality and Social Psychology, 5,* 389–399.

Alloy, L. B., & Abramson, L. Y. (1988). Depressive realism: Four theoretical perspectives. In L. B. Alloy (Ed.), *Cognitive processes in depression* (pp. 223–265). New York: Guilford Press.

Alloy, L. B., & Tabachnik, N. (1984). Assessment of covariation by humans and animals: The joint influence of prior expectations and current situational information. *Psychological Review, 91,* 112–149.

Alloy, L. B., Abramson, L. Y., & Viscusi, D. (1981). Induced mood and the illusion of control. *Journal of Personality and Social Psychology, 41,* 1129–1140.

Allport, G. (1954). *The nature of prejudice.* Reading, MA: Addison-Wesley.

Allport, G. W. (1985). The historical background of social psychology. In G. Lindzey & E. Aronson (Eds.), *The handbook of social psychology* (Vol. 1, pp. 1–46). Reading, MA: Addison-Wesley.

Amabile, T. M. (1983). Brilliant but cruel: Perceptions of negative evaluators. *Journal of Experimental Social Psychology, 19,* 146–156.

Amabile, T. M., Hennessey, B. A., & Grossman, B. S. (1986). Social influences on creativity: The effects of contracted-for reward. *Journal of Personality and Social Psychology, 50,* 14–23.

Amato, P. R. (1983). Helping behavior in urban and rural environments: Field studies based on a taxonomic organization of helping episodes. *Journal of Personality and Social Psychology, 45,* 571–586.

American Psychological Association. (1992). Ethical principles of psychologists and code of conduct. *American Psychologist, 47,* 1597–1611.

Amir, I. (1969). Contact hypothesis in ethnic relations. *Psychological Bulletin, 71,* 319–342.

Amir, Y. (1976). The role of intergroup contact in change of prejudice and ethnic relations. In P. Katz (Ed.), *Towards the elimination of racism.* New York: Pergamon Press.

Andersen, S. M., & Bem, S. L. (1981). Sex typing and androgyny in dyadic interaction: Individual differences in responsiveness to physical attractiveness. *Journal of Personality and Social Psychology, 41,* 74–86.

Andersen, S. M., & Klatzky, R. L. (1987). Traits and social stereotypes: Levels of categorization in person perception. *Journal of Personality and Social Psychology, 53,* 235–246.

Anderson, C. A., & Anderson, D. C. (1984). Ambient temperature and violent crime: Tests of the linear and curvilinear hypotheses. *Journal of Personality and Social Psychology, 46,* 91–97.

Anderson, C. A., & Sechler, E. S. (1986). Effects of explanation and counterexplanation on the development and use of social theories. *Journal of Personality and Social Psychology, 50,* 24–34.

Anderson, C. A., & Sedikides, C. (1990). Thinking about people: Contributions of a typological alternative to associationistic and dimensional models of person perception. *Journal of Personality and Social Psychology, 60,* 203–217.

Anderson, C. A., Lepper, M. R., & Ross, L. (1980). The perseverance of social theories: The role of explanation in the persistence of discredited information. *Journal of Personality and Social Psychology, 39,* 1037–1049.

Ann Landers, Dear (1991, September 10). *Boston Globe,* p. 52.

Archer, D. (1994). American violence: How high and why? *Law Studies,* Albany: New York State Bar Association, *19,* 12–20.

Archer, D., & Akert, R. M. (1977a, October). How well do you read body language? *Psychology Today*, pp. 68–69, 72, 119–120.

Archer, D., & Akert, R. M. (1977b). Words and everything else: Verbal and nonverbal cues in social interaction. *Journal of Personality and Social Psychology, 35,* 443–449.

Archer, D., & Akert, R. M. (1980). The encoding of meaning: A test of three theories of social interaction. *Sociological Inquiry, 50*(3–4), 393–419.

Archer, D., & Akert, R. M. (1984). Problems of context and criterion in nonverbal communication: A new look at the accuracy issue. In M. Cook (Ed.), *Issues in person perception* (pp. 114–144). London and New York: Methuen.

Archer, D., & Akert, R. M. (in press). *The interpretation of behavior: Verbal and nonverbal factors in person perception.* Cambridge, England: Cambridge University Press.

Archer, D., & Gartner, R. (1976). Violent acts and violent times: A comparative approach to postwar homicide rates. *American Sociological Review, 41,* 937–963.

Archer, D., & Gartner, R. (1984). *Violence and crime in cross-national perspective.* New Haven, CT: Yale University Press.

Archer, D., Iritani, B., Kimes, D. D., & Barrios, M. (1983). Face-ism: Five studies of sex differences in facial prominence. *Journal of Personality and Social Psychology, 45,* 725–735.

Archer, D. & McDaniel, P. (1995). Violence and gender: Differences and similarities across societies. In R. B. Ruback & N. A. Weiner (Eds.), *Interpersonal violent behaviors: social and cultural aspects* (pp. 63–88). New York: Springer Publishing.

Arendt, H. (1965). *Eichmann in Jerusalem: A report on the banality of evil.* New York: Viking.

Argyle, M. (1975). *Bodily communication.* New York: International Universities Press.

Arkin, R. M., & Baumgardner, A. H. (1985). Self-handicapping. In J. H. Harvey & G. Weary (Eds.), *Basic issues in attribution theory and research* (pp. 169–202). New York: Academic Press.

Arkin, R. M., & Maruyama, G. M. (1979). Attribution, affect, and college exam performance. *Journal of Educational Psychology, 71,* 85–93.

Arms, R. L., Russell, G. W., & Sandilands, M. L. (1979). Effects on the hostility of spectators of viewing aggressive sports. *Social Psychology Quarterly, 42,* 275–279.

Arnett, J. (1995). The young and the reckless: Adolescent reckless behavior. *Current Directions in Psychological Science, 4,* (June), 67–71.

Aron, A., Aron, E. N., & Smollan, D. (1990). The Inclusion of Other in the Self (IOS) scale and the structure of interpersonal closeness. *Journal of Personality and Social Psychology, 63,* 596–612.

Aron, A., Dutton, D. G., Aron, E. A., & Iverson, A. (1989). Experiences of falling in love. *Journal of Social and Personal Relationships, 6,* 243–257.

Aronson, E. (1968). Dissonance theory: Progress and problems. In R. P. Abelson, E. Aronson, W. J. McGuire, T. M. Newcomb, M. J. Rosenberg, and P. H. Tannenbaum (Eds.), *Theories of Cognitive Consistency: A Sourcebook* (pp. 5–27). Chicago: Rand McNally.

Aronson, E. (1969). The theory of cognitive dissonance: A current perspective. In L. Berkowitz (Ed.), *Advances in experimental social psychology* (Vol. 4, pp. 1–34). New York: Academic Press.

Aronson, E. (1978). *The jigsaw classroom.* Beverly Hills, CA: Sage.

Aronson, E. (1990). Applying social psychology to prejudice reduction and energy conservation. *Personality and Social Psychology Bulletin, 16,* 118–132.

Aronson, E. (1992a). *The social animal.* New York: Freeman.

Aronson, E. (1992b). The return of the repressed: Dissonance theory makes a comeback. *Psychological Inquiry, 3,* 303–311.

Aronson, E., & Bridgeman, D. (1979). Jigsaw groups and the desegregated classroom: In pursuit of common goals. *Personality and Social Psychology Bulletin, 5,* 438–446.

Aronson, E., & Carlsmith, J. M. (1962). Performance expectancy as a determinant of actual performance. *Journal of Abnormal and Social Psychology, 65,* 178–182.

Aronson, E., & Carlsmith, J. M. (1963). Effect of severity of threat in the devaluation of forbidden behavior. *Journal of Abnormal and Social Psychology, 66,* 584–588.

Aronson, E., & Carlsmith, J. M. (1968). Experimentation in social psychology. In G. Lindzey & E. Aronson (Eds.), *The handbook of social psychology* (Vol. 2, pp. 1–79). Reading, MA: Addison-Wesley.

Aronson, E., Fried, C., & Stone, J. (1991). Overcoming denial and increasing the intention to use condoms through the induction of hypocrisy. *American Journal of Public Health, 81,* 1636–1638.

Aronson, E., & Gonzalez, A. (1988). Desegregation, jigsaw, and the Mexican-American experience. In P. A. Katz & D. Taylor (Eds.), *Towards the elimination of racism: Profiles in controversy.* New York: Plenum.

Aronson, E., & Gonzales, M. (1990). The social psychology of energy conservation. In J Edwards (Ed.), *Social influence processes and prevention.* New York: Plenum.

Aronson, E., & Linder, D. (1965). Gain and loss of esteem as determinants of interpersonal attractiveness. *Journal of Experimental Social Psychology, 1,* 156–171.

Aronson, E., & Mettee, D. (1968). Dishonest behavior as a function of differential levels of induced self-esteem. *Journal of Personality and Social Psychology, 9,* 121–127.

Aronson, E., & Mills, J. (1959). The effect of severity of initiation on liking for a group. *Journal of Abnormal and Social Psychology, 59,* 177–181.

Aronson, E., & Thibodeau, R. (1992). The jigsaw classroom: A cooperative strategy for reducing prejudice. In J. Lynch, C. Modgil, & S. Modgil (Eds.), *Cultural diversity in the schools.* London: Falmer Press.

Aronson, E., & Worchel, P. (1966). Similarity versus liking as determinants of interpersonal attractiveness. *Psychonomic Science, 5,* 157–158.

Aronson, E., & Yates, S. (1985). Social psychological aspects of energy conservation. In D. Hafemeister, H. Kelly, & B. Levi, (Eds.), *Energy sources: Conservation and renewables* (pp. 81–91). New York: American Institute of Physics Press.

Aronson, E., Ellsworth, P., Carlsmith, J. M., & Gonzales, M. (1989). *Methods of research in social psychology* (2nd ed.). New York: Random House.

Aronson, E., Stephan, C., Sikes, J., Blaney, N., & Snapp, M. (1978). *The jigsaw classroom.* Beverly Hills, CA: Sage.

Aronson, E., Willerman, B., & Floyd, J. (1966). The effect of a pratfall on increasing interpersonal attractiveness. *Psychonomic Science, 4,* 227–228.

Aronson, J. M., & Jones, E. E., (1992). Inferring abilities after influencing performance. *Journal of Experimental Social Psychology, 28,* 277–299.

Asch, S. E. (1951). Effects of group pressure upon the modification and distortion of judgment. In H. Guetzkow (Ed.), *Groups, leadership, and men.* Pittsburgh, PA: Carnegie Press.

Asch, S. E. (1955). Opinions and social pressure. *Scientific American, 193,* 31–35.

Asch, S. E. (1956). Studies of independence and conformity: A minority of one against a unanimous majority. *Psychological Monographs, 70* (9, Whole No. 416).

Asch, S. E. (1957). An experimental investigation of group influence. In *Symposium on preventive and social psychiatry* (pp. 15–17). Walter Reed Army Institute of Research. Washington, DC: U.S. Government Printing Office.

Asch, S. E. (1959). A perspective on social psychology. In S. Koch (Ed.), *Psychology: A study of science* (Vol. 3, pp. 363–383). New York: McGraw-Hill.

Asendorf, J. (1987). Videotape reconstruction of emotions and cognitions related to shyness. *Journal of Personality and Social Psychology, 53,* 542–549.

Ashmore, R. D., & DelBoca, F. K. (1976). Psychological approaches to understanding intergroup conflict. In P. A. Katz (Ed.), *Towards the elimination of racism.* Elmsford, NY: Pergamon Press.

Aspinwall, L. G., & Taylor, S. E. (1993). Effects of social comparison direction, threat, and self-esteem on affect, evaluation, and expected success. *Journal of Personality and Social Psychology, 64,* 708–722.

Axelrod, R. (1984). *The evolution of cooperation.* New York: Basic Books.

Axsom, D. (1989). Cognitive dissonance and behavior change in psychotherapy. *Journal of Experimental Social Psychology, 25,* 234–252.

Ayres, I. (1991). Fair driving: Gender and race discrimination in retail car negotiations. *Harvard Law Review, 104,* 817–872.

Azrin, N. H. (1967, May). Pain and aggression. *Psychology Today,* pp. 27–33.

Baldwin, M. W., Carrell, S. E., & Lopez, D. F. (1990). Priming relationship schemas: My advisor and the pope are watching me from the back of my mind. *Journal of Experimental Social Psychology, 26,* 435–454.

Banaji, M. R., & Prentice, D. A. (1984). The self in social contexts. *Annual Review of Psychology, 45,* 297–332.

Bandura, A. (1973). *Aggression: A social learning analysis.* Englewood Cliffs, NJ: Prentice Hall.

Bandura, A. (1986). *Social foundations of thought and action.* Englewood Cliffs, NJ: Prentice Hall.

Bandura, A., Ross, D., & Ross, S. (1961). Transmission of aggression through imitation of aggressive models. *Journal of Abnormal and Social Psychology, 63,* 575–582.

Bandura, A., Ross, D., & Ross, S. (1963). Imitation of film-mediated aggressive models. *Journal of Abnormal and Social Psychology, 66,* 3–11.

Bar-Tal, D., & Saxe, L. (1976). Perceptions of similarly and dissimilarly attractive couples and individuals. *Journal of Personality and Social Psychology, 33,* 772–781.

Bargh, J. A., & Pietromonaco, P. (1982). Automatic information processing and social perception: The influence of trait information presented outside of conscious awareness on impression formation. *Journal of Personality and Social Psychology, 43,* 437–449.

Bargh, J. A., Chaiken, S., Raymond, P., & Hymes, C. (in press). The automatic evaluation effect: Unconditional automatic attitude activation with a pronunciation task. *Journal of Experimental Social Psychology.*

Bargh, J. A., & Raymond, P. (1995). The naive misuse of power: Nonconscious sources of sexual harassment. *Journal of Social Issues, 51,* 85–96.

Bargh, J. A., Raymond, P., Pryor, J. B., & Strack, F. (1995). Attractiveness of the underling: An automatic power-sex association and its consequences for sexual harassment and aggression. *Journal of Personality and Social Psychology, 68,* 768–781.

Barker, R., Dembo, T., & Lewin, K. (1941). Frustration and aggression: An experiment with young children. *University of Iowa Studies in Child Welfare, 18,* 1–314.

Baron, L., & Straus, M. A. (1984). Sexual stratification, pornography, and rape. In N. M. Malamuth & E. Donnerstein (Eds.), *Pornography and sexual aggression* (pp. 186–209). New York: Academic Press.

Baron, R. A. (1972). Reducing the influence of an aggressive model: The restraining effects of peer censure. *Journal of Experimental Social Psychology, 8,* 266–275.

Baron, R. A. (1976). The reduction of human aggression: A field study on the influence of incompatible responses. *Journal of Applied Social Psychology, 6,* 95–104.

Baron, R. A. (1988). Negative effects of destructive criticism: Impact on conflict, self-efficacy, and task performance. *Journal of Applied Psychology, 73,* 199–207.

Baron, R. A. (1990). Countering the effects of destructive criticism: The relative efficacy of four interventions. *Journal of Applied Psychology, 75,* 235–245.

Baron, R. A., & Richardson, D. R. (1994). *Human aggression* (2nd ed.). New York: Plenum.

Baron, R. S. (1986). Distraction/conflict theory: Progress and problems. In L. Berkowitz (Ed.), *Advances in experimental social psychology* (Vol. 19, pp. 1–40). Orlando, FL: Academic Press.

Baron, R., & Rodin, J. (1978). Personal control as a mediator of crowding. In A. Baum, J. S. Singer, & S. Valins (Eds.), *Advances in environmental psychology* (Vol. 1, pp. 145–190). Hillsdale, NJ: Erlbaum.

Bartlett, D. C. (1932). *Remembering.* Cambridge: Cambridge University Press.

Bass, E., & Davis, L. (1994). *The courage to heal: A guide for women survivors of child sexual abuse* (3rd ed.). New York: HarperCollins.

Basu, J. E. (1989, August). Why no one's safe: Effects of smog on residents in Los Angeles Basin. *American Health,* 64.

Batson, C. D. (1991). *The altruism question: Toward a social-psychological answer.* Hillsdale, NJ: Erlbaum.

Batson, C. D. (1993). Communal and exchange relationships: What's the difference? *Personality and Social Psychology Bulletin, 19,* 677–683.

Batson, C. D., & Shaw, L. L. (1991). Evidence for altruism: Toward a pluralism of prosocial motives. *Psychological Inquiry, 2,* 107–122.

Batson, C. D., & Weeks, J. L. (in press). Mood effects of unsuccessful helping: Another test of the empathy-altruism hypothesis. *Personality and Social Psychology Bulletin.*

Batson, C. D., Batson, J. G., Griffit, C. A., Barrientos, S., Brandt, J. R., Sprengelmeyer, P., & Bayly, M. J. (1989). Negative-state relief and the empathy-altruism hypothesis. *Journal of Personality and Social Psychology, 56,* 922–933.

Batson, C. D., Bolen, M. H., Cross, J. A., & Neuringer-Benefiel, H. E. (1986). Where is the altruism in the altruistic personality? *Journal of Personality and Social Psychology, 50,* 212–220.

Batson, C. D., Coke, J. S., Jasnoski, M. L., & Hanson, M. (1978). Buying kindness: Effect of an extrinsic incentive for helping on perceived altruism. *Personality and Social Psychology Bulletin, 4,* 86–91.

Batson, C. D., Duncan, B. D., Ackerman, P., Buckley, T., & Birch, K. (1981). Is empathic emotion a source of altruistic motivation? *Journal of Personality and Social Psychology, 40,* 290–302.

Batson, C. D., Dyck, J. L., Brandt, J. R., Batson, J. G., Powell, A. L., McMaster, M. R., & Griffit, C. (1988). Five studies testing two new egoistic alternatives to the empathy-altruism hypothesis. *Journal of Personality and Social Psychology, 55,* 52–77.

Batson, C. D., Sympson, S. C., Hindman, J. L., Decruz, P., Todd, R. M., Weeks, J. L., Jennings, G., & Burris, C. T. (in press). "I've been there too": Effect on empathy of prior experience with a need. *Personality and Social Psychology Bulletin.*

Battle for your brain. (1991, August). *Consumer Reports*, pp. 520–521.

Baum, A., & Valins, S. (1977). *Architecture and social behavior: Psychological studies of social density.* Hillsdale, NJ: Erlbaum.

Baum, A., & Valins, S. (1979). Architectural mediation of residential density and control: Crowding and the regulation of social contract. In L. Berkowitz (Ed.), *Advances in experimental social psychology* (Vol. 12, pp. 131–175). New York: Academic Press.

Baumeister, R. (1987). How the self became a problem: A psychological review of historical research. *Journal of Personality and Social Psychology, 52,* 163–176.

Baumeister, R. (Ed.) (1993). *Self-esteem: The puzzle of low self-regard.* New York: Plenum.

Baumeister, R. F. (1991). *Escaping the self: Alcoholism, spirituality, masochism, and other flights from the burden of selfhood.* New York: Basic Books.

Baumeister, R. F., & Leary, M. R. (1995). The need to belong: Desire for interpersonal attachments as a fundamental human motive. *Psychological Bulletin, 117,* 497–529.

Baumgardner, A. H., Lake, E. A., & Arkin, R. M. (1985). Claiming mood as a self-handicap. *Personality and Social Psychology Bulletin, 11,* 349–357.

Baxter, L. (1986). Gender differences in the heterosexual relationship rules embedded in break-up accounts. *Journal of Social and Personal Relationships, 3,* 289–306.

Baxter, L. (1988). A dialectical perspective on communication strategies in relationship development. In S. W. Duck, D. F. Hay, S. E. Hobfoll, W. Ickes, & B. M. Montgomery (Eds.), *Handbook of personal relationships: Theory, research and interventions* (pp. 257–273). New York: Wiley.

Baxter, L. (1990). Dialectical contradictions in relationship development. *Journal of Social and Personal Relationships, 7,* 69–88.

Baxter, L. A. (1986). Gender differences in the heterosexual relationship rules embedded in break-up accounts. *Journal of Social and Personal Relationships, 3,* 289–306.

Baxter, L. A. (1993). The social side of personal relationships: A dialectical perspective. In S. W. Duck (Ed.), *Social contexts of relationships* (Understanding relationship processes series, Vol. 3, pp. 139–165). Newbury Park, CA: Sage.

Bazerman, M., & Neale, M. (1992). *Negotiating rationally.* New York: Free Press.

Beach, S. R. H., & Tesser, A. (1995). Self-esteem and the extended self-evaluation maintenance model. In M. H. Kernis (Ed.), *Efficacy, agency, and self-esteem* (pp. 145–170). New York: Plenum.

Beaman, A. L., Barnes, P. J., Klentz, B., & McQuirk, B. (1978). Increasing helping rates through informational dissemination: Teaching pays. *Personality and Social Psychology Bulletin, 4,* 406–411.

Beaman, A. L., Klentz, B., Diener, E., & Svanum, S. (1979). Objective self-awareness and transgression in children: A field study. *Journal of Personality and Social Psychology, 37,* 1835–1846.

Becker, B. J. (1986). Influence again: Another look at studies of gender differences in social influence. In J. S. Hyde & M. C. Linn (Eds.), *The psychology of gender: Advances through meta-analysis* (pp. 178–209). Baltimore, MD: Johns Hopkins University Press.

Becker, M. H., & Josephs, J. G. (1988). AIDS and behavioral change to reduce risk: A review. *American Journal of Public Health, 78,* 394–410.

Belansky, E. S., & Boggiano, A. K. (1994). Predicting helping behaviors: The role of gender and instrumental/expressive self-schemata. *Sex Roles, 30,* 647–661.

Bell, P. A. (1980). Effects of heat, noise, and provocation on retaliatory evaluative behavior. *Journal of Social Psychology, 110,* 97–100.

Belli, R. F. (1989). Influences of misleading postevent information: Misinformation interference and acceptance. *Journal of Experimental Psychology: General, 118,* 72–85.

Bem, D. J. (1967). Self-perception: An alternative interpretation of cognitive dissonance phenomena. *Psychological Review, 74,* 183–200.

Bem, D. J. (1972). Self-perception theory. In L. Berkowitz (Ed.), *Advances in experimental social psychology* (Vol. 6, pp. 1–62). New York: Academic Press.

Berger, P. L. (1963). *Invitation to sociology: A humanistic perspective.* Garden City, NY: Anchor Books.

Berger, P. L., & Luckmann, T. (1967). *The social construction of reality: A treatise on the sociology of knowledge.* Garden City, NY: Anchor Books.

Berglas, S., & Jones, E. E. (1978). Drug choice as a self-handicapping strategy in response to noncontingent success. *Journal of Personality and Social Psychology, 36,* 405–417.

Berkow, J. H. (1989). *Darwin, sex, and status: Biological approaches to mind and culture.* Toronto: University of Toronto Press.

Berkowitz, L. (1962). *Aggression: A social psychological analysis.* New York: McGraw-Hill.

Berkowitz, L. (1968, September). Impulse, aggression, and the gun. *Psychology Today,* pp. 18–22.

Berkowitz, L. (1971). *Control of aggression.* Unpublished manuscript, University of Wisconsin.

Berkowitz, L. (1973, September). The case for bottling up rage. *Psychology Today,* pp. 24–31.

Berkowitz, L. (1978). Whatever happened to the frustration-aggression hypothesis? *American Behavioral Scientist, 21,* 691–708.

Berkowitz, L. (1981, June). How guns control us. *Psychology Today,* pp. 11–12.

Berkowitz, L. (1983). Aversively simulated aggression. *American Psychologist, 38,* 1135–1144.

Berkowitz, L. (1987). Mood, self-awareness, and willingness to help. *Journal of Personality and Social Psychology, 52,* 721–729.

Berkowitz, L. (1988). Frustrations, appraisals, and aversively stimulated aggression. *Aggressive Behavior, 14,* 3–11.

Berkowitz, L. (1989). Frustration-aggression hypothesis: Examination and reformulation. *Psychological Bulletin, 106,* 59–73.

Berkowitz, L. (1993). *Aggression.* New York: McGraw-Hill.

Berkowitz, L., & Frodi, A. (1979). Reactions to a child's mistakes as affected by her/his looks and speech. *Social Psychology Quarterly, 42,* 420–425.

Berkowitz, L., & Green, J. A. (1962). The stimulus qualities of the scapegoat. *Journal of Abnormal and Social Psychology, 64,* 293–301.

Berkowitz, L., & LePage, A. (1967). Weapons as aggression-eliciting stimuli. *Journal of Personality and Social Psychology, 7,* 202–207.

Berkowitz, L., & Troccoli, B., (1990). Feelings, direction of attention, and expressed evaluations of others. *Cognition and Emotion, 4,* 305–325.

Berman, J. S., & Kenny, D. A. (1976). Correlational bias in observer ratings. *Journal of Personality and Social Psychology, 34,* 263–273.

Berry, D. S., & McArthur, L. Z. (1986). Perceiving character in faces: The impact of age-related craniofacial changes in social perception. *Psychological Bulletin, 100,* 3–18.

Berry, J. W. (1967). Independence and conformity in subsistence-level societies. *Journal of Personality and Social Psychology, 7,* 415–418.

Berscheid, E. (1983). Emotion. In H. H. Kelley, E. Berscheid, A. Christensen, J. H. Harvey, T. L. Huston, G. Levinger, E. McClintock, L. A. Peplau, & D. R. Peterson (Eds.), *Close relationships* (pp. 110–168). New York: Freeman.

Berscheid, E. (1985). Interpersonal attraction. In G. Lindzey & E. Aronson (Eds.), *The handbook of social psychology* (pp. 413–484). New York: Random House.

Berscheid, E. (1988). Some comments on love's anatomy: Or, whatever happened to old-fashioned lust? In R. J. Sternberg & M. L. Barnes (Eds.), *The psychology of love* (pp. 359–374). New Haven, CT: Yale University Press.

Berscheid, E. (1994). Interpersonal relationships. *Annual Review of Psychology, 45,* 79–129.

Berscheid, E., & Peplau, L. A. (1983). The emerging science of relationships. In H. H. Kelley, E. Berscheid, A. Christensen, J. H. Harvey, T. L. Huston, G. Levinger, E. McClintock, L. A. Peplau, & D. R. Peterson (Eds.), *Close relationships* (pp. 1–19). New York: Freeman.

Berscheid, E., & Walster (Hatfield), E. (1978). *Interpersonal attraction.* Reading, MA: Addison-Wesley.

Berscheid, E., Boye, D., & Walster (Hatfield), E. (1968). Retaliation as a means of restoring equity. *Journal of Personality and Social Psychology, 10,* 370–376.

Berscheid, E., Snyder, M., & Omoto, A. M. (1989). Issues in studying close relationships: Conceptualizing and measuring closeness. In C. Hendrick (Ed.), *Close relationships: Review of personality and social psychology* (Vol. 10, pp. 63–91). Newbury Park, CA: Sage.

Bertenthal, B. I., & Fisher, K. W. (1978). Development of self-recognition in the infant. *Developmental Psychology, 14,* 44–50.

Bickman, L. (1974). The social power of a uniform. *Journal of Applied Social Psychology, 4,* 47–61.

Blaskovich, J., Ginsburg, G. P., & Veach, T. L. (1975). A pluralistic explanation of choice shifts on the risk dimension. *Journal of Personality and Social Psychology, 31,* 422–429.

Blau, P. M. (1964). *Exchange and power in social life.* New York: Wiley.

Bless, H., Bohner, G., Schwarz, N., & Strack, F. (1990). Mood and persuasion: A cognitive response analysis. *Personality and Social Psychology Bulletin, 16,* 331–345.

Blumberg, H. H. (1994). Bargaining, coalitions, and games. In A. P. Hare, H. H. Blumberg, M. F. Davies, & M. V. Kent (Eds.), *Small group research: A handbook* (pp. 237–257). Norwood, NJ: Ablex.

Bodenhausen, G. V. (1988). Stereotypic biases in social decision making and memory: Testing process models of stereotype use. *Journal of Personality and Social Psychology, 55,* 726–737.

Bodenhausen, G. V., & Lichenstein, M. (1987). Social stereotypes and information-processing strategies. The impact of task complexity. *Journal of Personality and Social Psychology, 52,* 871–880.

Bodenhausen, G. V., & Wyer, R. (1985). Effects of stereotypes on decision making and information processing strategies. *Journal of Personality and Social Psychology, 48,* 267–282.

Bond, C. F., & Titus, L. J. (1983). Social facilitation: A meta-analysis of 241 studies. *Psychological Bulletin, 94,* 264–292.

Bond, C., DiCandia, C., & McKinnon, J. R. (1988). Response to violence in a psychiatric setting. *Personality and Social Psychology Bulletin, 14,* 448–458.

Bond, M. (1991). Chinese values and health: A culture-level examination. *Psychology and Health, 5,* 137–152.

Bond, M. H. (Ed.). (1988). *The cross-cultural challenge to social psychology.* Newbury Park, CA: Sage.

Bonora, D., & Huteau, M. (1991). L'efficience comparée des garçons et des filles en mathematiques. *Orientation Scolaire et Professionnelle, 20,* 269–290.

Borgida, E., & Howard-Pitney, B. (1983). Personal involvement and the robustness of perceptual salience effects. *Journal of Personality and Social Psychology, 45,* 560–570.

Bornstein, R. F. (1992). Inhibitory effects of awareness on affective responding: Implications for the affect-cognition relationship. In M. S. Clark (Ed.), *Emotion: Review of personality and social psychology* (Vol. 13, pp. 235–255). Newbury Park, CA: Sage.

Bornstein, R. F., & D'Agostino, P. R. (1992). Stimulus recognition and the mere exposure effect. *Journal of Personality and Social Psychology, 63,* 545–552.

Bornstein, R. F., Leone, D. R., & Galley, D. J. (1987). The generalizability of subliminal mere exposure effects: Influence of stimuli perceived without awareness on social behavior. *Journal of Personality and Social Psychology, 53,* 1070–1079.

Bossard, J. H. S. (1932). Residential propinquity as a factor in marriage selection. *American Journal of Sociology, 38,* 219–224.

Bothwell, R. K., Brigham, J. C., & Malpass, R. S. (1989). Cross-racial identification. *Personality and Social Psychology Bulletin, 15,* 19–26.

Bothwell, R. K., Deffenbacher, K. A., & Brigham, J. C. (1987). Correlation of eyewitness accuracy and confidence: Optimality hypothesis revisited. *Journal of Applied Psychology, 72,* 691–695.

Bouchard, T. J., Barsaloux, J., & Drauden, G. (1974). Brainstorming procedure, group size, and sex as determinants of the problem-solving effectiveness of groups and individuals. *Journal of Applied Psychology, 59,* 135–138.

Bower, G. H., & Hilgard, E. R. (1981). *Theories of learning* (15th ed.). Englewood Cliffs, NJ: Prentice Hall.

Bowlby, J. (1969). *Attachment and loss: Vol. 1. Attachment.* New York: Basic Books.

Bowlby, J. (1973). *Attachment and loss: Vol. 2. Separation: Anxiety and anger.* New York: Basic Books.

Bowlby, J. (1980). *Attachment and loss: Vol. 3. Loss.* New York: Basic Books.

Boyden, T., Carroll, J. S., & Maier, R. A. (1984). Similarity and attraction in homosexual males: The effects of age and masculinity-femininity. *Sex Roles, 10,* 939–948.

Bragg, R. (1995, August 4). "A killer's only confidant: The man who caught Susan Smith." *New York Times,* p. A10.

Brandon, R., & Davies, C. (1973). *Wrongful imprisonment: Mistaken convictions and their consequences.* London: Allen & Unwin.

Brannon, L. A., & Brock, T. C. (1994). The subliminal persuasion controversy. In S. Shavitt & T. C. Brock (Eds.), *Persuasion: Psychological insights and perspectives* (pp. 279–293). Boston: Allyn & Bacon.

Bransford, J. D., & Johnson, M. K. (1973). Considerations of some problems of comprehension. In W. G. Chase (Ed.), *Visual information processing* (pp. 383–438). New York: Academic Press.

Breckler, S. J. (1984). Empirical validation of affect, behavior, and cognition as distinct components of attitude. *Journal of Personality and Social Psychology, 47,* 1191–1205.

Breckler, S. J., & Wiggins, E. C. (1989). On defining attitude and attitude theory: Once more with feeling. In A. R. Pratkanis, S. J. Breckler, & A. G. Greenwald (Eds.), *Attitude structure and function* (pp. 407–427). Hillsdale, NJ: Erlbaum.

Brehm, J. W. (1956). Postdecision changes in the desirability of alternatives. *Journal of Abnormal and Social Psychology, 52,* 384–389.

Brehm, J. W. (1966). *A theory of psychological reactance.* New York: Academic Press.

Brehm, J. W., & Cohen, A. R. (1962). *Explorations in cognitive dissonance.* New York: Wiley.

Brehm, S. S. (1992). *Intimate relationships* (2nd ed.). New York: McGraw-Hill.

Brewer, M. B. (1979). In-group bias in the minimal intergroup situation: A cognitive-motivational analysis. *Psychological Bulletin, 86,* 307–324.

Brewer, M. B., & Miller, N. (1984). Beyond the contact hypothesis: Theoretical perspectives on desegregation. In N. Miller & M. B. Brewer (Eds.), *Groups in contact: The psychology of desegregation* (pp. 281–302). New York: Academic Press.

Brigham, J. C. (1980). Limiting conditions of the "physical attractiveness stereotype": Attributions about divorce. *Journal of Research in Personality, 14,* 365–375.

Bringle, R. G. (1981). Conceptualizing jealousy as a disposition. *Alternative Lifestyles, 4,* 274–290.

Brislin, R. (1993). *Understanding culture's influence on behavior.* Fort Worth, TX: Harcourt Brace.

Brock, T. C., Edelman, S., Edwards, S., & Schuck, J. (1965). Seven studies of performance expectancy as a determinant of actual performance. *Journal of Experimental Social Psychology, 1,* 295–310.

Brophy, J. E. (1983). Research on the self-fulfilling prophecy and teacher expectations. *Journal of Educational Psychology, 75,* 631–661.

Brown, J. D. (1990). Evaluating one's abilities: Shortcuts and stumbling blocks on the road to self-knowledge. *Journal of Experimental Social Psychology, 26,* 149–167.

Brown, R. (1965). *Social psychology.* New York: Free Press.

Brown, R. (1986). *Social psychology: The second edition.* New York: Free Press.

Browning, D. L. (1983). Aspects of authoritarian attitudes in ego development. *Journal of Personality and Social Psychology, 45,* 137–144.

Bruch, H. (1973). *Eating disorders.* New York: Basic Books.

Bruch, H. (1978). *The golden cage.* Cambridge, MA: Harvard University Press.

Buck, R. (1984). *The communication of emotion.* New York: Guilford Press.

Buckhout, R. (1974). Eyewitness testimony. *Scientific American, 231,* 23–31.

Buehler, R., & Griffin, D. (1994). Change-of-meaning effects in conformity and dissent: Observing construal processes over time. *Journal of Personality and Social Psychology, 67,* 984–996.

Burger, J. M. (1981). Motivational biases in the attribution of responsibility for an accident: A meta-analysis of the defensive-attribution hypothesis. *Psychological Bulletin, 90,* 496–512.

Burger, J. M. (1986). Increasing compliance by improving the deal: The that's-not-all technique. *Journal of Personality and Social Psychology, 51,* 277–283.

Burnstein, E., & Vinokur, A. (1977). Persuasive argumentation and social comparison as determinants of attitude polarization. *Journal of Experimental Social Psychology, 13,* 315–332.

Burnstein, E., & Worchel, P. (1962). Arbitrariness of frustration and its consequences for aggression in a social situation. *Journal of Personality, 30,* 528–540.

Burnstein, E., Crandall, C., & Kitayama, S. (1994). Some neo-Darwinian decision rules for altruism: Weighing cues for inclusive fitness as a function of the biological importance of the decision. *Journal of Personality and Social Psychology, 67,* 773–789.

Burr, W. R. (1973). *Theory construction and the sociology of the family.* New York: Wiley.

Burt, M. R. (1980). Cultural myths and supports for rape. *Journal of Personality and Social Psychology, 38,* 217–230.

Busby, L. J. (1975). Defining the sex-role standard in commercial network television programming directed at children. *Journalism Quarterly, 51,* 690–696.

Buss, D. M. (1985). Human mate selection. *American Scientist, 73,* 47–51.

Buss, D. M. (1988a). The evolution of human intrasexual competition. *Journal of Personality and Social Psychology, 54,* 616–628.

Buss, D. M. (1988b). Love acts: The evolutionary biology of love. In R. J. Sternberg & M. L. Barnes (Eds.), *The psychology of love* (pp. 110–118). New Haven, CT: Yale University Press.

Buss, D. M. (1989). Sex differences in human mate preferences: Evolutionary hypotheses tested in 37 cultures. *Behavioral and Brain Sciences, 12,* 1–49.

Buss, D. M., & Barnes, M. (1986). Preferences in human mate selection. *Journal of Personality and Social Psychology, 50,* 559–570.

Buss, D. M., & Schmitt, D. P. (1993). Sexual strategies theory: An evolutionary perspective on human mating. *Psychological Bulletin, 100,* 204–232.

Buss, D. M., Abbott, M., Angleitner, Aerian, A., Biaggio, A., Blanco-Villasenor, A., Bruchon-Schweitzer, M., Ch'U, H., Czapinski, J., Deraad, B., Ekehammar, B., El Lohamy, N., Fioravanti, M., Georgas, J., Gjerde, P., Guttman, R., Hazan, F., Iwawaki, S., Janakiramaiah, N., Khosroshani, F., Kreitler, S., Lachenicht, L., Lee, M., Liik, K., Little, B., Mika, S., Moadel-Shahid, M., Moane, G., Montero, M., Mundy-Castle, A. C., Niit, T., Nsenduluka, E., Pienkowski, R., Pirttila-Backman, A., Ponce de Leon, J., Rousseau, J., Runco, M., Safir, M. P., Samuels, C., Sanitioso, R., Serpell, R., Smid, N., Spencer, C., Tadinac, M., Todorova, E. N., Troland, K., Van Den Brande, L., Van Heck, G., Van Langenhove, L., & Yang, K. (1990). International preferences in selecting mates: A study of 37 cultures. *Journal of Cross-Cultural Psychology, 21,* 5–47.

Buss, D. M., Larsen, R. J., Westen, D., & Semmelroth, J. (1992). Sex differences in jealousy: Evolution, physiology, and psychology. *Psychological Science, 3,* 251–255.

Butler, D., & Geis, F. L. (1990). Nonverbal affect responses to male and female leaders: Implications for leadership evaluations. *Journal of Personality and Social Psychology, 58,* 48–59.

Buunk, B. (1982). Anticipated sexual jealousy: Its relationship to self-esteem, dependency, and reciprocity. *Personality and Social Psychology Bulletin, 8,* 310–316.

Buunk, B., & Hupka, R. B. (1987). Cross-cultural differences in the elicitation of sexual jealousy. *Journal of Sex Research, 23,* 12–22.

Buzbee, S. S. (1995, March 3). "Earn to Learn" pays children to read. *Cavalier Daily,* p. 4.

Byrne, D. (1961). Interpersonal attraction and attitude similarity. *Journal of Abnormal and Social Psychology, 62,* 713–715.

Byrne, D. (1971). *The attraction paradigm.* New York: Academic Press.

Byrne, D., & Clore, G. L. (1970). A reinforcement model of evaluative processes. *Personality: An International Journal, 1,* 103–128.

Byrne, D., & Nelson, D. (1965). Attraction as a linear function of positive reinforcement. *Journal of Personality and Social Psychology, 1,* 659–663.

Byrne, D., Clore, G. L., & Smeaton, G. (1986). The attraction hypothesis: Do similar attitudes affect anything? *Journal of Personality and Social Psychology, 51,* 1167–1170.

Cacioppo, J. T., Marshall-Goodell, B. S., Tassinary, L. G., & Petty, R. E. (1992). Rudimentary determinants of attitudes: Classical conditioning is more effective when prior knowledge about the attitude stimulus is low than high. *Journal of Experimental Social Psychology, 28,* 207–233.

Cacioppo, J. T., Petty, R. E., Feinstein, J., & Jarvis, B. (1996). Dispositional differences in cognitive motivation: The life and times of individuals low versus high in need for cognition. *Psychological Bulletin, 119,* 197–253.

Calder, B. J., & Staw, B. M. (1975). Self-perception of intrinsic and extrinsic motivation. *Journal of Personality and Social Psychology, 31,* 599–605.

Calhoun, J. B. (1973). Death squared: The explosive growth and demise of a mouse population. *Proceedings of the Royal Society of Medicine, 66,* 80–88.

Calvert, J. D. (1988). Physical attractiveness: A review and reevaluation of its role in social skill research. *Behavioral Assessment, 10,* 29–42.

Campbell, D. T. (1967). Stereotypes and the perception of group differences. *American Psychologist, 22,* 817–829.

Campbell, D. T., & Stanley, J. C. (1967). *Experimental and quasi-experimental designs for research.* Chicago: Rand McNally.

Campbell, E. Q., & Pettigrew, T. F. (1959). Racial and moral crisis: The role of Little Rock ministers. *American Journal of Sociology, 64,* 509–516.

Campbell, J. (1980). Complementarity and attraction: A reconceptualization in terms of dyadic behavior. *Representative Research in Social Psychology, 11,* 74–95.

Campos, J. J., & Sternberg, C. (1981). Perception, appraisal, and emotion: The onset of social referencing. In M. E. Lamb & L. R. Sherrod (Eds.), *Infant social cognition: Empirical and theoretical considerations* (pp. 273–314). Hillsdale, NJ: Erlbaum.

Cannon, W. B. (1942). "Voodoo" death. *American Anthropologist, 44,* 169–181.

Cantor, N., & Kihlstrom, J. F. (1987). *Personality and social intelligence.* Englewood Cliffs, NJ: Prentice Hall.

Cantril, H. (1940). *The invasion from Mars: A study in the psychology of panic.* New York: Harper & Row.

Carlsmith, J. M., & Anderson, C. A. (1979). Ambient temperature and the occurrence of collective violence: A new analysis. *Journal of Personality and Social Psychology, 37,* 337–344.

Carlson, J., & Davis, D. M. (1971). Cultural values and the risky shift: A cross-cultural test in Uganda and the United States. *Journal of Personality and Social Psychology, 20,* 392–399.

Carlson, M., & Miller, N. (1987). Explanation of the relationship between negative mood and helping. *Psychological Bulletin, 102,* 91–108.

Carlson, M., Charlin, V., & Miller, N. (1988). Positive mood and helping behavior: A test of six hypotheses. *Journal of Personality and Social Psychology, 55,* 211–229.

Carlyle, T. (1841). *On heroes, hero-worship, and the heroic in history: Six lectures.* New York: Appleton.

Carnevale, P. J. (1986). Strategic choice in mediation. *Negotiation Journal, 2,* 41–56.

Carretta, T. R., & Moreland, R. L. (1982). Nixon and Watergate: A field demonstration of belief perseverance. *Personality and Social Psychology Bulletin, 6,* 446–453.

Cartwright, D. (1979). Contemporary social psychology in historical perspective. *Social Psychology Quarterly, 42,* 82–93.

Cartwright, D., & Zander, A. (Eds.). (1968). *Group dynamics: Research and theory* (3rd ed.). New York: Harper & Row.

Carver, C. S. (1975). Physical aggression as a function of objective self-awareness and attitudes toward punishment. *Journal of Experimental Social Psychology, 11,* 510–519.

Carver, C. S., & Scheier, M. F. (1981). *Attention and self-regulation: A control-theory approach to human behavior.* New York: Springer-Verlag.

Carver, C. S., DeGregorio, E., & Gillis, R. (1980). Ego-defensive attribution among two categories of observers. *Personality and Social Psychology Bulletin, 6,* 4–50.

Cash, T. F., & Derlega, V. J. (1978). The matching hypothesis: Physical attractiveness among same-sex friends. *Personality and Social Psychology Bulletin, 4,* 240–243.

Cervone, D., & Peake, P. (1986). Anchoring, efficacy, and action: The influence of judgmental heuristics on self-efficacy judgments and behavior. *Journal of Personality and Social Psychology, 50,* 492–501.

Chaiken, S. (1980). Heuristic versus systematic information processing and the use of source versus message cues in persuasion. *Journal of Personality and Social Psychology, 39,* 752–766.

Chaiken, S. (1987). The heuristic model of persuasion. In M. P. Zanna, J. M. Olson, & C. P. Herman (Eds.), *Social influence: The Ontario Symposium* (Vol. 5, pp. 3–39). Hillsdale, NJ: Erlbaum.

Chaiken, S., & Baldwin, M. W. (1981). Affective-cognitive consistency and the effect of salient behavioral information on the self-perception of attitudes. *Journal of Personality and Social Psychology, 41,* 1–12.

Chaiken, S., Liberman, A., & Eagly, A. H. (1989). Heuristic and systematic information processing within and beyond the persuasion context. In J. S. Uleman & J. A. Bargh (Eds.), *Unintended thought* (pp. 212–252). New York: Guilford Press.

Chapman, L. J. (1967). Illusory correlation in observational report. *Journal of Verbal Learning and Verbal Behavior, 5,* 151–155.

Chapman, L. J., & Chapman, J. P. (1967). Genesis of popular but erroneous psychodiagnostic observations. *Journal of Abnormal Psychology, 72,* 193–204.

Chassin, L., Presson, C. G., & Sherman, S. J. (1990). Social psychological contributions to the understanding and prevention of adolescent cigarette smoking. *Personality and Social Psychology Bulletin, 16,* 133–151.

Cheek, J. M., & Buss, A. H. (1981). Shyness and sociability. *Journal of Personality and Social Psychology, 41,* 330–339.

Cheek, J. M., & Melchoir, L. A. (1990). Shyness, self-esteem, and self-consciousness. In H. Leitenberg (Ed.), *Handbook of social and evaluation anxiety.* New York: Plenum.

Chemers, M. M., Hays, R. G., Rhodewalt, F., & Wysocki, J. (1985). A person-environment analysis of job stress: A contingency model explanation. *Journal of Personality and Social Psychology, 49,* 628–635.

Cheng, P. W., Holyoak, K. J., Nisbett, R. E., & Oliver, L. M. (1986). Pragmatic versus syntactic approaches to training deductive reasoning. *Cognitive Psychology, 18,* 293–328.

Christensen, L. (1988). Deception in psychological research: When is its use justified? *Personality and Social Psychology Bulletin, 14,* 664–675.

Christian, J. J. (1963). The pathology of overpopulation. *Military Medicine, 128,* 571–603.

Christianson, S. (1992). Emotional stress and eyewitness memory: A critical review. *Psychological Bulletin, 112,* 284–309.

Cialdini, R. B. (1991). Altruism or egoism? That is (still) the question. *Psychological Inquiry, 2,* 124–126.

Cialdini, R. B. (1993). *Influence: Science and practice* (3rd ed.). New York: HarperCollins.

Cialdini, R. B., & Fultz, J. (1990). Interpreting the negative mood-helping literature via "mega"-analysis: A contrary view, *Psychological Bulletin, 107,* 210–214.

Cialdini, R. B., Borden, R. J., Thorne, A., Walker, M. R., Freeman, S., & Sloan, L. R. (1976). Basking in reflected glory: Three (football) field studies. *Journal of Personality and Social Psychology, 34,* 366–375.

Cialdini, R. B., Darby, B. L., & Vincent, J. E. (1973).

Transgression and altruism: A case for hedonism. *Journal of Experimental Social Psychology, 9,* 502–516.

Cialdini, R. B., Kallgren, C. A., & Reno, R. R. (1991). A focus theory of normative conduct: A theoretical refinement and reevaluation of the role of norms in human behavior. In M. P. Zanna (Ed.), *Advances in experimental social psychology* (Vol. 24, pp. 201–234). San Diego, CA: Academic Press.

Cialdini, R. B., Schaller, M., Houlihan, D., Arps, K., Fultz, J., & Beaman, A. L. (1987). Empathy-based helping: Is it self-lessly or selfishly motivated? *Journal of Personality and Social Psychology, 52,* 749–758.

Cialdini, R. B., Vincent, J. E., Lewis, S. K., Catalan, J., Wheeler, D., & Darby, B. L. (1975). Reciprocal concessions proce-dure for inducing compliance: The door-in-the-face tech-nique. *Journal of Personality and Social Psychology, 31,* 206–215.

Cialdini, R. L., Cacioppo, J., Basset, R., & Miller, J. (1978). Low-ball procedure for producing compliance: Commitment then cost. *Journal of Personality and Social Psychology, 36,* 463–476.

Clark, K., & Clark, M. (1947). Racial identification and prefer-ence in Negro children. In T. M. Newcomb & E. L. Hartley (Eds.), *Readings in social psychology* (pp. 169–178). New York: Holt.

Clark, M. S. (1984). Record keeping in two types of relation-ships. *Journal of Personality and Social Psychology, 47,* 549–577.

Clark, M. S. (1986). Evidence of the effectiveness of manipula-tions of communal and exchange relationships. *Personality and Social Psychology Bulletin, 12,* 414–425.

Clark, M. S., & Isen, A. M. (1982). Toward understanding the relationship between feeling states and social behavior. In A. H. Hastorf & A. M. Isen (Eds.), *Cognitive social psychology* (pp. 73–108). New York: Elsevier.

Clark, M. S., & Mills, J. (1979). Interpersonal attraction in exchange and communal relationships. *Journal of Personality and Social Psychology, 37,* 12–24.

Clark, M. S., & Mills, J. (1993). The difference between communal and exchange relationships: What it is and is not. *Personality and Social Psychology Bulletin, 19,* 684–691.

Clark, M. S., & Waddell, B. (1985). Perception of exploitation in communal and exchange relationships. *Journal of Social and Personal Relationships, 2,* 403–413.

Clark, M. S., Mills, J., & Corcoran, D. M. (1989). Keeping track of needs and inputs of friends and strangers. *Personality and Social Psychology Bulletin, 15,* 533–542.

Clark, M. S., Ouellette, R., Powell, M. C., & Milberg, S. (1987). Recipient's mood, relationship type, and helping. *Journal of Personality and Social Psychology, 53,* 94–103.

Clark, R. D. III, & Maass, A. (1988). The role of social categori-zation and perceived source credibility in minority influ-ence. *European Journal of Social Psychology, 18,* 347–364.

Clark, R. D. III, & Word, L. E. (1972). Why don't bystanders help? Because of ambiguity? *Journal of Personality and Social Psychology, 24,* 392–400.

Clarke, A. C. (1952). An examination of the operation of resid-ual propinquity as a factor in mate selection. *American Sociological Review, 27,* 17–22.

Clary, E. G., Snyder, M., Ridge, R. D., Miene, P. K., & Haugen, J. A. (1994). Matching messages to motives in persuasion: A functional approach to promoting volunteerism. *Journal of Applied Social Psychology, 24,* 1129–1149.

Cline, V. B., Croft, R. G., & Courrier, S. (1973). Desensitization of children to television violence. *Journal of Personality and Social Psychology, 27,* 360–365.

Cody, M. J. (1982). A typology of disengagement strategies and an examination of the role intimacy reactions to inequity and relational problems play in strategy selection. *Communication Monographs, 49,* 148–170.

Cohen, A. R. (1962). An experiment on small rewards for discrepant compliance and attitude change. In J. W. Brehm & A. R. Cohen (Eds.), *Explorations in cognitive dissonance* (pp. 73–78). New York: Wiley.

Cohen, C. E. (1981). Person categories and social perception: Testing some boundary conditions of the processing effects of prior knowledge. *Journal of Personality and Social Psychology, 40,* 441–452.

Cohen, C. E. (1983). Inferring the characteristics of other people: Categories and attribute accessibility. *Journal of Personality and Social Psychology, 44,* 34–44.

Cohen, D. (Ed.). (1977). *Psychologists on psychology.* New York: Taplinger.

Cohen, D. J., Whitmyer, J. W., & Funk, W. H. (1960). Effect of group cohesiveness and training upon group thinking. *Journal of Applied Psychology, 44,* 319–322.

Cohen, D., & Nisbett, R. E. (1994). Self-protection and the culture of honor: Explaining Southern violence. *Personality and Social Psychology Bulletin, 20,* 551–567.

Cohen, L. J. (1981). Can human rationality be experimentally demonstrated? *The Behavioral and Brain Sciences, 4,* 317–370.

Cohen, S. (1978). Environmental load and the allocation of attention. In A. Baum, J. S. Singer, & S. Valins (Eds.), *Advances in environmental psychology* (Vol. 1, pp. 1–29). Hillsdale, NJ: Erlbaum.

Cohen, S., & Hebert, T. B. (in press). Health psychology: Psychological factors and physical disease from the perspec-tive of human psychoneuroimmunology. *Annual Review of Psychology, 47.*

Cohen, S., & Williamson, G. M. (1991). Stress and infectious disease in humans. *Psychological Bulletin, 109,* 5–24.

Cohen, S., & Wills, T. A. (1985). Stress, social support, and the buffering hypothesis. *Psychological Bulletin, 98,* 310–357.

Cohen, S., Evans, G. W., Krantz, D. S., & Stokols, D. (1980). Physiological, motivational, and cognitive effects of aircraft noise on children. *American Psychologist, 35,* 231–243.

Cohen, S., Evans, G. W., Krantz, D. S., Stokols, D., & Kelly, S. (1981). Aircraft noise and children: Longitudinal and cross-sectional evidence on adaptation to noise and the effective-ness of noise abatement. *Journal of Personality and Social Psychology, 40,* 331–345.

Cohen, S., Glass, D. C., & Singer, J. E. (1973). Apartment noise, auditory discrimination, and reading ability in chil-dren. *Journal of Experimental Social Psychology, 9,* 407–422.

Cohen, S., Kaplan, J. R., Cunnick, J. E., Manuck, S. B., & Rabin, B. S. (1992). Chronic social stress, affiliation, and cellular immune response in nonhuman primates. *Psychological Science, 3,* 301–304.

Cohen, S., Tyrrell, D. A. J., & Smith, A. P. (1991). Psychological stress in humans and susceptibility to the common cold. *New England Journal of Medicine, 325,* 606–612.

Cohen, S., Tyrrell, D. A. J., & Smith, A. P. (1993). Negative life events, perceived stress, negative affect, and susceptibility to the common cold. *Journal of Personality and Social Psychology, 64,* 131–140.

Cohen, S., Tyrrell, D. A. J., & Smith, A. P. (1993). Negative life events, perceived stress, negative affect, and susceptibility to the common cold. *Journal of Personality and Social Psychology, 64,* 131–140.

Cole, B. L. (1991, September 15). I greet each day as a gift. *Parade Magazine*, pp. 20–21.

Colligan, M. J., & Murphy, L. R. (1979). Mass psychogenic illness in organizations: An overview. *Journal of Occupational Psychology, 52,* 77–90.

Colligan, M. J., Pennebaker, J. W., & Murphy, L. R. (Eds.). (1982). *Mass psychogenic illness: A social psychological analysis.* Hillsdale, NJ: Erlbaum.

Collins, N. L., & Read, S. J. (1990). Adult attachment, working models, and relationship quality in dating couples. *Journal of Personality and Social Psychology, 58,* 644–663.

Coltrane, S., Archer, D., & Aronson, E. (1986). The social-psychological foundations of successful energy conservation programs. *Energy Policy, 14,* 133–148.

Condon, J. W., & Crano, W. D. (1988). Inferred evaluation and the relation between attitude similarity and interpersonal attraction. *Journal of Personality and Social Psychology, 54,* 789–797.

Conway, M., & Ross, M. (1984). Getting what you want by revising what you had. *Journal of Personality and Social Psychology, 47,* 738–748.

Cook, S. W. (1984). Cooperative interaction in multiethnic contexts. In N. Miller & M. Brewer (Eds.), *Groups in contact: The psychology of desegregation.* New York: Academic Press.

Cook, S. W. (1985). Experimenting on social issues: The case of school desegregation. *American Psychologist, 40,* 452–460.

Cooley, C. H. (1902). *Human nature and social order.* New York: Scribner's.

Cooper, J. (1980). Reducing fears and increasing assertiveness: The role of dissonance reduction. *Journal of Experimental Social Psychology, 47,* 738–748.

Cosmides, L., & Tooby, J. (1992). Cognitive adaptations for social exchange. In J. H. Barkow, L. Cosmides, & J. Tooby (Eds.), *The adapted mind: Evolutionary psychology and the generation of culture* (pp. 163–228). New York: Oxford University Press.

Cotton, J. L. (1981). *Ambient temperature and violent crime.* Paper presented at the meeting of the Midwestern Psychological Association, Chicago.

Cotton, J. L. (1986). Ambient temperature and violent crime. *Journal of Applied Social Psychology, 16,* 786–801.

Cottrell, N. B., Wack, K. L., Sekerak, G. J., & Rittle, R. (1968). Social facilitation in dominant responses by the presence of an audience and the mere presence of others. *Journal of Personality and Social Psychology, 9,* 245–250.

Crandall, C. S. (1988). Social contagion of binge eating. *Journal of Personality and Social Psychology, 55,* 588–598.

Crocker, J. (1981). Judgment of covariation by social perceivers. *Psychological Bulletin, 90,* 272–292.

Crocker, J., & Major, B. (1989). Social stigma and self-esteem: The self-protective properties of stigma. *Psychological Review, 96,* 608–630.

Crocker, J., Hannah, D. B., & Weber, R. (1983). Personal memory and causal attributions. *Journal of Personality and Social Psychology, 44,* 55–56.

Crosby, F., Bromley, S., & Saxe, L. (1980). Recent unobtrusive studies of black and white discrimination and prejudice: A literature review. *Psychological Bulletin, 87,* 546–563.

Crouse, B. B., & Mehrabian, A. (1977). Affiliation of opposite-sexed strangers. *Journal of Research in Personality, 11,* 38–47.

Croyle, R. T., & Jemmott, J. B. III. (1990). Psychological reactions to risk factor testing. In J. A. Skelton & R. T. Croyle (Eds.), *The mental representation of health and illness* (pp. 121–157). New York: Springer-Verlag.

Croyle, R., & Cooper, J. (1983). Dissonance arousal: Physio-logical evidence. *Journal of Personality and Social Psychology, 45,* 782–791.

Crutchfield, R. A. (1955). Conformity and character. *American Psychologist, 10,* 191–198.

Csikszentmihalyi, M. (1975). *Beyond boredom and anxiety.* San Francisco: Jossey-Bass.

Csikszentmihalyi, M. (1979). The concept of flow. In B. Sutton-Smith (Ed.), *Play and learning.* New York: Gardner Press.

Csikszentmihalyi, M. (1988). The flow experience and its significance for human psychology. In M. Csikszentmihalyi & I. S. Csikszentmihalyi (Eds.), *Optimal experience: Psychological studies of flow in consciousness* (pp. 15–35). New York: Cambridge University Press.

Csikszentmihalyi, M., & Figurski, T. J. (1982). Self-awareness and aversive experience in everyday life. *Journal of Personality, 50,* 15–28.

Curtis, R. C., & Miller, K. (1986). Believing another likes or dislikes you: Behaviors making the beliefs come true. *Journal of Personality and Social Psychology, 51,* 284–290.

Curtiss, S. (1977). *Genie: A psycholinguistic study of a modern-day "wild child."* New York: Academic Press.

Dabbs, James M., Carr, Timothy S., Frady, Robert L., & Riad, Jasmin K. (1995). Testosterone, crime, and misbehavior among 692 male prison inmates. *Personality & Individual Differences, 18,* 627–633.

Dabbs, J. M., Jr., Ruback, R. B., Frady, R. L., Hopper, C. H., & Sgoutas, D. S. (1988). Saliva testosterone and criminal violence among women. *Personality and Individual Differences, 7,* 269–275.

Dansereau, F., Graen, G., & Haga, W. J. (1975). A vertical dyad linkage approach to leadership within formal organizations: A longitudinal investigation of the role making process. *Organizational Behavior, 13,* 46–78.

Darley, J. M., & Akert, R. M. (1993). *Biographical interpretation: The influence of later events in life on the meaning of and memory for earlier events.* Unpublished manuscript, Princeton University.

Darley, J. M., & Batson, C. D. (1973). From Jerusalem to Jericho: A study of situational and dispositional variables in helping behavior. *Journal of Personality and Social Psychology, 27,* 100–108.

Darley, J. M., & Fazio, R. H. (1980). Expectancy confirmation processes arising in the social interaction sequence. *American Psychologist, 35,* 867–881.

Darley, J. M., & Gilbert, D. T. (1985). Social psychological aspects of environmental psychology. In G. Lindzey & E. Aronson (Eds.), *Handbook of social psychology* (3rd ed., Vol. 2, pp. 949–991). New York: Random House.

Darley, J. M., & Gross, P. H. (1983). A hypothesis-confirming bias in labeling effects. *Journal of Personality and Social Psychology, 44,* 20–33.

Darley, J. M., & Latané, B. (1968). Bystander intervention in emergencies: Diffusion of responsibility. *Journal of Personality and Social Psychology, 8,* 377–383.

Darwin, C. (1872). *The expression of emotions in man and animals.* London: John Murray.

Darwin, C. R. (1859). *The origin of species.* London: John Murray.

Davidson, A. R., & Jaccard, J. J. (1979). Variables that moderate the attitude behavior relation: Results of a longitudinal survey. *Journal of Personality and Social Psychology, 37,* 1364–1376.

Davies, R. (1988). *The lyre of Orpheus.* New York: Penguin Books.

Davis, C. G., Lehman, D. R., Wortman, C. B., Silver, R. C., & Thompson, S. C. (1995). The undoing of traumatic life events. *Personality and Social Psychology Bulletin, 21,* 109–124.

Davis, J. H. (1992). Some compelling intuitions about group consensus decisions, theoretical and empirical research, and interpersonal aggregation phenomena: Selected examples, 1950–1990. *Organizational Behavior and Human Decision Processes, 52,* 3–38.

Davis, K. E., & Jones, E. E. (1960). Changes in interpersonal perception as a means of reducing cognitive dissonance. *Journal of Abnormal and Social Psychology, 61,* 402–410.

Davis, M. H., & Stephan, W. G. (1980). Attributions for exam performance. *Journal of Applied Social Psychology, 10,* 235–248.

Davitz, J. (1952). The effects of previous training on post-frustration behavior. *Journal of Abnormal and Social Psychology, 47,* 309–315.

Dawes, R. M. (1980). Social dilemmas. *Annual Review of Psychology, 31,* 169–193.

Dawkins, R. (1976). *The selfish gene.* New York: Oxford University Press.

Deaux, K. (1993). Reconstructing social identity. *Personality and Social Psychology Bulletin, 19,* 4–12.

Deaux, K., & Emsweiler, T. (1974). Explanations of successful performance of sex-linked tasks: What is skill for male is luck for the female. *Journal of Personality and Social Psychology, 29,* 80–85.

Deaux, K., & Major, B. (1987). Putting gender into context: An interactive model of gender-related behavior. *Psychological Review, 94,* 369–389.

Deaux, K., & Taynor, J. (1973). Evaluation of male and female ability: Bias works two ways. *Psychological Reports, 32,* 261–262.

DeBono, K. G., & Snyder, M. (1995). Acting on one's attitudes: The role of a history of choosing situations. *Personality and Social Psychology Bulletin, 21,* 629–636.

Deci, E. L., & Ryan, R. M. (1985). *Intrinsic motivation and self-determination in human behavior.* New York: Plenum.

Deffenbacher, K. (1983). The influence of arousal on reliability of testimony. In S. Lloyd-Bostock & B. Clifford (Eds.), *Evaluating witness testimony* (pp. 235–251). London: Wiley.

DeJong, W. (1979). An examination of self-perception mediation of the foot-in-the-door effect. *Journal of Personality and Social Psychology, 37,* 2221–2239.

DeJong, W., & Winsten, J. A. (1989). *Recommendations for future mass media campaigns to prevent preteen and adolescent substance abuse.* Unpublished manuscript, Center for Health Communication, Harvard School of Public Health.

DeMarco, P. (1994, September 28). "Dear diary," *New York Times,* p. C2.

Dennett, D. C. (1991). *Consciousness explained.* Boston: Little, Brown.

DePaulo, B. M. (1983). Perspectives on help-seeking. In B. M. DePaulo, A. Nadler, & J. D. Fisher (Eds.), *New directions in helping: Help seeking* (Vol. 2, pp. 3–12). New York: Academic Press.

DePaulo, B. M. (1992). Nonverbal behavior and self-presentation. *Psychological Bulletin, 111,* 203–243.

DePaulo, B. M. (1994). Spotting lies: Can humans learn to do better? *Current Directions in Psychological Science, 3,* 83–86.

DePaulo, B. M., & Pfeiffer, R. L. (1986). On-the-job experience and skill at detecting deception. *Journal of Applied Social Psychology, 16,* 249–267.

DePaulo, B. M., & Rosenthal, R. (1979). Telling lies. *Journal of Personality and Social Psychology, 37,* 1713–1722.

DePaulo, B. M., Kenny, D. A., Hoover, C. W., Webb, W., & Oliver, P. (1987). Accuracy of person perception: Do people know what kinds of impressions they convey? *Journal of Personality and Social Psychology, 52,* 303–315.

DePaulo, B. M., Stone, J. I., & Lassiter, G. D. (1985). Deceiving and detecting deceit. In B. R. Schlenker (Ed.), *The self and social life* (pp. 323–370). New York: McGraw-Hill.

Dermer, M., & Thiel, D. L. (1975). When beauty may fail. *Journal of Personality and Social Psychology, 31,* 1168–1176.

Desmond, E. W. (1987, November 30). Out in the open. *Time,* pp. 80–90.

Deutsch, F. M., & Lamberti, D. M. (1986). Does social approval increase helping? *Personality and Social Psychology Bulletin, 12,* 149–157.

Deutsch, M. (1973). *The resolution of conflict: Constructive and destructive processes.* New Haven, CT: Yale University Press.

Deutsch, M. (1990). Cooperation, conflict, and justice. In S. A. Wheelan, E. A. Pepitone, & V. Abt (Eds.), *Advances in field theory* (pp. 149–164). Newbury Park, CA: Sage.

Deutsch, M., & Collins, M. E. (1951) *Interracial housing: A psychological evaluation of a social experiment.* Minneapolis: University of Minnesota Press.

Deutsch, M., & Gerard, H. G. (1955). A study of normative and informational social influence upon individual judgment. *Journal of Abnormal and Social Psychology, 51,* 629–636.

Deutsch, M., & Krauss, R. M. (1960). The effect of threat upon interpersonal bargaining. *Journal of Abnormal and Social Psychology, 61,* 181–189.

Deutsch, M., & Krauss, R. M. (1962). Studies of interpersonal bargaining. *Journal of Conflict Resolution, 6,* 52–76.

Devine, P. G. (1989a). Automatic and controlled processes in prejudice: The roles of stereotypes and personal beliefs. In A. R. Pratkanis, S. J. Breckler, & A. G. Greenwald (Eds.), *Attitude structure and function* (pp. 181–212). Hillsdale, NJ: Erlbaum.

Devine, P. G. (1989b). Stereotypes and prejudice: Their automatic and controlled components. *Journal of Personality and Social Psychology, 56,* 5–18.

Dickerson, C., Thibodeau, R., Aronson, E., & Miller, D. (1992). Using cognitive dissonance to encourage water conservation. *Journal of Applied Social Psychology, 22,* 841–854.

Diddling the subconscious: Subliminal advertising. (1957, October 5). *Nation,* p. 206.

Diehl, M., & Stroebe, W. (1987). Productivity loss in brainstorming groups: Toward the solution of a riddle. *Journal of Personality and Social Psychology, 53,* 497–509.

Diener, E. (1980). Deindividuation: The absence of self-awareness and self-regulation in group members. In P. B. Paulus (Ed.), *Psychology of group influence* (pp. 209–242). Hillsdale, NJ: Erlbaum.

Diener, E., & Wallbom, M. (1976). Effects of self-awareness on antinormative behavior. *Journal of Research in Personality, 10,* 107–111.

Dienesch, R. M., & Liden, R. C. (1986). Leader-member exchange model of leadership: A critique and further development. *Academy of Management Review, 11,* 618–634.

Dietz, P. D., & Evans, B. E. (1982). Pornographic imagery and prevalence of paraphilia. *American Journal of Psychiatry, 139,* 1493–1495.

Dillard, J. P., Hunter, J. E., & Burgoon, M. (1984). Sequential-request persuasive strategies: Meta-analysis of foot-in-the-door and door-in-the-face. *Human Communications Research, 10,* 461–488.

Dion, K. (1972). Physical attractiveness and evaluations of children's transgressions. *Journal of Personality and Social Psychology, 24,* 207–213.

Dion, K., Berscheid, E., & Walster (Hatfield), E. (1972). What is beautiful is good. *Journal of Personality and Social Psychology, 24,* 285–290.

Dodge, M. K. (1984). Learning to care: Developing prosocial behavior among one- and two-year-olds in group settings. *Journal of Research and Development in Education, 17,* 26–30.

Dollard, J. (1938). Hostility and fear in social life. *Social Forces, 17,* 15–26.

Dollard, J., Doob, L., Miller, N., Mowrer, O. H., & Sears, R. R. (1939). *Frustration and aggression.* New Haven, CT: Yale University Press.

Donnerstein, E. (1980). Aggressive erotica and violence against women. *Journal of Personality and Social Psychology, 39,* 269–277.

Donnerstein, E., & Berkowitz, L. (1981). Victim reactions in aggressive erotic films as a factor in violence against women. *Journal of Personality and Social Psychology, 41,* 710–724.

Donnerstein, E., & Donnerstein, M. (1976). Research in the control of interracial aggression. In R. G. Green & E. C. O'Neal (Eds.), *Perspectives on aggression* (pp. 133–168). New York: Academic Press.

Donnerstein, E., Linz, D., & Penrod, S. (1987). *The question of pornography: Research findings and policy implications.* New York: Free Press.

Dovidio, J. F. (1984). Helping behavior and altruism: An empirical and conceptual overview. In L. Berkowitz (Ed.), *Advances in experimental social psychology* (Vol. 17, pp. 361–427). New York: Academic Press.

Dovidio, J. F., Evans, N., & Tyler, R. B. (1986). Racial stereotypes: The contents of their cognitive representations. *Journal of Experimental Social Psychology, 22,* 22–37.

Dovidio, J. F., Piliavin, J. A., Gaertner, S. I., Schroeder, D. A., & Clark, R. D. III. (1991). The arousal: cost-reward model and the process of intervention. In M. S. Clark (Ed.), *Review of personality and social psychology* (Vol. 12, pp. 86–118). Newbury Park, CA: Sage.

Duck, S. (1982). A typography of relationship disengagement and dissolution. In S. Duck (Ed.), *Personal relationships 4: Dissolving personal relationships* (pp. 1–30). London: Academic Press.

Duke: The ex-Nazi who would be governor. (1991, November 10). *New York Times,* pp. 1, 26.

Dunn, D. S., & Wilson, T. D. (1990). When the stakes are high: A limit to the illusion of control effect. *Social Cognition, 8,* 305–323.

Dunning, D., & Stern, L. B. (1994). Distinguishing accurate from inaccurate eyewitness identifications via inquiries about decision processes. *Journal of Personality and Social Psychology, 67,* 818–835.

Dunning, D., Griffin, D. W., Milojkovic, J., & Ross, L. (1990). The overconfidence effect in social prediction. *Journal of Personality and Social Psychology, 58,* 568–581.

Dutton, D. G., & Aron, A. P. (1974). Some evidence for heightened sexual attraction under conditions of high anxiety. *Journal of Personality and Social Psychology, 30,* 510–517.

Duval, S., & Wicklund, R. A. (1972). *A theory of objective self-awareness.* New York: Academic Press.

Eagly, A. H. (1987). *Sex differences in social behavior: A social-role interpretation.* Hillsdale, NJ: Erlbaum.

Eagly, A. H., & Carli, L. L. (1981). Sex of researchers and sex-typed communications as determinants of sex differences in influenceability: A meta-analysis of social influence studies. *Psychological Bulletin, 90,* 1–20.

Eagly, A. H., & Chaiken, S. (1975). An attribution analysis of communicator characteristics on opinion change: The case of communicator attractiveness. *Journal of Personality and Social Psychology, 32,* 136–244.

Eagly, A. H., & Chaiken, S. (1993). *The psychology of attitudes.* Fort Worth, TX: Harcourt Brace Jovanovich.

Eagly, A. H., & Crowley, M. (1986). Gender and helping behavior: A meta-analytic review of the social psychological literature. *Psychological Bulletin, 100,* 283–308.

Eagly, A. H., & Johnson, B. T. (1990). Gender and leadership style: A meta-analysis. *Psychological Bulletin, 108,* 233–256.

Eagly, A. H., & Karau, S. J. (1991). Gender and the emergence of leaders: A meta-analysis. *Journal of Personality and Social Psychology, 60,* 685–710.

Eagly, A. H., & Steffen, V. J. (1984). Gender stereotypes stem from the distribution of women and men into social roles. *Journal of Personality & Social Psychology, 46,* 735–754.

Eagly, A. H., & Steffen, V. J. (1986). Gender and aggressive behavior: A meta-analytic review of the social psychological literature. *Psychological Bulletin, 100,* 309–330.

Eagly, A. H., & Wood, W. (1991). Explaining sex differences in social behavior: A meta-analytic perspective. *Personality and Social Psychology Bulletin, 17,* 306–315.

Eagly, A. H., Ashmore, R. D., Makhijani, M. G., & Longo, L. C. (1991). What is beautiful is good, but . . . : A meta-analytic review of research on the physical attractiveness stereotype. *Psychological Bulletin, 110,* 109–128.

Eagly, A. H., Karau, S. J., & Makhijani, M. G. (1995). Gender and the effectiveness of leaders: A meta-analysis. *Psychological Bulletin, 117,* 125–145.

Eagly, A. H., Makhijani, M. G., & Klonsky, B. G. (1992). Gender and the evaluation of leaders: A meta-analysis. *Psychological Bulletin, 111,* 3–22.

Ebbesen, E., Duncan, B., & Konecni, V. (1975). Effects of content of verbal aggression: A field experiment. *Journal of Experimental and Social Psychology, 11,* 192–204.

Economos, J. (1989). Altruism, nativism, chauvinism, racism, schism, and jizzum. *Behavioral and Brain Sciences, 12,* 521–523.

Edwards, K. (1990). The interplay of affect and cognition in attitude formation and change. *Journal of Personality and Social Psychology, 59,* 202–216.

Edwards, K., & von Hippel, W. (1995). Hearts and minds: The priority of affective versus cognitive factors in person perception. *Personality and Social Psychology Bulletin, 21,* 996–1011.

Edwards, W. (1968). Conservatism in human information processing. In B. Kleinmutz (Ed.), *Formal representation of human judgment* (pp. 17–52). New York: Wiley.

Eibl-Eibesfeldt, I. (1963). Aggressive behavior and ritualized fighting in animals. In J. H. Masserman (Ed.), *Science and psychoanalysis: Vol. 6. Violence and war.* New York: Grune & Stratton.

Eisenberg, N., & Fabes, R. A. (1991). Prosocial behavior and empathy: A multimethod developmental perspective. In M. S. Clark (Ed.), *Review of personality and social psychology* (Vol. 12, pp. 34–61). Newbury Park, CA: Sage.

Ekman, P. (1965). Communication through nonverbal behavior: A source of information about an interpersonal relationship. In S. S. Tomkins & C. E. (Eds.), *Affect, cognition, and personality* (pp. 390–442). New York: Springer-Verlag.

Ekman, P. (1985). *Telling lies.* New York: Norton.

Ekman, P. (1992). *Telling lies: Clues to deceit in the marketplace, politics, and marriage* (rev. ed.). New York: Norton.

Ekman, P., & Friesen, W. V. (1969). The repertoire of nonverbal behavior: Categories, origins, usage, and coding. *Semiotica, 1,* 49–98.

Ekman, P., & Friesen, W. V. (1971). Constants across cultures in the face and emotion. *Journal of Personality and Social Psychology, 17,* 124–129.

Ekman, P., & Friesen, W. V. (1975). *Unmasking the face.* Englewood Cliffs, NJ: Prentice Hall.

Ekman, P., & O'Sullivan, M. (1991). Who can catch a liar? *American Psychologist, 46,* 913–920.

Ekman, P., Friesen, W. V., & Ellsworth, P. (1982a). Does the face provide accurate information? In P. Ekman (Ed.), *Emotion in the human face* (pp. 56–97). Cambridge, England: Cambridge University Press.

Ekman, P., Friesen, W. V., & Ellsworth, P. (1982b). What are the similarities and differences in facial behavior across cultures? In P. Ekman (Ed.), *Emotion in the human face* (pp. 128–143). Cambridge, England: Cambridge University Press.

Ekman, P., Friesen, W. V., O'Sullivan, M., Chan, A., Diacoyanni-Tarlatzis, I., Heider, K., Krause, R., LeCompre, W. A., Pitcairn, T., Ricci-Bitti, P. E., Scherer, K., Tomita, M., & Tzavras, A. (1987). Universals and cultural differences in the judgments of facial expressions of emotions. *Journal of Personality and Social Psychology, 53,* 712–717.

Elig, T. W., & Frieze, I. H. (1979). Measuring causal attributions for success and failure. *Journal of Personality and Social Psychology, 38,* 270–277.

Elkin, R., & Leippe, M. (1986). Physiological arousal, dissonance, and attitude change: Evidence for a dissonance-arousal link and a "don't remind me" effect. *Journal of Personality and Social Psychology, 51,* 55–65.

Elliot, A. J., & Devine, P. G. (1994). On the motivational nature of cognitive dissonance: Dissonance as psychological discomfort. *Journal of Personality and Social Psychology, 67,* 382–294.

Elliot, G. R., & Eisdorfer, C. (1982). *Stress and human health: Analysis and implications of research.* New York: Springer.

Ellsworth, P. C. (1994). William James and emotion: Is a century of fame worth a century of misunderstanding? *Psychological Review, 101,* 222–229.

Elms, A. C., & Milgram, S. (1966). Personality characteristics associated with obedience and defiance toward authoritative command. *Journal of Experimental Research in Personality, 1,* 282–289.

Emanuelson, I., & Fischbein, S. (1986). Vive la difference? A study on sex and schooling. *Scandinavian Journal of Educational Research, 30,* 71–84.

Emerson, R. W. (1929). *The complete works of Ralph Waldo Emerson.* New York: Wm. H. Wise.

Emery, R. E., & Wyer, M. M. (1987). Divorce mediation. *American Psychologist, 42,* 472–480.

Eron, L. D. (1982). Parent-child interaction, television violence, and aggression of children. *American Psychologist, 37,* 197–211.

Eron, L. D. (1987). The development of aggressive behavior from the perspective of a developing behaviorism. *American Psychologist, 42,* 425–442.

Esser, J. K., & Lindoerfer, J. S. (1989). Groupthink and the space shuttle *Challenger* accident: Toward a quantitative case analysis. *Journal of Behavioral Decision Making, 2,* 167–177.

Falck, R., & Craig, R. (1988). Classroom-oriented, primary prevention programming for drug abuse. *Journal of Psychoactive Drugs, 20,* 403–408.

Faranda, J. A., Kaminski, J. A., & Giza, B. K. (1979). *An assessment of attitudes toward women with the bogus pipeline.* Paper presented at the meeting of the American Psychological Association.

Fazio, R. H. (1989). On the power and functionality of attitudes: The role of attitude accessibility. In A. R. Pratkanis, S. J. Breckler, & A. G. Greenwald (Eds.), *Attitude structure and function* (pp. 153–179). Hillsdale, NJ: Erlbaum.

Fazio, R. H. (1990). Multiple processes by which attitudes guide behavior: The MODE model as an integrative framework. In M. P. Zanna (Ed.), *Advances in experimental social psychology* (Vol. 23, pp. 75–109). San Diego: Academic Press.

Fazio, R. H. (1995). Attitudes as object-evaluation associations: Determinants, consequences, and correlates of attitude accessibility. In R. Petty, & J. Krosnick (Eds.), *Attitude strength: Antecedents and consequences* (pp. 247–282). Hillsdale, NJ: Erlbaum.

Fazio, R. H., & Zanna, M. P. (1981). Direct experience and attitude-behavior consistency. In L. Berkowitz (Ed.), *Advances in experimental social psychology* (Vol. 14, pp. 162–202). New York: Academic Press.

Fazio, R. H., Effrein, E. A., & Falender, V. J. (1981). Self-perceptions following social interaction. *Journal of Personality and Social Psychology, 41,* 232–242.

Fazio, R. H., Jackson, J. R., Dunton, B. C., & Williams, C. J. (in press). Variability in automatic activation as an unobtrusive measure of racial attitudes: A bona fide pipeline? *Journal of Personality and Social Psychology.*

Fazio, R. H., Powell, M. C., & Williams, C. J. (1989). The role of attitude accessibility in the attitude-to-behavior process. *Journal of Consumer Research, 16,* 280–288.

Fazio, R. H., Sanbonmatsu, D. M., Powell, M. C., & Kardes, F. R. (1986). On the automatic activation of attitudes. *Journal of Personality and Social Psychology, 50,* 229–238.

Fazio, R. H., Zanna, M. P., & Cooper, J. (1977). Dissonance and self-perception: An integrative view of each theory's proper domain of application. *Journal of Experimental Social Psychology, 13,* 464–479.

Feeney, J. A., & Noller, P. (1990). Attachment style as a predictor of adult romantic relationships. *Journal of Personality and Social Psychology, 58,* 281–291.

Feldman-Summers, S., & Kiesler, S. B. (1974). Those who are number two try harder: The effect of sex on attributions of causality. *Journal of Personality and Social Psychology, 38,* 846–855.

Feshbach, N. (1978, March). *Empathy training: A field study in affective education.* Paper presented at the meetings of the American Educational Research Association, Toronto, Ontario, Canada.

Feshbach, N., & Feshbach, S. (1969). The relationship between empathy and aggression in two age groups. *Developmental Psychology, 1,* 102–107.

Feshbach, S. (1971). Dynamics and morality of violence and aggression: Some psychological considerations. *American Psychologist, 26,* 281–292.

Festinger, L. (1954). A theory of social comparison processes. *Human Relations, 7,* 117–140.

Festinger, L. (1957). *A theory of cognitive dissonance.* Stanford, CA: Stanford University Press.

Festinger, L. (1980). Looking backward. In L. Festinger (Ed.), *Restrospections on social psychology* (pp. 236–254). New York: Oxford University Press.

Festinger, L., & Aronson, E. (1960). The arousal and reduction of dissonance in social contexts. In D. Cartwright & A. Zander (Eds.), *Group dynamics* (pp. 214–231). Evanston, IL: Row, Peterson.

Festinger, L., & Carlsmith, J. M. (1959). Cognitive consequences of forced compliance. *Journal of Abnormal and Social Psychology, 58,* 203–211.

Festinger, L., & Maccoby, N. (1964). On resistance to persuasive communications. *Journal of Abnormal and Social Psychology, 68,* 359–366.

Festinger, L., & Thibaut, J. (1951). Interpersonal communication in small groups. *Journal of Abnormal and Social Psychology, 46,* 92–99.

Festinger, L., Riecken, H. W., & Schachter, S. (1956). *When prophecy fails.* Minneapolis: University of Minnesota Press.

Festinger, L., Schachter, S., & Back, K. (1950). *Social pressures in informal groups: A study of human factors in housing.* New York: Harper & Bros.

Fiedler, F. (1967). *A theory of leadership effectiveness.* New York: McGraw-Hill.

Fiedler, F. (1978). The contingency model and the dynamics of the leadership process. In L. Berkowitz (Ed.), *Advances in experimental social psychology* (Vol. 11, pp. 59–112). Orlando, FL: Academic Press.

Fiedler, K., & Semin, G. R. (1992). Attribution and language as a socio-cognitive environment. In G. R. Semin & K. Fiedler (Eds.), *Language, interaction, and social cognition* (pp. 79–101). London: Sage.

Fiedler, K., Semin, G. R., Finkenauer, C., & Berkel, I. Actor-observer bias in close relationships: The role of self-knowledge and self-related language. *Personality and Social Psychology Bulletin, 21,* 525–538.

Fincher, J. (1981, October). Presumed guilty: The ordeal of Robert Dillen. *Reader's Digest,* pp. 104–109.

Fischhoff, B. (1975). Hindsight ≠ foresight: The effect of outcome knowledge on judgment under uncertainty. *Journal of Experimental Psychology: Human Perception and Performance, 1,* 288–299.

Fishbein, M., & Ajzen, I. (1975). *Belief, attitude, intention, and behavior: An introduction to theory and research.* Reading, MA: Addison-Wesley.

Fiske, S. T. (1989). Examining the role of intent: Toward understanding its role in stereotyping and prejudice. In J. S. Uleman & J. A. Bargh (Eds.), *Unintended thought* (pp. 253–283). New York: Guilford.

Fiske, S. T. (1989). *Interdependence and stereotyping: From the laboratory to the Supreme Court (and back).* Invited address, American Psychological Association, New Orleans.

Fiske, S. T. (1993). Social cognition and social perception. *Annual Review of Psychology, 44,* 155–194.

Fiske, S. T., & Taylor, S. E. (1991). *Social cognition* (2nd ed.). New York: McGraw-Hill.

Flink, C., & Park, B. (1991). Increasing consensus in trait judgments through outcome dependency. *Journal of Experimental Social Psychology, 27,* 453–467.

Flowers, M. L. (1977). A lab test of some implications of Janis' groupthink hypothesis. *Journal of Personality and Social Psychology, 35,* 888–897.

Fong, G. T., Krantz, D. H., & Nisbett, R. E. (1986). The effects of statistical training on thinking about everyday problems. *Cognitive Psychology, 18,* 253–292.

Ford, C. S., & Beach, F. A. (1952). *Patterns of sexual behavior.* New York: Ace Books.

Forgas, J. P. (1995). Mood and judgment: The affect infusion model (AIM). *Psychological Bulletin, 117,* 39–66.

Forgas, J. P., & Bower, G. H. (1987). Mood effects on person-perception judgments. *Journal of Personality and Social Psychology, 53,* 53–60.

Forsterling, F. (1989). Models of covariation and attribution: How do they relate to the analogy of analysis of variance? *Journal of Personality and Social Psychology, 57,* 615–625.

Four year study of girls shows concern over weight. (1992, January 5). *Boston Globe* , West Weekly Section, pp. 1, 4.

Frager, R. (1970). Conformity and anticonformity in Japan. *Journal of Personality and Social Psychology, 15,* 203–210.

Frank, J. D. (1978). *Psychotherapy and the human predicament: A psychosocial approach.* Ed. P. E. Dietz, New York: Schocken Books.

Freedman, D., Pisani, R., Purves, R., & Adhikari, A. (1991). *Statistics* (2nd ed.). New York: Norton.

Freedman, J. (1965). Long-term behavioral effects of cognitive dissonance. *Journal of Experimental and Social Psychology, 1,* 145–155.

Freedman, J. L., & Fraser, S. C. (1966). Compliance without pressure: The foot-in-the-door technique. *Journal of Personality and Social Psychology, 4,* 195–202.

Freud, S. (1930). *Civilization and its discontents* (Joan Riviere, Trans.). London: Hogarth Press.

Freud, S. (1933). *New introductory lectures on psycho-analysis.* New York: Norton.

Fried, C. B., & Aronson, E. (1995). Hypocrisy, misattribution, and dissonance reduction. *Personality and Social Psychology Bulletin, 21,* 925–933.

Friedman, L. (1977). *Sex-role stereotyping in the mass media: An annotated bibliography.* New York: Garland Press.

Friesen, W. V. (1972). *Cultural differences in facial expressions in a social situation: An experimental test of the concept of display rules.* Unpublished dissertation, University of California, San Francisco.

Frijda, N. H. (1986). *The emotions.* Cambridge, England: Cambridge University Press.

Funder, D. C., & Colvin, C. R. (1988). Friends and strangers: Acquaintanceship, agreement, and the accuracy of personality judgment. *Journal of Personality and Social Psychology, 55,* 149–158.

Furnham, A., & Gunter, B. (1984). Just world beliefs and attitudes toward the poor. *British Journal of Social Psychology, 23,* 265–269.

Gaertner, S. L., & Dovidio, J. F. (1986). The aversive form of racism. In J. F. Dovidio & S. L. Gaertner (Eds.), *Prejudice, discrimination, and racism: Theory and research* (pp. 61–89). New York: Academic Press.

Gaertner, S. L., Mann, J. A., Dovidio, J. F., & Murrell, A. J. (1990). How does cooperation reduce intergroup bias? *Journal of Personality & Social Psychology, 59,* 692–704.

Gallup, G. G. (1977). Self-recognition in primates: A comparative approach to the bidirectional properties of consciousness. *American Psychologist, 32,* 329–338.

Gallup, G. G. (1993). Mirror, mirror on the wall which is the most heuristic theory of them all? *New Ideas in Psychology, 11,* 327–335.

Gallup, G. G., & Suarez, S. D. (1986). Self-awareness and the emergence of mind in humans and other primates. In J. Suls & A. G. Greenwald (Eds.), *Psychological perspectives on the self* (Vol. 3, pp. 3–26). Hillsdale, NJ: Erlbaum.

Gangestad, S. W. (1989). Uncompelling theory, uncompelling data. *Behavioral and Brain Sciences, 12,* 525–526.

Garcia, L. T., & Milano, L. (1990). A content analysis of erotic videos. *Journal of Psychology and Human Sexuality, 3,* 95–103.

Garfinkle, H. (1967). *Studies in ethnomethodology.* Englewood Cliffs, NJ: Prentice Hall.

Garner, D. M., Garfinkel, P. E., Schwartz, D., & Thompson, M. (1980). Cultural expectations of thinness in women. *Psychological Reports, 47*, 483–491.

Gates, H. L., Jr. (1995, October 23). Thirteen ways of looking at a black man. *New Yorker*, pp. 56–65.

Gavanski, I., & Hoffman, C. (1987). Awareness of influences on one's own judgments: The roles of covariation detection and attention. *Journal of Personality and Social Psychology, 52*, 453–463.

Geen, R. G. (1989). Alternative conceptions of social facilitation. In P. B. Paulus (Ed.), *Psychology of group influence* (2nd ed., pp. 15–51). Hillsdale, NJ: Erlbaum.

Geen, R., & Quanty, M. (1977). The catharsis of aggression: An evaluation of an hypothesis. In L. Berkowitz (Ed.), *Advances in experimental social psychology* (Vol. 10, pp. 1–36). New York: Academic Press.

Geen, R., Stonner, D., & Shope, G. (1975). The facilitation of aggression by aggression: A study in response inhibition and disinhibition. *Journal of Personality and Social Psychology, 31*, 721–726.

George, J. M., & Brief, A. P. (1992). Feeling good–doing good: A conceptual analysis of the mood at work—organizational spontaneity relationship. *Psychological Bulletin, 112*, 310–329.

Gerard, H. B. (1953). The effect of different dimensions of disagreement on the communication process in small groups. *Human Relations, 6*, 249–271.

Gerard, H. B., & Mathewson, G. C. (1966). The effects of severity of initiation on liking for a group: A replication. *Journal of Experimental Social Psychology, 2*, 278–287.

Gerard, H. B., Wilhelmy, R. A., & Conolley, E. S. (1968). Conformity and group size. *Journal of Personality and Social Psychology, 8*, 79–82.

Gerbner, G., Gross, L., Morgan, M., & Signorielli, N. (1980). The "mainstreaming" of America: Violence profile no. 11. *Journal of Communication, 30*(3), 10–29.

Gerdes, E. P. (1979). College students' reactions to social psychological experiments involving deception. *Journal of Social Psychology, 107*, 99–110.

Gergen, K. J. (1971). *The concept of self*. New York: Holt, Rinehart & Winston.

Gergen, K. J., Gergen, M. M., & Barton, W. H. (1973). Deviance in the dark. *Psychology Today, 7*, 129–130.

Gerstein, L. H., & Tesser, A. (1987). Antecedents and responses associated with loneliness. *Journal of Social and Personal Relationships, 4*, 329–363.

Gibbons, F. X. (1978). Sexual standards and reactions to pornography: Enhancing behavioral consistency through self-focused attention. *Journal of Personality and Social Psychology, 36*, 976–987.

Gigerenzer, G. (1993). The bounded rationality of probabilistic mental models. In K. I. Manktelow & D. E. Over (Eds.), *Rationality: Psychological and philosophical perspectives* (pp. 284–313). London: Routledge.

Gigone, D., & Hastie, R. (1993). The common knowledge effect: Information sharing and group judgment. *Journal of Personality and Social Psychology, 65*, 959–974.

Gilbert, B. (1990, April). Earth Day plus 20, and counting. *Smithsonian*, pp. 47–55.

Gilbert, D. T. (1989). Thinking lightly about others: Automatic components of the social inference process. In J. S. Uleman & J. A. Bargh (Eds.), *Unintended thought* (pp. 189–211). New York: Guilford Press.

Gilbert, D. T. (1991). How mental systems believe. *American Psychologist, 46*, 107–119.

Gilbert, D. T. (1993). The assent of man: Mental representation and the control of belief. In D. M. Wegner & J. W.

Pennebaker, (Eds.), *The handbook of mental control* (pp. 57–87). Englewood Cliffs, NJ: Prentice Hall.

Gilbert, D. T., & Malone, P. S. (1995). The correspondence bias. *Psychological Bulletin, 117*, 21–38.

Gilbert, D. T., & Osborne, R. E. (1989). Thinking backward: Some curable and incurable consequences of cognitive busyness. *Journal of Personality and Social Psychology, 57*, 940–949.

Gilbert, D. T., Giesler, R. B., & Morris, K. A. (1995). When comparisons arise. *Journal of Personality and Social Psychology, 69*, 227–236.

Gilbert, D. T., Pelham, B. W., & Krull, D. S. (1988). On cognitive busyness: When person perceivers meet persons perceived. *Journal of Personality and Social Psychology, 54*, 733–740.

Gilbert, D. T., Tafarodi, R. W., & Malone, P. S. (1993). You can't not believe everything you read. *Journal of Personality and Social Psychology, 65*, 221–233.

Gilbert, G. M. (1951). Stereotype persistence and change among college students. *Journal of Abnormal and Social Psychology, 46*, 245–254.

Gilovich, T. (1991). *How we know what isn't so: The fallibility of human reasoning in everyday life*. New York: Free Press.

Glass, D. C. (1964). Changes in liking as a means of reducing cognitive discrepancies between self-esteem and aggression. *Journal of Personality, 32*, 531–549.

Glass, D. C., & Singer, J. E. (1972). *Urban stress: Experiments on noise and social stressors*. New York: Academic Press.

Goethals, G. R. (1986). Social comparison theory: Psychology from the lost and found. *Personality and Social Psychology Bulletin, 12*, 261–278.

Goethals, G. R., & Darley, J. M. (1977). Social comparison theory: An attributional approach. In J. M. Suls & R. L. Miller (Eds.), *Social comparison processes: Theoretical and empirical perspectives* (pp. 259–278). Washington, DC: Hemisphere/Halsted.

Goffman, E. (1955). On face-work: An analysis of ritual elements in social interaction. *Psychiatry, 18*, 213–231.

Goffman, E. (1959). *Presentation of self in everyday life*. Garden City, NY: Doubleday Anchor Books.

Goffman, E. (1967). *Interaction ritual*. Garden City, NY: Doubleday.

Goffman, E. (1971). *Relations in public*. New York: Basic Books.

Goffman, E. (1976). *Gender advertisements*. New York: Harper & Row.

Gold, J. A., Ryckman, R. M., & Mosley, N. R. (1984). Romantic mood induction and attraction to a dissimilar other: Is love blind? *Personality and Social Psychology Bulletin, 10*, 358–368.

Goldberg, P. (1968, April). Are women prejudiced against women? *Trans-Action*, pp. 28–30.

Goldstein, J. H., & Arms, R. L. (1971). Effect of observing athletic contests on hostility. *Sociometry, 34*, 83–90.

Goleman, D. (1982, January). Make-or-break resolutions. *Psychology Today*, p. 19.

Gollwitzer, P. M. (1986). *Public vs. private self-symbolizing*. Unpublished manuscript, Max-Planck Institute for Psychological Research, Munich, Germany.

Gollwitzer, P. M., & Wicklund, R. A. (1985). Self-symbolizing and the neglect of others' perspectives. *Journal of Personality and Social Psychology, 48*, 702–715.

Gologor, E. (1977). Group polarization in a non-risk-taking culture. *Journal of Cross-Cultural Psychology, 8*, 331–346.

Gonzales, M. H., Aronson, E., & Costanzo, M. (1988). Using social cognition and persuasion to promote energy conservation: A quasi-experiment. *Journal of Applied Social Psychology, 18*, 1049–1066.

Gonzalez, R., Ellsworth, P. C., & Pembroke, M. (1993). Response biases in lineups and showups. *Journal of Personality and Social Psychology, 64,* 525–537.

Goodman, N. G. (Ed.). (1945). *A Benjamin Franklin reader.* New York: Thomas Y. Crowell.

Granberg, D., & Brown, T. (1989). On affect and cognition in politics. *Social Psychology Quarterly, 52,* 171–182.

Greeley, A., & Sheatsley, P. (1971). The acceptance of desegregation continues to advance. *Scientific American, 225*(6), 13–19.

Greenberg, J. (1983). *Difficult goal choice as a self-handicapping strategy.* Unpublished manuscript, Ohio State University.

Greenberg, J., & Pyszczynski, T. (1985). The effect of an overheard slur on evaluations of the target: How to spread a social disease. *Journal of Experimental Social Psychology, 21,* 61–72.

Greenberg, J., Pyszczynski, T., & Paisley, C. (1984). The role of extrinsic incentives in the use of test anxiety as an anticipatory attributional defense: Playing it cool when the stakes are high. *Journal of Personality and Social Psychology, 47,* 1136–1145.

Greenberg, J., Pyszczynski, T., & Solomon, S. (1982). The self-serving attributional bias: Beyond self-presentation. *Journal of Experimental Social Psychology, 18,* 56–67.

Greenberg, J., Pyszczynski, T., & Solomon, S. (1986). The causes and consequences of the need for self-esteem: A terror management theory. In R. F. Baumeister (Ed.), *Public self and private self* (pp. 189–212). New York: Springer-Verlag.

Greenberg, L. (1979). Genetic component of bee odor in kin recognition. *Science, 206,* 1095–1097.

Greene, D., Sternberg, B., & Lepper, M. R. (1976). Overjustification in a token economy. *Journal of Personality and Social Psychology, 34,* 1219–1234.

Greenwald, A. G. (1980). The totalitarian ego: Fabrication and revision of personal history. *American Psychologist, 35,* 603–618.

Greenwald, A. G., & Banaji, M. R. (1989). The self as a memory system: Powerful, but ordinary. *Journal of Personality and Social Psychology, 57,* 41–54.

Greenwald, A. G., & Ronis, D. L. (1978). Twenty years of cognitive dissonance: Case study of the evolution of a theory. *Psychological Review, 85,* 53–57.

Greenwald, A. G., Spangenberg, E. R., Pratkanis, A. R., & Eskenazi, J. (1991). Double-blind tests of subliminal self-help audiotapes. *Psychological Science, 2,* 119–122.

Grice, H. P. (1975). Logic as conversation. In P. Cole & J. L. Morgan (Eds.), *Syntax and semantics: Vol. 3. Speech acts.* (pp. 365–372). New York: Seminar Press.

Griffin, D. W., & Ross, L. (1991). Subjective construal, social inference, and human misunderstanding. In L. Berkowitz (Ed.), *Advances in experimental social psychology* (Vol. 24, pp. 319–359). San Diego, CA: Academic Press.

Griffin, D. W., Dunning, D., & Ross, L. (1990). The role of construal processes in overconfident predictions about the self and others. *Journal of Personality and Social Psychology, 59,* 1128–1139.

Griffitt, W., & Veitch, R. (1971). Hot and crowded: Influences of population density and temperature on interpersonal affective behavior. *Journal of Personality and Social Psychology, 17,* 92–98.

Griffitt, W., & Veitch, R. (1974). Preacquaintance attitude similarity and attraction revisited: Ten days in a fall-out shelter. *Sociometry, 37,* 163–173.

Grusec, J. E. (1991). The socialization of altruism. In M. S. Clark (Ed.), *Review of personality and social psychology* (Vol. 12, pp. 9–33). Newbury Park, CA: Sage.

Grusec, J. E., Kuczynski, L., Rushton, J. P., & Simutis, Z. M. (1979). Modeling, direct instruction, and attributions: Effects on altruism. *Developmental Psychology, 14,* 51–57.

Gudykunst, W. B. (1988). Culture and intergroup processes. In M. H. Bond (Ed.), *The cross-cultural challenge to social psychology* (pp. 165–181). Newbury Park, CA: Sage.

Guerin, B. (1986). Mere presence effects in humans: A review. *Journal of Experimental Social Psychology, 22,* 38–77.

Guerin, B. (1993). *Social facilitation.* Cambridge, England: Cambridge University Press.

Gustafson, R. (1989). Frustration and successful vs. unsuccessful aggression: A test of Berkowitz' completion hypothesis. *Aggressive Behavior, 15,* 5–12.

Hackman, J. R., & Morris, C. G. (1978). Group process and group effectiveness: A reappraisal. In L. Berkowitz (Ed.), *Group processes* (pp. 57–66). New York: Academic Press.

Hagestad, G. O., & Smyer, M. A. (1982). Dissolving long-term relationships: Patterns of divorcing in middle age. In S. Duck (Ed.), *Personal relationships 4: Dissolving personal relationships* (pp. 155–188). London: Academic Press.

Haggard, E. A., & Issacs, F. S. (1966). Micromomentary facial expressions as indicators of ego mechanisms in psychotherapy. In L. A. Gottschalk & A. H. Auerback (Eds.), *Methods of research in psychotherapy* (pp. 154–165). New York: Appleton-Century-Crofts.

Halberstam, D. (1972). *The best and the brightest.* New York: Random House.

Hall, E. T. (1969). *The hidden dimension.* Garden City, NY: Doubleday.

Hall, J. A. (1979). *A cross-national study of gender differences in nonverbal sensitivity.* Unpublished manuscript, Northeastern University.

Hall, J. A. (1984). *Nonverbal sex differences: Communication accuracy and expressive style.* Baltimore, MD: Johns Hopkins University Press.

Hamill, R. C., Wilson, T. D., & Nisbett, R. E. (1980). Ignoring sample bias: Inferences about populations from atypical cases. *Journal of Personality and Social Psychology, 39,* 578–589.

Hamilton, D. L. (1970). The structure of personality judgments: Comments on Kuusinen's paper and further evidence. *Scandinavian Journal of Psychology, 11,* 261–265.

Hamilton, D. L. (1981a). Cognitive representations of persons. In E. T. Higgins, C. P. Herman, & M. P. Zanna (Eds.), *Social cognition: The Ontario Symposium* (Vol. 1, pp. 135–159). Hillsdale, NJ: Erlbaum.

Hamilton, D. L. (1981b). Illusory correlation as a basis for stereotyping. In D. L. Hamilton (Ed.), *Cognitive Processes in Stereotyping and Intergroup Behavior.* Hillsdale, NJ: Erlbaum.

Hamilton, D. L., & Gifford, R. K. (1976). Illusory correlation in interpersonal perception: A cognitive basis of stereotypic judgments: *Journal of Experimental Social Psychology, 12,* 392–407.

Hamilton, D. L., & Sherman, S. J. (1989). Illusory correlations: Implications for stereotype theory and research. In D. Bar-Tal, C. F. Graumann, A. W. Kruglanski, & W. Stroebe (Eds.), *Stereotypes and prejudice: Changing conceptions* (pp. 59–82). New York: Springer-Verlag.

Hamilton, W. D. (1964). The genetical evolution of social behavior. *Journal of Theoretical Biology, 7,* 1–52.

Han, S., & Shavitt, S. (1994). Persuasion and culture: Advertising appeals in individualistic and collectivistic societies. *Journal of Experimental Social Psychology, 30,* 326–350.

Haney, C., Banks, C., & Zimbardo, P. (1973). Interpersonal

dynamics in a simulated prison. *International Journal of Criminology and Penology, 1,* 69–97.

Hansen, C. H., & Hansen, R. D. (1988). Finding the face in the crowd: An anger superiority effect. *Journal of Personality and Social Psychology, 17,* 917–924.

Harackiewicz, J. M. (1979). The effects of reward contingency and performance feedback on intrinsic motivation. *Journal of Personality and Social Psychology, 37,* 1352–1363.

Harackiewicz, J. M. (1989). Performance evaluation and intrinsic motivation processes: The effects of achievement orientation and rewards. In D. Buss & N. Cantor (Eds.), *Personality psychology: Recent trends and emerging directions* (pp. 128–137). New York: Springer-Verlag.

Harackiewicz, J. M., Manderlink, G., & Sansone, C. (1984). Rewarding pinball wizardry: Effects of evaluation and cue value on intrinsic interest. *Journal of Personality and Social Psychology, 47,* 287–300.

Hardin, G. (1968). The tragedy of the commons. *Science, 162,* 1243–1248.

Haritos-Fatouros, M. (1988). The official torturer: A learning model for obedience to the authority of violence. *Journal of Applied Social Psychology, 18,* 1107–1120.

Harkins, S. G., & Szymanski, K. (1987). Social loafing and social facilitation: Old wine in new bottles. In C. Hendrick (Ed.), *Group processes and intergroup relations* (Vol. 9, pp. 167–188). Newbury Park, CA: Sage.

Harkness, A. R., DeBono, K. G., & Borgida, E. (1985). Personal involvement and strategies for making contingency judgments: A stake in the dating game makes a difference. *Journal of Personality and Social Psychology, 49,* 22–32.

Harries, K. D., & Stadler, S. J. (1988). Heat and violence: New findings from Dallas field data, 1980–1981. *Journal of Applied Social Psychology, 18,* 129–138.

Harris, B. (1986). Reviewing 50 years of the psychology of social issues. *Journal of Social Issues, 42,* 1–20.

Harris, M. (1974). Mediators between frustration and aggression in a field experiment. *Journal of Experimental and Social Psychology, 10,* 561–571.

Harris, M. B., Benson, S. M., & Hall, C. (1975). The effects of confession on altruism. *Journal of Social Psychology, 96,* 187–192.

Hart, A. J. (1995). Naturally occurring expectation effects. *Journal of Personality and Social Psychology, 68,* 109–115.

Hart, D., & Damon, W. (1986). Developmental trends in self-understanding. *Social Cognition, 4,* 388–407.

Hartshorne, H., & May, M. A. (1929). *Studies in the nature of character: Studies in service and self-control* (Vol. 2). New York: Macmillan.

Harvey, J. H., Flanary, R., & Morgan, M. (1986). Vivid memories of vivid loves gone by. *Journal of Personal and Social Relationships, 3,* 359–373.

Hassebrauck, M. (1988). Beauty is more than "name" deep: The effect of women's first names on ratings of physical attractiveness and personality attributes. *Journal of Applied Social Psychology, 18,* 721–726.

Hastie, R. (1980). Memory for behavioral information that confirms or contradicts a personality impression. In R. Hastie, T. M. Ostrom, E. B. Ebbesen, R. S. Wyer, D. L. Hamilton, & D. E. Carlston (Eds.), *Person memory: The cognitive basis of social perception* (pp. 141–172). Hillsdale, NJ: Erlbaum.

Hastie, R., Penrod, S. D., & Pennington, N. (1983). *Inside the jury.* Cambridge MA: Harvard University Press.

Hastorf, A., & Cantril, H. (1954). They saw a game: A case study. *Journal of Abnormal and Social Psychology, 49,* 129–134.

Hatfield, E. (1988). Passionate and companionate love. In R. J. Sternberg & M. L. Barnes (Eds.), *The psychology of love* (pp. 191–217). New Haven, CT: Yale University Press.

Hatfield, E., & Sprecher, S. (1986a). *Mirror, mirror: The importance of looks in everyday life.* Albany: State University of New York Press.

Hatfield, E., & Sprecher, S. (1986b). Measuring passionate love in intimate relationships. *Journal of Adolescence, 9,* 383–410.

Hatfield, E., & Walster, G. W. (1978). *A new look at love.* Reading, MA: Addison-Wesley.

Hatfield, E., Greenberger, E., Traupmann, J., & Lambert, P. (1982). Equity and sexual satisfaction in recently married couples. *Journal of Sex Research, 18,* 18–32.

Hays, R. B. (1984). The development and maintenance of friendship. *Journal of Social and Personal Relationships, 1,* 75–98.

Hazan, C., & Shaver, P. (1987). Romantic love conceptualized as an attachment process. *Journal of Personality and Social Psychology, 52,* 511–524.

Hazelwood, J. D., & Olson, J. M. (1986). Covariation information, causal questioning, and interpersonal behavior. *Journal of Experimental Social Psychology, 22,* 276–291.

Hearold, S. (1986). A synthesis of 1043 effects of television on social behavior. In G. Comstock (Ed.), *Public communication and behavior,* (Vol. 1, pp. 65–133). Orlando, FL: Academic Press.

Heckhausen, J., & Schulz, R. (1995). A life-span theory of control. *Psychological Review, 102,* 284–304.

Hedge, A., & Yousif, Y. H. (1992). Effects of urban size, urgency, and cost on helpfulness. *Journal of Cross-Cultural Psychology, 23,* 107–115.

Hedges, L. V., & Nowell, A. (1995). Sex differences in mental test scores, variability, and numbers of high-scoring individuals. *Science, 269,* 41–45.

Heider, F. (1958). *The psychology of interpersonal relations.* New York: Wiley.

Helgeson, V. S., & Cohen, S. (in press). Social support and adjustment to cancer: Reconciling descriptive, correlational, and intervention research. *Health Psychology.*

Henley, N. M. (1977). *Body politics: Power, sex, and nonverbal communication.* Englewood Cliffs, NJ: Prentice Hall.

Hennessey, B. A., & Zbikowski, S. M. (1993). Immunizing children against the negative effects of reward: A further examination of intrinsic motivation focus sessions. *Creativity Research Journal, 6,* 297–307.

Hennessey, B. A., Amabile, T., & Martinage, M. (1989). Immunizing children against the negative effects of reward. *Contemporary Educational Psychology, 14,* 212–227.

Henrick, S. S., & Henrick, C. (1986). A theory and method of love. *Journal of Personality and Social Psychology, 50,* 392–402.

Hepworth, J. T., & West, S. G. (1988). Lynchings and the economy: A time-series reanalysis of Hovland and Sears (1940). *Journal of Personality and Social Psychology, 55,* 239–247.

Herbert, T. B., & Cohen, S. (1993). Stress and immunity in humans: A meta-analytic review. *Psychosomatic Medicine, 55,* 364–379.

Herrnstein, R. J., & Murray, C. A. (1994). *The bell curve: Intelligence and class structure in American life.* New York: Free Press.

Hersh, S. M. (1970). *My Lai 4: A report on the massacre and its aftermath.* New York: Vintage Books.

Heunemann, R. L., Shapiro, L. R., Hampton, M. C., & Mitchell, B. W. (1966). A longitudinal study of gross body composition and body conformation and their association with food and activity in the teenage population. *American Journal of Clinical Nutrition, 18,* 325–338.

Hewstone, M., & Jaspars, J. (1987). Covariation and causal attribution: A logical model of the intuitive analysis of variance. *Journal of Personality and Social Psychology, 53,* 663–672.

Higgins, E. T. (1987). Self-discrepancy: A theory relating self and affect. *Psychology Review, 94,* 319–340.

Higgins, E. T. (1989). Knowledge accessibility and activation: Subjectivity and suffering from unconscious sources. In J. S. Uleman & J. A. Bargh (Eds.), *Unintended thought* (pp. 75–123). New York: Guilford Press.

Higgins, E. T. (1989). Self-discrepancy theory: What patterns of self-beliefs cause people to suffer? In L. Berkowitz (Ed.), *Advances in experimental social psychology* (Vol. 22, pp. 93–136). New York: Academic Press.

Higgins, E. T. (in press). Knowledge application: Accessibility, applicability, and salience. In E. T. Higgins and A. R. Kruglanski (Eds.), *Social psychology: Handbook of basic principles.* New York: Guilford.

Higgins, E. T., & Bargh, J. A. (1987). Social cognition and social perception. *Annual Review of Psychology, 38,* 369–425.

Higgins, E. T., Bond, R. N., Klein, R., & Strauman, T. (1986). Self-discrepancies and emotional vulnerability: How magnitude, accessibility, and type of discrepancy influence affect. *Journal of Personality and Social Psychology, 51,* 5–15.

Higgins, E. T., Klein, R., & Strauman, T. (1987). Self-discrepancies: Distinguishing among self-states, self-state conflicts, and emotional vulnerabilities. In K. M. Yardley & T. M. Honess (Eds.), *Self and identity: Psychosocial perspectives* (pp. 173–186). New York: Wiley.

Higgins, E. T., Rholes, W. S., & Jones, C. R. (1977). Category accessibility and impression formation. *Journal of Experimental Social Psychology, 13,* 141–154.

Higgins, R. L., & Harris, R. N. (1988). Strategic "alcohol" use: Drinking to self-handicap. *Journal of Social and Clinical Psychology, 6,* 191–202.

Hill, C. T., Rubin, Z., & Peplau, L. A. (1976). Breakups before marriage: The end of 103 affairs. *Journal of Social Issues, 32,* 147–168.

Hilton, J. L., & Darley, J. M. (1991). The effects of interaction goals on person perception. In M. P. Zanna (Ed.), *Advances in experimental social psychology* (Vol. 24, pp. 235–267). San Diego, CA: Academic Press.

Hinds, M. deCourcy. (1993, October 19). Not like the movie: 3 take a dare, and lose. *New York Times,* pp. A1, A22.

Hippler, H. J., Schwarz, N., & Sudman, S. (Eds.). (1987). *Social information processing and survey methodology.* New York: Springer-Verlag.

Hirt, E. R., Deppe, R. K., & Gordon, L. J. (1991). Self-reported versus behavioral self-handicapping: Empirical evidence for a theoretical distinction. *Journal of Personality and Social Psychology, 61,* 981–991.

Hobbes, T. (1986). *Leviathan.* Harmondsworth, England: Penguin Press. (Original work published 1651)

Hobfoll, S. E., & Vaux, A. (1993). Social support: Social resources and social context. In L. Goldberger & S. Breznitz (Eds.), *Handbook of stress: Theoretical and clinical aspects* (2nd ed., pp. 685–705). New York: Free Press.

Hoffman, C., Lau, I., & Johnson, D. R. (1986). The linguistic relativity of person cognition: An English-Chinese comparison. *Journal of Personality and Social Psychology, 51,* 1097–1105.

Hofstede, G. (1986). Cultural differences in teaching and learning. *International Journal of Intercultural Relations, 10,* 301–320.

Hogg, M. A., & Abrams, D. (1988). *Social identifications.* London: Routledge. (cf. Chapter 3)

Hollander, E. P. (1958). Conformity, status, and idiosyncrasy credit. *Psychological Review, 65,* 117–127.

Hollander, E. P. (1960). Competence and conformity in the acceptance of influence. *Journal of Abnormal and Social Psychology, 61,* 361–365.

Hollander, E. P. (1985). Leadership and power. In G. Lindzey & E. Aronson (Eds.), *Handbook of social psychology* (3rd ed., Vol. 2, pp. 485–537). New York: Random House.

Holmes, T. H., & Rahe, R. H. (1967). The social readjustment rating scale. *Journal of Psychosomatic Research, 11,* 213–218.

Homans, G. C. (1961). *Social behavior: Its elementary forms.* New York: Harcourt Brace & World.

Hong, G. W. (1992). Contributions of "culture-absent" cross-cultural psychology. Paper presented at annual meeting of Society for Cross-Cultural Research, Santa Fe, New Mexico.

Honts, C. R. (1994). Psychophysiological detection of deception. *Current Directions in Psychological Science, 3,* 77–82.

Hornstein, H. A. (1991). Empathic distress and altruism: Still inseparable. *Psychological Inquiry, 2,* 133–135.

Hornstein, H. A., LaKind, E., Frankel, G., & Manne, S. (1975). Effects of knowledge about remote social events on prosocial behavior, social conception, and mood. *Journal of Personality and Social Psychology, 32,* 1038–1046.

House, R. J., Spangler, W. D., & Woycke, J. (1991). Personality and charisma in the U.S. presidency: A psychological theory of leader effectiveness. *Administrative Science Quarterly. 36,* 364–396.

Houston, D. A., & Fazio, R. H. (1989). Biased processing as a function of attitude accessibility: Making objective judgments subjectively. *Social Cognition, 7,* 51–66.

Hovland, C. I., & Sears, R. R. (1940). Minor studies in aggression: 6. Correlation of lynchings with economic indices. *Journal of Psychology, 9,* 301–310.

Hovland, C. I., & Weiss, W. (1951). The influence of source credibility on communication effectiveness. *Public Opinion Quarterly, 15,* 635–650.

Hovland, C. I., Janis, I. L., & Kelley, H. H. (1953). *Communication and persuasion: Psychological studies of opinion change.* New Haven, CT: Yale University Press.

Hovland, C. I., Lumsdaine, A. A., & Sheffield, F. D. (1949). *Experiments on mass communication.* Princeton, NJ: Princeton University Press.

Hsu, F. L. K. (1981). The self in cross-cultural perspective. In A. J. Marsella, B. De Vos, & F. L. K. Hsu (Eds.), *Culture and self* (pp. 24–55). London: Tavistock.

Hsu, S. S. (1995, April 8). Fredericksburgh searches its soul after clerk is beaten as 6 watch. *Washington Post,* pp. A1, A13.

Huesmann, L. R. (1982). Television violence and aggressive behavior. In D. Pearly, L. Bouthilet, & J. Lazar (Eds.), *Television and behavior: Vol. 2. Technical reviews* (pp. 220–256). Washington, DC: National Institute of Mental Health.

Hull, J. G. (1981). A self-awareness model of the causes and effects of alcohol consumption. *Journal of Personality and Social Psychology, 90,* 586–600.

Hull, J. G., & Young, R. D. (1983). Self-consciousness, self-esteem, and success-failure as determinants of alcohol consumption in male social drinkers. *Journal of Personality and Social Psychology, 44,* 1097–1109.

Hunt, G. T. (1940). *The wars of the Iroquois.* Madison: University of Wisconsin Press.

Hurley, D., & Allen, B. P. (1974). The effect of the number of people present in a nonemergency situation. *Journal of Social Psychology, 92,* 27–29.

Hutchinson, R. R. (1983). The pain-aggression relationship and its expression in naturalistic settings. *Aggressive Behavior, 9*, 229–242.

Hyman, J. J., & Sheatsley, P. B. (1956; 1964). Attitudes toward desegregation. *Scientific American, 195*(6), 35–39, and *211*(1), 16–23.

Ickes, W., & Layden, M. A. (1978). Attributional styles. In J. H. Harvey, W. Ickes, & R. F. Kidd (Eds.), *New directions in attribution research* (Vol. 2, pp. 119–152). Hillsdale, NJ: Erlbaum.

Ickes, W., Patterson, M. L., Rajecki, D. W., & Tanford, S. (1982). Behavioral and cognitive consequences of reciprocal versus compensatory responses to preinteraction expectancies. *Social Cognition, 1*, 160–190.

Ickes, W., Robertson, E., Tooke, W., & Teng, G. (1986). Naturalistic social cognition: Methodology, assessment, and validation. *Journal of Personality and Social Psychology, 51*, 66–82.

Ingham, A. G., Levinger, G., Graves, J., & Peckham, V. (1974). The Ringelmann effect: Studies of group size and group performance. *Journal of Experimental Social Psychology, 10*, 371–384.

Insko, C. A., Schopler, J., Graetz, K. A., Drigotas, S. M., Currey, D. P., Smith, S. L., & Brazil, D. (1994). Interindividual-intergroup discontinuity in the Prisoner's Dilemma game. *Journal of Conflict Resolution, 38*, 87–116.

Isen, A. M. (1987). Positive affect, cognitive processes, and social behavior. In L. Berkowitz (Ed.), *Advances in experimental social psychology* (Vol. 20, pp. 203–253). San Diego, CA: Academic Press.

Isen, A. M. (1987). Positive affect, cognitive processes, and social behavior. In L. Berkowitz (Ed.), *Advances in experimental social psychology* (Vol. 21, pp. 203–253). New York: Academic Press.

Isen, A. M., & Levin, P. A. (1972). Effect of feeling good on helping: Cookies and kindness. *Journal of Personality and Social Psychology, 21*, 384–388.

Isenberg, D. J. (1986). Group polarization: A critical review and meta-analysis. *Journal of Personality and Social Psychology, 50*, 1141–1151.

Izard, C. (1969). The emotions and emotion constructs in personality and culture research. In R. B. Cattell (Ed.), *Handbook of modern personality theory* (pp. 496–510). Chicago: Aldine.

Izard, C. (1977). *Human emotions.* New York: Plenum.

Jackson, J. (1981, July 19). Syndicated newspaper column.

Jackson, J. M., & Williams, K. D. (1985). Social loafing on difficult tasks: Working collectively can improve performance. *Journal of Personality and Social Psychology, 49*, 937–942.

Jacobs, P., & Landau, S. (1971). *To serve the devil* (Vol. 2, p. 71). New York: Vintage Books.

Jacobson, M., & Hacker, G. (1985, May 6). The case for curbing alcohol advertising. *Broadcasting*, p. 19.

Jacobson, N. S., Waldron, H., & Moore, D. (1980). Toward a behavioral profile of marital distress. *Journal of Consulting and Clinical Psychology, 48*, 696–703.

Jacoby, L. L., Lindsay, S. D., & Toth, J. P. (1992). Unconscious influences revealed: Attention, awareness, and control. *American Psychologist, 47*, 802–809.

James, W. (1890). *The principles of psychology.* New York: Holt.

James, W. (1910). *The principles of psychology* (Vols. 1–2). London: Macmillan.

"Jammy man" actor's plight. (1988, October 18). *New York Times*, p. A25.

Janis, I. L. (1972). *Victims of groupthink.* Boston: Houghton Mifflin.

Janis, I. L. (1982). *Groupthink* (2nd ed.). Boston: Houghton Mifflin.

Janis, I. L., & Feshbach, S. (1953). Effects of fear-arousing communications. *Journal of Abnormal and Social Psychology, 49*, 78–92.

Janoff-Bulman, R., Timko, C., & Carli, L. L. (1985). Cognitive biases in blaming the victim. *Journal of Experimental Social Psychology, 21*, 161–177.

Jeavons, C. M., & Taylor, S. P. (1985). The control of alcohol related aggression: Redirecting the inebriate's attention to socially appropriate conduct. *Aggressive Behavior, 11*, 93–101.

Jecker, J., & Landy, D. (1969). Liking a person as a function of doing him a favor. *Human Relations, 22*, 371–378.

Jellison, J. M., & Riskind, J. A. (1970). A social comparison of abilities interpretation of risk-taking behavior. *Journal of Personality and Social Psychology, 15*, 375–390.

Jennings, D. J., Amabile, T. M., & Ross, L. (1982). Informal covariation assessment: Data-based versus theory-based judgments. In D. Kahneman, P. Slovic, & A. Tversky (Eds.), *Judgment under uncertainty: Heuristics and biases* (pp. 211–230). New York: Cambridge University Press.

Jepson, C., & Chaiken, S. (1990). Chronic issue-specific fear inhibits systematic processing of persuasive communications. *Journal of Social Behavior and Personality, 5*, 61–84.

Job, R. F. S. (1988). Effective and ineffective use of fear in health promotion campaigns. *American Journal of Public Health, 78*, 163–167.

Johnson, B. T., & Eagly, A. H. (1989). Effects of involvement on persuasion: A meta-analysis. *Psychological Bulletin, 106*, 290–314.

Johnson, B. T., & Eagly, A. H. (1990). Involvement and persuasion: Types, traditions, and evidence. *Psychological Bulletin, 107*, 375–384.

Johnson, D. M. (1945). The phantom anesthetist of Mattoon: A field study of mass hysteria. *Journal of Abnormal and Social Psychology, 40*, 175–186.

Johnson, D. W., & Johnson, R. T. (1987). *Learning together and alone: Cooperative, competitive, and individualistic learning* (2nd ed.). Englewood Cliffs, NJ: Prentice Hall.

Johnson, D. W., & Johnson, R. T. (1989). *A meta-analysis of cooperative, competitive, and individualistic goal structures.* Hillsdale, NJ: Erlbaum.

Johnson, J. T. (1986). The knowledge of what might have been: Affective and attributional consequences of near outcomes. *Personality and Social Psychology Bulletin, 12*, 136–153.

Johnson, L. B. (1971). *The vantage point: Perspectives of the presidency, 1963–69.* New York: Holt, Rinehart & Winston.

Johnson, M. K., & Raye, C. L. (1981). Reality monitoring. *Psychological Review, 88*, 67–85.

Johnson, M. K., Hashtroudi, S., & Lindsay, D. S. (1993). Source monitoring. *Psychological Bulletin, 114*, 3–28.

Johnson, R. D., & Downing, R. L. (1979). Deindividuation and valence of cues: Effects of prosocial and antisocial behavior. *Journal of Personality and Social Psychology, 37*, 1532–1538.

Johnson, T. E., & Rule, B. G. (1986). Mitigating circumstance information, censure, and aggression. *Journal of Personality and Social Psychology, 50*, 537–542.

Jones, C., & Aronson, E. (1973). Attribution of fault to a rape victim as a function of the respectability of the victim. *Journal of Personality and Social Psychology, 26*, 415–419.

Jones, E., & Kohler, R. (1959). The effects of plausibility on the learning of controversial statements. *Journal of Abnormal and Social Psychology, 57*, 315–320.

Jones, E. E. (1964). *Ingratiation: A social psychological analysis.* New York: Appleton-Century-Crofts.

Jones, E. E. (1979). The rocky road from acts to dispositions. *American Scientist, 34*, 107–117.

Jones, E. E. (1990). *Interpersonal perception.* New York: Freeman.

Jones, E. E., & Berglas, S. (1978). Control of attributions about the self through self-handicapping strategies: The appeal of alcohol and the role of underachievement. *Personality and Social Psychology Bulletin, 4,* 200–206.

Jones, E. E., & Davis, K. E. (1965). From acts to dispositions: The attribution process in social psychology. In L. Berkowitz (Ed.), *Advances in experimental social psychology* (Vol. 2, pp. 219–266). New York: Academic Press.

Jones, E. E., & Harris, V. A. (1967). The attribution of attitudes. *Journal of Experimental Social Psychology, 3,* 1–24.

Jones, E. E., & McGillis, D. (1976). Correspondent inferences and the attribution cube: A comparative reappraisal. In J. H. Harvey, W. J. Ickes, & R. F. Kidd (Eds.), *New directions in attribution research* (Vol. 1, pp. 389–420). Hillsdale, NJ: Erlbaum.

Jones, E. E., & Nisbett, R. E. (1972). The actor and the observer: Divergent perceptions of the causes of behavior. In E. E. Jones, D. E. Kanouse, H. H. Kelley, R. E. Nisbett, S. Valins, & B. Weiner (Eds.), *Attribution: Perceiving the causes of behavior* (pp. 79–94). Morristown, NJ: General Learning Press.

Jones, E. E., & Pittman, T. S. (1982). Toward a general theory of strategic self-presentation. In J. Suls (Ed.), *Psychological perspectives on the self* (pp. 231–262). Hillsdale, NJ: Erlbaum.

Jones, E. E., & Sigall, H. (1971). The bogus pipeline: A new paradigm for measuring affect and attitude. *Psychological Bulletin, 76,* 349–364.

Jones, E. E., & Wortman, C. B. (1973). *Ingratiation: An attributional approach.* Morristown, NJ: General Learning Press.

Jones, E. E., Davis, K. E., & Gergen, K. J. (1961). Role playing variations and their informational value for person perception. *Journal of Abnormal and Social Psychology, 63,* 302–310.

Jones, E. E., Rhodewalt, F., Berglas, S., & Skelton, J. A. (1981). Effects of strategic self-presentation on subsequent self-esteem. *Journal of Personality and Social Psychology, 41,* 407–421.

Jones, E. E., Rock, L., Shaver, K. G., Goethals, G. R., & Ward, L. M. (1968). Pattern of performance and ability attribution: An unexpected primacy effect. *Journal of Personality and Social Psychology, 10,* 317–340.

Jordan, M., & Sullivan, K. (1995, September 8). A matter of saving face: Japanese can rent mourners, relatives, friends, even enemies to buff an image. *Washington Post,* pp. A1, A28.

Josephson, W. D. (1987). Television violence and children's aggression: Testing the priming, social script, and disinhibition prediction. *Journal of Personality and Social Psychology, 53,* 882–890.

Judd, C. M., & Park, B. (1988). Out-group homogeneity: Judgments of variability at the individual and group levels. *Journal of Personality and Social Psychology, 54,* 778–788.

Jussim, L. (1986). Self-fulfilling prophecies: A theoretical and integrative review. *Psychological Review, 93,* 429–445.

Jussim, L., & Eccles, J. S. (1992). Teacher expectations: II: Construction and reflection of student achievement. *Journal of Personality and Social Psychology, 63,* 947–961.

Kahn, M. (1966). The physiology of catharsis. *Journal of Personality and Social Psychology, 3,* 278–298.

Kahneman, D., & Miller, D. T. (1986). Norm theory: Comparing reality to its alternatives. *Psychological Review, 93,* 136–153.

Kahneman, D., & Tversky, A. (1973). On the psychology of prediction. *Psychological Review, 80,* 237–251.

Kahneman, D., & Tversky, A. (1982). The simulation heuristic. In D. Kahneman, P. Slovic, & A. Tversky (Eds.), *Judgment under uncertainty: Heuristics and biases* (pp. 201–208). New York: Cambridge University Press.

Kahneman, D., & Tversky, A. (1983). Can irrationality be intelligently discussed? *The Behavioral and Brain Sciences, 6,* 509–510.

Kalick, S. M. (1977). *Plastic surgery, physical appearance, and person perception.* Unpublished doctoral dissertation, Harvard University.

Kalven, H., Jr., & Zeisel, H. (1966). *The American jury.* Boston: Little, Brown.

Karau, S. J., & Williams, K. D. (1993). Social loafing: A meta-analytic review and theoretical integration. *Journal of Personality and Social Psychology, 65,* 681–706.

Karlins, M., Coffman, T. L., & Walters, G. (1969). On the fading of social stereotypes: Studies in three generations of college students. *Journal of Personality and Social Psychology, 13,* 1–16.

Kassarjian, H., & Cohen, J. (1965). Cognitive dissonance and consumer behavior. *California Management Review, 8,* 55–64.

Katz, A. M., & Hill, R. (1958). Residential propinquity and marital selection: A review of theory, method, and fact. *Marriage and Family Living, 20,* 237–335.

Katz, D. (1960). The functional approach to the study of attitudes. *Public Opinion Quarterly, 24,* 163–204.

Katz, D., & Braly, K. W. (1933). Racial stereotypes of 100 college students. *Journal of Abnormal and Social Psychology, 28,* 280–290.

Kauffman, D. R., & Steiner, I. D. (1968). Conformity as an ingratiation technique. *Journal of Experimental Social Psychology, 4,* 404–414.

Kelley, H. H. (1950). The warm-cold variable in first impressions of persons. *Journal of Personality, 18,* 431–439.

Kelley, H. H. (1955). The two functions of reference groups. In G. E. Swanson, T. M. Newcomb, & E. L. Hartley (Eds.), *Readings in social psychology* (2nd ed., pp. 410–414). New York: Holt.

Kelley, H. H. (1967). Attribution theory in social psychology. In D. Levine (Ed.), *Nebraska Symposium on Motivation* (Vol. 15, pp. 192–238). Lincoln: University of Nebraska Press.

Kelley, H. H. (1972). Attribution in social interaction. In E. E. Jones, D. E. Kanouse, H. H. Kelley, R. E. Nisbett, S. Valins, & B. Weiner (Eds.), *Attribution: Perceiving the causes of behavior* (pp. 1–26). Morristown, NJ: General Learning Press.

Kelley, H. H. (1983). Love and commitment. In H. H. Kelley, E. Berscheid, A. Christensen, J. H. Harvey, T. L. Huston, G. Levinger, E. McClintock, L. A. Peplau, & D. R. Peterson (Eds.), *Close relationships* (pp. 265–314). New York: Freeman.

Kelley, H. H., & Thibaut, J. W. (1978). *Interpersonal relations: A theory of interdependence.* New York: Wiley.

Kelly, J. G., Ferson, J. E., & Holtzman, W. H. (1958). The measurement of attitudes toward the Negro in the South. *Journal of Social Psychology, 48,* 305–312.

Keltner, D. (1995). Signs of appeasement: Evidence for the distinct displays of embarrassment, amusement, and shame. *Journal of Personality and Social Psychology, 68,* 441–454.

Kenny, D. A. (1991). A general model of consensus and accuracy in interpersonal perception. *Psychological Review, 98,* 155–163.

Kenny, D. A., & La Voie, L. (1982). Reciprocity of interpersonal attraction: A confirmed hypothesis. *Social Psychology Quarterly, 45,* 54–58.

Kenny, D. A., & Nasby, W. (1980). Splitting the reciprocity correlation. *Journal of Personality and Social Psychology, 38,* 249–256.

Kenny, D. A., & Zaccaro, S. L. (1983). An estimate of variance due to traits in leadership. *Journal of Applied Psychology, 68,* 678–685.

Kenny, D. A., Albright, A., Malloy, T. E. & Kashy, D. A. (1994). Consensus in interpersonal perception: Acquaintance and the big five. *Psychological Bulletin, 116,* 245–258.

Kenny, D. A., Horner, C., Kashy, D. A., & Chu, L. (1992). Consensus at zero acquaintance: Replication, behavioral cues, and stability. *Journal of Personality and Social Psychology, 62,* 88–97.

Kenrick, D. T., & MacFarlane, S. W. (1986). Ambient temperature and horn honking: A field study of the heat/aggression relationship. *Environment and Behavior, 18,* 179–191.

Kent, M. V. (1994). The presence of others. In A. P. Hare, H. H. Blumberg, M. F. Davies, & M. V. Kent (Eds.), *Small group research: A handbook* (pp. 81–105). Norwood, NJ: Ablex.

Kerckhoff, A. C., & Back, K. W. (1968). *The June bug: A study of hysterical contagion.* New York: Appleton-Century-Crofts.

Kerckhoff, A. C., & Davis, K. E. (1962). Value consensus and need complementarity in mate selection. *American Sociological Review, 27,* 295–305.

Key, W. B. (1973). *Subliminal seduction.* Englewood Cliffs, NJ: Signet.

Key, W. B. (1989). *Age of manipulation: The con in confidence and the sin in sincere.* New York: Holt.

Kiesler, C. A., & Kiesler, S. B. (1969). *Conformity.* Reading, MA: Addison-Wesley.

Kihlstrom, J. F. (1987). The cognitive unconscious. *Science, 237,* 1445–1452.

Kihlstrom, J. F. (in press). Exhumed memory. In S. J. Lynn & N. P. Spanos (Eds.), *Truth in memory.* New York: Guilford.

Killen, J. D. (1985). Prevention of adolescent tobacco smoking: The social pressure resistance training approach. *Journal of Child Psychology and Psychiatry, 26,* 7–15.

Killian, L. M. (1964). Social movements. In R. E. L. Farris (Ed.), *Handbook of modern sociology* (pp. 426–455). Chicago: Rand McNally.

Kim, M. P., & Rosenberg, S. (1980). Comparison of two structural models of implicit personality theory. *Journal of Personality and Social Psychology, 38,* 375–389.

Kimura, D. (1987). Are men's and women's brains really different? *Canadian Psychology, 28,* 133–147.

Kinder, D. R., & Sears, D. O. (1981). Prejudice and politics: Symbolic racism versus racial threats to the good life. *Journal of Personality and Social Psychology, 40,* 414–431.

King, A. S. (1971, September). Self-fulfilling prophecies in training the hard-core: Supervisors' expectations and the underprivileged workers' performance. *Social Science Quarterly,* pp. 369–378.

Kipnis, D. M. (1957). Interaction between members of bomber crews as a determinant of sociometric choice. *Human Relations, 10,* 263–270.

Kirschner, R. H., Eckner, F., & Baron, R. C. (1986). The cardiac pathology of sudden unexplained nocturnal death in Southeast Asian refugees. *Journal of the American Medical Association, 256,* 2819–2918.

Kitayama, S., & Markus, H. R. (1994). Culture and the self: How cultures influence the way we view ourselves. In D. Matsumoto (Ed.), *People: Psychology from a cultural perspective* (pp. 17–37). Pacific Grove, CA: Brooks/Cole.

Kitayama, S., & Markus, H. R. (in press). Culture, self, and emotion: A cultural perspective to "self-conscious" emotions. In J. P. Tangney & K. W. Fisher (Eds.), *Shame, guilt, embarrassment, and pride: Empirical studies of self-conscious emotions.* New York: Guilford.

Knapp, M. L. (1980). *Essentials of nonverbal communication.* New York: Holt, Rinehart & Winston.

Knapp, M. L., & Comadena, M. E. (1979). Telling it like it isn't: A review of theory and research on deceptive communications. *Human Communication Research, 5,* 270–285.

Knox, R., & Inkster, J. (1968). Postdecision dissonance at post time. *Journal of Personality and Social Psychology, 8,* 319–323.

Kobak, R. R., & Hazan, C. (1991). Attachment in marriage: Effects of security and accuracy of working models. *Journal of Personality and Social Psychology, 60,* 861–869.

Koditz, T. A., & Arkin, R. M. (1982). An impression management interpretation of the self-handicapping strategy. *Journal of Personality and Social Psychology, 43,* 492–502.

Koehler, J. J. (1993). The base rate fallacy myth. *PSYCOLO-QUY, 4*(49).

Koestler, A. (1959). The initiates. In R. Crossman (Ed.), *The god that failed.* New York: Bantam.

Kogan, N., & Wallach, M. A. (1964). *Risk-taking: A study in cognition and personality.* New York: Holt.

Kohn, A. (1986). *No contest.* Boston: Houghton Mifflin.

Kohn, A. (1993). *Punished by rewards.* Boston: Houghlin Mifflin.

Komorita, S. S. (1995). Interpersonal relations: Mixed-motive interaction. *Annual Review of Psychology, 46,* 183–207.

Koriat, A., Lichtenstein, S., & Fischhoff, B. (1980). Reasons for confidence. *Journal of Experimental Psychology: Human Learning and Memory, 6,* 107–118.

Korte, C. (1980). Urban-nonurban differences in social behavior and social psychological models of urban impact. *Journal of Social Issues, 36,* 29–51.

Kramer, G. P., Kerr, N. L., & Carroll, J. S. (1990). Pretrial publicity, judicial remedies, and jury bias. *Law and Human Behavior, 14,* 409–438.

Kramer, T. H., Buckhout, R., & Eugenio, P. (1990). Weapon focus, arousal, and eyewitness memory: Attention must be paid. *Law and Human Behavior, 14,* 167–184.

Krantz, D. S., Grunberg, N. E., & Baum, A. (1985). Health psychology. *Annual Review of Psychology, 36,* 349–383.

Krauss, R. M., & Deutsch, M. (1966). Communication in interpersonal bargaining. *Journal of Personality and Social Psychology, 4,* 572–577.

Krauss, R. M., Freedman, J. L., & Whitcup, M. (1978). Field and laboratory studies of littering. *Journal of Experimental Social Psychology, 14,* 109–122.

Kremer, J. F., & Stephens, L. (1983). Attributions and arousal as mediators of mitigation's effects on retaliation. *Journal of Personality and Social Psychology, 45,* 335–343.

Kressel, K., & Pruitt, D. G. (1989). A research perspective on the mediation of social conflict. In K. Kressel & D. G. Pruitt (Eds.), *Mediation research: The process and effectiveness of third party intervention* (pp. 394–435). San Francisco: Jossey-Bass.

Krosnick, J. A., & Abelson, R. P. (1991). The case for measuring attitude strength in surveys. In J. Tanur (Ed.), *Questions about survey questions* (pp. 177–203). New York: Russell Sage.

Krosnick, J. A., & Alwin, D. F. (1989). Aging and susceptibility to attitude change. *Journal of Personality and Social Psychology, 57,* 416–425.

Kruglanski, A. W. (1989). *Lay epistemics and human knowledge.* New York: Plenum.

Kruglanski, A. W. (1989). The psychology of being "right": The problem of accuracy in social perception and cognition. *Psychological Bulletin, 106,* 395–409.

Kruglanski, A. W., & Mayseless, O. (1990). Classic and current social comparison research: Expanding the perspective. *Psychological Bulletin, 108,* 195–208.

Kuhn, D., Weinstock, M., & Flaton, R. (1994). How well do jurors reason? Competence dimensions of individual variation in a juror reasoning task. *Psychological Science, 5,* 289–296.

Kulik, J., & Brown, R. (1979). Frustration, attribution of blame, and aggression. *Journal of Experimental Social Psychology, 15*, 183–194.

Kunda, Z. (1990). The case for motivated reasoning. *Psychological Bulletin, 108*, 480–498.

Kunda, Z., & Nisbett, R. E. (1986). The psychometrics of everyday life. *Cognitive Psychology, 18*, 195–224.

Kunda, Z., Fong, G. T., Sanitioso, R., & Reber, E. (1993). Directional questions about self-conceptions. *Journal of Experimental Social Psychology, 29*, 63–86.

Kunz, P. R., & Woolcott, M. (1976). Season's greetings: From my status to yours. *Social Science Research, 5*, 269–278.

Kuo, Z. Y. (1961). Genesis of the cat's response to the rat. In *Instinct* (p. 24). Princeton, NJ: Van Nostrand.

Kuusinen, J. (1969). Factorial invariance of personality ratings. *Scandinavian Journal of Psychology, 10*, 33–44.

Kuykendall, D., & Keating, J. P. (1990). Altering thoughts and judgments through repeated association. *British Journal of Social Psychology, 29*, 79–86.

Kytle, C. (1969). *Gandhi, soldier of nonviolence: His effect on India and the world today.* New York: Grosset & Dunlap.

Laird, J. D. (1974). Self-attribution of emotion: The effects of expressive behavior on the quality of emotional experience. *Journal of Personality and Social Psychology, 33*, 475–486.

Laird, J. D., & Bressler, C. (1992). The process of emotional experience: A self-perception theory. In M. S. Clark (Ed.), *Review of personality and social psychology* (pp. 213–234). Newbury Park, CA: Sage.

Lamm, H., Schaude, E., & Trommsdorff, G. (1971). Risky shift as a function of group members' value of risk and need for approval. *Journal of Personality and Social Psychology, 20*, 430–435.

Lammers, H. B., & Becker, L. A. (1980). Distraction: Effects on the perceived extremity of a communication and on cognitive responses. *Personality and Social Psychology Bulletin, 6*, 261–266.

Langer, E. J. (1975). The illusion of control. *Journal of Personality and Social Psychology, 32*, 311–328.

Langer, E. J. (1989). Minding matters: The consequences of mindlessness-mindfulness. In L. Berkowitz (Ed.), *Advances in experimental social psychology* (Vol. 22, pp. 137–174). San Diego, CA: Academic Press.

Langer, E. J., & Rodin, J. (1976). The effects of choice and enhanced personal responsibility for the aged: A field experiment. *Journal of Personality and Social Psychology, 34*, 191–198.

Langer, E. J., Blank, A., & Chanowitz, B. (1978). The mindlessness of ostensibly thoughtful action: The role of "placebic" information in interpersonal interaction. *Journal of Personality and Social Psychology, 36*, 635–642.

Langer, P. A. (1986). *Preventing domestic violence against women.* Washington, DC: U.S. Department of Justice, U.S. Government Printing Office.

LaPiere, R. T. (1934). Attitudes vs. actions. *Social Forces, 13*, 230–237.

Larson, J. R., Jr., Foster-Fishman, P. G., & Keys, C. B. (1994). Discussion of shared and unshared information in decision-making groups. *Journal of Personality and Social Psychology, 67*, 446–461.

Latané, B. (1981). The psychology of social impact. *American Psychologist, 36*, 343–356.

Latané, B. (1987). From student to colleague: Retracing a decade. In N. E. Grunberg, R. E. Nisbett, J. Rodin, & J. E. Singer (Eds.), *A distinctive approach to psychological research: The influence of Stanley Schachter* (pp. 66–86). Hillsdale, NJ: Erlbaum.

Latané, B. (Ed.). (1966). Studies in social comparison: Introduction and overview. *Journal of Experimental Social Psychology, Supplement 1*, 1–5.

Latané, B., & Dabbs, J. M. (1975). Sex, group size, and helping in three cities. *Sociometry, 38*, 108–194.

Latané, B., & Darley, J. M. (1968). Group inhibition of bystander intervention. *Journal of Personality and Social Psychology, 10*, 215–221.

Latané, B., & Darley, J. M. (1970). *The unresponsive bystander: Why doesn't he help?* Englewood Cliffs, NJ: Prentice Hall.

Latané, B., & Nida, S. (1981). Ten years of research on group size and helping. *Psychological Bulletin, 89*, 308–324.

Latané, B., & Wolf, S. (1981). The social impact of majorities and minorities. *Psychological Review, 88*, 438–453.

Latané, B., Williams, K., & Harkins, S. (1979). Many hands make light work: The causes and consequences of social loafing. *Journal of Personality and Social Psychology, 37*, 822–832.

Lau, R. R., & Russell, D. (1980). Attributions in the sports pages: A field test of some current hypotheses about attribution research. *Journal of Personality and Social Psychology, 39*, 29–38.

Laughlin, P. R. (1980). Social combination processes of cooperative problem-solving groups as verbal intellective tasks. In M. Fishbein (Ed.), *Progress in social psychology* (Vol. 1, pp. 127–155). Hillsdale, NJ: Erlbaum.

Lazarsfeld, P. (Ed.). *Radio and the printed page.* New York: Duell, Sloan & Pearce.

Lazarus, R. S. (1966). *Psychological stress and the coping process.* New York: McGraw-Hill.

Lazarus, R. S. (1993). Why we should think of stress as a subset of emotion. In L. Goldberger & S. Breznitz (Eds.), *Handbook of stress: Theoretical and clinical aspects* (2nd ed., pp. 21–39). New York: Free Press.

Lazarus, R. S., & Folkman, S. (1984). *Stress, appraisal, and coping.* New York: Springer-Verlag.

LeBon, G. (1895). *The crowd.* London: F. Unwin.

Lee, D. (1959). *Freedom and culture.* Englewood Cliffs, NJ: Prentice Hall.

Lee, J. A. (1973). *The colors of love: An exploration of the ways of loving.* Don Mills, Ontario: New Press.

Lee, J. A. (1977). A typology of styles of loving. *Personality and Social Psychology Bulletin, 3*, 173–182.

Lee, J. A. (1988). Love-styles. In R. J. Sternberg & M. L. Barnes (Eds.), *The psychology of love* (pp. 38–67). New Haven, CT: Yale University Press.

Lehman, D. R., Davis, C. G., DeLongis, A., & Wortman, C. B. (1993). Positive and negative life changes following bereavement and their relations to adjustment. *Journal of Social and Clinical Psychology, 12*, 90–112.

Lehman, D. R., Lempert, R. O., & Nisbett, R. E. (1988). The effects of graduate training on reasoning. *American Psychologist, 43*, 431–442.

Leippe, M. R., Manion, A. P., & Romanczyk, A. (1992). Eyewitness persuasion: How and how well do fact finders judge the accuracy of adults' and children's memory reports? *Journal of Personality and Social Psychology, 63*, 181–197.

Leippe, M. R., & Eisenstadt, D. (1994). Generalization of dissonance reduction: Decreasing prejudice through induced compliance. *Journal of Personality and Social Psychology, 67*, 395–413.

Leishman, K. (1988, February). Heterosexuals and AIDS. *Atlantic Monthly.*

Leo, J. (1991, July 15). Hostility among the ice cubes. *U.S. News and World Report*, p. 18.

Lepper, M. R. (in press). Theory by numbers? Some concerns about meta-analysis. *Applied Cognitive Psychology.*

Lepper, M. R., & Greene, D. (1978). *The hidden costs of reward*. Hillsdale, NJ: Erlbaum.

Lepper, M. R., Greene, D., & Nisbett, R. E. (1973). Undermining children's intrinsic interest with extrinsic reward: A test of the overjustification hypothesis. *Journal of Personality and Social Psychology, 28,* 129–137.

Lepper, M. R., Keavney, M., & Drake, M. (in press). Intrinsic motivation and extrinsic rewards: A commentary on Cameron and Pierce's meta analysis. *Review of Educational Research, 64,* 363–423.

Lerner, M. J. (1980). *The belief in a just world: A fundamental decision*. New York: Plenum.

Lerner, M. J., & Simmons, C. H. (1966). Observers' reaction to the innocent victim: Compassion or rejection? *Journal of Personality and Social Psychology, 4,* 203–210.

Leventhal, H. (1970). Findings and theory in the study of fear communications. In L. Berkowitz (Ed.), *Advances in experimental social psychology* (Vol. 5, pp. 119–186). New York: Academic Press.

Leventhal, H., Watts, J. C., & Pagano, F. (1967). Effects of fear and instructions on how to cope with danger. *Journal of Personality and Social Psychology, 6,* 313–321.

Levi, P. (1986). *"Survival in Auschwitz"; and "The Reawakening: Two memoirs."* New York: Summit Books.

Levine, J., Resnick, L., & Higgins, E. T. (1993). Social foundations of cognition. *Annual Review of Psychology, 44,* 585–612.

Levine, J. M., & Moreland, R. L. (1990). Progress in small group research. *Annual Review of Psychology, 41,* 585–634.

Levine, J. M., & Moreland, R. L. (1995). Group processes. In A. Tesser (Ed.), *Advanced social psychology* (pp. 419–465). New York: McGraw-Hill.

Levine, J. M., & Russo, E. M. (1987). Majority and minority influence. In C. Hendrick (Ed.), *Group processes: Review of personality and social psychology* (Vol. 8, pp. 13–54). Newbury Park, CA: Sage.

Levine, R. A., & Campbell, D. T. (1972). *Ethnocentrism: theories of conflict, ethnic attitudes, and group behavior*. New York: Wiley.

Levine, R. V., Martinez, T. S., Brase, G., & Sorenson, K. (1994). Helping in 36 U.S. cities. *Journal of Personality and Social Psychology, 67,* 69–82.

Levinger, G. (1964). Note on need complementarity in marriage. *Psychological Bulletin, 61,* 153–157.

Levinger, G., Senn, D. J., & Jorgensen, B. W. (1970). Progress toward permanence in courtship: A test of the Kerckhoff-Davis hypothesis. *Sociometry, 33,* 427–433.

Levitas, M. (1969). *America in crisis*. New York: Holt, Rinehart & Winston.

Levy, J. S., & Morgan, T. C. (1984). The frequency and seriousness of war: An inverse relationship? *Journal of Conflict Resolution, 28,* 731–749.

Levy, S. (1979). Authoritarianism and information processing. *Bulletin of the Psychonomic Society, 13,* 240–242.

Levy-Leboyer, C. (1988). Success and failure in applying psychology. *American Psychologist, 43,* 779–785.

Lewin, K. (1943). Defining the "field at a given time." *Psychological Review, 50,* 292–310.

Lewin, K. (1948). *Resolving social conflicts: Selected papers in group dynamics*. New York: Harper.

Lewin, K. (1951). Problems of research in social psychology. In D. Cartwright (Ed.), *Field theory in social science* (pp. 155–169). New York: Harper & Row.

Lewis, C. S. (1952). *Mere Christianity*. New York: Macmillan.

Lewis, M. (1986). Origins of self-knowledge and individual differences in early self-recognition. In J. Suls & A. G. Greenwald (Eds.), *Psychological perspectives on the self* (Vol. 3, pp. 55–78). Hillsdale, NJ: Erlbaum.

Lewis, M., & Brooks, J. (1978). Self-knowledge and emotional development. In M. Lewis & L. Rosenblum (Eds.), *The development of affect* (pp. 205–226). New York: Plenum.

Leyens, J. P., Camino, L., Parke, R. D., & Berkowitz, L. (1975). Effects of movie violence on aggression in a field setting as a function of group dominance and cohesion. *Journal of Personality and Social Psychology, 32,* 346–360.

Leyens, J. P., Cisneros, T., & Hossay, J. F. (1976). Decentration as a means of reducing aggression after exposure to violent stimuli. *European Journal of Social Psychology, 6,* 459–473.

Liang, D. W., Moreland, R., & Argote, L. (1995). Group versus individual training and group performance: The mediating role of transactive memory. *Personality and Social Psychology Bulletin, 21,* 384–393.

Liberman, A., & Chaiken, S. (1992). Defensive processing of personally relevant health messages. *Personality and Social Psychology Bulletin, 18,* 669–679.

Lichtenstein, S., Fischhoff, B., & Phillips, L. D. (1982). Calibration of probabilities: The state of the art to 1980. In D. Kahneman, P. Slovic, & A. Tversky (Eds.), *Judgment under uncertainty: Heuristics and biases* (pp. 306–334). New York: Cambridge University Press.

Liebert, R. M., & Baron, R. A. (1972). Some immediate effects of televised violence on children's behavior. *Developmental Psychology, 6,* 469–475.

Liebrand, W. B. G., Messick, D. M., & Wilke, H. A. M. (Eds.). (1992). *Social dilemmas: Theoretical issues and research findings*. Oxford, England: Pergamon Press.

Lindsay, D. S. (1994). Memory source monitoring and eyewitness testimony. In D. F. Ross, J. D. Read, & M. P. Toglia (Eds.), *Adult eyewitness testimony: Current trends and developments* (pp. 27–55). New York: Cambridge University Press.

Lindsay, D. S., & Johnson, M. K. (1989). The eyewitness suggestibility effect and memory for source. *Memory and Cognition, 17,* 349–358.

Lindsay, R. C. L. (1994). Expectations of eyewitness performance: Jurors' verdicts do not follow from their beliefs. In D. F. Ross, J. D. Read, & M. P. Toglia (Eds.), *Adult eyewitness testimony: Current trends and developments* (pp. 362–384). New York: Cambridge University Press.

Lindsay, R. C. L., & Wells, G. L. (1985). Improving eyewitness identifications from lineups: Simultaneous versus sequential lineup presentation. *Journal of Applied Psychology, 70,* 556–564.

Linville, P. W., & Carlston, D. E. (1994). Social cognition and the self. In P. G. Devine, D. L. Hamilton, & T. M. Ostrom (Eds.), *Social cognition: Impact on social psychology* (pp. 144–193). San Diego: Academic Press.

Linville, P. W., Fischer, G. W., & Salovey, P. (1989). Perceived distributions of characteristics of in-group and out-group members: Empirical evidence and a computer simulation. *Journal of Personality and Social Psychology, 57,* 165–188.

Linz, D., Donnerstein, E., & Penrod, S. (1984). The effects of multiple exposure of filmed violence against women. *Journal of Communication, 34,* 130–137.

Linz, D., Donnerstein, E., & Penrod, S. (1988). Effects of long-term exposure to violent and sexually degrading depictions of women. *Journal of Personality and Social Psychology, 55,* 758–768.

Littlepage, G. E. (1991). Effects of group size and task characteristics on group performance: A test of Steiner's model. *Personality and Social Psychology Bulletin, 17,* 449–456.

Livesley, W. J., & Bromley, D. B. (1973). *Person perception in childhood and adolescence.* New York: Wiley.

Lloyd Morgan, C. (1961). C. Lloyd Morgan. In C. Murchison (Ed.), *History of psychology in autobiography* (Vol. 2, pp. 237–264). New York: Russell & Russell. (Original work published 1930)

Lloyd, S. A., & Cate, R. M. (1985). The developmental course of conflict in dissolution of premarital relationships. *Journal of Social and Personal Relationships, 2,* 179–194.

Loftus, E. F. (1979). *Eyewitness testimony.* Cambridge, MA: Harvard University Press.

Loftus, E. F. (1993). The reality of repressed memories. *American Psychologist, 48,* 518–537.

Loftus, E. F., & Hoffman, H. G. (1989). Misinformation and memory: The creation of new memories. *Journal of Experimental Psychology: General, 118,* 100–104.

Loftus, E. F., & Ketcham, K. (1994). *The myth of repressed memory: False memories and allegations of sexual abuse.* New York: St. Martin's Press.

Loftus, E. F., & Palmer, J. C. (1974). Reconstruction of automobile destruction: An example of the interaction between language and memory. *Journal of Verbal Learning and Verbal Behavior, 13,* 585–589.

Loftus, E. F., Loftus, G. R., & Messo, J. (1987). Some facts about "weapons focus." *Law and Human Behavior, 11,* 55–62.

Loftus, E. F., Miller, D. G., & Burns, H. J. (1978). Semantic integration of verbal information into a visual memory. *Journal of Experimental Psychology: Human Learning and Memory, 4,* 19–31.

London, P. (1970). The rescuers: Motivational hypotheses about Christians who saved Jews from the Nazis. In J. R. Macaulay & L. Berkowitz (Eds.), *Altruism and helping behavior* (pp. 241–250). New York: Academic Press.

Lonner, W., & Berry, J. (Eds.). (1986). *Field methods in cross-cultural research.* Beverly Hills, CA: Sage.

Lord, C. G., Lepper, M. R., & Preston, E. (1984). Considering the opposite: A corrective strategy for social judgment. *Journal of Personality and Social Psychology, 47,* 1231–1243.

Lord, C. G., Ross, L., & Lepper, M. (1979). Biased assimilation and attitude polarization: The effects of prior theories on subsequently considered evidence. *Journal of Personality and Social Psychology, 37,* 2098–2109.

Lore, R. K., & Schultz, L. A. (1993). Control of human aggression. *American Psychologist, 48,* 16–25.

Lorenz, K. (1966). *On aggression* (M. Wilson, Trans.). New York: Harcourt, Brace & World.

Losch, M., & Cacioppo, J. (1990). Cognitive dissonance may enhance sympathetic tonus, but attitudes are changed to reduce negative affect. *Journal of Experimental Social Psychology, 26,* 289–304.

Lott, A. J., & Lott, B. E. (1961). Group cohesiveness, communication level, and conformity. *Journal of Abnormal and Social Psychology, 62,* 408–412.

Lott, A. J., & Lott, B. E. (1974). The role of reward in the formation of positive interpersonal attitudes. In T. Huston (Ed.), *Foundations of interpersonal attraction.* New York: Academic Press.

Lowry, D. T., Love, G., & Kirby, M. (1981). Sex on the soap operas: Patterns of intimacy. *Journal of Communication, 31,* 90–96.

Luus, C. A. E., & Wells, G. L. (1994a). Eyewitness identification confidence. In D. F. Ross, J. D. Read, & M. P. Toglia (Eds.), *Adult eyewitness testimony: Current trends and developments* (pp. 348–361). New York: Cambridge University Press.

Luus, C. A. E., & Wells, G. L. (1994b). The malleability of eyewitness confidence: Co-witness and perserverance effects. *Journal of Applied Psychology, 79,* 714–723.

Lykken, D. T. (1984). Polygraphic interrogation. *Nature, 307,* 681–684.

Lynn, M., & Shurgot, B. A. (1984). Responses to lonely hearts advertisements: Effects of reported physical attractiveness, physique, and coloration. *Personality and Social Psychology Bulletin, 10,* 349–357.

Lysak, H., Rule, B. G., & Dobbs, A. R. (1989). Conceptions of aggression: Prototype or defining features? *Personality and Social Psychology Bulletin, 15,* 233–243.

Maass, A., & Clark, R. D. III. (1984). Hidden impact of minorities: Fifteen years of research. *Psychological Bulletin, 95,* 428–450.

Maccoby, E. E., & Jacklin, C. N. (1974). *The psychology of sex differences.* Stanford, CA: Stanford University Press.

MacCoun, R. J. (1989). Experimental research on jury decision-making. *Science, 244,* 1046–1050.

MacKinnon, C. (1993, July–August). "Turning rape into pornography: Postmodern genocide." *Ms.,* pp. 24–30.

Maclean, N. (1983). *A river runs through it.* Chicago: University of Chicago Press.

Madaras, G. R., & Bem, D. J. (1968) Risk and conservatism in group decision making. *Journal of Experimental Social Psychology, 4,* 350–366.

Magoo, G., & Khanna, R. (1991). Altruism and willingness to donate blood. *Journal of Personality and Clinical Studies, 7,* 21–24.

Maier, N. R. F., & Solem, A. R. (1952). The contribution of a discussion leader to the quality of group thinking: The effective use of minority opinions. *Human Relations, 5,* 277–288.

Main, M., Kaplan, N., & Cassidy, J. (1985). Security in infancy, childhood, and adulthood: A move to the level of representation. In T. Bretherton & E. Waters (Eds.), *Growing points of attachment theory and research. Monographs of the Society for Research on Child Development, 50,* 66–104.

Maio, G. R., & Olson, J. M. (1995). Relations between values, attitudes, and behavioral intentions: The moderating role of attitude function. *Journal of Experimental Social Psychology, 31,* 266–285.

Major, B. (1980). Information acquisition and attribution process. *Journal of Personality and Social Psychology, 39,* 1010–1023.

Malamuth, N. M. (1981). Rape fantasies as a function of exposure to violent stimuli. *Archives of Sexual Behavior, 10,* 33–47.

Malamuth, N. M. (1986). Predictors of naturalistic sexual aggression. *Journal of Personality and Social Psychology, 50,* 953–962.

Malamuth, N. M., & Briere, J., (1986). Sexual violence in the media: Indirect effects on aggression against women. *Journal of Social Issues, 42(3),* 75–92.

Malamuth, N. M., & Donnerstein, E. (1983). The effects of aggressive-pornographic mass media stimuli. In L. Berkowitz (Ed.), *Advances in experimental social psychology* (Vol. 15, pp. 103–136). New York: Academic Press.

Malamuth, N. M., Check, J., & Briere, J. (1986). Sexual arousal in response to aggression: Ideological, aggressive, and sexual correlates. *Journal of Personality and Social Psychology, 50,* 330–350.

Malpass, R. S., & Devine, P. G. (1981). Eyewitness identification: Lineup instructions and the absence of the offender. *Journal of Applied Psychology, 66,* 482–489.

Mandler, G. (1975). *Mind and emotion.* New York: Wiley.

Manis, M., Shedler, J., Jonides, J., & Nelson, T. E. (1993). Availability heuristic in judgments of set size and frequency of occurrence. *Journal of Personality and Social Psychology, 65,* 448–457.

Maracek, J., & Mettee, D. R. (1972). Avoidance of continued success as a function of self-esteem, level of esteem certainty, and responsibility for success. *Journal of Personality and Social Psychology, 22,* 90–107.

Markus, H. (1977). Self-schemata and processing information about the self. *Journal of Personality and Social Psychology, 35,* 63–78.

Markus, H., & Kitayama, S. (1991). Culture and the self: Implications for cognition, emotion, and motivation. *Psychological Review, 98,* 224–253.

Markus, H., & Nurius, P. (1986). Possible selves. *American Psychologist, 41,* 954–969.

Marlowe, D., & Gergen, K. J. (1970). Personality and social behavior. In K. J. Gergen & D. Marlowe (Eds.), *Personality and social behavior* (p. 1–75). Reading, MA: Addison-Wesley.

Marshall, G. D., & Zimbardo, P. G. (1979). Affective consequences of inadequately explained physiological arousal. *Journal of Personality and Social Psychology, 37,* 970–988.

Martz, J. M. (1991). Giving Batson's strawman a brain . . . and a heart. *American Psychologist, 20,* 162–163.

Maslach, C. (1979). Negative emotional biasing of unexplained arousal. *Journal of Personality and Social Psychology, 37,* 953–969.

Matthews, K. A. (1988). Coronary heart disease and Type A behaviors: Update on and alternative to the Booth-Kewley and Friedman (1987) quantitative review. *Psychological Bulletin, 104,* 373–380.

McAlister, A., Perry, C., Killen, J., Slinkard, L. A., & Maccoby, N. (1980). Pilot study of smoking, alcohol, and drug abuse prevention. *American Journal of Public Health, 70,* 719–721.

McArthur, L. (1972). The how and what of why: Some determinants and consequences of causal attribution. *Journal of Personality and Social Psychology, 22,* 171–193.

McArthur, L. Z. (1990). *Social perception.* Pacific Grove, CA: Brooks/Cole.

McArthur, L. Z., & Baron, R. M. (1983). Toward an ecological theory of social perception. *Psychological Review, 90,* 215–238.

McArthur, L. Z., & Resko, G. B. (1975). The portrayal of men and women in American television commercials. *Journal of Social Psychology, 97,* 209–220.

McAuley, E., & Gross, J. G. (1983). Perceptions of causality in sport: An application of the Causal Dimension Scale. *Journal of Sport Psychology, 5,* 72–76.

McCarthy, J. F., & Kelly, B. R. (1978). Aggressive behavior and its effect on performance over time in ice hockey athletes: An archival study. *International Journal of Sport Psychology, 9,* 90–96.

McCauley, C. (1989). The nature of social influence in groupthink: Compliance and internalization. *Journal of Personality and Social Psychology, 57,* 250–260.

McClelland, D. C. (1975). *Power: The inner experience.* New York: Irvington.

McClintock, C. G., & Liebrand, W. B. G. (1988). Role of interdependence structure, individual value orientation, and another's strategy in social decision making: A transformational analysis. *Journal of Personality and Social Psychology, 55,* 396–409.

McCloskey, M., & Zaragoza, M. (1985). Misleading postevent information and memory for events: Arguments and evidence against memory impairment hypotheses. *Journal of Experimental Psychology: General, 114,* 1–16.

McConahay, J. B. (1981). Reducing racial prejudice in desegregated schools. In W. D. Hawley (Ed.), *Effective school desegregation.* Beverly Hills, CA: Sage.

McConahay, J. B. (1986). Modern racism, ambivalence, and the Modern Racism Scale. In J. F. Dovidio & S. L. Gaertner (Eds.), *Prejudice, discrimination, and racism: Theory and Research* (pp. 91–125). New York: Academic Press.

McFarland, C., & Miller, D. T. (1994). The framing of relative performance feedback: Seeing the glass as half empty or half full. *Journal of Personality and Social Psychology, 66,* 1061–1073.

McFarland, C., & Ross, M. (1987). The relation between current impressions and memories of self and dating partners. *Personality and Social Psychology Bulletin, 13,* 228–238.

McGowan, W. (1993, May 7). Class ads. *Scholastic Update,* pp. 14–15.

McGrath, J. E. (1984). *Groups: Interaction and performance.* Englewood Cliffs, NJ: Prentice Hall.

McGuire, A. M. (1994). Helping behaviors in the natural environment: Dimensions and correlates of helping. *Personality and Social Psychology Bulletin, 20,* 45–56.

McGuire, W. J. (1964). Inducing resistance to persuasion. In L. Berkowitz (Ed.), *Advances in experimental social psychology* (Vol. 1, pp. 192–229). New York: Academic Press.

McGuire, W. J. (1968). Personality and susceptibility to social influence. In E. F. Borgatta & W. W. Lambert (Eds.), *Handbook of personality theory and research* (pp. 1130–1187). Chicago: Rand McNally.

McGuire, W. J. (1985). Attitudes and attitude change. In G. Lindzey & E. Aronson (Eds.), *Handbook of social psychology* (3rd ed., Vol. 2, pp. 233–346). New York: Random House.

McGuire, W. J., & McGuire, C. V. (1981). The spontaneous self-concept as affected by personal distinctiveness. In M. D. Lynch, A. A. Norem-Hebeisen, & K. J. Gergen (Eds.), *Self-concept: Advances in theory and research* (pp. 147–171). Cambridge, MA: Ballinger.

McGuire, W. J., & Padawer-Singer, A. (1976). Trait salience in the spontaneous self-concept. *Journal of Personality and Social Psychology, 33,* 743–754.

McGuire, W. J., McGuire, C. V., Child, P., & Fujioka, T. (1978). Salience of ethnicity in the spontaneous self-concept as a function of one's ethnic distinctiveness in the social environment. *Journal of Personality and Social Psychology, 36,* 511–520.

McNamara, Robert S. In retrospect: the tragedy and lessons of Vietnam / Robert S. McNamara with Brian VanDeMark. New York: Times Books, 1995.

McPherson, J. M. (1983). The size of voluntary associations. *American Sociological Review, 61,* 1044–1064.

Mead, G. H. (1934). *Mind, self, and society.* Chicago: University of Chicago Press.

Mead, M. (1977). Jealousy: Primitive and socialized. In G. Clanton & L. G. Smith (Eds.), *Jealousy* (pp. 115–127). Englewood Cliffs, NJ: Prentice Hall.

Medalia, N. Z., & Larsen, O. N. (1969). Diffusion and belief in a collective delusion: The Seattle windshield pitting epidemic. In R. Evans (Ed.), *Readings in collective behavior* (pp. 247–258). Chicago: Rand McNally.

Meier, D. (1995). *The power of their ideas.* New York: Beacon.

Meindl, J. R., & Lerner, M. J. (1985). Exacerbation of extreme responses to an out-group. *Journal of Personality and Social Psychology, 47,* 71–84.

Melara, R. D., DeWitt-Rickards, T. S., & O'Brien, T. P. (1989). Enhancing lineup identification accuracy: Two codes are better than one. *Journal of Applied Psychology, 74,* 706–713.

Menec, V. H., Perry, R. P., Struthers, C. W., Schonwetter, D. J., Hechter, F. J., & Eichholz, B. L. (1994). Assisting at-risk college students with attributional retraining and effective teaching. *Journal of Applied Social Psychology, 24,* 675–701.

Menninger, W. (1948). Recreation and mental health. *Recreation, 42,* 340–346.

Merikle, P. M. (1988). Subliminal auditory messages: An evaluation. *Psychology and Marketing, 5,* 355–372.

Merton, R. K. (1948). The self-fulfilling prophecy. *Antioch Review, 8,* 193–210.

Messick, D., & Liebrand, W. B. G. (1995). Individual heuristics and the dynamics of cooperation in large groups. *Psychological Review, 102,* 331–145.

Mettee, D., & Aronson, E. (1974). Affective reactions to appraisal from others. In T. L. Huston (Ed.), *Foundations of interpersonal attraction.* New York: Academic Press.

Mettee, D., Taylor, S. E., & Friedman, H. (1973). Affect conversion and the gain-loss effect. *Sociometry, 36,* 505–519.

Meyer, J. P. (1980). Causal attributions for success and failure: A multivariate investigation of dimensionality, formation, and consequences. *Journal of Personality and Social Psychology, 38,* 704–715.

Meyer, J. P., & Pepper, S. (1977). Need compatibility and marital adjustment in young married couples. *Journal of Personality and Social Psychology, 35,* 331–342.

Michaels, J. W., Blommel, J. M., Brocato, R. M., Linkous, R. A., & Rowe, J. S. (1982). Social facilitation and inhibition in a natural setting. *Replications in Social Psychology, 2,* 21–24.

Milgram, S. (1961). Nationality and conformity. *Scientific American, 205,* 45–51.

Milgram, S. (1963). Behavioral study of obedience. *Journal of Abnormal and Social Psychology, 67,* 371–378.

Milgram, S. (1970). The experience of living in cities. *Science, 167,* 1461–1468.

Milgram, S. (1974). *Obedience to authority: An experimental view.* New York: Harper & Row.

Milgram, S. (1976). Obedience to criminal orders: The compulsion to do evil. In T. Blass (Ed.), *Contemporary social psychology: Representative readings* (pp. 175–184). Itasca, IL: F. E. Peacock.

Milgram, S. (1977). *The individual in a social world.* Reading, MA: Addison-Wesley.

Milgram, S., & Sabini, J. (1978). On maintaining urban norms: A field experiment in the subway. In A. Baum, J. E. Singer, & S. Valins (Eds.), *Advances in environmental psychology* (Vol. 1, pp. 9–40). Hillsdale, NJ: Erlbaum.

Mill, J. S. (1974). *A system of logic ratiocinative and inductive.* Toronto: University of Toronto Press. (Original work published 1843)

Millar, M. G., & Tesser, A. (1986). Effects of affective and cognitive focus on the attitude-behavior relationship. *Journal of Personality and Social Psychology, 51,* 270–276.

Miller, C. (1972). *Women in policing.* Washington, DC: Police Foundation.

Miller, C. E., & Anderson, P. D. (1979). Group decision rules and the rejection of deviates. *Social Psychology Quarterly, 42,* 354–363.

Miller, C. T. (1982). The role of performance-related similarity in social comparison of abilities: A test of the related attributes hypothesis. *Journal of Experimental Social Psychology, 18,* 513–523.

Miller, D. T., & Ross, M. (1975). Self-serving biases in the attribution of causality: Fact or fiction? *Psychological Bulletin, 82,* 213–225.

Miller, D. T., Turnbull, W., & McFarland, C. (1990). Counterfactual thinking and social perception: Thinking about what might have been. In M. P. Zanna (Ed.), *Advances in experimental social psychology* (Vol. 23, pp. 305–331). San Diego, CA: Academic Press.

Miller, J. G. (1984). Culture and the development of everyday social explanation. *Journal of Personality and Social Psychology, 46,* 961–978.

Miller, N., & Bugelski, R. (1948). Minor studies in aggression: The influence of frustrations imposed by the in-group on attitudes expressed by the out-group. *Journal of Psychology, 25,* 437–442.

Miller, N., & Campbell, D. T. (1959). Recency and primacy in persuasion as a function of the timing of speeches and measurements. *Journal of Abnormal and Social Psychology, 59,* 1–9.

Mills, J. (1958). Changes in moral attitudes following temptation. *Journal of Personality, 26,* 517–531.

Mills, J., & Clark, M. S. (1982). Communal and exchange relationships. In L. Wheeler (Ed.), *Review of personality and social psychology* (Vol. 2, pp. 121–144). Beverly Hills, CA: Sage.

Minard, R. D. (1952). Race relations in the Pocohontas coal field. *Journal of Social Issues, 8,* 29–44.

Mischel, W. (1968). *Personality and assessment.* New York: Wiley.

Mita, T. H., Dermer, M., & Knight, J. (1977). Reversed facial images and the mere-exposure hypothesis. *Journal of Personality and Social Psychology, 35,* 597–601.

Moghaddam, F. M., Taylor, D. M., & Wright, S. C. (1993). *Social psychology in cross-cultural perspective.* New York: W. H. Freeman and Company.

Montemayor, R., & Eisen, M. (1977). The development of self-conceptions from childhood to adolescence. *Developmental Psychology, 13,* 314–319.

Montgomery, B. M. (1993). Relationship maintenance versus relationship change: A dialectical dilemma. *Journal of Social and Personal Relationships, 10,* 205–224.

Moore, J. S., Graziano, W. G., & Millar, M. C. (1987). Physical attractiveness, sex role orientation, and the evaluation of adults and children. *Personality and Social Psychology Bulletin, 13,* 95–102.

Moore, T. E. (1982). Subliminal advertising: What you see is what you get. *Journal of Marketing, 46,* 38–47.

Moore, T. E. (1992). Subliminal perception: Facts and fallacies. *Skeptical Inquirer, 16,* 273–281.

Moos, R. H., & Schaefer, J. A. (1993). Coping resources and processes: Current concepts and measures. In L. Goldberger & S. Breznitz (Eds.), *Handbook of stress: Theoretical and clinical aspects* (2nd ed., pp. 234–257). New York: Free Press.

Moreland, R. L., & Beach, R. (1992). Exposure effects in the classroom: The development of affinity among students. *Journal of Experimental Social Psychology, 28,* 255–276.

Moreland, R. L., & Zajonc, R. B. (1982). Exposure effects in person perception: Familiarity, similarity, and attraction. *Journal of Experimental Social Psychology, 18,* 395–415.

Morris, E. (Director). (1988). *Thin blue line* [Film]. New York: HBO Videos.

Morris, M. W., & Peng, K. (1994). Culture and cause: American and Chinese attributions for social and physical events. *Journal of Personality and Social Psychology, 67,* 949–971.

Morris, W. N., & Miller, R. S. (1975). The effects of consensus-breaking and consensus-preempting partners on reduction of conformity. *Journal of Experimental Social Psychology, 11,* 215–223.

Morsbach, H. (1973). Aspects of nonverbal communication in Japan. *Journal of Nervous and Mental Disease, 157,* 262–277.

Morse, D. R., Martin, J., & Moshonov, J. (1991). Psycho-somatically induced death: Relative to stress, hypnosis, mind control, and voodoo: Review and possible mechanisms. *Stress Medicine, 7,* 213–232.

Moscovici, S. (1980). Toward a theory of conversion behavior. In L. Berkowitz (Ed.), *Advances in experimental social psychology* (Vol. 13, pp. 209–239). Orlando, FL: Academic Press.

Moscovici, S. (1985). Social influence and conformity. In G. Lindzey & E. Aronson (Eds.), *Handbook of social psychology* (Vol. 2, pp. 347–412). New York: Random House.

Moscovici, S., & Nemeth, C. (1974). Minority influence. In C. Nemeth (Ed.), *Social psychology: Classic and contemporary integrations* (pp. 217–249). Chicago: Rand McNally.

Moyer, K. E. (1976). *The psychobiology of aggression.* New York: Harper & Row.

Moyer, K. E. (1983). The physiology of motivation: Aggression as a model. In C. J. Scheier & A. M. Rogers (Eds.), *G. Stanley Hall Lecture Series* (Vol. 3). Washington, DC: American Psychological Association.

Mullen, B. (1986). Atrocity as a function of lynch mob composition: A self-attention perspective. *Personality and Social Psychology Bulletin, 12,* 187–197.

Mullen, B., & Baumeister, R. F. (1987). Group effects on self-attention and performance: Social loafing, social facilitation, and social impairment. In C. Hendrick (Ed.), *Group processes and intergroup relations* (Vol. 9, pp. 189–206). Newbury Park, CA: Sage.

Mullen, B., & Johnson, C. (1988). *Distinctiveness-based illusory correlation and stereotyping: A meta-analytic integration.* Unpublished manuscript, Syracuse University.

Mullen, B., Anthony, T., Salas, E., & Driskell, J. E. (1994). Group cohesiveness and quality of decision making: An integration of tests of the groupthink hypothesis. *Small Group Research, 25,* 189–204.

Mullen, B., Johnson, C., & Salas, E. (1991). Productivity loss in brainstorming groups. *Basic and Applied Social Psychology, 12,* 3–24.

Münsterberg, H. (1908). *On the witness stand: Essays on psychology and crime.* New York: Doubleday, Page.

Murphy, S. T., & Zajonc, R. B. (1993). Affect, cognition, and awareness: Affective priming with optimal and suboptimal stimulus exposures. *Journal of Personality and Social Psychology, 64,* 723–739.

Mussen, P., & Eisenberg-Berg, N. (1977). *Roots of caring, sharing, and helping: The development of prosocial behavior in children.* San Francisco: Freeman.

My Lai: An American tragedy. (1969, December 5). *Time,* pp. 26–32.

Myers, D. G., & Arenson, S. J. (1972). Enhancement of dominant risk tendencies in group discussion. *Psychological Reports, 30,* 615–623.

Nadler, A. (1991). Help-seeking behavior: Psychological costs and instrumental benefits. In M. S. Clark (Ed.), *Prosocial behavior: Review of personality and social psychology* (Vol. 12, pp. 290–311). Newbury Park, CA: Sage.

Nadler, A., & Fisher, J. D. (1986). The role of threat to self-esteem and perceived control in recipient reactions to help: Theory development and empirical validation. In

L. Berkowitz (Ed.), *Advances in experimental social psychology* (Vol. 19, pp. 81–123). New York: Academic Press.

Nahemow, L., & Lawton, M. P. (1975). Similarity and propinquity in friendship formation. *Journal of Personality and Social Psychology, 32,* 205–213.

Nathanson, S. (1987). *An eye for an eye? The morality of punishing by death.* Totowa, NJ: Roman & Littlefield.

Neil v. Biggers, 409 U.S. 188 (1972).

Neisser, U. (1976). *Cognition and reality: Principles and implications of cognitive psychology.* San Francisco: Freeman.

Nel, E., Helmreich, R., & Aronson, E. (1969). Opinion change in the advocate as a function of the persuasibility of his audience: A clarification of the meaning of dissonance. *Journal of Personality and Social Psychology, 12,* 117–124.

Nemeth, C. J. (1986). Differential contributions of majority and minority influence. *Psychological Review, 93,* 23–32.

Nemeth, C. J., & Chiles, C. (1988). Modeling courage: The role of dissent in fostering independence. *European Journal of Social Psychology, 18,* 275–280.

Nemeth, C. J., Mayseless, O., Sherman, J., & Brown, Y. (1990). Exposure to dissent and recall of information. *Journal of Personality and Social Psychology, 58,* 429–437.

Neuberg, S. L. (1988). Behavioral implications of information presented outside of awareness: The effect of subliminal presentation of trait information on behavior in the Prisoner's Dilemma game. *Social Cognition, 6,* 207–230.

Neuberg, S. L. (1989). The goal of forming accurate impressions during social interactions: Attenuating the impact of negative expectancies. *Journal of Personality and Social Psychology, 56,* 374–386.

Neuberg, S. L. (in press). Expectancy-confirmation processes in stereotype-tinged social encounters: The moderating role of social goals. In M. P. Zanna & J. M. Olson (Eds.), *Psychology of prejudice: The seventh annual Ontario Symposium on Personality and Social Psychology.* Hillsdale, NJ: Erlbaum.

New Yorker (1957, September 21), p. 33.

New Yorker (1991, November 4), p. 106.

Newcomb, T. M. (1947). Autistic hostility and social reality. *Human Relations, 1,* 69–86.

Newcomb, T. M. (1961). *The acquaintance process.* New York: Holt, Rinehart & Winston.

Newcomb, T. M. (1963). Persistence and regression of changed attitudes: Long-range studies. *Journal of Social Issues, 19,* 3–14.

Newtson, D. (1974). Dispositional inferences from effects of actions: Effects chosen and effects forgone. *Journal of Experimental Social Psychology, 10,* 489–496.

Newtson, D. (1990). Alternatives to representation or alternative representations: Comments on the ecological approach. *Contemporary Social Psychology, 14,* 163–174.

Ng, W., & Lindsay, R. C. L. (1994). Cross-racial facial recognition: Failure of the contact hypothesis. *Journal of Cross-Cultural Psychology, 25,* 217–232.

Nichols, J. G. (1975). Casual attributions and other achievement-related cognitions: Effects of task outcome, attainment value, and sex. *Journal of Personality and Social Psychology, 31,* 379–389.

Nicholson, N., Cole, S. G., & Rocklin, T. (1985). Conformity in the Asch situation: A comparison between contemporary British and U.S. university students. *British Journal of Social Psychology, 24,* 59–63.

Niedenthal, P. M., & Kitayama, S. (1994). (Eds.). *The heart's eye: Emotional influences in perception and attention.* San Diego, CA: Academic Press.

Niedenthal, P. M., Tangney, J. P., & Gavanski, I. (1994). "If only

I weren't" versus "If only I hadn't": Distinguishing shame and guilt in counterfactual thinking. *Journal of Personality and Social Psychology, 67*, 585–595.

Nietzsche, F. W. (1918). *The genealogy of morals.* New York: Modern Library.

Nisbett, R. E. (1993). Violence and U.S. regional culture. *American Psychologist, 48*, 441–449.

Nisbett, R. E., & Ross, L. (1980). *Human inference: Strategies and shortcomings of human judgment.* Englewood Cliffs, NJ: Prentice Hall.

Nisbett, R. E., & Valins, S. (1972). Perceiving the causes of one's own behavior. In E. E. Jones, D. E. Kanouse, H. H. Kelley, R. E. Nisbett, S. Valins, & B. Weiner (Eds.), *Attribution: Perceiving the causes of behavior* (pp. 63–78). Morristown, NJ: General Learning Press.

Nisbett, R. E., & Wilson, T. D. (1977a). Telling more than we can know: Verbal reports on mental processes. *Psychological Review, 84*, 231–259.

Nisbett, R. E., & Wilson, T. D. (1977b). The halo effect: Evidence for unconscious alteration of judgments. *Journal of Personality and Social Psychology, 35*, 250–256.

Nisbett, R. E., Caputo, C., Legant, P., & Marecek, J. (1973). Behavior as seen by the actor and by the observer. *Journal of Personality and Social Psychology, 27*, 154–164.

Nisbett, R. E., Fong, G. T., Lehman, D. R., & Cheng, P. W. (1987). Teaching reasoning. *Science, 238*, 625–631.

Nisbett, R. E., Krantz, D. H., Jepson, C., & Kunda, Z. (1983). The use of statistical heuristics in everyday inductive reasoning. *Psychological Review, 90*, 339–363.

Nivison, M. E., & Endresen, I. M. (1993). An analysis of relationships among environmental noise, annoyance and sensitivity to noise, and the consequences for health and sleep. *Journal of Behavioral Medicine, 16*, 257–276.

Nixon, R. M., (1990). *In the arena: a memoir of victory, defeat, and renewal.* New York: Simon & Schuster.

Nolen-Hoeksema, S., Girgus, J. S., & Seligman, M. E. P. (1986). Learned helplessness in children: A longitudinal study of depression, achievement, and explanatory style. *Journal of Personality and Social Psychology, 51*, 435–442.

Nowak, A., Szamrej, J., & Latané, B. (1990). From private attitude to public opinion: A dynamic theory of social impact. *Psychological Review, 97*, 362–376.

Oakes, P. J., & Turner, J. C. (1980). Social categorization and intergroup behavior: Does minimal intergroup discrimination make social identity more positive? *European Journal of Social Psychology, 10*, 295–301.

Ofshe, R., & Watters, E. (1994). *Making monsters: False memories, psychotherapy, and sexual hysteria.* New York: Charles Scribner's Sons.

Ogloff, J. R., & Vidmar, N. (1994). The impact of pretrial publicity on jurors: A study to compare the relative effects of television and print media in a child sex abuse case. *Law and Human Behavior, 18*, 507–525.

Ohbuchi, K., Kamdea, M., & Agarie, N. (1989). Apology as aggression control: Its role in mediating appraisal of and response to harm. *Journal of Personality and Social Psychology, 56*, 219–227.

O'Leary, A. (1990). Stress, emotion, and human immune function. *Psychological Bulletin, 108*, 363–382.

Olson, J. M. (1990). Self-perception of humor: Evidence for discounting and augmentation effects. *Journal of Personality and Social Psychology, 62*, 369–377.

Olson, J. M., & Zanna, M. P. (1993). Attitudes and attitude change. *Annual Review of Psychology, 44*, 117–154.

Olweus, D. (1991). Bully/victim problems among schoolchildren: Basic facts and effects of a school-based intervention program. In D. Pepler & K. Rubin (Eds.), *The development and treatment of childhood aggression* (pp. 411–448). Hillsdale, NJ: Erlbaum.

Olzak, S., & Nagel, J. (1986). *Competitive ethnic relations.* New York: Academic Press.

Orbell, J. M., van de Kragt, A. J. C., & Dawes, R. M. (1988). Explaining discussion-induced comparison. *Journal of Personality and Social Psychology, 54*, 811–819.

Ortony, A., Clore, G., & Collins, A. (1988). *The cognitive structure of emotions.* Cambridge, England: Cambridge University Press.

Osborn, A. F. (1957). *Applied imagination.* New York: Scribner.

Osherow, N. (1988). Making sense of the nonsensical: An analysis of Jonestown. In E. Aronson (Ed.), *Readings about the social animal* (pp. 68–86). New York: Freeman.

O'Sullivan, C. S., & Durso, F. T. (1984). Effects of schema-incongruent information on memory for stereotypical attributes. *Journal of Personality and Social Psychology, 47*, 55–70.

Otten, C. A., Penner, L. A., & Waugh, G. (1988). That's what friends are for: The determinants of psychological helping. *Journal of Social and Clinical Psychology, 7*, 34–41.

Otto, A. L., Penrod, S. D., & Dexter, H. R. (1994). The biasing impact of pretrial publicity on juror judgments. *Law and Human Behavior, 18*, 453–469.

Ovcharchyn, C. A., Johnson, H. H., & Petzel, T. P. (1981). Type A behavior, academic aspirations, and academic success. *Journal of Personality, 49*, 248–256.

Overmeier, J. B., & Seligman, M. E. P. (1967). Effects of inescapable shock upon subsequent escape and avoidance learning. *Journal of Comparative and Physiological Psychology, 63*, 23–33.

Packard, V. (1957). *The hidden persuaders.* New York: D. McKay.

Palazzoli, M. P. (1974). *Anorexia nervosa.* London: Chaucer.

Pallak, M. S., & Pittman, T. S. (1972). General motivation effects of dissonance arousal. *Journal of Personality and Social Psychology, 21*, 349–358.

Pandey, J. (1990). The environment, culture, and behavior. In R. Brislin (Ed.), *Applied cross-cultural psychology* (pp. 254–277). Thousand Oaks, CA: Sage.

Park, B., & Rothbart, M. (1982). Perception of out-group homogeneity and levels of social categorization: Memory for the subordinate attributes of in-group and out-group members. *Journal of Personality and Social Psychology, 42*, 1051–1068.

Parke, R. D., Berkowitz, L., Leyens, J. P., West, S. G., & Sebastian, R. J. (1977). Some effects of violent and nonviolent movies on the behavior of juvenile delinquents. In L. Berkowitz (Ed.), *Advances in experimental social psychology* (Vol. 10, pp. 135–172). New York: Academic Press.

Parsons, J. E., Kaczala, C. M., & Meece, J. L. (1982). Socialization of achievement attitudes and beliefs: Classroom influences. *Child Development, 53*, 322–339.

Patch, M. E. (1986). The role of source legitimacy in sequential request strategies of compliance. *Personality and Social Psychology Bulletin, 12*, 199–205.

Patterson, A. (1974, September). *Hostility catharsis: A naturalistic quasi-experiment.* Paper presented at the meeting of the American Psychological Association, New Orleans.

Patton, P. (1989, August 6). Steve Jobs out for revenge. *New York Times Magazine*, pp. 23, 52, 56, 58.

Paulus, P. B., Dzindolet, M. T., Poletes, G., & Camacho, L. M. (1993). Perception of performance in group brainstorming: The illusion of group productivity. *Personality and Social Psychology Bulletin, 19*, 78–89.

Paulus, P. B., McCain, G., & Cox, V. (1981). Prison standards: Some pertinent data on crowding. *Federal Probation, 15,* 48–54.

Pedersen, D. M. (1965). The measurement of individual differences in perceived personality-trait relationships and their relation to certain determinants. *Journal of Social Psychology, 65,* 233–258.

Pennebaker, J. W. (1982). *The psychology of physical symptoms.* New York: Springer-Verlag.

Pennebaker, J. W. (1990). *Opening up: The healing powers of confiding in others.* New York: William Morrow.

Pennebaker, J. W., & Beale, S. K. (1986). Confronting a traumatic event: Toward an understanding of inhibition and disease. *Journal of Abnormal Psychology, 95,* 274–281.

Pennebaker, J. W., & Harber, K. D. (1993). A social stage model of collective coping: The Loma Prieta earthquake and the Persian Gulf War. *Journal of Social Issues, 49,* 125–145.

Pennebaker, J. W., & Sanders, D. Y. (1976). American graffiti: Effects of authority and reactance arousal. *Personality and Social Psychology Bulletin, 2,* 264–267.

Pennebaker, J. W., Barger, S. D., & Tiebout, J. (1989). Disclosure of traumas and health among Holocaust survivors. *Psychosomatic Medicine, 51,* 577–589.

Pennebaker, J. W., Colder, M., & Sharp, L. K. (1990). Accelerating the coping process. *Journal of Personality and Social Psychology, 58,* 528–537.

Pennington, N., & Hastie, R. (1988). Explanation-based decision making: Effects of memory structure on judgment. *Journal of Experimental Psychology: Learning, Memory, and Cognition, 14,* 521–533.

Pennington, N., & Hastie, R. (1990). Practical implications of psychological research on juror and jury decision making. *Personality and Social Psychology Bulletin, 16,* 90–105.

Pennington, N., & Hastie, R. (1992). Explaining the evidence: Tests of the story model for juror decision making. *Journal of Personality and Social Psychology, 62,* 189–206.

Pennington, N., & Hastie, R. (1993). Reasoning in explanation-based decision making. *Cognition, 49,* 123–163.

Peplau, L. A., & Perlman, D. (1982). Perspectives on loneliness. In L. A. Peplau & D. Perlman (Eds.), *Loneliness: A sourcebook of current theory, research, and therapy.* New York: Wiley.

Perrin, S., & Spencer, C. (1981). Independence or conformity in the Asch experiment as a reflection of cultural or situational factors. *British Journal of Social Psychology, 20,* 205–209.

Pertman, A. (1995, February 3). "Gestures aren't body of evidence," Ito warns. *Boston Globe,* p. 3.

Peters, L. H., Hartke, D. D., & Pohlmann, J. T. (1985). Fiedler's contingency theory of leadership: An application of the meta-analysis procedures of Schmidt and Hunter. *Psychological Bulletin, 97,* 274–285.

Peterson, C., & Seligman, M. E. P. (1984). Causal explanations as a risk factor for depression: Theory and evidence. *Psychological Review, 91,* 347–374.

Peterson, C., Seligman, M. E. P., & Vaillant, G. E. (1988). Pessimistic explanatory style is a risk factor for physical illness: A thirty-five-year longitudinal study. *Journal of Personality and Social Psychology, 55,* 23–27.

Peterson, R. D., & Bailey, W. C. (1988). Murder and capital punishment in the evolving context of the post-Furman era. *Social Forces, 66,* 774–807.

Pettigrew, T. F. (1958). Personality and sociocultural factors and intergroup attitudes: A cross-national comparison. *Journal of Conflict Resolution, 2,* 29–42.

Pettigrew, T. F. (1969). Racially separate or together? *Journal of Social Issues, 25,* 43–69.

Pettigrew, T. F. (1979). The ultimate attribution error: Extending Allport's cognitive analysis of prejudice. *Personality and Social Psychology Bulletin, 5,* 461–476.

Pettigrew, T. F. (1981). Extending the stereotype concept. In D. L. Hamilton (Ed.), *Cognitive processes in stereotyping and intergroup behavior.* Hillsdale, NJ: Erlbaum.

Pettigrew, T. F. (1985). New black-white patterns: How best to conceptualize them? *Annual Review of Sociology, 11,* 329–346.

Pettigrew, T. F., & Meertens, R. W. (1995). Subtle and blatant prejudice in western Europe. *European Journal of Social Psychology, 25,* 57–75.

Petty, R. E. (1995). Attitude change. In A. Tesser (Ed.), *Advanced social psychology* (pp. 195–255). New York: McGraw-Hill.

Petty, R. E., & Brock, T. C. (1981). Thought disruption and persuasion: Assessing the validity of attitude change experiments. In R. E. Petty, T. M. Ostrom, & T. C. Brock (Eds.), *Cognitive responses in persuasion* (pp. 55–79). Hillsdale, NJ: Erlbaum.

Petty, R. E., & Cacioppo, J. T. (1981). *Attitudes and persuasion: Classic and contemporary approaches.* Dubuque, IA: William C. Brown.

Petty, R. E., & Cacioppo, J. T. (1986). *Communication and persuasion: Central and peripheral routes to attitude change.* New York: Springer-Verlag.

Petty, R. E., & Krosnick, J. A. (1995). *Attitude strength: Antecedents and consequences.* Hillsdale, NJ: Erlbaum.

Petty, R. E., Cacioppo, J. T., & Goldman, R. (1981). Personal involvement as a determinant of argument-based persuasion. *Journal of Personality and Social Psychology, 41,* 847–855.

Petty, R. E., Wells, G. L., & Brock, T. C. (1976). Distraction can enhance or reduce yielding to propaganda: Thought disruption versus effort justification. *Journal of Personality and Social Psychology, 34,* 874–884.

Phillips, D. P. (1983). The impact of mass media violence on U.S. homicides. *American Sociological Review, 48,* 560–568.

Phillips, D. P. (1986). Natural experiments on the effects of mass media violence on fatal aggression: Strengths and weaknesses of a new approach. In L. Berkowitz (Ed.), *Advances in experimental social psychology* (Vol. 19, pp. 207–250). Orlando, FL: Academic Press.

Piliavin, I. M., Piliavin, J. A., & Rodin, J. (1975). Costs, diffusion, and the stigmatized victim. *Journal of Personality and Social Psychology, 32,* 429–438.

Piliavin, I. M., Rodin, J., & Piliavin, J. (1969). Good Samaritanism: An underground phenomenon? *Journal of Personality and Social Psychology, 13,* 289–299.

Piliavin, J. A., & Charng, H. (1990). Altruism: A review of recent theory and research. *Annual Review of Sociology, 16,* 27–65.

Piliavin, J. A., & Piliavin, I. M. (1972). The effect of blood on reactions to a victim. *Journal of Personality and Social Psychology, 23,* 253–261.

Piliavin, J. A., Dovidio, J. F., Gaertner, S., & Clark, R. D. III. (1981). *Emergency intervention.* New York: Academic Press.

Pines, A., & Aronson, E. (1983). Antecedents, correlates, and consequences of romantic jealousy. *Journal of Personality, 51,* 108–136.

Pleban, R., & Tesser, A. (1981). The effects of relevance and quality of another's performance on interpersonal closeness. *Social Psychology Quarterly, 44,* 278–285.

Plous, S. (1993). *The psychology of judgment and decision making.* New York: McGraw-Hill.

Pomerantz, E. M., Chaiken, S., & Tordesillas, R. S. (1995). Attitude strength and resistance processes. *Journal of Personality and Social Psychology 69,* 408–419.

Porter, J. R. (1971). *Black child, white child: The development* of racial attitudes. Cambridge, MA: Harvard University Press.

Porter, J. R., & Washington, R. E. (1979). Black identity and self-esteem, 1968–1978. Annual Review of Sociology. Stanford, CA: Annual Reviews.

Povinelli, D. J. (1993). Reconstructing the evolution of mind. American Psychologist, 48, 493–509.

Powledge, F. (1991). Free at last? The civil rights movement and the people who made it. Boston: Little, Brown.

Pratkanis, A. R. (1992). The cargo-cult science of subliminal persuasion. Skeptical Inquirer, 16, 260–272.

Pratkanis, A. R., & Aronson, E. (1991). Age of propaganda: The everyday use and abuse of persuasion. New York: Freeman.

Prentice-Dunn, S., & Rogers, R. W. (1989). Deindividuation and the self-regulation of behavior. In P. B. Paulus (Ed.), Psychology of group influence (2nd ed., pp. 87–109). Hillsdale, NJ: Erlbaum.

Priest, R. F., & Sawyer, J. (1967). Proximity and peership: Bases of balance in interpersonal attraction. American Journal of Sociology, 72, 633–649.

Proust, M. (1934). Remembrance of things past (C. K. Scott-Moncrieff, Trans.). New York: Random House.

Pruitt, D. G., & Carnevale, P. J. (1993). Negotiation in social conflict. Buckingham, England: Open University Press.

Pruitt, D. G., & Kimmel, M. J. (1977). Twenty years of experimental gaming: Critique, synthesis, and suggestions for the future. Annual Review of Psychology, 28, 363–392.

Pryor, J. B. (1980). Self-reports and behavior. In D. M. Wegner & R. R. Vallacher (Eds.), The self in social psychology (pp. 206–228). New York: Oxford University Press.

Pyszczynski, T. A., & Greenberg, J. (1987). Toward an integration of cognitive and motivational perspectives on social inference: A biased hypothesis-testing model. In L. Berkowitz (Ed.), Advances in experimental social psychology (Vol. 20, pp. 297–340). San Diego, CA: Academic Press.

Pyszczynski, T. A., Greenberg, J., & LaPrelle, J. (1985). Social comparison after success and failure: Biased search for information consistent with a self-serving conclusion. Journal of Experimental Social Psychology, 21, 195–211.

Quattrone, G. A. (1982). Behavioral consequences of attributional bias. Social Cognition, 1, 358–378.

Quattrone, G. A. (1986). On the perception of a group's variability. In S. Worchel & W. G. Austin (Eds.), Psychology of intergroup relations (2nd ed.). Chicago: Nelson-Hall.

Quattrone, G. A., & Jones, E. E. (1980). The perception of variability within ingroups and outgroups: Implications for the law of small numbers. Journal of Personality and Social Psychology, 38, 141–152.

Quattrone, G. A., Lawrence, C. P., Finkel, S. E., & Andrus, D. C. (1984). Explorations in anchoring: The effects of prior range, anchor extremity, and suggestive hints. Unpublished manuscript, Stanford University.

Rajecki, D. W., Kidd, R. F., & Ivins, B. (1976). Social facilitation in chickens: A different level of analysis. Journal of Experimental Social Psychology, 12, 233–246.

Ramsey, S. J. (1981). The kinesics of femininity in Japanese women. Language Sciences, 3, 104–123.

Rapoport, A., & Chammah, A. M. (1965). Prisoner's Dilemma: A study in conflict and cooperation. Ann Arbor: University of Michigan Press.

Raps, C. S., Peterson, C., Jonas, M., & Seligman, M. E. P. (1982). Patient behavior in hospitals: Helplessness, reactance, or both? Journal of Personality and Social Psychology, 42, 1036–1041.

Raskin, D. C. (1986). The polygraph in 1986: Scientific, profes-sional, and legal issues surrounding applications and acceptance of polygraph evidence. Utah Law Review, 29–74.

Reagan, R. (1990). An American life. New York: Simon & Schuster.

Rehm, J., Steinleitner, M., & Lilli, W. (1987). Wearing uniforms and aggression: A field experiment. European Journal of Social Psychology, 17, 357–360.

Reifman, A. S., Larrick, R., & Fein, S. (1988). The heat-aggression relationship in major-league baseball. Paper presented at the meeting of the American Psychological Association, San Francisco.

Reis, H. T., Nezlek, J., & Wheeler, L. (1980). Physical attractiveness in social interaction. Journal of Personality and Social Psychology, 38, 604–617.

Reis, H. T., Wheeler, L., Speigel, N., Kernis, M. H., Nezlek, J., & Perri, M. (1982). Physical attractiveness in social interaction 2: Why does appearance affect social experience? Journal of Personality and Social Psychology, 43, 979–996.

Reis, T. J., Gerrard, M., & Gibbons, F. X. (1993). Social comparison and the pill: Reactions to upward and downward comparison of contraceptive behavior. Personality and Social Psychology Bulletin, 19, 13–20.

Reiter, S. M., & Samuel, W. (1980). Littering as a function of prior litter and the presence or absence of prohibitive signs. Journal of Applied Social Psychology, 10, 45–55.

Reitzes, D. C. (1952). The role of organizational structures: Union versus neighborhood in a tension situation. Journal of Social Issues, 9, 37–44.

Reno, R., Cialdini, R., & Kallgren, C. A. (1993). The trans-situational influence of social norms. Journal of Personality and Social Psychology, 64, 104–112.

Rheingold, H. L. (1982). Little children's participation in the work of adults: A nascent prosocial behavior. Child Development, 53, 114–125.

Rhodes, R. (1995, June 19). The general and World War III. New Yorker, pp. 47–59.

Rhodewalt, F., & Davison, J. (1984). Self-handicapping and subsequent performance: The role of outcome valence and attitudinal certainty. Unpublished manuscript, University of Utah.

Richmond, V. P., McCroskey, J. C., & Payne, S. K. (1991). Nonverbal behavior in interpersonal relations. Englewood Cliffs, NJ: Prentice Hall.

Richter, C. P. (1957). On the phenomenon of sudden death in animals and man. Psychosomatic Medicine, 19, 191–198.

Rigby, K. (1988). Sexist attitudes and authoritarian personality characteristics among Australian adolescents. Journal of Research in Personality, 22, 465–473.

Ringelmann, M. (1913). Recherches sur les moteurs animés: Travail de l'homme. Annales de l'Institut National Argonomique, 2e série, tom 12, 1–40.

Riordan, C. A. (1978). Equal-status interracial contact: A review and revision of a concept. International Journal of Intercultural Relations, 2, 161–185.

Rodin, J. (1985). The application of social psychology. In G. Lindzey & E. Aronson (Eds.), Handbook of social psychology (3rd. ed., Vol. 2, pp. 805–881). New York: Random House.

Rodin, J. (1986). Aging and health: Effects of the sense of control. Science, 233, 1271–1276.

Rodin, J., & Langer, E. J. (1977). Long-term effects of a control-relevant intervention with the institutional aged. Journal of Personality and Social Psychology, 35, 897–902.

Rogers, R. (1983). Cognitive and physiological processes in fear appeals and attitude change: A revised theory of protection motivation. In J. T. Cacioppo & R. E. Petty (Eds.), Social *psychophysiology: A sourcebook* (pp. 153–176). New York: Guilford Press.

Rogers, R., & Prentice-Dunn, S. (1981). Deindividuation and anger-mediated interracial aggression: Unmasking regressive racism. *Journal of Personality and Social Psychology, 41,* 63–73.

Rohrer, J. H., Baron, S. H., Hoffman, E. L., & Swander, D. V. (1954). The stability of autokinetic judgments. *Journal of Abnormal and Social Psychology, 49,* 595–597.

Rosch, E., & Lloyd, B. (1978). (Eds.) *Cognition and categorization.* Hillsdale, NJ: Erlbaum.

Rosen, S., Bergman, M., Plester, D., El-Mofty, A., & Satti, M. (1962). Prebycusis study of a relatively noise-free population in the Sudan. *Annals of Otology, Rhinology, and Laryngology, 71,* 727–743.

Rosenbaum, M. E. (1986). The repulsion hypothesis: On the nondevelopment of relationships. *Journal of Personality and Social Psychology, 51,* 1156–1166.

Rosenberg, L. A. (1961). Group size, prior experience, and conformity. *Journal of Abnormal and Social Psychology, 63,* 436–437.

Rosenberg, M. J., Davidson, A. J., Chen, J., Judson, F. N., & Douglas, J. M. (1992). Barrier contraceptives and sexually transmitted diseases in women: A comparison of female-dependent methods and condoms. *American Journal of Public Health, 82,* 669–674.

Rosenberg, S., Nelson, S., & Vivekananthan, P. S. (1968). A multidimensional approach to the structure of personality impressions. *Journal of Personality and Social Psychology, 9,* 283–294.

Rosenhan, D. L. (1970). The natural socialization of altruistic autonomy. In J. R. Macaulay & L. Berkowitz (Eds.), *Altruism and helping behavior* (pp. 251–268). New York: Academic Press.

Rosenhan, D. L. (1973). On being sane in insane places. *Science, 179,* 250–258.

Rosenman, R. H. (1993). Relationship of the Type A behavior pattern with coronary heart disease. In L. Goldberger & S. Breznitz (Eds.), *Handbook of stress: Theoretical and clinical aspects* (2nd ed., pp. 449–476). New York: Free Press.

Rosenthal, A. M. (1964). *Thirty-eight witnesses.* New York: McGraw-Hill.

Rosenthal, R. (1994). Interpersonal expectancy effects: A 30-year perspective. *Current Directions in Psychological Science, 3,* 176–179.

Rosenthal, R., & DePaulo, B. M. (1979). Sex differences in accommodation in nonverbal communication. In R. Rosenthal (Ed.), *Skill in nonverbal communication: Individual differences* (pp. 68–103). Cambridge, MA: Oelgeschlager, Gunn & Hain.

Rosenthal, R., & Jacobson, L. (1968). *Pygmalion in the classroom: Teacher expectation and student intellectual development.* New York: Holt, Rinehart & Winston.

Rosenthal, R., Hall, J. A., DiMatteo, M. R., Rogers, P. L., & Archer, D. (1979). *Sensitivity to nonverbal communication: The PONS test.* Baltimore, MD: Johns Hopkins University Press.

Ross, L. (1977). The intuitive psychologist and his shortcomings: Distortions in the attribution process. In L. Berkowitz (Ed.), *Advances in experimental social psychology* (Vol. 10, pp. 173–220). Orlando, FL: Academic Press.

Ross, L., & Nisbett, R. E. (1991). *The person and the situation.* New York: McGraw-Hill.

Ross, L., & Samuels, S. M. (1993). *The predictive power of personal reputation versus labels and construal in the Prisoner's Dilemma game.* Unpublished manuscript, Stanford University.

Ross, L., & Ward, A. (1995). Psychological barriers to dispute resolution. In M. P. Zanna (Ed.), *Advances in experimental social psychology* (Vol. 27, pp. 255–304). San Diego, CA: Academic Press.

Ross, L., & Ward, A. (1996). Naive realism: Implications for social conflict and misunderstanding. In T. Brown, E. Reed, & E. Turiel (Eds.), *Values and knowledge.* Hillsdale, NJ: Erlbaum.

Ross, L., Amabile, T. M., & Steinmetz, J. L. (1977). Social roles, social control, and biases in social perception. *Journal of Personality and Social Psychology, 35,* 485–494.

Ross, L., Lepper, M. R., & Hubbard, M. (1975). Perseverance in self perception and social perception: Biased attributional processes in the debriefing paradigm. *Journal of Personality and Social Psychology, 32,* 880–892.

Ross, M. (1989). Relation of implicit theories to the construction of personal histories. *Psychological Review, 96,* 341–357.

Ross, M., & Conway, M. (1985). Remembering one's own past: The construction of personal histories. In R. Sorrentino & E. T. Higgins (Eds.), *Handbook of motivation and cognition* (pp. 122–144). New York: Guilford Press.

Ross, M., & McFarland, C. (1988). Constructing the past: Biases in personal memories. In D. Bar-Tel & A. Kruglanski (Eds.), *The social psychology of knowledge* (pp. 299–314). New York: Cambridge University Press.

Ross, M., & Olson, J. M. (1981). An expectancy-attribution model of the effects of placebos. *Psychological Review, 88,* 408–437.

Rothbart, M., & John, O. P. (1985). Social categorization and behavioral episodes: A cognitive analysis of the effects of intergroup contact. *Journal of Social Issues, 41*(3), 81–104.

Rothbart, M., & Park, B. (1986). On the confirmability and disconfirmability of trait concepts. *Journal of Personality and Social Psychology, 50,* 131–142.

Rotton, J., & Frey, J. (1985). Air pollution, weather, and violent crimes: Concomitant time-series analysis of archival date. *Journal of Personality and Social Psychology, 49,* 1207–1220.

Rousseau, J. J. (1930). *The social contract and discourses.* New York: Dutton.

Rubin, J., & Brown, B. (1975). *The social psychology of bargaining and negotiation.* New York: Academic Press.

Rubin, Z. (1970). Measurement of romantic love. *Journal of Personality and Social Psychology, 16,* 265–273.

Rubin, Z. (1973). *Liking and loving: An invitation to social psychology.* New York: Holt, Rinehart & Winston.

Rubin, Z., Peplau, L. A., & Hill, C. T. (1981). Loving and leaving: Sex differences in romantic attachments. *Sex Roles, 7,* 821–835.

Ruble, D. N., & Feldman, N. S. (1976). Order of consistency, distinctiveness, and consistency information and causal attribution. *Journal of Personality and Social Psychology, 31,* 930–937.

Rudolfsky, M. P. (1972). *The unfashionable human body.* New York: Doubleday.

Rule, B. G., Taylor, B. R., & Dobbs, A. R. (1987). Priming affects of heat on aggressive thoughts. *Social Cognition, 5,* 131–143.

Rusbult, C. E. (1980). Commitment and satisfaction in romantic associations: A test of the investment model. *Journal of Experimental Social Psychology, 16,* 172–186.

Rusbult, C. E. (1983). A longitudinal test of the investment model: The development (and deterioration) of satisfaction and commitment in heterosexual involvements. *Journal of Personality and Social Psychology, 45,* 101–117.

Rusbult, C. E. (1991). *Commitment processes in close relationships: The investment model.* Paper presented at the meeting of the American Psychological Association, San Francisco.

Rusbult, C. E., & Buunk, A. P. (1993). Commitment processes in close relationships: An interdependence analysis.

Journal of Social and Personal Relationships, 10, 175–204.

Rusbult, C. E., & Martz, J. (1995). Remaining in an abusive relationship: An investment model analysis of nonvoluntary dependence. *Personality and Social Psychology Bulletin, 21,* 558–571.

Rusbult, C. E., & Zembrodt, I. M. (1983). Responses to dissatisfaction in romantic involvements: A multidimensional scaling analysis. *Journal of Experimental Social Psychology, 43,* 1230–1242.

Rusbult, C. E., Johnson, D. J., & Morrow, G. D. (1986). Impact of couple patterns of problem solving on distress and nondistress in dating relationships. *Journal of Personal and Social Psychology, 50,* 744–753.

Rushton, J. P. (1975). Generosity in children: Immediate and long-term effects of modeling, preaching, and moral judgment. *Journal of Personality and Social Psychology, 31,* 459–466.

Rushton, J. P. (1989). Genetic similarity, human altruism, and group selection. *Behavioral and Brain Sciences, 12,* 503–559.

Russell, B., & Branch, T. (1979). *Second wind: The memoirs of an opinionated man.* New York: Ballantine Books.

Russell, D. (1982). The Causal Dimension Scale: A measure of how individuals perceive causes. *Journal of Personality and Social Psychology, 42,* 1137–1145.

Russell, G. W. (1983). Psychological issues in sports aggression. In J. H. Goldstein (Ed.), *Sports violence.* New York: Springer-Verlag.

Russell, J. A., Ward, L. M., & Pratt, G. (1981). Affective quality attributed to environments: A factor analytic study. *Environment and Behavior, 13,* 259–288.

Ryle, G. (1949). *The concept of mind.* London: Hutchinson.

Sacks, O. (1987). *The man who mistook his wife for a hat and other clinical tales.* New York: Harper & Row.

Sadik, N. (1991). World population continues to rise. *Futurist, 25,* 9–14.

Sadker, M., & Sadker, D. (1985, March). Sexism in the schoolroom of the '80s. *Psychology Today,* pp. 54–57.

Sadker, M., & Sadker, D. (1994). *Failing at fairness: How America's schools cheat girls.* New York: Charles Scribner's Sons.

Sakurai, M. M. (1975). Small group cohesiveness and detrimental conformity. *Sociometry, 38,* 340–357.

Salovey, P., & Rodin, J. (1985). Cognitions about the self: Connecting feeling states and social behavior. In P. Shaver (Ed.), *Self, situations, and social behavior: Review of personality and social psychology* (Vol. 6, pp. 143–166). Beverly Hills, CA: Sage.

Salovey, P., & Rodin, J. (1989). Envy and jealousy in close relationships. In C. Hendrick (Ed.), *Close relationships: Review of personality and social psychology* (pp. 221–246). Newbury Park, CA: Sage.

Salovey, P., & Rodin, J. (1991). Provoking jealousy and envy: Domain relevance and self-esteem threat. *Journal of Social and Clinical Psychology, 10,* 395–413.

Salovey, P., Mayer, J. D., & Rosenhan, D. L. (1991). Mood and helping: Mood as a motivator of helping and helping as a regulator of mood. In M. S. Clark (Ed.), *Prosocial behavior: Review of personality and social psychology* (Vol. 12, pp. 215–237). Newbury Park, CA: Sage.

Sanders, G. S. (1983). An attentional process model of social facilitation. In A. Hare, H. Bumberg, V. Kent, & M. Davies (Eds.), *Small groups.* London: Wiley.

Sanger, D. E. (1993, May 30). The career and the kimono. *New York Times Magazine,* pp. 18–19.

Sarason, I. G., Sarason, B. R., & Pierce, G. R. (1990). (Eds.). *Social support: An interactional view.* New York: Wiley.

Saxe, L. (1994). Detection of deception: Polygraph and integrity tests. *Current Directions in Psychological Science, 3,* 69–73.

Saxe, L., Dougherty, D., & Cross, T. (1985). The validity of polygraph testing: Scientific analysis and public controversy. *American Psychologist, 40,* 355–366.

Schachter, S. (1951). Deviation, rejection, and communication. *Journal of Abnormal and Social Psychology, 46,* 190–207.

Schachter, S. (1959). *The psychology of affiliation.* Stanford, CA: Stanford University Press.

Schachter, S. (1964). The interaction of cognitive and physiological determinants of emotional state. In L. Berkowitz (Ed.), *Advances in experimental social psychology* (Vol. 1, pp. 49–80). New York: Academic Press.

Schachter, S. (1977). Nicotine regulation in heavy and light smokers. *Journal of Experimental Psychology: General, 106,* 5–12.

Schachter, S., & Singer, J. E. (1962). Cognitive, social, and physiological determinants of emotional states. *Psychological Review, 69,* 379–399.

Schachter, S., & Singer, J. E. (1979). Comments on the Maslach and Marshall-Zimbardo experiments. *Journal of Personality and Social Psychology, 37,* 989–995.

Schacter, D. L. (1995, April). Memory wars. *Scientific American,* pp. 135–139.

Schafer, R. B., & Keith, P. M. (1980). Equity and depression among married couples. *Social Psychology Quarterly, 43,* 430–435.

Schaufeli, W. B. (1988). Perceiving the causes of unemployment: An evaluation of the Causal Dimension Scale in a real-life situation. *Journal of Personality and Social Psychology, 54,* 347–356.

Scheier, M. F., & Carver, C. S. (1987). Dispositional optimism and physical well-being: The influence of generalized outcome expectancies on health. *Journal of Personality, 55,* 169–210.

Scheier, M. F., Matthews, K. A., Owens, J., Magovern, G. J., Lefebvre, R. C., Abbott, R. A., & Carver, C. S. (1990). Dispositional optimism and recovery from coronary artery bypass surgery: The beneficial effects of physical and psychological well-being. *Journal of Personality and Social Psychology, 57,* 1024–1040.

Scheier, M. F., Weintraub, J. K., & Carver, C. (1986). Coping with stress: Divergent strategies of optimists and pessimists. *Journal of Personality and Social Psychology, 51,* 1257–1264.

Scherer, K. R. (1988). Cognitive antecedents of emotion. In V. Hamilton, G. H. Bower, & N. H. Frijda (Eds.), *Cognitive perspectives on emotion and motivation* (pp. 89–126). Dordrecht, the Netherlands: Kluwer.

Schlenker, B. R. (1980). *Impression management: The self-concept, social identity, and interpersonal relations.* Monterey, CA: Brooks/Cole.

Schmidt, D. E., & Keating, J. P. (1979). Human crowding and personal control: An integration of the research. *Psychological Bulletin, 86,* 680–700.

Schmitt, B. H., Gilovich, T., Goore, N., & Joseph, L. (1986). Mere presence and social facilitation: One more time. *Journal of Experimental Social Psychology, 22,* 228–241.

Schneider, D. J. (1973). Implicit personality theory: A review. *Psychological Bulletin, 79,* 294–309.

Schneider, D. J., Hastorf, A. H., & Ellsworth, P. C. (1979). *Person perception* (2nd ed.). Reading, MA: Addison-Wesley.

Schoeneman, T. J., & Rubanowitz, D. E. (1985). Attributions in the advice columns: Actors and observers, causes and reasons. *Personality and Social Psychology Bulletin, 11,* 315–325.

Schofield, J. W. (1986). Causes and consequences of the color-blind perspective. In J. F. Dovidio & S. L. Gaertner (Eds.), *Prejudice, discrimination, and racism* (pp. 231–253). Orlando, FL: Academic Press.

Schooler, J. W., & Engstler-Schooler, T. Y. (1990). Verbal overshadowing of visual memories: Some things are better left unsaid. *Cognitive Psychology, 22,* 36–71.

Schopler, J., & Insko, C. A. (1992). The discontinuity effect: Generality and mediation. In W. Stroebe & M. Hewstone (Eds.), *European review of social psychology* (Vol. 3, pp. 121–151). Chichester, England: John Wiley & Sons.

Schopler, J., Insko, C. A., Graetz, K. A., Kennedy, J., Cox, C., & Bornstein, G. (1993). Individual-group discontinuity: Further evidence for mediation by fear and greed. *Personality and Social Psychology Bulletin, 19,* 419–431.

Schroeder, D. A., Dovidio, J. F., Sibicky, M. E., Matthews, L. L., & Allen, J. L. (1988). Empathy concern and helping behavior: Egoism or altruism? *Journal of Experimental Social Psychology, 24,* 333–353.

Schroeder, D. H., & Costa, P. T., Jr. (1984). Influence of life event stress on physical illness: Substantive effects or methodological flaws? *Journal of Personality and Social Psychology, 46,* 853–863.

Schuler, E. A., & Parenton, V. J. (1943). A recent epidemic of hysteria in a Louisiana high school. *Journal of Social Psychology, 17,* 221–235.

Schulz, R. (1976). Effects of control and predictability on the physical and psychological well-being of the institutionalized aged. *Journal of Personality and Social Psychology, 33,* 563–573.

Schulz, R., & Hanusa, B. H. (1978). Long-term effects of control and predictability-enhancing interventions: Findings and ethical issues. *Journal of Personality and Social Psychology, 36,* 1202–1212.

Schuman, H., & Kalton, G. (1985). Survey methods. In G. Lindzey & E. Aronson (Eds.), *Handbook of social psychology* (3rd ed., Vol. 1, pp. 635–697). New York: Random House.

Schwartz, S. H. (1992). Universals in the content and structure of values: Theoretical advances and empirical tests in 20 countries. In M. P. Zanna (Ed.), *Advances in experimental social psychology* (Vol. 25, pp. 1–65). San Diego, CA: Academic Press.

Schwartz, S. H., & Gottlieb, A. (1976). Bystander reactions to a violent theft: Crime in Jerusalem. *Journal of Personality and Social Psychology, 34,* 1188–1199.

Schwarz, N., & Clore, G. L. (1988). How do I feel about it? Informative functions of affective states. In K. Fiedler & J. Forgas (Eds.), *Affect, cognition, and social behavior* (pp. 44–62). Toronto: Hogrefe.

Schwarz, N., Bless, H., Strack, F., Klumpp, G., Rittenauer-Schatka, H., & Simmons, A. (1991). Ease of retrieval as information: Another look at the availability heuristic. *Journal of Personality and Social Psychology, 61,* 195–202.

Scott, J. E., & Cuvelier, S. J. (1993). Violence and sexual violence in pornography: Is it increasing? *Archives of Sexual Behavior, 22,* 357–371.

Scott, J. P. (1958). *Aggression.* Chicago: University of Chicago Press.

Sears, D. O. (1981). Life stage effects on attitude change, especially among the elderly. In S. B. Kiesler, J. N. Morgan, & V. K. Oppenheimer (Eds.), *Aging: Social change* (pp. 183–204). New York: Academic Press.

Secord, P. F., & Backman, C. W. (1964). *Social psychology.* New York: McGraw-Hill.

Segal, M. W (1974). Alphabet and attraction: An unobtrusive measure of the effect of propinquity in a field setting. *Journal of Personality and Social Psychology, 30,* 654–657.

Seligman, M. E. P. (1975). *Helplessness: On depression, development, and death.* San Francisco: Freeman.

Seligman, M. E. P., & Maier, S. F. (1967). Failure to escape traumatic shock. *Journal of Experimental Psychology, 74,* 1–9.

Seligman, M. E. P., & Schulman, P. (1986). Explanatory style as a predictor of productivity and quitting among life insurance agents. *Journal of Personality and Social Psychology, 50,* 832–838.

Selye, H. (1956). *The stress of life.* New York: McGraw-Hill.

Selye, H. (1976). *Stress in health and disease.* Woburn, MA: Butterworth.

Semin, G. R., & Fiedler, K. (1989). Relocating attributional phenomena within a language-cognition interface: The case of actors' and observers' perspectives. *European Journal of Social Psychology, 19,* 491–508.

Semin, G. R., & Fiedler, K. (1991). The linguistic category model, its bases, applications, and range. In W. Stroege & M. Hewstone (Eds.), *European review of social psychology* (Vol. 1, pp. 1–30). Chichester, England: Wiley.

Sergios, P. A., & Cody, J. (1985). Physical attractiveness and social assertiveness skills in male homosexual dating behavior and partner selection. *Journal of Social Psychology, 125,* 505–514.

Seta, J. J., Seta, C. E., & Wang, M. A. (1990). Feelings of negativity and stress: An averaging-summation analysis of impressions of negative life experiences. *Personality and Social Psychology Bulletin, 17,* 376–384.

Shaffer, D. R. (1986). Is mood-induced altruism a form of hedonism? *Humboldt Journal of Social Relations, 13,* 195–216.

Sharan, S. (1980). Cooperative learning in small groups. *Review of Educational Research, 50,* 241–271.

Sharp, F. C. (1928). *Ethics.* New York: Century.

Shaver, K. (1970). Defensive attribution: Effects of severity and relevance on the responsibility assigned for an accident. *Journal of Personality and Social Psychology, 14,* 101–113.

Shaver, P. R., Hazan, C., & Bradshaw, D. (1988). Love as attachment: The integration of three behavioral systems. In R. J. Sternberg & M. L. Barnes (Eds.), *The psychology of love* (pp. 68–99). New Haven, CT: Yale University Press.

Shaver, P. R., Schwartz, J., Kirson, D., & O'Connor, C. (1987). Emotion knowledge: Further exploration of a prototype approach. *Journal of Personality and Social Psychology, 52,* 1061–1086.

Shavitt, S. (1989). Operationalizing functional theories of attitude. In A. R. Pratkanis, S. J. Breckler, & A. G. Greenwald (Eds.), *Attitude structure and function* (pp. 311–337). Hillsdale, NJ: Erlbaum.

Shavitt, S. (1990). The role of attitude objects in attitude function. *Journal of Experimental Social Psychology, 26,* 124–148.

Shaw, M. E. (1971). *Group dynamics: The psychology of small group behavior.* New York: McGraw-Hill.

Sheehan, S. (1975). Profiles: A welfare mother in Brooklyn. *New Yorker,* pp. 42–46.

Sheehan, S. (1982). *Is there no place on earth for me?* Boston: Houghton Mifflin.

Sheppard, B. H., Hartwick, J., & Warshaw, P. R. (1988). The theory of reasoned action: A meta-analysis of past research with recommendations for modifications and future research. *Journal of Consumer Research, 15,* 325–343.

Shepperd, J. A. (1993). Productivity loss in performance groups: A motivation analysis. *Psychological Bulletin, 113,* 67–81.

Sherif, M. (1966). *In common predicament: Social psychology of intergroup conflict and cooperation.* Boston: Houghton Mifflin.

Sherif, M., & Sherif, C. W. (1969). *Social psychology.* New York: Harper & Row.

Sherif, M., Harvey, O. J., White, J., Hood, W., & Sherif, C. (1961). Intergroup conflict and cooperation: The robber's cave experiment. Norman: University of Oklahoma, Institute of Intergroup Relations.

Sherman, I. W., & Berk, R. A. (1984). The specific deterrent effects or arrest for domestic assault. *American Sociological Review, 49*, 261–272.

Sherman, L. W. (1992). The influence of criminology on criminal law: Evaluating arrests for misdemeanor domestic violence. *Journal of Criminal Law and Criminology, 83*, 1–45.

Sherrod, D. R. (1974). Crowding, perceived control, and behavioral aftereffects. *Journal of Applied Social Psychology, 4*, 171–186.

Sherrod, D. R., & Cohen, S. (1979). Density, personal control, and design. In A. Baum & J. R. Aiello (Eds.), *Residential crowding and design* (pp. 217–227). New York: Plenum.

Shettel-Neuber, J., Bryson, J. B., & Young, L. E. (1978). Physical attractiveness of the "other person" and jealousy. *Personality and Social Psychology Bulletin, 4*, 612–615.

Shotland, R. L., & Straw, M. K. (1976). Bystander response to an assault: When a man attacks a woman. *Journal of Personality and Social Psychology, 34*, 990–999.

Shupe, L. M. (1954). Alcohol and crimes: A study of the urine alcohol concentration found in 882 persons arrested during or immediately after the commission of a felony. *Journal of Criminal Law and Criminology, 33*, 661–665.

Sigall, H., & Aronson, E. (1969). Liking for an evaluator as a function of her physical attractiveness and nature of the evaluations. *Journal of Experimental Social Psychology, 5*, 96–100.

Sigall, H., & Ostrove, N. (1975). Beautiful but dangerous: Effects of offender attractiveness and nature of the crime on juridic judgment. *Journal of Personality and Social Psychology, 31*, 410–414.

Sigall, H., & Page, R. (1971). Current stereotypes: A little fading, a little faking. *Journal of Personality and Social Psychology, 18*, 247–255.

Silver, L. B., Dublin, C. C., & Lourie, R. S. (1969). Does violence breed violence? Contributions from a study of the child abuse syndrome. *American Journal of Psychiatry, 126*, 404–407.

Silverstein, B., Perdue, L., Peterson, B., & Kelly, E. (1986). The role of the mass media in promoting a thin standard of bodily attractiveness for women. *Sex Roles, 14*, 519–532.

Silverstein, B., Peterson, B., & Perdue, L. (1986). Some correlates of the thin standard of bodily attractiveness for women. *International Journal of Eating Disorders, 5*, 895–906.

Sime, J. D. (1983). Affiliative behavior during escape to building exits. *Journal of Environmental Psychology, 3*, 21–41.

Simmons, C. H., Vom Kolke, A., & Shimizu, H. (1986). Attitudes toward romantic love among American, German, and Japanese students. *Journal of Social Psychology, 126*, 327–336.

Simon, H. A. (1990). A mechanism for social selection and successful altruism. *Science, 250*, 1665–1668

Simonton, D. K. (1984). *Genius, creativity, and leadership: Historiometric inquiries.* Cambridge, MA: Harvard University Press.

Simonton, D. K. (1985). Intelligence and personal influence in groups: Four nonlinear models. *Psychological Review, 92*, 532–547.

Simonton, D. K. (1987). *Why presidents succeed: A political psychology of leadership.* New Haven, CT: Yale University Press.

Simonton, D. K. (1992). Presidential greatness and personality: A response to McCann (1992). *Journal of Personality and Social Psychology, 63*, 676–679.

Simpson, G., & Yinger, J. M., (1885). *Racial and cultural minorities.* New York: Plenum.

Simpson, J. A. (1987). The dissolution of romantic relationships: Factors involved in relationship stability and emotional distress. *Journal of Personality and Social Psychology, 53*, 683–692.

Simpson, J. A. (1990). Influence of attachment styles on romantic relationships. *Journal of Personality and Social Psychology, 59*, 971–980.

Simpson, J. A., Rholes, W. S., & Nelligan, J. S. (1992). Support seeking and support giving within couples in an anxiety-provoking situation: The role of attachment styles. *Journal of Personality and Social Psychology, 62*, 434–446.

Sinclair, R. C., Hoffman, C., Mark, M. M., Martin, L. L., & Pickering, T. L. (1994). Construct accessibility and the misattribution of arousal: Schachter and Singer revisited. *Psychological Science, 5*, 15–19.

Sinclair, R. C., Mark, M. M., & Clore, G. L. (1994). Mood-related persuasion depends on (mis)attributions. *Social Cognition, 12*, 309–326.

Singelis, T. M. (1994). The measurement of independent and interdependent self-construals. *Personality and Social Psychology Bulletin, 20*, 580–591.

Singer, J. E., Baum, C. S., Baum, A., & Thew, B. D. (1982). Mass psychogenic illness: The case for social comparison. In M. J. Colligan, J. W. Pennebaker, & L. R. Murphy (Eds.), *Mass psychogenic illness: A social psychological analysis* (pp. 155–169). Hillsdale, NJ: Erlbaum.

Singer, M. (1990, January 29). Talk of the town. *New Yorker*, pp. 25–26.

Sirois, F. (1982). Perspectives on epidemic hysteria. In M. J. Colligan, J. W. Pennebaker, & L. R. Murphy (Eds.), *Mass psychogenic illness: A social psychological analysis* (pp. 217–236). Hillsdale, NJ: Erlbaum.

Skinner, B. F. (1938). *The behavior of organisms.* New York: Appleton-Century-Crofts.

Slavin, R. E. (1980). Cooperative learning and desegregation. Paper presented at the meeting of the American Psychological Association.

Sloan, J. H., Kellerman, A. L., Reay, D. T., Ferris, J. A., Koepsell, T., Rivara, F. P., Rice, C., Gray, L., & LoGerfo, J. (1988). Handgun regulations, crime, assaults, and homicide: A tale of two cities. *New England Journal of Medicine, 319*, 1256–1261.

Slovic, P., & Lichtenstein, S. (1971). Comparison of Bayesian and regression approaches to the study of information processing in judgment. *Organizational Behavior and Human Performance, 6*, 649–744.

Slovic, P., Fischhoff, B., & Lichtenstein, S. (1976). Cognitive processes and societal risk taking. In J. S. Carroll & J. W. Payne (Eds.), *Cognition and social behavior* (pp. 165–184). Hillsdale, NJ: Erlbaum.

Slusher, M. P., & Anderson, C. A. (1989). Belief perseverance and self-defeating behavior. In R. Curtis (Ed.), *Self-defeating behaviors: Experimental research, clinical impressions, and practical implications* (pp. 11–40). New York: Plenum.

Smith, D. D. (1976). The social content of pornography. *Journal of Communication, 26*, 16–24.

Smith, K. D., Keating, J. P., & Stotland, E. (1989). Altruism reconsidered: The effect of denying feedback on a victim's status to empathic witnesses. *Journal of Personality and Social Psychology, 57*, 641–650.

Smith, M. B., Bruner, J., & White, R. W. (1956). *Opinions and personality.* New York: Wiley.

Smith, R. E., Wheeler, G., & Diener, E. (1975). Faith without works: Jesus people, resistance to temptation, and altruism. *Journal of Applied Psychology, 5*, 320–330.

Smith, S. S., & Richardson, D. (1983). Amelioration of deception and harm in psychological research: The important role of debriefing. *Journal of Personality and Social Psychology, 44,* 1075–1082.

Smith, V. L. (1991). Prototypes in the courtroom: Lay representation of legal concepts. *Journal of Personality and Social Psychology, 61,* 857–872.

Smith, V. L., & Ellsworth, P. C. (1987). The social psychology of eyewitness accuracy: Misleading questions and communicator expertise. *Journal of Applied Psychology, 72,* 294–300.

Smith, V. L., Kassin, S. M., & Ellsworth, P. C. (1989). Eyewitness accuracy and confidence: Within- versus between-subjects correlations. *Journal of Applied Psychology, 74,* 356–359.

Snyder, C. R., & Higgins, R. L. (1988). Excuses: Their effective role in the negotiation of reality. *Psychological Bulletin, 104,* 23–35.

Snyder, C. R., Irving, L. M., & Anderson, J. R. (1991). Hope and health. In C. R. Snyder & D. R. Forsyth (Eds.), *Handbook of clinical and social psychology* (pp. 285–305). New York: Pergamon.

Snyder, C. R., Smith, T. W., Augelli, R. W., & Ingram, R. E. (1985). On the self-serving function of social anxiety: Shyness as a self-handicapping strategy. *Journal of Personality and Social Psychology, 48,* 970–980.

Snyder, M. (1984). When belief creates reality. In L. Berkowitz (Ed.), *Advances in experimental social psychology* (Vol. 18, pp. 247–305). Orlando, FL: Academic Press.

Snyder, M., & DeBono, K. G. (1989). Understanding the functions of attitudes: Lessons for personality and social behavior. In A. R. Pratkanis, S. J. Breckler, & A. G. Greenwald (Eds.), *Attitude structure and function* (pp. 339–359). Hillsdale, NJ: Erlbaum.

Snyder, M., & Ickes, W. (1985). Personality and social behavior. In G. Lindzey & E. Aronson (Eds.), *The handbook of social psychology* (3rd ed., Vol. 2, pp. 883–947). Hillsdale, NJ: Erlbaum.

Snyder, M., & Ickes, W. (1985). Personality and social behavior. In G. Lindzey & E. Aronson (Eds.), *Handbook of social psychology* (3rd ed., pp. 883–947). New York: Random House.

Snyder, M., & Swann, W. B., Jr. (1978). Hypothesis-testing procedures in social interaction. *Journal of Personality and Social Psychology, 36,* 1202–1212.

Snyder, M., Tanke, E. D., & Berscheid, E. (1977). Social perception and interpersonal behavior: On the self-fulfilling nature of social stereotypes. *Journal of Personality and Social Psychology, 35,* 656–666.

Soames, R. F. (1988). Effective and ineffective use of fear in health promotion campaigns. *American Journal of Public Health, 78,* 163–167.

Solomon, L. Z., Solomon, H., & Stone, R. (1978). Helping as a function of number of bystanders and ambiguity of emergency. *Personality and Social Psychology Bulletin, 4,* 318–321.

Sontag, S. (1978). *Illness as metaphor.* New York: Farrar, Straus & Giroux.

Sontag, S. (1988). *AIDS and its metaphors.* New York: Farrar, Straus & Giroux.

Sorenson, T. C. (1966). *Kennedy.* New York: Bantam.

Sorrentino, R. M. (1991). Evidence for altruism: The lady is still in waiting. *Psychological Inquiry, 2,* 147–150.

Sorrentino, R. M., & Field, N. (1986). Emergent leadership over time: The functional value of positive motivation. *Journal of Personality and Social Psychology, 50,* 1091–1099.

Span, P. (1994, December 14). The gene team: Innocence project fights injustice with DNA testing. *Washington Post,* pp. C1, C14.

Spencer, S. J., & Steele, C. M. (1996). *Under suspicion of inability: Stereotype vulnerability and women's math perfor-*

mance. Unpublished manuscript, State University of New York at Buffalo.

Spencer, S. J., Josephs, R. A., & Steele, C. M. (in press). Low self-esteem: The uphill battle for self-integrity. In R. F. Baumeister (Ed.), *Self-esteem and the puzzle of low self-regard* (pp. 21–36). New York: Wiley.

Spiegel, D., Bloom, J. R., Krawmer, H. C., & Gottheil, E. (1989). Psychological support for cancer patients. *Lancet, 2,* 1447.

Sporer, S. L. (1994). Decision times and eyewitness identification accuracy in simultaneous and sequential lineups. In D. F. Ross, J. D. Read, M. P. Toglia (Eds.), *Adult eyewitness testimony: Current trends and developments* (pp. 300–327). New York: Cambridge University Press.

Sporer, S. L., Penrod, S., Read, D., & Cutler, B. (1995). Choosing, confidence, and accuracy: A meta-analysis of the confidence-accuracy relation in eyewitness identification studies. *Psychological Bulletin, 118,* 315–327.

Stahyl, S. M., & Lebedun, M. (1974). Mystery gas: An analysis of mass hysteria. *Journal of Health and Social Behavior, 15,* 44–50.

Stangor, C., & McMillan, D. (1992). Memory for expectancy-congruent and expectancy-incongruent information: A review of the social and social developmental literatures. *Psychological Bulletin, 111,* 42–61.

Stasser, G., & Titus, W. (1985). Pooling of unshared information in group decision making: Biased information sampling during discussion. *Journal of Personality and Social Psychology, 48,* 1467–1478.

Stasser, G., Stella, N., Hanna, C., & Colella, A. (1984). The majority effect in jury deliberations: Number of supporters versus number of supporting arguments. *Law and Psychology Review, 8,* 115–127.

Stasser, G., Taylor, L. A., & Hanna, C. (1989). Information sampling in structured and unstructured discussions in three- and six-person groups. *Journal of Personality and Social Psychology, 57,* 67–78.

Stasson, M., & Fishbein, M. (1990). The relation between perceived and preventive action: A within-subject analysis of perceived driving risk and intentions to wear seatbelts. *Journal of Applied Social Psychology, 20,* 1541–1557.

Staub, E. (1974). Helping a distressed person: Social, personality, and stimulus determinants. In L. Berkowitz (Ed.), *Advances in experimental social psychology* (Vol. 7, pp. 293–341). New York: Academic Press.

Steblay, N. M. (1987). Helping behavior in rural and urban environments: A meta-analysis. *Psychological Bulletin, 102,* 346–356.

Steele, C. M. (1988). The psychology of self-affirmation: Sustaining the integrity of the self. In L. Berkowitz (Ed.), *Advances in experimental social psychology* (Vol. 21, pp. 261–302). New York: Academic Press.

Steele, C. M. (1992, April). Race and the schooling of black Americans. *Atlantic Monthly,* pp. 68–78.

Steele, C. M., & Aronson, J. (1995). Stereotype-threat and the intellectual test performance of African-Americans. *Journal of Personality and Social Psychology, 69,* 797–811.

Steele, C. M., & Josephs, R. A. (1990). Alcohol myopia: Its prized and dangerous effects. *American Psychologist, 45,* 921–933.

Steele, C. M., & Liu, T. J. (1981). Making the dissonance act unreflective of the self: Dissonance avoidance and the expectancy of a value affirming response. *Personality and Social Psychology Bulletin, 7,* 383–387.

Steele, C. M., & Liu, T. J. (1983). Dissonance processes as self affirmation. *Journal of Personality and Social Psychology, 45,* 5–19.

Steele, C. M., & Southwick, L. (1985). Alcohol and social

behavior I: The psychology of drunken excess. *Journal of Personality and Social Psychology, 48,* 18–34.

Steele, C. M., Hoppe, H., & Gonzales, J. (1986). *Dissonance and the lab coat: Self-affirmation and the free choice paradigm.* Unpublished manuscript, University of Washington.

Steele, C. M., Spencer, S. J., & Josephs, R. (1992). *Seeking self-relevant information: The effects of self-esteem and stability of the information.* Unpublished manuscript, University of Michigan.

Steele, C. M., Spencer, S. J., & Lynch, M. (1993). Self-image resilience and dissonance: The role of affirmational resources. *Journal of Personality and Social Psychology, 64,* 885–896.

Steele, C. M., Spencer, S. J., & Lynch, M. (in press). Dissonance and self-affirmation resources: Resilience against self-image threats. *Journal of Personality and Social Psychology.*

Steffen, V. J. (1990). Men's motivation to perform the testicle self-exam: Effects of prior knowledge and an educational brochure. *Journal of Applied Social Psychology, 20,* 681–702.

Steinbeck, J. (1988/1961). *Travels with Charley: In search of America.* New York: Penguin Books.

Steiner, I. D. (1972). *Group process and productivity.* New York: Academic Press.

Steiner, I. D. (1974). Whatever happened to the group in social psychology? *Journal of Experimental Social Psychology, 10,* 94–108.

Steiner, I. D., & Rajaratnam, N. A. (1961). A model for the comparison of individual and group performance scores. *Behavioral Science, 11,* 273–283.

Stephan, W. G. (1978). School desegregation: An evaluation of predictions made in Brown vs. Board of Education. *Psychological Bulletin, 85,* 217–238.

Stephan, W. G. (1985). Intergroup relations. In G. Lindzey & E. Aronson (Eds.), *Handbook of social psychology* (Vol. 2, pp. 599–658). New York:. Random House.

Stern, L. B., & Dunning, D. (1994). Distinguishing accurate from inaccurate eyewitness identifications: A reality monitoring approach. In D. F. Ross, J. D. Read, & M. P. Toglia (Eds.), *Adult eyewitness testimony: Current trends and developments* (pp. 273–299). New York: Cambridge University Press.

Stern, M., & Hildebrandt, K. A. (1986). Prematurity stereotyping: Effects on mother-infant interaction. *Child Development, 57,* 308–315.

Stern, P. C., & Aronson, E. (1984). *Energy use: The human dimension.* New York: Freeman.

Sternberg, R. J. (1986). A triangular theory of love. *Psychological Review, 93,* 119–135.

Sternberg, R. J. (1988). *The triangle of love.* New York: Basic Books.

Sternberg, R. J., & Grajek, S. (1984). The nature of love. *Journal of Personality and Social Psychology, 47,* 312–329.

Stewart, D. D., & Stasser, G. (in press). Expert role assignment and information sampling during collective recall and decision making. *Journal of Personality and Social Psychology.*

Stich, S. (1990). *The fragmentation of reason: Preface to a pragmatic theory of cognitive evaluation.* Cambridge, MA: MIT Press.

Stogdill, R. M. (1974). *Handbook of leadership.* New York: Free Press.

Stokols, D., & Altman, I. (1987). *Handbook of environmental psychology.* New York: Wiley.

Stone, J., Aronson, E., Crain, A. L., Winslow, M. P., & Fried, C. (1994). Inducing hypocrisy as a means of encouraging young adults to use condoms. *Personality and Social Psychology Bulletin, 20,* 116–128.

Storms, M. (1973). Videotape and the attribution process: Reversing actors' and observers' points of view. *Journal of Personality and Social Psychology, 27,* 165–175.

Storms, M. D., & McCaul, K. D. (1976). Attribution processes and emotional exacerbation of dysfunctional behavior. In J. H. Harvey, W. J. Ickes, & R. F. Kidd (Eds.), *New directions in attribution research* (Vol. 1, pp. 143–164). Hillsdale, NJ: Erlbaum.

Storms, M. D., & Nisbett, R. E. (1970). Insomnia and the attribution process. *Journal of Personality and Social Psychology, 16,* 319–328.

Stouffer, S. A., Suchman, E. A., DeVinney, L. C., Star, S. A., & Williams, R. M., Jr. (1949). *The American soldier: Adjustment during army life* (Vol. 1). Princeton, NJ: Princeton University Press.

Strack, F., Martin, L. L., & Stepper, S. (1988). Inhibiting and facilitating conditions of the human smile: A nonobtrusive test of the facial feedback hypothesis. *Journal of Personality and Social Psychology, 54,* 768–777.

Strauman, T. J., & Higgins, E. T. (1987). Automatic activation of self-discrepancies and emotional syndromes: When cognitive structures influence affect. *Journal of Personality and Social Psychology, 53,* 1004–1014.

Strauss, M. A., & Gelles, R. J. (1980). *Behind closed doors: Violence in the American family.* New York: Anchor/ Doubleday.

Stretch, R. H., & Figley, C. R. (1980). Beauty and the boast: Predictors of interpersonal attraction in a dating experiment. *Psychology, A Quarterly Journal of Human Behavior, 17,* 34–43.

Stroebe, W., & Diehl, M. (1994). Why groups are less effective than their members: On productivity losses in idea-generating groups. *European Review of Social Psychology, 5,* 271–303.

Strube, M., & Garcia, J. (1981). A meta-analysis investigation of Fiedler's contingency model of leadership effectiveness. *Psychological Bulletin, 90,* 307–321.

Struckman-Johnson, C., Struckman-Johnson, D., Gilliland, R. C., & Ausman, A. (1994). Effect of persuasive appeals in AIDS PSAs and condom commercials on intentions to use condoms. *Journal of Applied Social Psychology, 24,* 2223–2244.

Suls, J. M., & Miller, R. L. (Eds.). (1977). *Social comparison processes: Theoretical and empirical perspectives.* Washington, DC: Hemisphere/Halstead.

Suls, J., & Fletcher, B. (1983). Social comparison in the social and physical sciences: An archival study. *Journal of Personality and Social Psychology, 44,* 575–580.

Suls, J., & Wills, T. A. (1991). (Eds.). *Social comparison: Contemporary theory and research.* Hillsdale, NJ: Erlbaum.

Summers, G., & Feldman, N. S. (1984). Blaming the victim versus blaming the perpetrator: An attributional analysis of spouse abuse. *Journal of Social and Clinical Psychology, 2,* 339–347.

Swann, W. B., Jr. (1984). Quest for accuracy in person perception: A matter of pragmatics. *Psychological Review, 91,* 457–477.

Swann, W. B., Jr. (1990). To be adored or to be known? The interplay of self-enhancement and self-verification. In R. M. Sorrentino & E. T. Higgins (Eds.), *Motivation and cognition* (pp. 404–448). New York: Guilford Press.

Swann, W. B., Jr., & Ely, R. J. (1984). A battle of the wills: Self-verification versus behavioral confirmation. *Journal of Personality and Social Psychology, 46,* 1287–1302.

Swann, W. B., Jr., & Hill, C. A. (1982). When our identities are mistaken: Reaffirming self-conceptions through social interaction. *Journal of Personality and Social Psychology, 43,* 59–66.

Swann, W. B., Jr., & Pelham, B. W. (1988). *The social construction of identity: Self-verification through friend and intimate selection.* Unpublished manuscript, University of Texas-Austin.

Swann, W. B. Jr., & Schroeder, D. B. (1995). The search for beauty and truth: A framework for understanding reactions to evaluations. *Personality and Social Psychology Bulletin, 21,* 1307–1318.

Swann, W. B., Jr., Hixon, G., & De La Ronde, C. (1992). Embracing the bitter "truth": Negative self-concepts and marital commitment. *Psychological Science, 3,* 118–121.

Swap, W. C. (1977). Interpersonal attraction and repeated exposure to rewarders and punishers. *Personality and Social Psychology Bulletin, 3,* 248–251.

Sweeney, P. D., Anderson, K., & Bailey, S. (1986). Attributional style in depression: A meta-analytic review. *Journal of Personality and Social Psychology, 50,* 974–991.

Swim, J., Borgida, E., Maruyama, G., & Myers, D. G. (1989). Joan McKay vs. John McKay: Do gender stereotypes bias evaluations? *Psychological Bulletin, 105,* 409–429.

Tajfel, H. (1982a). *Social identity and intergroup relations.* Cambridge, England: Cambridge University Press.

Tajfel, H. (1982b). Social psychology of intergroup relations. *Annual Review of Psychology, 33,* 1–39.

Tajfel, H., & Billig, M. (1974). Familiarity and categorization in intergroup behavior. *Journal of Experimental Social Psychology, 10,* 159–170.

Tajfel, H., & Turner, J. C. (1979). An integrative theory of social contact. In W. Austin & S. Worchel (Eds.), *The social psychology of intergroup relations.* Monterey, CA: Brooks/Cole.

Tanford, S., & Penrod, S. (1984). Social influence model: A formal integration of research on majority and minority influence processes. *Psychological Bulletin, 95,* 189–225.

Tang, S., & Hall, V. C. (in press). The overjustification effect: A meta-analysis. *Applied Cognitive Psychology.*

Tavris, C. (1989). *Anger: The misunderstood emotion.* New York: Touchstone/Simon & Schuster.

Taylor, S. E. (1981). A categorization approach to stereotyping. In D. L. Hamilton (Ed.), *Cognitive processes in stereotyping and intergroup relations* (pp. 418–429). Hillsdale, NJ: Erlbaum.

Taylor, S. E. (1981). The interface of cognitive and social psychology. In J. Harvey (Ed.), *Cognition, social behavior, and the environment* (pp. 189–211). Hillsdale, NJ: Erlbaum.

Taylor, S. E. (1985). *Health psychology.* New York: Random House.

Taylor, S. E. (1989). *Positive illusions: Creative self-deception and the healthy mind.* New York: Basic Books.

Taylor, S. E., & Aspinwall, L. G. (1993). Coping with chronic illness. In L. Goldberger & S. Breznitz (Eds.), *Handbook of stress: Theoretical and clinical aspects* (2nd ed., pp. 511-531). New York: Free Press.

Taylor, S. E., & Brown, J. (1988). Illusion and well-being: A social psychological perspective on mental health. *Psychological Bulletin, 103,* 193–210.

Taylor, S. E., & Crocker, J. (1981) Schematic bases of social information processing. In E. T. Higgins, C. P. Herman, & M. P. Zanna (Eds.), *Social cognition: The Ontario Symposium* (Vol. 1, pp. 89–134). Hillsdale, NJ: Erlbaum.

Taylor, S. E., & Fiske, S. T. (1975). Point of view and perceptions of causality. *Journal of Personality and Social Psychology, 32,* 439–445.

Taylor, S. E., Lichtman, R. R., & Wood, J. V. (1984). Attributions, beliefs about control, and adjustment to breast cancer. *Journal of Personality and Social Psychology, 46,* 489–502.

Taylor, S. P., & Leonard, K. E. (1983). Alcohol and human physical aggression. In R. Geen & E. Donnerstein (Eds.), *Aggression: Theoretical and empirical reviews.* New York: Academic Press.

Taylor, S. P., & Sears, J. D. (1988). The effects of alcohol and persuasive social pressure on human physical aggression. *Aggressive Behavior, 14,* 237–243.

Tedeschi, J. T. (Ed.). (1981). *Impression management theory and social psychological research.* New York: Academic Press.

Teger, A. L., & Pruitt, D. G. (1967). Components of group risk taking. *Journal of Experimental Social Psychology, 3,* 189–205.

Tesser, A. (1980). Self-esteem maintenance in family dynamics. *Journal of Personality and Social Psychology, 39,* 77–91.

Tesser, A. (1988). Toward a self-evaluation maintenance model of social behavior. In L. Berkowitz (Ed.), *Advances in experimental social psychology* (Vol. 21, pp. 181–227). Orlando, FL: Academic Press.

Tesser, A. (1991). Emotion in social comparison and reflection processes. In J. Suls & T. A. Wills (Eds.), *Social comparison: Contemporary theory and research* (pp. 117–148). Hillsdale, NJ: Erlbaum.

Tesser, A., & Brodie, M. (1971). A note on the evaluation of a computer date. *Psychonomic Science, 23,* 300.

Tesser, A., & Cornell, D. P. (1991). On the confluence of self processes. *Journal of Experimental Social Psychology, 27,* 501–526.

Tesser, A., & Paulus, D. (1983). The definition of self: Private and public self-evaluation management strategies. *Journal of Personality and Social Psychology, 44,* 672–682.

Tesser, A., & Smith, J. (1980). Some effects of friendship and task relevance on helping: You don't always help the one you like. *Journal of Experimental Social Psychology, 16,* 582–590.

Tetlock, P. E. (1981). The influence of self-presentational goals on attributional reports. *Social Psychology Quarterly, 44,* 300–311.

Tetlock, P. E. (1992). The impact of accountability on judgment and choice: Toward a social contingency model. In M. P. Zanna (Ed.), *Advances in experimental social psychology* (Vol. 25, pp. 331–376). San Diego, CA: Academic Press.

Tetlock, P. E., Peterson, R. S., McGuire, C., Chang, S., & Field, P. (1992). Assessing political group dynamics: A test of the groupthink model. *Journal of Personality and Social Psychology, 63,* 403–425.

Thibaut, J. W., & Kelley, H. H. (1959). *The social psychology of groups.* New York: Wiley.

Thibodeau, R., & Aronson, E. (1992). Taking a closer look: Reasserting the role of the self-concept in dissonance theory. *Personality and Social Psychology Bulletin, 18,* 591–602.

Thomas, M. H., Horton, R., Lippincott, E., & Drabman, R. (1977). Desensitization to portrayals of real-life aggression as a function of exposure to television violence. *Journal of Personality and Social Psychology, 35,* 450–458.

Thomas, W. I. (1928). *The child in America.* New York: Alfred A. Knopf.

Thompson, L. (1990). Negotiation behavior and outcomes: Empirical evidence and theoretical issues. *Psychological Bulletin, 108,* 515–532.

Thompson, L. (1991). Information exchange in negotiation. *Journal of Experimental Social Psychology, 27,* 161–179.

Thompson, L. (1995). They saw a negotiation: Partisanship and involvement. *Journal of Personality and Social Psychology, 68,* 839–853.

Thompson, L., Peterson, E., & Brodt, S. E. (in press). Team

negotiation: An examination of integrative and distributive bargaining. *Journal of Personality and Social Psychology.*

Thompson, L., Peterson, E., & Kray, L. (in press). Social context in negotiation: An information-processing perspective. In R. Kramer & D. Messick (Eds.), *Social context in negotiations.* Beverly Hills, CA: Sage.

Thompson, S. C. (1981). Will it hurt less if I can control it? A complex answer to a simple question. *Psychological Bulletin, 90,* 89–101.

Thompson, S. C., Nanni, C., & Levine, A. (1994). Primary versus secondary and central versus consequence-related control in HIV-positive men. *Journal of Personality and Social Psychology, 67,* 540–547.

Thompson, S. C., Sobolew-Shubin, A., Galbraith, M. E., Schwankovsky, L., & Cruzen, D. (1993). Maintaining perceptions of control: Finding perceived control in low-control circumstances. *Journal of Personality and Social Psychology, 64,* 293–304.

Thornton, D., & Arrowood, A. J. (1966). Self-evaluation, self-enhancement, and the locus of social comparison. *Journal of Experimental Social Psychology,* (Suppl. 1), 40–48.

Thornton, W. (1984). Defensive attribution of responsibility: Evidence for an arousal-based motivational bias. *Journal of Personality and Social Psychology, 46,* 721–734.

Tice, D. M., & Baumeister, R. F. (1990). Self-esteem, self-handicapping, and self-presentation: The strategy of inadequate practice. *Journal of Personality, 58,* 443–464.

Timaeus, E. (1968). Untersuchungen zum sogenannten konformen Verhatten. *Zeitschrift fur Experimentelle und Angewandte Psychologie, 15,* 176–194.

Tindale, R. S. (1993). Decision errors made by individuals and groups. In N. J. Castellan, Jr. (Ed.), *Individual and group decision making* (pp. 109–124). Hillsdale, NJ: Erlbaum.

Toch, H. (1965). *The social psychology of social movements.* Indianapolis: Bobbs-Merrill.

Toch, H. (1980). *Violent men* (rev. ed.). Cambridge, MA: Schenkman.

Toch, T. (1992, November 9). Homeroom sweepstakes. *U.S. News & World Report,* pp. 86–89.

Toi, M., & Batson, C. D. (1982). More evidence that empathy is a source of altruistic motivation. *Journal of Personality and Social Psychology, 43,* 281–292.

Tollestrup, P. A., Turtle, J. W., & Yuille, J. C. (1994). Expectations of eyewitness performance: Jurors' verdicts do not follow from their beliefs. In D. F. Ross, J. D. Read, & M. P. Toglia (Eds.), *Adult eyewitness testimony: Current trends and developments* (pp. 144–162). New York: Cambridge University Press.

Toobin, J. (1995, October 23). A horrible human event. *New Yorker,* pp. 40–49.

Topf, M. (1992). Stress effects of personal control over hospital noise. *Behavioral Medicine, 18,* 84–94.

Traupmann, J., Petersen, R., Utne, M., & Hatfield, E. (1981). Measuring equity in intimate relations. *Applied Psychology Measurement, 5,* 467–480.

Triandis, H. C. (1995). *Individualism and collectivism.* Boulder, CO: Westview.

Triandis, H. C. (1989). The self and social behavior in differing cultural contexts. *Psychological Review, 96,* 506–520.

Triandis, H. C. (1990). Cross-cultural studies of individualism and collectivism. In J. J. Berman (Ed.), *Nebraska Symposium on Motivation, 1989* (pp. 41–133). Lincoln: University of Nebraska Press.

Triplett, N. (1898). The dynamogenic factors in pace making and competition. *American Journal of Psychology, 9,* 507–533.

Trivers, R. (1985). *Social evolution.* Menlo Park, CA: Benjamin-Cummings.

Trolier, T. K., & Hamilton, D. L. (1986). Variables influencing judgments of correlational relations. *Journal of Personality and Social Psychology, 50,* 879–888.

Turner, C. W., Hesse, B. W., & Peterson-Lewis, S. (1986). Naturalistic studies of the long-term effects of television violence. *Journal of Social Issues, 42*(3), 51–74.

Turner, F. J. (1932). *The significance of sections in American history.* New York: H. Holt.

Turner, M. E., Pratkanis, A. R., Probasco, P., & Leve, C. (1992). Threat, cohesion, and group effectiveness: Testing a social identity maintenance perspective on groupthink. *Journal of Personality and Social Psychology, 63,* 781–796.

Tversky, A., & Kahneman, D. (1973). Availability: A heuristic for judging frequency and probability. *Cognitive Psychology, 5,* 207–232.

Tversky, A., & Kahneman, D. (1974). Judgment under uncertainty: Heuristics and biases. *Science, 185,* 1124–1131.

Tversky, A., & Kahneman, D. (1983). Extensional versus intuitive reasoning: The conjunction fallacy in probability judgment. *Psychological Review, 90,* 293–315.

Tversky, B., & Tuchin, M. (1989). A reconciliation of the evidence on eyewitness testimony: Comments on McCloskey and Zaragoza. *Journal of Experimental Psychology: General, 118,* 86–91.

Uranowitz, S. W. (1975). Helping and self-attributions: A field experiment. *Journal of Personality and Social Psychology, 32,* 852–854.

Valacich, J. S., Dennis, A. R., & Connolly, T. (1994). Idea generation in computer-based groups: A new ending to an old story. *Organizational Behavior and Human Decision Processes, 57,* 448–467.

Valins, S. (1966). Cognitive effects of false heart-rate feedback. *Journal of Personality and Social Psychology, 4,* 400–408.

Vallerand, R. J., & Richer, F. (1988). On the use of the Causal Dimension Scale in a field setting: A test with confirmatory factor analysis in success and failure situations. *Journal of Personality and Social Psychology, 54,* 704–712.

Vallone, R. P., Griffin, D. W., Lin, S., & Ross, L. (1990). The overconfident prediction of future actions and outcomes by self and others. *Journal of Personality and Social Psychology, 58,* 582–592.

Vallone, R. P., Ross, L., & Lepper, M. R. (1985). The hostile media phenomenon: Biased perception and perceptions of media bias in coverage of the Beirut massacre. *Journal of Personality and Social Psychology, 49,* 577–585.

Van Overwalle, F., & De Metsenaere, M. (1990). The effects of attribution-based intervention and study strategy training on academic achievement in college freshmen. *British Journal of Educational Psychology, 60,* 299–311.

Vance, C. S. (1986, August 2–9). The Meese Commission on the road. *Nation,* pp. 65, 76.

Vanneman, R. D., & Pettigrew, T. (1972). Race and relative deprivation in the urban United States. *Race, 13,* 461–486.

Video news releases. (1995, July). *Public Relations Tactics,* p. 15.

Voissem, N. H., & Sistrunk, F. (1971). Communication schedules and cooperative game behavior. *Journal of Personality and Social Psychology, 19,* 160–167.

Vonnegut, K. (1963). *Cat's Cradle.* New York: Delacorte Press.

Wagner, R. C. (1975). Complementary needs, role expectations, interpersonal attraction, and the stability of work relationships. *Journal of Personality and Social Psychology, 32,* 116–124.

Wagstaff, G. (1982). Attitudes to rape: The "just world" strikes again? *Bulletin of the British Psychological Society, 35,* 277–279.

Wallach, M. A., Kogan, N., & Bem, D. J. (1962). Group influences on individual risk taking. *Journal of Abnormal and Social Psychology, 65,* 75–86.

Walster, E. (1966). Assignment of responsibility for an accident. *Journal of Personality and Social Psychology, 3,* 73–79.

Walster, E., & Festinger, L. (1962). The effectiveness of "overheard" persuasive communication. *Journal of Abnormal and Social Psychology, 65,* 395–402.

Walster, E., Aronson, V., Abrahams, D., & Rottman, L. (1966). Importance of physical attractiveness in dating behavior. *Journal of Personality and Social Psychology, 5,* 508–516.

Walster, E., Walster, G. W., & Berscheid, E. (1978). *Equity: Theory and research.* Boston: Allyn & Bacon.

Walster, E., Walster, G. W., & Traupmann, J. (1978). Equity and premarital sex. *Journal of Personality, 36,* 82–92.

Walster, E., Walster, G. W., Piliavin, J., & Schmidt, L. (1973). "Playing hard to get": Understanding an elusive phenomenon. *Journal of Personality and Social Psychology, 26,* 113–121.

Warren, B. L. (1966). A multiple variable approach to the assortive mating phenomenon. *Eugenics Quarterly, 13,* 285–298.

Washburn, S., & Hamburg, D. (1965). The implications of primate research In I. DeVore (Ed.), *Primate behavior: Field studies of monkeys and apes* (pp. 607–622). New York: Holt, Rinehart & Winston.

Watson, D. (1982). The actor and the observer: How are their perceptions of causality divergent? *Psychological Bulletin, 92,* 682–700.

Watson, D., & Pennebaker, J. W. (1989). Health complaints, stress, and distress: Exploring the central role of negative affectivity. *Psychological Review, 96,* 234–254.

Watson, J. (1924). *Behaviorism.* Chicago: University of Chicago Press.

Watson, J. (1950). Some social and psychological situations related to change in attitude. *Human Relations, 3,* 15–56.

Watson, R. I. (1973). Investigation into deindividuation using a cross-cultural survey technique. *Journal of Personality and Social Psychology, 25,* 342–345.

Wattenberg, M. P. (1987). The hollow realignment: Partisan change in a candidate-centered era. *Public Opinion Quarterly, 51,* 58–74.

Weary, G., & Arkin, R. C. (1981). Attributional self-presentation. In J. H. Harvey, W. Ickes, & R. F. Kidd (Eds.), *New directions in attribution research* (Vol. 3, pp. 223–246). New York: Erlbaum.

Weatherly, D. (1961). Anti-Semitism and the expression of fantasy aggression. *Journal of Abnormal and Social Psychology, 62,* 454–457.

Webber, R., & Crocker, J. (1983). Cognitive processes in the revision of stereotypic beliefs. *Journal of Personality and Social Psychology, 45,* 961–977.

Wegener, D. T., & Petty, R. E. (1994). Mood management across affective states: The hedonic contingency hypothesis. *Journal of Personality and Social Psychology, 66,* 1034–1048.

Wegener, D. T., Petty, R. E., & Smith, S. M. (1995). Positive mood can increase or decrease message scrutiny: The hedonic contingency view of mood and message processing. *Journal of Personality and Social Psychology, 69,* 5–15.

Wegner, D. M. (1986). Transactive memory: A contemporary analysis of the group mind. In B. Mullen & G. R. Goethals (Eds.), *Theories of group behavior* (pp. 185–208). New York: Springer-Verlag.

Wegner, D. M. (1989). *White bears and other unwanted thoughts: Suppression, obsession, and the psychology of mental control.* New York: Viking.

Wegner, D. M. (1992). You can't always think what you want: Problems in the suppression of unwanted thoughts. In M. P. Zanna (Ed.), *Advances in experimental social psychology* (pp. 193–225). San Diego, CA: Academic Press.

Wegner, D. M. (1994). Ironic processes of mental control. *Psychological Review, 101,* 34–52.

Wegner, D. M., Bowman, R. E., & Erber, R. (1995). *Sexism and mental control: When thought and speech betray egalitarian beliefs.* Unpublished manuscript, University of Virginia.

Wegner, D. M., Erber, R., & Raymond, P. (1991). Transactive memory in close relationships. *Journal of Personality and Social Psychology, 61,* 923–929.

Wegner, D. M., Quillan, F., & Houston, C. (1995). *Memories out of order: Thought suppression and the disassembly of remembered experience.* Unpublished manuscript, University of Virginia.

Wegner, D. M., Wenzlaff, R., Kerker, M., & Beattie, A. E. (1981). Incrimination through innuendo: Can media questions become public answers? *Journal of Personality and Social Psychology, 40,* 822–832.

Weinberg, R. S., Richardson, P. A., & Jackson, A. (1983). Effect of situation criticality on tennis performance of males and females. *Newsletter of the Society of the Advancement of Social Psychology, 9,* 8–9.

Weiner, B. (1985). "Spontaneous" causal thinking. *Psychological Bulletin, 97,* 74–84.

Weiner, B. (1986). *An attributional theory of emotion and motivation.* New York: Springer-Verlag.

Weiner, B. (Ed.). (1974). *Achievement motivation and attribution theory.* Morristown, NJ: General Learning Press.

Weiner, B., Amirkhan, J., Folkes, V. S., & Verette, J. A. (1987). An attributional analysis of excuse giving: Studies of a naive theory of emotion. *Journal of Personality and Social Psychology, 52,* 316–324.

Weiner, B., Frieze, L., Kukla, A., Reed, L., Rest, S. & Rosenbaum, R. M. (1972). Perceiving the causes of success and failure. In E. E. Jones, H. H. Kelley, R. E. Nisbett, S. Valins, & B. Weiner (Eds.), *Attribution: Perceiving the causes of behavior.* Morristown, NJ: General Learning Press.

Weiner, B., Nierenberg, R., & Goldstein, M. (1976). Social learning (locus of control) versus attributional (causal stability) interpretations of expectancy for success. *Journal of Personality, 44,* 52–68.

Weingardt, K. R., Toland, H. K., & Loftus, E. F. (1994). Reports of suggested memories: Do people truly believe them? In D. F. Ross, J. D. Read, & M. P. Toglia (Eds.), *Adult eyewitness testimony: Current trends and developments* (pp. 3–26). New York: Cambridge University Press.

Weinstein, N. D. (1980). Unrealistic optimism about future life events. *Journal of Personality and Social Psychology, 39,* 806–820.

Weir, W. (1984, October 15). Another look at subliminal "facts." *Advertising Age,* p. 46.

Weiss, R. S. (1973). *Loneliness: The experience of emotional and social isolation.* Cambridge, MA: MIT Press.

Wells, G. L. (1984). The psychology of lineup identifications. *Journal of Applied Social Psychology, 14,* 89–103.

Wells, G. L. (1993). What do we know about eyewitness identification? *American Psychologist, 48,* 553–571.

Wells, G. L., & Luus, C. A. E. (1990). Police lineups as experiments: Social methodology as a framework for properly conducted lineups. *Personality and Social Psychology Bulletin, 16,* 106–117.

Wells, G. L., Lindsay, R. C. L., & Ferguson, T. J. (1979).

Accuracy, confidence, and juror perceptions in eyewitness identification. *Journal of Applied Psychology, 64,* 440–448.

Wells, G. L., Seelau, E. P., Rydell, S. M., & Luus, S. M. (1994). Recommendations for properly conducted lineup identification tasks. In D. F. Ross, J. D. Read, & M. P. Toglia (Eds.), *Adult eyewitness testimony: Current trends and developments* (pp. 223–244). New York: Cambridge University Press.

West, S. G., Gunn, S. P., & Chernicky, P. (1975). Ubiquitous Watergate: An attributional analysis. *Journal of Personality and Social Psychology, 32,* 55–62.

Wheeler, L., & Kunitate, M. (1992). Social comparison in everyday life. *Journal of Personality and Social Psychology, 62,* 760–773.

Wheeler, L., Koestner, R., & Driver, R. (1982). Related attributes in the choice of comparison others: It's there, but it isn't all there is. *Journal of Experimental Social Psychology, 18,* 489–500.

White, G. L. (1980). Physical attractiveness and courtship progress. *Journal of Personality and Social Psychology, 39,* 660–668.

White, G. L. (1981a). A model of romantic jealousy. *Motivation and Emotion, 5,* 295–310.

White, G. L. (1981b). Some correlates of romantic jealousy. *Journal of Personality, 49,* 129–147.

White, R. K. (1977). Misperception in the Arab-Israeli conflict. *Journal of Social Issues, 33,* 190–221.

Whitly, B. E., & Frieze, I. H. (1985). Children's causal attributions for success and failure in achievement settings: A meta-analysis. *Journal of Educational Psychology, 77,* 608–616.

Whittaker, J. O., & Meade, R. D. (1967). Social pressure in the modification and distortion of judgment: A cross-cultural study. *International Journal of Psychology, 2,* 109–113.

Whorf, B. L. (1956). *Language, thought, and reality.* New York: Wiley.

Wicker, A. W. (1969). Attitudes versus actions: The relationship between verbal and overt behavioral responses to attitude objects. *Journal of Social Issues, 25,* 41–78.

Wicklund, R. A. (1975). Objective self-awareness. In L. Berkowitz (Ed.), *Advances in experimental social psychology* (Vol. 8, pp. 233–275). New York: Academic Press.

Wicklund, R. A., & Frey, D. (1980). Self-awareness theory: When the self makes a difference. In D. Wegner & R. Vallacher (Eds.), *The self in social psychology* (pp. 31–54). New York: Oxford University Press.

Wicklund, R. A., & Gollwitzer, P. M. (1982). *Symbolic self-completion.* Hillsdale, NJ: Erlbaum.

Wiedenfeld, S. A., O'Leary, A., Bandura, A., Brown, S., Levine, S., & Raska, K. (1990). Impact of perceived self-efficacy in coping with stressors on components of the immune system. *Journal of Personality and Social Psychology, 59,* 1082–1094.

Wilder, D. A. (1981). Perceiving persons as a group: Categorization and intergroup relations. In D. L. Hamilton (Ed.), *Cognitive processes in stereotyping and intergroup behavior.* Hillsdale, NJ: Erlbaum.

Wilder, D. A. (1984). Intergroup contact: The typical member and the exception to the rule. *Journal of Experimental Psychology, 20,* 177–194.

Wilder, D. A. (1986). Social categorization: Implications for creation and reduction of intergroup bias. In L. Berkowitz (Ed.), *Advances in experimental social psychology* (Vol. 19, pp. 291–355). New York: Academic Press.

Wilder, D. A., & Shapiro, P. N. (1989). Role of competition-induced anxiety in limiting the beneficial impact of positive behavior by an out-group member. *Journal of Personality and Social Psychology, 56,* 60–69.

Williams, K., Harkins, S., & Latané, B. (1981). Identifiability as a deterrent to social loafing: Two cheering experiments. *Journal of Personality and Social Psychology, 40,* 303–311.

Williams, K., Karau, S., & Bourgeois, M. (1993). Working on collective tasks: Social loafing and social compensation. In M. A. Hogg & D. Abrams (Eds.), *Group motivation: Social psychological perspectives* (pp. 130–148). New York: Harvester Wheatsheaf.

Williams, R. B., Jr. (1987). Refining the Type A hypothesis: Emergence of the hostility complex. *American Journal of Cardiology, 60,* 27J–32J.

Williams, R. H., & Ross, M. H. (1980, March–April). Drilling for oil and gas in our houses. *Technology Review,* pp. 24–36.

Williams, R. L. (1983, December). For the all-too-common cold, we are perfect, if unwilling, hosts. *Smithsonian,* pp. 47–55.

Williamson, G. M., & Clark, M. S. (1989). Providing help and desired relationship type as determinants of changes in moods and self-evaluations. *Journal of Personality and Social Psychology, 56,* 722–734.

Williamson, G. M., Clark, M. S., Pegalis, L. J., & Behan, A. (in press). Affective consequences of refusing to help in communal and exchange relationships. *Personality and Social Psychology Bulletin.*

Wills, T. A., Weiss, R. L., & Patterson, G. R. (1974). A behavioral analysis of the determinants of marital satisfaction. *Journal of Consulting and Clinical Psychology, 42,* 802–811.

Wilson, D. K., Purdon, S. E., & Wallston, K. A. (1988). Compliance in health recommendations: A theoretical overview of message framing. *Health Education Research, 3,* 161–171.

Wilson, E. O. (1975). *Sociobiology: The new synthesis.* Cambridge, MA: Belknap Press of Harvard University Press.

Wilson, E. O. (1978). *On human nature.* Cambridge, MA: Harvard University Press.

Wilson, J. Q., & Hernstein, R. J. (1985). *Crime and human nature.* New York: Simon & Schuster.

Wilson, T. D. (1985). Strangers to ourselves: The origins and accuracy of beliefs about one's own mental states. In J. H. Harvey & G. Weary (Eds.), *Attribution in contemporary psychology* (pp. 9–36). New York: Academic Press.

Wilson, T. D., & Brekke, N. C. (1994). Mental contamination and mental correction: Unwanted influences on judgments and evaluations. *Psychological Bulletin, 116,* 117–142.

Wilson, T. D., & Hodges, S. D. (1992). Attitudes as temporary constructions. In A. Tesser & L. Martin (Eds.), *The construction of social judgment* (pp. 37–65). Hillsdale, NJ: Erlbaum.

Wilson, T. D., & Kraft, D. (1993). Why do I love thee? Effects of repeated introspections about a dating relationship on attitudes toward the relationship. *Personality and Social Psychology Bulletin, 19,* 409–418.

Wilson, T. D., & LaFleur, S. J. (1995). Knowing what you'll do: Effects of analyzing reasons on self-prediction. *Journal of Personality and Social Psychology, 68,* 21–35.

Wilson, T. D., & Linville, P. W. (1982). Improving the academic performance of college freshmen: Attribution therapy revisited. *Journal of Personality and Social Psychology, 42,* 367–376.

Wilson, T. D., & Linville, P. W. (1985). Improving the performance of college freshmen using attributional techniques. *Journal of Personality and Social Psychology, 49,* 287–293.

Wilson, T. D., & Stone, J. I. (1985). Limitations of self-knowledge: More on telling more than we can know. In P. Shaver (Ed.), *Review of personality and social psychology* (Vol. 6, pp. 167–183). Beverly Hills, CA: Sage.

Wilson, T. D., Dunn, D. S., Bybee, J. A., Hyman, D. B., & Rotondo, J. A. (1984). Effects of analyzing reasons on attitude-behavior consistency. *Journal of Personality and Social Psychology, 47,* 5–16.

Wilson, T. D., Dunn, D. S., Kraft, D., & Lisle, D. J. (1989). Introspection, attitude change, and attitude-behavior consistency: The disruptive effects of explaining why we feel the way we do. In L. Berkowitz (Ed.), *Advances in experimental social psychology* (Vol. 19, pp. 123–205). Orlando, FL: Academic Press.

Wilson, T. D., Hodges, S. D., & LaFleur, S. J. (1995). Effects of introspecting about reasons: Inferring attitudes from accessible thoughts. *Journal of Personality and Social Psychology, 69,* 16–28.

Wilson, T. D., Houston, C., Etling, K. M., & Brekke, N. (1995). A new look at anchoring effects: Basic anchoring and its antecedents. Manuscript submitted for publication.

Wilson, T. D., Laser, P. S., & Stone, J. I. (1982). Judging the predictors of one's own mood: Accuracy and the use of shared theories. *Journal of Experimental Social Psychology, 18,* 537–556.

Wilson, T. D., Lisle, D. J., Schooler, J., Hodges, S. D., Klaaren, K. J., & LaFleur, S. J. (1993). Introspecting about reasons can reduce post-choice satisfaction. *Personality and Social Psychology Bulletin, 19,* 331–339.

Winch, R. (1958). *Mate selection: A study of complementary needs.* New York: Harper & Row.

Winter, D. G. (1987). Leader appeal, leader performance, and the motive profiles of leaders and followers: A study of American presidents and elections. *Journal of Personality and Social Psychology, 52,* 196–202.

Wiseman, F. (Director). (1967). *Titicut follies* [Film]. Cambridge, MA: Zipporah Films.

Witelson, S. F. (1992). Cognitive neuroanatomy: A new era. *Neurology, 42,* 709–713.

Wittenbaum, G. W., & Stasser, G. (in press). Management of information in small groups. In J. L. Nye & A. M. Brower (Eds.), *What's social about social cognition? Social cognition research in small groups.* Newbury Park, CA: Sage.

Wolf, S. (1985). Manifest and latent influence of majorities and minorities. *Journal of Personality and Social Psychology, 48,* 899–908.

Woll, S. (1986). So many to choose from: Decision strategies in videodating. *Journal of Social and Personal Relationships, 3,* 43–52.

Wood, J. V. (1989). Theory and research concerning social comparisons of personal attributes. *Psychological Bulletin, 106,* 231–248.

Wood, J. V., Taylor, S. E., & Lichtman, R. R. (1985). Social comparison in adjustment to breast cancer. *Journal of Personality and Social Psychology, 49,* 1169–1183.

Wood, W. (1982). Retrieval of attitude-relevant information from memory: Effects on susceptibility to persuasion and on intrinsic motivation. *Journal of Personality and Social Psychology, 42,* 798–810.

Wood, W. (1987). Meta-analytic review of sex differences in group performance. *Psychological Bulletin, 102,* 53–71.

Word, C. O., Zanna, M. P., & Cooper, J. (1974). The nonverbal mediation of self-fulfilling prophecies in interracial interaction. *Journal of Experimental Social Psychology, 10,* 109–120.

Worth, L T., & Mackie, D. M. (1987). Cognitive mediation of positive affect in persuasion. *Social Cognition, 5,* 76–94.

Wortman, C. B., & Brehm, J. W. (1975). Response to uncontrollable outcomes: An integration of reactance theory and the learned helplessness model. In L. Berkowitz (Ed.), *Advances in experimental social psychology* (Vol. 8, pp. 277–336). New York: Academic Press.

Wright, J. C., & Murphy, G. L. (1984). The utility of theories in intuitive statistics: The robustness of theory-based judgments. *Journal of Experimental Psychology: General, 113,* 301–322.

Wright, L. (1994). *Remembering Satan.* New York: Knopf.

Wrightsman, L. S. (1987). *Psychology and the legal system.* Pacific Grove, CA: Brooks/Cole.

Wuthnow, R. (1991). *Acts of compassion: Caring for others and helping ourselves.* Princeton, NJ: Princeton University Press.

Wyer, R. S., & Srull, T. K. (1989). *Memory and cognition in its social context.* Hillsdale, NJ: Erlbaum.

Wyer, R. S., Jr. (1988). Social memory and social judgment. In P. R. Solomon, G. R. Goethals, C. M. Kelley, & B. R. Stephens (Eds.), *Perspectives on memory research.* New York: Springer-Verlag.

Yamaguchi, K., & Kandel, D. B. (1984). Patterns of drug use from adolescence to young adulthood: III. Predictors of progression. *American Journal of Public Health, 74,* 673–681.

Yee, D., & Eccles, J. S. (1988). Parent perceptions and attributions for children's math achievement. *Sex Roles, 19,* 317–333.

Yuille, J. C., & Cutshall, J. L. (1986). A case study of eyewitness memory of a crime. *Journal of Applied Psychology, 71,* 291–301.

Zaccaro, S. J., Foti, R. J., & Kenny, D. A. (1991). Self-monitoring and trait-based variance in leadership: An investigation of leader flexibility across multiple group situations. *Journal of Applied Psychology, 76,* 308–315.

Zahn-Waxler, C., Radke-Yarrow, M., & King, R. A. (1979). Child rearing and children's prosocial initiations toward victims of distress. *Child Development, 50,* 319–330.

Zajonc, R. B. (1965). Social facilitation. *Science, 149,* 269–274.

Zajonc, R. B. (1968). Attitudinal effects of mere exposure. *Journal of Personality and Social Psychology, 9,* Monograph Suppl. No. 2, Pt. 2.

Zajonc, R. B. (1980). Compresence. In P. B. Paulus (Ed.), *Psychology of group influence* (pp. 35–60). Hillsdale, NJ: Erlbaum.

Zajonc, R. B., & Sales, S. M. (1966). Social facilitation of dominant and subordinate responses. *Journal of Experimental Social Psychology, 2,* 160–168.

Zajonc, R. B., Heingartner, A., & Herman, E. M. (1969). Social enhancement and impairment of performance in the cockroach. *Journal of Personality and Social Psychology, 13,* 83–92.

Zander, A. (1979). The psychology of group processes. *Annual Review of Psychology, 30,* 417–451.

Zanna, M., & Cooper, J. (1974). Dissonance and the pill: An attribution approach to studying the arousal properties of dissonance. *Journal of Personality and Social Psychology, 29,* 703–709.

Zanna, M., & Cooper, J. (1976). Dissonance and the attribution process. In J. H. Harvey, W. Ickes, & R. F. Kidd (Eds.),

New directions in attribution research (Vol. 1, pp. 199–217). New York: Erlbaum.

Zanna, M., & Rempel, J. K. (1988). Attitudes: A new look at an old concept. In D. Bar-Tal & A. W. Kruglanski (Eds.), *The social psychology of attitudes* (pp. 315–334). New York: Cambridge University Press.

Zanna, M., Goethals, G. R., & Hill, J. (1975). Evaluating a sex-related ability: Social comparison with similar others and standard setters. *Journal of Experimental Social Psychology, 11,* 86–93.

Zanot, E. J., Pincus, J. D., & Lamp, E. J. (1983). Public perceptions of subliminal advertising. *Journal of Advertising, 12,* 39–45.

Zanna, M. P., & Fazio, R. H. (1982). The attitude-behavior relation: Moving toward a third generation of research. In M. P. Zanna, E. T. Higgins, & C. P. Herman (Eds.), *Consistency in social behavior: The Ontario Symposium* (Vol. 2, pp. 283–301). Hillsdale, NJ: Erlbaum.

Zebrowitz-McArthur, L. (1988). Person perception in cross-cultural perspective. In M. H. Bond (Ed.), *The cross-cultural challenge to social psychology* (pp. 245–265). Newbury Park, CA: Sage.

Zillmann, D. (1978). Attribution and misattribution of excitatory reactions. In J. H. Harvey, W. J. Ickes, & R. F. Kidd (Eds.), *New directions in attribution research* (Vol. 2, pp. 335–370). Hillsdale, NJ: Erlbaum.

Zillmann, D. (1994). Erotica and family values. In J. Bryant, D. Zillmann, & A. C. Huston (Eds.), *Media, children, and the family: Social scientific, psychodynamic, and clinical perspectives* (pp. 199–213). Hillsdale, NJ: Erlbaum.

Zillmann, D., & Bryant, J. (1984). Effects of massive exposure to pornography. In N. M. Malamuth & E. Donnerstein (Eds.), *Pornography and sexual aggression* (pp. 115–138). New York: Academic Press.

Zimbardo, P. G. (1970). The human choice: Individuation, reason, and order versus deindividuation, impulse, and chaos. In W. J. Arnold & D. Levine (Eds.), *Nebraska Symposium on Motivation: 1969* (Vol. 17, pp. 237–307). Lincoln: University of Nebraska Press.

Zimbardo, P. G., Weisenberg, M., Firestone, I., & Levy, B. (1965). Communicator effectiveness in producing public conformity and private attitude change. *Journal of Personality, 33,* 233–255.

Zimbardo, P., & Andersen, S. (1993). Understanding mind control: Exotic and mundane mental manipulations. In M. D. Langone (Ed.), *Recovery from cults* (pp. 104–125). New York: Norton.

Zubek, J. P. (Ed.). (1969). *Sensory deprivation: Fifteen years of research.* New York: Appleton-Century-Crofts.

Zuber, J. A., Crott, H. W., & Werner, J. (1992). Choice shift and group polarization: An analysis of the status of arguments and social decision schemes. *Journal of Personality and Social Psychology, 62,* 50–61.

Zuckerman, M. (1978). Actions and occurrences in Kelley's cube. *Journal of Personality and Social Psychology, 36,* 647–656.

Zuckerman, M., DePaulo, B. M., & Rosenthal, R. (1981). Verbal and nonverbal communication of deception. In L. Berkowitz (Ed.), *Advances in experimental social psychology* (Vol. 14, pp. 1–59). New York: Academic Press.

CREDITS

Unless otherwise acknowledged, all photographs are the property of Addison Wesley Educational Publishers, Inc. Page abbreviations are as follows: (**T**) top, (**C**) center, (**B**) bottom, (**L**) left, (**R**) right, (**INS**) inset, (**BG**) background.

CHAPTER 1

Text and Art: p. 3: From *The New York Times,* July 3, 1981. Copyright © 1981. **p. 14:** Figure 1.1 from "Reputations Versus Labels: The power of situational effects in the Prisoner's Dilemma Game." Copyright © 1993. Reprinted by permission of Steven Samuels.
Photos and Cartoons: p. 2: George Dillon/Stock Boston; **p. 4:** © Willie Hill, Jr/The Image Works. **p. 6:** AP/Wide World; **p. 6INS:** Waco Tribune Herald/Sygma; **p. 8BG:** Greg Smith (Salsa)/TIME Magazine. **p. 13:** © Mike Mazzaschi/Stock Boston. **p. 17C:** Archives of the History of American Psychology, University of Akron. **p. 17R:** AP/Wide World. **p. 18:** The Bettmann Archive. **p. 21:** The Kobal Collection. **p. 22:** Innervision. **p. 25L:** © M. Greenlar/The Image Works; **p. 25C:** © David Weintraub/Stock Boston. **p. 25R:** © PETA.

CHAPTER 2

Text and Art: p. 34: From Latane and Darley, *Witness of the Genovese Murder,* p. 78. Copyright © 1987. **p. 39:** From "Pornographic imagery and prevalence of pararphilia," *American Journal of Psychiatry.* Copyright © 1982.
p. 43: From "Correlation and an Earthquake," *The New Yorker,* October 19, 1987. **p. 51:** Figure 2.4 from Donnerstein, "Aggressive erotica and violence against women," *Journal of Personality and Social Psychology,* 39. Copyright © 1980 by the American Psychological Association. Adapted with permission.
p. 60: Figure 2.5 from "Ethical principles of psychologists and code of conduct," *American Psychologist,* 47, pp. 1597–1611. Copyright © 1992 by the American Psychological Association. Adapted with permission.
Photos and cartoons: p. 28: © John Coletti/The Picture Cube; **p. 30:** AP/Wide World. **p. 33:** DOONESBURY © 1986 G. B. Trudeau. Reprinted with permission of Univeral Press Syndicate. All rights reserved. **p. 34:** Photo from European; **p. 37:** Univeral Press Syndicate. **p. 38:** Innervisions. **p. 39:** © C. Gatewood/The Image Works. **p. 42R:** *Literary Digest.* **p. 42L:** *Literary Digest.* **p. 44:** © Michael Newman/PhotoEdit. **p. 55:** © Paul Mozell/Stock Boston. **p. 61:** Universal Press Syndicate.

CHAPTER 3

Text and Art: p. 88: From John Steinbeck, *Travels with Charley,* p. 77. Copyright © 1988 Penguin USA. **p. 75:** Figure 3.1 from Jones, et al., "Pattern of performance and ability attribution: An unexpected primary effect," *Journal of Personality and Social Psychology,* 10, pp. 317–340. Copyright © 1968 by the American Psychological Association. Adapted by permission.
p. 76: Figure 3.2 from Ross, et al., "Perseverance in self-perception and social perception: Biased attributional processes in the debriefing paradigm," *Journal of Personality and Social Psychology,* 32, pp. 880–892. Copyright © 1975 by the American Psychological Association. Adapted by permission.
p. 77: Figure 3.3 from Rosenthal and Jacobson, *Pygmalion in the Classroom: Teacher Expectation and Student Intellectual*

Development. Copyright © 1968 Holt, Rinehart & Winston. **p. 82:** Figure 3.5 from Schwarz, et al., "Ease of retrieval as information: Another look at the availability heuristic," *Journal of Personality and Social Psychology,* 61, pp. 195–202. Copyright © 1991 by the American Psychological Association. Adpated by permission. **p. 88:** Figure 3.6 from Hamill, et al., "Ignoring sample bias: Inferences about population from atypical cases," *Journal of Personality and Social Psychology,* 39, pp. 578–589. Copyright © 1980 by the American Psychology Association. Adapted by permission. **p. 94:** Figure 3.8 from Gilbert, et al., "You can't believe everything you read," *Journal of Personality and Social Psychology,* 65. Copyright © 1993 by the American Psychological Association. Adapted by permission. **p. 98:** Figure 3.9 from Lehman, et al., "The effects of graduate training on reasoning: Formal discipline and thinking about everyday-life events," *American Psychologist,* 43, pp. 431–442. Copyright © 1988 by the American Psychological Association. Adapted by permission. **p. 99:** Figure 3.10 reprinted with permission from Nisbett, et al., "Teaching Reason," *Science,* 239, pp. 625–631. Copyright © 1987 American Association for the Advancement of Science.
Photos and cartoons: p. 64: © Arnold Kaplan/The Picture Cube. **p. 66:** © Mary Kate Denny/PhotoEdit. **p. 69:** The Kobal Collection. **p. 70L:** A. J. Warner from "The Darker Brother"; **p. 70R:** A. J. Warner from "The Darker Brother". **p. 73:** Princeton University. **p. 81:** "Comstock, Inc.". **p. 83:** Daemmrich/Stock Boston. **p. 86L:** E. R. Degginger. **p. 86R:** Joe Sohm/The Image Works. **p. 89:** © Jim Steinberg. **p. 95:** © MONKMEYER/Collins.

CHAPTER 4

Text and Art: p. 103: Exccrpt from "The Metropolitan Diary," by Ron Alexander, *New York Times,* January 17, 1996. Copyright © 1996 by The New York Times Company. Reprinted by permission. **p. 114:** Figure 4.1 from Rosenberg, et al., "A multidimensional approach to the structure of personality impressions," *Journal of Personality and Social Psychology,* 9, pp. 283–294. Copyright © 1968 by the American Psychological Association. Adapted by permission. **p. 115:** Figure 4.2 from Hoffman, "The linguistic relativity of person cognition: An English/Chinese comparison," *Journal of Personality and Social Psychology,* 51. Copyright © 1986 by the American Psychological Association. Adapted by permission.
p. 118: Figure 4.4 adapted from Higgins, et al., "Strategic alcohol use: Drinking to self-handicap," *Journal of Experimental Social Psychology,* 13. Copyright © 1977. Reprinted by permission of Academic Press. **p. 125:** Figure 4.7 adapted from Weiner. **p. 127:** Figure 4.8 adapted from Jones and Harris, "Attribution of attitudes," *Journal of Experimental Psychology,* 3. Copyright © 1967. Reprinted by permission of Academic Press. **p. 128:** Figure 4.9 from Taylor, et al., "Point of view and perception of causality," *Journal of Personality and Social Psychology,* 32. Copyright © 1975 by the American Psychological Association. Adapted by permission.
p. 129: Figure 4.10 adapted from Taylor and Fiske, 1975. **p. 130:** Figure 4.11 from Taylor, et al., "Point of view and perception of causality," *Journal of Personality and Social Psychology,* 32. Copyright © 1975 by the American Psychological Association. Adapted by permission.
p. 132: Figure 4.12 from Storms, "Videotape and the attribution process: Reversing actors' and observers' points of view,"

CHAPTER 5

CHAPTER 6

CHAPTER 7

CHAPTER 8

Melanie Carr/Uniphoto. **p. 385L:** UPI/Bettmann. **p. 388:** Elizabeth Crews/The Image Works. **p. 391:** © M. Antman/ The Image Works.

CHAPTER 11
Text and Art: p. 400: From *Time,* January 25, 1982. **p. 407:** Figure 11.1 from Baton, *The Altruism Question: Toward a Social Psychological Answer.* 1991 Lawrence Erlbaum Associates. **p. 409:** Figure 11.2 from M. Toi and C. D. Batson, "More evidence that empathy is a source of altruistic motivation," *Journal of Personality and Social Psychology,* 43, pp. 281–292. Copyright © 1982. Reprinted by permission. **p. 418:** Figure 11.3 adapted from R. B. Cialdini, "Transgression and altrusim," *Journal of Experimental Social Psychology,* 9, pp. 502–516. Copyright © 1973. Reprinted by permission of Academic Press. **p. 422:** Figure 11.4 from Darley, et al., "Bystander intervention in emergencies: Diffusion and responsibility," *Journal of Personality and Social Psychology,* 8. Copyright © 1968 by the American Psychological Association. Adapted by permission. **p. 423:** Figure 11.5 adapted from Latane & Darley, *The Unresponsive Bystander: Why Doesn't He Help?* Copyright © 1970. Reprinted by permission of Simon & Schuster. **p. 429:** Figure 11.6 from Hendrick, et al., *Romantic Love,* p. 69. Copyright © 1992 by Sage Publications, Inc. Reprinted by permission of Sage Publications, Inc.
Photos and cartoons: p. 398: Mel DiGiacomo/The Image Bank; **p. 400:** AP/Wide World. **p. 402:** Rhoda Sidney/The Image Works. **p. 405:** Agostini/Gamma-Liaison. **p. 408:** CALVIN AND HOBBES ©1995 Watterson. Dist. by Universal Press Syndicate. **p. 408:** United Press International, Inc.. **p. 411:** © Tony Freeman/PhotoEdit. **p. 412:** © Michael Newman/PhotoEdit; **p. 414:** Martha Taber/Impact Visuals. **p. 419L:** © John Coletti/The Picture Cube. **p. 419R:** © 1991 Kindra Clineff/The Picture Cube. **p. 420R:** New York Times Pictures. **p. 420L:** New York Times Pictures. **p. 424:** Steve McCurry/Magnum Photos; **p. 427:** © Charles Gupton/Stock Boston. **p. 431:** © Tony Freeman/PhotoEdit.

CHAPTER 12
Text and Art: p. 444: Figure 12.1 from Carlsmith, et al., "Ambient temperature and the occurence of collective violence," *Journal of Personality and Social Psychology,* 37. Copyright © 1979 by the American Psychological Association. Adapted by permission. **p. 449:** Figure 12.2 from Berkowitz, et al., "Weapons as aggression eliciting stimuli," *Journal of Personality and Social Psychology,* 7. Copyright © 1967 by the American Psychological Association. Adapted by permission. **p. 451:** Figure 12.3 from Liebert, et al., "Some immediate effects of televised violence on children's behavior," *Developmental Psychology,* 6. Copyright © 1972 by the American Psychological Association. Adapted by permission. **p. 454:** From Donald Goddard, *The New York Times,* February 27, 1977. **p. 459:** Figure 12.4 from Archer, et al., *Violence and Crime in Cross National Perspective.* Copyright © 1984. Reprinted by permission of Yale University Press. **p. 464:** Figure 12.5 from Archer and Gartner, "Violent Acts and Violent Times: A Comparative Approach to Postwar Incident Rates," *American Sociological Review,* 41. Copyright © 1976. Reprinted by permission. **p. 469:** Figure 12.6 from Baron, "The Reduction of Human Aggression: A Field Study on the Influence of Incompatible Responses," *Journal of Applied Social Psychology,* 6. Copyright © 1976. Reprinted by permission.
Photos and cartoons: p. 434: © 1992 Stanley Rowin/The Picture Cube. **p. 436** © Dr. Philip G. Zimbardo. **p. 438:** Drawing by D. Reilly, ©1994 The New Yorker Magazine, Inc.. **p. 440:** © N. R. Rowan/Stock Boston. **p. 442:** © 1975 The New Yorker

Magazine, Inc.. **p. 445:** © Jonathan Nourok/PhotoEdit. **p. 448:** © 1940 The New Yorker Magazine, Inc.. **p. 450:** Albert Bandura/Stanford University. **p. 453:** Michael Baytoff. **p. 455:** John Coletti/Stock Boston. **p. 456:** © 1973 Universal Press Syndicate. **p. 457:** Catherine Ursillo/Photo Researchers. **p. 463L:** U. S. Army Photo. **p. 463R:** From "Faces of the Enemy" by Sam Keen/Harper & Row © 1986. **p. 468:** Charles Moore/Black Star.

CHAPTER 13
Text and Art: p. 473: From NPR, June 28, 1991. **p. 482:** Figure 13.1 adapted from Bond, et al., "Response to violence in a psychiatric setting," *Personality and Social Psychology Bulletin,* 14, pp. 448–458. Copyright © 1988. Reprinted by permission of Sage Publications. **p. 486:** Figure 13.2 from Quattrone, et al., "The perception of variability within ingroups and outgroups: Implications for the law of small numbers," *Journal of Personality and Social Psychology,* 38. Copyright © 1980 by the American Psychological Association. Adapted by permission. **p. 487:** Excerpts from G. Allport, *The Nature of Prejudice.* Copyright © 1979 by Addison-Wesley Publishing Company, Inc. Reprinted by permission of Addision-Wesley Publishing Company, Inc. **p. 490:** Figure 13.3 from Rogers, et al., "Deindividuation and anger-mediated interracial aggression," *Journal of Personality and Social Psychology,* 41. Copyright © 1981 by the American Psychological Association. Adapted by permission. **p. 494:** Figure 13.5 adapted from Hamilton & Gifford, "Illusory correlation in interpersonal perception," *Journal of Experimental Social Psychology,* 12. Copyright © 1976. Reprinted by permission of Academic Press. **p. 505:** Figure 13.7 from *Journal of Psychology,* 9, pp. 301–310 (1940). Reprinted with permission of the Helen Dwight Reid Educational Foundation. Published by Heldref Publications, 1319 Eighteenth St., NW, Washington, D.C. 20036-1802. Copyright © 1940. **p. 508:** Figure 13.8 from Rogers, et al., "Deindividuation and anger-mediated interracial aggression, *Journal of Personality and Social Psychology,* 41. Copyright © 1981 by the American Psychological Association. Adapted by permission. **p. 515:** Figure 13.9 adapted from Sherif, "Intergroup conflict and cooperation: The Robber's Cave Experiment." Copyright © 1961. Reprinted by permission of O. J. Harvey.
Photos and cartoons: p. 472: © B. Daemmrich/The Image Works. **p. 474:** UPI/Bettmann. **p. ???:** Larry Fisher, Quad City Times. **p. 477:** © Michael Newman/PhotoEdit. **p. 479:** Drawing by Ziegler, ©1994 The New Yorker Magazine, Inc.. **p. 480:** © 1992 Gary Hallgren. **p. 484:** © M. Cassidy/The Picture Cube; **p. 496:** Moshe Shandiz/Sygma. **p. 498:** The Kobal Collection; **p. 500:** © 1951 The New Yorker: 25th Annual Album, Harper & Bros.. **p. 511L:** The Bettmann Archive. **p. 511R:** University of Alabama Archives. **p. 516:** © 1978 Simon & Shuster.

MODULE 1
Text and Art: p. 530: Table M1.1 reprinted by permission of the publisher from "The social readjustment rating scale," by Holmes and Rahe, *Journal of Psychosomatic Research,* 11, pp. 213–218. Copyright © 1967 by Elsevier Science, Inc. **p. 531:** Figure M1.1 from Cohen, et al., "Psychological Stress and Susceptibility to the Common Cold," *New England Journal of Medicine,* 325. Copyright © 1991. Reprinted by permission. **p. 534:** From Langer, et al., "The effects of choice and enhanced personal responsibility for the aged: A field experiment," *Journal of Personality and Social Psychology,* 34. Copyright © 1976 by the American Psychological Association. Adapted by permission. **p. 534:** Figure M1.2 from Seligman, et al., "Failure to escape traumatic shock," *Journal of Experimental Psychology,* 74. Copyright © 1967 by the American Psychological Association. Adapted by permission. **p. 539:** Figure M1.5 from Wilson, et al.,

NAME INDEX

Impressions
  accuracy of, 137–40
  first, 74, 75, 137–40, 375
  mental shortcuts in forming, 116–18
Incentives, overjustification effect and,
    159–63
Independent variables, 48–49
Independent view of self, 147–48
Indians, Iroquois, 440
Individual differences, 11, 17
  prosocial behavior and, 410–14
Infancy, attachment style and, 387–90
Inferences. *See also* Attribution
  correcting of, 96–99
  error in, 90–91
Influence, social. *See* Social influence
Information
  base rate, 84
  consensus, 122–24
  consistency, 122
  distinctiveness, 122–24
  failure to share, 334–36
Informational social influence, 271–79
  bystander intervention and, 424–25
  in conversions or crises, 273–75
  dangers in, 275–76
  Milgram experiment and, 304–5
  resisting of, 277–79
  situations producing, 276–77
Information availability
  actor/observer difference and, 133–34
  self-serving attributions and, 135–36
Information processing
  automatic vs. controlled, 490–93
  during trial, 589–92
Informed consent, 60
Ingram, Paul, 170
Ingratiation, 177, 370
In-group, 484–85
In-group bias, 485
Injunctive norms, 567, 568
Inoculation, attitude, 249–51
Institutionalized racism, 509
Institutionalized sexism, 509
Instructor-watching experiment, on attrac-
    tiveness, 364–65
Instrumental aggression, 437
Instrumental conditioning, 231
Insufficient justification, 195–205
Insufficient punishment, 199–202
Integrative solutions, 349, 350
Intelligence
  leadership and, 327
  self-fulfilling prophecy and, 23–24
  stereotype vulnerability and, 499–500
Interdependence
  cooperation and, 516–19
  mutual, 515
Interdependent view of self, 147–48
Interjudge reliability, 37
Internal (dispositional) attribution, 119, 538.
    See also Attribution
  correspondent inference model and,
    119–22
  covariation model and, 122–23, 124
  culture and, 130–31
  emphasis on, 129–30
  self-serving, 135–37
  stereotypes and, 497–501
Internal justification, 196–97, 201, 234–35
Internal validity, 49–52, 57–58
Interpersonal attraction. *See* Attraction
Interpersonal conflict, 341–42
Interpersonal process, relationships as,
    390–92
Interpersonal relationships, and self-evalua-
    tion maintenance theory, 217–18

Interpretation
  of environment, 5–6
  Gestalt psychology and, 16–17
  of negative life events, 529–42
Intervention of bystanders. *See* Bystander
    intervention
Interview experiments on self-fulfilling
    prophecy, 503–4
Intimacy
  attachment style and, 388–90
  in triangular theory of love, 378
Intimate relationships. *See* Love and long-
    term relationships
Intrapersonal conflict, 341
Intrinsic interest, overjustification hypothesis
    and, 160–61
Intrinsic motivation, 159, 161–63
Introspection, 149–56
Investment model of close relationships,
    382–84
Involvement of bystanders. *See* Bystander
    intervention
IQ tests, self-fulfilling prophecies and, 76–77
Iraq, war against, 233, 440, 464, 486
Ironic processing, 94–96
Iroquois Indians, aggressive behavior
    and, 440
Isolation, development of self-concept in, 172
Ito, Lance, 105

Jagger, Mick, 121
Japanese
  conformity among, 291
  definition of self, 146–49
  dissonance-reducing behavior, 223
  emotional display by, 108
  saving face, 176
  stereotypes of, 488
Jealousy, 392–93
Jews
  blaming the victim and, 501
  as scapegoats, 507, 508
  stereotypes of, 487, 488, 494–95, 498
Jigsaw classroom, 516–19
Job interview experiments, on self-fulfilling
    prophecy, 503–4
Jobs, Steve, 327
Jogging, stretching prior to, 181–83
Johnson, Lyndon, and Vietnam War, 18,
    19, 337
Jones, Reverend Jim, and Jonestown, 4, 7, 9,
    11, 267–68, 269, 277
Judgmental heuristics, 80–89
  anchoring and adjustment heuristic,
    85–88, 92, 129
  availability heuristic, 80–82, 88
  counterfactual thinking, 82–84
  representativeness heuristic, 84–85
  schemas and, 88
Jury deliberations, 590–92
Jury system, 586–92
Justice system, American, 573. *See also* Law
    and psychology
Justification. *See also* Self-justification
  of effort, 193–95, 196
  external, 196, 201, 234
  insufficient, 195–205
  internal, 196–97, 201, 234–35
  of past behavior, 19–21
Just world, belief in, 136, 137

Keech, Marian, 187–88
Kennedy, John F., 511
  Bay of Pigs fiasco and, 34, 311–12, 331,
    336–37
  Cuban missile crisis and, 338–39
Kennedy, Robert, 337

Khomeini, Ayatollah, 475
Killeen, Texas, cafeteria shooting as, 453
King, Rodney, 435
Kin selection, 402
Koffka, Kurt, 16
Kohler, Wolfgang, 16
Koresh, David, 7–8, 268, 269
Korsakov's syndrome, 69
Ku Klux Klan, 176, 321, 485

Lambert, Gerald, 258
Landers, Ann, 131, 240, 460, 465
Language
  actor/observer difference and, 134
  in implicit personality theories, 113–15
Law and psychology, 523
  American justice system and, 573
  detecting of deception and, 584–86
  eyewitness testimony and, 572, 573–86
  "inadmissible evidence," 74
  jury system and, 586–92
Law enforcement officials, detection of
    deception by, 584–85
Leadership, 327–31
  gender and, 330–31
Learned helplessness, 537–42, 557, 558
  stereotype vulnerability and, 540–42
Learning theory
  conditioning, 231
  social, 449–50, 509–11
Lewin, Kurt, 16
Liddy, G. Gordon, 436
Lie-detector test, 585–86
Lie-telling payment experiment, on counter-
    attitudinal advocacy, 197
Liking, reciprocal, 368–70. *See also*
    Attraction
Lincoln, Abraham, 328, 406
Line-length experiment, on conformity,
    280–82
Literary Digest poll (1936), 42
Litter reduction, 566–68
Loafing, social, 318–21, 331
Locus in taxonomy of success and failure
    attributions, 124, 125
Logic, prejudice and failure of, 487–88
Looking-glass self, 172
Los Angeles
  pollution in, 561
  riot, 435
    Reginald Denny and, 283, 405
Love and long-term relationships, 356. *See
    also* Attraction
  breakup of, 393–96
  causes of, 381–96
    attachment styles and, 387–90
    equity theory and, 384–85
    evolution and sociobiological approach
      to, 386–87
    physical attractiveness, 387
    social exchange, 381–84
  companionate, 376–77, 378
  culture and, 380–81
  defining love, 375–80
  falling-in-love accounts, 371
  jealousy and, 392–93
  love styles, 379–80, 381
  passionate, 377–78
  self-awareness and, 152–53
  triangular theory of, 378
Love Attitudes Scale, 381
Lowballing, 190–91
Ludus (love style), 379
Lying. *See* Deception or lying
Lynching, 321–22, 323, 474
  cotton prices and, 505–6, 507
  diminishing of, 508